D0404873

ESSENTIAL
GREAT
BRITAIN

Excerpted from *Fodor's England* and *Fodor's Scotland*.

WELCOME TO GREAT BRITAIN

Great Britain packs spectacular landscapes, as well as rich history, into the compact borders of England, Wales, and Scotland. From the southern coast up to the Highlands, its lush countryside and jagged mountains may surprise you. In London and other urban centers, explore iconic sights and great museums—and also discover cutting-edge cultural scenes that tweak tradition. Beyond the cities, ancient castles and pretty villages entice. Britain's iconic products and customs—from pubs to tartans—may travel the globe, but there's nothing like experiencing them firsthand.

TOP REASONS TO GO

★ **Cool Cities:** London's celebrated landmarks, Edinburgh's innovative festivals, and more.

★ **History:** Sites from Stonehenge to Stirling Castle bring the nation's past to life.

★ **Pubs:** For a pint or a chat, a visit to one of "Britain's living rooms" is essential.

★ **Landscapes:** Wooded hills, sparkling lakes, rugged mountains, wide-open moors.

★ **Idyllic Towns:** Cozy cottages with flowerbeds, pastel-painted seaside charmers.

★ **Great Walks:** In England's Lake District, Scotland's Highlands, and along Wales' coast.

Fodor's ESSENTIAL GREAT BRITAIN

Publisher: Amanda D'Acierno, *Senior Vice President*

Editorial: Arabella Bowen, *Editor in Chief*; Linda Cabasin, *Editorial Director*

Design: Fabrizio La Rocca, *Vice President, Creative Director*; Tina Malaney, *Associate Art Director*; Chie Ushio, *Senior Designer*; Ann McBride, *Production Designer*

Photography: Melanie Marin, *Associate Director of Photography*; Jessica Parkhill and Jennifer Romains, *Researchers*

Maps: Rebecca Baer, *Senior Map Editor*; Mark Stroud (Moonstreet Cartography), *Cartographers*

Production: Linda Schmidt, *Managing Editor*; Evangelos Vasilakis, *Associate Managing Editor*; Angela L. McLean, *Senior Production Manager*

Sales: Jacqueline Lebow, *Sales Director*

Marketing & Publicity: Heather Dalton, *Marketing Director*; Katherine Punia, *Senior Publicist*

Business & Operations: Susan Livingston, *Vice President, Strategic Business Planning*; Sue Daulton, *Vice President, Operations*

Fodors.com: Megan Bell, *Executive Director, Revenue & Business Development*; Yasmin Marinaro, *Senior Director, Marketing & Partnerships*

Copyright © 2015 by Fodor's Travel, a division of Random House LLC

Writers: Robert Andrews, Nick Bruno, Mike Gonzalez, Julius Honnor, Kate Hughes, Jack Jewers, James O'Neill, Shona Main, Ellin Stein, Alex Wijeratna

Editors: Linda Cabasin, lead project editor; Daniel Mangin

Editorial Contributor: Steven Montero

Production Editors: Teddy Minford, Evangelos Vasilakis

1st Edition

ISBN 978-0-8041-4209-0

ISSN 2373-9169

SPECIAL SALES

This book is available at special discounts for bulk purchases for sales promotions or premiums. For more information, e-mail specialmarkets@penguinrandomhouse.com

PRINTED IN THE UNITED STATES OF AMERICA

10 9 8 7 6 5 4 3 2 1

CONTENTS

CONTENTS

CONTENTS

MAPS

CONTENTS

ABOUT THIS GUIDE

Fodor's Recommendations

Everything in this guide is worth doing—we don't cover what isn't—but exceptional sights, hotels, and restaurants are recognized with additional accolades. Fodor's Choice★ indicates our top recommendations; and **Best Bets** call attention to notable hotels and restaurants in various categories. Care to nominate a new place? Visit Fodors.com/contact-us.

Trip Costs

We list prices wherever possible to help you budget well. Hotel and restaurant price categories from **$** to **$$$$** are noted alongside each recommendation. For hotels, we include the lowest cost of a standard double room in high season. For restaurants, we cite the average price of a main course at dinner or, if dinner isn't served, at lunch. For attractions, we always list adult admission fees; discounts are usually available for children, students, and senior citizens.

Hotels

Our local writers vet every hotel to recommend the best overnights in each price category, from budget to expensive. Unless otherwise specified, you can expect private bath, phone, and TV in your room. For expanded hotel reviews, visit Fodors.com.

Restaurants

Unless we state otherwise, restaurants are open for lunch and dinner daily. We mention dress code only when there's a specific requirement and reservations only when they're essential or not accepted. To make restaurant reservations, visit Fodors.com.

Credit Cards

The hotels and restaurants in this guide typically accept credit cards. If not, we'll say so.

Top Picks
★ Fodor's Choice

Listings
⊠ Address
✉ Branch address
☎ Telephone
🖷 Fax
⊕ Website
✎ E-mail
📧 Admission fee
⊙ Open/closed times
Ⓜ Subway
⊹ Directions or Map coordinates

Hotels & Restaurants
🏨 Hotel
🛏 Number of rooms
🍽 Meal plans
✕ Restaurant
☝ Reservations
👗 Dress code
⊟ No credit cards
$ Price

Other
⇨ See also
☞ Take note
⛳ Golf facilities

EXPERIENCE GREAT BRITAIN

GREAT BRITAIN TODAY

Great Britain and the United Kingdom—what's the difference? Historically the United Kingdom (or U.K.) has consisted of the countries of England, Scotland, Wales, and Northern Ireland; the Channel Islands; and the Isle of Man. Great Britain is the land mass occupied by England, Scotland, and Wales. "Britain" is a synonym of the U.K., and "the British" refers to its citizens.

At the time of this writing, Scotland was part of the U.K., but the 2014 constitutional referendum on Scottish independence may have drastically changed the picture. Whatever the outcome of the referendum, it's worth noting that Wales and Scotland have never been part of England, and vice versa. Get that one wrong at your peril—you haven't seen angry until you've seen a Welshman referred to as English.

The Royals Reinvented

How things have changed for the Windsor family. Essentially a figurehead monarchy with a symbolic political role, the Royal Family has teetered on the brink of obsolescence. After the royal scandals of the last century and the death of Princess Diana in 1997, the idea of scaling down or even ending the monarchy was widely discussed. Maintaining the Royal Family costs the country around £35 million (about $60 million) each year, a figure increasingly difficult to justify as the popularity of the family—aside from the beloved Queen—plummeted.

It's not surprising, then, that some maintain that Prince William saved the monarchy when he married the appealing Catherine Middleton. The young couple's popularity is enormous, particularly after the birth of their son, George, Prince of Cambridge, in July 2013. Meanwhile, the Queen, now in her late eighties and

with no thought of retiring, is reducing her public engagements, gradually transferring duties to her son, Prince Charles, and other members of the Royal Family. A significant swath of opinion, however, would like the succession to skip the slightly tainted Prince Charles and go directly to his son William, symbolizing a complete rejuvenation of this media-savvy institution.

Coalition Country

Until the next general election in May 2015, Britain is ruled by a coalition government. After the 2010 election, when no single party won an absolute majority of the vote, the leading vote-winner, the Conservative Party, teamed up with the small, politically moderate Liberal Democrat party to form a coalition government led by Prime Minister David Cameron, a Conservative, and Deputy Prime Minister Nick Clegg, a Liberal Democrat. Inevitably, this uncomfortable alliance has produced some controversial compromises on a range of complex issues. Matters were complicated in local and European Union elections in 2013 and 2014 by the heavy losses suffered by the Liberal Democrats and the significant gains made by the relatively new UKIP (U.K. Independence Party), led by Nigel Farage, favoring tighter control on immigration and an "amicable divorce" from the European Union (and sharing, too, in a Europe-wide disillusionment with mainstream politics).

However, the promise by all three major parties to hold a referendum on E.U. membership after 2015 may cut away at UKIP support, while the relative recovery of the U.K. economy has strengthened the coalition's hand. The next realignment of British politics could change the game still further in this volatile and unpredictable

phase; not for many years has Britain's future appeared so uncertain.

London-centricity

Dynamic, complex, and cosmopolitan, London is undoubtedly a success story. Economically vibrant, it is Europe's financial hub, it holds by far the nation's greatest concentration of the arts, and it is continually expanding, with an ongoing debate about how to increase the capacity of its airports. But London is also, in the words of Business Secretary Vince Cable, "a giant suction machine draining the life out of the rest of the U.K." For while the capital was spearheading the U.K.'s belated recovery from the global economic crisis in 2014, it was often at the expense of the rest of the country, where the majority of people were still mired in the reality of "austerity Britain." Nor is London's preeminence always good news for Londoners, many of whom have been priced out of a skyrocketing property market by investors and foreign buyers (and London is, by some distance, the most expensive British city to live in). London is in a category of its own—for better or worse.

Scotland: A Nation Apart

It's hardly surprising that visitors to Scotland who have first experienced England will find much that is familiar. After all, the two countries have had a common history since their crowns were united in 1603 and their parliaments merged a hundred years later. Scotland's distinctiveness soon becomes apparent, however, as does the country's fiery pride in its own identity. Although it may have just 5.3 million people (to England's 53 million), Scotland today has some big ideas about where it's headed socially, culturally, and economically.

This self-confidence is immediately evident in its thriving arts scene, with arts festivals proliferating and such companies as the National Theatre of Scotland continuing to enjoy international success. But the arguments surrounding Scotland's independence referendum in 2014 (the result not known at time of writing) have hinged on more nitty-gritty issues, such as whether an independent Scotland could afford to fund itself, and what weight it would have internationally. Robbie Burns himself might have appreciated this collision of romance and pragmatism.

Fashionable Britannia

Known for their quirky, creative, and bold style, British fashion designers have been influential on the global stage for decades. Whether it's from top-of-the-line companies like Burberry and Mulberry or from individual designers such as Paul Smith, Stella McCartney, Victoria Beckham, and the late Alexander McQueen, clothes made by British designers are sought after. According to the 2014 British Fashion Week, the British fashion industry is worth £26 billion and is still growing.

Catherine, the Duchess of Cambridge, commands attention as ambassador for British fashion. The "Kate effect," first fired by her wedding dress, has not diminished. Even the Queen takes note; Kate was reportedly advised by her grandmother-in-law to adopt lower hemlines for her 2014 tour of Australia and New Zealand. She continues to mix high fashion with high-street clothing, causing such chains as Reiss, LK Bennett, Hobbs, and Whistles to sell out when she dons their garments. Kate also helps keep designers such as Jenny Packham, Alice Temperley and Jimmy Choo in the spotlight.

WHAT'S WHERE

The following numbers refer to chapters.

2 London. Not only Britain's financial and governmental center but also one of the world's great cities, London has mammoth museums, posh palaces, sprawling parks, village-like neighborhoods, and iconic sights such as Big Ben.

3 The Southeast. This compact, green, and pleasant region within day-trip distance of London takes in Canterbury and its cathedral, funky seaside Brighton, charming Rye and Lewes, Dover's white cliffs, and castles such as Bodiam, Leeds, and Hever.

4 The South. Hampshire, Dorset, and Wiltshire have quintessential English countryside, with gentle hills and green pastures. Explore the stone circles at Stonehenge and Avebury, take in Winchester and Salisbury, and discover Highclere Castle and Lyme Regis.

5 The West Country. Somerset, Devon, and Cornwall are sunnier and warmer than the rest of England. Cornwall has a stunning coast. Of the cities, Bristol is the most vibrant; Wells and Exeter are attractive and compact.

6 Oxford and the Thames Valley. London's commuter belt takes in Windsor, where

the Queen spends time. Other draws are Oxford's university buildings, river towns such as Henley and Marlow, and Blenheim Palace.

7 Bath, the Cotswolds, and Stratford-upon-Avon. The stately Georgian town of Bath is one of England's highlights, including the Roman Baths. Nearby, the towns of the Cotswolds are famously pretty. See Shakespeare's birth-place and watch his plays in Stratford-upon-Avon.

8 Manchester, Liverpool, and the Peak District. Liverpool rides the Beatles' coattails but, like Manchester, has buzzing nightlife, sleek restaurants, and excellent museums. The Peak District has stately homes such as Chatsworth and Haddon Hall.

9 The Lake District. A popular national park, this is a beautiful area of craggy hills, wild moorland, stone cottages, and glittering silvery lakes. Literary high points are the homes of Wordsworth and Beatrix Potter.

10 Cambridge and East Anglia. The big lure in this low-key region is Cambridge, with its medieval halls of learning. The countryside has time-warp towns such as Lavenham, and salty coastal spots like Aldeburgh.

WHAT'S WHERE

11 Yorkshire and the Northeast. The ancient city of York is a center of attention, as are the Yorkshire moors and dales that inspired the Brontës. In the Northeast, medieval Durham, Hadrian's Wall, and coastal castles are highlights.

12 Wales. Clinging to the western edge of England, Wales is green and ruggedly beautiful, with mountains and magnificent coastline. Except for Cardiff and Swansea, this is a rural country. Wales is also known for its stunning castles.

13 Edinburgh. Scotland's captivating capital is its most popular city, famous for its high-perched castle, Old Town and 18th-century New Town, ultramodern Parliament building, and the Edinburgh International Festival and the Fringe.

14 Glasgow. The largest city in Scotland has earned a strong artistic, architectural, and culinary reputation. Museums and galleries such as the Kelvingrove are here, along with Arts and Crafts architecture by Charles Rennie Mackintosh.

15 The Borders and the Southwest. Scotland's southern gateway from England, the Borders region is rustic but historically rich, with stately homes such as Floors Castle

and ruined abbeys including Melrose. The Southwest is perfect for scenic drives and hiking.

16 The Central Highlands, Fife, and Angus. Convenient to Edinburgh and Glasgow, this area has some of Scotland's most beautiful terrain, including Loch Lomond and the Trossachs. In Fife, St. Andrews has world-famous golf courses.

17 Aberdeen and the Northeast. Malt-whisky buffs can use the port city of Aberdeen as a base for exploring fine distilleries. It's also a starting point for touring Royal Deeside, with its castles, moors, and hills.

18 Argyll and the Isles. This less visited region of the southwestern coastline has excellent gardens, religious sites, and distilleries. If you like whisky, a trip to Islay is a must.

19 The Great Glen, Skye, and the Northern Highlands. An awe-inspiring valley laced with rivers defines the Great Glen. Inverness, capital of the Highlands, is near Loch Ness. The beautiful Isle of Skye is a highlight for visitors, and the north's rugged highlands have wild moors.

NEED TO KNOW

AT A GLANCE

Capital: London

Population: 61,350,000

Currency: Pound

Money: ATMs are common; credit cards accepted widely

Language: English

Country Code: ☏ 44

Emergencies: ☏ 999

Driving: On the left

Electricity: 220–240v/50 cycles; electrical plugs have two or three square prongs

Time: Five hours ahead of New York

Documents: Six months with valid passport; Schengen rules apply

Mobile Phones: GSM (900 and 1800 bands)

Major Mobile Companies: EE, 3, Vodafone, O2

WEBSITES

Official Tourism site: ⊕ www.visitbritain.com

The National Trust: ⊕ www.nationaltrust.org.uk

London Theatre Guide: ⊕ www.officiallondontheatre.co.uk

GETTING AROUND

✈ **Air Travel:** The major airports are London Heathrow, London Gatwick, Manchester, and Edinburgh.

🚌 **Bus Travel:** An extensive network of long-distance buses (called "coaches") offers such luxuries as sleeper seats on some routes.

🚗 **Car Travel:** Rent a car to explore at your own pace, but never in London. Gas can be very expensive; also be sure to check regulations if you park in a town.

🚆 **Train Travel:** There are good fast train links between major cities and slower trains to smaller towns, however, fares can be high.

PLAN YOUR BUDGET

	HOTEL ROOM	MEAL	ATTRACTIONS
Low Budget	£120	£15	Tate Modern, free
Mid Budget	£200	£27	Tower of London ticket, £21.45
High Budget	£300	£100	West End Theatre ticket, £80

WAYS TO SAVE

Go for a fixed-price lunch. Many restaurants offer good prix-fixe lunch deals (Indian restaurants especially).

Book a B&B. If you're touring towns or the countryside, bed-and-breakfasts offer reasonably priced rooms and contact with locals.

Buy a Visitor Oyster Card for London. This is the easiest and cheapest way to pay for public transport around the capital. ⊕ www.visitorshop.tfl.gov.uk.

Go to a free museum. National museums—including London's British Museum, V&A, and National Gallery—are free, but charge for temporary exhibitions.

Scotland

GREAT BRITAIN

Wales

England

London

PLAN YOUR TIME

Hassle Factor	Low. Flights to London are frequent, and travel links for onward travel are good.
3 days	You can see some of London's historic sights and perhaps take a day trip out to Windsor Castle or Oxford.
1 week	Combine a short trip to London with a one-day trip to Stonehenge, and then travel on to Salisbury Cathedral and the grand estates of Stourhead and Longleat, or else head south to Jane Austen's house, the New Forest, and Lyme Regis.
2 weeks	This gives you time for a stop in London plus excursions farther north to the beautiful Lake District, the wild moors of Brontë Country in Yorkshire, and Scotland.

WHEN TO GO

High Season: You'll find good weather, sports events, and a busy music festival calendar from June through August. This is also the most expensive and popular time to visit Britain, though the natives tend to desert London in August.

Low Season: Rain and cold make this the best time for airfares and hotel deals—and to escape the crowds. But London is mobbed with Christmas shoppers in December.

Value Season: September has the most settled weather, plus saner airfares and the buzz of the new season's cultural events. The weather is still good in October, though temperatures start to drop in November. Late April or May is a great time to visit: fewer crowds, lower prices, and a glorious display of flowers. March and early April weather can be changeable and wet.

BIG EVENTS

May: Meet leading writers at the huge Hay Festival in Wales's lovely Brecon Beacon National Park. ⊕ www.hayfestival.com.

June: Wimbledon starts the last week and goes into July. ⊕ www.wimbledon.com.

August: A galaxy of arts luminaries perform at the Edinburgh International Festival. ⊕ www.edinburghfestivals.co.uk.

September: The Open House Weekend is a rare chance to explore many of London's most beautiful structures. ⊕ www.londonopenhouse.org.

READ THIS

■ *London: The Biography,* Peter Ackroyd. A magisterial history of the city.

■ *The English: A Portrait of a People,* Jeremy Paxman. A BBC star wryly examines his compatriots.

■ *Notes from a Small Island,* Bill Bryson. An American's look at his adopted home.

WATCH THIS

■ *Notting Hill.* A rose-colored view of London.

■ *Local Hero.* A close-knit Scottish community tries to fend off developers.

■ *Tamara Drewe.* Comical, modern reworking of Hardy's *Far from the Madding Crowd.*

EAT THIS

■ **Roast lamb with mint:** a traditional Sunday lunch

■ **"Full English/British" breakfast:** eggs, back bacon, beans, toast, mushrooms, and tomatoes

■ **British asparagus:** If you're in G. B. during May and June, don't miss it.

■ **Shepherd's pie:** minced lamb with vegetables under a mashed potato crust

■ **Cheese:** Blue Stilton and Wensleydale are especially prized.

■ **Fish-and-chips:** cod or haddock fried in a beer-batter crust with fries

GREAT BRITAIN TOP ATTRACTIONS

London
(A) Packed with treasures and pleasures, London entices with superb museums, royal pageantry, and exciting theater, shopping, and nightlife. Its iconic sights include the Houses of Parliament, Westminster Abbey, the Tower of London, and the British Museum, but parks and pubs offer memorable diversions as well. *(⇨ See Chapter 2.)*

Cotswold Villages
(B) Marked by rolling uplands, green fields, and mellow limestone cottages with prim flower beds, the Cotswolds, 100 miles west of London, make a peaceful getaway. There's little to do in idyllic villages, but that's exactly the point. Exquisite gardens and stately homes add further charm. *(⇨ See Chapter 7.)*

Stonehenge and Avebury
(C) Prehistoric monuments dot England's landscape, silent but tantalizing reminders of the distant past. Of these, the great circle of stones at Stonehenge is one of the country's icons. Nearby, the Avebury Stone Circles surround part of a village and are also deeply intriguing. *(⇨ See Chapter 4.)*

Oxford and Cambridge
(D) It's hard to choose a favorite between these two ancient university towns. Oxford is larger and more cosmopolitan, but lovely with its fairytale cityscape of steeples and towers. In Cambridge you can stroll through the colleges, visit the university's museums, and relax in the city's pubs. *(⇨ See Chapters 6 and 10.)*

Lake District
(E) Sprawling across northwest England, this area of 16 major lakes and jagged mountains inspired Romantic poets. You can hike the trails or view the mountains from a boat, or visit the retreats of William Wordsworth and Beatrix Potter. *(⇨ See Chapter 9.)*

Coastal Cornwall

(F) The coasts of Cornwall, in the far southwest, are beloved by many. The rugged northern coast has cliffs that drop to tiny coves and beaches; ruined, cliff-top Tintagel Castle and Padstow with its lively harbor are here. The south coast has resort towns such as arty St. Ives. *(⇨ See Chapter 5.)*

Castles in Wales

(G) Spread around the country, the more than 600 castles in Wales are among the world's finest. Some magnificent examples, such as Caernarfon and Conwy in North Wales, were built by the English in the 13th century. Others like Raglan are fascinating ruins. *(⇨ See Chapter 12.)*

Edinburgh and Glasgow

(H) Scotland's capital, Edinburgh, turns on the charm with sights from Edinburgh Castle to the Royal Mile to Old Town; the Edinburgh International Festival and the Fringe keep the city lively. In Glasgow, an urban renaissance has brought great shopping and nightlife to complement the city's rich architectural heritage and museums. *(⇨ See Chapters 13 and 14.)*

Loch Lomond and the Trossachs

(I) Sparkling water, lush woodlands, jagged mountains, and open skies make Loch Lomond a coveted—and accessible from Glasgow and Edinburgh—weekend retreat for visitors and locals. Loch Lomond and the Trossachs, Scotland's first national park, is ideal for hiking, biking, and more. *(⇨ See Chapter 16.)*

Isle of Skye

(J) With the misty Cuillin Mountains and aged stone crofts, and a dramatic coastline, the Isle of Skye is a place to linger over sunsets, explore meadows of heather, and savor fresh-caught seafood. The island's romantic past is linked to the saga of Bonnie Prince Charlie. *(⇨ See Chapter 19.)*

QUINTESSENTIAL GREAT BRITAIN

Pints and Pubs

Pop in for a pint at a pub to encounter what has been the center—literally the "public house"—of British social life for centuries. The basic pub recipe calls for a variety of beers on draft—dark creamy stouts like Guinness; bitter, including brews such as Tetley's and Bass; and lager, the blondest and blandest of the trio— a dartboard, oak paneling, and paisley carpets. In Scotland, there isn't a pub that doesn't sell whisky, too. Throw in a bunch of young suits in London, a generous dash of undergrads in places such as Oxford or Glasgow, and, in rural areas, a healthy helping of blokes around the television and ladies in the corner sipping their *halves* (half pints) and having a *natter* (gossip). In smaller pubs, listen in and enjoy the banter among the regulars. Join in if you care to, but remember not to take anything too seriously—a severe breach of pub etiquette. Make your visit soon: the encroachment of gastro-pubs (bar-restaurant hybrids) is just one of the forces challenging traditional pub culture.

Daily Rags

To blend in with the British, stash your smartphone and slide a newspaper under your arm. If you're on the move, pick up free copies of the *Evening Standard* (in London) and *Metro* (in London and on local trains and buses in various other cities), or head for a park bench or café and lose yourself in one of the national dailies for insight into Britain's worldview. The ramifications of the Leveson Inquiry into the role and relationships of the media in 2012 rumble on in the press from the tabloid *Sun,* the biggest-selling daily (though many wish that the topless model on Page 3 would be dropped), to the *i,* the cheapest and shortest of the dailies, and the Sunday papers, such as the *Observer* and the more conservative *Sunday Telegraph.* For a more satirical view, the fortnightly

If you want to get a sense of contemporary British culture and indulge in some of its pleasures, start by familiarizing yourself with the rituals of daily life. Here are a few highlights—things you can take part in with relative ease.

Private Eye, with its hallmark cartoons and parodies, offers British wit at its best.

A Lovely Cuppa

For almost four centuries the British and tea have been immersed in a love affair passionate enough to survive revolutions, rations, tariffs, and lattes, but also soothing, as "putting the kettle on" heralds moments of quiet comfort in public places and in homes and offices across the nation. The ritual known as "afternoon tea" had its beginnings in the early 19th century, in the private chambers of the duchess of Bedford, where she and her "ladies of leisure" indulged in afternoons of pastries and fragrant blends. Department stores, hotels, and tearooms offer everything from simple tea and biscuits to shockingly overpriced spreads with sandwiches and cakes that would impress even the duchess herself. Some restaurants are now even offering a different tea with each course of the meal. But, if tea isn't your cup of tea, coffee is fine, too.

Sports Fever

Whoever says Great Britain isn't an overtly religious country hasn't considered the sports mania here, and not merely because of the effects of the 2012 Olympic Games, Andy Murray winning Wimbledon in 2013, or the 2014 Commonwealth Games in Glasgow. Whether water events (such as Henley and the Head of the River Race) or a land competition (the Grand National steeplechase, a good football match anywhere), most bring people to the edge of their seats—or more often the living room couch. To partake in the rite, you'll need Pimm's (the drink for swank spectators of the Henley Royal Regatta) or beer (the drink for most everything else). You may experience the exhilaration yourself—which, you'll probably sense, is not for the love of *a* sport, but for the love of *sport* itself.

IF YOU LIKE

Castles

Whether a jumble of stones or intact, whether in private ownership or under the care of a preservation group—Britain's castles demonstrate the country's lavish past, military history, and the once-uneasy relationships of England and Scotland, and England and Wales.

Bamburgh Castle, Yorkshire and the Northeast. Views of the North Sea make this well-worn cliff-top fortress memorable.

Caerlaverock Castle, Borders and the Southwest. This 13th-century fortress with red-sandstone walls was a bastion in the 17th-century struggle for religious reform.

Caernarfon Castle, Wales. This is the best preserved of the mighty castles Edward I built in the 13th century.

Conwy Castle, Wales. The partially ruined castle has eight imposing towers that rise above the town of Conwy.

Dover Castle, Southeast. Towering above Dover's white cliffs, this Norman castle helped protect England for centuries and even played a role in World War II.

Edinburgh Castle, Edinburgh. Built atop a volcanic plug, this royal palace dominates the capital's history and skyline.

Eilean Donan Castle, Great Glen, Skye, and the Northern Highlands. A photogenic ruin, the castle sits on the edge of Loch Long, framed by views of three great sea lochs.

Stirling Castle, Central Highlands, Fife, and Angus. Stirling was the childhood home of Mary, Queen of Scots. One of the finest Renaissance palaces in Britain, it's also unmistakably a fortress.

Warwick Castle, Bath, the Cotswolds, and Stratford-upon-Avon. Packed with exhibits and entertainments, this magnificent medieval fortress offers a fun day out.

Palaces and Historic Houses

Exploring the diversity and magnificence of Britain's palaces and historic houses can occupy most of a blissful vacation. In England, you'll find clusters in the southeast, west of Salisbury, and in the Cotswolds. Note that many historic houses are open from spring through fall.

Abbotsford, Borders and the Southwest. Sir Walter Scott's beautiful home overlooks the River Tweed and has a fine museum.

Blair Castle, Central Highlands, Fife, and Angus. This impressive palace in northern Scotland has rooms that reflect the changes from medieval castle to Victorian mansion.

Blenheim Palace, Oxford and the Thames Valley. This baroque extravaganza is touted as England's only rival to Versailles.

Buckingham Palace, London. Glimpse royal life in the magnificent state rooms, open in August and September.

Chatsworth House, Manchester, Liverpool, and the Peak District. Lovely grounds surround this grand house with a monumental Palladian facade.

Palace of Holyroodhouse, Edinburgh and the Lothians. You can visit the state rooms, many used by Mary, Queen of Scots, as well as the gardens and ruins of the 12th-century abbey.

Petworth House, Southeast. One of the National Trust's glories, it's known for art by J. M. W. Turner.

Wilton House, South. The Double Cube room designed by Inigo Jones is one of the country's best interior designs.

Windsor Castle, Oxford and the Thames Valley. The Queen's favorite residence has a fabulous art collection.

Villages and Towns

Year after year, armies of tourists with images of green meadows flock to Britain's countryside. Most find their way to adorable towns along the Thames and a few fairy-tale hamlets in the Cotswolds. But there's more to discover, including tranquil villages in Wales and Scotland's coastal gems.

Chipping Campden, Bath, the Cotswolds, and Stratford-upon-Avon. Tucked in a slight valley, this lovely Cotswolds town has frozen-in-time streets.

Crail, Central Highlands, Fife, and Angus. Clustered around a sheltered harbor, this Fife coast fishing village is delightfully picturesque.

Clovelly, Southwest. A steep cobbled street threads between flower-bedecked cottages down to the tiny harbor.

Henley-on-Thames, Oxford and the Thames Valley. Famous for its regatta, affluent Henley has a lovely position on the Thames and is ideal for strolling.

Lavenham, Cambridge and East Anglia. The Tudor buildings here are the former houses of wool merchants and weavers.

Haworth, Yorkshire and the Northeast. Besides the Brontë sights, Haworth has a steep, cobblestone main street; it's close to memorable walks on the moors.

Rye, Southeast. Writers and artists have always been drawn to the cobbled streets and timber houses of this historic town.

Tenby, Wales. Besides its golden sandy beaches, Tenby still has ancient walls and charming Georgian houses.

Tobermory, Argyll and the Isles. The pastel-color houses around the harbor may enamor any visitor to the Isle of Mull.

Cities Small and Large

London has everything a world capital should have. It's not to be missed, but those who like cities should look further. In Scotland, Edinburgh and Glasgow offer different experiences from each other, and British cities of all sizes have everything from deep history to a modern multicultural vibe.

Aberdeen, Aberdeen and the Northeast. The city has impressive neoclassical granite buildings. Shops and services reflect its renaissance as an oil city.

Bath, Bath, the Cotswolds, and Stratford-upon-Avon. Well-preserved but entertaining, this small Georgian city still centers on the hot springs that made it a fashionable spa.

Brighton, Southeast. Bold, bright, and boisterous are the words to describe a seaside charmer that has everything from the dazzling Royal Pavilion to trendy shops.

Bristol, West Country. With its lively waterfront and music and food culture, this youthful city has vibrant nightlife as well as a long history.

Liverpool, Liverpool, Manchester, and the Peak District. Dramatic regeneration, a historic waterfront, Beatles sites, and the museums of the Albert Dock are stars.

Manchester, Liverpool, Manchester, and the Peak District. Much more than football, the city offers chic urban shopping, bars and clubs, and fabulous museums.

St. Andrews, Central Highlands, Fife, and Angus. Perched above the North Sea, the city with its university spans centuries of history. It's also the birthplace of golf.

York, Yorkshire and the Northeast. Besides York Minster, Britain's largest Gothic cathedral, this engaging city has a historic core that includes ancient town walls.

Glorious Gardens

A pilgrimage to a garden is an essential part of any spring or summer trip. Green havens thrive in many places, but fertile hunting grounds are Oxfordshire, Gloucestershire (including the Cotswolds), and Kent (the "Garden of England").

Alnwick Gardens, Yorkshire and the Northeast. This ambitious contemporary garden with traditional and modern sections was created with families in mind.

Eden Project, Southwest. Much ingenious thought has gone into presenting the world's plants from three climate zones in huge geodesic domes in Cornwall.

Hidcote Manor Garden, Bath, the Cotswolds, and Stratford-upon-Avon. A masterful example of the Arts and Crafts garden, it is divided into garden rooms and contains the stunning Red Border.

Kew Gardens, London. A treetop walk, 19th-century greenhouses, and a pagoda, as well as colorful flower beds, adorn this center of academic research.

National Botanic Garden of Wales, Wales. An awesome Norman Foster–designed conservatory adds to 568 acres of spectacular collections.

Sissinghurst Castle Garden, Southeast. Vita Sackville-West's masterpiece, set within the remains of a Tudor castle, is busy in summer and spectacular in autumn.

Stourhead, South. One of the country's most impressive house-and-garden combinations is an artful 18th-century sanctuary with a lake and grottoes.

Logan Botanic Gardens, Borders and the Southwest. A location in southwestern Scotland warmed by the Gulf Stream supports plants from both hemispheres.

Wonderful Walks

Britain seems to be designed with walking in mind, whether the trail is easy or rugged—footpaths wind through the contours of the land, and many popular routes are well endowed with cozy bed-and-breakfasts and pubs. You can walk the whole or small chunks of the many long-distance trails or ramble through a national park.

Borrowdale, Lake District. In this wonderful walking spot in the Lake District National Park, have a color-pencil kit handy to capture the beauty of the verdant valleys and jagged peaks.

Brecon Beacons National Park, Wales. The windswept uplands here are crossed with easy paths that are pleasantly uncrowded.

Cotswolds Way, Bath, the Cotswolds, and Stratford-upon-Avon. Hike the Cotswold Way and combine open grassland, pretty villages, and sweeping views.

Glen Nevis, Great Glen, Skye, and the Northern Highlands. Home of the magnificent peak Ben Nevis, Glen Nevis has moderate hikes past waterfalls and forested gorges, as well as more challenging climbs.

South West Coast Path, West Country. Spectacular is the word for the 630-mile trail that winds from Minehead in Somerset to Poole Harbour in Dorset.

Thames Path, Thames Valley. Follow the Thames from its source through water meadows and riverside villages to the heart of London.

West Highland Way, Central Highlands, Fife, and Angus. From Milngavie in Glasgow through the Central Highlands to Fort William, this well-marked 95-mile trek follows old coaching roads.

Mountains and Lakes

Britain may not be known for the highest mountains by international standards, but it has its share of impressive peaks and landscapes. For the snowcapped mountains and glassy lochs (lakes) for which Scotland is famous, you have to leave the south and the cities behind you.

Cairngorms National Park, Great Glen, Skye, and the Northern Highlands. The Great Glen is home to half of Scotland's highest peaks, many of them in this park.

Lake District National Park, Lake District. Whether you favor the gentler landscapes of southern lakes such as Windermere or the starker scenery in the north, including Derwentwater, the lakes and mountains here are majestic.

Loch Katrine, Central Highlands, Fife, and Angus. In the heart of the Trossachs, this lake in the Central Highlands was the setting of Walter Scott's narrative poem *The Lady of the Lake.*

Loch Lomond, Central Highlands, Fife, and Angus. Among Scotland's most famous lakes, Loch Lomond's shimmering shores, beautiful vistas, and plethora of water-sport options are 20 minutes from Glasgow.

Loch Ness, Great Glen, Skye, and the Northern Highlands. Don't let dubious tales of the monster distract you from the beauty of this dark deep loch with waters that reflect the thick surrounding woods.

Peak District, Manchester, Liverpool, and the Peak District. Its rocky outcrops and vaulting meadows make some people say this is England's most beautiful national park.

Snowdonia National Park, Wales. Ferocious peaks in the national park offer scenic delights and spectacular views.

Country-House Hotels

In all their luxurious glory, country-house hotels are an essential part of the British landscape, and some occupy the grand houses of the landed gentry of the past. Some hotels are traditional, but a modern breed has spas, pools, and sports available. If you can't spend a night, consider dinner or afternoon tea.

Calcot Manor, Bath, the Cotswolds, and Stratford-upon-Avon. Luxury and opulence join with family-friendly amenities here where traditional and modern mix.

Cliveden House, Oxford and the Thames Valley. This very grand stately pile, once the Astors' home, offers champagne boat trips on the River Thames.

Flodigarry Country House Hotel, Great Glen, Skye, and the Northern Highlands. Coastal views and the atmosphere of a grand country house distinguish this Skye hotel.

Gidleigh Park, West Country. Beautiful grounds in a wooded valley on the edge of Dartmoor are the backdrop for superb food and antiques-filled rooms.

Lime Wood, South. This woodland hideaway in a Regency house has the added treat of a fabulous spa.

Miller Howe, Lake District. Stunning views of Windermere, Arts and Crafts touches, and superior service are the appeal here.

Taychreggan Hotel, Argyll and the Isles. An unpretentious but lovely hideaway on the shores of Loch Awe offers activities and sunsets over the loch.

Thornbury Castle, West Country. A stay in this 16th-century castle with a royal pedigree connects you to history but also includes plenty of modern pampering.

Ynyshir Hall, Wales. Deep in the countryside, this Georgian house offers luxury and excellent cuisine.

FLAVORS OF GREAT BRITAIN

The New Food Scene

Britain has never lacked a treasure store of nature's bounty: lush green pastures, fruitful orchards, and the encompassing sea. Over the past few decades, dowdy images of British cooking have been sloughed off. A new focus on the land and a new culinary confidence and expertise are exemplified by the popularity and influence of celebrity chefs such as Rick Stein, Heston Blumenthal, Gordon Ramsay, Jamie Oliver, and Mary Berry.

The famous chefs are only one indicator of change: all over the country, artisanal food producers and talented professional and home cooks are indulging their passion for high-quality, locally sourced ingredients. Whether restaurants are riding the green wave or just following good food sense, they are trying their best to buy from local suppliers; many proudly advertise their support. And in another sign of change, television programs on home baking have proved phenomenally popular.

Food festivals, farmers' markets (some organic), and farm shops have sprung up in more cities and towns. Alongside the infiltration of supermarkets, much opposed by some people, comes a more discriminating attitude to food supplies. Outdoors-reared cows, sheep, and pigs; freshly caught fish; and seasonal fruits and vegetables provide a bedrock upon which traditional recipes are tempered with cosmopolitan influences. The contemporary British menu takes the best of Mediterranean and Asian cuisines and reinterprets them with new enthusiasm.

Natural Bounty

Cask ales. The interest in the provenance of food extends to beer, encouraging microbreweries to develop real or cask ales: beer that's unfiltered and unpasteurized, and that contains live brewer's yeast. The ales can be from kegs, bottles, or casks, and they range from pale amber to fullbodied. The Casque Marque outside pubs signals their availability. These ales are quickly making their mark on the British beverage scene.

Dairy produce. The stalwart Cheddar, Cheshire, Double Gloucester, and Stilton cheeses are complemented by traditional and experimental cheeses from small, local makers. Some cheeses come wrapped in nettles or vine leaves, others stuffed with apricots, cranberries, or herbs. Dairies are producing more sheep and goat cheeses, yogurts, and ice creams.

Game. In the fall and winter, pheasant, grouse, partridge, and venison are prominent on restaurant menus, served either roasted, in rich casseroles, or in pies. Duck (particularly the Gressingham and Aylesbury breeds), rabbit, and hare are available all year round.

Meat. Peacefully grazing cattle, including Aberdeen Angus, Herefordshire, and Welsh Black varieties, are an iconic symbol of the countryside. When hung and dry-aged for up to 28 days, British beef is at its most flavorsome. Spring lamb is succulent, and salt-marsh lamb from Wales and the Lake District, fed on wild grasses and herbs, makes for a unique taste. Outdoors-reared and rare breeds of pig, such as Gloucester Old Spot, often provide the breakfast bacon.

Preserved foods. Marmalade is a fixed item on the breakfast menu, and a wide variety of jams, including the less usual quince, find their place on the tea-shop table. Chutneys made from apples or tomatoes mixed with onions and spices are served with cheese at the end of a meal or as part of a pub lunch.

Seafood. The traditional trio of cod, haddock, and plaice is still in evidence, but declining fishing stocks have brought other varieties to prominence. Hake, bream, freshwater trout, wild salmon, sardines, pilchards, and mackerel are on the restaurant table, along with crab, mussels, and oysters. The east and Cornish coasts are favored fishing grounds in England.

Some of the most coveted fish and seafood in the world live in the rivers and lakes, as well as off the coasts, of Scotland. Smoked fish (haddock, salmon, and trout, notably) is the national specialty—so much so that the process of both hot and cold smoking has developed to a fine art. Scots eat smoked fish for breakfast and lunch, and as an appetizer with their evening meal. For a special treat, grilled, sautéed, or baked langoustines offer the ultimate seafood indulgence, succulent and tasty.

Whiskies

"Uisge beatha," translated from Scottish Gaelic, means "water of life," and in Scotland it most certainly is. Whisky helps weave together the country's essence, capturing the aromas of earth, water, and air in a single sip.

Whiskies differ greatly between single malts and blends. This has to do with the ingredients, specialized distillation processes, and type of oak cask. Whisky is made predominantly from malted barley that, in the case of blended whiskies, can be combined with grains and cereals like wheat or corn. Malts or single malts can come only from malted barley.

The five main whisky regions in Scotland produce distinctive tastes, though there are variations even within a region: the Lowlands (lighter in taste), Speyside

(sweet, with flower scents), the Highlands (fragrant, smooth, and smoky), Campbeltown (full-bodied and slightly salty), and Islay (strong peat flavor). Do sample these unique flavors; distillery tours are a good place to begin.

Traditional Dishes

Good international fare is available, and you shouldn't miss the Indian food in England. But do try some classics.

Black pudding. In this dish, associated with Lancashire, Yorkshire, and the Midlands, onions, pork fat, oatmeal, herbs, and spices are blended with the blood from a pig. In Scotland, where black pudding is also popular, it may be made with cooked sheep's- or goat's blood. At its best this dish has a delicate, crumbly texture and can be served at breakfast or as a starter to a meal.

Fish-and-chips. This number-one seaside favorite not only turns up in every seaside resort around Britain, but in fish-and-chip shops and restaurants throughout the land. Fish, usually cod, haddock, or plaice, is deep-fried in a crispy batter and served with thick french fries (chips) and, if eaten out, wrapped up in paper. The liberal sprinkling of salt and vinegar, and "mushy" (processed) peas are optional.

Haggis. Food in Scotland is steeped in history, and a rich story lies behind many traditional dishes. Once the food of peasants, haggis—a mixture of sheep's heart, lungs, and liver cooked with onions, oats, and spices, and then boiled in a sheep's stomach—has made a big comeback in more formal Scottish restaurants. You'll find "neeps and tatties" alongside haggis. Neeps are yellow turnips, potatoes are the tatties, and both are boiled and then mashed.

Meat pies and pasties. Pies and pasties make a filling lunch. Perhaps the most popular is steak-and-kidney pie, combining chunks of lean beef and kidneys mixed with braised onions and mushrooms in a thick gravy, topped with a light puff- or short-pastry crust. Other combinations are chicken with mushrooms or leek and beef slow-cooked in ale (often Guinness). Cornish pasties are filled with beef, potato, rutabaga, and onions, all enveloped in a circle of pastry folded in half.

Sausages. "Bangers and mash" are sausages, most commonly made with pork but sometimes beef or lamb, served with mashed potatoes and onion gravy. Lincolnshire sausage consists of pork flavored with sage. Cumberland sausage comes in a long coil and has a peppery taste.

Shepherd's and cottage pie. These classic pub dishes have a lightly browned mashed-potato topping over stewed minced meat and onions in a rich gravy. Shepherd's pie uses lamb, cottage pie beef.

Tempting Baked Goods

The British love their cakes, biscuits, breads, and pies. There's always something sweet and most likely crumbly to indulge in, whether after a meal or with a nice cup of tea. Bakeries are the perfect places to sample fresh goodies. Some local favorites include scones, butter-based shortbreads, empire biscuits (two shortbread cookies with jam in between, glazed in white icing and topped with a bright red cherry), and mince pies (small pies filled with brandy, stewed dried fruits, and nuts). Treacle tarts, gingerbread, butterscotch apple pie, and oatcakes (more a savory cracker than a sweet cake) with local cheese are also popular.

Meals Not to Be Missed

Full English breakfast. The "full English" (or Scottish or Welsh) is a three-course affair. Starting with orange juice, cereals, porridge, yogurt, or stewed fruit, it's followed by any combination of sausages, eggs, bacon, tomatoes, mushrooms, black pudding, baked beans, and fried bread. Fried potato scones are part of the Scottish breakfast. The feast finishes with toast and marmalade and tea or coffee. Alternatives to the aptly named fry-up are kippers, smoked haddock, or boiled eggs. Some cafés serve an all-day breakfast.

Ploughman's lunch. Crusty bread, British cheese (perhaps farmhouse Cheddar, blue Stilton, crumbly Cheshire, or waxy red Leicester), and tangy pickles with a side-salad garnish make up a delicious light lunch, found in almost every pub.

Roast dinners. On Sunday, the traditional roast dinner is still popular. The meat, either beef, pork, lamb, or chicken, is served with roast potatoes, carrots, seasonal green vegetables, and Yorkshire pudding, a savory batter baked in the oven until crisp, and then topped with a rich, dark, meaty gravy. Horseradish sauce and mustard are on hand for beef; a mint sauce accompanies lamb; and an applesauce enhances pork.

Tea in the afternoon. Tea, ideally served in a country garden on a summer afternoon, ranks high on the list of Britain's must-have experiences. You may simply have a scone with your tea, or you can opt for a more ample feast: dainty sandwiches with the crusts cut off; scones with jam and clotted cream; and an array of homemade cakes.

GREAT BRITAIN LODGING PRIMER

If your dreams of Britain involve staying in a cozy cottage with a lovely garden, here's some good news: you won't have to break the bank. Throughout the country you'll find stylish lodging options—from good-value hotels and intimate bed-and-breakfasts to chic apartments and unique historic houses—in all price ranges.

For resources and contacts, and information on hotel grading and booking, see Travel Smart Great Britain.

Apartments and House Rentals

For a home base with cooking facilities that's roomy enough for a family, consider renting furnished "flats" (the word for apartments in Great Britain). These are popular in cities and towns throughout the country and can save you money. They also provide more privacy than a hotel or B&B.

Cottages and other houses are available for weekly rental in all areas. These vary from quaint older homes to brand-new buildings in scenic surroundings. For families and large groups they offer the best value-for-money accommodations, but because they're often in isolated locations, a car is vital. Living Architecture offers stays in one-of-a-kind architect-designed country houses. Lists of rental properties are available free of charge from VisitBritain. You may find discounts of up to 50% on rentals during the off-season (October through March).

Bed-and-Breakfasts

A special British tradition, and the backbone of budget travel, B&Bs are usually in a family home. Typical prices (outside London) range from £45 to £100 a night. They vary in style and grace, but these days most have private bathrooms. B&Bs range from the ordinary to the truly elegant. The line between B&Bs and guesthouses is growing increasingly blurred, but the latter are often larger.

Some Tourist Information Centres in cities and towns can help you find and book a B&B even on the day you show up in town. Many private services also deal with B&Bs.

Farmhouses

Over the years farmhouses have become popular; their special appeal is the rural experience, whether in Cornwall, Yorkshire, or the Scottish Highlands. Consider this option only if you are touring by car, because farmhouses may be in remote locations. Prices are generally reasonable. Ask VisitBritain for the booklet "Stay on a Farm" or contact Farm Stay UK. Regional tourist boards may have information as well.

Historic Buildings

Looking for a unique experience and want to spend your vacation in a Gothic banqueting house, an old lighthouse, or maybe in an apartment at Hampton Court Palace? Several organizations, such as the Landmark Trust, National Trust, English Heritage, National Trust for Scotland, and Vivat Trust, have specially adapted historic buildings to rent. Many of these have kitchens, and some may require minimum stays.

Hotels

Britain is a popular vacation destination, so be sure to reserve hotel rooms weeks (months for London) in advance. The country has everything from budget chain hotels to luxurious retreats in converted country houses. In many towns and cities, you'll find old inns that are former coaching inns; these served travelers as they journeyed around the country in horse-drawn carriages and stagecoaches.

PLAYING GOLF IN SCOTLAND

There are some 550 golf courses in Scotland and only 5.3 million residents, so the country has probably the highest ratio of courses to people anywhere in the world. If you're visiting Scotland, you'll probably want to play the "famous names" sometime in your career.

So by all means play the championship courses such as the Old Course at St. Andrews, but remember they *are* championship courses. You may enjoy the game itself much more at a less challenging course. Remember, too, that everyone else wants to play the big names, so booking can be a problem at peak times in summer. Reserving three to four months ahead is not too far for the famous courses, although it's possible to get a time up to a month (or even a week) in advance if you are relaxed about your timing. If you're staying in a hotel attached to a course, get the concierge to book a tee time for you.

Happily, golf has always had a peculiar classlessness in Scotland. It's a game for everyone, and for centuries Scottish towns and cities have maintained courses for the enjoyment of their citizens. Admittedly, a few clubs have always been noted for their exclusive air, and some newer golf courses are losing touch with the game's inclusive origins, but these are exceptions to the tradition of recreation for all. Golf here is usually a democratic game, played by ordinary folk as well as the wealthy.

Tips About Playing

Golf courses are everywhere in Scotland. Most courses welcome visitors with a minimum of formalities, and some at a surprisingly low cost. Other courses are very expensive, but a lot of great golf can be played for between £30 to £100 a round. Online booking at many courses has made arranging a golf tour easier, too.

Be aware of the topography of a course. Scotland is where the distinction between "links" and "parkland" courses was first made. Links courses are by the sea and are subject to the attendant sea breezes— some quite bracing—and mists, which can make them trickier to play. The natural topography of sand dunes and long, coarse grasses can add to the challenge. A parkland course is in a wooded area and its terrain is more obviously landscaped. A "moorland" course is found in an upland area.

Here are three pieces of advice, particularly for North Americans: (1) in Scotland the game is usually played fairly quickly, so don't dawdle if others are waiting; (2) caddy carts are hand-pulled carts for your clubs and driven golf carts are rarely available; and (3) when they say "rough," they really mean "rough."

Unless specified otherwise, hours are generally sunrise to sundown, which in June can be as late as 10 pm. Note that some courses advertise the SSS, "standard scratch score," instead of par (which may be different). This is the score a scratch golfer could achieve under perfect conditions.

Rental clubs, balls, and other gear are generally available from clubhouses, except at the most basic municipal courses. Don't get caught by the dress codes enforced at many establishments: in general, untailored shorts, round-neck shirts, jeans, and sneakers are frowned upon.

The prestigious courses may ask for evidence of your golf skills by way of a handicap certificate; check in advance and carry this with you.

Costs and Courses

Many courses lower their rates before and after peak season—at the end of September, for example. It's worth asking about this. ■**TIP**→ Some areas offer regional golf passes that save you money. Check with the local tourist board.

For a complete list of courses, contact local tourist offices or VisitScotland's official and comprehensive golf website, ⊕ *golf.visitscotland.com*. It has information about the country's golf courses, special golf trails, regional passes, special events, and tour operators, as well as on conveniently located accommodations. U.K. Golf Guide (⊕ *www.uk-golfguide. com*) has reviews by recent players. *For information about regional courses, also see individual chapters; see Tours in Travel Smart Great Britain for some golf tour operators.*

Best Bets Around Scotland

If your idea of heaven is teeing off on a windswept links, then Scotland is for you. Dramatic courses, many of them set on sandy dunes alongside the ocean, are just one of the types you'll encounter. Highland courses that take you through the heather and moorland courses surrounded by craggy mountains have their own challenges.

Boat of Garten Golf Club, Inverness-shire. With the Cairngorm Mountain as a backdrop, this beautiful course has rugged terrain that requires even seasoned players to bring their A game. As an added bonus, a steam railway runs alongside the course.

Carnoustie Golf Links, Angus. Challenging golfers for nearly 500 years, Carnoustie is on many golfers' must-do list. The iconic Championship Course has tested many of the world's top players, while the

Burnside and Buddon courses attract budding Players and Watsons.

Castle Stuart Golf Links, Inverness-shire. A more recent addition to Scotland's world-class courses offers cliff-top hazards, sprawling bunkers, and rolling fairways overlooking the Moray Firth.

Cruden Bay Golf Club, Aberdeenshire. This challenging and enjoyable links course was built by the Great North of Scotland Railway Company in 1894. Its remote location beside a set of towering dunes makes it irresistible.

Gleneagles, Perthshire. Home of the 2014 Ryder Cup championship, Gleneagles has three 18-hole courses that challenge the pros and a nine-hole course that provides a more laid-back game. It's also home to the PGA National Golf Academy.

Machrihanish Golf Club, Argyll. A dramatic location on the Mull of Kintyre and some exciting match play makes these links well worth a journey.

Nairn Golf Club, Inverness-shire. The regular home of Scotland's Northern Open has huge greens, aggressive gorse, and distracting views across the Moray Firth.

St. Andrews Links, Fife. To approach the iconic 18th hole in the place where the game was invented remains the holy grail of golfers worldwide.

Turnberry, Ayrshire. Along the windswept Ayrshire coast, Turnberry's famous Ailsa Course pits golfers against the elements and, on one hole, a stretch of ocean.

Western Gailes Golf Club, near Glasgow. This splendid links course is a final qualifying course for the British Open. Sculpted by Mother Nature, it's the country's finest natural links course.

TIPS FOR VISITING HISTORIC HOUSES

Touring Britain's historic houses and castles isn't just a procession of beautiful photo ops; it's a living history lesson. From modest manor houses to the sprawling stately homes of the aristocracy, each building has something to tell about private life or the history of the nation, and often the story is presented in an entertaining way.

These places reveal the evolution of the country, from medieval fortresses planned for defense to architectural wonders that displayed the owner's power. Times, however, changed, and the aristocratic rewards of owning tracts of countryside, art, and family treasures encountered reality in the 20th century. Private owners opened homes to the public for a fee; hundreds of other homes and castles are now owned by organizations such as the National Trust or English Heritage, which raise part of the money needed to maintain them through entrance fees.

Keep in mind that houses and castles are unique. You may be free to wander at will, or you may be organized into groups like prisoners behind enemy lines. Sometimes the exterior of a building may be spectacular, but the interior dull. And the gardens and grounds may be just as interesting as (or more so than) the house. The individual reviews alert you to these instances, but you should study websites. You can often pay separately for the house and grounds.

Consider the kids (and those who don't love house tours). Some houses have activities or special events aimed at kids, especially in summer; some even have playgrounds. And many houses have gardens and extensive grounds that make a great day out for garden lovers or walkers.

Look into money-saving passes. If you plan to see lots of historic houses and castles, it might be cheaper to buy a pass, such as the ones from the National Trust, English Heritage, or National Trust for Scotland; Wales has the Cadw/Welsh Historic Monuments Explorer Pass. Or you can join an organization such as the National Trust (⇨ *See Sightseeing Passes in Essentials in Travel Smart Great Britain)* and thus get free entry.

Check seasonal opening hours. Hours can change abruptly, so call the day before or check online. Many houses are open only from April to October, and they may have unpredictable hours. In other cases the houses have celebrated parks and gardens that are open much of the year. Consider a trip in shoulder seasons if you can't take the crowds that pack the most popular houses. Some places are open during December.

Plan your transportation. Some places are very hard to reach without a car. Plan your transportation in advance—and remember that rural bus and train services can finish early!

Consider a stay at a property. You can rent a cottage from places such as the **National Trust** (⊕ *www.nationaltrustcottages. co.uk*) or **English Heritage** (⊕ *www. english-heritage.org.uk/holidaycottages*). Options include the servants' quarters, a lodge, or even a lighthouse. Some privately owned houses have cottages for rent on their estates; their websites generally have this information. The **Landmark Trust** (⊕ *www.landmarktrust.org. uk*) and **Vivat Trust** (⊕ *www.vivat-trust. org*) also have properties for rent. Some of these places are very popular, so plan well ahead.

TOP FESTIVALS AND EVENTS

1

Aldeburgh Festival. Classical music concerts, walks and talks takes place on the Suffolk coast in June. ⊕ *www.aldeburgh. co.uk.*

Burns Night. Ceremonial dinners are held throughout Scotland to celebrate poet Robert Burns on his birthday, January 25.

Celtic Connections. During the last two weeks of January, musicians gather in Glasgow to play Celtic-inspired music. ⊕ *www.celticconnections.com.*

Chelsea Flower Show. This five-day floral extravaganza is also a society event, held in London's Chelsea neighborhood. ⊕ *www.rhs.org.uk/chelsea.*

Edinburgh Festival. Taking over Scotland's capital every August, this cultural cornucopia is an amalgam of festivals running concurrently. Most prominent are the **Edinburgh International Festival**, featuring everything from opera to cutting-edge theater, and the rowdier **Edinburgh Fringe**, which highlights comedy and cabaret. ⊕ *www.eif.co.uk* and ⊕ *www.edfringe. co.uk.*

Eisteddfod. The **International Musical Eisteddfod** is a gathering of choirs and dancers from around the world in the Welsh town of Llangollen in July. The **National Eisteddfod of Wales** in August focuses on Welsh culture, alternating between venues in north and south Wales. ⊕ *www. international-eisteddfod.co.uk* and ⊕ *www.eisteddfod.org.uk.*

Glastonbury Festival. Iconic and idiosyncratic, this music event sprawls across Somerset farmland and features hundreds of bands over three days. ⊕ *www. glastonburyfestivals.co.uk.*

Guy Fawkes Day. A foiled attempt in 1605 to blow up Parliament is remembered every November 5, when fireworks are set off all over the country. Lewes and York stage some of the biggest festivities.

Hay Festival. As Britain's center for secondhand books, Hay-on-Wye makes a fitting venue for a lively literary jamboree in May. ⊕ *www.hayfestival.com*

Highland Games. This annual shindig takes place in Highland locations between May and September, and includes hammer throwing, caber tossing, and highland dancing. ⊕ *www.shga.co.uk.*

Hogmanay. Scotland's ancient, still-thriving New Year's bash extends over three days, with celebrations especially exuberant in Edinburgh. ⊕ *www. edinburghshogmanay.com*

Notting Hill Carnival. West London's Caribbean community takes to the streets at the end of August, with spectacular floats, costumes, and steel bands. ⊕ *www. thenottinghillcarnival.com*

The Proms. The main venue for this distinguished July–September series of classical-music concerts is in London's Royal Albert Hall. ⊕ *www.bbc.co.uk/proms*

Royal Henley Regatta. High society lines the banks of the Thames to cheer on rowers from around the world during this five-day event in early July. ⊕ *www.hrr.co.uk.*

St. David's Day. Leeks and daffodils are ubiquitous on Wales' national day on 1 March, with carnivals and processions in Cardiff and other places.

Shakespeare Birthday Celebrations. In late April, the Bard is celebrated with full pageantry and drama in his home town of Stratford-upon-Avon. ⊕ *www. shakespearescelebrations.com .*

Trooping the Colour. Queen Elizabeth's official birthday is marked in majestic style in mid-June in London's Horse Guards Parade. ⊕ *www.royal.gov.uk.*

GREAT ITINERARIES

HIGHLIGHTS OF BRITAIN: UNFORGETTABLE IMAGES

16 days

London

Days 1 and 2. The capital is just the jumping-off point for this trip, so choose a few highlights that grab your interest. If it's the Changing of the Guard at Buckingham Palace, check the time to be sure you catch the pageantry. If Westminster Abbey and the Tower of London appeal to your sense of history, arrive early. Pick a museum (many are free, so you needn't linger if you don't want to), whether it's the National Gallery in Trafalgar Square or the British Museum in Bloomsbury. Stroll Hyde Park or take a boat ride on the Thames before you find a pub or Indian restaurant for dinner. End with a play; the experience of theatergoing is not to be missed.

Salisbury and Stourhead

Day 3. Visible for miles around, Salisbury Cathedral's soaring spire is an unforgettable image of rural England. See the Magna Carta in the cathedral's Chapter House as you explore this marvel of medieval engineering, and walk the town path to get the view John Constable painted. Pay an afternoon visit to Stourhead to experience the finest example of the naturalistic 18th-century landscaping for which England is famous; the grand Palladian mansion is a bonus.

Logistics: For trains to Salisbury, use London's Waterloo Station.

Bath and Stonehenge

Day 4. Bath's immaculately preserved, golden-stone Georgian architecture helps you recapture the late 18th century. Take time to stroll; don't miss the Royal Crescent (you can explore the period interior of No. 1), and like a Jane Austen character, sip the Pump Room's natural water, which some say is vile-tasting. The Roman Baths are an amazing remnant of the ancient empire. Today you can do as the Romans did as you relax in the warm mineral waters at the Thermae Bath Spa. There's plenty to do in Bath (museums, shopping, theater), but you might make an excursion to Stonehenge (by car or tour bus). Go early or late to avoid the worst crowds at Stonehenge, and use your imagination—and the good audio guide—to appreciate this enigma.

Logistics: Trains and buses leave hourly from Salisbury to Bath.

Oxford and Blenheim Palace

Day 5. Join a guided tour of Oxford's glorious quadrangles, chapels, and gardens to get the best access to these centuries-old academic treasures. This leaves time for a jaunt to Blenheim, a unique combination of baroque opulence (inside and out) and naturalistic parkland, the work of the great 18th-century landscape designer Capability Brown. For classic Oxford experiences, rent a punt or join students and go pub-crawling around town.

Logistics: Hourly trains depart from Bath for Oxford. Buses frequently depart from Oxford's Gloucester Green for Blenheim Palace.

Stratford-upon-Avon and the Cotswolds

Days 6 and 7. In Stratford, fans of Shakespeare can see his birthplace and Anne Hathaway's Cottage, and then finish with a memorable performance at the Royal Shakespeare Company's main stage. Start the day early and be prepared for crowds. Use Stratford as a base to explore some pretty villages of the northern Cotswolds. See beautiful Chipping Campden, with its lost-in-time streets, and visit Hidcote Manor Garden. Antique-shop in fairy-tale Stow-on-the-Wold and feed the ducks at the brook in Lower Slaughter.

Logistics: From Oxford there are direct trains and a less frequent Stagecoach bus service. In the Cotswolds, drive to make the best of the beautiful scenery. Alternatively, opt for a guided tour bus.

North Wales and Chester

Days 8 and 9. Gain perspective on North Wales from the top of Conwy's medieval city walls, and take a tour to appreciate its awesome ruined castle, built by Edward I to intimidate the Welsh. Peruse the delights of Bodnant Garden, set against the backdrop of the mountains of Snowdonia. Head to the pleasantly old-fashioned Victorian resort town of Llandudno for a classic seaside stay, and take the cable car up Great Orme for great views. On the way back to England, stop in Chester, with its ancient (and some newer) half-timber buildings. The Rows, a series of two-story shops with medieval crypts beneath, and the fine city walls are sights you can't pass by. You can walk part or all of the city walls.

Logistics: The train to Conwy from Stratford takes about 4 hours and involves some changes.

The Lake District

Days 10 and 11. In the area extending around Windermere, explore the English lakes and beautiful surrounding mountains on foot in the Lake District National Park. This area is jam-packed with hikers in summer and on weekends, so rent a car to seek out the more isolated routes. Take a cruise on Windermere or Coniston Water, or rent a boat, for another classic Lakeland experience. If you have time for one Wordsworth-linked site, head to

Dove Cottage; you can even have afternoon tea there.

Logistics: Take the train to Oxenholme with a change at Warrington Bank Quay. At Oxenholme you can switch to Windermere. The trip takes about 2.5 hours.

Glasgow

Day 12. Scotland has astonishing variety in a small area. Glasgow, its largest city, hums with creative energy today. Check out its striking Victorian architecture downtown and take in the treasures at the Kelvingrove Art Gallery and Museum in the West End. Leave the city for Loch Lomond, Scotland's largest loch in terms of surface area; it's less than an hour's drive north of Glasgow. You can stop at Balloch and the Lochmond and the Trossachs National Park Headquarters. The winding banks of Loch Lomond can be easily followed by foot, car, or even boat.

Logistics: Take the train to Oxenholme and change for Glasgow; the trip is about 2.5 hours. You can take a tour or rent a car to see Loch Lomond.

Inverness and Loch Ness

Day 13 and 14. Inverness, about 175 miles north of Glasgow, is a useful base for exploring nearby sights in the Highlands. Here you are in the Great Glen, a valley crisscrossed by sparking rivers and ringed by brooding mountains. This is castle country, and rich in history. Possible excursions near Inverness are Culloden Moor, site of a major defeat for Bonnie Prince Charlie in 1746, as well as Cawdor Castle. Urquhart Castle, near famous Loch Ness, is a favorite spot.

Logistics: The train to Inverness takes about 3 hours and may involve changing in Perth. For the excursions, it's easiest to take a tour or rent a car.

Edinburgh

Day 15 and 16. Finish your trip in grand style in Scotland's capital; you'll most likely need to transfer to Glasgow Airport for your flight home. Three sights are critical to understanding the city and Scotland: Edinburgh Castle, the Palace of Holyroodhouse, and the new Scottish Parliament. But don't let sightseeing exhaust you. Just take a stroll among the ancient buildings along the Royal Mile in Old Town or explore the neoclassical grandeur of New Town to appreciate the lasting legacies of the city's influence and prosperity. Be sure to stop in one of the city's pubs for a well-deserved beer or a wee dram of whisky.

Logistics: The train to Edinburgh takes about 3.5 to 4 hours.

TIPS

■ Train travelers should keep in mind that regional "Rovers" and "Rangers" offer unlimited train travel in one-day, three-day, or weeklong increments. See ⊕ *www. nationalrail.co.uk* for details. Also check out BritRail passes, which must be purchased before your trip.

■ Buses are time-consuming, but more scenic and cheaper than train travel. National Express offers discounts including fun fares—fares to and from London to various cities for as low as £5 if booked more than 24 hours in advance. Or check out low-cost Megabus.

■ You can adjust this itinerary to your interests. If Scotland is important, for example, you might skip Wales and proceed to Glasgow from the Lake District. Or you can pass up Glasgow for excursions from Inverness. You can add the time to your London stay or another place you want to linger.

■ It's easy to visit Stonehenge from Salisbury, as well as from Bath, whether you have a car or want a guided excursion.

■ Buy theater tickets well in advance for Stratford-upon-Avon. And if you are in Edinburgh during festival season in August, plan ahead.

GREAT ITINERARIES

HISTORIC HOUSES AND LANDSCAPES OF ENGLAND

11 days

Hampton Court Palace

Day 1. Start your trip royally at this palace a half hour from London by train. It's two treasures in one: a Tudor palace with magnificent baroque additions by Christopher Wren. As you walk through cobbled courtyards, Henry VIII's State Apartments, and the enormous kitchens, you may feel as if you've been whisked back to the days of the Tudors and William and Mary. A quiet stroll through the 60 acres of immaculate gardens—the sculpted yews look like huge green gumdrops—is recommended. Be sure to get lost in the 18th-century maze—if it's open (diligent maintenance leads to occasional closures). It's easy to spend a whole day here, so start early.

Logistics: Tube to Richmond, then Bus R68; or catch the train from Waterloo to Hampton Court Station.

Knole and Ightham Mote

Days 2 and 3. Clustered around Royal Tunbridge Wells south of London is the highest concentration of stately homes in England, and, as if that weren't enough, the surrounding fields and colorful orchards are often wrapped in clouds of mist, creating a picture-perfect scene. These two homes are very different and you'll have plenty of time to tour each one at a leisurely pace. Knole, Vita Sackville-West's sprawling childhood home, has dark, baroque rooms and a famous set of silver furniture. Ightham Mote, a smaller, moated house, is a vision from the Middle Ages. Its rooms are an ideal guide to style changes from the Tudor to Victorian eras. Spend the evening at one of the many good restaurants in Royal Tunbridge Wells.

Logistics: Take the train from London's Charing Cross to Sevenoaks, from which it's a 20-minute walk to Knole. There's no public transportation to Ightham Mote.

Petworth House

Day 4. Priceless paintings by Gainsborough, Reynolds, and Turner (19 by Turner alone) embellish the august rooms of Petworth House, present-day home to Lord and Lady Egremont and one of the National Trust's treasures. Check out Capability Brown's 700-acre deer park or the Victorian kitchens, and for the perfect lunch peruse the offerings in the winding lanes of Petworth town. Head to Chichester for the evening, along a route passing through the rolling grasslands and deep valleys of the South Downs.

Logistics: Train to Chichester, switching in Redhill, then bus to Petworth.

Wilton House

Day 5. Base yourself in Salisbury for two days, taking time to see the famous cathedral with its impressively tall spire and to walk the town path from the Long Bridge for the best view of it. Visit neoclassical Wilton House (in nearby Wilton) first, where the exquisite Double Cube Room contains a spectacular family portrait by Van Dyck and gilded furniture that accommodated Eisenhower when he contemplated the Normandy invasion here. On your way back make a detour to Stonehenge to view the wide-open Salisbury Plain and ponder the enigmatic stones.

Logistics: Take a train from Chichester to Salisbury, with a switch in Cosham or Southampton; then bus it to Wilton House.

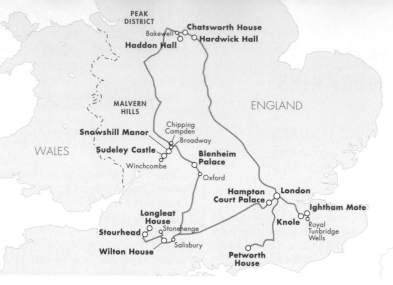

Stourhead to Longleat House

Day 6. Day-trip west from Salisbury to Stourhead to experience perhaps the most stunning house-garden combination in the country, and either spend the day here (climb Alfred's Tower for a grand view of the house) or leave some time for nearby Longleat House—a vast, treasure-stuffed Italian Renaissance palace complete with safari park and a devilish maze. If you want to see the safari park, you'll need plenty of time here. Once back in Salisbury, relax in one of New Street's many cafés.

Logistics: Bus to Warminster and then take a taxi for the 5-mile journey to Longleat; for Stourhead, take the train to Gillingham from Salisbury, followed by a short cab ride.

Blenheim Palace

Day 7. Home of the dukes of Marlborough and birthplace of Winston Churchill, Blenheim Palace uniquely combines exquisitely designed parklands (save time to walk) and one of the most ornate baroque structures in the world. Overnight in Oxford; do your own pub crawl.

Logistics: From Salisbury by train, change at Basingstoke for Oxford, then catch a bus to Blenheim.

Snowshill Manor and Sudeley Castle

Days 8 and 9. Here you can take in the idyllic Cotswold landscape, a magical mix of greenery and mellow stone cottages and ancient churches (built with wool-trade money), along with some famous buildings. Spend the first night in Broadway to explore nearby Snowshill Manor—with its delightfully eccentric collection of Tibetan scrolls, Persian lamps, and samurai armor—in the unspoiled village of Snowshill. If you have a car, don't linger in busy Broadway. Instead, head to Chipping Campden, one of the best-preserved Cotswolds villages, which nestles in a secluded valley. Nearby, visit Sudeley Castle, once home to Catherine Parr (Henry VIII's last wife), a Tudor-era palace with romantic gardens.

Logistics: Take a train from Oxford to Moreton-in-Marsh for the bus to Broadway; from Broadway, walk the 2½ miles to Snowshill Manor; for Sudeley Castle, take a bus from Broadway to Winchcombe, then walk.

Chatsworth House, Haddon Hall, and Hardwick Hall

Days 10 and 11. For the final stops, head north, east of Manchester, to a more dramatic landscape. In or near the craggy

Peak District, where the gentle slopes of the Pennine Hills begin their ascent to Scotland, are three of England's most renowned historic homes. Base yourself in Bakewell, and spend your first day taking in the art treasures amassed by the dukes of Devonshire at Chatsworth House. The gardens, grounds, shops, and farmyard exhibits make it easy to spend a day here. If you have any time left over, get out of Bakewell and take a walk in the hills of the Peak District National Park (maps are available at the town's tourist information center).

On the second day, devote the morning to the crenellations and boxy roofs of medieval Haddon Hall, a quintessentially English house. Give your afternoon to Hardwick Hall, an Elizabethan stone mansion with a facade that's "more glass than wall"—a truly innovative idea in the 16th century. Its collections of period tapestries and embroideries are remarkable reminders of the splendor of the age.

Logistics: Take a train back to Oxford and then up to Manchester for the connection to Buxton; then catch a bus to Bakewell.

TIPS

■ All stately homes in this itinerary, with the exception of Hampton Court Palace and Longleat House, are closed for winter, though gardens may remain open. Even homes open April through October may not be open every day. It's best to confirm all hours before visiting.

■ A car is best for this itinerary, as some houses are remote. Use GPS or get good maps.

■ Country roads around the Peak District are hard to negotiate; be especially careful when driving to Chatsworth House, Haddon Hall, and Hardwick Hall. Drives will take longer than you expect.

■ Look into discount passes, such as those from the National Trust or English Heritage (⇨ *See Sightseeing Passes in Essentials in Travel Smart Great Britain*), which provide significant savings on visits to multiple sites. Memberships are also available.

GREAT ITINERARIES

HIGHLIGHTS OF SCOTLAND: CASTLES, LOCHS, GOLF, AND WHISKY

10 days
Edinburgh

Days 1 and 2. The capital of Scotland is loaded with iconic sights in its Old Town and New Town. Visit Edinburgh Castle and the National Gallery of Scotland, and take tours of the National Museum of Scotland and the modern Scottish Parliament building. Walk along Old Town's Royal Mile and New Town's George Street for some fresh air and retail therapy. When the sun goes down, feast on the food of your choice and seek out a traditional pub with live music that will keep your toes tapping.

Logistics: Fly into Edinburgh Airport if you're flying via London and take a taxi or bus to the city center. If you're flying directly into Glasgow from overseas, make your way from Glasgow Airport to Queen Street Station via taxi or bus. It takes an hour to travel from Glasgow to Edinburgh by car or bus, about 45 minutes to an hour by train. Once in the city, explore on foot or by public transportation or taxi. There's no need to rent a car.

Stirling to St. Andrews

Day 3. Rent a car in Edinburgh and drive to the historic city of Stirling. Spend the day visiting Stirling Castle and the National Wallace Monument. Then drive to the legendary seaside town of St. Andrews, famous for golf. Have dinner at one of the city's seafood restaurants.

Logistics: Leave Edinburgh after 9 am to miss the worst of the rush-hour traffic. It's 35 miles or a one-hour drive to

Stirling from Edinburgh, and 50 miles and 90 minutes from Stirling to St. Andrews. You can easily take a train or bus to these destinations.

St. Andrews to Inverness

Day 4. Spend the morning exploring St. Andrews, known for its castle and the country's oldest university as well as its famous golf courses. The British Golf Museum is here, too. If you've booked well in advance (the time varies by season), play a round of golf. After lunch, drive to Inverness. Along the way, stretch your legs at one of Scotland's notable sights, Blair Castle (just off the A9 and 10 miles north of Pitlochry), a turreted white treasure with a war-torn past. Head to Inverness in the Highlands for the night.

Logistics: It's 150 miles from St. Andrews to Inverness via the A9, a drive that will take 3½ hours. This is a scenic journey, so do stop along the way. You can also take a train or bus.

Around Inverness and Castle Country

Day 5. Use Inverness as a base for exploring the Northeast, a region known for tempting castles and whisky distilleries. Don't visit too many sights or your day may become a forced march; two to three castles or distilleries are a good number. Some of the region's most interesting castles are Balmoral, popular because of its royal connection to Queen Elizabeth, and Castle Fraser, which has beautiful gardens. Keep Inverness as your base because of the number of restaurants and entertainment venues.

Alternatives: Prefer whisky to castles? Explore distilleries both on and off the Malt Whisky Trail in Speyside, near Inverness. Balvenie, Glenlivet, and Glen Grant are good choices; check hours and tour times, and note that some distilleries

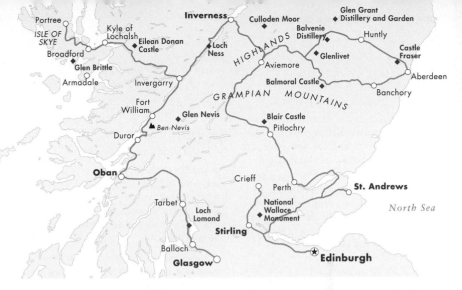

require prebooking. Another option for the day is to visit Loch Ness, though it's not one of Scotland's prettiest lochs; still, perhaps you'll spot Nessie. It's a 20-minute drive from Inverness. Just east of Inverness is Culloden Moor, where Bonnie Prince Charlie's forces were destroyed by the Duke of Cumberland's army.

Logistics: A car is best for this part of your journey. Rent one in Inverness or sign up for an organized tour; public transportation is not a viable option. Castles are often closed in winter; check in advance. It's about 1½ hours from Inverness to Balmoral, and Castle Fraser is 40 miles (90 minutes) from Balmoral. The distilleries are about 90 minutes from Inverness. Some distances between distilleries are 18 miles (50 minutes) from Balvenie to Glenlivet; 17 miles (30 minutes) from Glenlivet to Glen Grant.

The Isle of Skye

Day 6. Leave Inverness early and head south to Skye. The drive to the island is peaceful and full of raw landscapes and big, open horizons. Stop at Eilean Donan Castle on the way. Set on an island among three lochs, the castle is the stuff postcards are made of. Explore Skye; Glen Brittle is the perfect place to enjoy mountain scenery; and Armadale is a good place to go

crafts shopping. End up in Portree for dinner and the night.

Logistics: It's 80 miles (a two-hour drive) from Inverness to Skye. Public transportation is possible but connections can take time, so it's best to have the freedom of a car.

Oban via Ben Nevis

Day 7. Leave Skye no later than 9 am and head for Fort William. The town isn't worth stopping for, but the view of Britain's highest mountain, the 4,406-foot Ben Nevis, is. If time permits, take a hike in Glen Nevis. Continue on to Oban, a traditional Scottish resort town on the water. At night, feast on fish-and-chips in a local pub.

Logistics: It's nearly 100 miles from Skye to Oban; the drive is 3½ hours without stopping. Public transportation is an option but a challenging one.

Loch Lomond to Glasgow

Days 8 and 9. Enjoy a leisurely morning in Oban and take a waterfront stroll. Mid-morning, set off for Glasgow via Loch Lomond. Stop at the Loch Lomond and the Trossachs National Park Headquarters in Balloch on the loch and take a walk along the bonnie banks. Arrive in Glasgow in time for dinner; take in a play or concert. Spend the next day and night visiting the sights: Kelvingrove Art Gallery and Museum and the new Riverside Museum are a couple of highlights.

Logistics: It's 127 miles (a three-hour drive) from Oban to Glasgow via Balloch. Traveling by train is a possibility, but you won't be able to go via Balloch. Return your rental car in Glasgow; it's easy to travel around the city on foot or by subway or train.

Glasgow and Home

Day 10. On your final day, stow your suitcases at your hotel and hit Buchanan and Sauchiehall Streets for some of Britain's best shopping. Clothes, whisky, and tartan items are good things to look for.

Logistics: It's less than 10 miles (15 minutes) by taxi to Glasgow's international airport in Paisley but more than 30 miles (40 minutes) to the international airport in Prestwick. Be sure you have the correct airport information.

TIPS

■ You can begin this itinerary in Glasgow and finish in Edinburgh, or adjust the timing to your interests. For example, if you enjoy castles, you might stay in Inverness longer; if you like golf, St. Andrews may deserve more time.

■ August is festival season in Edinburgh; make reservations there well in advance during that month.

■ Remember to drive on the left side of the road and keep alert, especially on small, narrow country roads. Travel will take longer on smaller roads.

■ Weather is unpredictable; always dress in layers. Hikers should bring a map and compass for anything other than a ramble and always tell someone where they're going. Golfers and everyone else should carry rain gear.

■ Pack bug repellent for the midges (small, biting insects that travel in swarms). These insects breed in stagnant water, but they are *everywhere* from May through September.

■ Check distillery tour times and book arrangements in advance. When visiting distilleries, choose a designated driver or take a bus tour. Drunken drivers aren't tolerated.

THE MARKET PORTER

Bar Meals

FINE WINES
Continental Lagers

TRADITIONAL
ALES

FULL MENU

SEE YOU AT THE PUB

Pubs have been called "Britain's living rooms": more than just a bar or a place to drink, they are gathering places, conversation zones. A trip to a pub ranks high on most visitors' list of things to do, and that's not surprising: in many ways, pubs *are* Britain. You simply haven't experienced the country properly until you've been to one.

Pubs started appearing in the late 15th century, when whole communities would gather at the pub to meet and swap news. The very name—pub is short for "public house"—sums up their role. As towns grew into cities, the humble pub came to be seen as an antidote to the anonymity of modern life. Today many pubs are places to relax and socialize. It's not always all about drinking. Pubs can be good places for lunch as well, and during the day they're often family environ-

ments, before giving way to a lively, adults-only crowd at night.

Despite all this, the pub industry faces changing times and tastes, and competition from modern entertainment. In 2014 pubs were closing at the rate of around 26 per week. Although the adage about British town centers having a pub on every corner still just about rings true, times are tough. But still, the pub endures.

—by Jack Jewers

(Top) People gather outside the Market Porter pub at Borough Market in London, (bottom) Discovery Blonde Beer, Fuller's

CHOOSING A PUB

Pubs vary enormously, and that's a wonderful thing: in cities you may find splendid Victorian survivors; in England there are Tudor pubs with atmospheric wood beams and warm fires. In Scotland they may be attached to rural hotels.

To find a pub, ask the locals: everyone knows the good ones. Otherwise, if a pub looks attractive and well kept, check it out. Telltale signs that it's probably not the best include banners advertising lagers and "2-for-1" deals, or TV sports channels. Some basic definitions are useful:

A **freehouse** is a pub that is not tied to a single brewery, which means it can sell as many varieties of beer and wine as it likes. **Chain pubs** affiliated with particular breweries are middle-of-the-road, inexpensive franchises that serve decent food and drink. Bass, Wetherspoons, Courage, Whitbread, and Young's are chains; you will see their names on the pub's sign. **Gastropubs** serve very high-quality food, but a pub with good food isn't necessarily a gastropub: the name implies culinary aspirations, and some expense. In England **"the local"** is shorthand for a favorite pub in your community, though the term is also used generally to refer to any pub that's good for cozy, convivial conversation.

CAN I TAKE MY KIDS TO THE PUB?

As pubs emphasize what's coming out of the kitchen rather than what's flowing out of the tap, whether to bring the kids has become a question. By law, patrons must be 18 in order to drink alcohol in a pub. Children 14 to 17 may enter a pub, but, children under 14 are not permitted in the bar area of a pub unless it has a "children's certficate" and they are accompanied by an adult. In general, however, some pubs have a section set aside for families—especially during the day. Check with the bartender. Some pubs actively encourage families and have play areas and a kid-friendly menu.

(Left) The Flask, Hampstead, London, (Right) Lamb and Flag pub, Covent Garden, London

PUB ETIQUETTE AND BASICS

Ordering: You order drinks from the bartender, known in Britain as the "barman" or "barmaid"—and pay up front. Don't be put off by a crowd at the bar. Never be impatient; wait as close to the bar as possible and they'll get to you. At most pubs you also order food from the bar and it is brought to you. Credit cards are common but likely require a minimum of £10.

Tipping: If you're only buying drinks, don't tip. They will think you've forgotten your change.

The round: If you're with friends, generally everyone takes turns buying drinks for the group. This is called a "round."

Smoking: Sorry, no: smoking has been banned since 2007.

Hours: In small towns, most pubs stick to the traditional hours of 11 am–11 pm (10:30 pm on Sunday), with the exception of Friday and Saturday nights. In large towns and cities, a few stay open past midnight, sometimes as late as 2 am.

Music: Some pubs have live music, usually local bands that vary in quality; but even big stars started out like this. You're not usually expected to pay.

Conversation: People don't generally get involved in a stranger's discussions, but for the best chance to chat with locals, hang out at the bar.

"Last orders please!": This is the traditional call of a landlord 20 minutes before closing, usually accompanied by a bell and a rush to buy drinks. When 20 minutes is up, they'll yell "Time please!" Then you have a few minutes to finish up.

DO I HAVE TO DRINK?

It's fine to go to a pub and not drink alcohol. They're social places first, watering holes second. All pubs serve soft drinks and most have tea and coffee. Other popular alternatives include lime and soda water; orange juice and lemonade; and mineral water (with ice and lemon).

WHEN TO GO?

The British take their drink seriously, and pubs are where people go to hang out and, sometimes, drink heavily. Unless you're checking a place out on recommendation (a good idea), you may want to pick a midweek night for your first pub experience. On Friday and Saturday nights, rowdy young drinkers can take over some pubs.

KNOW YOUR BEER

Whether you're ordering a pint (the usual quantity), or a "half" (for half-pint), you have plenty of options, including draft picks and more expensive imported bottled beers. You can discuss your choice with the barman and then turn to your neighbor and utter that amiable toast, "Cheers!"

ALE. The most quintessentially English type of beer is brewed from barley and hops and usually served at cellar (cooler than room, but not chilled) temperature. The term *real ale* distinguishes the traditionally made product, containing only authentic ingredients and no carbonation, from mass-produced alternatives; real ales have a devoted following. The flavor of ales varies greatly, from nutty and bitter to light and sweet. *Common varieties include Adnams Broadside; Belhaven; Greene King I.P.A.; Newcastle Brown Ale.*

Adnams Broadside

BITTER. This is the generic name for bitter ales in England; in Scotland they are called "heavy." They vary greatly in strength; bitters with the word "best" after their name are medium; "premium," "strong," or "special" are the strongest. *Bitters to try include Leuchars London Pride, and Courage Directors.*

LAGER. Often imported, these carbonated, light, pale beers are usually mass produced, and they're extremely popular. Lager is always served chilled. What Americans call beer, the British call lager.

London Pride

STOUT. Stouts are dark beers made with roasted barley or malt. These days the market seems to have been cornered by Guinness, now served cold and on tap. *Try Guinness (the Irish favorite) or Fuller's London Porter.*

WHEAT BEER. These beers brewed from wheat are mostly imported from Europe. They are often white in color and have a malty taste. *Try Hoegaarden or Erdinger.*

Fuller's
London Porter

MORE CHOICES

CIDER. Made with apples, cider is like its American namesake—but alcoholic. Ciders can be sweet or dry. Try Magners or Strongbow.

LAGER TOPS. A pint of lager with a splash of lemonade on top is a lager top. A 50/50 version of the same thing is called a shandy; this traditional summer afternoon drink is worth a try.

SNAKEBITE. Half lager and half cider, snakebite is usually served with a splash of blackcurrant cordial as a "snakebite and black."

(top) Magners cider, (bottom) Newcastle Brown Ale

EATING AT THE PUB

(left) Traditional ploughman's lunch, (right) Steak and kidney pie

In the 1980s, the best you might hope for in a pub was a sandwich or a plate of cold meats and cheese. The gastropub revolution of the 1990s forced everybody to raise their game. Popular chain pubs, such as Wetherspoons and The Slug and Lettuce, offer decent meals, especially at lunchtime. Don't want a full meal? Most pubs will fix you a bowl of chips (thick-cut French fries) or other hot nibbles. If pubs have specials boards or a menu prominently displayed outside, they're probably worth a shot for a meal. Pub fare includes anything from lasagna to burgers, but look for these traditional favorites:

■ Savory pies, such as steak and ale or chicken and bacon. Just make sure they're homemade.

■ Bangers and mash (sausage links and mashed potato), especially if the sausages are "butchers" or "local."

■ Ploughman's lunch, with cheese, pickles, and crackers.

■ Fish and chips may seem like a good pick, but avoid it in city pubs because proper fish and chips shops are usually better. Near the coast, though, pubs that advertise local seafood may be the best place for fish and chips.

■ Sunday roasts, another culinary tradition, are hearty feasts—and pubs are usually the best places to sample them. Even pubs not noted for their food can pull out excellent roasts at Sunday lunchtime, and the best places get packed; you may need a reservation. The centerpiece is roast beef, chicken, pork, or lamb, served with roast potatoes and vegetables, covered in thin, rich, dark gravy. Each meat has its traditional accompaniment; Yorkshire pudding (light, fluffy batter, resembling a soufflé) and horseradish sauce with beef; mint jelly with lamb. It's a treat to savor.

PUB QUIZZES AND GAMES

Many pubs hold general knowledge quizzes on a weekday evening, and anybody can enter. It's usually a pound each, which goes into a pot as prize money. Quizzes are a fun and relaxed way to socialize with locals, although it helps to know some British sports and pop culture.

Video gaming machines are a common, if jarringly modern feature, in many pubs. They're the latest additions to a longtime custom, though. Traditional pub games include darts, dominoes, and chess—plus more arcane pastimes now found only rarely in the countryside. These include bar billiards, a miniature version of pool crossed with skittles; and Nine Men's Morris, similar to backgammon.

LONDON

WELCOME TO LONDON

TOP REASONS TO GO

★ **The abbey and the cathedral:** That Gothic splendor, Westminster Abbey, soars above the final resting place of some of Britain's most distinguished figures. To the east, St. Paul's Cathedral is a beautiful English baroque cathedral.

★ **Buckingham Palace:** Although not the prettiest royal residence, this is the public face of the monarchy and the place to watch the culmination of the Changing the Guard ceremony.

★ **Tower of London:** Parts of this complex date back 11 centuries. The tower has been a prison, an armory, and a mint—now it houses the Crown Jewels.

★ **Majestic museums:** From the old masters at the National Gallery to the cutting-edge works at Tate Modern and the historical artifacts of the British Museum, the choices overwhelm.

★ **A city of villages:** Each of London's dozens of neighborhoods has its own personality, with parks, shops, and pubs.

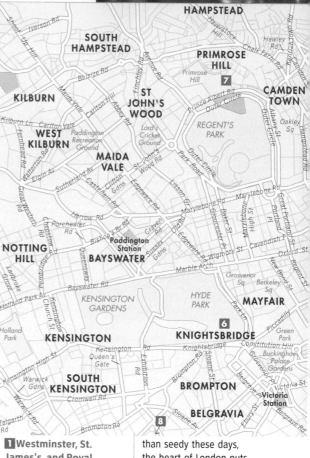

1 Westminster, St. James's, and Royal London. Embrace your inner tourist. Take pictures of the mounted Horse Guards, and drink in the old masters at the National Gallery. It's well worth braving the crowds to visit historic Westminster Abbey.

2 Soho and Covent Garden. More sophisticated than seedy these days, the heart of London puts Theatreland, strip joints, Chinatown, and notable restaurants side by side.

3 Bloomsbury and Holborn. The University of London dominates the city's historical intellectual center, Bloomsbury. Allow for long visits to the incomparable British Museum.

2

GETTING ORIENTED

London grew from a wooden bridge built over the Thames in the year AD 43 to its current 600 square miles and 8.3 million inhabitants in haphazard fashion, expanding from two centers of power: Westminster, seat of government and royalty, to the west, and the City, site of finance and commerce, to the east. The patchwork of urban villages is ever evolving, though the great parks, described by Lord Chatham as "the lungs of London," and the River Thames remain constants.

filled with treasures. Shopaholics should head for Bond Street and Sloane Street, Selfridges, and Harvey Nichols.

7 Regent's Park and Hampstead. London becomes noticeably calmer and greener as you head north from Euston Road. Come here to experience just how laid-back moneyed Londoners can be.

8 Up and Down the Thames. Maritime Greenwich boasts masterpieces by Wren and Inigo Jones. Other river excursions take you to Kew Gardens and Hampton Court Palace.

4 The City. London's Wall Street might be the oldest part of the capital, but thanks to the futuristic skyscrapers and a sleek Millennium Bridge, it looks like the newest. There's plenty for architecture buffs as well: St. Paul's Cathedral, Westminster Abbey, and the Tower of London.

5 The South Bank. The National Theatre, Old Vic, Royal Festival Hall, BFI Southbank, Shakespeare's Globe, and Tate Modern make this area a cultural hub. Get a bird's-eye view of the whole city from the Shard or the London Eye.

6 Kensington, Knightsbridge, and Mayfair. Kensington's museums are

Updated by
Julius Honnor,
Jack Jewers,
James O'Neill,
Ellin Stein,
and Alex
Wijeratna

If London's only attraction were its famous landmarks, it would still be unmissable. But London is so much more. Though its long history is evident at every turn, it's also one of the world's most modern and vibrant cities.

London beckons with great museums, royal pageantry, and historically significant buildings. Unique Georgian terraces perch next to cutting-edge modern skyscrapers, and parks and squares provide unexpected oases of greenery amid the dense urban landscape. Modern central London still largely follows its winding medieval street pattern. Even Londoners armed with the indispensable *London A–Z* street finder or equivalent app can get lost in their own city.

As well as visiting landmarks like St. Paul's Cathedral and the Tower of London, set aside time for random wandering; the city repays every moment spent exploring its backstreets and mews on foot. Go to lesser-known but thoroughly rewarding sites such as Kensington Palace and the unique home of 19th-century architect Sir John Soane, which houses his outstanding collection of antiquities and art.

Today the city's art, style, fashion, and restaurant scenes make headlines around the world. London's chefs have become internationally influential, its fashion designers and art stars set global trends, its nightlife continues to produce exciting new acts, and its theater remains celebrated for superb classical and innovative productions.

Then there's that greatest living link with the past—the Royal Family. Don't let fear of looking like a tourist stop you from enjoying the pageantry of the Changing the Guard at Buckingham Palace, one of the greatest free shows in the world.

As the eminent 18th-century man of letters Samuel Johnson said, "When a man is tired of London, he is tired of life, for there is in London all that life can afford." Armed with energy and curiosity, you can discover its riches.

LONDON PLANNER

2

WHEN TO GO

The heaviest tourist season runs from mid-April through mid-October, with another peak around Christmas—though the tide never really ebbs. Spring is the time to see the royal London parks and gardens at their freshest, fall to enjoy near-ideal exploring conditions. In late summer, be warned: air-conditioning is rarely found in places other than department stores, modern restaurants, hotels, and cinemas, although it's really needed for only a few days. Winter can be rather dismal, but all the theaters, concerts, and exhibitions go full speed ahead.

Avoid the February and October "half-terms" when schools in the capital take a break for a week and children flood nearly all the attractions. The start of August can be a very busy time, and the weather makes Tube travel a nightmare. Shopping in central London the week before Christmas is an idea best left only to desperate Londoners who have forgotten to buy presents.

GETTING HERE AND AROUND

ADDRESSES

Central London and its surrounding inner suburbs are divided into 32 boroughs—33, counting the City of London. More useful for finding your way around, however, are the subdivisions of London into postal districts. The first one or two letters give the location: N means north, NW means northwest, and so on.

AIR TRAVEL

For information about airports and airport transfers, see Getting Here and Around in Travel Smart Great Britain.

BUS TRAVEL

In central London, Transport for London (TfL) buses are traditionally bright red double- and single-deckers. Not all buses run the full length of their route at all times, so check with the driver. In central London you must purchase tickets from machines at bus stops along the routes before you board. The main bus stops have a red TfL symbol on a white background. When the word "Request" is written across the sign, you must flag the bus down. Buses are a good way to see the town, but don't take one if you're in a hurry.

All journeys cost £2.40, and there are no transfers. If you plan to make a number of journeys in one day, consider buying a Day Travelcard, good for both Tube and bus travel. Weekly Travelcards are also available. Prepaid Oyster cards can offer a considerable saving, with single journeys costing £1.45. Visitor Oyster cards cost £10 and can be topped up. They are available from the Gatwick Express desks at Gatwick airport and Victoria Station, or in advance through VisitBritain (⊕ *www.visitbritainshop.com*). Traveling without a valid ticket makes you liable for a fine (£20).

Night buses, denoted by an "N" before their route numbers, run from midnight to 5 am on a more restricted route than day buses. However, some night bus routes should be approached with caution and the top deck avoided. All night buses run by request stop, so flag them down if you're waiting, or push the button if you want to alight.

Buses, or "coaches," as privately operated bus services are known here, operate mainly from London's Victoria Coach Station to more than 1,200 major towns and cities. *For information, see Getting Here and Around in Travel Smart Great Britain.*

Contact Transport for London ☎ *0843/222–1234* ⊕ *www.tfl.gov.uk.*

CAR TRAVEL

The major approach roads to London are six-lane motorways. Motorways (from Heathrow, M4; from Gatwick, M23 to M25, then M3; Stansted, M11) are usually the faster option for getting in and out of town, although rush-hour traffic is horrendous. Stay tuned to local radio stations for updates.

The simple advice about driving in London is: don't. If you must drive, remember to drive on the left and stick to the speed limit (30 mph on some city streets, in the process of changing to 20 mph in several boroughs).

To encourage public-transit use and reduce traffic congestion, the city charges drivers of most vehicles entering central London £10 on weekdays from 7 am to 6 pm (excluding public holidays). Traffic signs designate the entrance to congestion-charge zones, and cameras read car license plates and send the information to a database. Drivers who don't pay up by midnight of the next charging day are penalized £120 (reduced to £60 if paid within 14 days).

TAXI TRAVEL

Taxis are expensive, but if you're with several people they can be practical. Hotels and main tourist areas have taxi ranks; you can also hail taxis on the street. If the yellow "For Hire" sign is lighted on top, the taxi is available. Fares start at £2.20, and there are per-minute charges— a journey of a mile that takes five minutes will cost £4.90, one that takes 12 minutes will cost £8.60. Taxi fares increase between 10 pm and 6 am, and a £2 surcharge is applied to telephone bookings. You don't have to tip taxi drivers, but it's advised; 10% of the fare is the norm, and most passengers round up to the nearest pound.

TRAIN TRAVEL

London has eight major train stations, each serving a different area of the country, and all are accessible by Underground or bus. Various private companies operate trains, but National Rail Enquiries acts as a central rail information number. *For more information on train travel, see Getting Here and Around in Travel Smart Great Britain.*

Contact National Rail Enquiries ☎ *0845/748–4950, 020/7278–5240 outside U.K.* ⊕ *www.nationalrail.co.uk.*

UNDERGROUND (TUBE) TRAVEL

London's extensive Underground (Tube) system has color-coded routes, clear signs, and far-reaching connections. Trains run out into the suburbs, and all stations are marked with the London Underground circular symbol. (In Britain, subway means "pedestrian underpass.") Some lines have branches (Central, District, Northern, Metropolitan, and Piccadilly), so be sure to note which branch is needed for your destination. Electronic platform signs indicate the final stop and route of the next train and how many minutes until it arrives. The London Overground now travels in a loop around Zone 2, calling at Shepherd's Bush in the west, Hampstead Heath in the North, Shoreditch High Street in the east, and Clapham Junction in the south, plus stations in between.

London is divided into six concentric zones (ask at Underground ticket booths for a map and booklet, which give details of the ticket options). For one-way fares paid in cash, a flat £4.70 price per journey applies between Zones 1 and 3, whether you're traveling for one stop or 12. If you're planning several trips in one day, it's much cheaper to buy a Visitor Oyster card or Day Travelcard, which are good for unrestricted travel on the Tube, buses, and Overground trains. The off-peak Oyster-card fare for Zones 1 and 2, for example, is £2.20. A one-day Travelcard for Zones 1 and 2 costs £9 if purchased before 9:30 am, and £8.90 if bought after 9:30 am. The more zones included in your travel, the more the Travelcard will cost.

Daily except Sunday, trains begin running just after 5 am; the last services leave central London between midnight and 12:30 am. On Sunday, trains start two hours later and finish about an hour earlier. The frequency of trains depends on the route and the time of day, but normally you won't have to wait more than 10 minutes in central areas.

DISCOUNTS AND DEALS

All national collections (such as the Natural History Museum, Science Museum, Victoria & Albert Museum) are free, a real bargain for museumgoers. *For other discounts, see Sightseeing Passes in Essentials in Travel Smart Great Britain.*

TOUR OPTIONS

BIKE TOURS

A 24-hour cycle-for-hire scheme, the Barclays Cycle Hire, introduced in 2010 to enable Londoners to pick up a bicycle at one of more than 570 docking stations and return it at another, has proved very popular. The first 30 minutes are free. After that, charges rise incrementally from £1 for one hour up to £50 for 24 hours. There is also a £2 per-day access charge. Fees are payable online, by phone, and at docking stations, by credit or debit card only—cash is not accepted. But whether you join the scheme or just rent a bike from a shop, remember that London is still a busy metropolis: the best way to see it on two wheels is probably to contact one of the excellent cycle tour companies.

Tour Operators Barclays Cycle Hire ☏ *0845/026–3630 within U.K., 208/216-6666 from outside U.K.* ⊕ *www.tfl.gov.uk/roadusers.*
Cycle Tours of London ☏ *0778/899-4430* ⊕ *www.biketoursoflondon.com.*
Fat Tire Bike Tours ☏ *0788/233-8779* ⊕ *www.fattirebiketours.com.*
London Bicycle Tour Company ☏ *020/3318-3088* ⊕ *www.londonbicycle.com.*

BOAT TOURS

Year-round, but more frequently from April to October, tour boats cruise the Thames, offering a singular view of the London skyline. Most leave from Westminster Pier, Charing Cross Pier, and Tower Pier. Boats on downstream routes pass by the Tower of London, Greenwich, and the Thames Barrier. Upstream destinations include Kew, Richmond, and

Hampton Court (mainly in summer). Depending upon the destination, river trips may last from one to four hours.

London's tranquil side can be experienced on narrow boats that cruise the city's two canals, the Grand Union and the Regent's Canal; most vessels operate on the latter, which runs between Little Venice in the west (nearest Tube: Warwick Avenue, on the Bakerloo Line) and Camden Lock (about 200 yards north of the Camden Town Tube station). Fares start at £9 for 1½-hour round-trip cruises.

Contacts Bateaux London ☎ *020/7695–1800* ⊕ *www.bateauxlondon.com.* **Canal Cruises** ☎ *020/8440–8962* ⊕ *www.londoncanalcruises.com.* **Jason's Trip** ☎ *020/7286–3428* ⊕ *www.jasons.co.uk.* **London Duck Tours** ☎ *020/7928–3132* ⊕ *www.londonducktours.co.uk.* **Thames Cruises** ☎ *020/7928–9009* ⊕ *www. thamescruises.com.* **Thames River Boats** ☎ *020/7930–2062* ⊕ *www.wpsa.co.uk.* **Thames River Services** ☎ *020/7930–4097* ⊕ *www.thamesriverservices.co.uk.*

BUS TOURS

Guided sightseeing tours on hop-on, hop-off double-decker buses— open-top in summer—cover the main central sights. Many companies run daily bus tours that depart, usually between 8:30 and 9 am, from central points. Best Value and other outfits conduct guided tours in traditional coach buses. Tickets can be bought from the driver and are good all day. Prices vary according to the type of tour, although £25 is the benchmark. Other guided bus tours, such as those offered by Golden, take place on enclosed (and more expensive) coach buses and are not hop-on, hop off excursions.

Contacts Best Value Tours ☎ *0870/803–1316* ⊕ *www.bestvaluetours.co.uk.* **Big Bus Tours** ☎ *020/7233–9533* ⊕ *www.bigbustours.com.* **Black Taxi Tour of London** ☎ *020/7935–9363* ⊕ *www.blacktaxitours.co.uk.* **Golden Tours** ☎ *0844/880–5050 in U.K., 800/509–2507 in U.S.* ⊕ *www.goldentours.com.* **Original London Sightseeing Tour** ☎ *020/8877–1722* ⊕ *www.theoriginaltour. com.* **Premium Tours** ☎ *020/7713–1311, 888/990-1209 from the US* ⊕ *www.premiumtours.co.uk.*

WALKING TOURS

One of the best ways to get to know London is on foot, and there are many guided and themed walking tours, which cover everything from Jack the Ripper's East End to Dickens's West End. Context London's expert docents lead small groups on walks with art, architecture, and similar themes. The London Walks Company hosts more than 100 walks every week.

Contacts Blood and Tears Walk ☎ *07905/746–733* ⊕ *www.shockinglondon. com.* **Blue Badge** ☎ *020/7403–1115* ⊕ *www.blue-badge-guides.com.* **Context London** ☎ *020/3514–1780, 800/691–6036 in U.S.* ⊕ *www.contexttravel.com/ london.* **London Walks** ☎ *020/7624–3978* ⊕ *www.walks.com.* **Richard Jones's London Walking Tours** ☎ *020/8530–8443* ⊕ *www.walksoflondon.co.uk.* **Shakespeare City Walk** ☎ *07905/746–733* ⊕ *www.shakespeareguide.com.*

VISITOR INFORMATION

You can get good information at the Travel Information Centres at Victoria Station and St. Pancras International train station. These are helpful if you're looking for brochures for London sights and if you need a hotel. Travel Information Centres can also be found at the Euston and Liverpool Street train stations, Heathrow Airport, St. Paul's Cathedral churchyard, and Piccadilly Circus, as well as in Greenwich and some other Outer London locations.

Information ⊕ *www.visitlondon.com.*

EXPLORING LONDON

Westminster and the City contain many of Britain's most historically significant buildings: the Tower of London, St. Paul's Cathedral, Westminster Abbey, the Houses of Parliament, and Buckingham Palace. Within a few-minutes' walk of Buckingham Palace lie St. James's and Mayfair, neighboring quarters of elegant town houses built for the nobility during the 17th and early 18th centuries and now notable for shopping opportunities.

Hyde Park and Kensington Gardens, originally Henry VIII's hunting ground, create an oasis of greenery in congested west London. Just south of the parks is South Kensington's museum district, with the Natural History Museum, the Science Museum, and the Victoria & Albert Museum. Another cultural center is the South Bank and Southwark: the concert halls of the South Bank Centre, the National Theatre, Tate Modern, and the reconstructed Shakespeare's Globe. Farther downstream is Maritime Greenwich, home of the meridian and a World Heritage Site, with its gorgeous Wren and Inigo Jones landmarks.

WESTMINSTER, ST. JAMES'S, AND ROYAL LONDON

This is postcard London at its best. Crammed with historic churches, grand state buildings, and major art collections, the area unites politics, high culture, and religion. (Oh, and the Queen lives here, too.) World-class monuments such as Buckingham Palace, the Houses of Parliament, Westminster Abbey, and the National Gallery sit alongside lesser-known but lovingly curated museums redolent of British history. If you only have time to visit one part of London, this is it. This is concentrated sightseeing, so pace yourself. For much of the year a large portion of Royal London is floodlighted at night, adding to the theatricality of the experience.

GETTING HERE Trafalgar Square—easy to access and in the center of the action—is a good place to start. Take the Tube to Embankment (District, Circle, Bakerloo, and Northern lines) and walk north until you cross the Strand, or alight at Charing Cross (Bakerloo, Jubilee, and Northern lines), where the Northumberland Avenue exit deposits you on the southeast corner of the Square.

PLANNING YOUR TIME A lifetime of exploring may still be insufficient to cover this historically rich part of London, but two to three days can take in the highlights: Begin with Buckingham Palace then move on to Westminster Abbey and the Houses of Parliament to the south, or east to the art of the National Gallery.

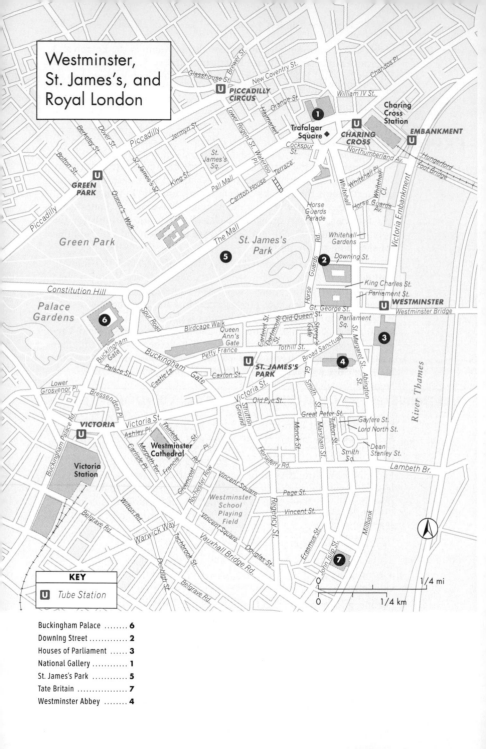

Westminster, St. James's, and Royal London

KEY

🇺 *Tube Station*

TOP ATTRACTIONS

Fodor's Choice **Buckingham Palace.** When the Queen heads off to Scotland on her
★ annual summer holiday, the palace's 19 State Rooms open up to visitors, although the north wing's private apartments remain behind closed
doors. With fabulous gilt moldings and walls adorned with masterpieces
by Rembrandt, Rubens, and other old masters, the State Rooms are the
grandest of the palace's 775 rooms.

The **Grand Hall, Grand Staircase,** and **Guard Room** are laden with
the marble, gold leaf, and massive chandeliers that characterize the
palace's grandeur. Don't miss the theatrical **Throne Room,** with the
original 1953 coronation throne, or, in the **Ballroom,** the sword used
by the Queen to bestow knighthoods and other honors. Royal portraits
line the **State Dining Room,** and the **Blue Drawing Room** is a superb
example of Georgian sumptuousness. The bow-shape **Music Room** has
lapis lazuli columns between arched floor-to-ceiling windows. The 19th-
century design whiz John Nash was responsible for the alabaster-and-
gold plasterwork of the **White Drawing Room's** ceiling. Save some time
to visit the splendid gardens.

The **Changing the Guard,** also known as **Guard Mounting,** culminates
in front of the palace. Marching to music provided by military bands,
the old guard proceeds up the Mall from St. James's Palace to Buckingham Palace. Shortly afterward, the new guard approaches from Wellington Barracks. Then within the forecourt, the captains of the old
and new guards symbolically transfer the keys to the palace. Arrive an
hour early for a good view. Changing the Guard (⊕ *www.changing-the-
guard.com) takes place daily at 11:30 from May until the end of July
(varies according to troop-deployment requirements) and on alternate
days for the rest of the year, weather permitting.* ⊠ *Buckingham Palace
Rd., St. James's* ☎ *020/7766–7300* ⊕ *www.royalcollection.org.uk/visit*
⊠ *£19 (includes audio tour)* ☉ *Open Aug. daily 9:30–7 (last admission 4:45); Sept. daily 9:30–6:30 (last admission 3:45). Times subject
to change; check website* Ⓜ *Victoria, St. James's Park, Green Park.*

Houses of Parliament. If you want to understand some of the centuries-
old traditions and arcane idiosyncrasies that make up constitutionless
British parliamentary democracy, a visit to the Palace of Westminster,
as the complex is still properly called, will enlighten. Edward the Confessor established the first palace here in the 11th century. William II
(also known as William Rufus) started building a new palace in 1087,
and this gradually became the seat of English administrative power.
All that remains of this palace is **Westminster Hall,** with its remarkable
hammer-beam roof. It's one of the largest remaining Norman halls in
Europe, and its dramatic interior was the scene of the trial of Charles
I. Fire destroyed most of the palace in 1834, and the current complex
dates largely from the middle of the 19th century.

After the 1834 fire, the Clock Tower—renamed the **Elizabeth Tower**
in 2012, in honor of the Queen's Diamond Jubilee—was completed in
1858 and contains the 13-ton bell known as **Big Ben.** At the southwest
end of the main Parliament building is the 323-foot-high Victoria Tower.
Visitors aren't allowed to roam at will, but the **Visitors' Galleries** of the

House of Commons afford a view of democracy in process when the green-leather benches are filled by MPs (members of Parliament) during debates. Nonresidents can only take one tour, which is offered year-round on Saturday and daily except Sunday in August and September. The tour costs £15; book through ⊕ *www.ticketmaster.co.uk*. The most romantic view of the Houses is from the opposite (south) bank, across Lambeth Bridge. It is especially dramatic at night when floodlighted green and gold. ⊠ *St. Stephen's Entrance, St. Margaret St., Westminster* ☎ *020/7219–4272 Information, 0844/847–1672 Public Tours* ⊕ *www.parliament.uk/visiting* ⊠ *Free; tours £15 (must book ahead)* ⊙ *Tours: Aug., Mon., Tues., Fri., and Sat. 9:15–4:30, Wed. and Thurs. 1:15–4:30; Sept., Mon., Fri., and Sat. 9:15–4:30, Tues., Wed., and Thurs. 1:15–4:30. Call to confirm hrs for Visitors Galleries.* Ⓜ *Westminster.*

FAMILY
Fodor's Choice
★
National Gallery. Standing proudly on the north side of Trafalgar Square, this is truly one of the world's outstanding art collections, with more than 2,300 masterpieces on exhibit, among them works by Picasso, Van Gogh, Michelangelo, Leonardo, Monet, and Turner.

This brief selection is your jumping-off point, but there are hundreds of other paintings to see, enough to fill a full day. In chronological order: (1) **Van Eyck** (circa 1395–1441), *The Arnolfini Portrait*—a solemn couple holds hands, the fish-eye mirror behind them subtly illuminating what lies behind them. (2) **Holbein** (1497–1543), *The Ambassadors*—two wealthy visitors from France stand surrounded by what were considered luxury goods at the time. Note the elongated skull at the bottom of the painting, which takes shape when viewed from an angle. (3) **Leonardo da Vinci** (1452–1519), *The Virgin and Child*—this exquisite black-chalk "Burlington Cartoon" depicts the Renaissance master's most haunting Virgin. (4) **Velazquez** (1599–1660), *Christ in the House of Martha and Mary*—in this enigmatic masterpiece the painter plays with perspective and the role of the viewer. (5) **Turner** (1775–1851), *Rain, Steam and Speed: The Great Western Railway*—the whirl of rain, mist, steam, and locomotion is nothing short of astonishing (spot the hare). (6) **Caravaggio** (1573–1610), *The Supper at Emmaus*—a freshly resurrected Christ blesses bread in an astonishingly domestic vision from the master of chiaroscuro. (7) **Van Gogh** (1853–1890), *Sunflowers*—painted during his sojourn with Gauguin in Arles, this is quintessential Van Gogh. (8) **Seurat** (1859–91), *Bathers at Asnières*—this summer day's idyll is one of the best-known works of pointillism. One-hour free, guided tours start at the Sainsbury Wing daily at 11:30 and 2:30 (also Friday at 7pm). ⊠ *Trafalgar Sq., Westminster* ☎ *020/7747–2885* ⊕ *www.nationalgallery.org.uk* ⊠ *Free; charge for special exhibitions; audio guide £3.50* ⊙ *Sun.–Thurs. 10–6, Fri. 10–9* Ⓜ *Charing Cross, Embankment, Leicester Sq.*

FAMILY
Fodor's Choice
★
St. James's Park. London's oldest park is also its smallest and most ornamental. Henry VIII acquired this former marshland in 1532 as a royal hunting ground. In the 17th century Charles II had more formal gardens modeled on Versailles laid out, but John Nash redesigned the landscape in the early 19th century in a more naturalistic, romantic style. If you gaze down the lake toward Buckingham Palace, you can believe you are on a country estate. From April to September the deck chairs (charge levied) come out, crammed with lunching office workers. The Inn the

A classic photo op: don't miss the cavalry from the Queen's Life Guard at Buckingham Palace.

Park restaurant is a wood-and-glass pavilion with a turf roof that blends in beautifully with the surrounding landscape; it's an excellent stopping place for a meal or a snack on a nice day. ✉ *The Mall or Horse Guards approach or Birdcage Walk, St. James's* ⊕ *www.royalparks.gov. uk* ☺ *Daily 5 am–midnight* Ⓜ *St. James's Park, Westminster.*

FAMILY
Fodor's Choice
★

Tate Britain. The stately neoclassical institution may not be as well known as its sibling Tate Modern on the South Bank, but Tate Britain's bright galleries are a great place to explore British art from 1500 to the present. The museum, which opened in 1897, displays portions of its magnificent permanent collection, with Van Dyck, Hogarth, Gainsborough, and Reynolds rubbing shoulders with Walter Sickert, David Hockney, and Francis Bacon. Not to be missed are the Pre-Raphaelite works, the Constable landscapes, and the outstanding Turners in the Clore Gallery, including many vaporous and light-infused works such as *Sunrise with Sea Monsters*. The Contemporary British Art galleries contain more recent works such as Damien Hirst's *Away from the Flock*. From about October to January, the galleries host an exhibition of works by the four finalists for the Turner Prize, awarded annually to a contemporary artist under age 50. Details of activities for families are on the website.

■**TIP→** Craving more art? Head down the river on the Tate to Tate boat (£5.50 one way) to Tate Modern, running between the two museums every 40 minutes. A River Roamer ticket (£13.60) permits a day's travel, with stops including the London Eye and the Tower of London. ✉ *Millbank, Westminster* ☎ *020/7887–8888* ⊕ *www.tate.org.uk/britain* 🎫 *Free, special exhibitions £9–£15* ☺ *Sat.–Thurs. 10–6 (last entry at 5:15), Fri. 10–10 (last entry at 9:15)* Ⓜ *Pimlico.*

CLOSE UP

Where to See the Royals

The Queen and the Royal Family attend hundreds of functions a year, and if you want to know what they are doing on any given date, turn to the Court Circular, printed in the major London dailies, or check out the Royal Family website, ⊕ *www.royal.gov. uk*, for the latest events on the Royal Diary. Trooping the Colour is usually held on the second Saturday in June, to celebrate the Queen's official birthday. This spectacular parade begins when she leaves Buckingham Palace in her carriage and rides down the Mall to arrive at Horse Guards Parade at 11 exactly. Just turn up along the Mall with your binoculars.

You can also view the Queen in full regalia when she and the Duke of Edinburgh ride in state to open the Houses of Parliament. The black and gilt-trimmed Irish State Coach travels from Buckingham Palace—ideally on a clear day, as this ceremony takes place in late October or early November. The fairy-tale Gold State Coach is used for coronations and jubilees only. You can also see the Queen riding in an open carriage with foreign heads of state during official visits.

Perhaps the most relaxed, least formal time to see the Queen is during Royal Ascot, held at the racetrack near Windsor Castle—a short train ride out of London—usually during the third week of June (Tuesday–Friday). The Queen may walk down to the paddock on a special path, greeting race goers along the way. If you meet her, remember to address her as "Your Majesty."

Fodor's Choice
★
Westminster Abbey. A monument to the nation's rich—and often bloody—history, the abbey is one of London's most iconic sites. The lofty medieval interior, with the highest Gothic nave in England, contains more than 600 statues, tombs, and commemorative tablets. About 3,300 British notables, from kings to composers to literary giants are buried here. Thirty-eight coronations—beginning in 1066 with William the Conqueror—have been held here, along with 16 royal weddings, the latest in 2011, when Prince William married Kate Middleton.

Enter by the north door, then turn around and look up to see the **painted-glass rose window,** the largest of its kind. As you walk east toward the apse, you'll see the **Coronation Chair** at the foot of the Henry VII Chapel. The chair has been used in every ceremony since Edward I ordered it in 1301. Elizabeth I is buried above half-sister Mary Tudor in the tomb just to the north; Mary, Queen of Scots rests in the tomb to the south. In front of the **High Altar,** which was used for the funerals of Princess Diana and the Queen Mother, is a black-and-white marble floor laid in 1268. The intricate Italian Cosmati work contains three Latin inscriptions, one of which states that the world will last for 19,683 years.

Continue through the South Ambulatory to the **Chapel of St. Edward the Confessor,** which contains a shrine dedicated to the Anglo-Saxon king. Because of its great age, to see the chapel you must join the vergers' tours (✉ £3; details available at the admission desk) or attend Holy Communion within the shrine on Tuesday at 8 am. To the left, you'll find **Poets' Corner.** Geoffrey Chaucer was the first poet to be buried here, in 1400, and William Shakespeare, D.H. Lawrence, T.S. Eliot, and Oscar Wilde, as well as Laurence Olivier and George Frederick Handel, are among those also commemorated here. Keep an eye out for the 700-year-old frescoes.

The medieval Chapter House, where the King's Council met between 1257 and 1547, is adorned with 14th-century frescoes. Its 13th-century tiled floor is one of the country's finest. Near the entrance is Britain's oldest door, dating from the 1050s. Continuing toward the Abbey's nave, in the choir screen to the north of the entrance to the choir, you'll see a marble **monument to Sir Isaac Newton.** Toward the West Entrance is **a plaque to Franklin D. Roosevelt**—one of the Abbey's very few tributes to a foreigner. The poppy-wreathed **Grave of the Unknown Warrior** commemorates soldiers who lost their lives in both world wars.

Arrive early if possible, but be prepared to wait in line to tour the abbey. Photography is not permitted. ⊠ *Broad Sanctuary, Westminster* ☎ *020/7222–5152* ⊕ *www.westminster-abbey.org* ✉ *Abbey and museum £16; audio tour free* ☉ *Abbey: Mon., Tues., Thurs., Fri. 9:30– 4:30; Wed. 9:30–7; Sat. 9:30–2:30; last admission is one hour before closing time; Sun. open for worship only. Museum: Mon.–Sat. 10:30–4. Cloisters: daily 8–6. College Garden: Apr.–Sept., Tues.–Thurs. 10–6; Oct.–Mar., Tues.–Thurs. 10–4. Chapter House: daily 10:30–4. Services may cause changes to hrs, so call ahead* Ⓜ *Westminster, St James's Park.*

WORTH NOTING

Downing Street. Looking like an unassuming side street but for the iron gates at both its Whitehall and Horse Guards Road approaches, this is the location of **No. 10,** London's relatively modest equivalent of the White House. A combination of a cottage, a Queen Anne mansion, and a town house, No. 10 actually has about 100 rooms and an interior courtyard behind its unassuming Georgian frontage. ⊠ *Whitehall* Ⓜ *Westminster.*

SOHO AND COVENT GARDEN

Soho has long been the media and nightlife center of London, its narrow, winding streets unabashedly devoted to pleasure. Wardour Street bisects the neighborhood. Many interesting boutiques and some of London's best-value restaurants can be found to the west, especially around Foubert's Place and on Brewer and Lexington streets. Nightlife central lies to the east—including London's gay mecca and Old Compton Street. Beyond that is the city's densest collection of theaters, on Shaftesbury Avenue, with London's compact Chinatown just past it. A bit of erudition surfaces to the east on Charing Cross Road, still with a couple of the secondhand bookshops it was once known for, and on tiny Cecil Court, a pedestrianized passage lined with small antiquarian booksellers.

To the east of Charing Cross Road you'll find Covent Garden, once a wholesale fruit and vegetable market and now more of a shopping mall. Although boutiques and outposts of high-end chains line the surrounding streets, many Londoners come to Covent Garden for two notable arts venues: the Royal Opera House and the Donmar Warehouse, one of London's best and most innovative theaters. To the south, the Strand leads to the huge, stately piazza of Somerset House, home to the many masterpieces on view at the Courtauld Gallery, a fine small art museum.

GETTING HERE Almost all Tube lines cross the Covent Garden and Soho areas, so it's easy to hop off for a dinner or show in this lively part of London. For Soho, take any train to Piccadilly Circus, or Leicester Square, Oxford Circus, or Tottenham Court Road. For Covent Garden, get off at the Covent Garden station on the Piccadilly Line. It might be easier to exit the Tube at Leicester Square or Holborn and walk. Thirty buses connect to the Covent Garden area from all over London.

PLANNING YOUR TIME You can comfortably tour all the sights in Covent Garden in a day. Visit the small but perfect Courtauld Gallery on Monday before 2 pm, when it's free. That leaves plenty of time to visit the market, watch the street entertainers, do a bit of shopping, and have energy left over for a night on the town in Soho.

TOP ATTRACTIONS

Courtauld Gallery. The gallery, part of the Courtauld Institute of Art, is to your right as you pass through the archway to enter the grounds of **Somerset House,** a grand, 18th-century neoclassical structure. Founded in 1931 by the textile magnate Samuel Courtauld to house his remarkable private collection, this world-class impressionist and postimpressionist gallery contains key works by Van Gogh, Manet, Monet, Gauguin, and other masters. ⊠ *Somerset House, Strand, Covent Garden* ☎ *020/7848–2526* ⊕ *www.courtauld.ac.uk* ⊠ *£6, free Mon. 10–2, except holidays* ⊙ *Daily 10–6; last admission 5:30* Ⓜ *Temple, Covent Garden.*

Covent Garden Piazza. The central square, or piazza, of Covent Garden was once home to London's central produce market, including the flower market where *My Fair Lady*'s Eliza Doolittle peddled her wares. The fine original market building now houses stalls and shops selling clothing, plus several restaurants and cafés and knickknack stores that are good for gifts. One particular gem is Benjamin Pollock's Toyshop, at No. 44. Established in the 1880s, it sells delightful toy theaters. The **Apple Market** has good crafts stalls on most days, too. On the south side of the piazza, the indoor **Jubilee Market,** with its stalls of clothing, army-surplus gear, and more crafts and knickknacks, has the feel of a flea market. Londoners who shop in the area tend to head for Neal Street and the area north of the Covent Garden Tube station rather than to the market itself. In the piazza, street performers—from world music artists to jugglers and mimes—play to the crowds, as they have done since the first English Punch and Judy Show, staged here in the 17th century. ⊠ *Covent Garden* ⊕ *www.coventgardenlondonuk.com* Ⓜ *Covent Garden.*

FAMILY **London Transport Museum.** Housed in the old flower market at the southeast corner of Covent Garden, this stimulating museum (for children and adults) is filled with impressive vehicle, poster, and photograph collections. The exhibits include a Tube-train simulation, horse-drawn trams, and steam locomotives. ■TIP→ **Tickets are valid for unlimited entry for 12 months.** ⊠ *Covent Garden Piazza, Covent Garden* ☎ *020/7565–7298* ⊕ *www.ltmuseum.co.uk* ⊠ *£13.50* ⊙ *Sat.–Thurs. 10–6 (last admission 5:15), Fri. 11–6 (last admission 5:15)* Ⓜ *Covent Garden, Leicester Sq.*

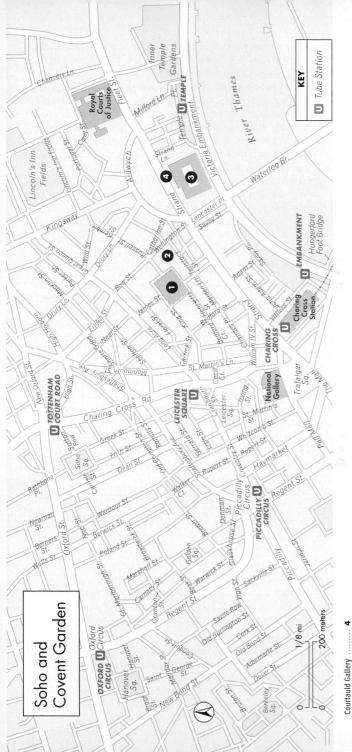

Soho and
Covent Garden

Courtauld Gallery **4**
Covent Garden Piazza **1**
London Transport
Museum **2**
Somerset House **3**

FAMILY   **Somerset House.** In recent years this huge complex—the work of Sir
Fodor's Choice   William Chambers (1726–96), built during the reign of George III to
★   house offices of the Navy—has completed its transformation from dusty
government space to buzzing center of culture and the arts. At any given
time it's apt to be hosting several interesting exhibitions. The **Courtauld
Gallery** (⇨ *see above*) occupies most of the north building, facing the
busy Strand. Across the courtyard are the Embankment Galleries, with
a vibrant calendar of design, fashion, architecture, and photography
exhibitions. Creative activities for children are a regular feature (the
website has details). The East Wing has another fine exhibition space,
and events are sometimes held in the cellars below the Fountain Court.
✉ *Strand, Covent Garden* ☎ *020/7845–4600* ⊕ *www.somersethouse.
org.uk* 🎟 *Embankment Galleries price varies, Courtauld Gallery £6,
other areas free* 🕙 *Daily 10–6; last admission 5:30* Ⓜ *Charing Cross,
Waterloo, Blackfriars.*

BLOOMSBURY AND HOLBORN

The character of London can change visibly from one area to the next.
There's a distinct difference between fun-loving Soho and intellectual
Bloomsbury, a mere 100 yards to the northeast, or between the diversions of Covent Garden and the sober businesslike Holborn (pronounced *hoe*-bun) on the other side of Kingsway.

The British Museum, the British Library, and the University of London
anchor the neighborhood that lent its name to the Bloomsbury Group,
the clique who personified early-20th-century literary bohemia. The
circle's mainstays included the writers Virginia Woolf, E. M. Forster,
and Lytton Strachey and the painter Vanessa Bell.

Originally a notorious red-light district, these days Holborn is legal
London's center. Because the neighborhood's buildings were among
the few structures spared during the Great Fire of 1666, its serpentine
alleys, cobbled courtyards, and the Inns of Court, where most British
trial lawyers still have offices, ooze history.

GETTING HERE   You can easily get to where you need to be in Bloomsbury on foot, and
the Russell Square Tube stop on the Piccadilly Line leaves you right at
the corner of Russell Square. The best Tube stops for Holborn are on
the Central and Piccadilly lines and Chancery Lane on the Central Line.
Tottenham Court Road on the Northern and Central lines and Russell
Square (Piccadilly Line) are best for the British Museum.

PLANNING   Bloomsbury can be seen in a day, or in half a day, depending on your
YOUR TIME   interests. If you plan to visit the Inns of Court as well as the British
Museum, and you'd like to walk through the quiet, leafy squares, then
you might want to devote an entire day to Bloomsbury and Holborn.

TOP ATTRACTIONS

FAMILY   **British Library.** This collection of around 18 million volumes, formerly
in the British Museum, now has a home in state-of-the-art surroundings. The library's greatest treasures are on view to the general public:
the Magna Carta, a Gutenberg Bible, Jane Austen's writings, Shakespeare's First Folio, and musical manuscripts by G.F. Handel as well as

The massive, glass-roofed Great Court in the British Museum has a couple of cafés.

Sir Paul McCartney are on display in the Sir John Ritblat Gallery. ✉ 96 *Euston Rd., Bloomsbury* ☎ *0843/208–1144* ⊕ *www.bl.uk* ✉ *Free, donations appreciated; charge for special exhibitions* ⊙ *Mon. and Wed.–Fri. 9:30–6, Tues. 9:30–8, Sat. 9:30–5, Sun. and public holidays 11–5* Ⓜ *Euston, Euston Sq., King's Cross/St Pancras.*

Fodor's Choice
★

British Museum. With a facade like a great temple, this celebrated treasure house, filled with plunder of incalculable value and beauty from around the globe, occupies an immense, imposing, neoclassical building in the heart of Bloomsbury. Inside are some of the greatest relics of humankind: the Parthenon Sculptures (Elgin Marbles), the Rosetta Stone, the Sutton Hoo Treasure—almost everything, it seems, but the Ark of the Covenant. The three rooms that comprise the **Sainsbury African Galleries** are a must-see in the Lower Gallery—together they present 200,000 objects, highlighting such ancient kingdoms as Benin and Asante. The museum's focal point is the **Great Court**, a brilliant modern design with a vast glass roof that reveals the museum's covered courtyard. The revered **Reading Room** has a blue-and-gold dome and hosts temporary exhibitions. If you want to navigate the highlights of the almost 100 galleries, join the free **eyeOpener** 30- to 40-minute tours by museum guides (details at the information desk). Or alternatively, hire a multimedia guide for £5.

The collection began when Sir Hans Sloane, physician to Queen Anne and George II, bequeathed his personal collection of antiquities to the nation. It grew quickly, thanks to enthusiastic kleptomaniacs after the Napoleonic Wars—most notoriously the seventh Earl of Elgin, who acquired the marbles from the Parthenon and Erechtheion in Athens

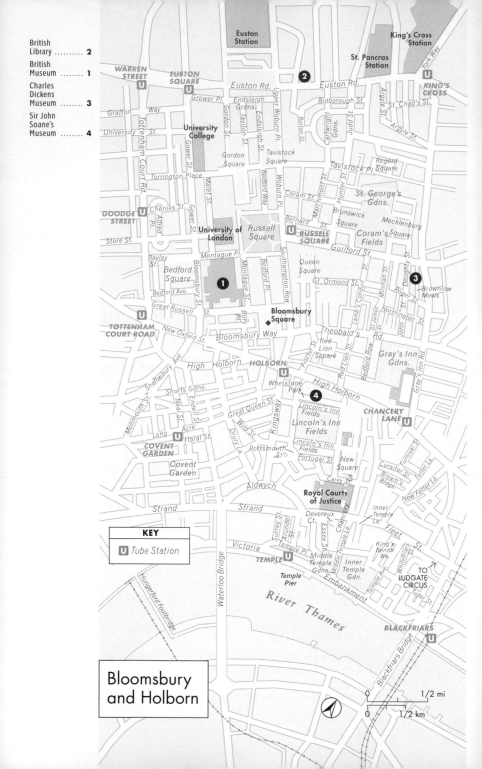

Euston
Station

King's Cross
Station

St. Pancras
Station

York Way

WARREN
STREET
U

EUSTON
SQUARE
U

KING'S
CROSS

Euston Rd.

Euston Rd.

2

Grower Pl.

Bidborough St.

Cartwright
Gdns.

St. Chad's St.

Argyle St.

Grafton

Way

Endsleigh
Grdns.

Upper Woburn Pl.

Burton St.

Judd St.

Argyle St.

University

St.

Tottenham Court Rd.

Gower St.

Taviton St.

Endsleigh St.

University
College

Gordon St.

Gordon
Square

Tavistock
Square

Woburn Pl.

Bedford Way

Tavistock Pl.

Marchmont St.

Hunter St.

Regent
Square

St. George's
Gdns.

Torrington Place

Malet St.

Coram St.

Brunswick
Square

Mecklenburg
Square

GOODGE
STREET
U

Chenies St.

Alfred
Pl.

Gower St.

University of
London
U

Russell
Square

Bernard
St.

RUSSELL
SQUARE
U

Coram's
Fields

Store St.

Bayley
St.

Bedford
Square

Gower St.

Montague Pl.

Montague St.

Bedford Pl.

Southampton Row

Guilford St.

Doughty St.

3

Bedford Ave.

1

Queen
Square

Gt. Ormond St.

Milman St.

Roger St.

Northington

Brownlow
Mews

Great Russell

St.

Bury

St.

Bloomsbury St.

TOTTENHAM
COURT ROAD
U

New Oxford St.

Bloomsbury Way

Bloomsbury
Square

Lamb's Conduit
St.

Gt. James
St.

Gray's Inn
Gdns.

Gray's Inn Rd.

Theobald's

Red
Lion
Square

Bedford Row

High

Holborn

HOLBORN
U

Procter St.

Red Lion St.

High Holborn

Shaftesbury Ave.

Shorts Gdns.

Neal St.

Endell St.

Whetstone
Park

4

Kingsway

CHANCERY
LANE
U

Monmouth St.

Great Queen St.

Lincoln's Inn
Fields

Cursitor St.

Fetter La.

Long
Acre

Floral St.

Wild St.

Drury La.

Lincoln's Inn
Fields

Bream's
Bldgs.

New Fetter La.

COVENT
GARDEN
U

Covent
Garden

Portsmouth
St.

Lincoln's Inn
Fields

Portugal St.

New
Square

Carey St.

Aldwych

Royal Courts
of Justice

Strand

Strand

Surrey St.

Arundel
St.

Devereux
Ct.

Essex St.

Chancery La.

Inner
Temple
La.

Fleet

St.

Whitefriars
St.

TO
LUDGATE
CIRCUS

Victoria

Temple Pl.

TEMPLE
U

Middle
Temple
Gdns.

Middle Temple La.

Inner
Temple
Gdn.

King's
Bench
Wk.

Temple Ave.

Embankment

Tudor St.

Waterloo Bridge

Hungerford Footbridge

Temple
Pier

River Thames

BLACKFRIARS
U

Blackfriars Bridge

KEY

U *Tube Station*

Bloomsbury
and Holborn

0 ————— 1/2 mi

0 ————— 1/2 km

during his term as British ambassador in Constantinople. Here follows a highly edited résumé (in order of encounter) of the British Museum's greatest hits: close to the entrance hall, in Room 4, is the **Rosetta Stone,** found by French soldiers in 1799, and carved in 196 BC by decree of Ptolemy V in Egyptian hieroglyphics, demotic (a cursive script developed in Egypt), and Greek. This inscription provided the French Egyptologist Jean-François Champollion with the key to deciphering hieroglyphics. Also in Room 4 is the colossal statue of Ramesses II, a 7-ton likeness of this member of the 19th dynasty's (ca. 1270 BC) upper half. Maybe the **Parthenon Sculptures** should be back in Greece, but while the debate rages on, you can steal your own moment with the Elgin Marbles in Room 18. Carved in about 400 BC, these graceful decorations are displayed along with a high-tech exhibit of the Acropolis. Upstairs are some of the most popular galleries, especially beloved by children: Rooms 62–63, where the **Egyptian mummies** live. Nearby are the glittering 4th-century **Mildenhall Treasure** and the equally splendid 8th-century Anglo-Saxon **Sutton Hoo Treasure** (with magnificent helmets and jewelry). A more prosaic exhibit is that of Pete Marsh, sentimentally named by the archaeologists who unearthed the **Lindow Man** from a Cheshire peat marsh; poor Pete was ritually slain in the 1st century, and lay perfectly pickled in his bog until 1984. ⊠ *Great Russell St., Bloomsbury* ☎ *020/7323–8299* ⊕ *www.britishmuseum.org* 🖲 *Free; donations encouraged* ☉ *Galleries Sat.–Thurs. 10–5:30, Fri. 10–8:30. Great Court Sat.–Thurs. 9–6, Fri. 9–8:30* Ⓜ *Russell Sq., Holborn, Tottenham Court Rd.*

Charles Dickens Museum. This is one of the few London houses Charles Dickens (1812–70) inhabited that is still standing—and is the place where the master wrote *Oliver Twist* and *Nicholas Nickleby* and finished *Pickwick Papers.* The house looks exactly as it would have in Dickens's day, complete with first editions, letters, and a tall clerk's desk (where the master wrote standing up, often while chatting with visiting friends and relatives). ⊠ *48 Doughty St., Bloomsbury* ☎ *020/7405–2127* ⊕ *www.dickensmuseum.com* 🖲 *£8* ☉ *Daily 10–5 (last admission 4:30)* Ⓜ *Chancery La., Russell Sq.*

Fodor's Choice   **Sir John Soane's Museum.** A wonderful, eccentric jewel of a place, Sir
★   John (1753–1837), architect of the Bank of England, bequeathed his house to the nation on one condition: that nothing be changed. It's a house full of surprises. In the Picture Room, for instance, two of Hogarth's *Rake's Progress* series are among the paintings on panels that swing away to reveal secret gallery pockets with even more paintings. Everywhere, mirrors and colors play tricks with light and space, and split-level floors worthy of a fairground fun house disorient you. ⊠ *13 Lincoln's Inn Fields, Bloomsbury* ☎ *020/7405–2107* ⊕ *www. soane.org* 🖲 *Free; tours £10* ☉ *Tues.–Sat. 10–5; also 6–9 on 1st Tues. of month* Ⓜ *Holborn.*

THE CITY

The City, as opposed to the city, is the capital's economic engine room. But the "Square Mile" captures attention for more than its role as London's Wall Street. Wren's masterpiece, the English baroque St. Paul's Cathedral, still stuns, as does the medieval Tower of London (full name: Her Majesty's Royal Palace and Fortress), which has served many functions during its more than 1,000-year history. Off the main roads, the City's winding lanes and courtyards are rich in historic churches and pubs.

The City has twice nearly been destroyed, first by the Great Fire of 1666—after which Sir Christopher Wren was put in charge of a total reconstruction that resulted in St. Paul's Cathedral and 49 lovely parish churches—and later by German bombing raids during World War II. Following the raids the area was rebuilt over time, but with no grand plan. Consequently, the City is a mishmash of the old, the new, the innovative, the distinguished, and the flagrantly awful. A walk across the Millennium Bridge from Tate Modern to St. Paul's offers a superb view of the river and the cathedral that presides over it.

GETTING HERE   The Underground serves the City at several stops. St Paul's and Bank, on the Central Line, and Mansion House, Cannon Street, and Monument, on the District and Circle lines, deliver visitors to its center. Liverpool Street and Aldgate border the City's eastern edge, and Chancery Lane and Farringdon lie to the west. Barbican and Moorgate provide easy access to the theaters and galleries of the Barbican, and Blackfriars, to the south, leads to Ludgate Circus and Fleet Street.

PLANNING   The City is compact, making it ideal for an afternoon's exploration. For
YOUR TIME   full immersion in the Tower of London, set aside half a day, especially if seeing the Crown Jewels is a priority. Allow an hour minimum each for the Museum of London and St. Paul's Cathedral. Weekdays are best, since on weekends the City is nearly deserted, with shops and restaurants closed. At the same time, this is when the major attractions are at their busiest.

TOP ATTRACTIONS

FAMILY   **Museum of London.** If there's one place to absorb the history of London, from 450,000 BC to the present day, it's here: Oliver Cromwell's death mask, Queen Victoria's crinoline gowns, Selfridges' art deco elevators, the *London's Burning* exhibition, fans, guns and jewelry, an original Newgate Prison door, and the incredible late-18th-century Blackett Dolls House— 7,000 objects to wonder at in all. The museum appropriately shelters a section of the 2nd- to 4th-century London wall, which you can view through a window, and permanent displays highlight Pre-Roman, Roman, Medieval, and Tudor London. The Galleries of Modern London are equally enthralling: experience the Expanding City, People's City, and World City, each gallery dealing with a section of London's history from 1666 until the 21st century. Innovative interactive displays abound, and you can even wander around a 19th-century London street with impressively detailed shop fronts and interiors, including a pawnbroker's, a pub, a barber's, and a bank manager's office, in case you're running short on holiday money. There's also a fine schedule of temporary exhibitions. ⊠ *London Wall, The City* ☎ *020/7001–9844* ⊕ *www.museumoflondon.org.uk* ✆ *Free* ⊙ *Mon.–Sun. 10–6; last admission 5:30* Ⓜ *Barbican, St. Paul's.*

The City

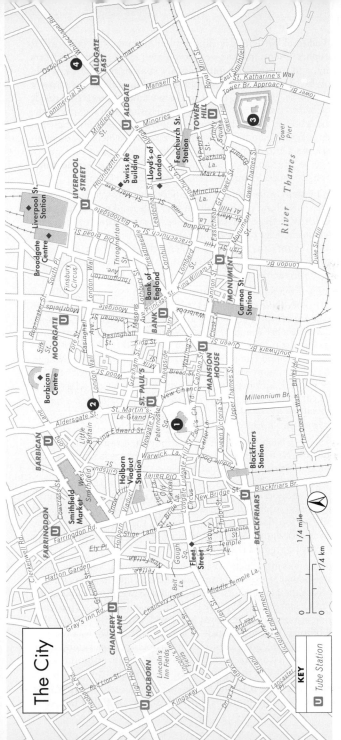

Fodor'sChoice **St. Paul's Cathedral.** St. Paul's is simply breathtaking. The structure is
★ Sir Christopher Wren's masterpiece, completed in 1710 after 35 years
of building, and, much later, miraculously spared (mostly) by World
War II bombs. St. Paul's simply would not be St. Paul's as we know it
without the dome, the third largest in the world. Even so, from inside
the vast cathedral the dome may seem smaller than you'd expect—the
inner dome is 60 feet lower than the lead-covered outer dome. Beneath
the lantern is Wren's famous and succinct epitaph, which his son composed and had set into the pavement: "Lector, si monumentum requiris,
circumspice"—"Reader, if you seek his monument, look around you."
The epitaph also appears on Wren's memorial in the Crypt.

Up 163 spiral steps is the **Whispering Gallery,** an acoustic phenomenon;
you whisper something to the wall on one side, and a second later it
transmits clearly to the other side, 107 feet away. Ascend to the **Stone
Gallery,** which encircles the base of the dome. Farther up (280 feet from
ground level) is the small **Golden Gallery,** the dome's highest point.
From both these galleries (if you have a head for heights) you can walk
outside for a spectacular panorama of London.

The remains of the poet John Donne, who was Dean of St. Paul's for
his final 10 years (he died in 1631), are in the south choir aisle. The
vivacious choir-stall carvings nearby are the work of Grinling Gibbons,
as are those on the **great organ,** which Wren designed. Behind the high
altar is the **American Memorial Chapel,** dedicated to the 28,000 GIs
stationed in the United Kingdom who lost their lives in World War II.
Among the famous figures whose remains lie in the **Crypt** are the Duke
of Wellington and Admiral Lord Nelson. The Crypt also has a gift
shop and a café. ⊠ *St. Paul's Churchyard, The City* ☎ *020/7236–4128*
⊕ *www.stpauls.co.uk* 💷 *£15 (includes multimedia guides and guided
tours)* ⊙ *Mon.–Sat. 8:30–4; Shop Mon.–Sat. 9–5, Sun. 10–4:30; Crypt
Café Mon.–Sat. 9–5, Sun. 12–4* Ⓜ *St. Paul's.*

Fodor'sChoice **Tower of London.** Nowhere else does London's history come to life so
★ vividly as it does in this complex of 20 towers filled with heraldry and
treasure. This is one of Britain's most popular sights, so consider buying
a ticket in advance online, by phone, at any Tube station, or from the
automatic kiosks on arrival. The Crown Jewels, housed in the Jewel
House in Waterloo Barracks, are well worth the inevitable wait, the
White Tower is essential, and the Medieval Palace and Bloody Tower
should at least be breezed through.

The visitor center's introduction can help you plan your visit, but allow
at least three hours for exploring and leave time to take in the wonderful
overview from the battlements. Although the Tower has served many
functions in its more than 1,000-year history—including as a palace, a
barracks, an armory, and the Royal Mint and Menagerie (the last one
the kernel of today's London Zoo)—it is primarily known as a place of
imprisonment, torture, and execution for aristocrats, royalty, and those
who served or plotted against them. Some were traitors, some innocent,
and several left their last thoughts etched on these walls.

The fortunate few were beheaded in the peace and seclusion of **Tower
Green** instead of in front of the baying mob at Tower Hill. In fact, only

seven people ever enjoyed this privilege—among them Anne Boleyn and Catherine Howard, wives two and five of Henry VIII; Elizabeth I's intimate and frenemy Robert Devereux, Earl of Essex; and the teenage Lady Jane Grey, whose crime was to be queen to Henry's short-lived son, Edward VI for only nine days. Lady Jane was imprisoned in **Beauchamp Tower, where** you can still see the Latin graffiti about her on the walls. Other famous (though not necessarily executed) Tower prisoners include Elizabeth I while still a princess, Sir Walter Raleigh, and Sir Thomas More.

The Tower's Yeoman Warders, better known as Beefeaters and designated warders of the Tower sometime after 1509, conduct free tours that depart every half hour or so from the Middle Tower. The Yeoman Warder Raven Master looks after the resident ravens (six plus reserves) that live in **Lanthorn Tower.** If the ravens were to desert the Tower, legend has it, the kingdom would fall, so even today the birds' wings are clipped.

The oldest part of the Tower, the **White Tower,** is the earliest stone keep in England, built by William I as part of the Norman Conquest. The name derives from a whitewashing ordered by Henry III (1207–72). Inside you'll find the **Armouries,** a splendid collection of arms and armor. Across the moat, **Traitors' Gate** lies to the right. Opposite Traitors' Gate is the former Garden Tower, better known since about 1570 as the **Bloody Tower,** so called because it was here the young "princes in the Tower," the heirs to Edward IV, were imprisoned in 1483 by their uncle, later Richard III. In 1674 two little skeletons, thought to be those of the two princes, were found under the White Tower's stairs.

The most famous exhibits, though, are the **Crown Jewels.** Symbolizing the power of the English monarchy since the 14th century, these crowns, staffs, and orbs are encrusted with magnificent precious stones, such as the legendary Indian diamond the Koh-i-noor, or "Mountain of Light," which now adorns a crown that belonged to Queen Elizabeth, the Queen Mother.

The little **Chapel Royal of St. Peter ad Vincula** is the final resting place of six beheaded Tudor bodies. Visitors are welcome for services or after 4:30 daily.

For free tickets to the 700-year-old Ceremony of the Keys (locking of main gates, nightly between 9:30 and 10), write several months in advance; check the tower website for details. Also, check for winter twilight tours of the Tower on selected evenings. ⊠ *Tower Hill, The City* ☎ *0844/482–7777, 0844/482–7799* ⊕ *www.hrp.org.uk* 🎟 *£19.50* ⊙ *Mar.–Oct., Tues.–Sat. 9–5:30, Sun. and Mon. 10–5:30 (last admission at 5); Nov.–Feb., Tues.–Sat. 9–4:30, Sun. and Mon. 10–4:30 (last admission at 4)* Ⓜ *Tower Hill.*

WORTH NOTING

Whitechapel Art Gallery. Established in 1897 and recently expanded, this large, independent East End gallery is one of London's most innovative and consistently interesting exhibition spaces. Jeff Wall, Bill Viola, Gary Hume, and Mark Rothko have exhibited here and there is an interesting program of events as well as an excellent restaurant. ✉ *80–82 Whitechapel High St., Shoreditch* ☎ *020/7522–7888* ⊕ *www.whitechapel. org* ✄ *Free* ⊙ *Tues., Wed., Fri.–Sun. 11–6, Thurs. 11–9* Ⓜ *Aldgate East.*

THE SOUTH BANK

Culture, history, markets—the South Bank has them all. Installed in a converted 1930s power station, Tate Modern is the star attraction, with the eye-catching Millennium Bridge connecting it to the City across the river. Near the National Theatre and the concert halls of the South Bank Centre, the London Eye observation wheel gives you a bird's-eye view of the city.

Traditionally, Southwark was a rough area known for its inns, prisons, bear-baiting arenas, and theaters. The Globe, which housed the company Shakespeare wrote for and performed with, was one of several here. It has been reconstructed on the original site, so you can experience watching the Bard's plays as the Elizabethans would have. Be sure to take a stroll along Queen's Walk, the embankment along the Thames from Southwark to Blackfriars Bridge, taking in Tate Modern along the way.

GETTING HERE For the South Bank, use Embankment on the District, Circle, Northern, and Bakerloo lines. From here you can walk across the Queens Jubilee footbridges. Another option is Waterloo—on the Northern, Jubilee, and Bakerloo lines—from where it's a five-minute walk to the Royal Festival Hall (slightly longer from the Jubilee Line station). London Bridge on the Northern and Jubilee lines is a five-minute walk from Borough Market and Southwark Cathedral.

PLANNING YOUR TIME Don't attempt to explore the area south of the Thames all in one go. Not only will you exhaust yourself, but you'll also miss out on the varied delights that it has to offer. Tate Modern alone deserves a whole morning or afternoon, especially if you want to do justice to both the temporary exhibitions and the permanent collection. The Globe requires about two hours for the exhibition theater tour and two to three hours for a performance.

TOP ATTRACTIONS

FAMILY **London Eye.** To mark the start of the new millennium, architects David Marks and Julia Barfield conceived a beautiful and celebratory structure that would allow people to see this great city from a completely new perspective. They came up with a giant Ferris wheel, which, as well as representing the turn of the century, would also be a symbol of regeneration. The London Eye is the largest cantilevered observation wheel ever built and among the tallest structures in London. The 25-minute slow-motion ride inside one of the enclosed passenger capsules is so smooth you'd hardly know you were suspended over the Thames. ■ **TIP→ Buy your ticket online to avoid the long lines and get a 10% discount.** ✉ *Westminster Bridge Rd., Riverside Bldg., County Hall, South Bank* ☎ *0870/990–8883* ⊕ *www.londoneye.com* ✄ *£18.90; cruise £12.50* ⊙ *June and Sept., daily 10–9; July and Aug., daily 10–9:30; Oct.–Mar., daily 10–8:30* Ⓜ *Waterloo.*

FAMILY **Shakespeare's Globe Theatre.** This spectacular theater is a replica of
Fodor'sChoice Shakespeare's open-roof, wood-and-thatch Globe Playhouse (built
★ in 1599 and burned down in 1613), where most of the Bard's greatest works premiered. American actor and director Sam Wanamaker
worked ceaselessly for several decades to raise funds for the theater's
reconstruction 200 yards from its original site, using authentic materials and techniques, a dream realized in 1997. "Groundlings"—patrons
with £5 standing-only tickets—are not allowed to sit during the performance. Fortunately, you can reserve an actual seat on any one of
the theater's three levels, but you will want to rent a cushion for £1 (or
bring your own) to soften the backless wooden benches. The show must
go on, rain or shine, warm or chilly—so come prepared for anything.
Umbrellas are banned, but you can bring a raincoat or buy a cheap
Globe rain poncho, which doubles as a great souvenir. In winter, the
Sam Wanamaker Playhouse, a 350-seat recreation of an indoor Jacobean theater, lit mostly by candles, presents plays and concerts in a less
exposed though still atmospheric setting.

Shakespeare's Globe Exhibition, a museum under the theater (the
entry is adjacent), provides background material on the Elizabethan
theater and the construction of the modern-day Globe. Admission to
the museum also includes a tour of the theater. On matinee days the
tour visits the archaeological site of the nearby (and older) Rose Theatre. ⊠ *21 New Globe Walk, Bankside* ☏ *020/7902–1400 box office,
020/7401–9919 Exhibition* ⊕ *www.shakespearesglobe.com* ✉ *Exhibition and Globe Theatre tour £13.50 (£2 reduction with valid performance ticket); ticket prices for plays vary, £5–£39* ☉ *Exhibition:
May–early Oct., daily 10–5; mid-Oct.–Apr., daily 9–12:30 and 1–5;
plays: April 23–Oct., call for performance schedule* Ⓜ *London Bridge;
Mansion House, then cross Southwark Bridge.*

FAMILY **Tate Modern.** This spectacular renovation of a mid-20th-century power
Fodor'sChoice station is one of the most-visited museums of modern art in the world.
★ Its great permanent collection, which starts in 1900 and ranges from
modern masters like Matisse to the most cutting-edge contemporary
artists, is arranged thematically—Landscape, Still Life, and the Nude.
Its blockbuster temporary exhibitions showcase the work of individual
artists like Gauguin, Roy Lichtenstein, and Gerhard Richter. The vast
Turbine Hall is a dramatic entrance point used to showcase big, auda-
cious installations that tend to generate a lot of publicity. The **Material
Gestures** galleries on Level 3 feature an impressive offering of post–
World War II painting and sculpture. Room 7 contains a breathtaking
collection of Rothkos and Monets; there are also paintings by Matisse,
Pollock, and Picasso, and newer works from the likes of the sculptor
Anish Kapoor. Head to the Restaurant on Level 7 or the Espresso Bar
on Level 3 for stunning vistas of the Thames. The view of St. Paul's from
the Espresso Bar's balcony is one of the best in London. An extension to
the front of the building is not only ambitious but also controversial—
you won't be alone if you don't care for it. ⊠ *Bankside* ☏ *020/7887–
8888* ⊕ *www.tate.org.uk/modern* ✉ *Free, charge for special exhibitions*
☉ *Sun.–Thurs. 10–6, Fri. and Sat. 10–10 (last admission to exhibitions
45 mins before closing)* Ⓜ *Southwark, Mansion House, St. Paul's.*

WORTH NOTING

IWM London. The exhibitions at the former Imperial War Museum, one of five IWM branches around the country, do not glorify bloodshed but rather analyze the impact of 20th- and 21st-century warfare on citizens and soldiers alike. A dramatic six-story atrium, part of a major renovation to mark the centenary of the First World War, encloses an impressive amount of hardware—including a Battle of Britain Spitfire—and accompanying interactive material. The *Trench Experiences* in the new First World War Galleries use sights, sounds, and smells to re-create the grimness of life in no-man's-land, while an equally effective *Blitz Experience* in the revamped Second World War Galleries puts you on a "street" filled with acrid smoke for a vivid 10-minute glimpse of an air raid. Also in these galleries is an extensive and haunting Holocaust exhibition. Other galleries contain war art by Henry Moore and John Singer Sargent, among others, along with conflict-related documentary film footage. James Bond fans won't want to miss the intriguing Secret War Gallery, which charts the work of secret agents. ⊠ *Lambeth Rd., South Bank* ☎ *020/7416–5000* ⊕ *www.iwm.org.uk* 🎫 *Free (charge for special exhibitions)* ⊙ *Daily 10–6* Ⓜ *Lambeth North.*

Southwark Cathedral. Pronounced "Suth-uck," this is the oldest Gothic church in London, with parts dating back to the 12th century. It remains off the beaten track, despite being the site of some remarkable memorials and a concert program that offers recitals of works for the organ at lunchtime on Monday (except in August and December) and classical music at 3:15 on Tuesday (except in December). Originally the priory church of St. Mary Overie (as in "over the water"—on the South Bank), it became a palace church under Henry VIII and was only promoted to cathedral status in 1905. Look for the gaudily renovated 1408 tomb of the poet John Gower, friend of Chaucer, and for the Harvard Chapel. Another notable buried here is Edmund Shakespeare, brother of William. ■TIP➔ The Refectory serves full English breakfasts, light lunches, and tea 8:30–6 Monday–Friday, 10–6 weekends. ⊠ *London Bridge, Bankside* ☎ *020/7367–6700* ⊕ *www. southwark.anglican.org* 🎫 *Free, suggested donation £4* ⊙ *Daily 8–6* Ⓜ *London Bridge.*

The View from the Shard. At 1,016 feet, this 2012 addition to the London skyline is currently the tallest building in Western Europe and, as a design of noted architect Renzo Piano, has attracted both admiration and opprobrium. Although the building itself is generally highly regarded, many feel it would be better sited in Canary Wharf (or, indeed, Dubai), as it spoils views of St. Paul's Cathedral from traditional vantage points such as Hampstead's Parliament Hill. No matter how you feel about the building, there's no denying that it offers a spectacular 360-degree view *over* London (extending to 40 miles on a clear day) from viewing platforms on floors 68, 69, and 72—almost twice as high as any other vantage point in the city. ⊠ *32 London Bridge St., Borough* ☎ *0844/499–7111* ⊕ *www.theviewfromtheshard.com* 🎫 *£24.95* ⊙ *Daily 9 am–10 pm, last admission 8:30* Ⓜ *London Bridge.*

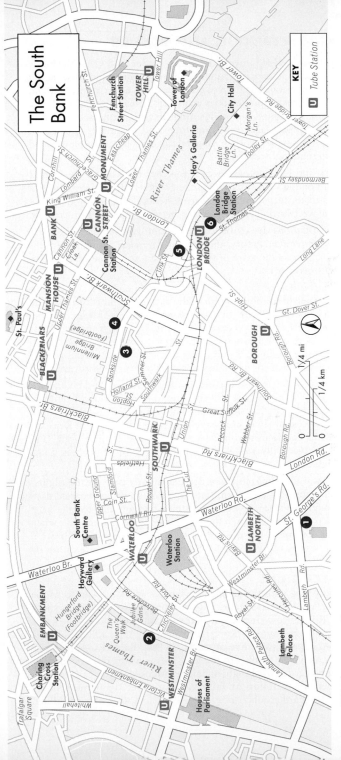

The South Bank

Fenchurch St.

Fenchurch
Street Station

TOWER HILL U

MONUMENT U

Eastcheap

Lower Thames St.

Tower Hill

Tower of
London

City Hall

River Thames

Hay's Galleria ◆

Morgan's
Ln.

Cornhill

Lombard St.

King William St.

Gracechurch St.

CANNON STREET U

BANK U

Cannon St.

Queen St.

Cannon St.
Station

Crook
La.

Clink St.

⑤

LONDON BRIDGE U

⑥

London
Bridge
Station

St. Thomas St.

Battle
Bridge
Ln.

Tooley St.

Bermondsey St.

Tower Bridge Rd.

Tower Br.

London Br.

MANSION HOUSE U

Upper Thames St.

BLACKFRIARS U

St. Paul's ◆

Millennium
Bridge
(Footbridge)

Bankside

Southwark Br.

④

③

Holland St.

Hopton
St.

Sumner St.

Southwark St.

BOROUGH U

High St.

Long Lane

Gt. Dover St.

1/4 mi

1/4 km

0

0

Blackfriars Br.

Blackfriars Rd

SOUTHWARK

Union
St.

Great Suffolk St.

Peacock
St.

Webber St.

The Cut

Southwark Br. Rd.

Borough Rd.

Borough Rd.

London Rd.

St. George's Rd.

①

LAMBETH NORTH U

Hatfields

Upper
Ground

Coin St.

Stamford
St.

Roupell St.

Cornwall Rd

Waterloo Rd.

Baylis Rd

Waterloo Br.

South Bank
Centre ◆

WATERLOO U

Waterloo
Station

Westminster Br.

Hayward
Gallery ◆

Hungerford
Bridge
(Footbridge)

EMBANKMENT U

Charing
Cross
Station

Trafalgar
Square

Whitehall

The
Queen's
Walk

Jubilee
Gdns.

Belvedere Rd.

York Rd.

Chicheley St.

②

River Thames

WESTMINSTER U

Victoria Embankment

Westminster Br.

Houses of
Parliament

Lambeth Palace Rd.

Royal St.

Lambeth
Rd.

Hercules Rd.

Lambeth
Palace

KENSINGTON, KNIGHTSBRIDGE, AND MAYFAIR

The Royal Borough of Kensington & Chelsea (or "K&C" as the locals call it) is London at its richest, and not just in the moneyed sense. South Kensington has a concentration of great museums near Cromwell Road, while within Kensington Gardens is historic Kensington Palace, home to royal family members including Queen Victoria, Princess Diana, and now Prince William, Duke of Cambridge and Catherine, Duchess of Cambridge (plus baby George). Knightsbridge has become a playground for the international wealthy.

Hyde Park and Kensington Gardens together form by far the biggest of central London's royal parks. As the property of the Crown, which still owns them, they were spared from being devoured by London's inexorable westward development that began in the late 18th century.

With world-famous department stores, boutiques selling the biggest names in international luxury, and expensive jewelers, London's wealthiest enclave reflects the taste of those who can afford the best and are prepared to pay for it.

Around the borders of Hyde Park are several of London's most elegant and upscale neighborhoods. South of the park and a short carriage ride from Buckingham Palace are the cream-stucco terraces of Belgravia, one of the most impressive set pieces of 19th-century urban planning, in this case by the developer Thomas Cubitt. On the eastern border of Hyde Park lies the most fashionable shopping area in London, Mayfair, which gives Belgravia a run for its money as London's wealthiest district.

GETTING HERE Several useful Tube stations are nearby: Knightsbridge and Hyde Park Corner on the Piccadilly Line will take you to Knightsbridge, Belgravia, and Hyde Park; South Kensington and Gloucester Road on the District, Circle, and Piccadilly lines are convenient stops for the South Kensington museums and Kensington Palace; Bond Street (Central Line) and Green Park (Piccadilly and Victoria lines), both on the Jubilee Line, serve Mayfair.

PLANNING The best way to approach these neighborhoods is to treat Knights-
YOUR TIME bridge shopping and the South Kensington museums as separate days out, although the three vast museums may be too much to take in at once. The parks are best when the leaves are out and during fall, when the foliage is turning. On the rare hot day, you may want to brave a dip in the waters of Hyde Park's Serpentine. Otherwise, explore by rented pedalo.

TOP ATTRACTIONS

FAMILY **Hyde Park.** Along with the smaller St. James's and Green parks to the
Fodor's Choice east, Hyde Park started as Henry VIII's hunting grounds. Along its south
★ side runs Rotten Row, once Henry's royal path to the hunt—the name is a corruption of *Route du Roi* (route of the king). It's still used by the Household Cavalry, who live at the Hyde Park Barracks—a high-rise and a low, ugly, red block—to the left. This is where the brigade that mounts the guard at Buckingham Palace resides, and you can see them leave to perform their duty, in full regalia, at about 10:30, or await the return of the guard around noon. Hyde Park is wonderful for strolling,

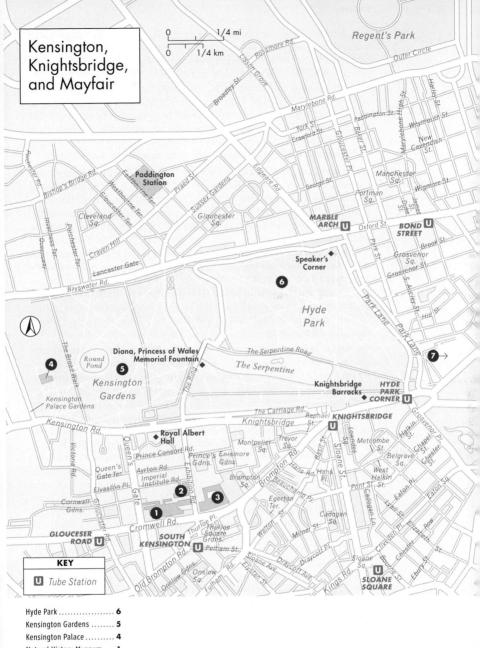

Kensington, Knightsbridge, and Mayfair

0 ···· 1/4 mi
0 ···· 1/4 km

Regent's Park

Outer Circle

Rossmore Rd.

Lisson Grove

Broadley St.

Marylebone Rd.

Harley St.

York St.

Crawford St.

Gloucester Pl.

Baker St.

New Cavendish St.

Weymouth St.

Manchester Sq.

Wigmore St.

Portman Sq.

George St.

Paddington Station

Praed St.

Sussex Gardens

Eastbourne Ter.

Westbourne Ter.

Gloucester Ter.

Bishop's Bridge Rd.

Porchester Rd.

Cleveland Sq.

Gloucester Sq.

Craven Hill

Lancaster Gate

Inverness Ter.

Porchester Ter.

Queensway

Bayswater Rd.

Edgware Rd.

MARBLE ARCH U

Oxford St.

BOND STREET U

Brook St.

Grosvenor Sq.

Grosvenor St.

Park St.

Park Lane

Duke St.

James St.

Speaker's Corner

Hyde Park

S. Audley St.

Hill St.

Hill St.

The Broad Walk

Round Pond

Diana, Princess of Wales Memorial Fountain

The Ring

The Serpentine Road

The Serpentine

Kensington Gardens

Kensington Palace Gardens

Kensington Rd.

Knightsbridge Barracks

HYDE PARK CORNER U

The Carriage Rd.

Knightsbridge

Raphael St.

KNIGHTSBRIDGE U

Grosvenor Pl.

Halkin St.

Chapel St.

Chester St.

Belgrave Sq.

Royal Albert Hall

Prince Consort Rd.

Prince's Gdns

Ennismore Gdns

Montpelier Sq.

Trevor Sq.

Basil St.

Sloane St.

Metcombe St.

West Halkin St.

Eaton Pl.

Eaton Sq.

Queen's Gate Ter.

Ayrton Rd.

Imperial Institute Rd.

Brompton Sq.

Brompton Rd.

Hans Rd.

Hans Pl.

Pont St.

Cadogan Lane

Cliveden Pl.

Elizabeth St.

Elvaston Pl.

Beauchamp Pl.

Egerton Ter.

Cadogan Sq.

Eaton Ter.

Cornwall Gdns.

Queen's Gate

Cromwell Rd.

GLOUCESTER ROAD U

SOUTH KENSINGTON U

Thurloe Pl.

Thurloe Square Gdns.

Pelham St.

Watton St.

Milner St.

Draycott Pl.

Sloane Ave.

Bourne St.

Chester Row

Chester St.

Ebury St.

Victoria Rd.

Gloucester Rd.

Old Brompton Rd.

Onslow Gdns.

Onslow Sq.

Fulham Rd.

Sloane Ave.

Elstan St.

Draycott Ave.

Kings Rd.

SLOANE SQUARE U

KEY

U Tube Station

watching the locals, or just relaxing by the Serpentine, the long body of water near its southern border. On the south side, by the 1930s **Serpentine Lido**, is the site of the **Diana, Princess of Wales Memorial Fountain**, which opened in 2003 and is a good spot to refuel at one of the cafés. On Sunday, close to Marble Arch, you'll find the uniquely British tribute to free speech, Speakers' Corner, a live variation on an Internet comments board, with orators expressing thoughts ranging from sensible to silly, rational to raving, and appalling to admirable. ⊠ *Hyde Park* ☎ *030/0061–2000* ⊕ *www.royalparks.gov.uk* ◇ *Daily 5 am–midnight* Ⓜ *Hyde Park Corner, Knightsbridge, Lancaster Gate, Marble Arch.*

FAMILY

Fodor's Choice

★

Kensington Gardens. Laid out in 1689 by William III, who commissioned Christopher Wren to build Kensington Palace, the gardens are a formal counterpart to neighboring Hyde Park. Just to the north of the palace itself is the Dutch-style **Sunken Garden**. Nearby, the 1912 bronze statue of *Peter Pan* commemorates the boy in J.M. Barrie's story who lived on an island in the Serpentine and never grew up. The **Diana, Princess of Wales Memorial Playground** also has sections inspired by Barrie's book. Nearby, the **Serpentine Gallery, along with its nearby second space, the Serpentine Sackler Gallery,** is noted for its shows by major contemporary artists and its annual outdoor summer pavilion designed by leading architects. ⊠ *Kensington* ☎ *030/0061–2000* ⊕ *www.royalparks.gov.uk* ◇ *Daily 6–dusk* Ⓜ *High Street Kensington, Lancaster Gate, Queensway, South Kensington.*

Kensington Palace. Neither as imposing as Buckingham Palace nor as charming as Hampton Court, Kensington Palace is something of a Royal Family commune, with various close relatives of the Queen occupying large apartments in the private part of the palace. Bought in 1689 by Queen Mary and King William III, it was converted into a palace by Sir Christopher Wren and Nicholas Hawksmoor, and royals have been in residence ever since. Its most famous resident, Princess Diana, lived here with her sons after her divorce, and this is where Prince William now lives with his wife, Catherine, Duchess of Cambridge. The State Apartments, however, are open to the public, and galleries showcase three permanent exhibitions that delve into palace history: *Victoria Revealed* is devoted to the private life of Queen Victoria (who was born and grew up here); the Queen's State Apartments tell the story of royal couple William and Mary and the Glorious Revolution; and the lavish King's State Apartments explore the world of the Georgian Court. Also not to be missed is the King's Staircase, with its panoramic trompe l'oeil painting, and the King's Gallery, where royal artworks are displayed in a jewel box setting under a beautiful painted ceiling. Through summer 2015, look for *Fashion Rules*, a temporary exhibition of gowns worn by Queen Elizabeth and Princesses Margaret and Diana. The palace's grounds are almost as lovely as the structure itself. ⊠ *The Broad Walk, Kensington Gardens, Kensington* ☎ *0844/482–7799 advance booking, 0844/482–7777 information, 0203/166–6000 from outside U.K.* ⊕ *www.hrp.org.uk* ☞ *£14.50 (subject to change)* ◇ *Mar.–Sept., daily 10–6; Oct.–Feb., daily 10–5; last admission 1 hr before closing* Ⓜ *Queensway, High Street Kensington.*

These ice-skaters outside the Natural History Museum in South Kensington are making the best of London's winter.

FAMILY **Natural History Museum.** The ornate terra-cotta facade of this enormous
Fodor's Choice Victorian museum is strewn with relief panels depicting living creatures to
★ the left of the entrance and extinct ones to the right (though some species
since changed categories). Within these walls lie more than 70 million
different specimens. Only a small percentage is on public display, but you
could still spend a day here and not come close to seeing everything. The
museum is full of cutting-edge exhibits with all the wow power and interactive displays necessary to interest younger visitors. You'll also come face
to face with a giant animatronic *Tyrannosaurus rex*—who is programmed
to sense when human prey is near and "respond" in character. When
he does, you can hear the shrieks of fear and delight all the way across
the room. A dizzyingly tall escalator takes you into a giant globe in the
Earth Galleries, where there's a choice of levels—and Earth surfaces—to
explore. Don't leave without checking out the earthquake simulation
in Gallery 61. ⊠ *Cromwell Rd., South Kensington* ☎ *0207/942–5000*
⊕ *www.nhm.ac.uk* ⌗ *Free (some fees for special exhibitions)* ☉ *Daily
10–5:50, last admission at 5:30* Ⓜ *South Kensington.*

Fodor's Choice **Royal Academy of Arts.** Burlington House was built in 1664, with later
★ Palladian additions for the 3rd Earl of Burlington in 1720. The house
itself is home to the drawing-card tenant, the Royal Academy of Arts.
The statue of the academy's first president, Sir Joshua Reynolds, palette in
hand, is prominent in the piazza of light stone with fountains by Sir Phillip King. Within the house and up the stairs are statues of creative giants
J.W.M. Turner and Thomas Gainsborough. Free tours show off part of
the academy's collection, some of it housed in the John Madejski Fine
Rooms, and the RA hosts excellent temporary exhibitions. ⊠ *Burlington*

House, Piccadilly, Mayfair ☎ 020/7300–8000, 0207/300–5839 lectures, 0207/300–5995 family programs ⊕ www.royalacademy.org.uk ✉ Prices vary with exhibition from £7–£15 ⊙ Sat.–Thurs. 10–6, Fri. 10–10; tours Tues. 1, Wed.–Fri. 1 and 3, Sat. 11:30 Ⓜ Piccadilly Circus, Green Park.

FAMILY
Fodor's Choice
★
Victoria & Albert Museum. Known to all as the V&A, this huge museum is devoted to the applied arts of all disciplines, all periods, and all nationalities. Full of innovation, it's a wonderful, generous place in which to get lost. First opened as the South Kensington Museum in 1857, it was renamed in 1899 in honor of Queen Victoria's late husband and has since grown to become one of the country's best-loved cultural institutions. Many collections at the V&A are presented not by period but by category—textiles, sculpture, jewelry, and so on. Nowhere is the benefit of this more apparent than in the **Fashion Gallery** (Room 40), where formal 18th-century court dresses are displayed alongside the haute couture styles of contemporary designers, creating an arresting sense of visual continuity. The **British Galleries** (rooms 52–58 and 118–125), devoted to British art and design from 1500 to 1900, are full of beautiful diversions—among them the Great Bed of Ware (immortalized in Shakespeare's *Twelfth Night*). Other cultures are represented in the galleries devoted to China, Korea, and the Islamic Middle East—check out the ornate samurai armor in the Japanese Gallery (Room 44). More recent installations include the Buddhist Sculpture Gallery, the Ceramics Gallery, and the Medieval and Renaissance Galleries, which have the largest collection of works from the period outside of Italy.

The V&A is a tricky building to navigate, so be sure to use the free map. ✉ Cromwell Rd., South Kensington ☎ 020/7942–2000 ⊕ www.vam. ac.uk ✉ Free; charge for some special exhibitions (from £5) ⊙ Sat.– Thurs. 10–5:45, Fri. 10–10 Ⓜ South Kensington.

WORTH NOTING

Science Museum. This, one of the three great South Kensington museums, stands next to the Natural History Museum in a far plainer building. It has lots of hands-on, painlessly educational exhibits, with entire schools of children apparently decanted inside to interact with them, but don't dismiss the Science Museum as just for kids. Highlights include the Launch Pad gallery, which demonstrates basic laws of physics; *Puffing Billy*, the oldest steam locomotive in the world; and the actual *Apollo 10* capsule. ✉ Exhibition Rd., South Kensington ☎ 0870/870–4868 ⊕ www.sciencemuseum.org.uk ✉ Free; charge for special exhibitions, cinema shows and simulator rides ⊙ Daily 10–6, 10–7 during school holidays (check website) Ⓜ South Kensington.

REGENT'S PARK AND HAMPSTEAD

Regent's Park, Primrose Hill, and Hampstead are three of London's prettiest and most civilized neighborhoods. The city becomes noticeably peaceable as you wind your way up from Marylebone Road through Regent's Park, with its elegant Nash terraces, to the well-tended lawns of Primrose Hill and the handsome Georgian streets of Hampstead.

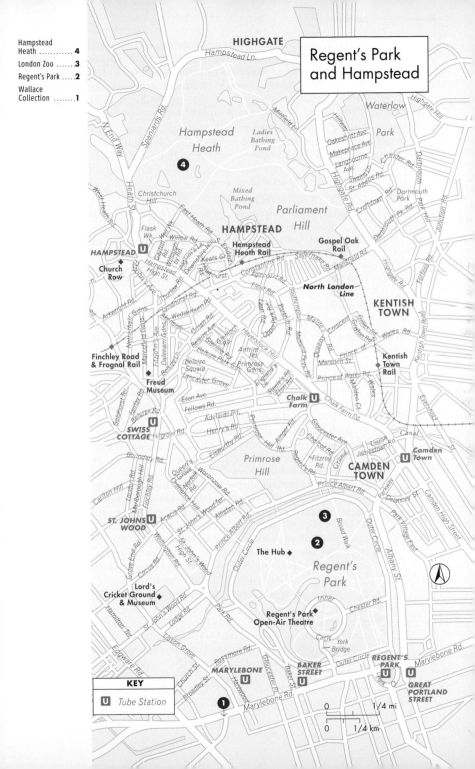

Regent's Park and Hampstead

HIGHGATE

Hampstead Ln.

Waterlow

Park

N. End Way

Spaniards Rd.

Hampstead
Heath

Ladies
Bathing
Pond

❹

West Heath Rd.

Heath St.

Christchurch
Hill

Mixed
Bathing
Pond

Parliament
Hill

Oakeshott Ave.

Makepeace Ave.

Langbourne
Ave.

Swains La.

St. Albans Rd.

Highgate Hill

Chester Rd.

Dartmouth
Park

Croftdown Rd.

Dartmouth Park Hill

Junction Rd.

Flask
Wk.

Well Wk.

Willow Rd.

HAMPSTEAD Ⓤ

Church
Row ◆

HAMPSTEAD

East Heath Rd.

Keats Gro.

**Hempstead
Heath Rail**

**Gospel Oak
Rail**

Mansfield Rd.

Downshire Hill

Garden Rd.

Windmill Hill

Hampstead High St.

Heath St.

Frognal

Rosslyn Hill

Constantine Rd.

Agincourt Rd.

Savernake Rd.

Highgate Rd.

**KENTISH
TOWN**

Fortess Rd.

Kentish Town Rd.

Frognal

Arkwright Rd.

Church Row

Fitzjohn's Ave.

Nethethall Gdns.

Maresfield Gdns.

Lyndhurst Rd.

Thurlow Rd.

Wedderburn Rd.

Fleet Rd.

Southampton Rd.

Mansfield Rd.

**North London
Line**

**Finchley Road
& Frognal Rail** ◆

Finchley Rd.

Netherhall Gdns.

Fairfax Rd.

Belsize Ave.

Belsize La.

Daleham Gdns.

Fitzjohn's Ave.

Glenloch Rd.

Glenilla Rd.

Belsize Park Gdns.

**Belsize
Square**

Lancaster Grove

Adamson Rd.

Aartrim
Rd.

Haverstock Hill

**Primrose
Gdns.**

England's La.

Queens Crescent

Malden Rd.

Grafton Rd.

Prince of
Wales Rd.

Marsden St.

**Kentish
Town
Rail** ◆

**Freud
Museum** ◆

Eton Ave.

Fellows Rd.

Lancaster Grove

Steele's Rd.

Eton Rd.

Prince of Wales Rd.

Malden Rd.

Wates Rd.

**SWISS
COTTAGE** Ⓤ

Belsize Rd.

Hilgrove Rd.

Adelaide Rd.

Henry's Rd.

**Chalk
Farm** Ⓤ

Chalk Farm Rd.

Eversholt St.

Boundary Rd.

Loudoun Rd.

Abbey Rd.

Queen's
Grove

Elsworthy Rd.

Primrose
Hill Rd.

Ainger Rd.

**Primrose
Hill**

Gloucester Ave.

Regent's Park Rd.

Fitzroy
Rd.

Chalcot Rd.

Jamestown Rd.

Union Rd.

Canal

**Camden
Town** Ⓤ

Camden High Street

Marlborough Hill

Finchley Rd.

Carlton Hill

Norfolk Rd.

Queen's
Grove

Watoonzow Rd.

Oppidans Rd.

Gloucester Ave.

Gloucester Gate

Grand Union

**CAMDEN
TOWN**

Parkway

Delancey St.

Camden High Street

Parkway Vintage East

**ST. JOHNS
WOOD** Ⓤ

Grove End Rd.

Wellington Rd.

Acacia Rd.

St. John's Wood Ter.

Attison Rd.

Prince Albert Rd.

Prince Albert Rd.

Camden Town Market

Albany St.

**Lord's
Cricket Ground
& Museum** ◆

Hamilton Ter.

St. John's Wood Rd.

Lodge Rd.

St. John's Wood High St.

Prince Albert Rd.

❸

The Hub ◆

❷

Broad Walk

**Regent's
Park**

Outer Circle

Chester Rd.

Outer Circle

Edgware Rd.

Lisson Grove

Rossmore Rd.

Park Rd.

Gloucester Pl.

Circle

Inner Circle

**Regent's Park
Open-Air Theatre** ◆

York
Bridge

Chester Rd.

**REGENT'S
PARK** Ⓤ

Marylebone Rd.

Church St.

Broadley St.

MARYLEBONE
Ⓤ

Harewood Av.

Gloucester Pl.

Baker St.

**BAKER
STREET** Ⓤ

Marylebone Rd.

Outer Circle

Ⓤ

Ⓤ

**GREAT
PORTLAND
STREET**

❶

KEY

Ⓤ *Tube Station*

0 ———— 1/4 mi

0 ———— 1/4 km

GETTING HERE   To get to Hampstead by Tube, take the Northern Line (make sure you get on the Edgware branch, not High Barnet) to Hampstead station, or take the London Overground to Hampstead Heath station. To get to Regent's Park, take the Bakerloo Line to Regent's Park Tube station or, for the Zoo, the Camden Town stop on the Northern Line. St. John's Wood has its own stop on the Jubilee Line.

PLANNING   Depending on your pace and inclination, Regent's Park and Hamp-
YOUR TIME   stead can realistically be covered in a day. It might be best to spend the morning in Hampstead, then head south toward Regent's Park in the afternoon so that you're closer to central London come nightfall, if that is where your hotel is located.

TOP ATTRACTIONS

FAMILY   **Hampstead Heath.** For an escape from the ordered prettiness of Hamp-
Fodor'sChoice   stead, head to the Heath—a unique remnant of London's preindustrial
★   countryside, with habitats ranging from wide grasslands to ancient woodlands spread over some 791 acres. **Parliament Hill,** one of the highest points in London, offers a stunning panorama over the city. ⊠ *Hampstead* ☎ *020/7482–7073 Heath Education Centre* ⊕ *www. cityoflondon.gov.uk/hampstead* ⌷ *Free* Ⓜ *Gospel Oak, Hampstead Heath for south of Heath; Hampstead for east of Heath; Golders Green, then Bus 210, 268 to Whitestone Pond for north and west of Heath.*

FAMILY   **London Zoo.** A modernization program at this facility that opened in
Fodor'sChoice   1828 has seen the introduction of several big attractions and a shift in
★   focus to wildlife conservation, education, and the breeding of endangered species. The huge **BUGS** pavilion (Biodiversity Underpinning Global Survival) is a self-sustaining, contained ecosystem with 140 species including spiders and millipedes, along with some reptiles and fish. At **Gorilla Kingdom** you can watch the four residents at close range. **Rainforest Life** is an indoor tropical rainforest populated by the likes of armadillos, monkeys, and sloths—a special nighttime section provides glimpses of nocturnal creatures such as slow lorises and bats. The new Animal Adventures Children's Zoo facilitates close encounters with animals that include mongooses, llamas, sheep, and goats. Don't miss feeding time at the popular Penguin Beach or the chance to watch the inhabitants of Meerkat Manor standing guard over their domain. ■**TIP**➔ **Check the website or the information board on-site for free events, including creature close encounters and "ask the keeper" sessions.** ⊠ *Outer Circle, Regent's Park* ☎ *020/7722–3333* ⊕ *www.zsl. org* ⌷ *£20* ⊘ *Mid-Nov.–Feb., daily 10–4; Mar.–early Sept., daily 10–6; early-Sept.–Oct., daily 10–5:30; early–mid-Nov., daily 10–4:30; last admission 1 hr before closing* Ⓜ *Camden Town, then Bus 274.*

FAMILY   **Regent's Park.** Cultivated and formal, compared with the relative wildness of Hampstead Heath, Regent's Park was laid out in 1812 by John Nash in honor of the Prince Regent, who was later crowned George IV. The idea was to re-create the feel of a grand country residence close to the center of town. Your nose should lead you to **Queen Mary's Gardens,** a 17-acre circle fragrant with 400 different varieties of roses in summer. ⊠ *Marylebone Rd., Regent's Park* ☎ *0300/061–2000* ⊕ *www.royalparks.gov.uk* ⌷ *Free* ⊘ *5 am–dusk* Ⓜ *Baker St., Regent's Park, Great Portland St.*

A TRIP TO ABBEY ROAD

The black-and-white crossroads (known as a "zebra crossing") near the Abbey Road Studios at No. 3 is a place of pilgrimage for Beatles' fans from around the world, many of them teenagers born long after the band split up. They converge here to recreate the cover of the Beatles' 1969 *Abbey Road* album, posing on the crossing despite the onrushing traffic. ■**TIP**➔ **Be very careful if you're going to attempt this. Abbey Road is a dangerous intersection.** The studio is where the Beatles recorded their entire output, from "Love Me Do" onward. A safer way to explore landmarks in the Beatles' story is to take one of the excellent walking tours

offered by **Original London Walks** (☎ *020/7624–3978* ⊕ *www.walks. com*), including **The Beatles In-My-Life Walk** (Saturday and Tuesday at 11:20 am outside Marylebone Underground) and **The Beatles Magical Mystery Tour** (Thursday and Sunday at 11 am year-round, Wednesday at 2 pm from February to November; Underground Exit 3, Tottenham Court Road), which cover landmark Beatles' spots in the city.

Abbey Road is in the elegant neighborhood of St. John's Wood, a 10-minute ride on the Tube from central London. Take the Jubilee Line to the St. John's Wood Tube stop and head southwest three blocks down Grove End Road.

FAMILY **Wallace Collection.** This exquisitely labyrinthine gallery is housed in Hertford House, an 18th-century mansion bequeathed to the nation along
Fodor's Choice with its contents, a stunning collection of classical European masters.
★ Rubens, Rembrandt, Van Dyck, Canaletto, Titian, and Velázquez are all represented. English works include paintings by Gainsborough and Turner, plus a dozen by Joshua Reynolds. ⊠ *Hertford House, Manchester Sq., Marylebone* ☎ *020/7563–9500* ⊕ *www.wallacecollection.org* 🖾 *Free* ☉ *Daily 10–5* Ⓜ *Bond St.*

UP AND DOWN THE THAMES

Downstream—meaning seaward, or east—from central London, Greenwich will require a day to explore, especially if you have any interest in maritime history or technology. Upstream to the west, are the royal palaces and grand houses that were built as country residences with easy access to London by river. Hampton Court Palace, with its famous maze, is the most notable.

GREENWICH

8 miles east of central London.

Greenwich makes an ideal day out from central London. Maritime Greenwich is a UNESCO World Heritage Site and includes Inigo Jones's Queens House, the first Palladian building in England; the Old Royal Observatory, home of the Greenwich Meridian that is the baseline for the world's time zones and the dividing line between the two hemispheres (you can stand astride it with one foot in either one); and the National Maritime Museum, which tells the story of how Britain came to rule the waves. Landlubbers, meanwhile, can explore the surrounding

Royal Park, laid out in the 1660s and thus the oldest of the royal parks, or central Greenwich with its attractive 19th-century houses.

The monorail-like Docklands Light Railway (DLR) will take you to Cutty Sark station from Canary Wharf and Bank Tube stations in the City. Or take the DLR to Island Gardens and walk the old Victorian Foot Tunnel under the river. But the most appropriate way to travel is—time and weather permitting—by water via River Bus.

Fodor's Choice

★ **National Maritime Museum.** From the time of Henry VIII until the 1940s, Britain was the world's preeminent naval power, and the collections here trace half a millennium of that seafaring history. The story is as much about trade as it is warfare; the Atlantic Worlds gallery explores how trade in goods—and people—helped shape the New World, and Voyagers: Britons and the Sea focuses on stories of the ordinary people who took to the waves over the centuries. One gallery is devoted to Admiral Lord Nelson, Britain's most famous naval commander, and among the exhibits is the uniform he was wearing, complete with bloodstains, when he died at the Battle of Trafalgar in 1805. The adjacent **Queen's House, designed by Inigo Jones,** is home to the museum's art collection, the largest collection of maritime art in the world, including works by William Hogarth, Canaletto, and Joshua Reynolds. ⌂ *Romney Rd., Greenwich* ☎ *020/8858–4422* ⊕ *www.rmg. co.uk* ☛ *Free* ⊙ *Daily 10–5; last admission 30 mins before closing* Ⓜ *DLR: Greenwich.*

QUICK BITES

Trafalgar Tavern. With its excellent vista of the Thames, there is no more handsomely situated pub in Greenwich than the Trafalgar Tavern. Featured in Charles Dickens's *Our Mutual Friend*, it's still as grand a place to have a pint and some (upscale) pub grub as it ever was. ⌂ *Park Row, Greenwich* ☎ *020/8858–2909* ⊕ *www.trafalgartavern.co.uk.*

FAMILY **Royal Observatory.** The baseline for world time was established here in 1884, when Britain was the world's largest and most important maritime power, and so the prime meridian at 0° longitude is found at Greenwich. A brass line laid between the cobblestones marks the meridian, with the Eastern Hemisphere on one side of it and the Western Hemisphere on the other. The observatory is similarly split into two sections, a short walk apart—one devoted to astronomy, the other to the study of time. The enchanting **Peter Harrison Planetarium,** London's only planetarium, has shows on black holes and how to interpret the night sky that are enthralling and enlightening. The cutting-edge touch screens and interactive programs of the **Astronomy Galleries** give young explorers the chance to run their own space missions to Ganymede, one of Jupiter's moons. Across the way is **Flamsteed House,** designed by Christopher Wren in 1675 for John Flamsteed, the first Royal Astronomer. The **Time Galleries** display the fine **Maritime Clocks** of John Harrison (1693–1776), which won him the Longitude Prize for finding a way to keep time accurately at sea and greatly improved navigation. ⌂ *Romney Rd., Greenwich* ☎ *020/8858–4422* ⊕ *www.rog.nmm.ac.uk* ☛ *Astronomy Galleries free; Flamstead house and Meridian Line courtyard £7; planetarium*

DAY TRIP TO HARRY POTTER STUDIO TOUR

Families and any fan of Harry Potter visiting the city may want to allow time for this entertaining studio tour outside London.

Warner Bros. Studio Tour London: The Making of Harry Potter. Muggles, take note: this spectacular attraction opened for wizarding business just outside Watford in 2012. From the Great Hall of Hogwarts to magical props, each section of this attraction showcases the real sets, props, and special effects used in the eight movies. Visitors enter the Great Hall, a fitting stage for costumes from each Hogwarts house. The spooky charm of the Defense Against the Dark Arts Classroom will tempt some to start experimenting, but others will hurry on to the comforting confines of Dumbledore's office. Tickets, pegged to a 30-minute arrival time slot, must be prebooked online. The studio tour is a 20-minute drive from St. Albans. You can also get here by taking a 20-minute train ride from London's Euston Station (then a 15-minute shuttle bus ride). Via car from London, use M1 and M25 and enjoy the free parking. ⊠ *Studio Tour Dr., Leavesden* ☎ *0845/084-0900* ⊕ *www.wbstudiotour.co.uk* ⊠ *£31* ⊗ *Daily 10–4 (until 6:30 at some times of year).*

shows £6.50; combined ticket £11.50. ⊗ *Daily 10–5 (May–Aug., Meridian courtyard until 6); last entry 30 mins before closing; last planetarium show 4* Ⓜ *DLR: Greenwich.*

HAMPTON COURT PALACE
20 miles southwest of central London.

FAMILY
Fodor's Choice
★

Hampton Court Palace. The beloved seat of Henry VIII's court, sprawled elegantly beside the languid waters of the Thames, this beautiful palace really gives you two beauties for the price of one: the magnificent Tudor red-brick mansion, begun in 1514 by Cardinal Wolsey to curry favor with the young Henry, and the larger 17th-century baroque building, which was partly designed by Christopher Wren (of St. Paul's fame). The earliest buildings on this site belonged to a religious order founded in the 11th century and were expanded over the years by its many subsequent residents, until George II moved the royal household closer to London in the early 18th century.

Wander through the **State Apartments,** decorated in the Tudor style, complete with priceless paintings, and on to the wood-beamed magnificence of **Henry's Great Hall,** before taking in the strikingly azure ceiling of the **Chapel Royal.** Well-handled reconstructions of Tudor life take place all year, from live appearances by "Henry VIII" and his elaborately-costumed court, to a small retinue of cook-historians preparing authentic Tudor feasts in the 15th-century **Henry's Kitchens.** Latter-day masters of the palace, the joint rulers William and Mary (reigned 1689–1702), were responsible for the beautiful **King's and Queen's Apartments** and the elaborate baroque of the **Georgian Rooms.** Don't miss the famous **maze** (the oldest hedge maze in the world), its half mile of pathways among clipped hedgerows still fiendish to negotiate. There's a trick, but we won't give it away here: It's

Among the botanical splendors of Kew Gardens is the Waterlily House.

much more fun just to go and lose yourself. ⊠ *Hampton Court Rd.,*
East Molesley, Surrey ☎ *0844/482–7799 tickets, 0844/482–7777*
information (24 hr.) ⊕ *www.hrp.org.uk/hamptoncourtpalace* 🖾 *Pal-*
ace, maze, and gardens £17; maze only £3.85; gardens only £5.50
(free Oct.-Mar.) ☉ *Late Mar.–Oct., daily 10–6; Nov.–late Mar., daily*
10–4:30; last admission one hr before closing; last entry to maze
45 mins before closing); check website before visiting Ⓜ *Richmond,*
then bus R68; National Rail: Hampton Court Station, 35 mins from
Waterloo (most trains require change at Surbiton).

KEW GARDENS
6 miles southwest of central London.

FAMILY **Kew Gardens.** Enter the Royal Botanic Gardens, as Kew Gardens are
also known, and you are enveloped by blazes of color, extraordinary
blooms, hidden trails, and lovely old follies. Beautiful though it all is,
Kew's charms are secondary to its true purpose as a major center for
serious research. Kew has been supported by royalty and nurtured by
landscapers, botanists, and architects since the 1720s. First opened to
the public in 1840, the gardens, now a UNESCO World Heritage Site,
hold more than 30,000 species of plants, from every corner of the globe.
Although the plant houses make Kew worth visiting even in the depths
of winter, the flower beds are, of course, best enjoyed in the fullness
of spring and summer. Architect Sir William Chambers built a series
of temples and follies, of which the crazy 10-story **Pagoda,** visible for
miles around, is the star turn. Two great 19th-century greenhouses—the
Palm House and the **Temperate House**—are filled with exotic blooms,
and many of the plants have been there since the final glass panel was

fixed into place. The Princess of Wales Conservatory houses 10 climate zones, and the Rhizotron and Xstrata Treetop Walkway takes you 59 feet up into the air. ⊠ *Kew Rd. at Lichfield Rd., for Victoria Gate entrance, Kew* ☎ *020/8332–5655* ⊕ *www.kew.org* ⊒ *£16* ⊙ *Mid-Feb.–mid Mar., daily 9:30–5:30; mid-Mar.–Aug., weekdays 9:30–6:30, weekends 9:30–7:30; Sept. and Oct., daily 9:30–6; Nov.–mid-Feb. daily 9:30–4:15. Glasshouses and galleries close 5:30 (3:45 Nov.–mid-Feb., 5 mid-Feb.–late Mar.); Palm House closes 2 on Tues.* Ⓜ *Kew Gardens. National Rail: Kew Gardens, Kew Bridge.*

QUICK BITES

The Original Maids of Honour. This most traditional of Old English tearooms, is named for a type of jam tart invented here and still baked by hand on the premises. Tea is served daily from 2:30 to 6, lunch in two sittings, at 12:30 and 1:30. Or opt for take-out to picnic at Kew Gardens or on Kew Green. ⊠ *288 Kew Rd., Kew* ☎ *020/8940–2752* ⊕ *www.theoriginalmaidsofhonour.co.uk.*

WHERE TO EAT

Use the coordinate (✛ B2) at the end of each listing to locate a site on the corresponding map.

For many years English food was a joke, especially to England's near neighbors, the French. But the days of steamed suet puddings and over-boiled brussels sprouts are long gone. For a good two decades London's restaurant scene has been booming, with world-class chefs—Jamie Oliver, Gordon Ramsay, Heston Blumenthal, and Jason Atherton among them—pioneering concepts that quickly spread overseas. Whether you're looking for bistros that rival their Parisian counterparts, five-star fine-dining establishments, fantastic fried-chicken and burger joints (American diner food is a current trend), gastro-pubs serving "Modern British," or places serving Peruvian–Japanese fusion, gourmet Indian, or nouveau greasy spoon, you'll be spoiled for choice. And that's just as well because you'll be spending, on average, 25% of your travel budget on dining out.

The British now take pride in the best of authentic homegrown food—local, seasonal, regional, and foraged are the buzzwords of the day. But beyond reinterpretations of native dishes, London's dining revolution is built on its incredible ethnic diversity, with virtually every international cuisine represented.

PRICES AND SAVING MONEY

In pricey London a modest meal for two can easily cost £40, and the £110-a-head meal is not unknown. Damage-control strategies include making lunch your main meal—the top places have bargain midday menus—going for early- or late-evening deals, or sharing an à la carte entrée and ordering an extra appetizer. Seek out fixed-price menus, and watch for hidden extras on the menu—that is, bread or vegetables charged separately.

TIPPING AND TAXES

Do not tip bar staff in pubs and bars—though you can always offer to buy them a drink. In restaurants, tip 12.5% of the check for full meals if service is not already included; tip a small token if you're just having coffee or tea. If paying by credit card, double-check that a tip (aka "service charge") has not already been included in the bill. If you leave cash it's more likely to go to the server rather than into a pool.

WHAT IT COSTS IN POUNDS				
	$	$$	$$$	$$$$
Restaurants	under £16	£16–£23	£24–£32	over £32

Prices are the average cost of a main course at dinner or, if dinner isn't served, at lunch.

WESTMINSTER, ST. JAMES'S, AND ROYAL LONDON

ST. JAMES'S

$$
MODERN
EUROPEAN
Fodor's Choice
★

✕ **Le Caprice.** Grande dame Le Caprice commands the deepest loyalty of any restaurant in London. The reasons include the three-decade celebrity history—going back to Liz Taylor and Princess Diana—the atmospheric David Bailey black-and-white portraits, the perfect service, and a menu that adroitly navigates the realm between traditional and trendy. Sit at the raised counter or at a corner table and enjoy calf's liver with crispy bacon or roast pheasant with caramelized quince, all served with a dollop of star spotting. $ *Average main: £23* ⊠ *Arlington House, Arlington St., St. James's* ☏ *020/7629–2239* ⊕ *www.caprice-holdings. co.uk* ⤷ *Reservations essential* Ⓜ *Green Park* ✛ *D4.*

$$$
BRITISH

✕ **Wiltons.** Aristocrats and the merely very-well-to-do blow the family fortune at this bastion of fine dining that began life as a shellfish stall in 1742. Jackets are required for gentlemen at this clubby time capsule, where signet ring–wearing patrons partake of half a dozen Colchester oysters, followed by grilled Dover sole on the bone or fabulous native game—the seasonal choices might include grouse, woodcock, partridge, or teal. There are antediluvian savories such as anchovies or mushrooms on toast, and sherry trifle, bread-and-butter pudding, and other traditional offerings for dessert. The wines weigh heavily towards Bordeaux and Burgundy, and the service, naturally, would put Jeeves to shame. $ *Average main: £32* ⊠ *55 Jermyn St., St. James's* ☏ *020/7629–9955* ⊕ *www.wiltons.co.uk* ⤷ *Reservations essential* ⓘ *Jacket required* ☾ *Closed weekends* Ⓜ *Green Park* ✛ *D3.*

$$
AUSTRIAN
FAMILY
Fodor's Choice
★

✕ **The Wolseley.** The home of the London power breakfast—and lunch, tea, and dinner—this former Wolseley car showroom on Piccadilly a few doors down from the Ritz has been transformed into a soaringly elegant yet relaxed Viennese-style *Mitteleuropa* grand café, the perfect stage set for the city's see-and-be-seen crowd to enjoy Hungarian goulash, Austrian pork belly, chicken soup with salt beef sandwich, eggs Benedict, kedgeree, and breaded Wiener schnitzel, all exemplary. The all-day brasserie opens for breakfast at 7 am and serves until midnight. Don't be afraid to just turn up—seats are held back for walk-ins—but you might want to book to savor the pastries included in the snazzy

BEST BETS: LONDON DINING

2

Fodor'sChoice★

10 Greek Street, $$, p. 93
Berners Tavern, $, p. 99
Brasserie Zédel, $, p. 96
Bubbledogs, $, p. 99
Chez Bruce, $$$, p. 102
Dabbous, $$, p. 99
The Delaunay, $$, p. 97
Dinner by Heston Blumenthal, $$$, p. 104
J Sheekey, $$$, p. 98
The Harwood Arms, $$, p. 104
The Ledbury, $$$, p. 108
Le Caprice, $$, p. 92

Petrus, $$$, p. 104
Pitt Cue Co., $, p. 97
Pollen Street Social, $$$, p. 107
Roti Chai, $, p. 100
Rules, $$$, p. 98
Scott's, $$$, p. 107
Spuntino, $, p. 97
St. John, $$, p. 101
The Wolseley, $$, p. 92
Zucca, $$, p. 102

Best by Cuisine

BRITISH

Berners Tavern, $, p. 99

The Harwood Arms, $$, p. 104
Hereford Road, $$, p. 108
St. John, $$, p. 101

FRENCH

The Delaunay, $$, p. 97
The Ledbury, $$$, p. 108
Petrus, $$$, p. 104
The Riding House Café, $, p. 107

ITALIAN

Bocca di Lupo, $$, p. 96
Cecconi's, $$, p. 106

---

afternoon teas. Attentive service will make you feel special even if you're not a boldface name. $ *Average main: £18* ✉ *160 Piccadilly, St. James's* ☎ *020/7499–6996* ⊕ *www.thewolseley.com* ✍ *Reservations essential* Ⓜ *Green Park* ✛ *D4.*

SOHO AND COVENT GARDEN

SOHO

$$
MODERN
EUROPEAN
Fodor'sChoice
★

✕ **10 Greek Street.** There may only be 28 seats and 9 counter stools overlooking the open kitchen at this stripped-back Modern European hideaway, but talented Aussie chef Cameron Emirali delivers with great food, *reasonable* wine, appealing service, decent prices *and* plenty of buzz. The only negative is the no-reservations policy in the evenings, but you can pass the time in the pub three doors down and wait for a call on your cell phone. Once seated, expect simple starters or mains such as grilled sardines with salsify and salsa verde, or octopus carpaccio with caperberries, chili, and lemon. Gutsy meats—including Welsh Black rib eye, hare, venison—are big and bold, as are the desserts, among them lemon delicious, rum panna cotta, and quince and apple pie. $ *Average main: £16* ✉ *10 Greek Street, Soho* ☎ *020/7734–4677* ⊕ *www.10greekstreet.com* ☯ *Closed Sun.* ✛ *E3.*

$$
MEDITERRANEAN

✕ **Andrew Edmunds.** Shabby chic, *intime*, and candlelit, Andrew Edmunds is a permanently packed, deeply romantic Soho institution—though it could be larger, less creaky underfoot, and the reclaimed wooden bench seats more forgiving. It's a cozy favorite with the Soho media crowd enticed by the daily-changing fixed-price lunch menus and the quirky, historic vibe. Satisfyingly rustic starters and mains draw on the tastes

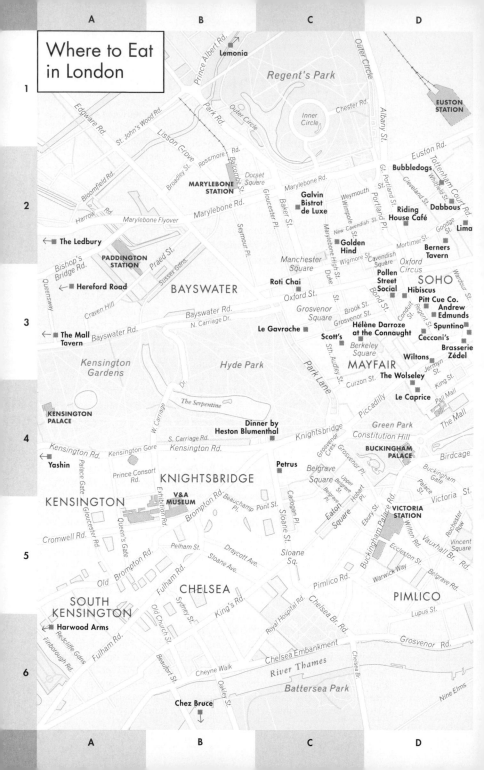

Where to Eat in London

Lemonia

Regent's Park

Prince Albert Rd.

Outer Circle

Inner Circle

Chester Rd.

Albany St.

EUSTON STATION

Edgware Rd.

St. John's Wood Rd.

Lisson Grove

Park Rd.

Outer Circle

Euston Rd.

Tottenham Court Rd.

Bloomfield Rd.

Rossmore Rd.

Balcombe St.

Dorset Square

Broadley St.

Gloucester Pl.

Gt. Portland St.

Cleveland St.

Whitfield St.

Bubbledogs

MARYLEBONE STATION

Marylebone Rd.

Weymouth St.

Portland Pl.

Dabbous

Riding House Café

Lima

Harrow Rd.

Marylebone Flyover

Marylebone Rd.

Baker St.

Wimpole St.

New Cavendish St.

Galvin Bistrot de Luxe

Goodge St.

Praed St.

Seymour Pl.

Berners Tavern

The Ledbury

Marylebone High St.

Wigmore St.

Cavendish Square

Mortimer St.

Oxford Circus

Golden Hind

PADDINGTON STATION

Stussex Gdns.

BAYSWATER

Manchester Square

Duke St.

SOHO

Bishop's Bridge Rd.

Hereford Road

Pollen Street Social

Hibiscus

Wardour St.

Queensway

Roti Chai

Oxford St.

Bond St.

Conduit St.

Pitt Cue Co.

Andrew Edmunds

Craven Hill

Bayswater Rd.

Grosvenor Square

Brook St.

Regent St.

Hélène Darroze at the Connaught

Spuntino

The Mall Tavern

Bayswater Rd.

N. Carriage Dr.

Le Gavroche

Grosvenor St.

Cecconi's

Scott's

Berkeley Square

Brasserie Zédel

Kensington Gardens

Hyde Park

Sth. Audley St.

Wiltons

Jermyn St.

King St.

KENSINGTON PALACE

The Serpentine

Park Lane

MAYFAIR

The Wolseley

Pall Mall

The Mall

W. Carriage Dr.

S. Carriage Rd.

Dinner by Heston Blumenthal

Knightsbridge

Curzon St.

Piccadilly

Le Caprice

Green Park

Constitution Hill

BUCKINGHAM PALACE

Birdcage

Kensington Rd.

Kensington Gore

Kensington Rd.

Petrus

Grosvenor Cres.

Grosvenor Pl.

Buckingham Gate

Yashin

Palace Gate

Prince Consort Rd.

Belgrave Square

Upper Belgrave St.

Hobart Pl.

Buckingham Palace Rd.

Palace St.

Victoria St.

Rochester Row

KENSINGTON

Exhibition Rd.

V&A MUSEUM

Brompton Rd.

Beauchamp Pl.

Pont St.

Cadogan Pl.

Eaton Square

Belgrave Pl.

VICTORIA STATION

Witton Rd.

Vauxhall Br. Rd.

Vincent Square

Gloucester Rd.

Cromwell Rd.

KNIGHTSBRIDGE

Queen's Gate

Pelham St.

Draycott Ave.

Sloane St.

Sloane Sq.

Ebury St.

Eccleston St.

Warwick Way

Belgrave Rd.

Old Brompton Rd.

Fulham Rd.

Sloane Ave.

Pimlico Rd.

PIMLICO

SOUTH KENSINGTON

CHELSEA

King's Rd.

Chelsea Br. Rd.

Lupus St.

Harwood Arms

Redcliffe Gdns.

Old Church St.

Sydney St.

Royal Hospital Rd.

Chelsea Br. Rd.

Grosvenor Rd.

Finborough Rd.

Fulham Rd.

Beaufort St.

Cheyne Walk

Chelsea Embankment

Chelsea Br.

Nine Elms

Chez Bruce

Oakley St.

River Thames

Battersea Park

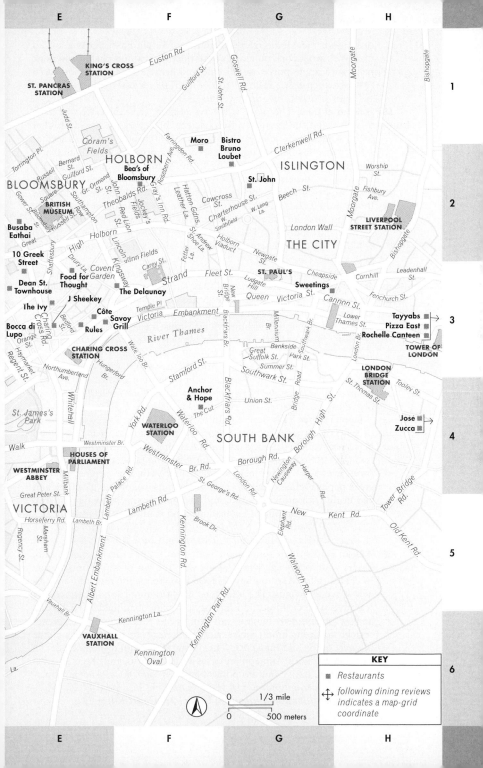

of Ireland, the Mediterranean, and the Middle East. Harissa-spiced mackerel, woodcock on toast, goose rillettes, seafood paella, and pork belly with apple purée are all hale and hearty. [$] *Average main: £16* ✉ *46 Lexington St., Soho* ☎ *020/7437–5708* ✍ *Reservations essential* [M] *Oxford Circus, Piccadilly Circus* ✥ *D3.*

$$ ITALIAN 🍴 **Bocca di Lupo.** The place is always packed, the tables are too close together, and the acoustics are deficient, but everyone applauds chef Jacob Kenedy's punchy, rustic Italian fare. On one of Soho's seedier side streets, this family-run place serves up a procession of small plates and peasant-based dishes hailing from Piedmont, Emilia, Lombardy, Campania, and elsewhere. Try yummy buffalo mozzarella, suckling pig, teal, polenta with anchovies, Sicilian lobster spaghetti, or *baccalà* (home-salted cod). Limber up with a colorful Aperol spritzer before plunging into the Italo-centric wine list, which weaves from Gavi di Gavi to rare Barolos. [$] *Average main: £16* ✉ *12 Archer St., Soho* ☎ *020/7734–2223* 🌐 *www.boccadilupo.com* ✍ *Reservations essential* [M] *Piccadilly Circus* ✥ *D3.*

$ BRASSERIE FAMILY Fodor's Choice ★ 🍴 **Brasserie Zédel.** The prices are *pas cher* (that's French for inexpensive) at this *magnifique* take on an all-day Parisian-style brasserie. Inside a glamorous art deco former underground ballroom with gilded ceilings and marble pillars, restaurateurs Corbin and King serve up vichyssoise with sliced baguette and butter for £2-plus; steak *haché* and *frites* for around £9; and a three-course daily meal with *salade mâche*, duck confit, a glass of red, and coffee for £20. Save centimes on a classic celery-root rémoulade or *soupe de poisson* (fish soup), and spend the difference at the swanky Bar Américain or the in-house cabaret, the Crazy Coqs. [$] *Average main: £8* ✉ *20 Sherwood St., Soho* ☎ *020/7734–4888* 🌐 *www.brasseriezedel.com* [M] *Piccadilly Circus* ✥ *D3.*

$ THAI FAMILY 🍴 **Busaba Eathai.** This sleek and sultry modern Thai canteen in the heart of Soho offers great food at reasonable prices. Fitted with dark-wood bench seats and hardwood communal-dining tables, this chain flagship is known for its rapid service, low lighting, and fast-moving queues out front. Menu mainstays include ginger beef with Thai pepper, crunchy green papaya salad, chicken with shiitake mushrooms, jungle curry, and vermicelli with prawns, squid, and scallops. At this top-value pit stop you'll escape for about £15 a head, not bad at all. [$] *Average main: £11* ✉ *106–110 Wardour St., Soho* ☎ *020/7255–8686* 🌐 *www.busaba.com* ✍ *Reservations not accepted* [M] *Tottenham Court Rd.* ✥ *E2.*

$$ PERUVIAN 🍴 **Lima.** Frisky pisco sours made with clear grape brandy, sugar syrup, bitters, and foamy egg white, along with the out-of-this-world cuisine by chef Virgilio Martinez have blasted Lima to the top rank of London's new-wave Peruvians. The informal, sky-lit dining room is attractively scattered with cushions and Inca-style stitched banquettes. Kick back and let the famously bubbly staff bring you a killer raw-fish sea bream ceviche doused in lime-y white tiger's milk (*leche de tigre*), with a tangle of sweet onion and Inka corn. The outstanding main dishes include the suckling pig with Amazonian cashews and lentils and the crab with purple corn, native *huayro* potato, and red *kiwich* (an Andean supergrain). [$] *Average main: £18* ✉ *31 Rathbone Pl., Soho* P020/3002–2640🌐 *www.limalondon.com* [M] *Tottenham Court Rd.* ✥ *D2.*

$ BARBECUE Fodor's Choice ★ 🍴 **Pitt Cue Co.** London's gone big for Southern-style BBQ, one reason the no-reservations hipster hangout Pitt Cue often has lines snaking out the door. That and the fact that there are only 18 basement seats, plus a few pavement berths and eight counter stools in the ground-level bourbon-and-rye crush bar. The pulled-pork sliders come with authentic slaw and house pickles, and you can order charred beef or pork ribs—or sausages or pulled pork—and sides such as baked beans and bone-marrow mash. It's a long way from Memphis, but even BBQ experts will likely approve. [$] *Average main: £12* ✉ *1 Newburgh St., Soho*P*020/7287–5578* 🌐 *www.pittcue.co.uk* ✍ *Reservations not accepted* ⏲ *Closed Sun.* [M] *Oxford Circus* ✥ *D3.*

$ DINER Fodor's Choice ★ 🍴 **Spuntino.** With its tin ceilings, tattooed waiters, moody low-wattage lighting from dangling filament bulbs, and bluegrass tunes, this Soho diner embodies the trend for American retro. Seating is tight, with a mere 26 raised counter stools at a pewter-topped rectangular bar. Adding to the speakeasy vibe, there's no phone, minimal signage, and reservations aren't accepted. The truffled egg toast, grits, soft-shell crab, and sliders—including spiced mackerel and ground beef and bone marrow—are worth the inevitable wait. Mac and cheese, steak and eggs, and a beloved peanut butter and jelly sandwich are among the other stateside comfort-food staples. You can wash your meal down with a shot or two of Elijah Craig or Knob Creek bourbon. [$] *Average main: £12* ✉ *61 Rupert St., Soho* P*no telephone* 🌐 *www.spuntino.co.uk* ✍ *Reservations not accepted* [M] *Piccadilly Circus* ✥ *D3.*

COVENT GARDEN

$ BISTRO FAMILY 🍴 **Côte.** Part of a chain, this brasserie serves up great two-course French meals for a mere £9.95, daily from noon until early evening (7 pm on weekdays, 6 pm on weekends). You'll find all the greatest hits: tuna Niçoise salad, bœuf Bourguignon, charcoal-grilled Breton chicken, *moules marinières* (mussels in white wine), steak haché, and, for dessert, crème caramel. Softly lit and nattily decked out with gray-and-white striped awnings, banquettes, and Parisian-style round café tables, Côte is perfect for pre-*or* post-theater dining. [$] *Average main: £10* ✉ *17-21 Tavistock St., Covent Garden* ☎ *020/7379–9991* 🌐 *www.cote-restaurants.co.uk* ✍ *Reservations essential* [M] *Covent Garden* ✥ *E3.*

$$ AUSTRIAN Fodor's Choice ★ 🍴 **The Delaunay.** Sister property of the Wolseley and with a similar aesthetic, this stylish, art deco–ish take on a grand all-day Central European café and Viennese coffeehouse has an impressive 60-item menu that includes delicious Weiner schnitzel, goulash, and Viennese hot dogs, served with sauerkraut and onions. Desserts such as apple strudel and an evocative three-peaked Salzburg soufflé delight as well. If you can't manage a full meal, the breakfasts, brunch, Viennese pastries, and afternoon teas provide other excellent options at this restaurant that's convenient to Drury Lane and its theaters. [$] *Average main: £21* ✉ *55 Aldwych, Covent Garden* ☎ *020/7499 8558* 🌐 *www.thedelaunay.com* [M] *Covent Garden, Charring Cross, Aldwych* ✥ *F3.*

$$ BRITISH 🍴 **The Ivy.** Ultra A-listers may prefer the Ivy's private members' club upstairs but there is still a heavy celebrity quotient at this longtime showbiz hangout. Diners famous and otherwise enjoy the salt beef hash, squash risotto, Thai-baked sea bass, salmon fish cakes, pork meatballs,

eggs Benedict, and English classics such as shepherd's pie and kedgeree (curried rice with smoked haddock, egg, and parsley) in a handsome mullioned stained-glass and oak-paneled dining salon. Service is flawless, and for low-to-mid wattage West End star spotting this is a prime spot. ■ TIP→ Even if you've been unable to reserve a table by phone, try your luck walking in off the street—it's been known to work. $ *Average main: £21* ✉ *1–5 West St., Covent Garden* ☎ *020/7836–4751* ⊕ *www. the-ivy.co.uk* ✍ *Reservations essential* Ⓜ *Covent Garden* ✛ *E3.*

$$$ ✕ **J Sheekey.** This atmospheric seafood specialist, decorated with warm
SEAFOOD wood paneling, vintage showbiz black-and-white portraits, and a lava-
Fodor'sChoice rock bar top, is a good alternative to Scott's and Nobu. Dating back
★ to 1896 and forever linked to the surrounding Theatreland district, J Sheekey has been a favorite haunt of West End theater and Hollywood stars for generations. The choices include bitingly fresh Atlantic prawns, pickled Arctic herring, crab bisque, slip sole, scallop, shrimp, and salmon burgers, and the famous Sheekey fish pie. For a lighter but still elegant repast, combine Gaston Chiquet Champagne with half a dozen Lindisfarne rock oysters at the mirrored raised-counter oyster bar. If here for weekend lunch, you can take advantage of the £26.50 three-course deals. $ *Average main: £24* ✉ *28–32 St. Martin's Ct., Covent Garden* ☎ *020/7240–2565* ⊕ *www.j-sheekey.co.uk* ✍ *Reservations essential* Ⓜ *Leicester Sq.* ✛ *E3.*

$$$ ✕ **Rules.** Opened by Thomas Rule in 1798, London's oldest restaurant
BRITISH and, according to some, still its most beautiful, Rules has fed Charles
Fodor'sChoice Dickens, Laurence Olivier, and many other luminaries. The main din-
★ ing salons exude period charm, with plush red banquettes, lacquered yellow walls, and spectacular etched-glass skylights, plus an abundance of vintage needlepoint, antique clocks, stuffed pheasants, and framed prints. The restaurant specializes in traditional British classics such as steak-and-kidney pie, jugged hare, and roast beef and Yorkshire pudding. In season, don't miss daily specials of acclaimed game—including grouse, partridge, snipe, and woodcock—from the restaurant's own High Pennines estate. $ *Average main: £29* ✉ *35 Maiden La., Covent Garden* ☎ *020/7836–5314* ⊕ *www.rules.co.uk* ✍ *Reservations essential* 🏛 *Jacket required* Ⓜ *Covent Garden* ✛ *E3.*

$$$ ✕ **The Savoy Grill.** The sense of history is palpable at this glamorous 1889
BRITISH power-dining salon that has hosted notables from Oscar Wilde to Frank
FAMILY Sinatra and Marilyn Monroe. Nowadays—buffed up with Swarovski chandeliers, velvet coverings, gold leaf-backed tortoiseshell walls, and period photos and mirrors—it caters to business barons and top-end tourists who come for the Grill's famous table-side trolley that's laden with saddle of lamb, crown of pork, and traditional beef Wellington. Other classics include the impressively executed T-bone, chateaubriand, and porterhouse steaks and, from the sea, Dover sole and lobster thermidor. Among the Savoy's specialties are the omelet Arnold Bennett (with smoked haddock, Parmesan, and cream) and egg cocotte with smoked bacon, wild mushrooms, and red wine sauce. $ *Average main: £30* ✉ *The Savoy, 100 Strand, Covent Garden* ☎ *020/7592–1600* ⊕ *www.gordonramsay.com/thesavoygrill* ✍ *Reservations essential* Ⓜ *Charing Cross, Covent Garden* ✛ *E3.*

BLOOMSBURY AND HOLBORN

BLOOMSBURY

$ AMERICAN

🍴 **Bea's of Bloomsbury.** With its on-site bakery, Bea's churns out such freshly baked sugary delights as a blackberry-topped vanilla sponge cupcake with a butter-cream filling and a chocolate fudge cupcake with fudge icing. Don't miss the brightly colored chocolate and peanut butter cupcakes, and try not to drool over the New York–style cheesecakes topped with lemon curd and berries—or the nine-layer chocolate cakes or the three-layer chocolate-truffle ones. The choices at afternoon tea (£19, with Champagne £26.50) include cupcakes, scones, mini-meringues, flavored marshmallows, and Valrhona-chocolate brownies. The tea is served from 2 to 7 on weekdays and noon to 7 pm on weekends. [$] *Average main: £6* ✉ *44 Theobald's Rd., Bloomsbury* ☎ *020/7242–8330* 🌐 *wwww.beasofbloomsbury.com* ✥ *F2.*

$ MODERN BRITISH FAMILY Fodor's Choice ★

🍴 **Berners Tavern.** All the cool cats converge at this grand brasserie at Ian Schrager's trendy London Edition hotel. It's hard not to feel like a million dollars as you enter the triple-height all-day dining salon, crammed with 1835 ornate plasterwork, bronze chandeliers, candles, and 150-odd stately home–style paintings. Bag a half-moon banquette and start the day with an impeccable £13 Full English breakfast (with Stornaway black pudding) and return for a light lunch of crispy rock-shrimp roll or pulled Old Spot pork with chips and slaw for £12. Reemerge refreshed for dinner, and swoon over a deep-fried duck egg, Cumbrian ham, and pea appetizer, and then ponder an entrée: perhaps Creedy Carver duck, Cornish sea bass, or Buccleuch Estates bavette. [$] *Average main: £15* ✉ *The London Edition, 10 Berners St., Bloomsbury* ☎ *020/7908–7979* 🌐 *www.bernerstavern.com* ✍ *Reservations essential* [M] *Oxford Circus, Tottenham Court Rd.* ✥ *D2.*

FITZROVIA

$ AMERICAN FAMILY Fodor's Choice ★

🍴 **Bubbledogs.** Husband-and-wife team Sandia Chang and chef James Knappett hit the jackpot by combining their respective loves of Champagne and New York–style hot dogs. Their menu pairs all-British pork and beef hot dogs—there are also vegetarian ones—with keenly priced (£6.50) Champagnes by the glass from distinguished smaller producers such as Gaston Chiquet. The dogs are served in baskets and toppings range from the superior BLT (bacon bits, caramelized lettuce, and truffle mayonnaise) to the Sloppy Joe (with chili, onions, and cheese) and even one with kimchi and red-bean paste. Reservations are only taken for groups of six or more. [$] *Average main: £7* ✉ *70 Charlotte St., Fitzrovia* ☎ *020/7637–7770* 🌐 *www.bubbledogs.co.uk* ✍ *Reservations not accepted* ⏲ *Closed Sun. and Mon.* [M] *Goodge St.* ✥ *D2.*

$$ MODERN EUROPEAN Fodor's Choice ★

🍴 **Dabbous.** Wunderkind chef Ollie Dabbous serves up startlingly stripped-back, inventive, and seasonal dishes at this industrial-chic restaurant (complete with exposed concrete and overhead ducts) off Charlotte Street. Frozen mint tea, edible violets, and broad-bean flowers enliven dishes such as peas and mint, and a coddled hen's egg with woodland mushrooms and smoked butter comes atop a bowl of hay. The phenomenal barbecued Ibèrico pork is flavored with acorn praline, turnip tops, and apple vinegar; halibut with coastal herbs (sea aster and oyster leaf); and brittle and crumbly chocolate ganache with green basil moss. Book months ahead. $ *Average main: £18* ✉ *39 Whitfield St., Fitzrovia* ☎ *020/7323–7323* ⊕ *www.dabbous.co.uk* ⌖ *Reservations essential* ⊙ *Closed Sun. and Mon.* Ⓜ *Goodge St.* ✛ *D2.*

$ ✕ **Roti Chai.** Incredible Indian street food hits the spot at this bright,

MODERN INDIAN   yellow-ceilinged, superior curry canteen found behind Selfridges. The

Fodor's Choice   kitchen specializes in snacks inspired by the ones served by Indian street-

★   cart vendors and at roadside "dhaba" cafés—spicy dishes such as *bhel puri* (puffed rice with onion, cumin, and tamarind), fiery white cubes of "Hakka" chili paneer cheese, and Keralan chicken "lollipops" that come with an irresistible coriander dip. Among the other must-try plates are Punjabi *aloo* (potato) *bun tikki* mini-burgers and a tomato-based "railway" lamb curry that's straight out of Bombay's Victoria Terminus station. This is a trip to India for which you need no passport. $ *Average main: £12* ✉ *3 Portman Mews S, Fitzrovia* ☎ *020/7408–0101* ⊕ *www.rotichai.com* Ⓜ *Marble Arch* ✛ *C3.*

THE CITY AND ENVIRONS

THE CITY

$$ ✕ **Moro.** Husband-and-wife chefs Sam and Sam Clark blend Spanish and

MEDITERRANEAN   Moorish North African flavors at their restaurant Moro, which helped spawn a mini restaurant row at Exmouth Market. Rustic tapas such as baba ghanoush, Syrian lentils, sardines, and grilled chorizo compete for attention with medium-size plates that might include a warm seafood and seaweed salad and smoked duck breast with pickles and hummus. Wood-fired sea bass with hispi cabbage and grilled sea bream with chickpea salad are among the standout mains. It can be very noisy at Moro, but it's always fun. $ *Average main: £19* ✉ *34–36 Exmouth Market, The City* ☎ *020/7833–8336* ⊕ *www.moro.co.uk* ⌖ *Reservations essential* ⊙ *Closed Sun.* Ⓜ *Farringdon, Angel* ✛ *F1.*

$$ ✕ **Sweetings.** A time-warp City seafood institution, Sweetings was estab-

SEAFOOD   lished in 1889 and it powers serenely on as if the sun never set on the British Empire, eschewing newfangled notions such as serving dinner or coffee, taking reservations, or opening on weekends. Not far from St. Paul's Cathedral, it's a favorite with bankers who down pewter tankards of Black Velvets (Guinness and Champagne) along with lobster salad, roe on toast, Dover sole, Cornish brill, and succulent skate wings with black butter sauce, all served on linen-covered raised counters or tables. The long-serving waiters wear whites, the oysters are plump and fresh, and the desserts, among them fruit crumble and baked jam roll, are old boarding school favorites. $ *Average main: £19* ✉ *39 Queen Victoria St., The City* ☎ *020/7248–3062* ⌖ *Reservations not accepted* ⊙ *Closed weekends. No dinner* Ⓜ *Mansion House* ✛ *H3.*

$ ✕ **Tayyabs.** Expect queues after dark at this noisy, neon-lit, BYO Paki-

PAKISTANI   stani curry specialist near Whitechapel and Banglatown. Amid the often-maddening chaos you can gorge handsomely for under £20 on a mixed charcoal-grilled extravaganza, which might include fiery Tandoori chicken and fish tikka. Other good bets include Kara-chi okra, minced meat *seekh* kebabs, Karachi prawns, hot steam-ing naan, and the restaurant's spicy secret-recipe charcoal-grilled

Karachi lamb chops. [$] *Average main: £12* ✉ *83 Fieldgate St., The City* ☎ *020/7247–9543* 🌐 *www.tayyabs.co.uk* ✍ *Reservations not accepted* [M] *Aldgate East* ⊕ *H3.*

2

CLERKENWELL

$$ FRENCH 🍴 **Bistrot Bruno Loubet.** The noted French chef Bruno Loubet is behind this buzzy dining room and bistro at the Zetter hotel in Clerkenwell. He creates so many must-try dishes it's genuinely hard to pick: deliciously pink quail comes with prune, Roquefort, and sautéed wild mushrooms, and guinea fowl *boudin blanc* sausages sit perfectly with leeks and chervil sauce, to name just two. Other menu delights might include wonderful sea bream with Pernod *beurre blanc,* yummy Mauricette snails and meatballs, and rabbit *royale,* followed by tarragon-poached pear. [$] *Average main: £19* ✉ *The Zetter, 86–88 Clerkenwell Rd.Clerkenwell* ☎ *020/7324–4455* 🌐 *www.bistrotbrunoloubet.com* ✍ *Reservations essential* [M] *Farringdon St., Barbican* ⊕ *G2.*

$ PIZZA FAMILY 🍴 **Pizza East.** This fashionable East London gourmet pizza parlor serves up chewy, 10-inch, wood-fired, thin-crust, crispy pizzas in a former tea warehouse. Don't come expecting candles stuck into raffia-covered wine bottles—the decor is achingly trendy, with concrete walls, raw brickwork, and long refectory-style shared tables. Starters include broad beans with pecorino and sea bass carpaccio with fennel and chili. The semolina-crust pizzas might be topped with San Daniele ham, ricotta and pesto, or pancetta, eggplant, and *scamorza* (an Italian cow's-milk cheese). Wine is served from the tap, cocktails come by the jug, and the music plays loud. [$] *Average main: £12* ✉ *56 Shoreditch High St., East End* ☎ *020/729–1888* 🌐 *www.pizzaeast.com* [M] *Rail: Shoreditch High Street* ⊕ *H3.*

$$ BRITISH 🍴 **Rochelle Canteen.** You'll feel quite the foodie insider once you've finally located quirky Rochelle Canteen—it's off the beaten path in a renovated bicycle shed, part of the restored Victorian Rochelle School (off Arnold Circus in Shoreditch). Ring a buzzer next to a pale blue door and enter chef Margot Henderson's white, austere "canteen," with its open kitchen and two long Formica tables. Gloriously understated British fare arrives at a convivial pace, from simple deviled kidneys on toast to a retro plate of Yorkshire ham, carrots, and parsley sauce. Join the art, architecture, and designer crowd enjoying seasonal guinea fowl with bacon and skate and capers, and finish with quince jelly or lemon posset. The restaurant is BYO (£5 corkage), and is open only on weekdays for breakfast, midmorning snacks, lunch, and tea. [$] *Average main: £16* ✉ *Rochelle School, Arnold Circus, Shoreditch* ☎ *020/7729 5677* 🌐 *www.arnoldandhenderson.com* ⏲ *No dinner. Closed weekends* [M] *Liverpool St.* ⊕ *H3.*

$$ MODERN BRITISH Fodor's Choice ★ 🍴 **St. John.** Foodies from around the world come to sample chef Fergus Henderson's "nose-to-tail" cooking at this no-frills, stark-white converted smokehouse near Clerkenwell's historic Smithfield Market. Henderson famously uses *all* parts of a carcass, so one appetizer might be pig's skin, while others, such as pig's ear and calf's brain and chicory, come off as marginally less extreme. St. John signature dishes, among them bone marrow and parsley salad, chitterlings with dandelion, and pheasant and pig's trotter pie, might appear stark on

the plate but represent accomplished cooking. The all-French wine selections complement the menu perfectly. Among the desserts are apple pie with custard, Eccles cakes, Lancashire cheese, and golden madeleines by the dozen or half dozen. $ *Average main: £23* ⊠ *26 St. John St., Clerkenwell* ☎ *020/3301–8069* ⊕ *www.stjohnrestaurant. com* ⌕ *Reservations essential* ⊘ *No dinner Sun.* Ⓜ *Farringdon, Barbican* ✛ *G2.*

THE SOUTH BANK

$$
MODERN BRITISH

✗ **Anchor & Hope.** Hearty, meaty dishes at wallet-friendly prices emerge from the open kitchen at this permanently packed, informal gastropub on The Cut (between Waterloo and Southwark Tube), a few doors down from the Young Vic theater. The menu is highly original, and there are great dishes for groups—slow-roasted shoulder of lamb, for example—along with individual orders such as pot roast duck, Herefordshire beef, deep-fried pig's head, pumpkin gratin, and cuttlefish with bacon. Be prepared to share the wooden dining tables. $ *Average main: £17* ⊠ *36 The Cut, South Bank* ☎ *020/7928–9898* ⌕ *Reservations not accepted* ⊘ *No dinner Sun. No lunch Mon.* Ⓜ *Waterloo, Southwark* ✛ *F4.*

$$$
MODERN FRENCH
Fodor's Choice
★

✗ **Chez Bruce.** Deeply flavorful French and Mediterranean cuisine, faultless service, a winning wine list, and a glossy neighborhood vibe have made Chez Bruce one of London's all-time favorite destination restaurants. Take a train or cab south of the Thames to chef Bruce Poole's cozy, gimmick-free haunt overlooking Wandsworth Common, and prepare for a procession of wonders, from homemade charcuterie and offal to lighter grilled fish dishes. Pot-roast pig's cheek with polenta, pollack with wild mushrooms, and roast monkfish with scallops, ham hock, and Jerusalem artichokes are among the other immaculately styled dishes you might find on the menu. The wine and desserts are stunning and the sommelier is superb. Pound-for-pound, Chez Bruce is nigh impossible to beat. Weekday lunches cost £27.50, three-course dinners £45. $ *Average main: £26* ⊠ *2 Bellevue Rd., Wandsworth* ☎ *020/8672–0114* ⊕ *www.chezbruce.co.uk* ⌕ *Reservations essential* Ⓜ *Tube: Wandsworth Common rail* ✛ *B6.*

$
TAPAS

✗ **José.** Rising Spanish chef José Pizarro packs 'em in like so many slices of *jamón* at his tapas-and-sherry establishment on happening Bermondsey Street, south of the river near London Bridge station. With only 30 seats, you'll be hard-pressed to find a spot at the tapas bar or a perch at an upturned barrel after 6 pm, but persevere—the tapas are astounding, among them *patatas bravas* (fried potatoes with a spicy tomato sauce), croquettes, hake and aioli, razor clams with chorizo, and paprika-specked Ibérico pork fillets You'll either love or hate the crush. $ *Average main: £7* ⊠ *104 Bermondsey St., South Bank* ☎ *020/7403–4902* ⊕ *www.josetapasbar.com* ⌕ *Reservations not accepted* Ⓜ *London Bridge* ✛ *H4.*

$$
ITALIAN
Fodor's Choice
★

✗ **Zucca.** River Café alumnus Sam Harris helms this excellent and commendably inexpensive modern Italian spot on London's latest restaurant row, Bermondsey Street. Harris's sure touch is evident throughout, from the white melamine tables and open kitchen to the

2

BRITISH TO A "T": TOP TEAS IN TOWN

The 7th Duchess of Bedford made taking an elaborate afternoon tea a fashionable pastime in the 1840s, a trend that has recently swung back into favor. Here are the best places to indulge, including a few that are gently priced.

Tea at the Palm Court at the **Ritz** (⊠ The Ritz, 150 Piccadilly ☎ 020/7300–2345 ⊕ www.theritzlondon.com) remains the ultimate afternoon tea experience, with a rococo starburst of gilt work, crystal chandeliers, and floral displays. Expect egg and cress-and-cucumber sandwiches on three-tiered silver cake stands, plus fruit scones, cakes, and dainty British pastries (£45–£64).

Across Piccadilly in Mayfair, the green-and-white-striped porcelain tea service at **Claridge's** (⊠ Brook St. ⊕ www.claridges.co.uk ☎ 020/7107–8872) is straight out of the Mad Hatter's Tea Party. You'll find 40 loose-leaf teas to choose from, including rare Darjeeling First Flush tea (prices from £39, or £63 for a rosé Champagne tea). At a the soigné **Connaught** (⊠ Carlos Pl. ⊕ www.the-connaught.co.uk

☎ 020/7107–8861) in nearby Carlos Place, fashionistas favor flourless caramel sponge cake, while traditionalists enjoy the log fires, Laurent-Perrier bubbly, smoked-salmon finger sandwiches, and loose-leaf Ceylon tea.

Even if you can't afford to stay at London's best hotels, you can still take tea for an hour or two and be part of the fantasy for a fraction of the cost. At the legendary **Savoy** (⊠ Strand ⊕ www.fairmont.com/savoy-london ☎ 020/7420–2111) on the Strand, you can savor afternoon Champagne and high teas (£40–£60), all served in the exceptionally pretty glass-cupola-covered Upper Thames Foyer, with its pink orchids and monochrome chinoiserie textiles. For eminently affordable (£16.75) afternoon tea, join the Soho crowd sinking into comfy velvet chairs in the parlor of the **Dean Street Townhouse** (⊠ 69–71 Dean St. ⊕ www.deanstreettownhouse.com ☎ 020/7434–1775) to enjoy Battenberg cake, buttered crumpets, or a cheesy Welsh rarebit topped with a poached egg.

homemade Italian breads, pastas, and ice creams. Start off sharing a punchy £5.50 antipasto—salt cod with chickpeas, perhaps—then experience the Piedmontese egg-yolk-colored pappardelle pasta with veal ragout, or the incredible Le Marche white truffle *vincisgrassi* pasta bake. You'll only find three fish or meat mains to choose from, but with dishes such as black ink squid with white polenta and the perfect blush-pink veal chop with spinach and lemon, quality makes up for the lack of quantity. The desserts and all-Italian wine list are superior, too. $ *Average main: £16* ⊠ *184 Bermondsey St., South Bank* ☎ *020/7378–6809* ⊕ *www.zuccalondon.com* ⊘ *Closed Mon. No dinner Sun.* Ⓜ *London Bridge* ✛ *H4.*

KENSINGTON, KNIGHTSBRIDGE, AND MAYFAIR

KENSINGTON

$$ JAPANESE

🍴 **Yashin.** Cofounder Yashuhiro Mineo and his fellow chefs create dish after awesome dish of fresh, colorful, exquisite sashimi, carpaccios, and omakase sushi spreads. A definite contender for the title of London's best sushi bar, Yashin sits right off Ken High Street. In addition to sushi, the chefs prepare ponzu-spiked salmon, Japanese sea bream with rice-cracker dust, salted Wagyu beef, and other delicacies. The tofu-topped miso cappuccino soup comes in a Victoriana cup-and-saucer, and the deep-fried soft-shell blue crab salad is a tangle of zingy mizuna leaves. For a bargain, come during the day for the five-piece salmon sushi lunch (£12.50). [$] *Average main: £22* ✉ *1A Argyll Road, Kensington* ☎ *020/7938 1536* 🌐 *www.yashinsushi.com* [M] *High Street Kensington* ✥ *A4.*

CHELSEA

$$ MODERN BRITISH Fodor's Choice ★

🍴 **The Harwood Arms.** Game cooked with a Modern British twist doesn't get any better—or more inventive—than it does at this exceptional gastro-pub off Fulham Broadway. Enthusiast and co-owner Mike Robinson shoots and bags all the wild venison on the menu, and you'll find a variety of terrific game-based seasonal dishes such as haunch of Berkshire roe deer with tarragon mustard and North Yorkshire grouse with Earl Grey–soaked prunes. Tuck into game pie with Somerset cider jelly or Herdwick lamb with rosemary curd in a comfy-sofas-and-newspapers type setting. If you're with a group, try the popular carve-your-own whole roast beef, lamb, or pork joints for the table. [$] *Average main: £19* ✉ *27 Walham Grove, Chelsea* ☎ *020/7386–1847* 🌐 *www.harwoodarms.com* ✍ *Reservations essential* ⏲ *No lunch Mon. Last dinners served 9 to 9:30pm* [M] *Fulham Broadway* ✥ *A6.*

KNIGHTSBRIDGE

$$$$ BRITISH Fodor's Choice ★

🍴 **Dinner by Heston Blumenthal.** The dishes at the Mandarin Oriental's award-winning restaurant may be inspired by historical English recipes, but Ashley Palmer-Watts, a Heston Blumenthal protégé, executes them with ultramodern precision. The signature dish, a Meat Fruit starter (circa 1500), appears to be a mandarin orange but it's actually an exceptionally smooth, creamy chicken-liver parfait. Another starter, Rice and Flesh (circa 1390) combines yellow saffron rice with calf's tail and red wine, and snails, girolles, fennel, and garlic go into the Savoury Porridge (circa 1660). Entrées such as the tender cod in cider (circa 1940), served with smoked artichokes, onions, and chard venture a bit closer to the present. Finish up with the marvelous spit-roasted pineapple Tipsy cake (circa 1810). For conversation-piece cuisine that delights the palate, you can do no better than this elegant eatery. [$] *Average main: £32* ✉ *Mandarin Oriental Hyde Park, 66 Knightsbridge, Knightsbridge* ☎ *020/7201–3833* 🌐 *www.dinnerbyheston.com* ✍ *Reservations essential* [M] *Knightsbridge* ✥ *C4.*

$$$ MODERN FRENCH Fodor's Choice ★

🍴 **Petrus.** Gordon Ramsay protégé Sean Burbidge presides over a flawless, world-class, modern French experience in posh Belgravia. The softly carpeted dining salon and central circular glass wine cellar may have dated a bit, but with the impeccable *bonnes bouches* and petit

LOCAL CHAINS WORTH A TASTE

When you're on the go or don't have time for a leisurely meal, consider visiting a local chain restaurant or sandwich bar. *The ones listed below have reasonable prices and are the best in their category.*

Byron: Bright and child-friendly, these hamburger joints serve delicious Scotch beef hamburgers, onion rings, Cobb salads, and french fries. 🌐 *www.byronhamburgers.com.*

Busaba Eathai: It's always jam-packed at these sultry dark-wood canteens where you'll find Thai noodles, rice dishes, and spicy all-in-one meals in a bowl. 🌐 *www.busaba.com.*

Carluccio's Caffè: The ingredients are freshly sourced at this family-friendly chain of combination Italian cafés, bars, and food shops. Carluccio's makes for a fine pasta and salad stop during a wild shopping spree. 🌐 *www.carluccios.com.*

Côte: High-quality and very reliable classic French brasserie meals are served up at this upmarket chain's smartly decked out locations. 🌐 *www.cote-restaurants.co.uk.*

Ed's Easy Diner: Overdose on milk shakes, ice-cream floats, chili dogs, and made-to-order hamburgers at this chain of shiny, retro-'50s-theme, American-style diners. 🌐 *www.edseasydiner.com.*

Gail's Artisan Bakery: Stop by upscale Gail's for take-outs that include chunky sandwiches made with artisanal breads and salads with ingredients such as chorizo, butternut squash, and quinoa. 🌐 *www.gailsbread.co.uk.*

Le Pain Quotidien: The worldwide chain's many London branches include a very busy one at St. Pancras International. Order a Belgian tartine open sandwich, a soup, a salad, or some cake and sit at the communal wooden tables. 🌐 *www.lepainquotidien.co.uk.*

Pret a Manger: The High Street take-out colossus isn't just for wholesome store-made sandwiches: it also sells great-tasting wraps, toasties, noodles, sushi, salads, fruit, porridge, and tea cakes. 🌐 *www.pret.com.*

Wagamama: Londoners love the bowls of Asian ramen and noodle soups served at this high-tech, child-friendly chain. 🌐 *www.wagamama.com.*

fours, assured sommelier, and charming, efficient service, you're in for a true event. Burbidge's mastery of technique is on display in starters such as the exemplary Les Landes duck foie gras with grape jelly, and in the perfect lobster ravioli swimming in creamed leeks and Champagne velouté. Bliss out on a pink Casterbridge beef fillet, aged for 25 days and served with braised shin and sticky Barolo sauce, and save room for the honeycomb-and-dark-chocolate sphere that theatrically melts in front of your eyes or white-chocolate popsicles that emerge from a bowl of dry ice. [$] *Average main: £28* ✉ *1 Kinnerton St., Belgravia, Knightsbridge* ☎ *020/7592–1609* 🌐 *www.gordonramsay.com/petrus* [M] *Knightsbridge* ✢ *C4.*

MAYFAIR

$$ ITALIAN 🍴 **Cecconi's.** Spot the odd A-list celeb and revel in the all-day buzz at this ever-fashionable Italian brasserie in the stealth wealth heartland between Old Bond and Cork streets, near the Royal Academy of Arts' rear entrance. In good weather, the private jet–set clientele takes to the outdoor tables for breakfast, brunch, and *cicchetti* (Italian tapas), then returns later in the day for something more substantial. The tasteful green-and-brown interior provides a stylish backdrop for classics such as stuffed baby squid, Umbrian sausages, lobster spaghetti, and a flavorful, pick-me-up tiramisu. This is just the spot for a high-end pit stop if you've shopped till you're ready to drop. [$] *Average main: £23* ✉ *5A Burlington Gardens, Mayfair* ☎ *020/7434–1500* 🌐 *www.cecconis.co.uk* ✍ *Reservations essential* [M] *Green Park, Piccadilly Circus* ✣ *D3.*

$$$$ FRENCH 🍴 **Hélène Darroze at the Connaught.** London's crème de la crème flocks to the exclusive Connaught hotel's sumptuous wood-paneled dining salon to sample Hélène Darroze's dazzling French haute cuisine. Taking inspiration from Les Landes in southwestern France, Darroze produces a procession of magical dishes, from caviar d'Aquitaine, served in a sleek martini glass with oyster tartare, black caviar jelly, and white haricot-bean velouté, to spit-roasted and flambéed pigeon with duck foie gras and mini–brussels sprouts. The desserts include pear jelly or apple compote accompanied by black Sawarak pepper cream. Darroze can be perfect for special occasions but beware the high prices: £35 for lunch, £55 for Saturday brunch, and £80 to £115 for dinner. [$] *Average main: £35* ✉ *The Connaught, Carlos Place, Mayfair* ☎ *020/7107-8880* 🌐 *www.the-connaught.co.uk* ✍ *Reservations essential* 👔 *Jacket required* ⏲ *Closed Sun. and Mon.* [M] *Green Park* ✣ *C3.*

$$$$ MODERN FRENCH 🍴 **Hibiscus.** Chef Claude Bosi has put this disarmingly neutral Mayfair spot on the culinary map with peerless, nouvelle cuisine dishes such as carpaccio of Isle of Skye scallops with blobs of truffle and pickled radish, and Cornish John Dory with Morteau sausage and girolle mushrooms. The desserts, among them an unlikely but flavorsome cep (porcini) mushroom tart, are equally original. The copious wine list includes top-rank "orange" biodynamic and organic fine wines. [$] *Average main: £35* ✉ *29 Maddox St., Mayfair* ☎ *020/7629–2999* 🌐 *www.hibiscusrestaurant.co.uk* ✍ *Reservations essential* ⏲ *Closed Sun. and Mon.* [M] *Oxford Circus, Piccadilly* ✣ *D3.*

$$$$ FRENCH 🍴 **Le Gavroche.** Carrying on a family tradition, Michel Roux Jr. works the floor at this clubby Mayfair fixture, which was established by his uncle and father in 1967 and which many feel provides London's best formal dining experience. Roux's mastery of technically precise and classical French cuisine is evident in signature dishes such as foie gras with a cinnamon-scented crispy-duck pancake, langoustine with snails and Hollandaise, and saddle of rabbit with Parmesan cheese. Desserts that include a chocolate-omelet soufflé and an upside-down apple tart are equally accomplished. The weekday three-course set lunches (£52)—with a half bottle of wine, water, coffee, and petit fours thrown in—are the best way to introduce yourself to this local landmark. [$] *Average main: £40* ✉ *43 Upper Brook St., Mayfair*

☎ 020/7408–0881 🌐 www.le-gavroche.co.uk ✍ Reservations essential 👔 Jacket required ⏲ Closed Sun. and 10 days at Christmas [M] Marble Arch, Bond St. ✣ C3.

$$$ MODERN EUROPEAN Fodor's Choice ★ 🍴 **Pollen Street Social.** Chef Jason Atherton became a culinary star thanks to this highly regarded restaurant on a cobbled lane off Regent Street. His cuisine is edgy, witty, and refined, beginning with an appetizer consisting of a poached egg, bacon, morels, tomato purée, and croutons that deconstructs in miniature a full English breakfast, followed by mains such as the sublime pork belly and tender Atlantic hake with cod cheeks and seaweed. The desserts, including a creamy goat-milk rice pudding with hay ice cream and the sensational, sashimi-like pressed watermelon with basil sorbet, are prepared at an open dessert bar. The £27.50 three-course lunches are, relatively speaking, a very good value. *[$] Average main: £26 ✉ 8–10 Pollen St., Mayfair ☎ 020/7290–7600 🌐 www.pollenstreetsocial.com ✍ Reservations essential [M] Oxford Circus, Piccadilly Circus ✣ D3.*

$ BURGER FAMILY 🍴 **The Riding House Café.** Stuffed-squirrel lamp holders peer down on trendy diners at this New York–style all-day café behind Oxford Circus in Noho (north of Soho). The aesthetic is funky and reclaimed, so you might find yourself sitting on a repurposed theater seat or a bright-orange leather banquette. At a mere £5, small plates such as sea bass ceviche and veal or pork meatballs with pomarola sauce are a good choice for a light meal, but if you want something more substantial, try the poached-egg chorizo hash browns, the pearl-barley salt-marsh lamb broth, the decadent cheeseburger with gherkin and chips, or the hearty lobster lasagna. The other draws here include the all-day breakfasts, sundaes for the kids, and cocktails and alcoholic milkshakes for the adults. *[$] Average main: £14 ✉ 43-51 Great Titchfield St., Noho ☎ 020/7927 🌐 www.ridinghousecafe.co.uk ✍ Reservations essential [M] Oxford Circus ✣ D2.*

$$$ SEAFOOD Fodor's Choice ★ 🍴 **Scott's.** Liveried doormen greet the rich and fancy with a discreet nod at this glamorous seafood restaurant on fashionable Mount Street in Mayfair. Dating back to 1851 and a haunt of the late James Bond author Ian Fleming—he adored the potted shrimps—today it draws the likes of Bill Clinton, Nigella Lawson, Kate Winslet, and other movers and shakers, who dine on day-boat fresh Lindisfarne oysters, baked crab, cod cheeks, shrimp burgers, and lobster thermidor. Standouts such as sautéed razor clams with wild boar sausage and Dover sole meunière are worth the cost, which is astronomical. But this crowd can afford it. *[$] Average main: £32 ✉ 20 Mount St., Mayfair ☎ 020/7495–7309 🌐 www.scotts-restaurant.com ✍ Reservations essential [M] Bond St., Green Park ✣ C3.*

MARYLEBONE

$$ BRASSERIE 🍴 **Galvin Bistrot de Luxe.** The accomplished chef-brothers Chris and Jeff Galvin conceived this handsome Parisian-style salon, complete with slate floors, bentwood chairs, and dark-wood paneling. Seasoned fans and discerning newcomers appreciate the impeccable cuisine and sterling service. There's no finer Dorset crab lasagna in town, and mains such as Cornish brill, calf's liver with Alsace bacon, stuffed pig's trotter, and sumptuous daube of venison with quince and chestnuts consistently

please. For the best value, order a three-course set lunch (£19.50) or the early evening dinner (£21.50), served between 6 and 7. [$] *Average main: £19* ✉ *66 Baker St., Marylebone* ☎ *020/7935–4007* 🌐 *www.galvinrestaurants.com* ✍ *Reservations essential* [M] *Baker St.* ✣ *C2.*

$ SEAFOOD 🍴 **The Golden Hind.** Partisans of this century-old, ultra-British chippy (traditional fish-and-chip shop) in Marylebone claim that it serves the best fish-and-chips in London. Tourists and locals chow down on homemade cod fish cakes, skate wings, feta fritters, and breaded scampi tails, but the truly big draws are the battered and deep-fried cod, plaice, and haddock, the classic hand-cut Maris Piper chips, and the traditional mushy peas. The café, run by a Greek family, is BYO and sells meals to go. [$] *Average main: £6* ✉ *73 Marylebone La., Marylebone* ☎ *020/7486–3644* ✍ *Reservations not accepted* ⏲ *No lunch Sat. Closed Sun.* [M] *Bond St.* ✣ *C2.*

NOTTING HILL AND BAYSWATER

NOTTING HILL

$$$ MODERN FRENCH Fodor's Choice ★ 🍴 **The Ledbury.** Sensational Aussie chef Brett Graham has won accolades for the cuisine at his high-ceilinged Notting Hill restaurant that's decked out with long, flowing drapes, mirrored walls, and plush seating. You won't find a more inventive vegetable dish than the ash-baked celeriac with hazelnut and wood sorrel. Mains such as roast quail with walnut cream, roe deer with bone marrow, and Cornish turbot with fennel and elderflower, are similarly outstanding. Game is a particular strength, as are desserts that include fig-leaf ice cream and thinly sliced figs with ewe's milk yogurt. All this plus professional service and a polished sommelier have helped make the Ledbury a top foodie destination. [$] *Average main: £31* ✉ *127 Ledbury Rd., Notting Hill* ☎ *0207/7792–9090* 🌐 *www.theledbury.com* ✍ *Reservations essential* ⏲ *No lunch Mon.* [M] *Westbourne Park, Ladbroke Grove* ✣ *A2.*

$ MODERN BRITISH FAMILY 🍴 **The Mall Tavern.** It's all things British at this charming 1856 Notting Hill gastro-pub that overflows with relaxed but discerning Notting Hill locals and Sloanes. Check out the coronation mugs, royal-wedding trinkets, and Prince Charles and Lady Di memorabilia before sampling great British bar snacks such as pork scratchings, soda bread, and lop-eared sausage rolls. Move through to the simple dark-oak-floored dining room to feast on hearty beef pie with bone marrow poking through the crust, or wallow in nostalgia with chicken Kiev, mac and cheese, or high-quality smoked-salmon fish cakes with spinach and a coddled egg. Dessert choices include salted-caramel chocolate Rolos and Victoria plum cheesecake, plus some stonking (very good) British farmhouse cheeses, like Shorrock's Bomb, Isle of Avalon, or Leagram blue. Note the bargain £10 weekday lunches. [$] *Average main: £13* ✉ *71–73 Palace Gardens Terr., Notting Hill* ☎ *020/7229–3374* 🌐 *www.themalltavern.com* ✍ *Reservations essential* [M] *Notting Hill Gate* ✣ *A3.*

BAYSWATER

$$ MODERN BRITISH 🍴 **Hereford Road.** Chef Tom Pemberton mans the front-of-house grill station at this Bayswater favorite renowned for straightforward British fare made from well-sourced regional, seasonal ingredients. Work

your way through pared-down combinations such as steamed mussels with cider and thyme, lemon sole with dulse (red seaweed), duck breast with pickled walnuts, and English rice pudding and jam. ■ TIP→ The express £9.50 and set £13 and £15.50 lunches are arguably the best midday deals in town. $ *Average main: £16* ⊠ *3 Hereford Rd., Bayswater* ☎ *020/7727–1144* ⊕ *www.herefordroad.org* ⊱ *Reservations essential* Ⓜ *Bayswater, Queensway* ✛ *A3.*

REGENT'S PARK AND HAMPSTEAD

$ ✕ **Lemonia.** A neighborhood gem, this vine-covered Greek Cypriot taverna is large, light, and always packed with local families. Along with an endless supply of small-dish dips and starters, the chefs prepare rustic mains such as slow-baked *kleftiko* lamb, eggplant, and potato moussaka, and beef stewed in red wine. Expect generous Greek hospitality, lots of noise, and the odd sighting of one of Primrose Hill's numerous resident movie stars. At £12.50, the weekday luncheons are a bargain. $ *Average main: £14* ⊠ *89 Regent's Park Rd., Regent's Park* ☎ *020/7586–7454* ⊱ *Reservations essential* ☉ *No lunch Sat. No dinner Sun.* Ⓜ *Chalk Farm* ✛ *B1.*

GREEK

PUBS

The city's public houses, more popularly known as pubs or "locals," dispense beer, good cheer, and simple food in structures that range from atmospheric old ones with authentic low wood-beamed ceilings and Victorian spots with ornate etched glass to modern shabby-chic hangouts and sticky-carpeted dens. Following the repeal in 2003 of some antiquated licensing laws and the prohibition on smoking that went into effect four years later, a surge in gastro-pubs occurred. The emphasis shifted as much toward eating as drinking, with alternatives such as Moroccan chicken replacing the usually mediocre "ploughman's lunch." But whatever you order, don't neglect the beer. American-style beer is called "lager" in Britain, whereas the real British brew is "bitter" and usually served at cellar temperature, which is cooler than room temperature but not actually chilled. Beer comes in two sizes—pints or half pints. Some London pubs also sell "real ale," which is less gassy than bitter and, many would argue, has a better flavor.

The list *below* offers a few pubs selected for their central location, historical interest, pleasant garden, music, or good food, but you might just as happily adopt your own temporary local.

SOHO AND COVENT GARDEN

Lamb & Flag. This refreshingly ungentrified 17th-century pub was once known as the Bucket of Blood because the upstairs room was used as a ring for bare-knuckle boxing. Now it's a convivial spot, serving food (lunch only) and real ale. It's on the edge of Covent Garden, up a hidden alley off Garrick Street. ⊠ *33 Rose St., Covent Garden* ☎ *020/7497–9504* ⊕ *www.lambandflagcoventgarden.co.uk* Ⓜ *Covent Garden.*

White Hart. Claiming to be the oldest licensed pub in London, this elegant, family-owned pub on Drury Lane had already been here for more than 500 years when it served highwayman Dick Turpin in 1739, just before he was hanged. Nowadays it is one of the best places to mix with theater cast-and-crew members having a post-show pint. A female-friendly environment, a cheery skylight above the lounge area, and above-average pub fare make the White Hart a sociable spot for a drink. ⊠ *191 Drury La., Covent Garden* ☎ *020/7242–2317* Ⓜ *Holborn, Covent Garden, Tottenham Court Rd.*

BLOOMSBURY AND HOLBORN

The Lamb. Charles Dickens and his contemporaries drank here, but today's enthusiastic clientele makes sure this intimate and eternally popular pub avoids the pitfalls of feeling too old-fashioned. For private chats at the bar, you can close a delicate etched-glass "snob screen" to the bar staff, opening it only when you fancy another pint. ⊠ *94 Lamb's Conduit St., Bloomsbury* ☎ *020/7405–0713* ⊕ *www.youngs. co.uk* Ⓜ *Russell Sq.*

Museum Tavern. Across the street from the British Museum, this friendly and classy Victorian pub makes an ideal resting place after the rigors of the cultural trail. Karl Marx himself unwound here after a hard day in the library. Seven well-kept beers are available on tap. ⊠ *49 Great Russell St., Bloomsbury* ☎ *020/7242–8987* Ⓜ *Tottenham Court Rd.*

THE CITY AND ENVIRONS

Fodor'sChoice ★ **Black Friar.** A step from Blackfriars Tube station, this spectacular pub has an Arts and Crafts interior that is entertainingly, satirically ecclesiastical, with inlaid mother-of-pearl, wood carvings, stained glass, and marble pillars all over the place. Despite the finely lettered temperance tracts on view just below reliefs of monks, fairies, and friars, the taps here dispense fine ales from independent brewers. The 20th-century poet Sir John Betjeman led a successful campaign to save the pub from demolition. ⊠ *174 Queen Victoria St., The City* ☎ *020/7236–5474* ⊕ *www. nicholsonspubs.co.uk/theblackfriarblackfriarslondon* Ⓜ *Blackfriars.*

Fodor'sChoice ★ **Craft Beer Company.** With 37 beers on tap and 300 more in bottles—some brewed exclusively for Craft Beer—the main problem at this pub is figuring out where to start. Luckily, you can get advice from the friendly and knowledgeable staff, or you can sign up for a guided tasting session. Tourists and beer pilgrims mingle with Leather Lane workers and locals at this worthwhile stop whose chandelier and mirrored ceiling lend it an antique charm. ⊠ *82 Leather La., Clerkenwell* ⊕ *thecraftbeerco. com* Ⓜ *Chancery La.*

Fodor'sChoice ★ **Jerusalem Tavern.** Owned by the well-respected St. Peter's Brewery of Suffolk, the Jerusalem is small and endearingly eccentric. Ancient Delft-style tiles meld with wood and concrete in a converted watchmaker and jeweler's shop that dates back to the 18th century. The beer, both bottled and on tap, is among London's best. Beloved by locals, the pub is often busy, especially after work. ⊠ *55 Britton St.,*

Clerkenwell ☎ *020/7490–4281* ⊕ *www.stpetersbrewery.co.uk/london-pub* Ⓜ *Farringdon.*

Ye Olde Cheshire Cheese. An extremely historic pub that opened in 1667, the year after the Great Fire of London, the Cheshire attracts many tourists, but it still deserves a visit for its sawdust-covered floors, low wood-beam ceilings, and the 14th-century crypt of Whitefriars' monastery under the cellar bar. This was the most regular of Dr. Johnson's and Dickens's many locals. Food is served except on Sunday, when the pub is open only from noon to 3. ✉ *145 Fleet St., The City* ☎ *020/7353–6170* Ⓜ *Blackfriars.*

SOUTH BANK

Market Porter. Opposite the foodie treasures of Borough Market, this atmospheric pub opens at 6 am for the stallholders and always seems busy. Remarkably, the place manages to remain relaxed, with helpful staff and happy customers spilling out onto the road year-round. The wide selection of real ales is lovingly tended. The pub was used as a set for one of the Harry Potter movies. ✉ *9 Stoney St., Borough* ☎ *020/7407–2495* ⊕ *www.markettaverns.co.uk* Ⓜ *London Bridge.*

KENSINGTON, KNIGHTSBRIDGE, AND MAYFAIR

The Nag's Head. The landlord of this idiosyncratic little mews pub in Belgravia runs a tight ship, and no cell phones are allowed. If that sounds like misery, the fondly collected artifacts (including antique penny arcade games) that decorate every inch of the place, high-quality beer, and old-fashioned pub grub should make up for it. ✉ *53 Kinnerton St., Belgravia* ☎ *020/7235–1135* Ⓜ *Knightsbridge, Hyde Park Corner.*

Fodor'sChoice ★ **Punch Bowl.** In a quiet corner of Mayfair, the cozy little Punch Bowl has a worn wood floor and well-spoken staff dressed in pale, checkered shirts. The pub dates from 1750, and the interior remains steadfastly old-fashioned, with a painting of Churchill, candles, polished dark wood, and engraved windows. Try the eponymous ale, made in Scotland by Caledonian. A special dining area at the rear buzzes at lunchtime with locals, who come for the upscale pub grub. ✉ *41 Farm St., Mayfair* ☎ *020/7493–6841* ⊕ *www.punchbowllondon.com* Ⓜ *Green Park, Bond St.*

WHERE TO STAY

Use the coordinate (✛ B2) at the end of each listing to locate a site on the corresponding map.

Her Majesty hasn't offered you a bed? No matter. London's grande-dame hotels are the next best thing—and possibly better. If your budget won't stretch to five-star luxury, don't worry. There are plenty of comfortable, clean, friendly options available for a relatively reasonable price. The key word is relatively. In recent years London has seen a welcome growth in the value-for-money sector, but overall, accommodations here still remain on the costly side.

If money is no object, London has some of the world's most luxurious hotels, ranging from blingtastic newcomers such as the Corinthia to the quirkily charming Firmdale Hotels, run by Tim and Kit Kemp. Even these high-end places have deals, and you can sometimes find a bargain, particularly during January and February. Other worthy recent arrivals in this sector include the gorgeous remodeled Victorian landmark, St. Pancras Renaissance.

Meanwhile, several midrange hotels have dropped their average prices, which has made some desirable options such as Hazlitt's more affordable. As well, large business-oriented hotels frequently offer weekend packages. Those on a budget should check out the stylish and super-cheap hotels that have shaken up the lodging scene of late. The downside is that these places tend to be a little out of the way, but you may find this a price worth paying. Another attractive alternative includes hotels in the Premier and Millennium chains, which offer sleek, modern rooms, many up-to-date conveniences, and discount prices that sometimes fall below £100 a night.

You should confirm *exactly* what your room costs before checking in. The usual practice in all but the less expensive hotels is for quoted prices to cover room alone; breakfast, whether Continental or "full English" (i.e. cooked), costs extra. Also check whether the quoted rate includes V.A.T. (sales tax), which is a hefty 20%. Most expensive hotels include it in the initial quote, but some middle-of-the-range and budget places may not. *Hotel reviews have been shortened. For full information and additional choices, visit Fodors.com.*

WHAT IT COSTS IN POUNDS			
$	$$	$$$	$$$$
Hotels under £100	£100–£200	£201–£300	over £300

Prices are the lowest cost of a standard double room in high season, including 20% V.A.T.

WESTMINSTER, ST. JAMES'S, AND ROYAL LONDON

WESTMINSTER

$$
B&B/INN

B&B Belgravia. At this modern guesthouse near Victoria Station, a clean, chic white color scheme, simple modern furniture, and a lounge where a fire crackles away in the winter are all geared to stylish comfort. **Pros:** nice extras such as free use of a laptop in the hotel lounge; coffee and tea always available. **Cons:** rooms and bathrooms are small; unimaginative breakfasts; can be noisy, especially on lower floors. $ *Rooms from: £135* ⊠ *64–66 Ebury St., Victoria* ☎ *020/7259–8570* ⊕ *www.bb-belgravia.com* 🗫 *17 rooms* ⦿ *Breakfast* Ⓜ *Sloane Square, Victoria* ✛ *E5.*

$$$$
HOTEL
Fodor's Choice
★

The Corinthia. Part of the international top-end luxury chain, this hotel provides service that makes everyone feel like a VIP. **Pros:** so much luxury and elegance you'll feel like royalty. **Cons:** prices leap once the least expensive rooms sell out. $ *Rooms from: £420* ⊠ *Whitehall Pl.,*

WHERE SHOULD I STAY?

	NEIGHBORHOOD VIBE	PROS	CONS
Westminster, St. James's, and Royal London	This historic area is home to major tourist attractions like Buckingham Palace.	Central and near tourist sites; easy Tube access; considered a safe area to stay.	Mostly expensive lodging options; few restaurants and entertainment venues nearby.
Soho and Covent Garden	A tourist hub with endless entertainment on the streets and in theaters and clubs—it's party central for young adults.	Buzzing area with plenty to see and do; late-night entertainment abounds; wonderful shopping district.	The area tends to be noisy at night; few budget hotels; keep your wits about you at night, and watch out for pickpockets.
Bloomsbury and Holborn	Diverse area that is part bustling business center and part tranquil respite with tree-lined streets and squares.	Easy access to Tube, and 15 minutes to city center; major sights, like British Museum are here.	Busy streets filled with honking trucks and roving students; the area around King's Cross can be sketchy—particularly at night.
The City and South Bank	London's financial district, where most of the city's banks and businesses are headquartered.	Central location with easy transportation access; great hotel deals in South Bank; many major sights nearby.	It can be as quiet as a tomb after 8 pm; many nearby restaurants and shops close over the weekend.
East London	Hipster central, with great art, restaurant, and nightlife scenes.	Great for art lovers, shoppers, and business execs with meetings in Canary Wharf.	Still a transitional area around the edges, parts of Hackney can be a bit dodgy at night; 20-minute Tube ride from central London.
Kensington, Knightsbridge, and Mayfair	This is one of London's most upscale neighborhoods, with designer boutiques and five-star hotels designed to appeal to those who can afford the best.	Diverse hotel selection; great area for meandering walks; London's capital of high-end shopping.	Depending on where you are, the nearest Tube might be a hike; residential area might be too quiet for some. Few budget hotel or restaurant options.
Notting Hill and Bayswater	This is an upscale, fashionable area favored by locals, with plenty of good hotels.	Hotel deals abound in Bayswater if you know where to look; gorgeous greenery in Hyde Park; great independent boutiques.	Choose the wrong place and you may end up in a flea pit; residential areas may be too quiet at night for some.
Regent's Park and Hampstead	Village-like enclaves where successful actors and intellectuals go to settle down.	Good access to central London; bucolic charm.	Some distance from center; lack of hotel and dining options.

Westminster ☎ *020/7930–8181* ⊕ *www.corinthia.com* ⤵ *294 rooms* ⦵| *Breakfast* Ⓜ *Embankment* ✛ *F4.*

$$$$
HOTEL
Fodor'sChoice
★

⛨ **Hotel 41.** Designer credentials and high-tech gadgets are in evidence everywhere in the impeccably coordinated black-and-white rooms, some split-level and all gorgeously furnished with extraordinary pieces drawn from every corner of the globe. **Pros:** unique place opposite Buckingham Palace; great service; free Wi-Fi. **Cons:** unusual design is not for everyone. ⓢ *Rooms from: £323* ⊠ *41 Buckingham Palace Rd., Victoria* ☎ *020/7300–0041* ⊕ *www.41hotel.com* ⤵ *26 rooms, 4 suites, 2 apartments* ⦵| *Breakfast* Ⓜ *Victoria* ✛ *E5.*

$$
HOTEL

⛨ **The Luna Simone Hotel.** This delightful and friendly little family-run hotel, a short stroll from Buckingham Palace, is a real find for the price in central London. **Pros:** friendly and well run; family rooms are outstanding value; superb location. **Cons:** dated style; tiny bathrooms; no elevator or air-conditioning. ⓢ *Rooms from: £120* ⊠ *47–49 Belgrave Rd., Pimlico* ☎ *020/7834–5897* ⊕ *www.lunasimonehotel.com* ⤵ *36 rooms* ⦵| *Breakfast* Ⓜ *Pimlico, Victoria* ✛ *E6.*

$
RENTAL

⛨ **Studios @ 82.** A great little side operation from B&B Belgravia, these self-catering apartments represent fantastic value for the money; they're pleasant, contemporary spaces that have everything you need, plus useful extras such as free Wi-Fi. **Pros:** great price; lovely location; all the independence of self-catering. **Cons:** lots of stairs; no elevator. ⓢ *Rooms from: £99* ⊠ *64–66 Ebury St., Victoria* ☎ *020/7259–8570* ⊕ *www. bb-belgravia.com* ⤵ *9 apartments* ⦵| *Breakfast* Ⓜ *Knightsbridge* ✛ *E5.*

ST. JAMES'S

$$$$
HOTEL
FAMILY
Fodor'sChoice
★

⛨ **Claridge's.** The original art deco public spaces of this super-glamorous London institution are gloriously unspoiled, down to the grand staircase and elevator, complete with upholstered sofa. **Pros:** serious luxury everywhere; comics, books, and DVDs to help keep kids amused. **Cons:** better pack your designer wardrobe—guests in the hotel bar can be almost cartoonishly snobbish. ⓢ *Rooms from: £390* ⊠ *Brook St., St. James's* ☎ *020/7629–8860, 866/599–6991 in U.S.* ⊕ *www.claridges. co.uk* ⤵ *203 rooms* ⦵| *Breakfast* Ⓜ *Bond St.* ✛ *E3.*

$$$
HOTEL
Fodor'sChoice
★

⛨ **The Stafford London by Kempinski.** This is a rare find: a posh hotel that's equal parts elegance and friendliness, and it's in one of the few peaceful spots in the area, down a small lane behind Piccadilly. **Pros:** great staff; big, luxurious rooms; quiet location. **Cons:** traditional style is not to all tastes; men must wear jackets in the bar. ⓢ *Rooms from: £260* ⊠ *St. James's Pl., St. James's* ☎ *020/7493–0111* ⊕ *www.kempinski.com/ london* ⤵ *81 rooms* ⦵| *Breakfast* Ⓜ *Green Park* ✛ *E4.*

SOHO AND COVENT GARDEN

SOHO

$$
HOTEL
Fodor'sChoice
★

⛨ **Dean Street Townhouse.** Discreet and unpretentious, but stylish and right in the heart of Soho, this place has a bohemian vibe and an excellent Modern British restaurant, hung with art by, among others, Peter Blake and Tracey Emin. **Pros:** über-cool; resembles an upper-class pied-à-terre. **Cons:** full rate reflects location rather than what you get; some rooms are small; rooms at the front can be noisy, especially on weekends;

BEST BETS: LONDON LODGING

2

occasional two-night minimum stay. **$** *Rooms from: £188* ✉ *69–71 Dean St., Soho* ☎ *020/7434–1775* ⊕ *www.deanstreettownhouse.com* ⇨ *39 rooms* ⚑ *Breakfast* Ⓜ *Leicester Sq., Tottenham Court Rd.* ✦ *F3.*

$$$ ⚀ **Hazlitt's.** This disarmingly friendly place, full of personality, robust
HOTEL antiques, and claw-foot tubs, occupies three connected early-18th-century houses, one of which was the last home of essayist William Hazlitt (1778–1830). **Pros:** great for lovers of art and antiques; atmospheric, with small sitting rooms and wooden staircases; truly beautiful and relaxed. **Cons:** no in-house restaurant; breakfast costs £12 extra; no elevators. **$** *Rooms from: £216* ✉ *6 Frith St., Soho* ☎ *020/7434–1771* ⊕ *www.hazlittshotel.com* ⇨ *20 rooms, 3 suites* ⚑ *No meals* Ⓜ *Tottenham Court Rd.* ✦ *F3.*

COVENT GARDEN

$$$$ ⚀ **Covent Garden Hotel.** With a Covent Garden location and quirkily
HOTEL stylish guest rooms, it's little wonder this is a favorite of off-duty movie
Fodor's Choice stars and style mavens. **Pros:** great for star-spotting, supertrendy. **Cons:**
★ you can feel you don't matter if you're not famous; Covent Garden setting can be boisterous. **$** *Rooms from: £315* ✉ *10 Monmouth St., Covent Garden* ☎ *020/7806–1000, 800/553–6674 in U.S.* ⊕ *www.firmdale. com* ⇨ *55 rooms, 3 suites* ⚑ *Some meals* Ⓜ *Covent Garden* ✦ *F3.*

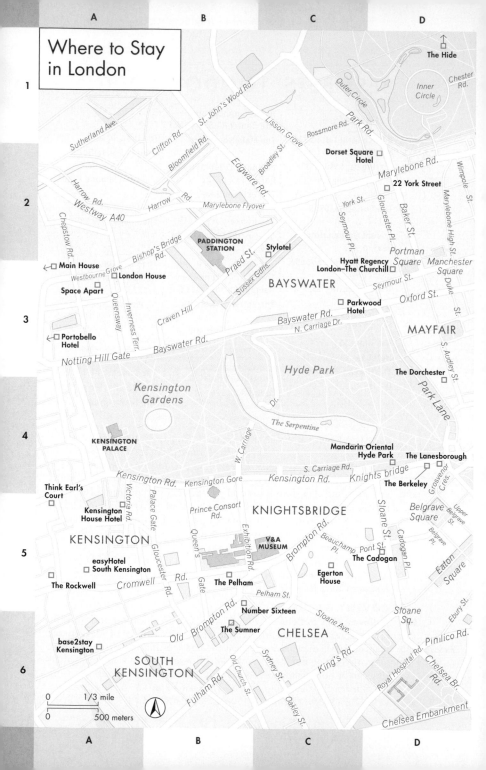

Where to Stay in London

The Hide

Dorset Square Hotel

22 York Street

Stylotel

Main House

London House

Space Apart

Hyatt Regency
London–The Churchill

Portobello Hotel

Parkwood Hotel

BAYSWATER

MAYFAIR

The Dorchester

Hyde Park

Kensington Gardens

The Serpentine

KENSINGTON PALACE

Mandarin Oriental Hyde Park

The Lanesborough

The Berkeley

Think Earl's Court

Kensington House Hotel

KNIGHTSBRIDGE

Belgrave Square

KENSINGTON

V&A MUSEUM

The Cadogan

easyHotel South Kensington

The Rockwell

The Pelham

Egerton House

Number Sixteen

base2stay Kensington

The Sumner

CHELSEA

SOUTH KENSINGTON

Sloane Sq.

0   1/3 mile
0   500 meters

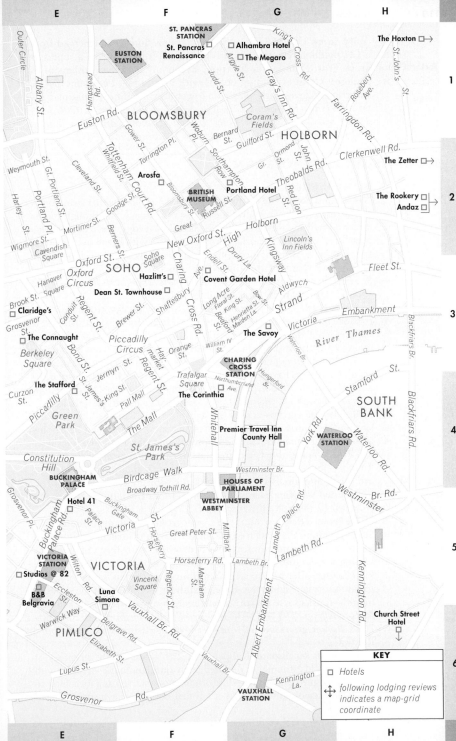

$$$$ **HOTEL** **Fodor's Choice ★** 🏨 **The Savoy.** One of London's most famous hotels has emerged from a £220 million renovation, and the old girl is looking like a superstar again. **Pros:** Thames-side location; less snooty than many others of its pedigree. **Cons:** everything comes with a price tag; bedrooms can be surprisingly noisy, particularly on lower floors; right off the superbusy Strand. [$] *Rooms from: £375* ✉ *Strand, Covent Garden* ☎ *020/7836–4343, 800/257–7544 in U.S.* 🌐 *www.fairmont.com/savoy-london* 🛏 *268* 🍴 *Breakfast* [M] *Covent Garden, Charing Cross* ✥ *G3.*

BLOOMSBURY AND HOLBORN

BLOOMSBURY

$ **B&B/INN** 🏨 **Alhambra Hotel.** One of the best bargains in Bloomsbury is a stone's throw from King's Cross and the Eurostar terminal, and though rooms are very small and the neighborhood is still a bit edgy, few places are this cheery and clean for the price. **Pros:** low price, with breakfast included; friendly service; central location. **Cons:** zero frills; stairs to climb; some rooms have shared bathrooms. [$] *Rooms from: £75* ✉ *17–19 Argyle St., Bloomsbury* ☎ *020/7837–9575* 🌐 *www.alhambrahotel.com* 🛏 *52 rooms* 🍴 *Breakfast* [M] *King's Cross* ✥ *G1.*

$$ **B&B/INN** 🏨 **Arosfa Hotel.** Simple, friendly, and pleasantly quirky, this little B&B, once the home of the pre-Raphaelite painter Sir John Everett Millais, is on an elegant Georgian street within walking distance of the West End and the British Museum. **Pros:** friendly staff; check-in from 7 am; convenient to museums and theaters; free Wi-Fi. **Cons:** some rooms are very small; bathrooms have showers only; few services. [$] *Rooms from: £110* ✉ *83 Gower St., Bloomsbury* ☎ *020/7636–2115* 🌐 *www.arosfalondon.com* 🛏 *15 rooms* 🍴 *Breakfast* [M] *Goodge St., Euston Sq.* ✥ *F2.*

$$ **HOTEL** 🏨 **The Megaro.** Directly across the street from St. Pancras International station (for Eurostar), this hotel has snazzy, well-designed bedrooms whose modern amenities include espresso machines and powerful showers. **Pros:** comfortable beds; great location for Eurostar; short hop on Tube to city center. **Cons:** neighborhood isn't great; standard rooms are small; interiors may be too stark for some. [$] *Rooms from: £160* ✉ *Belgrove St., King's Cross* ☎ *020/7843–2222* 🌐 *www.hotelmegaro.co.uk* 🛏 *49 rooms* 🍴 *Breakfast* ✥ *G1.*

$ **HOTEL** 🏨 **The Portland Hotel.** Around the corner from leafy Russell Square and an easy walk to the British Museum and Covent Garden, the Portland offers spacious and comfortable bedrooms, with large bathrooms, seating areas, and kitchenettes. **Pros:** great location; large rooms; kitchenettes offer alternative to restaurants; staff is friendly. **Cons:** restaurant is in neighboring hotel, requiring a walk down the street to breakfast; prices rise sharply after the least expensive rooms sell out. [$] *Rooms from: £91* ✉ *31–32 Bedford Pl., Bloomsbury* ☎ *020/7580–7088* 🌐 *www.grangehotels.com* 🛏 *18 rooms* 🍴 *Breakfast* [M] *Holborn Rd.* ✥ *G2.*

$$$ **HOTEL** **Fodor's Choice ★** 🏨 **St. Pancras Renaissance.** Reopened in 2011 after nearly a century of dereliction, this stunningly restored Victorian landmark—replete with gingerbread turrets and castle-like ornaments—started as a love letter to the golden age of railways; now it's one of London's most sophisticated places to stay. **Pros:** Victorian heaven (in public areas); unique and beautiful; faultless service; an elevator ride away from the Eurostar. **Cons:** the guest rooms lack the period grandeur of the public rooms; streets outside are always busy. [$] *Rooms from: £230* ✉ *Euston Rd., King's Cross* ☎ *020/7841–3540* 🌐 *www.marriott.com* 🛏 *207 rooms, 38 suites* 🍴 *Breakfast* [M] *Kings Cross St. Pancras. National Rail: Kings Cross St. Pancras* ✣ *F1.*

2

HOLBORN

$$$ HOTEL Fodor's Choice ★

🏨 **The Zetter.** The dizzying five-story atrium, art deco staircase, and slick European restaurant hint at the delights to come in this converted warehouse—a breath of fresh air with its playful color schemes, elegant wallpapers, and wonderful views of the City from the higher floors. **Pros:** character to spare; big rooms; free Wi-Fi; gorgeous "rain forest" showers. **Cons:** rooms with good views are expensive. [$] *Rooms from: £234* ✉ *86–88 Clerkenwell Rd., Holborn* ☎ *020/7324–4444* 🌐 *www.thezetter.com* 🛏 *59 rooms* 🍴 *Breakfast* [M] *Farringdon* ✣ *H2.*

THE CITY

$$ HOTEL Fodor's Choice ★

🏨 **The Rookery.** A unique and beautiful 1725 town house, the Rookery is the kind of place where you want to allow quality time to enjoy and soak up the atmosphere. **Pros:** helpful staff; free Wi-Fi; good deals in the off-season. **Cons:** breakfast costs extra; short Tube ride to tourist sites. [$] *Rooms from: £144* ✉ *12 Peter's La., at Cowcross St., The City* ☎ *020/7336–0931* 🌐 *www.rookeryhotel.com* 🛏 *30 rooms, 3 suites* 🍴 *No meals* [M] *Farringdon* ✣ *H2.*

THE EAST END

$$ HOTEL

🏨 **Andaz.** Swanky and upscale, this hotel boasts a modern, masculine design, and novel check-in procedure—instead of standing at a desk, guests sit in a lounge while a staff member with a handheld computer takes their information. **Pros:** attention to detail; guests can borrow an iPod from the front desk; no standing in line to check in; "healthy" minibars are stocked with nuts, fruit, and yogurt. **Cons:** sparse interior design is not for everyone; rates rise significantly for midweek stays. [$] *Rooms from: £154* ✉ *40 Liverpool St., East End* ☎ *020/7961–1234, 800/492–8804 in U.S.* 🌐 *www.andaz.hyatt.com* 🛏 *267 rooms* 🍴 *Breakfast* [M] *Liverpool St.* ✣ *H2.*

$ HOTEL Fodor's Choice ★

🏨 **The Hoxton Hotel.** The design throughout this trendy East London lodging is contemporary, but not so modern as to be absurd. **Pros:** cool vibe; neighborhood known for funky galleries and boutiques; sizable weekend discounts; way-cool restaurant; one hour of free international calls. **Cons:** high prices during the week; away from tourist sights; least-expensive rooms sell out months ahead. [$] *Rooms from: £90* ✉ *81 Great Eastern St., East End* ☎ *020/7550–1000* 🌐 *www.hoxtonhotels.com* 🛏 *205* 🍴 *Breakfast* ✣ *H1.*

THE SOUTH BANK

$ HOTEL Fodor's Choice ★ **Church Street Hotel.** Like rays of sunshine in gritty South London, these rooms above a popular tapas restaurant are individually decorated in rich, bold tones and have authentic Central American touches—elaborately painted crucifixes; tiles handmade in Guadalajara; homemade iron bed frames. **Pros:** unique and arty; great breakfasts; lovely staff; closer to central London than it might appear. **Cons:** a trendy but not great part of town; might suit adventurous young travelers more than families; a mile from a Tube station (though bus connections are handier); some rooms share a bathroom. [$] *Rooms from: £90 ✉ 29–33 Camberwell Church St., Camberwell, South East ☎ 020/7703–5984 🌐 www.churchstreethotel.com 🛏 28 rooms 🍴 Breakfast [M] Oval St. ✥ H6.*

$$ HOTEL FAMILY **Premier Travel Inn County Hall.** The small but nicely decorated rooms at this budget choice share the County Hall complex with the grander London Marriott Hotel County Hall, and though they lack its spectacular river views they occupy the same convenient location at a decidedly lower price. **Pros:** good location for the South Bank; bargains for booking in advance, including inexpensive breakfast and dinner rates; kids stay free. **Cons:** no river views; limited services. [$] *Rooms from: £132 ✉ Belvedere Rd., South Bank ☎ 0871/527–8648 🌐 www.premiertravelinn.com 🛏 313 rooms 🍴 Breakfast [M] Westminster, Waterloo. National Rail: Waterloo ✥ G4.*

KENSINGTON, KNIGHTSBRIDGE, AND MAYFAIR

KENSINGTON

$$ RENTAL **base2stay Kensington.** This near-budget option in a creamy white Georgian town house offers comfortable double rooms that have a stylish, modern look and tiny kitchenettes; some rooms have bunk beds for traveling friends or children. **Pros:** great value alternative to hotel; attractive rooms; handy mini-kitchens; free Wi-Fi. **Cons:** bathrooms are small (though well designed); 15-minute Tube ride to central London. [$] *Rooms from: £135 ✉ 25 Courtfield Gardens, South Kensington ☎ 020/7244–2255, 800/511–9821 in U.S. 🌐 www.base2stay.com 🛏 67 rooms 🍴 No meals [M] Earls Court ✥ A6.*

$ HOTEL **easyHotel South Kensington.** London's first "pod hotel" has tiny rooms with a double bed, private shower room, and little else, each brightly decorated in the easyGroup's trademark orange and white (to match the budget airline easyJet). **Pros:** amazing price; safe and pleasant space. **Cons:** not for the claustrophobic; most rooms have no windows; six floors and no elevator. [$] *Rooms from: £44 ✉ 14 Lexham Gardens, Kensington ☎ 020/7216–1717 🌐 www.easyhotel.com 🛏 34 rooms 🍴 No meals [M] Gloucester Rd. ✥ A5.*

$$ HOTEL **Kensington House Hotel.** A short stroll from High Street Kensington and Kensington Gardens, this refurbished 19th-century town house has streamlined, contemporary rooms with large windows that let in plenty of light. **Pros:** attractive design; comfortable beds with luxurious fabrics; relaxing setting; free Wi-Fi. **Cons:** rooms are small; bathrooms are minuscule; the elevator is Lilliputian. [$] *Rooms from: £144*

✉ *15–16 Prince of Wales Terr., Kensington* ☎ *020/7937–2345* 🌐 *www.kenhouse.com* 🛏 *39 rooms, 2 suites* 🍴 *Breakfast* [M] *High Street Kensington* ✥ *A5.*

$$$ HOTEL **Number Sixteen.** Guest rooms at this luxury guesthouse around the corner from the Victoria & Albert Museum look as though they've sprung from the pages of *Architectural Digest.* **Pros:** just the right level of helpful service; interiors are gorgeous; delightful garden. **Cons:** no restaurant; small elevator. [$] *Rooms from: £285* ✉ *16 Sumner Pl., South Kensington* ☎ *020/7589–5232, 888/559–5508 in U.S.* 🌐 *www.firmdale.com* 🛏 *42 rooms* 🍴 *Breakfast* [M] *South Kensington* ✥ *B5.*

$$$ HOTEL Fodor's Choice ★ **The Pelham Hotel.** One of the first and most stylish of London's boutique hotels, this still-chic choice is a short stroll away from the Natural History, Science, and V&A museums. **Pros:** great location for museum-hopping; gorgeous marble bathrooms; soigné interior design; lovely staff; good package deals for online booking. **Cons:** taller guests will find themselves cursing the top-floor rooms with sloping ceilings. [$] *Rooms from: £252* ✉ *15 Cromwell Pl., South Kensington* ☎ *020/7589–8288, 888/757–5587 in U.S.* 🌐 *www.pelhamhotel.co.uk* 🛏 *47 rooms, 4 suites* 🍴 *Breakfast* [M] *South Kensington* ✥ *B5.*

$$ HOTEL **The Rockwell.** Despite being on traffic-clogged Cromwell Road, the Rockwell is one of the best boutique hotels in this part of London—and the windows have good soundproofing. **Pros:** large bedrooms; stylish surroundings; helpful staff. **Cons:** on a busy, unattractive road; 20-minute Tube ride to central London. [$] *Rooms from: £180* ✉ *181 Cromwell Rd., South Kensington* ☎ *020/7244–2000* 🌐 *www.therockwell.com* 🛏 *38 rooms, 2 suites* 🍴 *Breakfast* ✥ *A5.*

$$ HOTEL **The Sumner.** You can feel yourself relaxing the minute you enter this elegant Georgian town house. **Pros:** excellent location for shopping; small enough that the staff knows your name; attractive conservatory and garden. **Cons:** services are limited but prices high. [$] *Rooms from: £180* ✉ *54 Upper Berkley St., Marble Arch, Marylebone* ☎ *020/7723–2244* 🌐 *www.thesumner.com* 🛏 *20 rooms* 🍴 *Breakfast* [M] *Marble Arch* ✥ *B6.*

$$ RENTAL **Think Earl's Court.** These serviced apartments are a stone's throw from Kensington High Street and a short walk from both Earl's Court and Olympia. **Pros:** brand-new building; self-catering offers greater independence. **Cons:** payment is made when you book; bland, officelike exterior. [$] *Rooms from: £168* ✉ *26A Adam and Eve Mews, Kensington* ☎ *020/3465–9100* 🌐 *www.think-apartments.com* 🛏 *133 rooms* 🍴 *No meals* [M] *High Street Kensington* ✥ *A5.*

CHELSEA

$$$ HOTEL **The Cadogan Hotel.** This elegant and luxurious hotel is one of London's most historically naughty hotels—once the home of scandalous actress Lillie Langtry (King Edward's mistress in the 1890s), and where Oscar Wilde was staying (in Room 118) when he was arrested for "indecency" with a young man on April 6, 1895. **Pros:** luxurious but not stuffy; friendly staff; great location for shopping; good advance discounts online. **Cons:** rooms are quite small. [$] *Rooms from: £234* ✉ *75 Sloane St., Chelsea* ☎ *020/7235–7141* 🌐 *www.cadogan.com* 🛏 *65 rooms* 🍴 *Breakfast* [M] *Sloane Sq.* ✥ *D5.*

KNIGHTSBRIDGE

$$$$ HOTEL 🏨 **The Berkeley.** Convenient for Knightsbridge shopping, the very elegant Berkeley is renowned for its restaurants and luxuries that culminate—literally—in a splendid penthouse swimming pool. **Pros:** lavish and elegant; attentive service; prices aren't quite as stratospheric as some high-end places. **Cons:** you'll need your best designer clothes to fit in. [$] *Rooms from: £390* ✉ *Wilton Pl., Knightsbridge* ☎ *020/7235–6000, 800/637–2869 in U.S.* 🌐 *www.the-berkeley.co.uk* 🛏 *103 rooms, 55 suites* 🍴 *Breakfast* [M] *Knightsbridge* ✥ *D4.*

$$$ HOTEL 🏨 **Egerton House.** The gorgeous pluses at this sensationally chic option include guest rooms lavishly decorated with luxurious, richly colored fabrics and a knockout white-on-gold dining room. **Pros:** lovely staff; great location; magnificent interiors that make guests feel as if they're staying in a private London home; striking art. **Cons:** some style touches a little too frou-frou, though Toulouse-Lautrec would have approved. [$] *Rooms from: £281* ✉ *17–19 Egerton Terr., Knightsbridge* ☎ *020/7589–2412, 877/955–1515 in U.S.* 🌐 *www.egertonhousehotel.co.uk* 🛏 *23 rooms, 6 suites* 🍴 *Breakfast* [M] *Knightsbridge, South Kensington* ✥ *C5.*

$$$$ HOTEL 🏨 **The Lanesborough.** A gilded cocoon for the seriously wealthy, this hotel exudes a spectacular richness and, when built by a Texan heiress, was the talk of the town, thanks to the magnificent 19th-century antiques, the personal butler service, and that 1770 cognac on the menu. **Pros:** lap of luxury; your wish is their command. **Cons:** prices are extraordinary; not everybody appreciates the constantly hovering service. [$] *Rooms from: £495* ✉ *Hyde Park Corner, Belgravia* ☎ *020/7259–5599, 800/999–1828 in U.S.* 🌐 *www.lanesborough.com* 🛏 *52 rooms, 43 suites* 🍴 *Breakfast* [M] *Hyde Park Corner* ✥ *D4.*

$$$$ HOTEL Fodor's Choice ★ 🏨 **Mandarin Oriental Hyde Park.** Built in 1880, the Mandarin welcomes you with its exuberantly Victorian facade, but the striking and luxurious guest rooms are ultra-contemporary and furnished with numerous high-tech gadgets. **Pros:** great shopping at your doorstep; amazing views of Hyde Park; excellent service. **Cons:** nothing comes cheap; you must dress for dinner (and lunch and breakfast). [$] *Rooms from: £570* ✉ *66 Knightsbridge, Knightsbridge* ☎ *020/7235–2000* 🌐 *www.mandarinoriental.com/london* 🛏 *177 rooms, 23 suites* 🍴 *Breakfast* [M] *Knightsbridge* ✥ *D4.*

MAYFAIR

$$ B&B/INN 🏨 **22 York Street.** This Georgian town house has a cozy, family feel, with polished pine floors and plenty of quilts and French antiques in the individually furnished bedrooms. **Pros:** outstanding location for shoppers; friendly hosts; flexible check-in times; entirely nonsmoking. **Cons:** the location aside, the rates are high for a B&B; socializing with strangers over breakfast isn't for everyone. [$] *Rooms from: £130* ✉ *22 York St., Mayfair* ☎ *020/7224–2990* 🌐 *www.22yorkstreet.co.uk* 🛏 *10 rooms* 🍴 *Breakfast* [M] *Baker St.* ✥ *D2.*

$$$$ HOTEL Fodor's Choice ★ 🏨 **The Connaught.** A huge favorite of the "we wouldn't dream of staying anywhere else" moneyed set since opening in 1917, the Connaught complements its period grace notes with thoroughly up-to-date amenities. **Pros:** legendary hotel; great for star-spotting. **Cons:** history comes at a

price; bathrooms are small. [$] *Rooms from: £400* ✉ *Carlos Pl., Mayfair* ☎ *020/7499–7070, 866/599–6991 in U.S.* 🌐 *www.the-connaught.co.uk* 🛏 *92 rooms* 🍴 *Breakfast* [M] *Bond St.* ✥ *E3.*

$$$$ HOTEL Fodor's Choice ★ 🏨 **The Dorchester.** The glamour level is off the scale at the Dorchester, with gold leaf and marble public rooms, guest quarters awash in English country-house-style furnishings, and more than a hint of art deco splendor, but few hotels this opulent manage to be as charming. **Pros:** historic luxury in a 1930s building; lovely views of Hyde Park; top-notch star-spotting; plenty of modern technology, including Web TVs. **Cons:** prices are high; some rooms are rather small. [$] *Rooms from: £365* ✉ *Park La., Mayfair* ☎ *020/7629–8888* 🌐 *www.thedorchester.com* 🛏 *195 rooms, 55 suites* 🍴 *Breakfast* [M] *Marble Arch, Hyde Park Corner* ✥ *D4.*

MARYLEBONE

$$$ HOTEL Fodor's Choice ★ 🏨 **Dorset Square Hotel.** Reopened in 2012 after extensive renovations, this boutique hotel occupies a charming town house in one of London's most fashionable neighborhoods. **Pros:** ideal location; enchanting design; welcoming vibe. **Cons:** some rooms are small; no bathtub in some rooms; fee for Wi-Fi. [$] *Rooms from: £260* ✉ *39 Dorset Sq., Marylebone* ☎ *020/7723–7874* 🌐 *www.firmdalehotels.com* 🛏 *35 rooms, 3 suites* 🍴 *Breakfast* [M] *Baker St.* ✥ *D2.*

$$$ HOTEL Fodor's Choice ★ 🏨 **Hyatt Regency London – The Churchill.** Even though it's one of London's largest hotels, the Churchill is always abuzz with guests basking in the perfection they find here, including warmly personalized service and calmly alluring guest rooms. **Pros:** comfortable and stylish; efficient service; up to three can stay in one room. **Cons:** feels more geared to business than to leisure travelers. [$] *Rooms from: £260* ✉ *30 Portman Sq., Marylebone* ☎ *020/7486–5800* 🌐 *www.london.churchill.hyatt.com* 🛏 *389 rooms, 45 suites* 🍴 *Breakfast* [M] *Marble Arch* ✥ *D3.*

NOTTING HILL AND BAYSWATER

NOTTING HILL

$$ B&B/INN Fodor's Choice ★ 🏨 **The Main House.** A stay in this welcoming B&B feels more like sleeping over at a friend's house than in a hotel—albeit a particularly wealthy and well-connected friend. **Pros:** unique and unusual place; charming and helpful owners. **Cons:** few services; two-night minimum stay. [$] *Rooms from: £110* ✉ *6 Colvile Rd., Notting Hill* ☎ *020/7221–9691* 🌐 *www.themainhouse.com* 🛏 *4 rooms* 🍴 *Breakfast* [M] *Notting Hill Gate* ✥ *A3.*

$$ HOTEL 🏨 **The Portobello Hotel.** The quirky little Portobello, formed from two adjoining Victorian houses, is seriously hip, attracting scores of celebrities to small but stylish rooms that are decorated with joyous abandon. **Pros:** stylish; celebrity vibe; guests have use of nearby gym and pool. **Cons:** most rooms are quite small; place may be too eccentric for some. [$] *Rooms from: £174* ✉ *22 Stanley Gardens, Notting Hill* ☎ *020/7727–2777* 🌐 *www.portobello-hotel.co.uk* 🛏 *24 rooms* 🕓 *Closed 10 days at Christmas* 🍴 *Breakfast* [M] *Notting Hill Gate* ✥ *A3.*

BAYSWATER

$$ HOTEL 🏨 **London House Hotel.** Set in a row of white Georgian town houses, this excellent budget option in hit-or-miss Bayswater is friendly, well run, and spotlessly clean. **Pros:** friendly and efficient; emphasis on value for money; good location. **Cons:** some public areas feel too clinical; smallest rooms are tiny. [$] *Rooms from: £105* ✉ *81 Kensington Garden Sq., Bayswater* ☎ *020/7243–1810* 🌐 *www.londonhousehotels.com* 🛏 *100 rooms* 🍴 *Breakfast* [M] *Queensway, Bayswater* ✥ *A3.*

$ B&B/INN 🏨 **Parkwood Hotel.** Seconds from Hyde Park in a quiet, upscale enclave, this sweet little guesthouse, a good value, has bright bedrooms tended by warm and helpful hosts. **Pros:** warm hosts; free Wi-Fi; great rates. **Cons:** often booked up far in advance; no elevator; front-facing rooms can be noisy. [$] *Rooms from: £85* ✉ *4 Stanhope Pl., Bayswater* ☎ *020/7402–2241* 🌐 *www.parkwoodhotel.com* 🛏 *18 rooms* 🍴 *Breakfast* [M] *Marble Arch* ✥ *C3.*

$$ RENTAL 🏨 **Space Apart Hotel.** These studio apartments near Hyde Park are decorated in soothing tones of white and gray and have polished wood floors and attractive modern kitchenettes equipped with all you need to make small meals. **Pros:** handy location; exceptional value; the larger suites have space for four people. **Cons:** no in-house restaurant or bar; minimum two-night stay required. [$] *Rooms from: £140* ✉ *32–37 Kensington Gardens Sq., Bayswater* ☎ *020/7908–1340* 🌐 *www.aparthotel-london.co.uk* 🛏 *30 rooms* 🍴 *No meals* [M] *Bayswater* ✥ *A3.*

$ HOTEL 🏨 **Stylotel.** Around the corner from Paddington station, this funky-looking place has small, functional rooms—done to death in contemporary style—and even tinier bathrooms, but it's clean, cheerful, and perfectly comfortable. **Pros:** bargain price; helpful staff; unique style. **Cons:** style will be too unique for some; small bedrooms and bathrooms. [$] *Rooms from: £95* ✉ *160–162 Sussex Gardens Sq., Bayswater* ☎ *0207/223-1026* 🌐 *www.stylotel.com* 🛏 *40 rooms* 🍴 *Breakfast* [M] *Paddington, Edgware Rd. National Rail: Paddington* ✥ *C2.*

REGENT'S PARK AND HAMPSTEAD

$$ HOTEL Fodor's Choice ★ 🏨 **The Hide.** This cozy, chic, little hideaway is an excellent value, exceeding virtually anything you could hope to find in central London at this price; the big downside is that the half-hour Tube ride into town can start to feel like penance at the end of a long day's sightseeing. **Pros:** excellent value; great service; free Wi-Fi; close to Tube station. **Cons:** far from the center; dull neighborhood. [$] *Rooms from: £100* ✉ *230 Hendon Way, Hendon, Hampstead* ☎ *020/8203–1670* 🌐 *www.thehidelondon.com* 🛏 *22 rooms* 🍴 *Breakfast* [M] *Hendon Central* ✥ *D1.*

NIGHTLIFE AND THE ARTS

London is a must-go destination for both nightlife enthusiasts and culture vultures. Whether you prefer a refined evening at the opera or ballet, funky rhythm and blues in a Soho club, hardcore techno in East London, a pint and gourmet pizza at a local gastro-pub, or cocktails and sushi at a chic Mayfair bar, Great Britain's capital has entertainment to suit all tastes. Admission prices are not always low, but when you consider how much a London hotel room costs, the city's arts and nightlife diversions seem like a bargain.

NIGHTLIFE

There isn't *one* London nightlife scene—there are many. As long as there are audiences for obscure indie bands, cabaret comedy, or the latest trend in dance music, someone will create a venue to satisfy the need. The result? London is more than ever party central.

WESTMINSTER, ST. JAMES'S, AND ROYAL LONDON

BARS

American Bar. Festooned with club ties, signed celebrity photographs, sporting mementos, and baseball caps, this sensational hotel cocktail bar serves superb martinis. The name dates from the 1930s, when hotel bars in London started to cater to growing numbers of Americans crossing the Atlantic in ocean liners, but it wasn't until the 1970s, when a customer left a small carved wooden eagle, that the vast paraphernalia collection was started. ⊠ *Stafford Hotel, 16–18 St. James's Pl., St. James's* ☎ *020/7493–0111* ⊕ *www.thestaffordhotel.co.uk* ☙ *Daily 11:30 am–1 am* Ⓜ *Green Park.*

Bedford and Strand. The wine bar enjoyed a London renaissance as the 21st century dawned, and this is among the best of a new generation. It's sunk atmospherically down below the streets of Covent Garden, with dark wood and hanging shades; the wine list is short but well chosen, the service is faultless, and the bistro food is created with plenty of care. ⊠ *1A Bedford St., Charing Cross* ☎ *020/7836–3033* ⊕ *www. bedford-strand.com* ☙ *Mon.–Fri. noon–midnight; Sat. 5 pm–midnight* Ⓜ *Charing Cross.*

SOHO AND COVENT GARDEN

BARS

Le Salon Bar. Renowned chef Joël Robuchon's intimate, relaxed, and elegant bar is in the same premises as his L'Atelier and La Cuisine restaurants. The drink menu changes every six months, with new flavors and textures sure to entice your taste buds. ⊠ *13–15 West St., Soho* ☎ *020/7010–8600* ⊕ *www.joel-robuchon.com* ☙ *Mon.–Sat. noon–2 am, Sun. noon–10:30 pm* Ⓜ *Leicester Sq.*

Nordic. With shooters called "Husky Poo" and "Danish Bacon Surprise" and crayfish tails and meatballs on the smorgasbord menu, Nordic takes its Scandinavian feel the whole way. This secluded, shabby-chic bar serves many couples cozied up among travel brochures promoting the Viking lands. If you can't decide what to drink, the cocktail roulette wheel on the wall may help. ⊠ *25 Newman St.,*

Soho ☎ *020/7631–3174* ⊕ *www.nordicbar.com* ☾ *Mon.–Wed. 5 pm–midnight, Thurs. noon–midnight, Fri. noon–2am, Sat. 5 pm–midnight* Ⓜ *Tottenham Court Rd.*

Sketch. One seat never looks like the next at this collection of esoteric living-room bars. The exclusive Parlour, a patisserie during the day, exudes plenty of rarefied charm; the intimate East Bar at the back is reminiscent of a sci-fi film set; and in the Glade it's permanently sunset in a forest. ⊠ *9 Conduit St., Soho* ☎ *020/7659–4500* ⊕ *www.sketch. uk.com* ☾ *Parlour Mon.–Fri. 8 am–2 am, Sat. 10 am–2 am; The Glade 6:30 pm–2 am* Ⓜ *Oxford Circus.*

COMEDY AND CABARET

Comedy Store. Known as the birthplace of alternative comedy, this is where the U.K.'s funniest stand-ups have cut their teeth before being launched onto prime-time TV. The Comedy Store Players, a team with six comedians doing improvisation based on audience suggestions, entertain on Wednesday and Sunday; the Cutting Edge steps in every Tuesday. Thursday, Friday, and Saturday see the best stand-up acts. There's also a bar with food. Children under 18 are not admitted. ⊠ *1A Oxendon St., Soho* ☎ *0844/847–1728* ⊕ *www.thecomedystore.co.uk* 🎟 *£14–£28* ☾ *Shows daily 7:30 or 8 pm, with extra shows Fri. and Sat. at 11 pm* Ⓜ *Piccadilly Circus, Leicester Sq.*

Fodor's Choice ★ **Soho Theatre.** This innovative theater's programs include comedy shows by established acts and up-and-coming comedians and new writers. The relaxed Soho Theatre Bar has food, free Wi-Fi, simple tables, and a license to stay open until 1 am for members and ticket holders. ⊠ *21 Dean St., Soho* ☎ *020/7478–0100* ⊕ *www.sohotheatre.com* 🎟 *£10–£30* ☾ *Mon.–Sat. usually 7–11 although show times vary* Ⓜ *Tottenham Court Rd.*

JAZZ AND BLUES

Fodor's Choice ★ **Pizza Express Jazz Club Soho.** One of the capital's most ubiquitous pizza chains also runs a great Soho jazz venue. The dimly lighted restaurant hosts top-quality international jazz acts every night. The Italian-style thin-crust pizzas are good, too, though on the small side. ⊠ *10 Dean St., Soho* ☎ *0845/602–7017* ⊕ *www.pizzaexpresslive.com* 🎟 *£10–£25* ☾ *Daily 11:30 am–midnight for food; music after 7:30 pm (timings vary)* Ⓜ *Tottenham Court Rd.*

THE GAY SCENE

Fodor's Choice ★ **Friendly Society.** This haute moderne hot spot hops with activity almost any night of the week; with its white-leather pod seats the basement feels like something out of *Star Trek.* The place is known for being gay yet female-friendly. ⊠ *79 Wardour St., Soho* ☎ *020/7434–3805* ☾ *Weekdays 4–11, Sat. 2–11, Sun. 2–10:30* Ⓜ *Leicester Sq.*

Fodor's Choice ★ **Heaven.** With the best light show on any London dance floor, Heaven is huge, loud, and unpretentious, with a labyrinth of rooms, bars, and live-music parlors. Gay comedians perform (£10 in advance) on Friday and Saturday night from 7 to 10, and the club often hosts live performances from Tuesday through Thursday. If you go to just one gay club in London, Heaven should be it. ⊠ *The Arches, Villiers St., Covent Garden* ☎ *020/7930–2020* ⊕ *www.heavennightclub-london.*

2

com ✉ *£4–£12* ⊙ *Mon. 11 pm–5:30 am, Tues.–Fri. 11 pm–5 am, Sat. 10:30 pm–5 am* Ⓜ *Charing Cross, Embankment.*

The Shadow Lounge. This fabulous little lounge and dance club glitters with faux jewels and twinkling fiber-optic lights over its sunken dance floor, which comes complete with pole for those inclined to do their thing around it. It has a serious A-list celebrity factor, with the glamorous London glitterati camping out in the VIP booth. Members are given entrance priority when the place gets full, especially on weekends, so show up early, book onto the guest list online, or prepare to wait in line. ✉ *5–7 Brewer St., Soho* ☏ *020/7317-9270* ⊕ *www.theshadowlounge. co.uk* ✉ *Mon. free, Tues.–Thurs. £5, Fri.–Sat. £10* ⊙ *Mon.–Sat. 10 pm–3 am* Ⓜ *Leicester Sq.*

BLOOMSBURY AND HOLBORN

BARS

All Star Lanes. Surrounded by 1950s Americana in a retro bowling alley in the heart of literary Bloomsbury, you can sit on the red leather seats and choose from London's largest selection of bourbons. DJs play on Friday and Saturday night; there are also locations in Bayswater, Brick Lane, and Stratford. ✉ *Victoria House, Bloomsbury Pl., Bloomsbury* ☏ *020/7025-2676* ⊕ *www.allstarlanes.co.uk* ⊙ *Mon.–Wed. 4–11:30, Thurs. 4 midnight, Fri. noon–2 am, Sat. 11 am–2 am, Sun. 11–11* Ⓜ *Holborn.*

THE EAST END

DANCE CLUBS

Cargo. Housed under a series of old railroad arches, this vast brick-wall bar, restaurant, dance floor, and live-music venue pulls a young, international crowd with its hip vibe and diverse selection of music. Long tables bring people together, as does the food, which draws on global influences and is served tapas-style. Drinks, though, are expensive. ✉ *83 Rivington St., Shoreditch* ☏ *020/7739-3440* ⊕ *www.cargo-london.com* ✉ *Free–£20* ⊙ *Mon.–Thurs. 6 pm–1 am, Fri. 6 pm–3 am, Sat. 6 pm–3 am, Sun. 6 pm–midnight (restaurant opens at noon)* Ⓜ *Old St.*

Fabric. This sprawling subterranean club opposite Smithfield Meat Market is a firm fixture on the London scene and is regularly voted as one of the top clubs in the world. "FabricLive" hosts drum 'n' bass, dubstep, and hip-hop crews and live acts on Friday; international big-name DJs play slow, sexy bass lines and cutting-edge music on Saturday. The devastating sound system and vibrating "bodysonic" dance floor ensure that bass lines vibrate through your entire body. ■**TIP→** Get here early to avoid a lengthy queue, and don't wear a suit. ✉ *77A Charterhouse St., The City* ☏ *020/7336-8898* ⊕ *www.fabriclondon.com* ✉ *£15–£20; discounts after 3 or 4 am* ⊙ *Fri. 10 pm–6 am, Sat. 11 pm–8 am, Sun. 11 pm–6 am* Ⓜ *Farringdon.*

THE SOUTH BANK

BARS

The Dogstar. This popular South London hangout, frequented by local hipsters, was the first DJ bar in the world and has since enjoyed the resulting kudos. The vibe at this "surrealist boudoir" is down-to-earth, with top-name DJs playing cutting-edge sounds every night (no cover from Tuesday through Thursday) and pizza available until midnight. ⊠ *389 Coldharbour La., Brixton* ☎ *020/7733–7515* ⊕ *www. antic-ltd.com/dogstar* ☎ *Free–£8* ⊗ *Tues.–Wed. 4 pm–11 pm, Thurs. 4 pm–2 am, Fri. 4 pm–4 am, Sat. noon–4 am, Sun. noon–10:30 pm* Ⓜ *Brixton.*

DANCE CLUBS

Ministry of Sound. Ministry is more of an industry than a club, with its own record label, online radio station, and international DJs. Though it's too much a part of the establishment these days to be at the forefront of cool, the stripped-down warehouse-style club has a super sound system and still pulls in the world's most legendary names in dance music. There are chill-out rooms, two bars, and three dance floors. ⊠ *103 Gaunt St., Borough* ☎ *020/740–8600* ⊕ *www.ministryofsound.com* ☎ *£15–£23* ⊗ *Fri. 10 pm–5 am, Sat. 11 pm–7 am* Ⓜ *Elephant & Castle.*

ECLECTIC MUSIC

Fodor's Choice ★ **O2 Academy Brixton.** This legendary Brixton venue has seen it all—mods and rockers, hippies and punks—and it remains one of the city's top indie and rock venues. Despite a capacity of almost 5,000, this refurbished Victorian hall with original art deco fixtures retains a clublike charm; it has plenty of bars and upstairs seating. ⊠ *211 Stockwell Rd., Brixton* ☎ *020/7771–3000* ⊕ *www.o2academybrixton.co.uk* ☎ *£10–£50* ⊗ *Opening hrs vary* Ⓜ *Brixton.*

KENSINGTON, KNIGHTSBRIDGE, AND MAYFAIR

BARS

Fodor's Choice ★ **The Blue Bar at the Berkeley Hotel.** With low-slung dusty-blue walls, this hotel bar is sophisticated but sexy. Immaculate service, an excellent cocktail list, and a sleek decor by the late David Collins make this an ideal spot for a romantic tête-à-tête, complete with jazzy music in the background. ⊠ *Wilton Pl., Knightsbridge* ☎ *020/7235–6000* ⊕ *the-berkeley.co.uk* ⊗ *Mon.–Sat. 9 am–1 am, Sun. 9 am–11 pm* Ⓜ *Knightsbridge.*

Fodor's Choice ★ **Claridge's Bar.** This elegant Mayfair meeting place remains unassuming even when it brims with beautiful people. The bar has an art deco heritage made hip by the sophisticated touch of the late designer David Collins. A library of rare Champagnes and brandies as well as a delicious choice of traditional and exotic cocktails—try the Flapper or the Black Pearl—will occupy your taste buds. Request a glass of vintage Cristal in the darkly moody Fumoir. ⊠ *55 Brook St., Mayfair* ☎ *020/7629–8860* ⊕ *www.claridges.co.uk* ⊗ *Mon.–Sat. noon–1 am, Sun. noon–midnight* Ⓜ *Bond St.*

JAZZ AND BLUES

Dover Street Restaurant & Jazz Bar. Dance the night away after you've feasted from the French Mediterranean menu. Fun for dates as well as groups, Dover Street has three bars, a DJ, and a stage with the latest live bands performing everything from jazz to soul to R&B, all this encircling linen-covered tables with a friendly staff catering to your every whim. ⊠ *8–10 Dover St., Mayfair* ☎ *020/7491–7509* ⊕ *www. doverst.co.uk* ☎ *£7–£15* ⊗ *Mon.–Thurs. 5:30 pm–3 am, Fri.–Sat. 7 pm–3 am* Ⓜ *Green Park.*

NOTTING HILL

BARS

Beach Blanket Babylon. In a Georgian house in Notting Hill, close to Portobello Market, this always-packed bar is notable for its eclectic indoor-outdoor spaces full of Gaudí-esque curves and snuggly corners—like a fairy-tale grotto or a medieval dungeon. A sister restaurant-bar-gallery offers a slightly more modern take on similar themes in an ex-warehouse in Shoreditch (✉ *19–23 Bethnal Green Rd.* ☎ *020/7749–3540*). ✉ *45 Ledbury Rd., Notting Hill* ☎ *020/7229–2907* ⊕ *www.beachblanket. co.uk* ☉ *Daily noon–midnight* Ⓜ *Notting Hill Gate.*

DANCE CLUBS

Notting Hill Arts Club. What this small basement club-bar lacks in looks it makes up for in mood, and an alternative crowd swills beer to eclectic music that spans Asian underground, hip-hop, Latin-inspired funk, deep house, and jazzy grooves. ✉ *21 Notting Hill Gate, Notting Hill* ☎ *020/7460–4459* ⊕ *www.nottinghillartsclub.com* 🎫 *Free–£8* ☉ *Tues. noon–2 am, Wed.–Thurs. 7 pm–2 am, Fri.–Sat. 7 pm–midnight* Ⓜ *Notting Hill Gate.*

REGENT'S PARK AND HAMPSTEAD

DANCE CLUBS

KOKO. This Victorian theater, formerly known as Camden Palace, has hosted acts from Charlie Chaplin to Madonna, and genres from punk to rave, and it remains one of London's most stunning venues. Sounds of live indie rock, cabaret, funky house, and club classics keep the big dance floor moving, even when it's not heaving. ✉ *1A Camden High St., Camden Town* ☎ *0870/432–5527* ⊕ *www.koko.uk.com* 🎫 *£6–£25* ☉ *Opening hrs vary, depending on shows* Ⓜ *Mornington Crescent.*

ECLECTIC

Union Chapel. The beauty of this sublime old chapel and its impressive multicultural programming make this one of London's best musical venues, especially for acoustic shows. Performers have included Björk, Beck, and Goldfrapp, though now you're more likely to hear lower-key alternative country, world music, and jazz, alongside poetry and literary events. ✉ *Compton Terr., Islington* ☎ *020/7226–1686 venue (no box office; ticket sales numbers vary with each event)* ⊕ *www.unionchapel. org.uk* 🎫 *Free–£25* ☉ *Opening hrs vary* Ⓜ *Highbury & Islington.*

JAZZ AND BLUES

Jazz Café. A mainstay of bohemian Camden, this is an essential venue for fans of classic jazz as well as hip-hop, funk, world music, and Latin fusion. It's also the unlikely venue for Saturday "I Love the 80s" nights. Book ahead if you want a prime table in the balcony restaurant overlooking the stage, the only way to avoid standing. ✉ *5 Parkway, Camden Town* ☎ *020/7688–8899 restaurant reservations, 020/7485–6834 venue info, 0844/847–2514 tickets (Ticketmaster)* ⊕ *venues.meanfiddler.com/jazz-cafe/home* 🎫 *£6–£35* ☉ *Daily 7 pm–2 am* Ⓜ *Camden Town.*

ROCK

Barfly Club. At one of the finest small clubs in the capital, punk, indie guitar bands, and new metal rock attract a non-mainstream crowd. Weekend club nights upstairs host DJs (and live bands) who rock the decks. ✉ *49 Chalk Farm Rd., Camden Town* ☎ *020/7424-0800 venue, 0870/9070-999 tickets* ⊕ *www.barflyclub.com* ✉ *£5–£11* ⊙ *Mon. and Tues. 7–midnight, Wed. and Thurs. 7 pm–2 am, Fri. and Sat. 7 pm–3 am* Ⓜ *Camden Town, Chalk Farm.*

THE ARTS

Whether you prefer your art classical or contemporary, you'll find that London's vibrant cultural scene has as much to offer as any in the world. The Royal Opera House hosts world-class productions of opera and ballet, the reconstructed Shakespeare's Globe re-creates seeing the Bard's work as its original audience would have, and the National Theatre, the Royal Court, and several other subsidized theaters produce challenging new plays and reimagined classics.

To find out what's showing now, the free weekly magazine *Time Out* (issued every Tuesday in print and online at ⊕ *www.timeout.com*) is invaluable. The free *Evening Standard* carries listings, many of which are also available online at ⊕ *www.thisislondon.co.uk*. *Metro*, London's other widely available free newspaper, is also worth checking out. You can pick up the free fortnightly *London Theatre Guide* from hotels and tourist-information centers.

MAIN PERFORMING ARTS CENTERS

FAMILY **Barbican Centre.** Opened in 1982, the Brutalist-style Barbican is the largest performing arts center in Europe. The main concrete theater is most famous as the home of the London Symphony Orchestra. As well as the LSO (⊕ *www.lso.co.uk*), the Barbican is also the frequent host of the English Chamber Orchestra and the BBC Symphony Orchestra, and has an excellent concert season of big-name virtuosos. Performances by British and international theater companies make up part of its year-round **BITE** (Barbican International Theatre Events), which also features groundbreaking performance, dance, drama, and musical theater. Innovative exhibitions of 20th-century and current art and design are shown in the Barbican Gallery and the Curve (usually free). In addition to Hollywood films, obscure classics and film festivals with Screen Talks are programmed in the three movie theaters here. Saturday Family Film Club has adventure and animation to please all ages. ✉ *Silk St., The City* ☎ *020/7638–8891 box office* ⊕ *www.barbican.org.uk* ⊙ *Mon.–Sat. 9 am–11 pm, Sun. noon–11 pm* Ⓜ *Barbican.*

Southbank Centre. The Royal Festival Hall is one of London's best spaces for large-scale choral and orchestral works and is home to the Philharmonia and London Philharmonic orchestras. Other venues in the Southbank Centre host smaller-scale music performances: The Queen Elizabeth Hall is a popular venue for chamber orchestras and top-tier soloists, and the intimate Purcell Room is known for chamber music and solo recitals. The Southbank also hosts everything from the London International Mime Festival to large-scale dance performances, including a diverse and exciting season of international and British-based contemporary dance companies. Also part of the complex is the **Hayward Gallery** (open daily from 10 to 6), a landmark Brutalist-style 1960s building and one of London's major venues for contemporary art exhibitions. ⊠ *Belvedere Rd., South Bank* ☎ *020/7960–4200, 0844/875–0073 box office* ⊕ *www.southbankcentre.co.uk* Ⓜ *Waterloo, Embankment.*

CLASSICAL MUSIC

Whether it's a concert by cellist Yo-Yo Ma or Mozart's Requiem by candlelight, it's possible to hear first-rate musicians in world-class venues almost every day of the year. If you can't book in advance, arrive at the hall an hour before the performance for a chance at returns.

■**TIP**➡ Lunchtime concerts take place all over the city in smaller concert halls, the big arts-center foyers, and churches; they usually cost less than £5 or are free, and feature string quartets, singers, jazz ensembles, or gospel choirs. St. John's, Smith Square, and St. Martin-in-the-Fields are popular locations. Performances usually begin about 1 pm and last one hour.

A great British tradition since 1895, the **Henry Wood Promenade Concerts** (more commonly known as the "Proms" ⊕ *www.bbc.co.uk/proms*) run eight weeks, from July to September, at the Royal Albert Hall. Despite an extraordinary quantity of high-quality concerts, it's renowned for its (atypical) last night: a madly patriotic display of singing "Land of Hope and Glory," and Union Jack–waving. For regular Proms, tickets run from £5 to £90, with hundreds of standing tickets for £5 available at the hall on the night of the concert. ■**TIP**➡ The last night is broadcast in Hyde Park on a jumbo screen, but even a seat on the grass requires a paid ticket (around £25).

Royal Albert Hall. Built in 1871, this splendid iron-and-glass–dome auditorium hosts music programs in a wide range of genres. Its terra-cotta exterior surmounted by a mosaic frieze depicting figures engaged in artistic, scientific, and cultural pursuits, this domed, circular 5,223-seat auditorium was made possible by the Victorian public, who donated the money to build it. The RAH hosts everything from pop and classical headliners to Cirque du Soleil, ballet on ice, awards ceremonies, and Sumo wrestling championships, but is best known as the venue for the annual July–September BBC Promenade Concerts—the "Proms." ⊠ *Kensington Gore, Kensington* ☎ *020/7589–8212, 0845/401–5034 box office* ⊕ *www.royalalberthall.com* Ⓜ *South Kensington.*

St. Martin-in-the-Fields. Popular lunchtime concerts (free but £3.50 donation suggested) are held in this lovely 1726 church, as are regular evening concerts. ■**TIP**➡ Stop for a snack at the Café in the Crypt. ⊠ *Trafalgar Sq., Westminster* ☎ *020/7766–1100* ⊕ *www.stmartin-in-the-fields.org* Ⓜ *Charing Cross.*

Fodor'sChoice ★ **Wigmore Hall.** Hear chamber music and song recitals in this charming hall with near-perfect acoustics. Don't miss the Sunday morning concerts (11:30 am). ⊠ *36 Wigmore St., Marylebone* ☎ *020/7935–2141* ⊕ *www.wigmore-hall.org.uk* Ⓜ *Bond St.*

The Royal Opera House is simply dazzling inside and out, including at night.

DANCE

Dance aficionados in London can enjoy the classicism of the world-renowned Royal Ballet, innovative works by the Rambert Dance Company, Matthew Bourne's New Adventures, the Wheeldon Company, and other groups, and the latest pieces by scores of independent choreographers. The English National Ballet and visiting international companies perform at the Coliseum and at Sadler's Wells, which also hosts various other ballet companies and dance troupes. Encompassing the refurbished Royal Festival Hall, the Southbank Centre has a seriously good contemporary dance program that hosts top international companies and important U.K. choreographers, as well as multicultural offerings ranging from Japanese Butoh and Indian Kathak to hip-hop. The Place and the Lilian Bayliss Theatre at Sadler's Wells are where you'll find the most daring, cutting-edge performances. Also check ⊕ *www.londondance.com* for performances and fringe venues.

Dance Umbrella. The biggest annual event is Dance Umbrella, ten days in October that host international and British-based artists at various venues across the city. ☎ *020/7407–1200* ⊕ *www.danceumbrella.co.uk.*

The Place. The Robin Howard Dance Theatre at The Place is London's only theater dedicated to contemporary dance, and with tickets often under £15 it's good value, too. "Resolution!" is the United Kingdom's biggest platform event for new choreographers. ✉ *17 Duke's Rd., Bloomsbury* ☎ *020/7121–1100* ⊕ *www.theplace.org.uk* Ⓜ *Euston.*

Fodor's Choice ★ **Sadler's Wells.** This gleaming building opened in 1998, the seventh on the site in its 300-year history, and is devoted to presenting leading classical and contemporary dance companies. The Random Dance Company is in residence, and the little Lilian Bayliss Theatre hosts avant-garde work. ✉ *Rosebery Ave., Islington* ☎ *0844/412–4300 tickets, 020/7863-8198 general enquiries* ⊕ *www.sadlerswells.com* Ⓜ *Angel.*

FILM

There are many lovely movie theaters in London and several that are committed to non-mainstream cinema, notably the BFI Southbank and the Curzon and Everyman mini-chains. Most of the big cinemas, such as the Odeon Leicester Square and the Empire, are in the Leicester Square–Piccadilly Circus area, where tickets average £15. Tickets on Monday and for matinees are often cheaper (from £6 to £10), and there are fewer crowds.

FAMILY **BFI Southbank.** With the best repertory programming in London, the three movie theaters and studio at what was previously known as the National Film Theatre are effectively a national film center run by the British Film Institute. They show more than 1,000 titles each year, favoring art-house, foreign, silent, overlooked, classic, noir, and short films. The center also has a gallery, a bookshop, and a "mediatheque" (closed on Monday), where visitors can watch film and television from the National Archive for free. ✉ *Belvedere Rd., South Bank* ☎ *020/7928-3535 information, 020/7928-3232 box office* ⊕ *www. bfi.org.uk* Ⓜ *Waterloo.*

Curzon Soho. This popular, comfortable movie theater runs a vibrant and artsy program of mixed repertoire and mainstream films, with a good calendar of director talks and other events, too. There are branches in Mayfair, Bloomsbury, Chelsea, and Richmond. ✉ *99 Shaftesbury Ave., Soho* ☎ *0330/500–1331* ⊕ *www.curzoncinemas.com* Ⓜ *Piccadilly Circus, Leicester Sq.* ✉ *38 Curzon St., Mayfair* ☎ *0330/500–1331* Ⓜ *Green Park.*

FAMILY **The Electric Cinema.** This refurbished Portobello Road art house screens mainstream and international movies. The emphasis is on comfort, with leather sofas for two, armchairs, footstools, and mini–coffee tables for your tapas-style food and wine. Saturday matinees for kids are popular. Edible Cinema combines experimental food and cocktails with the cinema experience. The Electric also has another sumptuous movie theater in East London—the Aubin, on Redchurch Street, with sofas and wine coolers. ✉ *191 Portobello Rd., Notting Hill* ☎ *020/7908–9696* ⊕ *www.electriccinema.co.uk* ✉ *£12.50–£22.50* Ⓜ *Ladbroke Grove, Notting Hill Gate.*

OPERA

The two key players in London's opera scene are the Royal Opera House (which ranks with the Metropolitan Opera House in New York) and the more innovative English National Opera (ENO), which presents English-language productions at the London Coliseum. Only the Theatre Royal, Drury Lane, has a longer theatrical history than the Royal Opera House—the third theater to be built on the site since 1858.

Despite occasional performances by the likes of Björk, the Royal Opera House struggles to shrug off its reputation for elitism and ticket prices that can rise to £800. It is, however, more accessible than it used to be—the cheapest tickets cost less than £10. Prices for the ENO range from around £20 to £95.

In summer, the increasingly adventurous Opera Holland Park presents the usual chestnuts, along with some obscure works, under a canopy in leafy Holland Park. International touring companies often perform at Sadler's Wells, the Barbican, the Southbank Centre, and Wigmore Hall, so check the weekly listings for details.

The London Coliseum. An extravaganza of Edwardian architectural exoticism, the restored baroque-style theater (1904) has a magnificent auditorium and a rooftop glass dome with a bar and great views. As one of the city's largest and most venerable theaters, the Coliseum functions mainly as the home of the English National Opera. Seemingly in better financial shape than it has been for some time, ENO continues to produce innovative opera, sung in English, for lower prices than the Royal Opera House. During opera's off-season, the house hosts dance troupes, including the English National Ballet (⊕ *www.ballet.org.uk*). Guided tours (every Saturday at 11:30 am) cost £10. ⊠ *St. Martin's La., Covent Garden* ☎ *0871/911–0200 box office, 020/7836–0111 enquiries* ⊕ *www.eno.org* Ⓜ *Leicester Sq.*

Opera Holland Park. In summer, well-loved operas and imaginative productions of relatively unknown works are presented under a spectacular new canopy against the remains of Holland House, one of the first great houses built in Kensington. Ticket prices range from £12 to £67.50, with 1,100 tickets offered free every season to young people ages 9 to 18. Tickets go on sale in April. ⊠ *Holland Park, Kensington High St., Kensington* ☎ *0300/999–1000 box office (opens late Apr.), 020/7361–3570 enquiries* ⊕ *www.operahollandpark.com* Ⓜ *High Street Kensington, Holland Park.*

Fodor's Choice
★ **Royal Opera House.** Along with Milan's La Scala, New York's Metropolitan, and the Palais Garnier in Paris, this is one of the world's greatest opera houses. The resident troupe has mounted famously spectacular productions in the past, though recent productions have tended toward starker, more contemporary operas. Tickets range in price from £8 to £800. The box office opens at 10 am, but lines for popular productions can start as early as 7 am; unsold tickets are offered at half price four hours before a performance. There are free lunchtime recitals on most Mondays in the Crush Room—arrive early to get a ticket, between 11 am and noon; some tickets are available online from nine days before the event. ROH2, the Opera House's contemporary arm, stages more experimental dance and voice performances in locations including the Linbury Studio Theatre, a 400-seater space below the Opera House. ⊠ *Bow St., Covent Garden* ☎ *020/7304–4000* ⊕ *www.roh.org. uk* ☉ *Public areas generally 10–3:30; auditorium tours daily at 4; backstage tours Mon.–Fri. 10:30, 12:30, and 2:30, Sat. 10:30, 11:30, 12:30, and 1:30* Ⓜ *Covent Garden.*

THEATER

The London theater scene encompasses long-running popular musicals, the most recent work from leading contemporary playwrights, imaginative physical theater from experimental companies, lavish Disney spectacles, and small fringe productions above pubs. Glitzy West End jukebox musicals and star-studded revivals of warhorses continue to pull in the audiences, but more challenging productions do so as well—only in London will a Tuesday matinee of the Royal Shakespeare Company's *Henry IV* sell out a 1,200-seat theater. In London, the words "radical" and "quality," or "classical" and "experimental," are not mutually exclusive. The Royal Shakespeare Company (⊕ *www. rsc.org.uk*) and the National Theatre (⊕ *www.nationaltheatre.org.uk*) often stage contemporary interpretations of the classics. The Almeida, Battersea Arts Centre (BAC), Donmar Warehouse, Royal Court Theatre, Soho Theatre, and Old Vic attract famous actors and have excellent reputations for showcasing new writing and innovative theatrical approaches. These are the venues where you'll see an original production before it becomes a hit in the West End or on Broadway (and for a fraction of the cost). During the summer you can take in an open-air production of Shakespeare at the Globe Theatre or under the stars in Regent's Park's Open Air Theatre.

Though less pricey than Broadway, theatergoing here isn't cheap. Tickets under £10 are a rarity, although designated productions at the National Theatre have seats at this price. At the commercial theaters you should expect to pay from £15 for a seat in the upper balcony to at least £25 for a good one in the stalls (orchestra) or dress circle (mezzanine). However, last-minute returns available on the night may provide some good deals. Tickets may be booked through ticket agents, at individual theater box offices, or over the phone by credit card. Be sure to inquire about any extra fees—prices can vary enormously, but agents are legally obliged to reveal the face value of the ticket if you ask. All the larger hotels offer theater bookings, but they tack on a hefty service charge. ■ TIP→ Be very wary of ticket touts (scalpers) and unscrupulous ticket agents outside theaters.

Ticketmaster (☎ *0844/277–4321* ⊕ *www.ticketmaster.co.uk*) sells tickets to a number of different theaters, although it charges a booking fee. For discount tickets, **Society of London Theatre** (☎ *020/7557–6700* ⊕ *www. tkts.co.uk*) operates "tkts," a half-price ticket booth on the southwest corner of Leicester Square, and sells the best available seats to performances at about 25 theaters. It's open daily from 9 to 7 except Sunday (10:30 to 4:30). A £3 service charge is included in the price. Major credit cards are accepted.

THEATERS

Almeida Theatre. This Off–West End venue premieres excellent new plays and exciting twists on the classics, often featuring high-profile actors. It has a good café and a bar that serves "sharing dishes" as well as tasty main courses. ✉ *Almeida St., Islington* ☎ *020/7359–4404* ⊕ *www. almeida.co.uk* Ⓜ *Angel, Highbury & Islington.*

BAC. Battersea Arts Centre has a reputation for producing innovative new work. Check out Scratch events, low-tech cabaret theater by emerging artists where the audience provides feedback on works-in-progress. Tuesday shows often have pay-what-you-can entry. ✉ *176 Lavender Hill, Battersea* ☎ *020/7223–2223* ⊕ *www.bac.org.uk* Ⓜ *National Rail: Clapham Junction.*

Fodor's Choice   **Donmar Warehouse.** Stars of the caliber of Nicole Kidman, Gwyneth Pal-
★   trow, and Chiwetel Ejiofor often perform at this not-for-profit theater
that presents diverse and daring new works, bold interpretations of
the classics, and small-scale musicals. ⊠ *41 Earlham St., Seven Dials,
Covent Garden* ☎ *0844/871–7624* ⊕ *www.donmarwarehouse.com*
Ⓜ *Covent Garden.*

National Theatre. When this theater designed by Sir Denys Lasdun first
opened in 1976, many Londoners weren't enraptured by the low-
rise, multilayered Brutalist block. But the inside is better. Interspersed
with the three theaters—the 1,120-seat Olivier, the 890-seat Lyttelton,
and the 300-seat Cottesloe—is a multilayered foyer with exhibitions,
bars, and restaurants, and free entertainment. Musicals, classics, and
new plays are all performed by top-flight professionals. Some shows
offer £12 ticket deals. ⊠ *Belvedere Rd., South Bank* ☎ *020/7452–3000
box office, 020/7452–3400 information* ⊕ *www.nationaltheatre.org.
uk* 🎟 *Tour £8.50* ⊙ *Foyer Mon.–Sat. 9:30 am–11 pm; 75-min tour
backstage up to 6 times daily weekdays, twice on Sat., often on Sun.*
Ⓜ *Waterloo.*

The Old Vic. In early 2015, the American actor Kevin Spacey is scheduled
to end a dozen-year run as the artistic director of this grand old theater
whose stage was frequently graced by such legends as John Gielgud,
Vivien Leigh, Peter O'Toole, Richard Burton, and Judi Dench. The
theater had suffered decades of decline before being brought under the
ownership of a dedicated trust headed by Spacey, whose tenure is largely
regarded as having been a success, both artistically and financially.
⊠ *The Cut, Southwark* ☎ *0844/871–7628 box office, 020/7928–2651*
⊕ *www.oldvictheatre.com* Ⓜ *Waterloo, Southwark.*

Fodor's Choice   **Open Air Theatre.** On a warm summer evening, open-air classical theater
★   in the pastoral and royal Regent's Park is hard to beat for a magical
adventure. Enjoy a supper before the performance, a bite during the
intermission on the picnic lawn, or drinks in the spacious bar. The only
downside is that warm summer nights in London are not always entirely
reliable. ⊠ *Inner Circle, Regent's Park* ☎ *0844/826–4242* ⊕ *www.
openairtheatre.com* Ⓜ *Baker St., Regent's Park.*

Royal Court Theatre. With an unparalleled reputation for finding exciting new theatrical voices since the 1950s (John Osborne, Caryl
Churchill, and Martin McDonagh are among the playwrights who
have had premieres here), the RCT continues to produce compelling original British and international drama. ■TIP→ Don't miss the
best deal in town—four 10-pence standing tickets go on sale one hour
before each performance, and £10 tickets are available on Monday.
⊠ *Sloane Sq., Chelsea* ☎ *020/7565–5000* ⊕ *www.royalcourttheatre.
com* Ⓜ *Sloane Sq.*

Soho Theatre. This sleek theater in the heart of Soho is devoted to foster-
ing new work and is a prolific presenter of plays by emerging writers,
comedy performances, cabaret shows, and other entertainment. ⊠ *21
Dean St., Soho* ☎ *020/7478–0100* ⊕ *www.sohotheatre.com* Ⓜ *Tottenham Court Rd.*

Tricycle Theatre. Committed to representing the cultural diversity of its community, the Tricycle shows the best in black, Irish, Jewish, Asian, and South African drama, and also promotes new work. ✉ *269 Kilburn High Rd., Kilburn* ☎ *020/7372 6611 information, 020/7328–1000 box office* ⊕ *www.tricycle.co.uk* Ⓜ *Kilburn.*

Young Vic. In a venue near Waterloo, big names perform alongside young talent, often in daring, innovative productions of classic plays that appeal to a more diverse audience than is traditionally found in London theaters. ✉ *66 The Cut, Waterloo, South Bank* ☎ *020/7922–2800, 020/7922–2922 box office* ⊕ *www.youngvic.org* Ⓜ *Southwark, Waterloo.*

SHOPPING

You can try on underwear fit for a queen at Her Majesty's lingerie supplier, track down a leather-bound Brontë classic at an antiquarian bookseller, or find a bargain antique on Portobello Road. Whether you're just browsing or on a fashion-seeking mission, London shopping offers something for all tastes and budgets.

Although it's impossible to pin down one particular look that defines the city, London style tends to fall into two camps: one is the quirky, individualistic, somewhat romantic look exemplified by homegrown designers such as Vivienne Westwood. The other reflects Britain's celebrated tradition of classic knitwear and suiting, with labels such as Oswald Boateng and Paul Smith taking tradition and giving it a very modern twist. If your budget can't stretch to the custom-made shirts and suits of Jermyn Street and Savile Row or the classic handbags at Mulberry, Asprey, and Anya Hindmarch, no problem; the Topshop chain, aimed at the younger end of the market, is an excellent place to pick up designs copied straight from the catwalk at a fraction of the price, and midmarket chains such as Reiss and Jigsaw offer smart design and better quality for the more sophisticated shopper.

If there's anything that unites London's designers, it's a commitment to creativity and originality, underpinned by a strong sense of heritage. This combination of posh and rock 'n' roll sensibilities is exemplified by designers like Sarah Burton—the late Alexander McQueen's successor at his eponymous label and designer of the Duchess of Cambridge's wedding dress—Stella McCartney, the creative milliner Philip Treacy, and the imaginative shoemakers United Nude. If anything, London is even better known for its vibrant street fashion found at the stalls at Portobello, Camden, and Spitalfields markets.

London's shopping districts are spread all over the city, so pace yourself and take in only one or two areas in a day. Or visit one of the grand department stores such as Selfridges, Liberty, or Harvey Nichols, where you can find a wide assortment of designers, from mass to class, all under one roof.

WESTMINSTER, ST. JAMES'S, AND ROYAL LONDON

BEAUTY

Fodor's Choice ★ **Floris.** What do Queen Victoria and Marilyn Monroe have in common? They both used fragrances from Floris, one of the most beautiful shops in London, with gleaming glass-and-Spanish-mahogany showcases salvaged from the Great Exhibition of 1851. In addition to scents for both men and women, Floris makes its own shaving products, reflecting its origins as a barbershop. Other gift possibilities include goose-down powder puffs, a famous rose-scented mouthwash, and beautifully packaged soaps and bath essences. There's another branch in Belgravia. ⊠ *89 Jermyn St., St. James's* ☎ *020/7930–2885* ⊕ *www.florislondon. com* ⊗ *Closed Sun.* Ⓜ *Piccadilly Circus, Green Park.*

BOOKS AND STATIONERY

Fodor's Choice ★ **Hatchards.** This is London's oldest bookshop, open since 1797 and beloved by writers themselves (customers have included Oscar Wilde, Rudyard Kipling, and Lord Byron). Despite its wood-paneled, "gentleman's library" atmosphere, and eclectic selection of books, Hatchards is owned by the large Waterstone's chain. Nevertheless, the shop retains its period charm, aided by the staff's old-fashioned helpfulness and expertise. Look for the substantial number of books signed by notable contemporary authors on the well-stocked shelves. ⊠ *187 Piccadilly, St. James's* ☎ *020/7439–9921* ⊕ *www.hatchards.co.uk* Ⓜ *Piccadilly Circus.*

CLOTHING: MENSWEAR

Fodor's Choice ★ **Turnbull & Asser.** This is *the* custom shirtmaker, dripping exclusivity from every fiber—after all, Prince Charles is a client and every filmic James Bond has worn shirts from here. At least 15 separate measurements are taken, and the cloth, woven to the company's specifications, comes in 1,000 different patterns—the cottons feel as good as silk. The first order must be for a minimum of six shirts, which start at £195 each. As well as jackets, cashmeres, suits, ties, pajamas, and accessories perfect for the billionaire who has everything, the store also carries less expensive, though still exquisite, ready-to-wear shirts. There's another branch in the City. ⊠ *71–72 Jermyn St., St. James's* ☎ *020/7808–3000* ⊕ *www. turnbullandasser.com* ⊗ *Closed Sun.* Ⓜ *Green Park.*

FOOD

Fodor's Choice ★ **Berry Bros. & Rudd.** Nothing matches Berry Bros. & Rudd for rare offerings and a unique shopping experience. A family-run wine business since 1698, "BBR" stores its vintage bottles and casks in vaulted cellars that are more than 300 years old. The shop has an offbeat charm, and the staff is extremely knowledgeable—and not snooty if you're on a budget. ⊠ *3 St. James's St., St. James's* ☎ *020/396–9600* ⊕ *www.bbr. com* ⊗ *Closed Sun.* Ⓜ *Green Park.*

Fodor's Choice ★ **Fortnum & Mason.** Although F&M is popularly known as the Queen's grocer and the impeccably mannered staff wear traditional tailcoats, its celebrated food hall stocks gifts for all budgets, among them irresistibly packaged luxury foods stamped with the gold "By Appointment" crest for less than £5. Try the teas, preserves (unusual products include rosepetal jelly), condiments, or Gentleman's Relish (anchovy paste). If you

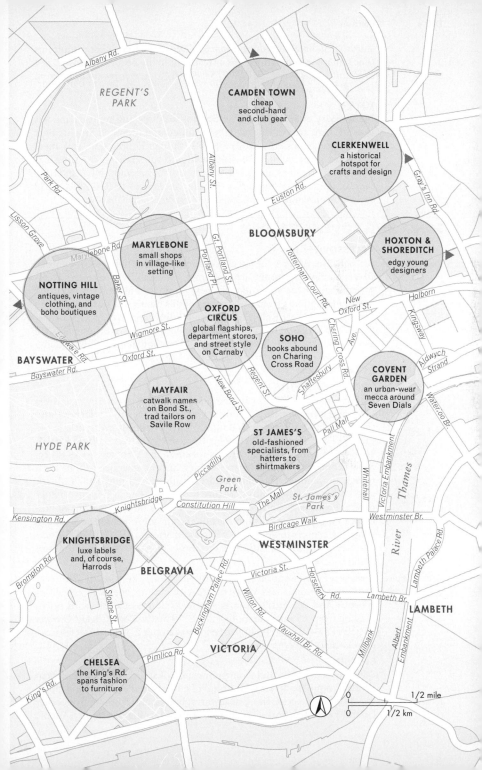

CAMDEN TOWN
cheap
second-hand
and club gear

CLERKENWELL
a historical
hotspot for
crafts and design

REGENT'S
PARK

Albany Rd.

Albany St.

Euston Rd.

Gt. Portland St.

Portland Pl.

Park Rd.

Lisson Grove

BLOOMSBURY

MARYLEBONE
small shops
in village-like
setting

**HOXTON &
SHOREDITCH**
edgy young
designers

Gray's Inn Rd.

Holborn

Kingsway

Marylebone Rd.

Baker St.

NOTTING HILL
antiques, vintage
clothing, and
boho boutiques

**OXFORD
CIRCUS**
global flagships,
department stores,
and street style
on Carnaby

New
Oxford St.

Tottenham Court Rd.

SOHO
books abound
on Charing
Cross Road

Charing Cross Rd.

Aldwych

Strand

Edgware Rd.

Wigmore St.

BAYSWATER

Oxford St.

Bayswater Rd.

Regent St.

Shaftesbury

**COVENT
GARDEN**
an urban-wear
mecca around
Seven Dials

Waterloo Br.

MAYFAIR
catwalk names
on Bond St.,
trad tailors on
Savile Row

New Bond St.

HYDE PARK

ST JAMES'S
old-fashioned
specialists, from
hatters to
shirtmakers

Pall Mall

Piccadilly

Green
Park

Whitehall

Victoria Embankment

Thames

Knightsbridge

Constitution Hill

The Mall

St. James's
Park

Kensington Rd.

KNIGHTSBRIDGE
luxe labels
and, of course,
Harrods

Birdcage Walk

WESTMINSTER

Westminster Br.

River

Lambeth Palace Rd.

Brompton Rd.

Sloane St.

BELGRAVIA

Buckingham Palace Rd.

Victoria St.

Horseferry
Rd.

Lambeth Br.

LAMBETH

Millbank

Albert
Embankment

Wilton Rd.

CHELSEA
the King's Rd.
spans fashion
to furniture

Pimlico Rd.

VICTORIA

Vauxhall Br. Rd.

King's Rd.

0   1/2 mile

0   1/2 km

start to flag, break for afternoon tea at one of the four other restaurants (one's an ice-cream parlor)—or a treatment in the Beauty Rooms. ⊠ *181 Piccadilly, St. James's* ☎ *020/7734–8040* ⊕ *www.fortnumandmason. com* Ⓜ *Green Park.*

TOYS

The Armoury of St. James's. The fine toy soldiers and military models in stock here are collectors' items. Painted and mounted knights only 6 inches high can cost up to £1,200 (though figures start at a mere £7.50 for a toy soldier). Besides lead and tin soldiers, the shop has regimental brooches, porcelain figures, military memorabilia, and military antiques. ⊠ *17 Piccadilly Arcade, St. James's* ☎ *020/7493–5082* ⊕ *www.armoury.co.uk* ☉ *Closed Sun.* Ⓜ *Piccadilly Circus.*

SOHO AND COVENT GARDEN

ACCESSORIES

Fodor's Choice
★
Peckham Rye. Among the specialist boutiques that line the cobblestone streets fanning out from Carnaby Street, Peckham Rye sells men's accessories—handmade silk and twill ties, bow ties, and scarves, all using traditional patterns from the archives of this family-run business that go back to 1799. More Ralph Lauren than Ralph Lauren, the socks, striped shirts, and handkerchiefs here entice modern-day Beau Brummells such as musician-producer Mark Ronson and ex-footballer David Beckham. ⊠ *11 Newburgh St., Soho* ☎ *0207/734–5181* ⊕ *www.peckhamrye.com* Ⓜ *Oxford Street.*

BOOKS AND PRINTS

Fodor's Choice
★
Foyles. Founded in 1903 by the Foyle brothers after they failed the Civil Service exam, this family-owned store, recently relocated into this historic 1930s art deco building, carries almost every title imaginable. The largest bookstore in Europe, with over 200,000 titles, and one of London's best sources for textbooks, Foyles stocks everything from popular fiction to military history, sheet music, medical tomes, graphic novels, and handsome illustrated fine arts books. It also houses the store-within-a-store Ray's Jazz (one of London's better outlets for music) and a cool café. Foyles has branches in the Southbank Centre, St. Pancras International train station, and the Westfield shopping centers in Shepherd's Bush and Stratford. ⊠ *107–109 Charing Cross Rd., Soho* ☎ *020/7437–5660* ⊕ *www.foyles.co.uk* Ⓜ *Tottenham Court Rd.*

Fodor's Choice
★
Grosvenor Prints. London's largest collection of 17th- to-early 20th-century prints emphasizes views of the city and architecture as well as sporting and decorative motifs. The selection is eclectic, with prices ranging from £5 into the thousands. ⊠ *19 Shelton St., Covent Garden* ☎ *020/7836–1979* ⊕ *www.grosvenorprints.com* ☉ *Closed Sun.* Ⓜ *Covent Garden, Leicester Sq.*

CLOTHING

Other. Aimed at men and women in search of stylish cool, this independent boutique stocks its own brand of entirely made-in-England clothing, as well as accessories, housewares, books, and clothing from other carefully selected brands such as b store, Opening Ceremony, Sophie

LONDON'S SPECTATOR SPORTS

Sport in the capital comes into its own when it's watched, rather than participated in. You'll most easily witness London's fervent sporting passions in front of a screen in a pub with a pint in hand. And those passions run deep.

FOOTBALL

London's top teams—Chelsea, Arsenal, Tottenham Hotspur—are world-class (especially the first two) and often progress in the European Champions League. It's unlikely you'll be able to get tickets for anything except the least popular Premier League games during the August–May season, despite absurdly high ticket prices—as much as £41 for a standard, walk-up, match-day seat at Chelsea, and a whopping £126 for the dearest match-day tickets at Arsenal!

Arsenal. Arsenal (aka the Gunners) is historically London's most success-ful club. Under the managerial reign of Arsene Wenger they have shed their boring image to become proponents of tippy-tappy, attractive, free-flowing football—while hardly ever employing any English players. ⊠ *Emirates Stadium, 75 Drayton Park* ☎ *020/7619-5000* ⊕ *www.arsenal. com* Ⓜ *Arsenal.*

Chelsea. Chief rivals of Manches-ter United in the Premier League, Champions League winners in 2012, and Premier League title and FA Cup winners in 2009 and 2010, Chelsea (aka the Blues) is owned by one of Russia's richest oligarchs, Roman Abramovich. In recent years the team has been forged into a formidable and ruthless footballing machine. ⊠ *Stamford Bridge, Fulham Rd.,*

Fulham ☎ *0871/984-1905* ⊕ *www. chelseafc.com* Ⓜ *Fulham Broadway.*

Tottenham Hotspur. Tottenham Hotspur (aka Spurs)—bitter North London rivals of Arsenal—has underperformed for decades but there are strong hints of a revival with a bevy of England national team regulars. ⊠ *White Hart La., 748 High Rd.* ☎ *0844/499-5000* ⊕ *www. tottenhamhotspur.com* Ⓜ *National Rail: White Hart Lane.*

West Ham. Known as "The Hammers," West Ham, despite the name, is the team of the East End. The Hammers have created a more consistent team, but one unlikely to claim many trophies. ⊠ *Boleyn Ground, Green St., Upton Park* ☎ *0871/222-2700* ⊕ *www.whufc. com* Ⓜ *Upton Park.*

TENNIS

Wimbledon Lawn Tennis Champi-onships. The Wimbledon Lawn Tennis Championships are famous for the green grass of Centre Court and an old-school insistence on players wearing white. Whether you can get Centre Court tickets is liter-ally down to the luck of the draw, because there's a ballot system (lottery) for advance purchase. For more information, see their website. You can also buy entry to roam matches on the outside courts, where even the top-seeded players compete early on. Five hundred show court tickets are also sold daily, but these usually go to those prepared to stand in line all night. ⊠ *The All England Lawn Tennis Club, Church Rd.* ☎ *020/8944-1066* ⊕ *www.wimbledon.com.*

Hulme, and Peter Jensen. The look is understated, slightly geeky, and totally contemporary. ⊠ *21 Kingly St., Soho* ☎ *020/7734–6846* ⊕ *www. other-shop.com* Ⓜ *Oxford Circus.*

Fodor's Choice **Paul Smith.** British classics with an irreverent twist define Paul Smith's
★ collections for women, men, and children. Beautifully tailored suits for men and women take hallmarks of traditional British style and turn them on their heads with humor and color, combining exceptional fabrics with flamboyant linings or unusual detailing. There are several branches throughout London, in Notting Hill, South Kensington, Chelsea, and Borough Market, plus a vintage furniture shop at 9 Albemarle Street in Mayfair and a shoes and accessories shop on Marylebone High Street. ⊠ *40–44 Floral St., Covent Garden* ☎ *020/7379–7133* ⊕ *www. paulsmith.co.uk* Ⓜ *Covent Garden.*

CLOTHING: WOMEN'S WEAR

Poste Mistress. The Office chain's more glamorous sibling, this boudoir-styled boutique features fashion-forward but wearable styles from some 40 brands including Stella McCartney, Acne, and Miu Miu. Casual alternatives such as Vivienne Westwood rubber booties and Converse sneakers are also available, and the prices are not eye-watering. There's a branch devoted to men's designer shoes at 10 South Moulton Street in Mayfair. ⊠ *61–63 Monmouth St., Covent Garden* ☎ *020/7379–4040* ⊕ *www.office.co.uk* Ⓜ *Covent Garden.*

Reiss. With an in-house design team whose experience includes stints at Gucci and Calvin Klein and customers like Beyoncé and the Duchess of Cambridge (formerly Kate Middleton), who wore a Reiss dress for her official engagement picture, this hot chain brings luxury standards of tailoring and details to mass-market women's and menswear. The sleek and contemporary style is not cheap, but does offer value for the price. There are branches in Knightsbridge, The City, Covent Garden, Chelsea, Hampstead, Notting Hill, Soho, and basically all over London. ⊠ *10 Barrett St., Fitzrovia* ☎ *020/7486–6557* ⊕ *www.reiss.com* Ⓜ *Oxford Street.*

Fodor's Choice **Topshop.** A hot spot for straight-from-the-runway affordable fashion,
★ Topshop is destination shopping for teenagers and fashion editors alike. Clothes and accessories are geared to the youthful end of the market, although women who are young at heart and girlish of figure can find plenty of wearable items here. However, you will need a high tolerance for loud music and busy dressing rooms. The store also features collections designed by a rotating roster of high-end designers as well as offering its own premium designer line called Topshop Unique. Topman brings the same fast-fashion approach to clothing for men. ■ **TIP→ If the crowds become too much at this location, head to one of the smaller Topshops in Kensington High Street, Knightsbridge, Victoria, Marble Arch, or Holborn.** ⊠ *36–38 Great Castle St., Fitzrovia* ☎ *0844/848–7487* ⊕ *www.topshop.com* Ⓜ *Oxford Circus.*

Fodor's Choice **United Nude.** Co-created by noted architect Rem D. Koolhaas (who also
★ designed this Covent Garden flagship store) and Galahad Clark (of the Clark's shoes dynasty), these distinctive, futuristic designs that use up-to-the-minute techniques such as carbon fiber heels and injection-molded

soles are flattering and surprisingly comfortable. There's another branch in Knightsbridge. ⊠ *13 Floral St., Covent Garden* ☎ *0207/240-7106* ⊕ *www.unitednude.com* Ⓜ *Covent Garden.*

DEPARTMENT STORES

FodorśChoice **Liberty.** The wonderful black-and-white mock-Tudor facade, created
★ from the timbers of two Royal Navy ships, reflects this store's origins in the late-19th-century's Arts and Crafts movement. Leading designers were recruited from this and the Aesthetic movement to create the classic art nouveau Liberty prints that are still a centerpiece of the brand, gracing everything from cushions and silk kimonos to embossed leather bags and photo albums. Inside, Liberty's is a labyrinth of nooks and crannies stuffed with thoughtfully chosen merchandise. ⊠ *Regent St., Soho* ☎ *020/7734–1234* ⊕ *www.liberty.co.uk* Ⓜ *Oxford Circus.*

TOYS

FAMILY **Benjamin Pollock's Toyshop.** This landmark shop still carries on the tra-
FodorśChoice dition of its eponymous founder, who sold miniature theater stages
★ made from richly detailed paper from the late-19th century until his death in 1937. Today the antique model theaters tend to be expensive, but there are plenty of magical reproductions for under £10. There's also an extensive selection of new but nostalgic puppets, marionettes, teddy bears, spinning tops, jack-in-the-boxes, and similar traditional children's toys from the days before batteries were required. ⊠ *44 Clare Market, The Piazza, Covent Garden* ☎ *020/7379–7866* ⊕ *www. pollocks-coventgarden.co.uk* Ⓜ *Covent Garden.*

FAMILY **Hamleys.** Besieged by pester power? Don't worry, help is at hand—this London institution has six floors of the latest dolls, soft toys, video games, and technological devices (plus such old-fashioned pleasures as train sets, drum kits, and magic tricks), with every must-have on the preteen shopping list. It's a madhouse at Christmastime, but Santa's grotto is one of the best in town. There's a smaller branch in St. Pancras International train station. ⊠ *188–196 Regent St., Soho* ☎ *0800/280–2444* ⊕ *www.hamleys.com* Ⓜ *Oxford Circus, Piccadilly Circus.*

BLOOMSBURY AND HOLBORN

ACCESSORIES

James Smith & Sons Ltd. This has to be the world's ultimate umbrella shop, and a must for anyone interested in real Victorian London. The family-owned shop has been in this location on a corner of New Oxford Street since 1857, and sells every kind of umbrella, cane, and walking stick imaginable. The interior is unchanged since the 19th century; you will feel as if you have stepped back in time. If the umbrellas are out of your price range, James Smith also sells smaller accessories and handmade wooden bowls. ⊠ *Hazelwood House, 53 New Oxford St., Bloomsbury* ☎ *020/7836–4731* ⊕ *www.james-smith.co.uk* ⊗ *Closed Sun.* Ⓜ *Tottenham Court Rd., Holborn.*

ANTIQUES

FodorśChoice **London Silver Vaults.** Housed in a basement vault, this extraordinary
★ space holds stalls from more than 30 silver dealers. Products range from the spectacularly over-the-top costing thousands to smaller

items—among them teaspoons, candlesticks, and Victorian cake forks—starting at £25. ■TIP→ Most of the silver merchants operate out of room-size, underground vaults that were originally rented out to London's upper crust to store their valuables. ⊠ *53–64 Chancery La., Holborn* ☎ *020/7242–3844* ⊕ *www.thesilvervaults.com* ⊘ *Closed Sat. after 1 and Sun.* Ⓜ *Chancery La.*

THE CITY

JEWELRY

Fodor'sChoice **Lesley Craze Gallery.** This serene gallery displays unique pieces by some
★ 100 innovative designers from around the world (with a strong British bias). A textiles room showcases colorful handmade scarves. Prices start at £45. ⊠ *33–35A Clerkenwell Green, Clerkenwell* ☎ *020/7608–0393* ⊕ *www.lesleycrazegallery.co.uk* ⊘ *Closed Sun.; open Mon. in Nov. and Dec. only* Ⓜ *Farringdon.*

THE EAST END

CLOTHING

Fodor'sChoice **Junky Styling.** This brand was launched by designers Annika Sanders and
★ Kerry Seager, who used to "deconstruct" old clothing when they wanted something unique to wear clubbing. They recycled traditional suits and shirts into wild outfits, and the business grew from there. ⊠ *21 Hackney Road, Shoreditch* ☎ *020/7247–1883* ⊕ *www.junkystyling.co.uk* Ⓜ *Old St. London Overground: Hoxton, Shoreditch High St.*

Fodor'sChoice **The Laden Showroom.** Sienna Miller and Victoria Beckham are among the
★ celebs who regularly check out emerging talent at this East End show-room for young designers. The store retails the work of more than 50 new designers, some selling one-off items—so the look you find is likely to be original. ⊠ *103 Brick La., Spitalfields* ☎ *020/7247–2431* ⊕ *www. laden.co.uk* Ⓜ *London Overground: Shoreditch High St.*

HATS

Fodor'sChoice **Bernstock Speirs.** Here since 1982, Paul Bernstock and Thelma Speirs
★ turn traditional hats on their head with street-smart trilbies and knitted hats that feature unusual colors and quirky details. ⊠ *234 Brick La., Spitalfields* ☎ *020/7739–7385* ⊕ *www.bernstockspiers.com* ⊘ *Closed Mon.* Ⓜ *London Overground: Shoreditch High Street.*

HOUSEHOLD

Fodor'sChoice **Labour & Wait.** Although such household items as colanders and clothes-
★ pins may not sound like ideal souvenirs, this shop may make you recon-sider. The owners are on a mission to revive functional, old-fashioned British goods, such as enamel kitchenware, "Brown Betty" glazed tea-pots, Guernsey sweaters, and vintage Welsh blankets. ⊠ *85 Redchurch St., Shoreditch* ☎ *020/7729–6253* ⊕ *www.labourandwait.co.uk* Ⓜ *London Overground: Shoreditch High St.*

MUSIC

Fodor'sChoice **Rough Trade East.** While many London record stores are struggling, this
★ veteran indie-music specialist seems to have gotten the formula right. The spacious surroundings are as much a hangout as a shop, complete

with a stage for live gigs, a café, and Internet access. There's another branch on Portobello Road in Notting Hill. ⊠ *Dray Walk, Old Truman Brewery, 91 Brick La., Spitalfields* ☎ *020/7392–7788* Ⓜ *Liverpool St. London Overground: Shoreditch High St.*

STREET MARKETS

Old Spitalfields Market. This fine example of a Victorian market hall (once the East End's wholesale fruit and vegetable market), now restored to its original splendor, is at the center of the area's gentrified revival. The original building is now largely occupied by shops with traders' stalls in the courtyard, and a modern shopping precinct under a Norman Foster–designed glass canopy adjoins the old building, home to a large number of independent traders' stalls. Thursday is particularly good for antiques. And, from Spanish tapas to Thai satays, the food outlets (mostly small, upscale chains but some independent stallholders as well) offer cuisines from around the world. ⊠ *16 Horner Sq., Brushfield St., Spitalfields* ☎ *020/7247–8556* ⊕ *www.spitalfields.co.uk* ⊗ *Stalls Tues.–Fri. 10–5, Sun. 9–5; restaurants weekdays 11–11, Sun. 9–11; retail shops daily 10–7* Ⓜ *Liverpool St. London Overground: Shoreditch High Street.*

THE SOUTH BANK

STREET MARKETS

Fodor's Choice ★ **Borough Market.** There's been a market in Borough since Roman times. This one, spread under the arches and railroad tracks leading to London Bridge Station, is the successor to a medieval market once held on London Bridge. Postmillennium, it has been transformed from a noisy collection of local produce stalls to a trendy foodie center that attracts some of London's best merchants of comestibles. Fresh coffees, gorgeous cheeses, olives, and baked goods complement the organically farmed meats, fresh fish, fruit, and veggies. Seven of the original Borough Market traders, including the celebrated Kappacasein Swiss raclette stand that serves heaping plates of melted Ogleshield cheese over new potatoes, baby pickles, and onion, have established a breakaway market on nearby Maltby Street, which operates on Saturday morning from 9 am. ⊠ *Southwark St., Borough* ☎ *020/7402–1002* ⊕ *www.boroughmarket.org.uk* ⊗ *Mon.–Wed. 10–3 (lunch stalls only), Thurs. 11–5, Fri. noon–6, Sat. 8–5* Ⓜ *London Bridge.*

KENSINGTON, KNIGHTSBRIDGE, AND MAYFAIR

ANTIQUES

Fodor's Choice ★ **Alfie's Antique Market.** This four-story, bohemian-chic labyrinth is London's largest indoor antiques market, housing dealers specializing in art, lighting, glassware, textiles, jewelry, furniture, and collectibles, with a particular strength in vintage clothing and 20th-century design. Come here to pick up Victorian and Edwardian clothes and textiles at Melinda Colthurst, 19th- and 20th-century furniture and decorative objects from Christopher, or a spectacular mid-20th-century Italian lighting fixture at Vincenzo Caffarrella. There's also a rooftop restaurant if you need a coffee break. In addition to the market, this end of Church Street is lined with excellent antiques shops. ⊠ *13–25 Church St., Marylebone* ☎ *020/7723–6066* ⊕ *www.alfiesantiques.com* ☉ *Closed Sun. and Mon.* Ⓜ *Marylebone.*

Fodor's Choice
★ **Rupert Cavendish.** This most elevated of Chelsea dealers had the Biedermeier market cornered so has now expanded to Empire and art deco antiques. The shop is a museum experience. ⊠ *610 King's Rd., Fulham* ☎ *020/7731–7041* ⊕ *www.rupertcavendish.co.uk* Ⓜ *Fulham Broadway.*

ACCESSORIES

Fodor's Choice
★ **Anya Hindmarch.** Exquisite leather bags and personalized, printed canvas totes are what made Hindmarch famous, along with her "I'm Not A Plastic Bag" eco-creation. Her designs are sold at Harrods, Liberty, and Harvey Nichols, but in her stores you can see her complete collection of bags and shoes, or order a bespoke piece such as the "Be A Bag," a tote bag imprinted with your chosen photo. There are also branches around the corner on Pont Street, in Mayfair, and in Notting Hill. ⊠ *157–158 Sloane St., Knightsbridge* ☎ *020/7730–0961* ⊕ *www.anyahindmarch. com* Ⓜ *Sloane Sq., Knightsbridge.*

Fodor's Choice
★ **Lulu Guinness.** Famous for her flamboyantly themed bags (think the satin "bucket" topped with roses and the elaborately beaded red snakeskin "lips" clutch), Guinness also showcases vintage-inspired luggage and beauty accessories in this frilly little shop, which is just as whimsical as her designs. There are other branches in Mayfair and the City. ⊠ *3 Ellis St., Belgravia* ☎ *020/7823–4828* ⊕ *www.luluguinness.com* ☉ *Closed Sun.* Ⓜ *Sloane Sq.*

Mulberry. Staying true to its roots in rural Somerset, this luxury goods company epitomizes *le style Anglais*, a sophisticated take on the earth tones and practicality of English country style. Best-known for highly desirable luxury handbags such as the Alexa and the Bayswater, the company also produces gorgeous leather accessories, from wallets to luggage, as well as shoes and clothing. ⊠ *50 New Bond St., Mayfair* ☎ *020/7491–3900* ⊕ *www.mulberry.com* Ⓜ *Bond St.*

Fodor's Choice
★ **Philip Treacy.** Magnificent hats by Treacy are annual showstoppers on Ladies Day at the Royal Ascot races and regularly grace the glossy magazines' society pages. In addition to the extravagant, haute couture hats handmade in the atelier, ready-to-wear hats and bags are also for sale. ⊠ *69 Elizabeth St., Belgravia* ☎ *020/7730–3992* ⊕ *www.philiptreacy. co.uk* ☉ *Closed Sun.* Ⓜ *Sloane Sq.*

Fodor's Choice
★ **Swaine Adeney Brigg.** Providing practical supplies for country pursuits since 1750, this store, now in new Mayfair premises, carries beautifully crafted umbrellas, walking sticks, and hip flasks, and ingenious combinations of same, such as the umbrella with a slim tipple-holding flask secreted inside the stem. The same level of quality and craftsmanship applies to leather goods, which include attaché cases and wallets. You'll find scarves, caps, and the Herbert Johnson "Poet Hat," the iconic headgear (stocked since 1890) worn by Harrison Ford in every Indiana Jones film. Satellite branches are in the Piccadilly Arcade and the City. ⊠ *41 S. Audley St., Mayfair* ☎ *020/7409–7277* ⊕ *www.swaineadeney. co.uk* ☉ *Closed Sun.* Ⓜ *Green Park.*

2

BOOKS AND STATIONERY

Smythson of Bond Street. Hands down, this is the most elegant stationer in Britain. No hostess of any standing would consider having a leather-bound guest book made by anyone else, and the shop's social stationery and distinctive diaries, with their pale blue pages, are thoroughly British. Smythson also produces a small range of leather handbags and purses. You'll find other branches in Chelsea, Notting Hill, and the City. ⌧ *40 New Bond St., Mayfair* ☎ *020/7629–8558* ⊕ *www.smythson.com* Ⓜ *Bond St., Oxford Circus.*

Waterstone's. At this mega-bookshop (Europe's largest) in an art deco former department store building near Piccadilly Circus, browse through your latest purchase or admire the view while sipping a glass of bubbly or getting a bite to eat at the sixth-floor Champagne and Seafood Bar, which is open until 9. Waterstone's is the country's leading book chain, and its flagship as comfortable and welcoming as a bookstore can be. Several smaller branches operate throughout the city. ⌧ *203–206 Piccadilly, Mayfair* ☎ *0843/290–8549* ⊕ *www.waterstones. com* Ⓜ *Piccadilly Circus.*

CERAMICS

Emma Bridgewater. Here's where you'll find fun and funky casual plates, mugs, jugs, and breakfast tableware embellished with polka dots, hens, hearts and flowers, amusing mottoes, and matter-of-fact labels (sugar or coffee). There's another branch in Fulham. ⌧ *81a Marylebone High St., Marylebone* ☎ *020/7486–6897* ⊕ *www.emmabridgewater.co.uk* Ⓜ *Regent's Park.*

CLOTHING

Fodor'sChoice ★ **Dover Street Market.** Visiting this six-floor emporium isn't just about buying; with its creative displays and eclectic, well-chosen mix of merchandise, it's as much art installation as store. The creation of Comme des Garçons' Rei Kawakubo, it showcases all of the label's collections for men and women alongside a changing roster of other designers, including Erdem, Alaia, and YSL—all of whom have their own customized mini-boutiques—plus avant-garde art books, vintage couture, and curiosities such as antique plaster anatomy models. With the merchandise and configuration changing every six months, you never know what you will find, which is half the fun. ■ TIP→ An outpost of the Rose Bakery on the top floor makes for a yummy break. ⌧ *17–18 Dover St., Mayfair* ☎ *020/7518–0680* ⊕ *www.doverstreetmarket.com* ☉ *Closed Sun.* Ⓜ *Green Park.*

Jack Wills. The British preppie's answer to Abercrombie & Fitch, Jack Wills specializes in heritage and country sports-inspired styles for men and women but gives them a youthful, sexy edge. Branches are in Notting Hill, Covent Garden, Islington, and Soho. ⌧ *72 Kings Rd., Chelsea* ☎ *020/7581–0347* ⊕ *www.jackwills.com* Ⓜ *Sloane Sq.*

CLOTHING: MENSWEAR

Fodor'sChoice ★ **Ozwald Boateng.** The dapper menswear by Ozwald Boateng (pronounced Bwa-teng) combines contemporary funky style with traditional Savile Row quality. His made-to-measure suits have been worn by trendsetters such as Jamie Foxx, Mick Jagger, and Laurence Fishburne, who appreciate the sharp cuts, luxurious fabrics, and occasionally vibrant colors (even the more conservative choices sport jacket linings in bright silk). ✉ *30 Savile Row, Mayfair* ☎ *020/7437–2030* ⊕ *www. ozwaldboateng.co.uk* ☉ *Closed Sun.* Ⓜ *Piccadilly Circus.*

CLOTHING: WOMEN'S WEAR

Fodor's Choice **Alexander McQueen.** Since McQueen's death in 2010, his right-hand
★ woman Sarah Burton has been at the helm, receiving raves for continuing his tradition of theatrical, darkly romantic, and beautifully cut clothes incorporating corsetry, lace, embroidery, and hourglass silhouettes, all of which were exemplified in Burton's celebrated wedding dress for Kate Middleton. Can't afford a gala gown? Go home with a skull-printed scarf. ✉ *4–5 Old Bond St., Mayfair* ☎ *020/7355–0088* ⊕ *www.alexandermcqueen.com* Ⓜ *Bond St.*

Fodor's Choice **Browns.** This shop—actually a collection of small shops—was a pio-
★ neer designer boutique in the 1970s and continues to talent-spot the newest and best around. You may find the windows showcasing the work of top graduates from this year's student shows or displaying well-established designers such as Marni, Chloé, Dries Van Noten, and Temperley. The men's store at No. 23 has a similar designer selection, while Browns Focus, across the street at Nos. 38–39, showcases youthful, hip designs and denim. A bargain outlet operates in Marylebone and there's a smaller boutique on Sloane Street. ✉ *24–27 South Molton St., Mayfair* ☎ *020/7514–0000* ⊕ *www.brownsfashion.com* ☉ *Closed Sun.* Ⓜ *Bond St.*

Fodor's Choice **Jigsaw.** Jigsaw specializes in clothes that are classic yet trendy, ladylike
★ without being dull. The style is epitomized by the former Kate Middleton, who was a buyer for the company before her marriage. The quality of fabrics and detailing belie the reasonable prices, and the cuts are kind to the womanly figure. Although there are numerous branches across London, no two stores are the same. The pre-teen set has its own line, Jigsaw Junior. ✉ *The Chapel, Duke of York Sq., King's Rd., Chelsea* ☎ *020/730–4404* ⊕ *www.jigsaw-online.com* Ⓜ *Sloane Sq.*

Rigby & Peller. Lovers of luxury lingerie shop here for brands like Prima Donna and Aubade, as well as R&P's own line. If the right fit eludes you and you fancy being fitted by the Queen's *corsetiére*, the made-to-measure service starts at around £300. Many of London's most affluent women shop here, not only because of the royal appointment but also because the quality is excellent and the service impeccably knowledgeable while being much friendlier than you might expect. There are also branches in Mayfair, Chelsea, and the City. ✉ *2 Hans Rd., Knightsbridge* ☎ *020/7225–4760* ⊕ *www.rigbyandpeller.com* Ⓜ *Knightsbridge.*

Fodor's Choice **Stella McCartney.** It's not easy to emerge from the shadow of a Beatle
★ father, but Stella McCartney has become a major force in fashion. Her signature jumpsuits and tuxedo pantsuits embody her design philosophy, combining minimalist tailoring with femininity and sophistication with ease of wear. ✉ *30 Bruton St., Mayfair* ☎ *020/7518–3100* ⊕ *www. stellamccartney.com.uk* Ⓜ *Bond St.*

Vivienne Westwood. From beginnings as the most shocking and outré designer around, Westwood has become a standard bearer for high-style British couture. The Chelsea boutique is where it all started: the lavish corseted ball gowns, the dandified nipped-waist jackets, and the tartan with a punk edge that formed the core of her signature look. Here you can still buy ready-to-wear, mainly the more casual Anglomania diffusion line and the exclusive Worlds End label based on the archives. The small Davies Street boutique sells only the more exclusive, expensive Gold Label and Couture collections (plus bridal), while the flagship Conduit Street store carries all of the above. ⊠ *44 Conduit St., Mayfair* ☎ *020/7439–1109* ⊕ *www.viviennewestwood. co.uk* ⊙ *Closed Sun.* Ⓜ *Oxford Circus* ⊠ *World's End Shop, 430 King's Rd., Chelsea* ☎ *020/7352–6551* ⊕ *www.worldsendshop.co.uk* ⊙ *Closed Sun.* Ⓜ *West Brompton.*

DEPARTMENT STORES

Harrods. With an encyclopedic assortment of luxury brands, this Knightsbridge institution has more than 300 departments and 20 restaurants spread over 1 million square feet on a 5-acre site. If you approach Harrods as a tourist attraction rather than as a fashion hunting ground, you won't be disappointed. Focus on the spectacular food halls, the huge ground-floor perfumery, the revamped toy and technology departments, the excellent Urban Retreat spa, and the Vegas-like Egyptian Room. ∎TIP➔ Be prepared to brave the crowds (avoid visiting on a Saturday if you can), and be prepared to pay if you want to use the bathroom on some floors. ⊠ *87–135 Brompton Rd., Knightsbridge* ☎ *020/7730–1234* ⊕ *www.harrods.com* Ⓜ *Knightsbridge.*

Harvey Nichols. While visiting tourists flock to Harrods, true London fashionistas shop at Harvey Nichols, aka "Harvey Nicks." The womenswear and accessories departments are outstanding, featuring of-the-moment designers like Roland Mouret, Peter Pilotto, and 3.1 Phillip Lim. The furniture and housewares are equally gorgeous (and pricey), though they become somewhat more affordable during the annual sales in January and July. The Fifth Floor restaurant is a place to see and be seen, but if you're just after a quick bite, the choices include a more informal café on the same floor and sushi-to-go from Yo! Sushi. ⊠ *109–125 Knightsbridge, Knightsbridge* ☎ *020/7235–5000* ⊕ *www. harveynichols.com* Ⓜ *Knightsbridge.*

Marks & Spencer. You'd be hard-pressed to find a Brit who doesn't have something in the closet from Marks & Spencer (or "M&S," as it's affectionately known). This major chain is known for its classic, dependable clothing for men, women, and children—affordable cashmere and lambswool sweaters are particularly good buys—and occasionally scores a fashion hit with its Per Una and Autograph lines. The food department at M&S is consistently superb, especially for frozen food, and a great place to pick up a sandwich or premade salad on the go (look for M&S Simply Food stores all over town). The flagship branch at Marble Arch and the Pantheon location at 173 Oxford Street have extensive fashion departments. ⊠ *458 Oxford St., Marylebone* ☎ *020/7935–7954* ⊕ *www.marksandspencer.com* Ⓜ *Marble Arch.*

Choices, choices: there are plenty of prints—and much else—at the Portobello Road Market.

Fodor'sChoice ★ **Selfridges.** This giant, bustling store (the second-largest in the U.K. after Harrods) gives Harvey Nichols a run for its money as London's most fashionable department store. Packed to the rafters with clothes ranging from mid-price lines to the latest catwalk names, the store continues to break ground with its innovative retail schemes, especially the high-fashion Superbrands section, the ground-floor Wonder Room showcasing extravagant jewelry and luxury gifts, and the Concept Store, which features a rotating series of themed displays. ■ **TIP➜ Take a break with a glass of wine from the Wonder Bar, or pick up some rare tea in the Food Hall as a gift.** ✉ *400 Oxford St., Marylebone* ☎ *0800/123–400* ⊕ *www.selfridges.com* Ⓜ *Bond St.*

HOUSEHOLD

Fodor'sChoice ★ **The Conran Shop.** This is the brainchild of Sir Terence Conran, who has been informing British taste since he opened Habitat in the 1960s. Although he is no longer associated with Habitat, his eponymous stores are still bastions of similarly clean, unfussy modernist design. Both the flagship store and the branch on Marylebone High Street are bursting with great gift ideas. ✉ *Michelin House, 81 Fulham Rd., South Kensington* ☎ *020/7589–7401* ⊕ *www.conranshop.co.uk* Ⓜ *South Kensington.*

Fodor'sChoice ★ **Mint.** Owner Lina Kanafani has scoured the globe to curate an eclectic mix of conceptual statement furniture, art, ceramics, and home accessories. Mint also showcases works by up-and-coming designers and sells limited edition and one-off pieces. If you don't want to ship a couch home, consider a miniature flower vase or a handmade ceramic pitcher. ✉ *2 North Terr., South Kensington* ☎ *020/7225–2228* ⊕ *www.mintshop.co.uk* Ⓜ *South Kensington.*

JEWELRY

Asprey. Created by architect Norman Foster and interior designer David Mlinaric, this "global flagship" store displays exquisite jewelry—as well as silver and leather goods, watches, china, and crystal—in a discreet, very British setting that oozes quality, expensive good taste, and hushed comfort And, for the really well-heeled, there's a custom-made jewelry service available as well. ⊠ *167 New Bond St., Mayfair* ☎ *020/7493– 6767* ⊕ *www.asprey.com* Ⓜ *Green Park.*

Fodor's Choice **Butler & Wilson.** Long before anybody ever heard the word "bling,"
★ this shop was marketing the look—in diamanté, colored rhinestones, and crystal—to movie stars and secretaries alike. There's also another shop at 20 South Molton Street. ⊠ *189 Fulham Rd., South Kensington* ☎ *020/7352–3045* ⊕ *www.butlerandwilson.co.uk* Ⓜ *South Kensington.*

Fodor's Choice **Kabiri.** A dazzling array of exciting contemporary jewelry by emerg-
★ ing and established designers from around the world is packed into this small shop. There is something to suit most budgets and tastes, from flamboyant statement pieces to subtle, delicate adornment. Look out for British talent Johanne Mills, among many others. There's another branch in Chelsea. ⊠ *37 Marylebone High St., Marylebone* ☎ *020/7317–2150* ⊕ *www.kabiri.co.uk* Ⓜ *Baker St.*

SHOES

Fodor's Choice **Rupert Sanderson.** Designed in London and made in Italy, Sanderson's
★ elegant shoes have been a huge hit in fashion circles. Ladylike styles, bright colors, smart details, and a penchant for peep toes are signature elements. Prices reflect the impeccable craftsmanship. There's now a tiny outpost next to Harrods at 2A Hans Road. ⊠ *19 Bruton Pl., Mayfair* ☎ *0207/491–2260* ⊕ *www.rupertsanderson.com* ☽ *Closed Sun.* Ⓜ *Bond St., Green Park.*

NOTTING HILL

BOOKS

Books for Cooks. It may seem odd to describe a bookshop as delicious-smelling, but the aromas wafting out of Books for Cooks' test kitchen will whet your appetite even before you've opened one of the 8,000 cookbooks. Just about every world cuisine is represented along with a complete lineup of books by celebrity chefs. A tiny café at the back offers lunch dishes drawn from recipes on the shelves, as well as desserts and coffee. Menus change daily. ■ TIP➔ Before you come to London, visit the shop's website to sign up for a cooking class. ⊠ *4 Blenheim Crescent, Notting Hill* ☎ *020/7221–1992* ⊕ *www.booksforcooks.com* ☽ *Closed Sun. and Mon.* Ⓜ *Notting Hill Gate, Ladbroke Grove.*

CLOTHING

Aimé. French-Cambodian sisters Val and Vanda Heng-Vong launched this shop to showcase the best of French clothing and designer housewares. Expect to find fashion by Isabel Marant, Forte Forte, and A.P.C. You can also pick up A.P.C. candles, Rice housewares, and a well-edited collection of ceramics. Just next door, Petit Aimé sells children's clothing. ⊠ *32 Ledbury Rd., Notting Hill* ☎ *020/7221–7070* ⊕ *www. aimelondon.com* Ⓜ *Notting Hill Gate.*

MUSIC

Music & Video Exchange. This store is a music collector's treasure trove, with a constantly changing stock refreshed by customers selling and exchanging as well as buying. The main store focuses on rock, pop, soul, and dance, both mainstream and obscure, in a variety of formats ranging from vinyl to CD, cassette, and even mini-disk. Don't miss the discounts in the basement and the rarities upstairs. Classical music is at No. 40, and there are branches in Soho and Greenwich. ⊠ *38 Notting Hill Gate, Notting Hill* ☏ *020/7243–8574* ⊕ *www.mgeshops.com* Ⓜ *Notting Hill Gate.*

STREET MARKETS

Portobello Market. London's most famous market still wins the prize (according to some) for the all-round best, stretching almost two miles from fashionable Notting Hill to the lively cultural melting pot of North Kensington, changing character as it goes. The southern end, starting at Chepstow Villas, is lined with shops, stalls, and arcades selling antiques, silver, and bric-a-brac on Saturday; the middle, above Westbourne Grove, is devoted on weekdays to fruit and veg, interspersed with excellent hot food stalls. On Friday and Saturday, the area between Talbot Road and the elevated highway (called the Westway) becomes more of a flea market specializing in household and mass-produced goods sold at a discount. North of the Westway are more stalls selling even cheaper household goods. Some say Portobello Road has become a tourist trap, but if you acknowledge that it's a circus and get into the spirit, it's a lot of fun. Saturday is when the market is in full swing. Serious shoppers avoid the crowds and go on Friday morning. ■TIP→ Bring cash (some vendors don't take credit cards) but keep an eye on it. ⊠ *Portobello Rd., Notting Hill* ⊕ *www.portobellomarket.org* ⊘ *Mon.–Wed., Fri.–Sat. 8–6:30, Thurs. 8–1 pm* Ⓜ *Notting Hill Gate.*

THE SOUTHEAST

WELCOME TO THE SOUTHEAST

TOP REASONS TO GO

★ **Amazing gardens:** Gardens of all kinds are an English specialty, and at Sissinghurst, as well as in the gardens of Hever Castle and Chartwell, you can easily spend an entire afternoon wandering through acres of floral exotica.

★ **Bodiam, Dover, Hever, and Herstmonceux castles:** Take your pick: the most evocative castles in a region filled with them dazzle you with their fortitude and fascinate you with their histories.

★ **Brighton:** With its nightclubs, sunbathing scene, and funky atmosphere, this is the quintessential modern English seaside city.

★ **Canterbury Cathedral:** This massive building, a textbook case of medieval architecture, inspires awe with its soaring towers and flagstone corridors.

★ **Treasure houses:** Here is one of England's richest concentrations of historic homes: among the superlatives are Petworth House, sprawling Knole, Ightham Mote, and Chartwell.

1 **Canterbury, Dover, and Environs.** Dover's distinctive chalk-white cliffs plunging hundreds of feet into the sea are just a part of this region's dramatic coastal scenery. Don't miss Canterbury's medieval town center, dominated by its massive cathedral.

2 **Rye, Lewes, and Environs.** Medieval villages dot the hills along this stretch of Sussex coastline. The centerpiece is Rye, a pretty hill town of cobbled streets lined with timbered homes. Lewes, with its crumbling castle, is another gem.

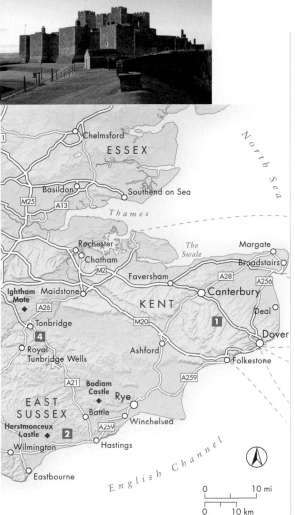

GETTING ORIENTED

3

For sightseeing purposes, the Southeast can be divided into four sections. The eastern part of the region takes in the cathedral town of Canterbury, as well as the port city of Dover. The next section stretches along the southern coast from the medieval hill town of Rye to picturesque Lewes. A third area reaches from the coastal city of Brighton west to Chichester. The fourth section takes in the spa town of Royal Tunbridge Wells and western Kent, where stately homes and castles dot the farmland. Larger towns in the area can be easily reached by train or bus from London for a day trip. To visit most castles, grand country homes, or quiet villages, though, you need to rent a car or join a tour.

3 Brighton and the Sussex Coast. Funky, lively Brighton perfectly melds Victorian architecture with a modern vibe that includes the best shopping and dining on the coast. Outside town are a Roman villa and beautiful old homes such as Petworth House.

4 Tunbridge Wells and Environs. From Anne Boleyn's regal childhood abode at Hever Castle to the medieval manor at Ightham Mote, this area is rich with grand houses. Spend a couple of days exploring them; Tunbridge Wells is a comfortable base.

Updated by
Jack Jewers

Kent and Sussex are part of the breadbasket of England, where bucolic farmland stretches as far as the eye can see. Once a favorite destination of English nobility, this region is rich with history, visible in the great castles and stately homes that dot the countryside. Its cities are similarly historic, especially ancient Canterbury, with its spectacular cathedral and medieval streets. Along the coast, funky seaside towns have a more relaxed attitude, especially artsy Brighton, where artists and musicians use the sea as inspiration for their work.

Although it's close to London (Kent reaches all the way to London's suburbs) and is one of the most densely populated areas of Britain, the Southeast feels far away from the big city. In Kent, acres of orchards burst into a mass of pink-and-white blossoms in spring, while Dover's white cliffs and brooding castle have become symbols of Britain. Historic mansions, such as Petworth House and Knole, are major draws for travelers, and lush gardens such as Vita Sackville-West's Sissinghurst attract thousands to their vivid floral displays.

Because the English Channel is at its narrowest here, a great deal of British history has been forged in the Southeast. The Romans landed in this area and stayed to rule Britain for four centuries. So did the Saxons—*Sussex* means "the land of the South Saxons." The biggest invasion of them all took place here when William ("the Conqueror") of Normandy defeated the Saxons at a battle near Hastings in 1066, changing the island forever.

SOUTHEAST PLANNER

WHEN TO GO

It's best to visit in spring, summer, or early fall. Many privately owned castles and mansions are open only between April and September or October. Failing that, the parks surrounding the stately houses are often open all year. If crowds tend to spoil your fun, avoid August, Sunday, and national holidays, particularly in Canterbury and the seaside towns.

3

PLANNING YOUR TIME

With the exception of Brighton, you can easily see the highlights of each of the towns in less than a day. Brighton has more to offer, and you should allot at least two days to take it all in. Consider basing yourself in one town while exploring a region. For example, you could stay in Brighton and take in Lewes on a day trip. Base yourself in Rye for a couple of days while exploring Battle, Hastings, and Herstmonceux Castle. Tunbridge Wells is a great place to overnight if you plan on exploring the many stately homes and castles nearby.

GETTING HERE AND AROUND

AIR TRAVEL

Heathrow is convenient for London, but Gatwick Airport is a more convenient gateway for Kent. The rail station inside Gatwick has trains to Brighton and other major towns.

BUS TRAVEL

National Express buses serve the region from London's Victoria Coach Station. Trips to Brighton and Canterbury take two hours; to Chichester, three hours. Megabus runs buses at budget prices from Victoria Coach Station to many of the same destinations as National Express and can be cheaper, although luggage limits are strict.

Bus service between towns can be useful but is often intermittent. Out in the country, don't expect buses more often than once every half hour or hour. Sometimes trains are a better option; sometimes they're much worse. Traveline is the best central place to call for bus information, and local tourist information centers can be a big help.

Contacts Megabus ☎ 0900/160–0900 ⊕ uk.megabus.com. **National Express** ☎ 0871/781–8178 ⊕ www.nationalexpress.com. **Traveline** ☎ 0871/200–2233 ⊕ traveline.info.

CAR TRAVEL

Traveling by car is the best way to get to the stately homes and castles in the region. Having a car in Canterbury or Brighton, however, is a nuisance; you'll need to park and walk. Major routes radiating outward from London to the Southeast are, from west to east, M23/A23 to Brighton (52 miles); A21, passing by Royal Tunbridge Wells to Hastings (65 miles); A20/M20 to Folkestone (58 miles); and A2/M2 via Canterbury (56 miles) to Dover (71 miles).

TRAIN TRAVEL

Trains are the fastest and most efficient way to travel to major cities in the region, but they don't stop in many small towns. From London, Southeastern trains serve Sussex and Kent from Victoria and Charing Cross stations. Getting to Brighton takes about 1 hour, to Canterbury about 1½ hours, and to Dover between 1½ and 2 hours. A Network Railcard costing £28, valid throughout the southern and southeastern regions for a year, entitles you and three companions to one-third off many off-peak fares.

Contacts National Rail Enquiries ☎ 0845/748–4950 ⊕ www.nationalrail.co.uk.

RESTAURANTS

If you're in a seaside town, look for that great British staple, fish-and-chips. Perhaps "look" isn't the word—just follow your nose. On the coast, seafood, much of it locally caught, is a specialty. Try local smoked fish (haddock and mackerel) or the succulent local oysters. Inland, sample fresh local lamb and beef. In cities such as Brighton and Tunbridge Wells there are numerous restaurants and cafés, but out in the countryside the best options are often pubs.

HOTELS

All along the coast, resort towns stretch along beaches, their hotels standing cheek by jowl. Of the smaller hotels and guesthouses not all remain open year-round; many do business only from mid-April to September or October. Some hotels have all-inclusive rates for a week's stay. Prices rise in July and August, when the seaside resorts can get solidly booked, especially Brighton. (On the other hand, hotels may drop rates by up to 40% off season.) Places in Brighton may not take a booking for a single night in summer or on weekends. *Hotel reviews have been shortened. For full information, visit Fodors.com.*

WHAT IT COSTS IN POUNDS			
	$	$$	$$$	$$$$
Restaurants	Under £15	£15–£19	£20–£25	over £25
Hotels	Under £100	£100–£160	£161–£220	over £220

Restaurant prices are the average cost of a main cost at dinner or, if dinner isn't served, at lunch. Hotel prices are the lowest cost of a standard double room in high season, including 20% V.A.T.

VISITOR INFORMATION

Tourist boards in the main towns can help with information, and many will also book local accommodations.

Contacts Southeast England Tourist Board
⊕ www.visitsoutheastengland.com.

CANTERBURY, DOVER, AND ENVIRONS

The cathedral city of Canterbury is an ancient place that has attracted travelers since the 12th century. Its magnificent cathedral, the Mother Church of England, remains a powerful draw. Even in prehistoric times, this part of England was relatively well settled. Saxon settlers, Norman conquerors, and the folk who lived here in late-medieval times all left their mark. From Canterbury there's rewarding wandering to be done in the gentle Kentish countryside between the city and the busy port of Dover. Here the landscape ravishes the eye in spring with apple blossoms, and in autumn with lush fields ready for harvest. It's a county of orchards, market gardens, and round oast houses with their tilted, pointed roofs. They were once used for drying hops, but now many are expensive homes.

CANTERBURY

56 miles southeast of London.

Just mention Canterbury, and most people are taken back to memories of high-school English classes and Geoffrey Chaucer's *Canterbury Tales,* about medieval pilgrims making their way to Canterbury Cathedral. Judging from the tales, however, in those days Canterbury was as much a party town as it was a spiritual center.

The city has been the seat of the Primate of All England, the archbishop of Canterbury, since Pope Gregory the Great dispatched St. Augustine to convert the pagan hordes of Britain in 597. The height of Canterbury's popularity came in the 12th century, when thousands of pilgrims flocked here to see the shrine of the murdered archbishop St. Thomas à Becket. This southeastern town became one of the most visited in England, if not Europe. Buildings that served as pilgrims' inns (and that survived World War II bombing of the city) still dominate the streets of Canterbury's center, though it's tourists who flock to this city of about 40,000 people today.

Prices at city museums are higher than average, so if you plan to see more than one, ask at the tourist office if a combination ticket might be cheaper.

GETTING HERE AND AROUND

The fastest way to reach Canterbury from London is by train. Southeastern trains to Canterbury run every half hour in peak times from London's Charing Cross Station. The journey takes around 1½ hours. Canterbury has two centrally located train stations, Canterbury East Station (a five-minute walk from the cathedral square) and Canterbury West Station (a 10-minute walk from the cathedral).

National Express and Megabus buses bound for Canterbury depart several times a day from London's Victoria Coach Station. Trips to Canterbury take around two hours, and drop passengers near the train stations. If you're driving, take the A2/M2 to Canterbury from London (56 miles). Park in one of the signposted parking lots at the edge of the town center.

Canterbury has a small, walkable town center. Although the town has good local bus service, you're unlikely to need it. Most major tourist sites are on one street that changes name three times—beginning as St. George's Street and then becoming High Street and St. Peter's Street. Canterbury Guild of Guides provides walking tours with expert guides. Tours (£6.50) are at 11 am daily, with an additional tour at 2 pm from April to October. VisitBritain offers an MP3 tour of Canterbury ($8.50) that you can download from its website.

TIMING

The town tends to get crowded around religious holidays—particularly Easter weekend—and on other national holiday weekends. If you'd rather avoid the tour buses, try visiting midweek.

ESSENTIALS

Visitor and Tour Information Canterbury Guild of Guides ⊠ *Arnett House, Hawks La.* ☎ *01227/459779* ⊕ *www.canterburyguidedtours.com.* **Canterbury Visitor Centre** ⊠ *18 High St.* ☎ *01227/378100* ⊕ *www.canterbury.co.uk.* **VisitBritain** ⊕ *www.visitbritain.com.*

EXPLORING
TOP ATTRACTIONS

Fodor's Choice
★

Canterbury Cathedral. The focal point of the city was the first of England's great Norman cathedrals. Nucleus of worldwide Anglicanism, the Cathedral Church of Christ Canterbury (its formal name) is a living textbook of medieval architecture. The building was begun in 1070, demolished, begun anew in 1096, and then systematically expanded over the next three centuries. When the original choir section burned to the ground in 1174, another replaced it, designed in the new Gothic style, with tall, pointed arches. The cathedral is popular, so arrive early or late in the day to avoid the crowds.

The cathedral was only a century old and still relatively small when Thomas Becket, the archbishop of Canterbury, was murdered here in 1170. Becket, as head of the church, had been engaged in a political struggle with his old friend Henry II. Four knights supposedly overheard Henry scream, "Will no one rid me of this troublesome priest?" But there is no evidence that those were his actual words. The only contemporary record has him saying, "What miserable drones and traitors have I nourished and brought up in my household, who let their lord be treated with such shameful contempt by a low-born cleric?"

Thinking they were carrying out the king's wishes, the knights went immediately to Canterbury and hacked Becket to pieces in one of the side chapels. Henry, racked with guilt, went into deep mourning. Becket was canonized and Canterbury's position as the center of English Christianity was assured.

For almost 400 years Becket's tomb was one of the most extravagant shrines in Christendom, until it was destroyed by Henry VIII's troops during the Reformation. In **Trinity Chapel,** which held the shrine, you can still see a series of 13th-century stained-glass windows illustrating Becket's miracles. (The actual site of Becket's murder is down a flight of steps just to the left of the nave.) Nearby is the tomb of Edward,

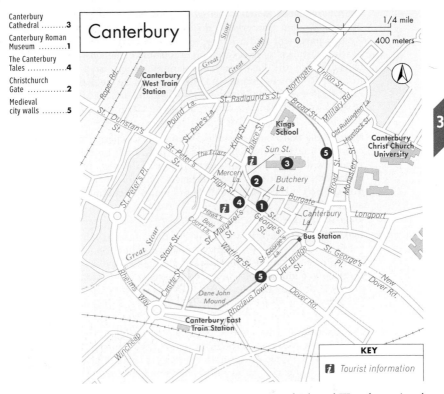

3

the Black Prince (1330–76), warrior son of Edward III and a national hero. In the corner of Trinity Chapel, a second flight of steps leads down to the enormous Norman **undercroft,** or vaulted cellar, built in the early 12th century. A row of squat pillars engraved with dancing beasts (mythical and otherwise) supports the roof.

To the north of the Cathedral are the **cloisters** and a small compound of monastic buildings. The 12th-century octagonal water tower is still part of the cathedral's water supply. The Norman staircase in the northwest corner of the Green Court dates from 1167 and is a unique example of the architecture of the times. ⊠ *Cathedral Precincts* ☎ *01227/762862* ⊕ *www.canterbury-cathedral.org* ⊠ *£9.50, free for services and ½ hr before closing; £5 tour; £3.50 for audio guide* ☉ *Cathedral: Mon.–Sat. 9–5:30 (9–5, Oct.–Easter), Sun. 12:30–2:30. Last entry ½ hr before closing. Restricted access during services. Tours: Apr.–Oct., weekdays 10:30, noon, and 2, Sat. 10:30, noon, and 1; Nov.–Mar., weekdays 10:30 (not Jan.), noon, and 2, Sat. 10:30, noon, and 1.*

QUICK BITES

The Custard Tart. A short walk from the cathedral, the Custard Tart serves freshly made sandwiches, pies, tarts, and cakes, along with steaming cups of tea and coffee. You can take your selection upstairs to the seating area. Arrive early, as it's not open for dinner. ⊠ *35A St. Margaret's St.* ☎ *01227/785178.*

Canterbury Roman Museum. Below ground, at the level of the remnants of Roman Canterbury, this museum features colorful mosaic Roman pavement and a hypocaust—the Roman version of central heating. Displays of excavated objects (some of which you can hold in the **Touch the Past** area) and computer-generated reconstructions of Roman buildings and the marketplace help re-create the past. ■ **TIP→ Up to four kids get in free with an adult.** ✉ *Butchery La.* ☎ *01227/785575* 🌐 *www.canterbury.co.uk* 🎟 *£6* 🕑 *Daily 10–5; last admission 4:15. Closed last wk in Dec.*

Medieval city walls. For an essential Canterbury experience, follow the circuit of the 13th- and 14th-century walls, built on the line of the Roman walls. Roughly half survive; those to the east are intact, towering some 20 feet high and offering a sweeping view of the town. You can access these from a number of places, including Castle Street and Broad Street.

WORTH NOTING

FAMILY **The Canterbury Tales.** Take an audiovisual tour of the sights, sounds (and smells) of 14th-century England at this cheesy but popular attraction. You'll "meet" Chaucer's pilgrims and view tableaus illustrating five of his tales. In summer, costumed actors perform scenes from the town's history. ✉ *St. Margaret's St.* ☎ *01227/479227* 🌐 *canterburytales.org.uk* 🎟 *£8.50* 🕑 *Nov.–Feb., daily 10–4:30; Mar.–June, Sept., and Oct., daily 10–5; July and Aug., daily 9:30–5.*

Christchurch Gate. This immense gate, built in 1517, leads into the cathedral close. As you pass through, look up at the sculpted heads of two young figures: Prince Arthur, elder brother of Henry VIII, and the young Catherine of Aragon, to whom Arthur was betrothed. After Arthur's death, Catherine married Henry. Her failure to produce a male heir after 25 years of marriage led to Henry's decision to divorce her, creating an irrevocable breach with the Roman Catholic Church and altering the course of English history.

WHERE TO EAT

$ BRITISH 🍴 **City Fish Bar.** Long lines and lots of satisfied finger-licking attest to the deserved popularity of this excellent fish-and-chip shop in the center of town. Everything is freshly fried, the batter crisp, and the fish tasty; the fried mushrooms are also surprisingly good. There's no seating, so your fish is wrapped up in paper and you eat it where you want, perhaps in the park. This place closes at 7. [$] *Average main: £7* ✉ *30 St. Margaret's St.* ☎ *01227/760873* 💳 *No credit cards.*

$$ BRITISH 🍴 **The Goods Shed.** Next to Canterbury West Station, this vaulted wooden space with stone-and-brick walls was a storage shed in Victorian times. Now it's a farmers' market with a restaurant that has wooden tables and huge arched windows overlooking the market and a butchers' stall. It's well known for offering fresh Kentish food—think locally caught fish and smoked meats, local cider, and freshly baked bread. Whatever is freshest that day appears on the menu, whether it's John Dory with garlic, or steak with blue cheese butter. [$] *Average main: £15* ✉ *Station Rd. W.* ☎ *01227/459153* 🌐 *thegoodsshed.co.uk* 🕑 *Closed Mon. No dinner Sun.*

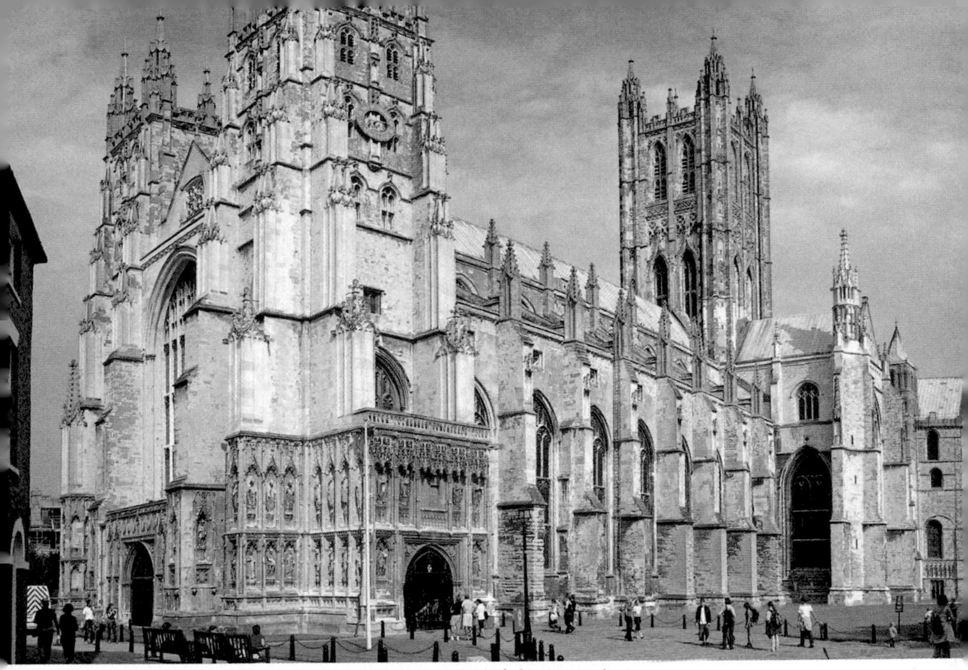

Impressive both inside and out, ancient Canterbury Cathedral dominates the town.

$$$ MODERN FRENCH Fodor's Choice ★ 🍴 **Michael Caines at ABode.** Canterbury's most sought-after tables are at Michael Caines (not the actor, the eminent British chef with a similar name). Occupying a light-filled corner of the trendy ABode Canterbury, with its pine tables, white walls, and sophisticated country style, this place is hugely popular with local foodies. The modern French cuisine is excellent; dishes change weekly but could include slow poached then roasted pheasant with pumpkin and cumin purée, or monkfish and braised oxtail with porcini mushroom fricassée. Leave room for a dessert of pistachio soufflé, or perhaps chestnut mousse with chocolate crémeux, meringue, and chestnut ice cream. The seven-course tasting menu (£72, or £110 with matching wine) is great for special occasions. **TIP→ True aficionados will want to reserve the chef's table in the kitchen to watch the staff in action.** [$] *Average main: £24* ✉ *ABode Canterbury, 30–33 High St.* ☎ *01227/766266* 🌐 *www.michaelcaines.com* ✍ *Reservations essential.*

$ BRITISH 🍴 **Old Buttermarket.** A colorful, friendly old pub near the cathedral, the Buttermarket is a great place to grab a hearty lunch and sample some traditional English fare with a modern inflection. You can indulge in a fresh English ale from the changing selection while sampling a beef rib puff pastry pie with creamy mashed potato, or perhaps a wild boar and chorizo burger if you're feeling more adventurous. There's been a pub on this site for more than 500 years, so although the current building is a few hundred years younger than that, it's carrying on a fine tradition. [$] *Average main: £11* ✉ *39 Burgate* ☎ *01227/462170* 🌐 *www.nicholsonspubs.co.uk.*

WHERE TO STAY

$$ HOTEL **ABode Canterbury.** This glossy boutique hotel inside the old city walls offers an up-to-date style in traditional Canterbury. **Pros:** central location; luxurious handmade beds; great restaurants and bars. **Cons:** one of the priciest hotels in town; bar gets quite crowded; breakfast is extra. [$] *Rooms from: £135* ✉ *30–33 High St.* ☎ *01227/766266* 🌐 *www.abodehotels.co.uk* 🛏 *73 rooms* 🍴 *No meals.*

$$ HOTEL **Canterbury Cathedral Lodge.** Small and modern, this hotel tucked away within the grounds of the cathedral has quiet, soothingly decorated rooms with creamy white walls and exposed oak trim. **Pros:** outstanding location; incredible views; free access to the cathedral. **Cons:** no restaurant; few services. [$] *Rooms from: £120* ✉ *The Precincts* ☎ *01227/865350* 🌐 *www.canterburycathedrallodge.org* 🛏 *35 rooms* 🍴 *Breakfast.*

$$ HOTEL **Ebury Hotel.** Family-run, this hotel earns rave reviews for its laid-back attitude and comfortable accommodations inside two big Victorian buildings. **Pros:** cozy lounge; comfortable rooms; free Wi-Fi. **Cons:** a bit of a walk to the town center; no elevator. [$] *Rooms from: £140* ✉ *65–67 New Dover Rd.* ☎ *01227/768433* 🌐 *www.ebury-hotel.co.uk* 🛏 *15 rooms* 🍴 *Breakfast.*

$ B&B/INN **The White House.** Reputed to have been the place in which Queen Victoria's head coachman came to live upon retirement, this handsome Regency building sits on a quiet road off St. Peter's Street. **Pros:** historic house; spacious rooms; family-friendly atmosphere. **Cons:** a bit outside the center; no restaurant; no elevator. [$] *Rooms from: £90* ✉ *6 St. Peter's La.* ☎ *01227/761836* 🌐 *www.whitehousecanterbury.co.uk* 🛏 *7 rooms* 💳 *No credit cards* 🍴 *Breakfast.*

NIGHTLIFE AND THE ARTS

NIGHTLIFE

Canterbury is home to a popular university, and the town's many pubs and bars are busy, often crowded with college-age folks.

Parrot. Built in 1370, the Parrot is an atmospheric old pub known for its real ale. They also offer good food; Sunday lunch here is popular. ✉ *3–9 Church La.* ☎ *01227/762355* 🌐 *www.theparrotcanterbury.com.*

Thomas Becket. A traditional English pub, Thomas Becket has a fire crackling in winter, copper pots hanging from the ceiling, and a friendly crowd. They also serve decent pub grub. ✉ *21 Best La.* ☎ *01227/464384.*

THE ARTS

Canterbury Festival. The two-week-long Canterbury Festival fills the town with music, dance, theater, and other colorful events every October. ☎ *01227/787787* 🌐 *www.canterburyfestival.co.uk.*

Gulbenkian Theatre. Outside the town center, the Gulbenkian Theatre mounts all kinds of plays, particularly experimental works, and is a venue for dance performances, concerts, comedy shows, and films. ✉ *University of Kent, Giles La.* ☎ *01227/769075* 🌐 *www.kent.ac.uk/gulbenkian.*

SHOPPING

Canterbury's medieval streets are lined with shops, perfect for an afternoon of rummaging. The best are in the district just around the cathedral. The King's Mile, which stretches past the cathedral and down Palace Street and Northgate, is a good place to start.

925. This shop has a great selection of handmade silver jewelry. ✉ *57 Palace St.* ☎ *01227/785699* ⊕ *www.925-silver.co.uk.*

Burgate Antiques. This rambling shop is full of fine British and French antiques, mostly Georgian and Victorian, with both high-end and less expensive selections. It's a great place to nose around on a rainy day. ✉ *23a Palace St.* ☎ *01227/456500.*

OAST HOUSES

Take a drive through the Kent and Sussex countryside and you'll soon notice a distinctive feature of the landscape: oast houses, tall brick buildings with conical roofs, looking somewhat like witch's hats with a weathervane on top. These were built for drying hops, with a kiln at ground level heating the floors above. Dating as far back as the mid-18th century, most have now been converted into private houses.

3

BROADSTAIRS

17 miles east of Canterbury.

Like other Victorian seaside towns such as Margate and Ramsgate, Broadstairs was once the playground of vacationing Londoners, and grand 19th-century houses line the waterfront. In the off-season Broadstairs is peaceful, but day-trippers pack the town in July and August.

Park your car in one of the town lots and strike out for the crescent beach or wander down the residential Victorian streets. Make your way down to the amusement pier and try your hand in one of the game arcades. You can grab fish-and-chips to go and dine on the beach.

Charles Dickens spent many summers in Broadstairs between 1837 and 1851 and wrote glowingly of its bracing freshness.

GETTING HERE AND AROUND

By car, Broadstairs is about a two-hour drive (78 miles) from London, off A256 on the southeast tip of England. Trains run from London's St. Pancras and Victoria stations to Broadstairs once or twice an hour; it's a two-hour trip and sometimes involves a change in Rochester. Broadstairs Station is off the Broadway in the town center. National Express buses travel to Broadstairs from London several times a day; the journey takes about three hours.

EXPLORING

Dickens House Museum. This house was originally the home of Mary Pearson Strong, on whom Dickens based the character of Betsey Trotwood, David Copperfield's aunt. Dickens lived here from 1837 to 1839 while writing *The Pickwick Papers* and *Oliver Twist.* Some rooms have been decorated to look as they would have in Dickens' day, and there's a reconstruction of Miss Trotwood's room as described by Dickens. The house is in Broadstairs, 18 miles northeast of Canterbury. ☒ *2 Victoria Parade* ☎ *01843/861232* ⊕ *www.dickensfellowship.org* ▨ *£3.50* ⊙ *Apr. and May, daily 2–5; June–Oct., daily 10–5.*

NIGHTLIFE AND THE ARTS

Dickens Festival. For a week every June, Broadstairs is taken over by a sea of people in Victorian costumes, as the town hosts its annual Dickens Festival—a tradition going back to 1937. The fun includes readings, a Dickensian cricket match, a Victorian bathing party, and vaudeville acts. ☎ *01843/861827* ⊕ *www.broadstairsdickensfestival.co.uk.*

DOVER

21 miles south of Broadstairs, 78 miles east of London.

The busy passenger port of Dover has for centuries been Britain's gateway to Europe and is known for its famous white cliffs. You may find the town itself disappointing; the savage bombardments of World War II and the shortsightedness of postwar developers left the city center an unattractive place. Roman legacies include a lighthouse adjoining a stout Anglo-Saxon church.

GETTING HERE AND AROUND

National Express buses depart from London's Victoria Coach Station for Dover about every 1½ hours. The journey takes about three hours. Drivers from London take the M20; the 76-mile journey should take around two hours. Southeastern trains leave London's Charing Cross, Victoria, and St. Pancras stations about every 30 minutes for Dover Priory Station in Dover. The trip is between one and two hours; some services require a change in Ashford.

For the best views of the cliffs, you need a car or taxi; it's a long way to walk from town.

ESSENTIALS

Visitor Information Dover Visitor Information Centre ☒ *Dover Museum, Market Sq.* ☎ *01304/201066* ⊕ *www.whitecliffscountry.org.uk.*

EXPLORING

FAMILY

Fodor's Choice

★

Dover Castle. Spectacular and with plenty to explore, Dover Castle, towering high above the ramparts of the white cliffs, is a mighty medieval castle that has served as an important strategic center over the centuries. Most of the castle, including the keep, dates to Norman times. It was begun by Henry II in 1181 but incorporates additions from almost every succeeding century. There's a lot to see besides the castle rooms themselves, most notably the recently opened **secret wartime tunnels**. Dover Castle played a surprisingly dramatic role in World War II, and these well-thought-out interactive galleries tell the complete story. The tunnels themselves, originally built during the Napoleonic Wars, were used as a top-secret nerve center in the fight against Hitler. ☒ *Castle Rd.* ☎ *01304/211067* ⊕ *www.english-heritage.org.uk* ▨ *£16.50* ⊙ *Apr.–July and Sept., daily 10–6; Aug., daily 9:30–6; Oct.–early Nov., daily 10–5; mid-Nov.–Mar., weekends 10–4.*

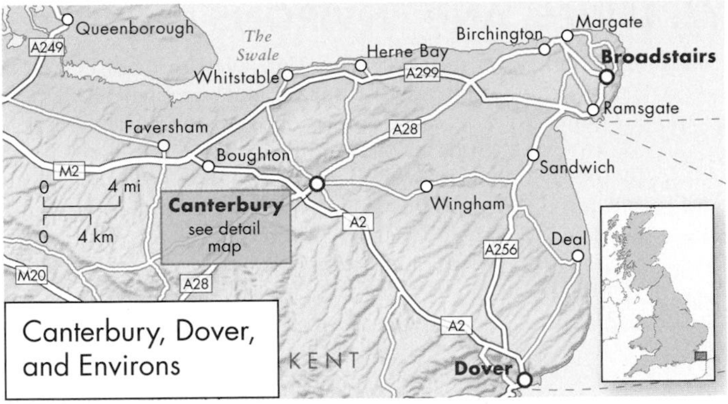
Queenborough
A249
The Swale
Whitstable
Herne Bay
A299
Birchington
Margate
Broadstairs
Ramsgate
Faversham
A28
Boughton
M2
0 4 mi
0 4 km
Canterbury
see detail map
A2
Wingham
Sandwich
Deal
A256
M20
A28
A2
KENT
Dover
Canterbury, Dover, and Environs

Roman Painted House. Believed to have been a hotel, the remains of this nearly 2,000-year-old structure were excavated in the 1970s. There are some Roman wall paintings (mostly dedicated to Bacchus, the god of revelry), along with the remnants of an ingenious heating system. ✉ *New St.* ☎ *01304/203279* 🌐 *www.theromanpaintedhouse.co.uk* 🎟 *£3* 🕒 *Early–mid-Apr., Tues.–Sun. 10–5; late Apr.–May, Tues. and Sat. 10–5; June–late Sept, Tues.–Sun. 10–5; last admission 30 mins before closing.*

Fodor's Choice ★ **White Cliffs.** Plunging hundreds of feet into the sea, Dover's chalk-white cliffs are an inspirational site and a symbol of England. They stay white because of the natural process of erosion. Because of this, you must be cautious when walking along the cliffs—experts recommend staying at least 20 feet from the edge. The best places to see the cliffs are at Samphire Hoe, St. Margaret's Bay, or East Cliff and Warren Country Park. Signs will direct you from the roads to scenic spots. **■ TIP→ The visitor center at Langdon Cliffs has 5 miles of walking trails with some spectacular views.**

WHERE TO STAY

$ HOTEL 🏨 **Premier Inn Dover.** By the waterfront, this modern hotel has spacious, quiet rooms, and a handy restaurant and bar. **Pros:** affordable rates; great location. **Cons:** busy neighborhood; no character; hotel restaurant is only so-so. [$] *Rooms from: £72* ✉ *Marine Court, Marine Parade* ☎ *0871/527–8306* 🌐 *www.premierinn.com* 🛏 *100 rooms* 🍴 *Breakfast.*

$$ B&B/INN 🏨 **White Cliffs Hotel.** Literally in the shadow of the famous White Cliffs of Dover, this colorful little hotel is attached to a high-end housewares store and a good restaurant. **Pros:** bags of character; beautiful location; guests can use the spa at another local hotel. **Cons:** far from central Dover; difficult to get here without a car. [$] *Rooms from: £119* ✉ *High St., St. Margaret's-at-Cliffe* ☎ *01304/852229* 🌐 *www.thewhitecliffs.com* 🛏 *15 rooms* 🍴 *Breakfast.*

3

RYE, LEWES, AND ENVIRONS

From Dover the coast road winds west through Folkestone (a genteel resort, small port, and Channel Tunnel terminal), across Romney Marsh (famous for its sheep and, at one time, its ruthless smugglers), and on to the delightful medieval town of Rye. The region along the coast is noted for the history-rich sites of Hastings, Herstmonceux, and Bodiam, and the Glyndebourne Opera House festival, based outside Lewes, a town celebrated for its architectural heritage. One of the three steam railroads in the Southeast services part of the area: the Romney, Hythe, and Dymchurch Railway.

RYE

34 miles southwest of Dover, 68 miles southeast of London.

Fodor's Choice With cobbled streets and ancient timbered dwellings, Rye is an artist's
★ dream. It was an important port town until the harbor silted up and the waters retreated more than 150 years ago; now the nearest harbor is 2 miles away. Virtually every building in the little town center is intriguingly historic. Rye is known for its many antiques stores and also for its sheer pleasantness. This place can be easily walked without a map, but the local tourist office has an interesting audio tour of the town as well as maps.

GETTING HERE AND AROUND

If you're driving to Rye, take the M20 to A2070. Trains from London's St. Pancras station leave once an hour and take an hour, with a change in Ashford.

ESSENTIALS

Visitor Information Rye Tourist Information Centre ⊠ *4 Lion St.*
☎ *01797/229049* ⊕ *www.ryesussex.co.uk.*

EXPLORING
TOP ATTRACTIONS

FAMILY   **Bodiam Castle.** Immortalized in paintings, photographs, and films, Bodiam Castle rises out of the distance like a piece of medieval legend. From the outside it's one of Britain's most impressive castles, with turrets, battlements, a glassy moat, and 2-foot-thick walls. Once you cross the drawbridge to the interior there's little to see but ruins, albeit on an impressive scale. Built in 1385 to withstand a threatened French invasion, it was partly demolished during the English Civil War of 1642–46 and has been uninhabited ever since. Still, you can climb the towers to take in sweeping countryside views, and kids love running around the keep. The castle, 12 miles west of Rye, schedules organized activities for kids during school holidays. ⊠ *Off B2244, Bodiam* ☎ *01580/830196* ⊕ *www.nationaltrust.org.uk* ⚲ *£7* ⊗ *Mid-Feb.–Oct., daily 10:30–5; Nov. and Dec., Wed.–Sun. 11–4 or dusk; Jan.–mid-Feb., weekends 11–4; last admission 1 hr before closing.*

Church of St. Mary the Virgin. At the top of the hill at the center of Rye, this classic English village church is more than 900 years old and encompasses a number of architectural styles. The turret clock

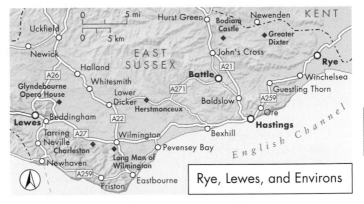

Rye, Lewes, and Environs

3

dates to 1561 and still keeps excellent time. Its huge pendulum swings inside the church nave. ■TIP→ Climb the tower for amazing views of the surrounding area. ⊠ *Church Sq.* ☎*01797/224935* ⊕*www. ryeparishchurch.org.uk* ⊠*Free* ⊙ *Daily 10–4.*

Fodor's Choice
★
Great Dixter House and Gardens. Combining a large timber-frame hall with a cottage garden on a grand scale, this place will get your green thumbs twitching. The house dates to 1464 (you can tour a few rooms) and was restored in 1910 by architect Edwin Lutyens, who also designed the garden. From these beginnings, the late horticulturist and writer Christopher Lloyd, whose home this was, developed a series of creative, colorful "garden rooms" and a dazzling herbaceous Long Border. The house is 9 miles northwest of Rye. ⊠ *Off A28, Northiam* ☎*01797/252878* ⊕ *www.greatdixter.co.uk* ⊠*£10.50; gardens only £8.50* ⊙ *Apr.–Oct., Tues.–Sun. and holiday Mon. 11–5 (house 2–5).*

Mermaid Street. One of the town's original cobbled streets (with perhaps its most quintessential view) heads steeply from the top of the hill to the former harbor. Its name supposedly came from the night a drunken sailor swore he heard a mermaid call him down to the sea. The houses here date from between the medieval and Georgian periods; a much-photographed pair have the delightfully fanciful names "The House with Two Front Doors" and "The House Opposite." Be careful on your feet—the cobbles are very uneven.

Ypres Tower. Down the hill past Church Square, Ypres Tower was originally built as part of the town's fortifications (now all but disappeared) in 1249; it later served as a prison. The stone chambers hold a rather random collection of local items, such as smuggling bric-a-brac and shipbuilding mementos. A row of defensive cannons are fixed to the rampart, which used to overlook the sea. ⊠ *Gungarden* ☎*01797/226728* ⊕ *www.ryemuseum.co.uk* ⊠*£3; £4 combined ticket with Rye Castle Museum* ⊙ *Apr.–Oct., daily 10:30–5; Nov.–Mar., daily 10:30–3:30; last admission 30 mins before closing.*

WORTH NOTING

Lamb House. Something about Lamb House, an early-18th-century dwelling, attracts writers. The novelist Henry James lived here from 1898 to 1916. E. F. Benson, onetime mayor of Rye and author of the witty *Lucia* novels (written in the 1920s and 1930s), was a later resident. The ground-floor rooms contain some of James's furniture and personal belongings. ✉ *West St.* ☎ *01580/762334* 🌐 *www.nationaltrust.org.uk* 🎟 *£4.80* 🕒 *Apr.–Oct., Tues. and Sat. 2–6; last admission at 5:30.*

WHERE TO EAT

$ ITALIAN 🍴 **Simply Italian.** In a prime location near the marina, this popular Italian eatery packs in the crowds on weekend nights with its inexpensive classic pasta and pizza dishes. The atmosphere is cheerful and bright, and the food is straightforward and unfussy. Try tagliatelle with salmon in a creamy sauce, or grilled lemon sole with white wine sauce. Good pizza picks are the *quarto stagioni,* with mushrooms, salami, and peppers on a crisp crust, and pizza *reale* with red peppers, spinach, goat cheese, and red onion. [$] *Average main: £8* ✉ *The Strand* ☎ *01797/226024* 🌐 *www.simplyitalian.co.uk.*

$$ SEAFOOD Fodor's Choice ★ 🍴 **Webbes at the Fish Café.** One of Rye's most popular restaurants occupies a brick building that dates to 1907, but the interior has been redone in a sleek, modern style. The ground-floor café has a relaxed atmosphere, and upstairs is a more formal dining room. Most of the seafood here is caught nearby, so it's very fresh. Sample the shellfish platter with oysters, whelks, winkles, shrimp, and crab claws, or try the grilled squid with bok choi. Reservations are recommended for dinner. [$] *Average main: £15* ✉ *17 Tower St.* ☎ *01797/222226* 🌐 *www.webbesrestaurants.co.uk* 🕒 *Closed Mon. Oct.–Apr. No dinner Sun.*

WHERE TO STAY

$ B&B/INN 🏨 **Jeake's House.** Antiques fill the cozy bedrooms of this rambling 1689 house, where the snug, painted-and-paneled parlor has a wood-burning stove for cold days. **Pros:** pleasant atmosphere; delicious breakfasts; winter discounts. **Cons:** Mermaid Street is steep and cobbled; cheapest room has bathroom across the hall. [$] *Rooms from: £90* ✉ *Mermaid St.* ☎ *01797/222828* 🌐 *www.jeakeshouse.com* 🛏 *11 rooms, 10 with bath* 🍽 *Breakfast.*

$$ HOTEL Fodor's Choice ★ 🏨 **The Mermaid.** Steeped in a history of smuggling, the Mermaid is Rye's most historic inn, and one of the oldest in the country—it's been in business for 600 years. **Pros:** dripping in atmosphere; good restaurant; 24-hour room service. **Cons:** price is high for what's on offer; allegedly haunted. [$] *Rooms from: £150* ✉ *Mermaid St.* ☎ *01797/223065* 🌐 *www.mermaidinn.com* 🛏 *31 rooms* 🍽 *Multiple meal plans.*

$$ B&B/INN 🏨 **White Vine House Hotel.** Occupying a building from the late 1500s, this small hotel embraces tradition with features such as wood-paneled lounges with warming fireplaces. **Pros:** beautiful building; one of the area's best restaurants. **Cons:** main street location can be a bit noisy; few services. [$] *Rooms from: £130* ✉ *24 High St.* ☎ *01797/224748* 🌐 *www.whitevinehouse.co.uk* 🛏 *7 rooms* 🍽 *Breakfast.*

SHOPPING

Rye has great antiques shops, perfect for an afternoon of rummaging, with the biggest cluster at the foot of the hill near the tourist information center.

Britcher & Rivers. This traditional candy store is like something out of a bygone age. Choose from row upon row of tall jars packed with every imaginable type of candy, measured out into little paper bags. ⊠ *89 High St.* ☎ *01797/227152.*

David Sharp Pottery. Like the distinctive ceramic name plaques that are a feature of the town? They are on offer at this sweet little shop. ⊠ *55 The Mint* ☎ *01797/222620* ⊕ *www.studiopottery.com.*

Glass Etc. A glorious collection of quality antique glass can be found in this colorful, friendly shop by the train station. ⊠ *18–22 Rope Walk* ☎ *01797/226600* ⊕ *www. decanterman.com.*

The Paper Place. This little stationery boutique sells beautiful handmade paper and cards with intricate, Asian-influenced designs. ⊠ *12 Market Rd.* ☎ *01797/222688* ⊕ *www.thepaperplaceonline.co.uk.*

THE BATTLE OF HASTINGS

When William of Normandy attacked King Harold's army in 1066, a vicious battle ensued. Harold's troops had just successfully fended off the Vikings near York and marched across the country to take on the Normans. Utterly exhausted, Harold was no match, and William became known as William the Conqueror. It's worth noting that, though it was called the Battle of Hastings, the skirmish actually took place 6 miles away at a town now called, well, Battle.

HASTINGS

12 miles southwest of Rye, 68 miles southeast of London.

In the 19th century Hastings became one of England's most popular spa resorts. Tall Victorian row houses painted in lemony hues still cover the cliffs around the deep blue sea, and the views from the hilltops are extraordinary. The pretty Old Town, on the east side of the city, offers a glimpse into the city's 16th-century past. Hastings has been through difficult times in recent decades, and the town developed a reputation as a rough place. It's currently trying hard to reinvent itself—a clutch of trendy new boutique B&Bs has opened, also an important new art gallery—but the town center can still be quite rowdy after dark. Expect a handsome but tattered town, with a mix of traditional English seaside amusements: miniature golf, shops selling junk, fish-and-chip stands, and a rocky beach that stretches for miles.

GETTING HERE AND AROUND

If you're driving to Hastings from London (70 miles), take A21. Trains travel to Hastings every 30 minutes or so from London's Charing Cross and St. Pancras stations; the journey takes about 1½ hours. The station, Hastings Warrior Square, is in the town center, within easy walking distance of most sights. National Express buses travel from London to Hastings about twice a day in about 3½ hours.

ESSENTIALS

Visitor Information **Hastings Tourist Information Centre** ✉ *Queens Sq.* ☎ *01424/451111* 🌐 *www.visit1066country.com.*

EXPLORING

FAMILY **Hastings Castle.** Take a thrilling ride up the West Hill Cliff Railway from George Street precinct to the atmospheric ruins of the Norman fortress now known as Hastings Castle, built by William the Conqueror in 1069. All that remains are fragments of the fortifications, some ancient walls, and a number of gloomy dungeons. Nevertheless, you get an excellent view of the chalky cliffs, the rocky coast, and the town below. ✉ *West Hill* ☎ *01424/201609* 🎟 *£4.50* ⏲ *Mid.–late Feb. and Apr.–Sept., daily 10–5; Mar., weekends 10–5; last admission 30 mins before closing.*

Fodor's Choice ★ **The Jerwood Gallery.** A symbol of the town's slow but growing regeneration after decades of neglect, this new exhibition space in the Old Town became one of the most talked about new galleries outside London when it opened in 2012. The permanent collection includes works by Augustus John, Walter Sickert, and Stephen Lowry, and temporary exhibitions change every couple of months. The glazed tile building on the seafront was designed to reflect the row of distinctive old, blackened fishing sheds it sits alongside. ✉ *Rock-a-Nore Rd.* ☎ *01424/728377* 🌐 *www.jerwoodgallery.org* 🎟 *£7* ⏲ *Tues.–Fri., 11–5, weekends 11–6.*

WHERE TO EAT AND STAY

$ SEAFOOD 🍴 **Blue Dolphin.** The crowds line up all day to make their way into this small fish-and-chips shop just off the seafront, down near the fish shacks. Although the decor is humble, reviewers consistently rank the battered fish and huge plates of double-cooked chips (chunky fries) as among the best in the country. Everything is steaming fresh and it's all cheaper if you get it to go. [$] *Average main: £6* ✉ *61 High St.* ☎ *01424/425778* 💳 *No credit cards* ⏲ *No dinner.*

$ B&B/INN 🏨 **The Cloudesley.** No TVs and a general Zen vibe at this boutique B&B in the quieter St. Leonard's district of Hastings make it a thoroughly relaxing place to stay. **Pros:** oasis of calm; great spa treatments; impeccable eco credentials. **Cons:** super-chilled vibe won't be for everyone; two-night minimum at certain times. [$] *Rooms from: £75* ✉ *7 Cloudesley Rd., St. Leonards-on-Sea* ☎ *07507/000148* 🌐 *www.thecloudesley.co.uk* 🛏 *5 rooms.*

$$ B&B/INN Fodor's Choice ★ 🏨 **Swan House.** Originally a bakery, this extraordinary 15th-century building has been beautifully converted into a welcoming, stylish B&B. **Pros:** beautiful, historic building; welcoming hosts; delicious breakfasts. **Cons:** some bathrooms have shower only. [$] *Rooms from: £120* ✉ *1 Hill St.* ☎ *01424/430014* 🌐 *www.swanhousehastings.co.uk* 🛏 *27 rooms* 🍽 *Breakfast.*

$$ HOTEL 🏨 **Zanzibar International Hotel.** This spacious, light-filled hotel overlooking the sea has guest rooms designed as a playful, yet restrained homage to exotic destinations. **Pros:** great facilities for a small hotel; sea views; champagne is served with breakfast. **Cons:** a bit over the top for some tastes; pricey for Hastings; nonrefundable deposit. [$] *Rooms from: £125* ✉ *9 Everfield Pl., St. Leonards-on-Sea* ☎ *01424/460109* 🌐 *www.zanzibarhotel.co.uk* 🛏 *9 rooms* 🍽 *Breakfast.*

BATTLE

7 miles northwest of Hastings, 61 miles southeast of London.

Battle is the actual site of the crucial Battle of Hastings, at which, on October 14, 1066, William of Normandy and his army trounced King Harold's Anglo-Saxon army. Today it's a sweet, quiet town, and a favorite of history buffs.

GETTING HERE AND AROUND

Southeastern trains arrive from London's Charing Cross and Cannon Street stations every half hour. The journey takes 90 minutes. National Express buses travel once daily in the early evening from London's Victoria Coach Station. The trip takes around 2½ hours.

ESSENTIALS

Visitor Information Battle Information Point ⊠ *Yesterdays World, 89–90 High Street* ☎ *01797/229049* ⊕ *www.visit1066country.com.*

EXPLORING

Battle Abbey. This great Benedictine abbey was erected by William the Conqueror on the site of the Battle of Hastings—one of the most decisive turning points in English history and the last time the country was successfully invaded. A memorial stone marks the high altar, which in turn was supposedly laid on the spot where Harold II, the last Saxon king, was killed. All of this meant little to Henry VIII, who didn't spare the building from his violent dissolution of the monasteries. Today the abbey is just a ruin, but films and interactive exhibits help bring it all to life. You can also take the mile-long walk around the edge of the battlefield and see the remains of the abbey's former outbuildings. ⊠ *High St.* ☎ *01424/775705* ⊕ *www.english-heritage.org.uk* ⊠ *£7.60* ⊙ *Apr.–Sept., daily 10–6; Oct.– early Nov., daily 10–4; early Nov.–Mar., weekends 10–4.*

FAMILY
Fodor's Choice
★

Herstmonceux. A banner waving from one tower and a glassy moat crossed by what was once a drawbridge: this fairy-tale castle has everything except knights in shining armor. The redbrick structure was originally built by Sir Roger Fiennes (ancestor of actor Ralph Fiennes) in 1444, although it was altered in the Elizabethan Age and again early in the 20th century, after it had largely fallen to ruin. Canada's Queen's University owns the castle, so only part of it is open for guided tours once or twice a day (except Saturday). Highlights include the magnificent ballroom, a medieval room, and the stunning Elizabethan-era staircase. Explore the formal walled garden, lily-covered lakes, and miles of woodland—the perfect place for a picnic on a sunny afternoon. There's a hands-on science center for kids. When school isn't in session, the castle rents out its small, plain guest rooms from £40 per night. The castle is 8 miles southwest of Battle. ⊠ *Off A271, Hailsham* ☎ *01323/833816* ⊕ *www.herstmonceux-castle.com* ⊠ *Castle and grounds £6; castle, grounds, and science center £12.50; castle tours £2.50* ⊙ *Mid-Apr.–Sept., daily 10–6; Oct., daily 10–5; last admission 1 hr before closing.*

Long Man of Wilmington. Wilmington, 9 miles southwest of Herstmonceux Castle on A27, has a famous landmark that people drive for miles to see. High on the downs to the south of the village (signposted off

A27), a 226-foot-tall white figure with a staff in each hand, known as the Long Man of Wilmington, is carved into the chalk. His age is a subject of great debate, but some researchers think he might have originated in Roman times.

WHERE TO EAT

$$$ ✕ **The Sundial.** This 17th-century brick farmhouse with views of the
MODERN FRENCH South Downs is home to a popular Modern French restaurant. Wood-beamed rooms and white tablecloths provide a backdrop for the imaginative menu, which may include rack of lamb with rosemary cream sauce, or steak fillet with shallot tarte Tatin and Madeira sauce. Dessert may be pineapple carpaccio marinated in Malibu and star anise, or perhaps mascarpone mousse with plum compote. The Sundial is near the castle in Herstmonceux, 8 miles southwest of Battle. $ *Average main: £21* ⊠ *Gardner St., Herstmonceux* ☎ *01323/832217* ⊕ *www. sundialrestaurant.co.uk* ⊗ *Closed Mon. No dinner Sun.*

LEWES

24 miles east of Battle, 8 miles northeast of Brighton, 54 miles south of London.

Fodor's Choice The town nearest to the celebrated Glyndebourne Opera House, Lewes
★ is so rich in architectural history that the Council for British Archaeology has named it one of the 50 most important English towns. A walk is the best way to appreciate its steep streets and appealing jumble of building styles and materials—flint, stone, brick, tile—and the secret lanes (called "twittens") behind the castle, with their huge beeches. Here and there are smart antiques shops, good eateries, and secondhand-book dealers. Most of the buildings in the center date to the 18th and 19th centuries.

Something about this town has always attracted rebels. It was once the home of Thomas Paine (1737–1809), whose pamphlet *Common Sense* advocated that the American colonies break with Britain. It was also favored by Virginia Woolf and the Bloomsbury Group, early-20th-century countercultural artistic innovators.

Today Lewes's beauty and proximity to London mean that the counter-culture crew can't really afford to live here anymore, but its rebel soul still peeks through, particularly on Guy Fawkes Night (November 5), the anniversary of Fawkes's foiled attempt to blow up the Houses of Parliament in 1605. Flaming tar barrels are rolled down High Street and into the River Ouse; costumed processions fill the streets.

GETTING HERE AND AROUND

If you're driving to Lewes from London, take the M23 south. The 57-mile journey takes around an hour and 45 minutes. Southern trains run direct to Lewes from Victoria Station every 30 minutes or so on the Brighton line. It may be faster to take a train to Brighton and change to the regional service for Lewes. There's no easy way to get to Lewes by bus; you need to take a National Express or Megabus to Brighton and change to a regional bus line.

A mixture of architectural styles and good shops make Lewes a wonderful town for a stroll.

ESSENTIALS

Visitor Information Lewes Tourist Information Centre ☒ *187 High St.* ☎ *01273/483448* ⊕ *www.lewes.gov.uk.*

EXPLORING

FAMILY **Anne of Cleves House.** This 16th-century structure, a fragile-looking, timber-frame building, holds a small collection of Sussex ironwork and other items of local interest, such as Sussex pottery. The house was part of Anne of Cleves's divorce settlement from Henry VIII, although she never lived in it. There are medieval dress-up clothes for kids. To get to the house, walk down steep, cobbled Keere Street, past lovely Grange Gardens, to Southover High Street. ☒ *52 Southover High St.* ☎ *01273/474610* ⊕ *www.sussexpast.co.uk* ☒ *£4.90* ☉ *Feb.–Nov., Tues.–Sat. 10–5, Sun. and Mon. 11–5.*

Charleston. Art and life mixed at Charleston, the farmhouse Vanessa Bell—sister of Virginia Woolf—bought in 1916 and fancifully decorated, along with Duncan Grant (who lived here until 1978). The house became a refuge for the writers and artists of the Bloomsbury Group. On display are colorful ceramics and textiles of the Omega Workshop, in which Bell and Grant participated. There are also paintings by Picasso and Renoir, as well as by Bell and Grant themselves. You view the house on a guided tour except on Sunday. On Friday there's a special 90-minute tour that focuses on a different aspect of Charleston's history, such as the great influence French culture had on the Bloomsbury Group. ☒ *Off A27, 7 miles east of Lewes, Firle* ☎ *01323/811626* ⊕ *www.charleston.org.uk* ☒ *£10; gardens only £4* ☉ *Late Mar.–June and Sept.–late Oct., Wed.–Sat. 1–6, Sun. and holiday Mon. 1–5:30; July and Aug., Wed.–Sat. noon–6, Sun. 1–5:30.*

Lewes Castle. High above the valley of the River Ouse stand the majestic ruins of Lewes Castle, begun in 1100 by one of the country's Norman conquerors, and completed 300 years later. The castle's barbican holds a small museum with archaeology collections, a changing temporary exhibition gallery, and a bookshop. There are panoramic views of the town and countryside. ✉ *169 High St.* ☎ *01273/486290* 🌐 *www.sussexpast.co.uk* 🎟 *£6.80* 🕘 *Tues.–Sat. 10–5:30, Sun. and Mon. 11–5:30.*

WHERE TO EAT

$ CAFÉ 🍴 **The Real Eating Company.** This light-filled restaurant has big windows overlooking the bustling shopping street outside. The heavy wood tables are perfect for lingering over the home-style cooking. Come at breakfast for the waffles with bacon and maple syrup, or perhaps some raspberry granola. For lunch you may opt for beer-battered cod and chips, or perhaps a grilled chicken Caesar. Great cakes and strong tea help to make this an ideal afternoon pit stop. [$] *Average main: £11* ✉ *18 Cliff High St.* ☎ *01273/402650* 🌐 *www.real-eating.co.uk* 🕘 *No dinner Sun.*

$ CAFÉ 🍴 **Robson's of Lewes.** Good coffee, fresh produce, and delicious pastries have made this coffee shop very popular with locals. A light-filled space with wood floors and simple tables creates a pleasant, casual spot to enjoy a cup of coffee with breakfast, a scone, or a light sandwich or salad lunch. You can also order to go. [$] *Average main: £5* ✉ *22A High St.* ☎ *01273/480654* 🌐 *www.robsonsoflewes.co.uk* 🕘 *No dinner.*

WHERE TO STAY

$$ HOTEL 🏨 **Crossways Hotel.** Near the Long Man of Wilmington, this small "restaurant with rooms" in a whitewashed house with 2 acres of gardens is decorated in warm, upbeat colors that contrast with the lovely antique furniture. **Pros:** lovely location near Glyndebourne; spacious bedrooms. **Cons:** few frills. [$] *Rooms from: £145* ✉ *Lewes Rd., Polegate* ☎ *01323/482455* 🌐 *www.crosswayshotel.co.uk* 🛏 *7 rooms, 1 cottage* 🍽 *Breakfast.*

$$$ B&B/INN 🏨 **Horsted Place.** On 1,100 acres, this luxurious Victorian manor house was built as a private home in 1850; it was owned by a friend of Queen Elizabeth until the 1980s, and she was a regular visitor. **Pros:** historic building; amazing architecture; lovely gardens. **Cons:** too formal for some; creaky floors bother light sleepers. [$] *Rooms from: £180* ✉ *Off A26, Little Horsted* ☎ *01825/750581* 🌐 *www.horstedplace.co.uk* 🛏 *15 rooms, 5 suites* 🍽 *Breakfast.*

$ B&B/INN 🏨 **The Ram Inn.** Roaring fires, cozy rooms, and friendly locals give this 500-year-old inn its wonderful feeling of old-world authenticity. **Pros:** proper village pub atmosphere; good food; cozy, well-designed rooms. **Cons:** you need a car to get here from Lewes. [$] *Rooms from: £90* ✉ *The Street, West Firle* ☎ *01273/858222* 🌐 *www.raminn.co.uk* 🛏 *4 rooms.*

$$ B&B/INN 🏨 **The Shelleys.** The lounge and dining room in this 17th-century building are on the grand scale, furnished with antiques that set the tone for the rest of the lovely building. **Pros:** historic atmosphere; good, French-influenced cuisine. **Cons:** service a bit spotty;

securing a table at the restaurant can be tough. $ *Rooms from: £130* ✉ *High St.* ☎ *01273/472361* ⊕ *www.the-shelleys.co.uk* ⇥ *19 rooms* ❍❙ *Breakfast.*

NIGHTLIFE AND THE ARTS

NIGHTLIFE

Lewes has a relatively young population and a nightlife scene to match; there are also many lovely old pubs.

Brewers' Arms. On High Street, this is a good pub with a friendly crowd. The half-timbered building dates from 1906, but a pub has stood on this spot since the 16th century. ✉ *91 High St.* ☎ *01273/475524* ⊕ *www. brewersarmslewes.co.uk.*

King's Head. A traditional pub, the King's Head has a good menu with locally sourced fish and meat dishes. ✉ *9 Southover High St.* ☎ *01273/474628* ⊕ *www.thekingsheadlewes.co.uk.*

THE ARTS

Glyndebourne Opera House. Nestled beneath the Downs, this world-famous opera house combines first-class productions, a state-of-the-art auditorium, and a beautiful setting. Seats are *very* expensive (the cheapest are around £50) and you have to book months in advance, but it's worth every penny to aficionados, who traditionally wear evening dress and bring a hamper to picnic in the gardens. The main season runs from mid-May to the end of August. ■ **TIP➜** If you can't afford a seat, standing room costs about £10. The Glyndebourne Touring Company performs here in October, when seats are cheaper. ✉ *New Rd., off A26, Ringmer* ⚓ *Near Lewes* ☎ *01273/813813* ⊕ *www.glyndebourne.com.*

SHOPPING

Antiques shops offer temptation along the busy High Street. Lewes also has plenty of tiny boutiques and independent clothing stores vying for your pounds.

Cliffe Antiques Centre. This center carries a fine mix of vintage English prints, estate jewelry, and art at reasonable prices. ✉ *47 Cliffe High St.* ☎ *01273/473266.*

The Fifteenth Century Bookshop. A wide collection of rare and vintage books can be found at this ancient, timber-framed building in the center of Lewes. Antique children's books are a specialty. ✉ *99–100 High St.* ☎ *01273/474160* ⊕ *www.oldenyoungbooks.co.uk.*

Louis Potts & Co. From frivolous knickknacks to full-on formal dining sets, Louis Potts specializes in stylish bone china and glassware. ✉ *43 Cliffe High St.* ☎ *01273/472240* ⊕ *www.louispotts.com.*

BRIGHTON AND THE SUSSEX COAST

The self-proclaimed belle of the coast, Brighton is upbeat, funky, and endlessly entertaining. Outside town the soft green downs of Sussex hold stately homes you can visit, including Arundel Castle and Petworth House. Along the way, you'll discover the largest Roman villa in Britain, and Chichester, whose cathedral is a poem in stone.

BRIGHTON

9 miles southwest of Lewes, 54 miles south of London.

Fodor's Choice ★ For more than 200 years, Brighton has been England's most interesting seaside city, and today it's more vibrant, eccentric, and cosmopolitan than ever. A rich cultural mix—Regency architecture, specialty shops, sidewalk cafés, lively arts, and a flourishing gay scene—makes it unique and unpredictable.

In 1750 physician Richard Russell published a book recommending sea-water treatment for glandular diseases. The fashionable world flocked to Brighton to take Dr. Russell's "cure," and sea bathing became a popular pastime. Few places in the south of England were better for it, since Brighton's broad beach of smooth pebbles stretches as far as the eye can see. It's been popular with sunbathers ever since.

The next windfall for the town was the arrival of the Prince of Wales (later George IV). "Prinny," as he was called, created the Royal Pavilion, a mock-Asian pleasure palace that attracted London society. This triggered a wave of villa building, and today the elegant terraces of Regency houses are among the town's greatest attractions. The coming of the railway set the seal on Brighton's popularity: the *Brighton Belle* brought Londoners to the coast in an hour.

Londoners still flock to Brighton. Add them to the many local university students, and you have a trendy, young, laid-back city that does, occasionally, burst at its own seams. Property values have skyrocketed, but all visitors may notice is the good shopping and restaurants, attractive (if pebbly) beach, and wild nightlife. Brighton is also the place to go if you're looking for hotels with offbeat design and party nights.

GETTING HERE AND AROUND

Brighton-bound National Express and Megabus buses depart from London's Victoria Coach Station. The trip takes about two hours. South-eastern trains leave from London's Victoria and Charing Cross stations four or five times an hour. The journey takes 75 minutes, and the trains stop at Gatwick Airport. By car from London, head to Brighton on the M23/A23. The journey should take about 1½ hours.

Brighton (and the adjacent Hove) sprawls in all directions, but the part of interest to travelers is fairly compact. None of the sights is more than a 10-minute walk from the train station. You can pick up a town map at the station. City Sightseeing has a hop-on, hop-off tour bus that leaves Brighton Pier every 20 to 30 minutes. It operates May through mid-September (plus weekends, March and April) and costs £11.

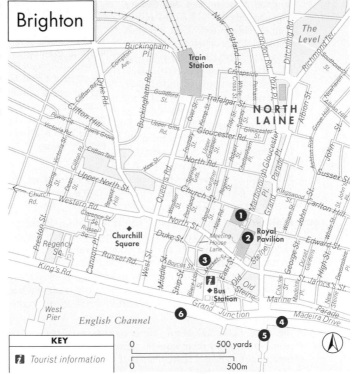

KEY

i Tourist information

TIMING

On summer weekends the town is packed with Londoners looking for a day by the sea. Oceanfront bars can be rowdy, especially on national holidays when concerts and events bring in crowds. But summer is also when Brighton looks its best, and revelers pack the shops, restaurants, and bars. At other times, it's much quieter. The Brighton Festival in May fills the town with music and other performances.

ESSENTIALS

Visitor and Tour Information Brighton Visitor Information Centre ✉ *Royal Pavilion Shop, Royal Pavilion* ☎ *01273/290337* ⊕ *www.visitbrighton.com.* **City Sightseeing** ☎ *01273/886200* ⊕ *www.city-sightseeing.com.*

EXPLORING
TOP ATTRACTIONS

Brighton Beach. Brighton's most iconic landmark is its famous beach, which sweeps smoothly from one end of town to the other. In summer sunbathers, swimmers, and hawkers selling ice cream and toys pack the shore; in winter people stroll at the water's stormy edge, walking their dogs and searching for seashells. The water is bracingly cold, and the beach is covered in a thick blanket of large, smooth pebbles (615 billion of them, according to the tourism office). ■ **TIP→ Bring a pair of rubber swimming shoes if you're taking a dip—the stones are hard on bare feet.**

Brighton Museum and Art Gallery. The grounds of the Royal Pavilion contain this museum, in a former stable block designed for the Prince Regent (1762–1830), son of George III. The museum has particularly interesting art nouveau and art deco collections. Look out for Salvador Dalí's famous sofa in the shape of Mae West's lips. The Fashion & Style Gallery has clothes from the Regency period to the present day, and the Performance gallery has a collection of masks, puppets, and other theatrical curiosities. ✉ *Royal Pavilion, Church St.* ☎ *0300/029–0900* ⊕ *www.brighton-hove-rpml. org.uk* ✍ *Free* ⊗ *Tues.–Sun. and holiday Mon., 10–5.*

> **WE DO NOT APPROVE**
>
> When Queen Victoria came to the throne in 1837, she so disapproved of the Royal Pavilion that she stripped it of its furniture and planned to demolish it. Fortunately, the local council bought it from her and today the palace looks much as it did in its Regency heyday.

FAMILY **Brighton Pier.** Opened in 1899, the pier is an amusement park set above the sea. In the early 20th century it had a music hall and entertainment; today it has roller coasters and other carnival rides, as well as game arcades, clairvoyants, candy stores, and greasy-food stalls. In summer it's packed with children by day and teenagers by night. The skeletal shadow of a pier you can see off in the water is all that's left of the old West Pier. ✉ *Madeira Dr.* ☎ *01273/609361* ⊕ *www.brightonpier.co.uk* ⊗ *Daily 10–10.*

The Lanes. This maze of tiny alleys and passageways was once the home of fishermen and their families. Closed to vehicular traffic, the area's narrow cobbled streets are filled with interesting restaurants, boutiques, and antiques shops. Fish and seafood restaurants line the heart of the Lanes, at Market Street and Market Square. ✉ *Bordered by West, North, East, and Prince Albert Sts.*

Fodor's Choice **Royal Pavilion.** The city's most remarkable building is this delightfully ★ over-the-top domed and pinnacled fantasy. Built as a simple seaside villa in the fashionable classical style of 1787 by architect Henry Holland, the Pavilion was rebuilt between 1815 and 1822 by John Nash for the Prince Regent (later George IV). The result was an exotic, foppish Eastern design with opulent Chinese interiors. The two great set pieces are the **Music Room,** styled in the form of a Chinese pavilion, and the **Banqueting Room,** with its enormous flying-dragon "gasolier," or gas-light chandelier, a revolutionary invention in the early 19th century. The gardens, too, have been restored to Regency splendor, following John Nash's naturalistic design of 1826. ■TIP→ For an elegant time-out, a tearoom serves snacks and light meals. ✉ *Old Steine* ☎ *03000/290900* ⊕ *www.royalpavilion.org.uk* ✍ *£10* ⊗ *Oct.–Mar., daily 9:30–5:15; Apr.–Sept., daily 9:30–5:45; last admission 45 mins before closing.*

WORTH NOTING

FAMILY **Brighton Wheel.** Brighton's answer to the London Eye, this 50-metre (164-foot) Ferris wheel gives you a spectacular panorama of the town and the sea, from air-conditioned capsules. VIP tickets, including rides where wine or champagne is served, cost from £25 to £60 per person.

3

■ **TIP→ There's a discount on all tickets if you book online.** ✉ *Daltons Bastion, Madeira Dr.* ☎ *01273/722822* 🌐 *www.brightonwheel.com* 🎫 *£8* 🕐 *Sun.–Thurs. 10–9, Fri. and Sat. 10–11.*

WHERE TO EAT

$ CAFÉ 🍴 **Bill's Produce.** Even groceries seem attractive at this casual, pleasant coffee shop–restaurant–deli. On tall shelves all around the light-filled dining room, bottles of olive oil and vinegars glisten alongside stacks of fresh fruit, vegetables, baskets, and flowers. Blackboards near the counter list the day's specials: these usually include a variety of salads, sandwiches (your choice of fresh breads), and a few hot dishes. Comfort food mains include burgers, fish pie, and mac and cheese. Breakfast is popular here, too. [$] *Average main: £10* ✉ *The Depot, 100 North Rd.* ☎ *01273/692894* 🌐 *www.bills-website.co.uk.*

$ VEGETARIAN 🍴 **Iydea.** This popular café-restaurant is a must for visiting vegetarians, though even the most ardent carnivores are likely to leave satisfied. The food is laid out canteen style; choose from imaginitive, well-prepared mains like potato, cheese, and caramelized onion galette, or pea and goat cheese *arancini* (breaded and fried rice balls), and maybe a side of giant couscous with lemon and mustard dressing, or the tamari potato wedges. They also do a very popular vegetarin breakfast. A second branch, at 105 Western Rd., stays open until 10 pm. [$] *Average main: £6* ✉ *17 Kensington Gardens* ☎ *01273/667992* 🌐 *www.iydea.co.uk* ✍ *Reservations not accepted.*

$ MIDDLE EASTERN 🍴 **Pomegranate.** A contemporary Kurdish restaurant, Pomegranate takes a lighthearted, fun approach to Middle Eastern cuisine. Its small dining area spreads over two floors and has large windows and exposed brick walls. The sprawling menu includes lamb with rosemary and lemon juice, and grilled chicken in a grape-and-honey sauce. For dessert, try the figs stuffed with walnuts and pomegranate seeds. The lunch menu (£12.50 for three courses) is particularly good value. [$] *Average main: £13* ✉ *10 Manchester St.* ☎ *01273/628386* 🌐 *www.eatpomegranates.com.*

$$ SEAFOOD Fodor's Choice ★ 🍴 **Riddle and Finns.** White tiles, bare metal tables, and sparkling chandeliers set the tone as soon as you walk through the door of this casually elegant restaurant—the more laid-back sister to ⇨ *Arch 139*. The house specialty is oysters, fresh and sustainably sourced, served with or without a tankard of Black Velvet (Champagne and Guinness) on the side. Other options include sea bass with bubble and squeak (a traditional dish of fried vegetables and potatoes), or lobster served with garlic and herb butter or thermidor. They don't take bookings, so come early or be prepared to wait. It's also open weekends for breakfast (and, yes, they serve oysters and Champagne). [$] *Average main: £16* ✉ *12B Meeting House La.* ☎ *01273/323008* 🌐 *www.riddleandfinns.co.uk* ✍ *Reservations not accepted.*

$$ VEGETARIAN 🍴 **Terre à Terre.** This inspiring vegetarian restaurant is incredibly popular, so come early for a light lunch or later for a more sophisticated evening meal. Dishes have a pan-Asian influence, so you may start with Indian tandoori-spiced halloumi, before moving on to aubergine with tahini, sesame, and white miso. There's also an excellent collection of wines from around the globe. [$] *Average main: £15* ✉ *71 East St.* ☎ *01273/729051* 🌐 *www.terreaterre.co.uk* 🕐 *No lunch Tues. and Wed. in winter.*

CLOSE UP

Brighton and the Regent

The term "Regency" comes from the last 10 years of the reign of George III (1811–20), who was deemed unfit to rule because of his mental problems. Real power was officially given to the Prince of Wales, also known as the Prince Regent, who became King George IV and ruled until his death in 1830.

Throughout his regency, George spent grand sums indulging his flamboyant tastes in architecture and interior decorating—while failing in affairs of state.

The distinctive architecture of the Royal Pavilion is a prime, if extreme, example of the Regency style, popularized by architect John Nash (1752–1835) in the early part of the 19th century. The style is characterized by a diversity of influences—French, Greek, Italian, Persian, Japanese, Chinese, Roman, Indian—you name it. Nash was George IV's favorite architect, beloved for his interest in Indian and Asian art and for his neoclassical designs, as evidenced in his other most famous work—Regent's Park and its terraces in London.

WHERE TO STAY

$ B&B/INN **Brightonwave.** Chic and sleek, this hotel off the seafront but near Brighton Pier is all about relaxation. **Pros:** big, comfy beds; soothing decor. **Cons:** rooms on the small side; few extras. [$] *Rooms from: £95* ✉ *10 Madeira Pl.* ☎ *01273/676794* 🌐 *www.brightonwave.com* 🛏 *8 rooms* 🍴 *Breakfast.*

$$ HOTEL **Grand Brighton.** The city's most famous hotel, this seafront landmark is a huge, creamy Victorian wedding cake of a building dating from 1864. **Pros:** as grand as its name; lovely sea views. **Cons:** a bit impersonal; prices can rise sharply at weekends. [$] *Rooms from: £160* ✉ *97–99 Kings Rd.* ☎ *01273/224300* 🌐 *www.devere-hotels.co.uk* 🛏 *200 rooms, 3 suites* 🍴 *Breakfast.*

$ HOTEL **Granville Hotel.** Three grand Victorian buildings facing the sea make up this hotel where the themed guest quarters include the pink-and-white Brighton Rock Room and the art deco Noël Coward Room. **Pros:** creative design; friendly staff; rambunctious atmosphere. **Cons:** rooms are a bit too quirky; can get noisy. [$] *Rooms from: £89* ✉ *124 King's Rd.* ☎ *01273/326302* 🌐 *www.granvillehotel.co.uk* 🛏 *24 rooms* 🍴 *Breakfast.*

$$ HOTEL **Hotel du Vin.** In the Lanes area, this outpost of a snazzy boutique chain has chic modern rooms. **Pros:** gorgeous rooms; comfortable beds; excellent restaurant. **Cons:** bar can get crowded; big price fluctuations in summer. [$] *Rooms from: £140* ✉ *Ship St.* ☎ *01273/718588* 🌐 *www.hotelduvin.com* 🛏 *40 rooms, 3 suites* 🍴 *No meals.*

$ HOTEL **Oriental Brighton.** With a casual elegance that typifies Brighton, this Regency-era hotel sits close to the seafront. **Pros:** close to the beach; beautiful rooms. **Cons:** no restaurant; busy bar; minimum stay on weekends. [$] *Rooms from: £85* ✉ *9 Oriental Pl.* ☎ *01273/205050* 🌐 *www.orientalbrighton.co.uk* 🛏 *9 rooms* 🍴 *Breakfast.*

$ HOTEL **Pelirocco.** Here the imaginations of designers have been given free rein, and the result is a vicarious romp through pop culture and rock and roll. **Pros:** quirky design; laid-back atmosphere; near the beach. **Cons:** too form-over-function; no restaurant. [$] *Rooms from: £99* ✉ *10 Regency Sq.* ☎ *01273/327055* 🌐 *www.hotelpelirocco.co.uk* 🛏 *18 rooms, 1 suite* 🍴 *Breakfast.*

NIGHTLIFE AND THE ARTS

NIGHTLIFE

Brighton is a techno hub, largely because so many DJs have moved here from London. Clubs and bars present live music most nights, and on weekends the entire place can be a bit too raucous for some tastes. There's a large and enthusiastic gay scene.

Above Audio. The popular Above Audio, in an art deco building east of Brighton Pier, serves up a mix of house and underground music. ✉ *10 Marine Parade* ☎ *01273/606906* 🌐 *www.audiobrighton.com.*

The Jazz Lounge at the Bohemia Grand Café. Every Thursday the best local jazz acts take over this upscale café-bar. It's arranged like a traditional jazz club, with table service and an old-school vibe. ✉ *54 Meeting House La.* ☎ *01273/777770* 🌐 *www.bohemiabrighton.co.uk.*

Proud Cabaret. A mixture of vintage and avant-garde cabaret and burlesque is on offer at this stylish nightclub, which also serves a 1920s-style three-course dinner from Thursday to Saturday. Booking is advisable. ✉ *83 St. Georges Rd.* ☎ *01273/605789* 🌐 *www.brightoncabaret.com.*

The Tube. Underneath the Victorian arches on the seafront is one of Brighton's hottest nightclubs, with an eclectic range of dance, hip-hop, funk, soul, and indie playing until 6 am Wednesday to Saturday. ✉ *169 King's Rd. Arches* ☎ *01273/725541.*

THE ARTS

Brighton Dome. West of the Royal Pavilion, the Brighton Dome was converted from the prince regent's stables in the 1930s. It includes a theater and a concert hall that stage pantomime (a traditional British children's play with songs and dance, usually featuring low-rent TV stars), and classical and pop concerts. ✉ *Church St.* ☎ *01273/709709* 🌐 *brightondome.org.*

Brighton Festival. The three-week-long Brighton Festival, one of England's biggest and liveliest arts festivals, takes place every May in venues around town. The more than 600 events include drama, music, dance, and visual arts. ☎ *01273/709709* 🌐 *www.brightonfestival.org.*

Theatre Royal. Close to the Royal Pavilion, the Theatre Royal has a gem of an auditorium that's a favorite venue for shows on their way to or fresh from London's West End. ✉ *35 Bond St.* ☎ *01273/328488.*

SHOPPING

Brighton Lanes Antique Centre. Although this shop specializes in gold and jewelry, it also has a good selection of furniture and ornaments. ✉ *12 Meeting House La.* ☎ *01273/823121* 🌐 *www.brightonlanesantiques.co.uk.*

Colin Page. At the western edge of the Lanes, Colin Page stocks a wealth of antiquarian and secondhand books at all prices. ⊠ *36 Duke St.* ☎ *01273/325954.*

Cologne & Cotton. This lovely little bed-and-bath emporium sells vintage bed linens, blankets, bath products, and tableware. ⊠ *13 Pavilion Bldgs.* ☎ *01273/729666* ⊕ *www.cologneandcotton.com.*

Curiouser & Curiouser. This shop is filled with unique handmade jewelry, mostly sterling silver pieces with semiprecious stones. ⊠ *2 Sydney St.* ☎ *01273/673120* ⊕ *www.curiousersilverjewellery.co.uk.*

The Lanes. The main shopping area is the Lanes, especially for antiques or jewelry. It also has clothing boutiques, coffee shops, and pubs.

Lavender Room. This relaxing boutique tempts with scented calendars, glittery handmade jewelry, and little things you just can't live without. ⊠ *16 Bond St.* ☎ *01273/220380* ⊕ *www.lavender-room.co.uk.*

North Laine. Across North Street from the Lanes lies the North Laine, a network of narrow streets full of little stores. They're less glossy than those in the Lanes, but are fun, funky, and exotic.

Pavilion Shop. Next door to the Royal Pavilion, the Pavilion Shop carries well-designed toys, trinkets, books, and cards, all with a loose Regency theme. There are also high-quality fabrics, wallpapers, and ceramics based on material in the Pavilion itself. ⊠ *4–5 Pavilion Bldgs.* ☎ *03000/290900.*

Pecksniff's Bespoke Perfumery. The old-fashioned Pecksniff's Bespoke Perfumery mixes and matches ingredients to suit your wishes. ⊠ *45–46 Meeting House La.* ☎ *01273/723292.*

ARUNDEL

23 miles west of Brighton, 60 miles south of London.

The little hilltop town of Arundel is dominated by its great castle, the much-restored home of the dukes of Norfolk for more than 700 years, and an imposing neo-Gothic Roman Catholic cathedral (the duke is Britain's leading Catholic peer). The town itself is full of interesting old buildings and well worth a stroll.

GETTING HERE AND AROUND

Arundel is on the A27, about a two-hour drive south of central London. Trains from London's Victoria Station leave every half hour and take 90 minutes. No direct buses run from London, but you can take a National Express bus to Worthing or Chichester and change to a local bus going to Arundel, though that journey could easily take five hours.

ESSENTIALS

Visitor Information Arundel Museum and Visitor Information Point ⊠ *1–3 Crown Yard Mews, off River Rd.* ☎ *01903/882419* ⊕ *www.sussexbythesea.com.*

EXPLORING

FAMILY

Fodor's Choice

★

Arundel Castle. You've probably already seen Arundel Castle without knowing it—the striking resemblance to Windsor means that it's frequently used as a stand-in for its more famous cousin in movies

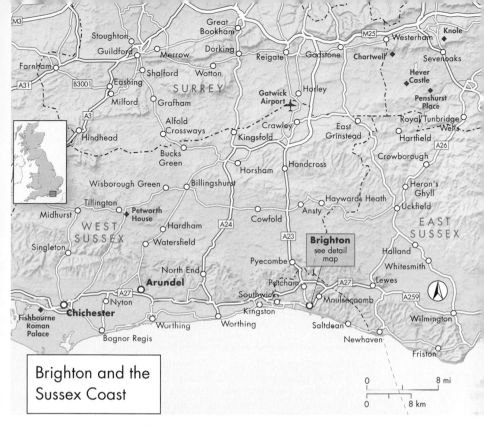

Brighton and the Sussex Coast

and television. Begun in the 11th century, this vast castle remains rich with the history of the Fitzalan and Howard families and with paintings by Van Dyck, Gainsborough, and Reynolds. During the 18th century and in the Victorian era it was reconstructed in the fashionable Gothic style—although the keep, rising from its conical mound, is as old as the original castle (climb its 130 steps for great views of the River Arun), and the barbican and the Barons' Hall date from the 13th century. Among the treasures are the rosary beads and prayer book used by Mary, Queen of Scots, in preparing for her execution. The newly redesigned formal garden is a triumph of order and beauty. Although the castle's ceremonial entrance is at the top of High Street, you enter at the bottom, close to the parking lot. ⊠ *Mill Rd.* ☎ *01903/882173* ⊕ *www.arundelcastle.org* ⊠ *£17; grounds only £8* ⊙ *Easter–early Nov., Tues.–Sun. and holiday Mon. 10–5 (keep closes 4:30); last admission 4.*

WHERE TO EAT AND STAY

$$$

EUROPEAN

✕ **The Town House.** This small but elegant restaurant in a beautifully converted Regency town house (look up—the dining room ceiling is quite something) serves top-notch British and European cuisine. The fixed-price lunch and dinner menus change regularly, but could include roast partridge with spinach and wild mushrooms, or local sea bass with caramelized shallots and potato rosti. If you want to see more of the place, they also do bed and breakfast accommodation from £95 per night. $ *Average main: £24* ⊠ *65 High St.* ☎ *01903/883847* ⊕ *www. thetownhouse.co.uk.*

$$$$
HOTEL
Fodor's Choice
★

⚏ **Amberley Castle.** The lowering of the portcullis every night at midnight is a sure sign that you're in a genuine medieval castle. **Pros:** sleep in a real castle; lovely gardens and grounds. **Cons:** you have to dress for dinner. $ *Rooms from: £315* ⊠ *Off B2139, Amberley* ☎ *01798/831992* ⊕ *www.amberleycastle.co.uk* ⇨ *19 rooms* |○| *Breakfast.*

$
HOTEL

⚏ **Norfolk Arms Hotel.** Like the cathedral and the castle in Arundel, this 18th-century coaching inn on the main street was built by one of the dukes of Norfolk. **Pros:** charming building; historic setting. **Cons:** older rooms on the small side; a little old-fashioned. $ *Rooms from: £94* ⊠ *22 High St.* ☎ *01903/882101* ⇨ *34 rooms* |○| *Breakfast.*

NIGHTLIFE AND THE ARTS

Arundel Festival. The popular Arundel Festival presents dramatic productions and classical and pop concerts in and around the castle grounds for 10 days in late August or early September. ☎ *01903/883690* ⊕ *www. arundelfestival.co.uk.*

CHICHESTER

10 miles west of Arundel, 66 miles southwest of London.

The Romans founded Chichester, the capital city of West Sussex, on the low-lying plains between the wooded South Downs and the sea. The city walls and major streets follow the original Roman plan. This cathedral town, a good base for exploring the area, is a well-respected theatrical hub, with a reputation for attracting good acting talent during its summer repertory season. North of town is Petworth House, one of the region's finest stately homes.

GETTING HERE AND AROUND

From London, take A3 south and follow exit signs for Chichester. The 67-mile journey takes slightly more than two hours; much of it is on smaller highways. Southern trains run to Chichester several times an hour from Victoria Station, with a travel time of about 90 minutes. Buses leave from London's Victoria Coach Station every two hours and take just over three hours.

ESSENTIALS

Visitor Information Chichester Tourist Information Centre ⊠ *29A South St.* ☎ *01243/775888* ⊕ *www.visitchichester.org.*

EXPLORING

Chichester Cathedral. Standing on Roman foundations, 900-year-old Chichester Cathedral has a glass panel that reveals Roman mosaics uncovered during restorations. Other treasures include the wonderful Saxon limestone reliefs of the raising of Lazarus and Christ arriving in Bethany, both in the choir area. Among the outstanding contemporary artworks are a stained-glass window by Marc Chagall and a colorful tapestry by John Piper. Free guided tours begin every day except Sunday at 11:15 and 2:30. You can also prebook tours that concentrate on subjects including the English Civil War and the cathedral's art collection; call or go online for details. ⊠ *West St.* ☎ *01243/782595* ⊕ *www.chichestercathedral. uk* 🖾 *Free; £3 suggested donation* ☉ *Easter–Sept., daily 7:15–7; Oct.– Easter, daily 7:15–6.*

3

> **A TEMPTING TOWN**
>
> After you visit Petworth House, take time to explore the small town of Petworth, with its narrow old streets and timbered houses. Temptation awaits, too: this is a center for fine antiques and collectibles, with many excellent shops.

Fodor's Choice ★ **Fishbourne Roman Palace.** In 1960, workers digging a water-main ditch uncovered a Roman wall; so began nine years of archaeological excavation of this site, the remains of the largest, grandest Roman villa in Britain. Intricate mosaics (including Cupid riding a dolphin) and painted walls lavishly decorate what is left of many of the 100 rooms of the palace, built in the 1st century AD, possibly for local chieftain Tiberius Claudius Togidubnus. You can explore the sophisticated bathing and heating systems, along with the only example of a Roman garden in northern Europe. An expansion has added many modern attributes, including a video reconstruction of how the palace might have looked. The site is half a mile west of Chichester. ⊠ *Salthill Rd., Fishbourne* ☎ *01243/785859* ⊕ *www.sussexpast.co.uk* 🖾 *£8.50* ☉ *Feb. and Nov. mid-Dec., daily 10–4; Mar.–Oct., daily 10–5; mid-Dec.–Jan., weekends 10–4.*

Fodor's Choice ★ **Pallant House Gallery.** This small but important collection of mostly modern British art includes work by Henry Moore and Graham Sutherland. It's in a modern extension to Pallant House, a mansion built for a wealthy wine merchant in 1712, and considered one of the finest surviving examples of Chichester's Georgian past. At that time its state-of-the-art design showed the latest in complicated brickwork and superb wood carving. Appropriate antiques and porcelains furnish the faithfully restored rooms. Admission includes entry to the **Hans Feibusch Studio,** nearby in St. Martin's Square, with an exact re-creation of the London studio of this exiled German artist (1898–1998) who was the last member of the so-called degenerate art group. ⊠ *9 N. Pallant* ☎ *01243/774557* ⊕ *www.pallant.org.uk* 🖾 *£9* ☉ *Tues., Wed., Fri., and Sat. 10–5, Thurs. 10–8, Sun. and holiday Mon. 11–5.*

Fodor's Choice ★ **Petworth House.** One of the National Trust's greatest treasures, Petworth is the imposing 17th-century home of Lord and Lady Egremont and holds an outstanding collection of English paintings by Gainsborough, Reynolds, and Van Dyck, as well as 19 oil paintings by J. M. W. Turner, the great proponent of romanticism who often visited Petworth and immortalized it in luminous drawings. A 13th-century chapel is all that remains of the original manor house. The celebrated landscape architect Capability Brown (1716–83) added a 700-acre deer park. Other highlights include Greek and Roman sculpture and Grinling Gibbons wood carvings, such as those in the spectacular Carved Room. Six rooms in the servants' quarters, among them the old kitchen, are also open to the public. A restaurant serves light lunches. You can reach the house off A283; Petworth House is 13 miles northeast of Chichester and 54 miles south of London. ✉ *A283, Petworth* ☎ *01798/342207* 🌐 *www.nationaltrust.org.uk* 🎟 *£12.10; gardens only £4.70* 🕒 *House mid-Mar.–early Nov., Sat.–Wed. 11–5. Gardens Mar.–late Oct., Sat.–Wed. 11–6; Nov.–mid-Dec., Wed.–Sat. 10:30–6. Park daily 8–dusk.*

WHERE TO EAT AND STAY

$$$$ FRENCH 🍴 **Comme Ça.** The location, about a five-minute walk across the park from the Chichester Festival Theatre, makes this a popular spot for pre- and post-theater dinners. The dining room is relaxed and homey, with big windows and ceiling fans. The owner, Michel Navet, is French, and his chef produces sophisticated, authentic French dishes using fresh local produce. The prix-fixe menu changes regularly, but includes dishes like halibut wrapped in smoked salmon served with a horseradish and white wine velouté; or saddle of lamb in a brioche crust with thyme *jus*. The fixed-price lunch menu offers two courses for £22. [$] *Average main: £30* ✉ *67 Broyle Rd.* ☎ *01243/788724* 🌐 *www.commeca.co.uk* 🕒 *Closed Mon. No dinner Sun. No lunch Tues.*

$$ HOTEL 🏨 **Ship Hotel.** Originally the home of Admiral George Murray, one of Admiral Nelson's right-hand men, this architecturally interesting hotel is known for its flying (partially freestanding) staircase and colonnade. **Pros:** well-restored building; good location. **Cons:** rooms are small; not many amenities. [$] *Rooms from: £120* ✉ *North St.* ☎ *01243/778000* 🌐 *www.theshiphotel.net* 🛏 *36 rooms* 🍽 *Multiple meal plans.*

NIGHTLIFE AND THE ARTS

Chichester Festival Theatre. The modernist Chichester Festival Theatre presents classics and modern plays from May through September and is a venue for touring companies the rest of the year. Built in 1962, it has an international reputation for innovative performances and attracts theatergoers from across the country. ✉ *Oaklands Park, Broyle Rd.* ☎ *01243/781312* 🌐 *www.cft.org.uk.*

TUNBRIDGE WELLS AND ENVIRONS

England is famous for its magnificent stately homes and castles, but many of them are scattered across the country, presenting a challenge for travelers. Within a 15-mile radius of Tunbridge Wells, however, in that area of hills and hidden dells known as the Weald, lies a wealth of architectural wonder in historic homes, castles, and gardens: Penshurst Place, Hever Castle, Chartwell, Knole, Ightham Mote, Leeds Castle, and lovely Sissinghurst Castle Garden.

ROYAL TUNBRIDGE WELLS

53 miles east of Chichester, 39 miles southeast of London.

Nobody much bothers with the "Royal" anymore, but Tunbridge Wells is no less regal because of it. Because of its wealth and political conservatism, this historic bedroom community has been the subject of (somewhat envious) British humor for years. Its restaurants and lodgings make it a convenient base for exploring the many homes and gardens nearby.

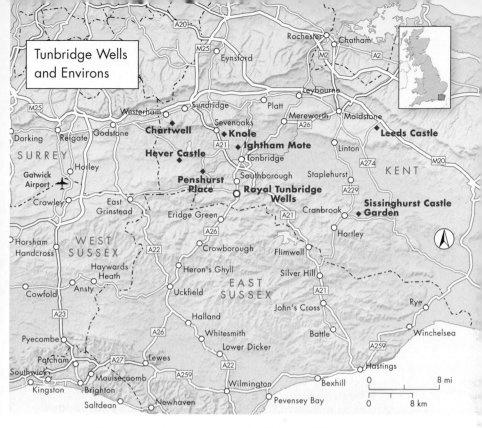

The city owes its prosperity to the 17th- and 18th-century passion for spas and mineral baths. In 1606 a mineral-water spring was discovered here, drawing legions of royal visitors looking for eternal health. Tunbridge Wells reached its zenith in the mid-18th century, when Richard "Beau" Nash presided over its social life. The buildings at the lower end of High Street are mostly 18th century, but as the street climbs the hill north, changing its name to Mount Pleasant Road, structures become more modern.

GETTING HERE AND AROUND

Southeastern trains leave from London's Charing Cross Station every 15 minutes. The journey to Tunbridge Wells takes just under an hour. If you're traveling by car from London, head here on the A21; travel time is about an hour.

Tunbridge Wells sprawls in all directions, but the historic center is compact. None of the sights is more than a 10-minute walk from the main train station. You can pick up a town map at the station.

ESSENTIALS

Visitor Information Royal Tunbridge Wells Tourist Information Centre
✉ *The Old Fish Market, The Pantiles* ☎ *01892/515675*
⊕ *www.visittunbridgewells.com.*

EXPLORING

All Saints Church. This modest 13th-century church holds one of the glories of 20th-century church art. The building is awash with the luminous yellows and blues of 12 windows by Marc Chagall (1887–1985), commissioned as a tribute by the family of a young girl who was drowned in a sailing accident in 1963. The church is 4 miles north of Tunbridge Wells; turn off A26 before Tonbridge and continue a mile or so east along B2017. ⊠ *B2017, Tudeley* ☎ *01732/808277* 🖃 *Free; £2.50 donation requested* ⊘ *Late Mar.–late Oct., daily 9–6; late Oct.–late Mar., daily 9–4.*

Church of King Charles the Martyr. Across the road from the Pantiles, this church dates from 1678, when it was dedicated to Charles I, who had been executed by Parliament in 1649. Its plain exterior belies its splendid interior, with a particularly beautiful plastered baroque ceiling. ⊠ *Chapel Pl.* ☎ *01892/511745* ⊕ *www.kcmtw.org* 🖃 *Free* ⊘ *Mon.–Sat., 11–3.*

Pantiles. A good place to begin a visit is at the Pantiles, a famous promenade with colonnaded shops near the spring on one side of town. Its odd name derives from the Dutch "pan tiles" that originally paved the area. Now sandwiched between two busy main roads, the Pantiles remains an elegant, tranquil oasis, and the site of the actual well of the town's name. ■ TIP→ You can still drink the waters when a "dipper" (the traditional water dispenser) is in attendance, from Easter through September.

WHERE TO EAT

$ ✕ **Himalayan Gurkha.** It's not what you might expect to find in the cozy
NEPALESE   confines of Tunbridge Wells, but the Nepalese cuisine at this friendly spot is popular with locals. Spicy mountain dishes are cooked with care in traditional clay ovens or barbecued on flaming charcoal. The vegetarian options are appealing, too. $ *Average main: £8* ⊠ *31 Church Rd.* ☎ *01892/527834* ⊕ *www.himalayangurkha.com.*

$ ✕ **Kitsu.** Good Japanese food is often difficult to come by in England,
JAPANESE   so this tiny, unassuming restaurant seems an unlikely venue for the best
Fodor's Choice   sushi you're likely to find for miles. Everything is fresh and delicious,
★   from the fragrant miso soup to the light tempura to the sushi platters that are big enough to share. For something heartier, try a bowl of steaming fried noodles or a katsu curry. There are only two drawbacks: the place doesn't take credit cards and doesn't serve alcohol, although you're welcome to bring your own. $ *Average main: £6* ⊠ *82a Victoria Rd.* ☎ *01892/515510* ⊕ *www.kitsu.co.uk* ⊟ *No credit cards.*

$$$$ ✕ **Thackeray's House.** Once the home of Victorian novelist William
FRENCH   Makepeace Thackeray, this mid-17th-century tile-hung house is now an elegant restaurant known for creative French cuisine. The menu changes daily, but often lists such dishes as roast beef with black truffle creamed potato, or poached lemon sole with pistachio crust and caramelized Belgium endive. $ *Average main: £25* ⊠ *85 London Rd.* ☎ *01892/511921* ⊕ *www.thackerays-restaurant.co.uk* ⊘ *Closed Mon. and last wk in Dec. No dinner Sun.*

WHERE TO STAY

$$ HOTEL **Hotel du Vin.** An elegant sandstone house dating from 1762 has been transformed into a chic boutique hotel with polished wood floors and luxurious furnishings. **Pros:** historic building; luxurious linens. **Cons:** restaurant can get booked up; bar can be crowded. [$] *Rooms from: £130* ✉ *Crescent Rd., near Mount Pleasant Rd.* ☎ *01892/526455* 🌐 *www.hotelduvin.com* 🛏 *34 rooms* 🍴 *Breakfast.*

$ HOTEL **Smart & Simple Hotel.** This small place near the train station takes a contemporary approach with rooms that are small but nicely decorated. **Pros:** handy location; free Wi-Fi. **Cons:** few services; no frills at all. [$] *Rooms from: £75* ✉ *54–57 London Rd.* ☎ *01892/552700* 🌐 *www.smartandsimple.co.uk* 🛏 *40 rooms* 🍴 *Some meals.*

$$ HOTEL **Spa Hotel.** Carefully chosen furnishings and period-perfect details help maintain the country-house flavor of this 1766 Georgian mansion. **Pros:** lap-of-luxury feel; gorgeous views. **Cons:** breakfast is extra; very formal atmosphere; can be a bit stuffy. [$] *Rooms from: £160* ✉ *Mount Ephraim* ☎ *01892/520331* 🌐 *www.spahotel.co.uk* 🛏 *70 rooms* 🍴 *No meals.*

PENSHURST PLACE

7 miles northwest of Royal Tunbridge Wells, 33 miles southeast of London.

One of the best preserved of the great medieval houses in Britain, and surrounded by stunning landscaped gardens, Penshurst Place is like an Elizabethan time machine.

GETTING HERE AND AROUND

To get to Penshurst, take the A26 north to Penshurst Road. The drive from Tunbridge Wells takes about 12 minutes. Buses 231 and 233 run from Tunbridge Wells to Penshurst; also 235 weekdays and 237 Saturdays only.

EXPLORING

Fodor's Choice ★ **Penshurst Place.** At the center of the adorable hamlet of Penshurst stands this fine medieval manor house, hidden behind tall trees and walls. Although it has a 14th-century hall, Penshurst is mainly Elizabethan and has been the family home of the Sidneys since 1552. The most famous Sidney is the Elizabethan poet Sir Philip, author of *Arcadia*. The **Baron's Hall,** topped with a chestnut roof, is the oldest and one of the grandest halls to survive from the early Middle Ages. Family portraits, furniture, tapestries, and armor help tell the story of this house that was first inhabited in 1341 by Sir John de Pulteney, the very wealthy four-time London mayor. On the grounds are a toy museum, a gift shop, and the enchanting 11-acre walled Italian Garden, which displays tulips and daffodils in spring, roses in summer. Take time to study the village's late-15th-century half-timber structures adorned with soaring brick chimneys. To get here from Tunbridge Wells, take the A26 and B2176. ✉ *Rogues Hill, off Leicester Square* ☎ *01892/870307* 🌐 *www.penshurstplace.com* 🎟 *£10; grounds only £8* ⏲ *Mid-Feb.–late Mar., weekends 10:30–6; late Mar.–early Nov., daily 10:30–6. Last entry 1 hr before closing.*

WHERE TO EAT

$ BRITISH 🍴 **Spotted Dog.** This pub first opened its doors in 1520 and hardly appears to have changed. Its big inglenook fireplace and heavy beams give it character, the views from the hilltop are lovely, and the good food and friendly crowd make it a pleasure. Many ingredients are locally sourced, as is the ale. There's seating in the sunny garden in the summertime. The pub, which sells locally made ales, is a mile from Penshurst via the narrow B2188. [$] *Average main: £10* ✉ *Smarts Hill* ☎ *01892/870253* 🌐 *www.spotteddogpub.co.uk.*

HEVER CASTLE

3 miles west of Penshurst, 10 miles northwest of Royal Tunbridge Wells, 30 miles southeast of London.

A fairy-tale medieval castle on the outside, and a Tudor mansion within, Hever contains layer on layer of history. It's one of the most unusual and romantic of the great English castles.

GETTING HERE AND AROUND

Hever Castle is best reached via the narrow, often one-lane B2026. From Tunbridge Wells, take A264 east then follow signs directing you north toward Hever.

EXPLORING

Fodor's Choice ★ **Hever Castle.** For some, 13th-century Hever Castle fits the stereotype of what a castle should look like: all turrets and battlements, the whole encircled by a water lily–bound moat. Here, at her childhood home, the unfortunate Anne Boleyn, second wife of Henry VIII and mother of Elizabeth I, was courted and won by Henry. He loved her dearly for a time but had her beheaded in 1536 after she failed to give birth to a son. He then gave Boleyn's home to his fourth wife, Anne of Cleves, as a present. Famous though it was, the castle fell into disrepair in the 19th century. When American millionaire William Waldorf Astor acquired it in 1903, he built a Tudor village to house his staff (it's now used for private functions) and created the stunning gardens, which today include an excellent yew maze, ponds, playgrounds, tea shops, gift shops, plant shops—you get the picture. There's a notable collection of Tudor portraits, and in summer activities are nonstop here, with jousting, falconry exhibitions, and country fairs, making this one of southern England's most rewarding castles to visit. In one of the Victorian wings, B&B rooms go for about £100 per night. ✉ *Off B2026* ☎ *01732/865224* 🌐 *www.hevercastle.co.uk* 🎟 *£15; grounds only £12.50* ⏲ *Castle: Mar., Wed.–Sun., noon–5; Apr.–Oct., daily noon–6; Nov. and Dec., Wed.–Sun. 11–5. Grounds: Mar., Wed.–Sun. 10:30–4; Apr.–Oct., daily 10:30–6; Nov. and Dec., Thurs.–Sun. 10:30–4; last admission 1 hr before closing.*

CHARTWELL

9 miles north of Hever Castle, 12 miles northwest of Royal Tunbridge Wells, 28 miles southeast of London.

Beloved of Winston Churchill, Chartwell retains a homely warmth despite its size and grandeur. Almost as lovely are the grounds, with a rose garden and magnificent views across rolling Kentish hills.

GETTING HERE AND AROUND

From Tunbridge Wells, take A21 north toward Sevenoaks, then turn east onto A25 and follow signs from there. You can travel to Chartwell by bus from the town of Sevenoaks. Take Go Coach 401, but check with the driver to make sure the bus passes near the mansion.

3

EXPLORING

Chartwell. A grand Victorian mansion with views over the Weald, Chartwell was the home of Sir Winston Churchill from 1924 until his death in 1965. Virtually everything has been kept as it was when he lived here, with his pictures, books, photos, and maps. There's even a half-smoked cigar that the World War II prime minister never finished. Churchill was an amateur artist, and his paintings show a softer side of the stiff-upper-lipped statesman. Admission to the house is by timed ticket available only the day of your visit. ■ **TIP→** Be sure to explore the rose gardens and take one of the walks in the nearby countryside. ⊠ *Off B2026* ☎ *01732/866368* ⊕ *www.nationaltrust.org.uk* 🖾 *£12; garden only £6* ⊙ *House Mar.–Oct., daily 11–5. Gardens Mar.–Oct., daily 10–5; Nov.–Feb., daily 11–4; last admission 45 mins before closing.*

KNOLE

8 miles east of Chartwell, 11 miles north of Royal Tunbridge Wells, 27 miles southeast of London.

Perhaps the quintessential Tudor mansion, Knole is as famous for its literary connections and impressive collection of furniture and tapestries as it is for its elegant 15th and 16th century architecture.

GETTING HERE AND AROUND

To get to the town of Sevenoaks from Chartwell, drive north to Westerham, then pick up A25 and head east for 8 miles to A225. The route is well signposted. Southeastern trains travel from London's Charing Cross Station to Sevenoaks every few minutes and take about half an hour. Knole is a 20-minute walk from the train station.

EXPLORING

Fodor's Choice **Knole.** The town of Sevenoaks lies in London's commuter belt, a ★ world away from the baronial air of its premier attraction, the grand, beloved home of the Sackville family since the 16th century. Begun in the 15th century and enlarged in 1603 by Thomas Sackville, Knole, with its complex of courtyards and buildings, resembles a small town. You'll need most of an afternoon to explore it thoroughly. The house is noted for its tapestries, embroidered furnishings, and an extraordinary set of 17th-century silver furniture. Most of the salons are in the pre-baroque mode, rather dark and armorial. The magnificently florid staircase was a novelty in its Elizabethan heyday. Vita Sackville-West grew up here and used it as the setting for her novel *The Edwardians*, a witty account of life among the gilded set. Encircled by a 1,000-acre park where herds of deer roam free, the house lies in the center of Sevenoaks, opposite St. Nicholas Church. ⊠ *Knole La., off A225* ☎ *01732/462100* ⊕ *www.nationaltrust.org.uk* ⊠ *House £10.40, gardens £5; parking £4* ☉ *House Mar., weekends noon–4; Apr.–Oct., Tues.–Sun., noon–4. Gardens Apr.–Sept., Tues. 11–4. Last admission 30 mins before closing.*

IGHTHAM MOTE

7 miles southeast of Knole, 10 miles north of Royal Tunbridge Wells, 31 miles southeast of London.

Almost unique among medieval manor houses in that it still has a moat (although that has nothing to do with the name) Ightham is a captivating, unreal-looking place reached down a warren of winding country lanes.

GETTING HERE AND AROUND

The house sits 6 miles south of Sevenoaks. From Sevenoaks, follow A25 east to A227 and then follow the signs. At the village of Ivy Hatch follow signs to tiny Mote Road, which winds its way to the house. The 404 bus from Sevenoaks stops here on Thursday and Friday only; otherwise you'll have to get off in Ivy Hatch and walk just under a mile from there.

EXPLORING

Fodor's Choice ★ Ightham Mote. Finding Ightham (pronounced "Item") Mote requires careful navigation, but it's worth the effort to see a vision right out of the Middle Ages. To enter this outstanding example of a small manor house, you cross a stone bridge over a dry moat. This moat, however, doesn't relate to the "mote" in the name, which refers to the role of the house as a meeting place, or "moot." Built nearly 700 years ago, Ightham's magical exterior has changed little since the 14th century, but within you'll find that it encompasses styles of several periods, Tudor to Victorian. The Great Hall, Tudor chapel, and drawing room are all highlights. ⊠ *Mote Rd., off A227, Sevenoaks* ☎ *01732/810378* ⊕ *www.nationaltrust.org.uk* ⊠ *£11.50; £5.75 in winter.* ☉ *Mid-Mar.–Oct., Wed.–Mon. 11–5; Dec. (to 23rd), daily 11–3. Closed Nov., Jan., and Feb.*

LEEDS CASTLE

17 miles east of Ightham Mote, 19 miles northwest of Royal Tunbridge Wells, 40 miles southeast of London.

Every inch the grand medieval castle, Leeds is a like a storybook illustration of what an English castle should look like—from the fortresslike exterior to the breathtaking rooms within.

GETTING HERE AND AROUND

Just off the M20 motorway, signs direct you to Leeds Castle from every road in the area, so it's hard to miss.

One of England's most notable stately homes, sprawling Knole displayed the power of the Sackvilles.

EXPLORING

Fodor's Choice
★ **Leeds Castle.** The bubbling River Medway runs through Maidstone, Kent's county seat, with its backdrop of chalky downs. Nearby, the fairy tale stronghold of Leeds Castle commands two small islands on a peaceful lake. Dating to the 9th century and rebuilt by the Normans in 1119, Leeds (not to be confused with the city in the north of England) became a favorite home of many medieval English queens. Henry VIII liked it so much he had it converted from a fortress into a grand palace. The interior doesn't match the glories of the much-photographed exterior, although there are fine paintings and furniture, including many pieces from the 20th-century refurbishment by the castle's last private owner, Lady Baillie. The outside attractions are more impressive and include a maze, a grotto, an aviary of native and exotic birds, and woodland gardens. The castle is 5 miles east of Maidstone. ⊠ A20 ☎ 01622/765400 ⊕ www. leedscastle.org.uk ☜ £20 ⊗ Apr.–Sept., daily 10:30–6 (last admission 4:30); Oct.–Mar., daily 10:30–4 (last admission 3).

SISSINGHURST CASTLE GARDEN

10 miles south of Leeds Castle, 53 miles southeast of London.

Impeccable literary credentials go hand in hand with enchanting grounds, magnificent countryside views, and even a working kitchen garden at this beautiful home in the Sussex countryside.

GETTING HERE AND AROUND

For those without a car, take a train from London's Charing Cross Station and transfer to a bus in Staplehurst. Direct buses operate on Tuesday, Friday, and Sunday between May and August; at other times, take the bus to Sissinghurst village and walk the remaining 1¼ mile. From Leeds Castle, make your way south on B2163 and A274 through Headcorn, and then follow signs.

EXPLORING

Fodor's Choice ★ **Sissinghurst Castle Garden.** One of the most famous gardens in the world, unpretentiously beautiful and quintessentially English, Sissinghurst rests deep in the Kentish countryside. The gardens, with 10 themed "rooms," were laid out in the 1930s around the remains of part of a moated Tudor castle by writer Vita Sackville-West (one of the Sackvilles of Knole, her childhood home) and her husband, diplomat Harold Nicolson. ■ **TIP→ Climb the tower to see Sackville-West's study and to get wonderful views of the garden and surrounding fields. The view is best in June and July, when the roses are in bloom.** The beautiful White Garden is filled with snow-color flowers and silver-gray foliage, while the herb and cottage gardens reveal Sackville-West's encyclopedic knowledge of plants. There are woodland and lake walks, too, making it easy to spend a half day or more here. Stop by the big tea shop for lunch made with the farm's fruits and vegetables. If you'd like to linger, the National Trust rents the Priest's House on the property for a minimum stay of three nights. ✉ *A262* ☎ *01580/710700* 🌐 *www.nationaltrust.org.uk* 🎟 *Jan.–Nov., £10.80; Dec., £5.40* 🕓 *Garden: Mar.–early Nov., daily 11–5:30; Dec., 11–3:30; last admission at 4:30. Closed early–late Nov. Estate: daily dawn–dusk.*

WHERE TO STAY

$ B&B/INN 🏨 **Bishopsdale Oast.** This converted 18th-century double-kiln oast house (used for drying hops) makes an atmospheric place to stay in tiny Biddenden, near Sissinghurst. **Pros:** quiet and restful setting; owner is a chef, so breakfasts are great; nice garden. **Cons:** some rooms are small; car needed to get around. [$] *Rooms from: £90* ✉ *Off Tenterden Rd., Biddenden* ☎ *01580/291027* 🌐 *www.bishopsdaleoast.co.uk* 🛏 *5 rooms* 🍴 *Breakfast.*

$$$ B&B/INN Fodor's Choice ★ 🏨 **Sissinghurst Castle Farmhouse.** On the grounds of Sissinghurst Castle Garden, this beautiful 1885 farmhouse was lovingly restored by the National Trust in 2009; bedrooms are simple but quite spacious, decorated in historical color schemes, and boast sumptuous views across the estate. **Pros:** beautiful location on the grounds of a historic home; lovely hosts; elevator makes building more accessible than most older B&Bs; discounts for two or more nights. **Cons:** few amenities; need a car to get here. [$] *Rooms from: £165* ✉ *The Street, Sissinghurst* ☎ *01580/720992* 🌐 *www.sissinghurstcastlefarmhouse.com* 🛏 *7 rooms* 🍴 *Breakfast.*

THE SOUTH

WELCOME TO THE SOUTH

TOP REASONS TO GO

★ **Salisbury Cathedral:** This impressive Early English cathedral offers spectacular views over the surrounding countryside from its roof and spire, England's tallest.

★ **Stonehenge:** The power and mystery of this Neolithic stone circle on Salisbury Plain remain spellbinding.

★ **House and garden at Stourhead:** The cultivated English landscape is at its finest here, with an 18th-century Palladian stately home and beautiful gardens adorned with neoclassical temples.

★ **The New Forest:** Get away from it all in the South's most extensive woodland, crisscrossed by myriad trails that are ideal for horseback riding, hiking, and biking.

★ **Literary trails:** Jane Austen, Thomas Hardy, John Fowles, and Ian McEwan have made this area essential for book buffs, with a concentration of sights in Chawton, Dorchester, Chesil Beach, and Lyme Regis.

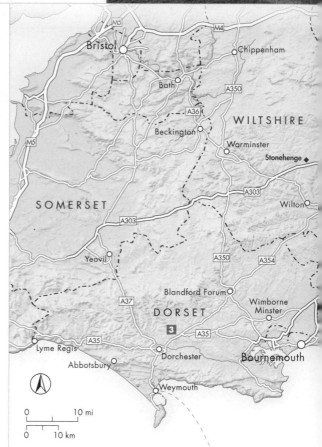

1 Winchester, Portsmouth, and Environs. One of the region's most culturally and historically significant towns, Winchester lies a short distance from the genteel village of Chawton, home to Jane Austen, and the great south-coast port of Portsmouth.

2 Salisbury, Stonehenge, and Salisbury Plain. Wiltshire's great cathedral city of Salisbury is close to the prehistoric monuments of Stonehenge and Avebury, as well as Wilton House, a Palladian estate. Farther afield are more great estates, Stourhead and Longleat.

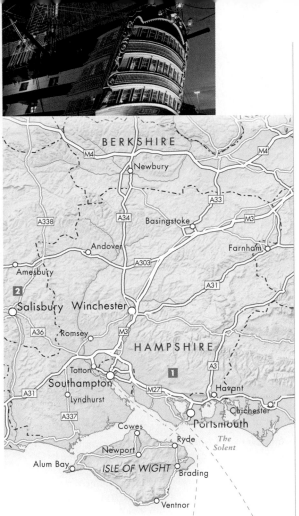

4

GETTING ORIENTED

In the south of England, the inland county of Wiltshire's wide-open Salisbury Plain offers a sharp contrast to the sheltered villages of coastal Hampshire and Dorset and the bustle of the port city of Portsmouth. Spend your nights in the culturally compelling towns of Salisbury and Winchester. Salisbury puts you within easy reach of Stonehenge and also the equally ancient stone circles at Avebury. From there you can swing south to the New Forest. Lyme Regis, on the southern coast of Dorset at the center of the wide arc of Lyme Bay, is a vacation favorite. It provides a gateway to the Jurassic Coast, a World Heritage Site that stretches between Swanage in the east and Exmouth in Devon.

3 New Forest, Dorset, and the South Coast.
The sparsely populated New Forest stretches south of Salisbury to the coast. The route west passes ruined Corfe Castle. Also worth a stop is the market town of Sherborne, as well as Dorchester and coastal Weymouth and Lyme Regis.

Updated by
Ellin Stein

The South—made up of Hampshire, Dorset, and Wiltshire counties—has played a central role in England's history for over 4,000 years, occupied successively by prehistoric man, the Celts, the Romans, the Saxons, the Normans, and the modern British. The area contains notable attractions as well as quieter pleasures. Two important cathedrals, Winchester and Salisbury (pronounced *sawls*-bree), are here, as are classic stately homes—such as Longleat, Stourhead, and Wilton House—and prehistoric sites, two of which, Avebury and Stonehenge, are of world-class significance.

These are just the tourist-brochure highlights. Anyone spending time in these parts should rent a bike or a car and set out to discover the back-road villages and larger market towns. Close to London, the green fields of Hampshire divide the cliffs and coves of the West Country from the sprawl of the suburbs. Even if you have a coastal destination in mind, hit the brakes—there's plenty to see. Originally a Roman town, historic Winchester was made capital of the ancient kingdom of Wessex in the 9th century by Alfred the Great, a pioneer in establishing the rule of law and considered to be the first king of a united England. The city is dominated by its imposing cathedral, the final resting place of notables ranging from Saxon kings to the son of William the Conqueror to Jane Austen. It's a good base for visiting the villages associated with several of England's literary greats, including Chawton, home to Jane Austen.

North of Hampshire and the New Forest lies the somewhat harsher terrain of Salisbury Plain, part of it owned by the British army and used for training and weapons testing. Two monuments, millennia apart, dominate the plain. One is the 404-foot-tall stone spire of Salisbury Cathedral, the subject of one of John Constable's finest paintings. Not far away is the most imposing and dramatic prehistoric structure in Europe: Stonehenge. The many theories about its construction and purpose only add to its otherworldly allure. Other sub-regions have their own appeal, and many are of literary or historical interest. The Dorset countryside immortalized in the novels of Thomas Hardy, composed of grass-covered chalk hills (downs), wooded valleys, meandering rivers, and meadows, is interspersed with unspoiled market towns and villages. Busy beach resorts such as Lyme Regis perch next to hidden coves on the fossil-rich Jurassic Coast. Though short on historic buildings due to wartime bombing, the port city of Portsmouth is rich in history itself; from here Nelson sailed to the Battle of Trafalgar, Allied forces to Normandy on D-Day, and British forces to the Falklands.

SOUTH PLANNER

WHEN TO GO

In summer the coastal resorts are crowded; it may be difficult to find the accommodations you want. The New Forest is most alluring in spring and early summer (for the foaling season) and fall (for the colorful foliage), whereas summer can be busy with walkers and campers. In all seasons, take waterproof boots for the mud and puddles. Major attractions such as Stonehenge and Longleat House attract plenty of people at all times; bypass such sights on weekends, public holidays, or school vacations. Don't plan to visit the cathedrals of Salisbury and Winchester on a Sunday, when your visit will be restricted, or during services, when it won't be appreciated by worshippers.

PLANNING YOUR TIME

The South has no obvious hub, though many people base themselves in one or both of the cathedral cities of Winchester and Salisbury and make excursions to nearby destinations. The coastal city of Portsmouth has its charms but is not particularly attractive as an overnight stop. To escape the bustle, the New Forest, west of Portsmouth, offers space and semi-wilderness. It's easy to take a morning or afternoon break to enjoy the activities it offers, whether on foot, by bike, or on horseback.

GETTING HERE AND AROUND

BUS TRAVEL

National Express buses at London's Victoria Coach Station on Buckingham Palace Road depart every one to two hours for Portsmouth (1¾ hours), and every two to three hours for Winchester (1¾ hours). There are five buses daily to Salisbury (about 3 hours). Bluestar operates a comprehensive service in the Winchester area, and Stagecoach South has service in Portsmouth and around Hampshire. Salisbury Red serves Salisbury, and First serves Portsmouth and Dorchester. More and Salisbury Reds both offer one-day Dayrider passes as well as weekly and monthly Period passes valid on all routes. Ask about the Megarider tickets offered by Stagecoach. Contact Traveline for all information on routes and tickets.

Bus Contacts Bluestar ☎ 023/8023–1950 ⊕ www.bluestarbus.co.uk. **First** ☎ 0871/200–2233 ⊕ www.firstgroup.com. **More** ☎ 0845/072–7093 ⊕ www.morebus.co.uk. **National Express** ☎ 0871/781–8178 ⊕ www. nationalexpress.com. **Salisbury Reds** ☎ 0845/072–093 ⊕ www.salisburyreds. co.uk. **Stagecoach South** ☎ 0845/121–0190 ⊕ www.stagecoachbus.com. **Traveline** ☎ 0871/200–2233 ⊕ www.traveline.org.uk.

CAR TRAVEL

On the whole, the region is easily negotiable using public transportation. But for rural spots, especially the grand country estates, a car is useful. The well-developed road network includes M3 to Winchester (70 miles from London); A3 to Portsmouth (77 miles); and M27 along the coast, from the New Forest and Portsmouth. For Salisbury, take M3 to A303, then A30. For Dorchester and Lyme Regis, take A35; A350 runs north to Dorset's inland destinations.

TRAIN TRAVEL

South West Trains serves the South from London's Waterloo Station. Travel times average 1 hour to Winchester, 1½ hours to Salisbury, and 1¾ hours to Portsmouth. A yearlong Network Railcard, valid throughout the South and Southeast, entitles you and up to three accompanying adults to one-third off most train fares, and up to four accompanying children ages 5–15 to a 60% discount off each child fare. It costs £30.

Train Contacts National Rail Enquiries ☏ *0845/748–4950*
⊕ *www.nationalrail.co.uk.* **South West Trains** ☏ *0845/600–0650*
⊕ *www.southwesttrains.co.uk.*

TOURS

The Guild of Registered Tourist Guides maintains a directory of qualified Blue Badge guides who can meet you anywhere in the region for private tours. Local organizations such as Wessexplore can also arrange Blue Badge tours.

Tour Information Guild of Registered Tourist Guides ☏ *0207/403–1115*
⊕ *www.britainsbestguides.org.* **Wessexplore** ☏ *01722/326304*
⊕ *www.dmac.co.uk/wessexplore.*

RESTAURANTS

In summer, and especially on summer weekends, visitors can overrun the restaurants in small villages, so either book a table in advance or be prepared to wait. The more popular or upscale the restaurant, the more critical a reservation is. For local specialties, try fresh-grilled river trout or sea bass poached in brine, or dine like a king on New Forest's renowned venison. Hampshire is noted for its pig and sheep farming, and you might zero in on pork and lamb dishes on local restaurant menus. The region places a strong emphasis on seasonal produce, so venison, for example, is best sampled between September and February.

HOTELS

Modern hotel chains are well represented, and in rural areas you can choose between elegant country-house hotels, traditional coaching inns (updated to different degrees), and modest guesthouses. Some seaside hotels don't accept one-night bookings in summer. *Hotel reviews have been shortened. For full information, visit Fodors.com.*

WHAT IT COSTS IN POUNDS				
	$	**$$**	**$$$**	**$$$$**
Restaurants	under £15	£15–£19	£20–£25	over £25
Hotels	under £100	£100–£160	£161–£220	over £220

Restaurant prices are the average cost of a main course at dinner or, if dinner isn't served, at lunch. Hotel prices are the lowest cost of a standard double room in high season, including 20% V.A.T.

VISITOR INFORMATION
Visitor Information Southwest Tourism Alliance ☎ *0117/230–262* ⊕ *www.visitsouthwest.co.uk.* **Tourism South East** ☎ *023/8062–5400* ⊕ *www.visitsoutheastengland.com.*

4

WINCHESTER, PORTSMOUTH, AND ENVIRONS

From the cathedral city of Winchester, 70 miles southwest of London, you can meander southward to the coast, stopping at the bustling port of Portsmouth to explore its maritime heritage.

WINCHESTER

66 miles southwest of London, 29 miles northwest of Portsmouth.

Winchester is among the most historic of English cities, and as you walk the graceful streets and wander the many public gardens, a sense of the past envelops you. Although it's now merely the county seat of Hampshire, for more than four centuries Winchester served first as the capital of the ancient kingdom of Wessex and then of England. The first king of England, Egbert, was crowned here in AD 827, and the court of his successor, Alfred the Great, was based here until Alfred's death in 899. After the Norman Conquest in 1066, William I ("the Conqueror") had himself crowned in London, but took the precaution of repeating the ceremony in Winchester. William also commissioned the local monastery to produce the Domesday Book, a land survey begun in 1085. The city remained the center of ecclesiastical, commercial, and political power until the 13th century, when that power shifted to London. Despite its deep roots in the past, Winchester is also a thriving market town living firmly in the present, with numerous shops and restaurants on High Street.

GETTING HERE AND AROUND
On a main train line and on the M3 motorway, Winchester is easily accessible from London. The train station is a short walk from the sights; the bus station is in the center, opposite the tourist office. The one-way streets are notoriously confusing, so find a parking lot as soon as possible. The city center is very walkable, and most of High Street is closed to vehicular traffic. A walk down High Street and Broadway will bring you to St. Giles Hill, which has a panoramic view of the city.

TIMING

The city is busier than usual during the farmers' market, the largest in the country, held on the second and last Sunday of each month.

ESSENTIALS

Visitor and Tour Information Winchester Tourist Guides
⊕ www.winchestertouristguides.com. **Winchester Tourist Information Centre**
✉ The Guildhall, Broadway ☎ 01962/840500 ⊕ www.visitwinchester.co.uk.

EXPLORING
TOP ATTRACTIONS

Great Hall. A short walk west of the cathedral, this hall is all that remains of the city's Norman castle, and it's still used today for events and ceremonies. It's thought the English Parliament had one of its first meetings here in 1246; Sir Walter Raleigh was tried for conspiracy against King James I in 1603; and Dame Alice Lisle was sentenced to death by the brutal Judge Jeffreys for sheltering fugitives, after Monmouth's Rebellion in 1685. The hall's greatest artifact hangs on its west wall: King Arthur's Round Table has places for 24 knights and a portrait of Arthur bearing a remarkable resemblance to King Henry VIII. In fact, the oak table dates back only to the 13th century and was painted by order of Henry in 1522 on the occasion of a visit by the Holy Roman Emperor Charles V; one theory is that the real Arthur was a Celtic chieftain who held off the invading Saxons after the fall of the Roman Empire in the 5th or 6th century. The Tudors were among several British monarchs who periodically revived the Arthurian legend for political purposes. Take time to wander through the garden named for two Queens, Eleanor of Provence and Eleanor of Castille—a re-creation of a medieval shady retreat. ✉ Castle Hill ☎ 01962/846476 ⊕ www.hants.gov.uk/greathall ☞ Free ☉ Daily 10–5.

Fodor's Choice ★ **Highclere Castle.** Set in 1,000 acres of parkland designed by Capability Brown, the historic home of the actual Earls of Carnarvon—as opposed to the imaginary Earls of Grantham of period television drama *Downton Abbey*, which is shot here—owes its appearance to Sir Charles Barry, architect of the Houses of Parliament. Commissioned by the 3rd Earl to transform a simpler Georgian mansion, Barry used golden Bath stone to create this fantasy castle bristling with Gothic turrets. Like its fictional counterpart, it served as a hospital during World War I. Highlights of the state rooms include Van Dyke's equestrian portrait of Charles I in the dining room and the imposing library (Lord Grantham's retreat). There's also an exhibit of Egyptian antiquities collected by the 5th Earl, known for his pivotal role in the 1920s excavation of ancient Egyptian tombs, notably Tutankhamen's. Get good views of the house and countryside by walking the gardens and grounds. The house is 25 miles north of Winchester and 5 miles south of Newbury; there's train service from London and Winchester to Newbury, and taxis can take you the 5 miles to Highclere. ✉ Off A34, Highclere Park, Newbury ☎ 01635/253204 ⊕ www.highclerecastle.co.uk ☞ £16 castle, exhibition, and gardens; £9.50 castle and gardens or exhibition; £5 gardens only ☉ July–mid-Sept., Sun.–Thurs. 10:30–6; last admission at 4. Also selected days Apr.–June.

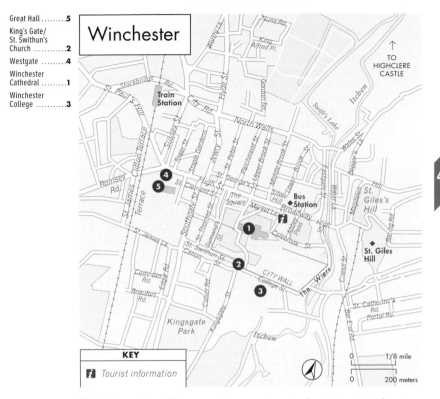

King's Gate. One of two surviving gateways in the city's original ancient walls, this structure to the south of the Close is thought to date back to 1300. The tiny medieval **St. Swithun's Church** is on the upper floor. ⊠ *South of the Close.*

Fodor's Choice ★ **Winchester Cathedral.** The city's greatest monument, begun in 1079 and consecrated in 1093, presents a sturdy, chunky appearance in keeping with its Norman construction, so that the Gothic lightness within is even more breathtaking. Its tower, transepts, and crypt, and the inside core of the great Perpendicular nave, reveal some of the world's best surviving examples of Norman architecture. Other features, such as the arcades, the presbytery (behind the choir, holding the high altar), and the windows, are Gothic alterations carried out between the 12th and 14th centuries. Little of the original stained glass has survived, except in the large window over the entrance. When Cromwell's troops ransacked the cathedral in the 17th century, locals hid away bits of stained glass they found on the ground so that it could later be replaced. The Library and Triforium Gallery contains the Winchester Bible, one of the finest remaining 12th-century illuminated manuscripts.

Among the many well-known people buried in the cathedral are William the Conqueror's son, William II ("Rufus"), mysteriously murdered in the New Forest in 1100; Izaak Walton (1593–1683), author of *The Compleat Angler,* whose memorial window in Silkestede's Chapel was paid for by "the fishermen of England and America"; and Jane Austen, whose grave lies in the north aisle of the nave. The tombstone makes no mention of Austen's literary status, though a brass plaque in the wall, dating from 80 years after her death, celebrates her achievements, and modern panels provide an overview of her life and work. Firmly in the 20th century, Antony Gormley's evocative statue *Sound II* (1986) looms in the crypt, as often as not standing in water (as it was designed to do), because of seasonal flooding. You can also explore the bell tower—with far-reaching views in fair weather—and other recesses of the building on a tour. Special services or ceremonies may mean the cathedral is

ST. SWITHUN WEATHER

St. Swithun (died AD 862) is interred in Winchester Cathedral, although he requested outdoor burial. Legend says that when his body was transferred inside from the cathedral's churchyard, it rained for 40 days. Since then, folk wisdom says that rain on St. Swithun's Day (July 15) means 40 more days of wet weather. (Elsewhere in England the name is usually spelled "Swithin.") Near St. Swithun's Church at King's Gate, 8 College Street, is the house where Jane Austen died on July 18, 1817, three days after writing a comic poem about the legend of St. Swithun's Day (copies are usually available in the cathedral).

closed to visits, so call ahead. Outside the cathedral, explore the Close, the area to the south of the cathedral that boasts neat lawns and the Deanery, Dome Alley, and Cheyney Court. ⊠ *The Close, Cathedral Precincts* 🕾 *01962/857200* ⊕ *www.winchester-cathedral.org.uk* 🖂 *Cathedral £7.50; bell tower £6; cathedral and bell tower £9.50* ☉ *Cathedral Mon.–Sat. 10–4 (last admission 3), Sun. 12:30–2:30. Library and Triforium Gallery Apr.–Oct., Mon. 2–4, Tues.–Sat. and national holidays 10:30–4; Nov.–Mar., Sat. 10:30–3:30. Free tours on the hr Mon.–Sat. 10–3, bell tower tours May–Sept., Mon. and Fri. 2:15, Sat. 11:30 and 2:15; Oct.–mid-Nov., Jan.–Apr., Wed. 2:15, Sat. 11:30 and 2:15; late Nov.–Dec., "twilight tower tour," see website for details.*

WORTH NOTING

FAMILY **Westgate.** This atmospheric fortified medieval gateway with its stunning Tudor ceiling was a debtor's prison for 150 years, and now holds a motley assortment of artifacts relating to Tudor and Stuart times, displayed among the 16th-century graffiti by former prisoners. Child-size replicas of authentic 16th-century armor that can be tried on, as well as the opportunity to make brass rubbings, make it popular with kids. You can take in a view of Winchester from the roof. ⊠ *Upper High St.* 🕾 *01962/869864* 🖂 *Free* ☉ *Apr.–Oct., Sat. 10–5, Sun. noon–5; early Nov.–Mar., Sat. 10–4, Sun. noon–4.*

Winchester College. One of England's oldest "public" (meaning private) schools was founded in 1382 by Bishop William of Wykeham, whose alabaster tomb sits in a chapel dedicated to him in Winchester Cathedral. The school's own chapel is notable for its delicately vaulted ceiling. Among the buildings still in use is Chamber Court, center of college life for six centuries. Notice the "scholars"—students holding academic scholarships—clad in their traditional gowns. Call about tours, sometimes canceled due to college events. ✉ *College St.* ☎ *01962/621209* 🌐 *www.winchestercollege.org* 🎟 *£6* 🕒 *1-hr tours Mon., Wed., Fri., and Sat. 10:45, noon, 2:15, and 3:30, Tues. and Thurs. 10:45 and noon, Sun. 2:15 and 3:30.*

WHERE TO EAT

$$ MODERN BRITISH

🍴 **The Bistro at Hotel du Vin.** Classic French and British fare is served with modern touches in this stylish bistro paneled in light wood, converted from a redbrick Georgian town house. Such dishes as sea bass *en papillote* are complemented by the many eclectic wine selections. In summer, meals are served on a terrace and in a walled garden. The hotel's luxurious rooms are richly furnished in crisp modern style. [$] *Average main: £18* ✉ *14 Southgate St.* ☎ *01962/841414* 🌐 *www.hotelduvin.com.*

$$ MODERN BRITISH

🍴 **Chesil Rectory.** The timbered and gabled building may be Old English—it dates back to the mid-15th century—but the cuisine is Modern British, using locally sourced ingredients. Dishes might include venison carpaccio for a starter, followed by slow-cooked pork rib eye or oven-roasted halibut. Good-value fixed-price lunches and early-evening dinners are available. Service and the heritage charm of the surroundings enhance the quality of the food. [$] *Average main: £17* ✉ *1 Chesil St.* ☎ *01962/851555* 🌐 *www.chesilrectory.co.uk.*

$ CAFÉ

🍴 **Ginger Two for Tea.** This bright and airy corner café is the place to come for a relaxed afternoon tea. White walls and wooden furniture lend it a modern, rustic feel. The kitchen serves simple lunches, locally baked cakes and pastries, and a variety of teas and coffees. The cakes and coffees are acclaimed, the sandwiches and service less so. Try such seasonal dishes as butternut squash soup or crepes with salmon. You'll find this place on a quiet road off High Street. [$] *Average main: £6* ✉ *29 St. Thomas St.* ☎ *01962/877733* 🕒 *No dinner.*

$ BRITISH

🍴 **Green's Wine Bar.** Everything is served cafeteria style at this local favorite, which offers delicious comfort food like chicken and leek pie, lamb stew with dumplings, and panini at reasonable prices. The space is small, but sidewalk seating means there's plenty of space in good weather. In the evening, the place transforms into a busy bar, and there's a DJ and dancing on weekends. Despite the name, the atmosphere and beverage selection make the place more like a lively pub than a sophisticated wine bar. [$] *Average main: £8* ✉ *4 Jewry St.* ☎ *01962/869630.*

WHERE TO STAY

$$$ HOTEL Fodor's Choice ★

🏨 **Lainston House.** The 63 acres surrounding this elegant 17th-century country house retain many original features, including the walls of the kitchen garden (still in use), the apple trees in the former orchard, and a mile-long avenue of linden trees, the longest in Europe. **Pros:** beautiful setting; atmospheric guest rooms. **Cons:** lower-priced modern rooms small; country house "shabby chic" not to everyone's taste. [$] *Rooms from: £165* ✉ *Woodman La., off B3049, Sparsholt* ☎ *01962/776088* 🌐 *www.lainstonhouse.com* 🛏 *25 rooms, 25 suites or Jr. suites* 🍽 *Some meals.*

$$
B&B/INN

⌂ **Old Vine.** Blessed with an ideal location opposite the cathedral, this 18th-century inn, now a gastro-pub with rooms, has received a smart, modern makeover without losing any of its character. **Pros:** elegant rooms; delicious food; attentive service. **Cons:** rooms over the bar may be noisy on weekends. $ *Rooms from: £105* ⌂ *8 Great Minster St.* ☎ *01962/854616* ⊕ *www.old vinewinchester.com* 🛏 *6 rooms* ⫩*Breakfast.*

$$
B&B/INN

⌂ **Wykeham Arms.** A watering hole since 1755, this pub with rooms near the cathedral and the college wears its Britishness proudly, with decor that features photos of such national heroes as Nelson and Churchill, military artifacts, and an assortment of pewter mugs hanging from the ceiling. **Pros:** quirky charm; lively bar; good food. **Cons:** rooms above the bar can be noisy; no kids under 14; small portions at restaurant. $ *Rooms from: £129* ⌂ *75 Kingsgate St.* ☎ *01962/853834* ⊕ *www.fullershotels.com* 🛏 *13 rooms, 1 suite* ⫩*Breakfast.*

> **OPEN-AIR MARKETS**
>
> Among the best open-air markets is the Winchester Farmers' Market held in Winchester's Middle Brook Street on the second and the last Sunday of each month. It specializes in local produce and goods. Also worth a look are Salisbury's traditional Charter Market (Tuesday and Saturday); and Dorchester's large market (Wednesday) and Farmers' Market (fourth Saturday).

SHOPPING

Kingsgate Books and Prints. This is a good stop for a selection of secondhand books, maps, and prints. ⌂ *Kingsgate Arch, College St.* ☎ *01962/864710.*

King's Walk. Off Friarsgate, King's Walk has a number of stalls selling antiques, crafts, and bric-a-brac.

P&G Wells. The oldest bookshop in the country, P&G Wells has numerous books by and about Jane Austen, who had an account here and died almost next door in 1817. It also has the region's largest selection of children's books. ⌂ *11 College St.* ☎ *01962/852016.*

CHAWTON

16 miles northeast of Winchester.

In Chawton you can visit the home of Jane Austen (1775–1817), who lived the last eight years of her life in the village, moving to Winchester only during her final illness. The site has always drawn literary pilgrims, but with the ongoing release of successful films based on her novels, the town's popularity among visitors has grown enormously.

GETTING HERE AND AROUND

Hourly Stagecoach bus X64 service connects Winchester and New Alresford with Chawton. It's a 10-minute walk from the bus stop to Jane Austen's House. By car, take A31. Alternatively, take a 40-minute stroll along the footpath from Alton.

IN SEARCH OF JANE AUSTEN

Jane Austen used this tiny writing table at her home in Chawton.

Jane Austen country—verdant countryside interspersed with relatively unspoiled villages—still bears traces of the decorous early-19th-century life the writer described with wry wit in novels such as *Emma, Persuasion, Sense and Sensibility,* and *Pride and Prejudice.* You can almost hear the clink of teacups raised by the likes of Elinor Dashwood and Mr. Darcy. Serious Janeites will want to retrace her life in the towns of Bath (*see Chapter 7*), Chawton, Winchester, and Lyme Regis.

BATH
Bath is the elegant setting that served as a backdrop for the society Austen observed with such razor sharpness. She lived in Bath between 1801 and 1806, and although she wrote relatively little while she was here, she used it as a setting for *Northanger Abbey* and *Persuasion.* Bath's Jane Austen Centre explores her relationship to the city.

CHAWTON
About 83 miles southeast of Bath is this tiny Hampshire village, the heart of Jane Austen country. Here you'll find the elegant but understated house, a former bailiff's cottage on her brother's estate, where Austen worked on three of her novels. It's now a museum that effectively evokes her life there.

WINCHESTER
Driving southwest from Chawton, take the A31 for about 15 miles to Winchester, where you can visit Austen's austere grave within the cathedral and view an exhibit about her life; then see the commemorative plaque on No. 8 College Street, where her battle with Addison's disease ended with her death on July 18, 1817.

LYME REGIS
Heading 110 miles southwest of Winchester you can visit Lyme Regis, the 18th-century seaside resort on the Devon border where Austen spent the summers of 1804 and 1805. Here, at the Cobb, the stone jetty that juts into Lyme Bay, poor Louisa Musgrove jumps off the steps known as Granny's Teeth—a turning point in Chapter 12 of *Persuasion.*

EXPLORING

Fodor's Choice ★ **Jane Austen's House.** Here, in an unassuming redbrick house, Jane Austen wrote *Emma, Persuasion,* and *Mansfield Park,* and revised *Sense and Sensibility, Northanger Abbey,* and *Pride and Prejudice.* Now a museum, the house retains the modest but genteel atmosphere suitable to the unmarried daughter of a clergyman. In the drawing room there's a piano similar to the one Jane would play every morning before repairing to a small writing table in the family dining parlor—leaving her sister, Cassandra, to do the household chores ("I find composition impossible with my head full of joints of mutton and doses of rhubarb," Jane wrote). In the early 19th century the road near the house was a bustling thoroughfare, and one traveler reported that a window view proved that the Misses Austen were "looking very comfortable at breakfast." Jane was famous for working through interruptions, but one protection against the outside world was the famous door that creaked. She asked that its hinges remain unattended to because they gave her warning that someone was coming. It's often closed for special events, so call ahead. ✉ *Winchester Rd., signed off A31/A32 roundabout* ☎ *01420/83262* 🌐 *www.jane-austens-house-museum.org.uk* 🎟 *£7.50* 🕒 *Jan.–mid-Feb., weekends 10:30–4:30; mid-Feb.–May and Sept.–Dec., daily 10:30–4:30; June–Aug., daily 10–5; last admission 30 mins before closing.*

WHERE TO STAY

$$$$ HOTEL 🏨 **Four Seasons Hotel Hampshire.** Although deep in the peaceful British countryside, this country-house hotel on a 500-acre estate is only a half hour from Heathrow. **Pros:** peaceful location; great spa; plenty of activities. **Cons:** dogs are welcome (a pro or a con); not in the center of any action. [$] *Rooms from: £225* ✉ *Dogmersfield Park, Chalky La., Hook* ☎ *01252/853000* 🌐 *www.fourseasons.com/hampshire* 🛏 *111 rooms, 22 suites* 🍴 *No meals.*

PORTSMOUTH

24 miles south of Chawton, 77 miles southwest of London.

Besides a historic harbor and revitalized waterfront, Portsmouth has the energy of a working port. At the newly developed Gunwharf Quays, you'll find the soaring Spinnaker Tower as well as shops, restaurants, bars, and a contemporary art gallery. The main attraction for many visitors is Admiral Nelson's well-preserved HMS *Victory,* the flagship from which he won the Battle of Trafalgar (on view at the Portsmouth Historic Dockyard), and the extraordinary record of seafaring history at the Royal Navy museum. For others, Portsmouth is primarily of interest for the ferries that set off from here to the Isle of Wight and more distant destinations.

GETTING HERE AND AROUND

The M27 motorway from Southampton and the A3 from London take you to Portsmouth. There are also frequent buses and trains that drop you off at the Hard, the main transport terminus, which is only a few steps from the Historic Dockyard and Gunwharf Quays. Regular passenger ferries cross Portsmouth Harbour from the Hard

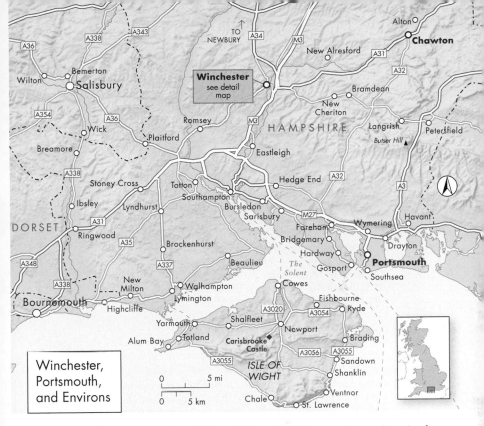

Winchester
see detail
map

Winchester,
Portsmouth,
and Environs

0   5 mi

0   5 km

for Gosport's Royal Navy Submarine Museum. Attractions in the nearby town of Southsea are best reached by car or by buses departing from the Hard.

ESSENTIALS

Visitor Information Portsmouth Visitor Information Centre ✉ *D-Day Museum, Clarence Esplanade, Southsea* ☎ *023/9282–6722* ⊕ *www.visitportsmouth.co.uk.*

EXPLORING

TOP ATTRACTIONS

FAMILY **D-Day Museum.** In the absorbing D-Day Museum in nearby Southsea, an eclectic range of exhibits illustrates the planning and logistics involved in the D-Day landings, as well as the actual invasion on June 6, 1944. The museum's centerpiece is the Overlord Embroidery ("Overlord" was the code name for the invasion), a 272-foot-long embroidered cloth with 34 panels illustrating the history of World War II, from the Battle of Britain in 1940 to D-Day and the first days of the liberation. ✉ *Clarence Esplanade, Southsea* ☎ *023/9282-7261* ⊕ *www.ddaymuseum. co.uk* ✍ *£6.50* ⊙ *Apr.–Sept., daily 10–5:30; Oct.–Mar., daily 10–5; last admission 30 mins before closing.*

FAMILY
Fodor's Choice
★

Portsmouth Historic Dockyard. The city's most impressive attraction includes an unrivaled collection of historic ships. The dockyard's youngest ship, **HMS** *Warrior* (1860), was England's first ironclad battleship. British naval hero Admiral Lord Horatio Nelson's flagship, **HMS** *Victory,* is in the process of being painstakingly restored to appear as it did at the battle at Trafalgar (1805). You can inspect the cramped gun decks, visit the cabin where Nelson entertained his officers, and stand on the spot where he was mortally wounded by a French sniper. A museum opened in 2013 houses the *Mary Rose,* the former flagship of the Tudor navy. Built in this very dockyard more than 500 years ago, the boat sank in the harbor in 1545 before being raised in

> ## RULING THE WAVES
>
> England invested heavily in its Royal Navy, to defend its island shores and later to access its far-flung empire. In 1495, Henry VII ordered the building of Europe's first dry dock, still located in Portsmouth. Henry VIII built up the navy (his warship the *Mary Rose* is on view at the Historic Dockyard), but it was still considered no match for the Spanish Armada, which attacked in 1588. Nevertheless, the English Navy beat back the invaders. Over the next two centuries, Britain made its navy the world's largest and most powerful, a distinction it held up to World War II.

1982. Described in the 16th century as "the flower of all the ships that ever sailed," it's berthed in a special enclosure where water continuously sprays the timbers to prevent them from drying out and breaking up.

The **National Museum of the Royal Navy** has extensive exhibits about Nelson and the battle of Trafalgar, a fine collection of painted figureheads, and galleries of paintings and mementos recalling naval history from King Alfred to the present. **Action Stations,** an interactive attraction, gives insight into life in the modern Royal Navy and tests your sea legs with tasks such as piloting boats through gales. **Dockyard Apprentice** showcases the skills of the shipbuilders and craftsmen who constructed and maintained the naval vessels, with illustrations of rope making, sail making, caulking, signals, and knots. You should allow one or two days to tour all the attractions in the Historic Dockyard. ■**TIP**➔ The entrance fee includes a boat ride around the harbor. ⊠ *Historic Dockyard, Victory Gate* ☎ *023/9283–9766* ⊕ *www. historicdockyard.co.uk* ⊠ *£26 includes harbor tour* ☉ *Apr.–Oct., daily 10–5:30; Nov.–Mar., daily 10–5; last admission 1 hr before closing.*

QUICK
BITES

Boathouse No. 7. In the heart of the Historic Dockyard, Boathouse No. 7 is a family-friendly eatery in a converted 18th-century boathouse a stone's throw from the HMS *Victory*. The kitchen dishes out traditional favorites like shepherd's pie and baked potatoes, as well as lighter options like freshly made sandwiches, salads, and soups. Kids can enjoy the "treasure trove" lunchbox filled with healthy snacks. You can eat here without purchasing a ticket to the museums. ⊠ *Historic Dockyard, Victory Gate* ☎ *023/9283– 8060* ⊕ *www.historicdockyard.co.uk.*

You can tour Admiral Nelson's famous flagship, the HMS *Victory*, at Portsmouth's Historic Dockyard.

WORTH NOTING

Millennium Promenade. Starting at the Spinnaker Tower, the Millennium Promenade meanders through Old Portsmouth and along the seafront. The 4-mile self-guided walk, marked by a rope pattern on the sidewalk, passes though the original port, where fishing boats still dock, and where press gangs forcibly enlisted young men for the Royal Navy in the 18th century. Follow it to Clarence Pier in Southsea. ⊠ *Gunwharf Quays.*

FAMILY **Royal Navy Submarine Museum.** The highlight here is a tour of the World War II submarine HMS *Alliance,* from the cramped quarters to the engine room. The museum fills you in on submarine history and lets you view Portsmouth Harbour through a periscope. There are plenty of submarine-related artifacts, as well as three actual subs spread around the large site. From Portsmouth Harbour, take the ferry to Gosport and walk along Millennium Promenade past the huge sundial clock. ⊠ *Halsar Jetty Rd., Gosport* ☎ *023/9251–0354* ⊕ *www.submarine-museum. co.uk* ✑ *£12.50* ☉ *Apr.–Oct., daily 10–5:30; Nov.–Mar., Wed.–Sun.10– 4:30; last tour 1 hr before closing.*

WHERE TO EAT

$ ✕ **Abarbistro.** A relaxed, modern bistro midway between Old Portsmouth and Gunwharf Quays, this place is ideal for a snack, a full MODERN BRITISH meal, or just a glass from the thoughtfully chosen wine list. The changing Modern British menu specializes in seafood dishes, mostly sourced from Portsmouth's fish market right opposite, and may include *moules marinière,* fish cakes, or salmon Wellington; alternatively, opt for the sirloin steak and fries, or mushroom risotto. You can sit indoors, in a garden at the back, or at Continental-style tables on the pavement. $ *Average main: £12* ⊠ *58 White Hart Rd.* ☎ *023/9281–1585* ⊕ *www.abarbistro.co.uk.*

$$$$ × **Montparnasse.** Modern photographs on cinnamon walls add a con-
BRITISH temporary touch to this relaxed restaurant. The fixed-price menus (£32.50 and £37.50) specialize in British classics with a twist, like pork belly with homemade sausage rolls or a mushroom-and-potato pavé with poached tomatoes. Desserts such as a macadamia with praline parfait are to die for. The service is discreet but attentive and knowledgeable. $ *Average main: £35* ⊠ *103 Palmerston Rd., Southsea* ☎ *023/9281–6754* ⊕ *www.bistromontparnasse.co.uk* ⊗ *Closed Sun. and Mon.*

SALISBURY, STONEHENGE, AND SALISBURY PLAIN

This area is filled with sites of cultural and historical interest, including the handsome city of Salisbury, renowned for its spectacular cathedral, and the iconic prehistoric sites at Stonehenge and Avebury. A trio of stately homes reveals the ambitions and wealth of their original aristocratic inhabitants—Wilton House with its Inigo Jones–designed state rooms, Stourhead and its exquisite neoclassical gardens, and the Elizabethan splendor of Longleat. Your own transportation is essential to get to anything beyond Salisbury, other than Stonehenge or Avebury.

SALISBURY

36 miles southeast of Portsmouth, 20 miles west of Winchester, 79 miles southwest of London.

The silhouette of Salisbury Cathedral's majestic spire signals your approach to this historic city long before you arrive. Although the cathedral is the principal focus of interest here (and its Cathedral Close is one of the country's most atmospheric spots, especially on a foggy night), Salisbury has much more to see, not least its largely unspoiled—and relatively traffic-free—old center. Here are stone shops and houses that over the centuries grew up in the shadow of the great church. You're never far from any of the five rivers that meet here, or from the bucolic water meadows that stretch out to the west of the cathedral and provide the best views of it. Salisbury didn't become important until the early 13th century, when the seat of the diocese was transferred here from Old Sarum, the original settlement 2 miles to the north, of which only ruins remain. In the 19th century, novelist Anthony Trollope based his tales of ecclesiastical life, notably Barchester Towers, on life here, although his fictional city of Barchester is really an amalgam of Salisbury and Winchester. The local tourist office organizes walks—of differing lengths for varying levels of stamina—to guide you to the must-sees. And speaking of must-sees, prehistoric Stonehenge is less than 10 miles away and easily visited from the city.

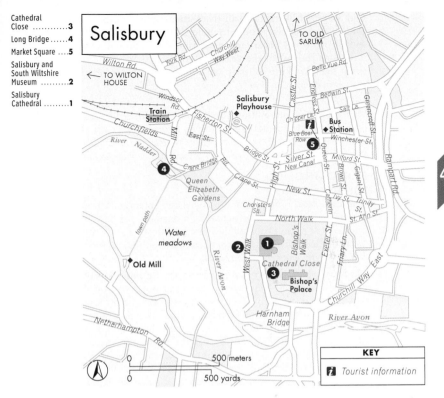

GETTING HERE AND AROUND

Salisbury is on main bus and train routes from London and South-ampton; regular buses also connect Salisbury with Winchester. The bus station is centrally located on Endless Street; trains stop west of the center. After negotiating a ring-road system, drivers will want to park as soon as possible. The largest of the central parking lots is by Salisbury Playhouse. The city center is compact, so you won't need to use local buses for most sights. For Wilton House, take Bus Red 3 from New Canal, near Market Square.

TIMING

Market Square hosts general markets every Tuesday and Saturday and farmers' markets on the first and third Wednesday of the month. It's also the venue for other fairs and festivals, notably the one-day Food & Drink Festival in mid-September and the three-day Charter Fair in October. The city gets busy during the arts festival in May and June, when accommodations may be scarce.

TOURS

The Stonehenge Tour has hop-on, hop-off open-top buses leaving once or twice an hour all year from the train station and the bus station, and the route includes Old Sarum and Salisbury Cathedral as well as Stonehenge. Tickets cost £12; £20 includes a tour of Stonehenge and

Old Sarum, £24 includes all three attractions. Salisbury City Guides offers 90-minute city tours by Blue Badge guides, departing from the tourist office at 11 every morning from April through October and on weekends the rest of the year. The cost is £5. Wessexplore has everything from walking tours to trips in luxury cars to a helicopter ride over Stonehenge.

ESSENTIALS

Visitor and Tour Information Salisbury City Guides ☎ *07873/212941* ⊕ *www.salisburycityguides.co.uk.* **Salisbury Information Centre** ⊠ *Fish Row, off Market Sq.* ☎ *01722/342860* ⊕ *www.visitwiltshire.co.uk/salisbury.* **Stonehenge Tour** ☎ *0845/072–7093* ⊕ *www.thestonehengetour.co.uk.*

EXPLORING
TOP ATTRACTIONS

Cathedral Close. With its smooth lawns and splendid examples of architecture from many periods creating a harmonious background, Salisbury's Close forms probably the finest backdrop of any British cathedral. Some of the historic houses are open to the public. ⊠ *Bounded by West Walk, North Walk, and Exeter St.*

Old Sarum. Massive earthwork ramparts in a bare sweep of Wiltshire countryside are all that remain of this impressive Iron Age hill fort, which was successively taken over by Romans, Saxons, and Normans (who built a castle and cathedral within the earthworks). The site was still fortified in Tudor times, though the population had mostly decamped in the 13th century for the more amenable site of New Sarum, or Salisbury. You can clamber over the huge banks and ditches and take in the bracing views over the chalk downland to Salisbury Cathedral. ⊠ *Off A345, 2 miles north of Salisbury* ☎ *01722/335398* ⊕ *www.english-heritage.org.uk* ⊠ *£3.90* ☉ *Apr.–June and Sept., daily 10–5; July and Aug., daily 9–6; Oct. and Mar., daily 10–4; Nov., Jan., and Feb., daily 11–4.*

Salisbury and South Wiltshire Museum. Opposite the cathedral's west front, this excellent museum is in the King's House, parts of which date back to the 15th century (James I stayed here in 1610 and 1613). Models and exhibits in the Stonehenge Gallery provide helpful background information for a visit to the famous stones. Also on view are skeletons, collections of costumes, lace, embroidery, Wedgwood pottery, and a collection of Turner watercolors, all dwarfed by the medieval pageant figure of St. Christopher, a 14-foot-tall giant, and his companion hobbyhorse, Hob Nob. A cozy café (closed Sunday) is in one of the oldest sections of the building. ⊠ *The King's House, 65 The Close* ☎ *01722/332151* ⊕ *www.salisburymuseum.org.uk* ⊠ *£6* ☉ *July and Aug., Mon.–Sat. 10–5, Sun. noon–5; Sept.–June, Mon.–Sat. 10–5.*

Fodor's Choice ★ **Salisbury Cathedral.** Salisbury is dominated by the towering cathedral, a soaring hymn in stone. It is unique among cathedrals in that it was conceived and built as a whole in the amazingly short span of 38 years (1220–58). The spire, added in 1320, is the tallest in England and a miraculous feat of medieval engineering—even though the point, 404 feet above the ground, is 2½ feet off vertical. For a fictional, keenly

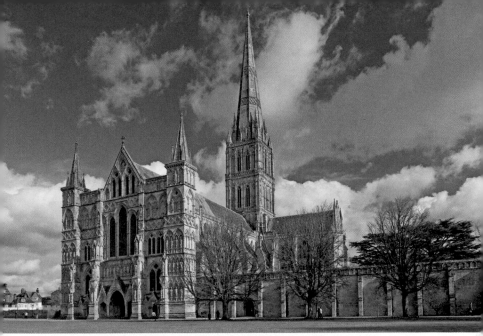

Salisbury Cathedral has a towering spire—the tallest in England—that you can tour.

imaginative reconstruction of the drama underlying such an achievement, read William Golding's novel *The Spire*. The excellent model of the cathedral in the north nave aisle, directly in front of you as you enter, shows the building about 20 years into construction, and makes clear the ambition of Salisbury's medieval builders. For all their sophistication, the height and immense weight of the great spire have always posed structural problems. In the late 17th century Sir Christopher Wren was summoned from London to strengthen the spire, and in the mid-19th century Sir George Gilbert Scott, a leading Victorian Gothicist, undertook a major program of restoration. He also initiated a clearing out of the interior and removed some less-than-sympathetic 18th-century alterations, returning a more authentically Gothic feel. Despite this, the interior seems spartan and a little gloomy, but check out the remarkable lancet windows and sculpted tombs of crusaders and other medieval notables. Next to the cathedral model in the north aisle is a medieval clock—probably the oldest working mechanism in Europe, if not the world—made in 1386.

The **cloisters** are the largest in England, and the octagonal **Chapter House** contains a marvelous 13th-century frieze showing scenes from the Old Testament. Here you can also see one of the four original copies of the **Magna Carta**, the charter of rights the English barons forced King John to accept in 1215; it was sent here for safekeeping in the 13th century. ■ TIP➔ **Join a free 45-minute tour of the church, leaving two or more times a day. There are also daily tours of the roof and spire (except on Sunday morning) that vary in frequency—check website.** For a peaceful break, the café in the cloister offers freshly baked cakes and pastries, plus hot lunches. ✉ *Cathedral Close* ☎ *01722/555150* ⊕ *www.salisburycathedral.org.uk* ✎ *Cathedral and Chapter House free; suggested donation £6.50; tower tour £10* ⊙ *Cathedral: Apr.–Sept., Mon.–Sat. 9–5, Sun. noon–4; Oct.–Mar., daily 10–4:30. Chapter House: Mon.–Sat. 9:30–4:30, Sun. 12:45–3:45.*

Fodor's Choice

★

Wilton House. This is considered to be one of the loveliest stately homes in England and, along with its grounds, a fine example of the English Palladian style. The seat of the earls of Pembroke since Tudor times, the south wing of the current building was rebuilt in the early 17th century by Isaac de Caus, with input from Inigo Jones, Ben Jonson's stage designer and the architect of London's Banqueting House. It was completed by James Webb, again with input from Jones, Webb's uncle-by-marriage, after the recently finished south wing was ravaged by fire in 1647. Most noteworthy are the seven state room in the south wing, among them the Single Cube Room (built as a perfect 30-foot cube) and one of the most extravagantly beautiful rooms in the history of interior decoration, the aptly named Double Cube Room. The name refers to its proportions (60 feet long by 30 feet wide and 30 feet high), evidence of Jones's classically inspired belief that beauty in architecture derives from harmony and balance. The room's headliner is the spectacular Van Dyck portrait of the Pembroke family. Elsewhere at Wilton House, the art collection includes several other old master paintings, including works by Rembrandt and members of the Brueghel family. Also of note are the lovely grounds, which have sweeping lawns dotted with towering oaks; the gardens; and the Palladian bridge crossing the small River Nadder, designed by the 9th Earl after the Rialto Bridge in Venice. ■TIP➜ **Be sure to explore the extensive gardens; children will appreciate the large playground.** The town of Wilton is 3 miles west of Salisbury. Buses 2, 13, 25, 26, 27, and Red 3 from Salisbury stop outside Wilton House. They depart every 10 to 15 minutes. ✉ *Off A36, Wilton* ☎ *01722/746714* ⊕ *www.wiltonhouse.co.uk* ✎ *£14; grounds only £5.50* ⊙ *House: Easter and May–Aug., Sun.–Thurs. 11:30–5. Grounds: early Apr.–mid-Apr. and May–mid-Sept., daily 11–5:30.*

DOUBLE CUBE ROOM

Adorned with gilded furniture by William Kent, Wilton House's Double Cube was where Eisenhower and Churchill prepared plans for the D-Day landings during World War II. It has been used in many films, including *The Madness of King George, Mrs. Brown,* the 2005 version of *Pride and Prejudice,* Emma Thompson's adaptation of *Sense and Sensibility,* and *The Young Victoria.*

WORTH NOTING

Long Bridge. For a classic view of Salisbury, head to the Long Bridge and the Town Path. From the main street walk west to Mill Road, which leads you across Queen Elizabeth Gardens. Cross the bridge and continue on the Town Path through the water meadows from which you can see the vista John Constable painted to create that 19th-century icon, *Salisbury Cathedral,* now hung in the Constable Room of London's National Gallery.

Market Square. One of southern England's most popular markets fills this square on Tuesday and Saturday. Permission to hold an annual fair here was granted in 1221, and that right is still exercised for three days every October, when the Charter Fair takes place. A narrow side street links Poultry Cross to Market Square. ✉ *Market Sq.*

FOOD AND DRINK FESTIVAL

Salisbury forces you to squeeze a lot in during its one-day **Food & Drink Festival** (☎ *01722/332241* 🌐 *www.salisburyfestival.co.uk*) in mid-September. There are wine and beer tents, a waiters' race, cooking demonstrations, barbecues, and festival menus in the restaurants. The main venue is Market Square.

QUICK BITES

Fisherton Mill. A former grain mill, Fisherton Mill houses artist studios and exhibition spaces showcasing paintings, sculptures, textiles, and jewelry. Enjoy a light lunch or Wiltshire cream tea in the well-regarded café. It shuts down for the day at 5, except for Sunday when it's closed. ✉ ***108 Fisherton St.*** ☎ ***01722/415121*** 🌐 ***www.fishertonmill.co.uk.***

WHERE TO EAT

$ CAFÉ 🍴 **Boston Tea Party.** Specializing in quick, nourishing meals, this relaxed and child-friendly café serves hot and cold breakfasts, lunches, and afternoon snacks. Homemade meat and vegetarian burgers with interesting toppings like red-onion marmalade or chili sauce, come with potato wedges. The huge vegan Super Salad is enlivened with mango and grapefruit. Freshly roasted coffee and a wide selection of teas are a nice complement to the freshly baked cakes. You can eat upstairs in the spectacular Tudor great hall or the quieter side room. [$] *Average main: £7* ✉ *13 High St.* ☎ *01722/238116* 🌐 *www.bostonteaparty.co.uk* 🕑 *No dinner.*

$ BRITISH 🍴 **Haunch of Venison.** This wood-paneled pub opposite the Poultry Cross has been going strong for more than six centuries. It brims with character, thanks to details such as the mummified hand of an 18th-century card player still clutching his cards and the last pewter-top bar in England. You can fortify yourself with one of the 80 or so malt whiskies or repair to the upstairs restaurant for dishes such as panfried sea bass or venison and bacon casserole. The pub can be crowded and the service (to nonlocals) brusque. [$] *Average main: £13* ✉ *1 Minster St.* ☎ *01722/411313* 🌐 *www.restaurant-salisbury.com.*

$$$$ MODERN BRITISH 🍴 **Howard's House.** If you're after complete tranquillity, head for this early-17th-century house set on 2 acres of grounds in the Nadder Valley. The style is traditional and smart, and a terrace provides alfresco dining overlooking the tidy lawns in summer. Sophisticated contemporary fare makes up most of what's on the set-price menus, such as fillet of wild turbot with goat cheese gnocchi, and breast of guinea fowl with seared foie gras. Nine luxuriously furnished guest rooms may tempt you into forgoing the 10-mile drive back to Salisbury. [$] *Average main: £32* ✉ *Off B3089, Teffont Evias* ☎ *01722/716392* 🌐 *www.howardshousehotel.co.uk.*

Salisbury, Stonehenge, and Salisbury Plain

WHERE TO STAY

$
B&B/INN
Cricket Field House. Located halfway between Wilton and Salisbury, this comfortable ex-gamekeeper's cottage overlooks a cricket ground and has a large, peaceful garden of its own. **Pros:** efficient, helpful management; well-maintained rooms; good breakfasts. **Cons:** dated decor; on a busy road; lacks charm. $ *Rooms from: £85* ✉ *Wilton Rd.* ☎ *01722/322595* ⊕ *www.cricketfieldhouse.co.uk* ⇄ *18 rooms* ❍| *Breakfast.*

$
B&B/INN
Rokeby Guest House. Easy to find on the east side of town, this four-story Edwardian B&B represents good value for your money with its spic-and-span, tastefully decorated interiors and a large, landscaped garden with a summerhouse. **Pros:** convenient location; helpful hosts; abundant and tasty breakfasts. **Cons:** not central. $ *Rooms from: £65* ✉ *3 Wain-a-Long Rd.* ☎ *01722/329800* ⊕ *www.rokebyguesthouse. co.uk* ⇄ *10 rooms* ❍| *Breakfast.*

$
B&B/INN
Wyndham Park Lodge. This simple Victorian house in a quiet part of town (off Castle Street) provides an excellent place to rest and a delicious breakfast, as well as a garden. **Pros:** efficient and hospitable owners; convenient location; good breakfast; handy parking. **Cons:** spotty Wi-Fi connection. $ *Rooms from: £55* ✉ *51 Wyndham Rd.* ☎ *01722/416517* ⊕ *www.wyndhamparklodge.co.uk* ⇄ *3 rooms* ❍| *Breakfast.*

STONEHENGE

8 miles north of Salisbury, 20 miles south of Avebury.

The famous stone circles on the Salisbury Plain still hold mysteries after many centuries. The surrounding landscape, too, is dotted with ancient earthworks and ceremonial pathways, all related to the rituals held here, a testament to the sophisticated belief system of these early Britons.

GETTING HERE AND AROUND

Stonehenge Tour buses leave from Salisbury's train and bus stations every half hour starting at 9:30 am from June to August and hourly beginning at 10 between September and May. Tickets cost £12, or £20 with a tour of Stonehenge. Other options are a taxi or a custom tour. Drivers will find the monument near the junction of A303 and A344.

EXPLORING

Fodor'sChoice **Stonehenge.** Almost five millennia after their construction, the stone
★ circles on the Salisbury Plain continue to fascinate people from around the world: more than a million visitors come each year to this UNESCO World Heritage Site. Stonehenge—the name derives from the Anglo-Saxon term for "hanging stones"—was begun as early as 3000 BC with the construction of a circular earthwork enclosure. The nearby Cursus, long rectangular earthwork banks, were also created around this time. The stone circle itself was completed in stages, beginning around 2500 BC with the inner circle of bluestones. It underwent changes and remained in use until around 1600 BC. The early inner circle was later (c. 2300 BC) surrounded by an outer circle of 30 sarsen stones, huge sandstone blocks weighing up to 25 tons, which are believed to have originated from the Marlborough Down. Within these two circles was a horseshoe-shape group of sarsen trilithons (two large vertical stones supporting a third stone laid horizontally across it), each sarsen averaging 45 tons, and within that another horseshoe-shape grouping of bluestones. It's still not known how the huge stones were brought here from as far away as Wales before the invention of the wheel. Similarly, the primary reason for their erection remains unknown. It's fairly certain that Stonehenge was a religious site, and that worship here involved the cycles of the sun, but why the stones were aligned with the midsummer sunrise and the midwinter sunset remains unclear. Stonehenge is not an isolated monument, but part of a much larger complex of ceremonial structures. You can sort through the latest theories by picking up an audio guide, viewing an exhibition of artifacts found at the site, or by picking up some books at the visitor center. The surrounding landscape, which you can explore on foot, is dotted with ancient earthworks and ceremonial pathways, all connected to the rituals held here. The improved visitor center is located 1½ miles away (access is via a frequent 10-minute shuttle), with parking, audio-guide rental, a café, and an exhibition of prehistoric objects found at the site. There's also a dramatic display using time-lapse photography that puts you (virtually) in the center of the circle as the seasons change. ■TIP➜ English Heritage arranges access to the stone circle outside of normal hours. These tours cost £21. Book well in advance. ⊠ *Junction of A303 and*

A344/A360, Amesbury ☎ *0870/333–1181, 01722/343830 for private tours* ⊕ *www.english-heritage.org.uk* ☑ *£14.90* ☉ *Late Mar.–May and Sept.–mid-Oct., daily 9:30–7; June–Aug., daily 9–8; mid-Oct.–mid-Mar., daily 9:30–5. Last admission 2 hours before closing.*

AVEBURY

24 miles north of Stonehenge, 34 miles north of Salisbury, 25 miles northeast of Longleat, 27 miles east of Bath.

The village of Avebury was built much later than the stone circles that bring the visitors; it has an informative museum with an outstanding collection of Bronze Age artifacts from the area around Stonehenge. You can also explore a cluster of other prehistoric sites nearby.

4

GETTING HERE AND AROUND

From Salisbury, follow A345 north to Upavon and take the A342 to Devizes; then continue 7 miles northeast on the A361. You can also take the hourly Stagecoach bus No. 49 from Swindon to Avebury (30 minutes).

EXPLORING

TOP ATTRACTIONS

FAMILY **Alexander Keiller Museum.** Archaeological finds from the Avebury area, and charts, photos, models, and home movies taken by archaeologist Alexander Keiller himself, put the Avebury Stone Circles and the site into context. Recent revelations suggest that Keiller, responsible for the excavation of Avebury in the 1930s, may have adapted the site's layout more in the interests of presentation than authenticity. The exhibits are divided between the **Stables Gallery,** showing excavated finds, and the more child-friendly, interactive **Barn Gallery.** You can also visit the Elizabethan manor house where Keiller lived, which has interactive exhibits on his work and the excavation. ✉ *1 mile north of A4* ☎ *01672/539250* ⊕ *www.nationaltrust.org.uk* ☑ *£4.90* ☉ *Apr.–Oct., daily 10–6; Nov.–Mar., daily 10–4.*

Fodor's Choice **Avebury Stone Circles.** Surrounding part of Avebury village, the Avebury
★ Stone Circles are one of England's most evocative prehistoric monuments—not so famous as Stonehenge, but all the more powerful for their lack of commercial exploitation. The stones were erected around 2600 BC, about the same time as the better-known monument. As with Stonehenge, the purpose of this stone circle has never been ascertained, although it most likely was used for similar ritual purposes. Unlike Stonehenge, however, there are no certain astronomical alignments at Avebury, at least none that have survived. The main site consists of a wide, circular ditch and bank, about 1,400 feet across and more than half a mile around. Entrances break the perimeter at roughly the four points of the compass, and inside stand the remains of three stone circles. The largest one originally had 98 stones, although only 27 remain. Many stones on the site were destroyed centuries ago, especially in the 14th century when they were buried for unclear reasons, possibly religious fanaticism. Others were later pillaged in the 18th century to build the thatched cottages you see flanking the fields. You can walk around the circles at any time; early morning and early evening are recommended. ✉ *1 mile north of A4* ⊕ *www.nationaltrust.org.uk* ☑ *Free* ☉ *Daily.*

TIPS FOR VISITING STONEHENGE

WHEN TO VISIT

Come early before the crowds arrive, or in the evening when the light is low. Summer weekends and school holidays can be especially crowded. Stonehenge is packed at Summer Solstice, when visitors stay all night to watch the sun rise. If you want to visit at this time, use the dedicated bus service from Salisbury.

English Heritage can arrange access to the inner circle (not a guided tour) outside of regular hours; each group is 26 people maximum. This requires application and payment of £21 well in advance, as Stone Circle Access visits are popular. Apply by mail or fax, call the booking office at ☎ 0870/333–0605, or email 📠 stonecircleaccess@english-heritage.org.uk. The booking form is available at ⊕ www.english-heritage.org.uk.

The visitor center is 1.5 miles from the stones. Frequent shuttles take you to the circle itself, a 10-minute trip.

WHAT TO BRING

Since the stones are roped off, bring binoculars to see the prehistoric carvings on them. Spend a few hours: walk all around the site to get that perfect photo and to see the equally ancient earthworks. The free audio guide is essential, and the shop sells plenty of books.

MAKING A DAY OF IT

The Salisbury and South Wiltshire Museum in Salisbury has finds from the site and burial reconstructions that help put Stonehenge into perspective. The smaller Alexander Keiller Museum in Avebury has finds from the area. It's an easy drive between nearby prehistoric sites. Stonehenge is set in 1,500 acres of National Trust land with excellent walks.

GETTING HERE

By car, Stonehenge is 2 miles west of Amesbury off A344. The **Stonehenge Tour Bus** (⊕ www.thestonehengetour.info) departs from Salisbury rail and bus stations frequently; buses leave every half hour or hour. Tickets cost £12, or £20 with Stonehenge and Old Sarum admission. Other options are a taxi or an organized tour. **Salisbury and Stonehenge Guided Tours** (⊕ www.salisbury guided tours.com ☎ 07775/674816) operates tours from Salisbury and London.

VISITOR INFORMATION

✉ Off A303 at Airman's Corner, near Amesbury ☎ 0870/333–1181, 0870/333–0605 for after-hours access ⊕ www.english-heritage.org.uk 🎟 £14.90 ⊙ Mid-Mar.–May and Sept.–mid-Oct., daily 9:30–7; June–Aug., daily 9–8; mid-Oct.–mid-Mar., daily 9:30–5. Last admission 2 hours before closing.

WORTH NOTING

Cherhill Down. Four miles west of Avebury, Cherhill Down is a prominent hill carved with a vivid white horse and topped with a towering obelisk. It's one of a number of hillside etchings in Wiltshire, all but two of which date back no farther than the late 18th century. This one was put there in 1780 to indicate the highest point of the downs between London and Bath. The views from the top are well worth the half-hour climb. The best view of the horse is from A4, on the approach from Calne. ✉ A4.

Kennet Stone Avenue. The Avebury monument lies at the end of the Kennet Stone Avenue, a sort of prehistoric processional way leading to the stone circles. The avenue's stones were spaced 80 feet apart, but only the half mile nearest the main monument survives intact. The lost stones are marked with concrete obelisks.

Silbury Hill. Rising 130 feet and comparable in height and volume to the roughly contemporary pyramids in Egypt, the largest man-made mound in Europe dates from about 2400 BC. Though there have been periodic excavations of the mound since the 17th century, its original purpose remains unknown. The viewing area, less than 1 mile east of Avebury, is accessible only during daylight hours. ✉ *A4.*

West Kennet Long Barrow. One of the largest Neolithic chambered tombs in Britain, West Kennet Long Barrow was built around 3400 BC. You can explore all around the site and also enter the tomb, which was used for more than 1,000 years before the main passage was blocked and the entrance closed, around 2000 BC. More than 300 feet long, it has an elevated position with a great view of Silbury Hill and the surrounding countryside. It's about 1 mile east of Avebury. ✉ *A4.*

4

WHERE TO EAT AND STAY

$ BRITISH 🍴 **Waggon and Horses.** A 16th-century thatched building, this traditional inn and pub is a two-minute drive from the prehistoric circle. Dickens mentioned the building in the *Pickwick Papers*. Excellent lunches and dinners are served beside a fire. Homemade dishes include steak, kidney, and ale pie, pork terrine, and goat's cheese and spinach risotto. In high season it's something of a tourist hub. [$] *Average main: £10* ✉ *A4, east of A361, Beckhampton* ☎ *01672/539418.*

$$$ B&B/INN 🏨 **The Lodge.** The spacious rooms of this charming B&B are full of character, thanks to the eclectic decor, rare prints, and antique furnishings, but its special appeal is its one-of-a-kind location within the Avebury Stone Circles, which the two guest rooms look out on. **Pros:** great views; comfortable rooms; friendly host. **Cons:** can book up. [$] *Rooms from: £175* ✉ *High St.* ☎ *01672/539023* 🌐 *www.aveburylodge.co.uk* 🛏 *2 rooms* 🍽 *Breakfast.*

LONGLEAT HOUSE

31 miles southwest of Avebury, 6 miles north of Stourhead, 19 miles south of Bath, 27 miles northwest of Salisbury.

With its popular safari park and a richly decorated High Elizabethan-style house to explore, Longleat can provide a day of diversions.

GETTING HERE AND AROUND

Longleat House is off A36 between Bath and Salisbury. The nearest train station is Warminster, about 5 miles away. Your best option is to take a taxi from there.

ESSENTIALS

Visitor Information Warminster Information Centre ✉ *Central car park, off Station Rd.* ☎ *01985/218548* 🌐 *www.visitwiltshire.co.uk.*

EXPLORING

FAMILY **Longleat House.** Home of the Marquess of Bath, Longleat House is one of southern England's most famous private estates, and possibly the most ambitiously, even eccentrically, commercialized, as evidenced by the presence of a drive-through safari park (open since 1966) with giraffes, zebras, monkeys, rhinos, and lions. The Italian Renaissance-style building was largely completed in 1580 (for more than £8,000, an astronomical sum at the time) and contains outstanding tapestries, paintings, porcelain, and furniture, as well as notable period features such as the Victorian kitchens, an Elizabethan minstrels' gallery, and the great hall with its massive wooden beams. Giant antlers of the extinct Irish elk decorate the walls, as do the present marquess's occasionally raunchy murals—described as "keyhole glimpses into my psyche" that range from philosophical subjects to depictions of the Kama Sutra. Besides the safari park, Longleat has a butterfly garden, a miniature railway, an extensive (and fairly fiendish) hedge maze, and an adventure castle, all of which make it extremely popular, particularly in summer and during school vacations. ■ **TIP→ You can easily spend a whole day here. Visit the house in the morning, when tours are more relaxed, and the safari park in the afternoon.** A safari bus service is available (£4) for those arriving without their own transport. ✉ *Off A362* ☎ *01985/844400* 🌐 *www.longleat.co.uk* 🎟 *£29.50; house and grounds only, £14.50* ⏲ *Mar., daily 10–5; Apr.–mid-July and mid-Sept.–late Oct., daily 10–6; late July–early Sept., daily 10–7:30; Nov. and Dec., call in advance.*

WHERE TO STAY

$$ HOTEL 🏨 **Bishopstrow House.** This ivy-covered Georgian manor house set in 27 acres has been converted into a relaxed country-house hotel that combines well-chosen antiques with modern amenities such as DVD players. **Pros:** country-house ambience; impressive suites; excellent leisure facilities. **Cons:** expensive extras; restaurant lacks charm; some standard rooms dark; unpredictable heating. [$] *Rooms from: £145* ✉ *Boreham Rd.* ☎ *01985/212312* 🌐 *www.bishopstrow.co.uk* 🛏 *29 rooms, 3 suites* 🍴 *Breakfast.*

STOURHEAD

9 miles southwest of Longleat, 15 miles northeast of Sherborne, 30 miles west of Salisbury.

England has many memorable gardens, but Stourhead is one of the most glorious. Its centerpiece is a magnificent artificial lake surrounded by neoclassical temples, mysterious grottoes, and rare trees. The Palladian stately home is also worth a look.

GETTING HERE AND AROUND

By car, you can reach Stourhead via B3092; it's signposted off the main road. From London, board a train to Gillingham and take a five-minute cab ride to Stourton.

EXPLORING

Fodor's Choice ★ **Stourhead.** Close to the village of Stourton lies one of Wiltshire's most breathtaking sights—Stourhead, a country-house-and-garden combination that has few parallels for beauty anywhere in Europe. Most of Stourhead was built between 1721 and 1725 by Henry the Magnificent, the wealthy banker Henry Hoare. A fire gutted the center of the house in 1902, but it was reconstructed with only a few differences. Many rooms in the Palladian mansion contain Chinese and French porcelain, and some have furniture by Chippendale. The elegant Regency library and picture gallery were built for the cultural enrichment of this cultivated family. Still, the house takes second place to the adjacent gardens designed by Henry Hoare II, which are the most celebrated example of the English 18th-century taste for "natural" landscaping. Temples, grottoes, and bridges have been placed among shrubs, trees, and flowers to make the grounds look like a three-dimensional oil painting. A walk around the artificial lake (1½ miles) reveals changing vistas that conjure up the 17th-century landscapes of Claude Lorrain and Nicolas Poussin; walk counterclockwise for the best views. **■TIP→ The best time to visit is early summer, when the massive banks of rhododendrons are in full bloom, or mid-October for autumn color, but the gardens are beautiful at any time of year.** You can get a fine view of the surrounding area from Alfred's Tower, a 1772 folly (a structure built for picturesque effect). A restaurant and a plant shop are on the grounds. All in all, it's easy to spend half a day here. ✉ *Off B3092, northwest of Mere* ☎ *01747/841152* 🌐 *www.nationaltrust.org.uk* 🎟 *House £14.20 house; gardens £8.50; Alfred's Tower £3.50* 🕒 *House: mid-Mar.–Oct., daily 11–4:30. Gardens: Apr.–Sept., daily 9–7; Oct., daily 9–5. Alfred's Tower: Mar.–Oct., weekends noon–4.*

WHERE TO STAY

$$ B&B/INN 🏨 **The Spread Eagle.** You can't stay at Stourhead, but you can stay at this popular inn built at the beginning of the 19th century just inside the main entrance. **Pros:** period character; lovely rooms; free access to Stourhead. **Cons:** needs some modernization; food can be disappointing and service brusque. $ *Rooms from: £120* ✉ *Off B3092, northwest of Mere* ☎ *01747/840587* 🌐 *www.spreadeagleinn.com* 🛏 *5 rooms* 🍴 *Breakfast.*

NEW FOREST, DORSET, AND THE SOUTH COAST

Just southeast of Salisbury, the New Forest was once a hunting preserve of William the Conqueror and his royal descendants. Thus protected from the deforestation that has befallen most of southern England's other forests, this relatively wild, scenic expanse offers great possibilities for walking, riding, and biking. West of here stretches the green, hilly, and largely unspoiled county of Dorset, the setting for most of the books of Thomas Hardy, author of *Far from the Madding Crowd* and other classic Victorian-era novels. "I am convinced that it is better for a writer to know a little bit of the world remarkably well than to know a great part of the world remarkably little," Hardy wrote. The bit he chose to examine was the towns, villages, and fields of this rural area, not least the county capital, Dorchester, an ancient agricultural center. North of here is the scenic market town of Sherborne with its impressive 15th-century abbey church and Sherborne Castle. Other places of historic interest such as Maiden Castle and the chalk-cut giant of Cerne Abbas are close to bustling seaside resorts. You may find Lyme Regis (associated with the 20th-century novelist John Fowles) and the villages along the route close to your ideal of coastal England. The Jurassic Coast is the place to search for fossils.

LYNDHURST

37 miles southeast of Stourhead, 26 miles southeast of Stonehenge, 18 miles southeast of Salisbury.

Lyndhurst is famous as the capital of the New Forest. Although some popular spots can get crowded in summer, there are ample parking lots, picnic areas, and campgrounds. Miles of trails crisscross the region.

GETTING HERE AND AROUND
From Salisbury, follow A36, B3079, and continue along A337 another 4 miles or so. To explore the depths of the New Forest, take A35 out of Lyndhurst or A337 south. The New Forest Tour, a hop-on, hop-off open-top bus, runs a circular route through the New Forest between mid-June and mid-September (adults £10 per day, tickets on board). There are eight departures daily, and the bus will stop anywhere. Regular bus services are operated by Bluestar and Wilts & Dorset.

Many parts of the New Forest are readily accessible by train from London via the centrally located Brockenhurst Station.

ESSENTIALS
Visitor and Tour Information Lyndhurst Visitor Information Centre ⊠ *Main Car Park, High St.* ☎ *023/8028–2269* ⊕ *www.thenewforest.co.uk.* **New Forest Tour** ⊕ *www.thenewforesttour.info.*

EXPLORING
Fodor's Choice ★ **New Forest.** This area consists of 150 square miles of open countryside interspersed with dense woodland, a natural haven for herds of free-roaming deer, cattle, and, most famously, hardy New Forest ponies. The forest was "new" in 1079, when William the Conqueror cleared the area of farms and villages and turned it into his private hunting grounds. An extensive network of trails makes it a wonderful place for biking, walking, and horseback riding. ⊕ *www.thenewforest.co.uk.*

FAMILY **New Forest Centre.** This visitor complex contains fascinating and informative background on the region. The exhibits focus on the area's fauna, flora, and social traditions and are linked by quizzes, and there are other interactive elements that will keep children engaged. ⊠ *Main car park, High St.* ☎ *023/8028–3444* ⊕ *www.newforestcentre.org.uk* ⊠ *£4* ⊙ *Daily 10–5; last entry at 4.*

New Forest, Dorset, and the South Coast

WHERE TO EAT AND STAY

$$

MODERN BRITISH

Fodor's Choice

★

✕ **The Pig.** Funkier sister of glamorous Lime Wood, this New Forest "restaurant with rooms" puts the emphasis on localism and seasonality and is a local favorite. Lunch and dinner are served in a large conservatory overlooking lawns, and 95% of the ingredients come from the kitchen garden or other sources within 15 miles. The frequently changing menu may include dishes like honey and smoked chili crispy pork belly salad or Lyme Bay scallops with bacon. As the name suggests, porcine dishes feature prominently. You can overnight in one of the 26 comfortable rooms in the main building (an 18th-century former royal hunting lodge) or the converted stable block. All combine a slightly retro, shabby-chic style with modern bathrooms. You may accompany the "staff forager" on expeditions to find edible fauna like wild garlic. $ *Average main: £16* ✉ *Beaulieu Rd., Brockenhurst* ☎ *01590/622354* ⊕ *www.thepighotel.com.*

$$$$

HOTEL

Fodor's Choice

★

⊞ **Chewton Glen Hotel and Spa.** This grand early-19th-century country-house hotel and spa on extensive manicured grounds ranks among Britain's most acclaimed—and most expensive—lodgings. **Pros:** classic English luxury; top-notch leisure facilities; high staff-to-guest ratio. **Cons:** expensive rates. $ *Rooms from: £325* ✉ *Christchurch Rd., New Milton* ☎ *01425/275341, 800/344–5087 in U.S.* ⊕ *www.chewtonglen. com* ⟿ *35 rooms, 35 suites* ❡❍❘ *No meals.*

$$$$ HOTEL Fodor's Choice ★ 🏨 **Lime Wood.** If you're looking for a discreet, luxurious hideaway in a woodland setting with uninterrupted views and an excellent spa, this hugely relaxing country-house hotel is hard to beat. **Pros:** great location; stylish decor; friendly staff. **Cons:** hard to reach without a car; breakfast not included [$] *Rooms from: £295* ✉ *Beaulieu Rd.* ☎ *02380/287177* 🌐 *www.limewoodhotel.co.uk* 🛏 *14 rooms, 15 suites* 🍴 *No meals.*

$ B&B/INN 🏨 **Rufus House.** Personal service and easy access to the New Forest are the draws at this turreted Victorian house run by a Japanese-Italian couple. **Pros:** friendly owners; delicious breakfasts; great location. **Cons:** traffic noise in front rooms; some rooms and beds are small. [$] *Rooms from: £80* ✉ *Southampton Rd.* ☎ *023/8028–2930* 🌐 *www.rufushouse.co.uk* 🛏 *10 rooms* 🍴 *Breakfast.*

SPORTS AND THE OUTDOORS

Largely unspoiled and undeveloped, yet accessible even to those not normally given to long walks or bike rides, the New Forest offers abundant opportunities to explore the outdoors. Bike rental and horseback riding are widely available. Numerous trails lead through thickly wooded country, across open heaths, and through the occasional bog. With very few hills, it's fairly easy terrain and rich with animals. You're almost guaranteed to see ponies and deer, and occasionally free-roaming cattle and pigs.

BIKING

Cycle Experience. The range of trails weaving through the New Forest makes this one of Britain's best terrains for off-road biking. For £16 per day you can rent bikes at Cycle Experience. ✉ *2–4 Brookley Rd., Brockenhurst* ☎ *01590/624204.*

HORSEBACK RIDING

Burley Manor Riding Stables. There are rides for all levels at Burley Manor Riding Stables. Hour-long rides are £33. ✉ *Burley Manor Hotel, Ringwood Rd., Burley* ☎ *01425/403489.*

Forest Park Riding Centre. You can arrange a ride at Forest Park Riding Centre for £33 per hour. ✉ *Rhinefield Rd., Brockenhurst* ☎ *01590/623429.*

WALKING

New Forest walks. The area is crisscrossed with short, easy trails, as well as longer hikes. For an easy walk (about 4 miles), start from Lyndhurst and head directly south for Brockenhurst, a commuter village. The path goes through woods, pastureland, and heath—and you'll see plenty of New Forest ponies. ✉ *Lyndhurst.*

BEAULIEU

7 miles southeast of Lyndhurst.

The unspoiled village of Beaulieu (pronounced *byoo*-lee) has three major attractions in one.

GETTING HERE AND AROUND

Beaulieu is best reached by car on B3056 from Lyndhurst or B3054 from Lymington. Bus 112 has a limited service (twice daily on Tuesday and Thursday, once on Saturday) between Beaulieu and Lymington and Hythe.

EXPLORING

FAMILY **Beaulieu.** With a ruined abbey, a stately home, and an automobile museum, Beaulieu can satisfy different interests. In 1204 King John established **Beaulieu Abbey** for the Cistercian monks, who gave their new home its name, which means "beautiful place" in French. It was badly damaged as part of the suppression of Catholicism during the reign of Henry VIII, leaving only the cloister, the doorway, the gatehouse, and two buildings. A well-planned exhibition in one building re-creates daily life in the monastery. **Palace House** incorporates the abbey's 14th-century gatehouse and has been the home of the Montagu family since they purchased it in 1538, after the dissolution of the monasteries. Inside you can see drawing rooms, dining halls, and fine family portraits. The present Lord Montagu is noted for his work in establishing the **National Motor Museum,** which traces the development of motor transport from 1895 to the present. You can see more than 250 classic cars and motorcycles. Museum attractions include a monorail, audiovisual presentations, and a trip in a 1912 London bus. ⊠ *Off B3056* ☎ *01590/612345* ⊕ *www.beaulieu.co.uk* 🎫 *Abbey, Palace House, and Motor Museum £20* ⊙ *Late May–late Sept., daily 10–6; late Sept.–late May, daily 10 5.*

CORFE CASTLE

29 miles southwest of Beaulieu, 21 miles east of Dorchester.

The village of Corfe Castle is best known for the ancient, ruined castle that overlooks it.

ESSENTIALS

Visitor Information Discover Purbeck Information Centre ⊠ *Wareham Library, South St.* ☎ *01929/552740* ⊕ *www.visitswanageandpurbeck.co.uk.*

EXPLORING

Corfe Castle. One of the most impressive ruins in Britain, Corfe Castle overlooks the appealing gray limestone village of the same name. The castle site guards a gap in the surrounding Purbeck Hills. The present ruins are of the castle built between 1086, when the great central keep was erected by William the Conqueror, and the 1270s, when the outer walls and towers were built. Cromwell's soldiers blew up the castle in 1646 during the civil war, after a long siege during which its Royalist chatelaine, Lady Bankes, led its defense. ⊠ *A351* ☎ *01929/477060* ⊕ *www.nationaltrust.org.uk* 🎫 *£8.50* ⊙ *Mar. and Oct., daily 10–5; Apr.–Sept., daily 10–6; Nov.–Feb., daily 10–4.*

OFF THE
BEATEN
PATH
Clouds Hill. This brick-and-tile cottage near the Tank Museum served as the retreat of T. E. Lawrence (Lawrence of Arabia) before he was killed in a motorcycle accident on the road from Bovington in 1935. The house remains very much as he left it, with photos and memorabilia from the Middle East. It's particularly atmospheric on a gloomy day, as there's no electric light. Clouds Hill is 8 miles northwest of Corfe. ⊠ *Off B3390, Morton* ☎ *01929/405616* ⊕ *www.nationaltrust. org.uk* 🎫 *£5.50* ⊙ *Mid-Mar.–Oct., Wed.–Sun. and national holiday Mon. 11–5, last admission 4:30 or dusk.*

Swanage Railway. Largely volunteer-run, this railroad makes 25-minute scenic trips in vintage train carriages (steam and diesel engines) across the Isle of Purbeck—more a peninsula—from Norden in the center to the seaside town of Swanage via Corfe Castle. Small, pretty stations with details like flower baskets, painted signs, and water bowls for dogs add to the excursion's charm. Trains leave approximately every 80 minutes in low season, and every 40 minutes in high season. ⊠ *Station House, Springfield Rd., Swanage* ☎ *01929/425800* ⊕ *www. swanagerailway.co.uk* 🎫 *£1–£6.20* ⊘ *Apr.–Oct., daily 10–5:20; Nov.– Mar., weekends 10–5:20.*

DORCHESTER

21 miles west of Corfe Castle, 43 miles southwest of Salisbury.

The traditional county market town of Dorchester was immortalized as Casterbridge by Thomas Hardy in his 19th-century novel *The Mayor of Casterbridge*. In fact, the whole area around here, including a number of villages tucked away in the rolling hills of Dorset, has become known as "Hardy Country" because of its connection with the author. Hardy was born in a cottage in the hamlet of Higher Bockhampton, about 3 miles northeast of the town, and his bronze statue looks westward from a bank on Colliton Walk. Two important historical sites, as well as the author's birthplace and a former residence, are a short drive from Dorchester.

Dorchester has many reminders of its Roman heritage. A walk along Bowling Alley Walk, West Walk, and Colliton Walk follows the approximate lines of the original Roman town walls, part of a city plan laid out around AD 70. On the north side of Colliton Park is an excavated Roman villa with a marvelously preserved mosaic floor. While the high street in the center of town can be busy with vehicular traffic, the tourist office has walking itineraries that cover the main points of interest along quieter routes to help you appreciate the character of Dorchester today.

GETTING HERE AND AROUND

Dorchester can be reached from Corfe Castle via A351 and A352, and from Sherborne via A37. From Salisbury take A354. Park wherever you can (pay parking lots are scattered around the center) and explore the town on foot.

ESSENTIALS

Visitor Information Dorchester Tourist Information Centre ⊠ *11 Antelope Walk* ☎ *01305/267992* ⊕ *www.visit-dorset.com.*

EXPLORING
TOP ATTRACTIONS

Athelhampton House and Gardens. Fine 19th-century gardens enhance an outstanding example of 15th-century domestic Tudor architecture at Athelhampton House and Gardens. Thomas Hardy called this place Athelhall in some of his writings, referring to the legendary King Aethelstan, who had a palace on this site. The current house includes the Great Hall, with much of its original timber roof intact, the King's Room, and the Library, with oak paneling and more than 3,000

Hardy's Dorset

Among this region's proudest claims is its connection with Thomas Hardy (1840–1928), one of England's most celebrated novelists. If you read some of Hardy's novels before visiting Dorset—evoked by Hardy's part-fact, part-fiction county of Wessex—you may well recognize some places immediately from his descriptions. The tranquil countryside surrounding Dorchester is lovingly described in *Far from the Madding Crowd*, and Casterbridge, in *The Mayor of Casterbridge*, stands in for Dorchester itself.

Any pilgrimage to Hardy's Wessex begins at the author's birthplace in Higher Bockhampton, 3 miles east of Dorchester. Salisbury makes an appearance as "Melchester" in *Jude the Obscure*. North of Dorchester, walk in the footsteps of Jude Fawley by visiting the village of Shaftesbury—"Shaston"—and its steep Gold Hill, a street lined with cottages. It is still possible get a sense of the landscapes and streetscapes that inspired the writer, and any trip will give his books a greater resonance for readers.

books. The 10 acres of landscaped gardens have a dozen giant yew pyramids. ⊠ *A35, 5 miles east of Dorchester* ☎ *01305/848363* ⊕ *www. athelhampton.co.uk* ☞ *£12.50* ☉ *Mar.–Oct., Sun.–Thurs. 10:30–5; Nov.–Feb., Sun. 11–dusk.*

Maiden Castle. This castle is one of the most important pre-Roman archaeological sites in England. It's not an actual castle but an enormous Iron Age hill fort of stone and earth with ramparts that enclose about 45 acres. England's Neolithic inhabitants built the fort some 4,000 years ago, and many centuries later it was a Celtic stronghold. In AD 43 invading Romans, under the general (later emperor) Vespasian, stormed the fort. Finds from the site are on display in the Dorset County Museum in Dorchester. To experience an uncanny silence and sense of mystery, climb Maiden Castle early in the day. Leave your car in the lot at the end of Maiden Castle Way, a 1½-mile lane. ⊠ *A354, 2 miles southwest of Dorchester.*

WORTH NOTING

FAMILY **Dinosaur Museum.** The popular Dinosaur Museum has life-size models, interactive displays, and a hands-on Discovery Gallery. ⊠ *Icen Way, off High East St.* ☎ *01305/269880* ⊕ *www.thedinosaurmuseum.com* ☞ *£6.99* ☉ *Apr.–Sept., daily 10–5; Oct.–Mar., daily 10–4. Closed mid–late Dec.*

Hardy's Cottage. The small thatch-and-cob cottage, where the writer was born in 1840, was built by his grandfather and is little altered since that time. From here Thomas Hardy would make his daily 6-mile walk to school in Dorchester. Among other things, you can see the desk at which the author completed *Far from the Madding Crowd*. Access is on foot only, via a woodland walk, or country lane from the parking lot. ⊠ *Brockhampton Ln., ½ mile south of Blandford Rd., Higher Bockhampton* ☎ *01305/262366* ⊕ *www.nationaltrust.org.uk* ☞ *£5* ☉ *Mid-Mar.–Oct., Wed.–Sun. and holiday Mon. 11–5 or dusk.*

Max Gate. Thomas Hardy lived in Max Gate from 1885 until his death in 1928. An architect by profession, Hardy designed the house himself, and visitors can now see the study where he wrote *Tess of the d'Urbevilles, The Mayor of Casterbridge,* and *Jude the Obscure.* The dining room, the drawing room, and the garden are open to the public. ⊠ *Allington Ave., 1 mile east of Dorchester on A352* ☎ *01305/262538* ⊕ *www.nationaltrust.org.uk* 🖼 *£5.50* ☉ *Mar.–Oct., Wed.–Sun. and holiday Mon. 11–5, last entry 4:30.*

WHERE TO EAT AND STAY

$$$
MODERN BRITISH
✕ **Yalbury Cottage.** Oak-beamed ceilings, exposed stone walls, and inglenook fireplaces add to the charm of this restaurant in a 300-year-old cottage. It specializes in superior Modern British cooking using locally sourced produce, such as Portland dressed crab, roast loin of lamb with a mustard and herb crust, and panfried Dorset Coast sea bass. A three-course fixed-price dinner menu (£36) offers good value. Eight comfortable bedrooms are available in an extension overlooking gardens or fields. Lower Bockhampton is signposted off the A35, 1½ miles east of Dorchester. $ *Average main: £24* ⊠ *Bockhampton La., Lower Bockhampton* ☎ *01305/262382* ⊕ *www.yalburycottage.com* ☉ *No dinner Sun. or Mon.*

$$
B&B/INN
🛏 **The Casterbridge.** Small but full of character, this family-owned inn in a Georgian building dating from 1790 is elegantly decorated with period antiques. **Pros:** central location; period setting; good breakfasts. **Cons:** traffic noise in front rooms; annex rooms are small and lack character; limited parking. $ *Rooms from: £110* ⊠ *49 High East St.* ☎ *01305/264043* ⊕ *www.thecasterbridge.co.uk* ⇦ *14 rooms* ⍩ *Breakfast.*

SHOPPING

Wednesday Market. You can find Dorset delicacies such as Blue Vinney cheese (which some connoisseurs prefer to Blue Stilton) in the market. ⊠ *Fairfield parking lot, off Weymouth Ave.*

THE OUTDOORS

Thomas Hardy Society. From April through October, the Thomas Hardy Society organizes guided walks that follow in the steps of Hardy's novels. Readings and discussions accompany the walks, which range from a couple of hours to most of a day. ☎ *01305/251501* ⊕ *www. hardysociety.org.*

CERNE ABBAS

6 miles north of Dorchester.

The village of Cerne Abbas, worth a short exploration on foot, has some Tudor houses on the road beside the church. Nearby you can also see the original village stocks.

GETTING HERE AND AROUND

Cerne Abbas is best reached by car from Dorchester to the south or Sherborne to the north via A352.

EXPLORING

Cerne Abbas Giant. This colossal and unblushingly priapic figure, 180 feet long, dominates a hillside overlooking the village of Cerne Abbas. The giant carries a huge club and may have originated as a pre-Roman tribal fertility symbol. Alternatively, historians have tended to believe he is a representation of Hercules dating back to the 2nd century AD, but more recent research suggests he may be a 17th-century gibe at Oliver Cromwell. The figure's outlines are formed by 1-foot-wide trenches cut into the ground to reveal the chalk beneath. The best place to view the figure is from the A352 itself, where you can park in one of the numerous nearby turnouts. ⊠ *A352* ⊕ *www.nationaltrust.org.uk.*

SHERBORNE

4

12 miles north of Cerne Abbas, 20 miles north of Dorchester, 43 miles west of Salisbury.

Originally the capital of Wessex (the actual Saxon kingdom, not Hardy's retro conceit), this unspoiled market town is adorned with medieval buildings that use the local honey-colored stone. The focal point of the winding streets is Sherborne Abbey, where King Alfred's older brothers are buried. Also worth visiting is Sherborne Castle, a Tudor mansion originally built by Sir Walter Raleigh.

GETTING HERE AND AROUND

Hourly trains from Salisbury take 45 minutes to reach Sherborne. The station is at the bottom of Digby Road, near the abbey. Drivers should take A303, A37 to Yeovil, and A30 from there.

ESSENTIALS

Visitor Information Sherborne Tourist Information Centre ⊠ *3 Tilton Ct., Digby Rd.* ☎ *01935/815341* ⊕ *www.visit-dorset.com.*

EXPLORING

Shaftesbury. The model for the town of Shaston in Thomas Hardy's *Jude the Obscure* is still a small market town. It sits on a ridge overlooking Blackmore Vale—you can catch a sweeping view of the surrounding countryside from the top of Gold Hill, a steep street lined with cottages, so picturesque it was used in an iconic TV commercial to evoke the quintessential British village of yore. Shaftesbury is 20 miles west of Salisbury and 15 miles east of Sherborne.

Sherborne Abbey. The glory of Sherborne Abbey, a warm, "old gold" stone church, is the delicate and graceful 15th-century fan vaulting that extends the length of the soaring nave and choir. ("I would pit Sherborne's roof against any contemporary work of the Italian Renaissance," enthused Simon Jenkins in his *England's Thousand Best Churches.*) If you're lucky, you might hear "Great Tom," one of the heaviest bells in the world, pealing out from the bell tower. Guided tours are offered from April through September on Tuesday (10:30) and Friday (2:30), or by prior arrangement. ⊠ *Abbey Close* ☎ *01935/812452* ⊕ *www.sherborneabbey.com* ⊡ *Free* ☉ *Apr.–Sept., daily 8–6; Oct.–Mar., daily 8–4.*

Sherborne Castle. Built by Sir Walter Raleigh in 1594, this castle remained his home for 10 years before it passed to the custodianship of the Digby family. The castle has interiors from a variety of periods, including Tudor, Jacobean, and Georgian. The Victorian Gothic rooms are notable for their splendid plaster moldings on the ceiling. After admiring the extensive collections of Meissen and Asian porcelain, stroll around the lake and landscaped grounds, the work of Capability Brown. The house is less than a mile southeast of town. ✉ *Off A352* ☎ *01935/812072* 🌐 *www.sherbornecastle.com* 🎫 *£10; gardens only, £5* 🕒 *Castle Apr.–Oct., Tues.–Thurs. and Sun. 11–5, Sat. 2–5. Gardens Apr.–Oct., Tues.–Thurs. and Sun. 11–5, Sat. 11–5.*

WEYMOUTH

28 miles south of Sherborne, 8 miles south of Dorchester.

West Dorset's main coastal resort, Weymouth, is known for its sandy and pebble beaches and its royal connections. King George III began bathing here for his health in 1789, setting a trend among the wealthy and fashionable people of the day. Popularity left Weymouth with many fine buildings, including the Georgian row houses lining the Esplanade. Striking historical details command attention: a wall on Maiden Street holds a cannonball that was embedded in it during the English Civil War. Not far away, a column commemorates the launching of U.S. forces from Weymouth on D-Day.

Weymouth and its lively harbor offer the full bucket-and-spade seaside experience: donkey rides, sand castles, and plenty of fish-and-chips.

GETTING HERE AND AROUND

You can reach Weymouth on frequent local buses and trains from Dorchester. The bus and train stations are close to each other near King's Statue, on the Esplanade. If you're driving, take A354 from Dorchester and park on or near the Esplanade—an easy walk from the center—or in a lot near the harbor.

EXPLORING

Chesil Beach. A 5-mile-long spit jutting south from Weymouth leads to the Isle of Portland, well known for its limestone and as the setting for Ian McEwan's novel of the same name. The spit is the eastern end of the unique geological curiosity known as Chesil Beach—a 200-yard-wide, 30-foot-high bank of pebbles that decrease in size from east to west. The beach extends for 18 miles. A powerful undertow makes swimming dangerous, and tombstones in local churchyards attest to the many shipwrecks the beach has caused. There are walking and cycle trails along the rugged coastline.

WHERE TO EAT

$ BRITISH 🍴 **Old Rooms Inn.** This popular pub has great views over the harbor. The extensive menu ranges from wraps and salads to grilled steaks, curries, burgers, and comfort food. There are two separate dining areas and tables outside, or you can mix with the locals at the bar. [$] *Average main: £8* ✉ *2 Cove Row* ☎ *01305/771130.*

Sunrise is lovely at the Cobb, the harbor wall built by Edward I in Lyme Regis.

LYME REGIS

23 miles west of Weymouth, 25 miles west of Dorchester.

"A very strange stranger it must be, who does not see the charms of the immediate environs of Lyme," wrote Jane Austen in *Persuasion*. Judging from the summer crowds, most people appear to agree with her. The scenic seaside town of Lyme Regis and the so-called Jurassic Coast are the highlights of southwest Dorset. The crumbling Channel-facing cliffs in this area are especially fossil rich.

GETTING HERE AND AROUND

Lyme Regis is off the A35. Drivers should park as soon as possible—there are lots at the top of town—and explore the town on foot. First buses run here from Dorchester and Axminster, 6 miles northwest; the latter town is on the main rail route from London Waterloo and Salisbury, as is Exeter, from which you can take the X53 bus.

ESSENTIALS

Visitor Information Lyme Regis Tourist Information Centre ✉ *Guildhall Cottage, Church St.* ☎ *01297/442138* ⊕ *www.lymeregis.org.*

EXPLORING

Cobb. Lyme Regis is famous for its curving stone harbor breakwater, the Cobb, built by King Edward I in the 13th century to improve the harbor. The duke of Monmouth landed here in 1685 during his ill-fated attempt to overthrow his uncle James II, and the Cobb figured prominently in the movie of John Fowles's novel *The French Lieutenant's Woman*, as well as in the film version of Jane Austen's *Persuasion*.

FAMILY **Dinosaurland Fossil Museum.** Located in a former church, this compact museum displays an excellent collection of local fossils and gives the background on regional geology and how fossils develop. It also provides information on guided fossil-hunting walks. The shop on the ground floor sells minerals and fascinating fossils. ✉ *Coombe St.* ☎ *01297/443541* 🌐 *www.dinosaurland.co.uk* 🎟 *£5* 🕒 *Mid-Feb.–mid-Oct., daily 10–5; mid-Oct.–mid-Feb., hrs vary.*

Lyme Regis Philpot Museum. In a gabled and turreted Edwardian building, this lively museum contains engaging items that illustrate the town's maritime and domestic history, as well as a section on local writers and a good selection of local fossils. It also offers a series of fossil hunting and local history walks throughout the year. ✉ *Bridge St.* ☎ *01297/443370* 🌐 *www.lymeregismuseum.co.uk* 🎟 *£3.95* 🕒 *Easter–Oct., Mon.–Sat. 10–5, Sun. 11–5; Nov.–Easter, Wed.–Sun. 11–4.*

WHERE TO EAT AND STAY

$ BRITISH 🍴 **The Bell Cliff Restaurant and Tea Rooms.** This cozy, welcoming, child-friendly place in a 17th-century building at the bottom of Lyme Regis's main street makes a great spot for a light lunch or tea, although it can get noisy and cramped. Apart from teas and coffees, you can order seafood, including salmon, cod, and breaded plaice, or a gammon steak (a thick slice of cured ham) or vegetarian lasagna. [$] *Average main: £9* ✉ *5–6 Broad St.* ☎ *01297/442459* 🕒 *No dinner Nov.–Mar.*

$$ SEAFOOD 🍴 **Hix Oyster & Fish House.** This coastal outpost of one of London's trendiest restaurants combines stunning views from a height overlooking the Cobb with the celebrity chef's trademark high standards and originality. Simply cooked and beautifully presented seafood rules here, including Portland whole sea bass with creamed wild garlic. As the name suggests, the variety of local oysters is a particular specialty. Non-fish-eaters have limited choices, but the dessert menu is extensive. Book well ahead to sit by the floor-to-ceiling windows or on the small terrace. [$] *Average main: £17* ✉ *Cobb Rd.* ☎ *01297/446910* 🌐 *www.hixoysterandfishhouse.co.uk* ✍ *Reservations essential* 🕒 *Closed Sun. and Mon. evenings in Jan. and Feb.*

$$$ HOTEL 🏨 **Alexandra.** Magnificently sited above the Cobb, the family-owned Alexandra combines contemporary decor with genteel charm. **Pros:** great garden; deck overlooking the sea; central location. **Cons:** cheaper rooms have no sea views; small bathrooms; restricted parking. [$] *Rooms from: £177* ✉ *Pound St.* ☎ *01297/442010* 🌐 *www.hotelalexandra.co.uk* 🛏 *24 rooms* 🕒 *Closed late Dec.–late Jan.* 🍽 *Breakfast.*

SPORTS AND THE OUTDOORS

Dorset Coast Path. The 72-mile Dorset Coast Path—a section of the 630-mile-long Southwest Coast Path—runs east from Lyme Regis to Poole, bypassing Weymouth and taking in the quiet bays, shingle beaches, and low chalk cliffs of the coast. Some highlights are Golden Cap, the highest point on the south coast; the Swannery at Abbotsbury; Chesil Beach; Durndle Door; and Lulworth Cove (between Weymouth and Corfe Castle). Villages and isolated pubs dot the route, as do many rural B&Bs. ☎ *01392/383560* 🌐 *www.southwestcoastpath.com.*

THE WEST COUNTRY

WELCOME TO
THE WEST COUNTRY

TOP REASONS
TO GO

★ **A coastal walk:** For high, dramatic cliff scenery, choose the Exmoor coast around Lynmouth or the coast around Tintagel. Another option is a walk on part of the 630-mile-long South West Coast Path.

★ **Seafood in Padstow:** Celebrity chef Rick Stein rules the roost in this small, pretty Cornish port, and any of his establishments will strongly satisfy.

★ **Tate St. Ives:** There's nowhere better to absorb the local arts scene than this offshoot of London's Tate in the pretty seaside town of St. Ives. A roof-top café claims views over Porthmeor Beach.

★ **A visit to Eden:** It's worth the journey west for Cornwall's Eden Project alone: a wonderland of plant life in a former clay pit. Two gigantic geodesic "biomes" are filled with flora.

★ **Wells Cathedral:** A perfect example of medieval craftsmanship, the building is a stunning spectacle.

1 Bristol, Wells, and North Devon. Bristol is filled with remnants of its long history, but you need to explore small towns like Wells and Glastonbury to get the full flavor of the region.

2 Cornwall. You're never more than 20 miles from the sea in this western outpost of Britain, and the maritime flavor imbues such port towns as Padstow and Falmouth. A string of good beaches and resort towns such as St. Ives pull in the summer crowds.

GETTING ORIENTED

Going from east to west, the counties of Somerset, Devon, and Cornwall make up the West Country. A circular tour of the West Country peninsula covers stark contrasts, from the bustling city of Bristol in the east to the remote and rocky headlands of Devon and Cornwall to the west. On the whole, the northern coast is more rugged, the cliffs dropping dramatically to tiny coves and beaches, whereas the south coast shelters many more resorts and wider expanses of sand. The crowds gravitate to the southern shore, but there are many remote inlets and estuaries, and you don't need to go far to find a degree of seclusion. The national park of Dartmoor, with its wilder landscape, adds even more variety.

3 Plymouth and Dartmoor. Though modern in appearance, Plymouth has some important historical sights. To the northeast, the open heath and wild moorland of Dartmoor National Park invite walking and horseback riding; towns such as Chagford make a good base for exploring.

4 Exeter and South Devon. A sturdy cathedral dominates the historic city of Exeter. To the south, on the River Dart, are relaxed Totnes and bustling Dartmouth.

Updated by Robert Andrews

England's West Country is a land of granite promontories, windswept moors, hideaway hamlets, and—above all—the sea. Leafy, narrow country roads lead through miles of buttercup meadows and cider-apple orchards to heathery heights and mellow villages. With their secluded beaches and dreamy backwaters, Somerset, Devon, and Cornwall can be some of England's most relaxing regions to visit.

The counties of the West Country each have their own distinct flavor, and each comes with a regionalism that borders on patriotism. Somerset is noted for its rolling green countryside; Devon's wild and dramatic moors—bare, boggy, upland heath dominated by heathers and gorse—contrast with the restfulness of its many sandy beaches and coves; and Cornwall has managed to retain a touch of its old insularity, despite the annual invasion of thousands of people lured by the Atlantic waves or the ripples of the English Channel.

The historic port of Bristol is where you come across the first unmistakable burrs of the western brogue. Its Georgian architecture and a dramatic gorge create a backdrop to what has become one of Britain's most dynamic cities. To the south lie the cathedral city of Wells and Glastonbury, with its ruined abbey and Arthurian associations.

There's wild moorland in Devon, where Dartmoor is famed for its ponies roaming amid an assortment of strange tors: rocky outcroppings eroded into weird shapes. Devon's coastal towns are as interesting for their cultural and historical appeal—many were smuggler havens—as for their scenic beauty.

Cornwall, England's westernmost county, has always regarded itself as separate from the rest of Britain, and the Arthurian legends really took root here, not least at Tintagel Castle, the legendary birthplace of Arthur. The south coast is filled with sandy beaches, delightful coves, and popular resorts.

WEST COUNTRY PLANNER

WHEN TO GO

In July and August, traffic chokes the roads leading into the West Country. Somehow the region squeezes in all the "grockles," or tourists, and the chances of finding a remote oasis of peace and quiet are severely curtailed. The beaches and resort towns are either bubbling with zest or unbearably tacky, depending on your point of view. In summer your best option is to find a secluded hotel and make brief excursions from there. Avoid traveling on Saturday, when weekly rentals start and finish and the roads are jammed. Most properties that don't accept business year-round open for Easter and close in late September or October. Those that remain open have reduced hours. Winter has its own appeal: the Atlantic waves crash dramatically against the coast, and the austere Cornish cliffs are at their most spectacular.

The most notable festivals are Padstow's Obby Oss, a traditional celebration of the arrival of summer that takes place around May 1; and the St. Ives September Festival of music and art in mid-September. In addition, many West Country maritime towns host regattas over summer weekends. The best times to visit Devon are late summer and early fall, during the end-of-summer festivals.

PLANNING YOUR TIME

The elongated shape of Britain's southwestern peninsula means that you may well spend more time traveling than seeing the sights. The key is to base yourself in one or two places and make day trips to the surrounding region. The cities of Bristol, Exeter, and Plymouth make handy bases from which to explore the region, but they can also swallow up a lot of time, at the expense of smaller, less demanding places. The same is true of the resorts of Newquay and Falmouth, which can get very busy. Choose instead towns and villages such as Wells, Lynmouth, and Fowey to soak up local atmosphere. If you stick to just a few towns in Somerset and Devon (Bristol, Wells, and Exeter) you could get a taste of the area in four or five days. If you intend to cover Cornwall, at the end of the peninsula, you'll need at least a week. Allow time for aimless rambling—the best way to explore the moors and the coast—and leave enough free time for doing nothing at all.

GETTING HERE AND AROUND

AIR TRAVEL

Bristol International Airport, a few miles southwest of the city, has frequent flights from London, as well as from Dublin, Amsterdam, and other international cities. Exeter International Airport is 5 miles east of the city. Newquay Cornwall Airport, 5 miles northeast of town, has daily flights to London Gatwick.

Airport Information Bristol International Airport ⊠ *A38, Lulsgate Bottom* ☎ *0871/334–4444* ⊕ *www.bristolairport.co.uk.* **Exeter International Airport** ⊠ *A30, Clyst Honiton* ☎ *01392/367433* ⊕ *www.exeter-airport.co.uk.* **Newquay Cornwall Airport** ⊠ *Off A3059, St. Mawgan, Newquay* ☎ *01637/860600* ⊕ *www.newquaycornwallairport.com.*

5

BUS TRAVEL

National Express buses leave London's Victoria Coach Station for Bristol (2 hours), Exeter (4–5 hours), and Plymouth (5½ hours). Megabus (book online to avoid premium-line costs) offers cheap service to Bristol, Exeter, Plymouth, and Newquay. There's also a good network of regional bus services. First buses serve Somerset, Devon, and Cornwall, and Stagecoach South West covers mainly south Devon and the north Devon coast. Western Greyhound operates mostly in Cornwall. All three companies offer moneysaving one- or seven-day passes good for unlimited bus travel. Traveline can help you plan your trip.

Bus Contacts First ☎ *0845/600–1420* ⊕ *www.firstgroup.com.* **Megabus** ☎ *0900/160–0900* ⊕ *www.megabus.com.* **National Express** ☎ *0871/781–8178* ⊕ *www.nationalexpress.com.* **Stagecoach South West** ☎ *01392/427711* ⊕ *www.stagecoachbus.com.* **Traveline** ☎ *0871/200–2233* ⊕ *www.travelinesw.com.* **Western Greyhound** ☎ *01637/871871* ⊕ *www.westerngreyhound.com.*

CAR TRAVEL

Unless you confine yourself to a few towns—for example, Exeter and Plymouth—you'll be at a huge disadvantage without your own transportation. The region has a few main arteries, but you should take minor roads whenever possible, if only to see the real West Country at a leisurely pace.

The fastest route from London to the West Country is via the M4 and M5 motorways. Allow at least two hours to drive to Bristol, three to Exeter. The main roads heading west are the A30 (burrowing through the center of Devon and Cornwall all the way to the tip of Cornwall), the A39 (near the northern shore), and the A38 (near the southern shore, south of Dartmoor and taking in Plymouth).

TRAIN TRAVEL

Rail travelers can make use of a fast service connecting Exeter, Plymouth, and Penzance (for Cornwall). First Great Western and South West Trains serve the region from London's Paddington and Waterloo stations. Average travel time to Exeter is 2½ hours, to Plymouth 3½ hours, and to Penzance about 5½ hours. Once you've arrived, however, you'll find trains to be of limited use in the West Country, as only a few branch lines leave the main line between Exeter and Penzance.

Regional Rail Rover tickets provide three days of unlimited travel throughout the West Country in any seven-day period, or eight days in any 15-day period; localized Ranger passes cover Devon or Cornwall.

Train Contacts National Rail Enquiries ☎ *0845/748–4950* ⊕ *www.nationalrail.co.uk.*

RESTAURANTS

The last several years have seen a food renaissance in England's West Country. In the top restaurants the accent is firmly on local and seasonal products. Seafood is the number one choice along the coasts, from Atlantic pollock to Helford River oysters, and it's available in places from haute restaurants to harborside fish shacks. Celebrity chefs have marked their pitch all over the region, including Michael Caines in Exeter and Dartmoor, the Tanner brothers in Plymouth,

Rick Stein in Padstow, and Jamie Oliver in Newquay. Better-known establishments are often completely booked on Friday or Saturday, so reserve well in advance.

HOTELS

Accommodations include national hotel chains, represented in all of the region's principal centers, as well as ancient inns and ubiquitous bed-and-breakfast places. Availability can be limited on the coasts during August and during the weekend everywhere, so book well ahead. Many farmhouses also rent out rooms—offering tranquil rural surroundings—but these lodgings are often difficult to reach without a car. If you have a car, though, renting a house or cottage with a kitchen may be ideal. It's worth finding out about weekend and winter deals that many hotels offer. *Hotel reviews have been shortened. For full information, visit Fodors.com*

WHAT IT COSTS IN POUNDS				
	$	**$$**	**$$$**	**$$$$**
Restaurants	under £15	£15–£19	£20–£25	over £25
Hotels	under £100	£100–£160	£161–£220	over £220

Restaurant prices are the average cost of a main course at dinner or, if dinner isn't served, at lunch. Hotel prices are the lowest cost of a standard double room in high season, including 20% V.A.T.

Visitor Information Contacts South West Tourism ⊕ www.visitsouthwest. co.uk. **Visit Cornwall** ✉ Pydar House, Pydar St., Truro ☎ 01872/322900 ⊕ www.visitcornwall.com. **Visit Devon** ⊕ www.visitdevon.co.uk. **Visit Somerset** ☎ 01934/750833 ⊕ www.visitsomerset.co.uk.

BRISTOL, WELLS, AND NORTH DEVON

On the eastern side of this region is the vibrant city of Bristol. From here you might head south to the pretty cathedral city of Wells and continue on via Glastonbury, which just might be the Avalon of Arthurian legend. Proceed west along the Somerset coast into Devon, skirting the moorlands of Exmoor and tracing the northern shore via Clovelly.

BRISTOL

120 miles west of London, 46 miles south of Birmingham, 45 miles east of Cardiff, 13 miles northwest of Bath.

The West Country's biggest city (population 430,000), Bristol has in recent years become one of the country's most vibrant centers, with a thriving cultural scene encompassing some of the best contemporary art, theater, and music in the country. Buzzing bars, cafés, and restaurants, and a largely youthful population make it an attractive place to spend time.

Now that the city's industries no longer rely on the docks, the historic harbor along the River Avon has been given over to recreation. Arts and entertainment complexes, museums, and galleries fill the quayside. The pubs and clubs here draw the under-25 set and make the area fairly boisterous (and best avoided) on Friday and Saturday night.

Bristol also trails a great deal of history in its wake. It can be called the "birthplace of America" with some confidence, for John Cabot and his son Sebastian sailed from the old city docks in 1497 to touch down on the North American mainland, which he claimed for the English crown. The city had been a major center since medieval times, but in the 17th and 18th centuries it became the foremost port for trade with North America, and played a leading role in the Caribbean slave trade. Bristol was the home of William Penn, developer of Pennsylvania, and a haven for John Wesley, who founded the Methodist movement.

GETTING HERE AND AROUND

Bristol has good connections by bus and train to most cities in the country. From London, calculate about 2½ hours by bus or 1 hours by train. From Cardiff it's about 50 minutes by bus or train. By train, make sure you get tickets for Bristol Temple Meads Station (not Bristol Parkway), which is a short bus or taxi ride from the center. The bus station is more central, near the Broadmead shopping center. Most sights can be visited on foot, though a bus or a taxi is necessary to reach the Clifton neighborhood.

ESSENTIALS

Visitor Information Bristol Tourist Information Centre ⊠ *E Shed, Canon's Rd.* ☎ *0906/711–2191* ⊕ *www.visitbristol.co.uk.*

EXPLORING
TOP ATTRACTIONS

FAMILY

Fodor's Choice

★

At-Bristol. One of the country's top family-friendly science centers, this multimedia attraction provides a "hands-on, minds-on" exploration of science and technology in more than 300 interactive exhibits and displays. *All About Us* is dedicated to the inner workings of the human body. Another section allows you to create your own animations. A planetarium in a gleaming stainless-steel sphere takes you on a 25-minute voyage through the galaxy. There are up to 10 shows a day, bookable when you buy your ticket. A popular exhibit lets kids test their skills at creating animations. Allow at least three hours to see it all. ⊠ *Anchor Rd., Harbourside* ☎ *0845/345–1235* ⊕ *www.at-bristol.org. uk* ⊠ *£11.70* ☉ *Weekdays 10–5; weekends, holiday Mon., and school vacations 10–6.*

Church of St. Mary Redcliffe. Built by Bristol merchants who wanted a place in which to pray for the safe (and profitable) voyages of their ships, this rib-vaulted, 14th-century church was called "the fairest in England" by Queen Elizabeth I. High up on the nave wall hang the arms and armor of Sir William Penn, father of the founder of Pennsylvania. The church is a five-minute walk from Temple Meads train station toward the docks. ⊠ *Redcliffe Way* ☎ *0117/929–1487* ⊕ *www. stmaryredcliffe.co.uk* ⊠ *Free* ☉ *Mon.–Sat. 8:30–5, Sun. 8–8.*

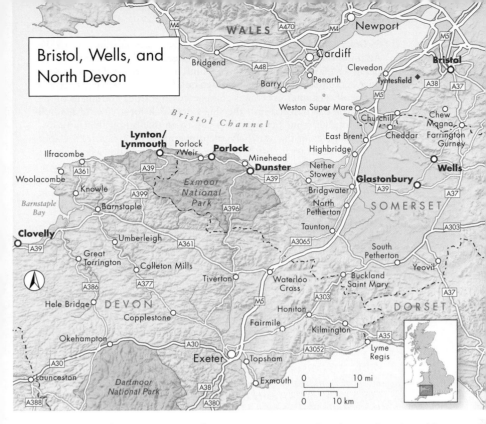

Bristol, Wells, and North Devon

Clifton Suspension Bridge. A monument to Victorian engineering, this 702-foot-long bridge spans the Avon Gorge. Work began on Isambard Kingdom Brunel's design in 1831, but the bridge wasn't completed until 1864. Free hour-long guided tours usually take place at 3 on weekends between April and October, departing from the tollbooth at the Clifton end of the bridge. At the far end of the bridge, the **Clifton Suspension Bridge Interpretation Centre** has a small exhibition on the bridge and its construction, including a 10-minute video. Near the bridge lies **Clifton Village,** studded with boutiques, antiques shops, and smart crafts shops in its lanes and squares. Bus number 8 from Bristol Temple Meads Station and the city center stops in Clifton Village. ⊠ *Bridge Rd., Leigh Woods* ☎ *0117/974–4664* ⊕ *www.cliftonbridge.org.uk* 🎫 *Free* ☉ *Daily 10–5.*

Fodor's Choice ★ **M Shed.** In a refurbished transit shed on the harbor side, this museum is dedicated to the city's history. The collection comprises three main galleries—Bristol People, Bristol Places, and Bristol Life—that focus on everything from the slave trade to scientific inventions to recent cultural innovations associated with the city. Check out the artifacts, photos, and sound and video recordings of and by Bristolians, all jazzed up with the latest interactive technology. ⊠ *Princes Wharf, Wapping Rd.* ☎ *0117/352–6600* ⊕ *mshed.org* 🎫 *Free* ☉ *Tues.–Fri. 10–5, weekends and holiday Mon. 10–6.*

SS *Great Britain*. On view in the harbor is the first iron ship to cross the Atlantic. Built by the great English engineer Isambard Kingdom Brunel in 1843, it remained in service until 1970, first as a transatlantic liner and ultimately as a coal storage hulk. Everything from the galley to the officers' quarters comes complete with sounds and smells of the time. You can descend into the ship's dry dock for a view of the hull and propeller. Your ticket admits you to an exhibit on the ship's history. A replica of the *Matthew,* the tiny craft that carried John Cabot to North America in 1497, may be moored alongside (when it's not sailing on the high seas). ✉ *Great Western Dockyard, Gas Ferry Rd.* ☎ *0117/926–0680* 🌐 *www.ssgreatbritain.org* 🎟 *£12.95* 🕒 *Apr.–Oct., daily 10–5:30; Nov.–Mar., daily 10–4:30; last entry 1 hr before closing.*

WORTH NOTING

Fodor's Choice ★ **Tyntesfield.** The National Trust is gradually restoring this extravagant, 35-bedroom Victorian–Gothic Revival mansion. Every ornate detail of this decorative-arts showcase compels attention. Besides magnificent woodwork, stained glass, tiles, and original furniture and fabrics, the house contains the modern conveniences of the 1860s, such as a heated billiards table. The servants' quarters are equally absorbing. There's a restaurant and family play area, too. You can see the house, garden, and chapel at your own pace. ■ **TIP→ Arrive early in the day to avoid the crowds competing for timed tickets—Monday and Tuesday are the quietest days.** Tyntesfield is 7 miles southwest of Bristol; take Bus 354 or 361 from the city every day except Sunday. ✉ *B3128, Wraxall* ☎ *01275/461900* 🌐 *www.nationaltrust.org.uk* 🎟 *£13.20; gardens only £8.10* 🕒 *House: early Feb.–early Mar., Sat.–Wed. 11–3; early Mar.–early July, Sat.–Wed. 11–5; early July–Oct., Fri.–Wed. 11–5; early Dec.–mid-Dec., Mon.–Wed. and Fri. 11–3. Gardens: early Mar.–early Nov., daily 10–6, early Nov.–early Mar., 10–5 or dusk.*

WHERE TO EAT

$$ MODERN BRITISH 🍴 **Riverstation.** Occupying a former police station, this modern, clean-lined restaurant affords serene views over the passing swans and boats. Book early for a window seat. Upstairs, the more formal restaurant serves such delicately cooked dishes as braised rabbit haunch and pan-fried brill, and some irresistible desserts, including pistachio crème brûlée with marinated figs. The bar has a more rough-and-ready menu that includes warm savory tarts and Thai-spiced mussels. With its terrace seating, this place also makes a great spot for breakfast, afternoon coffee, or evening drinks. [$] *Average main: £17* ✉ *The Grove, Harbourside, Bristol* ☎ *0117/914–4434* 🌐 *www.riverstation.co.uk* 🕒 *No dinner Sun.*

$$ MODERN BRITISH 🍴 **Source Food Hall.** In the heart of the old city, this trendy eatery benefits from its location in the St. Nicholas Market by offering a range of fresh seasonal produce, either to eat in or take out from the deli, meat, or fish counters. The wholesome lunch menu might feature asparagus soup with cream and chives or Hereford beef burgers, while the evening menu includes a range of steaks and seafood. The breakfasts and coffees are energizing, making this an ideal place to kick off a sightseeing excursion or take a pause en route. The attractive Bath-stone building has an airy, high-ceilinged interior. [$] *Average main: £15* ✉ *St. Nicholas*

EATING WELL IN THE WEST COUNTRY

From cider to cream teas, many specialties tempt your palate in the West Country. Lamb, venison, and, in Devon and Cornwall, seafood, are favored in restaurants, which have risen to heights of gastronomic excellence, notably through the influence of Rick Stein's seafood-based culinary empire in Padstow, in Cornwall. Seafood is celebrated at fishy frolics that include the Newlyn Fish Festival (late August) and Falmouth's Oyster Festival (early or mid-October).

WHAT TO EAT

Cheddar. Somerset is the home of Britain's most famous cheese—the ubiquitous cheddar, originally from the Mendip Hills village of the same name. Make certain that you sample a real farmhouse cheddar, made in the traditional barrel shape known as a truckle.

Cream teas. Devon's caloric cream teas consist of a pot of tea, homemade scones, and lots of strawberry jam and thickened clotted cream (a regional specialty, which is sometimes called Devonshire cream).

Pasties. Cornwall's specialty is the pasty, a pastry shell filled with chopped meat, onions, and potatoes. The pasty was devised as a handy way for miners to carry their dinner to work; today's versions are generally pale imitations of the original, though you can still find delicious home-cooked pasties if you're willing to search a little.

Seafood. In many towns in Devon and Cornwall, the day's catch is unloaded from the harbor and transported directly to eateries. The catch varies by season, but lobster is available year-round, as is crab, stuffed into sandwiches at quayside stalls and in pubs.

WHAT TO DRINK

Perry. This is similar to cider but made from pears.

Scrumpy. For liquid refreshment, try scrumpy, a homemade dry cider that's refreshing but carries a surprising kick.

Cream tea: A pot of tea with scones, clotted cream, and jam is compulsory in the West Country.

Wine and mead. English wine, similar to German wine, is made in all three counties (you may see it on local menus), and in Devon and Cornwall you can find a variant of age-old mead made from local honey.

5

Market, 1–3 Exchange Ave. ☎ *0117/927–2998* ⊕ *www.source-food. co.uk* ⊗ *Closed Sun. No dinner Mon.–Wed.*

WHERE TO STAY

$$ ⛭ **Hotel du Vin.** This hip chain has brought high-tech flair to six for-
HOTEL mer sugar-refining warehouses, built in 1728 when the River Frome ran outside the front door. **Pros:** tastefully restored old building; great bathrooms; excellent bar and bistro. **Cons:** traffic-dominated location; dim lighting in rooms; limited parking. Ⓢ *Rooms from: £129* ⊠ *Narrow Lewins Mead* ☎ *0844/736–4252* ⊕ *www.hotelduvin.com* ⇗ *36 rooms, 4 suites* ⦿ *No meals.*

$$$ ☐ **Thornbury Castle.** An impressive lodging, Thornbury has everything a
HOTEL   genuine 16th-century Tudor castle needs: huge fireplaces, moody paint-
Fodor's Choice   ings, mullioned windows, and a large garden. **Pros:** grand medieval
★   surroundings; sumptuous rooms; doting service. **Cons:** many steps to
climb; village is dull. $ *Rooms from: £170* ⊠ *Castle St., off A38, Thorn-
bury* ☎ *01454/281182* ⊕ *www.thornburycastle.co.uk* ↩ *22 rooms, 5
suites* 📄*Breakfast.*

NIGHTLIFE AND THE ARTS

Arnolfini. In a converted warehouse on the harbor, the Arnolfini is one
of the country's most prestigious contemporary-art venues, known
for uncovering innovative yet accessible art. There are galleries, a cin-
ema, a bookshop, and a lively bar and bistro. ⊠ *16 Narrow Quay*
☎ *0117/917–2300* ⊕ *www.arnolfini.org.uk.*

St. George's. A church built in the 18th century, St. George's now serves
as one of the country's leading venues for classical, jazz, and world
music. Stop by for lunchtime concerts. ⊠ *Great George St., off Park
St.* ☎ *0845/402–4001* ⊕ *www.stgeorgesbristol.co.uk.*

Watershed. A contemporary arts center by the harbor, the Watershed
also has a movie theater that screens excellent international films. ⊠ *1
Canon's Rd., Harbourside* ☎ *0117/927–5100* ⊕ *www.watershed.co.uk.*

WELLS

22 miles south of Bristol, 132 miles west of London.

England's smallest cathedral city, with a population of 10,000, lies
at the foot of the Mendip Hills. Set in what feels like a quiet country
town, the great cathedral is a masterpiece of Gothic architecture—the
first to be built in the Early English style. The city's name refers to the
underground streams that bubble up into St. Andrew's Well within
the grounds of the Bishop's Palace. Spring water has run through
High Street since the 15th century. Seventeenth-century buildings sur-
round the ancient marketplace, which hosts market days on Wednes-
day and Saturday.

GETTING HERE AND AROUND

Regular First buses from Bristol take 1 hours to reach Wells; the bus
station is a few minutes south of the cathedral. Drivers should take A37,
and park outside the compact and eminently walkable center.

ESSENTIALS

Visitor Information Wells Visitor Information Service ⊠ *Wells Museum,
8 Cathedral Green* ☎ *01749/671770* ⊕ *www.wellssomerset.com.*

EXPLORING

Bishop's Palace. The Bishop's Eye gate leading from Market Place takes
you to the magnificent, moat-ringed Bishop's Palace, which retains
parts of the original 13th-century residence. Most rooms are closed to
the public, but you can see the private chapel, the gatehouse, and the
ruins of a late-13th-century great hall in the peaceful grounds. The hall
lost its roof in the 16th century because Edward VI needed the lead it
contained. ⊠ *Market Pl.* ☎ *01749/988111* ⊕ *www.bishopspalacewells.*

Harmonious and stately, Wells Cathedral has a monumental west front decorated with medieval statues of kings and saints.

co.uk ✉ *£6.35* ⊙ *Early Feb.–Mar. and Nov.–late Dec., daily 10–4; Apr.–Oct., daily 10–6; last admission 1 hr before closing.*

Fodor's Choice **Cathedral Church of St. Andrew.** The great west towers of this medieval struc-
★ ture, the oldest surviving English Gothic church, can be seen for miles. Dating from the 12th century, the cathedral derives its beauty from the perfect
harmony of all of its parts, the glowing colors of its original stained-glass
windows, and its peaceful setting among stately trees and majestic lawns.
To appreciate the elaborate west-front facade, approach the building from
the cathedral green, accessible from Market Place through a great medieval
gate called "penniless porch" (named after the beggars who once waited
here to collect alms from worshippers). The cathedral's west front is twice
as wide as it is high, and some 300 statues of kings and saints adorn it.
Inside, vast inverted arches—known as scissor arches—were added in 1338
to stop the central tower from sinking to one side.

The cathedral has a rare and beautiful medieval clock, the second-
oldest working clock in the world, consisting of the seated figure of a
man called Jack Blandifer, who strikes a bell on the quarter hour while
mounted knights circle in a joust. Near the clock is the entrance to the
Chapter House—a small wooden door opening onto a great sweep of
stairs worn down on one side by the tread of pilgrims over the centuries. Free guided tours lasting up to an hour begin at the back of the
cathedral. A cloister restaurant serves snacks and teas. ✉ *Cathedral
Green* ☎ *01749/674483* ⊕ *www.wellscathedral.org.uk* ✉ *£6 suggested
donation* ⊙ *Apr.–Sept., daily 7–7; Oct.–Mar., daily 7–6. Tours: Apr.–
Oct., Mon.–Sat. at 10, 11, 1, 2, and 3; Nov.–Mar., Mon.–Sat. at 11,
noon, and 2.*

WHERE TO EAT AND STAY

$$

MEDITERRANEAN

✕ **The Old Spot.** For relaxed but top-notch dining in the heart of Wells, this sociable bistro with wood paneling and creamy white walls hits all the right notes. The Modern British and Mediterranean dinner menu varies seasonally, but might include a starter of smoked haddock fritters with tartar sauce, followed by a main course of tagine of lamb with hummus, eggplant, and North African spicy sausage. Set-price two-course lunches are £15.50. Arrive early for a table at the back, where there are views of the cathedral's west front. $ *Average main: £17 ⊠ 12 Sadler St.* ☎ *01749/689099* ⊕ *www.theoldspot.co.uk* ☉ *Closed Mon. No lunch Tues. No dinner Sun.*

$$

HOTEL

☷ **Swan Hotel.** A former coaching inn built in the 15th century, the Swan has an ideal spot facing the cathedral. **Pros:** professional service; some great views; good restaurant. **Cons:** some rooms need updating; occasional noise issues; parking lot tricky to negotiate. $ *Rooms from: £147 ⊠ 11 Sadler St.* ☎ *01749/836300* ⊕ *www.swanhotelwells.co.uk* ⊷ *51 rooms, 1 suite* ⏺ *Breakfast.*

GLASTONBURY

5 miles southwest of Wells, 27 miles south of Bristol, 27 miles southwest of Bath.

Fodor's Choice
★

A town steeped in history, myth, and legend, Glastonbury lies in the lea of Glastonbury Tor, a grassy hill rising 520 feet above the drained marshes known as the Somerset Levels. The Tor is supposedly the site of crossing ley lines (hypothetical alignments of significant places), and, in legend, Glastonbury is identified with Avalon, the paradise into which King Arthur was reborn after his death.

Partly because of these associations but also because of its world-class rock-music festival, the town has acquired renown as a New Age center, mixing crystal gazers with druids, yogis, and hippies, variously in search of Arthur, Merlin, Jesus—and even Elvis. ■**TIP**➔ **Between April and September, a shuttle bus runs every half hour between all of Glastonbury's major sights. Tickets are £3, and are valid all day.**

GETTING HERE AND AROUND

Frequent buses link Glastonbury to Wells and Bristol, pulling in close to the abbey. Drivers should take the A39. You can walk to all the sights or take the shuttle bus, though you'll need a stock of energy for ascending the tor.

ESSENTIALS

Visitor Information Glastonbury Tourist Information Centre ⊠ *The Tribunal, 9 High St.* ☎ *01458/832954* ⊕ *www.glastonburytic.co.uk.*

EXPLORING

Glastonbury Abbey. The ruins of this great abbey, in the center of town, are on the site where, according to legend, Joseph of Arimathea built a church in the 1st century. A monastery had certainly been erected here by the 9th century, and the site drew many pilgrims. The ruins are those of the abbey completed in 1524 and destroyed in 1539, during Henry VIII's dissolution of the monasteries. A sign south of the Lady Chapel marks the sites where Arthur and Guinevere were supposedly buried. Between April and October, guides in period costumes are on hand to point out some of the abbey's most interesting features. The visitor center has a scale model of the abbey as well as carvings and decorations salvaged from the ruins. ✉ *Magdalene St.* ☎ *01458/832267* 🌐 *www.glastonburyabbey.com* 🎟 *£6* 🕒 *Mar.–May, Sept., and Oct., daily 9–6; June–Aug., daily 9–8; Nov.–Feb., daily 9–4; last admission 30 mins before closing.*

TALE OF THE GRAIL

According to tradition, Glastonbury was where Joseph of Arimathea brought the Holy Grail, the chalice used by Jesus at the Last Supper. Centuries later, obtaining the Grail was said to be the objective of the quests of King Arthur and the Knights of the Round Table. When monks claimed to have found the bones of Arthur and Guinevere at Glastonbury in 1191, the popular association of the town with the mythical Avalon was sealed. Arthur and Guinevere's presumed remains were lost to history after Glastonbury Abbey was plundered for its riches in 1539.

WHERE TO EAT AND STAY

$ BRITISH 🍴 **Who'd a Thought It.** As an antidote to the natural-food cafés of Glastonbury's High Street, try this traditional backstreet inn for some more down-to-earth fare that doesn't compromise on quality. Bar classics such as beef-and-ale pie with a suet pastry appear alongside sizzling steaks and the chef's special "curry of the day." The beers and ciders are local, and the pub's quirky decor—including ancient radios, a red telephone box, and a bicycle on the ceiling—has a definite entertainment quotient. [$] *Average main: £12* ✉ *17 Northload St.* ☎ *01458/834460* 🌐 *www.whodathoughtit.co.uk.*

$ HOTEL 🏨 **George and Pilgrim Hotel.** Pilgrims en route to Glastonbury Abbey stayed here in the 15th century. **Pros:** historic surroundings; steps from the abbey. **Cons:** limited parking; some rooms need refreshing. [$] *Rooms from: £90* ✉ *1 High St.* ☎ *01458/831146* 🌐 *www.relaxinnz.co.uk* 🛏 *14 rooms* 🍽 *Breakfast.*

NIGHTLIFE AND THE ARTS

Glastonbury Festival. Held a few miles away in Pilton, the Glastonbury Festival is England's biggest and perhaps best annual rock festival. For five days over the last weekend in June, it hosts hundreds of bands—established and up-and-coming—on three main stages and myriad smaller venues. Tickets are steeply priced—over £200—and sell out months in advance; they include entertainment, and access to a camping area and service facilities. ✉ *Pilton* 🌐 *www.glastonburyfestivals.co.uk.*

DUNSTER

35 miles west of Glastonbury, 43 miles north of Exeter.

Lying between the Somerset coast and the edge of Exmoor National Park, Dunster is a picture-book village with a broad main street. The eight-sided Yarn-Market building on High Street dates from 1589.

GETTING HERE AND AROUND

To reach Dunster by car, follow the A39. By bus, there are frequent departures from nearby Minehead and Taunton. Dunster Castle is a brief walk from the village center. In the village is the Exmoor National Park Visitor Centre, which can give you plenty of information about local activities.

ESSENTIALS

Visitor Information Exmoor National Park Visitor Centre ✉ *Dunster Steep* ☎ *01643/821835* 🌐 *www.exmoor-nationalpark.gov.uk.*

EXPLORING

Fodor's Choice ★ **Dunster Castle.** A 13th-century fortress remodeled in 1868, Dunster Castle dominates the village from its site on a hill. Parkland and unusual gardens with subtropical plants surround the building, which has fine plaster ceilings, stacks of family portraits (including one by Joshua Reynolds), 17th-century Dutch leather hangings, and a magnificent 17th-century oak staircase. The climb to the castle from the parking lot is steep. ✉ *Off A39* ☎ *01643/821314* 🌐 *www.nationaltrust.org.uk* 🎫 *£9; gardens only £5.20* 🕐 *Castle: early Mar.–early Nov., daily 11–5; early Dec.–late Dec., weekends 11–3. Gardens: early Mar.–early Nov., daily 10–5; early Nov.–early Mar., daily 11–4.*

WHERE TO STAY

$$ B&B/INN 🏨 **Luttrell Arms.** In style and atmosphere, this classic inn harmonizes perfectly with Dunster village and castle; it was used as a guesthouse by the abbots of Cleeve in the 14th century. **Pros:** central location; historic trappings; good dining options. **Cons:** some standard rooms are small and viewless; no parking. [$] *Rooms from: £130* ✉ *High St.* ☎ *01643/821555* 🌐 *www.luttrellarms.co.uk* 🛏 *28 rooms* 🍴 *Breakfast.*

PORLOCK

6 miles west of Dunster, 45 miles north of Exeter.

Buried at the bottom of a valley, with the slopes of Exmoor National Park all about, the small, unspoiled town of Porlock lies near "Doone Country," the setting for R. D. Blackmore's swashbuckling saga *Lorna Doone*. Porlock had already achieved a place in literary history by the late 1790s, when Samuel Taylor Coleridge declared it was a "man from Porlock" who interrupted his opium trance while the poet was composing "Kubla Khan."

GETTING HERE AND AROUND

Porlock is best reached via the A39 coastal route. Quantock Motor Services operates several buses between Porlock and Minehead. The village can be easily explored on foot.

ESSENTIALS

Visitor Information Porlock Visitor Centre ✉ *The Old School, High St.* ☎ *01643/863150* 🌐 *www.porlock.co.uk.* **Quantock Motor Services** ☎ *01823/430202* 🌐 *www.quantockmotorservices.co.uk.*

EXPLORING

Coleridge Way. The 36-mile Coleridge Way passes through the northern fringes of the Quantock Hills, the isolated villages of the Brendon Hills, and parts of Exmoor National Park on the way from Nether Stowey (site of Coleridge's home) to Porlock. ⊕ *www.coleridgeway.co.uk.*

Porlock Weir. Two miles west of Porlock, this tiny harbor is the starting point for an undemanding 2-mile walk along the coast through chestnut and walnut trees to **Culbone Church,** reputedly the smallest and most isolated church in England. Saxon in origin, it has a small Victorian spire and is lighted by candles. It would be hard to find a more enchanting spot.

WHERE TO EAT

$$

MODERN BRITISH

✕ **The Café.** Don't be put off by its unassuming name, because this self-styled "café-with-rooms" in a sea-facing Georgian building is a relaxed, English country house. The husband-and-wife team behind this establishment offer top-quality food and accommodations. You can settle down in the spacious dining room for a cream tea with warm scones, opt for a light lunch, or enjoy more ambitious fare, including a seafood platter with oysters, lobster, crab, and scallops (ordering a day ahead). The five reasonably priced guest rooms are done in restful hues. $ *Average main: £16* ⊠ *Dunster Steep, Porlock Weir* ☎ *01643/863300* ⊕ *www.thecafeatporlockweir.co.uk* ⊗ *Closed Mon. and Tues.*

LYNTON AND LYNMOUTH

13 miles west of Porlock, 60 miles northwest of Exeter.

A steep hill separates this pretty pair of Devonshire villages, which are linked by a Victorian cliff railway you can still ride. Lynmouth, a fishing village at the bottom of the hill, crouches below 1,000-foot-high cliffs at the mouths of the East and West Lyn rivers; Lynton is higher up. The poet Percy Bysshe Shelley visited Lynmouth in 1812, in the company of his 16-year-old bride, Harriet Westbrook. During their nine-week sojourn, the poet found time to write his polemical *Queen Mab.* The grand landscape of Exmoor lies all about, with walks to local beauty spots: Watersmeet, the Valley of Rocks, or Hollerday Hill, where rare feral goats graze.

GETTING HERE AND AROUND

These towns are best reached via the A39. Lynton is a stop on Quantock Motor Services Bus 300, which runs daily from Minehead between April and October. Lynton and Lynmouth are both walkable, but take the cliff railway to travel between them.

ESSENTIALS

Visitor Information Lynton and Lymouth Tourist Information Centre ⊠ *Lee Rd., Lynton* ☎ *0845/458–3775* ⊕ *lynton-lynmouth-tourism.co.uk.*

EXPLORING

Lynton and Lynmouth Cliff Railway. Water and a cable system power the 862-foot cliff railway that connects these two towns. As they ascend a rocky cliff, you are treated to fine views over the harbor. Inaugurated in 1890, it was the gift of publisher George Newnes, who also donated Lynton's imposing town hall, near the top station on Lee Road. ✉ *The Esplanade, Lynmouth* ☎ *01598/753908* 🌐 *www.cliffrailwaylynton.co.uk* 🎟 *£3.20 round-trip* 🕒 *Mar. and Oct., daily 10–5; Apr.–late May and mid-Sept.–late Sept., daily 10–6; late May–late July and early Sept.–mid-Sept., daily 10–7; late July–early Aug., daily 10–8; early Aug.–early Sept., daily 10–9; early Nov., daily 10–4.*

WHERE TO EAT AND STAY

$$ MODERN BRITISH 🍴 **Rising Sun.** A 14th-century inn and a row of thatched cottages make up this restaurant with great views over the Bristol Channel. The kitchen specializes in local cuisine with European influences, so expect such dishes as a smoked haddock tartlet, or duck confit with tomato-and-olive ragout. There's a superb game menu December to February. In the attached hotel, corridors and creaking staircases lead to cozy guest rooms decorated in stylish prints or solid fabrics. [$] *Average main: £16* ✉ *Riverside Rd., Lynmouth* ☎ *01598/753223* 🌐 *www.risingsunlynmouth.co.uk.*

$$ B&B/INN 🏨 **Shelley's Hotel.** Centrally located, this well-maintained hotel has bright and spacious rooms with generous windows and excellent views. **Pros:** harbor views from most rooms; great breakfasts; hospitable owners. **Cons:** some rooms overlook public car park; no restaurant; no kids under 12. [$] *Rooms from: £100* ✉ *8 Watersmeet Rd., Lynmouth* ☎ *01598/753219* 🌐 *www.shelleyshotel.co.uk* 🛏 *11 rooms* 🍽 *Breakfast.*

SPORTS AND THE OUTDOORS

West of Lynton, the Atlantic-facing beaches of Saunton Sands, Croyde Bay, and Woolacombe Bay are much beloved of surfers, with plenty of outlets renting equipment and offering lessons. Croyde Bay and Woolacombe Bay are more family-friendly.

CLOVELLY

40 miles southwest of Lynton, 60 miles northwest of Exeter.

Fodor's Choice ★ Lovely Clovelly always seems to have the sun shining on its flower-lined cottages and stepped and cobbled streets. Alas, its beauty is well known and day-trippers can overrun the village in summer. Perched precariously among cliffs, a steep, cobbled road—tumbling down at such an angle that it's closed to cars—leads to the toylike harbor with its 14th-century quay. Allow about two hours (more if you stop for a drink or a meal) to take in the village. Hobby Drive, a 3-mile cliff-top roadway laid out in 1829 through thick woods, gives scintillating views over the village and coast.

Donkey stables, donkey rides for kids, and abundant donkey souvenirs in Clovelly recall the days when these animals played an essential role in town life, carrying food, packages, and more up and down the village streets. Even in the 1990s, donkeys helped carry bags from the hotels. Today sleds do the work, but the animals' labor is remembered.

Clovelly may have it all: cobbled streets, quaint houses, and the endless blue sea.

GETTING HERE AND AROUND

To get to Clovelly by bus, take Stagecoach service 319 from Barnstaple or Bideford. If you're driving, take the A39 and park at the Clovelly Visitor Centre for £6.50. The center of town is steep and cobbled. The climb from the harbor to the parking lot can be exhausting, but from Easter through October a reasonably priced shuttle service brings you back.

EXPLORING

Clovelly Visitor Centre. Here you'll see a 20-minute film that puts Clovelly into context. In the village you can visit a 1930s-style fisherman's cottage and an exhibition about Victorian writer Charles Kingsley, who lived here as a child. The admission fee includes parking. ■**TIP→ To avoid the worst crowds, arrive early or late in the day.** ⌧ *Off A39* ☎ *01237/431781* ⊕ *www.clovelly.co.uk* 🎫 *£6.50* 🕙 *June–Sept., daily 9–6; late Mar.–May and Oct., daily 9:30–5:30; Nov.–late Mar., daily 10–4.*

WHERE TO STAY

$$
HOTEL
🛏 **Red Lion Hotel.** You can soak up the tranquillity of Clovelly after the day-trippers have gone home at the 18th-century Red Lion, located right on the harbor in this coastal village. **Pros:** superb location; clean and comfortable; good service. **Cons:** some rooms are small; food is inconsistent. 💲*Rooms from: £147* ⌧ *The Quay* ☎ *01237/431237* ⊕ *www.clovelly.co.uk* ⇥ *11 rooms* 🍴 *Breakfast.*

CORNWALL

Cornwall stretches west into the sea, with plenty of magnificent coastline to explore, along with tranquil towns and some bustling resorts. One way to discover it all is to travel southwest from the cliff-top ruins of Tintagel Castle, the legendary birthplace of Arthur, along the north Cornish coast to Land's End. This predominantly cliff-lined coast, interspersed with broad expanses of sand, has many tempting places to stop, including Padstow (for a seafood feast), Newquay (a surfing and tourist center), and St. Ives (a delightful artists' colony).

From Land's End, the westernmost tip of Britain, known for its savage land- and seascapes and panoramic views, return to the popular harbor town of Falmouth and the river port of Fowey. The Channel coast is less rugged than the northern coast, with more sheltered beaches. Leave time to visit the excellent Eden Project, with its surrealistic-looking conservatories in an abandoned clay pit, and to tour the magnificent house and grounds of Lanhydrock.

TINTAGEL

35 miles southwest of Clovelly.

The romance of Arthurian legend thrives around Tintagel's ruined castle on the coast. Ever since the somewhat unreliable 12th-century chronicler Geoffrey of Monmouth identified Tintagel as the home of Arthur, son of Uther Pendragon and Ygrayne, devotees of the legend cycle have revered the site. In the 19th century Alfred, Lord Tennyson described Tintagel's Arthurian connection in *The Idylls of the King*. Today the village has its share of tourist junk—including Excaliburgers. Never mind: the headland around Tintagel is splendidly scenic.

GETTING HERE AND AROUND

To drive to Tintagel, take the A39 to the B3263. Numerous parking lots are found in the village center. Between April and October a shuttle service brings mobility-impaired passengers to the castle from parking in town.

ESSENTIALS

Visitor Information **Tintagel Visitor Centre** ⊠ *Bossiney Rd.* ☎ *01840/779084.*

EXPLORING

Fodor'sChoice **Tintagel Castle.** Although all that remains of the ruined cliff-top Tintagel
★ Castle, legendary birthplace of King Arthur, is the outline of its walls, moats, and towers, it requires only a bit of imagination to conjure up a picture of Sir Lancelot and Sir Galahad riding out in search of the Holy Grail over the narrow causeway above the seething breakers. Archaeological evidence, however, suggests that the castle dates from much later than popularly believed—about 1150, when it was the stronghold of the earls of Cornwall. Long before that, Romans may have occupied the site. The earliest identified remains here are of Celtic (AD 5th century) origin, and these may have some connection with the legendary Arthur. Legends aside, nothing can detract from the castle ruins, dramatically set off by the wild, windswept Cornish coast, on an island joined to the mainland by a narrow isthmus. Paths lead down to the pebble

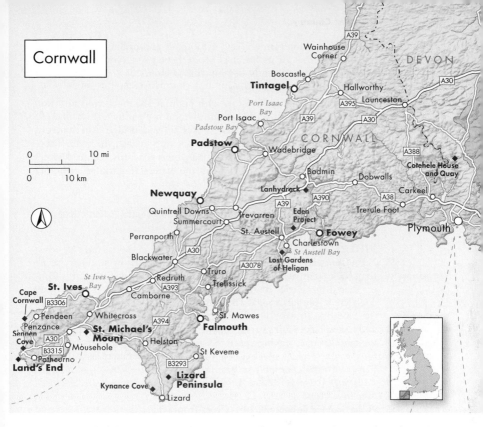

beach and a cavern known as **Merlin's Cave.** Exploring Tintagel Castle involves some arduous climbing on steep steps, but even on a summer's day, when people swarm over the battlements and a westerly Atlantic wind sweeps through Tintagel, you can feel the proximity of the distant past. ⊠ *Castle Rd., ½ mile west of the village* ☎ *01840/770328* ⊕ *www. english-heritage.org.uk* 🎟 *£5.90* ⊙ *Apr.–Sept., daily 10–6; Oct.–early Nov., daily 10–5; early Nov.–Mar., weekends 10–4.*

PADSTOW

16 miles southwest of Tintagel.

A small fishing port at the mouth of the River Camel, Padstow attracts attention and visitors as a center of culinary excellence, largely because of the presence here since 1975 of pioneering seafood chef Rick Stein. Stein's empire includes two restaurants, a café, a fish-and-chips joint, a delicatessen, a patisserie, and a cooking school where classes fill up months in advance.

Even if seafood isn't your favorite fare, Padstow is worth visiting. The cries of seagulls fill its lively harbor, a string of fine beaches lies within a short ride—including some choice strands highly prized by surfers—and two scenic walking routes await: the Saints Way across the peninsula to Fowey, and the Camel Trail, a footpath and cycling path that follows the river as far as Bodmin Moor. If you can avoid peak visiting times—summer weekends—so much the better.

GETTING HERE AND AROUND

Regular buses connect Padstow with Bodmin, the main transportation hub hereabouts, and on the main Plymouth–Penzance train line. To get here from Port Isaac, change buses at Wadebridge. Alternatively, take the bus to Rock and the passenger ferry across the river. There are numerous direct buses on the Newquay–Padstow route. Drivers should take A39/A389 and park in the waterside parking lot before reaching the harbor.

ESSENTIALS

Visitor Information Padstow Tourist Information Centre ⊠ *North Quay* ☎ *01841/533449* ⊕ *www.padstowlive.com.*

WHERE TO EAT

$$$$ ✕ **Paul Ainsworth at Number 6.** There is more to Padstow's culinary scene
MODERN BRITISH than Rick Stein, as this intimate bistro persuasively demonstrates. Diners seated in a series of small, stylish rooms can feast on ingeniously concocted dishes that make the most of local and seasonal produce. Try the blow-torched mackerel with celeriac and Parma ham for starters, and baked hake with saffron *Milanese* or Cornish saddleback pork for the main course, leaving space for some astounding desserts. Set-price lunches are a particularly good value. The atmosphere is warm and lively, with swift, amiable service. $ *Average main: £26* ⊠ *6 Middle St., Padstow* ☎ *01841/532093* ⊕ *www.number6inpadstow.co.uk* ☾ *Closed Sun. and Mon.*

$$$$ ✕ **The Seafood Restaurant.** Just across from where the lobster boats and
SEAFOOD trawlers unload their catches, Rick Stein's flagship restaurant has built
Fodor's Choice its reputation on the freshest fish and the highest culinary artistry. The
★ exclusively fish and shellfish menu includes everything from grilled Padstow lobster with herbs to monkfish in an Indonesian-style curry sauce. Choose either sitting formally at a table or grabbing a stool at the Seafood Bar in the center of the modern, airy restaurant (no reservations for bar). Don't want to move after your meal? Book one of the sunny, individually designed guest rooms overlooking the harbor. $ *Average main: £30* ⊠ *Riverside* ☎ *01841/532700* ⊕ *www.rickstein. com* ⚓ *Reservations essential.*

SPORTS AND THE OUTDOORS

BIKING

Trail Bike Hire. Bikes of all shapes and sizes can be rented at Trail Bike Hire, at the start of the Camel Trail. ⊠ *South Quay* ☎ *01841/532594* ⊕ *www.trailbikehire.co.uk.*

SURFING

Harlyn Surf School. This school can arrange two-hour to four-day surfing courses at its base in Harlyn Bay, 3 miles west of Padstow. ⊠ *Harlyn Bay Beach* ☎ *01841/533076* ⊕ *www.harlynsurfschool.co.uk.*

WALKING

Saints Way. This 30-mile inland path takes you between Padstow and the Camel Estuary on Cornwall's north coast to Fowey on the south coast. It follows a Bronze Age trading route, later used by Celtic pilgrims to cross the peninsula. Several relics of such times can be seen along the way.

NEWQUAY

14 miles southwest of Padstow, 30 miles southwest of Tintagel.

The biggest, most developed resort on the north Cornwall coast is a fairly large town established in 1439. It was once the center of the trade in pilchards (a small herringlike fish), and on the headland you can still see a white hut where a lookout known as a "huer" watched for pilchard schools and directed the boats to the fishing grounds. Newquay has become Britain's surfing capital and in summer young California-dreamin' devotees can pack the wide, cliff-backed beaches.

GETTING HERE AND AROUND

A branch line links Newquay with the main Plymouth–Penzance train line at Par, and there are regular buses from Padstow, Bodmin, and St. Austell. Train and bus stations are both in the center of town. Newquay has good road connections with the rest of the peninsula via the A30 and A39. The best beaches are a long walk or a short bus ride from the center.

ESSENTIALS

Visitor Information Newquay Tourist Information Centre ⊠ *Marcus Hill* ☎ *01637/854020* ⊕ *www.visitnewquay.org.*

WHERE TO EAT

$$$$
ITALIAN
Fodor's Choice
★

✕ **Fifteen Cornwall.** Bright and modern, this Italian restaurant has won plaudits both for its fabulous food and for its fine location overlooking magnificent Watergate Bay, a broad beach much beloved of water-sports enthusiasts. It's run by one of Britain's culinary heroes, Cockney chef Jamie Oliver, who trains local young people for careers in catering. To provide the staff with the widest possible repertoire, the £60 sampling menu changes frequently and lists five courses that might include a starter of gnocchi with oxtail and sage, followed by duck with polenta and *salsa verde* (green sauce) for a main course and *affogato al caffé* (ice cream soaked in black coffee) to finish. A fixed-price lunch is a cheaper option at £28. Watergate Bay lies 3 miles east of Newquay. ⓢ *Average main: £60* ⊠ *Watergate Rd., Watergate Bay* ☎ *01637/861000* ⊕ *www.fifteencornwall.co.uk.*

SPORTS AND THE OUTDOORS

Surfing is Newquay's raison d'être for many of the enthusiasts who flock here throughout the year. Great Western and Tolcarne beaches are most suitable for beginners, while Fistral Beach is better for those with more experience. There are dozens of surf schools around town, many offering accommodation packages; rental outlets are also ubiquitous.

Extreme Academy. One of the West Country's water-sports specialists, Extreme Academy offers courses in wave-skiing, kite-surfing, kite-buggying, paddle-surfing, and just plain old surfing, as well as equipment for hire. ⊠ *The Hotel, Trevarrian Hill, Watergate Bay* ☎ *01637/860543* ⊕ *www.watergatebay.co.uk.*

ST. IVES

25 miles southwest of Newquay.

Fodor's Choice ★ James McNeill Whistler came here to paint his landscapes, Barbara Hepworth to fashion her modernist sculptures, and Virginia Woolf to write her novels. Today sand, sun, and superb art continue to attract thousands of vacationers to the fishing village of St. Ives, named after Saint Ia, a 5th-century female Irish missionary said to have arrived on a floating leaf. Many come to St. Ives for the sheltered beaches; the best are Porthmeor, on the northern side of town, and, facing east, Porthminster—the choice for those seeking more space to spread out.

GETTING HERE AND AROUND
St. Ives has good bus and train connections with Bristol, Exeter, and Penzance. Train journeys usually involve a change at St. Erth (the brief St. Erth–St. Ives stretch is one of the West Country's most scenic train routes). The adjacent bus and train stations are within a few minutes' walk of the center. Drivers should avoid the center—parking lots are well marked in the higher parts of town.

ESSENTIALS
Visitor Information St. Ives Tourist Information Centre ⊠ *The Guildhall, Street-an-Pol* ☎ *0905/252-2250* ⊕ *www.stivestic.co.uk.*

EXPLORING
Barbara Hepworth Museum and Sculpture Garden. The studio and garden of Dame Barbara Hepworth (1903–75), who pioneered abstract sculpture in England, are now a museum and sculpture garden, managed by Tate St. Ives. The artist lived here for 26 years. ⊠ *Trewyn Studio, Barnoon Hill* ☎ *01736/796226* ⊕ *www.tate.org.uk* ᗌ *£6, £10 combined ticket with Tate St. Ives* ⊙ *Mar.–Oct., daily 10–5:20; Nov.–Feb., Tues.–Sun. 10–4:20.*

Tate St. Ives. The spectacular sister of the renowned London museum displays the work of artists who lived and worked in St. Ives, mostly from 1925 to 1975. There's also a selection of pieces from the museum's rich collection. It occupies a modernist building—a fantasia of seaside art deco–period architecture with a panoramic view of rippling ocean. The rooftop café is excellent for the food and views. ⊠ *Porthmeor Beach* ☎ *01736/796226* ⊕ *www.tate.org.uk* ᗌ *£7, £10 combined ticket with Barbara Hepworth Museum and Sculpture Garden* ⊙ *Mar.–Oct., daily 10–5:20; Nov.–Feb., Tues.–Sun. 10–4:20.*

WHERE TO EAT

$$$ MODERN BRITISH 🍴 **The Garrack.** This family-run restaurant is known for the panoramic sea views from its hilltop location and for relaxed fine dining. The pretheater (£13.50 and £17.50), set-price (£23 and £26.50), and à la carte menus specialize in local fish and seafood, including seared scallops, as well as Cornish beef. Breads are made on the premises, and the wine list features some Cornish vineyards. Some rooms at the attached hotel are furnished in traditional style; others are more modern. [$] *Average main: £21* ✉ *Burthallan La.* ☎ *01736/796199* 🌐 *www.garrack.com* 🕒 *No lunch Mon.–Sat.*

$$ MODERN BRITISH 🍴 **Gurnard's Head.** This pub with bright, homey furnishings and a relaxed ambience looks past green fields to the ocean beyond. The frequently changing menu features fresh, inventively prepared meat and seafood dishes; look for braised beef with orange and parsnip purée, or fish stew with saffron potatoes, spinach, and sprouting broccoli. Seven smallish rooms provide guest accommodations. The inn sits near the curvy coast road 6 miles west of St. Ives. [$] *Average main: £16* ✉ *B3306, near Zennor, Treen* ☎ *01736/796928* 🌐 *www.gurnardshead.co.uk* ✍ *Reservations essential.*

WHERE TO STAY

$ B&B/INN 🏨 **Cornerways.** Everything in St. Ives seems squeezed into the tiniest of spaces, and this cottage B&B in the quiet Downalong quarter is no exception. **Pros:** friendly owners and staff; stylish decor; excellent cooked breakfast. **Cons:** rooms are mostly small; narrow stairways to climb; very limited parking. [$] *Rooms from: £95* ✉ *1 Bethesda Pl.* ☎ *01736/796706* 🌐 *www.cornerwaysstives.com* 🛏 *6 rooms* 💳 *No credit cards* 🍽 *Breakfast.*

$$ HOTEL 🏨 **Primrose Valley Hotel.** Blending the elegance of an Edwardian villa with clean-lined modern style, this family-friendly hotel has the best of both worlds. **Pros:** close to beach and train and bus stations; friendly atmosphere; attention to detail. **Cons:** some rooms are small and lack views; tricky access to car park; steps to negotiate. [$] *Rooms from: £125* ✉ *Porthminster Beach* ☎ *01736/794939* 🌐 *www.primroseonline.co.uk* 🛏 *8 rooms, 1 suite* 🍽 *Breakfast.*

LAND'S END

17 miles southwest of St. Ives.

The coastal road, B3306, ends at the western tip of Britain at what is, quite literally, Land's End.

GETTING HERE AND AROUND

Frequent buses serve Land's End from St. Ives (taking around one hour, 40 minutes). In summer an open-top double-decker tracks the coast between St. Ives and Penzance, taking in Land's End en route.

EXPLORING

Land's End. The sea crashes against the rocks at Land's End and lashes ships battling their way around the point. **■TIP→ Approach from one of the coastal footpaths for the best panoramic view.** Over the years, sightseers have caused some erosion of the paths, but new ones are constantly being built, and Cornish "hedges" (granite walls covered with turf) have been planted to prevent erosion. The scenic grandeur of Land's End remains undiminished. The Land's End Hotel here is undistinguished, though the restaurant has good views.

Porthcurno Beach. Porthcurno Beach, 3 miles east of Land's End, has a stunning strip of cliff-backed sand that's good for both walkers (the coastal path is nearby) and anyone ready to relax on a beach. ⊠ *Off B3315, Porthcurno.*

Sennen Cove. Less than 2 miles north of Land's End, lovely Sennen Cove can be reached by car or by a walk on the South West Coast Path. You can enjoy the view or try the surfing. ⊠ *Off A30, Sennen.*

NIGHTLIFE AND THE ARTS

Fodor's Choice ★ **Minack Theatre.** The open-air Minack Theatre perches high above a beach 3 miles southeast of Land's End. The slope of the cliff forms a natural amphitheater, with bench seats on the terraces and the sea as a magnificent backdrop. Different companies present everything from classic dramas to modern comedies, as well as operas and concerts, on afternoons and evenings between Easter and late September. An exhibition center tells the story of the theater's creation. ⊠ *Off B3315, Porthcurno* ☎ *01736/810181* ⊕ *www.minack.com* 🎟 *Exhibition center £4, performances £8–£9.50* ⊙ *Apr.–Sept., daily 9:30–5:30; Oct.–Mar., daily 10–4.*

ST. MICHAEL'S MOUNT

15 miles east of Land's End, 7 miles south of St. Ives.

Walking the causeway to the castle dramatically set on an island is an appealing experience in itself, but there's plenty more to see.

GETTING HERE AND AROUND

Take the coastal road B3315 from Land's end to A394; the site is 3 miles east of Penzance.

Fodor's Choice ★ **St. Michael's Mount.** Rising out of Mount's Bay just off the coast, this spectacular granite-and-slate island is one of Cornwall's greatest natural attractions. The 14th-century castle perched at the highest point—200 feet above the sea—was built on the site of a Benedictine chapel founded by Edward the Confessor. In its time, the island has served as a church (Brittany's island abbey of Mont St. Michel was an inspiration), a fortress, and a private residence. The castle rooms you can tour include the Chevy Chase Room—a name probably associated with the Cheviot Hills or the French word *chevaux* (horses), after the hunting frieze that decorates the walls of this former monks' refectory. Family portraits include works by Reynolds and Gainsborough. Don't miss the wonderful views from the castle battlements. Around the base of the rock are buildings from medieval to Victorian, but they appear harmonious. Fascinating gardens surround the Mount, and many kinds of plants flourish in its microclimate.

To get to the island, walk the cobbled causeway from the village of Marazion or, when the tide is in during summer, take the £2 ferry. There are pubs and restaurants in the village, but the island also has a café and restaurant. ■ **TIP**→ **Wear stout shoes for your visit, which requires a steep climb.** Visits may be canceled in severe weather. ✉ *A394, 15 miles east of Land's End, Marazion* ☎ *01736/710507* ⊕ *www. stmichaelsmount.co.uk* ✆ *£9.60, castle only £7.60, garden only £4* ⊙ *Castle: mid-Mar.–June, Sept., and Oct., Sun.–Fri. 10:30–5; July and Aug., Sun.–Fri. 10:30–5:30; Nov.–mid-Mar., tours Tues. and Fri. 11 and 2. Garden: mid-Apr.–June, weekdays 10:30–5; July and Aug., Thurs. and Fri. 10:30–5:30; Sept., Thurs. and Fri. 10:30–5; last admission 45 mins before closing.*

LIZARD PENINSULA

20 miles southeast of St. Michael's Mount.

Fodor's Choice ★ The southernmost point on mainland Britain, this peninsula is a government-designated Area of Outstanding Natural Beauty, named so for the rocky, dramatic coast rather than the flat and boring interior. The huge, eerily rotating dish antennae of the Goonhilly Satellite Earth Station are visible from the road as it crosses Goonhilly Downs, the backbone of the peninsula. There's no coast road, unlike Land's End, but the coastal path offers marvelous opportunities to explore on foot—and is often the only way to reach the best beaches. With no large town (Helston at the northern end is the biggest, and isn't a tourist center), it's far less busy than the Land's End peninsula.

GETTING HERE AND AROUND

If you're driving, take A394 to reach Helston, gateway town to the Lizard Peninsula. From Helston, A3083 heads straight down to Lizard Point. Helston is the main public transport hub, but bus service to the villages is infrequent.

EXPLORING

Kynance Cove. A path close to the tip of the peninsula plunges down 200-foot cliffs to this tiny cove dotted with a handful of pint-size islands. The sands here are reachable only during the 2½ hours before and after low tide. The peninsula's cliffs are made of greenish serpentine rock, interspersed with granite; souvenirs of the area are carved out of the stone.

FALMOUTH

8 miles northeast of Lizard Peninsula.

The bustle of this resort town's fishing harbor, yachting center, and commercial port only adds to its charm. In the 18th century Falmouth was the main mail-boat port for North America, and in Flushing, a village across the inlet, you can see the slate-covered houses built by prosperous mail-boat captains. A ferry service now links the two towns. On Custom House Quay, off Arwenack Street, is the King's Pipe, an oven in which seized contraband was burned.

GETTING HERE AND AROUND

Falmouth can be reached from Truro on a branch rail line or on frequent buses, and is also served by local and National Express buses from other towns. Running parallel to the seafront, the long, partly pedestrianized main drag links the town's main sights. Visitors to

Pendennis Castle traveling by train should use Falmouth Docks Station, from which it's a short walk. Alternatively, drive or take a local bus to the castle to save legwork.

ESSENTIALS

Visitor Information Falmouth VIsitor Information Centre ⊠ *Prince of Wales Pier, 11 Market Strand* ☎ *0905/325–4534* ⊕ *www.falmouth.co.uk.*

EXPLORING

FAMILY **National Maritime Museum Cornwall.** The granite-and-oak-clad structure by the harbor is an excellent place to come to grips with Cornish maritime heritage, weather lore, and navigational science. You can view the collection of 140 or so boats, examine the tools associated with Cornish boat builders, and gaze down from the lighthouse-like lookout, which is equipped with maps, telescopes, and binoculars. In the glass-fronted Tidal Zone below sea level, you come face-to-face with the sea itself. ⊠ *Discovery Quay* ☎ *01326/313388* ⊕ *www.nmmc.co.uk* ⊠*£11* ☉ *Daily 10–5.*

FAMILY **Pendennis Castle.** At the end of its own peninsula stands this formi-
Fodor's Choice dable castle, built by Henry VIII in the 1540s and improved by his
★ daughter Elizabeth I. You can explore the defenses developed over the centuries. In the Royal Artillery Barracks, the *Pendennis Unlocked* exhibit explores the castle's history and its connection to Cornwall and England. The castle has sweeping views over the English Channel and across to St. Mawes Castle, designed as a companion fortress to guard the roads. There are also occasional performances, jousting, and shows for kids. ⊠ *Pendennis Head* ☎ *01326/316594* ⊕ *www.english-heritage.org.uk* ⊠ *£6.70* ☉ *Apr.–June, Sept., and Oct., Sun.–Fri. 10–5, Sat. 10–4; July and Aug., Sun.–Fri. 10–6, Sat. 10–4; Nov–Mar., weekends 10–4.*

WHERE TO EAT AND STAY

$$ ✕ **Gylly Beach Café.** For views and location, this beachside eatery with
MODERN BRITISH a crisp, modern interior and deck seating can't be beat. By day, it's a breezy café offering burgers, salads, and sandwiches, while the evening menu presents a judicious balance of meat, seafood, and vegetarian dishes, from a "seafood taster" of freshly caught fish to slow-braised saddle of lamb with garlic and rosemary mash. There are barbecues in summer and live music on Sunday evening. $ *Average main: £15* ⊠ *Gyllyngvase Beach, Cliff Rd.* ☎ *01326/312884* ⊕ *www.gyllybeach.com.*

$$$$ ☴ **St. Michael's Hotel.** A cool, contemporary ambience pervades this sea-
HOTEL side hotel and its lush, subtropical garden, both of which overlook Falmouth Bay. **Pros:** excellent facilities; attentive and amiable staff. **Cons:** cheapest rooms are small and viewless; 20-minute walk to center. $ *Rooms from: £230* ⊠ *Gyllyngvase Beach* ☎ *01326/312707* ⊕ *www.stmichaelshotel.co.uk* ⊅ *58 rooms, 3 suites* ¶⊙¶ *Breakfast.*

FOWEY

30 miles northeast of Falmouth.

Fodor's Choice
★ Nestled in the mouth of a wooded estuary, Fowey (pronounced Foy) is still very much a working china-clay port as well as a focal point for the sailing fraternity. Increasingly, it's also a favored home of the rich and famous. Good and varied dining and lodging options abound; these are most in demand during Regatta Week in mid- to late August and the annual Daphne du Maurier Festival in mid-May. The Bodinnick and Polruan ferries take cars as well as foot passengers across the river for the coast road on to Looe.

A few miles west of Fowey are a pair of very different gardens: the Eden Project, a futuristic display of plants from around the world, and the Lost Gardens of Heligan, a revitalized reminder of the Victorian age.

GETTING HERE AND AROUND

Fowey isn't on any train line, but the town is served by frequent buses from St. Austell. Don't attempt to drive into the steep and narrow-lane town center, which is ideal for strolling around. Parking lots are sign-posted on the approach roads.

ESSENTIALS

Visitor Information Fowey Tourist Information Centre ⊠ *Du Maurier Literary Centre, 5 South St.* ☎ *01726/833616* ⊕ *www.fowey.co.uk.*

EXPLORING

FAMILY
Fodor's Choice
★ **Eden Project.** Spectacularly set in a former china-clay pit, this garden presents the world's major plant systems in microcosm. The crater contains more than 70,000 plants—many of them rare or endangered species—from three climate zones. Plants from the temperate zone are outdoors, and those from other zones are housed in hexagonally paneled geodesic domes. In the Mediterranean Biome, olive and citrus groves mix with cacti and other plants indigenous to warmer climates. The Rainforest Biome steams with heat, resounds with the gushing of a waterfall, and blooms with exotic flora. The emphasis is on conservation and ecology, but is free of any editorializing. A free shuttle helps the footsore, and well-informed guides provide information. An entertaining exhibition in the visitor center gives you the lowdown on the project, and the Core, an education center, provides amusement and instruction for children. There are open-air concerts in summer and an ice-skating rink in winter. The Eden Project is 3 miles northeast of Charleston and 5 miles northwest of Fowey. There's frequent bus service from Fowey to St. Austell. ⊠ *Bodelva Rd., off A30, A390, and A391, St. Austell* ☎ *01726/811911* ⊕ *www.edenproject.com* 🎟 *£23.50, £19.50 if arriving by bike, on foot, or on public transport* ⊙ *Apr.–Oct., daily 9:30–6; Nov.–Mar., daily 10–4; last admission 90 mins before closing.*

Fodor's Choice
★ **Lanhydrock.** One of Cornwall's greatest country piles, Lanhydrock gives a look into the lives of the upper classes in the 19th century. The former home of the powerful, wealthy Robartes family was originally constructed in the 17th century but was totally rebuilt after a fire in 1881. Its granite exterior remains true to the house's original form, however, and the long picture gallery in the north wing, with its barrel-vaulted

plaster ceiling depicting 24 biblical scenes, survived the devastation. A small museum shows photographs and letters relating to the family. The house's endless pantries, sculleries, dairies, nurseries, and linen cupboards bear witness to the immense amount of work involved in maintaining this lifestyle. About 900 acres of wooded parkland border the River Fowey nearby, and in spring the gardens present an exquisite ensemble of magnolias, azaleas, and rhododendrons. Allow two hours to see the house and more time to stroll the grounds and park. The house is 9 miles north of Fowey. ✉ *Off A30, A38, and B3268Bodmin* ☎ *01208/265950* 🌐 *www.nationaltrust.org.uk* 🎟 *£11; grounds only £6.50* 🕒 *House: Apr.–Sept., Tues.–Sun. 11–5:30; Mar. and Oct., Tues.–Sun. 11–5. Garden: mid-Feb.–Oct., daily 10–6; park daily dawn–dusk; last admission 30 mins before closing.*

Fodor's Choice ★ **Lost Gardens of Heligan.** These sprawling grounds have something for all garden lovers, as well as an intriguing history. Begun by the Tremayne family in the late 18th century, they were rediscovered and spruced up in the early 1990s by former rock music producer Tim Smit (the force behind the Eden Project). In Victorian times the gardens displayed plants from around the British Empire. The Jungle Zone contains surviving plants from this era, including a lone Monterey pine, as well as giant redwood and clumps of bamboo. The Italian garden and walled flower gardens are delightful, but don't overlook the fruit and vegetable gardens or Flora's Green, bordered by a ravine. It's easy to spend half a day here. Guided tours cost £2 and are available daily at 11:30. ■ **TIP→ Travel via St. Austell to avoid confusing country lanes, then follow signs to Mevagissey.** ✉ *B3273, Pentewan* ☎ *01726/845100* 🌐 *www.heligan.com* 🎟 *£11* 🕒 *Apr.–Sept., daily 10–6; Oct.–Mar., daily 10–5; last entry 90 mins before closing.*

WHERE TO EAT AND STAY

$ AMERICAN 🍴 **Sam's.** This small and buzzing bistro has a rock-and-roll flavor, thanks to the walls adorned with posters of music icons. Diners squeeze onto benches and into booths to savor dishes made with local seafood, including a majestic bouillabaisse, or just a simple "Samburger." You may have to wait for a table, but there's a slinky lounge-bar upstairs for a preprandial drink. [$] *Average main: £12* ✉ *20 Fore St.* ☎ *01726/832273* 🌐 *www.samsfowey.co.uk* ✍ *Reservations not accepted.*

$$$$ HOTEL FAMILY 🏨 **Fowey Hall.** A showy Victorian edifice, all turrets and elaborate plasterwork, this hotel with 5 acres of gardens, a spa, and a pool is a great place for families. **Pros:** grand manorial setting; family-friendly rates. **Cons:** some rooms distant from the main house; not ideal for anyone seeking an adult ambience. [$] *Rooms from: £230* ✉ *Hanson Dr.* ☎ *01726/833866* 🌐 *www.foweyhallhotel.co.uk* 🛏 *24 rooms, 12 suites* 🍽 *Breakfast.*

SPORTS AND THE OUTDOORS

Fowey River Expeditions. Between June and September, Fowey River Expeditions runs daily canoe trips up the tranquil River Fowey, which is a good way to observe the area's abundant wildlife. Kayaks are also available to rent. ✉ *17 Passage St.* ☎ *01726/833627* 🌐 *www.foweyriverexpeditions.co.uk.*

PLYMOUTH AND DARTMOOR

Just over the border from Cornwall is Plymouth, an unprepossessing city but one with a historic old core and splendid harbor that recall a rich maritime heritage. North of Plymouth, you can explore the vast, boggy reaches of hilly Dartmoor, the setting for the Sherlock Holmes classic *The Hound of the Baskervilles*. This national park is a great place to hike or go horseback riding away from the crowds.

PLYMOUTH

48 miles southwest of Exeter, 124 miles southwest of Bristol, 240 miles southwest of London.

Devon's largest city has long been linked with England's commercial and maritime history. The Pilgrims sailed from here to the New World in the *Mayflower* in 1620. Although much of the city center was destroyed by air raids in World War II and has been rebuilt in an uninspiring style, there are worthwhile sights. A harbor tour is also a good way to see the city.

GETTING HERE AND AROUND

Frequent trains arrive from Bodmin and Penzance in Cornwall, and from Exeter. From London Paddington, trains take around four hours; Megabus and National Express buses from London's Victoria Coach Station take five to six hours. The train station is 1 mile north of the seafront, connected by frequent buses. Long-distance buses stop at the centrally located bus station off Royal Parade. Drivers can leave their cars in one of the numerous parking lots, including a couple right by the harbor. The seafront and central city areas are best explored on foot.

ESSENTIALS

Visitor Information Plymouth Tourism Information Centre ⊠ *Plymouth Mayflower, 3–5 The Barbican* ☎ *01752/306330* ⊕ *www.visitplymouth.co.uk.*

EXPLORING

Barbican. East of the Royal Citadel is the Barbican, the oldest surviving section of Plymouth. Here Tudor houses and warehouses rise from a maze of narrow streets leading down to the fishing harbor and marina. Many of these buildings have become antiques shops, art shops, and cafés. It's well worth a stroll for the atmosphere.

Hoe. From the Hoe, a wide, grassy esplanade with crisscrossing walkways high above the city, you can take in a magnificent view of the inlets, bays, and harbors that make up Plymouth Sound.

FAMILY **National Marine Aquarium.** This excellent aquarium on the harbor presents aqueous environments, from a freshwater stream to a seawater wave tank to a huge "shark theater." Not to be missed is the extensive collection of sea horses, part of an important breeding program, and the chance to walk under sharks in the Mediterranean tank. Feeding times are fun for the kids, and Waves café, with its harbor views, makes a good spot for a rest and refreshment. ⊠ *Rope Walk, Coxside* ☎ *0844/893–7938* ⊕ *www.national-aquarium.co.uk* ⊠ *£12.75* ⊙ *Apr.–Sept., daily 10–6; Oct.–Mar., daily 10–5; last admission 1 hr before closing.*

5

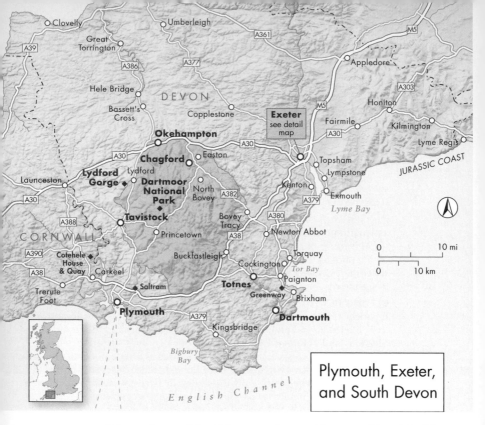

Plymouth, Exeter,
and South Devon

Saltram. An exquisite 18th-century home with many of its original furnishings, Saltram was built around the remains of a late-Tudor mansion. Its jewel is one of Britain's grandest neoclassical rooms, a vast, double-cube salon designed by Robert Adam and hung with paintings by Sir Joshua Reynolds, first president of the Royal Academy of Arts, who was born nearby in 1723. Fine plasterwork adorns many rooms and three have original Chinese wallpaper. The outstanding garden includes rare trees and shrubs, and there's a restaurant and a cafeteria. Saltram is 3½ miles east of Plymouth city center. ⊠ *South of A38, Plympton* ☎ *01752/333503* ⊕ *www.nationaltrust.org.uk* 🖃 *£9.70; garden only £5* ⊙ *House: early Mar.–early Nov., Sat.–Thurs. noon–4:30; last admission at 3:45. Garden: early Mar.–early Nov., daily 11–5; early Nov.–early Mar., daily 11–4.*

WHERE TO EAT AND STAY

$$$

MODERN BRITISH

✕ **Tanners.** One of the city's oldest buildings, the 15th-century Prysten House, is the setting for the highly regarded, inventive cuisine of brothers Chris and James Tanner. The seasonal à la carte and fixed-price menus may include slow-cooked shoulder of lamb, or whole lemon sole with sea greens, mussels, and clams. One of the two lattice-windowed dining rooms has a well inside it, and the other is hung with tapestries. A canopied courtyard is ideal for alfresco dining. The brothers also operate the Barbican Kitchen, a more casual, less pricey offshoot at the Black Friars Distillery on Southside Street. [$] *Average main: £20* ✉ *Finewell St.* ☎ *01752/252001* 🌐 *www.tannersrestaurant.com* ✍ *Reservations essential* ⏲ *Closed Sun. and Mon.*

$ HOTEL 🏨 **Holiday Inn.** Grandly sited in a tall block overlooking Plymouth Hoe, this modern chain hotel has a businesslike tone but doesn't skimp on comforts. **Pros:** excellent location; large rooms; fantastic views. **Cons:** impersonal feel; dated decor; tight parking. [$] *Rooms from: £83* ✉ *Armada Way* ☎ *01752/639988* 🌐 *www.ihg.com* 🛏 *211 rooms* 🍴 *Breakfast.*

NIGHTLIFE AND THE ARTS

Theatre Royal. Plymouth's Theatre Royal presents ballet, musicals, and plays by some of Britain's best companies. ✉ *Royal Parade* ☎ *01752/267222* 🌐 *www.theatreroyal.com.*

SHOPPING

Black Friars Distillery. At the Black Friars Distillery, Plymouth's most famous export, gin, has been distilled since 1793. You can purchase bottles of sloe gin, damson liqueur, fruit cup, or the fiery "Navy Strength" gin that traditionally was issued to the Royal Navy. Learn the full story on walking tours around the distillery, ending with a sampling in the wood-paneled Refectory Bar. The building originally housed a friary, and was where the Pilgrims spent their last night on English soil in 1620. ✉ *60 Southside St.* ☎ *01752/665292* 🌐 *www.plymouthdistillery.com.*

5

DARTMOOR NATIONAL PARK

10 miles north of Plymouth, 13 miles west of Exeter.

GETTING HERE AND AROUND

Public transport services are extremely sparse in Dartmoor, making a car indispensable for anywhere off the beaten track. The peripheral towns of Okehampton and Tavistock are well served by bus from Exeter and Plymouth. Chagford also has direct connections to Exeter, but central Princetown has only sporadic links with the outside world.

EXPLORING

Fodor's Choice ★ **Dartmoor National Park.** Even on a summer's day, the brooding hills of this sprawling wilderness appear a likely haunt for such monsters as the hound of the Baskervilles, and it seems entirely fitting that Sir Arthur Conan Doyle set his Sherlock Holmes thriller in this landscape. Sometimes the wet, peaty wasteland of Dartmoor National Park vanishes in rain and mist, although in clear weather you can see north to Exmoor, south over the English Channel, and west far into Cornwall. Much of Dartmoor consists of open heath and moorland, unspoiled by roads—wonderful walking and horseback-riding territory but an easy place to lose your bearings. Dartmoor's earliest inhabitants left behind stone monuments and burial mounds that help you envision prehistoric man roaming these pastures. Ponies, sheep, and birds are the main animals to be seen.

Several villages scattered along the borders of this 368-square-mile reserve—one-third of which is owned by Prince Charles—make useful bases for hiking excursions. Accommodations include simple inns and some elegant havens. **Okehampton** is a main gateway, and **Chagford** is a good base for exploring north Dartmoor. Other scenic spots include **Buckland-in-the-Moor,** a hamlet with thatch-roof cottages; **Widecombe-in-the-Moor,** whose church is known as the Cathedral of the Moor; and **Grimspound,** the Bronze Age site featured in Conan Doyle's most famous tale. Transmoor Link buses connect most of Dartmoor's towns and villages. The **High Moorland Visitor Centre** in Princetown is a good place to start your trip, as are centers in Postbridge and Haytor. You can also pick up information in Ivybridge, Okehampton, Moretonhampstead, Tavistock, and Buckfastleigh. ⊠ *High Moorland Visitor Centre, Tavistock Rd., Princetown* ☎ *01822/890414* ⊕ *www.dartmoor-npa.gov.uk.*

SPORTS AND THE OUTDOORS

Hiking is extremely popular in Dartmoor National Park. The areas around Widgery Cross, Becky Falls, and the Bovey Valley, as well as the short but dramatic walk along Lydford Gorge, have wide appeal, as do the many valleys around the southern edge of the moors. Guided hikes, typically costing £3 to £8, are available through the park's visitor information centers. Reservations are usually not necessary. Longer hikes in the bleak, less-populated regions—for example, the tors south of Okehampton—are appropriate only for the most experienced walkers. Dartmoor is a great area for horseback riding; many towns have stables for guided rides.

TAVISTOCK AND ENVIRONS

13 miles miles north of Plymouth.

On the River Tavy, the ancient town of Tavistock historically owed its importance to its Benedictine abbey (dissolved by Henry VIII in the 16th century) and to its status as a stannary town, where tin was weighed, stamped, and assessed. Today the town of 11,000 preserves a prosperous, predominantly Victorian appearance, especially at the bustling indoor Pannier Market off central Bedford Square. Tavistock makes a useful base for exploring Cotehele House, and for touring Dartmoor's western reaches.

GETTING HERE AND AROUND

Tavistock, on A386 and A390, is easily accessed via the frequent buses from Plymouth, which take about an hour. You'll need your own transportation to visit the attractions scattered around it, however.

ESSENTIALS

Visitor Information Tavistock Tourist Information Centre ⊠ *The Archway, Bedford Sq.* ☎ *01822/612938* ⊕ *www.dartmoor.co.uk.*

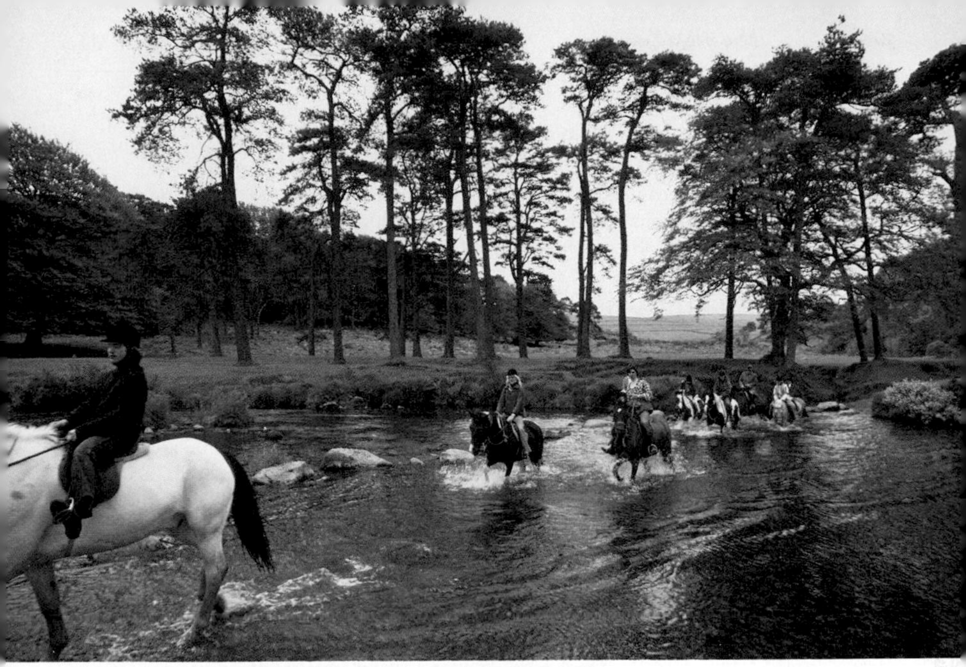

Pony trekking in Dartmoor National Park lets you get off the beaten path.

EXPLORING

Cotehele House and Quay. About 9 miles southwest of Tavistock, this area was a busy port on the River Tamar. Now it's usually visited for the well-preserved, atmospheric late-medieval manor, home of the Edgcumbe family for centuries. The house has original furniture, tapestries, embroideries, and armor, and you can also visit the impressive gardens, a quay museum, and a restored mill (usually in operation on Tuesday and Thursday). A limited number of visitors are allowed per day, so arrive early and be prepared to wait during busy periods. Choose a bright day, because the rooms have no electric light. Shops, crafts studios, a gallery, and a restaurant provide other diversions. **■TIP→ Take advantage of the shuttle bus that runs every half hour between the house, quay, and mill.** ✉ *Off A390, St. Dominick* ☎ *01579/351346* 🌐 *www.nationaltrust.org.uk* 🎫 *£9; gardens and mill only £5.40* 🕒 *House: mid-Mar.–early Nov., Sat.–Thurs. 11–4. Mill: early Mar.–Sept., daily 11–5; Oct–early Nov., daily 11–4:30. Gardens daily dawn–dusk.*

WHERE TO EAT

$$$$ MODERN BRITISH Fodor's Choice ★

🍴 **Horn of Plenty.** This restaurant within a Georgian house has magnificent views across the wooded, rhododendron-filled Tamar Valley. The sophisticated menu favors local and seasonal ingredients. Beef Rossini—roast sirloin with seared foie gras, Jerusalem artichoke purée, and truffle *jus*—is a typical main course. There are several fixed-price menus (lunch £19.50 and £24.50; dinner £49.50). The best value is Monday evening's potluck menu (£29). A converted coach house and the main house contain 10 sumptuously furnished guest rooms. It's 3 miles west of Tavistock. [$] *Average main: £49* ✉ *A390, Gulworthy* ☎ *01822/832528* 🌐 *www.thehornofplenty.co.uk.*

LYDFORD GORGE

7 miles north of Tavistock, 24 miles north of Plymouth.

GETTING HERE AND AROUND

The gorge is easily accessed on Beacon buses from Tavistock (which has frequent bus connections to Plymouth) and Okehampton (connected to Exeter). By car, take A386 between Tavistock and Okehampton.

EXPLORING

Fodor'sChoice ★ **Lydford Gorge.** The River Lyd carved a spectacular 1½-mile-long chasm through the rock at Lydford Gorge, outside the pretty village of Lydford, midway between Okehampton and Tavistock. Two paths follow the gorge past gurgling whirlpools and waterfalls with evocative names such as Devil's Cauldron and White Lady. ■ TIP→ Sturdy footwear is recommended. Although the walk can be quite challenging, the paths can still get congested during busy periods. In winter, access is restricted to the main waterfall and the top of the gorge. ⊠ *Off A386* ☎ *01822/820320* ⊕ *www.nationaltrust.org.uk* 🎫 *£6* ⊗ *Early Mar.–early Oct., daily 10–5; early Oct–early Nov., daily 10–4; early Nov.–early Mar., call for times.*

WHERE TO EAT AND STAY

$$ MODERN BRITISH ✗ **Dartmoor Inn.** Locals and visitors alike make a beeline for this gastropub in a 16th-century building with a number of small dining spaces done in spare, contemporary country style. The elegantly presented dishes may include pork belly, fish casserole with a ragout of leeks and saffron sauce, or fillet of duck with vanilla-apple purée, prunes, and toasted almonds. Set-price menus may be available, and there's a separate, reasonably priced bar menu. Three spacious guest rooms make it possible to linger. $ *Average main: £17* ⊠ *School Rd., off A386* ☎ *01822/820221* ⊕ *www.dartmoorinn.com* ⊗ *No dinner Sun. Closed Mon.*

$ B&B/INN 🏨 **Castle Inn.** In the heart of Lydford village, this 16th-century inn sits next to Lydford Castle. **Pros:** antique character; peaceful rural setting. **Cons:** shabby in places; some small rooms. $ *Rooms from: £70* ⊠ *School Rd., off A386* ☎ *01822/820241* ⊕ *www.castleinndartmoor.co.uk* ⇆ *8 rooms* ⫿○⫿ *Breakfast.*

$$$ HOTEL **Fodor'sChoice** ★ 🏨 **Lewtrenchard Manor.** Paneled rooms, stone fireplaces, leaded-glass windows, and handsome gardens outfit this spacious 1620 manor house on the northwestern edge of Dartmoor. **Pros:** beautiful Jacobean setting; conscientious service; outstanding food. **Cons:** rooms in outbuildings have less atmosphere; minimum stay on summer weekends; not very child-friendly. $ *Rooms from: £175* ⊠ *Off A30, Lewdown* ☎ *01566/783222* ⊕ *www.lewtrenchard.co.uk* ⇆ *10 rooms, 4 suites* ⫿○⫿ *Breakfast.*

OKEHAMPTON

8 miles northeast of Lydford Gorge, 28 miles north of Plymouth, 23 miles west of Exeter.

This town at the confluence of the rivers East and West Okement is a good base for exploring north Dartmoor. It has a fascinating museum dedicated to the moor, as well as a helpful tourist office.

GETTING HERE AND AROUND

There's good bus service to Okehampton from Tavistock and Exeter, and on summer Sundays you can travel by train from Exeter. If you're driving, the town is on A30 and A386; parking is easy in the center of town.

ESSENTIALS

Visitor Information Okehampton Tourist Information Centre ✉ *Museum Courtyard, 3 West St.* ☎ *01837/53020* 🌐 *www.okehamptondevon.co.uk.*

EXPLORING

FAMILY **Museum of Dartmoor Life.** The three floors of this informative museum contain historical artifacts, domestic knickknacks, traditional agricultural and mining tools, and fascinating insights into the lives of ordinary folks living on the moor. ✉ *Museum Courtyard, 3 West St.* ☎ *01837/52295* 🌐 *www.museumofdartmoorlife.org.uk* 🎫 *£2.50* ⏲ *Late Mar.–late Nov., weekdays 10:15–4:15, Sat. 10:15–1.*

Okehampton Castle. On the riverbank a mile southwest of the town center, the jagged ruins of this Norman castle occupy a verdant site with a picnic area and woodland walks. ✉ *Castle Lodge, off B3260* ☎ *01837/52844* 🌐 *www.english-heritage.org.uk* 🎫 *£3.90* ⏲ *Apr.–June and Sept.–early Nov., daily 10–5; July and Aug., daily 10–6.*

WHERE TO STAY

$ B&B/INN 🏨 **White Hart Hotel.** This venerable 17th-century coaching inn has counted the eminent statesman William Pitt the Elder among its guests, and little has changed since he visited in the 18th century: the rooms retain their low doors and sloping floors, for example. **Pros:** central location; historical character. **Cons:** breakfast costs extra; would benefit from a thorough updating; some street noise in front rooms. [$] *Rooms from: £80* ✉ *Fore St.* ☎ *01837/52730* 🌐 *www.thewhitehart-hotel.com* 🛏 *19 rooms* 🍴 *No meals.*

SPORTS AND THE OUTDOORS

Eastlake Riding Stables. A couple of miles outside Okehampton, Eastlake Riding Stables arranges horseback rides throughout the year. Trips last one or two hours or a full day. ✉ *Off A30, Belstone* ☎ *01837/52513* 🌐 *www.eastlakeridingstables.co.uk.*

CHAGFORD

9 miles southeast of Okehampton, 30 miles northeast of Plymouth.

Once a tin-weighing station, Chagford was an area of fierce fighting between the Roundheads and the Cavaliers during the English Civil War. Although officially a "town" since 1305, Chagford is more of a village, with taverns grouped around a seasoned old church and a curious "pepper-pot" market house on the site of the old Stannary Court. With a handful of cafés and shops to browse around, it makes a convenient base from which to explore north Dartmoor.

GETTING HERE AND AROUND

Infrequent local buses connect Chagford with Exeter (except on Sunday, when there's no service). The village is off A382; a car or bicycle is the best way to see its far-flung sights.

EXPLORING

Devon Guild of Craftsmen. The southwest's most important contemporary arts-and-crafts center, the Devon Guild is in a converted 19th-century coach house in the village of Bovey Tracey, 10 miles southeast of Chagford and 14 miles southwest of Exeter. The center has excellent exhibitions of local, national, and international crafts, as well as a shop and café. ✉ *Riverside Mill, Fore St., Bovey Tracey* ☎ *01626/832223* 🌐 *www.crafts.org.uk* 🎟 *Free* 🕓 *Daily 10–5:30.*

WHERE TO EAT AND STAY

$$$$ MODERN BRITISH Fodor's Choice ★ 🍴 **Gidleigh Park.** One of England's foremost country-house hotels, Gidleigh Park occupies an enclave of landscaped gardens and streams. It's reached via a lengthy, winding country lane and private drive at the edge of Dartmoor. The extremely pricey contemporary restaurant, directed by chef Michael Caines, has been showered with culinary awards. You may see why when you dig into the turbot and scallops with leeks, wild mushrooms, and chive butter sauce, one of the choices often on the prix-fixé menus (£42 for two courses at lunch, £110 for three courses at dinner). The locally pumped spring water is like no other. Antiques fill the long half-timber building, built in 1928 in Tudor style; there are 24 luxurious guest rooms. [$] *Average main: £105* ✉ *Gidleigh Park* ☎ *01647/432367* 🌐 *www.gidleigh.com* ✍ *Reservations essential.*

$ B&B/INN 🏨 **Easton Court.** Discerning travelers such as C.P. Snow, Margaret Mead, John Steinbeck, and Evelyn Waugh—who completed *Brideshead Revisited* here—made this their Dartmoor home-away-from-home. **Pros:** helpful hosts; peaceful ambience. **Cons:** minimum stay required on weekends in high season; rooms upstairs accessed by exterior stairs; a drive from the village. [$] *Rooms from: £75* ✉ *Easton Cross* ☎ *01647/433469* 🌐 *www.easton.co.uk* 🛏 *5 rooms* 🍽 *Breakfast.*

EXETER AND SOUTH DEVON

The ancient city of Exeter, Devon's county seat, has preserved some of its historical character despite wartime bombing and is worth exploring. To the south, on the banks of the River Dart, is the pretty market town of Totnes, while the well-to-do yachting center of Dartmouth lies south of Torbay (a coastal resort) at the river's estuary.

EXETER

18 miles east of Chagford, 48 miles northeast of Plymouth, 85 miles southwest of Bristol, 205 miles southwest of London.

Exeter has been the capital of the region since the Romans established a fortress here 2,000 years ago. Evidence of the Roman occupation remains in the city walls. Although it was heavily bombed in 1942, Exeter retains much of its medieval character, as well as examples of the gracious architecture of the 18th and 19th centuries. It's a convenient base for exploring Dartmoor, Totnes, and Dartmouth.

GETTING HERE AND AROUND

Hourly train service from London Paddington takes about two hours, 45 minutes; the cheaper Megatrain service takes 3 hours, 20 minutes and leaves London Waterloo four times daily. From London's Victoria Coach Station, National Express buses leave every two hours and Megabus has three daily departures, all taking around 4½ hours. Exeter is a major transportation hub for Devon. Trains from Bristol, Salisbury, and Plymouth stop at Exeter St. David's, and connect to the center by frequent buses. Some trains also stop at the more useful Exeter Central. The bus station is off Paris Street near the tourist office. Cars are unnecessary in town, so park yours as soon as possible—all the sights are within an easy walk.

TOURS Free 90-minute walking tours of Exeter by Red Coat Guided Tours take place daily all year, focusing on different aspects of the city. You can also pick up a leaflet on self-guided walks from the tourist office.

ESSENTIALS

Visitor Information and Tours Exeter Visitor Information and Tickets ⊠ *Dix's Field* ☎ *01392/665700* ⊕ *www.heartofdevon.com.* **Red Coat Guided Tours** ☎ *01392/265203* ⊕ *www.exeter.gov.uk/guidedtours.*

EXPLORING

Fodor'sChoice **Cathedral of St. Peter.** At the heart of Exeter, the great Gothic cathedral
★ was begun in 1275 and completed almost a century later. Its twin towers are survivors of an even earlier Norman cathedral. Rising from a forest of ribbed columns, the nave's 300-foot stretch of unbroken Gothic vaulting is the longest in the world. Myriad statues, tombs, and memorial plaques adorn the interior. In the minstrels' gallery, high up on the left of the nave, stands a group of carved figures singing and playing musical instruments, including bagpipes. Outside in Cathedral Close, don't miss the 400-year-old door to No. 10, the bishop of Crediton's house, ornately carved with angels' and lions' heads. ⊠ *Cathedral Close* ☎ *01392/255573* ⊕ *www.exeter-cathedral.org.uk* ☞ *£6* ☉ *Mon.–Sat. 9–5, Sun. open for services only. Guided tours: weekdays at 11, 12:30, and 2:30, Sat. at 11 and 12:30.*

Guildhall. On the city's main shopping street, this is said to be the oldest municipal building in the country still in use. The current hall, with its Renaissance portico, dates from 1330, although a guildhall has occupied this site since at least 1160. Its timber-braced roof, one of the earliest in England, dates from about 1460. ⊠ *High St.* ☎ *01392/665500* ☞ *Free* ☉ *Weekdays 10:30–1 and 2–4, Sat. 10–12:30.*

Quay House. This late-17th-century stone warehouse houses a visitor center where you can view documents on the city's maritime history and an audiovisual display. ⊠ *The Quay* ☎ *01392/271611* ☞ *Free* ☉ *Apr.–Oct., daily 10–5; Nov.–Mar., weekends 11–4.*

FAMILY **Royal Albert Memorial Museum.** This family-friendly museum is housed in
Fodor'sChoice a recently refurbished Victorian building. The centerpiece is the exten-
★ sive Making History gallery, a giddy mix of objects imaginatively illustrating the city's history and covering everything from Roman pottery to memorabilia from World War II. The geology section is thrillingly enhanced by the latest video technology, and there are also excellent ethnographical and archaeological collections, natural-history displays,

Cathedral of St. Peter 1
Guildhall 2
Quay House 5
Royal Albert Memorial Museum 3
Underground Passages 4

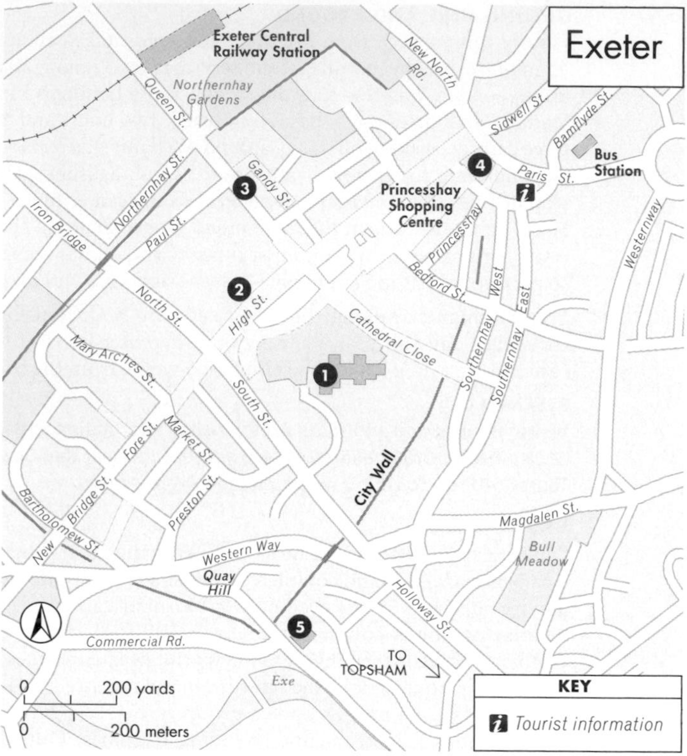

and works by West Country artists. ✉ *Queen St.* ☎ *01392/265858* 🌐 *www.rammuseum.org.uk* 🎟 *Free* 🕒 *Tues.–Sun. 10–5.*

FAMILY **Underground Passages.** Exeter's Underground Passages, which once served as conduits for fresh water, are the only medieval vaulted passages open to the public in Britain. They date to the mid-14th century, although some were enlarged by the Victorians. An exhibition and video precede the 25-minute guided tour. Many of the passages are narrow and low: be prepared to stoop. The tours often sell out during school vacations, so come early. Children under five are not permitted in the tunnels. ✉ *2 Paris St.* ☎ *01392/665887* 🌐 *www.exeter.gov.uk* 🎟 *£5.60* 🕒 *June–Sept. and school vacations, Mon.–Sat. 9:30–5:30, Sun. 10:30–4; Oct.–May, Tues.–Fri. 11:30–5:30, Sat. 9:30–5:30, Sun. 11:30–4; last tours 1 hr before closing.*

WHERE TO EAT

$ ITALIAN 🍴 **Ask.** This outpost of an Italian chain has secured an enviable site in a part-medieval, part-Georgian building opposite the cathedral. The large windows in the three dining areas offer superb views across the Close, and the courtyard is perfect for warm days. Among a typical menu of classic Italian dishes, choose from good antipasti, fresh salads, and a generous selection of pizzas and pastas. [$] *Average main: £11* ✉ *5 Cathedral Close* ☎ *01392/427127* 🌐 *www.askitalian.co.uk.*

$$$ ✕ **Michael Caines Restaurant.** Perfectly located within Cathedral Close,
MODERN BRITISH this ultrachic restaurant is in the centuries-old building that is now the
Fodor's Choice ABode Exeter hotel. Master chef Michael Caines oversees the kitchen,
★ which serves eclectic contemporary fare like glazed Creedy Carver duck
breast with a honey-rutabaga purée and orange confit, or Brixham sea
bass with stir-fried shiitake mushrooms, bean sprouts, and lemongrass
sauce. Fixed-price lunch and early evening menus are more afford-
able. Alternatively, a more relaxed (and more affordable) café-bar next
door serves meals all day, including good fixed-price lunches, and hosts
live jazz on alternate Friday evenings. $ *Average main: £24* ⊠ *ABode
Exeter, Cathedral Close* ☎ *01392/223638* ⊕ *www.michaelcaines.com*
☺ *Closed Sun.*

WHERE TO STAY

$$ ⊞ **ABode Exeter.** Claimed to be the first inn in England to be described
HOTEL as a "hotel," the 1769 Royal Clarence (the old name still appears out-
side) has been transformed into a strikingly modern boutique hotel.
Pros: superb central location; wonderful views from front rooms; mixes
old and new. **Cons:** some rooms are small and viewless; no parking.
$ *Rooms from: £160* ⊠ *Cathedral Close* ☎ *01392/319955* ⊕ *www.
abodehotels.co.uk* ⤵ *53 rooms* ⏅⃝ *No meals.*

$$$ ⊞ **Combe House.** Rolling parkland surrounds this luxurious Elizabethan
HOTEL manor house 16 miles east of Exeter. **Pros:** beautiful rural surroundings;
Fodor's Choice romantic ambience; attentive but informal staff. **Cons:** rather remote;
★ decor a bit tired in places. $ *Rooms from: £215* ⊠ *Off A30, Gittisham*
☎ *01404/540400* ⊕ *www.thishotel.com* ⤵ *13 rooms, 2 suites, 1 cot-
tage* ⏅⃝ *Breakfast.*

$ ⊞ **Raffles.** A 10-minute walk from the center, this quirky B&B in a quiet
B&B/INN neighborhood makes an ideal base for a night or two in town. **Pros:**
peaceful location; plenty of character; handy parking. **Cons:** not very
central for sights; occasional noise from trains in front-facing rooms.
$ *Rooms from: £78* ⊠ *11 Blackall Rd.* ☎ *01392/270200* ⊕ *www.
raffles-exeter.co.uk* ⤵ *6 rooms* ⏅⃝ *Breakfast.*

$ ⊞ **White Hart.** Guests have been welcome at this inn since the 15th cen-
HOTEL tury, and it is said that Oliver Cromwell stabled his horses here. **Pros:**
close to center; historic building; friendly service. **Cons:** can be noisy;
tight parking. $ *Rooms from: £84* ⊠ *66 South St.* ☎ *01392/279897*
⊕ *www.whitehartpubexeter.co.uk* ⤵ *55 rooms* ⏅⃝ *Breakfast.*

NIGHTLIFE AND THE ARTS
Northcott Theatre. Some of the country's most innovative companies
stage plays at the Northcott Theatre. ⊠ *Stocker Rd.* ☎ *01392/493493*
⊕ *www.exeternorthcott.co.uk.*

SHOPPING
Many of Exeter's most interesting shops are along Gandy Street, off
the main High Street drag, with several good food and clothes outlets.
Exeter was the silver-assay office for the West Country, and the earli-
est example of Exeter silver (now a museum piece) dates from 1218;
Victorian pieces are still sold. The Exeter assay mark is three castles.

Bruford's of Exeter. This shop stocks antique jewelry and silver. ⊠ *Guild-
hall Centre, Queen St.* ☎ *01392/254901* ⊕ *www.brufords.co.uk.*

5

SPORTS AND THE OUTDOORS

Saddles and Paddles. Renting bikes, kayaks, and canoes, this shop is handily placed for a 7-mile trip along the scenic Exeter Canal Trail, which follows the River Exe and the Exeter Ship Canal. ✉ *4 Kings Wharf* ☎ *01392/424241* 🌐 *www.sadpad.com.*

TOTNES

28 miles southwest of Exeter.

This busy market town on the banks of the River Dart preserves plenty of its medieval past, and on summer Tuesdays vendors dress in period costume for the Elizabethan Market. Market days are Friday and Saturday, when the town's status as a center of alternative medicine and culture becomes especially clear, and on the third Sunday of the month, when there's a local produce market on Civic Square. The historic buildings include a guildhall and St. Mary's Church.

GETTING HERE AND AROUND

Totnes is on a regular fast bus route between Plymouth and Torbay, and is a stop for main-line trains between Plymouth and Exeter. Buses pull into the center, and the train station is a few minutes' walk north of the center. Drivers should take A38 and A385 from Plymouth.

ESSENTIALS

Visitor Information **Totnes Tourist Information Centre** ✉ *The Town Mill, Coronation Rd.* ☎ *01803/863168* 🌐 *www.totnesinformation.co.uk.*

EXPLORING

Brixham. At the southern point of Tor Bay, Brixham has kept much of its original charm, partly because it still has an active fishing harbor. Much of the catch goes straight to restaurants as far away as London. Sample fish-and-chips on the quayside, where there's a (surprisingly petite) full-scale reproduction of the vessel on which Sir Francis Drake circumnavigated the world. The village is 10 miles southeast of Totnes by A385 and A3022. ✉ *Brixham.*

FAMILY **South Devon Railway.** Steam trains of this railway run through 7 miles of the wooded Dart Valley between Totnes and Buckfastleigh, on the edge of Dartmoor. Call about special trips around Christmas. ✉ *Dart Bridge Rd., Buckfastleigh* ☎ *0843/357–1420* 🌐 *www.southdevonrailway.co.uk* 🎟 *£12 round-trip* 🕒 *Mid-Mar.–Oct., daily; call for hours.*

Totnes Castle. You can climb up the hill in town to the ruins of this castle—a fine Norman motte-and-bailey design—for a wonderful view of Totnes and the River Dart. ✉ *Castle St.* ☎ *01803/864406* 🌐 *www.english-heritage.org.uk* 🎟 *£3.60* 🕒 *Apr.–Sept., daily 10–6; Oct., daily 10–5; Nov.–Mar., weekends 10–4.*

WHERE TO STAY

$$ HOTEL 🏨 **Royal Seven Stars Hotel.** Conveniently located at the bottom of the main street, this centuries-old coaching inn has counted Daniel Defoe and Edward VII among its former guests. **Pros:** central location; friendly staff; spotless rooms. **Cons:** some accommodations are small; rooms over bars can be noisy; busy public areas. [$] *Rooms from: £119* ✉ *The Plains* ☎ *01803/862125* 🌐 *www.royalsevenstars.co.uk* 🛏 *16 rooms* 🍴 *Breakfast.*

NIGHTLIFE AND THE ARTS

Dartington Hall. One of the foremost arts centers of the West Country, Dartington Hall lies 2 miles northwest of Totnes. There are concerts, film screenings, and exhibitions. The gardens, free year-round, are the setting for outdoor performances of Shakespeare in summer. There's a café, and you can stay overnight in rooms in the hall. ⊠ *Off A384 and A385, Dartington* ☎ *01803/847070* ⊕ *www.dartington.org/arts.*

SHOPPING

Shops at Dartington. Near Dartington Hall, 15 stores and two restaurants in and around an old cider press make up the Shops at Dartington. Open daily, it's a good place to find handmade Dartington crystal glassware, kitchenware, crafts, books, and toys. The farm shop sells fudge, ice cream, and cider, and Cranks is an excellent vegetarian restaurant. ⊠ *Shinners Bridge, Dartington* ☎ *01803/847500* ⊕ *www.dartington.org/shops.*

DARTMOUTH

13 miles southeast of Totnes, 35 miles east of Plymouth, 35 miles south of Exeter, 5 miles southwest of Brixham.

An important port in the Middle Ages, Dartmouth is today a favorite haunt of yacht owners. Traces of its past include the old houses in Bayard's Cove at the bottom of Lower Street, where the Mayflower made a stop in 1620; the 16th-century covered Butterwalk; and the two castles guarding the entrance to the River Dart. The Royal Naval College, built in 1905, dominates the heights above the town. A few miles south of Dartmouth on Start Bay there are a number of pretty beaches including Blackpool Sands, popular with families.

GETTING HERE AND AROUND

Frequent buses connect Dartmouth with Plymouth and Totnes. Drivers coming from the west should follow A381 and A3122. Approaching via A3022 and A379, you can save mileage by using the passenger and car ferries crossing the Dart. Travelers on foot can take advantage of a vintage steam train service operating between Paignton and Kingswear, where there are ferry connections with Dartmouth. River ferries also link Dartmouth with Totnes.

ESSENTIALS

Visitor Information Dartmouth Tourist Information Centre ⊠ *The Engine House, Mayors Ave.* ☎ *01803/834224* ⊕ *www.discoverdartmouth.com.*

EXPLORING

FAMILY **Dartmouth Steam Railway.** These lovingly restored trains chug along on tracks beside the River Dart between Paignton and Kingswear (across the river from Dartmouth). You can combine a train ride with a river excursion between Dartmouth and Totnes and a bus between Totnes and Paignton on a £23 Round Robin ticket. ⊠ *5 Lower St.* ☎ *01803/555872* ⊕ *www.dartmouthrailriver.co.uk* 🎫 *£11* ⊙ *Mid-Feb.–early Nov., call for departure times.*

Fodor's Choice **Greenway.** A rewarding way to experience the River Dart is to join a
★ cruise from Dartmouth's quay to visit Greenway, the 16th-century riverside home of the Gilbert family (Sir Humphrey Gilbert claimed

Newfoundland on behalf of Elizabeth I), more famous today for its association with the crime writer Agatha Christie. Mrs. Mallowan (Christie's married name) made it her holiday home beginning in 1938, and the house displays collections of archaeological finds, china, and silver. The gorgeous gardens are thickly planted with magnolias, camellias, and rare shrubs, and richly endowed with panoramic views. Beware, however, that the grounds are steeply laid out, and those arriving by boat face a daunting uphill climb. Allow three hours to see everything; timed tickets for the house are given on arrival. Parking spaces here are restricted and must be booked in advance. Alternatively, ask at the tourist office about walking and cycling routes to reach the house (non-car-users get discounted entry). ✉ *Greenway Rd., Galmpton* ☎ *01803/842382* 🌐 *www.nationaltrust.org.uk* 🎟 *£9* 🕒 *Mid-Feb.–late July and mid-Sept.–early Nov., Wed.–Sun. 10:30–5; late July–mid-Sept., Tues.–Sun. 10:30–5.*

Greenway Cruises. A round-trip ticket between Dartmouth and Greenway costs £7.50 on Greenway Cruises. ☎ *01803/882811* 🌐 *www.greenwayferry.co.uk*

WHERE TO EAT AND STAY

$$$ SEAFOOD 🍴 **The Seahorse.** In a prime riverside location, this seafood restaurant epitomizes the region's ongoing food revolution. The knowledgeable staff will guide you through the Italian-inspired menu, which primarily depends on the day's catch: look for scallops with garlic and white port, grilled monkfish, and poached skate wing. The meat dishes are equally enticing, while the formidable desserts are well worth leaving space for. The owner, celebrity chef Mitch Tonks, also runs a much more relaxed fish-and-chips restaurant a few doors down called RockFish, which is open daily. [$] *Average main: £24* ✉ *5 S. Embankment* ☎ *01803/835147* 🌐 *www.seahorserestaurant.co.uk* 🕒 *Closed Mon. No dinner Sun., no lunch Tues.*

$$$ HOTEL 🏨 **Royal Castle Hotel.** This hotel has truly earned the name "Royal"—several monarchs have slept here. **Pros:** historical resonance; central location; superb breakfasts. **Cons:** some cheaper rooms are nondescript; no elevator. [$] *Rooms from: £170* ✉ *11 The Quay* ☎ *01803/833033* 🌐 *www.royalcastle.co.uk* 🛏 *25 rooms* 🍽 *Breakfast.*

OXFORD AND THE THAMES VALLEY

WELCOME TO OXFORD AND THE THAMES VALLEY

TOP REASONS TO GO

★ **Blenheim Palace:** The birthplace of Sir Winston Churchill and the only British historic home to be named a World Heritage Site sits amid stunning parkland.

★ **Boating on the Thames:** Life is slower on the river, and renting a boat or taking a cruise is an ideal way to see verdant riverside pastures and villages. Windsor, Marlow, Henley, and Oxford are good options.

★ **Mapledurham House:** This is the house that inspired Toad Hall from *The Wind in the Willows;* you can picnic here on the grounds and drink in the views.

★ **Oxford:** While scholars' noses are buried in their books, you can wander among Oxford University's ancient stone buildings and memorable museums.

★ **Windsor Castle:** The mystique of eight successive royal houses of the British monarchy envelops Windsor and its famous castle, where a fraction of the current Queen's vast wealth is displayed.

1 **Windsor, Marlow, and Environs.** Gorgeous Windsor has its imposing and battlemented castle, stone cottages, and tea shops, and nearby Eton also charms. The meadows and villages around Marlow and Henley are delightful in summer when the flowers are in bloom. Mapledurham House near Henley-on-Thames is an idyllic stop; you can take a boat here.

2 **Oxford.** Wonderfully walkable, this university town has handsome, golden-stone buildings and one museum after another to explore. For a break, rent a flat-bottom boat, also known as a punt, and glide on the local waterways; after dark, experience the vibrant nightlife. Oxford provides easy access to the extravagant and fanciful Waddesdon Manor, along with Blenheim Palace and Stowe Landscape Gardens. Blenheim and Stowe each take the better part of the day to see.

GETTING ORIENTED

An ideal place to begin any exploration of the Thames Valley is the town of Windsor, about an hour's drive west of central London. From there you can follow the river to Marlow and Henley-on-Thames, site of the famous Henley Royal Regatta. To the north is Oxford, with its pubs, colleges, and museums; it can make a good base for exploring some of the area's small towns and stately homes. Blenheim Palace and Stowe Landscape Gardens lie northwest of Oxford, Waddesdon Manor northeast.

6

Updated by
Kate Hughes

Easy proximity to London made the Thames Valley enormously popular with the rich and powerful throughout England's history. They built the lavish country estates and castles, including Windsor, that form the area's most popular tourist attractions today. Some of these, as well as Oxford and its university, are easy day trips from London. Consider exploring this stretch of the River Thames by boat, either by boarding a cruiser or getting behind the oars. Windsor, Henley, and Marlow all make good starting points.

Traditionally, the area west of London is known as the Thames Valley (the area to the east is called the Thames Gateway). Once an aquatic highway connecting London to the rest of England and the world, the Thames was critical to the city's power when the sun never set on the British Empire. By the 18th century the Thames was one of the world's busiest water systems, declining in commercial importance only when the 20th century brought other means of transportation to the forefront. These days the railroads and motorways carrying traffic to and from London have turned much of this area into commuter territory, but you can still find timeless villages and miles of relaxing countryside.

Anyone who wants to understand the mystique of the British monarchy should visit Windsor, home to the medieval and massive Windsor Castle. Farther upstream, the green quadrangles and graceful spires of Oxford are the hallmarks of one of the world's most famous universities. Within reach of Oxford, Blenheim Palace, Waddesdon Manor, and Stowe Landscape Gardens provide insights into the grand lifestyle of the empire's elite, and the stretches of the Thames near Marlow and Henley-on-Thames are home to handsome rowing clubs and piers and sturdy waterside cottages and villas. It all conspires to make the Thames Valley a wonderful find, even for experienced travelers.

OXFORD AND THE THAMES VALLEY PLANNER

WHEN TO GO

High summer is lovely, but to avoid the tourist droves consider visiting in the less busy late spring or early fall. Book tickets and accommodations well in advance for the Henley Royal Regatta, on the cusp of June and July, and the Royal Ascot horse race, in mid-June. Visits to Eton and the Oxford colleges are more restricted during term time—generally from September to late March and late April to mid-July—than at other times. Most stately homes are open from March through September or October. Avoid driving from London during morning and afternoon rush hours.

PLANNING YOUR TIME

You can easily visit the major Thames Valley towns on a day trip from London. A train to Windsor, for example, takes about an hour, and you can tour Windsor and environs in a day. Base yourself in Oxford for a couple of days, though, if you want to explore the town fully.

GETTING HERE AND AROUND

BUS TRAVEL

Oxford and the area's main towns are convenient by bus from London, as is Windsor (although trains are faster. For information, contact Traveline. You can take a bus from Oxford to Blenheim, but to see Waddesdon Manor and Stowe Landscape Gardens you'll need to rent a car or join an organized tour.

Contacts Megabus ☎ *0871/266–3333 Inquiries, 0900/160–0900 booking line, calls cost 60p per minute* ⊕ *www.megabus.co.uk.* **Oxford Bus Company** ☎ *01865/785400* ⊕ *www.oxfordbus.co.uk.* **Stagecoach Oxford Tube** ☎ *01865/772250* ⊕ *www.oxfordtube.com.* **Traveline** ☎ *0871/200–2233* ⊕ *www.traveline.org.uk.*

CAR TRAVEL

Most towns in this area are within a one- or two-hour drive of central London—except during rush hour. Although the roads are good, this wealthy section of the commuter belt has heavy traffic, even on the secondary roads. Parking in towns can be a problem, so take advantage of public parking lots near the outskirts of town centers.

TRAIN TRAVEL

Trains to Oxford (one hour) and the region depart from London's Paddington Station. Trains bound for Ascot (50 minutes) leave from Waterloo every 30 minutes. National Rail Enquiries has information.

Contacts National Rail Enquiries ☎ *0845/748–4950* ⊕ *www.nationalrail.co.uk.*

RESTAURANTS

Londoners weekend here, and where they go, stellar restaurants follow. Bray (near Windsor), Marlow, and Great Milton (near Oxford) claim some excellent tables; you will need to book months ahead for these. Simple pub food, as well as classic French cuisine, can be enjoyed in waterside settings at many restaurants beside the Thames. Reservations are often not required but are strongly recommended, especially on weekends.

6

HOTELS

From converted country houses to refurbished Elizabethan inns, the region's accommodations are rich in history and distinctive in appeal. Many hotels cultivate traditional gardens and retain a sense of the past with impressive collections of antiques. Book ahead, particularly in summer. *Hotel reviews have been shortened. For full information, visit Fodors.com.*

WHAT IT COSTS IN POUNDS			
$	$$	$$$	$$$$
Restaurants	under £15	£15–£19	£20–£25	over £25
Hotels	under £100	£100–£160	£161–£220	over £220

Restaurant prices are the average cost of a main course at dinner or, if dinner isn't served, at lunch. Hotel prices are the lowest cost of a standard double room in high season, including 20% V.A.T.

VISITOR INFORMATION

Contacts River Thames Alliance ⊕ *www.visitthames.co.uk.*
Tourism Southeast ⊕ *www.visitsoutheastengland.com.*

WINDSOR, MARLOW, AND ENVIRONS

Windsor Castle is one of the jewels of the area known as Royal Windsor, but a journey around this section of the Thames has other classic pleasures. The town of Eton holds the eponymous private school, Ascot has its famous racecourse, and Cliveden is a stately home turned into a grand hotel.

The stretch of the Thames Valley from Marlow to Henley-on-Thames is enchanting. Walking through its fields and along its waterways, it's easy to see how it inspired Kenneth Grahame's 1908 children's book *The Wind in the Willows.* Lining each bank are fine wooded hills, with spacious homes, flower gardens, and neat lawns that stretch to the water's edge.

WINDSOR

21 miles west of London.

Only a small portion of old Windsor—the settlement that grew up around the town's famous castle during the Middle Ages—has survived. In the time of Sir John Falstaff and *The Merry Wives of Windsor,* the town was famous for its convivial inns—in 1650, it had about 70 of them. These days only a few remain. Windsor can feel overrun by tourists in summer, but despite this romantics will still appreciate cobbled Church Lane and noble Queen Charlotte Street, opposite the castle entrance.

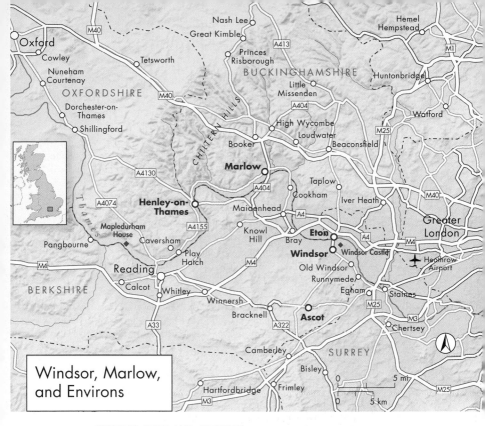

Windsor, Marlow,
and Environs

GETTING HERE AND AROUND

Fast Green Line buses leave from the Colonnades, opposite London's Victoria Coach Station, every half hour for the 70-minute trip to Windsor. First Group has frequent services from Heathrow Airport's Terminal 5; the journey takes less than an hour.

Trains travel from London Waterloo every 30 minutes, or you can catch a more frequent train from Paddington and change at Slough. The trip takes less than an hour from Waterloo and about 30 minutes from Paddington. By car, the drive on the M4 from London takes about an hour. Park in one of the public lots near the edge of the town center. Compact Windsor is easy to explore on foot.

TOURS City Sightseeing operates hop-on, hop-off tours (£10.50) of Windsor and Eton.

TIMING

Windsor is at its best in winter and fall, when there are fewer tour groups. In summer it can be uncomfortably packed.

ESSENTIALS

Bus Contacts First Group ☎ 0175/352–4144 ⊕ www.firstgroup.com.
Green Line ☎ 0844/801–7261 ⊕ www.greenline.co.uk.

Tour Information City Sightseeing ☎ *0780/871–3938* ⊕ *www. city-sightseeing.com.*

Visitor Information Royal Windsor Information Centre ⊠ *Old Booking Hall, Windsor Royal Station, Thames St.* ☎ *01753/743900, 01753/743907 for accommodations* ⊕ *www.windsor.gov.uk.*

EXPLORING

Fodor's Choice **Windsor Castle.** From William the Conqueror to Queen Victoria, the
★ kings and queens of England added towers and wings to this brooding, imposing castle, visible for miles and now the largest inhabited castle in the world. Despite the multiplicity of hands involved in its design, the palace manages to have a unity of style and character. The most impressive view of Windsor Castle is from the A332 road, coming into town from the south. Admission includes an audio guide and, if you wish, a guided tour of the castle precincts. Entrance lines can be long in season and you're likely to spend at least half a day here, so come early. When the Queen is in town, the guard and a regimental band parade through town to the castle gate; when she's away, a drum-and-fife band takes over.

William the Conqueror began work on the castle in the 11th century, and Edward III modified and extended it in the mid-1300s. One of Edward's largest contributions was the enormous and distinctive **Round Tower.** Between 1824 and 1837, George IV transformed the still essentially medieval castle into the fortified royal palace you see today. Most of England's kings and queens have demonstrated their undying attachment to the castle, the only royal residence in continuous use by the Royal Family since the Middle Ages.

As you enter the castle, **Henry VIII's gateway** leads uphill into the wide castle precincts, where you're free to wander. Across from the entrance is the exquisite **St. George's Chapel** (closed on Sunday). Here lie 10 of the kings of England, including Henry VI, Charles I, and Henry VIII (Jane Seymour is the only one of his six wives buried here). One of the noblest buildings in England, the chapel was built in the Perpendicular style popular in the 15th and 16th centuries, with stained-glass windows; a high, vaulted ceiling; and intricately carved choir stalls. The colorful heraldic banners of the Knights of the Garter—the oldest British Order of Chivalry, founded by Edward III in 1348—hang in the choir. The ceremony in which the knights are installed as members of the order has been held here with much pageantry for more than five centuries.

The **North Terrace** provides especially good views across the Thames to Eton College, perhaps the most famous of Britain's exclusive "public" boys' schools. From the terrace, you enter the **State Apartments,** which are open to the public most days. On display to the left of the entrance to the State Apartments in Windsor Castle, **Queen Mary's Dolls' House** is a perfect miniature Georgian palace-within-a-palace, created in 1923. Electric lights glow, the doors all have tiny keys, and a miniature library holds Lilliputian-size books written especially for the young queen by famous authors of the 1920s.

Although a fire in 1992 gutted some of the State Apartments, hardly any works of art were lost. Phenomenal repair work brought to new life the **Grand Reception Room,** the **Green and Crimson Drawing Rooms,** and the **State and Octagonal Dining Rooms.** A green oak hammer-beam (a short horizontal roof beam that projects from the tops of walls for support) roof looms over the 600-year-old **St. George's Hall,** where the Queen gives state banquets. The State Apartments contain priceless furniture, including an eye-catching Louis XVI bed and Gobelin tapestries; and paintings by Canaletto, Rubens, Van Dyck, Holbein, Dürer, and Brueghel. The tour's high points are the **Throne Room** and the **Waterloo Chamber,** where Sir Thomas Lawrence's portraits of Napoléon's victorious foes line the walls. You can also see arms and armor—look out for Henry VIII's ample suit. A visit between October and March also includes the Semi-State rooms, the private apartments of George IV, resplendent with gilded ceilings.

■**TIP➜** To see the castle come alive, view the Changing of the Guard, which takes place daily at 11 am from April through July and on alternate days at 11 am from August through March. Confirm the schedule before traveling to Windsor. ⊠ *Castle Hill* ☎ *020/7766–7304 tickets, 01753/831118 recorded information* ⊕ *www.royalcollection.org.uk* ☏ *£17.75 for Precincts, State Apartments, Gallery, St. George's Chapel, and Queen Mary's Dolls' House; £9.70 when State Apartments are closed* ⊙ *Mar.–Oct., daily 9:45–5:15, last admission at 4; Nov.–Feb., daily 9:45–4:15, last admission at 3.*

QUICK BITES

Crooked House of Windsor. With two tiny rooms in a 300-year-old house, this favorite for tea and plates of cakes and scones (£8.50) is open until 5:30. ⊠ *51 High St.* ☎ *01753/857534* ⊕ *www.crooked-house.com.*

Windsor Great Park. The remains of an ancient royal hunting forest, this park stretches for some 5,000 acres south of Windsor Castle. Much of it is open to the public and can be seen by car or on foot, including its geographical focal points, the romantic **Long Walk,** a 3-mile path designed by Charles II to join castle and park, and **Virginia Water,** a 2-mile-long lake. **Valley Gardens** is particularly vibrant in April and May, when the dazzling multicolored azaleas are in full bloom. ⊠ *Entrances on A329, A332, B383, and Wick La.* ☎ *01784/435544* ⊕ *www.theroyallandscape.co.uk* ☏ *Free* ⊙ *Daily dawn–dusk.*

Savill Garden. The main horticultural delight of Windsor Great Park, this exquisite garden is about 4 miles from Windsor Castle. The 35 acres of ornamental gardens contain an impressive display of 2,500 rose bushes and a tremendous diversity of trees and shrubs. The Savill Building, easily recognizable by its undulating roof in the shape of a leaf, holds a visitor center, restaurant, and terrace where you can dine overlooking the garden, as well as a large shopping area where there are plenty of gifts, cards, and original artworks. ⊠ *Wick Rd., Egham* ☎ *01784/435544* ⊕ *www.theroyallandscape.co.uk* ☏ *£9 Mar.–Oct., £6.50 Nov.–Feb.* ⊙ *Mar.–Oct., daily 10–6; Nov.–Feb., daily 10–4:30; parking charge.*

BOATING ON THE THAMES

"There is nothing—absolutely nothing—half so much worth doing as simply messing about in boats." So says the Water Rat in Kenneth Grahame's children's novel *The Wind in the Willows*. It's hard to beat gliding on the river and tying up for a picnic or lunch at a riverside pub. Putter about in a rowboat, or take one of the many organized trips. Your pace slows down: boats aren't allowed to travel above 5 mph.

CHOOSE A BOAT
Most boats rented by the hour accommodate four people. Motorboats are noisy, but you can opt for electric canoes or launches that have canopies. Punts (flat-bottom wooden boats) require a strong arm so you can maneuver the long pole and push the boat along. For information, see ⊕ *www.visitthames.co.uk*.

MESS ABOUT ON THE RIVER
The main hubs for hiring self-drive boats on the Thames are at Windsor, Henley-on-Thames, and Oxford. The cost varies from £15 an hour for a rowboat, £25 for an electric boat, and £60 for half a day with a punt, to £125 a day for a motor cruiser.

Hobbs of Henley ⊠ *Station Rd., Henley-on-Thames* ☎ *01491/572035* ⊕ *www.hobbs-of-henley.com*.

John Logie Motorboats ⊠ *The Promenade, Barry Ave., Windsor* ☎ *07774/983809*.

Oxford River Cruises ⊠ *Folly Bridge, Oxford* ☎ *01865/269889* ⊕ *www.oxfordrivercruises.com*.

PICK AN ORGANIZED CRUISE
Windsor Castle and Henley-on-Thames, where you can stop for the River and Rowing Museum, and Mapledurham all lie on the banks of the Thames. Thames River Cruise has outings to Mapledurham from Caversham, about six miles southwest of Henley-on-Thames, on weekends. Salter's Steamers runs short round-trips out of Windsor, Henley, Marlow, and Oxford, and French Brothers offers round-trips from Windsor. Oxford River Cruises *(see above)* conducts a one-hour cruise from Folly Bridge in Oxford and a longer trip (2½ hours) up to Godstow.

French Brothers ⊠ *The Promenade, Barry Ave., Windsor* ☎ *01753/851900* ⊕ *www.boat-trips. co.uk*.

Salter's Steamers ⊠ *Folly Bridge, Oxford* ☎ *01865/243421* ⊕ *www.salterssteamers.co.uk*.

Thames River Cruise ⊠ *Bridge St., Reading* ☎ *0118/948–1088* ⊕ *www.thamesrivercruise.co.uk*.

WHERE TO EAT
Bray, a tiny village 6 miles outside Windsor, is known for its restaurants more than anything else. Fat Duck, the restaurant of star chef Heston Blumenthal—an advocate of molecular gastronomy famed for bizarre taste combinations such as scrambled-egg-and-bacon ice cream—is scheduled to reopen by August 2015 after refurbishment.

$$
MODERN BRITISH ✕ **Bel and the Dragon.** Sit streetside and watch as village life streams by, or cozy up in the oak-beamed bar of this historic inn dating from the 11th century. Old meets new as inglenook fireplaces and stone walls are juxtaposed with colorfully painted chairs and paneling. The menu shows the same judicious mixture; served by a young and friendly staff,

the creative dishes might include wild garlic and white onion soup, pink peppercorn squid with chili jam, roasted suckling pig, or slow-cooked shoulder of lamb. Don't miss out on the delicious thyme and duck-fat roasted potatoes from the rotisserie. $ *Average main: £17* ⊠ *Thames St.* ☎ *01753/866056* ⊕ *www.belandthedragon-windsor.co.uk.*

$$$
MODERN BRITISH
✕ **Hinds Head.** Esteemed chef Heston Blumenthal owns this traditional pub across the road from his destination restaurant Fat Duck—expect less extreme dishes at more affordable prices. The atmosphere and dress code are relaxed, and the look of the place is historical, with exposed beams, polished wood-panel walls, and brick fireplaces. A brilliant modern take on traditional English cuisine, the menu includes tea-smoked salmon with soda bread as a starter, followed by lemon sole with samphire and pickled cucumber, and Hereford rib-eye steak with bone-marrow sauce and triple-cooked fries. $ *Average main: £23* ⊠ *High St., Bray-on-Thames* ☎ *01628/626151* ⊕ *www.hindsheadbray.com* ☾ *No dinner Sun.*

$$
BRITISH
✕ **Two Brewers.** Locals congregate in a pair of low-ceiling rooms at this 17th-century establishment by the gates of Windsor Great Park. Those under 18 aren't allowed inside the pub (though they can be served at a few outdoor tables), but adults will find a suitable collection of wine, espresso, and local beer, plus an excellent menu with such dishes as sausages with mash and pea gravy, fish cakes, and many sandwiches. On Sundays the pub serves a traditional, hearty lunchtime roast. $ *Average main: £15* ⊠ *34 Park St.* ☎ *01753/855426* ⊕ *www.twobrewerswindsor. co.uk* ⚑ *Reservations essential* ☾ *No dinner Fri.–Sun.*

WHERE TO STAY

$$$$
HOTEL
Fodor's Choice
★
🛏 **Cliveden.** If you've ever wondered what it would feel like to be an Edwardian grandee, then sweep up the drive to this stately home, one of Britain's grandest hotels. **Pros:** like stepping back in time; outstanding sense of luxury; beautiful grounds. **Cons:** airplanes fly overhead; no tea- or coffee-making facilities in rooms. $ *Rooms from: £265* ⊠ *Cliveden Rd.Taplow* ☎ *01628/668561* ⊕ *www.clivedenhouse.co.uk* ⚑ *22 rooms, 16 suites, 1 cottage* ⑩ *Breakfast.*

$$
B&B/INN
FAMILY
🛏 **Langton House.** A former residence for representatives of the crown, this Victorian mansion on a quiet, leafy road is a 10-minute walk from Windsor Castle. **Pros:** soothing decor; family-friendly environment. **Cons:** not for those who prefer privacy; a little out of town. $ *Rooms from: £110* ⊠ *46 Alma Rd.* ☎ *01753/858299* ⊕ *www.langtonhouse. co.uk* ⚑ *5 rooms* ⑩ *Breakfast.*

$$
HOTEL
🛏 **Mercure Windsor Castle Hotel.** You're treated to an exceptional view of Windsor Castle's Changing of the Guard ceremony from this former coaching inn, parts of which date back to the 16th century. **Pros:** excellent location; wonderful afternoon tea. **Cons:** older rooms are small; furniture is faux antique. $ *Rooms from: £140* ⊠ *18 High St.* ☎ *01753/252800* ⊕ *www.mercure.com* ⚑ *108 rooms, 4 suites* ⑩ *Breakfast.*

$
B&B/INN
🛏 **Rainworth House.** Ducks come a-calling at this country house that has an expansive green lawn. **Pros:** elegant rooms; peaceful setting 2 miles from Windsor; tennis court. **Cons:** out of town. $ *Rooms from: £98* ⊠ *Oakley Green Rd.* ☎ *01753/856749* ⊕ *www.rainworthhouse.com* ⚑ *7 rooms* ⑩ *Breakfast.*

6

The horses at Royal Ascot are beautiful, and so is the formal attire of the memorably dressed spectators.

NIGHTLIFE AND THE ARTS

Theatre Royal. Productions have been staged since 1910 at the Royal, one of Britain's leading provincial theaters. It presents plays and musicals year-round, including a pantomime for five weeks around Christmas. ⌧ *Thames St.* ☎ *01753/853888* ⊕ *www.theatreroyalwindsor.co.uk.*

SHOPPING

Check out Peascod Street, opposite the castle, for independent stores selling gifts, jewelry, toiletries, chocolates, and other items.

Windsor Royal Station. The highlights at this shopping center in a Victorian-era train station include men's and women's fashions from Jaeger, Viyella, Hobbs, Whistles, and other purveyors. ⌧ *5 Goswell Hill* ☎ *01753/797070.*

ETON

½ mile north of Windsor, 23 miles west of London.

Some observers may find it symbolic that almost opposite Windsor Castle—which embodies the continuity of the royal tradition—stands Eton, a school that for centuries has educated many of the country's leaders. With High Street, its single main street, leading from the river to the famous school, the old-fashioned town of Eton is much quieter than Windsor.

GETTING HERE AND AROUND

A footbridge across the Thames links Eton to Windsor. Most visitors barely notice passing from one to the other.

EXPLORING

Fodor'sChoice **Eton College.** Signs warn drivers of "Boys Crossing" on the approach to
★ the splendid Tudor-style buildings of Eton College, the distinguished
boarding school for boys ages 13 through 18 that was founded in
1440 by King Henry VI. It's all terrifically photogenic, because during the college semester students still dress in pinstriped trousers,
swallow-tailed coats, and stiff collars. Rivaling St. George's at Windsor in terms of size, the Gothic **Chapel** contains superb 15th-century
grisaille wall paintings juxtaposed against modern stained glass by
John Piper. Beyond the cloisters are the school's playing fields where,
according to the duke of Wellington, the Battle of Waterloo was really
won, since so many of his officers had learned discipline and strategy
during their school days. David Cameron is among the country's prime
ministers educated here. The **Museum of Eton Life** has displays on the
school's history and vignettes of school life. Public tours begin again in
2015 after completion of renovation work. ⊠ *Brewhouse Yard, Eton,
Berkshire* ☎ *01753/671177* ⊕ *www.etoncollege.com* ☉ *Call ahead for
open times.*

WHERE TO EAT

$$ ✗ **Gilbey's Eton.** Just over the bridge from Windsor, this restaurant at
MODERN BRITISH the center of Eton's Antiques Row serves a changing menu of imaginative fare, from quail, mushroom, and pistachio rillettes with pickled
rhubarb to mustard crust lamb with black-eyed beans and shallots.
The £19.50 lunch and early-dinner menu is a good deal. Well-priced
wines, both French and from the restaurant's own English vineyard
are a specialty, as are the savories—think meat, fish, and vegetarian
pâtés—and scrumptious cakes served with afternoon tea on weekends.
The conservatory, with its colorful scattering of cushions, is a pleasant
place to sit, as is the courtyard garden. $ *Average main: £17* ⊠ *82–83
High St., Eton, Berkshire* ☎ *01753/854921* ⊕ *www.gilbeygroup.com.*

ASCOT

8 miles southwest of Eton, 28 miles southwest of London.

The posh town of Ascot (pronounced *as*-cut) has for centuries been
famous for horse racing and for style. Queen Anne chose to have a
racecourse here, and the first race meeting took place in 1711: Royal
Meeting, or Royal Ascot. The impressive show of millinery at the race
was immortalized in *My Fair Lady,* in which a hat with osprey feathers and black-and-white silk roses transformed Eliza Doolittle into a
grand lady. Betting on the races at England's most prestigious course is
as important as dressing up; it's all part of the fun.

GETTING HERE AND AROUND

If you're driving, leave M4 at Junction 6 and take A332. Trains from
London leave Waterloo Station every half hour, and the journey takes 50
minutes. The racecourse is a seven-minute walk from the train station.

EXPLORING

Ascot Racecourse. The races run regularly throughout the year, and Royal Ascot takes place annually in mid-June. ■ **TIP➜** Tickets for Royal Ascot generally go on sale in November—buy them well in advance. Prices range from £13 for standing room on the heath to £73 for seats in the stands. Car parking costs £20. ✉ *A329* ☎ *0844/346–3000* ⊕ *www. ascot.co.uk.*

WHERE TO STAY

$$$$
HOTEL
Fodor'sChoice
★

Coworth Park. Much imagination and thoughtful renovation has transformed this 18th-century mansion, set in 240 acres of parkland, into a playful and contemporary lodging. **Pros:** country-house atmosphere; attentive and friendly service; free activities for kids. **Cons:** bathrobes weigh you down. $ *Rooms from: £305* ✉ *Blacknest Rd.* ☎ *01344/876600* ⊕ *www.coworthpark.com* ↝*55 rooms, 15 suites* ❑ *Breakfast.*

MARLOW

17 miles northwest of Ascot, 14 miles northwest of Windsor.

Just inside the Buckinghamshire border, Marlow and the surrounding area overflow with Thames-side prettiness. The unusual suspension bridge here, which dates to the early 1830s, was designed by William Tierney Clark, the architect of the bridge in Hungary linking Buda and Pest. Marlow has numerous striking old buildings, particularly the privately owned Georgian houses along Peter and West streets. In 1817 the Romantic poet Percy Bysshe Shelley stayed with friends at 67 West Street and then bought **Albion House** on the same street. His second wife, Mary, completed her Gothic novel *Frankenstein* here. Marlow hosts its own one-day regatta in mid-June. The town is a good base from which to join the **Thames Path** to Henley-on-Thames. On summer weekends tourists often overwhelm the town.

GETTING HERE AND AROUND

Trains leave London from Paddington every half hour and involve a change at Maidenhead; the journey takes an hour. By car, leave M4 at Junction 8/9, following A404 and then A4155. From M40, join A404 at Junction 4.

ESSENTIALS

Visitor Information Marlow Tourist Information Centre ✉ *55a High St.* ☎ *01628/483597* ⊕ *www.visitbuckingamshire.org.*

EXPLORING

Swan-Upping. This traditional event, which dates back 800 years, takes place in Marlow during the third week of July. By bizarre ancient laws, the Queen owns the country's swans, so each year swan-markers in skiffs start from Sunbury-on-Thames, catching the new cygnets and marking their beaks to establish ownership. The Queen's Swan Marker, dressed in scarlet livery, presides over this colorful ceremony. ☎ *01628/523030.*

WHERE TO EAT AND STAY

$$$$ FRENCH 🍴 **Vanilla Pod.** Discreet and intimate, this restaurant is a showcase for the French-inspired cuisine of chef Michael Macdonald, who, as the name implies, holds vanilla in high esteem. The fixed-price menu includes smoked salmon in Bourbon vanilla, and you can sample Tahitian vanilla in the desserts of rice pudding with spiced plums and bitter chocolate soup with spiced bread. The three-course lunch menu is a fantastic bargain at £19.50, and the seven-course *menu gourmand* for £55 is a tour de force. Vegetarians have a separate menu. [$] *Average main: £45* ✉ *31 West St.* ☎ *01628/898101* 🌐 *www.thevanillapod.co.uk* ✍ *Reservations essential* 🕓 *Closed Sun. and Mon.*

$$$ HOTEL 🏨 **Macdonald Compleat Angler.** Although fishing aficionados consider this luxurious 17th-century Thames-side inn the ideal place to stay, the place is stylish enough to attract those with no interest in casting a line. **Pros:** gorgeous rooms; great views of the Thames. **Cons:** river views cost more except Rooms 9 and 10; need a car to get around. [$] *Rooms from: £170* ✉ *Marlow Bridge, Bisham Rd.* ☎ *0844/879–9128* 🌐 *www.macdonaldhotels.co.uk/compleatangler* 🛏 *61 rooms, 3 suites* 🍽 *Breakfast.*

WALK THE CHILTERNS

Part of the Chiltern Hills is an **Area of Outstanding Beauty** (🌐 *www.chilternsaonb.org*), a nature reserve that stretches over 320 square miles, taking in chalk hills, valleys, forests, lakes, and pretty towns. Its springtime bluebell woods are famed, and its autumn colors are glorious. The chestnut-color birds soaring above will be red kites. You'll likely drive in and out of the Chilterns as you explore, or you could walk part of the circular 134-mile Chiltern Way. An easy 5-mile circular walk starts from Henley-on-Thames and takes in the picturesque Hambleden Valley.

6

HENLEY-ON-THAMES

7 miles southwest of Marlow, 36 miles west of central London.

Fodor's Choice ★ Henley's fame is based on one thing: rowing. The Henley Royal Regatta, held at the cusp of June and July on a long, straight stretch of the River Thames, has made the little riverside town famous throughout the world. Townspeople launched the Henley Regatta in 1839, initiating the Grand Challenge Cup, the most famous of many trophies. The best amateur oarsmen from around the globe compete in crews of eight, four, or two, or as single scullers. For many spectators, the event is on a par with Royal Ascot and Wimbledon.

The town is set in a broad valley between gentle hillsides. Henley's historic buildings, including half-timber Georgian cottages and inns—as well as one of Britain's oldest theaters, the Kenton—are all within a few minutes' walk of each other. The river near Henley is alive with boats of every shape and size, from luxury cabin cruisers to tiny rowboats.

GETTING HERE AND AROUND

Frequent First Great Western trains depart for Henley from London Paddington; journey time is around an hour. If you're driving from London or from the west, leave M4 at Junction 8/9 and follow A404(M) and then A4130 to Henley Bridge. From Marlow, Henley is a 7-mile drive southwest on A4155.

ESSENTIALS

Visitor Information Henley Visitor Information Centre ⊠ *Henley Town Hall, Market Pl.* ☎ *01491/578034* ⊕ *www.henley-on-thames.org.*

EXPLORING

Mapledurham House. The house anchors a section of the Thames that inspired Kenneth Grahame's 1908 *The Wind in the Willows*, which began as a bedtime story for Grahame's son Alastair while the family lived at Pangbourne. Some of E. F. Shepard's illustrations are of specific sites along the river—none more fabled than this redbrick Elizabethan mansion, bristling with tall chimneys, mullioned windows, and battlements. It became the inspiration for Shepard's vision of Toad Hall. Family portraits, elegant oak staircases, wood paneling, and plasterwork ceilings abound. Look out for the life-size deer guarding the fireplace in the entrance hall. There's also a 15th-century working grain mill on the river. Mapledurham House is 10 miles southwest of Henley-on-Thames. On summer weekend afternoons you can reach the house by boat from Caversham Promenade in Reading *(⇨ see Thames River Cruises in the Boating on the Thames sidebar).* ⊠ *Off A074, Mapledurham* ☎ *0118/972–3350* ⊕ *www.mapledurham.co.uk* ⊡ *House and mill £8.50; grounds £1* ⊘ *Easter–Sept., weekends and national holidays Mon. 2–5:30; Oct., Sun. 2–5:30; last admission 30 mins before closing.*

FAMILY **River & Rowing Museum.** Focusing on the history and sport of rowing, this absorbing museum includes exhibits devoted to actual vessels, from a Saxon log boat to a Victorian steam launch. Exhibits in one gallery tell the story of the Thames as it flows from its source to the ocean, and those in another explore the town's history and its regatta. A *Wind in the Willows* exhibit evokes the settings of the famous children's book. ⊠ *Mill Meadows* ☎ *01491/415600* ⊕ *www.rrm.co.uk* ⊡ *£8* ⊘ *May–Aug., daily 10–5:30; Sept.–Apr., daily 10–5.*

St. Mary's Church. With a 16th-century "checkerboard" tower, St. Mary's is a stone's throw from the bridge over the Thames. The adjacent, yellow-washed **Chantry House,** built in 1420, is one of England's few remaining merchant houses from the period. It's an unspoiled example of the rare timber-frame design, with upper floors jutting out. You can enjoy tea here on Sunday afternoons in summer. ⊠ *Hart St.* ☎ *01491/577340* ⊕ *www.stmaryshenley.org.uk* ⊡ *Free* ⊘ *Church daily 9–5.*

WHERE TO EAT AND STAY

$$
MODERN BRITISH

✕**Crooked Billet.** It's worth negotiating the maze of lanes leading to this 17th-century country pub 6 miles west of Henley-on-Thames. Menu choices might include cured salmon with celeriac slaw or roast pheasant with chestnuts and smoked bacon. British cheeses and filling desserts such as toffee pudding round out the meals here. There's a garden for open-air dining and live music on many evenings. Fixed-price lunches are a good deal. The restaurant is popular, so book ahead. $ *Average main: £18* ⊠ *Newlands La., Stoke Row* ☎ *01491/681048* ⊕ *www.thecrookedbillet.co.uk.*

$ ✕ **The Three Tuns.** Walk past the cozy bar in this traditional 17th-century
MODERN BRITISH pub to dine in the snug dining room with the clutch of locals who come nightly. Traditionalists among them are sampling pub grub like fish-and-chips or sausages and mash, while the more adventurous are tucking into squid, choirzo, and prawn with homemade sourdough toast or scallops with spiced crab cakes. Both types opt for the waist-expanding tarts and crumbles for dessert. The two-course lunch is a steal at £10. $ *Average main: £13* ⊠ *5 Market Pl.* ☎ *01491/410138* ⊕ *www.threetunshenley.co.uk* ⊘ *No dinner Sun.*

$ ⛫ **Falaise House.** The rooms in this B&B, a Georgian town house in the
B&B/INN center of Henley, are individually furnished in a soft and warm contemporary style that mixes traditional and modern pieces. **Pros:** family-run; great breakfasts; fluffy towels. **Cons:** on the main road; two-night minimum on summer weekends. $ *Rooms from: £95* ⊠ *37 Market Pl.* ☎ *01491/573388* ⊕ *www.falaisehouse.com* ↰ *6 rooms* ⦿| *Breakfast.*

$$ ⛫ **Hotel du Vin.** A sprawling brick brewery near the river has been trans-
HOTEL formed into a distinctively modern architectural showplace. **Pros:** striking decor; river views from upper floors; wine bar and bistro good for oenophiles. **Cons:** won't thrill traditionalists; a charge for parking. $ *Rooms from: £120* ⊠ *New St.* ☎ *01491/848400* ↰ *41 rooms, 2 suites* ⦿| *Breakfast.*

NIGHTLIFE AND THE ARTS

Henley Festival. A floating stage and spectacular musical events from classical to folk draw a dress-code-abiding crowd to this upscale July festival held the week after the regatta. ☎ *01491/843404* ⊕ *www.henley-festival.co.uk.*

SPORTS AND THE OUTDOORS

Henley Royal Regatta. A series of rowing competitions attracting participants from many countries, the regatta takes place over five days in late June and early July. Large tents are erected along both sides of a straight stretch of the Thames known as Henley Reach, and every surrounding field becomes a parking lot. There's plenty of space on the public towpath from which to watch the early stages of the races. ■**TIP→** If you want to attend, book a room months in advance—500,000 people turn out for the event. ☎ *01491/571900* ⊕ *www.hrr.co.uk.*

OXFORD

Fodor's Choice With arguably the most famous university in the world, Oxford has
★ been a center of learning since 1167, with only the Sorbonne preceding it. It doesn't take more than a day or two to explore its winding medieval streets, photograph its ivy-covered stone buildings and ancient churches and libraries, and even take a punt down one of its placid waterways. The town center is compact and walkable, and at its heart is Oxford University. Alumni of this prestigious institution include 48 Nobel Prize winners, 26 British prime ministers, and 28

foreign presidents, along with poets, authors, and artists such as Percy Bysshe Shelley, Oscar Wilde, and W. H. Auden.

Oxford is 55 miles northwest of London, at the junction of the rivers Thames and Cherwell. The city is larger, more interesting, and more cosmopolitan than Cambridge. All interest centers on the Old Town, which curls around the grand stone buildings, good restaurants, and historic pubs. The Victorian writer Matthew Arnold described Oxford's "dreaming spires," a phrase that has become famous. Students rush past you on the sidewalks on the way to their exams, clad with marvelous antiquarian style in their requisite mortar caps, flowing dark gowns, stiff collars, and crisp white bow ties. ■TIP➔ Watch your back when crossing roads, as bikes are everywhere.

GETTING HERE AND AROUND

Megabus, Oxford Bus Company, and Stagecoach Oxford Tube all have buses traveling from London 24 hours a day; the trip takes between 1 hour 40 minutes and 2 hours. In London, Megabus departs from Victoria Coach Station, Oxford Bus Company from nearby Buckingham Palace Road, and Stagecoach Oxford Tube has pickup points opposite Victoria Coach Station and the Marble Arch underground station. Oxford Bus Company also offers round-trip shuttle service from Gatwick (£32) every hour and Heathrow (£29) every half hour. Most of the companies have multiple stops in Oxford, with Gloucester Green, the final stop, being the most convenient for most travelers.

Trains to Oxford depart from London's Paddington Station for the one-hour trip. Oxford Station is at the western edge of the historic town center on Botley Road.

To drive, take the M40 northwest from London. It takes an hour, except during commute times, when it can take twice as long. In-town parking is notoriously difficult, so it's best to use one of the five free park-and-ride lots and pay for the bus to the city. The Thornhill Park and Ride and the St. Clement's parking lot before the roundabout that leads to Magdalen Bridge are convenient to the M40.

TOURS The Oxford Tourist Information Centre has information on the many guided walking tours of the city. The best way of gaining access to the collegiate buildings is to take the two-hour university and city tour, which leaves the center daily. City Sightseeing offers hop-on, hop-off bus tours (£13.50) with 19 stops around Oxford; your ticket, purchased from the driver, is good for 24 hours.

TIMING

You can explore Oxford's major sights in a day or so, but it takes longer to spend an hour each in the key museums and absorb the scene at the colleges. Some colleges are open only in the afternoons during university terms. When the undergraduates are in residence, access is often restricted to the chapels, dining rooms, and libraries, and picnicking in the quadrangles is discouraged. All the colleges are closed for exams on certain days from mid-April to late June.

ESSENTIALS

Bus Contacts Megabus ☎ *0871/266–3333 Inquiry line, 0960/160–900 booking line, calls cost 60p per minute* ⊕ *www.megabus.com.* **Oxford Bus Company** ☎ *01865/785400* ⊕ *www.oxfordbus.co.uk.* **Stagecoach Oxford Tube** ☎ *01865/772250* ⊕ *www.oxfordtube.com.*

Visitor and Tour Information City Sightseeing ☎ *01865/790522* ⊕ *www. citysightseeingoxford.com.* **Oxford Tourist Information Centre** ⊠ *15/16 Broad St.* ☎ *01865/252200* ⊕ *www.visitoxfordandoxfordshire.com.*

EXPLORING

Oxford University isn't one easily identifiable campus, but a sprawling mixture of 38 colleges scattered around the city center, each with its own distinctive identity and focus. Oxford students live and study at their own college, and also use the centralized resources of the overarching university. The individual colleges are deeply competitive. Most of the grounds and dining halls and chapels are open to visitors, though the opening times (displayed at the entrance gates) vary greatly.

The **city center** of Oxford is bordered by High Street, St. Giles, and Longwall Street. Most of Oxford University's most famous buildings are within this area. **Jericho,** the neighborhood where many students live, is west of St. Giles, just outside the city center. Its narrow streets are lined with quaint cottages. The area north of the center around Banbury and Marston Ferry Roads is called **Summertown,** and the area east of the center, along St. Clement's Street, is known as **St. Clement's.**

TOP ATTRACTIONS

Fodor'sChoice
★

Ashmolean Museum. Britain's oldest public museum displays its rich and varied collections from the Neolithic to the present day over five floors. Innovative and spacious galleries on the theme of "Crossing Cultures, Crossing Time" explore connections between the priceless Egyptian, Greek, Roman, Chinese, and Indian artifacts, and also display a superb art collection. Among the highlights are drawings by Raphael, the shell-encrusted mantle of Powhatan (father of Pocahontas), the lantern belonging to the early-17th-century political conspirator Guy Fawkes, and the Alfred Jewel, which dates from the reign (871–899) of King Alfred the Great. ■**TIP**→ There's too much to see in one visit, but admission is free, so you can return as often as you want. The Ashmolean Dining Room, Oxford's first rooftop restaurant, is a good spot for refreshments. ⊠ *Beaumont St.* ☎ *01865/278002* ⊕ *www.ashmolean. org* ⊡ *Free* ☉ *Tues.–Sun. and national holidays 10–6.*

Christ Church. Built in 1546, the college of Christ Church is referred to by its members as "The House." This is the site of Oxford's largest quadrangle, Tom Quad, named after the huge bell (6¼ tons) that hangs in the Christopher Wren–designed gate tower and rings 101 times at five past nine every evening in honor of the original number of Christ Church scholars. The vaulted, 800-year-old chapel in one corner has been Oxford's cathedral since the time of Henry VIII. The college's medieval dining hall, re-created for the Harry Potter films, contains portraits of many famous alumni, including 13 of Britain's prime ministers.

6

■TIP→ The dining hall is open on weekdays from 10:30 to 11:40 and 2:30 to 4:30, and on weekends from 2:30 to 4:30. Lewis Carroll, the author of *Alice in Wonderland,* was a teacher of mathematics here for many years; a shop opposite the meadows on St. Aldate's sells Alice paraphernalia. ⊠ *St. Aldate's* ☎ *01865/276492* ⊕ *www.chch.ox.ac.uk* ⊡ *£8; £8.50 in July and Aug.* ◷ *Mon.–Sat. 10–5, Sun. 2–5; last admission 30 mins before closing.*

Christ Church Picture Gallery. This connoisseur's delight in Canterbury Quadrangle exhibits works by the Italian masters as well as Hals, Rubens, and Van Dyck. Drawings in the 2,000-strong collection are shown on a changing basis. ⊠ *Oriel Sq.* ☎ *01865/276172* ⊕ *www.chch. ox.ac.uk* ⊡ *£3* ◷ *June, Mon. and Wed.–Sat. 10:30–5, Sun. 2–5; July–Sept., Mon.–Sat. 10:30–5, Sun. 2–5; Oct.–May, Mon. and Wed.–Sat. 10:30–1 and 2–4:30, Sun. 2–4:30.*

Fodor'sChoice ★ **Magdalen College.** Founded in 1458, with a handsome main quadrangle and a supremely monastic air, Magdalen (pronounced *maud*-lin) is one of the most impressive of Oxford's colleges and attracts its most artistic students. Alumni include P. G. Wodehouse, Oscar Wilde, and the poet John Betjeman. The school's large, square tower is a famous local landmark. ■TIP→ To enhance your visit, take a stroll around the Deer Park and along Addison's Walk; then have tea in the Old Kitchen, which overlooks the river. ⊠ *High St.* ☎ *01865/276000* ⊕ *www.magd. ox.ac.uk* ⊡ *£5* ◷ *July–Sept., daily noon–7 or dusk; Oct.–June, daily 1–6 or dusk.*

FAMILY **Oxford University Museum of Natural History.** This highly decorative Victorian Gothic creation of cast iron and glass, more a cathedral than a museum, is worth a visit for its architecture alone. Among the eclectic collections of entomology, geology, mineralogy, and zoology are the towering skeleton of a *Tyrannosaurus rex* and casts of a dodo's foot and head. There's plenty for children to explore and touch. ⊠ *Parks Rd.* ☎ *01865/272950* ⊕ *www.oum.ox.ac.uk* ⊡ *Free* ◷ *Daily 10–5.*

FAMILY Fodor'sChoice ★ **Pitt Rivers Museum.** More than half a million intriguing archaeological and anthropological items from around the globe, based on the collection bequeathed by Lieutenant-General Augustus Henry Lane Fox Pitt Rivers in 1884, are crammed into a multitude of glass cases and drawers. Items are organized thematically rather than geographically, an eccentric approach that's surprisingly thought provoking. Labels are handwritten, and children are given flashlights to explore the farthest corners and spot the world's smallest dolly. Give yourself plenty of time to wander through the displays of shrunken heads, Hawaiian feather cloaks, and fearsome masks. Children will have a field day. ⊠ *S. Parks Rd.* ☎ *01865/270927* ⊕ *www.prm.ox.ac.uk* ⊡ *Free, suggested donation £3* ◷ *Mon. noon–4:30, Tues.–Sun. and national holidays 10–4:30.*

Radcliffe Camera and Bodleian Library. A vast library and Oxford's most spectacular building, the domed Radcliffe Camera was erected between 1737 and 1749. Designed by architect James Gibbs in the Italian baroque style, it's usually surrounded by tourists with cameras trained at its golden-stone walls. The Camera contains part of the Bodleian Library's enormous collection, begun in 1602. Much like the Library

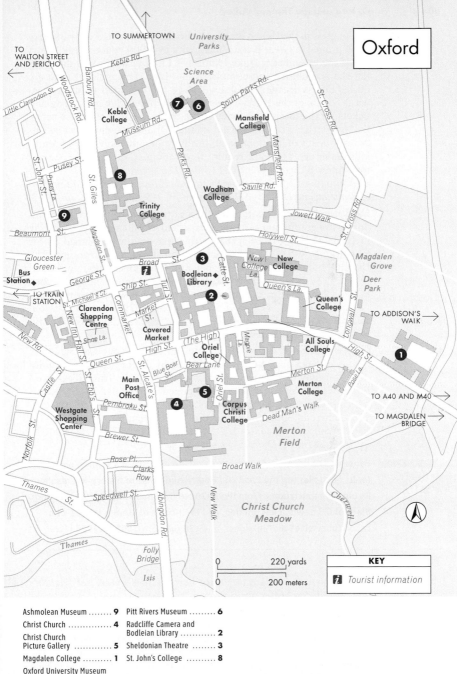

Oxford

TO SUMMERTOWN

TO WALTON STREET AND JERICHO

University Parks

Little Clarendon St.

Woodstock Rd.

Keble Rd.

Banbury Rd.

Science Area

7   **6**

South Parks Rd.

St. Cross Rd.

Keble College

Museum Rd.

Mansfield College

Mansfield Rd.

St. Giles

Pusey St.

St. John St.

Pusey La.

8

Parks Rd.

Wadham College

Savile Rd.

9

Beaumont St.

Magdalen St.

Trinity College

Jowett Walk

Holywell St.

Magdalen Grove

Deer Park

Gloucester Green

Bus Station

George St.

TO TRAIN STATION

New Inn Hall St.

St. Michael's St.

Ship St.

Cornmarket

Broad St.

3

Catte St.

Turl St.

Bodleian Library

2

New College La.

New College

Queen's La.

Queen's College

TO ADDISON'S WALK

Longwall

Clarendon Shopping Centre

Shoe La.

Market St.

Covered Market

High St.

(The High)

Oriel College

Bear Lane

Magpie La.

All Souls College

Merton St.

High St.

Rose La.

1

New Rd.

Queen St.

Blue Boar St.

St. Aldate's

Oriel St.

Merton College

TO A40 AND M40

Castle St.

St. Ebb's St.

Main Post Office

Pembroke St.

5

4

Corpus Christi College

Dead Man's Walk

TO MAGDALEN BRIDGE

Westgate Shopping Center

Norfolk St.

Brewer St.

Merton Field

Rose Pl.

Clarks Row

Broad Walk

Thames St.

Speedwell St.

Abingdon Rd.

New Walk

Christ Church Meadow

Cherwell

Thames

Folly Bridge

Isis

| 0 | 220 yards |
| 0 | 200 meters |

KEY

i *Tourist information*

of Congress in the United States, the Bodleian contains a copy of every book printed in Great Britain and grows by 5,000 items a week. Tours reveal the magnificent Duke Humfrey's Library, which was the original chained library and completed in 1488. (The ancient tomes are dusted once a decade.) Guides will show you the spots used for Hogwarts School in the Harry Potter films. ■TIP→ **Arrive early to secure tickets for the three to six daily tours. These are sold on a first-come, first-served basis (except for the extended tour on Wednesday and Saturday, which can be prebooked).** Audio tours, the only tours open to kids under age 11, don't require reservations. Call ahead to confirm tour times. ✉ *Broad St.* ☎ *01865/277216* ⊕ *www.bodleian.ox.ac.uk* ⏰ *Audio tour £2.50, minitour £5, standard tour £7, extended tour £13* ⊙ *Bodleian and Divinity School weekdays 9–5, Sat. 9–4:30, Sun. 11–5.*

Sheldonian Theatre. This fabulously ornate theater is where Oxford's impressive graduation ceremonies are held, conducted almost entirely in Latin. Dating to 1663, it was the first building designed by Sir Christopher Wren when he served as professor of astronomy. The D-shape auditorium has pillars, balconies, and an elaborately painted ceiling. The stone pillars outside are topped by 18 massive stone heads. Climb the stairs to the cupola for the best view of the city's "dreaming spires." ✉ *Broad St.* ☎ *01865/277299* ⊕ *www.sheldon. ox.ac.uk* ⏰ *£2.50* ⊙ *Mon.–Sat. 10–1 and 2–4:30. Closed for 10 days at Christmas and Easter.*

St. John's College. One of Oxford's most attractive campuses, St. John's has seven quiet quadrangles surrounded by elaborately carved buildings. You enter the first through a low wooden door. This college dates to 1555, when Sir Thomas White, a merchant, founded it. His heart is buried in the chapel (by tradition, students curse as they walk over it). The Canterbury Quad represented the first example of Italian Renaissance architecture in Oxford. ✉ *St. Giles* ☎ *01865/277300* ⊕ *www.sjc. ox.ac.uk* ⏰ *Free* ⊙ *Daily 1–5.*

QUICK BITES

Eagle and Child. Close to St. John's College, this pub is a favorite not only for its good ales (try the local Old Hooky) and sense of history, but also for its literary associations. From the 1930s to the 1960s this was the meeting place of C.S. Lewis, J.R.R. Tolkien, and their circle of literary friends who called themselves the "Inklings." ✉ *49 St. Giles* ☎ *01865/302925.*

WHERE TO EAT

In addition to the restaurants listed here, Oxford's pubs *(see Nightlife and Pubs, below)* offer options for a quick bite.

$$

FRENCH

✗ **Brasserie Blanc.** Raymond Blanc's sophisticated brasserie in the Jericho neighborhood, a hipper cousin of Le Manoir aux Quat' Saisons in Great Milton, is one of the best places to eat in Oxford. Wood floors, pale walls, and large windows keep the restaurant open and airy. The cuisine—innovative, visually striking adaptations of bourgeois French fare—sometimes incorporates Mediterranean or Asian influences. Try the pasta with Jervaulx blue cheese, chestnut, and apple or the chicken stuffed with Armagnac-soaked prunes. The selection of steaks impresses as well. The £11.50 fixed-price lunch is a good value, and there's a kids' menu. [$] *Average main: £15* ✉ *71–72 Walton St.* ☎ *01865/510999* 🌐 *www.brasserieblanc.com.*

$$ SEAFOOD 🍴 **Fishers.** Everything is remarkably fresh at what is widely viewed as the city's best fish restaurant. Seafood is prepared with a European touch and frequently comes with butter, cream, and other sauces: bream is served with fennel and black olive butter, for instance. Hot and cold shellfish platters are popular, as are the mussels in white wine and oysters in shallot vinegar. The interior has a casual nautical theme, with wooden floors and tables, porthole windows, and red sails overhead. Lunches are a very good value. [$] *Average main: £16* ✉ *36–37 St. Clement's St.* ☎ *01865/243003* 🌐 *www.fishers-restaurant.com.*

$$ MODERN BRITISH 🍴 **Gee's.** With its glass-and-steel framework, this former florist's shop just north of the town center makes a charming plant-filled conservatory dining room. The menu concentrates on the best of local produce. You could start with small bites of cured wild boar and salt-cod fritters and continue with such dishes as prosciutto and wild garlic pizzetta, bream with fennel and tapenade from the wood-fired oven, or pork, venison, and lamb chops from the charcoal grill. Chocolate and espresso tart and blood-orange sorbet make fine desserts. [$] *Average main: £16* ✉ *61 Banbury Rd.* ☎ *01865/553540* 🌐 *www.gees-restaurant.co.uk.*

6

$ CAFÉ 🍴 **Grand Café.** Golden-hue tiles and towering columns make this café both architecturally impressive and an excellent spot for sandwiches, salads, or other light fare. It's packed with tourists and the service can be slow, but this is a pretty spot for afternoon tea. From Thursday through Saturday night, it transforms into a popular cocktail bar. [$] *Average main: £8* ✉ *84 High St.* ☎ *01865/204463* 🌐 *www.thegrandcafe.co.uk.*

$$ ITALIAN 🍴 **Jamie's Italian.** Chef Jamie Oliver's mission to re-create the best rustic Italian fare manifests itself at his buzzing eatery in the diverting range of antipasti and mains. Among the latter are tuna fusilli slow-cooked with tomatoes and cinnamon, and steak *tagliata* with crunchy fennel and garlic. The various dishes served on a wood plank are a steal, and the desserts—including fruit sorbets and tutti frutti lemon meringue pie—are light and refreshing. [$] *Average main: £15* ✉ *24–26 George St.* ☎ *01865/838383* 🌐 *www.jamieoliver.com.*

$$$$ FRENCH Fodor's Choice ★ 🍴 **Le Manoir aux Quat' Saisons.** Standards are high at this 15th-century stone manor house, a hotel with a cooking school and one of the country's finest kitchens. Chef Raymond Blanc's epicurean touch shows at every turn. The innovative French creations include terrine of baby beetroot with horseradish sorbet and roasted duck breast with caramelized chicory, clementines, and jasmine tea sauce. You can dine à la carte, but if money is no object you might try one of the fixed-price dinner menus ranging from £134 to £154 (the five-course set-price lunch at £79 is easier on the wallet). There is a separate vegetarian menu, too. You need to book up to three months ahead in summer. A stroll through the hotel's herb and Japanese tea gardens is de rigueur. The pretty town of Great Milton is 7 miles southeast of Oxford. [$] *Average main: £50* ✉ *Church Rd., Great Milton* ☎ *01844/278881* 🌐 *www.manoir.com* ✍ *Reservations essential.*

WHERE TO STAY

Oxford is pricey; for the least expensive lodgings, inquire at the tourist information center about bed-and-breakfasts in locals' homes.

$ **Burlington House.** This Victorian guesthouse in Summertown, on
B&B/INN the outskirts of Oxford, shows flair in its decoration, creativity in its breakfasts, and attentiveness in its service. **Pros:** friendly staff; superior breakfasts; double-glazed windows throughout. **Cons:** 10-minute bus ride to the center; main-road location. $ *Rooms from: £94 ⊠ 374 Banbury Rd. ☎ 01865/513513 ⊕ www.burlington-hotel-oxford.co.uk ↝ 12 rooms ⟍⟋ Breakfast.*

$$$$ **Le Manoir aux Quat'Saisons.** One of the original gastronomy-focused
HOTEL hotels, Le Manoir was opened in 1984 by chef Raymond Blanc, whose
Fodor's Choice culinary talents have earned the hotel's restaurant two Michelin stars—
★ which it has held for an incredible three decades and running. **Pros:** Michelin-starred restaurant; attentive service; plush, but not stuffy, decor; perfect for romance, but accommodates kids; famous on-site cooking school. **Cons:** rooms vary—if you have specific requirements, reveal them when booking; tough on the wallet and waistline. $ *Rooms from: £545 ⊠ Church Road, Great Milton, Oxford, England ☎ 01844/278881 ⊕ www.manoir.com ↝ 32 rooms ⟍⟋ Breakfast.*

$$$ **Macdonald Randolph.** A 19th-century neo-Gothic landmark, this hotel
HOTEL is ideally situated near the Ashmolean Museum. **Pros:** handy location; grand building. **Cons:** on a busy street; some small bathrooms; formality can be a bit daunting. $ *Rooms from: £200 ⊠ Beaumont St. ☎ 0844/879–9132 ⊕ www.macdonaldhotels.co.uk/randolph ↝ 151 rooms ⟍⟋ Breakfast.*

$$$ **Malmaison Oxford Castle.** Housed in a 19th-century prison, this high-
HOTEL concept boutique hotel remains true to its unusual history by showing off the original metal doors and exposed-brick walls. **Pros:** modern luxury; historic building; great bar and restaurant. **Cons:** prison life isn't for everyone; expensive parking. $ *Rooms from: £210 ⊠ 3 Oxford Castle ☎ 01865/268400 ⊕ www.malmaison.com ↝ 86 rooms, 8 suites ⟍⟋ Breakfast.*

$$$ **Old Bank Hotel.** From the impressive collection of modern artworks
HOTEL throughout to the sleek furnishings in the guest rooms, this stately converted bank building offers contemporary style in a city that favors the traditional. **Pros:** excellent location; interesting artworks at every turn. **Cons:** standard rooms can be small; breakfast costs extra. $ *Rooms from: £220 ⊠ 91–94 High St. ☎ 01865/799599 ⊕ www.oldbank-hotel. co.uk ↝ 42 rooms ⟍⟋ Breakfast.*

$$$ **Old Parsonage.** A 17th-century gabled stone house in a small garden
HOTEL next to St. Giles Church, the Old Parsonage is a dignified retreat. **Pros:** interesting building; complimentary walking tours. **Cons:** pricey given what's on offer; some guest rooms on small side. $ *Rooms from: £220 ⊠ 1 Banbury Rd. ☎ 01865/310210 ⊕ www.oldparsonage-hotel.co.uk ↝ 26 rooms, 4 suites ⟍⟋ Breakfast.*

$$ **Royal Oxford Hotel.** This efficiently run hotel, a few steps from the train
HOTEL station, has bright, light, and modern rooms with simple contemporary furniture. **Pros:** comfortable rooms; good for travelers. **Cons:** not many amenities. $ *Rooms from: £150 ⊠ 17 Park End St. ☎ 01865/248432*

🌐 *www.royaloxfordhotel.co.uk* 🛏 *26 rooms* 🍴 *Breakfast.*

$ B&B/INN **Tilbury Lodge.** What this modern house on the city's western outskirts lacks in history it makes up for in hospitality; the homemade tea and scones that greet you on arrival set just the right tone. **Pros:** quiet location; free Wi-Fi; well-appointed bathrooms. **Cons:** away from the attractions; not good for families with young kids. [$] *Rooms from: £98* ✉ *5 Tilbury La., Botley* ☎ *01865/862138* 🌐 *www.tilburylodge.com* 🛏 *9 rooms* 🍴 *Breakfast.*

A LITTLE NIGHT MUSIC

Choral music. Choral music at the city's churches is a calming way to spend the early evening. Drop by weekdays during term time at 6 pm at Magdalen (except Monday), New College (except Wednesday), or Christ Church to hear evensong.

NIGHTLIFE AND THE ARTS

NIGHTLIFE AND PUBS

Nightlife in Oxford centers around student life, which in turn focuses on the local pubs. The popular Jericho area, around Walton Street north of the old city walls and within walking distance of the center of town, has good restaurants and pubs.

Head of the River. The terrace at this pub near Folly Bridge is the perfect place to watch life on the water. You can also enjoy a pint in the clubby interior. ✉ *St. Aldate's* ☎ *01865/721600.*

Kings Arms. The capacious Kings Arms, popular with students and fairly quiet during the day, carries excellent local brews as well as inexpensive pub grub. ✉ *40 Holywell St.* ☎ *01865/242369.*

Raoul's. This trendy cocktail bar is located in the equally trendy Jericho neighborhood. ✉ *32 Walton St.* ☎ *01865/553732.*

Turf Tavern. Off Holywell Street, the tavern has a higgledy-piggledy collection of little rooms and outdoor spaces where you can enjoy a quiet drink and inexpensive pub food. ✉ *Bath Pl.* ☎ *01865/243235.*

White Horse. The cozy White Horse, one of the city's oldest pubs, serves real ales and traditional food all day. ✉ *52 Broad St.* ☎ *01865/728318.*

THE ARTS

CONCERTS **Music at Oxford.** This acclaimed series of weekend classical concerts takes place from October through June in such esteemed venues as Christ Church Cathedral and the Sheldonian Theatre. ☎ *01865/244806 Box Office* 🌐 *www.musicatoxford.com.*

Oxford Coffee Concerts. Europe's oldest custom-built concert hall (1748) hosts this acclaimed chamber music series at 11:15 am on most Sunday mornings. Tickets cost £11. ✉ *Holywell Music Room, Holywell Rd.* ☎ *01865/305305* 🌐 *www.coffeeconcerts.co.uk.*

FESTIVALS Fodor's Choice ★ **Oxford Literary Festival.** The festival takes place during the last week of March at Christ Church College and other university venues. Leading authors come to give lectures and interviews. ✉ *Christ Church College, St. Aldate's* ☎ *0870/343–1001* 🌐 *oxfordliteraryfestival.org.*

THAMES VALLEY HIKING AND BIKING

The Thames Valley is a great area to explore on foot or by bike. It's not too hilly, and pubs and easily accessible lodgings dot the riverside and small towns. The Thames is almost completely free of car traffic along the Thames Path, a 184-mile national trail that traces the river from the London flood barrier to the river's source near Kemble, in the Cotswolds. The path follows towpaths from the outskirts of London, through Windsor, Oxford, and Lechlade.

Good public transportation in the region makes it possible to start and stop easily anywhere along this route. In summer the walking is fine and no special gear is necessary, but in winter the path often floods—check before you head out.

For the best information on the Thames paths, contact the National Trails Office or the Ramblers' Association, both good sources of information, advice, and maps. The Chiltern Conservation Board promotes walking in the Chilterns peaks.

Biking is perhaps the best way to see the Chilterns. Routes include the 99-mile Thames Valley Cycle Route from London to Oxford, and the 87-mile Ridgeway Path from Uffington that follows the Chilterns; the National Trails Office has information. The Thames Path also has plenty of biking opportunities.

CONTACTS AND RESOURCES
Chiltern Conservation Board
☎ 01844/355500
⊕ www.chilternsaonb.org.

Chiltern Way ☎ 01494/771250
⊕ www.chilternsociety.org.uk.

National Trails Office
⊕ www.nationaltrail.co.uk.

Ramblers' Association
☎ 020/7339-8500
⊕ www.ramblers.org.uk.

THEATER **New Theatre.** Oxford's main performance space, the New Theatre stages popular shows, comedy acts, and musicals. ⊠ *George St.* ☎ *0844/871–3020* ⊕ *www.newtheatreoxford.org.uk.*

Oxford Playhouse. This theater presents classic and modern dramas as well as dance and music performances. ⊠ *Beaumont St.* ☎ *01865/305305* ⊕ *www.oxfordplayhouse.com.*

SHOPPING

Small shops line High Street, Cornmarket, and Queen Street; the Clarendon and Westgate shopping centers, leading off them, have branches of several nationally known stores.

Alice's Shop. This store sells all manner of *Alice in Wonderland* paraphernalia. ⊠ *83 St. Aldate's* ☎ *01865/723793.*

Blackwell's. Family-owned and family-run since 1879, Blackwell's stocks an excellent selection of books. Inquire about the literary and historical walking tours that run from April through September. ⊠ *48–51 Broad St.* ☎ *01865/792792.*

Fodor's Choice ★ **Covered Market.** This is a fine place for a cheap sandwich and a leisurely browse; the smell of pastries and coffee follows you from cake shop to jeweler to cheesemonger. ⊠ *High St.* ⊕ *www.oxford-covered-market. co.uk.*

Scriptum Fine Stationery. Cards, stationery, handmade paper, and leather-bound journals can be found at Scriptum Fine Stationery, as well as quills, sealing wax, and Venetian masks. ⊠ *3 Turl St.* ☎ *01865/200042.*

Shepherd & Woodward. This traditional tailor specializes in university gowns, ties, and scarves. ⊠ *109–113 High St.* ☎ *01865/249491.*

Taylors Deli. If you're planning a picnic, Taylors Deli has everything you need. There are cakes and pastries, as well as first-rate teas and coffees. There's a shop on the High Street as well. ⊠ *31 St. Giles* ☎ *01865/558853.*

University of Oxford Shop. The university-run shop sells authorized clothing, ceramics, and tea towels emblazoned with university crests. ⊠ *106 High St.* ☎ *01865/247414* ⊕ *www.oushop.com.*

SPORTS AND THE OUTDOORS

PUNTING

Fodor's Choice ★ You may choose, like many an Oxford student, to spend a summer afternoon **punting,** while dangling your Champagne bottle in the water to keep it cool. Punts—shallow-bottom boats that are poled slowly up the river—can be rented in several places, including at the foot of the Magdalen Bridge.

Cherwell Boathouse. From mid-March through mid-October, the boathouse will rent you a boat and, if you wish, someone (usually an Oxford student) to punt it. Rentals are £14 (£17 on weekends) per hour or £70 (£85 on weekends) per day, and should be booked ahead. The facility, a mile north of the heart of Oxford, also includes a stylish restaurant. ⊠ *Bardwell Rd.* ☎ *01865/515978* ⊕ *www.cherwellboathouse.co.uk.*

SPECTATOR SPORTS

Eights Week. At the end of May, during Oxford's Eights Week, men and women from the university's colleges compete to be "Head of the River." Because the river is too narrow for the eight-member teams to race side by side, the boats set off one behind another. Each boat tries to catch and bump the one in front.

Oxford University Cricket Club. The highly regarded Oxford University Cricket Club competes against leading county teams in late spring and summer, as well as major foreign teams visiting Britain each summer. In the middle of the sprawling University Parks—itself worthy of a walk—the club's playing field is truly lovely. ⊕ *www.cricketintheparks.org.uk.*

SIDE TRIPS FROM OXFORD

BLENHEIM PALACE

8 miles northwest of Oxford.

The ducal palace of Blenheim, one of England's largest and grandest houses, lies at the edge of Woodstock, a mellow town of handsome 17th- and 18th-century houses and quiet lanes that seem to rise right out of a 19th-century etching.

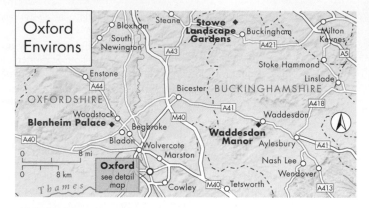

GETTING HERE AND AROUND

The public bus service S3 runs (usually every half hour) between Oxford and Woodstock and costs £3.40 one-way. It can drop you at the gates at Blenheim Palace. By car from Oxford, take the A44 heading north.

EXPLORING

Fodor's Choice

★

Blenheim Palace. This grandiose palace was named a UNESCO World Heritage Site, the only historic house in Britain to receive the honor. Designed by Sir John Vanbrugh in the early 1700s in collaboration with Nicholas Hawksmoor, Blenheim was given by Queen Anne and the nation to General John Churchill, first duke of Marlborough, in gratitude for his military victories (including the Battle of Blenheim) against the French in 1704. The exterior is mind-boggling, with its huge columns, enormous pediments, and obelisks, all exemplars of English baroque. Inside, lavishness continues in monumental extremes: to experience it all you can join a free guided tour or simply walk through on your own. In most of the opulent rooms, family portraits look down at sumptuous furniture, elaborate carpets, fine Chinese porcelain, and immense pieces of silver. Exquisite tapestries in the three state rooms illustrate the first duke's victories. ■TIP→ Book a tour of the current duke's private apartments for a more intimate view of ducal life. For some visitors, the most memorable room is the small, low-ceiling chamber where Winston Churchill (his father was the younger brother of the then-duke) was born in 1874; he's buried in nearby Bladon.

Sir Winston wrote that the unique beauty of Blenheim lay in its perfect adaptation of English parkland to an Italian palace. Its 2,000 acres of grounds, the work of Capability Brown, 18th-century England's best-known landscape gardener, are arguably the country's best example of the "cunningly natural" park. Blenheim's formal gardens include notable water terraces and an Italian garden with a mermaid fountain, all built in the 1920s.

The Pleasure Gardens, reached by a miniature train that stops outside the palace's main entrance, contain some child-pleasers, including a butterfly house, a hedge maze, and giant chess set. The herb-and-lavender garden is also delightful. Outdoor events during the summer include jousting tournaments. ⊠ *Off A4095* ☎ *0800/849–6500 information line*

Fountains and formal Italian gardens set off the monumental baroque pile that is Blenheim Palace.

⊕ *www.blenheimpalace.com* ✉ *Palace, park, and gardens £21; park and gardens £12* ⊙ *Palace: mid-Feb.–Oct., daily 10:30–4:45; Nov.–mid-Dec., Wed.–Sun. 10:30–4:45. Park: mid-Feb.–mid-Dec., daily 9–6 or dusk.*

WADDESDON MANOR
25 miles east of Blenheim, 26 miles northeast of Oxford.

Although firmly set in the Buckinghamshire countryside, opulent Waddesdon Manor bristles with the spires and turrets of a French chateau. It's one of the National Trust's most visited houses.

GETTING HERE AND AROUND
You will need to drive or join an organized tour to visit Waddesdon. The quickest route from Blenheim Palace to the house is to take the A34 south to the A41 and north to the town of Aylesbury.

EXPLORING
Fodor's Choice ★ **Waddesdon Manor.** Many of the regal residences created by the Rothschild family throughout Europe are gone now, but this one is still a vision of the 19th century at its most sumptuous. G. H. Destailleur designed the house in the 1880s for Baron Ferdinand de Rothschild in the style of a 16th-century French château, with perfectly balanced turrets and towers and walls of creamy stone. Although intended only for summer weekend house parties, it was lovingly furnished over the course of 35 years with Savonnerie carpets, Sèvres porcelain, furniture made by Riesener for Marie Antoinette, and paintings by Guardi, Gainsborough, and Reynolds. An exquisite 21st-century broken porcelain chandelier by Ingo Maurer in the Blue Dining Room brings the collection up-to-date. The gardens are equally extraordinary, with an

aviary, colorful plantings, and winding trails that provide panoramic views. In the restaurant you can dine on English or French fare and order excellent Rothschild wines if your pocketbook can take the hit. ■TIP→ **Admission is by timed ticket; arrive early or book in advance.** ✉ *Silk St., Waddesdon* ✛ *On A41 west of Aylesbury* ☎ *01296/653226* ⊕ *www.waddesdon.org.uk* ✉ *House and gardens £16.20; gardens only £7.20* ⊙ *House: Apr.–Oct. and mid-Nov.–Dec., Wed.–Fri. noon–4, weekends and national holidays Mon. 11–4. Gardens: Jan.–Mar., weekends 10–5; Apr.–Oct., Wed.–Sun. and national holidays Mon. 10–5; last admission 45 mins before closing.*

STOWE LANDSCAPE GARDENS

15 miles north of Waddesdon Manor, 30 miles northeast of Oxford.

Tourists have been visiting Stowe Landscape Gardens since the 18th century, and with its beautiful parkland full of marvelous views, monuments, and temples, it's really no wonder.

GETTING HERE AND AROUND

You can either reach the gardens by car or on an organized tour. By car from Waddesdon head due north. From Oxford drive north on the A34, M40, and A43, and east on A422. Buckingham is the closest town to Stowe.

EXPLORING

Fodor's Choice   **Stowe Landscape Gardens.** This superb example of a Georgian garden was ★   created for the Temple family by the most famous gardeners of the 18th century. Capability Brown, Charles Bridgeman, and William Kent all worked on the land to create pleasing greenery in the valleys and meadows. More than 40 striking monuments, follies, and temples dot the 250-acre landscape of lakes, rivers, and pleasant vistas; this is a historically important place, but it's not for those seeking primarily a flower garden. Allow at least half a day if you want to explore the grounds. Stowe House, at its center, is now a fancy school with some magnificently restored rooms; it's open for tours most afternoons from Sunday through Thursday, but call ahead. You enter the gardens through the New Inn visitor center, where there are period parlor rooms to explore. ✉ *New Inn Farm, off A422, Stowe, Buckingham* ☎ *01280/817156, 01280/818166 house information line, 01289/818002 house tours* ⊕ *www.nationaltrust.org.uk* ✉ *Gardens £8.20; house £5.50; house and gardens £13.25* ⊙ *Mar.–late Oct., daily 10–6; late Oct.–Feb., daily 10–4; last admission 90 mins before closing.*

BATH, THE COTSWOLDS, AND STRATFORD-UPON-AVON

WELCOME TO BATH, THE COTSWOLDS, AND STRATFORD-UPON-AVON

TOP REASONS TO GO

★ **Architecture of Bath:** Bath is perhaps the most perfectly preserved and harmonious English city. Close up, the elegance and finesse of the Georgian buildings is a perpetual delight.

★ **Shakespeare in Stratford:** To see a play by Shakespeare in the town where he was born—and perhaps after you've visited his birthplace or other sights—is a magical experience.

★ **Hidcote Manor Gardens:** In a region rich with imaginative garden displays, Hidcote lays good claim to eminence. Exotic shrubs from around the world and the famous "garden rooms" are the highlights of this Arts and Crafts masterpiece.

★ **Perfect villages:** With their stone cottages, Cotswold villages tend to be improbably picturesque; the hamlets of Upper and Lower Slaughter are among the most seductive.

★ **Roman Baths, Bath:** Return to Bath's Roman days on a tour around this ancient complex.

1 Bath and Environs. With the Roman Baths—renovated and embellished in the 18th century—and the late-medieval Bath Abbey at its heart, Bath is one of the country's comeliest towns. You can also soak up its thriving cultural scene and many shops.

2 The Cotswolds. With a scattering of picture-postcard towns and villages separated by sequestered valleys and woods, the Cotswolds are rural England at its best. Nearby Cheltenham, a larger town, with busy cafés and shops, provides a lively counterpoint.

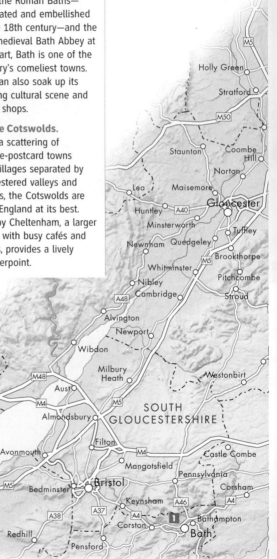

Hawbridge

Pershore

Evesham

A46 A44

Broadway

Teddington

Tewkesbury

Winchcombe

Arle   Cheltenham
A40
Andoversford

GLOUCESTERSHIRE

A417   A429

A419

Kemble

A419

A433
Tetbury   Crudwell

A429
Corston

WILTSHIRE

Chippenham

Lacock

A350

Stratford-upon-Avon **3**

Aldasminster   A429

Halford

Hidcote
Manor
Gardens

Chipping
Campden
A429

Moreton-in-
Marsh   A44
A424   Chastleton

A436

Upper Slaughter   Stow-on-the   Chipping
Lower Slaughter   Wold   Norton
Bourton-on- **2**
the-Water   A424

A40   Burford

Fossebridge

Bibury

Cirencester   A417
Lechlade

Latton

Swindon

M4

0   5 mi

0   5 km

GETTING ORIENTED

The major points of interest in this part of west-
central England—Bath, the
Cotswolds, and Stratford-
upon-Avon—are one way to
organize your explorations.
Bath, a two-hour car drive
west of London, is a good
place to start. North of
Bath about an hour by car,
and two hours northwest of
London, lie the Cotswolds.
The small roads here make
for wonderful exploring,
but public transportation is
limited. The elegant town
Cheltenham sits on the western edge of this region; to its
northeast, about a 45-minute
drive, is Stratford-upon-Avon,
the center of Shakespeare
Country. Tiny villages surround Stratford-upon-Avon,
and to the north stand
two magnificent castles,
Warwick and Kenilworth.

7

3 **Stratford-upon-Avon
and Environs.** The birthplace of Shakespeare,
the bustling historic town
of Stratford-upon-Avon
is liberally dotted with
16th-century buildings the
playwright would recognize.
Nearby Warwick Castle is
well worth a stop.

Updated by
Kate Hughes

The rolling uplands of the Cotswolds represent the quintessence of rural England, as immortalized in countless books, paintings, and films. In eloquently named settlements from Bourton-on-the-Water to Stow-on-the-Wold, you can experience the glories of the old English village—its stone slate roofs, low-ceiling rooms, and gardens; the atmosphere is as thick as honey, and equally as sweet. On the edge of the Cotswolds is Bath, among the most alluring small cities in Europe, and nothing evokes the England of the imagination more vividly than Stratford-upon-Avon, birthplace of perhaps the nation's most famous son, William Shakespeare.

Bath offers up "18th-century England in all its urban glory," to use a phrase by the writer Nigel Nicolson, and the city rightly boasts of being the best-planned town in England. The Romans founded Bath when they discovered here the only true hot springs in England, and its popularity during the 17th and 18th centuries luckily coincided with one of Britain's most creative architectural eras. Today people come to walk in the footsteps of Jane Austen, visit Bath Abbey and the excavated Roman baths, shop in an elegant setting, and have a modern spa treatment at the stunning Thermae spa.

North of Bath and occupying much of the county of Gloucestershire lie the blissfully unspoiled Cotswolds—a region that more than one writer has called the very soul of England. This idyllic place, which also includes slices of neighboring Oxfordshire, Worcestershire, and Somerset, grew prosperous on the wool trade from medieval times. Rich with time-defying churches, sleepy hamlets, and sequestered ancient farmsteads, it is home to such fabled abodes as Sudeley Castle. The Cotswolds can hardly claim to be undiscovered, but the area's poetic appeal has survived the tour buses and antiques shops.

Visits to Stratford-upon-Avon, William Shakespeare's birthplace, and the surrounding areas yield insights into the great playwright's life and inspirations. The sculpted, rolling farmland of Warwickshire may look nothing like the forested countryside of the 16th century, but many sturdy Tudor buildings that Shakespeare knew survive to this day, including his birthplace. With its Bard-related sights and the theaters of the Royal Shakespeare Company, Stratford-upon-Avon can sometimes feel like "Shakespeare World." But there's much more to see—magnificent castles, bucolic churches, and gentle countryside—in this famously picturesque part of England. Stop in at Charlecote, a grand Elizabethan manor house, and Baddesley Clinton, a superb example of late-medieval domestic architecture. The huge fortresses of Warwick and Kenilworth castles also provide glimpses into England's pre-Shakespearean past.

BATH, THE COTSWOLDS, AND STRATFORD-UPON-AVON PLANNER

WHEN TO GO

This area contains some of England's most popular destinations, and it's best to avoid weekends in the busier areas of the Cotswolds. During the week, even in summer, you may hardly see a soul in the more remote spots. Bath is particularly congested in summer, when students flock to its language schools. On the other hand, Cheltenham is a relatively workaday place that can absorb many tour buses comfortably. The sights in Shakespeare Country become very crowded on weekends and during school vacations; Warwick Castle usually brims with visitors, so arrive early in the day.

Book your room well ahead if you visit during the two weeks in May and June when the Bath International Music Festival hits town, or if you visit Cheltenham during the National Hunt Festival (horse racing), in mid-March. The private properties of Hidcote Manor, Snowshill Manor, and Sudeley Castle close in winter; Hidcote Manor Garden is at its best in spring and fall.

PLANNING YOUR TIME

You can get a taste of Bath and the Cotswolds in three hurried days; a weeklong visit allows you time for the slow wandering this small region deserves and rewards. Near Bath, it's an easy drive to Lacock and Castle Combe, two stately villages on the southern edge of the Cotswolds. At the heart of the Cotswolds, Stow-on-the-Wold, Bourton-on-the-Water, and Broadway should on no account be missed. Within a short distance of these, Chipping Campden has a beautiful high street and attractive wool church, and Bibury and Upper and Lower Slaughter are tiny settlements that can easily be appreciated on a brief passage. On the southern fringes of the area, Burford, Tetbury, and Cirencester have antiques and tea shops galore, yet for the most part you'll be avoiding the worst of the crowds.

Stratford-upon-Avon, on the northern border of the Cotswolds, is ideal for day visits from London or as a base for exploring the surrounding attractions. Warwick can be toured in an hour or two, but castle lovers could spend half a day at busy Warwick Castle. A drive through country lanes is a pleasant way to spend part of a day; stopping at a stately home will add a few hours.

GETTING HERE AND AROUND

AIR TRAVEL

Bristol and Birmingham have the closest regional airports.

BUS TRAVEL

National Express buses head to the region from London's Victoria Coach Station. It takes about three hours to get to Cheltenham, Bath, and Stratford-upon-Avon. The budget line Megabus (best booked online) also serves Cheltenham and Bath from London. Bus service between the smaller towns can be limited. Stagecoach serves local routes throughout the Stratford and Birmingham areas. Traveline has comprehensive information about all public transportation.

Contacts Megabus ☎ 0871/266–3333 for general inquiries, 0900/160–0900 for bookings; calls cost 60p per minute ⊕ www.megabus.com. **National Express** ☎ 0871/781–8178 ⊕ www.nationalexpress.com. **Stagecoach** ☎ 0871/200–2233 ⊕ www.stagecoachbus.com. **Traveline** ☎ 0871/200–2233 ⊕ www.traveline.info.

CAR TRAVEL

Traveling by car is the best way to make a thorough tour of Bath, the Cotswolds, and Stratford-upon-Avon. The M4 is the main route west from London to Bath and southern Gloucestershire; the drive takes about two hours. From London you can also take M40 and A40 to the Cotswolds, where minor roads link the villages. The M40 serves Stratford and Warwick as well. Journey time is about two hours.

TRAIN TRAVEL

First Great Western trains serve the region from London's Paddington Station; First Great Western and CrossCountry trains connect Cheltenham and Birmingham. Travel time from Paddington to Bath is about 90 minutes. Most trains to Cheltenham (two hours and 20 minutes) involve a change at Swindon or Bristol. Train service within the Cotswolds area is limited, with Kemble (near Cirencester) and Moreton-in-Marsh being the most useful stops, both serviced by regular trains from London Paddington. A three-day or seven-day Heart of England Rover pass is valid for unlimited travel on various lines within the region. Stratford has good train service and can be seen as a day trip from London if your time is limited (a matinee is your best bet if you want to squeeze in a play). Chiltern Railways trains depart from London Marylebone Station for Stratford and Warwick; the company sells one-day (£35) and four-day (£50) Shakespeare Explorer tickets for the region. London Midland serves the area from Birmingham (about 40 miles from Stratford). National Rail Enquiries can help with schedules and other information about all train lines.

Contacts Chiltern Railways ☎ 0845/600–5165 ⊕ www.chilternrailways.co.uk. **London Midland** ☎ 0121/634–2040, 0844/811–0133 ⊕ www.londonmidland. com. **National Rail Enquiries** ☎ 0845/748–4950 ⊕ www.nationalrail.co.uk.

RESTAURANTS

Noteworthy chefs catering to wealthy locals and waves of demanding visitors create memorable dining experiences in this area. Restaurants have never had a problem with a fresh food supply: excellent regional produce, salmon from the rivers Severn and Wye, local lamb and pork, venison from the Forest of Dean, and pheasant, partridge, quail, and grouse in season. Also look for Gloucestershire Old Spot pork, bacon (try a delicious Old Spot bacon sandwich), and sausage on area menus. Stratford-upon-Avon has many reasonably priced bistros and unpretentious eateries offering a broad choice of international fare.

HOTELS

The region's hotels are among Britain's most highly rated—from bed-and-breakfasts in village homes and farmhouses to luxurious country-house hotels. Many hotels present themselves as deeply traditional rural retreats, but some have opted for a sleeker, fresher style, with boldly contemporary or minimalist furnishings. Spas are popular at many of these hotels. Book ahead whenever possible and brace yourself for high prices. B&Bs are a cheaper alternative to the fancier hotels, and most places offer two- and three-day packages.

Most lodgings in Bath and many in the Cotswolds require a two-night minimum stay on weekends and holidays; rates are often higher on weekends. Accommodations in Cheltenham and the Cotswolds are especially hard to find during the week of Cheltenham's National Hunt Festival in March.Because Stratford is *so* popular with theatergoers, book well ahead and watch for theater packages. Top-notch country hotels near Stratford-upon-Avon provide discreet but attentive service, albeit at fancy prices. *Hotel reviews have been shortened. For full information, visit Fodors.com.*

WHAT IT COSTS IN POUNDS				
	$	$$	$$$	$$$$
Restaurants	under £15	£15–£19	£20–£25	over £25
Hotels	under £100	£100–£160	£161–£220	over £220

Restaurant prices are the average cost of a main course at dinner or, if dinner isn't served, at lunch. Hotel prices are the lowest cost of a standard double room in high season, including 20% V.A.T.

VISITOR INFORMATION

The Cotswolds website and the Heart of England Tourism Board concentrate on the entire region. Shakespeare Country covers Stratford-upon-Avon and environs, and South West Tourism provides information about Bath, Castle Combe, and Lacock. Local tourist offices can recommend day or half-day tours and will have the names of registered Blue Badge guides.

Contacts The Cotswolds ☏ *01452/328321* ⊕ *cotswolds.com.* **Heart of England Tourist Board** ☏ *01905/887690* ⊕ *www.visitheartofengland.com.* **Shakespeare Country** ☏ *0871/978–0800* ⊕ *www.shakespeare-country.co.uk.* **South West Tourism** ⊕ *www.visitsouthwest.co.uk.*

BATH AND ENVIRONS

On the eastern edge of the county of Somerset, the city of Bath has strong links with the Cotswolds stretching north, the source of the wool that for centuries underpinned its economy. The stone mansions and cottages of that region are recalled in Bath's Georgian architecture and in the mellow stone that it shares with two of the villages across the Wiltshire border, Lacock and Castle Combe.

BATH

13 miles southeast of Bristol, 115 miles west of London.

Fodor's Choice
★

"I really believe I shall always be talking of Bath. Oh! Who can ever be tired of Bath," enthuses Catherine Morland in Jane Austen's *Northanger Abbey*, and today many people agree with these sentiments. In Bath, a UNESCO World Heritage Site, you're surrounded by magnificent 18th-century architecture, a lasting reminder of the vanished world described by Austen. In the 19th century the city lost its fashionable luster and slid into a refined gentility that still remains. Bath is no museum, though: it's lively, with good dining and shopping, excellent art galleries and museums, the remarkable excavated Roman baths, and theater, music, and other performances all year. Many people rush through Bath in a day, but there's enough to do to merit an overnight stay—or more. In summer, the sheer volume of sightseers may hamper your progress.

The Romans put Bath on the map in the 1st century when they built a temple here, in honor of the goddess Minerva, and a sophisticated network of baths to make full use of the mineral springs that gush from the earth at a constant temperature of 116°F (46.5°C). ■**TIP→ Don't miss the remains of the baths, one of the city's glories.** Visits by Queen Anne in 1702 and 1703 brought attention to the town, and soon 18th-century "people of quality" took it to heart. Assembly rooms, theaters, and pleasure gardens were built to entertain the rich and titled when they weren't busy attending the parties of Beau Nash—the city's master of ceremonies and chief social organizer, who helped increase Bath's popularity—and having their portraits painted by Gainsborough.

GETTING HERE AND AROUND

Frequent trains from Paddington and National Express buses from Victoria connect Bath with London. The bus and train stations are close to each other south of the center. By car from London, take M4 to Exit 18, from which A46 leads 10 miles south to Bath.

Drivers should note that parking is extremely limited within the city, and any car illegally parked will be ticketed. Fees for towed cars can run hundreds of pounds. Public parking lots in the historic area fill up early, but the park-and-ride lots on the outskirts provide inexpensive shuttle service into the center, which is pleasant to stroll around.

TOURS
Free two-hour walking tours of Bath are offered year-round by the Mayor of Bath's Honorary Guides. Individuals can just show up outside the main entrance to the Pump Room. Tours take place daily at 10:30 and 2 except on Saturday (10:30 only), and from May to September there are also tours on Tuesday and Thursday at 7 pm. The

The remains of the Roman Baths evoke the days when the Romans gathered here to socialize and bathe.

Jane Austen Centre arranges Jane-themed walking tours on weekends. City Sightseeing runs 50-minute guided tours on open-top buses year-round, leaving two to four times an hour from High Street, near Bath Abbey. Tickets, valid for 24 hours, are good for discounted admission to some top attractions. During summer on Wednesday and Saturday, Mad Max Tours runs full-day Cotswolds tours, departing at 9 am; the stops include Tetbury, Burford, Bibury, and Arlington Row. The company conducts full-day tours year-round, starting at 8:30 am, that take in Castle Combe, Lacock, the Avebury Stone Circles, and Stonehenge.

TIMING
If possible, schedule a visit to Bath during the week, as weekends see an influx of visitors. The city also becomes crowded during its various festivals, though the conviviality and cultural activity during these events are draws in themselves.

ESSENTIALS
Visitor and Tour Information Bath Tourist Information Centre
✉ Abbey Chambers, Abbey Churchyard ☎ 0906/711–2000, 0844/847–5256 booking accommodation service ⊕ www.visitbath.co.uk. **City Sightseeing** ☎ 01225/444102 ⊕ www.city-sightseeing.com. **Mad Max Tours** ☎ 0799/050–5970 ⊕ www.madmaxtours.co.uk. **Mayor of Bath's Honorary Guides** ☎ 01225/477411 ⊕ www.bathguides.org.uk.

EXPLORING
TOP ATTRACTIONS
Bath Abbey. Dominating Bath's center, this 15th-century edifice of golden, glowing stone has a splendid west front, with carved figures of angels ascending ladders on either side. Notice, too, the miter, olive

tree, and crown motif, a play on the name of the building's founder, Bishop Oliver King. More than 50 stained-glass windows fill about 80% of the building's wall space, giving the interior an impression of lightness. The abbey was built in the Perpendicular (English late-Gothic) style on the site of a Saxon abbey, and the nave and side aisles contain superb fan-vaulted ceilings. Look for the expressively carved angels on the choir screens. There are five services on Sunday, including choral evensong at 3:30. Forty-five-minute **tower tours,** affording close-up views of the massive bells and panoramic cityscapes from the roof, take place daily except Sunday; the 212 steps demand a level of fitness. ⊠ *Abbey Churchyard* ☎ *01225/422462* ⊕ *www.bathabbey.org* 🖃 *Abbey £2.50 suggested donation, tower tours £6* ⊙ *Abbey: Mon. 9:30–6, Tues–Sat. 9–6, Sun. 1–2:30 and 4:30–5:30. Tower tours: Apr., May, Sept., and Oct., Mon.–Sat. 10–4 hourly; June–Aug., Mon.–Sat. 10–5 hourly; Nov.–Mar., Mon.–Sat. 11, noon, and 2.*

Circus. John Wood designed the masterful Circus, a circle of curving, perfectly proportioned Georgian houses interrupted just three times for intersecting streets. Wood died shortly after work began; his son, the younger John Wood, completed the project. Notice the carved acorns atop the houses: Wood nurtured the myth that Prince Bladud founded Bath, ostensibly with the help of an errant pig rooting for acorns (this is one of several variations on Bladud's story). A garden fills the center of the Circus. The painter Thomas Gainsborough (1727–88) lived at No. 17 from 1760 to 1774. ⊠ *Intersection of Bennett, Brock, and Gay Sts.*

QUICK BITES

Bea's Vintage Tea Rooms. After surveying the Royal Crescent and the Circus, fast forward into the 1940s with a visit to these charming tearooms. Breakfasts, light lunches, and afternoon teas are all served on vintage china set upon hand-embroidered tablecloths. Teapots come with egg timers for the correct length of brew. ⊠ *6–8 Saville Row, Bath* ☎ *01225/464552* ⊕ *www.beasvintagetearooms.com* ⊙ *No dinner.*

Fodor's Choice
★

Fashion Museum and Assembly Rooms. In its role as the **Assembly Rooms,** this neoclassical building was one of the leading centers for social life in 18th-century Bath. Jane Austen came here often, and it's in the Ballroom that Catherine Morland has her first, disappointing encounter with Bath's beau monde in *Northanger Abbey*; the Octagon Room is the setting for an important encounter between Anne Elliot and Captain Wentworth in *Persuasion*. Built by John Wood the Younger in 1771, the building was badly damaged by wartime bombing in 1942 but was faithfully restored. Its stunning chandeliers are the 18th-century originals. Throughout the year, classical concerts are given here, just as they were in bygone days. The Assembly Rooms are also known today for the entertaining **Fashion Museum,** displaying apparel from Jacobean times up to the present. You can see examples of what would have been worn during Bath's heyday, as well as glamorous frocks from the 20th century—a dress of the year is an annual addition. Besides admiring the exhibits, you can have fun trying on corsets and crinolines. An audio guide is included in the price of admission. ⊠ *Bennett St.* ☎ *01225/477789* ⊕ *www.museumofcostume.co.uk* 🖃 *£2.50 for*

Assembly Rooms; £8 for Assembly Rooms and Fashion Museum; £17 combined ticket includes Roman Baths ⊘ Mar.–Oct., daily 10:30–6; Nov.–Feb., daily 10:30–5; last admission 1 hr before closing.

Fodor's Choice **Holburne Museum.** One of Bath's gems, this elegant 18th-century building
★ and its modern extension house a superb collection of 17th- and 18th-century decorative arts, ceramics, and silverware. Highlights include paintings by Gainsborough (*The Byam Family,* on indefinite loan) and George Stubbs (*Reverend Carter Thelwall and Family*), and a hilarious collection of caricatures of the Georgian city's fashionable elite. In its original incarnation as the Sydney Hotel, the house was one of the pivots of Bath's high society, which came to perambulate in the pleasure gardens (Sydney Gardens) that still lie behind it. One visitor was Jane Austen, whose main Bath residence was No. 4 Sydney Place, a brief stroll from the museum. There's an excellent café and tea garden. ✉ *Great Pulteney St.* ☎ *01225/388569* ⊕ *www.holburne.org* 🎫 *Free* ⊘ *Mon.–Sat. 10–5, Sun. and national holidays 11–5.*

Jane Austen Centre. The center contains a diverting exhibition about the influence of Bath on Jane Austen's writings and connection to Bath. There's a 15-minute introductory talk, and displays give a pictorial overview of life in the city circa 1800. The cozy Georgian house, a few doors up from where the writer lived in 1805 (one of several addresses she had in Bath), also includes the Austen-themed Regency Tea Rooms, open to the public. ■TIP→ Buy tickets here for Jane Austen walking tours, which leave from the Abbey Churchyard at 11 on weekends and holidays (also at 4 on Friday and Saturday in July and August). A tour ticket entitles you to a 10% reduction for entry to the exhibition. ✉ *40 Gay St.* ☎ *01225/443000* ⊕ *www.janeausten.co.uk* 🎫 *£8, tours £12* ⊘ *Late Mar.–June, Sept., and Oct, daily 9:45–5:30; July and Aug., Sun.–Wed. 9:45–5:30, Thurs.–Sat. 9:45–7; Nov.–late Mar., Sun.–Fri. 11–4:30, Sat. 9:45–5:30.*

Fodor's Choice **No. 1 Royal Crescent.** The majestic arc of the Royal Crescent, much used
★ as a film location, is the crowning glory of Palladian architecture in Bath. The work of John Wood the Younger, these 30 houses fronted by 114 columns were laid out between 1767 and 1774. The first house to be built, on the corner of Brock Street and the Royal Crescent, was No. 1 Royal Crescent. Having undergone substantial refurbishment in 2013, it has been reunited with its original servants' annex, and the museum now crystallizes a view of the English class system in the 18th century—status, wealth and elegance of the main house reflected in and contrasted with the servants' quarters and kitchen, set apart in the service wing. ✉ *Royal Crescent* ☎ *01225/428126* ⊕ *www.bath-preservation-trust.org.uk* 🎫 *£8.50* ⊘ *Mid-Feb.–mid-Dec., Mon. 12–4:30, Tues.–Sun. 10:30–5:30; last admission 1 hr before closing.*

Pulteney Bridge. Florence's Ponte Vecchio inspired this 18th-century span, one of the most famous landmarks in the city and the only work of the neoclassical architect Robert Adam in Bath. It's unique in Great Britain because shops line both sides of the bridge. ✉ *Between Bridge St. and Argyle St.*

7

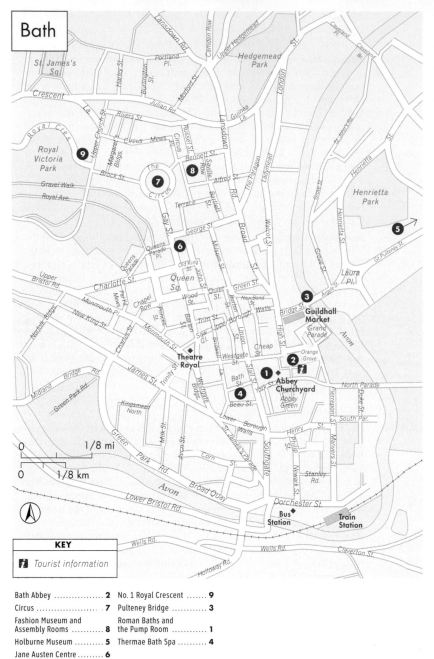

Fodor's Choice ★ **Roman Baths and the Pump Room.** The hot springs have drawn people here since prehistoric times, so it's quite appropriate to begin an exploration of Bath at this excellent museum on the site of the ancient city's primary "watering hole." Roman patricians would gather to immerse themselves, drink the mineral waters, and socialize. With the departure of the Romans, the baths fell into disuse. When bathing again became fashionable at the end of the 18th century, this magnificent Georgian building was erected.

Almost the entire Roman bath complex was excavated in the 19th century, and the museum displays relics that include a memorable mustachioed, Celtic-influenced Gorgon's head, fragments of colorful curses invoked by the Romans against their neighbors, and information about Roman bathing practices. The **Great Bath** is now roofless, and the statuary and pillars belong to the 19th century, but much remains from the original complex, and the steaming, somewhat murky waters are undeniably evocative. Free tours take place hourly, and you can visit after 6:30 pm in July and August to experience the baths lighted by torches.

Adjacent to the Roman bath complex is the famed **Pump Room,** built in 1792–96, a rendezvous for members of 18th- and 19th-century Bath society. Here Catherine Morland and Mrs. Allen "paraded up and down for an hour, looking at everybody and speaking to no one," to quote from Jane Austen's *Northanger Abbey.* Today you can take in the elegant space—or you can simply, for a small fee, taste the fairly vile mineral water. Charles Dickens described it as tasting like warm flatirons. ■TIP➜ The tourist office offers a £63.50 package that includes a visit to the Roman Baths, a three-course lunch or Champagne afternoon tea, and a two-hour spa session. ⊠ *Abbey Churchyard* ☎ *01225/477785* ⊕ *www.romanbaths.co.uk* ⊠ *Roman Baths £13.50 (£14 in July and Aug.); £17 combined ticket includes the Fashion Museum and Assembly Rooms* ☉ *Mar.–June, Sept., and Oct., daily 9–6; July and Aug., daily 9 am–10 pm; Nov.–Feb., daily 9:30–5:30; last admission 1 hr before closing.*

QUICK BITES **Pump Room.** You can linger in the Pump Room for morning coffee or afternoon tea after seeing the Roman Baths. ⊠ *Abbey Churchyard* ☎ *01225/444477.*

Thermae Bath Spa. The only place in Britain where you can bathe in natural hot-spring water—and in an open-air, rooftop location—this striking complex designed by the modernist architect Nicholas Grimshaw and completed in 2006 consists of a Bath-stone building surrounded by a glass curtain wall. The only difficulty is in deciding where to spend more time—in the sleekly luxurious, light-filled Minerva Bath, with its curves and gentle currents, or in the smaller, open-air rooftop pool for the unique sensation of bathing with views of Bath's operatic skyline (twilight is atmospheric here). Two 18th-century thermal baths, the Cross Bath and the Hot Bath, are back in use, too. Towels, robes, and slippers are available for rent (the changing rooms here are co-ed). ■TIP➜ It's essential to book spa treatments ahead; you must be at least 18 to reserve one. The separate, free **Spa Visitor Centre,** opposite the entrance, is open from April through October, daily from

7

A GOOD WALK IN BATH

For an hour-long stroll that takes in Bath's architectural showpieces, start in the traffic-free Abbey Churchyard, a lively piazza often filled with musicians and street artists and dominated by Bath Abbey and the Roman Baths complex. Work your way east to Grand Parade and look out over flower-filled gardens and the River Avon, crossed by the graceful, Italianate Pulteney Bridge.

Stroll over the shop-lined bridge to gaze up the broad thoroughfare of Great Pulteney Street; then cross back over the bridge and head east up Bridge Street, turning right at High Street to follow up Broad Street and its northern extension, Lansdown Road. Turn left onto Bennett Street, passing the 18th-century Assembly Rooms and the Fashion Museum. Bennett Street ends at the Circus, an architectural tour de force likened by some to an inverted Colosseum.

The graceful arc of Bath's most dazzling terrace, the Royal Crescent, embraces a swath of green lawns at one end of Brock Street. Return to the Circus and walk south down Gay Street, which brings you past dignified Queen Square, with its obelisk, to the Theatre Royal. Wander east from here along tiny alleys packed with stores, galleries, and eating places, back to your starting point at Abbey Churchyard, where you could have a well-earned sit-down and tea at the Pump Room. Alternatively, end your perambulation with a soak at Thermae Bath Spa.

10 to 5 except Sunday (11 to 4). Its exhibits chronicle the baths' history since Roman times. Audio guides (£2) are available. ✉ *Hot Bath St.* ☎ *0844/888–0844* 🌐 *www.thermaebathspa.com* 🎟 *£27 for 2 hrs, £37 for 4 hrs, £57 all day* 🕒 *Daily 9 am–10 pm; last admission at 7.*

WHERE TO EAT

$$ FRENCH 🍴 **Casanis.** Dappled sunlight on the stripped wood floor, small tables covered with white linens, and ProvenÁal antiques and bottles of pastis make this place seem like a chic corner of France. Chef Laurent Couvreur puts his stamp on the beautifully presented and amiably served classic dishes, including goat cheese with pear and pickled mushrooms, quail with lentil ragout, and an apple or chocolate tart. Round off your meal with a selection of tasty cheeses. The £16 two-course lunch menu is a relative steal. [$] *Average main: £16* ✉ *4 Saville Row* ☎ *01225/780055* 🌐 *www.casanis.co.uk* 🕒 *Closed Sun.*

$$ MODERN BRITISH 🍴 **Circus Cafe and Restaurant.** You could linger all day in this sophisticated eatery on the corner of the Circus. There's always a good crowd for morning coffee, elevenses (brunch), afternoon tea, and cocktails, let alone lunch and dinner, all of which are dispensed with efficient cordiality. If you can take your attention off the crumpets with Marmite, the spinach and sorrel soup, or the Wiltshire lamb under a marjoram crust, you can discuss the colorful modern art on the walls. Desserts include nutmeg crème brûlé with sherry-soaked raisins. Ingredients are locally sourced and wines come from small growers. [$] *Average main: £16* ✉ *34 Brock St.* ☎ *01225/466020* 🌐 *www.thecircuscafeandrestaurant.co.uk* 🕒 *Closed Sun.*

$ ✕**Jazz Café.** Snack to a background of jazz classics in this cramped
ECLECTIC but cozy café. Famous for its all-day breakfasts, the café is also a good
spot for a quick lunch, with soups, salads, sandwiches, and fine mezes.
Daily specials might include spicy beef chili, chicken and leek pie, or
Moroccan pork. Get here early, as the place closes at 5 pm (4 on Sunday). $ *Average main: £7* ✉ *Kingsmead Sq.* ☎ *01225/329002* ⊕ *www.
bathjazzcafe.co.uk* ⊘ *No dinner.*

$ ✕**Pump Room.** The 18th-century Pump Room, with views over the
BRITISH Roman Baths, serves morning coffee, substantial lunches, and afternoon
tea, to music by a pianist or string trio. The stately setting is the selling point rather than the food, but do sample the West Country cheese
board and the homemade cakes and pastries. There's a fixed-price menu
at lunchtime, and the place is usually open for dinners in July, August,
and December, and during the major festivals (reservations are essential). Be prepared to wait in line for a table during the day. $ *Average
main: £12* ✉ *Abbey Churchyard* ☎ *01225/444477* ⊕ *www.romanbaths.
co.uk* ⊘ *No dinner Jan.–June and Sept.–Nov.*

$ ✕**Rustico.** Favorite places to sit in this traditional and cozy corner of
ITALIAN Cotswold Italy are among the scatter of cushions in the window or,
on a sunny day, outside on the pavement. Befitting its name, Rustico
serves good old-fashioned country fare, including homemade pastas,
lashings of seafood casserole, handsome steaks, and pork in a creamy
white wine sauce. Leave room for the light and fluffy tiramisu. $ *Av-
erage main: £12* ✉ *2 Margaret's Bldgs., Cheltenham* ☎ *01225/310064*
⊕ *www.rusticobistroitaliano.co.uk* ⊘ *Closed Mon.*

$ ✕**Sally Lunn's.** Small and slightly twee, this tourist magnet near Bath
BRITISH Abbey occupies the oldest house in Bath, dating to 1482. It's famous
for the Sally Lunn bun, semisweet bread served here since 1680. You
can choose from more than 30 sweet and savory toppings to accompany
your bun, or turn it into a meal with such dishes as duck with orange-
and-cinnamon sauce. There are economical lunch and early-evening
menus. Daytime diners can view the small kitchen museum in the cellar (30p for nondining visitors). $ *Average main: £12* ✉ *4 N. Parade
Passage* ☎ *01225/461634* ⊕ *www.sallylunns.co.uk.*

$$ ✕**Tilleys Bistro.** This intimate, bow-windowed French eatery presents
FRENCH alluring meat, vegan, and vegetarian dishes offered in small, medium,
and large portions. Choices include medallions of pork *à la dijonnaise*
(fried tenderloin and mushrooms in a brandy, cream, and mustard
sauce), roasted *aubergine à la Tunisienne* (eggplant cooked with chick-
peas, dates, and apricots), and smoked haddock with a Cheddar cheese
sauce. Pretheater meals are available on weekdays between 6 and 7 pm.
$ *Average main: £16* ✉ *3 N. Parade Passage* ☎ *01225/484200* ⊕ *www.
tilleysbistro.co.uk* ⊘ *No lunch Sun.*

WHERE TO STAY

$$ 🛏 **Bath Paradise House.** Don't be put off by the 10-minute uphill walk
B&B/INN from the center of Bath—you'll be rewarded by a wonderful view of the
city from the garden and upper stories of this Georgian guesthouse. **Pros:**
great attention to detail; spectacular views from some rooms. **Cons:** uphill
walk; books up far in advance. $ *Rooms from: £130* ✉ *88 Holloway*
☎ *01225/317723* ⊕ *www.paradise-house.co.uk* ⤴ *11 rooms* 🍽 *Breakfast.*

7

$$
HOTEL

🖼 **Dukes Bath.** Georgian grandeur is evident throughout this Palladian-style mansion that was transformed into an elegant small hotel. **Pros:** central location; superb restaurant; friendly and helpful service. **Cons:** some rooms are small; steps to climb. Ⓢ *Rooms from: £120* ✉ *53–54 Great Pulteney St., entrance on Edward St.* ☎ *01225/787960* ⊕ *www.dukesbath.co.uk* ⇆ *11 rooms, 6 suites* ⦿ *Breakfast.*

$$
HOTEL

🖼 **Harington's Hotel.** It's rare to find a compact hotel in the cobblestone heart of Bath, and this informal three-story lodging converted from a group of Georgian town houses fits the bill nicely. **Pros:** good breakfasts; helpful staff. **Cons:** occasional street noise from revelers; steps to climb; many small rooms. Ⓢ *Rooms from: £145* ✉ *Queen St.* ☎ *01225/461728* ⊕ *www.haringtonshotel.co.uk* ⇆ *13 rooms* ⦿ *Breakfast.*

$$
B&B/INN

🖼 **Marlborough House.** The rooms at this Victorian establishment not far from the Royal Crescent charm with period furniture, fresh flowers, and antique beds. **Pros:** obliging and helpful hosts; immaculate rooms. **Cons:** walk to the center is along a busy road. Ⓢ *Rooms from: £125* ✉ *1 Marlborough La.* ☎ *01225/318175* ⊕ *www.marlborough-house.net* ⇆ *6 rooms* ⦿ *Breakfast.*

$$$
HOTEL

🖼 **Queensberry Hotel.** Intimate and elegant, this boutique hotel on a residential street near the Circus occupies three 1772 town houses built by John Wood the Younger for the marquis of Queensberry; it's a perfect marriage of chic sophistication, homey comforts, and attentive service. **Pros:** efficient service; tranquil ambience; valet parking. **Cons:** occasional street noise; no tea/coffee-making facilities in rooms; breakfast extra. Ⓢ *Rooms from: £165* ✉ *7 Russel St.* ☎ *01225/447928* ⊕ *www.thequeensberry.co.uk* ⇆ *26 rooms, 3 suites* ⦿ *No meals.*

$$
B&B/INN

🖼 **Three Abbey Green.** On a gorgeous square dominated by a majestic plane tree, this welcoming B&B is just steps from Bath Abbey. **Pros:** superb location; airy rooms. **Cons:** some noise from pub goers; only two suites have bathtubs; no parking. Ⓢ *Rooms from: £120* ✉ *3 Abbey Green* ☎ *01225/428558* ⊕ *www.threeabbeygreen.com* ⇆ *7 rooms* ⦿ *Breakfast.*

NIGHTLIFE AND THE ARTS

BARS AND PUBS

The Bell. Owned by a co-op, and a favorite among locals, the Bell has live music—jazz, blues, and folk—on Monday, Wednesday, and Sunday, as well as a selection of real ales, good food, computer access, and even a self-service laundry. ✉ *103 Walcot St* ☎ *01225/460426.*

Raven. Pub aficionados will relish the friendly, unspoiled ambience of the Raven, a great spot for a pint. There are regular poetry readings, and art, science, and storytelling nights upstairs. ✉ *Queen St.* ☎ *01225/425045* ⊕ *www.theravenofbath.co.uk.*

FESTIVALS

Bath Comedy Festival. A 10-day event in April, the festival presents comedy events at venues throughout the city. ✉ *Bath Box Office, Abbey Chambers, Abbey Courtyard* ☎ *01225/463362* ⊕ *www.bathcomedy.com.*

Fodor's Choice
★

Bath International Music Festival. For 12 days in May and June, the festival presents classical, jazz, and world-music concerts, dance performances, and exhibitions in and around Bath. ✉ *Bath Box Office, Abbey Chambers, Abbey Churchyard* ☎ *01225/463362* ⊕ *www.bathfestivals.org.uk.*

Bath Literature Festival. The 10-day early-March lit fest features readings and talks by writers, mostly in the 18th-century Guildhall, on High Street. ⊠ *Bath Box Office, Abbey Chambers, Abbey Churchyard* ☎ *01225/463362* ⊕ *www.bathfestivals.org.uk.*

Jane Austen Festival. Celebrating the great writer with films, plays, walks, and talks over nine days in mid-September, this fest is a feast for Janeites. ☎ *01225/443000* ⊕ *www.janeausten.co.uk/festival.*

THEATER **Theatre Royal.** A gemlike Regency playhouse from 1805, the Theatre Royal has a year-round program that often includes pre- or post-London tours. You must reserve the best seats well in advance, but you can line up for same-day standby seats or standing room. ■ **TIP→** Take care choosing your seat location—sight lines can be poor. ⊠ *Box Office, Saw Close* ☎ *01225/448844* ⊕ *www.theatreroyal.org.uk.*

SPORTS AND THE OUTDOORS

Bath Boating Station. To explore the River Avon by rented skiff, punt, or canoe, head for this facility behind the Holburne Museum. It's open from Easter through September. ⊠ *Forester Rd.* ☎ *01225/312900* ⊕ *www.bathboating.co.uk.*

SHOPPING

Bath has excellent small, family-run, and specialty shops; many close on Sunday. The shopping district centers on Stall and Union streets and the SouthGate shopping center near the train station (modern stores), Milsom Street (traditional stores), and Walcot Street (arts and crafts). Leading off these main streets are alleyways and passages lined with galleries and antiques shops.

Bartlett Street Antiques Centre. This place has more than 50 showcases and stands selling every kind of antique imaginable, including silver, porcelain, and jewelry. ⊠ *Bartlett St.* ☎ *01225/469785.*

Bath Christmas Market. For 18 days in late November and early December, vendors at this outdoor market sell gift items—from handcrafted toys to candles, cards, and edible delights—in 130 chalet-style stalls concentrated in the area just south of the abbey. ⊠ *York St.* ☎ *0844/847–5257* ⊕ *www.bathchristmasmarket.co.uk.*

Bath Sweet Shop. The city's oldest candy store stocks some 350 varieties of sweets, including traditional licorice torpedoes, pear drops, and aniseed balls. Sugar-free treats are sold, too. ⊠ *8 N. Parade Passage* ☎ *01225/428040.*

Beaux Arts Ceramics. This shop carries the work of prominent potters, sculptors, painters, and printmakers. ⊠ *12–13 York St.* ☎ *01225/464850* ⊕ *www.beauxartsbath.co.uk.*

Guildhall Market. The covered market, open daily except Sunday from 9 to 5, is the place for everything from jewelry and gifts to delicatessen food, secondhand books, bags, and batteries. There's a café, too. ⊠ *Entrances on High St. and Grand Parade* ⊕ *www.bathguildhall market.co.uk.*

7

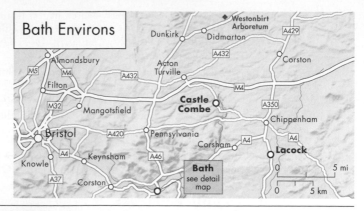

CASTLE COMBE

12 miles northeast of Bath, 5 miles northwest of Chippenham.

Fodor's Choice ★ This Wiltshire village lived a sleepy existence until 1962, when it was voted the "prettiest village" in England—without any of its inhabitants knowing that it had even been a contender. The village's magic is that it's so toylike, so delightfully all of a piece: you can see almost the whole town at one glance from any one position. Castle Combe consists of little more than a brook, a pack bridge, a street (called the Street) of simple stone cottages, a market cross from the 13th century, and the Perpendicular-style church of St. Andrew. The grandest house in the village, on its outskirts, is the Upper Manor House, said once to be the home of Sir John Fastolf (Falstaff, of Shakespeare fame) and now the Manor House Hotel.

GETTING HERE AND AROUND
Regular buses and trains serve Chippenham, where you can pick up a bus for Castle Combe, but it's easier to drive or join a tour.

WHERE TO STAY

$$$$
HOTEL
Fodor's Choice
★
🏨 **Manor House Hotel.** Secluded in a 23-acre park on the edge of the village, this manor house that dates in part to the 14th century has guest rooms—some in mews cottages—that brim with antique character. **Pros:** romantic getaway; rich historical setting; good golf course. **Cons:** some rooms not in main house. $ *Rooms from: £230* ☎ *01249/782206* ⊕ *www.manorhouse.co.uk* 🛏 *48 rooms.*

LACOCK

8 miles southeast of Castle Combe, 12 miles east of Bath.

Fodor's Choice ★ Owned by the National Trust, this lovely Wiltshire village is the victim of its own charm, its unspoiled gabled and stone-tile cottages drawing tour buses aplenty. Off-season, however, Lacock slips back into its profound slumber, the mellow stone and brick buildings little changed in 500 years and well worth a wander. Besides Lacock Abbey, there's the handsome church of St. Cyriac (built with money earned in the wool trade) and a 14th-century tithe barn and, in the village, a few antiques shops and a scattering of pubs that serve bar meals in atmospheric surroundings.

GETTING HERE AND AROUND
All buses from Bath to Lacock involve a change and take 60 to 110 minutes, so it's best to drive or join a tour.

EXPLORING
Lacock Abbey. Well-preserved Lacock Abbey reflects the fate of many religious establishments in England—a spiritual center became a home. The abbey, at the town's center, was founded in the 13th century and closed down during the dissolution of the monasteries in 1539, when its new owner, Sir William Sharington, demolished the church and converted the cloisters, sacristy, chapter house, and monastic quarters into a private dwelling. The house passed to the Talbot family, the most notable descendant of whom was William Henry Fox Talbot (1800–77), who developed the world's first photographic negative. You can see the oriel window, the subject of this photograph, in the upper rooms of the abbey, along with the rare 16th-century purpose-built strong room in the octagonal tower. The last descendant, Matilda Talbot, donated the property as well as Lacock itself to the National Trust in the 1940s. The abbey's grounds and Victorian woodland are also worth a wander. Harry Potter fans, take note: Lacock Abbey was used for some scenes at Hogwarts School in the film *Harry Potter and the Sorcerer's Stone*.

The **Fox Talbot Museum,** in a 16th-century barn at the gates of Lacock Abbey, commemorates the work of Fox Talbot and surveys the history of photography from "camera obscura to today's iPhone." ⊠ *High St.* ☎ *01249/730459* ⊕ *www.nationaltrust.org.uk* 🖃 *£11.20; excluding Abbey rooms £8.50* ⊙ *Abbey rooms: mid-Feb.–Oct., Wed.–Mon. 11–5; early Nov.–mid-Feb., weekends noon–4. Cloister, museum, and grounds: mid-Feb.–Oct., daily 10:30–5:30; Nov.–mid-Feb., daily 11–4. Last admission 30 mins before closing.*

THE COTSWOLDS

A gently undulating area of limestone uplands, the Cotswolds are among England's best-preserved rural districts, and the quiet but lovely grays and ambers of the stone buildings here are truly unsurpassed. Much has been written about the area's age-mellowed towns, but the architecture of the villages actually differs little from that of villages elsewhere in England. Their distinction lies in their surroundings: the valleys are lush and rolling, and cozy hamlets appear covered in foliage from church tower to garden gate.

Over the centuries, quarries of honey-color stone have yielded building blocks for many Cotswold houses and churches and have transformed little towns into realms of gold. Make Chipping Campden or Stow-on-the-Wold your headquarters and wander for a few days. Then ask yourself what the area is all about. Its secret seems shared by two things—sheep and stone. These were once the great sheep-rearing areas of England, and during the peak of prosperity in the Middle Ages, Cotswold wool was in demand the world over. This made the local merchants rich, but many gave back to the Cotswolds by restoring old churches (the famous "wool churches" of the region) or building rows of almshouses of limestone now seasoned to a glorious golden-gray. These days the wool merchants have gone but the wealth remains—the region includes some of the most exclusive real estate in the country.

One possible route is to begin with Cheltenham—the largest town in the area and a gateway to the Cotswolds, but slightly outside the boundaries and more of a small city in atmosphere—before moving on to Sudeley Castle and Snowshill Manor, among the most impressive houses of the region. Continue on to the oversold village of Broadway, Chipping Campden (the Cotswold cognoscenti's favorite), and Hidcote Manor, one of the most spectacular gardens in England. Then circle back south through Stow-on-the-Wold, Upper Slaughter, Lower Slaughter, and Bourton-on-the-Water, and end with Bibury and Tetbury. This is definitely a region where it pays to go off the beaten track to take a look at that village among the trees.

CHELTENHAM

50 miles north of Bath, 13 miles east of Gloucester, 99 miles west of London.

Although Cheltenham has acquired a reputation as being snooty—the population (around 110,000) is generally well-heeled and conservative—it's also cosmopolitan. The town has excellent restaurants and bars, fashionable stores, and a thriving cultural life. Its primary renown, however, derives from its architecture, rivaling Bath's in its Georgian elegance, with wide, tree-lined streets, crescents, and terraces with row houses, balconies, and iron railings.

Like Bath, Cheltenham owes part of its fame to mineral springs. By 1740 the first spa was built, and after a visit from George III and Queen Charlotte in 1788, the town dedicated itself to idleness and enjoyment. "A polka-, parson-worshipping place"—in the words of resident Lord Tennyson—Cheltenham gained its reputation for snobbishness when stiff-collared Raj majordomos returned from India to find that the springs—the only purely natural alkaline waters in England—were the most effective cure for their "tropical ailments."

Great Regency architectural set pieces—Lansdown Crescent, Pittville Spa, and the Lower Assembly Rooms, among them—were built solely to embellish the town. The Rotunda building (1826) at the top of Montpellier Walk—now a bank—contains the spa's original "pump room," in which the mineral waters were on tap. More than 30 statues adorn the storefronts of Montpellier Walk. Wander past Imperial Square, with its ironwork balconies, past the ornate Neptune's Fountain, and along the Promenade. In spring and summer lush flower gardens enhance the town's buildings, attracting many visitors.

GETTING HERE AND AROUND

Trains from London Paddington and buses from London Victoria head to Cheltenham. The train station is west of the center, and the bus station is centrally located off Royal Well Road. Drivers should leave their vehicles in one of the numerous parking lots. The town center is easily negotiable on foot. Cheltenham's tourist office, in the Wilson

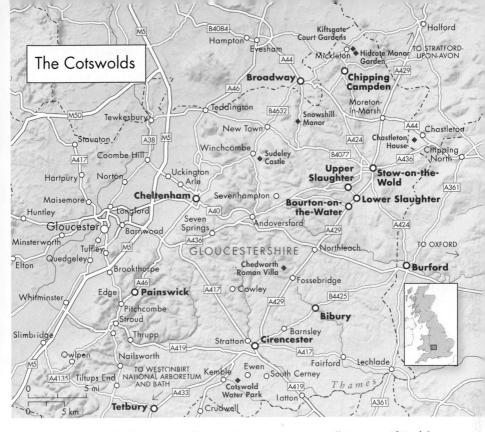

The Cotswolds

Cheltenham Art Gallery & Museum, arranges walking tours (£5) of the town at 11 am on Saturday from April until mid-November.

EXPLORING

Sudeley Castle. One of the grand showpieces of the Cotswolds, Sudeley Castle was the home and burial place of Catherine Parr (1512–48), Henry VIII's sixth and last wife, who outlived him by one year. Here Catherine undertook, in her later years, the education of the ill-fated Lady Jane Grey and the future queen, Princess Elizabeth. Sudeley, for good reason, has been called a woman's castle. The term "castle" is misleading, though, for it looks more like a Tudor-era palace, with a peaceful air that belies its turbulent history. In the 17th century Charles I took refuge here, causing Oliver Cromwell's army to besiege the castle. It remained in ruins until the Dent-Brocklehurst family renovated it during the 19th century.

The 14 acres of gardens, which include the spectacular roses of the Queen's Garden and a Tudor knot garden, are the setting for Tudor fun days in summer. Inside the castle, visitors see only the West Wing, whose Long Room contains exhibitions about the castle's history. The private apartments of Lord and Lady Ashcombe, where you can see paintings by Van Dyck, Rubens, Turner, and Reynolds, are viewable as well. The 11 cottages and apartments on the grounds can be booked for stays of three nights or longer. The castle is 8 miles northeast of Cheltenham. ✉ *Off B4632* ☎ *01242/602308, 01242/609481 Cottages* 🌐 *www.sudeleycastle.co.uk* 🎟 *£14; gardens £8* 🕐 *Apr.–Oct., daily 10–5.*

The Wilson, Cheltenham Art Gallery & Museum. Exhibits at this museum and art gallery inside a handsomely refurbished building document Cheltenham's position at the forefront of the Arts and Crafts movement from the 1880s onward. There are fine displays of William Morris textiles, furniture by Charles Voysey, and wood and metal pieces by Ernest Gimson. Decorative arts, such as Chinese ceramics, are also represented, and the works of British painters such as Stanley Spencer and Vanessa Bell are on display. Other exhibits focus on local archaeology and history. One is devoted to the museum's namesake, Edward Wilson, a Cheltenham native who accompanied Robert Scott on an ill-fated 1912 expedition to Antarctica during which both men and three others died. ✉ *Clarence St.* ☎ *01242/237431* 🌐 *www.cheltenhammuseum.org.uk* 🎟 *Free* 🕐 *Daily: Apr.–Oct. 10–5; Nov.–Mar. 10–4.*

QUICK BITES

Well Walk Tea Room. Squeeze past the antiques and knickknacks in this pretty bow-fronted shop and tearoom for a soup, pasta, or sandwich lunch, or treat yourself to an afternoon tea with crumpets and cakes. [$] ***Average main: £3*** ✉ ***5–6 Well Walk, Cheltenham*** ☎ ***01242/574546*** 🌐 ***www.wellwalktearoom.co.uk*** 🕐 ***Closed Mon. No dinner.***

WHERE TO EAT

$$ BISTRO

🍴 **Bistrot Coco.** Stone steps lead down to this intimate basement bistro where tassel-fringed red lamps, a wood-burning stove, and a little bar with a ceiling papered with the Eiffel Tower and other French icons provide the backdrop for dining on classic bistro cuisine. Menu selections might include warm goat-cheese salad, lamb stew, snails, and frogs' legs, which you can accompany with a glass or two from the carefully chosen wine list. The two-course lunch for £10 is worth checking out. [$] *Average main: £15* ✉ *30 Cambray Pl.* ☎ *01242/534000.*

$$ MODERN BRITISH

🍴 **The Daffodil.** This restaurant proves that turning up the wow quotient doesn't always mean a drop in culinary standards. Housed in a former art deco cinema, the place is themed along 1920s lines. It's dimly lighted, with sweeping staircases and an open kitchen where the screen once hung; the best view is from the Circle Bar. The menu features twice-baked Double Gloucester soufflé, oxtail pudding with beef fillet, and slow-roasted pork belly. Afterward, indulge in a popcorn panna cotta, or a platter of cheeses with quince chutney. There's live jazz on Monday evening and at lunchtime on Saturday. The early-evening and lunch menus are a good deal. [$] *Average main: £15* ✉ *18–20 Suffolk Parade* ☎ *01242/700055* 🌐 *www.thedaffodil.com* ✍ *Reservations essential* 🕐 *Closed Sun.*

$$ MODERN BRITISH

🍴 **Purslane.** Daughters treating their mothers, ladies who shop, and gentlemen cutting a dash all come here, lured by the imaginative and well-presented cuisine and cool, unfussy surroundings. The freshest of Cornish fish, smoked eel from the River Severn, and Dorset oysters are accompanied by unusual but delicious vegetables such as wild garlic, alexanders, and radish shoots. The accent is on fish, but you will also

As enchanting as the house, the gardens at Sudeley Castle provide a perfect backdrop for outdoor events in summer.

find Gloucestershire chorizo and hay-baked rabbit, and plenty of local cheeses. Service is friendly and knowledgeable. $ *Average main: £16* ✉ *16 Rodney Rd., Cheltenham* ☎ *01242/321639* ⊕ *www.purslane-restaurant.co.uk* ⊗ *Closed Sun and Mon.*

WHERE TO STAY

$
B&B/INN
🖭 **The Bradley.** The thoughtful and hospitable owners take great pride in this town house, near the center, that has been in the same family for more than 100 years. **Pros:** good value; attentive hosts; well-designed rooms. **Cons:** lots of stairs to top rooms; no private parking. $ *Rooms from: £85* ✉ *19 Bayshill Rd* ☎ *01242/519077* ⊕ *www.thebradleyhotel. co.uk* ⇆ *5 rooms, 1 suite* ⦿*Breakfast.*

$$$
HOTEL
🖭 **Cowley Manor.** Good-bye, floral prints: this Georgian mansion on 55 acres brings country-house style into the 21st century with a mellow atmosphere and modern fabrics and furnishings. **Pros:** beautiful grounds; excellent spa facilities; relaxed vibe. **Cons:** slightly corporate feel; some hitches with service. $ *Rooms from: £185* ✉ *Off A435, Cowley* ☎ *01242/870900* ⊕ *www.cowleymanor.com* ⇆ *30 rooms* ⦿*Breakfast.*

$$
B&B/INN
🖭 **Hanover House.** Centrally located, this family-run guesthouse dating from 1848 brims with character, and richly colored cushions, vases of flowers, and myriad books enliven the bright and airy rooms. **Pros:** fun; convenient location; award-winning breakfasts. **Cons:** not for those who wish to remain anonymous; all guests share one large table at breakfast. $ *Rooms from: £100* ✉ *65 St. George's Rd.* ☎ *01242/541297* ⊕ *www. hanoverhouse.org* ⇆ *3 rooms* ⦿*Breakfast.*

NIGHTLIFE AND THE ARTS

Cheltenham Festivals. The town's ambitious jazz (May), science (June), music (July), and literature (October) festivals draw more than 150,000 participants each year. ☒ *15 Suffolk Parade* ☎ *0844/880–8094 box office* ⊕ *www.cheltenhamfestivals.com.*

Everyman Theatre. The late-Victorian Everyman Theatre is an intimate venue for opera, dance, concerts, and plays. ∎**TIP→** You can often catch pre– or post–West End productions here, at a fraction of big-city prices. ☒ *Regent St.* ☎ *01242/572573.*

Fodor'sChoice
★ **Literature Festival.** The 10-day Literature Festival in October brings together world-renowned authors, actors, and critics for hundreds of readings, lectures, and other events. ☎ *0844/880–8094 box office* ⊕ *www.cheltenhamfestivals.com.*

SPORTS

Cheltenham Racecourse. Important steeplechase events take place at this racecourse north of the town center. ☒ *Prestbury Park* ☎ *0844/579–3003 ticket line, 01242/513014 tickets and inquiries* ⊕ *www.cheltenham.co.uk.*

SHOPPING

This is serious shopping territory. A stroll along Montpellier Walk and then along the flower-bedecked Promenade brings you to high-end specialty stores and boutiques. A bubble-blowing Wishing Fish Clock, designed by Kit Williams, dominates the Regent Arcade, a modern shopping area behind the Promenade. A farmers' market enlivens the Promenade on the second and last Friday of the month.

Cavendish House. This high-end department store stocks designer fashions. ☒ *32–48 The Promenade* ☎ *01242/521300.*

Feva. Eye-catching women's clothing in bright, splashy colors, as well as accessories like shoes, belts, and handbags, are on display at Feva. More formal wear is sold on the upper floor. ☒ *20 Regent St.* ☎ *01242/222998.*

Martin. This shop carries a good stock of classic and modern jewelry. ☒ *19 The Promenade* ☎ *01242/522821.*

Q and C Militaria. A find for military buffs, Q and C sells badges and medals, breastplates, helmets, coats of arms, and books. ☒ *22 Suffolk Rd.* ☎ *01242/519815.*

BROADWAY

17 miles northeast of Cheltenham.

The Cotswold town to end all Cotswold towns, Broadway has become a favorite of day-trippers. William Morris first discovered the delights of this village, and J.M. Barrie, Vaughan Williams, and Edward Elgar soon followed. Today you may want to avoid Broadway in summer, when it's clogged with cars and buses. Named for its handsome, wide main street (well worth a stroll), the village includes numerous antiques shops, tea parlors, and boutiques.

GETTING HERE AND AROUND

Broadway can be reached by car via A44; park in one of the parking lots signposted from the main street. The village is not easily reached by public transit.

ESSENTIALS

Visitor Information Broadway Tourist Information Centre ✉ *Russell Sq.* ☎ *01386/852937* 🌐 *www.beautifulbroadway.com.*

EXPLORING

FAMILY
Fodor's Choice ★

Snowshill Manor. Three miles south of Broadway and 13 miles northeast of Cheltenham, Snowshill is one of the most unspoiled of all Cotswold villages. Snuggled beneath Oat Hill, with little room for expansion, the hamlet is centered on an old burial ground, the 19th-century St. Barnabas Church, and Snowshill Manor, a 17th-century house whose rooms burst with Tibetan scrolls, spinners' tools, ship models, Persian lamps, and bric-a-brac; the Green Room displays 26 suits of Japanese samurai armor. Children love the place. Outside, an imaginative terraced garden frames the house exquisitely. **■ TIP→ Admission is by timed tickets issued on a first-come, first-served basis, so arrive early in peak season.** ✉ *Off A44, Snowshill* ☎ *01386/852410* 🌐 *www.nationaltrust.org.uk* 🎟 *£9.80; garden only £5.20* ⏲ *House: Apr.–June, Oct., Sept., Wed.–Sun. and national holidays noon–5; July and Aug., Tues.–Sun. 11:30–4:30. Garden: mid-Mar.–June, Sept., Oct., Wed.–Sun. and national holidays 11–5:30; July and Aug. 11:30–5. Last admission 1 hr before closing.*

WHERE TO EAT

$$$ MODERN BRITISH

🍴 **Russell's.** With a courtyard in back and a patio out front, this chic restaurant in a former furniture factory belonging to local designer George Russell is modern, airy, and stylish. The cuisine is Modern British, with such temptations as Warwickshire lamb with herb crust and wild mushrooms, mandarin soufflé, and peach Melba with coriander cress. The less expensive fixed-price menu is just as tempting, and there's also an attached fish-and-chip shop. [$] *Average main: £20* ✉ *20 High St.* ☎ *01386/853555* 🌐 *www.russellsofbroadway.co.uk* ⏲ *No dinner Sun.*

$ MODERN BRITISH

🍴 **The Swan.** In the center of Broadway, this pub-restaurant is a handy stop for a snack, lunch, a drink, or something more substantial. Service may be occasionally slapdash and the place can get congested, but on a weekday it's cozy and convivial, with an open fire in winter and comfortable seating. Menu items might include marinated sticky chicken with lemon, honey, and chili sauce, and duck breast in an orange sauce. Tapots (small British tapas-style dishes) and tasting platters are popular options as well. The wine cellar is well stocked, and there are plenty of cask ales. [$] *Average main: £14* ✉ *2 The Green* ☎ *01386/852278* 🌐 *www.theswanbroadway.co.uk.*

WHERE TO STAY

$$$$ HOTEL

🏨 **Buckland Manor.** As an alternative to the hustle and bustle of Broadway, you can travel the 2 miles to the idyllic hamlet of Buckland and splurge at this traditional country house, which has more of a feel of a genteel family home than a hotel. **Pros:** beautiful setting; elegant guest rooms; large bathrooms with high-quality toiletries. **Cons:** some rooms

7

are small; restaurant quite formal; steep prices. $ *Rooms from: £305* ⊠ *Off B4632, Buckland* ☎ *01386/852626* ⊕ *www.bucklandmanor. co.uk* ↩ *13 rooms* |○| *Breakfast.*

$$$ **Mill Hay House.** If the rose garden, trout-filled pond, and sheep on the
B&B/INN hill at this 18th-century Queen Anne house aren't appealing enough, then the stone-flagged floors, leather sofas, and grandfather clocks should satisfy. **Pros:** delightful owners; beautifully landscaped gardens; gourmet breakfasts. **Cons:** books up quickly; no young children admitted. $ *Rooms from: £175* ⊠ *Snowshill Rd.* ☎ *01386/852498* ⊕ *www. millhay.co.uk* ↩ *2 rooms, 1 suite* |○| *Breakfast.*

$ **The Olive Branch.** Right on the main drag, this 16th-century cottage
B&B/INN has authentic period charm and is strewn with antique knickknacks: a brass wind-up gramophone holds pride of place. **Pros:** cottage character; central location; hospitable hosts. **Cons:** small bathrooms; narrow stairs; low ceilings. $ *Rooms from: £98* ⊠ *78 High St.* ☎ *01386/853440* ⊕ *www.theolivebranch-broadway.com* ↩ *8 rooms* |○| *Breakfast.*

CHIPPING CAMPDEN

4 miles east of Broadway, 18 miles northeast of Cheltenham.

Fodor'sChoice One of the most beautiful towns in the area, Chipping Campden, with
★ its population of about 2,500, is the Cotswolds in a microcosm. It has St. James, the region's most impressive church; frozen-in-time streets; a silk mill that was once the center of the Guild of Handicraft; and pleasant, untouristy shops. One of the area's most seductive settings unfolds before you as you travel on B4081 through sublime English countryside and happen upon the town, tucked in a slight valley. North of town is lovely Hidcote Manor Garden. ■TIP→ Chipping Campden can easily be reached on foot along a level section of the Cotswold Way from Broadway Tower, outside Broadway; the walk takes about 75 minutes.

GETTING HERE AND AROUND

By car, Chipping Campden can be reached on minor roads from A44 or A429. There's a small car park in the center and spaces on the village outskirts. By bus, take Johnson's Coaches from Stratford-upon-Avon, Broadway, and Moreton-in-Marsh, or Pulham's Coaches from Bourton-on-the-Water and Cheltenham, changing at Moreton-in-Marsh (no Sunday service).

ESSENTIALS

Visitor Information Chipping Campden Tourism Information Centre ⊠ *The Old Police Station, High St.* ☎ *01386/841206* ⊕ *www.chippingcampdenonline.org.*

EXPLORING
TOP ATTRACTIONS

Fodor'sChoice **Hidcote Manor Garden.** Laid out around a fetching manor house, this is
★ arguably Britain's most interesting and attractive large garden. A horticulturist from the United States, Major Lawrence Johnston, created the garden in 1907 in the Arts and Crafts style. Johnston was an imaginative gardener and avid traveler who brought back specimens from all over the world. The formal part of the garden is arranged in "rooms" separated by hedges and often with fine topiary work and walls. The

variety of plants here impresses, as do the different effects created, from calm, open spaces to areas packed with flowers. ■TIP→ **Look for one of Johnston's earliest schemes, the red borders of dahlias, poppies, fuchsias, lobelias, and roses; the tall hornbeam hedges; and the Bathing Pool garden, where the pool is so wide there's scarcely space to walk.** If you have time, explore the tiny village of Hidcote Bartrim; it borders the garden and fills a storybook dell. ⊠ *Off B4081, 4 miles northeast of Chipping Campden, Hidcote Bartrim* ☎ *01386/438333* ⊕ *www. nationaltrust.org.uk* ✉ *£10* ⊘ *Mid-Mar.–Apr. and Sept., Mon.–Wed. and weekends 10–6; May–Aug., daily 9–7; Oct.–early Nov., Mon.– Wed. and weekends 10–5; early Nov.–mid-Dec., weekends 11–4; last admission 1 hr before closing.*

St. James. The soaring pinnacled tower of St. James, a prime example of a Cotswold wool church—it was rebuilt in the 15th century with money from wool merchants—announces Chipping Campden from a distance. The church recalls the old saying, which became popular because of the vast numbers of houses of worship in the Cotswolds, "As sure as God's in Gloucestershire." It's worth stepping inside to see the lofty nave. ⊠ *Church St.* ☎ *01386/841927* ⊕ *www.stjameschurchcampden.co.uk* ✉ *£3 donation suggested* ⊘ *Mar.–Oct., Mon.–Sat. 11–5, Sun. 2–5:45; Nov.–Feb., Mon.–Sat. 11–3 Sun. 2–3.*

WORTH NOTING

Guild of Handicraft. In 1902 the Guild of Handicraft took over this former silk mill. Arts and Crafts evangelist Charles Robert Ashbee (1863–1942) brought 150 acolytes from London, including 50 guildsmen, to revive and practice such skills as cabinetmaking and bookbinding. The operation folded in 1920, but the refurbished building now houses the intriguing and very full workshop of a silversmith and has a café and gallery. ⊠ *Sheep St.* ☎ *0787/041–7144* ✉ *Free* ⊘ *Workshops weekdays 9–5, Sat. 9–1; gallery daily 10–5.*

Kiftsgate Court Gardens. While not so spectacular as Hidcote Manor Garden, this intimate, privately owned garden, just a five-minute stroll away, still captivates. It's skipped by the majority of visitors to Hidcote, so you won't be jostled by the crowds. The interconnecting flower beds present harmonious arrays of color, and the contemporary formal water garden adds an elegant contrast. Don't miss the prized Kiftsgate rose, supposedly the largest in England, flowering gloriously in mid-July. ⊠ *Off B4081, Mickleton* ☎ *01386/438777* ⊕ *www.kiftsgate.co.uk* ✉ *£7.50* ⊘ *Apr. and Sept., Mon., Wed., and Sun. 2–6; May–July, Sat.– Wed. noon–6; Aug., Sat.–Wed. 2–6.*

Market Hall. The broad High Street, lined with stone houses and shops, follows a captivating curve; in the center, on Market Street, is the Market Hall, a gabled Jacobean structure built by Sir Baptiste Hycks in 1627 "for the sale of local produce." ⊠ *Market St.*

WHERE TO EAT

$ ✕ **Eight Bells.** Close to St. James Church, this traditional tavern has
BRITISH low beams, a flagstone floor, and a small courtyard. The long menu includes such enticing dishes as wild mushroom and spinach risotto, chicken, leek and gammon pie, and baked fillet of sea trout. Fixed-price

7

CLOSE UP

Arts and Crafts in the Cotswolds

The Arts and Crafts movement flourished throughout Britain in the late-19th and early-20th centuries, but the Cotswolds are most closely associated with it. The godfather of the movement was designer William Morris (1834–96), whose home for the last 25 years of his life, Kelmscott Manor in Gloucestershire, became the headquarters of the school. A lecture by Morris, "The Beauty of Life," delivered in Birmingham in 1880, included the injunction that became the guiding principle of the movement: "Have nothing in your houses which you do not know to be useful or believe to be beautiful."

Driven by the belief that the spirit of medieval arts and crafts was being degraded and destroyed by the mass production and aggressive capitalism of the Victorian era, and aided by a dedicated core of artisans, Morris revolutionized the art of house design and decoration. His work with textiles was particularly influential.

WHERE TO SEE IT
Many of Morris's followers were influenced by the Cotswold countryside, among them the designer and architect Charles Robert Ashbee, who transferred his Guild of Handicraft from London to Chipping Campden in 1902. The village's small Court Barn Museum, on Church Street, off Station Road, exhibits pieces by the original group and those who followed them. Their work can also be seen at The Wilson, Cheltenham Art Gallery & Museum and, in its original context, at Rodmarton Manor outside Tetbury—which Ashbee declared the finest application of the movement's ideals. To see the Arts and Crafts ethic applied to horticulture, visit Hidcote Manor Garden, near Chipping Campden.

---

menus at lunchtime are easy on the wallet. The service is swift, and the good local ales are worth a taste. $ *Average main: £14* ⊠ *Church St.* ☏ *01386/840371* ⊕ *www.eightbellsinn.co.uk.*

WHERE TO STAY

$
B&B/INN
Badgers Hall. Expect a friendly welcome at this antique B&B above a tearoom just across from the Market Hall, where the spacious, spotless rooms have beamed ceilings and exposed stonework. **Pros:** atmospheric building; attentive hosts; delicious breakfasts. **Cons:** low ceilings; entrance is through tea shop. $ *Rooms from: £98* ⊠ *High St.* ☏ *01386/840839* ⊕ *www.badgershall.com* ☜ *3 rooms* ⏍ *Breakfast.*

$$$
HOTEL
Charingworth Manor. Views of the countryside are limitless from this 14th-century manor house hotel where mullioned windows and oak beams enhance the sitting room. **Pros:** helpful and friendly staff; great breakfasts; lots of amenities. **Cons:** some low beams in bedrooms; birds leave messages on cars. $ *Rooms from: £180* ⊠ *Off B4035, Charingworth* ☏ *01386/593555* ⊕ *www.classiclodges.co.uk* ☜ *23 rooms, 3 suites* ⏍ *Breakfast.*

$$$
HOTEL
Cotswold House. This luxury hotel in the heart of Chipping Campden injects contemporary design into a stately 18th-century manor house, and from the swirling staircase in the entrance to the guest rooms studded with contemporary art and high-tech gadgetry, it's a winning

formula. **Pros:** plenty of pampering; pleasant garden. **Cons:** some bathrooms are small. [$] *Rooms from: £185* ✉ *The Square* ☎ *01386/840330* 🌐 *www.cotswoldhouse.com* 🛏 *21 rooms, 7 suites* 🍴 *Breakfast.*

$$$ HOTEL 🏨 **Noel Arms Hotel.** Dating to the 14th century, Chipping Campden's oldest inn was built to accommodate foreign wool traders, and even though it's been enlarged, the building retains its exposed beams and stonework. **Pros:** traditional character; friendly staff. **Cons:** rooms can be noisy and overheated; annex overlooks car park. [$] *Rooms from: £185* ✉ *High St.* ☎ *01386/840317* 🌐 *www.noelarmshotel.com* 🛏 *27 rooms* 🍴 *Breakfast.*

SHOPPING

Hart. Descendants of an original member of the Guild of Handicraft specialize in fashioning lovely items from silver at this shop. ✉ *Guild of Handicrafts, Sheep St.* ☎ *01386/841100.*

Stuart House Antiques. This shop has windows filled with silverware and copperware, porcelain, Doulton figurines, and Staffordshire figures, and there's plenty more inside. ✉ *High St.* ☎ *01386/840995.*

STOW-ON-THE-WOLD

10 miles south of Chipping Campden, 15 miles east of Cheltenham.

At an elevation of 800 feet, Stow is the highest town in the Cotswolds—"Stow-on-the-Wold, where the wind blows cold" is the age-old saying. Built around a wide square, Stow's imposing golden-stone houses have been discreetly converted into high-quality antiques stores, shops, and tea parlors. The Square, as it's known, has a fascinating history. In the 18th century Daniel Defoe, best known as the author of Robinson Crusoe, wrote that more than 20,000 sheep could be sold here on a busy day; such was the press of livestock that sheep runs, known as "tures," were used to control the sheep, and these narrow streets still run off the main square. Today pubs and antiques shops fill the area.

Also here are St. Edward's Church and the Kings Arms Old Posting House, its wide entrance still seeming to wait for the stagecoaches that used to stop here on their way to Cheltenham.

GETTING HERE AND AROUND

Stow-on-the-Wold is well connected by road (A429, A424, and A436). There are car parks off Sheep Street and Fosseway (A429). Chastleton House is only reachable by car.

ESSENTIALS

Visitor Information Stow-on-the-Wold Visitor Information Centre ✉ *12 Talbot Ct., off Sheep St.* ☎ *01451/870150* 🌐 *www.go-stow.co.uk.*

EXPLORING

Chastleton House. One of the most complete Jacobean properties in Britain opts for a beguilingly lived-in appearance, taking advantage of almost 400 years' worth of furniture and trappings accumulated by many generations of the single family that owned it until 1991. The house was built between 1605 and 1612 for William Jones, a wealthy wool merchant, and has an appealing authenticity: bric-a-brac

CLOSE UP

Which Cotswold Garden Is Right for You?

Perhaps it's the sheer beauty of this area that has inspired the creation of so many superb gardens. Gardening is an English passion, and even nongardeners may be tempted by the choices large and small. Here's a guide to your options if time forces you to be selective.

Hidcote Manor Garden. The Arts and Crafts movement in Britain transformed not only interior design but also the world of gardening; in this large, influential, much-visited masterpiece of the style, hedges and walls set off vistas and surround distinct themed garden rooms.

Kiftsgate Court Gardens. Three generations of women gardeners created this intimate but charming garden that has traditional and modern features with harmonious colors.

Painswick Rococo Garden. This 18th-century garden, with its Gothic screen and other intriguing structures, has a pleasant intimacy; it's a rare survivor of the rococo style.

Rodmarton Manor. Here you can tour an Art and Crafts–style house and notable garden rooms that reflect this style.

Sudeley Castle. In England, gardens often complement a stately home and deserve as close a look as the house. At the home of Catherine Parr (Henry VIII's last wife), the 19th-century Queen's Garden is beloved for its roses.

Westonbirt National Arboretum. The magnificent collection of trees here spreads over 600 acres; late spring and fall are colorful.

---

is strewn around, wood and pewter are unpolished, and upholstery is uncleaned. The top floor is a glorious, barrel-vaulted long gallery, and throughout the house you can see exquisite plasterwork, paneling, and tapestries. The gardens include rotund topiaries and the first croquet lawn (the rules of croquet were codified here in 1865). **■TIP→ Admission is by timed ticket on a first-come, first-served basis, so it's a good idea to arrive early.** There is no tearoom or shop here. ✉ *Off A436, 6 miles northeast of Stow, Moreton-in-Marsh* ☎ *01608/674981, 01494/755560 (info line)* 🌐 *www.nationaltrust.org.uk* 🎟 *£8.50; garden only £3.50* ⏲ *Mar. and Oct., Wed.–Sun. 1–4; Apr.–Sept., Wed.–Sun. 1–5.*

WHERE TO EAT AND STAY

$ BRITISH 🍴 **Queen's Head.** An excellent and convivial stopping-off spot for lunch or dinner, this pub has a courtyard out back that's a quiet retreat on a summer day. Expect to rub shoulders with the local painters and decorators as well as passing tourists. Besides standard pub grub, including sandwiches, baguettes, and sausage and mash, there are daily specials such as homemade fish pie, and liver and bacon with onion gravy. [$] *Average main: £9* ✉ *The Square* ☎ *01451/830563.*

$ B&B/INN 🏨 **Number Nine.** Beyond the traditional Cotswold stone exterior of this former coaching inn—now a bed-and-breakfast—are unfussy, spacious bedrooms done in soothing white and pale colors. **Pros:** helpful and amiable hosts; close to pubs and restaurants. **Cons:** two bathrooms have tubs, not showers; low ceilings; steps to climb. $ *Rooms from: £80* ✉ *9 Park St.* ☎ *01451/870333* ⊕ *www.number-nine.info* ⌖ *3 rooms* ⦿ *Breakfast.*

$$ ⟐ **Stow Lodge.** A former rectory, this stately, family-run hotel couldn't be
HOTEL better placed, separated from Stow's main square by a tidy garden. **Pros:** central location; hospitable service; good breakfasts. **Cons:** chiming church clock can be disturbing; steep steps to top-floor rooms. $ *Rooms from: £130* ✉ *The Square* ☎ *01451/830485* ⊕ *www.stowlodgehotel. co.uk* ⌖ *19 rooms, 1 suite* ⦿ *Breakfast.*

SHOPPING

Stow-on-the-Wold is the leading center for antiques stores in the Cotswolds, with more than 40 dealers centered on the Square, Sheep Street, and Church Street.

Baggott Church St. Limited. This shop displays fine old furniture, portraits and landscape paintings, silver, and toys, their price tags tied on with ribbon. ✉ *Church St.* ☎ *01451/830370.*

Durham House Antiques. Showcases of jewelry, silver items, and ceramics, along with antiquarian books, and period furniture are on display over two floors. ✉ *Sheep St.* ☎ *01451/870404.*

Roger Lamb Antiques. Specializing in objets d'art and small furnishings from the Georgian and Regency periods, the shop's strengths include lighting fixtures, bronze pieces, and Imari porcelain. ✉ *The Square* ☎ *01451/831371.*

BOURTON-ON-THE-WATER

4 miles southwest of Stow-on-the-Wold, 12 miles northeast of Cheltenham.

Off A429 on the eastern edge of the Cotswolds, Bourton-on-the-Water is deservedly famous as a classic Cotswold village. Like many others, it became wealthy in the Middle Ages because of wool. The little River Windrush runs through Bourton, crossed by low stone bridges; it's as pretty as it sounds. This village makes a good touring base and has a collection of quirky small museums, but in summer it can be overcrowded. A stroll through Bourton takes you past stone cottages, many converted to small stores, fish-and-chip shops, and tea houses.

GETTING HERE AND AROUND

By car, take A40 and A436 from Cheltenham. You may find parking in the center, but if not, use the lot outside the village.

ESSENTIALS

Visitor Information Bourton-on-the-Water Visitor Information Centre
✉ *Victoria St.* ☎ *01451/820211* ⊕ *www.bourtoninfo.com.*

EXPLORING

FAMILY Cotswold Motoring Museum and Toy Collection. Housed in an old mill, this museum has seven rooms crammed to the rafters with more than 50 shiny vintage and classic cars, delightful caravans from the 1920s and 1960s, ancient motorbikes and bicycles, road signs from past times, and a shepherd's hut on wheels. Motoring memorabilia is also displayed, and there are children's toys, pedal cars, models, and board games.

7

✉ *The Old Mill, Sherborne St.* ☎ *01451/821255* 🌐 *www.cotswoldmotoringmuseum.co.uk* 🎟 *£4.99* ⏲ *Mid-Feb.–Oct., daily 10–6.*

FAMILY **Model Village.** A knee-high, one-ninth-scale replica of Bourton-on-the-Water, the Model Village took five years in the 1930s to complete. As you walk its tiny lanes, you'll realize how little has changed during the intervening decades. Also here are Miniature World, with its depictions of a vegetable shack, a schoolroom, and other scenes, and seven precisely proportioned models of historic English cottages. ✉ *Old New Inn, High St.* ☎ *01451/820467* 🌐 *www.theoldnewinn.co.uk* 🎟 *£3.60; Miniature World £1 additional* ⏲ *Late Mar.–Oct., daily 10–6; Nov.–late Mar., daily 10–4; last admission 15 mins before closing.*

COTSWOLD WALKS

Short walks thread the gentle countryside of the Cotswolds, an **Area of Outstanding National Beauty** (🌐 *www.cotswoldsaonb.org.uk*). Tourist information centers have information about longer trails. You can also track the rivers on which many towns are built, following **footpaths** by the water. The **Cotswold Way** (🌐 *www.nationaltrail.co.uk*), a 100-mile national trail between Bath and Chipping Campden, traces the ridge marking the edge of the Cotswolds and the Severn Valley and has incomparable views. You can walk just part of it.

WHERE TO EAT AND STAY

$ BRITISH 🍴 **Rose Tree.** Plain wooden tables and understated decor provide the setting for the wholesome British dishes served in this traditional restaurant on the banks of the Windrush. Try the chicken liver and mushroom pâté for starters, moving on to lemon sole with caper butter or steak and kidney pie. Desserts include raspberry pavlova, and lemon meringue pie. Candlelight adds atmosphere in the evenings. Sip a cocktail on the riverside terrace while you wait for your order. [$] *Average main: £13* ✉ *Victoria St.* ☎ *01451/820635.*

$ HOTEL 🏨 **Chester House Hotel.** Just steps from the River Windrush, this traditional stone building has been tastefully adapted with contemporary fittings and style. **Pros:** friendly staff; stylish rooms. **Cons:** busy on weekends; coach-house rooms overlook car park. [$] *Rooms from: £95* ✉ *Victoria St.* ☎ *01451/820286* 🌐 *www.chesterhousehotel.com* 🛏 *22 rooms* 🍽 *Breakfast.*

LOWER SLAUGHTER AND UPPER SLAUGHTER

2 miles north of Bourton-on-the-Water, 15 miles east of Cheltenham.

Fodor's Choice ★ To see the quieter, more typical Cotswold villages, seek out the evocatively named Lower Slaughter and Upper Slaughter (the names have nothing to do with mass murder, but come from the Saxon word *sloh*, which means "a marshy place"). Lower Slaughter is one of the "water villages," with Slaughter Brook running down the town's center road. Little stone footbridges cross the brook, and the resident gaggle of geese can often be seen paddling through the sparkling water. Nearby, Lower and Upper Swell are two other quiet towns to explore.

GETTING HERE AND AROUND

Drivers should follow indications from A429 or B4068.

EXPLORING

Warden's Way. Connecting the two Slaughters is the Warden's Way, a mile-long pathway that begins in Upper Slaughter at the town-center parking lot and passes stone houses, green meadows, ancient trees, and a 19th-century corn mill with a waterwheel and brick chimney. The Warden's Way continues south to Bourton-on-the-Water; the full walk from Winchcombe to Bourton is 14 miles. You can pick up maps from local tourist offices.

WHERE TO STAY

$$$ HOTEL **Lords of the Manor Hotel.** You'll find refinement and a warm welcome in this rambling 17th-century manor house (with Victorian additions), tucked away in a quintessential Cotswold village. **Pros:** heavenly setting; understated elegance; outstanding food. **Cons:** some rooms on the small side; limited Wi-Fi. [$] *Rooms from: £200* ✉ *Off A429, Upper Slaughter* ☎ *01451/820243* 🌐 *www.lordsofthemanor.com* 🛏 *26 rooms* 🍴 *Breakfast.*

BURFORD

12 miles southeast of Upper Slaughter, 36 miles southeast of Cheltenham, 18 miles west of Oxford.

Burford's broad main street leads steeply down to a narrow bridge across the River Windrush. The village served as a stagecoach stop for centuries and has many historic inns; it's now a popular stop for tour buses and seekers of antiques.

GETTING HERE AND AROUND

If you're driving, A424 heads south from Stow-on-the Wold to Burford; A40 heads west from Oxford. There is bus service from Oxford (you may need to change at Witney). Once here, it's easy to stroll around.

ESSENTIALS

Visitor Information Burford Visitor Information Centre ✉ *33a High St.* ☎ *01993/823558* 🌐 *www.oxfordshirecotswolds.org.*

EXPLORING

St. John the Baptist. Hidden away on a lane at the bottom of High Street is the parish church of St. John the Baptist, its interior a warren of arches, chapels, and shrines. The church was remodeled in the 15th century from Norman beginnings. Among the monuments is one dedicated to Henry VIII's barber, Edmund Harman, that depicts four Amazonian Indians; it's said to be the first depiction of native people from the Americas in Britain. Look also for the elaborate Tanfield monument and its poignant widow's epitaph. ✉ *Lawrence La.* ☎ *01993/823788* 🌐 *www.burfordchurch.org* 🎫 *Free* 🕒 *Mon.–Sat. 9–5, Sun. 9–10 and 1–5.*

WHERE TO EAT AND STAY

$$ MODERN BRITISH 🍴 **The Angel at Burford.** At this informal eatery in a 16th-century coaching inn, contemporary dishes such as rainbow trout with beetroot and carrot coleslaw and risotto with cauliflower and roasted garlic are delivered

to farmhouse-style tables. A secluded, sunny garden is a perfect place for a lunchtime baguette. Upstairs, the three cheery guest rooms are furnished in different styles: Indian in rich reds, French with a wooden sleigh bed, and cool-green contemporary Italian. [$] *Average main: £15* ✉ *14 Witney St.* ☎ *01993/822714* 🌐 *www.theangelatburford.co.uk.*

$$$ HOTEL 🏨 **Burford House.** The family photographs, old books, and toys scattered throughout this 17th-century building make it feel more like home than a hotel. **Pros:** friendly, unobtrusive service; comfortable public rooms; great dinners. **Cons:** rooms at front subject to traffic noise; parking difficult at peak times; piped-in music. [$] *Rooms from: £170* ✉ *99 High St.* ☎ *01993/823151* 🌐 *www.burford-house.co.uk* 🛏 *8 rooms* 🍴 *Breakfast.*

BIBURY

10 miles southwest of Burford, 6 miles northeast of Cirencester.

The tiny town of Bibury, with a population of less than 1,000, sits idyllically beside the little River Coln. The famed Arts and Crafts designer William Morris called this England's most beautiful village. Fine old cottages, a river meadow, and the church of St. Mary's are among its delights.

GETTING HERE AND AROUND

Bibury, on B4425, is best visited by car; you'll also need one to reach Chedworth Roman Villa.

EXPLORING

Arlington Row. Bibury has a famously pretty and much-photographed group of stone cottages built in 1380 that were converted during the 17th century into wool-weavers' cottages.

FAMILY **Chedworth Roman Villa.** The remains of a mile of walls are what's left of one of England's largest Roman villas, beautifully set in a wooded valley on the eastern fringe of the Cotswolds. Thirty-two rooms, including two complete bath suites, have been identified, and covered walkways take you over the colorful mosaics, some of the most complete in England. Audio guides are available, and there's a small museum. Look out for the rare large snails, fattened on milk and herbs during Roman times, on the grounds. There's a café here, but this is also an ideal place for a picnic. ■ **TIP→ Look carefully for the signs for the villa: from Bibury, go across A429 to Yanworth and Chedworth. The villa is also signposted from A40. Roads are narrow.** ✉ *Off A429, 6 miles northwest of Bibury and 10 miles southeast of Cheltenham, Yanworth* ☎ *01242/890256* 🌐 *www.nationaltrust.org.uk* 🎟 *£9* 🕐 *Mid-Feb.–late Mar., Nov., and Dec., daily 10–4; late Mar.–Oct., daily 10–5.*

WHERE TO STAY

$$$ HOTEL 🏨 **Swan Hotel.** Few inns can boast of a more idyllic setting than this mid-17th-century coaching inn, originally a row of cottages on the banks of the gently flowing River Coln. **Pros:** idyllic spot; helpful staff. **Cons:** often busy with day-trippers and wedding parties; most standard rooms lack views. [$] *Rooms from: £170* ✉ *B4425* ☎ *01285/740695* 🌐 *www.cotswold-inns-hotels.co.uk* 🛏 *18 rooms, 4 suites* 🍴 *Breakfast.*

Blue skies, stone buildings, a peaceful brook: villages such as Upper Slaughter demonstrate the enduring appeal of the Cotswolds.

CIRENCESTER

6 miles southwest of Bibury, 14 miles southeast of Cheltenham.

A hub of the Cotswolds since Roman times, when it was called Corinium, Cirencester (pronounced *sirensester*) was second only to London in importance. Today this old market town is the area's largest, with a population of 19,000. It sits at the intersection of two major Roman roads, the Fosse Way and Ermin Street (now A429 and A417). In the Middle Ages Cirencester grew rich on wool, which funded its 15th-century parish church. It preserves many mellow stone buildings dating mainly from the 17th and 18th centuries, and bow-fronted shops that still have one foot in the past.

GETTING HERE AND AROUND

Cirencester has hourly bus service from Cheltenham, and less frequent service from Tetbury and Kemble (for rail links). By road, the town can be accessed on A417, A419, and A429. Its compact center is easily walkable.

ESSENTIALS

Visitor Information Cirencester Visitor Information Centre ✉ *Corinium Museum, Park St.* ☎ *01285/654180* ⊕ *www.cotswold.gov.uk.*

EXPLORING

FAMILY

Fodor'sChoice

★

Corinium Museum. Not much of the Roman town remains visible, but the museum displays an outstanding collection of Roman artifacts, including jewelry and coins, as well as mosaic pavements and full-scale reconstructions of local Roman interiors. Spacious and light-filled galleries that explore the town's history in Roman and Anglo-Saxon times and in the 18th century include plenty of hands-on exhibits for kids. ✉ *Park St.* ☎ *01285/655611* 🌐 *www.coriniummuseum.org* 🎫 *£4.95* 🕒 *Apr.–Oct., Mon.–Sat. 10–5, Sun. 2–5; Nov.–Mar., Mon.–Sat. 10–4, Sun. 2–4.*

St. John the Baptist. At the top of Market Place is this magnificent Gothic parish church, known as the cathedral of the "woolgothic" style. Its elaborate, three-tier, three-bay south porch, now gleaming gold after a renovation, is the largest in England and once served as the town hall. The chantry chapels and many coats of arms bear witness to the importance of the wool merchants as benefactors of the church. A rare example of a delicate 15th-century wineglass pulpit sits in the nave. ✉ *Market Pl.* ☎ *01285/659317* 🌐 *www.cirenparish.co.uk* 🎫 *£3 donation suggested* 🕒 *Mon.–Sat. 10–4:45 (10–4 in winter), Sun. 2–5.*

QUICK BITES

Made by Bob. The energy and buzz of this plate-glass and chrome eatery, right by the Corn Hall in the center of town, will set you up as much as the coffee and pastry, afternoon tea and a bun, or a soup and focaccia lunch. You can always pick something up from the delicatessen for a picnic if you prefer. ✉ ***Unit 6, The Corn Hall, 26 Market Place, Cirencester*** ☎ ***01285/641818*** 🕒 ***Closed Sun.***

WHERE TO EAT AND STAY

$$$ MODERN BRITISH

🍴 **Jesse's.** The fish is chilling on the counter and the charcoal is glowing in the oven as you sit at your mosaic-topped table and watch the chefs at work. The bistro, tucked away in a little courtyard, is intimate yet roomy, bustling yet snug. Treat yourself to a chilled sherry, then be tempted by soft-shell crab in a sushi roll, local Gatcombe lamb, or fish straight up from Cornwall. You'll be spoiled for choice by the excellent choices on the British cheese board. [$] *Average main: £20* ✉ *The Stableyard, Black Jack Street, Cirencester* ☎ *01285/641497* 🌐 *www.jessesbistro.co.uk* 🕒 *Closed Sun. No dinner Mon.*

$$$$ HOTEL

🏨 **Barnsley House.** A honey-and-cream Georgian mansion, the former home of garden designer Rosemary Verey has been discreetly modernized and converted into a luxurious retreat without sacrificing its essential charm. **Pros:** romantic setting; great attention to detail. **Cons:** some rooms at the top of three flights of stairs. [$] *Rooms from: £280* ✉ *B4425, Barnsley* ☎ *01285/740000* 🌐 *www.barnsleyhouse.com* 🛏 *9 rooms, 9 suites* 🍽 *Breakfast.*

$ B&B/INN

🏨 **Ivy House.** Delicious breakfasts, hospitable owners, and reasonable rates enhance a stay at this stone Victorian house, close to the center of town. **Pros:** homemade granola at breakfast; child-friendly atmosphere. **Cons:** on a main road; some rooms on the small side. [$] *Rooms from: £77* ✉ *2 Victoria Rd.* ☎ *01285/656626* 🌐 *www.ivyhousecotswolds.com* 🛏 *4 rooms* 🍽 *Breakfast.*

SPORTS AND THE OUTDOORS

FAMILY

Cotswold Water Park. You can indulge in water sports such as waterskiing and windsurfing at the Cotswold Water Park, 4 miles south of Cirencester. This group of 150 lakes covers 40 square miles and has multiple entrances. There's swimming from May through September, and plenty to do for walkers, cyclists, and kayakers as well. You pay individual charges for the activities, and you can rent equipment on-site. ⊠ *B4696, South Cerney* ☏ *01793/752413* ⊕ *www.waterpark.org* ⊒ *Free* ⊙ *Individual operators have varying opening hrs.*

SHOPPING

Corn Hall. This is the venue for a food market on Monday, Wednesday, and Thursday, an antiques market on Friday, and a crafts market on Saturday. ⊠ *Market Pl.* ⊕ *www.cornhallcirencester.com.*

Makers and Designers Emporium. Better known as MADE, this shop is a cornucopia of unusual designer items, including stationery, textiles, housewares, and jewelry. ⊠ *9 Silver St.* ☏ *01285/658225* ⊕ *www. made-gallery.com.*

Market Place. Every Monday and Friday, Cirencester's central Market Place is packed with vendors selling a motley assortment of goods, mainly household items but some local produce and crafts, too. A farmers' market takes place here on the second and fourth Saturday of the month.

PAINSWICK

16 miles northwest of Cirencester, 8 miles southwest of Cheltenham.

Fodor's Choice An old Cotswold wool town of about 2,000 inhabitants, Painswick has ★ become a chocolate-box picture of quaintness, attracting day-trippers and tour buses. Come during the week to discover the place in relative tranquillity. The huddled gray-stone houses and inns date from as early as the 14th century and include a notable group from the Georgian era. It's worth a stroll through the churchyard of St. Mary's, renowned for its table tombs and monuments and its 100 yew trees planted in 1792. The Cotswold Way passes near the center of the village, making it easy to take a pleasant walk in the countryside.

GETTING HERE AND AROUND

Painswick is on A46 between Stroud and Cheltenham. Buses serve the village hourly from Cheltenham.

ESSENTIALS

Visitor Information Painswick Visitor Information Centre ⊠ *Grave Digger's Hut, St. Mary's Church, Stroud Rd.* ☏ *0750/351–6924* ⊕ *www.visitthecotswolds.org.uk.*

EXPLORING

Painswick Rococo Garden. Half a mile north of town, this garden is a rare survivor from the exuberant rococo period of English garden design (1720–60). After 50 years in its original form, the 6-acre garden became overgrown, but the discovery of a 1748 Thomas Robins painting of the garden led to a restoration project that began in 1984. Now you can view the original structures—such as the pretty Gothic Eagle House and curved Exedra—take in the asymmetrical vistas, and try the modern maze, which, unusually, has three goals you can discover. A restaurant and a shop are also here. ⊠ *B4073* ☏ *01452/813204* ⊕ *www.rococogarden.org.uk* ⊒ *£6.50* ⊙ *Mid-Jan.–Oct., daily 11–5; last admission at 4.*

WHERE TO EAT AND STAY

$ ✕**Falcon Inn.** With views of the church of St. Mary's, this pub dating
BRITISH from 1554 provides a reassuringly traditional and charming milieu for
food and refreshment. Light meals are available at lunchtime, teas in the
afternoon, and for the evening meal you might start with scallops on a
pea and lentil purée, then move on to the trio of lamb with a tomato,
olive, and rosemary *jus* for your main course. The clotted cream rice
pudding makes for an indulgent conclusion. The inn's grounds hold
what is claimed to be the world's oldest bowling green. There are 11
well-furnished bedrooms upstairs. $ *Average main: £14* ✉ *New St.*
☎ *01452/814222* ⊕ *www.falconinn-cotswolds.co.uk.*

$$ ⌂ **Cardynham House.** In the heart of the village, this 15th- to 16th-cen-
HOTEL tury former wool merchant's house, which retains its beamed ceilings,
Jacobean staircase, and Elizabethan fireplace, has four-poster beds
in most rooms. **Pros:** romantic and quirky; great food in restaurant.
Cons: some low ceilings; mainly small bathrooms. $ *Rooms from: £100*
✉ *The Cross, Tibbiwell St.* ☎ *01452/814006, 01452/810030 restaurant*
⊕ *www.cardynham.co.uk* ⇄ *9 rooms* ⍟*Breakfast.*

TETBURY

12 miles south of Painswick, 8 miles southwest of Cirencester.

With about 5,300 inhabitants, Tetbury claims royal connections. Indeed,
the soaring spire of the church that presides over this Elizabethan market
town is within sight of Highgrove House, the Prince of Wales's abode.
The house isn't open to the public, but you can book well in advance
for a tour of the gardens. Tetbury is one of the area's antiques centers.

GETTING HERE AND AROUND

Take A46 south to A4135 east from Painswick; drive southwest on
A433 from Cirencester. Cotswold Green buses (no Sunday service) from
Cirencester serve Tetbury, which is easy to stroll around.

ESSENTIALS

Visitor Information Tetbury Tourist Information Centre ✉ *33 Church St.*
☎ *01666/503552* ⊕ *www.visittetbury.co.uk.*

EXPLORING

Fodor'sChoice **Highgrove House.** Prince Charles and the late Princess Diana made their
★ home at Highgrove House, 1 miles southwest of Tetbury. Charles set
about making the 37-acre estate his personal showcase for traditional
and organic growing methods and conservation of native plants and
animals. Here you can appreciate the amazing industry on the part of
the royal gardeners who have created the orchards, kitchen garden,
and woodland garden almost from nothing. Look for the stumpery,
the immaculate and quirky topiaries, and the national collection of
hostas. You can sample the estate's produce in the restaurant and shop,
or from its retail outlet in Tetbury. Allow three to four hours to tour
the garden. Visitors must be age 12 or older. ■**TIP**➔ **Tickets go on
sale in February and sell out quickly, so book well ahead.** ✉ *Off A433,
Doughton* ☎ *020/7766–7310 book tours* ⊕ *www.highgrovegardens.
com* ✉ *£24.50, prebooked only* ☉ *Early Apr.–late Oct., weekdays plus
occasional weekends.*

Market House. In the center of Tetbury, look for the eye-catching Market House, dating from 1655. Constructed of white-painted stone, it's built up on rows of Tuscan pillars. Various markets are held here during the week. ✉ *Market Sq.*

Rodmarton Manor. One of the last English country houses constructed using traditional methods and materials, Rodmarton, built between 1909 and 1929, is furnished with commissioned pieces in the Arts and Crafts style. Ernest Barnsley, a follower of William Morris, worked on the house and gardens. The notable gardens—wild, winter, sunken, and white—are divided into "rooms" bounded by hedges of holly, beech, and yew. ✉ *Off A433, 5 miles northeast of Tetbury, Rodmarton* ☎ *01285/841442* 🌐 *www.rodmarton-manor.co.uk* 🎟 *£8; garden only, £5* 🕒 *May–Sept., Wed., Sat., and national holidays 2–5.*

St. Mary the Virgin. This church, in 18th-century neo-Gothic style, has a galleried interior with pews. ✉ *Church St.* ☎ *01666/500088.*

QUICK BITES

Snooty Fox. Just steps from Market House and at the heart of village life, the Snooty Fox is a bustling inn and restaurant with leather armchairs and an open fire in winter and a patio to use in summer. Real ales and local ciders are served at the bar, and teas, coffees, and hot and cold meals are available all day. ✉ ***Market Pl.*** ☎ ***01666/502436*** 🌐 ***www.snooty-fox.co.uk.***

FAMILY **Westonbirt National Arboretum.** Spread over 600 acres, this arboretum contains one of the most extensive collections of trees and shrubs in Europe. A lovely place to spend an hour or two, it's 3 miles southwest of Tetbury and 10 miles north of Bath. The best times to come for color are in late spring, when the rhododendrons, azaleas, and magnolias are blooming, and in fall, when the maples come into their own. Open-air concerts take place in summer, and there are exhibitions throughout the year. A gift shop, café, and restaurant are on the grounds. ✉ *Off A433* ☎ *01666/880220* 🌐 *www.forestry.gov.uk/westonbirt* 🎟 *£8 Mar.–Aug.; £9 Sept.–Nov.; £5 Dec.–Feb.* 🕒 *Apr.–Aug., daily 9–8; Sept.–Mar., daily 9–5.*

WHERE TO STAY

$$$$ HOTEL FAMILY Fodor's Choice ★

🏨 **Calcot Manor.** In an ideal world everyone would sojourn in this oasis of opulence at least once; however, the luxury never gets in the way of the overall air of relaxation, a tribute to the warmth and efficiency of the staff. **Pros:** rural setting; excellent spa facilities; children love it. **Cons:** all but 12 rooms are separate from main building; not all rooms have separate shower units; steep prices. [$] *Rooms from: £280* ✉ *A4135* ☎ *01666/890391* 🌐 *www.calcotmanor.co.uk* 🛏 *26 rooms, 9 suites* 🍴 *Breakfast.*

SHOPPING

Tetbury is home to more than 30 antiques shops, some of which are incorporated into small malls.

Highgrove Shop. This pleasant, if pricey, shop sells organic products and gifts inspired by Prince Charles's gardens. ✉ *10 Long St.* ☎ *0845/521-4342* 🌐 *www.highgroveshop.com.*

House of Cheese. Fresh and flavorsome farm-produced cheeses are the specialty of this tiny shop that also sells pâtés, preserves, and other goodies. ⊠ *13 Church St.* ☎ *01666/502865* ⊕ *www.houseofcheese.co.uk.*

Long Street Antiques. The more than 40 dealers here sell everything from jewelry and kitchenalia to oak and mahogany furniture. ⊠ *14 Long St.* ☎ *01666/500850* ⊕ *www.longstreetantiques.com.*

STRATFORD-UPON-AVON AND ENVIRONS

Even under the weight of busloads of visitors, Stratford, on the banks of the slow-flowing River Avon, has somehow hung on to much of its ancient character and can, on a good day, still feel like an English market town. It doesn't take long to figure out who's the center of attention here. Born in a half-timber, early-16th-century building in the center of Stratford on April 23, 1564, William Shakespeare died on April 23, 1616, his 52nd birthday, in a more imposing house at New Place. Although he spent much of his life in London, the world still associates him with "Shakespeare's Avon."

The countryside around Stratford is marked by gentle hills, green fields, slow-moving rivers, quiet villages, churches, and castles—Warwick and Kenilworth are the best examples, and well worth visiting. Historic houses such as Baddesley Clinton and Packwood House Court are another reason to explore. All four of these sights are close enough to Stratford-upon-Avon that you can easily use the town as a base if you wish.

STRATFORD-UPON-AVON

100 miles northwest of London.

Here, in the years between his birth and 1587, playwright William Shakespeare played as a young lad, attended grammar school, and married Anne Hathaway; and here he returned, as a prosperous man. You can see Shakespeare's whole life here: his birthplace on Henley Street; his burial place in Holy Trinity Church; Anne Hathaway's Cottage; the home of his mother, Mary Arden, at Wilmcote; New Place; and the neighboring Nash's House, home of Shakespeare's granddaughter.

By the 16th century, Stratford was a prosperous market town with thriving guilds and industries. Half-timber houses from this era have been preserved, and they're set off by later architecture, such as the elegant Georgian storefronts on Bridge Street, with their 18th-century porticoes and arched doorways.

Most sights cluster around Henley Street (off the roundabout as you come in on the A3400 Birmingham road), High Street, and Waterside, which skirts the public gardens through which the River Avon flows. Bridge and Sheep streets (parallel to Bridge) are Stratford's main thoroughfares and the site of most banks, shops, and eateries. Bridgefoot, between the canal and the river, is next to Clopton Bridge—"a sumptuous new bridge and large of stone"—built in the 15th century by Sir Hugh Clopton, once lord mayor of London and one of Stratford's richest and most philanthropic residents.

GETTING HERE AND AROUND

Stratford lies about 100 miles northwest of London; take M40 to Junction 15. The town is 37 miles southeast of Birmingham by A435 and A46 or by M40 to Junction 15.

Chiltern Railways serves the area from London's Marylebone Station. Six direct trains a day take just over two hours to reach Stratford; other trains require changing at Birmingham. London Midland operates direct routes from Birmingham's Snow Hill Station (journey time under an hour). Stratford has two stations, Stratford Parkway, northwest of the center at Bishopton, and Stratford at the edge of the town center on Alcester Road, from which you can take a taxi or walk the short distance into town.

Stratford's center is small and easily walkable—it's unlikely you'd need to use the local bus service. You will need a car to visit Baddesley Clinton and Packwood House, but Warwick and Kenilworth can be reached by public transport.

TOURS AND
TICKETS

City Sightseeing runs hop-on, hop-off guided tours of Stratford (£12.50 for one day, £19 for two), and you can combine the tour (about an hour with no stops) with entry to either three (£25.50) or five (£29) Shakespeare houses. The Stratford Town Walk takes place all year and also offers ghost-themed walks and cruises.

The Shakespeare Birthplace Trust runs the main places of Shakespearean interest: Anne Hathaway's Cottage, Hall's Croft, Mary Arden's Farm, Nash's House and New Place, Shakespeare's Birthplace, and Shakespeare's Grave. ■TIP→ You can save money by purchasing the Shakespeare Five House Pass (£23.90) to all properties and by booking online. There are family discounts as well. The Shakespeare's Birthplace Pass (£15.90) includes admission to Hall's Croft Nash's House and New Place and the playwright's birthplace and grave.

TIMING

If you have only one day in Stratford, arrive early and confine your visit to two or three Shakespeare Birthplace Trust properties, a few other town sights, a pub lunch, and a walk along the river, capped off by a stroll to the cottage of Anne Hathaway. If you don't like crowds, avoid visiting on weekends and during school vacations, and take in the main Shakespeare shrines in the early morning to see them at their least frenetic. To see both Warwick and Kenilworth Castle you will need at least a day and a half.

ESSENTIALS

Tour Information City Sightseeing ☎ *01789/412680* ⊕ *www.city-sightseeing. com.* **Shakespeare Birthplace Trust** ☎ *01789/204016* ⊕ *www.shakespeare.org. uk.* **Stratford Town Walk** ☎ *01789/292478, 0785/576–0377* ⊕ *www.stratfordtownwalk.co.uk.*

Visitor Information Stratford-upon-Avon Tourist Information Centre ✉ *Bridgefoot* ☎ *01789/264293* ⊕ *www.shakespeare-country.co.uk.*

7

EXPLORING

TOP ATTRACTIONS

Fodor's Choice
★

Anne Hathaway's Cottage. The most picturesque of the Shakespeare Trust properties, on the western outskirts of Stratford, was the family home of the woman Shakespeare married in 1582. The "cottage," actually a substantial Tudor farmhouse, has latticed windows and a grand thatch roof. Inside is period furniture, including the settle where Shakespeare reputedly conducted his courtship, and a rare carved Elizabethan bed; outside is a garden planted in lush Victorian style with herbs and flowers. A stroll through the adjacent orchard takes you to willow cabins where you can listen to sonnets, view sculptures with Shakespearean themes, and try a yew and a heart-shaped lavender maze. ■TIP→ The best way to get here is on foot, especially in late spring when the apple trees are in blossom. The signed path runs from Evesham Place (an extension of Grove Road) opposite Chestnut Walk. Pick up a leaflet with a map from the tourist office; the walk takes a good half hour. ✉ *Cottage La., Shottery* ☎ *01789/295517* ⊕ *www.shakespeare.org. uk* ✆ *£9.50; £23.90 with the Five House Pass which includes Anne Hathaway's Cottage & Gardens, Hall's Croft, Mary Arden's Farm, Nash's House & New Place, Shakespeare's Birthplace, Shakespeare's Grave* ⊙ *Apr.–Oct., daily 9–5; Nov.–Mar., daily 10–4; last admission 30 mins before closing.*

Charlecote Park. A celebrated house in the village of Hampton Lucy, Charlecote Park was built in 1572 by Sir Thomas Lucy to entertain Queen Elizabeth I (in her honor, the house is shaped like the letter "E"). Shakespeare knew the house and may even have poached deer here. Overlooking the River Avon, the redbrick manor is striking and sprawling. It was renovated in neo-Elizabethan style by the Lucy family, represented here by numerous portraits, during the mid-19th century; a carved ebony bed is one of many spectacular pieces of furniture. The Tudor gatehouse is unchanged since Shakespeare's day, and a collection of carriages, a Victorian kitchen, and a small brewery occupy the outbuildings. Indulge in a game of croquet near the quirky, thatched, Victorian-era summer hut, or explore the deer park landscaped by Capability Brown. Interesting themed tours and walks take place in summer—call in advance to find out what's on offer. From Stratford by car take the B4086, or sign up there for City Sightseeing's Heart of Warwickshire tour. The house is 6 miles northeast of Stratford. ✉ *B4086, off A429, Hampton Lucy* ☎ *01789/470277* ⊕ *www.nationaltrust.org. uk* ✆ *£9.63, £7.50 in winter; grounds only £6.50* ⊙ *House: Mar.–Oct., Thurs.–Tues. 11–4:30; Nov.–Dec., weekends noon–3:30; mid- to late Feb., Thurs.–Tues. noon–3:30. Park and gardens: daily 10:30–5:30 or dusk. Last entry 30 mins before closing.*

Holy Trinity Church. The burial place of William Shakespeare, this 13th-century church sits on the banks of the Avon, with a graceful avenue of lime trees framing its entrance. Shakespeare's final resting place is in the chancel, rebuilt between 1465 and 1491 in the late Perpendicular style. He was buried here not because he was a famed poet but because he was a lay rector of Stratford, owning a portion of the township tithes. On the north wall of the sanctuary, over the altar steps, is the

With its thatch roof, half-timbering, and countryside setting, Anne Hathaway's Cottage is a vision from the past.

famous marble bust created by Gerard Jansen in 1623 and thought to be a true likeness of Shakespeare. The bust offers a more human, even humorous, perspective when viewed from the side. Also in the chancel are the graves of Shakespeare's wife, Anne; his daughter Susanna; his son-in-law John Hall; and his granddaughter's husband, Thomas Nash. Nearby, the Parish Register is displayed, containing Shakespeare's baptismal entry (1564) and his burial notice (1616). ⊠ *Trinity St.* ☎ *01789/266316* ⊕ *www.stratford-upon-avon.org* ✉ *£2 for chancel* ☼ *Mar. and Oct., Mon.–Sat. 9–5, Sun. 12:30–5; Apr.–Sept., Mon.–Sat. 8:30–6, Sun. 12:30–5; Nov.–Feb., Mon.–Sat. 9–4, Sun. 12:30–5; last admission 20 mins before closing.*

Fodor's Choice ★ **Royal Shakespeare Theatre.** Set amid gardens along the River Avon, the Stratford home of the world-renowned Royal Shakespeare Company has a viewing tower and well-regarded rooftop restaurant among its amenities. The company, which presents some of the world's finest productions of Shakespeare's plays, has existed since 1879. Shows are also staged in the Swan. ■**TIP**→ Book ahead for the popular backstage tour. ⊠ *Waterside* ☎ *0844/800–1110 ticket hotline* ⊕ *www.rsc. org.uk* ✉ *Backstage tour £7.50, front of house tour £5.50, open-air tour £6.50, tower visit £2.50.*

Fodor's Choice ★ **Shakespeare's Birthplace.** A half-timber house typical of its time, the playwright's birthplace is a much-visited shrine that has been altered and restored since he lived here. Entering through the modern visitor center, you are immersed in an entertaining but basic introduction to Shakespeare through a "Life, Love, and Legacy" visual and audio exhibition; this can be crowded. You can see a First Folio and

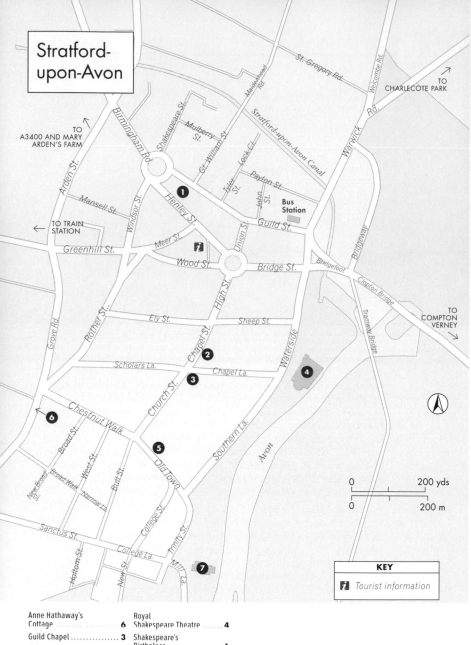

Stratford-upon-Avon

TO
A3400 AND MARY
ARDEN'S FARM

TO CHARLECOTE PARK

TO TRAIN STATION

Arden St.

Mansell St.

Birmingham Rd.

Windsor St.

Henley St.

Shakespeare St.

Mulberry St.

Gt. William St.

Tyler St.

Lock Cl.

John St.

Payton St.

Union St.

Guild St.

Bus Station

Mansehead Rd.

St. Gregory Rd.

Welcombe Rd.

Warwick Rd.

Stratford-upon-Avon Canal

Meer St.

Greenhill St.

Wood St.

High St.

Bridge St.

Bridgefoot

Bridgeway

Clopton Bridge

TO COMPTON VERNEY

Grove Rd.

Rother St.

Ely St.

Chapel St.

Sheep St.

Waterside

Scholars La.

Chapel La.

Church St.

Chestnut Walk

Broad St.

West St.

Bath St.

Old Town

Southern La.

Avon

Tramway Bridge

New Broad St.

Broad Walk

Narrow La.

College St.

Sanctus St.

Hottom St.

New St.

College La.

Trinity St.

Mill La.

200 yds

200 m

KEY

🛈 Tourist information

what is reputedly Shakespeare's signet ring, listen to the sounds of the Forest of Arden, and watch snippets of contemporary Shakespearean films. The house itself is across the garden from this large modern center. Colorful wall decorations and the furnishings in the actual house reflect comfortable, middle-class Elizabethan domestic life. Shakespeare's father, John, a glove maker and wool dealer, purchased the house; a reconstructed workshop shows the tools of the glover's trade. Mark Twain and Charles Dickens were earlier pilgrims here, and you can see the signatures of Thomas Carlyle and Walter Scott scratched into Shakespeare's windowpanes. In the garden, actors present excerpts from the plays. There's also a café and bookshop on the grounds. ⊠ *Henley St.* ☏ *01789/201822* ⊕ *www. shakespeare.org.uk* ⊠ *£15.90, includes entry to Hall's Croft and Nash's House* ⊗ *Apr.–June and Sept.–Oct., daily 9–5; July and Aug. daily 9–5:30; Nov.–Mar., daily 10–4.*

> **SHAKESPEARE FOR SALE**
>
> In 1847 two widowed ladies were maintaining Shakespeare's birthplace in a somewhat ramshackle state. With the approach of the tercentennial of the playwright's birth, and in response to a rumor that the building was to be purchased by P. T. Barnum and shipped across the Atlantic, the city shelled out £3,000 for the relic. It was tidied up and opened to a growing throng of Shakespeare devotees.

7

QUICK BITES

Hobsons Patisserie. Visitors and locals alike head for the half-timber Hobsons Patisserie to indulge in the famous savory pies and scrumptious afternoon teas. ⊠ *1 Henley St.* ☏ *01789/293330.*

WORTH NOTING

Compton Verney. A neoclassical country mansion remodeled in the 1760s by Robert Adam has been repurposed by the Peter Moores Foundation as an art museum with more than 800 works. The house is set in 120 acres of rolling parkland and lake landscaped by Capability Brown. The works of art are intriguingly varied and beautifully displayed in restored rooms: British folk art and portraits, textiles, Chinese pottery and bronzes, southern Italian art from 1600 to 1800, and German art from 1450 to 1600 are the main focus. Daily tours take place at noon and 2:30. From Stratford by car, take the B4086, or sign up in Stratford for City Sightseeing's Heart of Warwickshire tour. Compton Verney is 9 miles east of Stratford. ⊠ *Off B4086, near Kineton* ☏ *01926/645500* ⊕ *www.comptonverney.org.uk* ⊠ *£7.25; extra charge for exhibitions* ⊗ *Late Mar.–mid-Dec., Tues.–Sun. and national holidays 11–5. Last entry 30 mins before closing.*

Guild Chapel. This chapel is the noble centerpiece of Stratford's Guild buildings, including the Guildhall, the Grammar School, and the almshouses—all well known to Shakespeare. The ancient structure was rebuilt in the late Perpendicular style in the first half of the 15th century, thanks to the largesse of Stratford resident Hugh Clopton. Its otherwise plain interior includes fragments of a remarkable medieval fresco of the Last Judgment painted over in the 16th century and uncovered in a

20th-century reconstruction. The bell, also given by Sir Hugh, still rings as it did to tell Shakespeare the time of day. ✉ *Chapel La., at Church St.* ☎ *01789/207111* 🎟 *Free, donations welcome* 🕒 *Daily 10–4.*

Hall's Croft. One of the finest surviving Jacobean (early 17th-century) town houses, this impressive residence has a delightful walled garden. Hall's Croft was the home of Shakespeare's elder daughter, Susanna, and her husband, Dr. John Hall, a physician who, by prescribing an herbal cure for scurvy, was well ahead of his time. His consulting room and medical dispensary are on view along with the other rooms, all containing Jacobean furniture of heavy oak and some 17th-century portraits. The café serves light lunches and afternoon teas. ✉ *Old Town* ☎ *01789/292107* 🌐 *www.shakespeare.org.uk* 🎟 *£15.90, includes admission to Shakespeare's Birthplace and Nash's House* 🕒 *Apr.–Oct., daily 10–5; Nov.–Mar., daily 11–4.*

Nash's House. This heavily restored house was the residence of Thomas Nash, who married Shakespeare's last direct descendant, his granddaughter Elizabeth Hall. It has been furnished in 17th-century style and contains a museum containing finds from the excavations of **New Place,** the house in which Shakespeare died in 1616. Built in 1483 "of brike and tymber" for a lord mayor of London, New Place was Stratford's grandest piece of real estate when Shakespeare bought it in 1597 for £60. It was torn down in 1759 by the Reverend Francis Gastrell, who was angry at the hordes of Shakespeare-related sightseers. You can see an Elizabethan knot garden in the gardens. ✉ *Chapel St.* ☎ *01789/292325* 🌐 *www.shakespeare.org.uk* 🎟 *£15.90, includes admission to Shakespeare's Birthplace and Hall's Croft* 🕒 *Apr.–Oct., daily 10–5; Nov.–Mar., daily 11–4.*

WHERE TO EAT

$ BRITISH Fodor's Choice ★

🍴 **The Black Swan/The Dirty Duck.** The only pub in Britain to be licensed under two names (the more informal one came courtesy of American GIs who were stationed here during World War II), this is one of Stratford's most celebrated pubs—it's attracted actors since the 18th-century thespian David Garrick's days. A little veranda overlooks the theaters and the river here. Along with your pint of bitter, you can choose from the extensive menu of daily specials, wraps, ciabattas, steaks, burgers, and grills. Few people come here for the food, though you will need to book ahead for dinner: the real attraction is the ambience and your fellow customers. [$] *Average main: £10* ✉ *Waterside* ☎ *01789/297312* 🌐 *www.dirtyduck-pub-stratford-upon-avon.co.uk.*

$$ MODERN BRITISH

🍴 **Church Street Town House.** Theatergoers tucking into an early supper to the strains of the grand piano in the Blue Bar, grandmothers enjoying afternoon tea in the Library, and couples lingering over their candlelit suppers can all be found here. Plush armchairs, red drapes, oil paintings, and bookshelves add to the intimacy and refinement of this 18th-century town house. The chef uses local produce in such dishes as baked Camembert with chutney, sea bass with fennel, butterbean and chickpea cassoulet, and peach and almond trifle. A dozen bedrooms replete with silvered French furniture are available should you wish to linger. [$] *Average main: £15* ✉ *16 Church St.* ☎ *01789/262222* 🌐 *www.churchstreettownhouse.com.*

$ BRITISH 🍴 **Lambs of Sheep Street.** Sit downstairs to appreciate the hardwood floors and oak beams of this local epicurean favorite; upstairs, the look is a bit more contemporary. The updates of tried-and-true dishes include salmon cakes with sorrel sauce, and Cotswold lamb shank with creamed potatoes. Desserts are fantastic here, and daily specials keep the menu seasonal. The two- and three-course fixed-price menus (£13.50 and £17) for lunch or pretheater dining on weekdays are good deals. [$] *Average main: £14* ✉ *12 Sheep St.* ☎ *01789/292554* 🌐 *www.lambsrestaurant.co.uk* ✍ *Reservations essential* 🕒 *No lunch Mon. and Tues.*

$ FRENCH 🍴 **Le Bistrot Pierre.** There's always a satisfied hum in the air at this large, modern, and bustling bistro, part of a small chain, that's close to the river. It's French and make no mistake about it: olives from Provence, Alsace bacon, pâtés, free-range chickens from the Janzé region of Brittany, 21-day aged Scottish beef cooked overnight in Bordeaux wine, and rustic cheeses all appear on the menu. Croque Monsieur (toasted ham-and-cheese sandwich) is a popular lunchtime dish. Vegetarians are well catered to, and the service is amicable and attentive. [$] *Average main: £13* ✉ *Swan's Nest La.* ☎ *01789/264804* 🌐 *www.lebistrotpierre.co.uk.*

$ MODERN BRITISH 🍴 **Opposition.** Hearty, warming meals are offered at this informal, family-style restaurant in a 16th-century building on the main dining street near the theaters. The British and international dishes—chicken roasted with banana and served with curry sauce and basmati rice, for instance—win praise from the locals. There's a good range of lighter and vegetarian options and fixed-price menus as well. Make reservations a month ahead in summer. [$] *Average main: £14* ✉ *13 Sheep St.* ☎ *01789/269980* 🌐 *www.theoppo.co.uk* 🕒 *Closed Sun.*

$$ ITALIAN 🍴 **Sorrento.** Family-run, this Italian restaurant takes a respectable, old-fashioned approach to service. Upon arrival, sip an aperitif in the lounge before you're escorted to your table for a silver-service, white-tablecloth meal. The menu of traditional favorites is cooked from family recipes, and includes a starter of cured beef with rocket and flakes of Parmesan, and main dishes of deep-fried calamari or black linguine with crab and scallops. There's also a hearty risotto of the day. Pretheater dinners are a good value. [$] *Average main: £17* ✉ *8 Ely St.* ☎ *01789/297999* 🌐 *www.sorrentorestaurant.co.uk* 🕒 *Closed Sun. No lunch Mon.*

$ INDIAN 🍴 **Thespian's Indian Restaurant.** A buzzing crowd of regulars frequents this casual Indian restaurant, drawn by its extensive menu of spicy dishes from the subcontinent and its friendly atmosphere. Along with dishes like the creamy lamb *saqi* (barbecued lamb simmered in coconut milk with ginger and mint), there are baltis, tandooris, and fish specials. It's an excellent option when you're bored with meat and potatoes. [$] *Average main: £9* ✉ *26 Sheep St.* ☎ *01789/267187.*

$ BISTRO 🍴 **The Vintner.** The imaginative, bistro-inspired menu varies each day at this café and wine bar. Pork fillet with caper butter is a popular main course, as is the steak; a children's menu is available. To dine before curtain time, arrive early or make a reservation. The building, largely unaltered since the late 1400s, has lovely flagstone floors and oak beams. [$] *Average main: £14* ✉ *5 Sheep St.* ☎ *01789/297259* 🌐 *www.the-vintner.co.uk.*

WHERE TO STAY

$$$ HOTEL **Arden Hotel.** Bedrooms are spacious and discreet with splashes of green, violet, and dark crimson in this redbrick boutique hotel across the road from the Royal Shakespeare Theatre. **Pros:** convenient to the Shakespeare theater; crisp and modern style; large bathrooms. **Cons:** gets booked up quickly; plastic, not real, orchids. [$] *Rooms from: £170* ✉ *Waterside* ☎ *01789/298682* 🌐 *www.theardenhotelstratford.com* 🛏 *45 rooms* 🍴 *Breakfast.*

$$ B&B/INN **Cherry Trees.** Although it's nothing fancy from the outside, this modern house near the river offers three beautifully and individually furnished suites in a tranquil location with chic rear garden. **Pros:** welcoming hosts; great breakfasts; convenient to in-town sights. **Cons:** too small for some. [$] *Rooms from: £110* ✉ *Swan's Nest La.* ☎ *01789/292989* 🌐 *www.cherrytrees-stratford.co.uk* 🛏 *3 suites* 🍴 *Breakfast.*

$$ HOTEL FAMILY **Holiday Inn Stratford-upon-Avon.** This good-value hotel's selling points are an excellent location near the center of the historic district and views across the river. **Pros:** good location; handy for families; free accommodations and dinners for kids under 13. **Cons:** modern and featureless; big and impersonal. [$] *Rooms from: £130* ✉ *Bridgefoot* ☎ *0871/942–9270* 🌐 *www.holidayinn.com* 🛏 *259 rooms, 2 suites* 🍴 *Breakfast.*

$$ HOTEL **Legacy Falcon Hotel.** Licensed as an alehouse since 1640, this black-and-white timber-frame hotel in the center of town has an excellent location as well as a light, airy interior that looks out to a pleasant garden. **Pros:** great location; old portion of the building is charming; free parking. **Cons:** some rooms are a bit cramped; rooms can be a bit hot. [$] *Rooms from: £160* ✉ *Chapel St.* ☎ *0844/411–9005* 🌐 *www.legacy-hotels.co.uk* 🛏 *83 rooms* 🍴 *Breakfast.*

$$ HOTEL **Macdonald Alveston Manor.** This redbrick Elizabethan manor house across the River Avon has plenty of historic details, as well as a modern spa with a long list of treatments. **Pros:** nice mix of historic and modern; you can warm yourself by a fire in winter. **Cons:** modern rooms are less interesting; there's no elevator and lots of stairs; parking fee. [$] *Rooms from: £120* ✉ *Clopton Bridge* ☎ *0844/879–9138* 🌐 *www.macdonald-hotels.co.uk* 🛏 *110 rooms, 3 suites* 🍴 *Breakfast.*

$$$ HOTEL **Menzies Welcombe Hotel Spa & Golf Club.** With its mullioned bay windows, gables, and tall chimneys, this hotel in an 1886 neo-Jacobean-style building evokes the luxury of bygone days. **Pros:** great for golfers; good spa facilities; gorgeous grounds and gardens. **Cons:** dining too formal for some; need a car to get here. [$] *Rooms from: £180* ✉ *Warwick Rd.* ☎ *01789/295252* 🌐 *www.menzies-hotels.co.uk* 🛏 *78 rooms* 🍴 *Breakfast.*

$$ HOTEL **Mercure Shakespeare Hotel.** Built in the 1400s, this Elizabethan town house in the heart of town is a vision right out of *The Merry Wives of Windsor,* with its nine gables and long, stunning, black-and-white half-timber facade. **Pros:** historic building; relaxing lounge. **Cons:** some very small bedrooms; charge for parking. [$] *Rooms from: £130* ✉ *Chapel St.* ☎ *01789/294997* 🌐 *www.mercure.com* 🛏 *63 rooms, 10 suites* 🍴 *Breakfast.*

$
B&B/INN

Victoria Spa Lodge. This good-value B&B lies 1 miles outside town, within view of the Stratford Canal; the grand, clematis-draped building dates from 1837. **Pros:** beautiful building; full of character; family friendly. **Cons:** away from the town center. $ *Rooms from: £70* ✉ *Bishopton La., Bishopton* ☎ *01789/267985* ⊕ *www.victoria spa.co.uk* ⤳ *7 rooms* ❧ *Breakfast.*

$$
HOTEL
Fodor's Choice
★

White Swan. None of the character of this black-and-white timbered hotel, which claims to be the oldest building in Stratford, has been lost in its swanky, but sympathetic update. **Pros:** antiquity; generous bathrooms; friendly service. **Cons:** tricky to stop with car; no parking on-site; stripey carpet may cause dizziness. $ *Rooms from: £150* ✉ *Rother St.* ☎ *01789/297022* ⊕ *www.white-swan-stratford.co.uk* ⤳ *37 rooms, 4 suites* ❧ *Breakfast.*

COUNTRY WALKS

The gentle countryside rewards exploration on foot. Ambitious walkers can try the 26-mile Arden Way loop that takes in Henley-in-Arden and the Forest of Arden. On the 3-mile walk from Stratford to Wilmcote and Mary Arden's Farm, you can see beautiful scenery. Parkland with trails surrounds stately homes such as Charlecote Park. Even Stratford can be the base for easy walks along the River Avon or on the path bordering the Stratford-upon-Avon Canal. Stratford's Tourist Information Centre has pamphlets with walks.

NIGHTLIFE AND THE ARTS

Fodor's Choice
★

Royal Shakespeare Company. One of the finest repertory troupes in the world and long the backbone of the country's theatrical life, the company performs plays year-round in Stratford and at venues around Britain. The stunning Royal Shakespeare Theatre, home of the RSC, has a thrust stage based on the original Globe Theater in London. The Swan Theatre, part of the theater complex and also built in the style of Shakespeare's Globe, stages plays by Shakespeare and contemporaries such as Christopher Marlowe and Ben Jonson, as well as works by contemporary playwrights. Prices usually are £14 to £60. ■ **TIP→** Seats book up fast, but day-of-performance and returned tickets are often available. ✉ *Waterside* ☎ *0844/800–1110 ticket hotline* ⊕ *www.rsc.org.uk.*

SPORTS AND THE OUTDOORS

Avon Boating. From Easter to October, Avon Boating rents boats and punts and runs half-hour river excursions (£5.50). A Venetian gondola can be rented for £100 for 40 minutes. ✉ *The Boatyard, Swan's Nest La.* ☎ *01789/267073* ⊕ *www.avon-boating.co.uk.*

Bancroft Cruisers. A family-run business, Bancroft Cruises runs regular 45-minute guided excursions along the Avon (£5.50). ✉ *Moathouse, Bridgefoot* ☎ *01789/269669* ⊕ *www.bancroftcruisers.co.uk.*

SHOPPING

Chain stores and shops sell tourist junk, but this is also a good place to shop for high-quality (and high-price) silver, jewelry, and china. There's an open **market** (great for bargains) every Friday in the Market Place at Greenhill and Meer streets.

Antiques Centre. This building contains 50 stalls displaying jewelry, silver, linens, porcelain, and memorabilia. ⊠ *60 Ely St.*

B&W Thornton. Above Shakespeare's Birthplace, B&W Thornton stocks Moorcroft pottery and glass. ⊠ *23 Henley St.* ☎ *01789/269405.*

Chaucer Head Bookshop. This is the best of Stratford's many secondhand bookshops. ⊠ *21 Chapel St.* ☎ *01789/415691.*

Lakeland. A great range of kitchen and home wares are available at Lakeland. ⊠ *4/5 Henley St.* ☎ *01789/262100.*

Shakespeare Bookshop. Run by the Shakespeare Birthplace, the bookshop carries Elizabethan plays, Tudor history books, children's books, and general paraphernalia. ⊠ *Shakespeare's Birthplace, Henley St.* ☎ *01789/292176.*

HENLEY-IN-ARDEN

8 miles northwest of Stratford.

A brief drive out of Stratford will take you under the Stratford-upon-Avon Canal aqueduct to pretty Henley-in-Arden, whose wide main street is an architectural pageant of many periods. This area was once the Forest of Arden, where Shakespeare set one of his greatest comedies, *As You Like It.* Among the buildings to look for are the former Guildhall, dating from the 15th century, and the White Swan pub, built in the early 1600s. Near Henley-in-Arden are two stately homes worth a stop, Packwood House and Baddesley Clinton.

GETTING HERE AND AROUND

The town is on the A3400. London Midland trains for Henley-in-Arden depart every hour from Stratford; the journey takes about 15 minutes. Train service from Birmingham New Street takes about 45 minutes, and trains leave every hour.

EXPLORING

Fodor's Choice
★

Baddesley Clinton. The eminent architectural historian Sir Nikolaus Pevsner described this as "the perfect late medieval manor house. The entrance side of grey stone, the small, creeper-clad Queen Anne brick bridge across the moat, the gateway with a porch higher than the roof and embattled—it could not be better." Set off a winding back-road, this grand manor dating from the 15th century retains its great fireplaces, 17th-century paneling, and three priest holes (secret chambers for Roman Catholic priests, who were hidden by sympathizers when Catholicism was banned in the 16th and 17th centuries). The café is an idyllic spot. Admission to the house is by timed ticket; Baddesley Clinton is 2 miles east of Packwood House and 15 miles north of Stratford-upon-Avon. ⊠ *Rising La., off A4141 near Chadwick End* ☎ *01564/783294* ⊕ *www.nationaltrust.org.uk* ⊠ *£9.60; garden only £6.30* ⊙ *House and grounds: mid-Feb.–Oct., daily 11–5; Nov.–mid-Feb., daily 11–4; last admission 30 mins before closing.*

Packwood House. Garden enthusiasts are drawn to Packwood's re-created 17th-century gardens, highlighted by an ambitious topiary Tudor garden in which yew trees depict Jesus's Sermon on the Mount. With tall chimneys, the house combines redbrick and half-timbering.

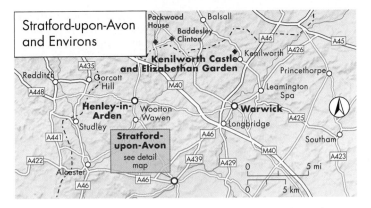

Exquisite collections of 16th-century furniture and textiles in the interior's 20th-century version of Tudor architecture make this one of the area's finest historic houses open to the public. It's 5 miles north of Henley-in-Arden and 12 miles north of Stratford-upon-Avon. ⊠ *Off B4439, 2 miles east of Hockley Heath* ☎ *01564/782024* ⊕ *www. nationaltrust.org.uk* ⊠ *£9.60; garden only £6.30* ⊙ *House and garden: mid-Feb.–mid-July, Sept., and Oct., Tues.–Sun. 11–5; mid-July and Aug. daily 11–5; last admission 30 mins before closing.*

WARWICK

8 miles east of Henley-in-Arden, 9 miles northeast of Stratford-upon-Avon.

Most famous for Warwick Castle—that vision out of the feudal ages—the town of Warwick (pronounced *war*-ick) is an interesting architectural mix of Georgian redbrick and Elizabethan half-timbering.

GETTING HERE AND AROUND
Frequent trains from London to Warwick leave London's Marylebone Station; travel time is about 90 minutes. The journey between Stratford-upon-Avon and Warwick takes around 30 minutes by train or bus. Stagecoach Bus 16 is more frequent, running every hour.

ESSENTIALS
Visitor Information Warwick Tourist Information Centre ⊠ *Court House, Jury St.* ☎ *01926/492212* ⊕ *www.visitwarwick.co.uk.*

EXPLORING
Collegiate Church of St. Mary. Crowded with gilded, carved, and painted tombs, the **Beauchamp Chapel** of this church is the essence of late-medieval and Tudor chivalry—although it was built (1443–64) to honor the somewhat-less-than-chivalrous Richard Beauchamp, who consigned Joan of Arc to the flames. Alongside his impressive effigy in gilded bronze lie the fine tombs of Robert Dudley, earl of Leicester, adviser and favorite of Elizabeth I, and Leicester's brother Ambrose. The church's chancel, distinguished by its flying ribs, a feature unique to a parish church, houses the alabaster table tomb of Thomas Beauchamp and his wife; the adjacent tiny Dean's chapel has exquisite

miniature fan vaulting. In the Norman crypt, look for the rare ducking stool (a chair in which people were tied for public punishment). There's a brass-rubbing center, and you can climb the tower in summer. The site is a five-minute walk from Warwick Castle. ⊠ *Old Sq., Church St.* ☎ *01926/403940* ⊕ *www.stmaryswarwick.org.uk* ✉ *£2 donation suggested; tower £2.50* ⊙ *Apr.–Oct., daily 10–6; Nov.–Mar., daily 10–4:30.*

Lord Leycester Hospital. Unattractive postwar development has spoiled much of Warwick's town center, but look for the 15th-century half-timber Lord Leycester Hospital, a home for old soldiers since the earl of Leicester dedicated it to that purpose in 1571. Within the complex are a chapel, an impressive beamed hall containing a small museum, and a fine courtyard with a wattle-and-daub balcony and 500-year-old gardens with a pineapple pit. Try a cream tea in the Brethren's Kitchen. ⊠ *High St.* ☎ *01926/491422* ⊕ *www.lordleycester.com* ✉ *£4.90* ⊙ *Apr.–Sept., Tues.–Sun. 10–5; Oct.–Mar., Tues.–Sun. 10.*

FAMILY
Fodor's Choice
★

Warwick Castle. The vast bulk of this medieval castle rests on a cliff overlooking the Avon—"the fairest monument of ancient and chivalrous splendor which yet remains uninjured by time," to use the words of Sir Walter Scott. Today the company that runs the Madame Tussauds wax museums owns the castle, and the exhibits and diversions can occupy a full day. Warwick is a great castle experience for kids, though it's pricey (there are family rates). Warwick's two soaring towers, bristling with battlements, can be seen for miles: the 147-foot-high Caesar's Tower, built in 1356, and the 128-foot-high Guy's Tower, built in 1380. The castle's most powerful commander was Richard Neville, Earl of Warwick, known during the 15th-century Wars of the Roses as the Kingmaker. Warwick Castle's monumental walls enclose an impressive armory of medieval weapons, as well as state rooms with historic furnishings and paintings by Peter Paul Rubens, Anthony Van Dyck, and other old masters. Twelve rooms are devoted to an imaginative wax exhibition, *A Royal Weekend Party—1898*. Other exhibits display the sights and sounds of a great medieval household as it prepares for an important battle, and of a princess's fairy-tale wedding; in the Dragon Tower, Merlin and a talking dragon breathe life into the Arthurian legend. At the Mill and Engine House you can see the turning water mill and the engines used to generate electricity early in the 20th century. In the spooky dungeon exhibit you can wander by wax re-creations of decaying bodies, chanting monks, witches, executions, and "the labyrinth of lost souls"—a modern mirror maze. Elsewhere, a working trebuchet (a kind of catapult), falconry displays, and rat-throwing (stuffed, not live) games add to the atmosphere. Below the castle strutting peacocks patrol the 60 acres of grounds elegantly landscaped by Capability Brown in the 18th century. ■ TIP→ Arrive early to beat the crowds. Book tickets online for a discount (sizable if a week or more ahead). Lavish medieval banquets (extra charge) and special events, including festivals, jousting tournaments, and a Christmas market, take place throughout the year, and plenty of food stalls serve lunches. ⊠ *Castle La., off Mill St.* ☎ *01926/495421, 0871/265–2000 24-hr information line* ⊕ *www. warwick-castle.com* ✉ *Castle, Dragon Tower and Dungeon £30.60,*

Castle and Dungeon £28.20, Castle £22.80; parking £6 ⊙ Late July and Aug., daily 10–6; mid-Sept.–mid-July, daily 10–5; last admission 30 mins before closing.

KENILWORTH CASTLE AND ELIZABETHAN GARDEN

5 miles north of Warwick.

Within the small town of Kenilworth stand the ruins of Kenilworth Castle, the site of an interlude between Elizabeth I and Robert Dudley, Earl of Leicester, which has been immortalized in print by Sir Walter Scott and in operas by Donizetti and others.

GETTING HERE AND AROUND

The local Stagecoach company offers bus services to and from Stratford and Warwick on the 16 and X17 route. The castle is a mile and a half from the town center.

ESSENTIALS

Visitor Information Kenilworth Library and Information Centre
⊠ *Kenilworth Library, 11 Smalley Pl.* ☎ *0300/555–8171* ⊕ *www.warwickshire. gov.uk/kenilworthlibrary*

EXPLORING

Fodor's Choice
★

Kenilworth Castle and Elizabethan Garden. The sprawling, graceful red ruins of the castle loom over the green fields of Warwickshire, surrounded by the low grassy impression of what was once a lake that surrounded it completely. The top of the keep (central tower) has commanding views of the countryside, one good indication of why this was such a formidable fortress from 1120 until Oliver Cromwell dismantled it after the civil war in the mid-17th century. Still intact are its keep, with 20-foot-thick walls; its great hall built by John of Gaunt in the 14th century; and its curtain walls, the low outer walls forming the castle's first line of defense. Even more than Warwick Castle, these ruins reflect English history. In 1326 King Edward II was imprisoned here and forced to renounce the throne, before he was transferred to Berkeley Castle and allegedly murdered with a red-hot poker. Here the ambitious Robert Dudley, Earl of Leicester, one of Elizabeth I's favorites, entertained her four times, most notably in 1575 with 19 days of revelry. An excellent exhibition in the restored gatehouse discusses the relationship between Leicester and Elizabeth, and a stunning re-created Elizabethan garden with arbors, aviary, and an 18-foot high Cararra marble fountain provides further interest for a visit for an hour or two. This is a good place for a picnic and contemplation of the passage of time. The fine gift shop sells excellent replicas of tapestries and swords. ⊠ *Off A452* ☎ *01926/852078* ⊕ *www.english-heritage.org.uk* ⬛ *£9* ⊙ *Apr.–Oct., daily 10–5; Nov.–Mar., weekends 10–4.*

7

MANCHESTER, LIVERPOOL, AND THE PEAK DISTRICT

WELCOME TO MANCHESTER, LIVERPOOL, AND THE PEAK DISTRICT

TOP REASONS TO GO

★ **Liverpool culture, old and new:** The Beatles' home city is already a must-see for fans of the Fab Four, but this once-rundown Victorian city has spent a decade reinventing itself as a cultural hub.

★ **Manchester nightspots:** Catch the city at night in any of its humming café-bars and pubs; or just enjoy a good beer in an ornate Victorian-era pub.

★ **Chatsworth House and Haddon Hall:** Engage the past and imagine yourself as a country landowner roaming the great pile that is Chatsworth, or as a Tudor noble strolling through the grounds of the quintessentially English Haddon Hall.

★ **Walking in the Peak District:** Even a short hike reveals the craggy, austere beauty for which the area is famous.

★ **Ironbridge Gorge:** Recall the beginnings of England's Industrial Revolution at this fine complex of industrial-heritage museums.

1 Manchester. The skies may be gray, but the vibrant city of Manchester is known for its modern urban design and its thriving music and club scenes. Great museums justify its status as the leading city of the northwest.

2 Liverpool. Now in the midst of a postindustrial rebirth, this city is more than the Beatles. The imposing waterfront and the grand architecture make this clear. Even so, the museums don't forget to mention the city's place in rock-and-roll history.

3 The Peak District. Britain's first national park, the Peak District is studded with an array of stately homes, the most impressive being Chatsworth House. Dramatic moors, sylvan dales, and atmospheric limestone caverns are just demanding to be explored.

4 Chester, Ludlow, and Environs. The southern part of the region, studded with its characteristic half-timber buildings, encompasses the World Heritage Site of Ironbridge Gorge, the ancient city of Chester, and medieval Ludlow with its top-class restaurants.

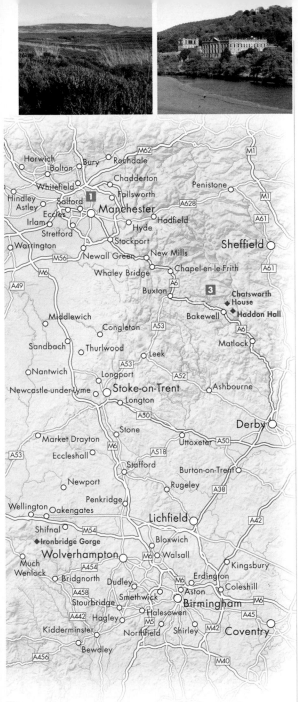

GETTING ORIENTED

Manchester lies at the heart of a tangle of motorways in the northwest of England, about a half hour across the Pennines from Yorkshire. It's 70 miles from the southern part of the Lake District. The city spreads west toward the coast and the mouth of the River Mersey, where Liverpool is still centered on its port. The Peak District National Park is less than an hour's drive southeast of Manchester. The dramatic, windswept Peaks are the only area of truly outstanding natural beauty in the northwest; also here are two of the grandest historic homes in Britain: Chatsworth and Haddon Hall. The southwestern part of the region, bordering Wales, is a gentler landscape; the medieval city of Chester is here, along with Ironbridge and its stunning industrial heritage museums.

8

Updated by
Jack Jewers

The northwest region of England encompasses notable urban areas and a few lovely areas inland. Manchester and Liverpool, the two big cities here, are bustling with redevelopment after years of decline. To their east, Derbyshire has the spectacular Peak District, and south of the cities are tranquil counties with small villages and market towns.

Manchester and Liverpool, with populations of about 450,000 each, were once the economic engines that propelled Britain in the 18th and 19th centuries. Now that rich industrial and maritime heritage is celebrated in excellent museums, Liverpool's within the city's Victorian edifices, and Manchester's in some thrustingly modern buildings.

The cities have also reestablished themselves as centers of sporting and musical excellence, and as hot spots for nightlife. Since 1962 the Manchester United, Everton, and Liverpool football (soccer in the United States) clubs have won everything worth winning in Britain and Europe. The Beatles launched the Mersey sound of the '60s; contemporary Manchester groups still punch above their weight on both sides of the Atlantic. Manchester is also the home of Britain's oldest leading orchestra, the Hallé (founded in 1857)—just one legacy of 19th-century industrialists' investments in culture.

Just 25 miles southeast of Manchester, the Peak District is a wild part of England, a region of crags that rear violently out of the plains. The Pennines, a line of hills that begins in this region and runs as far north as Scotland, are sometimes called "the backbone of England." In this landscape of rocky outcrops and undulating meadowland, you'll see nothing for miles but sheep, dry-stone (without mortar) walls, and farms, interrupted—spectacularly—by old villages and stately homes.

South of the cities, along the 108-mile border with Wales, are the counties of Herefordshire, Worcestershire, and Shropshire, dotted with market towns full of 13th- and 14th-century black-and-white, half-timber buildings. The medieval main streets of Chester are monuments to past wealth; more half-timbered structures are found in Ludlow, now a culinary center. In the 18th century, in a wooded stretch of the Severn Gorge in Shropshire, the coke blast furnace was invented and the first iron bridge was erected (1779), heralding the birth of the Industrial Revolution. You can get a sense of this history at the spectacular heritage museums at Ironbridge Gorge.

MANCHESTER, LIVERPOOL, AND THE PEAK DISTRICT PLANNER

WHEN TO GO

Manchester has a reputation as one of the wettest cities in Britain, and visiting in summer won't guarantee fine weather. Nevertheless, wet or cold weather shouldn't spoil a visit because of the many indoor sights and cultural activities here and in Liverpool. Summer is the optimum time to see the Peak District, especially because traditional festivities take place in many villages. The *only* time to see the great houses of Derbyshire's Wye Valley is from spring through fall. Most rural sights have limited opening hours in winter, and the majority of attractions close at 5. Some stately homes have limited hours even in summer, which is when the countryside is at its most appealing.

PLANNING YOUR TIME

It's possible to see the main sights of Manchester or Liverpool in a day each, but you'd have to take the museums at a gallop. In Manchester the Museum of Science and Industry and the Imperial War Museum could easily absorb a day, as could the Albert Dock and waterfront area of Liverpool, where the Beatles Story, Tate Liverpool, Merseyside Maritime, and International Slavery museums vie for attention. In Liverpool an additional half day is needed to see the homes of John Lennon and Paul McCartney. The buzzing nightlife of each city demands at least an overnight stay. You can explore the Peak District on a day trip from Manchester in a pinch, but you'd hardly do it justice—allow longer to visit the stately homes or to hike. In the south of the region, Ironbridge Gorge demands a full day. You could do Ludlow and Chester in a half day each, though it would be a shame to leave Ludlow without sampling its fine dining.

GETTING HERE AND AROUND
AIR TRAVEL
Both Manchester and Liverpool are well served by their international airports. Manchester, the third-largest airport in the country, has the greater number of flights, including some from the United States.

Airports **Liverpool John Lennon Airport** ☎ *0871/521–8484* ⊕ *www.liverpoolairport.com.* **Manchester Airport** ☎ *0871/271–0711* ⊕ *www.manchesterairport.co.uk.*

BUS TRAVEL
National Express buses serve the region from London's Victoria Coach Station. Average travel time to Manchester or Liverpool is five hours. To reach Bakewell, and Buxton you can take a bus from London to the city of Derby and change to TransPeak bus service, which also stops at Haddon Hall; local buses go from Bakewell to Chatsworth

House. Manchester is an alternative interchange to Derby when traveling from London.

Bus Contacts National Express ☎ 08717/818178 ⊕ www.nationalexpress.com. **TransPeak** ☎ 01773/712265 ⊕ www.trentbarton.co.uk. **Traveline** ☎ 0871/200–2233 ⊕ www.traveline.org.uk.

CAR TRAVEL

If you're traveling by road, expect heavy traffic out of London on weekends. Travel time to Manchester or Liverpool from London via the M6 is 3 to 3½ hours. Although a car may not be an asset in touring the centers of Manchester and Liverpool, it's helpful in getting around the Peak District. Bus service there is quite good, but a car allows the most flexibility.

Roads within the region are generally good. In Manchester and Liverpool, try to sightsee on foot to avoid parking problems. In the Peak District, park in signposted parking lots whenever possible. In summer, Peak District traffic is heavy; watch out for speeding motorbikes, especially on the A6. In winter, know the weather forecast, as moorland roads can quickly become impassable. To reach Ludlow and Chester from London, take M40.

TRAIN TRAVEL

Virgin Trains serves the region from London's Euston Station. Direct service to Manchester and Liverpool takes between 2 and 2½ hours. There are trains between Manchester's Piccadilly Station and Liverpool's Lime Street roughly three times an hour during the day; the trip takes 50 minutes. Get schedules and other information through National Rail Enquiries.

Travel time from Paddington Station in London to Ludlow is 3½ hours (changing at Newport); from Euston Station in London to Chester, with a change at Crewe, is 2¾ hours.

Train Contacts National Rail Enquiries ☎ 0845/748–4950 ⊕ www.nationalrail.co.uk.

TRANSPORTATION DISCOUNTS AND DEALS

A Wayfarer ticket (£11), which covers a day's travel on all forms of transportation in Manchester, Lancashire, Cheshire, Staffordshire, Derbyshire, and the Peak District, is a good deal. Contact National Rail Enquiries for information.

RESTAURANTS

Dining options in Manchester and Liverpool vary from smart cafés offering Modern British and Continental fare to excellent international restaurants. Manchester has one of Britain's biggest Chinatowns, and locals also favor the 40-odd Bangladeshi, Pakistani, and Indian restaurants along Wilmslow Road in Rusholme, a mile south of the city center, known as Curry Mile. In recent years, Ludlow has grown into something of a foodie town, with a burgeoning collection of great restaurants.

One local dish that has survived is Bakewell pudding (*never* called "tart" in these areas, as its imitations are elsewhere in England). Served with custard or cream, the pudding—a pastry covered with jam and a thin layer of almond-flavor filling—is the joy of Bakewell. Another regional creation is Lancashire hot pot, a hearty meat stew.

HOTELS

Because the larger city-center hotels in Manchester and Liverpool rely on business travelers during the week, they may markedly reduce their rates on weekends. Smaller hotels and guesthouses abound in nearby suburbs, many just a short bus ride from downtown. The Manchester and Liverpool visitor centers operate room-booking services. Also worth investigating are serviced apartments, which are becoming more popular in the cities. The Peak District has inns, bed-and-breakfasts, and hotels, as well as a network of youth hostels. Local tourist offices have details; reserve well in advance for Easter and summer. *Hotel reviews have been shortened. For full information, visit Fodors.com.*

WHAT IT COSTS IN POUNDS				
	$	$$	$$$	$$$$
Restaurants	under £15	£15–£19	£20–£25	over £25
Hotels	under £100	£100–£160	£161–£220	over £220

Restaurant prices are the average cost of a main course at dinner or, if dinner isn't served, at lunch. Hotel prices are the lowest cost of a standard double room in high season, including 20% V.A.T.

VISITOR INFORMATION

Contacts England's Northwest ⊕ *www.visitenglandsnorthwest.com.* **Heart of England Tourist Board** ☎ *01905/887690* ⊕ *www.visittheheart.co.uk.*

8

MANCHESTER

Today Manchester's center hums with the vibe of cutting-edge popular music and a swank café culture. The city's once-grim industrial landscape, redeveloped since the late 1980s, includes tidied-up canals, cotton mills transformed into loft apartments, and stylish contemporary architecture that has pushed the skyline ever higher. Beetham Tower, the ninth-tallest building in Britain (and the tallest outside London), can't be overlooked. Bridgewater Hall and the Lowry, as well as the Imperial War Museum North, are outstanding cultural facilities. Sure, it still rains here, but the rain-soaked streets are part of the city's charm, in a bleak, northern kind of way.

The now-defunct Haçienda Club marketed New Order to the world, and Manchester became the clubbing capital of England. Other bands formed in Manchester, like Joy Division, the Smiths, Stone Roses, Happy Mondays, and Oasis, have also enjoyed longevity at the top of the charts. The extraordinary success of the Manchester United football club (which now faces a stiff challenge from its newly rich neighbor, Manchester City, owing to a stupendous injection of cash from its oil-rich Middle Eastern owners) has kept the eyes of sports fans fixed firmly on Manchester.

GETTING HERE AND AROUND

Manchester Airport has many international flights, so you might not even have to travel through London. There are frequent trains from the airport to Piccadilly Railway Station (15–20 minutes) and buses to Piccadilly Gardens Bus Station (one hour). A taxi from the airport to Manchester city center costs around £20. For details about public transportation in Manchester, call the Greater Manchester Passenger Transport Executive information line.

Driving to Manchester from London (3 to 3½ hours), take M1 north to M6, then the M62 east, which becomes M602 as it enters Greater Manchester. Trains from London's Euston Station drop passengers at the centrally located Piccadilly Railway Station. The journey takes just over two hours. Chorlton Street Coach Station, a few hundred yards west of Piccadilly Railway Station, is the main bus station for regional and long-distance buses.

Most local buses leave from Piccadilly Gardens Bus Station, the hub of the urban bus network.

Metroshuttle operates three free circular routes around the city center; service runs every 5 to 10 minutes Monday to Saturday, from 7 to 7 and Sunday and public holidays from 10 to 6.

Metrolink electric tram service runs through the city center and out to the suburbs. The Eccles extension has stops for the Lowry (Harbour City) and for the Manchester United Stadium (Old Trafford). Buy a ticket from the platform machine before you board. SystemOne Travelcards, which allow unlimited travel on public transportation, cost between £5 and £8.60, depending on the times of day and the transport you want to include. Buy from the driver or any ticket machine.

Blue Badge Guides can arrange dozens of different tours of the city, and City Centre Cruises (☎ 0161/902–0222 ⊕ www.citycentrecruises. co.uk) offer a three-hour Sunday lunch round-trip on a barge in the Manchester Ship Canal.

ORIENTATION

Manchester is compact enough that you can easily walk across the city center in 40 minutes. Deansgate and Princess Street, the main thoroughfares, run roughly north–south and west–east; the lofty terra-cotta Victorian **Town Hall** sits in the middle, close to the visitor center and the fine **Manchester Art Gallery.** Dominating the skyline at the southern end of Deansgate is Manchester's highest building, Beetham Tower, which houses a Hilton Hotel and marks the beginning of the **Castlefield Urban Heritage Park,** with the Museum of Science and Industry and the canal system. The **Whitworth Art Gallery** is a bus ride from downtown; otherwise, all other central sights are within easy walking distance of the Town Hall. Take a Metrolink tram 2 miles south for the Salford Quays dockland area, with the **Lowry** and the **Imperial War Museum;** you can spend half a day or more in this area. ■TIP→ Keep in mind that the museums are both excellent and free.

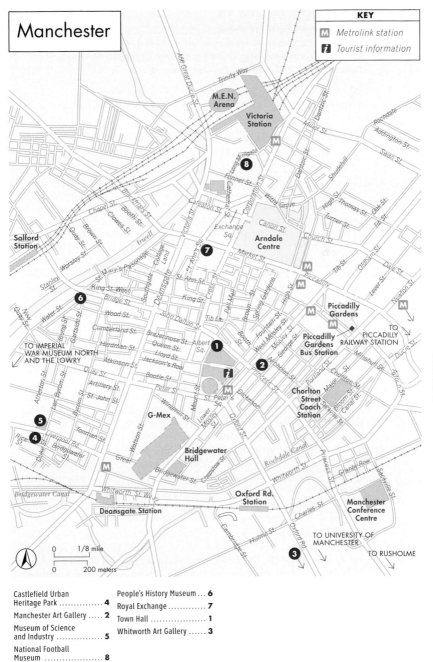

Manchester

ESSENTIALS

Transportation Contacts Metrolink ☏ *0161/205–2000*
⊕ *www.metrolink.co.uk.* **Metroshuttle** ☏ *0161/244–1000*
⊕ *www.tfgm.com/buses/Pages/metroshuttle.aspx.* **Transport for Greater Manchester** ☏ *0161/244–1000* ⊕ *www.tfgm.com.*

Tour Information Blue Badge Guides ☏ *0161/864–2640*
⊕ *www.britainsbestguides.org.* **City Centre Cruises** ☏ *0161/902–0222*
⊕ *www.citycentrecruises.co.uk.*

Visitor Information Manchester Visitor Information Centre ⊠ *40-50 Piccadilly Plaza, Portland St., City Centre* ☏ *0871/222–8223* ⊕ *www.visitmanchester.com.*

EXPLORING

TOP ATTRACTIONS

Castlefield Urban Heritage Park. Site of an early Roman fort, the district of Castlefield was later the center of the city's industrial boom, which resulted in the building of Britain's first modern canal in 1764 and the world's first railway station in 1830. It has been beautifully restored into an urban park with canal-side walks, landscaped open spaces, and refurbished warehouses. The 7-acre site contains the reconstructed gate to the Roman fort of Mamucium, the buildings of the **Museum of Science and Industry,** and several of the city's hippest bars and restaurants. You can spend half a day here. ⊠ *Off Liverpool Rd., Castlefield* ☏ *0161/834-4026.*

Imperial War Museum North. The thought-provoking exhibits in this striking, aluminum-clad building, which architect Daniel Libeskind described as representing three shards of an exploded globe, present the reasons for war and show its effects on society. Three Big Picture audiovisual shows envelop you in the sights and sounds of conflicts from 1914 to the present, and a storage system has trays of objects to examine, including artifacts from the 2003 war in Iraq. The Air Shard, a 100-foot viewing platform, gives a bird's-eye view of the city. The museum is on the banks of the Manchester Ship Canal in Salford Quays, across the footbridge from the Lowry. It's a 10-minute (often breezy) walk from the Harbour City stop of the Metrolink tram. ⊠ *Trafford Wharf Rd., Salford Quays* ☏ *0161/836–4000* ⊕ *www.iwm.org.uk* ▨ *Free* ☉ *Daily 10–5; last admission 30 mins before closing.*

The Lowry. Clad in perforated steel and glass and fronted by an illuminated canopy, this impressive arts center in Manchester is one of the highlights of the Salford Quays waterways. L. S. Lowry (1887–1976) was a local artist, and one of the few who painted the industrial landscape. Galleries showcase Lowry's and other contemporary artists' work. The theater, Britain's largest outside London, presents an impressive lineup of touring companies. The nearest Metrolink tram stop is Harbour City, a 10-minute walk from the Lowry. ⊠ *Pier 8, Salford Quays* ☏ *0843/208–6000* ⊕ *www.thelowry.com* ▨ *Free, tours £5* ☉ *Mon.–Sat. 10–8 (closes 6 on nights with no performance); Sun. and holiday Mon. 10–6. Galleries: Sun.–Fri. 11–5, Sat. 10–5.*

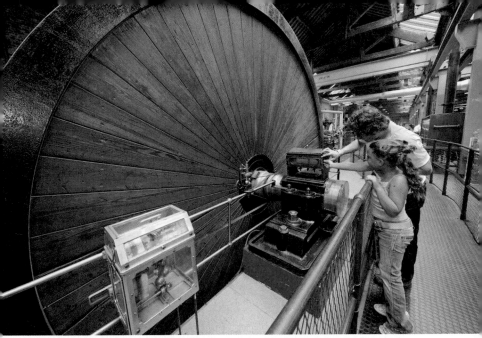

Manchester was an industrial powerhouse; learn all about this history at the engaging Museum of Science and Industry.

Manchester Art Gallery. Behind its impressive classical portico, this splendid museum presents its collections in both a Victorian and contemporary setting. Don't miss the outstanding collection of paintings by the Pre-Raphaelites and their circle, notably Ford Madox Brown's masterpiece *Work*, Holman Hunt's *The Hireling Shepherd*, and Dante Gabriel Rossetti's *Astarte Syriaca*. British artworks from the 18th and the 20th centuries are also well represented. The second-floor Craft and Design Gallery shows off the best of the decorative arts in ceramics, glass, metalwork, and furniture. ⊠ *Mosely St., City Centre* ☎ *0161/235–8888* ⊕ *www.manchestergalleries.org.uk* ⊠ *Free* ☉ *Fri.–Wed. 10–5; Thurs. 10–9; last admission 30 mins before closing.*

FAMILY
Fodor'sChoice
★

Museum of Science and Industry. The museum's five buildings, one of which is the world's oldest passenger rail station (1830), hold marvelous collections relating to the city's industrial past and present. You can walk through a reconstructed Victorian sewer, be blasted by the heat and noise of working steam engines, see cotton looms whirring in action, and watch a planetarium show. The Air and Space Gallery fills a graceful cast-iron-and-glass building, constructed as a market hall in 1877. ■TIP→ Allow at least half a day to get the most out of all the sites. ⊠ *Castlefield Urban Heritage Park, Liverpool Rd., main entrance on Lower Byrom St., Castlefield* ☎ *0161/832–2244* ⊕ *www.mosi.org. uk* ⊠ *Free, charges vary for special exhibits* ☉ *Daily 10–5.*

FAMILY **People's History Museum.** Not everyone in 19th-century Manchester owned a cotton mill or made a fortune on the trading floor. This museum recounts powerfully the struggles of working people in the city since the Industrial Revolution. Displays include the story of the 1819

Peterloo Massacre—when the army attacked a crowd of civil rights protesters in Manchester's St. Peter's Square, killing 15 and almost sparking revolution—together with an unrivaled collection of trade-union banners, tools, toys, utensils, and photographs, all illustrating the working lives and pastimes of the city's people. ⊠ *Left Bank, City Centre* ☎ *0161/838–9190* ⊕ *www. phm.org.uk* ☑ *Free* ☉ *Daily 10–5.*

Royal Exchange. Throughout the city's commercial heyday, the most important building was the cotton market. Built with Victorian exuberance in 1874, the existing structure accommodated 7,000 traders. The giant glass-dome roof was restored after a 1996 IRA bombing.

Visit to see the lunar module–inspired Royal Exchange Theatre, have a drink in the café, and browse the crafts shop or the clothes outlets in the arcade. ⊠ *St. Ann's Sq., City Centre* ☎ *0161/833–9833 (Theatre)* ⊕ *www.royalexchange.co.uk.*

Town Hall. Manchester's imposing Town Hall, with its 280-foot-tall clock tower, speaks volumes about the city's 19th-century sense of self-importance. Alfred Waterhouse designed the Victorian Gothic building (1867–76); extensions were added just before World War II. Over the main entrance is a statue of Roman general Agricola, who founded Mamucium in AD 79. Just inside the entrance, the Sculpture Hall has a magnificent low vaulted ceiling; now used as a café, the walls are lined with Gothic-style alcoves and statues of famous Mancunians. The Great Hall is decorated with murals of the city's history, painted between 1852 and 1865 by the Pre-Raphaelite Ford Madox Brown. You can view the murals for free when the room isn't being used; call ahead to check. ⊠ *Albert Sq., public entrance on Lloyd St., City Centre* ☎ *0161/234–5000* ☑ *Free* ☉ *Weekdays 9–5; Sculpture Hall also 11–4 Sat.*

Whitworth Art Gallery. This University of Manchester–run art museum has strong collections of British watercolors, old-master drawings, and postimpressionist works, as well as wallpapers. The excellent textile gallery—befitting a city built on textile manufacture—demonstrates the meaning and power of clothing in such items as a 16th-century Spanish funeral cope, 18th-century babies' vests, and a modern-day Turkish circumcision suit. There's's also a good bistro and a gift shop. To get to the museum, catch any southbound bus with a number in the 40s (except 47) on Oxford Road, or from St. Peter's Square or Piccadilly Gardens. ⊠ *University of Manchester, Oxford Rd., University Quarter* ☎ *0161/275–7450* ⊕ *www.whitworth.manchester.ac.uk* ☑ *Free* ☉ *Mon.–Sat. 10–5, Sun. noon–4.*

WORTH NOTING

National Football Museum. This huge museum is devoted to one of the biggest British exports of all time—football (soccer), the English national sport, and the most popular team game in the world. This striking, glass-skinned triangle of a building includes a galaxy of footballing memorabilia, from historic trophies, souvenirs, and shirts (many of them signed by legends of the sport) to such near-sacred items as the ball from the 1966 World Cup–the last time England won the sport's ultimate prize. Other exhibits explore football's role in British popular culture. In the interactive Football Plus zone you can pick up a microphone and develop your commentary style or test your ball skills in a range of activities, including a tense penalty shoot-out. ✉ *Urbis Bldg., Cathedral Gardens, Millennium Quarter* ☎ *0161/605–8200* 🌐 *www.nationalfootballmuseum.com* 🎫 *Free* 🕒 *Mon.–Sat. 10–5, Sun. 11–5.*

WHERE TO EAT

The city's dining scene, with everything from Indian (go to Rusholme) to Modern British fare, is lively. The Manchester Food and Drink Festival, held in late September or early October, showcases the city's chefs and regional products with special events. The city's pubs are also good options for lunch or dinner.

$ INDIAN 🍴 **Akbar's.** Locals line up for this big, bright, and buzzing contemporary restaurant just opposite the Museum of Science and Industry. If they're not tucking into sizzling, stir-fried balti dishes (a don't-miss), they might be enjoying a mild and creamy korma, *rogan josh* (with tomatoes and coriander), or a sweet-and-sour *dhansak* (with pineapple and lentils)—all popular staples. Vegetarians have plenty of choices, too. Be prepared to wait at busy times. [$] *Average main: £9* ✉ *73–83 Liverpool Rd., Castlefield* ☎ *0161/834–8444* 🌐 *www.akbars.co.uk* ✍ *Reservations not accepted* 🕒 *No lunch.*

$$ BRITISH 🍴 **Albert's Shed.** A relaxed canalside setting and an alluring contemporary interior with large plate-glass windows compensate for the uninspiring, brick box facade of this traditional Castlefield restaurant. Most of the dishes, which use produce from Lancashire farms, hark back to the English country-manor table: roast venison loin topped with Stilton cheese and a port and blackberry *jus,* for example. Other dishes, like gnocchi with a rabbit and pancetta sauce, bring a scent of the Mediterranean. There's also a wide selection of pizzas. An excellent-value two-course lunch menu is served until 5 pm. [$] *Average main: £16* ✉ *20 Castle St., Castlefield* ☎ *0161/839–9818* 🌐 *www.albertsshed.com.*

$$ MODERN BRITISH 🍴 **The Lime Tree.** Chef Patrick Hannity's unstuffy restaurant offers a seductive British menu with a hint of northern bohemia in the leafy suburb of West Didsbury. Expect Cheshire lamb in the exotic company of moussaka, couscous, and mint yogurt, or Morecambe Bay scallops in cannelloni. If you don't mind eating between 5:30 and 6:30 pm, the early-evening three-course menu is a superb value at £15.95. Wine can be ordered by the glass to suit each dish. You might need to book a week in advance. [$] *Average main: £17* ✉ *8 Lapwing La., West Didsbury* ☎ *0161/445–1217* 🌐 *www.thelimetreerestaurant.co.uk* ✍ *Reservations essential.*

8

$ ✕ **Mr. Thomas's Chophouse.** The city's oldest restaurant, dating from 1872,
BRITISH　dishes out good old British favorites such as brown onion soup, corned
beef hash, Lancashire hot pot, and spotted dick pudding to crowds
of city dwellers and shoppers. This hearty food is served in a Victo-
rian-style room with a black-and-white-checked floor and green tiling.
The wine list is exceptional. Mr. Sam's Chophouse in Chapel Walks
serves similar fare. $ *Average main: £14* ✉ *52 Cross St., City Centre*
☎ *0161/832–2245* ⊕ *www.tomschophouse.com.*

$ ✕ **Mughli Restaurant and Charcoal Pit.** Take your seat by the open charcoal
INDIAN　pit and be seduced by the sizzling tandoori or tikka dishes in
this fast-paced Indian restaurant on Rusholme's "Curry Mile." Specializing in Mughlai (northern Indian and Pakistani) cuisine, the restaurant
has a capacious, mood-lit interior with striking Indonesian murals and
Bollywood posters. It's been a local fixture for over 20 years. $ *Aver-
age main: £9* ✉ *28–32 Wilmslow Rd., Rusholme* ☎ *0161/248–0900*
⊕ *www.mughli.com.*

$$ ✕ **Sapporo Teppanyaki.** The emphasis is on riotous good fun at this mod-
JAPANESE　ern Japanese restaurant in Castlefield. Take your place around the chef's
Fodor's Choice　iron griddle and the theater begins; once you've had potato fritters
★　tossed into your mouth and seen other morsels caught and balanced
on the chef's spatula, you can enjoy a delicious and creative *teppanyaki*
(main courses served on an iron plate) of duck in raspberry sauce or
sole with lemon, ginger and coriander. For a quieter, lighter meal, take
a private table and peruse the sushi menu. Curiosity might tempt you
to try a Manchester roll, made of smoked swordfish with Lancashire
cheese, carrots, and crabmeat. $ *Average main: £17* ✉ *91–93 Liverpool
Rd., Castlefield* ☎ *0161/979–0578* ⊕ *www.sapporo.co.uk.*

$ ✕ **Sweet Mandarin.** Warm neon lights and floor-to-ceiling windows invite
CHINESE　you into this contemporary Chinese restaurant from the hip streets of
the Northern Quarter. Deliciously simple family recipes have earned it
a growing reputation; locals flock here to enjoy the famous salt-and-
pepper ribs, clay-pot chicken, Lily Kwok's curry, and crispy Szechuan
beef, all of which come on the fixed-price banquet menu at £20 per
head. On the ‡ la carte menu, try General Tse's sweet-and-sour chicken,
named after an uncle of the owner, whose protection of his secret recipe
virged on militant. $ *Average main: £11* ✉ *19 Copperas St., North-
ern Quarter* ☎ *0161/832–8848 after 5 pm, 0776/783–4583 daytime*
⊕ *www.sweetmandarin.com* ☉ *Closed Mon.*

$ ✕ **Umezushi.** A short walk from Manchester's Victoria train station,
JAPANESE　this tiny restaurant may not look like much from the outside—among
a row of industrial units inside converted railway arches—but it serves
some of the most exceptional sushi in Manchester. Traditional maki and
tempura are beautifully prepared, or you could opt for one of the more
experimental daily specials, such as stir-fried spaghetti with chili and
garlic, or Gressingham duck served with garlic and saki sauce. $ *Aver-
age main: £10* ✉ *Unit 4, Mirabel St., City Centre* ☎ *0161/832–1852*
⊕ *www.umezushi.co.uk.*

WHERE TO STAY

$ HOTEL 🏨 **Arora.** Opposite the Manchester Art Gallery, the centrally located Arora Hotel occupies one of the city's grand Victorian buildings; its interior design, however, is minimalist modern. **Pros:** fun theme rooms; good deals on weekends. **Cons:** no parking; smallish rooms. [$] *Rooms from: £80* ✉ *18–24 Princess St., City Centre* ☎ *0161/236-8999* 🌐 *www.arorainternational.com* 🛏 *141 rooms* 🍴 *No meals.*

$ HOTEL 🏨 **Castlefield Hotel.** This popular modern hotel near the water's edge in the Castlefield Basin, opposite the Museum of Science and Industry, has cheery and traditional public rooms. **Pros:** excellent leisure facilities; reasonable rates. **Cons:** gym can get very busy; walls a little thin. [$] *Rooms from: £99* ✉ *Liverpool Rd., Castlefield* ☎ *0161/832–7073* 🌐 *www.castlefield-hotel.co.uk* 🛏 *48 rooms* 🍴 *Breakfast.*

$$$$ HOTEL Fodor's Choice ★ 🏨 **Great John Street.** Once a Victorian schoolhouse, this plush boutique hotel next to the Granada TV studios now attracts well-heeled business executives, television stars, and anyone seeking something truly special. **Pros:** luxurious rooms; unique design. **Cons:** expensive valet parking. [$] *Rooms from: £238* ✉ *Great John St., City Centre* ☎ *0161/831–3211* 🌐 *www.greatjohnstreet.co.uk* 🛏 *14 rooms, 16 suites* 🍴 *No meals.*

$$ HOTEL 🏨 **The Lowry Hotel.** The strikingly modern design of this glass edifice overlooking the River Irwell and Santiago Calatrava's Trinity Bridge exudes luxury and spaciousness. **Pros:** luxury at every turn; spacious rooms. **Cons:** rather bleak views in rooms facing Chapel Street; cheapest rates don't include breakfast. [$] *Rooms from: £118* ✉ *50 Dearman's Pl., City Centre* ☎ *0161/827–4000* 🌐 *www.thelowryhotel.com* 🛏 *157 rooms, 7 suites* 🍴 *Multiple meal plans.*

$$ HOTEL 🏨 **The Midland Hotel.** The Edwardian splendor of the hotel's public rooms manages to shine through a contemporary makeover, evoking the days when this was the city's main railway station hotel. **Pros:** central location, close to Town Hall and a Metrolink stop; superb restaurant; good for business travelers. **Cons:** impersonal feel; rooms facing road can be noisy. [$] *Rooms from: £119* ✉ *Peter St., City Centre* ☎ *0161/236–3333* 🌐 *www.qhotels.co.uk* 🛏 *298 rooms, 14 suites* 🍴 *Breakfast.*

$ HOTEL 🏨 **The Oxnoble at Potato Wharf.** At the southern end of the city center opposite the Museum of Science and Industry, this friendly and relaxed gastro-pub comes with guestrooms that are simple, creamy cool, and modern in style. **Pros:** friendly staff; bargain prices. **Cons:** no-frills decor; noise from the bar reaches some of the rooms. [$] *Rooms from: £50* ✉ *71 Liverpool Rd., Castlefield* ☎ *0161/839–7760* 🌐 *www.theox.co.uk* 🛏 *9 rooms* 🍴 *No meals.*

$ RENTAL 🏨 **RoomZZZ.** Although the stylishly modern serviced apartments in this old cotton warehouse are all about self-contained autonomy, the lobby and corridors have the jazzed-up feel of a boutique hotel. **Pros:** bang in the center of town; on Chinatown's doorstep; smoothly run. **Cons:** bathrooms have glass doors; location can be noisy. [$] *Rooms from: £79* ✉ *36 Princess St., Chinatown* ☎ *0844/248–8075* 🌐 *www.roomzzz.co.uk* 🛏 *48 apartments* 🍴 *No meals.*

NIGHTLIFE AND THE ARTS

Manchester vies with London as Britain's capital of youth culture, but has vibrant nightlife and entertainment options for all ages. Spending time at a bar, pub, or club is definitely an essential part of any trip. For event listings, check out the free *Manchester Evening News* or *Manchester Metro News,* both widely available.

NIGHTLIFE

The action after dark centers on the Deansgate and Northern Quarter areas.

CAFÉ-BARS

Cloud 23. This swanky bar has a stunning 360-degree view of the city that's not for the vertiginous. It's popular, so book well ahead. ⊠ *Hilton Manchester Deansgate, 303 Deansgate, City Centre* ☎ *0161/870–1600* ⊕ *www.cloud23bar.com.*

Dry Bar. The Northern Quarter's original café-bar opened by Factory Records, Dry Bar is full of young people dancing and drinking. ⊠ *28–30 Oldham St., Northern Quarter* ☎ *0161/236–9840* ⊕ *www.drybar. co.uk.*

Kosmonaut. This funky new bar in the Northern Quarter has attracted a legion of fans since it opened in 2012. The stripped-down decor fits the hipster mood; exposed brick walls, leather benches, and the odd wry touch such as old barber chairs that form an intimate nook by the window. The wine list and beer selection are good, although the cocktail menu draws the biggest crowd. ⊠ *10 Tariff St., Northern Quarter* ☎ *0161/236–7171* ⊕ *www.kosmonaut.co.*

Living Room. For something a little more glamorous and intimate, the Living Room is one of the city's top spots; a pianist plays on the gorgeous white piano in the early evening. Book ahead. ⊠ *80 Deansgate, City Centre* ☎ *0161/832–0083* ⊕ *www.thelivingroom.co.uk.*

The Molly House. This lively bar has an outstanding selection of beers from around the world, in addition to good wine and cocktail lists. The tapas nibbles are delicious and surprisingly inexpensive. ⊠ *26 Richmond St., Northside* ☎ *0161/237–9329* ⊕ *www.themollyhouse.com.*

PUBS

Britons Protection. You can sample more than 230 whiskies and bourbons at this gorgeous pub with stained-glass windows, cozy back rooms, and a mural of the Peterloo Massacre. ⊠ *50 Great Bridgewater St., Peter's Fields* ☎ *0161/236–5895* ⊕ *www.britonsprotection.co.uk.*

Dukes 92. This spot has a great canal-side setting for a summer pub lunch or drink. ⊠ *18 Castle St., Castlefield* ☎ *0161/839–3522* ⊕ *www. dukes92.com.*

Peveril of the Peak. A throwback Victorian pub with a green-tile exterior, Peveril of the Peak draws a crush of locals to its tiny rooms. ⊠ *127 Great Bridgewater St., Peter's Fields* ☎ *0161/236–6364.*

Sinclair's Oyster Bar. In a half-timber pub built in the 17th century, Sinclair's Oyster Bar specializes in fresh oyster dishes. ⊠ *2 Cathedral Gates, Millennium Quarter* ☎ *0161/834–0430.*

DANCE CLUBS

42nd Street. Off Deansgate, 42nd Street plays retro, indie, sing-along anthems, and classic rock, with Manchester's proud musical heritage to the fore. ⊠ *2 Bootle St., City Centre* ☎ *0161/831–7108* ⊕ *www.42ndstreetnightclub.co.uk.*

Sankey's. Electro, techno, and hard-core music draw crowds of young people to Sankey's. ⊠ *Beehive Mill, Jersey St., Ancoats* ☎ *0161/236–5444* ⊕ *www.sankeys.info.*

GAY CLUBS

Gay Village. The Gay Village, which came to television in the British series *Queer as Folk,* has stylish bars and cafés along the Rochdale Canal; Canal Street is its heart. The area is not only the center of Manchester's good-size gay scene but also the nightlife center for the young and trendy.

Lammars. With colored-glass chandeliers, a mirrored grand piano, and other kitschy furnishings, the popular Lammars has stand-up comedy and live music. It's open late on weekends with a DJ playing Motown, soul, and disco classics. ⊠ *57 Hilton St., Northern Quarter* ☎ *0161/237–9058* ⊕ *www.lammars.co.uk.*

LIVE MUSIC

O2 Apollo Manchester. Housed in an art deco structure, the 3,500-seat venue (known by locals as just "the Apollo") showcases live rock and comedy acts before a mixed-age crowd. ⊠ *Stockport Rd., Ardwick Green* ☎ *0844/477–7677* ⊕ *www.o2apollomanchester.co.uk.*

Band on the Wall. A famous venue recently revamped, Band on the Wall has a reputation for hosting both established and pioneering music groups. Past performers include Joy Division, Simply Red, and Björk. ⊠ *25 Swan St., Northern Quarter* ☎ *0845/250–0500* ⊕ *www.bandonthewall.org.*

Manchester Arena. Major rock and pop stars appear at the Manchester Arena. ⊠ *21 Hunt's Bank, Hunt's Bank* ☎ *0844/847–8000 box office, 0161/950–5000 recorded information* ⊕ *www.men-arena.com.*

Roadhouse. An intimate venue for live bands, the Roadhouse hosts funk and indie nights. ⊠ *8 Newton St., City Centre* ☎ *0161/237–9789* ⊕ *www.theroadhouselive.co.uk.*

THE ARTS

PERFORMING ARTS VENUES

Bridgewater Hall. Dramatically modern Bridgewater Hall has concerts by Manchester's renowned Hallé Orchestra and hosts both classical music and a varied light-entertainment program. ⊠ *Lower Mosley St., Peter's Fields* ☎ *0161/907–9000* ⊕ *www.bridgewater-hall.co.uk.*

Opera House. The elegant Opera House is a venue for West End musicals, opera, and classical ballet. ⊠ *3 Quay St., City Centre* ☎ *0844/871–3018* ⊕ *www.manchesteroperahouse.org.uk.*

Palace Theatre. One of the city's largest houses, the Palace Theatre presents touring shows—plays, ballet, and opera. ⊠ *Oxford St., City Centre* ☎ *0844/871–3019* ⊕ *www.atgtickets.com.*

Royal Northern College of Music. Classical and contemporary music concerts—everything from opera to jazz—are on the bill at the Royal Northern College of Music. ⊠ *124 Oxford Rd., University Quarter* ☎ *0161/907–5200* ⊕ *www.rncm.ac.uk.*

THEATER

Royal Exchange Theatre. This futuristic glass-and-metal structure, cradling a theater-in-the-round space, serves as the city's main venue for innovative contemporary theater. ⊠ *St. Ann's Sq., City Centre* ☎ *0161/833– 9833* ⊕ *www.royalexchange.co.uk.*

SHOPPING

The city is nothing if not fashion conscious; take your pick from glitzy department stores, huge retail outlets, designer shops, and idiosyncratic boutiques. Famous names are centered on Exchange Square, Deansgate, and King Street; the Northern Quarter provides style for younger trendsetters.

Afflecks Palace. Young Mancunians head to Afflecks Palace for four floors of bohemian glam, ethnic crafts and jewelry, and innovative gift ideas. ⊠ *52 Church St., Northern Quarter* ☎ *0161/839–0718* ⊕ *www. afflecks.com.*

Barton Arcade. Inside a lovely Victorian arcade, Barton Arcade has plenty of specialty shopping. ⊠ *51–63 Deansgate, City Centre* ⊕ *www. bartonarcade.com.*

Corn Exchange. A stylish mall in the Victorian Corn Exchange, the Triangle has more than 30 stores, including independent designer shops. ⊠ *Longridge Pl., Millennium Quarter* ☎ *0161/834–8961* ⊕ *www. thetriangle.co.uk.*

Harvey Nichols. An outpost of London's chic luxury department store, Harvey Nichols is packed with designer goods and has an excellent second-floor restaurant and brasserie. ⊠ *21 New Cathedral St., City Centre* ☎ *0161/828–8888* ⊕ *www.harveynichols.com/manchester.*

Lowry Designer Outlet. With 80 stores, the Lowry Designer Outlet has good discounts on top brands at stores such as Nike and Karen Millen. ⊠ *11 The Quays, Salford Quays* ☎ *0161/848–1850* ⊕ *www. lowryoutletmall.com.*

Manchester Craft and Design Centre. Two floors of workshop-cum-retail outlets are found at the Manchester Craft and Design Centre. ⊠ *17 Oak St., Northern Quarter* ☎ *0161/832–4274* ⊕ *www.craftanddesign.com.*

Oldham Street. In the Northern Quarter, Oldham Street is littered with urban hip-hop boutiques and music shops.

FOOTBALL

Football (soccer in the United States) is *the* reigning passion in Manchester. Locals support the local club, Manchester City, and glory seekers come from afar to root for Manchester United, based in neighboring Trafford. Matches for both clubs are usually sold out months in advance, though you have more of a chance with Manchester City.

Manchester City. This football club, a favorite with locals, plays at the City of Manchester Stadium. ⊠ *Rowsley St., SportCity* ☎ *0161/444–1894* ⊕ *www.mcfc.co.uk.*

Manchester City Museum and Stadium Tours. Here you can see club memorabilia, visit the changing rooms, and go down the tunnel to pitch side. Excluding match days, there are three tours daily Monday through Saturday, and two on Sunday. ⊠ *Rowsley St., SportCity* ☎ *0161/444–1894* ⊕ *www.mcfc.co.uk* 🎫 *£13.*

Manchester United. One of the biggest clubs in Soccer (and the world's richest sports team), Manchester United has home matches at Old Trafford. ⊠ *Sir Matt Busby Way, Trafford Wharf* ☎ *0161/868–8000* ⊕ *www.manutd.com.*

Manchester United Museum and Tour. You can take a trip to the Theatre of Dreams at the Manchester United Museum and Tour, which tells the history of the football club. It's best to prebook the tour, which takes you behind the scenes, into the changing rooms and players' lounge, and down the tunnel. Take the tram to the Old Trafford stop and walk five minutes. ⊠ *Sir Matt Busby Way, Trafford Wharf* ☎ *0161/868–8000* ⊕ *www.manutd.com* 🎫 *£16* ⊙ *Daily 9:30–5, except game days.*

LIVERPOOL

A city lined with one of the most famous waterfronts in England, celebrated around the world as the birthplace of the Beatles, and still the place to catch that "Ferry 'Cross the Mersey," Liverpool reversed a downturn in its fortunes with developments in the late 1980s, such as the impressively refurbished Albert Dock area and Tate Liverpool. Its stint as the European Union's Capital of Culture in 2008 acted as a catalyst for further regeneration. UNESCO named six historic areas in the city center a World Heritage Site, in recognition of the city's maritime and mercantile achievements during the height of Britain's global influence. This heritage, together with the renowned attractions and a legacy of cultural vibrancy, now draws in an ever-increasing number of visitors.

The 1960s produced Liverpool's most famous export: the Beatles. The group was one of hundreds that copied the rock and roll they heard from visiting American GIs and merchant seamen in the late 1950s, and one of many that played local venues such as the Cavern (demolished but rebuilt nearby). All four Beatles were born in Liverpool, but the group's success dates from the time they left for London. Nevertheless, the city has milked the group's Liverpool connections for all they're worth, with a multitude of local attractions such as Paul McCartney's and John Lennon's childhood homes.

GETTING HERE AND AROUND

Liverpool John Lennon Airport, about 8 miles southeast of the city, receives mostly domestic and European flights. The Airlink 500 bus service runs to the city center every 30 minutes, and a taxi to the center of Liverpool costs around £15.

Long-distance National Express buses, including service from London, use the Norton Street Coach Station, and local buses depart from Sir Thomas Street, Queen Square, and the Paradise Street Interchange. Traveline has information on long-distance and local routes. Train service on Virgin Trains from London's Euston Station takes 2½ hours.

If you're walking (easier than driving), you'll find the downtown sights well signposted. Take care when crossing the busy inner ring road separating the Albert Dock from the rest of the city. The circular C4 bus ("Cumfybus") links Queen Square bus station with the Albert Dock (Gower Street stop).

TOURS
Blue Badge Guides can arrange dozens of different tours, which can be booked through the tourist office. Cavern City Tours offers a Beatles Magical Mystery Tour of Liverpool, departing from the Albert Dock visitor center. The two-hour bus tour, which costs £17, runs past Penny Lane, Strawberry Field, and other mop-top landmarks. Liverpool Beatles Tours has personalized tours of Beatles sites from two hours to all day. Yellow Duckmarine runs daily tours on amphibious vehicles from World War II. The trips, which cost between £12 and £16, depart from the Gower Street bus stop in Albert Dock.

ORIENTATION
Liverpool has a fairly compact center, and you can see most of the city highlights on foot. The skyline helps with orientation: the Radio City tower on **Queen Square** marks the center of the city. The Liver Birds, on top of the **Royal Liver Building,** signal the waterfront and River Mersey. North of the Radio City tower lie Lime Street Station and William Brown Street, a showcase boulevard of municipal buildings, including the outstanding **Walker Art Gallery** and **World Museum Liverpool.** The city's other museums, including the dazzling Museum of Liverpool and the **Beatles Story,** are concentrated westward on the waterfront in the **Albert Dock** area, a 20-minute walk or a 5-minute bus ride away. **Hope Street,** to the east of the center, connects the city's two cathedrals, both easily recognizable on the skyline. On nearby Berry Street the red, green, and gold **Chinese Arch,** the largest multiple-span arch outside China, marks the small Chinatown area. ■**TIP→** Allow extra time to tour the childhood homes of Paul McCartney and John Lennon, as they lie outside the city center.

ESSENTIALS
Bus Contacts Airlink 500 ☎ *0871/200–2233* ⊕ *www.arrivabus.co.uk.* **Traveline** ☎ *0871/200–2233* ⊕ *www.traveline.org.uk.*

Tour Contacts Blue Badge Guides ☎ *0794/093–3073 MerseyGuides Association* ⊕ *www.blue-badge-guides.com.* **Cavern City Tours** ✉ *Mathew St., City Centre* ☎ *0151/236–9091* ⊕ *www.cavernclub.org.* **Liverpool Beatles Tours** ✉ *25 Victoria St., City Centre* ☎ *0151/281–7738* ⊕ *www.beatlestours.co.uk.* **Yellow Duckmarine** ☎ *0151/708–7799* ⊕ *www.theyellowduckmarine.co.uk.*

Visitor Information Visit Liverpool ✉ *John Lennon Airport, South Terminal, Arrivals Hall* ☎ *0151/907–1057* ⊕ *www.visitliverpool.com* ✉ *Albert Dock, Anchor Courtyard, Waterfront* ☎ *0151/707–0729* ⊕ *www.visitliverpool.com.*

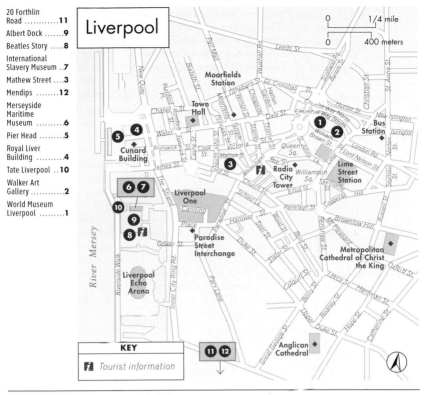

EXPLORING LIVERPOOL

TOP ATTRACTIONS

20 Forthlin Road. From 1955 to 1964, Paul McCartney lived with his family in this modest 1950s council house (a building rented from the local government). A number of the Beatles' songs, including "Love Me Do" and "When I'm Sixty-Four," were written here. The house is viewable only on a tour, leaving from the Jurys Inn next to Albert Dock or Speke Hall. ⊠ *20 Forthlin Rd., Allerton* ☎ *0844/800–4791* ⊕ *www. nationaltrust.org.uk* ⊠ *£20, includes Mendips and Speke Hall gardens* ⊗ *Mid-Mar.–Oct., Wed.–Sun. and holiday Mon., Jury's Inn departure 10, 11, 2:15, Speke Hall departure 3; early Mar. and Nov., Wed.–Sun., Jury's Inn departure, 10, 11 and 2:15.*

Albert Dock. To understand the city's prosperous maritime past, head for waterfront Albert Dock, 7 acres of restored warehouses built in 1846. Named after Queen Victoria's consort, Prince Albert, the dock provided storage for silk, tea, and tobacco from the Far East until it was closed in 1972. The fine colonnaded brick warehouse buildings contain the **Merseyside Maritime Museum,** the **International Slavery Museum, Tate Liverpool,** and the **Beatles Story.** When weather allows, you can sit at an outdoor café overlooking the dock or take a boat trip through the docks and onto the river. For a bird's-eye view of the Albert Dock area, take the rotating Echo Wheel—Liverpool's 60-meter-tall version of the London Eye—which has 42 capsules seating up to eight passengers. ■TIP→ Much of the pedestrian area of the Albert Dock and waterfront area is cobblestone, so wear comfortable shoes. ⊠ *Off Strand St. (A5036), Waterfront* ☎ *0151/707–0729 visitor center* ⊕ *www.albertdock.com.*

Fodor'sChoice   **Beatles Story.** You can follow in the footsteps of that most legendary
★   of British bands at one of the more popular attractions in the Albert Dock complex. Entertaining scenes re-create stages in the Beatles' story (and their later careers as solo artists), from the enthusiastic early days in Germany and the Cavern Club to the White Room, where "Imagine" seems to emanate from softly billowing curtains. Artifacts include the glasses John Lennon wore when he composed "Imagine" and the blue felt bedspread used in the famous "Bed-in" in 1969. ■TIP→ Avoid the crowds of July and August by visiting in the late afternoon. Purchase tickets, good for two days, online in advance. A shop sells every conceivable kind of souvenir a Fab Four fan could wish for. Included in the price is admission to a second location at the Mersey Ferries Terminal at Pier Head: *Fab4D*, a 3-D show with computer animation. Fans will Twist and Shout with delight. ⊠ *Albert Dock, Britannia Vaults, Waterfront* ☎ *0151/709–1963* ⊕ *www. beatlesstory.com* ⊠ *£16* ⊙ *Apr.–Oct., daily 9–7 (last admission 5); Nov.–Mar., daily 10–6 (last admission 5). Closed Dec. 25-26.*

International Slavery Museum. On the third floor of the Maritime Museum, this museum's three dynamic galleries recount the history of transatlantic slavery and trace its significance in contemporary society. "Life in West Africa" reproduces a Nigerian Igbo compound; life aboard slave ships bound for the Americas is revealed in the "Enslavement and the Middle Passage" section; and "Legacies of Slavery" examines the effect of the African diaspora on contemporary society. ⊠ *Albert Dock, Hartley Quay, off A5036, Waterfront* ☎ *0151/478–4499* ⊕ *www.liverpoolmuseums.org.uk* ⊠ *Free* ⊙ *Daily 10–5.*

Mathew Street. It was at the Cavern on this street that Brian Epstein, the Beatles' manager, first heard the group in 1961. The Cavern had opened at No. 10 as a jazz venue in 1957, but beat groups, of whom the Beatles were clearly the most talented, had taken it over. Epstein became their manager a few months after first visiting the club, and within two years the group was the most talked-about phenomenon in music. The club was demolished in 1973; it was rebuilt a few yards from the original site. At No. 5 is the Cavern Pub, opened in 1994, with Beatles memorabilia and plenty of nostalgia. ■TIP→ At No. 31, check out the well-stocked Beatles Shop.

Mendips. The National Trust maintains the 1930s middle-class, semi-detached house that was the home of John Lennon from 1946 to 1963—a must-see for Beatles pilgrims. After his parents separated, John joined his aunt Mimi here; she gave him his first guitar but banished him to the porch, saying, "The guitar's all very well, John, but you'll never make a living out of it." The house can be seen only on a tour, leaving from the Jury's Inn next to Albert Dock (mornings) or

Once a major shipping center and now transformed with museums, restaurants, and shops, the Albert Dock has views of the green dome of the Royal Liver Building.

Speke Hall (afternoons). ⊠ *251 Menlove Ave., Woolton* ☎ *0844/800–4791* ⊕ *www.nationaltrust.org.uk* ⊡ *£20, includes 20 Forthlin Rd. and Speke Hall gardens* ☉ *Mid-Mar.–Oct., Wed.–Sun. and holiday Mon., Jury's Inn departure 10, 11, 2:15, Speke Hall departure 3; early Mar. and Nov., Wed.–Sun., Jury's Inn departure, 10, 11, and 2:15.*

FAMILY
Fodor'sChoice
★

Merseyside Maritime Museum. Part of the Albert Dock complex, this is a wonderful place to explore the role of the sea in the life of the city. The museum captures the triumphs and tragedies of Liverpool's seafaring history over five floors. Besides exhibits of maritime paintings, models, ceramics, and ships in bottles, the main museum brings to life the ill-fated stories of the *Titanic* and *Lusitania*, the Battle of the Atlantic, and the city's role during World War II. The basement is home to the Customs and Excise National Museum, which explores the heroes and villains of the world of smuggling, together with the story of mass emigration from the port in the 19th century. In summer full-size vessels are on display. ⊠ *Albert Dock, Hartley Quay, off A5036, Waterfront* ☎ *0151/478–4499* ⊕ *www.liverpoolmuseums.org.uk* ⊡ *Free* ☉ *Daily 10–5.*

Pier Head. Here you can take a ferry across the River Mersey to Birkenhead and Seacombe. Mersey Ferries depart regularly and offer fine views of the city—a journey celebrated in "Ferry 'Cross the Mersey," Gerry and the Pacemakers' 1964 hit song. It was from Pier Head that 9 million British, Irish, and other European emigrants set sail between 1830 and 1930 for new lives in North America, Australia, and Africa. ■TIP➜ The ferry terminal is home to the Beatles Story, so you might want to make this the last stop on your Beatles tour. ⊠ *Pier Head Ferry Terminal, off A5036, Waterfront* ☎ *0151/330–1444* ⊕ *www.*

The Beatles and Liverpool

This distinctive northern English city was the birthplace of the Beatles, who changed rock music forever using recording techniques unheard of at the time. The Fab Four became counterculture icons who defined the look and sound of the 1960s; but despite their international success, they remained true sons of Liverpool.

When these four local rapscallions appeared on the Liverpool pop circuit in the early 1960s, they were just another group of lads struggling to get gigs on the city's "Merseybeat" scene. What followed was extraordinary: Beatlemania swept over fans around the world, including the United States, which the group first visited in 1964. Before their 1969 breakup, the Beatles achieved phenomenal commercial and creative success, bringing bohemianism to the masses and embodying a generation's ideals of social liberation and peace. They reinvented pop music, bridging styles and genres as diverse as Celtic folk, psychedelia, and Indian raga, starring in epoch-making movies such as *A Hard Day's Night* and *Help!*, and causing such hysteria they couldn't even hear their own guitars on stage. Though adulation followed them everywhere, the Beatles remained obstinate "Scousers," showing a grounded charm and irreverent humor characteristic of their native city.

IN THEIR OWN WORDS
"I knew the words to 25 rock songs, so I got in the group. 'Long Tall Sally' and 'Tutti Frutti,' that got me in. That was my audition." —Paul McCartney

"Paul wasn't quite strong enough, I didn't have enough girl appeal, George was too quiet, and Ringo was the drummer. But we thought that everyone would be able to dig at least one of us, and that's how it turned out." —John Lennon

---

merseyferries.co.uk ✉ *£4 round-trip, cruises £8; with U-Boat Story £12.* ⊙ *Ferries: every 20 mins weekdays 7:20–9:40 and 4:10–7:05. Cruises: hourly weekdays 10–3, weekends 10–6.*

Royal Liver Building. Best seen from the ferry, the 322-foot-tall Royal Liver (pronounced *lie-ver*) Building with its twin towers is topped by two 18-foot-high copper birds. They represent the mythical Liver Birds, the town symbol; local legend has it that if they fly away, Liverpool will cease to exist. For decades Liverpudlians looked to the Royal Liver Society for assistance—it was originally a burial club to which families paid contributions to ensure a decent send-off. ⊠ *Water St., off A5036, Waterfront.*

Fodor's Choice
★
Tate Liverpool. A handsome conversion of Albert Dock warehouses by the late James Stirling, one of Britain's leading 20th-century architects, hosts an offshoot of the London-based art galleries of the same name. There is no permanent collection; challenging exhibitions of modern art change every couple of months. A free introductory tour begins daily at 2:40. There's an excellent shop, a children's play area, and a dockside café-restaurant. ⊠ *Albert Dock, The Colonnades, Waterfront* ☎ *0151/702–7400* ⊕ *www.tate.org.uk* ✉ *Free; charges for special exhibitions vary* ⊙ *Apr.–Sept., daily 10–5:50; Oct.–Mar., Tues.–Sun. 10–5:50; last admission 5.*

Fodor's Choice ★ **Walker Art Gallery.** With a superb display of British art and some outstanding Italian and Flemish works, the Walker maintains its reputation as one of the best British art collections outside London. Don't miss the unrivaled collection of paintings by 18th-century Liverpudlian equestrian artist George Stubbs, and works by J. M. W. Turner, John Constable, Sir Edwin Henry Landseer, and the Pre-Raphaelites. Modern artists are included, too; on display is one of David Hockney's typically Californian pool scenes. Other excellent exhibits showcase china, silver, and furniture that once adorned the mansions of Liverpool's industrial barons. The Tea Room holds center stage in the airy museum lobby. ✉ *William Brown St., City Centre* ☎ *0151/478–4199* 🌐 *www.liverpoolmuseums.org.uk* 🎟 *Free* 🕑 *Daily 10–5.*

FAMILY **World Museum Liverpool.** You can travel from the prehistoric to the space age through stunning displays in these state-of-the-art galleries. Ethnology, the natural and physical sciences, and archaeology all get their due on five floors. Highlights include a collection of Egyptian mummies in the Ancient World Gallery, and a beautiful assemblage of Javanese shadow puppets in the World Culture Gallery. There's plenty to keep kids amused, from monster bugs in the Bug House, to life-size casts of prehistoric monsters in the Dinosaurs Gallery. ✉ *William Brown St., City Centre* ☎ *0151/478–4393* 🌐 *www.liverpoolmuseums.org.uk* 🎟 *Free* 🕑 *Daily 10–5.*

WHERE TO EAT

$$$ MODERN BRITISH 🍴 **60 Hope Street.** The combination of a ground-floor restaurant and a more informal basement bistro makes this a popular choice. A light, polished-wood floor and blue-and-cream walls help create an uncluttered backdrop for updated British dishes; baked lemon sole with saffron potatoes and crispy capers, for example, or braised ox cheek with celeriac purée and wood blewitts. For dessert you could try a rich chocolate fondant, or embrace the slightly mischievous spirit of the place with a deep-fried jam sandwich. [$] *Average main: £21* ✉ *60 Hope St., City Centre* ☎ *0151/707–6060* 🌐 *www.60hopestreet.com* 🕑 *Closed Sun. No lunch Sat. in restaurant.*

$ JAPANESE 🍴 **Etsu.** Minimalist decor, a friendly staff, and a polished Japanese menu greet you at this inconspicuous street-corner locale just off the Strand. Along with the traditional sushi, noodle soups, and tempuras, all served with the freshest ingredients, are some witty East-meets-West creations, including sushi pizzas and tuna burgers made of rice blocks. The bento box meals provide great value at lunchtime in between museum visits. Make sure you try a *shochu*, a stronger version of sake, served neat or with oolong tea. [$] *Average main: £14* ✉ *25 The Strand, entrance on Brunswick St., City Centre* ☎ *0151/236–7530* 🌐 *www.etsu-restaurant.co.uk* 🕑 *Closed Mon. No lunch Wed. and weekends.*

$ ASIAN 🍴 **Matou.** Expansive views of the historic waterfront are joined by the scent of Eastern spices at this popular spot on the second floor of the Mersey Ferry Terminal. The menu sticks to pan-Asian classics, such as Thai green curry, crispy aromatic lamb, and stir-fried beef in a black-bean sauce. Contemporary dark-wood furnishings sit beside huge slanting windows in the dining room. $ *Average main: £11* ⊠ *Mersey Ferry Terminal, Georges Parade, Pier Head* ☎ *0151/236–2928* ⊕ *www.matou.co.uk.*

$$$
MODERN
EUROPEAN
Fodor'sChoice
★

✗**Panoramic 34.** Watch the city lights glitter beyond the sweeping windows of this 34th-floor restaurant overlooking the waterfront. The boundless views and sleek decor are matched by head chef Parth Bhatt's voguish European menu. Fillet of halibut might be stewed with chorizo and clams; lamb could appear with sweetbreads, *dauphinoise* potatoes, and almond purée. Even if you're dining elsewhere, enjoy a cocktail here, especially at sunset. $ *Average main: £20* ⊠ *West Tower, Brook St., 34th fl., Waterfront* ☎ *0151/236–5534* ⊕ *www.panoramicliverpool. com* ☉ *Closed Mon.*

$$
INTERNATIONAL

✗**The Restaurant Bar and Grill.** An alluring cocktail bar beneath a glass-domed ceiling provides a glitzy habitat for local celebrities and high-fliers in this former banking house in the commercial district. Served in a dining room lined with wine racks and coffee-color leather seating, you can choose from international favorites, from Thai curries to Indian tandoori dishes, or perhaps just a simple rib-eye steak. Desserts include a delicious range of homemade sorbets. $ *Average main: £18* ⊠ *Halifax House, Brunswick St., City Centre* ☎ *0151/236–6703* ⊕ *www.therestaurantbarandgrill.co.uk.*

$$
BRITISH

✗**Side Door.** You'll often find couples enjoying a meal before a play or concert at this intimate and unpretentious bistro. The menu changes every week, but there are always plenty of fish choices, such as cod fillet with olive mash and *caponata*—a Sicilian eggplant and caper sauce—or brown trout with roast pepper and courgette. Sticky toffee pudding is a don't-miss dessert. The service is attentive, and the early evening fixed-price meals are a good value. $ *Average main: £16* ⊠ *29A Hope St., City Centre* ☎ *0151/707–7888* ⊕ *www.thesidedoor. co.uk* ☉ *Closed Sun.*

$
CAFÉ

✗**Tate Café.** The Tate Liverpool's café is a winner for daytime sustenance whenever you're visiting the Albert Dock area—especially on warm summer days when you can request dockside seating. Choose from among the salads and open sandwiches including steak with Wirral watercress, as well as main dishes such as spinach and feta patty with butterbean and chickpea stew. Fruit scones with jam and cream also make an appearance. $ *Average main: £8* ⊠ *Albert Dock, The Colonnades, Waterfront* ☎ *0151/702–7581* ⊕ *www.tate.org.uk* ☉ *Closed Mon. in winter. No dinner.*

WHERE TO STAY

$
HOTEL

Crowne Plaza Liverpool City Centre. Many of the city's main sights are at the doorstep of this handsome brick building, located on the waterfront next to the Royal Liver Building. **Pros:** on waterfront; friendly staff; plenty of activities. **Cons:** chain-hotel furnishings; no Wi-Fi in rooms. $ *Rooms from: £84* ⊠ *St. Nicholas Pl., off A5036, Waterfront* ☎ *0151/243–8000* ⊕ *www.cpliverpool.com* ⇥ *159 rooms* ❘○❘ *Multiple meal plans.*

$$ HOTEL **Hard Day's Night Hotel.** A marble-columned former office block on the corner of Mathew Street has been transformed into a giant homage in hotel form to Liverpool's most famous musical export. **Pros:** welcoming staff; sophisticated rooms; close to Beatles attractions. **Cons:** can't escape the gimmicky feel; street noise can be very loud in some rooms; no parking. [$] *Rooms from: £100* ✉ *Central Bldgs., N. John St., City Centre* ☎ *0151/236–1964* 🌐 *www.harddaysnighthotel.com* 🛏 *108 rooms, 2 suites* 🍴 *No meals.*

$ HOTEL **Hope Street Hotel.** Liverpool's first boutique hotel is in a converted carriage warehouse built in the style of a Venetian palazzo. **Pros:** beautiful design; plenty of space; attentive staff. **Cons:** rooms face a busy street. [$] *Rooms from: £94* ✉ *40 Hope St., City Centre* ☎ *0151/709–3000* 🌐 *www.hopestreethotel.co.uk* 🛏 *89 rooms* 🍴 *No meals.*

$ HOTEL **Hotel Indigo.** Combining the designer feel of a boutique hotel with the facilities of an established chain, Hotel Indigo is a slick option in the commercial district. **Pros:** talked-about restaurant; up-to-the-minute design; good location near Pier Head. **Cons:** not the most spacious rooms. [$] *Rooms from: £75* ✉ *10 Chapel St., City Centre* ☎ *0151/559–0111* 🌐 *www.hotelindigoliverpool.co.uk* 🛏 *151 rooms* 🍴 *Multiple meal plans.*

$ HOTEL **Malmaison.** The only purpose-built hotel in this chic chain—most are in renovated older buildings—the Malmaison combines glamorous furnishings with sleek industrial design and a great sense of space. **Pros:** buzzy atmosphere; rich decor. **Cons:** dark guest rooms; no parking; views to the back are disappointing. [$] *Rooms from: £69* ✉ *Princes Dock, Waterfront* ☎ *0151/229–5000* 🌐 *www.malmaison.com* 🛏 *128 rooms, 2 suites* 🍴 *Multiple meal plans.*

$ RENTAL **Staybridge Apartments.** These up-to-the-minute and well equipped apartments close to the Liverpool Echo Arena make for a great stay on the waterfront. **Pros:** upbeat atmosphere; complimentary receptions on weekday evenings; public spaces for socializing. **Cons:** limited parking; no nice views. [$] *Rooms from: £77* ✉ *21 Keel Wharf, Waterfront* ☎ *0151/703–9700 front desk, 0871/423–4942 central reservations* 🌐 *www.staybridge.co.uk* 🛏 *132 apartments* 🍴 *Breakfast.*

8

NIGHTLIFE AND THE ARTS

NIGHTLIFE

The many bars, clubs, and pubs of Liverpool, ranging from trendy to traditional, make for a unique experience.

Fodor's Choice ★ **Alma de Cuba.** A church transformed into a luxurious bar, Alma de Cuba uses a huge mirrored altar and hundreds of dripping candles to great effect. ✉ *Seel St., City Centre* ☎ *0151/702–7394* 🌐 *www.alma-de-cuba.com.*

Cavern Club. Despite not being the original venue—that was demolished years ago—the Cavern Club still draws in rock-and-roll fans with its Beatles tribute bands and other live acts on weekends. ✉ *8–10 Mathew St., City Centre* ☎ *0151/236–1965* 🌐 *www.cavernclub.org.*

Heebie Jeebies. A frequently changing roster of local indie bands and talented DJs makes this two-story club a top option with the young alternative crowd. ✉ *80–82 Seel St., City Centre* ☎ *0151/709–3678.*

Philharmonic Dining Rooms. Opposite Philharmonic Hall, the Philharmonic (commonly know as "The Phil") is a Victorian-era extravaganza decorated in rich woods and colorful marble. Choose a comfy spot in one of the dining rooms and order one of the award-winning ales and perhaps such pub grub as hand-battered fish-and-chips, which here is raised to a whole new level. ✉ *36 Hope St., City Centre* ☎ *0151/707–2837* ⊕ *www.nicholsonspubs.co.uk.*

Ye Cracke. One of the city's oldest pubs, Ye Cracke was much visited by John Lennon and his first wife, Cynthia, when they were at art school together. ✉ *13 Rice St., off Hope St., City Centre* ☎ *0151/709–4171.*

THE ARTS
PERFORMING ARTS VENUES
Liverpool Empire. This theater presents major ballet, opera, drama, and musical performances. ✉ *Lime St., City Centre* ☎ *0844/847–3017* ⊕ *www.liverpoolempire.org.uk.*

Philharmonic Hall. The well-regarded Royal Liverpool Philharmonic Orchestra plays its concert season at Philharmonic Hall. The venue also hosts contemporary music, jazz, and world concerts, and shows classic films. ✉ *Hope St., City Centre* ☎ *0151/709–3789* ⊕ *www. liverpoolphil.com.*

THEATER
Everyman Theatre. The Everyman Theatre focuses on works by British playwrights as well as experimental productions from around the world. Productions here frequently attract national attention. At this writing a two-year renovation was scheduled to be completed by the end of 2013. A second theater, the Everyman Playhouse in Williamson Square, stages more mainstream productions. ✉ *5–9 Hope St., City Centre* ☎ *0151/709–4776 box office (both theaters).*

SHOPPING

The Beatles Shop. All the mop-top knickknacks of your dreams are available at this hugely popular, official Beatles souvenir shop. ✉ *31 Mathew St., City Centre* ☎ *0151/236–8066* ⊕ *www.thebeatleshop.co.uk.*

Circa 1900. This shop specializes in authentic art nouveau and art deco pieces, from ceramics and glass to furniture, in an upmarket marble shopping arcade within the historic India Buildings. ✉ *Holts Arcade, Water St., City Centre* ☎ *0151/236–1282* ⊕ *www.classicartdeco.co.uk.*

Liverpool One. The city's largest shopping complex, Liverpool One has more than 160 stores, including John Lewis. ✉ *Paradise St., City Centre* ☎ *0151/232–3100* ⊕ *www.liverpool-one.com.*

Metquarter. With more than 40 stores, Metquarter is the place for upmarket boutiques, designer names, and the latest fashions. ✉ *35 Whitechapel, City Centre* ☎ *0151/224–2390* ⊕ *www.metquarter.com.*

SPORTS AND THE OUTDOORS

FOOTBALL

Football matches are played on weekends and, increasingly, weekdays. Tickets for Liverpool are sold out months in advance, but you should have more luck with Everton.

Everton Football Club. One of Liverpool's two great football teams, Everton plays at Goodison Park. ⊠ *Goodison Park, Goodison Rd.* ☎ *0871/663–1878* ⊕ *www.evertonfc.com.*

Liverpool Football Club. One of England's top teams, Liverpool plays at Anfield, 2 miles north of the city center. ⊠ *Anfield Rd., Anfield* ☎ *0844/844–0844* ⊕ *www.liverpoolfc.tv.*

Liverpool Museum and Stadium Tour. This trip into the dressing rooms and down the tunnel of Anfield Football Stadium gives you a sense of match day for the Liverpool Football Club. There are no tours on days that games are scheduled. ⊠ *Anfield Rd., Anfield* ☎ *0151/260–6677* ⊕ *www. liverpoolfc.tv* 🖾 *£16* ☉ *Daily 10–3.*

THE PEAK DISTRICT

Heading southeast, away from the urban congestion of Manchester and Liverpool, it's not far to the southernmost contortions of the Pennine Hills. Here, about an hour from Manchester, sheltered in a great natural bowl, is the spa town of Buxton: at an elevation of more than 1,000 feet, it's the second-highest town in England. Buxton makes a convenient base for exploring the 540 square miles of the Peak District, Britain's oldest—and, its fans say, most beautiful—national park. About 38,000 people live in the towns throughout the park.

"Peak" is perhaps misleading; despite being a hilly area, it contains only gentle rises that don't reach much higher than 2,000 feet. Yet a trip around the grand estates of Chatsworth House, Haddon Hall, and Hardwick Hall involves negotiating fairly perilous country roads, each of which repays the effort with enchanting views. Outdoor activities are popular in the Peaks, particularly caving (or "potholing"), walking, and hiking. Bring all-weather clothing and waterproof shoes.

BUXTON

46 miles east of Liverpool, 25 miles southeast of Manchester.

Buxton makes a good base for Peak District excursions, but it has its own attractions as well. The town's spa days left a notable legacy of 18th- and 19th-century buildings, parks, and open spaces that give the town an air of faded grandeur. The Romans arrived in AD 79 and named Buxton Aquae Arnemetiae, loosely translated as "Waters of the Goddess of the Grove." The mineral springs, which emerge from 3,500 to 5,000 feet below ground at a constant 82°F, were believed to cure assorted ailments; in the 18th century the town became established as a popular spa, a minor rival to Bath. You can still drink water from the ancient St. Anne's Well, and it's also sold throughout Britain.

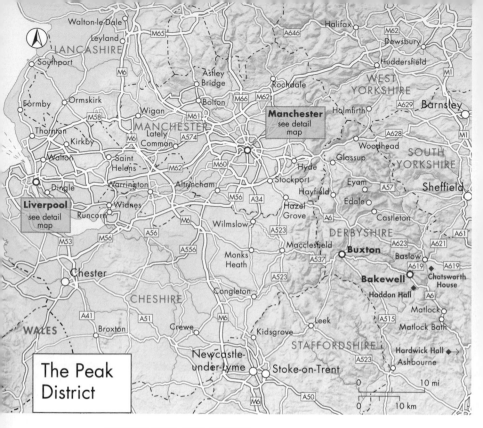

GETTING HERE AND AROUND

Both the National Express and TransPeak bus services from Manchester stop at Buxton. There are departures every two to three hours from Manchester's Chorlton Street Bus Station. If you're driving from Manchester, take A6 southeast to Buxton. The journey takes one hour. The hourly train from Manchester to Buxton takes an hour.

ESSENTIALS

Visitor Information Buxton Tourist Information Centre ✉ *Pavilion Gardens, St. John's Rd.* ☎ *01298/25106* ⊕ *www.visitpeakdistrict.com.*

EXPLORING

The Crescent. Almost all out-of-town roads lead toward this central green with its curving semicircle of buildings. The Georgian-era Crescent, with its arches, colonnades, and 378 windows, was built in 1780 by fashionable architect John Carr for the 5th Duke of Devonshire (of nearby Chatsworth House). At this writing, a large portion was being redeveloped as a luxury hotel. It's near where Terrace Road meets St. Johns Road. ✉ *Off Terrace Rd.*

Pavilion Gardens. Surrounded by 25 acres of pretty gardens, the Pavilion, with its ornate iron-and-glass roof, was originally a concert hall and ballroom. Erected in the 1870s, it remains a lively place that hosts local events, and also has a plant-filled conservatory, two cafés, and a restaurant. The Pavilion is adjacent to the Crescent and the Slopes on the west; the tourist office is here, too, with a food-and-crafts shop. ✉ *St. John's Rd.* ☎ *01298/23114* 🌐 *www.paviliongardens.co.uk.*

WORTH NOTING

Buxton Opera House. Built in 1903, the opera house is one of the most architecturally exuberant structures in town. Its marble bulk, bedecked with carved cupids, is even more impressive inside. The varied program of events includes classical music recitals, jazz, ballet, theater, and standup comedy. ✉ *Water St.* ☎ *0845/127–2190* 🌐 *www.buxtonoperahouse.org.uk.*

Poole's Cavern. The Peak District's extraordinary geology can be seen up close at this large limestone cave far beneath the 100 wooded acres of Buxton Country Park. The cave was inhabited in prehistoric times and contains, in addition to the standard stalactites and stalagmites, the source of the River Wye, which flows through Buxton. Admission includes a guided tour lasting nearly an hour. ✉ *Green La.* ☎ *01298/26978* 🌐 *www.poolescavern.co.uk* 🎟 *£8.80* 🕒 *Mar.–Oct., daily 9:30–5 (tours every 20 mins, last tour 4:30); Nov.–Feb., weekends 10–4 (tours every 20 mins, last tour 3:30), weekends tours at 10:30, 12:30, and 2:30 only.*

WHERE TO EAT AND STAY

$$ MODERN BRITISH 🍴 **Columbine.** The husband-and-wife team behind Columbine are known for their fine use of local ingredients and flavors, from pork tenderloin with a Sage Derby cheese glaze, to duck braised in port with wild mushrooms. The cozy venue, with upstairs and downstairs seating, is a good spot for pre- and posttheater meals. [$] *Average main: £16* ✉ *7 Hall Bank* ☎ *01298/78752* 🌐 *www.columbinerestaurant.co.uk* 🕒 *Closed Sun. Closed Tues. Nov.–Apr. No lunch Aug.–June.*

$ B&B/INN 🏨 **Buxton Victorian Guesthouse.** One of a group of row houses built by the duke of Devonshire in 1860, this handsomely decorated house stands in the center of Buxton. **Pros:** peaceful location on Pavilion Gardens; free Wi-Fi; delightful hosts. **Cons:** many stairs to climb. [$] *Rooms from: £94* ✉ *3A Broad Walk* ☎ *01298/78759* 🌐 *www.buxtonvictorian.co.uk* 🛏 *6 rooms, 1 suite* 🍽 *Breakfast.*

$$ B&B/INN 🏨 **Old Hall.** In a refurbished 16th-century building rumored to have once accommodated Mary Queen of Scots, this hotel overlooks the ornate Buxton Opera House. **Pros:** unpretentious atmosphere; good dining choices. **Cons:** conventional furnishings; no private parking. [$] *Rooms from: £100* ✉ *The Square* ☎ *01298/22841* 🌐 *www.oldhallhotelbuxton.co.uk* 🛏 *38 rooms* 🍽 *Breakfast.*

$ B&B/INN 🏨 **Stoneridge.** Built of stone, this Edwardian B&B has been richly restored. **Pros:** excellent food choices; secluded and tranquil garden. **Cons:** no tubs in bathrooms; two-night minimum at weekends. [$] *Rooms from: £75* ✉ *9 Park Rd.* ☎ *01298/26120* 🌐 *www.stoneridge.co.uk* 🛏 *4 rooms* 💳 *No credit cards* 🍽 *Breakfast.*

8

SHOPPING

Buxton has many kinds of stores, especially around Spring Gardens, the main shopping street.

Cavendish Arcade. Stores in the beautifully tiled Cavendish Arcade, on the site of the old thermal baths, sell antiques, jewelry, fashions, and leather goods in stylish surroundings. ⊠ *The Crescent.*

BAKEWELL

12 miles southeast of Buxton, 37 miles southeast of Manchester.

In Bakewell, a medieval bridge crosses the winding River Wye in five graceful arches, and the 9th-century Saxon cross that stands outside the parish church reveals the town's great age. Narrow streets and houses built out of the local gray-brown stone also make the town extremely appealing. Ceaseless traffic through the streets can take the shine off—though there's respite down on the quiet riverside paths.

This market town is the commercial hub of the Peak District, for locals and visitors. The crowds are really substantial on market day (Monday), attended by area farmers. For a self-guided hour-long stroll, pick up a map at the tourist office, where the town trail begins. A small exhibition upstairs explains the landscape of the Peak District.

GETTING HERE AND AROUND

TransPeak offers bus services from Manchester's Chorlton Street Bus Station to Bakewell. National Express covers the same route, but only once a day at 6:40 am. By car, Bakewell is a one-hour, 30-minute drive southeast on the A6 from Manchester.

ESSENTIALS

Visitor Information Bakewell Visitor Centre ⊠ *Old Market Hall, Bridge St.* ☎ *01629/816558* ⊕ *www.visitpeakdistrict.com.*

EXPLORING

FAMILY
Fodor's Choice
★

Chatsworth House. Glorious parkland leads to the ancestral home of the dukes of Devonshire and one of England's greatest country houses. The vast expanse of greenery, grazed by deer and sheep, sets off the Palladian-style elegance of "the Palace of the Peak." Originally an Elizabethan house, Chatsworth was conceived on a monumental scale. It was altered over several generations starting in 1686, and the architecture now has a hodgepodge look, though the Palladian facade remains untouched. The house is surrounded by woods, elaborate gardens, greenhouses, rock gardens, and the most famous water cascade in the country—all designed by two great landscape artists: Capability Brown in the 18th century and, in the 19th, Joseph Paxton, an engineer as well as a brilliant gardener. The gravity-fed Emperor Fountain can shoot as high as 300 feet. ■TIP→ **Plan on at least a half day to explore the grounds; avoid Sunday if you're allergic to heavy crowds.** Inside are intricate carvings, Van Dyck portraits, superb furniture, and a few fabulous rooms, including the Sculpture Gallery, the library, and the Blue Drawing Room, where you can see two of the most famous portraits in Britain, Sir Joshua Reynolds's *Georgiana, Duchess of Devonshire, and Her Baby,* and John Singer Sargent's enormous *Acheson Sisters.*

Chatsworth is 4 miles northeast of Bakewell. On the grounds are a farm with milking demonstrations at 3 and an adventure playground. ⊠ *Off B6012* ☎ *01246/565300* ⊕ *www.chatsworth.org* ⊠ *House, gardens, and farm £19; house and gardens £16; gardens only £10* ⊙ *House: daily 11–5:30; gardens: daily 11–6. Farmyard and adventure playground: daily 10:30–5:30. Last admission 1 hr before closing.*

Fodor's Choice
★

Haddon Hall. One of England's finest stately homes, and perhaps the most authentically Tudor of the great houses, Haddon Hall bristles with intricate period detail. Built between 1180 and 1565, the house passed into the ownership of the dukes of Rutland and remained largely untouched until the early 20th century, when the 9th duke undertook a superlative restoration. This revealed a series of early decorative 15th-century frescoes in the chapel. The finest of the intricate plasterwork and wooden paneling is best seen in the superb Long Gallery on the first floor. Baking is still done in the bread ovens in the well-preserved Tudor kitchen, using authentic Tudor methods. Here, too, is the unique collection of Gothic dole cupboards, some original to the house, which would have been filled with food and placed outside for those in need. Unsurprisingly the house is a popular filming location; its starring roles include *The Princess Bride* (1985), *Pride and Prejudice* (2005) and *The Other Boleyn Girl* (2008). ⊠ *A6* ☎ *01629/812855* ⊕ *www.haddonhall. co.uk* ⊠ *£9.50, parking £1.50* ⊙ *Apr. and Oct., Sat.–Mon. noon–5; May–Sept., daily noon–5 (closes 8 on Thurs., June and July; last admission 1 hr before closing.*

Fodor's Choice
★

Hardwick Hall. Few houses in England evoke the late Elizabethan era as vividly as Hardwick Hall, a beautiful stone mansion and treasure trove. The facade glitters with myriad windows, making it easy to see why the house came to be known as "Hardwick Hall, more glass than wall." ■TIP→ Choose a sunny day to see the rooms and their treasures at their best. The vast state apartments well befit their original chatelaine, Bess of Hardwick. By marrying a succession of four rich husbands, she had become second only to Queen Elizabeth in her wealth when work on this house began. She took possession in 1597, and four years later made an inventory of the important rooms and their contents—furniture, tapestries, and embroideries. Unique patchwork hangings, probably made from clerical copes and altar frontals taken from monasteries and abbeys, grace the entrance hall, and superb 16th- and 17th-century tapestries cover the walls of the main staircase and first-floor High Great Chamber. The collection of Elizabethan embroideries—table carpets, cushions, bed hangings, and pillowcases—is second to none. Outside, you can visit the walled gardens. The hall appeared as Malfoy Manor in the last two Harry Potter movies. Hardwick Hall is 21 miles east of Bakewell. Access is signposted from Junction 29 of the M1 motorway. ⊠ *Doe Lea, Chesterfield* ☎ *01246/850430* ⊕ *www.nationaltrust.org. uk* ⊠ *£11; gardens only, £5.50* ⊙ *House: mid-Mar.–Oct., Wed.–Sun. noon–4:30. Gardens: daily 9–6; last admission 30 mins before closing. Grounds: daily 8–dusk.*

8

The Emperor Fountain enhances the bucolic landscape at Chatsworth, one of England's most magnificent stately homes.

WHERE TO EAT AND STAY

$$ · MODERN BRITISH · Fodor's Choice ★

🍴 **Devonshire Arms.** This stone 18th-century coaching inn, which counts Charles Dickens as one of its many famous visitors, is divided into a cozy bar area and a modern brasserie, both serving impressive homemade fare. Alongside old favorites like bangers and mash, the menu offers such imaginative creations as roast partridge with Pinot Noir, potato purée, and Chatsworth estate venison with smoked aubergine (eggplant), churros, and chili chocolate sauce. For dessert, try the apple tarte tatin served with ice cream made from apple and bilberries—a native English fruit in the same family as (but different from) blueberries. The inn, 2 miles south of Chatsworth, also has eight bedrooms. [$] *Average main: £15* ✉ *B6012, Beeley* ☎ *01629/733259* 🌐 *www.devonshirebeeley.co.uk.*

$$$$ · MODERN BRITISH

🍴 **Fischer's.** The Fischer family bought this stately Edwardian manor on the edge of the Chatsworth estate, 4 miles north of Bakewell, to house their restaurant. Intimate and formal, the restaurant takes pride in using high-quality local products; on the fixed-price menus you'll find wild venison, Derbyshire pork and lamb, and Yorkshire rhubarb, all presented with care and aplomb. If you can't decide, there's a six-course tasting menu of specialty dishes (£72, or £120 with wines). With 11 elegant bedrooms here as well, you might consider staying the night. [$] *Average main: £34* ✉ *Baslow Hall, Calver Rd., Baslow* ☎ *01246/583259* 🌐 *www.fischers-baslowhall.co.uk.*

$ · BRITISH

🍴 **The Old Original Bakewell Pudding Shop.** Given the plethora of local rivals, it takes a bold establishment to claim its Bakewell puddings as "original," but there's certainly nothing wrong with those served here. A British favorite, the "pudding" in question is actually a dense, sugary pie with a jam and almond filling and a puff pastry crust, eaten cold or hot with custard or cream. A more common varient, the Bakewell tart, is made with shortcrust pastry, but aficionados consider the pudding to be more authentic. The oak-beam dining room also turns out commendable main courses of Yorkshireman (batter pudding with meat and vegetables) and steak-and-ale pie. $ *Average main: £8* ✉ *The Square* ☎ *01629/812193* ⊕ *www.bakewellpuddingshop.co.uk.*

$ 🏠 **Haddon House Farm.** This may be a working farm, but there's nothing
B&B/INN   workaday about the colourful and beautifully designed rooms (with themes such as Shakespeare and Monet's Garden) that the Nicholls husband-and-wife team have created. **Pros:** charming and obliging hosts; outdoor hot tub; easily accessible by bus. **Cons:** no credit cards; £10 surcharge for one-night stays. $ *Rooms from: £95* ✉ *Haddon Rd.* ☎ *01629/814024* ⊕ *www.great-place.co.uk* ⬎4 *rooms* ⊟ *No credit cards* ⫟ *Breakfast.*

CHESTER, LUDLOW, AND ENVIRONS

Rural Shropshire, one of the least populated English counties, is far removed from most people's preconceptions of the industrial Midlands. Within its spread are towns long famed for their beauty, such as Ludlow. Chester, one of the region's most important cities, is renowned for its medieval heritage. The 6-mile stretch of the Ironbridge Gorge, however, gives you the chance to experience the cradle of the Industrial Revolution with none of the reeking smoke that gave this region west of Birmingham its name—the Black Country—during the mid-19th century. Now taken over by the Ironbridge Gorge Museum Trust, the bridge, opened in 1781 and the first in the world to be built of iron, is the centerpiece of this vast museum complex.

8

CHESTER

51 miles west of Bakewell, 21 miles south of Liverpool, 50 miles north of Ironbridge.

Cheshire's thriving center is Chester, rich in black-and-white half-timber buildings (some built in Georgian and Victorian times), with still-standing medieval walls. History seems more tangible in Chester than in many other ancient cities, as modern buildings haven't been allowed to intrude on the center. A negative result of this perfection is that Chester has become a favorite tour bus destination, with gift shops, noise, and crowds aplenty.

Chester has been a prominent city since the late 1st century, when the Roman Empire expanded north to the banks of the River Dee. The original Roman town plan is still evident: the principal streets, Eastgate, Northgate, Watergate, and Bridge Street, lead out from the Cross—the site of the central area of the Roman fortress—to the four city gates. The partly excavated remains of what is thought to have been the country's largest Roman amphitheater lie to the south of Chester's medieval castle.

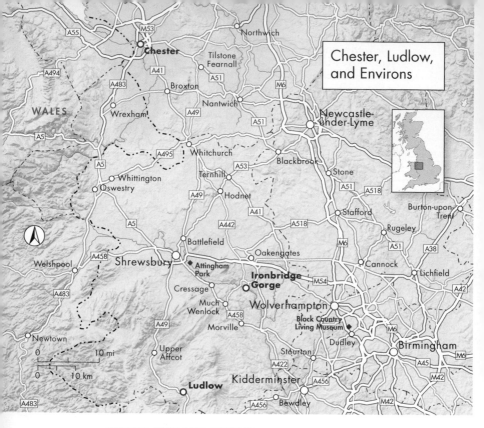

GETTING HERE AND AROUND

There's a free shuttle bus to the center if you arrive by train, and buses pull up at Vicar's Lane in the center (Monday to Saturday). Chester is 180 miles from London, and about 2 hours by train; some change at Crewe. If you're driving and here for a day only, use the city's Park and Ride lots, as central parking lots fill quickly, especially in summer.

Guided walks leave the town hall daily at 10:30, with an additional tour at 11:30 from May to October (£6). In summer the 10:30 tour ends with a proclamation from the Town Crier, in full traditional dress. City Sightseeing operates daily tours in open-top buses from April to October.

ESSENTIALS

Visitor and Tour Information Chester Tourist Information Centre ✉ *Town Hall, Northgate St.* ☎ *0845/647–7868* ⊕ *www.visitchester.com.* **City Sightseeing** ☎ *0845/6477868, 01244/381461 weekdays only* ⊕ *www.city-sightseeing.com.*

EXPLORING

TOP ATTRACTIONS

Chester Cathedral. Tradition has it that a church of some sort stood on the site of what is now Chester Cathedral in Roman times, but records indicate construction around AD 900. The earliest work traceable today, mainly in the north transept, is that of the 11th-century Benedictine abbey. After Henry VIII dissolved the monasteries in the

16th century, the abbey church became the cathedral church of the new diocese of Chester. The misericords (kneeling benches) in the choir stalls reveal carved figures of people and animals, both real and mythical, and above is a gilded and colorful vaulted ceiling. There are free guided tours daily at 2:30; meet inside under the big blue stained-glass window. ⊠ *St. Werburgh St., off Market Sq.* ☏ *01244/324756* ⊕ *www. chestercathedral.com* ▨ *Free; £3 suggested donation; audio guides £1* ⊙ *Mon.–Sat. 9–5, Sun. 1–4.*

City walls. Accessible from several points, the city walls provide splendid views of Chester and its surroundings. The whole circuit is 2 miles, but if your time is short, climb the steps at Newgate and walk along toward Eastgate to see the great ornamental **Eastgate Clock,** erected to commemorate Queen Victoria's Diamond Jubilee in 1897. Lots of small shops near this part of the walls sell old books, old postcards, antiques, and jewelry. Where the **Bridge of Sighs** (named after the enclosed bridge in Venice that it closely resembles) crosses the canal, descend to street level and walk up Northgate Street into Market Square.

Rows. Chester's unique Rows, which originated in the 12th and 13th centuries, are essentially double rows of stores, one at street level and the other on the second floor with galleries overlooking the street. The Rows line the junction of the four streets in the Old Town. They have medieval crypts below them, and some reveal Roman foundations. ■TIP➜ You can view some Roman foundations in the basement of fast-food restaurant Spudulike at 39 Bridge Street.

WORTH NOTING

ChesterBoat. This company runs excursions on the River Dee every 30 minutes daily (late March through October) and hourly on weekends (November through March). Saturday evening cruises in summer feature discos. ⊠ *Boating Station, Souters La.* ☏ *01244/325394* ⊕ *www. chesterboat.co.uk* ▨ *£6.50.*

FAMILY **Chester Zoo.** Well-landscaped grounds and natural enclosures make the 80-acre zoo one of Britain's most popular, as well as the largest. Highlights include Chimpanzee Island, the jaguar enclosure, and the Islands in Danger tropical habitat. Baby animals are often on display. Eleven miles of paths wind through the zoo, and you can use the waterbus boats or the overhead train to tour the grounds. Fun, 10-minute animal talks, aimed at kids, take place at various locations around the zoo throughout the day. The zoo is 2 miles north of Chester. ⊠ *A41* ☏ *01244/380280* ⊕ *www.chesterzoo.org* ▨ *Apr.–Oct. £18, Nov.–Mar. £14.50; waterbus £2, monorail £2* ⊙ *Daily 10–dusk.*

Grosvenor Museum. Start a visit to this museum with a look at the Roman Stones Gallery, which displays Roman-era tombstones previously used to repair city walls. (Keep an eye out for the wounded barbarian.) Afterward you can skip a few centuries to explore the period house for a tour from 1680 to the 1920s. ⊠ *27 Grosvenor St.* ☏ *01244/972197* ⊕ *www. grosvenormuseum.co.uk* ▨ *Free* ⊙ *Mon.–Sat. 10:30–5, Sun. 1–4.*

8

WHERE TO EAT

$ BRITISH 🍴 **Albion.** You feel as if you're stepping back in time at this Victorian pub; the posters, advertisements, flags, and curios tell you the idiosyncratic landlord keeps it as it would have been during World War I. The candlelit restaurant forms one of the three snug rooms and, unsurprisingly, serves up such traditional fare as corned beef hash, Staffordshire oatcakes, and gammon (thick-sliced ham) with pease pudding. You can stay overnight here as well. [$] *Average main: £9* ✉ *Park St.* ☎ *01244/340345* 🌐 *www.albioninnchester.co.uk* 💳 *No credit cards* 🕓 *No dinner Sun.*

$ BISTRO 🍴 **Chez Jules.** Once a fire station, this bustling bistro is now unashamedly French and rustic, with red-and-white-check tablecloths and a menu chalked up on the blackboard. Start perhaps with a chicken liver parfait, followed by grilled sea bass with warm artichoke and pea salad, or perhaps a classic rib-eye steak. The two-course early-bird menu is great value at £12. [$] *Average main: £13* ✉ *71 Northgate St.* ☎ *01244/400014* 🌐 *www.chezjules.com.*

$$$$ FRENCH Fodor's Choice ★ 🍴 **Simon Radley at the Chester Grosvenor.** Named for its noted chef, this restaurant has a sophisticated panache and prices to match. Expect the seasonal but not the usual, including named dishes: Herdwick is mutton with wild garlic, spearmint jelly, and ewe's curd, while Millionaire is a rich dessert made with several types of chocolate. There's a fixed-price dinner (£69) as well as a daily tasting menu (£90). The wine cellar has more than 1,000 bins. Reservations are essential on weekends, and children must be at least 12. [$] *Average main: £69* ✉ *Chester Grosvenor Hotel, Eastgate St.* ☎ *01244/324024* 🌐 *www.chestergrosvenor.com* ✍ *Reservations essential* 🕓 *No dinner Mon. and Sun. Closed 1st 3 wks in Jan.*

WHERE TO STAY

$ HOTEL Fodor's Choice ★ 🏨 **ABode.** Perched on a busy traffic intersection on the edge of Chester's Old Town, this gleaming new hotel from the trendy ABode chain may not occupy the city's most romantic spot, but it's well run and comfortable. **Pros:** modern and comfortable; good food; great bar. **Cons:** lacks historic charm of older hotels; parking lot is hard to find (take the almost-hidden exit from the roundabout that looks like it's just for deliveries). [$] *Rooms from: £89* ✉ *Grosvenor Rd.* ☎ *01244/347000* 🌐 *www.abodehotels.co.uk/chester* 🛏 *85 rooms.*

$ B&B/INN 🏨 **Chester Recorder House.** This Georgian redbrick house has the perfect location right on the city wall and overlooking the River Dee. **Pros:** within easy reach of the center; excellent breakfasts. **Cons:** no elevator. [$] *Rooms from: £80* ✉ *19 City Walls* ☎ *01244/326580* 🌐 *www.recorderhotel.co.uk* 🛏 *11 rooms* 🍽 *Breakfast.*

$$$ HOTEL Fodor's Choice ★ 🏨 **Green Bough Hotel.** This friendly little hotel, furnished with antiques including cast-iron beds, is in Chester's leafy outskirts, about a mile from the center. **Pros:** attentive service; well-designed rooms. **Cons:** no young children allowed. [$] *Rooms from: £185* ✉ *60 Hoole Rd.* ☎ *01244/326241* 🌐 *www.greenbough.co.uk* 🛏 *8 rooms, 7 suites* 🍽 *Breakfast.*

NIGHTLIFE AND THE ARTS

Oddfellows. This is the swankiest bar in town. Sip Champagne cocktails or afternoon tea and admire the big wallpaper and big candelabra. You can dine (and stay) here, too. ⊠ *20 Lower Bridge St.* ☏ *01244/895700.*

SHOPPING

Bluecoat Books. This book emporium specializes in travel, art, architecture, and history. ⊠ *1 City Walls* ☏ *01244/318752.*

Chester Market. This indoor market, near the Town Hall, is open every day except Sunday. ⊠ *6 Princess St.* ⊕ *www.chestermarket.com.*

IRONBRIDGE GORGE

50 miles southeast of Chester, 65 miles southwest of Bakewell, 26 miles northeast of Ludlow.

Fodor's Choice
★ The River Severn and its tree-cloaked banks make an attractive backdrop to this cluster of villages. Within a mile of the graceful span of the world's first iron bridge are a cluster of fascinating museums exploring the area's industrial past and the reasons why it's been described as the "cradle of the Industrial Revolution."

GETTING HERE AND AROUND

To drive here from Chester or Liverpool, take A41 south before following the brown signs for Ironbridge. On weekends and holidays from Easter to late October, the Gorge Connect Bus shuttles passengers between Ironbridge's museums every 30 minutes; it's free of charge to museum passport holders.

ESSENTIALS

Visitor Information Ironbridge Visitor Information ⊠ *Toll House, The Wharf-age* ☏ *01952/433424* ⊕ *www.ironbridge.org.uk.*

EXPLORING

FAMILY
Fodor's Choice
★
Ironbridge Gorge Museum. The 10 sites that make up the Ironbridge Gorge Museum—a World Heritage Site, spread over 6 square miles—preserve the area's fascinating industrial history in spectacular fashion. ■ TIP→ Allow at least a full day to appreciate all the major sights, and perhaps to take a stroll around the famous iron bridge or hunt for Coalport china in the stores clustered near it. On weekends and national holidays from April through October, a shuttle bus takes you between sites. The best starting point is the **Museum of the Gorge,** which has a good selection of literature and an audiovisual show on the gorge's history. In nearby Coalbrookdale, the **Museum of Iron** explains the production of iron and steel. You can see the blast furnace built by Abraham Darby, who developed the original coke process in 1709. The adjacent **Enginuity** exhibition is a hands-on, feet-on, interactive exploration of engineering; it's good for kids. From here, drive the few miles along the river until the arches of the **Iron Bridge** come into view. Designed by T.F. Pritchard, smelted by Darby, and erected between 1777 and 1779, this graceful arch spanning the River Severn can best be seen—and photographed or painted—from the towpath, a riverside walk edged with wildflowers and shrubs. The tollhouse on the far side houses an exhibition on the bridge's history and restoration.

8

A mile farther along the river is the **Jackfield Tile Museum,** a repository of decorative tiles from the 19th and 20th centuries. Another half mile brings you to the **Coalport China Museum.** Exhibits show some of the factory's most beautiful wares, and craftspeople give demonstrations; visit the restrooms for the unique communal washbasins. Above Coalport is **Blists Hill Victorian Town,** where you can see old mines, furnaces, and a wrought-iron works. But the main draw is the re-creation of the "town" itself, with its doctor's office, bakery, grocer's, candle maker's, sawmill, printing shop, and candy store. At the entrance you can change some money for specially minted pennies and make purchases from the shops. Shopkeepers, the bank manager, and the doctor's wife are on hand to give you advice. If you don't fancy the refreshments at the Fried Fish shop, you could drop into the **New Inn** pub (in Blists Hill) for a traditional ale or ginger beer, and join one of the sing-alongs around the piano that take place a couple of times every afternoon; or, for something more formal, try the **Club Room** restaurant next door. ✉ *B4380* ☎ *01952/433424* 🌐 *www.ironbridge.org.uk* 🎟 *Passport ticket (all attractions, valid 1 year) £24. Individual sites: Blists Hill £16; Enginuity £8.50; Coalport China Museum £8.50; Jackfield Tile Museum £8.50; Museum of Iron £8.25; Darby Houses £5; Museum of Iron and Darby Houses £9; Broseley Pipeworks £5; Museum of the Gorge £4; Tar Tunnel £3.* 🕒 *Daily 10–5; Blists Hill Apr.–Oct., daily 10–5; Nov.–Mar., daily 10–4; Tar Tunnel Apr.–Oct., daily 10:30-4; (tunnel closed Nov.–Mar).*

WHERE TO EAT AND STAY

$$$ MODERN BRITISH Fodor's Choice ★

🍴 **Restaurant Severn.** This discreet restaurant, set back from the main road in the center of Ironbridge, delivers fine-quality food prepared with care and attention. Chefs Beb and Eric Bruce prepare delicious fixed-price dinner menus of updated English fare; fillets of sole and sea bass with sorrel and vermouth, perhaps, or king scallops with bacon. You may round off the meal with a lemon meringue cheesecake with lavender and honey ice cream, or a damson and almond tart. [$] *Average main: £24* ✉ *33 High St., Ironbridge* ☎ *01952/432233* 🌐 *www.restaurantseven.co.uk* 🕒 *Closed Mon. and Tues. No dinner Sun. No lunch Wed.–Sat.*

$ HOTEL

🏨 **Hundred House Hotel.** The low beams, stained glass, wood paneling, and patchwork cushions that greet you as you enter this Georgian inn set the tone for the whimsical guest rooms. **Pros:** full of nooks and corners; good food. **Cons:** not for those who favor the plain and simple. [$] *Rooms from: £75* ✉ *Bidgnorth Rd. (A442), Norton* ☎ *01952/580240* 🌐 *www.hundredhouse.co.uk* 🛏 *10 rooms* 🍽 *Breakfast.*

$ B&B/INN

🏨 **Library House.** At one time the village's library, this small guesthouse on the hillside near the Ironbridge museums (and a few steps from the bridge) has kept its attractive Victorian style while allowing for more modern luxuries—a DVD library, for instance. **Pros:** welcoming hosts; good location; free parking passes for the town. **Cons:** not for families with young children; no restaurant. [$] *Rooms from: £90* ✉ *11 Severn Bank* ☎ *01952/432299* 🌐 *www.libraryhouse.com* 🛏 *4 rooms* 🍽 *Breakfast.*

LUDLOW

22 miles south of Ironbridge Gorge, 70 miles south of Chester.

Fodor'sChoice
★
Medieval, Georgian, and Victorian buildings jostle for attention in pretty Ludlow, which has a fine display of black-and-white half-timber buildings. Dominating the center is the Church of St. Lawrence, its extravagant size a testimony to the town's prosperous wool trade. Cross the River Teme and climb Whitcliffe for a spectacular view of the church and the Norman castle.

Several outstanding restaurants have given the town of just 10,000 a reputation as a culinary hot spot. Ludlow is now the national headquarters of the Slow Food movement, which focuses on responsible production and preserving regional traditions.

GETTING HERE AND AROUND

Ludlow has good train connections. From London Paddington, the journey time is 3 hours (changing at Newport), from Shrewsbury 30 minutes, and from Birmingham 2 hours with a change in Hereford. The train station is a 15-minute walk southwest to the center. Driving from London, take M40, M42, and then A448 to Kidderminster, A456, and A4117 to Ludlow. The town has good parking and is easily walkable.

ESSENTIALS

Visitor Information Ludlow Visitor Information Centre ✉ *Castle St.* ☎ *01584/875053* ⊕ *www.ludlow.org.uk.*

EXPLORING

Ludlow and the Marches Food Festival. The festival takes place over a weekend in mid-September and has demonstrations and tastings of local sausages, ale, and cider. ☎ *01584/873957* ⊕ *www.foodfestival.co.uk.*

Ludlow Castle. The "very perfection of decay," according to author Daniel Defoe, the ruins of this red sandstone castle date from 1085. No wonder the massive structure dwarfs the town: it served as a vital stronghold for centuries and was the seat of the Marcher Lords who ruled "the Marches," the local name for the border region. The two sons of Edward IV—the little princes of the Tower of London—spent time here before being dispatched to London and their death in 1483. Follow the terraced walk around the castle for a lovely view of the countryside. ✉ *Castle Sq.* ☎ *01584/873355* ⊕ *www.ludlowcastle.com* 🎫 *£5* ⊗ *Jan.–mid-Feb., weekends 10–4; mid-Feb.–Mar. and Oct.–Dec., daily 10–4; Apr.–July and Sept., daily 10–5; Aug. daily 10–6; last admission 30 mins before closing. Closed approx. 7 days in Sept. and Nov. and certain days in summer; call to confirm.*

OFF THE BEATEN PATH

Stokesay Castle. This 13th-century fortified manor house built by a wealthy merchant is arguably the finest of its kind in England. Inside the main hall, the wooden cruck roof and timber staircase (a rare survival) demonstrate state-of-the-art building methods of the day. Outside, the cottage-style garden creates a bewitching backdrop for the magnificent Jacobean timber-frame gatehouse. The castle is 7 miles northwest of Ludlow. ✉ *Off A49, Craven Arms* ☎ *01588/672544* ⊕ *www.englishheritage.org.uk* 🎫 *£6.50* ⊗ *Apr.–Oct., daily 10–5; Nov.–Mar., weekends 10–4.*

8

WHERE TO EAT AND STAY

Ludlow is known for some pricier fine-dining establishments, but options from excellent tearooms to pubs and ethnic restaurants are also available.

$$$$ FRENCH Fodor's Choice ★

🍴 **La Bécasse.** Dip into the past—the intimate building dates to 1349, the warm oak paneling merely to the 17th century—as you savor a fixed-price menu (£54–£65) of French food that's bang up to the minute. Rose-color glass chargers on crisp white table linens set the tone for such dishes as beef sirloin with Shropshire blue cheese *dauphinoise*, or crab with spiced fish cakes and papaya salsa. Vegetarians are well served with a separate menu. The two-course lunch menu is a great value at £26. Reservations are essential on weekends. [$] *Average main: £54* ✉ *17 Corve St.* ☎ *01584/872325* 🌐 *www.labecasse.co.uk* ⏲ *Closed Mon. No dinner Sun. No lunch Tues.*

$$$$ MODERN BRITISH Fodor's Choice ★

🍴 **Mr. Underhill's.** Occupying a converted mill building beneath the castle, this secluded establishment looks onto the wooded River Teme and is stylish, light, and informal. The superb Modern British, fixed-price menus take advantage of fresh seasonal ingredients. The daily changing menu could include roast duck breast with orange zest and peppercorn *jus*, or lemon sole with pistachio crust and smoked almond. Book well ahead, especially on weekends; rooms and suites are available should you want to make a night of it. [$] *Average main: £56* ✉ *Dinham Weir* ☎ *01584/874431* 🌐 *www.mr-underhills.co.uk* ✍ *Reservations essential* ⏲ *Closed Mon. and Tues. No lunch.*

$$ HOTEL

🏨 **The Feathers.** Even if you're not staying here, take time to admire the extravagant half-timber facade of this hotel, built in the early 17th century and described by the historian Jan Morris in the *New York Times* as "the most handsome inn in the world." **Pros:** ornate plasterwork; unpretentious feel. **Cons:** most guest rooms lack the old-fashioned feel. [$] *Rooms from: £115* ✉ *The Bull Ring* ☎ *01584/875261* 🌐 *www.feathersatludlow.co.uk* 🛏 *40 rooms* 🍽 *Multiple meal plans.*

$ B&B/INN Fodor's Choice ★

🏨 **Fishmore Hall.** Saved from dereliction in 2008, Fishmore Hall has been beautifully converted from a crumbling old mansion into a relaxing, contemporary place to stay. **Pros:** lovely location; well-designed rooms; beautiful views. **Cons:** restaurant is pricey; a little out of town. [$] *Rooms from: £99* ✉ *Fishmore Rd., Ludlow* ☎ *01584/875148* 🌐 *www.fishmorehall.co.uk* 🛏 *15 rooms.*

NIGHTLIFE AND THE ARTS

Ludlow Festival. The two-week Ludlow Festival, starting in late June, includes Shakespeare performed near the ruined castle, and opera, dance, and concerts around town. ☎ *0844/248–5165* 🌐 *www.ludlowfestival.co.uk.*

THE LAKE DISTRICT

WELCOME TO THE LAKE DISTRICT

TOP REASONS TO GO

★ **Hiking the trails:** Whether it's a demanding trek or a gentle stroll, walking is the way to see the Lake District at its best.

★ **Messing about in boats:** There's nowhere better for renting a small boat or taking a cruise. The Coniston Boating Centre and Derwent Water Marina near Keswick are possible places to start.

★ **Literary landscapes:** The Lake District has a rich literary history, in the children's books of Beatrix Potter, in the writings of John Ruskin, and in the poems of Wordsworth. Stop at any of the writers' homes to enrich your experience.

★ **Pints and pubs:** A pint of real ale in one of the region's inns, such as the Drunken Duck near Hawkshead, may never taste as good as after a day of walking.

★ **Sunrise at Castlerigg:** The stone circle at Castlerigg, in a hollow ringed by peaks, is a reminder of the region's ancient history.

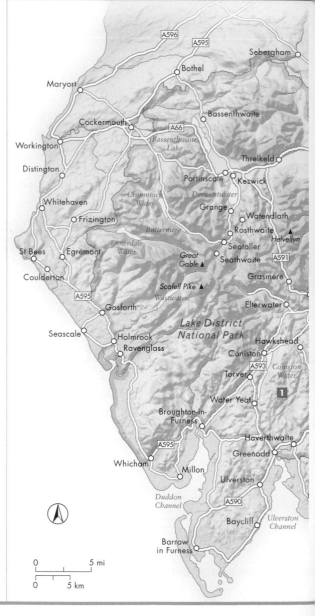

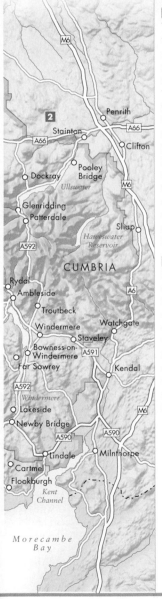

1 The Southern Lakes. The southern lakes and valleys contain the park's most popular, and thus most overcrowded in summer, destinations. The region incorporates the largest body of water, Windermere, as well as most of the quintessential Lakeland towns and villages: Bowness, Ambleside, Grasmere, Elterwater, Coniston, and Hawkshead. To the east and west of this cluster of habitation, the valleys and fells climb to some beautiful upland country.

2 The Northern Lakes. In the north, the landscape opens out across the bleaker fells to reveal challenging, spectacular walking country. Here, in the northern lakes, south of Keswick, you have the best chance to get away from the crowds. This region's northwestern reaches are largely unexplored.

GETTING ORIENTED

The Lake District is in northwest England, some 70 miles north of the industrial belt that stretches from Liverpool to Manchester, and south of Scotland. The major gateway from the south is Kendal, and from the north, Penrith. Both are near the M6 motorway. Windermere, in the south, is the most obvious starting point and has museums, cafés, and gift shops. But the farther (and higher) you can get from the southern towns, the more you'll appreciate the area's spectacular landscapes. The Lake District National Park breaks into two reasonably distinct sections: the gentler, rolling south and the craggier, wilder north, which includes towns such as Keswick.

9

Updated by
Julius Honnor

"Let nature be your teacher." Wordsworth's ideal comes true in this popular region of jagged mountains, waterfalls, wooded valleys, and stone-built villages. No mountains in Britain give a greater impression of majesty; deeper and bluer lakes can be found, but none that fit so readily into the surrounding scene. Outdoors enthusiasts flock to this region for boating or hiking, while literary types visit the homes of Beatrix Potter and other favorite writers.

In 1951 the Lake District National Park was created here from parts of the old counties of Cumberland, Westmorland, and Lancashire. The Lake District is a contour map come to life, covering an area of approximately 885 square miles and holding 16 major lakes and countless smaller stretches of water. The scenery is key to all the park's best activities: you can cross it by car in about an hour, but this is an area meant to be walked or boated or climbed. The mountains aren't high by international standards—Scafell Pike, England's highest peak, is only 3,210 feet above sea level—but they can be tricky to climb.

The poets Wordsworth and Coleridge, and other English writers, found the Lake District an inspiring setting for their work, and visitors have followed ever since, to walk, go boating, or just relax and take in the views. Seeing the homes and other sights associated with these writers can occupy part of a trip.

This area can be one of Britain's most appealing reservoirs of calm, though in summer the lakeside towns, however appealing, can lose their charm when cars and tour buses clog the narrow streets. Similarly, the walks and hiking trails that crisscross the region seem less inviting when you share them with a crowd. Despite the challenges of popularity, the Lake District has managed tourism and the landscape in a manner that retains the character of the villages and the natural environment.

Today, too, a new generation of hotel and restaurant owners is making more creative use of the local foods and other assets of the Lakeland fells, and chic modern or foodie-oriented establishments are springing up next to traditional tearooms and chintz-filled inns.

LAKE DISTRICT PLANNER

WHEN TO GO

The Lake District is one of the rainiest areas in Britain, but June, July, and August hold the best hope of fine weather and summer is the time for all the major festivals. You will, however, be sharing the lakes with thousands of other people. If you travel at this time, turn up early at popular museums and attractions, and expect to work to find parking. April and May, as well as September and October, are good alternatives. Later and earlier in the year there'll be even more space and freedom, but many attractions close, and from December to March, snow and ice can block roads and may preclude serious hill walking without heavy-duty equipment.

PLANNING YOUR TIME

You could spend months tramping the hills, valleys, and fells of the Lake District, or, in three days you could drive through the major towns and villages. The key is not to do too much in too short a time. If you're traveling by public transportation, many places will be off-limits. As a base, Windermere has the best transport links, but it can be crowded and it has less character than some of the smaller towns like Ambleside and Keswick, which also have plenty of sleeping and eating options. For a more intimate version of village life, try Coniston, Hawkshead, or Grasmere. Keep in mind that the northern and western lakes have the most dramatic scenery and offer the best opportunity to escape the summertime hordes.

GETTING HERE AND AROUND

AIR TRAVEL

Manchester Airport has its own rail station with direct service to Windermere. Manchester is 70 miles from the southern part of the Lake District.

Contact **Manchester Airport** ⊠ *M56, Near Junctions 5 and 6* ☎ *08712/710711* ⊕ *www.manchesterairport.co.uk.*

BOAT TRAVEL

Whether you rent a boat or take a ride on a modern launch or vintage vessel, getting out on the water is a fun (and often useful) way to see the Lake District. Windermere, Coniston Water, and Derwentwater all have boat rental facilities.

BUS TRAVEL

Stagecoach in Cumbria provides local service between Lakeland towns and through the valleys and high passes. Bus service between main tourist centers is fairly frequent on weekdays, but much reduced on weekends and holidays. Don't count on reaching the more remote parts of the area by bus. Off-the-beaten-track touring requires a car or strong legs. A one-week Cumbria Goldrider ticket (£23.50), available on the bus, is valid on all routes. Explorer tickets (£10) are valid for a day on all routes. Contact Traveline for up-to-date timetables.

Contacts Traveline ☎ *0871/200–2233* ⊕ *www.traveline.info.*

CAR TRAVEL

A car is almost essential in the Lake District; bus service is limited and trains can get you to the edge of the national park but no farther. You can rent cars in Penrith and Kendal. Roads within the region are generally good, although minor routes and mountain passes can be steep and narrow. Warning signs are often posted if snow or ice has made a road impassable; check local weather forecasts in winter before heading out. In July and August and during the long public holiday weekends, expect heavy traffic. The Lake District has plenty of parking lots; use them to avoid blocking narrow lanes.

Travel time to Windermere from London is about four to five hours, to Keswick five to six hours. Expect heavy traffic out of London on weekends.

TRAIN TRAVEL

There are direct trains from Manchester and Manchester airport to Windermere. For schedule information, call National Rail Enquiries. Two train companies serve the region from London's Euston Station: take a Virgin or Northern Rail train bound for Carlisle, Edinburgh, or Glasgow and change at Oxenholme for the branch line service to Windermere. Average travel time to Windermere (including the change) from London is 4½ hours. National Rail can handle all questions about trains.

Train connections are good around the edges of the Lake District, but you must take the bus or drive to reach the central Lakeland region. Trains are sometimes reduced, or nonexistent, on Sunday.

Contacts National Rail Enquiries ☎ *08457/484950* ⊕ *www.nationalrail.co.uk.* **Northern Rail** ☎ *0844/241–3454* ⊕ *www.northernrail.org.* **Virgin Trains** ☎ *08719/774222* ⊕ *www.virgintrains.co.uk.*

NATIONAL PARK

The Lake District National Park head office (and main visitor center) is at Brockhole, north of Windermere. It's closed November through mid-February. Helpful regional national-park information centers sell books and maps, book accommodations, and provide walking advice.

Contacts Bowness Bay Information Centre ✉ *Glebe Rd., Bowness-on-Windermere* ☎ *015394/42895.* **Keswick Information Centre** ✉ *Moot Hall, Main St., Keswick* ☎ *017687/72645.* **Lake District Visitor Centre** ✉ *Brockhole, Ambleside Rd., Windermere* ☎ *015394/46601* ⊕ *www.brockhole.co.uk.* **Ullswater Information Centre** ✉ *Beckside Car Park, off Greenside Rd., Glenridding* ☎ *017684/82414* ⊕ *www.lakedistrict.gov.uk.*

TOURS

Mountain Goat and Lakes Supertours provide minibus sightseeing tours with skilled local guides. Half- and full-day tours, some of which really get off the beaten track, depart from Bowness, Windermere, Ambleside, and Grasmere.

Walks range from gentle, literary-oriented strolls to challenging ridge hikes. The Lake District National Park or tourist information centers can put you in touch with qualified guides.

Contacts Cumbria Tourist Guides ☎ *01228/562096*
⊕ *www.cumbriatouristguides.org.* **English Lakeland Ramblers** ☎ *703/680–4276, 800/724–8801* ⊕ *www.ramblers.com.* **Lake District Walker** ☎ *0844/693–3389* ⊕ *www.thelakedistrictwalker.co.uk.* **Lakes Supertours** ✉ *1 High St., Windermere* ☎ *015394/42751* ⊕ *www.lakes-supertours.com.* **Mountain Goat** ✉ *Victoria St., Windermere* ☎ *015394/45161* ⊕ *www.mountain-goat.com.*

RESTAURANTS
Lakeland restaurants increasingly reflect a growing British awareness of good food. Local sourcing and international influences are common, and even old Cumberland favorites are being creatively reinvented. Pub dining in the Lake District can be excellent—the hearty fare often makes use of local ingredients such as Herdwick lamb, and real ales are a good accompaniment. If you're going walking, ask your hotel or B&B about making you a packed lunch. Some local delicatessens also offer this service.

HOTELS
Your choices include everything from small country inns to grand lakeside hotels; many hotels offer the option of paying a higher price that includes dinner as well as breakfast. The regional mainstay is the bed-and-breakfast, from the house on Main Street to an isolated farmhouse. Most country hotels and B&Bs gladly cater to hikers and can provide on-the-spot information. Wherever you stay, book well in advance for summer visits, especially those in late July and August. In winter many accommodations close for a month or two. On weekends and in summer it may be hard to get a reservation for a single night. Internet access is improving, and an increasing number of hotels and cafés offer Wi-Fi access. *Hotel reviews have been shortened. For full information, visit Fodors.com.*

WHAT IT COSTS IN POUNDS			
$	$$	$$$	$$$$
Restaurants	under £15	£15–£19	£20–£25	over £25
Hotels	under £100	£100–£160	£161–£220	over £220

Restaurant prices are the average cost of a main course at dinner or, if dinner isn't served, at lunch. Hotel prices are the lowest cost of a standard double room in high season, including 20% V.A.T.

VISITOR INFORMATION
Contacts Cumbria Tourism ✉ *Windermere Rd., Staveley* ☎ *01539/822222* ⊕ *www.golakes.co.uk.*

THE SOUTHERN LAKES

Among the many attractions here are the small resort towns clustered around Windermere, England's largest lake, and the area's hideaway valleys, rugged walking centers, and monuments rich in literary associations. This is the easiest part of the Lake District to reach. An obvious route from Kendal takes in Windermere, the area's natural touring center, before moving north through Ambleside and Rydal Water to Grasmere. Some of the loveliest Lakeland scenery is to be found by then turning south, through Elterwater, Hawkshead, and Coniston.

WINDERMERE AND BOWNESS-ON-WINDERMERE

90 miles north of Manchester.

For a natural touring base for the southern half of the Lake District, you don't need to look much farther than Windermere, though it does get crowded in summer. The resort became popular in the Victorian era when the arrival of the railway made the remote and rugged area accessible. Wordsworth and Ruskin opposed the railway, fearing an influx of tourists would ruin the tranquil place. Sure enough, the railway terminus in 1847 brought with it Victorian day-trippers, and the original hamlet of Birthwaite was subsumed by the new town of Windermere, named after the lake.

Windermere has continued to flourish, despite being a mile or so from the water; the development now spreads to envelop the slate-gray lakeside village of Bowness-on-Windermere. Bowness is the more attractive of the two, but they're so close it doesn't matter where you stay.

GETTING HERE AND AROUND

Windermere is easily reached by car, less than a half hour off the M6. There's also a train station at the eastern edge of town; change at Oxenholme for the branch line to Kendal and Windermere.

Bus 599, leaving every 20 minutes in summer (hourly the rest of the year) from outside the Windermere train station, links the town with Bowness.

The Windermere Ferry, carrying cars and pedestrians, crosses from Ferry Nab on the Bowness side of the lake to reach Far Sawrey and the road to Hawkshead. With year-round ferry service between Ambleside, Bowness, Brockhole, and Lakeside, Windermere Lake Cruises is a pleasant way to experience the lake.

ESSENTIALS

Contacts **Windermere Ferry** ☎ 01228/227653 ⊕ www.cumbria.gov.uk 💷 £4.30 one-way for cars; 50p one-way for foot passengers ⊙ Apr.–Oct., Mon.–Sat. 6:50 am–9:50 pm, Sun. 9:10 am–9:50 pm; Nov.–Mar., Mon.–Sat. 6:50 am–8:50 pm, Sun. 9:10 am–8:50 pm. Approx every 20 mins. **Windermere Lake Cruises** ✉ Windermere ☎ 015394/43360 ⊕ www.windermere-lakecruises.co.uk.

Visitor Information **Windermere Tourist Information Centre** ✉ Victoria St. ☎ 015394/46499 ⊕ www.exploresouthlakeland.co.uk.

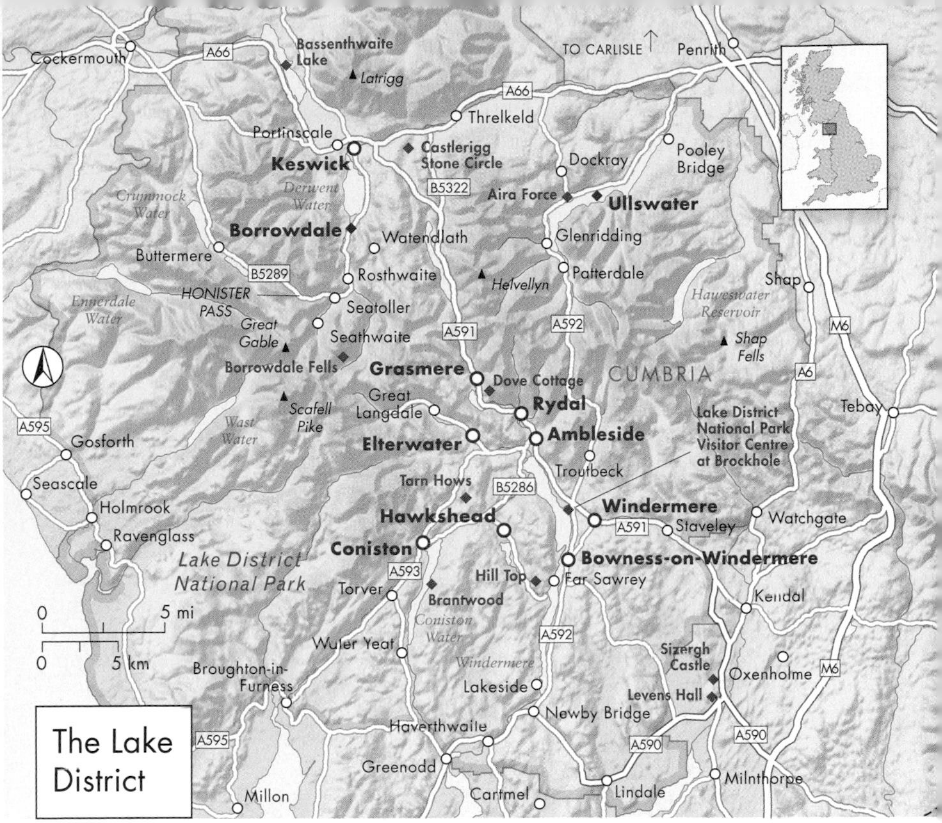
The Lake District
Cockermouth
A66
Bassenthwaite Lake
Latrigg
TO CARLISLE
Penrith
A66
Threlkeld
Portinscale
Keswick
Castlerigg Stone Circle
Dockray
Pooley Bridge
Crummock Water
Derwent Water
B5322
Aira Force
Ullswater
Borrowdale
Watendlath
Glenridding
Buttermere
B5289
Rosthwaite
Helvellyn
Patterdale
Shap
Ennerdale Water
HONISTER PASS
Seatoller
Haweswater Reservoir
Great Gable
Seathwaite
A591
A592
M6
Shap Fells
Borrowdale Fells
Grasmere
Dove Cottage
CUMBRIA
A6
Scafell Pike
Great Langdale
Rydal
Lake District National Park Visitor Centre at Brockhole
Tebay
A595
Wast Water
Elterwater
Ambleside
Gosforth
Troutbeck
Seascale
Tarn Hows
B5286
Holmrook
Hawkshead
Windermere
Watchgate
A591
Staveley
Ravenglass
Coniston
Bowness-on-Windermere
Lake District National Park
A593
Hill Top
Far Sawrey
Torver
Brantwood
Kendal
0
5 mi
Coniston Water
A592
0
5 km
Wuler Yeat
Sizergh Castle
Windermere
Oxenholme
M6
Broughton-in-Furness
Lakeside
Levens Hall
Newby Bridge
Haverthwaite
A595
A590
A590
Greenodd
Millon
Cartmel
Lindale
Milnthorpe

EXPLORING

TOP ATTRACTIONS

Fodor's Choice ★ **Abbot Hall.** The region's finest art gallery, Abbot Hall occupies a Palladian-style Georgian mansion built in 1759 in nearby Kendal, 10 miles east of Windermere. In the permanent collection are works by Victorian artist and critic John Ruskin, who lived near Coniston, and by 18th-century portrait painter George Romney, who worked in Kendal. *The Great Picture*, a grand 17th-century triptych of the life of Lady Ann Clifford, is attributed to Flemish painter Jan Van Belcamp. The gallery also owns some excellent contemporary art, including work by Barbara Hepworth, Ben Nicholson, Winifred Nicholson, and L. S. Lowry. There's also an excellent café. Abbot Hall is on the River Kent, next to the parish church. The **Museum of Lakeland Life,** with exhibits on blacksmithing and wheelwrighting and a wonderful re-creation of a period pharmacy, is in the former stable block of the hall, on the same site. ✉ *Off HighgateKendal* ☎ *01539/722464* 🌐 *www.abbothall.org.uk* 🎫 *Abbot Hall £6.20; Museum of Lakeland Life £5; combined ticket £8* ⏲ *Mar.–Oct., Mon.–Sat. 10:30–5; Nov.–mid-Dec. and mid-Jan.–Feb., Mon.–Sat. 10:30–4.*

Fodor's Choice **Blackwell.** From 1898 to 1900, architect Mackay Hugh Baillie Scott
★ (1865–1945) designed Blackwell, a quintessential Arts and Crafts house
with carved paneling, delicate plasterwork, and a startling sense of light
and space. Originally a retreat for a Manchester brewery owner, the house
is a refined mix of modern style and the local vernacular. Lime-washed
walls and sloping slate roofs make it fit elegantly into the landscape above
Windermere, and the artful integration of decorative features into stained
glass, stonework, friezes, and wrought iron gives the house a sleekly contemporary feel. Accessibility is wonderful here: nothing is roped off and
you can even play the piano. Peruse the shop and try the honey-roast ham
in the excellent tearoom. The grounds are also worth a visit: they often
host contemporary sculpture installations. ⊠ *B5360* ☎ *015394/46139*
⊕ *www.blackwell.org.uk* ☞ *£7.20; garden only £4* ☉ *Apr.–Oct., daily*
10:30–5; Nov., Dec., and mid-Jan.–Mar., daily 10:30–4.

FAMILY   **Lakes Aquarium.** On the quayside at the southern end of Windermere,
Fodor's Choice this excellent aquarium has wildlife and waterside exhibits. One high-
★ light is an underwater tunnel walk along a re-created lake bed, complete
with diving ducks and Asian short-clawed otters. Piranhas, rays, and
tropical frogs also have their fans, and there are some unexpected extra
treats such as marmosets, a caiman, and Cinder the boa constrictor.
Friendly, knowledgeable staff members are eager to talk about the animals. ∎**TIP→** Animal handling takes place daily at 12:45 in the rain-for-
est areas. ⊠ *C5062, Lakeside* ☎ *015394/30153* ⊕ *www.lakesaquarium.*
co.uk ☞ *£8.95; £12.15 combined ticket with Lakeside & Haverthwaite*
Railway Company ☉ *Apr.–Oct., daily 9–6; Nov.–Mar., daily 9–5; last*
entry 1 hr before closing.

∎OFF THE **Orrest Head.** To escape the traffic and have a view of Windermere, set
BEATEN out on foot and follow the signs to the left of the Windermere Hotel to
PATH Orrest Head. The shady, uphill path winds through Elleray Wood, and
after a 20-minute hike you arrive at a rocky little summit (784 feet) with
a panoramic view that encompasses the Yorkshire fells, Morecambe
Bay, and the beautiful Troutbeck Valley.

Windermere. No sights in Windermere or Bowness compete with that of
Windermere itself. At 11 miles long, 1 miles wide, and 220 feet deep,
the lake is England's largest and stretches from Newby Bridge almost
to Ambleside, filling a rocky gorge between thickly wooded hills. The
cold waters are superb for fishing, especially for Windermere char, a rare
lake trout. In summer, steamers and pleasure craft travel the lake, and a
trip across the island-studded waters, particularly the round-trip from
Bowness to Ambleside or down to Lakeside, is wonderful. Although the
lake's marinas and piers have some charm, you can bypass the busier
stretches of shoreline (in summer they can be packed solid) by walking
beyond the boathouses. Windermere Lake Cruises offers a variety of
excursions. ⊕ *www.windermere-lakecruises.co.uk.*

WORTH NOTING

FAMILY   **Brockhole.** A lakeside 19th-century mansion with 30 acres of terraced
gardens sloping down to the water, Brockhole serves as the park's official
visitor center and has exhibits about the local ecology, flora, and fauna.
Impressive aerial photography is good for orientation and inspiration,

making it a good stop at the start of your visit. The gardens, designed in the Arts and Crafts style by Thomas Mawson, are at their best in spring, when daffodils punctuate the lawns and azaleas burst into bloom. There's an adventure playground, croquet field, miniature golf course, rowboats for hire, an aerial walkway, and zipline through the trees. The bookstore carries hiking guides and maps, and you can picnic here or eat at the café-restaurant. Bus 555/559 goes to the visitor center from Windermere and boats from Waterhead stop at a pier. Windermere Lake Cruises has seasonal ferry service to Brockhole from Waterhead in Ambleside. ✉ *Ambleside Rd.* ☎ *015394/46601* 🌐 *www.brockhole.co.uk* 🎫 *Free* 🕒 *Mid-Feb.–Oct., daily 10–5. Gardens: daily dawn–dusk.*

FAMILY **Lakeside & Haverthwaite Railway Company.** Vintage steam trains chug along on the 4-mile branch line between Lakeside and Haverthwaite, giving you a great view of the lake's southern tip. You can add on a lake cruise for another perspective of the region's natural beauty. Departures from Lakeside coincide with ferry arrivals from Bowness and Ambleside. ✉ *A590, Haverthwaite* ☎ *015395/31594* 🌐 *www.lakesiderailway.co.uk* 🎫 *£6.40 round-trip; £12.15 combined ticket with Lakes Aquarium* 🕒 *Apr.–Oct., daily 10:30–6.*

FAMILY **World of Beatrix Potter.** A touristy attraction aimed at kids interprets the author's 23 tales with three-dimensional scenes of Peter Rabbit and more. Skip it if you can and visit Potter's former home at Hill Top and the Beatrix Potter Gallery in Hawkshead. ✉ *The Old Laundry, Crag Brow, Bowness-on-Windermere* ☎ *0844/504–1233* 🌐 *www.hop-skip-jump.com* 🎫 *£6.95* 🕒 *Apr.–Sept., daily 10–5:30; Oct.–Mar., daily 10–4:30; closed 1 week end of Jan.*

WHERE TO EAT

$ BRITISH 🍴 **Angel Inn.** Up the steep slope from the water's edge in Bowness, this spacious, stylish pub serves good home-cooked fare as well as a fine collection of beers that includes its own Hawkshead brew. Specials, chalked on a board, might be grilled sole with crushed crab and char-broiled steak with thyme-roasted tomatoes. Leather sofas and open fires make the Angel a cozy place; service is low-key and friendly, and the decoration is bright, minimal, and contemporary, with wooden floors and off-white walls. Thirteen comfortable, good-value bedrooms complete the picture. [$] *Average main: £14* ✉ *Helm Rd., Bowness-on-Windermere* ☎ *015394/44080* 🌐 *www.theangelinnbowness.com.*

$ BRITISH 🍴 **Lazy Daisy's.** Wooden floors, a big window onto the main street, displays of hops, and the smell of homemade bread: it's a Lakeland kitchen with a contemporary twist. Try the daily roast, slow cooked with herbs, or great sandwiches such as melted Brie, bacon, and tomato, and homemade soup. Good all day are cakes such as "lumpy bumpy"—a caloric mix of peanuts, sugar, and chocolate. This friendly and cozy coffee shop also serves a full dinner menu, and there's Wi-Fi, too. [$] *Average main: £12* ✉ *31–33 Crescent Rd.* ☎ *015394/43877* 🌐 *www.lazydaisyslakelandkitchen.co.uk* 🕒 *Closed Sun.*

$$ BRITISH 🍴 **Queen's Head Hotel.** An unpretentious 17th-century inn in the pretty little village of Troutbeck, the Queen's Head serves innovative pub food all through the day. Dishes may include free-range duck with cashews and watermelon, or fish-and-chips made with a vodka batter. It's also noted

for real ales served from what was once an Elizabethan four-poster bed. The intimate dining rooms have oak beams, flagged floors, and log fires. Lunches can be less hearty than the excellent evening meals. If you want to stay overnight, the 15 guest rooms have splendid views. [$] *Average main: £15* ✉ *A592, 3 miles north of Windermere, Troutbeck* ☎ *015394/32174* 🌐 *www.queensheadtroutbeck.co.uk.*

STAY ON A FARM

Sally's Cottages (🌐 *www.sallyscottages.co.uk*) is a good place to start checking out farm stays. Go Lakes (🌐 *www.golakes.co.uk*) has a wide range of less luxurious options. Prices can be reasonable, but you'll need a car for most.

WHERE TO STAY

$ B&B/INN Fodor's Choice ★ 🏨 **1 Park Road.** On a quiet street, this upmarket boutique B&B has spacious guest rooms with carefully chosen fabrics and contemporary touches such as iPod docking stations. **Pros:** welcoming and stylish; collects guests from the station; good food, wine, and beer. **Cons:** a 15-minute walk to the lake. [$] *Rooms from: £84* ✉ *1 Park Rd.* ☎ *015394/42107* 🌐 *www.1parkroad.com* 🛏 *6 rooms* 🍴 *Breakfast.*

$ B&B/INN 🏨 **Archway Guesthouse.** A chef and a restaurant manager make a friendly and well-qualified team running this excellent little guesthouse in a Victorian building near the train station. **Pros:** great value; uncluttered sitting area; rooms at front have good views. **Cons:** not as much space as you might find elsewhere. [$] *Rooms from: £75* ✉ *13 College Rd.* ☎ *015394/45613* 🌐 *www.the-archway.co.uk* 🛏 *4 rooms* 🍴 *Breakfast.*

$$$$ HOTEL Fodor's Choice ★ 🏨 **Gilpin Lodge.** Hidden among 22 acres of grounds with meandering paths leading to sleek, spacious lodges, this rambling country-house hotel pampers you in a low-key way. **Pros:** plenty of pampering; notable food; a policy of no weddings or conferences. **Cons:** a little out of the way; expensive rates. [$] *Rooms from: £310* ✉ *Crook Rd., 2 miles east of Windermere, Bowness-on-Windermere* ☎ *015394/88818* 🌐 *www.gilpinlodge.co.uk* 🛏 *26 rooms and suites* 🍴 *Some meals.*

$$$ HOTEL Fodor's Choice ★ 🏨 **Miller Howe.** A lovely location, lake views, and superb service help set this luxurious Edwardian country-house hotel apart. **Pros:** more than 5 acres of grounds; great lake views; staff takes care of the little extras. **Cons:** sometimes closes for a couple of weeks in winter. [$] *Rooms from: £210* ✉ *Rayrigg Rd., Bowness-on-Windermere* ☎ *015394/42536* 🌐 *www.millerhowe.com* 🛏 *15 rooms* 🍴 *Some meals.*

$$$ HOTEL Fodor's Choice ★ 🏨 **Punch Bowl Inn.** An outstanding inn and restaurant, the Punch Bowl is a stylish but down-to-earth retreat in the peaceful Lyth Valley, between Windermere and Kendal. **Pros:** contemporary design; relaxed atmosphere; excellent food. **Cons:** a little way from the area's main sights. [$] *Rooms from: £165* ✉ *Off A5074, Crosthwaite* ☎ *015395/68237* 🌐 *www.the-punchbowl.co.uk* 🛏 *9 rooms* 🍴 *Breakfast.*

$$$$ HOTEL 🏨 **The Samling.** On its own sculpture-dotted 67 acres above Windermere, this place oozes exclusivity from every carefully fashioned corner. **Pros:** you'll feel like a star, and may sit next to one at breakfast, too. **Cons:** exclusivity doesn't come cheap. [$] *Rooms from: £280* ✉ *Ambleside Rd.* ☎ *01539/431922* 🌐 *www.thesamlinghotel.co.uk* 🛏 *11 suites* 🍴 *Breakfast.*

SHOPPING

The best selection of shops is at the Bowness end of Windermere, on Lake Road and around Queen's Square: clothing stores, crafts shops, and souvenir stores of all kinds.

Fodor's Choice ★ **More? The Artisan Baker.** Between Kendal and Windermere, this bakery is the place to stop for mouthwatering, award-winning bread, cakes, and sandwiches. It also brews fine coffee. ⊠ *Mill Yard, Staveley* ☎ *015398/22297* ⊕ *www.moreartisan.co.uk.*

SPORTS AND THE OUTDOORS

BIKING

Country Lanes Cycle Hire. This shop rents a variety of bikes from £16 per day. ⊠ *Windermere Railway Station, off A591* ☎ *015394/44544* ⊕ *www.countrylaneslakedistrict.co.uk.*

BOATING

Windermere Lake Holidays. This company rents a wide range of vessels, from small sailboats to houseboats. ⊠ *Mereside, Ferry Nab, Bowness-on-Windermere* ☎ *015394/43415* ⊕ *www.lakewindermere.net.*

AMBLESIDE

7 miles northwest of Windermere.

Unlike Kendal and Windermere, Ambleside seems almost part of the hills and fells. Its buildings, mainly of local stone and many built in the traditional style that forgoes the use of mortar in the outer walls, blend perfectly into their setting. The small town sits at the northern end of Windermere along A591, making it a popular center for Lake District excursions. It has a better choice of restaurants than Windermere or Bowness, and the numerous outdoor shops are handy for fell walkers. Ambleside does, however, suffer from overcrowding in high season. Wednesday, when the local market takes place, is particularly busy.

9

GETTING HERE AND AROUND

An easy drive along A591 from Windermere, Ambleside can also be reached by ferry.

ESSENTIALS

Visitor Information Ambleside Tourist Information Centre ⊠ *The Hub, Central Bldgs., Market Cross, Rydal Rd.* ☎ *0844/225 0544* ⊕ *www.thehubofambleside.co.uk.*

EXPLORING

Armitt Museum. Ambleside's fine local-history gallery and library explores the town's past and its surroundings through the eyes of local people such as Beatrix Potter. A large collection of Beatrix Potter's natural-history watercolors and a huge number of photographic portraits can be viewed by appointment in the excellent library upstairs. Temporary exhibitions of art with a local connection are widely lauded. ⊠ *Rydal Rd.* ☎ *015394/31212* ⊕ *www.armitt.com* 🖼 *£2.50* ⊗ *Mon.–Sat. 10–5; last admission at 4:30.*

Bridge House. This tiny 17th-century stone building, once an apple store, perches on an arched stone bridge spanning Stone Beck. It may have been built here to avoid land tax. This much-photographed building holds a shop and an information center. ✉ *Rydal Rd.* ☎ *015394/35599* 🖾 *Free* ☉ *Easter–Oct., daily 10–5.*

WHERE TO EAT AND STAY

$ ✕ **Fellinis.** Billing itself as "Vegeterranean" to reflect its Mediterranean culinary influences, Fellinis is one of Cumbria's finest foodie destinations. Upstairs is a plush studio cinema screening art-house releases, while downstairs the restaurant rustles up sumptuous concoctions for a sophisticated crowd. The menu's imaginative dishes might start with sweet potato galettes, then continue with herb and three-cheese phyllo-dough pastries topped with a spiced tomato-and-coriander sauce. The large, open dining room has soft seating, bold patterns, oversize lamp shades, and a chill, jazzy soundtrack. White tablecloths, contemporary art, and fresh flowers enhance the modern sensibility. $ *Average main: £12* ✉ *Church St.* ☎ *01539/433845* ⊕ *www.fellinisambleside.com* ☉ *No lunch.*

VEGETARIAN
Fodor's Choice
★

$ ✕ **Lucy's on a Plate.** Ambleside's favorite informal eatery has survived various travails and remains a good spot to relax, whether with mushroom stroganoff for lunch, a chocolate almond torte for afternoon tea, or grilled char for dinner by candlelight. One room has scrubbed pine tables; a conservatory provides additional seating. Lucy's is famous for its wide selection of puddings (desserts), so make sure to save some room. $ *Average main: £9* ✉ *Church St.* ☎ *015394/31191* ⊕ *www.lucysofambleside.co.uk.*

BRITISH

$ ☷ **3 Cambridge Villas.** It's hard to find a more welcoming spot than this lofty Victorian house right in the center of town, thanks to hosts who know a thing or two about local walks. **Pros:** especially good value for single travelers; warm family welcome; central location. **Cons:** some rooms are a little cramped; can occasionally be noisy. $ *Rooms from: £75* ✉ *3 Church St.* ☎ *015394/32307* ⊕ *www.3cambridgevillas.co.uk* ⤵ *7 rooms, 5 with bath* ⦿| *Breakfast.*

B&B/INN

$ ☷ **Rooms at the Apple Pie.** Converted from what were once the offices of Beatrix Potter's solicitor husband, one of Ambleside's best cafés has accommodations. **Pros:** scrumptious breakfasts; central location. **Cons:** not staffed 24 hours a day. $ *Rooms from: £80* ✉ *Rydal Rd.* ☎ *015394/33679* ⊕ *www.roomsattheapplepie.co.uk* ⤵ *8 rooms* ⦿| *Breakfast.*

B&B/INN

SPORTS AND THE OUTDOORS

The fine walks in the vicinity include routes north to Rydal Mount or southeast over Wansfell to Troutbeck. Each walk will take up to a half day, there and back. Ferries from Bowness-on-Windermere dock at Ambleside's harbor, called Waterhead. ■**TIP**➜ **To escape the crowds, rent a rowboat at the harbor for an hour or two.**

CLOSE UP

Poetry, Prose, and the Lakes

The Lake District's beauty has whetted the creativity of many a famous poet and artist over the centuries. Here's a quick rundown of some of the writers inspired by the area's vistas.

William Wordsworth (1770–1850), one of the first English Romantics, redefined poetry by replacing the mannered style of his predecessors with a more conversational style. Many of his greatest works, such as *The Prelude,* draw directly from his experiences in the Lake District, where he spent the first 20 and last 50 years of his life. Wordsworth and his work had an enormous effect on Coleridge, Keats, Shelley, Byron, and countless other writers. Explore his homes in Rydal and Grasmere, among other sites.

John Ruskin (1819–1900), writer, art critic, and early conservationist, was an impassioned champion of new ways of seeing. He defended contemporary artists such as William Turner and the Pre-Raphaelites. His five-volume masterwork, *Modern Painters,* changed the role of the art critic from that of approver or naysayer to that of interpreter. Stop by Coniston to see his home and the Ruskin Museum.

Thomas De Quincey (1785–1859) wrote essays whose impressionistic style influenced many 19th-century writers, including Poe and Baudelaire. His most famous work, *Confessions of an English Opium-Eater* (1822), is an imaginative memoir of his young life, which indeed included opium addiction. He settled in Grasmere in 1809.

Beatrix Potter (1866–1943) never had a formal education; instead, she spent her childhood studying nature. Her love of the outdoors, and Lakeland scenery in particular, influenced her delightfully illustrated children's books, including *The Tale of Peter Rabbit* and *The Tale of Jemima Puddle-Duck.* Potter also became a noted conservationist who donated land to the National Trust. The story of her life was made into the 2006 film *Miss Potter,* starring Renée Zellweger and Ewan McGregor. Today you can visit Hill Top, the writer-artist's home in Hawkshead.

9

RYDAL

1 mile northwest of Ambleside.

The village of Rydal, on the small glacial lake called Rydal Water, is rich with Wordsworthian associations.

EXPLORING

Dora's Field. One famous beauty spot linked with Wordsworth is Dora's Field, below Rydal Mount next to the church of **St. Mary's** (where you can still see the poet's pew). In spring the field is awash in yellow daffodils, planted by William Wordsworth and his wife in memory of their beloved daughter Dora, who died in 1847. ✉ A591.

Rydal Mount. If there's one poet associated with the Lake District, it is Wordsworth, who made his home at Rydal Mount from 1813 until his death. Wordsworth and his family moved to these grand surroundings when he was nearing the height of his career, and his descendants still live here, surrounded by his furniture, his books, his barometer, and

One of the Lake District's literary landmarks, Dove Cottage near Grasmere was where poet William Wordsworth wrote many famous works.

portraits. You can see the study in which he worked, Dorothy's bedroom, and the 4-acre garden, laid out by the poet himself, that gave him so much pleasure. ■TIP→ Wordsworth's favorite footpath can be found on the hill past White Moss Common and the River Rothay. Spend an hour or two walking the paths and you may understand why the great poet composed most of his verse in the open air. A tearoom in the former saddlery provides cakes and drinks; in winter it moves into the dining room. ⊠ Off A591 ☎ 015394/33002 ⊕ www.rydalmount. co.uk ☜ £6.75; garden only £4.50 ⊙ Mar.–Oct., daily 9:30–5; Nov., Dec., and Feb., Wed.–Sun. 11–4.

GRASMERE

3 miles north of Rydal, 4 miles northwest of Ambleside.

Fodor's Choice ★ Lovely Grasmere, on a tiny, wood-fringed lake, is made up of crooked lanes in which Westmorland slate–built cottages hold shops and galleries. The village is a focal point for literary and landscape associations because this area was the adopted heartland of the Romantic poets, notably Wordsworth and Coleridge. The Vale of Grasmere has changed over the years, but many features Wordsworth wrote about are still visible. Wordsworth lived on the town's outskirts for almost 50 years and described the area as "the loveliest spot that man hath ever known."

GETTING HERE AND AROUND

On the main A591 between Ambleside and Keswick, Grasmere is easily reached by car.

ESSENTIALS

Visitor Information Grasmere Tourist Information Centre ⊠ *Church Stile* ☎ *015394/35665* ⊕ *www.nationaltrust.org.uk/allan-bank-and-grasmere.*

EXPLORING

FAMILY

Fodor's Choice

★

Allan Bank. Rope swings on the grounds, picnics in atmospheric old rooms, and walls you can write on: Allan Bank is unlike most other historic houses cared for by the National Trust. On a hill above the lake near Grasmere village, Allan Bank was once home to poet William Wordsworth. Seriously damaged by fire in 2011, it has been partially restored but also left deliberately undecorated. It offers a much less formal experience than other stops on the Wordsworth trail. There are frequent child-friendly activities. Red squirrels can be seen on the woodland walk through the grounds. ⊠ *Off A591, Grasmere* ⊕ *www. nationaltrust.org.uk* ⊠ *£4.80* ☯ *Mid-Mar.–Dec., daily 10–5.*

Dove Cottage and Wordsworth Museum. William Wordsworth lived in Dove Cottage from 1799 to 1808, a prolific and happy time for the poet. During this time he wrote some of his most famous works including, "Ode: Intimations of Immortality" and *The Prelude.* Built in the early 17th century as an inn, this tiny, dim, and, in some places, dark, house is beautifully preserved, with an oak-paneled hall and floors of Westmorland slate. It first opened to the public in 1891 and remains as it was when Wordsworth lived here with his sister, Dorothy, and wife, Mary. Bedrooms and living areas contain much of Wordsworth's furniture and many personal belongings. Coleridge was a frequent visitor, as was Thomas De Quincey, best known for his 1822 autobiographical masterpiece *Confessions of an English Opium-Eater.* De Quincey moved in after the Wordsworths left. You visit the house on a timed guided tour, and the ticket includes admission to the spacious, modern Wordsworth Museum, which documents the poet's life and the literary contributions of Wordsworth and the Lake Poets. The museum includes space for major art exhibitions. The **Jerwood Centre,** open to researchers by appointment, houses 50,000 letters, first editions, and manuscripts. Afternoon tea is served at **Villa Colombina.** ⊠ *A591, south of Grasmere* ☎ *015394/35544* ⊕ *www. wordsworth.org.uk* ⊠ *£7.50* ☯ *Mar.–Oct., daily 9:30–5:30; Nov.– Feb., daily 9:30–4:30.*

9

QUICK BITES

Heidi's. This bustling, cozy little café and deli is lined with jars of locally made jams and chutneys. Bang in the center of Grasmere, it's great for coffee and a homemade pastry or flapjack (bars made with syrup, butter, and oats). ⊠ *Red Lion Sq.* ☎ *015394/35248* ⊕ *www.heidisgrasmerelodge.co.uk.*

St. Oswald's. William Wordsworth, his wife Mary, his sister Dorothy, and four of his children are buried in the churchyard of this church on the River Rothay. The poet planted eight of the yew trees here. As you leave the churchyard, stop at the Gingerbread Shop, in a tiny cottage, for a special local treat. ⊠ *Stock La.* ⊕ *www.grasmereandrydal.org.uk.*

WHERE TO EAT AND STAY

$$
BRITISH
Fodor's Choice
★

✕ **The Jumble Room.** A small stone building dating to the 18th century, Grasmere's first shop is now a friendly, fashionable, and colorful place, with children's books, bold animal paintings, and hanging lamps. A dedicated local fan base means the place always buzzes, and the owners' enthusiasm is contagious. The food is an eclectic mix of international and traditional British: excellent fish-and-chips and beefsteak appear on the menu with polenta gnocchi with beetroot, pesto, and thyme-roasted pumpkin. Lunches are lighter and cheaper, with good soups and homemade desserts; bread is baked fresh every day. Note: hours change frequently, so call ahead. $ *Average main: £15* ✉ *Langdale Rd.* ☎ *015394/35188* ⊕ *www.thejumbleroom.co.uk* ⊙ *Closed Mon. and Tues.*

$$
MODERN BRITISH
Fodor's Choice
★

✕ **Tweedies Bar.** One of the region's best gastro-pubs, Tweedies attracts many locals as well as visitors. Delicious updated British classics include pork stuffed with apricots and wrapped in prosciutto, and venison with potato and beetroot *dauphinoise*. Everything is served in a smart, cozy, wood-filled contemporary pub with mellow music, flickering candles, a slate floor, and a fireplace. The Lodge Restaurant in the Dale Lodge Hotel next door serves the same menu in a more formal setting. Several of Cumbria's best beers are on tap alongside a good selection of world beers. $ *Average main: £16* ✉ *Langdale Rd.* ☎ *015394/35300* ⊕ *www.tweediesbargrasmere.co.uk.*

$
B&B/INN
Fodor's Choice
★

▦ **Heidi's Grasmere Lodge.** Small but sumptuous, this lodging has a distinctly feminine sensibility, with floral wallpaper, curly steel lamps, and painted woodwork. **Pros:** chic bathrooms with whirlpool tubs; warm welcome. **Cons:** no children allowed; so pristine you may worry about your muddy boots. $ *Rooms from: £89* ✉ *Red Lion Sq.* ☎ *015394/35248* ⊕ *www.heidisgrasmerelodge.co.uk* ⏎ *6 rooms* ❙◉❙ *Breakfast.*

$$$
B&B/INN

▦ **Moss Grove.** A Victorian building in the heart of Grasmere, the chic and spacious Moss Grove has an emphasis on environmental credentials. **Pros:** plenty of room; huge chunky furniture; modern design with a conscience. **Cons:** tight parking; not the place for a big fry-up breakfast. $ *Rooms from: £179* ✉ *Red Lion Sq.* ☎ *015394/35251* ⊕ *www.mossgrove.com* ⏎ *11 rooms* ❙◉❙ *Breakfast.*

SHOPPING

Fodor's Choice
★

Grasmere Gingerbread Shop. The smells wafting across the churchyard draw many people to the Grasmere Gingerbread Shop. Since 1854 Sarah Nelson's gingerbread has been sold from this cramped 17th-century cottage, which was once the village school. The delicious treats, still made from a secret recipe, are available in attractive tins for the journey home or to eat right away. ✉ *Church Cottage* ☎ *015394/35428* ⊕ *www.grasmeregingerbread.co.uk.*

SPORTS AND THE OUTDOORS

Loughrigg Terrace. The most panoramic views of lake and village are from the south of Grasmere, from the bare slopes of Loughrigg Terrace, reached along a well-signposted track on the western side of the lake or through the woods from parking lots on the A591 between Grasmere and Rydal Water. It's less than an hour's walk from the village, though your stroll can be extended by continuing around Rydal Water, passing Rydal Mount, detouring onto White Moss Common, before returning to Dove Cottage and Grasmere, a 4-mile (three-hour) walk in total.

ELTERWATER

2˝ miles south of Grasmere, 4 miles west of Ambleside.

The delightful village of Elterwater, at the eastern end of the Great Langdale Valley on B5343, is a good stop for hikers. It's barely more than a cluster of houses around a village green, but from here you can choose from a selection of excellent circular walks.

WHERE TO EAT AND STAY

$ BRITISH 🍴 **Sticklebarn.** The National Trust owns other pubs, but Sticklebarn is the first one it has run. With its own water supply and hydroelectric power, the pub's aim is sustainability. The kitchen uses as much produce as possible from the immediate area, and makes its own gin and vodka. Most of the menu is traditional pub fare—burgers, macaroni and cheese, and lamb stew, for example—aimed at the Langdale walkers that fill the rustic, wood-beamed dining room. Tables spill out onto the terrace in sunny weather. There's also a wood-fired pizza oven. [$] *Average main: £11* ✉ *Great Langdale* ☎ *01539/437356* 🌐 *www.nationaltrust.org.uk.*

$$ HOTEL 🏨 **Old Dungeon Ghyll Hotel.** There's no more comforting stop after a day outdoors than the Hiker's Bar of this 300-year-old hotel at the head of the Great Langdale Valley. **Pros:** ideally situated for walking; wonderfully isolated; spectacular views all around. **Cons:** no-nonsense approach not to everyone's taste. [$] *Rooms from: £116* ✉ *Off B5343, Great Langdale* ☎ *015394/37272* 🌐 *www.odg.co.uk* 🛏 *12 rooms* 🍽 *Breakfast.*

SPORTS AND THE OUTDOORS

There are access points to Langdale Fell from several spots along B5343, the main road; look for information boards at local parking places. You can also stroll up the river valley or embark on more energetic hikes to Stickle Tarn or to one of the summits of the Langdale Pikes. Beyond the Old Dungeon Ghyll Hotel, the Great Langdale Valley splits in two around a hill known as the Band—a path up its spine has particularly good views back down over the valley and can be continued to the summit of Scafell Pike.

CONISTON

5 miles south of Elterwater.

This small lake resort and boating center attracts climbers to the steep peak of the **Old Man of Coniston** (2,635 feet), which towers above the slate-roof houses. It also has sites related to John Ruskin and Arthur Ransome. Quieter than Windermere, Coniston is a good introduction to the pastoral and watery charms of the area, though the small town itself can get crowded in summer.

GETTING HERE AND AROUND

The Coniston Launch connects Coniston Pier with Ruskin's home at Brantwood and some other stops around the lake, offering hourly service (£10.50 for a day-long, "hop on and off" ticket; £17.15 including entry to Brantwood) on its wooden Ruskin and Ransome launches.

ESSENTIALS

Visitor Information Coniston Launch ⊠ *Coniston* ☎ *017687/75753* ⊕ *www.conistonlaunch.co.uk.* **Coniston Tourist Information Centre** ⊠ *Ruskin Ave.* ☎ *015394/41533* ⊕ *www.conistontic.org.*

EXPLORING

Fodor'sChoice
★
Brantwood. On the eastern shore of Coniston Water, Brantwood was the cherished home of John Ruskin (1819–1900), the noted Victorian artist, writer, critic, and social reformer, after 1872. The rambling 18th-century house (with Victorian alterations) is on a 250-acre estate that stretches high above the lake. Here, alongside mementos such as his mahogany desk, are Ruskin's own paintings, drawings, and books. On display is art that this great connoisseur collected, and in cerebral corners such as the Ideas Room visitors are encouraged to think about meaning and change. *Ruskin Rocks* explores his fascinations with stones and music with a brilliant bit of modern technology. A video on Ruskin's life shows the lasting influence of his thoughts, and the Severn Studio has rotating art exhibitions. Ruskin himself laid out the extensive grounds; take time to explore the gardens and woodland walks. Brantwood hosts a series of classical concerts on some Saturdays as well as talks, guided walks, and study days. ⊠ *Off B5285* ☎ *015394/41396* ⊕ *www.brantwood.org. uk* ☜ *£7.20; gardens only £4.95* ⊗ *Mid-Mar.–mid-Nov., daily 10:30–5; mid-Nov.–mid-Mar., Wed.–Sun. 10:30–4.*

Coniston Water. The lake came to prominence in the 1930s when Arthur Ransome made it the setting for *Swallows and Amazons,* one of a series of novels about a group of children and their adventures. The lake is about 5 miles long, a tempting stretch that drew Donald Campbell here in 1959 to set a water-speed record of 260 mph. He was killed when trying to beat it in 1967. His body and the wreckage of *Bluebird K7* were retrieved from the lake in 2001. Campbell is buried in St. Andrew's church in Coniston, and a stone memorial on the village green commemorates him.

Ruskin Museum. This repository of fascinating and thought-provoking manuscripts, personal items, and watercolors by John Ruskin illuminates his thinking and influence. There is also a focus on speedboat racer Donald Campbell; the tail fin of his *Bluebird K7,* dragged up from Coniston Water, is here. Good local-interest exhibits include copper mining, geology, lace, and more. ⊠ *Yewdale Rd.* ☎ *015394/41164* ⊕ *www.ruskinmuseum.com* ☜ *£5.25* ⊗ *Mid-Mar.–mid-Nov., daily 10–5:30; mid-Nov.–mid-Mar., Wed.–Sun. 10:30–3:30.*

Steam Yacht Gondola. The National Trust's Victorian steam yacht runs between Coniston Pier, Brantwood, and Park-a-Moor at the south end of Coniston Water, daily from April through October (£10.50). A stop at Monk Coniston jetty connects to the footpaths through the Monk Coniston Estate, linking Coniston Water to the beauty spot of Tarn

WALKING IN THE LAKE DISTRICT

You can choose gentle rambles near the most popular towns and villages or challenging hikes up some of England's most impressive peaks. The choice is yours, but going for a walk is an essential Lake District experience. Information boards at parking lots throughout the region point out a few possibilities.

British mountaineering began in the Lake District, with its notable hikes: the famous Old Man of Coniston, the Langdale Pikes, Scafell Pike (England's highest peak), Skiddaw, and Helvellyn are all popular, though these require experience, energy, and proper hiking boots and clothing. The Cumbria Way (70 miles) crosses the Lake District, starting at the market town of Ulverston and finishing at Carlisle. The Coast-to-Coast Walk (190 miles) runs from St. Bees on the Irish Sea through the Lake District and across the Yorkshire Dales and the North York Moors; it ends at Robin Hood's Bay at the edge of the North Sea in Yorkshire. Guidebooks to these and other Lakeland walks are available in local bookstores—check out Alfred Wainwright's classic guides. Ordnance Survey maps are helpful, too.

For short walks, consult the tourist information centers: those at Ambleside, Grasmere, Keswick, and Windermere provide maps and advice. The other main sources of information are the Lake District National Park information centers. Cumbria Tourism's website, 🌐 *www.golakes.co.uk*, is helpful for planning. Several climbing organizations offer guided hikes.

Hows. ■ **TIP→ You get a 10% discount if you book online.** ✉ *Coniston Pier* ☎ *015394/41288* 🌐 *www.nationaltrust.org.uk/gondola.*

WHERE TO EAT AND STAY

$ BRITISH 🍴 **Black Bull Inn.** Attached to the Coniston Brewing Company, whose ales are on tap here, the Black Bull is an old-fashioned pub in the heart of the village. It's a good pick for simple, hearty food and exemplary beer. Old photos of Donald Campbell's boat *Bluebird* decorate the walls, and there are wooden beams and benches. The menu lists daily specials as well as sandwiches for lunch or shrimp from Morecambe Bay. [$] *Average main: £10* ✉ *Coppermines Rd.* ☎ *015394/41335* 🌐 *www.conistonbrewery.com.*

$ BRITISH 🍴 **Jumping Jenny's.** Named after Ruskin's beloved boat, the wood-beamed tearoom at Brantwood occupies the converted coach house. It has an open-log fire and mountain views, and serves morning coffee, lunch (sophisticated soups, pastas, sandwiches, and salads), and afternoon tea with homemade cakes. You can sit on the terrace in season for a great view across Coniston Water. [$] *Average main: £8* ✉ *Off B5285* ☎ *015394/41715* 🌐 *jumpingjenny.net* 🕓 *No dinner.*

$ HOTEL Fodor's Choice ★ 🏨 **Bank Ground Farm.** Used by Arthur Ransome as the model for the setting for *Swallows and Amazons*, 15th-century Bank Ground is beautifully situated on the eastern shore of Coniston Water, opposite the village of Coniston on the western shore. **Pros:** stunning lake views; homey atmosphere; traditional welcome. **Cons:** a fair walk from the village. [$] *Rooms from: £90* ✉ *Off B5285* ☎ *015394/41264* 🌐 *www.bankground.com* 🛏 *7 rooms, 5 cottages* 🍽 *Breakfast.*

9

$ B&B/INN [icon] **Lakeland House.** In the middle of Coniston, Lakeland House has smart, modern rooms with bold wallpaper, beamed ceilings, and slate-floored bathrooms. **Pros:** café downstairs means drinks and snacks are never far away; good value. **Cons:** not as homey as a traditional B&B. [$] *Rooms from: £80* ✉ *Tilberthwaite Ave.* ☎ *015394/41303* 🌐 *www.lakelandhouse.co.uk* 🛏 *6 rooms* 🍴 *Breakfast.*

SPORTS AND THE OUTDOORS

BOATING

Coniston Boating Centre. Here you can rent launches, canoes, kayaks, and wooden rowboats, or even take a sailing lesson. Bikes are also available, and a picnic area and café are nearby. Rowboats are £10 an hour, while motorboats are £20 an hour. On weekends you can also walk on the water in a giant transparent plastic ball (£5). ✉ *Lake Rd.* ☎ *015394/41366* 🌐 *www.conistonboatingcentre.co.uk.*

HIKING

Steep tracks lead up from the village to the **Old Man of Coniston.** The trail starts near the Sun Hotel on Brow Hill and goes past an old copper mine to the peak, which you can reach in about two hours. It's one of the Lake District's most satisfying hikes—not too arduous but high enough to feel a sense of accomplishment and get fantastic views (west to the sea, south to Morecambe Bay, and east to Windermere). Experienced hikers include the peak in a seven-hour circular walk from the village, also taking in the heights and ridges of Swirl How and Wetherlam.

LAKE DISTRICT BIKING

Cycling along the numerous bicycle paths and quiet forest roads in Cumbria is pleasurable and safe. Some flat paths are beside the lakes, but the best routes involve plenty of ups and downs. The Cumbria Cycle Way circles the county, and for local excursions guided bike tours are often available, starting at about £25 per day. Contact local tourist offices or bike-rental places for details on cycle routes.

HAWKSHEAD

3 miles east of Coniston.

In the Vale of Esthwaite, this small market town is a pleasing hodgepodge of tiny squares, cobbled lanes, and whitewashed houses. There's a good deal more history here than in most local villages, however. The Hawkshead Courthouse, just outside town, was built by the monks of Furness Abbey in the 15th century. Hawkshead later derived much wealth from the wool trade, which flourished here in the 17th and 18th centuries.

As a thriving market center, Hawkshead could afford to maintain the **Hawkshead Grammar School,** at which William Wordsworth was a pupil from 1779 to 1787; he carved his name on a desk inside, now on display. In the village, Ann Tyson's House claims the honor of having provided the young William with lodgings. The twin draws of Wordsworth and Beatrix Potter—apart from her home, Hill Top, there's a Potter gallery—conspire to make Hawkshead crowded year-round.

GETTING HERE AND AROUND

Hawkshead is east of Coniston on B5285 and south of Ambleside via B5286. An alternative route is to cross Windermere via the car ferry from Ferry Nab, south of Bowness. Local buses link the village to others nearby.

ESSENTIALS

Visitor Information Hawkshead Tourist Information Centre ⊠ *Main St.* ☎ *015394/36946* ⊕ *www.hawksheadtouristinfo.org.uk.*

EXPLORING

FAMILY

Fodor'sChoice

★

Beatrix Potter Gallery. In the 17th-century solicitor's offices formerly used by Potter's husband, the Beatrix Potter Gallery displays a selection of the artist-writer's original illustrations, watercolors, and drawings. There's also information about her interest in conservation and her early support of the National Trust. The house looks almost as it would have in her day, though with touch screens in wooden frames and a children's play area upstairs. Admission is by timed ticket when the place gets busy. ⊠ *Main St.* ☎ *015394/36355* ⊕ *www.nationaltrust. org.uk* ☑ *£4.80* ⊙ *Mid-Feb.–mid-Mar., Sat.–Thurs. 10:30–3:30; mid-Mar.–Oct., Sat.–Thurs. 10:30–5.*

Fodor'sChoice

★

Hill Top. Children's author and illustrator Beatrix Potter (1866–1943), most famous for her *Peter Rabbit* stories, called this place home. The house looks much the same as when Potter bequeathed it to the National Trust, and fans will recognize details such as the porch and garden gate, old kitchen range, Victorian dollhouse, and four-poster bed, which were depicted in the book illustrations. ■**TIP**➔ **Admission to this often-crowded spot is by timed ticket; book in advance and avoid summer weekends and school vacations.** Hill Top lies 2 miles south of Hawkshead by car or foot, though you can also approach via the car ferry from Bowness-on-Windermere. ⊠ *Off B5285, near Sawrey* ☎ *015394/36269* ⊕ *www.nationaltrust.org.uk* ☑ *£8.50* ⊙ *House: mid-Feb.–Mar., Sat.–Thurs. 10:30–3:30; Apr., May, Sept., and Oct., Sat.–Thurs. 10:30–4:30; June–Aug., Sat.–Thurs. 10–5:30. Gardens: mid-Feb.–Mar., daily 10:15–4; Apr., May, Sept., and Oct., daily 10–5; June–Aug., daily 9:45–5:45; Nov. and Dec., daily 10–4.*

WHERE TO EAT AND STAY

$

BRITISH

Fodor'sChoice

★

✕**Tower Bank Arms.** With a porch that appears in a Beatrix Potter story and a location just a rabbit's hop from the author's home, you might expect this pub to be something of a tourist trap. It's anything but. There's a slate floor, a crackling open fire, and a bar that stocks some of the best beers around, usually including some great ales from the nearby Barngates Brewery. There's a friendly welcome and the meals are tasty and copious, making use of local ingredients; the beef-and-ale stew is especially good. Four bedrooms upstairs (starting at £95) offer a good-value alternative to pricier lodgings in the area. $ *Average main: £10* ⊠ *Off B5285, Near Sawrey* ☎ *015394/36334* ⊕ *www.towerbankarms.com.*

$$

HOTEL

Fodor'sChoice

★

⌂ **Drunken Duck Inn.** After four centuries, this friendly old coaching inn remains an outstanding place for both food and lodging. **Pros:** superchic rural style; excellent dining and drinking. **Cons:** hunting paraphernalia may put you off your beer; can feel isolated. $ *Rooms from: £140*

9

✉ *Off B5286, Barngates* ☎ *015394/36347* 🌐 *www.drunkenduckinn.co.uk* 🛏 *16 rooms* 🍴 *Some meals.*

$ B&B/INN Fodor's Choice ★ 🏨 **Yewfield.** With the laid-back friendliness of a B&B and the sophisticated style of a country house, Yewfield is a very good value—especially if you can score one of the rooms at the front of the house with a great view across the valley. **Pros:** out-of-the-way location; pretty garden; apartments are great for weeklong stays. **Cons:** not good for families with young kids. [$] *Rooms from: £98* ✉ *Hawkshead Hill* ☎ *015394/36765* 🌐 *www.yewfield.co.uk* 🛏 *10 rooms, 2 apartments* 🕒 *Closed Dec. and Jan.* 🍴 *Breakfast.*

SPORTS AND THE OUTDOORS

Grizedale Forest Park. Stretching southwest from Hawkshead and blanketing the hills between Coniston and Windermere, Grizedale Forest Park has a thick mix of oak, pine, and larch woods crisscrossed with biking and walking paths. Fifty permanent outdoor sculptures are scattered beside the trails. The **visitor center** has information, maps, a café, and an adventure playground. ✉ *Off B5286* ☎ *01229/860010* 🌐 *www.forestry.gov.uk/grizedaleforestpark.*

Grizedale Mountain Bikes. If you have the urge to explore the trails of the national park, Grizedale Mountain Bikes rents all the right equipment from £26 per day. ✉ *Grizedale Forest Park Visitor Centre, off B5286* ☎ *01229/860369* 🌐 *www.grizedalemountainbikes.co.uk.*

THE NORTHERN LAKES

The scenery of the northern lakes is considerably more dramatic—some would say bleaker—than much of the landscape to the south. The wild and desolate Shap Fells rise to a height of 1,304 feet. The 30-mile drive north along the A6 is one of the most notorious moorland crossings in the country: even in summer it's a lonely place to be, and in winter, snow on the road can be dangerous. From the red-sandstone town of Penrith, the road leads to Ullswater, possibly the grandest of all the lakes; then there's a winding route west past Keswick, south through the marvelous Borrowdale Valley, and on to Cockermouth. Outside the main towns such as Keswick, it can be easier to escape the summer crowds in the northern lakes.

ULLSWATER

12 miles north of Windermere.

Hemmed in by towering hills, Ullswater, the region's second-largest lake, is one of the least developed, drawing people for its calm waters and good access to the mountain slopes of Helvellyn. The A592 winds along the lake's pastoral western shore, through the adjacent hamlets of **Glenridding** and **Patterdale** at the southern end. Lakeside strolls, great views, tea shops, and rowboat rentals provide the full Lakeland experience.

ESSENTIALS

Visitor Information Ullswater Tourist Information Centre ✉ *Beckside Car Park, off A592, Glenridding* ☎ *017684/82414* 🌐 *www.visiteden.co.uk.*

EXPLORING

Aira Force. A spectacular 65-foot waterfall pounds under a stone bridge and through a wooded ravine to feed into Ullswater. From the parking lot it's a 10-minute walk to the falls, with more serious walks on Gowbarrow Fell and to the village of Dockray beyond. ■**TIP→** Bring sturdy shoes, especially in wet or icy weather, when the paths can be treacherous. ⊠ *A592, near A5091* ⊕ *www.nationaltrust.org.uk* ☞ *Parking £3.50–£5.50.*

Helvellyn. West of Ullswater's southern end, the brooding presence of Helvellyn (3,118 feet), one of the Lake District's most formidable mountains and England's third highest, recalls the region's fundamental character. It's an arduous climb to the top, especially via the challenging ridge known as Striding Edge, and the ascent shouldn't be attempted in poor weather or by inexperienced hikers. Signposted paths to the peak run from the road between Glenridding and Patterdale and pass by **Red Tarn,** at 2,356 feet the highest small mountain lake in the region. ⊠ *Glenridding.*

Fodor's Choice ★ **Ullswater Steamers.** These antique vessels, including a 19th-century steamer that is said to be the oldest working passenger ship in the world, run the length of Ullswater between Glenridding in the south and Pooley Bridge in the north, via Howtown on the eastern shore. It's a pleasant tour, especially if you combine it with a lakeside walk. One-way trips start from £6.20, or you can sail the entire day for £13.20. ⊠ *Pier House, off A592, Glenridding* ☎ *017684/82229* ⊕ *www.ullswater-steamers.co.uk.*

WHERE TO STAY

$$$
HOTEL
Howtown Hotel. Near the end of the road on the isolated eastern side of Ullswater, this gloriously quiet family-run hotel is low-key and low-tech. **Pros:** exceptionally quiet; spectacular location; dinner included in price. **Cons:** not for those who must be plugged in; a bit remote; books up fast. $ *Rooms from: £178* ⊠ *Howtown Rd., Howtown* ☎ *017684/86514* ⊕ *www.howtown-hotel.com* ⇆ *12 rooms, 4 cottages* ═ *No credit cards* ☉ *Closed Nov.–Mar.* ⊙*Some meals.*

$$$
HOTEL
Sharrow Bay. Sublime views and exceptional service and cuisine add distinction to this country house on the shores of Ullswater. **Pros:** great views across Ullswater; pretty garden; top-notch service. **Cons:** not for the faint of wallet; some distance from other facilities. $ *Rooms from: £200* ⊠ *Howtown Rd., Pooley Bridge* ☎ *017684/86301* ⊕ *www.sharrowbay.co.uk* ⇆ *16 rooms, 8 suites* ⊙*Some meals.*

KESWICK

14 miles west of Ullswater.

Fodor's Choice ★ The great mountains of Skiddaw and Blencathra brood over the gray slate houses of Keswick (pronounced *kezz*-ick), on the scenic shores of Derwentwater. The town is a natural base for exploring the rounded, heather-clad Skiddaw range to the north, while the hidden valleys of Borrowdale and Buttermere (the latter reached by stunning Honister Pass) take you into the rugged heart of the Lake District. Nearby, five beautiful lakes are set among the three highest mountain ranges in England. The tourist information center here has regional information and is the place to get fishing permits for Derwentwater.

Keswick's narrow, cobbled streets have a grittier charm compared to the refined Victorian elegance of Grasmere or Ambleside. Nevertheless, it's the best spot in the Lake District to purchase mountaineering gear and outdoor clothing. There are also many hotels, guesthouses, restaurants, and pubs.

GETTING HERE AND AROUND
It's easily reached along A66 from Penrith, though you can get to Keswick more scenically via Grasmere in the south. Buses run from the train station in Penrith to Keswick. The town center is pedestrianized. ■TIP→ Traffic can be horrendous in summer, so consider leaving your car in Keswick. The open-top Borrowdale bus service between Keswick and Seatoller (to the south) runs frequently, and the Honister Rambler minibus is perfect for walkers aiming for the high fells of the central lakes; it makes stops from Keswick to Buttermere. The Keswick Launch service on Derwentwater links to many walks as well as the Borrowdale bus service.

ESSENTIALS
Visitor Information Keswick Information Centre ⊠ *Moot Hall, Market Sq.* ☎ *017687/72645* ⊕ *www.keswick.org.*

EXPLORING
Fodor's Choice **Castlerigg Stone Circle.** A Neolithic monument about 100 feet in diameter, this stone circle was built around 3,000 years ago on a hill overlooking St. John's Vale. The brooding northern peaks of Skiddaw and Blencathra loom to the north, and there are views of Helvellyn to the south. The 38 stones aren't large, but the site makes them particularly impressive. Wordsworth described them as "a dismal cirque of Druid stones upon a forlorn moor." The site, always open to visitors, is 4 miles east of Keswick. There's usually space for cars to park beside the road that leads along the northern edge of the site. ⊠ *Off A66* ⊕ *www. english-heritage.org.uk* 🎫 *Free.*

Derwentwater. To understand why Derwentwater is considered one of England's finest lakes, take a short walk from Keswick's town center to the lakeshore and past the jetty, and follow the **Friar's Crag** path, about a 15-minute level walk from the center. This pine-tree-fringed peninsula is a favorite vantage point, with its view of the lake, the ring of mountains, and many tiny islands. Ahead, crags line the **Jaws of Borrowdale** and overhang a mountain ravine—a scene that looks as if it emerged from a Romantic painting.

Keswick Launch Company. For the best lake views, take a wooden-launch cruise around Derwentwater. Between late March and November, cruises set off every hour in each direction from a dock at the shore; there's also a limited winter timetable. You can also rent a rowboat here. Buy a hop-on, hop-off Around the Lake ticket (£9.50) and take advantage of the seven landing stages around the lake that provide access to hiking trails, such as the two-hour climb up and down Cat Bells, a celebrated lookout point on the western shore of Derwentwater. ⊠ *Lake Rd.* ☎ *017687/72263* ⊕ *www.keswick-launch.co.uk.*

Wordsworth House. Cockermouth was the birthplace of William Wordsworth (and his sister Dorothy), whose childhood home was this

CLOSE UP

Festivals in the Lake District

The Lake District hosts some of Britain's most unusual country festivals as well as some excellent but more typical ones.

Major festivals include the Keswick Film Festival (February), Words by the Water (a literary festival in Keswick, March), Keswick Jazz Festival (May), Cockermouth and Keswick carnivals (June), Ambleside and Grasmere rushbearing (August), and the Lake District Summer Music (regionwide, in August)—but there are many others. Horse racing comes to Cartmel over May and August holiday weekends.

A calendar of events is available at tourist information centers or on the Cumbria Tourism website, ⊕ www.golakes.co.uk.

18th-century town house. You see it complete with clutter, costumed interpreters, and period cooking in the kitchen. Young visitors can also dress up in period costumes. Harpsichord recitals take place regularly. Wordsworth's father is buried in the All Saints' churchyard, and the church has a stained-glass window in memory of the poet. Cockermouth is 12 miles west of Keswick. ⊠ *Main St., Cockermouth* ☎ *01900/824805* ⊕ *www.nationaltrust.org.uk* ⊜*£6.70* ⊙ *Mid-Mar.– Oct., Sat.–Thurs. 11–5; last admission at 4.*

WHERE TO EAT

$
BRITISH
✕**Café Bar 26.** A metropolitan bar in a town where cozy tearooms are more the norm, Café Bar 26 has wooden beams, mellow brick-color walls, flickering candlelight, an excellent coffee machine, and live music every Saturday. The wine list is on the short side, but there are tasty homemade pizzas and tapas. In the middle of the day, lunch options include potted shrimp, burgers, and fish cakes. The four spacious bedrooms upstairs are an excellent value for an overnight stop. $ *Average main: £6* ⊠ *26 Lake Rd.* ☎ *017687/80863* ⊕ *www.cafebar26.co.uk.*

$$
MODERN BRITISH
✕**Morrels.** One of the town's better eateries, Morrels has local art and wooden floors that give a contemporary edge to the bar and dining area. Updated British fare is the specialty at this mellow place: a tomato, olive, and pine-nut compote complements the mackerel fillet, and the fish cakes come with a bean-and-corn salsa. The restaurant opens at 5:30 for anyone going to the town's theater. A couple of stylish apartments upstairs are available for short-term rentals. $ *Average main: £15* ⊠ *34 Lake Rd.* ☎ *017687/72666* ⊕ *www.morrels.co.uk* ⊙ *Closed Mon. No lunch.*

WHERE TO STAY

$
B&B/INN
FAMILY
▦ **Ferndene.** Exceptionally friendly, this spotless B&B is carefully tended by its kindly owners. **Pros:** family-focused; good value; bicycle storage. **Cons:** lacks style of more expensive lodgings. $ *Rooms from: £72* ⊠ *6 St. John's Terr.* ☎ *017687/74612* ⊕ *www.ferndene-keswick.co.uk* ⊰*6 rooms* ⊙*Breakfast.*

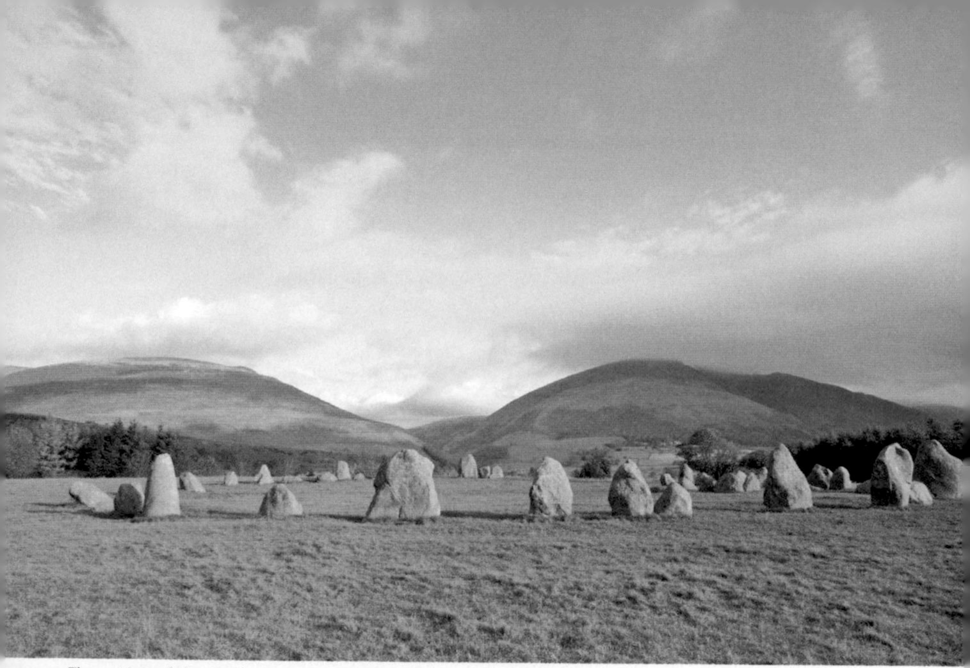

The setting of the Castlerigg Stone Circle, ringed by stunning mountains, makes this Neolithic monument deeply memorable.

$$ HOTEL **Highfield Hotel.** Slightly austere on the outside but charming within, this Victorian hotel overlooks the lawns of Hope Park and has accommodations with great character, including rooms in a turret and a former chapel. **Pros:** good service; tasty food; great views. **Cons:** some small downstairs bedrooms. [$] *Rooms from: £100* ✉ *The Heads* ☎ *017687/72508* 🌐 *www.highfieldkeswick.co.uk* 🛏 *18 rooms* 🕒 *Closed Jan.–mid-Feb.* 🍴 *Some meals.*

$$ B&B/INN Fodor's Choice ★ **The Pheasant.** Halfway between Cockermouth and Keswick at the northern end of Bassenthwaite Lake, this traditional 18th-century coaching inn exudes English coziness without the usual Lakeland fussiness. **Pros:** atmosphere of a well-loved local inn; fantastic bar; great food. **Cons:** a little out of the way. [$] *Rooms from: £150* ✉ *Off A66, Bassenthwaite Lake* ☎ *017687/76234* 🌐 *www.the-pheasant.co.uk* 🛏 *15 rooms, 3 suites* 🍴 *Some meals.*

NIGHTLIFE AND THE ARTS

Keswick Film Club. With an excellent festival in February and a program of international and classic films, the Keswick Film Club lights up the old redbrick Alhambra Cinema on St. John's Street and the Theatre by the Lake. ☎ *017687/72195* 🌐 *www.keswickfilmclub.org.*

Keswick Jazz Festival. Held each May, the popular Keswick Jazz Festival consists of four days of music. Reservations are accepted as early as before Christmas. ☎ *017687/74411* 🌐 *www.keswickjazzfestival.co.uk.*

Theatre by the Lake. The company at the Theatre by the Lake presents classic and contemporary productions year-round. The Keswick Music Society season runs from September through January, and the

Words on the Water literary festival takes place in March. ⊠ *Lake Rd.* ☎ *017687/74411* ⊕ *www.theatrebythelake.com.*

SHOPPING

Keswick has a good choice of bookstores, crafts shops, and wool-clothing stores tucked away in its cobbled streets, as well as excellent outdoor shops. Keswick's market is held Saturday.

George Fisher. The area's largest and best outdoor equipment store, George Fisher sells sportswear, travel books, and maps. Daily weather information is posted in the window. ⊠ *2 Borrowdale Rd.* ☎ *017687/72178* ⊕ *www.georgefisher.co.uk.*

Northern Lights Gallery. This well-lighted space carries a good selection of contemporary paintings, photography, sculpture, jewelry, and ceramics by around 80 local artists. ⊠ *22 St. John's St.* ☎ *01768/775402* ⊕ *www.northernlightsgallery.co.uk.*

Thomasons. A butcher and delicatessen, Thomasons sells some very good meat pies—just the thing for putting in your pocket before you climb a Lakeland fell. ⊠ *8–10 Station St.* ☎ *017687/80169.*

SPORTS AND THE OUTDOORS

BIKING

Keswick Bikes. This company rents bikes (from £20 per day) and provides information on all the nearby trails. Guided tours can be arranged with advance notice. ⊠ *133 Main St.* ☎ *017687/73355* ⊕ *www.keswickbikes.co.uk.*

WATER SPORTS

Derwent Water Marina. Rental boats in all shapes and sizes and instruction in canoeing, sailing, and windsurfing can be had at Derwent Water Marina. Other water-related activities include ghyll scrambling—the fine art of walking up or down a steep Lakeland stream. A two-day sailing or windsurfing course costs £185. ⊠ *Portinscale* ☎ *017687/72912* ⊕ *www.derwentwatermarina.co.uk.*

EN ROUTE The most scenic route from Keswick, B5289 south, runs along the eastern edge of Derwentwater, past turnoffs to natural attractions such as Ashness Bridge, the idyllic tarn of Watendlath, the Lodore Falls (best after a good rain), and the precariously balanced Bowder Stone. Farther south is the tiny village of **Grange,** a walking center at the head of Borrowdale, where there's a riverside café.

BORROWDALE

7 miles south of Keswick.

Fodor's Choice ★ South of Keswick and its lake lies the valley of Borrowdale, whose varied landscape of green valley floor and surrounding crags has long been considered one of the region's most magnificent treasures. **Rosthwaite,** a tranquil farming village, and **Seatoller,** the southernmost settlement, are the two main centers (both are accessible by bus from Keswick), though they're little more than clusters of aged buildings surrounded by glorious countryside.

GETTING HERE AND AROUND

The valley is south of Keswick on B5289. The Borrowdale bus service between Keswick and Seatoller runs frequently.

EXPLORING

Fodor's Choice ★ **Borrowdale Fells.** These steep fells rise up dramatically behind Seatoller. Get out and walk whenever inspiration strikes. Trails are well signposted, but you can pick up maps and any gear in Keswick.

Honister Pass. Beyond Seatoller, B5289 turns westward through Honister Pass (1,176 feet) and Buttermere Fell. Boulders line the road, which offers some of the most dramatic scenery in the region; at times the route channels through soaring rock canyons. The road sweeps down from the pass to the village of Buttermere, sandwiched between its namesake lake and Crummock Water at the foot of high, craggy fells. Just beyond the pass toward Buttermere, Syke Farm sells fantastic ice cream. To the north, Newlands Pass is an equally spectacular route back to Keswick.

Scafell Pike. England's highest mountain at 3,210 feet, Scafell (pronounced *scar*-fell) Pike is visible from Seatoller. One route up the mountain, for experienced walkers, is from the hamlet of Seathwaite, a mile south of Seatoller.

WHERE TO STAY

$$ HOTEL 🏨 **Langstrath Country Inn.** In the tranquil hamlet of Stonethwaite, the welcoming Langstrath was originally built as a miner's cottage in the 16th century but has expanded into a spacious inn with chunky wooden tables and logs burning on a slate open fire. **Pros:** great walks right out the door; children welcomed and looked after; wonderfully peaceful. **Cons:** few other places to eat or shop nearby. [$] *Rooms from: £106* ✉ *Off B5289, Stonethwaite* ☎ *017687/77239* 🌐 *www.thelangstrath.com* 🛏 *8 rooms* 🕒 *Closed Dec. and Jan.* 🍴 *Breakfast.*

CAMBRIDGE AND
EAST ANGLIA

WELCOME TO CAMBRIDGE AND EAST ANGLIA

TOP REASONS TO GO

★ **Cambridge:** A walk through the colleges is grand, but the best views of the university's colleges and immaculate lawns (and some famous bridges) are from a punt on the river.

★ **Constable country:** In the area where Constable grew up, you can walk or row downstream from Dedham straight into the setting of one of the English landscape painter's masterpieces at Flatford Mill.

★ **Ely Cathedral:** The highlight of Ely, north of Cambridge, is its beautiful cathedral, known for its octagonal Lantern Tower.

★ **Lavenham:** This medieval town is the most comely of the tight-knit cluster of places that did well from the wool trade, with architecture including timber-frame houses gnarled into crookedness by age.

★ **Aldeburgh:** A trip to Suffolk isn't complete without a stop by the seaside. Aldeburgh fills the bill and is also home to the famous Aldeburgh Festival, which includes music and more.

1 Cambridge. The home of the ancient university is East Anglia's liveliest town. The city center is perfect for ambling around the colleges, museums, and King's College Chapel, one of England's greatest monuments.

2 Central Suffolk. The towns and villages within a short drive of Cambridge remain largely unspoiled. Long Melford and Lavenham preserve their rich historical flavors.

3 The Suffolk Coast. Idyllic villages such as Dedham and Flatford form the center of what's been dubbed "Constable Country," while the nearby Suffolk Coast includes such atmospheric seaside towns as Aldeburgh.

TO LINCOLN

The Wash

Spalding

Sutton Crosses

A17

A149

LINCOLNSHIRE

King's Lynn

Stamford

Wisbech

A141

Downham Market

Peterborough

CAMBRIDGESHIRE

Chatteris

A1(M)

A10

Ely

Huntingdon

A142

A14

A1

A11

Newmarket

1

Cambridge

M11

Duxford

Audley End Home & Gardens

ESSEX

M11

Braintree

A120

A131

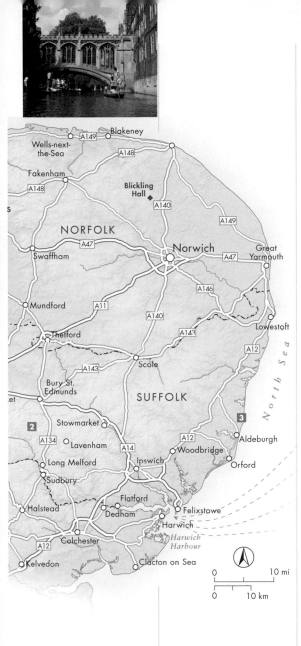

GETTING ORIENTED

East Anglia, in southeastern England, can be divided into distinct areas for sightseeing: the central area surrounding the ancient university city of Cambridge and including Ely, with its magnificent cathedral rising out of the flatlands; the towns of inland Suffolk; and the Suffolk Heritage Coast, with its historic small towns and villages.

10

Updated by
Jack Jewers

One of those beautiful English inconsistencies, East Anglia has no spectacular mountains or rivers to disturb the storied, quiet land, full of rural delights. Occupying an area of southeastern England that pushes out into the North Sea, its counties of Essex, Norfolk, Suffolk, and Cambridgeshire feel cut off from the pulse of the country. Among its highlights is Cambridge, a lovely and ancient university city.

In times past East Anglia was one of the most important centers of power in northern Europe. There were major Roman settlements here, and the medieval wool trade brought huge prosperity to places such as tiny Lavenham. Thanks to its relative lack of thoroughfares and canals, however, East Anglia was mercifully untouched by the Industrial Revolution. The area around Cambridge and Ely is set in an eerie, flat landscape that was once such treacherous marsh—or "fenland"—that the people had to cross the landscape on foot. A medieval term, "the fens," is still used informally to describe the surrounding region.

The area is rich in idyllic, quintessentially English villages: sleepy, sylvan settlements in the midst of otherwise deserted lowlands. Cambridge, with its ancient university, is the area's most famous draw. Notable buildings include the incomparable cathedral at Ely and one of the finest Gothic buildings in Europe, King's College Chapel in Cambridge.

And yet, despite all of these treasures, the real joy of exploring East Anglia is making your own discoveries. Spend a couple of days exploring the hidden byways of the fens, or just taking in the subtle beauties of the many England-like-it-looks-in-the-movies villages. If you find yourself driving down a small country lane and an old church or mysterious, ivy-covered ruin peeks out from behind the trees, give in to your curiosity and look inside. Such hidden places are East Anglia's best-kept secret.

CAMBRIDGE AND EAST ANGLIA PLANNER

WHEN TO GO

Summer and late spring are the best times to visit East Anglia. Late fall and winter can be cold, windy, and rainy, though this is England's driest region and crisp, frosty days here are beautiful. You can't visit most of the Cambridge colleges during exam period (late May to mid-June), and the competition for hotel rooms heats up during graduation week (late June). The Aldeburgh Festival of Music and the Arts, one of the biggest events on the British classical music calendar, takes place in June.

PLANNING YOUR TIME

Cambridge is the region's most interesting city, and ideally you should allow two days to absorb its various sights. (In a pinch you could do it as a day trip from London, but only with an early start and a good pair of walking shoes.) You could easily use the city as a base for exploring Ely Cathedral and Lavenham, although you'll also find good accommodations in the latter. If you're exploring inland around Suffolk and the coast, you can overnight in those towns.

GETTING HERE AND AROUND

BUS TRAVEL

National Express buses serve the region from London's Victoria Coach Station. The average travel time is 3 hours to Cambridge.

Long-distance buses are useful for reaching the region and traveling between its major centers, but for smaller hops, local buses are best. First and Stagecoach buses cover the Cambridge area. Traveline can answer public transportation questions.

Bus Contacts First ☎ *0845/410–4444* ⊕ *www.firstgroup.com.* **National Express East Anglia** ☎ *0845/600–7245* ⊕ *www.nationalexpresseastanglia. com.* **Stagecoach** ☎ *0871/834–0010* ⊕ *www.stagecoachbus.com/cambridge.* **Traveline** ☎ *0871/200–2233* ⊕ *www.traveline.org.uk.*

CAR TRAVEL

If you're driving from London, Cambridge (54 miles) is off M11. A12 from London goes through east Suffolk via Ipswich. East Anglia has few fast main roads besides those mentioned here. Once off the A roads, traveling within the region often means taking country lanes that have many twists and turns, and going even just a few miles can take much longer than you think.

TRAIN TRAVEL

The entire region is well served by trains from London's Liverpool Street and King's Cross stations. The quality and convenience of these services varies enormously, however. Cambridge trains leave from King's Cross and Liverpool Street, take around one hour, and cost between £15 and £22. A good way to save money on local trains in East Anglia is to buy an Anglia Plus Ranger Pass. It costs £17 for one day or £34 for three days, and allows unlimited rail travel in Norfolk, Suffolk, and part of Cambridgeshire. You can add up to four kids for an extra £2 each.

10

Train Contacts **East Midlands Trains** ☎ *0845/712–5678*
⊕ *www.eastmidlandstrains.co.uk.* **First Capital Connect** ☎ *0845/026–4700*
⊕ *www.firstcapitalconnect.co.uk.* **Greater Anglia** ☎ *0845/600–7245*
⊕ *www.greateranglia.co.uk.* **National Rail Enquiries** ☎ *0845/748–4950*
⊕ *www.nationalrail.co.uk.*

RESTAURANTS

In summer the coast gets so packed with people that reservations are essential at restaurants. Getting something to eat at other than regular mealtime hours isn't always possible in small towns; head to cafés if you want a midmorning or after-lunch snack. Look for area specialties, such as crab, lobster, duckling, Norfolk black turkey, hare, and partridge, on menus around the region.

HOTELS

The region is full of centuries-old, half-timber inns with rooms full of roaring fires and cozy bars. Bed-and-breakfasts are a good option in pricey Cambridge. It's always busy in Cambridge and along the coast in summer, so reserve well in advance. *Hotel reviews have been shortened. For full information, visit Fodors.com.*

WHAT IT COSTS IN POUNDS			
$	**$$**	**$$$**	**$$$$**
Restaurants	under £15	£15–£19	£20–£25	over £25
Hotels	under £100	£100–£160	£161–£220	over £220

Restaurant prices are the average cost of a main course at dinner or, if dinner isn't served, at lunch. Hotel prices are the lowest cost of a standard double room in high season, including 20% V.A.T.

VISITOR INFORMATION

East of England Tourism ✉ *Dettingen House, Dettingen Way, Bury St. Edmunds* ☎ *0333/3204202* ⊕ *www.visiteastofengland.com.*

CAMBRIDGE

Fodor's Choice ★ With the spires of its university buildings framed by towering trees and expansive meadows, its medieval streets and passages enhanced by gardens and riverbanks, the city of Cambridge is among the loveliest in England. The city predates the Roman occupation of Britain, but there's confusion over exactly how the university was founded. The most widely accepted story is that it was established in 1209 by a pair of scholars from Oxford, who left their university in protest over the wrongful execution of a colleague for murder.

Keep in mind there's no recognizable campus: the scattered colleges *are* the university. The town reveals itself only slowly, filled with tiny gardens, ancient courtyards, imposing classic buildings, alleyways that lead past medieval churches, and wisteria-hung facades. Perhaps the best views are from the Backs, the green parkland that extends along the River Cam behind several colleges. This sweeping openness, a result of the larger size of the colleges and from the lack of industrialization in the city center, is what distinguishes Cambridge from Oxford. This university town may be beautiful, but it's no museum. Well-preserved medieval buildings sit cheek-by-jowl next to the latest in modern architecture—the William Gates building, which houses Cambridge University's computer laboratory, is one such example. The student body, one-fifth of the city's 109,000 inhabitants, dominates this growing city, while the architecture, parks, gardens, and quietly flowing River Cam enhance its beauty.

GETTING HERE AND AROUND

Good bus (three hours) and train (one hour) services connect London and Cambridge. The long-distance bus terminal is on Drummer Street, very close to Emmanuel and Christ's colleges. Several local buses connect the station with central Cambridge, including the frequent Citi 7 and 8 services, although any bus listing City Centre or Emmanuel Street among its stops will do. The journey takes just under 10 minutes. If you're driving, don't attempt to venture very far into the center—parking is scarce and pricey. The center is amenable to explorations on foot, or you could join the throng by renting a bicycle.

Stagecoach sells Dayrider (£3.70) tickets for all-day bus travel within Cambridge, and Megarider tickets (£12.50) for seven days of travel within the city. You can extend these to cover the whole county of Cambridgeshire (£5.70 and £22.50, respectively). Buy any of them from the driver.

TOURS City Sightseeing operates open-top bus tours of Cambridge—the Backs, the colleges, the Imperial War Museum in Duxford, and the Grafton Centre, a covered shopping area in central Cambridge. Tours can be joined at marked bus stops in the city. Tickets are £13. Also ask the tourist office about tours.

TIMING

In summer and over the Easter and Christmas holidays, Cambridge is devoid of students, its heart and soul. To see the city in full swing, visit from October through June. In summer there are arts and music festivals, notably the Strawberry Fair and the Arts Festival (both June) and the Folk Festival (late July to early August). The May Bumps, intercollegiate boat races, are, confusingly, held the first week of June. This is also the month when students celebrate the end of exam season, so expect to encounter some boisterous nightlife.

ESSENTIALS

Visitor and Tour Information Cambridge University ☎ *01223/337733* ⊕ *www.cam.ac.uk.* **City Sightseeing** ✉ *Cambridge Train Station, Station Rd.* ☎ *01223/423578* ⊕ *www.city-sightseeing.com.* **Visit Cambridge** ✉ *Peas Hill* ☎ *0871/226–8006* ⊕ *www.visitcambridge.org.*

10

EXPLORING

Exploring the city means, in large part, exploring the university. Each of the 25 oldest colleges is built around a series of courts, or quadrangles, framing manicured, velvety lawns. Because students and fellows (faculty) live and work in these courts, access is sometimes restricted, and at *all* times you're asked not to picnic in the quadrangles.

Cricket, anyone? Audley End, a 17th-century house, serves as an idyllic backdrop for a cricket match.

Visitors aren't normally allowed into college buildings other than chapels, dining halls, and some libraries; some colleges charge admission for certain buildings. Public visiting hours vary from college to college, depending on the time of year, and it's best to call or to check with the city tourist office. Colleges close to visitors during the main exam time, late May to mid-June. Term time (when classes are in session) means roughly October to December, January to March, and April to June; summer term, or vacation, runs from July to September. ■ **TIP→ Bring a pair of binoculars as some college buildings have highly intricate details, such as the spectacular ceiling at King's College Chapel.** When the colleges are open, the best way to gain access is to join a walking tour led by an official Blue Badge guide—many areas are off-limits unless you do. The two-hour tours (£14 to £18.50) leave up to four times daily from the city tourist office. The other traditional view of the colleges is gained from a punt—the boats propelled by pole on the River Cam.

TOP ATTRACTIONS

OFF THE BEATEN PATH

Audley End House and Gardens. A famous example of early-17th-century architecture, Audley End was once owned by Charles II, who bought it as a convenient place to break his journey on the way to the Newmarket races. Although the palatial building was remodeled in the 18th and 19th centuries, the Jacobean style is still on display in the magnificent Great Hall. You can walk in the park, landscaped by Capability Brown in the 18th century, and the fine Victorian gardens. Two exhibits focus on the lives of domestic servants in the late 19th century. The Service Wing lets you look "below stairs" at the kitchen, scullery (where fish were descaled and chickens were plucked), and game larder (where pheasants, partridges, and rabbits were hung), while the Stable Yard gives kids the chance to see old saddles and tack, and don Victorian riding costumes. The house is in Saffron Waldon, 14 miles south of Cambridge. ✉ *Off London Rd., Saffron Waldon* ☎ *01799/522842* ⊕ *www.english-heritage. org.uk* ☞ *£13; Service Wing, Stable Yard, and gardens only £9* ☉ *House: Apr.–Sept., Wed.–Sun. noon–5; Oct., Wed.–Sun. 10–4. Service Wing, Stable Yard, and gardens: Apr.–June, Wed.–Sun. 10–6; July–Sept., daily 10–6; Oct., Wed.–Sun. 10–5; Nov.–Mar, weekends 10–4.*

OFF THE
BEATEN
PATH

Ely Cathedral. Sixteen miles north of Cambridge lies Ely, a modest town with one huge attraction: its magnificent cathedral. Known affectionately as the Ship of the Fens, Ely Cathedral can be seen for miles, towering above the flat landscape on one of the few ridges in the fens. In 1083 the Normans began work on the cathedral, which stands on the site of a Benedictine monastery founded by the Anglo-Saxon princess Etheldreda in 673. In the center of the cathedral you see a marvel of medieval construction—the unique octagonal **Lantern Tower,** a sort of stained-glass skylight of colossal proportions, built to replace the central tower that collapsed in 1322. The cathedral's **West Tower** is even taller; the view from the top (if you can manage the 288 steps) is spectacular. Tours of both towers are daily between April and October and on weekends between November and March. The cathedral is also notable for its 248-foot-long **nave,** with its simple Norman arches and Victorian painted ceiling. Much of the decorative carving of the 14th-century **Lady Chapel** was defaced during the Reformation (mostly by knocking off the heads of the statuary), but enough traces remain to show its original beauty.

The cathedral houses a superior **Stained Glass Museum,** up a flight of 42 steps. Exhibits trace the history of stained glass from medieval to modern times. Ely Cathedral is a popular location for films; it doubled for Westminster Abbey in *The King's Speech* (2010). Guided tours begin daily at 10:45, 1, and 2, with an additional tour at 3 on weekends and also weekdays between April and October. ■**TIP➔ Always call ahead about tours, as times are subject to change.** To reach Ely from Cambridge, take A10 north; the drive takes half an hour. Alternatively the 9 and 12 buses leave twice an hour from the Drummer Street bus station in Cambridge; trains leave three times an hour and take 15 minutes. ✉ *The Gallery, Ely* ☎ *01353/667735* ⊕ *www.elycathedral.org* ☞ *£7 including tour; with Octagon Tower or West Tower £8.50; with Stained Glass Museum £10.20; combined ticket £16.20* ☉ *May–Oct., daily 7–6:30; Nov.–Apr., Mon.–Sat. 7:30–6:30, Sun. 7:30–5:30.*

10

Emmanuel College. The master hand of architect Christopher Wren (1632–1723) is evident throughout much of Cambridge, particularly at Emmanuel, built on the site of a Dominican friary, where he designed the chapel and colonnade. A stained-glass window in the chapel has a likeness of John Harvard, founder of Harvard University, who studied here. The college, founded in 1584, was an early center of Puritan learning; a number of the Pilgrims were Emmanuel alumni, and they remembered their alma mater in naming Cambridge, Massachusetts. ✉ *St. Andrew's St.* ☎ *01223/334200* ⊕ *www.emma.cam.ac.uk* ☞ *Free* ☉ *Daily 9–6, except exam period.*

Fodor'sChoice
★

Fitzwilliam Museum. In a Classical Revival building renowned for its grand Corinthian portico, the Fitzwilliam, founded by the seventh viscount Fitzwilliam of Merrion in 1816, has one of Britain's most outstanding collections of art and antiquities. Highlights include two large Titians, an extensive collection of French impressionist painting, and many paintings by Matisse and Picasso. The opulent interior displays its treasures to marvelous effect, from Egyptian pieces such as inch-high figurines and painted coffins, to sculptures from the Chinese Han dynasty of the 3rd century BC. Other collections of note here are a fine assortment of medieval illuminated manuscripts and a fascinating room full of armor and muskets. ⊠ *Trumpington St.* ☎ *01223/332900* ⊕ *www.fitzmuseum.cam.ac.uk* ⊠ *Free* ☉ *Tues.–Sat. 10–5, Sun. noon–5.*

Great St. Mary's. Known as the "university church," Great St. Mary's has its origins in the 11th century, although the current building dates from 1478. The main reason to visit is to climb the 113-foot tower, which has a superb view over the colleges and marketplace. Also here is the Michaelhouse Centre, a small café, gallery, and performing arts venue with frequent free lunchtime concerts. Guided tours must be booked in advance. ⊠ *Market Hill, King's Parade* ☎ *01223/462914* ⊕ *www.gsm. cam.ac.uk* ⊠ *Free, tower £3.50, guided tours £10* ☉ *May–Aug., Mon.– Sat. 9:30–5, Sun. 12:30–5; Sept.–Apr., Mon.–Sat. 9:30–4, Sun. 12:30–4.*

**OFF THE
BEATEN
PATH**

Imperial War Museum Duxford. Europe's leading aviation museum houses a remarkable collection of 180 aircraft from Europe and the United States. The former airfield is effectively a complex of several museums under one banner. The **Land Warfare Hall** features tanks and other military vehicles. The striking **American Air Museum**, honoring the 30,000 Americans killed in action flying from Britain during World War II, contains the largest display of American fighter planes outside the U.S. **AirSpace** contains a vast array of military and civil aircraft in a 3-acre hangar. Directly underneath is the **Airborne Assault Museum**, which chronicles the history of airborne forces, such as the British Parachute Regiment, which played a pivotal role in the Normandy Landings. There are also hangars where you can watch restoration work on World War II planes and exhibitions on maritime warfare and the Battle of Britain. ⊠ *A505, Duxford* ☎ *01223/835000* ⊕ *duxford.iwm.org.uk* ⊠ *£17.50* ☉ *Mid-Mar.–late Oct., daily 10–6; late Oct.–mid-Mar., daily 10–4. Last admission 1 hr before closing.*

King's College. Founded in 1441 by Henry VI, King's College has a magnificent late-15th-century chapel that is its most famous landmark. Other notable architecture is the neo-Gothic Porters' Lodge, facing King's Parade, which was a relatively recent addition in the 1830s, and the classical Gibbs building. ■ **TIP→ Head down to the river, from where the panorama of college and chapel is one of the university's most photographed views.** Past students of King's College include the novelist E.M. Forster, the economist John Maynard Keynes, and the World War I poet Rupert Brooke. ⊠ *King's Parade* ☎ *01223/331100* ⊕ *www.kings. cam.ac.uk* ⊠ *£7.50, includes chapel* ☉ *Term time, weekdays 9:30–3:30, Sat. 9:30–3:15, Sun. 1:15–2:30; out of term, daily 9:30–4:30.*

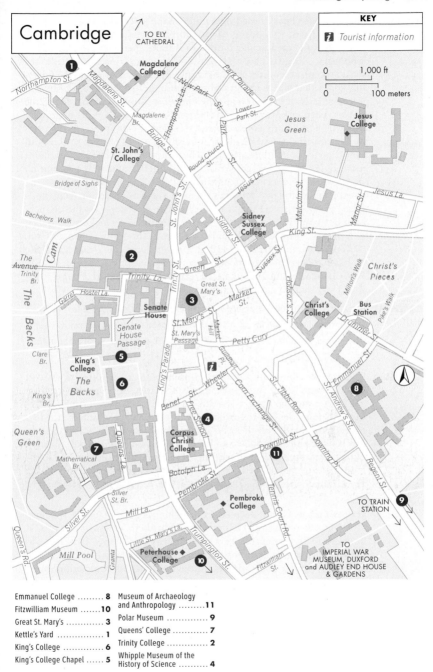

Cambridge

TO ELY
CATHEDRAL

KEY

🛈 *Tourist information*

0   1,000 ft

0   100 meters

Fodor's Choice
★

King's College Chapel. Based on Sainte-Chapelle, the 13th-century royal chapel in Paris, this house of worship is perhaps the most glorious flowering of Perpendicular Gothic in Britain. Henry VI, the king after whom the college is named, oversaw the work. From the outside, the most prominent features are the massive flying buttresses and the finger-like spires that line the length of the building. Inside, the most obvious impression is of great space—the chapel was once described as "the noblest barn in Europe"—and of light flooding in from its huge windows. The brilliantly colored bosses (carved panels at the intersections of the roof ribs) are particularly intense, although hard to see without binoculars. An exhibition in the chantries, or side chapels, explains more about the chapel's construction. Behind the altar is *The Adoration of the Magi,* an enormous painting by Peter Paul Rubens. ■ TIP→ The chapel, unlike the rest of King's College, stays open during exam periods. Every Christmas Eve a festival of carols is sung by the chapel's famous choir. To compete for the small number of tickets available, join the line at the college's main entrance early—doors open at 7 am. ⊠ *King's Parade* ☎ *01223/331212* ⊕ *www.kings.cam.ac.uk* 🖃 *£7.50, includes college and grounds* ☉ *Term time, weekdays 9:30–3:30, Sat. 9:30–3:15, Sun. 1:15–2:30; out of term, daily 9:30–4:30. Chapel occasionally closed for services and private events; call or check online.*

▌QUICK BITES

Pickerel Inn. The 600-year-old Pickerel Inn, one of the city's oldest pubs, makes for a good stop for an afternoon pint of real ale and a bowl of doorstop-sized potato wedges. Watch for the low beams. ⊠ *30 Magdalene St.* ☎ *01223/355068.*

Fodor's Choice
★

Polar Museum. Beautifully designed, this museum at the university's Scott Polar Research Institute chronicles the history of polar exploration. There's a particular emphasis on the British expeditions of the 20th century, including the ill-fated attempt by Robert Falcon Scott to be the first to reach the South Pole in 1912. Norwegian explorer Roald Amundsen reached the pole first; Scott and his men perished on the return journey, but his story became legendary. There are also collections devoted to the indigenous people of northern Canada, Greenland, and Alaska. ⊠ *Scott Polar Research Institute, Lensfield Rd.* ☎ *01223/336540* ⊕ *www.spri. cam.ac.uk/museum* 🖃 *Free* ☉ *Tues.–Sat. 10–4.*

Queens' College. One of the most eye-catching colleges, Queens' is named after Margaret, queen of Henry VI, and Elizabeth, queen of Edward IV. Founded in 1448, the college is tucked away on Queens' Lane, next to the wide lawns that lead down from King's College to the Backs. The secluded "cloister court" looks untouched since its completion in the 1540s. Queens' masterpiece is the **Mathematical Bridge,** the original version of which is said to have been built without any fastenings. The current bridge (1902) is securely bolted. The college is closed to visitors late May to late June. ⊠ *Queens' La.* ☎ *01223/335511* ⊕ *www. quns.cam.ac.uk* 🖃 *£2.50* ☉ *Mid-Mar.–mid-May and late June–Sept., daily 10–4:30; Oct., weekdays 2–4, weekends 10–4:30; Nov.–mid-Mar., daily 2–4.*

Trinity College. Founded in 1546 by Henry VIII, Trinity replaced a 14th-century educational foundation and is the largest college in either Cambridge or Oxford, with nearly 700 undergraduates. In the 17th-century great court, with its massive gatehouse, is **Great Tom**, a giant clock that strikes each hour with high and low notes. The college's greatest masterpiece is Christopher Wren's **library**, colonnaded and seemingly constructed with as much light as stone. Among the things you can see here is A. A. Milne's handwritten manuscript of *The House at Pooh Corner.* Trinity alumni include Isaac Newton, William Thackeray, Lord Byron, Alfred Tennyson, and 31 Nobel Prize winners. ⊠ *St. John's St.* ☎ *01223/338400* ⊕ *www.trin.cam.ac.uk* 🏷 *£1* ☉ *College and chapel: daily 10–4, except exam period and event days. Great court and library: weekdays noon–2, Sat. in term time 10:30–12:30.*

WORTH NOTING

Kettle's Yard. Originally a private house owned by a former curator of London's Tate galleries, Kettle's Yard contains a fine collection of 20th-century art, sculpture, furniture, and decorative arts, including works by Henry Moore, Barbara Hepworth, and Henri Gaudier-Brzeska. A separate gallery shows changing exhibitions of modern art and crafts, and weekly concerts and lectures attract an eclectic mix of enthusiasts. Ring the bell for admission. ⊠ *Castle St.* ☎ *01223/748100* ⊕ *www. kettlesyard.co.uk* 🏷 *Free* ☉ *House: Apr.–late Sept., Tues.–Sun. 2–5; Oct.–Mar., Tues.–Sun. 2–4. Gallery: Tues.–Sun. 1–5.*

Museum of Archaeology and Anthropology. The university maintains some fine museums in its research halls on Downing Street—the wonder is that they're not better known to visitors. At the recently renovated Museum of Archaeology and Anthropology, highlights include an array of objects brought back from Captain Cook's pioneering voyages to the Pacific; Roman and medieval-era British artifacts; and the oldest human-made tools ever discovered, from the African expeditions of British archaeologist Louis Leakey (1903–1972). ⊠ *Downing St.* ☎ *01223/333516* ⊕ *maa.cam.ac.uk* 🏷 *Free* ☉ *Tues.–Sat. 10:30–4:30.*

Whipple Museum of the History of Science. This rather delightful, dusty old cupboard of a museum contains all manner of scientific artifacts, instruments and doodads from the medieval period to the early 20th century. Most fun is the section on astronomy, including a beautiful 18th-century grand orrary—an elaborate three-dimensional model of the solar system, minus the planets that had yet to be discovered at the time. ⊠ *Free School La.* ☎ *01223/330906* ⊕ *www.hos.cam.ac.uk/ whipple* 🏷 *Free* ☉ *Weekdays 12:30–4:30.*

10

WHERE TO EAT

$ ✕ **Jamie's Italian.** Run by celebrity chef Jamie Oliver, this is one of the
ITALIAN busiest restaurants in Cambridge. In truth, the long queues probably have more to do with his star power and the no-reservations policy, but the food also deserves praise. The menu is a combination of authentic Italian flavors and modern variations on the classics; you could opt for the pasta *arrabiata,* made with bread crumbs and fiery peppers, or fillet of sea bream with garlic, wine, capers, and plum tomatoes. The

gorgeous building, a former library, is an attraction in itself. The atmosphere is relaxed and casual, and the prices are lower than you'd expect. [$] *Average main: £14* ✉ *Old Library, Wheeler St.* ☎ *01223/654094* 🌐 *www.jamieoliver.com/italian* ✍ *Reservations essential.*

$$ SEAFOOD 🍴 **Loch Fyne.** Part of a Scottish chain that harvests its own oysters, this airy, casual place across from the Fitzwilliam Museum is deservedly popular. The mussels and salmon are fresh and well prepared, and line-caught tuna is served with a mint-and-caper salsa. Try the smokey, sweet Bradan Rost smoked salmon flavored with Scotch whisky if it's on the menu. The place is open for breakfast, lunch, and dinner. [$] *Average main: £15* ✉ *37 Trumpington St.* ☎ *01223/362433* 🌐 *www.lochfyne-restaurants.com.*

$$$$ FRENCH 🍴 **Midsummer House.** Beside the River Cam on the edge of Midsummer Common, this gray-brick building holds an elegant restaurant with a comfortable conservatory and a handful of tables under fruit trees in a lush, secluded garden. Fixed-price menus for lunch and dinner include innovative French and Mediterranean dishes. Choices might include roasted sea bass or venison with blue cheese and cocoa nibs. [$] *Average main: £40* ✉ *Midsummer Common* ☎ *01223/369299* 🌐 *www.midsummerhouse.co.uk* ✍ *Reservations essential* ⏲ *Closed Sun. and Mon. No lunch Tues.*

$$ BRITISH 🍴 **The Oak.** This charming, intimate restaurant has fast become a local favorite. It's near an unpromisingly busy intersection, but the friendliness of the staff and classic bistro food more than make up for it. Typical mains include linguini with crab and spiced tomato sauce, or rib-eye steak with truffle butter and fries. Ask to be seated in the lovely walled garden if the weather's fine. [$] *Average main: £15* ✉ *6 Lensfield Rd.* ☎ *01223/323361* 🌐 *www.theoakbistro.co.uk.*

$$$$ BRITISH 🍴 **Restaurant 22 Chesterton Road.** Pretty stained-glass windows separate this sophisticated little restaurant from bustling Chesterton Road. The setting, in a terrace of houses, is low-key, but the food is creative and eye-catching. The fixed-price menu changes monthly and features such dishes as pork belly with bubble and squeak (a traditional dish made of fried potatoes and onions), and beef and chorizo stew with rosemary dumplings. [$] *Average main: £33* ✉ *22 Chesterton Rd.* ☎ *01223/351880* 🌐 *www.restaurant22.co.uk* ⏲ *Closed Sun. and Mon. No lunch.*

$$ MODERN BRITISH 🍴 **River Bar & Kitchen.** Across the river from Magdalene College, this popular waterfront bar and grill serves delicious steak and burgers, plus specialties such as lobster macaroni and cheese and blackened salmon with soy and ginger greens. Light lunches are served in the afternoon, and the evening cocktail list is small but elegant. Try the French 75, which is gin with lemon juice, sugar, and sparkling wine. [$] *Average main: £17* ✉ *Quayside, Thompsons Ln., off Bridge St.* ☎ *01223/307030* 🌐 *www.riverbarsteakhouse.com* ✍ *Reservations essential.*

$$ ITALIAN 🍴 **Three Horseshoes.** This early-19th-century pub-restaurant in a thatched cottage has an elegant dining space in the conservatory and more casual tables in the airy bar. The tempting, beautifully presented, and carefully sourced dishes are Modern Italian with a British accent. Appetizers might include beetroot risotto with creamed goat cheese and orange oil, and among the main courses you might find beef shin with risotto,

or haunch of venison with blackened leeks and *dauphinoise* potatoes. The wine list is enormous and predominantly Italian, but there are also some good New World choices. It's 5 miles west of Cambridge, about a 10-minute taxi ride. [$] *Average main: £18* ✉ *High St., Madingley* ☎ *01954/210221* 🌐 *www.threehorseshoesmadingley.co.uk.*

WHERE TO STAY

There aren't many hotels downtown. For more (and cheaper) options, consider one of the numerous guesthouses on the arterial roads and in the suburbs. These average around £30 to £80 per person per night and can be booked through the tourist information center.

$$ HOTEL 🏨 **DoubleTree by Hilton.** This modern establishment makes the most of its peaceful riverside location, and many rooms have sweeping views of the surrounding area. **Pros:** central position; good facilities and service; spacious rooms. **Cons:** price fluctuates wildly over summer season. [$] *Rooms from: £150* ✉ *Granta Pl. and Mill La.* ☎ *01223/259988* 🌐 *www.doubletreecambridge.com* 🛏 *118 rooms, 4 suites* 🍴 *Multiple meal plans.*

$$ B&B/INN Fodor's Choice ★ 🏨 **Duke House.** Guest rooms at this beautifully converted town house (home of the Duke of Gloucester when he was a student) look like they've been copied from the pages of a lifestyle magazine. **Pros:** beautiful house; great location; suites are quite spacious. **Cons:** gets booked up fast; cheaper rooms are small. [$] *Rooms from: £130* ✉ *1 Victoria St.* ☎ *01223/314773* 🌐 *www.dukehousecambridge.co.uk* 🛏 *4 rooms* 🍴 *Breakfast.*

$ B&B/INN 🏨 **Finches Bed and Breakfast.** Although it's in a rather inauspicious building, the diminutive Finches is a well-run B&B with prices that make it an excellent value. **Pros:** cheerful staff; quiet location; good level of service. **Cons:** away from the action; no tubs in bathrooms; no credit cards. [$] *Rooms from: £70* ✉ *144 Thornton Rd.* ☎ *01223/276653* 🌐 *www.finches-bnb.com* 🛏 *3 rooms* 💳 *No credit cards* 🍴 *Breakfast.*

$$ HOTEL 🏨 **Regent Hotel.** A rare small hotel in central Cambridge, this handsome Georgian town house has wooden sash windows that look out over a tree-lined park called Parker's Piece. **Pros:** good view from top rooms; close to bars and restaurants. **Cons:** no parking; a tad scruffy; disappointing breakfasts. [$] *Rooms from: £102* ✉ *41 Regent St.* ☎ *01223/351470* 🌐 *www.regenthotel.co.uk* 🛏 *22 rooms* 🍴 *Breakfast.*

$$$ HOTEL Fodor's Choice ★ 🏨 **The Varsity.** This stylish boutique hotel with an adjoining spa has wide windows that flood the place with light. **Pros:** beautiful location; gorgeous views; stylish design. **Cons:** not such great views in the cheap rooms. [$] *Rooms from: £165* ✉ *Thompson's La., off Bridge St.* ☎ *01223/306030* 🌐 *www.thevarsityhotel.co.uk* 🛏 *48 rooms* 🍴 *Multiple meal plans.*

$ B&B/INN 🏨 **Warkworth House.** The location of this sweet B&B could hardly be better, as the Fitzwilliam Museum and several of Cambridge's colleges are within a 15-minute walk. **Pros:** excellent location; lovely hosts; some free parking. **Cons:** few frills. [$] *Rooms from: £80* ✉ *Warkworth Terr.* ☎ *01223/363682* 🌐 *www.warkworthhouse.co.uk* 🛏 *5 rooms* 🍴 *Breakfast.*

NIGHTLIFE AND THE ARTS

NIGHTLIFE

The city's pubs provide the mainstay of Cambridge's nightlife and shouldn't be missed.

Eagle. This 16th-century coaching inn with a cobbled courtyard has lost none of its old-time character. It also played a minor role in scientific history when on February 28, 1953, a pair of excited Cambridge scientists announced to a roomful of rather surprised lunchtime patrons that they'd just discovered the secret of life: DNA. A plaque outside commemorates the event. ⊠ *8 Benet St.* ☎ *01223/505020.*

Fort St. George. Overlooking the university boathouses, Fort St. George gets the honors for riverside views. ⊠ *Midsummer Common* ☎ *01223/354327.*

Free Press. A favorite of student rowers, this small pub has an excellent selection of traditional ales. ⊠ *7 Prospect Row* ☎ *01223/368337* ⊕ *www.freepresspub.co.uk.*

THE ARTS

CONCERTS Cambridge supports its own symphony orchestra, and regular musical events are held in many colleges, especially those with large chapels.

Corn Exchange. The beautifully restored Corn Exchange presents classical and rock concerts, stand-up comedy, musicals, opera, and ballet. ⊠ *Wheeler St.* ☎ *01223/357851* ⊕ *www.cornex.co.uk.*

King's College Chapel. During regular terms, King's College Chapel has evensong services Monday through Saturday at 5:30, Sunday at 3:30. ■ TIP→ Your best chance of seeing the full choir is Thursday to Sunday. ⊠ *King's Parade* ☎ *01223/769340* ⊕ *www.kings.cam.ac.uk.*

THEATER **ADC Theatre.** Home of the famous *Cambridge Footlights Revue*, the ADC Theatre hosts mainly student and fringe theater productions. ⊠ *Park St.* ☎ *01223/300085* ⊕ *www.adctheatre.com.*

Arts Theatre. The city's main repertory theater, the Arts Theatre was built by economist John Maynard Keynes in 1936 and supports a full program of plays and concerts. It also has a good ground-floor bar and two restaurants. ⊠ *6 St. Edward's Passage* ☎ *01223/503333* ⊕ *www. cambridgeartstheatre.com.*

SHOPPING

Head to the specialty shops in the center of town, especially in and around Rose Crescent and King's Parade. Bookshops, including antiquarian stores, are Cambridge's pride and joy.

All Saints Garden Art & Craft Market. This market displays the wares of local artists outdoors on Saturday. It's also open Friday from June to August and Wednesday to Friday in December (weather permitting). ⊠ *Trinity St.* ⊕ *www.cambridge-art-craft.co.uk.*

Ryder & Amies. Need a straw boater? This shop carries official university wear, from hoodies to ties to cufflinks. ⊠ *22 King's Parade* ☎ *01223/350371* ⊕ *www.ryderamies.co.uk.*

Punting on the Cam

To punt is to maneuver a flat-bottom, wooden, gondolalike boat—in this case, through the shallow River Cam along the verdant Backs behind the colleges of Cambridge. One benefit of this popular activity is that you get a better view of the ivy-covered walls from the water. Mastery of the sport lies in your ability to control a 15-foot pole, used to propel the punt. With a bottle of wine, some food, and a few friends, you may find yourself saying things such as, "It doesn't get any better than this." One piece of advice: if your pole gets stuck, let go. You can use the smaller paddle to go back and retrieve it. Hang on to a stuck punt for too long and you'll probably fall in with it.

The lazier-at-heart may prefer chauffeured punting, with food supplied. Students from Cambridge often do the work, and you get a fairly informative spiel on the colleges. For a romantic evening trip, there are illuminated punts.

One university punting society once published a useful *Bluffer's Guide to Punting* featuring detailed instructions and tips on how to master the art. It has been archived online at ⊕ *duramecho.com/Misc/HowToPunt. html.*

BOOKS **Cambridge University Press Bookshop.** In business since at least 1581, the Cambridge University Press runs this store on Trinity Street. ⊠ *1 Trinity St.* ☎ *01223/333333* ⊕ *www.cambridge.org/uk/bookshop.*

G. David. Near the Arts Theatre, G. David sells antiquarian books. ⊠ *16 St. Edward's Passage* ☎ *01223/354619* ⊕ *www.gdavidbookseller.co.uk.*

Haunted Bookshop. This shop carries a great selection of old, illustrated books and British classics. And apparently it has a ghost, too. ⊠ *9 St. Edward's Passage* ☎ *01223/312913* ⊕ *www.sarahkeybooks.co.uk.*

Heffer's. With many rare and imported books, Heffner's boasts a particularly extensive arts section. ⊠ *20 Trinity St.* ☎ *01223/463200* ⊕ *bookshop.blackwell.co.uk.*

SPORTS AND THE OUTDOORS

BIKING

City Cycle Hire. This shop charges supercheap rates of £7 per half day, £10 per day, and £25 for a week. All bikes are mountain or hybrid bikes. Advance reservations are essential in July and August. ⊠ *61 Newnham Rd.* ☎ *01223/365629* ⊕ *www.citycyclehire.com.*

PUNTING

You can rent punts at several places, notably at Silver Street Bridge–Mill Lane, at Magdalene Bridge, and from outside the Rat and Parrot pub on Thompson's Lane on Jesus Green. Hourly rental costs £15 to £20. Chauffeured punting, usually by a Cambridge student, is also popular. It costs around £12 per person.

Scudamore's Punting Co. This company rents chauffeured and self-drive punts. It also offers various tours, ranging from a Ghost Tour to a Punt

10

& Cream Tea Tour, for about £18.50 per person. Private tours can be booked for the same price, but there's quite a hefty minimum charge. ⊠ *Granta Place, Mill La.* ☎ *01223/359750* ⊕ *www.scudamores.com.*

CENTRAL SUFFOLK

This central area of towns and villages within easy reach of Cambridge is testament to the amazing changeability of the English landscape. Parts of the landscape are comprised of marsh, or fenland, and appear eerie, flat, and apparently endless. Only a few miles south and east into Suffolk, however, all this changes to pastoral landscapes of gently undulating hills and clusters of villages, including pretty Long Melford and Lavenham.

LONG MELFORD

27 miles east of Cambridge,14 miles south of Bury St. Edmunds.

It's easy to see how this village got its name, especially if you walk the full length of its 2-mile-long main street, which gradually broadens to include green squares and trees, and finally opens into the large triangular green on the hill. Long Melford grew rich on its wool trade in the 15th century, and the town's buildings are an appealing mix, mostly Tudor half-timber or Georgian. Many house antiques shops. Away from the main road, Long Melford returns to its resolutely late-medieval roots.

GETTING HERE AND AROUND

Long Melford is just off the main A134. If you're driving from Sudbury, 2 miles to the south, take the smaller B1064; it's much quicker than it looks on the map. There are several bus connections with Sudbury and Bury St. Edmonds. The nearest train station is in Sudbury.

EXPLORING

Holy Trinity Church. This largely 15th-century church, founded by the rich clothiers of Long Melford, stands on a hill at the north end of the village. Close up, the delicate flint flush-work (shaped flints set into a pattern) and huge Perpendicular Gothic windows that take up most of the church's walls have great impact, especially because the nave is 150 feet long. The Clopton Chapel, with an ornate (and incredibly rare) painted medieval ceiling, predates the rest of the church by 150 years. The beautiful Lady Chapel has an unusual cloister; the stone on the wall in the corner is an ancient multiplication table, used when the chapel served as a school in the 17th and 18th centuries. ⊠ *Main St.* ☎ *01787/310845* ⊕ *www.longmelfordchurch.com* ⊗ *Apr.–Oct., daily 10–6; Nov.–Mar., daily 10–5.*

Melford Hall. Distinguished from the outside by its turrets and topiaries, Melford Hall is an Elizabethan house with its original banqueting room, a fair number of 18th-century additions, and pleasant gardens. Much of the porcelain and other fine pieces here come from the *Santissima Trinidad,* a ship loaded with gifts from the emperor of China and bound for Spain that was captured in the 18th century. Children's writer

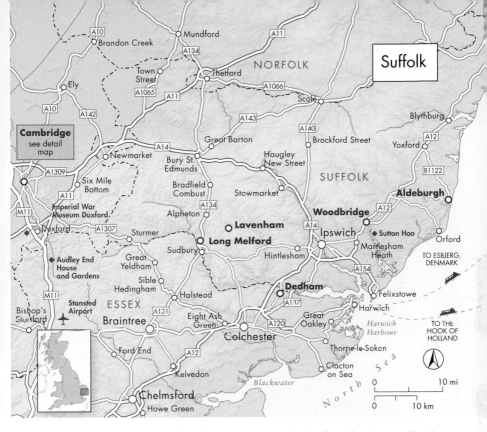

Beatrix Potter, related to the owners, visited often; there's a small collection of Potter memorabilia. ⊠ *Off A134* ☎ *01787/376395* ⊕ *www. nationaltrust.org.uk* 🎫 *£7* ⊗ *Mar.–Oct., Wed.–Sun. 1–5.*

WHERE TO STAY

$ 🏨 **The Bull.** This half-timber Elizabethan building reveals its long history
HOTEL with stone-flagged floors, bowed and twisted oak beams, and heavy antique furniture. **Pros:** historic atmosphere; comfortable bedrooms; friendly staff. **Cons:** minimum stay on summer weekends; popular with wedding parties. $ *Rooms from: £85* ⊠ *Hall St.* ☎ *01787/378494* ⊕ *www.thebull-hotel.com* 🛏 *25 rooms* ⫿⊙⫿ *Some meals.*

LAVENHAM

4 miles northeast of Long Melford.

Fodor'sChoice Virtually unchanged since the height of its wealth in the 15th and 16th
★ centuries, Lavenham is one of the most perfectly preserved examples of a Tudor village in England. The weavers' and wool merchants' houses occupy not just one show street but most of the town. The houses are timber-frame in black oak, the main posts looking as if they could last another 400 years, although their walls are often no longer entirely perpendicular to the ground. The town has many examples of Suffolk

pink buildings, in hues from pale pink to apricot, and many of these house small galleries selling paintings and crafts.

GETTING HERE AND AROUND

Lavenham is on the A1141 and B1071. Take the latter if possible, as it's a prettier drive. There are hourly buses from Sudbury (near Long Melford) and Bury St. Edmunds, and slightly less frequent buses from Ipswich. The nearest train station is in Sudbury.

ESSENTIALS

Visitor Information Lavenham Tourist Information Centre ☒ *Lady St.* ☎ *01787/248207* ⊕ *www.southandheartofsuffolk.org.uk* ☉ *Mid-Mar.–Oct., daily 10–4:45; Nov.–Dec., daily 11–3; Jan.–mid-Mar., weekends 11–3.*

EXPLORING

Church of St. Peter and St. Paul. Set apart from the village on a hill, this grand 15th-century church was built between 1480 and 1520 by cloth merchant Thomas Spring. The height of its tower (141 feet) was meant to surpass those of the neighboring churches—and perhaps to impress rival towns. The rest of the church is perfectly proportioned, with intricately carved wood. ☒ *Church St.* ☎ *01787/247244* ☒ *Free* ☉ *Daily; hrs vary but usually 10–5.*

Lavenham Guildhall. Also known as the Guildhall of Corpus Christi, this higgledy-piggledy timber-frame building dating from 1529 dominates Market Place, an almost flawlessly preserved medieval square. Upstairs is a rather dull exhibition on local agriculture and the wool trade, although looking around the building itself is well worth the admission charge. ☒ *Market Pl.* ☎ *01787/247646* ⊕ *www.nationaltrust.org. uk* ☒ *£4.85* ☉ *Early–late Mar., Wed.–Sun. 11–4; late Mar.–Oct., daily 11–5; Nov., weekends 11–4.*

Little Hall. This timber-frame wool merchant's house (brightly painted on the outside, in the local custom) contains a display showing the building's progress from its creation in the 14th century to its subsequent "modernization" in the 17th century. It also has a beautiful garden at the back. ☒ *Market Pl.* ☎ *01787/247019* ⊕ *www.littlehall. org.uk* ☒ *£3.50* ☉ *Apr.–Oct., Wed., Thurs., and weekends 2–5:30, Mon. 10–1, holidays 11–5:30.*

QUICK BITES

Tickled Pink Tea Room. In a haphazardly leaning house built in 1532, the Tickled Pink Tea Room serves fresh cakes and tea as well as soup and sandwiches. ☒ *17 High St.* ☎ *01787/249517.*

WHERE TO EAT

$$$

FRENCH

Fodor's Choice

★

✕ **Great House.** This excellent "restaurant-with-rooms" on the medieval market square serves Modern British cuisine with a slight French twist; dishes could include pork belly confit or turbot with vanilla butter and a Jerusalem artichoke sauce. The five spacious guestrooms have sloping floors, beamed ceilings, well-appointed bathrooms, and antique furnishings. $ *Average main: £21* ☒ *Market Pl.* ☎ *01787/247431* ⊕ *www. greathouse.co.uk* ☒ *Reservations essential* ☉ *Closed Mon. and Jan. No dinner Sun. No lunch Mon. and Tues.*

Colorful and ancient, the timbered houses in pretty towns such as Lavenham recall the days when these buildings housed weavers and wool merchants.

$ INDIAN Fodor's Choice ★ 🍴 **Memsaab.** In a town ready to burst with cream teas, it's a bit of a surprise to find an Indian restaurant, let alone such an exceptional one. Among the classics one would expect from a curry house—from mild kormas to spicy *madrases* and *jalfrezies* (traditional curries made with chili and tomato)—are some finely executed specialties, including Nizami chicken (a fiery dish prepared with yogurt and fresh ginger) and duck *bhujon* (with orange and Madeira sauce). The menu also contains regional specialties from Goa and Hyderabad. [$] *Average main: £11* ✉ *2 Church St.* ☎ *01787/249431* 🌐 *www.memsaaboflavenham.co.uk.*

WHERE TO STAY

$ B&B/INN 🏨 **Guinea House.** Still a private home after 600 years, Guinea House attracts travelers seeking more authenticity than your average B&B. **Pros:** quiet central location; intimate feel; one-of-a-kind atmosphere. **Cons:** low ceilings and hobbit-size doorways; no common areas. [$] *Rooms from: £75* ✉ *16 Bolton St.* ☎ *01787/249046* 🌐 *www.guineahouse.co.uk* 🛏 *2 rooms* 💳 *No credit cards* 🍽 *Breakfast.*

$$ B&B/INN 🏨 **Lavenham Priory.** You can immerse yourself in Lavenham's Tudor heritage at this sprawling house that dates back to the 13th century. **Pros:** historic ambience; charming rooms; lovely garden; free Wi-Fi. **Cons:** no locks on room doors; service can be surly; traffic noise in side rooms. [$] *Rooms from: £120* ✉ *Water St.* ☎ *01787/247404* 🌐 *www.lavenhampriory.co.uk* 🛏 *5 rooms, 1 suite* 🍽 *Breakfast.*

$$$ HOTEL 🏨 **Swan Hotel.** This half-timber 14th-century lodging has rambling public rooms, roaring fireplaces, and corridors so low that cushions are strategically placed on beams. **Pros:** lovely building; atmospheric rooms.

Cons: creaky floors; lots of steps to climb. [$] *Rooms from: £195* ✉ *High St.* ☎ *01787/247477* 🌐 *www.theswanatlavenham.co.uk* 🛏 *47 rooms, 2 suites* 🍴 *Some meals.*

THE SUFFOLK COAST

The 40-mile Suffolk Heritage Coast, which wanders northward from Felixstowe up to Kessingland, is one of the most unspoiled shorelines in the country. The lower part of the coast is the most impressive; however, some of the loveliest towns and villages, such as Dedham (in Essex, just over the Suffolk border) and the older part of Flatford, are inland. The best way to experience the countryside around here is to be willing to get lost along its tiny, ancient back roads. In places like Aldeburgh, on the coast, be sure to stop for fish and chips.

DEDHAM

17 miles southeast of Lavenham, 62 miles southeast of Cambridge, 15 miles southeast of Bury St. Edmund.

Fodor's Choice ★

Dedham, in Essex but on the Suffolk border, is the heart of Constable country. Here gentle hills and the cornfields of Dedham Vale, set under the district's delicate pale skies, inspired John Constable (1776–1837) to paint some of his most celebrated canvases. He went to school in Dedham, a picture-book village that did well from the wool trade in the 15th and 16th centuries and has retained a prosperous air ever since. A 15th-century church looms large over handsomely sturdy, pastel-color houses.

Nearby towns have several other sites of interest to Constable fans. About 2 miles from of Dedham is Flatford, where you can see Flatford Mill, one of the two water mills owned by Constable's father. Northeast of Dedham, off A12, the Constable trail continues in East Bergholt, where Constable was born in 1776. Although the town is mostly modern, the older part has some atmospheric buildings like the church of St. Mary-the-Virgin.

GETTING HERE AND AROUND

From the main A12, Dedham is easily reached by car via the B1029. Public transportation is extremely limited; there's no nearby train station.

EXPLORING

Bridge Cottage. On the north bank of the Stour, this 16th-century home in East Bergholt has a shop and an exhibition about Constable's life. You can also rent rowboats here. ✉ *Off B1070, East Bergholt* ☎ *01206/298260* 🌐 *www.nationaltrust.org.uk* 🎟 *Free* 🕒 *Mar., Wed.–Sun. 10:30–5; Apr. and Oct., daily 10:30–5; May–Sept., daily 10:30–5:30; Nov. and Dec., Wed.–Sun., 10:30–3:30; Jan. and Feb., weekends 10:30–3:30.*

St. Mary-the-Virgin. One of the most remarkable churches in the region, St. Mary-the-Virgin was started just before the Reformation. The doors underneath the ruined archways outside (remnants of a much older church) contain a series of mysterious symbols—actually a coded message left by Catholic sympathizers of the time. The striking interior contains a host of treasures, including an ancient wall painting of the Virgin Mary in one of the rear chapels, a 14th-century chest, and an extraordinary series of florid memorial stones on the nave wall opposite the main entrance. ✉ *Flatford Rd., East Bergholt* ☎ *01206/392646* 🎟 *Free* ⏲ *Daily; hrs vary but usually 10–5.*

Willy Lott's House. A five-minute stroll down the path from Bridge Cottage brings you to this 16th-century structure that is instantly recognizable from Constable's painting *The Hay Wain* (1821). Although the house itself is not open to the public, the road is a public thoroughfare, so you don't have to buy a ticket to see the famous—and completely unchanged—view for yourself. Just stand across from the two trees on the far bank, with the mill on your right, and look upstream. ■ **TIP→ On the outside wall of the mill is a handy reproduction of the painting** to help you compose your own photo. ✉ *Off B1070, East Bergholt.*

WHERE TO EAT AND STAY

$$$$ BRITISH Fodor's Choice ★

🍴 **Le Talbooth.** This sophisticated restaurant is set in a Tudor house beside the idyllic River Stour. There are lighted terraces where food and drinks are served on warm evenings and where jazz and steel bands play on summer Sunday evenings. Inside, original beams, leaded-glass windows, and a brick fireplace add to the sense of history. The superb British fare at lunch and dinner may include filet of John Dory with crayfish and anchovies, duck breast with red cabbage and parsley root, or Dedham Vale beef with Madeira *jus.* [$] *Average main: £26* ✉ *Gun Hill* ☎ *01206/323150* 🌐 *www.milsomhotels.com/letalbooth* ✍ *Reservations essential* ⏲ *No dinner Sun. Nov.–May.*

$ BRITISH

🍴 **Marlborough Head.** This friendly, 300-year-old pub across from Constable's school in Dedham serves traditional pub grub with a flourish. Dishes such as venison pie and bangers and mash share the menu with fish-and-chips and burgers. There are also rooms available, one with a four-poster bed. [$] *Average main: £10* ✉ *Mill La.* ☎ *01206/323250* 🌐 *www.marlborough-head.co.uk* ⏲ *No dinner Sun.*

$$$$ HOTEL

🏨 **Maison Talbooth.** Constable painted the rich meadowlands in which this luxurious Victorian country-house hotel is set. **Pros:** good food; lovely views over Dedham Vale; some private hot tubs. **Cons:** restaurant books up fast; perhaps a little snooty. [$] *Rooms from: £300* ✉ *Stratford Rd.* ☎ *01206/322367* 🌐 *www.milsomhotels.com* 🛏 *10 rooms* 🍽 *Breakfast.*

$$ HOTEL

🏨 **Milsoms.** This Victorian-era hotel combines an old-fashioned feel with a modern style. **Pros:** comfortable rooms; stylish surroundings; delicious food. **Cons:** occasionally poor service; breakfast is overpriced. [$] *Rooms from: £120* ✉ *Stratford Rd.* ☎ *01206/322795* 🌐 *www.milsomhotels.com/milsoms* 🛏 *15 rooms* 🍽 *Breakfast.*

SPORTS AND THE OUTDOORS

Boathouse Restaurant. From Dedham, on the banks of the River Stour, you can rent a rowboat from the Boathouse Restaurant. The cost is £14 per hour. ✉ *Mill La.* ☎ *01206/323153* 🌐 *www.dedhamboathouse.co.uk* 🎟 *£14 per hr* ⏲ *Easter–Sept., daily 10–5.*

WOODBRIDGE

18 miles northeast of Dedham.

One of the first good ports of call on the Suffolk Heritage Coast, Woodbridge is a town whose upper reaches center on a fine old market square, site of the 16th-century Shire Hall. Woodbridge is at its best around its old quayside, where boatbuilding has been carried out since the 16th century. The most prominent building is a white-clapboard mill, which dates from the 18th century and is powered by the tides.

GETTING HERE AND AROUND

Woodbridge is on A12. There are local buses, but they mostly serve commuters. By train, Woodbridge is 1½ hours from London, and just under 2 hours from Cambridge (with connections).

ESSENTIALS

Visitor Information Woodbridge Tourist Information Centre ⊠ *Woodbridge Library, New St.* ☎ *01394/446510* ⊕ *www.suffolkcoastal.gov.uk/tourism/tics.*

EXPLORING

Sutton Hoo. The visitor center at Sutton Hoo tells the story of one of Britain's most significant Anglo-Saxon archaeological sites. In 1938 a local archaeologist excavated a series of earth mounds and discovered a 7th-century burial ship, probably that of King Raedwald of East Anglia. A replica of the 90-foot-long ship stands in the visitor center, which has artifacts and displays about Anglo-Saxon society—although the best finds have been moved to the British Museum in London. Trails around the 245-acre site explore the area along the River Deben. ⊠ *Off B1083* ☎ *01394/389700* ⊕ *www.nationaltrust.org.uk* ⊠ *£7.50* ☉ *Mar.–Nov., daily 10:30–5; Nov.–Mar., weekends 11–4.*

WHERE TO EAT AND STAY

$ ✕ **Butley Orford Oysterage.** What started as a little café that sold oysters
SEAFOOD   and cups of tea is now a bustling restaurant. It has no pretenses to
Fodor'sChoice   grandeur but serves some of the best smoked fish you're likely to taste
★   anywhere. The fish pie is legendary in these parts, and the traditional English desserts are exceptional. The actual smoking (of fish, cheese, and much else) takes place in the adjacent smokehouse, and products are for sale in a shop around the corner. $ *Average main: £7* ⊠ *Market Hill, Orford* ☎ *01394/450277* ⊕ *www.butleyorfordoysterage. co.uk* ☉ *No dinner Sun.–Thurs., Nov.–Mar., and Sun.–Tues., Apr. and May.*

$$ ☵ **Crown and Castle.** Artsy, laid-back, and genuinely friendly, this little
B&B/INN   gem occupies an 18th-century building in the village of Orford, 10
Fodor'sChoice   miles east of Woodbridge. **Pros:** warm service; relaxed atmosphere;
★   good restaurant. **Cons:** need a car to get around. $ *Rooms from: £130* ⊠ *Market Hill, Orford* ☎ *01394/450205* ⊕ *www.crownandcastle.co.uk* ⇶ *19 rooms* ⧉⊙⧉ *Multiple meal plans.*

ALDEBURGH

15 miles northeast of Woodbridge, 37 miles northeast of Dedham.

Aldeburgh (pronounced *orl*-bruh) is a quiet seaside resort, except in June, when the town fills with people attending the noted Aldeburgh Festival. Its beach is backed by a promenade lined with candy-color dwellings. The 20th-century composer Benjamin Britten lived here for some time. He was interested in the story of Aldeburgh's native son, poet George Crabbe (1754–1832), and turned his life story into *Peter Grimes*, a celebrated opera that perfectly captures the atmosphere of the Suffolk Coast.

GETTING HERE AND AROUND

You have little choice but to drive to Aldeburgh; turn off the A12 near Farnham and follow signs. There's no train station and no bus service.

ESSENTIALS

Visitor Information Aldeburgh Tourist Information Centre ⊠ *48 High St.* ☎ *01728/453637* ⊕ *www.visit-suffolkcoast.co.uk.*

EXPLORING

Aldeburgh Museum. The Elizabethan Moot Hall, built of flint and timber, stood in the center of a thriving 16th-century town when first erected. Now it's just a few steps from the beach, a mute witness to the erosive powers of the North Sea. It's the home of the Aldeburgh Museum, a low-key collection that includes finds from an Anglo-Saxon ship burial. ⊠ *Market Cross Pl.* ☎ *01728/454666* ⊕ *www.aldeburghmuseumonline. co.uk* ⊠ *£2* ⊙ *Apr., May, Sept., and Oct., daily 2:30–5; June–Aug., daily noon–5.*

WHERE TO EAT AND STAY

$

BRITISH

Fodor'sChoice

★

✕ **Aldeburgh Fish and Chip Shop.** A frequent entry on "best fish-n-chips in Britain" lists, Aldeburgh's most celebrated eatery always has a long line of eager customers come frying time. The fish is fresh and local, the batter melts in your mouth, and the chips (from locally grown potatoes) are satisfyingly chunky. Upstairs you can bring your own wine or beer and sit at tables, but for the full experience, join the line and take out the paper-wrapped version. The nearby Golden Galleon, run by the same people, is a good alternative if this place is too crowded. $ *Average main: £5* ⊠ *226 High St.* ☎ *01728/452250* ⊕ *www.aldeburghfishandchips.co.uk* ⊟ *No credit cards.*

$

MODERN BRITISH

✕ **The Lighthouse.** An excellent value, this low-key brasserie with tightly packed wooden tables relies exclusively on local produce. The menu focuses on seafood, including oysters and Cromer crabs. All the contemporary British dishes are imaginatively prepared. Desserts, such as the Grand Marnier fudge cake, are particularly good. $ *Average main: £13* ⊠ *77 High St.* ☎ *01728/453377* ⊕ *www.lighthouserestaurant.co.uk.*

$

B&B/INN

Dunan House. A creative, friendly atmosphere pervades this pretty B&B, home to artists Ann Lee and Simon Farr, their cats, and their friendly dog. **Pros:** spacious rooms; delightful hosts; location near the beach. **Cons:** advance deposite required. $ *Rooms from: £80* ⊠ *41 Park Rd.* ☎ *01728/452486* ⊕ *www.dunanhouse.co.uk* ⋌ *3 rooms* ⎰ *Breakfast.*

10

$$ HOTEL **Wentworth Hotel.** The Pritt family has owned and managed the Wentworth since 1920, and the attention shows. **Pros:** good restaurant; sea views. **Cons:** small bathrooms; service can be impersonal. [$] *Rooms from: £159* ✉ *Wentworth Rd.* ☎ *01728/452312* 🌐 *www.wentworth-aldeburgh.com* *35 rooms* 🍴 *Breakfast.*

NIGHTLIFE AND THE ARTS

Fodor's Choice ★ **Aldeburgh Festival.** East Anglia's most important arts festival, and one of the best known in Britain, is the Aldeburgh Festival. It's held for two weeks in June in the small village of Snape, 5 miles west of Aldeburgh. Founded by Benjamin Britten, the festival concentrates on music but includes exhibitions, poetry readings, and lectures. A handful of events are aimed specifically at children. ✉ *Snape* ☎ *01728/687110* 🌐 *www.aldeburgh.co.uk.*

Snape Maltings. It's well worth a stop to take in the peaceful River Alde location of this cultural center. It includes art galleries and crafts shops in distinctive large brick buildings once used to malt barley. There are also a café, tearoom, and a pub, the Plough and Sail. There's a farmers' market on the first Saturday of the month, a major food festival in September, and a Benjamin Britten festival in October. Leisurely 45-minute river cruises (£7.50) leave from the quayside in summer. ✉ *Off B1069, Snape* ☎ *01728/688303* 🌐 *www.snapemaltings.co.uk* ⏲ *Late Mar.–July and Sept.–Nov., daily 10–5:30; Aug., daily 10–6; Dec.–late Mar., daily 10–5.*

YORKSHIRE AND THE NORTHEAST

WELCOME TO YORKSHIRE AND THE NORTHEAST

TOP REASONS TO GO

★ **York Minster:** The largest Gothic cathedral in Northern Europe helps make York one of the country's most visited towns. The building's history is told in its crypt, brilliantly converted into a museum.

★ **Brontë Country:** The wild plains and dark, rolling hills of the Pennine Moors encircle the atmospheric town of Haworth, where the Brontë sisters lived. Wander the hilly, cobbled streets and visit the parsonage where the noted writers lived.

★ **Hadrian's Wall:** The ancient Roman wall is a wonder for the wild countryside around it as well as for its stones and forts, such as Housesteads.

★ **Castles, castles, castles:** Fought over by the Scots and the English, and prey to Viking raiders, the Northeast was heavily fortified. Durham, Alnwick, and Bamburgh castles are spectacular.

★ **Medieval Durham:** A splendid Norman cathedral that dates back to the 11th century is just one of the city's charms.

1 York. Still enclosed within its medieval city walls, this beautifully preserved city makes the perfect introduction to Yorkshire. Its towering minster and narrow little streets entrance history buffs.

2 York Environs. This rural region contains the elegant Victorian spa town Harrogate, as well as the baroque splendor of Castle Howard.

3 West Yorkshire. Rocky and bleak, this windswept stretch of country provides an appropriate setting for the dark, dramatic narratives penned by the Brontë sisters in Haworth.

4 Durham. The historic city of Durham, set on a rocky spur, has a stunning castle and cathedral. South and west are scenic towns with castles and industrial heritage sites.

5 Hadrian's Wall and Environs. England's wildest countryside is traversed by the remains of the wall that marked the northern border of the Roman Empire. Hexham is a useful base, and Housesteads Roman Fort is a key site. It's stunning country for walking or biking.

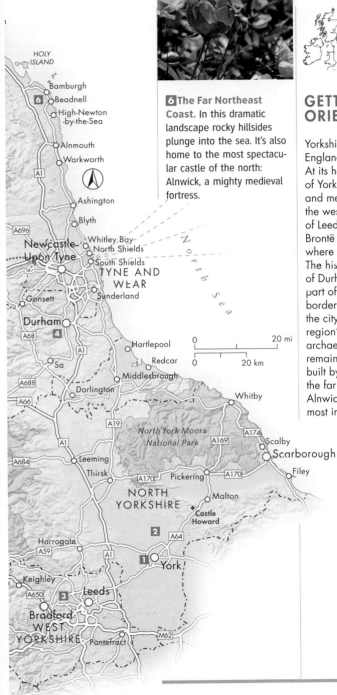

HOLY
ISLAND

Bamburgh
6 Beadnell
High-Newton
-by-the-Sea

Alnmouth

Warkworth

A1

Ashington

Blyth

A696

Whitley Bay
Newcastle-
Upon Tyne
North Shields
South Shields
**TYNE AND
WEAR**

Gonsett
Sunderland

Durham
A68 **4**

A1
Hartlepool
Sa
Redcar
A688
Middlesbrough
Darlington
A66
A19

Leeming
A1

A684
Thirsk

North York Moors
National Park
A169
A174
Scalby
Scarborough
Filey

A170
Pickering
A170
**NORTH
YORKSHIRE**
Malton
Castle
Howard

Harrogate
A59
A1
A64

2

1 York

Keighley
A650 **3**
Leeds

Bradford
**WEST
YORKSHIRE**
Pontefract
M62

Whitby

North Sea

0   20 mi
0   20 km

6 **The Far Northeast
Coast.** In this dramatic
landscape rocky hillsides
plunge into the sea. It's also
home to the most spectacular castle of the north:
Alnwick, a mighty medieval
fortress.

GETTING
ORIENTED

Yorkshire is the largest of
England's historic counties.
At its heart is the ancient city
of York, with its cathedral
and medieval city walls. To
the west of York, past the city
of Leeds, are the wild hills of
Brontë Country—Haworth,
where the Brontë family lived.
The historic cathedral city
of Durham is in the southern
part of the Northeast, which
borders Scotland. West of
the city of Newcastle is the
region's most important
archaeological wonder: the
remains of Hadrian's Wall,
built by the Romans. On
the far northeast coast is
Alnwick, one of the region's
most impressive castles.

HADRIAN'S WALL

Winding through the wild and windswept Northumberland countryside, Hadrian's Wall is Britain's most important Roman relic. It once formed the northern frontier of the Roman Empire—its most remote outpost and first line of defense against raiders from the north. Even today, as a ruin, the wall is an awe-inspiring structure.

(above) The wall is a dramatic sight in the countryside; (right, top) Roman writing tablet from Vindolanda; (right, bottom) Remains of a fort near Housesteads

One of the most surprising things about visiting the 73-mile-long wall is its openness and accessibility. Although many of the best-preserved sections are within managed tourist sites, Hadrian's Wall is also part of the landscape, cutting through open countryside. Signposted trails along the entire route allow you to hike or cycle along most of the wall for free. The area around the wall is also rich in archaeological treasures that paint a picture of a thriving, multicultural community. The soldiers and their families who were stationed here came from as far away as Spain and North Africa, and recent discoveries give us an insight into their daily lives. Artifacts displayed at the wall's museums provide fascinating perspective.

POSTCARDS FROM THE PAST

"Oh, how much I want you at my birthday party. You'll make the day so much more fun. Good-bye, sister, my dearest soul."

"I have sent you two pairs of sandals and two pairs of underpants. Greet all your messmates, with whom I pray you live in the greatest good fortune."

—From 1st-century writing tablets unearthed at Vindolanda

SEEING THE WALL'S HIGHLIGHTS

Hadrian's Wall has a handful of Roman-era forts, the best of which are concentrated near Housesteads, Vindolanda, and Chesters. Housesteads is the most complete, although getting there involves a quarter-mile walk up a hill; Chesters and Vindolanda have excellent museums. The separate Roman Army Museum near Greenhead offers a good overview of the wall's history and is near one of the best sections in open countryside, at Walltown Crags.

WHEN TO GO

The best time to visit is midsummer, when the long hours of daylight allow time to see a few of the wall's major attractions and fit in a short hike on the same day. Winter brings icy winds; not all the forts and museums stay open, but those that do can be all but deserted. The weather can change suddenly at any time of year, so always bring warm clothes.

GETTING AROUND BY CAR OR BUS

The tiny, winding B6318 road passes within a stone's throw of most of the forts. It's a true back road, so don't expect to get anywhere fast. Public transport is limited; the special AD 122 bus covers the highlights (but only during summer), and several local buses follow parts of the same route.

EXPLORING BY FOOT OR BIKE

Hadrian's Wall Path meanders along the wall's entire length; it's a seven-day hike. Joining it for a mile or so is a great way to see the wall and stunning scenery. Try the section around Walltown, or near Corbridge, where the path goes by the remains of a Roman garrison town. Hadrian's Cycleway, for bicyclists, follows roughly the same route.

SIGHTSEEING RESPONSIBLY

The wall is accessible, but vulnerable. Don't climb on it, and never break off or remove anything. In muddy weather you're encouraged not to stand directly next to the wall, as over time this can make the soil unstable.

WALL TIMELINE

55 BC Julius Caesar invades what's now southern England, but doesn't stay. He names the island Britannia.

AD 41–50 Full-scale invasion. The Romans establish fortified towns across the south, including Londinium (London).

75–79 The conquest of northern England is completed—but the Romans fail to take Caledonia (Scotland).

122 Emperor Hadrian orders the construction of a defensive wall along the territory's northern border.

208 After the Romans make another disastrous attempt to invade Caledonia, Hadrian's Wall is expanded.

410 The Romans leave Britain. Local tribes maintain the wall for at least a century.

1700s Stones from the ruined wall are plundered for road building.

1830s Local philanthropist John Clayton buys land around the wall to save it from further destruction.

1973 First Vindolanda tablets are found.

1987 Hadrian's Wall becomes a UNESCO World Heritage Site.

Updated by
Ellin Stein and
Jack Jewers

A hauntingly beautiful region, Yorkshire is known for its wide-open spaces and dramatic landscapes—both natural and man-made. Historic buildings line the narrow streets of towns like York and Harrogate, while ancient cathedrals, abbeys, and castles provide majestic backdrops to day-to-day life. England's northeast, a more remote and less-traveled area, has its own appeal, including the cathedral city of Durham and the Roman remains of Hadrian's Wall.

Indeed, some of the region's biggest attractions are the result of human endeavor. In Yorkshire these include the towering cathedral in York, as well as Castle Howard, Vanbrugh and Hawksmoor's baroque masterpiece near York. The Yorkshire landscape, however, is just as compelling. The West Yorkshire Pennines, with their moors and rocky crags punctuated by gray-stone villages, is the landscape that inspired the Brontës.

For many Britons, the words "the Northeast" provoke a vision of near-Siberian isolation. But although there are wind-hammered spaces and empty roads threading the wild high moorland, the area also has simple fishing towns, small villages of remarkable charm, and historic abbeys and castles that are all the more romantic for their often-ruinous state. This is also where you'll find two of England's most iconic sights: the medieval city of Durham and the stark remains of Hadrian's Wall.

Mainly composed of the two large counties of Durham and Northumberland, the Northeast includes English villages adjacent to the Scottish border area, renowned in ballads and romantic literature for feuds, raids, and battles. Fittingly, Durham Cathedral, the seat of bishops for nearly 800 years, was once described as "half church of God, half castle 'gainst the Scot." Hadrian's Wall, which marked the northern limit of the Roman Empire, stretches across prehistoric remains and moorland. Heading toward the far northeast coast are mighty castles such as Alnwick, with its beautiful gardens.

YORKSHIRE AND THE NORTHEAST PLANNER

11

WHEN TO GO

The best time to see the region is in summer. This ensures that the museums—and the roads—will be open, and you can take advantage of the countryside walks that are one of the area's greatest pleasures (but despite the season, be prepared for some cool days). Summer is also the best time to see the coast, as colorful regattas and arts festivals are under way. At the end of June, Alnwick hosts its annual fair, with a medieval market, art shows, and concerts. The Durham Regatta also takes place in June. York Minster makes a splendidly atmospheric focal point for the prestigious York Early Music Festival in early July.

Spring and fall bring their own rewards: far fewer crowds and crisp, clear days, although there's an increased risk of rain and fog. The harsh winter is tricky: while the moors and dales are beautiful covered in snow and the coast sparkles on a clear, bright day, storms and blizzards can set in quickly. Then the moorland roads become impassable and villages can be cut off entirely. The weather may be terrible, but on the other hand, there are few places in England so bleakly beautiful and remote.

PLANNING YOUR TIME

Yorkshire is a vast region, and difficult to explore in a short amount of time. If you're in a hurry, you could see the highlights of York as a day trip from London; the fastest trains take just two hours. But it's an awful lot to pack into one day, and you're bound to leave out places you'll probably regret missing. Proper exploration—especially of the countryside—requires time and effort. Anywhere in Northumberland is within relatively easy reach of Durham, with its lovely ancient buildings. If you're interested in exploring Hadrian's Wall and the Roman ruins, you'll probably want to base yourself at a guesthouse in or around Hexham. From there you can easily take in Housesteads and the other local landmarks.

GETTING HERE AND AROUND

AIR TRAVEL

Leeds Bradford Airport, 11 miles northwest of Leeds, has frequent flights from other cities in England and Europe. Look for cheap fares on British Airways, flybe, Jet2, or Ryanair. Another good choice for this region is Manchester Airport, about 40 miles southwest of Leeds. This larger airport is well served by domestic and international carriers.

Airports Leeds Bradford International Airport ⊠ *A658, Yeadon* ☎ *0871/288-2288* ⊕ *www.leedsbradfordairport.co.uk.* **Manchester Airport** ⊠ *M56, near Junctions 5 and 6, Manchester* ☎ *0871/271-0711* ⊕ *www.manchesterairport.co.uk.*

BUS TRAVEL

National Express and Megabus both have numerous daily departures from London's Victoria Coach Station to York and Durham. Average travel times are 6 hours to York and 7 hours to Durham. Local bus services run throughout the region, including Keighley & District services that connect York and Haworth. The farther you get into the northeastern countryside, the harder it is practically to get around without a car. But the aptly named AD122 public bus runs between Newcastle and Carlisle during the summer months, stopping near all the major Hadrian's Wall destinations along the way. A special Hadrian's Wall Bus has Rover Ticket passes (£9), offering unlimited travel on the route for one, three, and seven days. Several other local services go out from Newcastle and other towns in the region to various parts of the wall. Traveline has route information.

Bus Contacts Arriva ☎ *0844/800–4411* ⊕ *www.arrivabus.co.uk.* **Hadrian's Wall Country Bus** ☎ *01434/322002* ⊕ *www.hadrians-wall.org.***Harrogate & District** ☎ *01423/566061* ⊕ *www.harrogatebus.co.uk.* **Keighley & District** ☎ *01535/603284* ⊕ *www.keighleyanddistrict.co.uk.* **Megabus** ☎ *0900/160–0900* ⊕ *uk.megabus.com.* **National Express** ☎ *0871/781–8178* ⊕ *www.nationalexpress.com.* **Traveline** ☎ *0871/200–2233* ⊕ *www.traveline.info.*

CAR TRAVEL

If you're driving, the M1 is the principal route north from London. This major thoroughfare gets you to Leeds in about three hours. For York (204 miles), stay on M1 to Leeds (197 miles), and then take A64. For the Yorkshire Dales, take M1 to Leeds, then A65 north and west to Skipton. The trans-Pennine motorway, the M62, between Liverpool and Hull, crosses the bottom of this region. North of Leeds, A1 is the major north–south road, although narrow stretches, roadworks, and heavy traffic make this route slow going at times.

Some of the steep, narrow roads in the countryside off the main routes are difficult drives and can be perilous (or closed altogether) in winter. Main roads often closed by snowdrifts are the moorland A169 and the coast-and-moor A171.

If you're headed to small villages in the Northeast, remote castles, or Hadrian's Wall, traveling by car is the best option. The A1 highway links London and Newcastle (five to six hours). The A69 roughly follows Hadrian's Wall, although sometimes it's a few miles in either direction. The best sections of the wall are near the narrower B6318, including Vindolanda, Housesteads Roman Fort, and Chesters Roman Fort. The scenic route is the A697, which branches west off A1 north of Morpeth. For the coast, leave the A1 at Alnwick and follow the minor B1340 for spectacular views.

TRAIN TRAVEL

East Coast trains travel to York from London's King's Cross Station. Average travel time is 2 hours. Northern Rail trains operate throughout the region. East Coast also runs the train service from London to the Northeast. The average travel time to Durham from London is 3 hours. From the city of Newcastle (also 3 hours from London) you can catch local trains to Alnwick and Hexham; these journeys take about 30 minutes. Contact National Rail for train times, and to find out if any discounted Rover tickets are available for your journey.

Train Contacts East Coast ☎ *0845/722–5111* ⊕ *www.eastcoast.co.uk.* **National Rail Enquiries** ☎ *0845/748–4950* ⊕ *www.nationalrail.co.uk.* **Northern Rail** ☎ *0845/000–0125* ⊕ *www.northernrail.org.*

RESTAURANTS

Yorkshire is known for hearty food, though bacon-based breakfasts and lunches of pork pies do tend to pale fairly quickly. Indian restaurants (called curry houses) can be very good in northern cities. Out in the countryside, pubs are your best bet for dining. Many offer excellent home-cooked food and locally reared meat (especially lamb) and vegetables. Roast beef dinners generally come with Yorkshire pudding, the tasty, puffy, oven-baked dish made from egg batter known as a popover in the United States. It's generally served with lots of gravy. Be sure to sample local cheeses, especially Wensleydale, which has a delicate flavor and honey aftertaste.

Northumberland lags somewhat behind other parts of England in terms of good places to eat. Aside from the ubiquitous chains, the best bets are often small country pubs that serve traditional, hearty fare. Look for restaurants that serve game from the Kielder Forest, local lamb from the hillsides, salmon and trout from the rivers, and shellfish, crab, and oysters from the coast. Don't wait until 9 pm to have dinner, though, or you may have a hard time finding a place that's still serving.

HOTELS

Hotel chains don't have much of a presence in Yorkshire or the Northeast, outside the few cities such as York. Instead, you can expect to find country houses converted into welcoming hotels, old coaching inns that still greet guests after 300 years, and cozy bed-and-breakfasts convenient to hiking trails. Many budget accommodations close in winter. *Hotel reviews have been shortened. For full information, visit Fodors.com.*

WHAT IT COSTS IN POUNDS			
$	**$$**	**$$$**	**$$$$**
Restaurants	under £15	£15–£19	£20–£25	over £25
Hotels	under £100	£100–£160	£161–£220	over £220

Restaurant prices are the average cost of a main course at dinner or, if dinner isn't served, at lunch. Hotel prices are the lowest cost of a standard double room in high season, including 20% V.A.T.

VISITOR INFORMATION

Contact Welcome to Yorkshire ☎ *0113/322–3500* ⊕ *www.yorkshire.com.*
Visit North East England ⊕ *www.visitnortheastengland.com.*

YORK

Fodor's Choice
★

For many people, the first stop in Yorkshire is the historic cathedral city of York. Much of the city's medieval and 18th-century architecture has survived, making it a delight to explore. It's one of the most popular short-stay destinations in Britain, and only two hours by train from London's King's Cross Station.

Named "Eboracum" by the Romans, York was the military capital of Roman Britain, and traces of garrison buildings survive throughout the city. After the Roman Empire collapsed in the 5th century, the Saxons built "Eoforwic" on the ruins of a fort, but were soon defeated by Vikings who called the town "Jorvik" and used it as a base from which to subjugate the countryside. The Normans came in the 11th century and emulated the Vikings by using the town as a military base. It was during Norman times that the foundations of York Minster, the largest medieval cathedral in England, were laid. The only changes the 19th century brought were large houses, built mostly on the outskirts of the city center.

GETTING HERE AND AROUND

If you're driving, take the M1 north from London. Stay on it to Leeds, and then take the A64 northeast for 25 miles to York. The journey should take around 3½ hours. Megabus coaches leave from St. Pancras International station three times a day (4½ hours), and National Express buses depart from London's Victoria Coach Station three times a day (6 hours). East Coast trains run from London's King's Cross Station about every 30 minutes during the week (2 hours). York Station, just outside the city walls, has a line of taxis out front to take you to your hotel. If you don't have bags, the walk to town takes eight minutes.

York's city center is mostly closed to traffic and is very walkable. The old center is a compact, dense web of narrow streets and tiny medieval alleys called "snickleways." These provide shortcuts across the city center, but they're not on maps, so you never quite know where you'll end up, which in York is often a pleasant surprise.

TOURS

City Sightseeing runs frequent hop on, hop off bus tours of York that stop at the Castle Museum, Clifford's Tower, and Jorvik Viking Centre. The York Association of Voluntary Guides arranges short walking tours around the city at least once a day. The tours are free, but tips are appreciated.

Ghost Creeper runs "bloodcurdling" tours weekend nights from November to late December and March to June, and nightly from July through Halloween. Tours start at 7:30 pm outside the Jorvik Viking Centre and cost £5 per person. Ghost Trail of York guides take a straightforward approach to ghosts—telling you what other people have heard or seen, and what they've seen themselves. The hour-long tours commence at 7:30 pm by the minster and cost £4 per person.

11

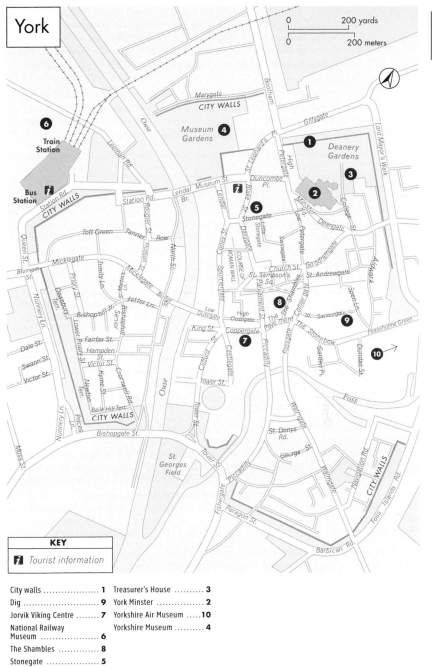

York

0 — 200 yards
0 — 200 meters

6 Train Station

i Bus Station

Station Rd.

CITY WALLS

Marygate
CITY WALLS

Museum Gardens **4**

Ouse

Leeman Rd.

Toft Green

Tanner Row

Rougier St.

Houser St.

North St.

Micklegate

Bridge

Blossom St.

Micklegate

Trinity Ln.

Priory St.

Dewsbury Terr.

Nunnery Ln.

St. Mary's

Bishophill Senior

Bishophill Jr.

Fetter Ln.

Fairfax St.

Hampden St.

Victor St.

Cromwell Rd.

Kyme St.

Newton Terr.

Baile Hill Terr.

CITY WALLS

Bishopgate St.

Prices

Moss St.

Dale St.

Swann St.

Victor St.

Nunnery Ln.

Lendal Br.

Museum St.

Station Rd.

Lendal

St. Leonard's Pl.

High Petergate

Duncombe Pl.

Blake St.

Stonegate **5**

Little Stonegate

Davygate

Swinegate

COURSE OF ROMAN WALL

Church St.

St. Sampson's Sq.

Spurriergate

Coney St.

Low Ousegate

High Ousegate

Coppergate **7**

King St.

Clifford St.

Castlegate

Tower St.

Ouse

Tower St.

St. Georges Field

Fishergate

Paragon St.

1 Deanery Gardens

2 York Minster

3 Treasurer's House

College St.

Minster Yd.

Low Petergate

Deangate

Goodramgate

St. Andrewgate

The Shambles

Pavement

The Stonebow

Fossgate

Piccadilly

The Stonebow

Garden Pl.

Dundas St.

8

9 Dig

10

Peasholme Green

Aldwark

Spen Ln.

St. Saviourgate

Foss

St. Denys Rd.

Walmgate

George St.

Walmgate

Navigation Rd.

CITY WALLS

Foss Islands Rd.

Barbican Rd.

Gillygate

Lord Mayor's Walk

Bootham

Ouse

KEY

i Tourist information

TIMING

In July and August tourists choke the narrow streets and form long lines at the minster. April, May, June, and September are less crowded, but the weather can be unpredictable. April is also the time to see the embankments beneath the city walls rippling with pale gold daffodils.

ESSENTIALS

Tour Information City Sightseeing ☎ 01904/634296 ⊕ www.city-sightseeing. com. **Ghost Creeper** ☎ 07947/325239 ⊕ www.ghostcreeper.com. **Ghost Trail of York** ☎ 01904/633276 ⊕ www.ghosttrail.co.uk. **York Association of Voluntary Guides** ✉ 1 Museum St. ☎ 01904/550098 ⊕ www.visityork.org.

Visitor Information York ✉ 1 Museum St. ☎ 01904/550099 ⊕ www.visityork.org.

EXPLORING

TOP ATTRACTIONS

City walls. York's almost 3 miles of ancient stone walls are among the best preserved in England. A walk on the narrow paved path along the top leads you through 1,900 years of history, from the time the earthen ramparts were raised by the Romans and York's Viking kings to repel raiders, to their fortification by the Normans, to their current colorful landscaping by the city council. The walls are crossed periodically by York's distinctive "bars," or fortified gates: the portcullis on Monk's Bar on Goodramgate is still in working order, and Walmgate Bar in the east is the only gate in England with an intact barbican. It also has scars from the cannon balls hurled at it during the civil war. Bootham Bar in Exhibition Square was the defensive bastion for the north road, and Micklegate Bar, in the city's southwest corner, was traditionally the monarch's entrance. To access the path and the lookout towers, find a staircase at one of the many breaks in the walls. ⬛ *Free* ⊘ *Daily 8 am–dusk.*

FAMILY **Dig.** This venture from the people behind the Jorvik Viking Centre is a great way to get young people inspired about history and archaeology. It's a reproduction of an archaeological dig in and beneath an old church; kids, supervised by knowledgeable experts, dig in the dirt and "find" Roman or Viking artifacts. After your exploration, head to the lab to learn what archaeological finds discovered on the site reveal about former inhabitants. ✉ *St. Saviour's Church, St. Saviourgate* ☎ *01904/615505* ⊕ *www.vikingjorvik.com* ⬛ *£5.50; joint admission to Jorvik Viking Centre £13.25* ⊘ *Daily 10–5, last admission at 4.*

FAMILY **Jorvik Viking Centre.** This kid-focused exhibition re-creates a 10th-century Viking village. A mixture of museum and carnival ride, you "travel through time" by climbing into a Disney-esque machine that propels you above straw huts and mannequins in Viking garb. Commentary is provided in six languages. Kids will get a lot out of it, but adults are unlikely to learn anything new. A small collection of Viking-era artifacts is on display at the end of the ride. ✉ *Coppergate* ☎ *01904/615505* ⊕ *www.vikingjorvik.com* ⬛ *£9.75; joint admission to Dig £13.25* ⊘ *Apr.–Oct., daily 10–5; Nov.–Mar., daily 10–4.*

The Shambles, a narrow medieval street in York, once held butchers' shops, but now has stores that serve the city's many shoppers and visitors.

FAMILY **National Railway Museum.** A must for train lovers, Britain's biggest railway museum houses part of the national collection of rail vehicles. Don't miss such gleaming giants of the steam era as the *Mallard*, holder of the world speed record for a steam engine (126 mph), and train-buff legend the *Flying Scotsman*. Passenger cars used by Queen Victoria are on display, as is the only Japanese bullet train to be seen outside Japan. You can climb aboard some of the trains and occasionally take a short trip on one. ⊠ *Leeman Rd.* ☎ *08448/153139* ⊕ *www.nrm.org.uk* ☛ *Free* ⊗ *Daily 10–6.*

The Shambles. York's best-preserved medieval street has shops and residences in half-timbered buildings with overhangs so massive you could almost reach across the narrow gap from one second-floor window to another. Once a hub of butchers (meat hooks are still fastened outside some of the doors), today it's mostly filled with independent shops and remains highly atmospheric.

Stonegate. This narrow, pedestrian-only street lined with Tudor and 18th-century storefronts retains considerable charm. It's been in daily use for almost 2,000 years, when it was first paved during Roman times. Today it's a vibrant shopping strip lined with upscale boutiques, jewelers, and quirky one-offs like the Eye of Newt at 35, your one-stop shop for "tarot, spells, candles, crystal balls, potions, and wands." A passage just off Stonegate, at 52A, leads to the remains of a 12th-century Norman stone house attached to a more recent structure. You can see the old Norman wall and window. ■TIP➜ Look out for the little red "printer's devil" at No. 33, a medieval symbol of a printer's premises. At the intersection of Stonegate and High Petergate, Minerva reclines on a stack of books, indicating they were once sold inside.

QUICK BITES

Betty's. Betty's has been a York institution since 1937. The plate-glass windows with art nouveau stained glass, the dessert trollies, and solicitous white-aproned staff contribute to an impression of stepping back in time. The traditional dishes (like pork schnitzel and fried haddock) are so-so, but the tea and cakes are excellent. An in-house store sells specialty coffees and teas plus pastries and old-fashioned sweets. There's a smaller branch at 46 Stonegate. ✉ *6–8 Helen's Sq., off Stonegate* ☎ *01904/659142.*

WHERE ARE THE GATES?

The Viking conquerors of northern England who held the region for more than a century made York their capital. *Gate* was the Viking word for "street," hence street names such as Goodramgate and Micklegate. Adding to the confusion, the city's entrances, or gates, are called "bars," from an Old English term. As local tour guides like to say, "In York, our streets are called gates, our gates are called bars, and our bars are called pubs."

Fodor's Choice
★

York Minster. Focal point of the city, this vast cathedral is the largest Gothic building north of the Alps and attracts almost as many visitors as London's Westminster Abbey. Inside, the effect created by its soaring pillars and lofty vaulted ceilings is almost overpowering. Come with binoculars if you wish to study the loftier of the 128 dazzling stained-glass windows. Glowing with deep wine reds and cobalt blues, they're bested only by those in Chartres Cathedral in France. Mere statistics can't convey the scale of the building; however, the central towers are 200 feet high, and the church is 519 feet long, 249 feet across its transepts, and 90 feet from floor to roof. Contributing to the spacious, uplifting splendor are the ornamentation of the 14th-century nave; the east window, one of the greatest pieces of medieval glazing in the world; the north transept's **Five Sisters** windows, five tall lancets of gray-tinged 13th-century glass; the enormous choir screen depicting somewhat stylized images of every king of England from William the Conqueror to Henry VI; and the masterful tracery of the **Rose Window,** with elements commemorating the marriage of Henry VII and Elizabeth of York in 1486 (the event that ended the Wars of the Roses and began the Tudor dynasty). Don't miss the exquisite 13th-century **Chapter House** and the **Undercroft, Treasury, and Crypt.** Finds uncovered during restoration work date back to Roman times, and include a Saxon child's coffin. After exploring the interior, you might take the 275 winding steps to the roof of the great **Central Tower** (strictly for those with a head for heights), not only for the close-up view of the cathedral's detailed carvings but for a panorama of York. Until 2016, a special elliptical exhibition in the cathedral's east end, called *The Orb*, displays the great east window's stained glass panels at eye level (a different panel every month), along with interactive galleries on the window's creation. ■**TIP→** To experience the cathedral at its most atmospheric, try to attend one of the evensong services with organ and choir. There's a charge for sightseers, but the minster is free for those who come to pray or attend services. ✉ *Duncombe Pl.*

A WALK IN YORK

York is a fine city for walking, especially along the walls embracing the old center. Start at the Minster and head down Stonegate, a lane dating back to the Middle Ages now lined with shops that leads directly to Betty's celebrated tearooms. Eventually you'll come to a highly atmospheric shopping street known as the Shambles and further along the remains of the old castle. Take time to shop if you wish; York has both antiques shops and spots with plenty of contemporary items, and draws many local shoppers.

To get a sense of where you are at any point, climb the steps up to the top of the city walls (they are also good for a walk). The River Ouse is bordered in places by walking paths that make for a pleasant stroll.

☎ *0844/939–0011* ⊕ *www.yorkminster.org* ✉ *Minster £10, Minster and Central Tower £15* ⊙ *Apr.–Oct., Mon.–Sat. 9–5, Sun. noon–5; Nov.–Mar., Mon.–Sat. 9:30–5, Sun. noon–5.*

FAMILY **Yorkshire Air Museum.** Located on 20 acres of parkland, this is the country's largest World War II airbase open to the public. The independent museum showcases numerous historic aircraft, many of which are still in working condition and are certain to delight aviation enthusiasts. Planes range from early-20th-century biplanes and gliders to Spitfires and other World War II-era planes to contemporary fighter jets. There are also exhibits devoted to military vehicles, aircraft weaponry, and Royal Air Force uniforms. The museum is home to a memorial and gardens commemorating British and Allied service members who lost their lives in the conflict. ✉ *Halifax Way, Elvington* ☎ *01904/608595* ⊕ *www.yorkshireairmuseum.org* ✉ *£8* ⊙ *April–mid-Nov., 10–5; mid-Nov.–Mar., 10–4.*

WORTH NOTING

Treasurer's House. Surprises await inside this large 17th-century house, the home from 1897 to 1930 of industrialist Frank Green. With a fine eye for texture, decoration, and pattern, Green re-created period rooms—including a medieval great hall—as a showcase for his collection of antique furniture. Delft tiles decorate the former kitchen (now a shop), copies of medieval stenciling cover the vibrant King's Room, and 17th-century stumpwork adorns the Tapestry Room. The cellar has displays about a ghostly Roman legion allegedly sighted there in the 1950s. ✉ *Minster Yard* ☎ *01904/624247* ⊕ *www.nationaltrust.org.uk* ✉ *House and garden £6.50, attic tour £3, cellar tour £2.40* ⊙ *Mar.–Oct., Sat.–Thurs. 11–5; Feb. and Nov., Sat.–Thurs. 11–3, by guided tour only; last admission at 4:30.*

Yorkshire Museum. The natural and archaeological history of the county, including material on the Roman, Anglo-Saxon, and Viking aspects of York, is the focus of this museum on the site of the medieval St. Mary's Abbey. The museum is divided into themed galleries focusing on the different time periods. On display in the early 19th-century Greek Revival–style building with its massive Doric column is the

DID YOU KNOW?

York Minster is the largest
Gothic cathedral in Britain.
The towers of its west front
rise 174 feet, and its nave
is an imposing 138 feet
wide and 276 feet long.
The west front includes the
window known as the Heart
of Yorkshire because of the
shape of the tracery near
its top.

15th-century Middleham Jewel, a pendant gleaming with a large sapphire, and the extremely rare Copperplate Helmet, a 1,200-year-old Viking artifact discovered during excavations of the city. ✉ *Museum Gardens, Museum St.* ☎ *01904/687687* 🌐 *www.yorkshiremuseum.org.uk* 🎟 *£7.50* 🕒 *Daily 10–5.*

WHERE TO EAT

$$ MODERN BRITISH 🍴 **Blue Bicycle.** One of York's best restaurants is in a building that once served as a brothel, a past reflected in its murals featuring undraped women. Downstairs are four intimate walled booths, and at street level is a lively room lighted with candles. The menu changes with the seasons and concentrates on local seafood. Typical dishes include pan-seared scallops with horseradish purée, seared sea bass with truffled potatoes, or grilled local beef sirloin with pink peppercorn mash. The wine list is impressive, and the service couldn't be friendlier. The restaurant has six self-contained apartments—called the Blue Rooms—in a courtyard to the rear. [$] *Average main: £18* ✉ *34 Fossgate* ☎ *01904/673990* 🌐 *www.thebluebicycle.com* ✍ *Reservations essential.*

$ BRITISH 🍴 **Café Concerto.** Music is the theme at this relaxed, intimate bistro in sight of York Minster where sheet music serves as wallpaper. The kitchen serves British classics with an emphasis on local ingredients. Dinner favorites include braised lamb shank with caramelized onion mash, panfried pork fillet with a Madeira cream sauce, or sirloin steak with field mushrooms and roast potatoes. Lunch is mostly soups, salads, and sandwiches, and you can always pop in for tea and cake. [$] *Average main: £14* ✉ *21 High Petergate* ☎ *01904/610478* 🌐 *www.cafeconcerto.biz.*

$$ ITALIAN 🍴 **Le Langhe.** So popular that it has already moved twice to larger premises, this combination café/restaurant/upscale deli has an emphasis on Italian, particularly Piedmontese, meats and cheeses. The deli sells take-out sandwiches incorporating a variety of both, as well as small-producer olive oils, wines, and other items sourced by the owners. The glass-roofed café offers a variety of house-made pastas, such as pasta with Whitby crab with shallots and potatoes. Entrées change daily and might include slow-cooked pork belly, lemon sole, or venison. There's a tasting menu at dinner, and fixed-price lunch menus. The upstairs restaurant serves dinner on Friday and Saturday. [$] *Average main: £18* ✉ *The Old Coach House, Peasholme Green* ☎ *01904/622584* 🌐 *www.lelanghe.co.uk* ✍ *Reservations essential.*

$$ MODERN BRITISH 🍴 **Melton's.** A converted Victorian shop, this unpretentious restaurant has work by local artists on the walls, but you'll more likely be trying to catch a glimpse of the open kitchen beyond a glass door. The excellent seasonal menus are highly imaginative takes on Modern British dishes using regional produce, such as chicken with apples and parsley mashed potatoes, venison in a red-wine sauce with fondant potatoes, or fish-and-mussel stew with potatoes and fennel. There's also a five-course "Yorkshire Tasting Menu" for £38. Melton's is a 10-minute walk from Clifford's Tower. There's an offshoot bar-bistro called Melton's Too on nearby Walmsgate. [$] *Average main: £18* ✉ *7 Scarcroft Rd.* ☎ *01904/634341* 🌐 *www.meltonsrestaurant.co.uk* ✍ *Reservations essential* 🕒 *Closed Sun. and Mon. and 3 wks at Christmas.*

$ CAFÉ 🍴 **Spurriergate Centre.** Churches aren't just for services, as this 15th-century house of worship proves. Resurrected as a cafeteria (there's also a café on the upper floor), St. Michael's is a favorite spot for both tourists and locals to refuel spiritually (you can request use of the prayer room upstairs) as well as physically. You may end up eating beef casserole on the spot where John Wesley prayed in 1768. Don't pass up the cream scones. [$] *Average main: £7* ✉ *Spurriergate* ☎ *01904/629393* 🌐 *www.thespurriergatecentre.com* 🕐 *Closed Sun. No dinner.*

WHERE TO STAY

$$ HOTEL 🏨 **Cedar Court Grand Hotel and Spa.** This handsome, comfortable hotel is near the train station—not surprising, considering it was formerly the headquarters of the regional railroad. **Pros:** beautiful building; spacious rooms; good location. **Cons:** Continental breakfast only average; unceasing soft rock in restaurant. [$] *Rooms from: £155* ✉ *Station Rise* ☎ *01904/380038* 🌐 *www.cedarcourtgrand.co.uk* 🛏 *107 rooms, 13 suites* 🍽 *Breakfast.*

$$ HOTEL 🏨 **Grange Hotel.** Built in the early 19th century as a home for a wealthy member of the York clergy, this luxurious boutique hotel is reminiscent of a grand country house. **Pros:** spacious rooms; lovely decor; good food. **Cons:** can feel a bit fussy; restaurant service uneven. [$] *Rooms from: £115* ✉ *1 Clifton* ☎ *01904/644744* 🌐 *www.grangehotel.co.uk* 🛏 *36 rooms* 🍽 *Breakfast.*

$ B&B/INN 🏨 **The Hazelwood.** These two tall, elegant Victorian town houses retain many of their original features and stand in a peaceful cul-de-sac; they're away from the hustle and bustle despite being a short walk from York Minster. **Pros:** good service; lovely building; convenient parking. **Cons:** thin walls; poor water pressure on upper floors. [$] *Rooms from: £80* ✉ *24–25 Portland St.* ☎ *01904/626548* 🌐 *www.thehazelwoodyork.com* 🛏 *14 rooms* 🍽 *Breakfast.*

$$ HOTEL 🏨 **Hotel Du Vin.** A 19th-century orphanage, this historic building has been converted into a swanky hotel that preserves the original exposed brick walls and arched doorways. **Pros:** makes great use of the space; friendly staff; comfortable beds. **Cons:** high parking charges; low bathroom lighting. [$] *Rooms from: £129* ✉ *89 The Mount* ☎ *01904/557350* 🌐 *www.hotelduvin.com* 🛏 *44 rooms* 🍽 *Breakfast.*

$$$ HOTEL 🏨 **Middlethorpe Hall & Spa.** Aimed at those who prize period details like oak-paneled walls, four-poster beds, carved wood banisters, and window seats and whose idea of luxury is a bowl of fresh daffodils, this splendidly restored Queen Anne–style mansion feels less like a country-house hotel than an actual country house. **Pros:** period luxury; gorgeous grounds; attentive staff. **Cons:** water pressure; outside the city center. [$] *Rooms from: £199* ✉ *Bishopthorpe Rd.* ☎ *01904/641241* 🌐 *www.middlethorpe.com* 🛏 *18 rooms, 11 suites* 🍽 *Breakfast.*

$$ HOTEL 🏨 **Mount Royale Hotel.** This hotel has the feel of a relaxing country house despite being close to the city center in an upscale residential neighborhood. **Pros:** large rooms; lovely pool and garden; good service. **Cons:** well outside the town center; some rooms dated. [$] *Rooms from: £125* ✉ *117–119 The Mount* ☎ *01904/628856* 🌐 *www.mountroyale.co.uk* 🛏 *14 rooms, 10 suites* 🍽 *Breakfast.*

NIGHTLIFE AND THE ARTS

NIGHTLIFE

York is full of historic pubs where you can while away an hour over a pint.

Black Swan. In a 14th-century Tudor building complete with flagstone floors and oak paneling, this pub serves home-cooked bar food and hosts a roster of local folk musicians. ⊠ *Peasholme Green* ☎ *01904/679131* ⊕ *www.blackswanyork.com.*

Old White Swan. Spreading across five medieval, half-timbered buildings on busy Goodramgate, the Old White Swan is known for good pub lunches and its ghosts—it claims to have more than the equally venerable Black Swan. ⊠ *80 Goodramgate* ☎ *01904/540911* ⊕ *www. nicholsonspubs.co.uk.*

Snickleway Inn. The 15th-century setting, complete with open fireplaces, gives the Snickleway Inn a real sense of history. ⊠ *Goodramgate* ☎ *01904/656138.*

THE ARTS

Early Music Festival. Featuring songs written before the 18th century, the Early Music Festival is held each July. There's also a Christmas version in early December. ☎ *01904/658338* ⊕ *www.ncem.co.uk.*

Viking Festival. Held every February, these celebrations include a parade and long-ship regatta. It ends with the Jorvik Viking combat reenactment, when Norsemen confront their Anglo-Saxon enemies. ⊠ *Jorvik Viking Centre, Coppergate* ☎ *01904/543400* ⊕ *www.vikingjorvik.com.*

York Theatre Royal. In a lovely 18th-century building, the York Theatre Royal hosts theater, dance, music, and comedy performances, as well as readings, lectures, and children's entertainment. ⊠ *St. Leonard's Pl.* ☎ *01904/623568* ⊕ *www.yorktheatreroyal.co.uk.*

SHOPPING

Stonegate is the city's main shopping street. Winding down from the minster toward the river, it's lined with a mix of unique shops and boutiques. Another good shopping street is Petergate, which has mostly chain stores. The Shambles is another prime shopping area, with an eclectic mix of shops geared towards locals and tourists.

Minster Gate Bookshop. This shop sells secondhand books, old maps, and prints. ⊠ *8 Minster Gate* ☎ *01904/621812* ⊕ *www.minstergatebooks. co.uk.*

Mulberry Hall. This store sells fine bone china from big names ranging from Royal Doulton to Donna Karan Lenox and glittering crystal from the likes of Baccarat and Lalique. There are also elegant ornaments, cookware, and kitchen essentials. An upstairs traditional tea room serves light lunches and snacks on Wedgwood china. ⊠ *Stonegate* ☎ *01904/620736* ⊕ *www.mulberryhall.co.uk.*

YORK ENVIRONS

West and north of York a number of sights make easy, appealing day trips from the city, starting with the spa town of Harrogate, with its still-thriving Victorian spa; the ruins of Fountain Abbey; and Castle Howard, one of the region's most magnificent stately homes.

HARROGATE

21 miles west of York, 16 miles north of Leeds.

During the Regency and early-Victorian periods, it became fashionable for the aristocratic and wealthy to "take the waters" at British spa towns, combining the alleged health benefits with socializing. In Yorkshire the most elegant spa destination was Harrogate, where today its mainly Victorian buildings, parks, and spas still provide a relaxing getaway.

GETTING HERE AND AROUND

Trains from York leave every hour or so, and the journey takes about 30 minutes. There's one direct train daily from London. National Express buses leave from York every hour most days; the journey takes about 40 minutes. By car, Harrogate is off A59, and is well marked. It's a walkable town, so you can park in one of its central parking lots and explore on foot.

Within and around Harrogate, the Harrogate and District bus company provides area services, and taxis are plentiful.

ESSENTIALS

Visitor Information Harrogate Tourist Information Centre ⊠ *Royal Baths, Crescent Rd.* ☎ *01423/537300* ⊕ *www.enjoyharrogate.com.*

EXPLORING

Royal Pump Room Museum. This octagonal structure was built in 1842 over the original sulfur well that brought great prosperity to the town. You can still sniff the evil-smelling spa waters here. The museum displays some equipment of spa days gone by, alongside a somewhat eccentric collection of fine 19th-century china, clothes, and bicycles. ⊠ *Crown Pl.* ☎ *01423/556188* ⊕ *www.harrogate.gov.uk* 🎫 *£3.80* ☉ *Apr.–Oct., Mon.–Sat. 10:30–5, Sun. 2–5; Nov.–Mar., Mon.–Sat. 10:30–4, Sun. 2–4.*

The Stray. At the edge of the town center, this 200-acre grassy parkland is a riot of color in spring. It contains many of the mineral springs that first made Harrogate famous. ⊕ *www.harrogate.gov.uk.*

Fodor'sChoice
★
Studley Royal Water Garden & Fountains Abbey. You can easily spend a day at this UNESCO World Heritage Site, an 822-acre complex made up of an 18th-century water garden and deer park, a Jacobean mansion, and, on the banks of the River Skell, Fountains Abbey, the largest monastic ruins in Britain. Here a neoclassical vision of an ordered universe—with spectacular terraces, classical temples, and a grotto—blends with the majestic Gothic abbey, which was founded in 1132 and completed in the early 1500s. It housed Cistercian monks, called "White Monks" for the color of their robes, who devoted their lives to silence, prayer,

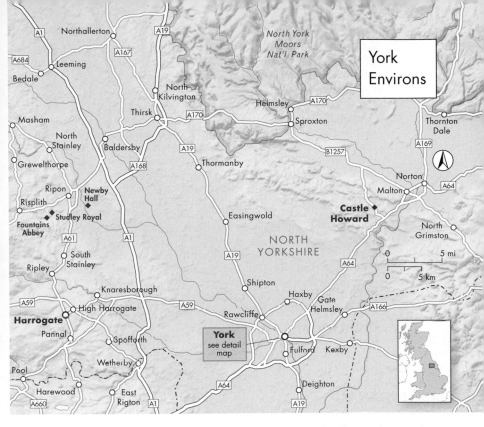

and work. Of the surviving buildings, the lay brothers' echoing refectory and dormitory are the most complete. The 12th-century Fountains Mill, perhaps the best-preserved in England, displays reconstructed machinery (wool was the abbey's profitable business). The 17th-century Fountains Hall is partially built with stones taken from the abbey. The water garden and Fountains Abbey are 10 miles north of Harrogate, 4 miles southwest of Ripon. ⊠ *Off B6265* ☎ *01765/608888* ⊕ *www. nationaltrust.org.uk/fountainsabbey* ⊠ *£9.50* ⊙ *Apr.–Sept., daily 10–5; Oct. and Mar., daily 10–4; Nov.–Jan., Sat.–Thurs. 10–4.*

Turkish Baths and Health Spa. Dating from 1897, the exotic and fully restored Turkish Baths allow you to experience what brought so many Victorians to Harrogate. After changing into your bathing suit, you can relax on luxurious lounge chairs in the stunning mosaic-tile warming room. Move on to increasingly hot sauna rooms, and then soak up eucalyptus mist in the steam room before braving the icy plunge pool. You can also book a massage or facial. Open hours are divided into women-only and mixed nights, so book in advance. ⊠ *Parliament St.* ☎ *01423/556746* ⊕ *www.turkishbathsharrogate.co.uk* ⊠ *£15–£20.50 per session* ⊙ *Daily; call for schedule.*

Valley Gardens. Southwest of the town center, these 17-acres of formal gardens include a children's boating lake, tennis courts, skate park, and a little café. ✉ *Valley Dr.* 🌐 *www.harrogate.gov.uk.*

WHERE TO EAT AND STAY

$ CAFÉ 🍴 **Betty's Cafe Tea Rooms.** This celebrated Yorkshire tearoom began life in Harrogate in 1919, when a Swiss restaurateur brought his Alpine pastries and chocolates to England. The welcoming decor has changed little since then, and the extensive array of teas not at all. In addition to omelets, quiches, sandwiches, and traditional cakes and pastries, the menu ranges from the Dales (sausages) to the Alps (rösti). A pianist plays nightly. Reservations are accepted only for afternoon tea served in the Imperial Room on weekends. *Average main: £11* ✉ *1 Parliament St.* ☎ *01423/814070* 🌐 *www.bettys.co.uk.*

$$ HOTEL 🏨 **Hotel du Vin.** This hip hotel sprawls through eight Georgian houses, with stripped-wood floors, clubby leather armchairs, and a purple billiard table setting the tone. **Pros:** tasty food; wonderful wine list; helpful staff; modern vibe. **Cons:** some rooms dark; housekeeping uneven; the bar can take over the lounge. [$] *Rooms from: £145* ✉ *Prospect Pl.* ☎ *01423/856800* 🌐 *www.hotelduvin.com* 🛏 *40 rooms, 8 suites* 🍽 *No meals.*

NIGHTLIFE AND THE ARTS

Harrogate Festival. This annual celebration of ballet, contemporary dance, music, film, comedy, street theater, and more takes place throughout July. ☎ *01423/562303* 🌐 *www.harrogate-festival.org.uk.*

CASTLE HOWARD

28 miles northeast of Harrogate, 15 miles northeast of York.

The baroque grandeur of Castle Howard is without equal in northern England. The grounds, enhanced by groves of trees, a twinkling lake, and a perfect lawn, add to the splendor.

GETTING HERE AND AROUND

There's a daily scheduled bus service between Malton and Castle Howard, which is well outside any town and several miles off any public road. The nearest train stop is Malton, and you can take a taxi from there. By car, follow signs off A64 from York.

EXPLORING

FAMILY Fodor's Choice ★ **Castle Howard.** Standing in the Howardian Hills to the west of Malton, Castle Howard is an outstanding example of English baroque, with a distinctive roofline punctuated by a magnificent central dome. It served as Brideshead, the home of the fictional Flyte family in Evelyn Waugh's tale of aristocratic woe, *Brideshead Revisited,* in both the 1981 TV and 2008 film adaptations. The house was the first commission for playwright-turned-architect Sir John Vanbrugh, who, assisted by Nicholas Hawksmoor, designed it for the 3rd Earl of Carlisle, a member of the Howard family. Started in 1701, the central portion took 25 years to complete, with a Palladian wing added subsequently, but the end result was a stately home of audacious grandeur.

The streets and houses of Haworth look much as they did when the Brontë sisters lived and wrote their famous novels in this village near the moors.

A spectacular central hallway with soaring columns supporting a hand-painted ceiling dwarfs all visitors, and there's no shortage of splendor elsewhere: vast family portraits, intricate marble fireplaces, immense tapestries, Victorian silver on polished tables, and a great many marble busts. Outside, the neoclassical landscape of carefully arranged woods, lakes, and lawns led 18th-century bon vivant Horace Walpole to comment that a pheasant at Castle Howard lived better than a duke elsewhere. Hidden throughout the 1,000 acres of formal and woodland gardens are temples, statues, fountains, and a grand mausoleum— even a fanciful children's playground. Hourly tours of the grounds, included in the admission price, fill you in on more background and history. ✉ *Off A64 and B1257, Malton, York* ☎ *01653/648333* ⊕ *www. castlehoward.co.uk* ✉ *£14; gardens only £9.50* ☉ *House: late Mar.– Oct., daily 11–5:30; last admission at 4. Grounds: daily 10–6:30 or dusk; last admission at 4:30.*

WEST YORKSHIRE: BRONTË COUNTRY

Out from the busy city of Leeds, the West Yorkshire countryside quickly becomes a landscape of wild moorland and picture-perfect villages. The traditional wool town of Saltaire is a UNESCO-protected gem, built as one of the first model communities in the Victorian heyday of the mid-1800s. But the main thrust of many visits to West Yorkshire is to the west of Leeds, where the stark hills north of the Calder Valley and south of the River Aire form the district immortalized in the equally unsparing novels of the Brontë sisters. Haworth, a gray-stone village,

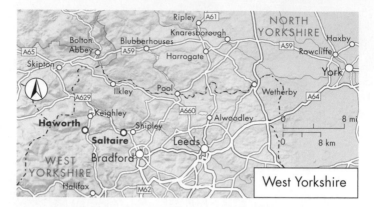

West Yorkshire

might have faded into obscurity were it not for the enduring fame of the literary sisters. Every summer, thousands toil up the steep main street to visit their former home. But to truly appreciate the setting that inspired their books you need to go farther afield to the ruined farm of Top Withins, which in popular mythology, if not in fact, was the model for Wuthering Heights.

SALTAIRE

41 miles southwest of Castle Howard, 12 miles west of Leeds, 8 miles east of Haworth.

GETTING HERE AND AROUND
An old wool-market town, Saltaire has regular bus and train services from the nearby town of Bradford. Drivers should take A650 from Bradford and follow the signs.

ESSENTIALS
Visitor Information Saltaire Visitor Information Centre ⊠ *Salt's Mill, Victoria Rd.* ☎ *01274/437942* ⊕ *www.visitsaltaire.com.*

EXPLORING
Fodor'sChoice **Saltaire.** A UNESCO World Heritage Site, the former model village of
★ Saltaire was built in the mid-19th century by textile magnate Sir Titus Salt. When he decided to relocate his factories from the dark mills of Bradford to the countryside, he hoped to create an ideal industrial community in which his workers would be happy. The Italianate village is remarkably well preserved, its former mills and houses now turned into shops, restaurants, and galleries. Part of Salt's Mill, built in 1853, resembles a palazzo. The largest factory in the world when it was built, today it holds an art gallery, along with crafts and furniture shops. One-hour guided tours (£4) of the village depart weekends and some holiday Mondays at 2 pm from the tourist information center. ⊠ *A657.*

   1853 Gallery. This gallery is devoted to a remarkable exhibition of some 400 works by Bradford-born artist David Hockney. There are two restaurants on-site. ⊠ *Salt's Mill, Victoria Rd.* ☎ *01274/531163* ⊠ *Free* ⊙ *Weekdays 10–5:30, weekends 10–6*

HAWORTH

8 miles west of Saltaire.

Whatever Haworth might have been in the past, today it's Brontë country. This old stone-built textile village on the edge of the Yorkshire Moors long ago gave up its own personality and allowed itself to be taken over by the literary sisters, their powerful novels, and their legions of fans. In 1820, when Anne, Emily, and Charlotte were very young, their father relocated them and their other three siblings away from their old home in Bradford to Haworth. The sisters—Emily (author of *Wuthering Heights*, 1847), Charlotte (*Jane Eyre*, 1847), and Anne (*The Tenant of Wildfell Hall*, 1848) were all affected by the stark, dramatic countryside.

These days, it seems that every building they ever glanced at has been turned into a memorial, shop, or museum. The Haworth Visitor Center has good information about accommodations, maps, books on the Brontës, and inexpensive leaflets to help you find your way to such outlying *Wuthering Heights* sites as Ponden Hall (Thrushcross Grange) and Ponden Kirk (Penistone Crag).

GETTING HERE AND AROUND

To reach Haworth by bus or train, buy a Metro Day Rover for bus and rail (£7.50) and take the Metro train from Leeds train station to Keighley, where you change to a Keighley & District bus to Haworth. On weekends you can opt to take the Keighley and Worth Valley Railway to continue on to Haworth.

By car, Haworth is a just over an hour's drive from York; take A64 southwest, bypass Leeds on M1, M62, and M606, and follow signs to Haworth. It's well signposted, and there's plenty of cheap parking in town.

ESSENTIALS

Visitor Information Haworth Visitor Information Centre ⊠ *2–4 Westlane* ☏ *01535/642329.*

EXPLORING

Fodor's Choice

★

Brontë Parsonage Museum. The best of Haworth's Brontë sights is this somber Georgian house where the sisters grew up. It displays original furniture (some bought by Charlotte after the success of *Jane Eyre*), portraits, and books. The Brontës moved here when the Reverend Patrick Brontë was appointed to the local church, but tragedy soon struck—his wife, Maria, and their two eldest children died within five years. The museum explores the family's tragic story, bringing it to life with a strong collection of enchanting mementos of the four children. These include tiny books they made when they were still very young; Charlotte's wedding bonnet; and the sisters' spidery, youthful graffiti on the nursery wall. Branwell, the Brontës' only brother, painted several of the portraits on display. ⊠ *Church St.* ☏ *01535/642323* ⊕ *www.bronte. org.uk* ⊠ *£7* ⊙ *Apr.–Sept., daily 10–5:30; Oct.–Mar., daily 11–5; last admission 30 mins before closing.*

Brontë Waterfall. If you have the time, pack a lunch and walk for 2¾ miles or so from Haworth along a field path, a lane, and a moorland track to the lovely, isolated waterfall that has, inevitably, been renamed in honor of the sisters. It was one of their favorite haunts, which they wrote about in poems and letters.

FAMILY **Keighley and Worth Valley Railway.** On this gorgeous 5-mile-long branch line, Haworth is one stop along the route on which handsome steam engines carry passengers between Keighley and Oxenhope. On special days, family fairs en route add to the fun. ✉ *Haworth Station, Station Rd.* ☎ *01535/645214* 🌐 *www.kwvr.co.uk* 🎟 *£10 round-trip, £15 Day Rover ticket* 🕒 *Sept.–May, weekends; June–Aug., daily.*

Main Street. Haworth's steep, cobbled high street has changed little in outward appearance since the early 19th century, but it now acts as a funnel for crowds heading for points of interest: the **Black Bull** pub, where the reprobate Branwell Brontë drank himself into an early grave; the former **post office** (now a bookshop) from which Charlotte, Emily, and Anne sent their manuscripts to their London publishers; and the **church,** with its atmospheric graveyard (Charlotte and Emily are buried in the family vault inside the church; Anne is buried in Scarborough).

Top Withins. A ruined, gloomy mansion on a bleak hilltop farm 3 miles from Haworth, Top Withins is often taken to be the inspiration for the fictional Wuthering Heights. Brontë scholars say it probably isn't; even in its heyday, the house never fit the book's description of Heathcliff's lair. Still, it's an inspirational walk across the moors. There and back from Haworth is a 3½-hour walk along a well-marked footpath that goes past the Brontë waterfall. ■ **TIP→ If you've read Wuthering Heights, you don't need to be reminded to wear sturdy shoes and protective clothing. .**

LANDSCAPE AS MUSE

The rugged Yorkshire Moors helped inspire Emily Brontë's 1847 *Wuthering Heights*; if ever a work of fiction grew out of the landscape in which its author lived, it was surely this. "My sister Emily loved the moors," wrote Charlotte. "Flowers brighter than the rose bloomed in the blackest of the heath for her; out of a sullen hollow in a livid hillside her mind could make an Eden. She found in the bleak solitude many and dear delights; and not the least and best loved was liberty."

WHERE TO STAY

$ B&B/INN 🏨 **Aitches.** In a 19th-century stone house very close to the Brontë Parsonage, this intimate B&B has cozy guest rooms decorated with pine furnishings and colorful quilts. **Pros:** excellent food; friendly staff. **Cons:** the traditional decor won't appeal to everyone. [$] *Rooms from: £60* ✉ *11 West La.* ☎ *01535/642501* 🌐 *www.aitches.co.uk* 🛏 *5 rooms* 🍴 *Breakfast.*

$ B&B/INN 🏨 **Ashmount Country House.** A short walk from the Parsonage, this charming stone building was once home to the Brontë sisters' physician, Amos Ingham. **Pros:** lovely period building; ideal location; great views. **Cons:** books up in advance. [$] *Rooms from: £95* ✉ *Mytholmes La.* ☎ *01535/645726* 🌐 *www.ashmounthaworth.co.uk* 🛏 *12 rooms* 🍴 *Breakfast.*

DURHAM

96 miles northeast of Haworth, 250 miles north of London, 15 miles south of Newcastle.

The great medieval city of Durham, seat of County Durham in Northumberland, stands dramatically on a rocky spur, overlooking the countryside. Its cathedral and castle, a World Heritage Site, rise together on a wooded peninsula almost entirely encircled by the River Wear (rhymes with "beer"). For centuries these two ancient structures have dominated Durham—a thriving university town, the Northeast's equivalent of Oxford or Cambridge. Steep, narrow streets overlooked by perilously angled medieval houses and 18th-century town houses make for fun exploring. In the most attractive part of the city, near the Palace Green and along the river, people go boating, anglers cast their lines, and strollers walk along the shaded paths. For great views, take a short stroll along the River Wear and cross the 17th-century Prebends Footbridge. You can return to town via the 12th-century Framwellgate Bridge.

Despite the military advantages of its location, Durham was founded surprisingly late, probably in about the year 1000, growing up around a small Saxon church erected to house the remains of St. Cuthbert. It was the Normans, under William the Conqueror, who put Durham on the map, building the first defensive castle and beginning work on the cathedral. From here Durham's prince-bishops, granted almost dictatorial local powers by William in 1072, kept a tight rein on the county, coining their own money and maintaining their own laws and courts; not until 1836 were these rights finally restored to the English Crown.

GETTING HERE AND AROUND

East Coast trains from London's King's Cross Station arrive at the centrally located Durham Station once an hour during the day. The journey takes about three hours. Trains from York arrive three to four times an hour; that journey takes roughly 50 minutes. A handful of National Express and Megabus buses make the seven-hour trip from London daily. The Durham Cathedral Bus (route 40) links parking lots and the train and bus stations with the cathedral, castle, and university. Between 10 and 4 Monday through Saturday, cars are charged £2 (on top of parking charges) to enter the Palace Green area. You pay the charge at an automatic tollbooth on exiting. ■TIP→ **If you don't have change for the tollbooth, press the button and an attendant will take down your information. Pay later, in person or over the phone, at the Parking Shop. Don't forget or you'll be fined.**

ESSENTIALS

Visitor Information Durham Visitor Contact Centre ✉ *Claypath* ☎ *03000/262–626* ⊕ *www.thisisdurham.com*. **Parking Shop** ✉ *Forster House, Finchdale Rd.* ☎ *0191/384–6633* ⊕ *www.durham.gov.uk.*

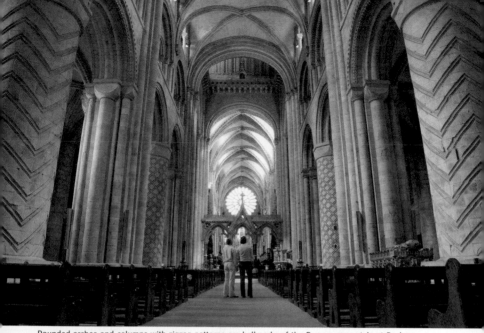

Rounded arches and columns with zigzag patterns are hallmarks of the Romanesque style at Durham Cathedral.

EXPLORING

Durham Castle. Facing the cathedral across Palace Green, Durham's stately, manorlike castle commands a strategic position above the River Wear. For almost 800 years the castle was the home of the enormously powerful prince-bishops; from here they ruled large tracts of the countryside and acted as the main line of defense against Scottish raiders from the north. Henry VIII was the first to curtail the bishops' autonomy, although it wasn't until the 19th century that they finally had their powers annulled. The castle was given over to University College, part of the University of Durham (founded 1832), the oldest in England after Oxford and Cambridge. You can visit the castle only on a 45-minute guided tour. Times can vary, especially on summer afternoons, so call ahead. ✉ *Palace Green* 🕾 *0191/334–2932* ⊕ *www. dur.ac.uk/university.college* 💷 *£5* ⊗ *Early Oct.–late June, weekdays at 2, 3, and 4; late June–early Oct., weekdays at 10, 11, noon, 2, and 5.*

QUICK BITES **9 Altars Café.** Down a narrow alleyway between the castle and the river, the tiny 9 Altars Café is an excellent spot for coffee and sandwiches. Eat on the river terrace if the weather's good—and you're lucky enough to get a seat. ✉ *River St.* 🕾 *0191/374–1120* ⊕ *www.9altars.com.*

Fodor's Choice ★ **Durham Cathedral.** A Norman masterpiece in the heart of the city, the cathedral is an amazing vision of solidity and strength, a far cry from the airy lightness of later Gothic cathedrals. Construction began about 1090, and the main body was finished about 1150. The round arches of the nave and the deep zigzag patterns carved into them typify the heavy, gaunt style of Norman, or Romanesque, building. The technology of Durham, however, was revolutionary. This was the first European cathedral to be given a stone, rather than a wooden, roof. When you consider the means of construction available to its builders—the stones that form the ribs of the roof had to be hoisted by hand and set on a wooden structure, which was then knocked away—the achievement seems staggering.

The story of the cathedral actually goes back 200 years before the first stones were laid. After a Viking raid on the monastery at Lindisfarne in 875, a group of monks smuggled away the remains of St. Cuthbert, patron saint of Northumbria. The remains were eventually interred in a shrine on this spot, which became a hugely popular destination for pilgrims. The wealth this brought the town was more than enough to pay for the building of the cathedral. Today Cuthbert's shrine is a relatively humble marble slab, although the enormous painting suspended from the ceiling is what the spectacular medieval coffin covering is thought to have looked like.

Note the enormous bronze **Sanctuary Knocker,** shaped like the head of a ferocious mythological beast, mounted on the massive northwestern door. By grasping the ring clenched in the animal's mouth, medieval felons could claim sanctuary; cathedral records show that 331 criminals sought this protection between 1464 and 1524. An unobtrusive tomb at the western end of the cathedral, in the Moorish-influenced **Galilee Chapel,** is the final resting place of the Venerable Bede, an 8th-century Northumbrian monk whose contemporary account of the English people made him the country's first reliable historian. In good weather you can climb the tower, which has spectacular views of Durham. From April to October, guided tours of the cathedral are offered daily at 10:30, 11, and 2.

After a long refurbishment, the cathedral's **museum** is due to reopen in early 2015. The collection includes the cathedral's beautiful illuminated manuscripts; there will also be a new space for talks and other public events, as well as an expanded program of tours.

A choral evensong service takes place Tuesday to Saturday at 5:15 and Sunday at 3:30. ☒ *Palace Green* ☎ *0191/386–4266* ⊕ *www. durhamcathedral.co.uk* ☜ *£5; tower £5; guided tours £5* ☉ *Cathedral: mid-July–Aug., daily 7:30 am–8 pm; Sept.–mid-July, Mon.–Sat. 7:30–6, Sun. 7:45–5:30. Tower: Apr.–Sept., Mon.–Sat. 10–4; Oct.–Mar., Mon.– Sat. 10–3.*

Durham University Oriental Museum. A 15-minute walk from the cathedral, this museum displays fine art and craftwork from all parts of Asia and the Middle East. Galleries are ordered by culture, including Ancient Egypt, China, and Korea. Among the highlights are beautiful Qing dynasty jade and lacquer ornaments, and a collection of Japanese woodblock prints from the Edo period. ☒ *Elvet Hill, off South Rd.* ☎ *0191/334–5694* ⊕ *www.dur.ac.uk/oriental.museum* ☜ *£1.50* ☉ *Weekdays 10–5, weekends noon–5.*

WHERE TO EAT

$$ FRENCH 🍴 **Bistro 21.** This fashionable restaurant, a few miles northwest of the center, is known for its eclectic menu of French classics with a modern twist. Signature dishes include rib-eye steak with tarragon and mustard butter, herb-encrusted salmon with creamed leeks, and black truffle gnocchi with wild mushrooms and Madeira cream. Get here by taxi, or take Bus 43 to Durham Hospital and walk five minutes. [$] *Average main: £17* ✉ *Aykley Heads* ☎ *0191/384–4354* 🌐 *www.bistrotwentyone.co.uk* 🕘 *No dinner Sun.*

$$ BRITISH 🍴 **Oldfields.** At this convivial restaurant, cheerful raspberry walls and unfussy walnut furnishings create a nicely laid-back vibe that complements the excellent food. Organic vegetables and free-range meat, sourced mostly from the surrounding region, are a specialty. The seasonal menu features such dishes as deviled kidneys with cauliflower, roasted chicken with garlic butter, and haddock and crab *kedgeree* (a rice dish with parsley and butter or cream). [$] *Average main: £16* ✉ *18 Clay Path* ☎ *0191/370–9595* 🌐 *www.oldfieldsrealfood.co.uk.*

$$ THAI 🍴 **Zen.** This popular restaurant mainly serves Thai food, but the menu is also scattered with Japanese, Chinese, and Indonesian dishes. This rather dizzying trip around the Far East can take you from Thai green curry to Mongolian lamb, or perhaps teriyaki beef or cod fillet wrapped in banana leaves served with chili and lime. Or, if you're feeling less adventurous, there's steak. [$] *Average main: £16* ✉ *Court La.* ☎ *0191/384–9588* 🌐 *www.zendurham.co.uk.*

WHERE TO STAY

$ B&B/INN 🏨 **Georgian Town House.** At the top of a cobbled street overlooking the cathedral and castle, this family-run guesthouse has small, snug bedrooms with pleasant city views. **Pros:** great location; jovial owners; good-value rooms. **Cons:** most rooms are small; decor won't please everyone. [$] *Rooms from: £75* ✉ *11 Crossgate* ☎ *0191/386–8070* 🌐 *www.thegeorgiantownhouse.co.uk* 🛏 *8 rooms* 💳 *No credit cards* 🕘 *Closed last wk of Dec.* 🍽 *Breakfast.*

$$ HOTEL Fodor's Choice ★ 🏨 **Lumley Castle Hotel.** This is a real Norman castle, right down to the dungeons and maze of dark flagstone corridors. **Pros:** great for antiques lovers; festive meals; good online deals. **Cons:** it's easy to get lost down the winding corridors. [$] *Rooms from: £100* ✉ *B1284, Chester-le-Street* ☎ *0191/389–1111* 🌐 *www.lumleycastle.com* 🛏 *59 rooms* 🍽 *Multiple meal plans.*

$ HOTEL 🏨 **Seven Stars Inn.** This early-18th-century coaching inn is cozy and surprisingly affordable. **Pros:** cozy lounge; reasonable rates; pleasant staff. **Cons:** on a main road; minimum two-night stay at peak times; very strict midnight curfew. [$] *Rooms from: £85* ✉ *High St. N, Shincliffe Village* ☎ *0191/384–8454* 🌐 *www.sevenstarsinn.co.uk* 🛏 *8 rooms* 🍽 *Breakfast.*

$ B&B/INN 🏨 **Victoria Inn.** An authentically Victorian air pervades at this cozy pub near Durham Cathedral, considered one of the country's best B&Bs. **Pros:** step-back-in-time atmosphere; lovely hosts; free Wi-Fi. **Cons:** few amenities; pub doesn't serve full meals. [$] *Rooms from: £70* ✉ *86 Hallgarth St.* ☎ *0191/386–5269* 🌐 *www.victoriainn-durhamcity.co.uk* 🛏 *6 rooms* 🍽 *Breakfast.*

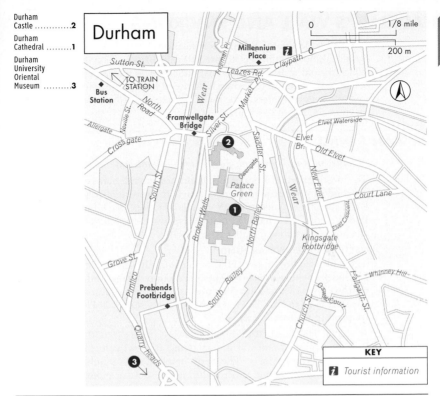

KEY

ℹ Tourist information

NIGHTLIFE AND THE ARTS

Durham's nightlife is geared to university students.

Half Moon. This handsome old pub is as popular for its excellent range of traditional ales as for its one-of-a-dying-breed atmosphere. ✉ *New Elvet* ☎ *0191/374–1918.*

SHOPPING

Bramwells Jewellers. The specialty here is a pendant copy of the gold-and-silver cross of St. Cuthbert. ✉ *24 Elvet Bridge* ☎ *0191/386–8006.*

Durham Indoor Market. The food and bric-a-brac stalls in Durham Indoor Market, a Victorian arcade, are open Monday through Saturday 9–5. An excellent farmers' market is held on the third Thursday of every month. ✉ *Market Pl.* ☎ *0191/384–6153* ⊕ *www.durhammarkets.co.uk.*

SPORTS AND THE OUTDOORS

Brown's Boat House. At the downtown Brown's Boat House, you can rent rowboats April through early November. You can also take short cruises from April to October. ✉ *Elvet Bridge* ☎ *0191/386–3779.*

HADRIAN'S WALL AND ENVIRONS

A formidable line of Roman fortifications, Hadrian's Wall was the Romans' most ambitious construction in Britain. The land through which the old wall wanders is wild and inhospitable in places, but that seems only to add to the powerful sense of history it evokes. Museums and information centers along the wall make it possible to learn as much as you want about the Roman era.

HADRIAN'S WALL

21 miles north of Durham, 73 miles from Wallsend.

The most important Roman relic in Britain extends across the countryside and can be accessed in many ways. In Northumberland National Park, about half a mile north of Vindolanda, the Once Brewed National Park Visitor Centre has informative displays about Hadrian's Wall and can advise about local walks.

GETTING HERE AND AROUND

The A69 roughly follows Hadrian's Wall, although sometimes it's a few miles in either direction. The best sections of the wall are near the narrower B6318, including Vindolanda, Housesteads Roman Fort, and Chesters Roman Fort. There's a small railway station at Hexham, with frequent trains from Newcastle.

A special Hadrian's Wall Bus offers day passes (£9.50) for service between Wallsend and Carlisle, stopping at Newcastle, Hexham, and the major Roman forts. The aptly named AD122 public bus runs between Newcastle and Carlisle during the summer months, stopping near all the major destinations along the way. Buses 10, 74, 93, 185, 685, 689, and 880 also pass parts of the wall.

ESSENTIALS

Visitor Information Hadrian's Wall Country Bus ☎ *01434/322002* ⊕ *www.hadrians-wall.org.*

EXPLORING

Fodor'sChoice ★ **Hadrian's Wall.** Dedicated to the Roman god Terminus, the massive span of Hadrian's Wall once marked the northern frontier of the Roman Empire. Today remnants of the wall wander across pastures and hills, stretching 73 miles from Wallsend in the east to Bowness-on-Solway in the west. The wall is a World Heritage Site, and excavating, interpreting, repairing, and generally managing the Roman wall remains a Northumbrian growth industry. ■TIP→ **Chesters, Housesteads, Vindolanda, and the Roman Army Museum near Greenhead give you a good introduction to the life led by Roman soldiers.** In summer there are talks, plays, and festivals; local tourist offices have details.

At Emperor Hadrian's command, three legions of soldiers began building the wall in AD 122, and finished it in four years. It was constructed by soldiers and masons after repeated invasions by troublesome Pictish tribes from what is now Scotland. During the Roman era it was the most heavily fortified wall in the world, with walls 15

11

feet high and 9 feet thick; behind it lay the vallum, a ditch about 20 feet wide and 10 feet deep. Spaced at 5-mile intervals along the wall were massive forts (such as those at Housesteads and Chesters), which could house up to 1,000 soldiers. Every mile was marked by a thick-walled milecastle (a fort that housed about 30 soldiers), and between each milecastle were two turrets, each lodging four men who kept watch. For more than 250 years the Roman army used the wall to control travel and trade and to fortify Roman Britain against the barbarians to the north.

During the Jacobite Rebellion of 1745, the English dismantled much of the Roman wall and used the stones to pave what is now the B6318 highway. The most substantial stretches of the remaining wall are between Housesteads and Birdoswald (west of Greenhead). Running through the southern edge of Northumberland National Park and along the sheer escarpment of Whin Sill, this section is also an area of dramatic natural beauty. The ancient ruins, rugged cliffs, dramatic vistas, and spreading pastures make it a great area for hiking.

SPORTS AND THE OUTDOORS

BIKING

Hadrian's Cycleway. Between Tynemouth and Whitehaven, Hadrian's Cycleway follows the River Tyne from the east coast until Newcastle, where it traces the entire length of Hadrian's Wall. It then continues west to the Irish Sea. Maps and guides are available at the Tourist Information Centre in Newcastle. ⊕ *www.cycle-routes.org/hadrianscycleway.*

HIKING

Hadrian's Wall Path. One of Britain's national trails, Hadrian's Wall Path runs the entire 73-mile length of the wall. If you don't have time for it all, take one of the less challenging circular routes. One of the most scenic but also most difficult sections is the 12-mile western stretch between Sewingshields and Greenhead. ⊕ *www.nationaltrail.co.uk/ hadrianswall.*

HEXHAM

31 miles northwest of Durham.

The area around the busy market town of Hexham is a popular base for visiting Hadrian's Wall. Just a few miles from the most significant remains, it's a bustling working town, but it has enough historic buildings and winding medieval streets to warrant a stop in its own right. First settled in the 7th century, around a Benedictine monastery, Hexham later became a byword for monastic learning, famous for its book painting, sculpture, and singing.

GETTING HERE AND AROUND

The A1 highway links London and the region (five to six hours). No major bus companies travel here, but the AD122 tourist bus from Newcastle and Carlisle does. East Coast trains take about three hours to travel from London's King's Cross to Newcastle. From there, catch a local train.

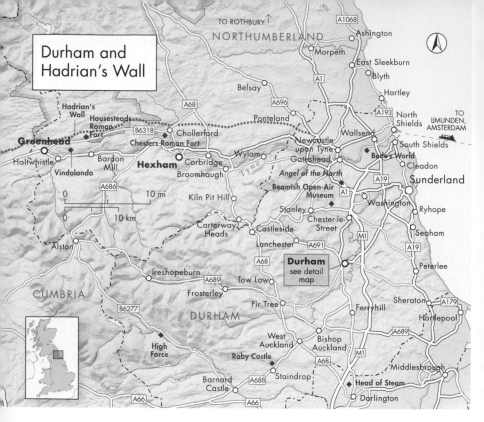

Durham and Hadrian's Wall

Hexham is a small, walkable town. It has infrequent local bus service, but you're unlikely to need it. If you're driving, park in the lot by the tourism office and walk into town. The tourism office has free maps and will point you in the right direction.

ESSENTIALS

Visitor Information Hexham Tourist Information Centre ⊠ *Wentworth Car Park, Wentworth Pl.* ☎ *01434/652220* ⊕ *www.visitnortheastengland.com.*

EXPLORING

Birdoswald Roman Fort. Beside the longest unbroken stretch of Hadrian's Wall, Birdoswald Roman Fort reveals the remains of gatehouses, a granary, and a parade ground. You can also see the line of the original turf wall, later rebuilt in stone. Birdoswald has a unique historical footnote: unlike other Roman forts along the wall, it was maintained by local tribes long after being abandoned by the Romans. The small visitor center has artifacts discovered at the site, a full-scale model of the wall, and a good café. ⊠ *Wallace Dr., Ravenglass, Cumbria* ⊕ *www. hadrians-wall.org* 🖾 *£5.50* ⊙ *Nov.–Mar., weekends 10–4; Apr.–Sept., daily 10–5:30; Oct., daily 10–4.*

Chesters Roman Fort. In a wooded valley on the banks of the North Tyne River, this cavalry fort was known as Cilurnum in Roman times, when it protected the point where Hadrian's Wall crossed the river. Although the site cannot compete with Housesteads for its setting, the museum holds a fascinating collection of Roman artifacts, including statues of river and water gods, altars, milestones, iron tools, weapons, and jewelry. The military bathhouse by the river is supposedly the best-preserved Roman structure of its kind in the British Isles. The fort is 4 miles north of Hexham. ✉ *B6318, Chollerford* ☎ *01434/681379* 🌐 *www.english-heritage.org.uk* 🎫 *£5.50* 🕒 *Apr.–Oct., daily 10–6; Nov.–Mar., weekends 10–4.*

Hexham Abbey. A site of Christian worship for more than 1,300 years, ancient Hexham Abbey forms one side of the town's main square. Inside, you can climb the 35 worn stone "night stairs," which once led from the main part of the abbey to the canon's dormitory, to overlook the whole ensemble. Most of the current building dates from the 12th and 13th centuries, and much of the stone, including that of the Anglo-Saxon crypt, was taken from the Roman fort at Corbridge. Note the portraits on the 16th-century wooden rood screen and the four panels from a 15th-century *Dance of Death* in the sanctuary. In September the abbey hosts the renowned Festival of Music and the Arts, which hosts classical musicians from around the world. ✉ *Beaumont St.* ☎ *01434/602031* 🌐 *www.hexhamabbey.org.uk* 🎫 *£3* 🕒 *Daily 9:30–5.*

Market Place. Since 1239 this has been the site of a weekly market, held each Tuesday (although there are usually a handful of sellers during the rest of the week, aside from Sunday). Crowded stalls are set out under the long slate roof of the Shambles; others, protected only by bright awnings, take their chances with the weather.

FAMILY **Old Gaol.** Dating from 1330, Hexham's Old Gaol houses fascinating exhibits about the history of the borderlands, including tales of the terrifying "reavers" and their bloodthirtsty raids into Northumberland from Scotland during the 16th and 17th centuries. Photographs, weapons, and a reconstructed house interior give a full account of what the region was like in medieval times. A glass elevator takes you to four floors, including the dungeon. ✉ *Hallgate* ☎ *01434/652439* 🎫 *£4* 🕒 *Apr.–June and Sept., Tues.–Sat. 11–4:30; July and Aug., Mon.–Sat. 11–4:30; Feb., Mar., Oct., and Nov., Tues. and Sat. 11–4:30.*

WHERE TO EAT AND STAY

$$$$ BRITISH 🍴 **Langley Castle.** This lavish 14th-century castle with turrets and battlements offers an elegant fine-dining experience. The baronial dining room is romantic, with little candlelit alcoves draped in rich fabric. Choose from an excellent five-course prix-fixe menu of traditional English dishes—perhaps the beef shin and pheasant breast served with oyster mushrooms and Madeira *jus*, or the Dover sole with parsley and caper butter. There's also a lighter (and cheaper) snack menu. If you're really taken with the place, rooms start at around £160 per night. Langley Castle is 6 miles west of Hexham. [$] *Average main: £40* ✉ *A686, Langley-on-Tyne* ☎ *01434/688888* 🌐 *www.langleycastle.com.*

$ B&B/INN **Battlesteads Hotel.** On the outer edge of Hexham, this delightful old inn combines three virtues: good food, cozy rooms, and eco-friendly credentials, with a string of awards to prove it (including "Green Pub of the Year" in 2010). **Pros:** lovely staff; good food; green ethos. **Cons:** some rooms on the small side; no mobile phone reception. [$] *Rooms from: £90* ✉ *Wark on Tyne* ☎ *01434/230209* 🌐 *www.battlesteads.com* 🛏 *17 rooms* 🍴 *Breakfast.*

$ B&B/INN **Dene House.** This former farmhouse on 9 acres of lovely countryside has beamed ceilings and homey rooms with pine pieces and colorful quilts. **Pros:** tasty breakfasts; warm atmosphere; reasonable rates. **Cons:** no restaurant. [$] *Rooms from: £70* ✉ *B6303, Juniper* ☎ *01434/673413* 🌐 *www.denehouse-hexham.co.uk* 🛏 *3 rooms, 1 with bath* 🍴 *Breakfast.*

NIGHTLIFE AND THE ARTS

Queen's Hall Arts Centre. Theater, dance, and art exhibitions are on the bill at the Queen's Hall Arts Centre. ✉ *Beaumont St.* ☎ *01434/652477* 🌐 *www.queenshall.co.uk.*

GREENHEAD

18 miles west of Hexham, 49 miles northwest of Durham.

In and around tiny Greenhead you'll find a wealth of historical sites related to Hadrian's Wall, including the fascinating Housesteads Roman Fort, the Roman Army Museum, and Vindolanda. In Northumberland National Park, about half a mile north of Vindolanda, the Once Brewed National Park Visitor Centre has informative displays about Hadrian's Wall and can advise about local walks.

GETTING HERE AND AROUND

Greenhead is on the A69 and B6318. The nearest train station is 3 miles east, in Haltwhistle.

ESSENTIALS

Visitor Information Once Brewed National Park Visitor Centre ✉ *Northumberland National Park, Military Rd., Bardon Mill, Once Brewed* ☎ *01434/344396* 🌐 *www.northumberlandnationalpark.org.uk* 🕒 *Apr.–Oct., daily 9:30–5; Nov.–Mar., weekends 10–3.*

EXPLORING

Fodor's Choice ★ **Housesteads Roman Fort.** If you have time to visit only one Hadrian's Wall site, Housesteads Roman Fort, Britain's most complete example of a Roman fort, is your best bet. It includes long sections of the wall, an excavated fort, and a new visitor center with a collection of artifacts discovered at the site and computer-generated images of what the fort originally looked like. The fort itself is a 10-minute walk uphill from the parking lot (not for those with mobility problems), but the effort is worth it to see the surprisingly extensive ruins, dating from around AD 125. Excavations have revealed the remains of granaries, gateways, barracks, a hospital, and the commandant's house. ■ **TIP→ The northern tip of the fort, at the crest of the hill, has one of the best views of Hadrian's Wall, passing beside you before disappearing over hills and crags in the distance.** ✉ *B6318, Haydon Bridge*

☎ 01434/344363 🌐 www.english-heritage.org.uk 🎟 £6.50 🕒 Apr.–Oct., daily 10–6; Nov.–Mar., weekends 10–4.

FAMILY **Roman Army Museum.** At the garrison fort of Carvoran, this museum makes an excellent introduction to Hadrian's Wall. Full-size models and excavations bring this remote outpost of the empire to life; authentic Roman graffiti adorns the walls of an excavated barracks. There's a well-designed museum with Roman artifacts and a 3-D film that puts it all into historical context. Opposite the museum, at Walltown Crags on the Pennine Way (one of Britain's long-distance national hiking trails), are 400 yards of the best-preserved section of the wall. The museum is 1 mile northeast of Greenhead. *✉ Off B6318 ☎ 01697/747485 🌐 www.vindolanda.com 🎟 £5; £10 with admission to Vindolanda 🕒 Mid-Feb–Mar. and Oct., daily 10–5; Apr.–Sept., daily 10–6; Nov.–mid-Feb., weekends 10–4.*

Vindolanda. About 8 miles east of Greenhead, this archaeological site holds the remains of eight successive Roman forts and civilian settlements, providing an intriguing look into the daily life of a military compound. Most of the visible remains date from the 2nd and 3rd centuries, and new excavations are constantly under way. A reconstructed Roman temple, house, and shop provide context, and the museum displays rare artifacts, such as a handful of extraordinary wooden tablets with messages about everything from household chores to military movements. A full-size reproduction of a section of the wall gives a sense of its massiveness. The site is sometimes closed in bad weather. *✉ Off B6318, Bardon Mill ☎ 01434/344277 🌐 www.vindolanda.com 🎟 £6.50; £10 includes admission to Roman Army Museum 🕒 Mid-Feb.–Mar. and Oct., daily 10–5; Apr.–Sept., daily 10–6; Nov.–mid-Feb., weekends 10–4.*

WHERE TO EAT AND STAY

$ BRITISH 🍴 **Milecastle Inn.** The snug bar and restaurant of this remote, peaceful 17th-century pub make an excellent place to dine. Fine local meat goes into its famous pies; take your pick from wild boar and duckling. The unfussy menu also features such staples as fish-and-chips or lasagna with garlic bread. Two cottages are available for rent. The inn is on the north side of Haltwhistle on B6318. *[$] Average main: £11 ✉ Military Rd., Haltwhistle ☎ 01434/321372 🌐 www.milecastle-inn.co.uk.*

$ B&B/INN 🏨 **Holmhead Guest House.** Talk about a feel for history—this former farmhouse in open countryside, graced with stone arches and exposed beams, is not only built *on* Hadrian's Wall but also partly *from* it. **Pros:** full of atmosphere; close to Hadrian's Wall; reasonable rates. **Cons:** rooms are a bit of a squeeze; you need a car out here. *[$] Rooms from: £68 ✉ Off A69 ☎ 01697/747402 🌐 www.bandbhadrianswall.com 🛏 4 rooms, 8 beds, 1 apartment 🍽 Breakfast.*

THE FAR NORTHEAST COAST

Extraordinary medieval fortresses and monasteries line the final 40 miles of the northeast coast before England gives way to Scotland—none of them more impressive than Alnwick, for centuries the main seat of dynastic power in the far north of England. The region also has some magnificent beaches, though because of the cold water and rough seas they're far better for walking than swimming.

ALNWICK

71 miles northeast of Greenhead, 30 miles north of Newcastle, 46 miles north of Durham.

Dominated by a grand castle, the little market town of Alnwick (pronounced *ahn*-ick) is the best base from which to explore the dramatic coast and countryside of northern Northumberland.

GETTING HERE AND AROUND

If you're driving, Alnwick is just off the A1. The nearest train station is 4 miles away in Alnmouth; trains travel between here and Durham roughly every hour and take 45 minutes.

Buses X15 and X18 connect Alnwick with Newcastle.

ESSENTIALS

Visitor Information Visit Alnwick ⊠ *2 The Shambles* ☎ *01665/511333* ⊕ *www.visitalnwick.org.uk.*

EXPLORING

FAMILY

Fodor'sChoice

★

Alnwick Castle. Sometimes called the "Windsor of the North," the imposing Alnwich Castle is more familiar to many as a location in the Harry Potter movies. (The castle grounds appear as the exterior of Hogwarts School.) The building is still home to the dukes of Northumberland, whose family, the Percys, dominated in the Northeast for centuries. Family photos and other knickknacks are scattered around the lavish staterooms, a subtle reminder that this is a family home rather than a museum. Highlights include the extraordinary gun room, lined with hundreds of antique pistols in swirling patterns; the formal dining room, its table set as if guests are due at any minute; and the magnificent galleried library, containing 14,000 books in floor-to-ceiling cases.

There's plenty here for younger visitors: **Knights' Quest** lets kids dress up and complete interactive challenges; **Dragon's Quest** is a labyrinth designed to teach a bit of medieval history; and for the very young there are Harry Potter–style **Broomstick Lessons,** on the exact spot used in the movie. Spooky ghost stories are told by costumed actors in the **Lost Cellars.** In addition, the staff hides a toy owl somewhere in each room of the castle, and kids get a certificate if they spot them all. ■TIP➔ Tickets are valid for one year, so you can come back if you don't see everything in a day. ⊠ *Narrowgate* ☎ *01665/511350* ⊕ *www.alnwickcastle.com* ⊠ *£14; combined ticket with Alnwick Gardens £23* ⊙ *Late Mar.–late Oct., castle daily 11–5; grounds daily 10–6. Last admission at 4:15.*

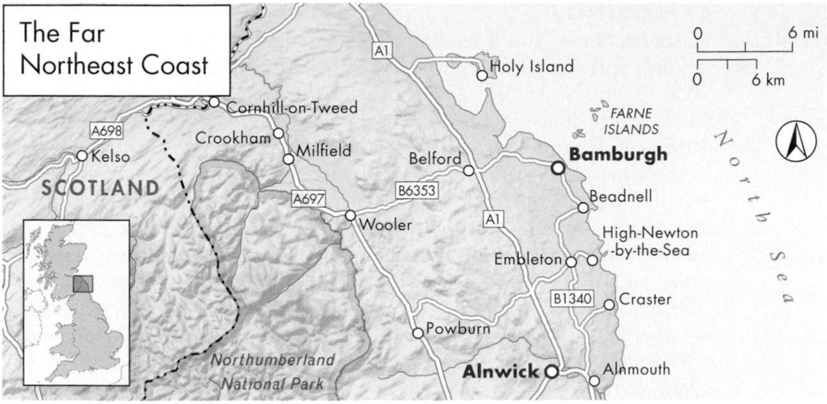
The Far Northeast Coast
0 6 mi
0 6 km
A1
Holy Island
Cornhill-on-Tweed
FARNE ISLANDS
A698
Crookham
Kelso
Milfield
Belford
Bamburgh
North Sea
SCOTLAND
A697
B6353
Beadnell
Wooler
A1
High-Newton -by-the-Sea
Embleton
B1340
Craster
Powburn
Northumberland National Park
Alnwick
Alnmouth

FAMILY
Fodor's Choice ★

Alnwick Garden. A marvelous flight of fancy, Alnwick Garden was designed by Capability Brown in 1750. Centering on modern terraced fountains by Belgian designers Jacques and Peter Wirtz, the gardens include traditional features (shaded woodland walks, a rose garden) and funkier, kid-appealing elements such as a Poison Garden and a labyrinth of towering bamboo. **■TIP→ You can buy clippings of the unique varieties of roses in the shop.** This is the location of one of the area's most unusual restaurants, the Treehouse. ✉ *Denwick La.* ☎ *01665/511350* 🌐 *www.alnwickgarden.com* 🎫 *£12; combined ticket with Alnwick Castle £24* 🕓 *Apr.–Oct., daily 10–6; Nov.–Mar., Mon.–Sat. 10–3, Sun. 11–5. Closed 3rd wk in Jan. Last admission 45 mins before closing.*

WHERE TO EAT

$$
BRITISH
Fodor's Choice ★

🍴 **The Treehouse.** You don't have to visit Alnwick Garden to eat at this extraordinary restaurant set among the treetops. The location may sound gimmicky, but the effect is quite magical, especially when the place is lit up at night. The Modern British fare is excellent—honey-glazed duck in a peppercorn and brandy sauce, perhaps, or roasted cod with tomato and chorizo gnocchi. From July to September, the kitchen only serves prix-fixe menus at night; the rest of the year there's an à la carte selection. You can grab a light lunch or tea and cake at the Potting Shed bar, which is also open for predinner drinks. [$] *Average main: £18* ✉ *Alnwick Garden, Denwick La.* ☎ *01665/511852* 🌐 *www.alnwickgarden.com/eat* 🕓 *No dinner Mon.–Wed.*

BAMBURGH

14 miles north of Alnwick.

Tiny Bamburgh has a splendid castle, and several beaches are a few minutes' walk away.

GETTING HERE AND AROUND

Bamburgh can be reached by car on B3140, B3141, or B3142. Buses run from Alnwick to Bamburgh every two hours at quarter to the hour. The nearest train station is in Chathill, about 7 miles away.

EXPLORING

Fodor's Choice ★ **Bamburgh Castle.** You'll see Bamburgh Castle long before you reach it: a solid, weather-beaten cliff-top fortress that dominates the coastal view for miles around. A fortification of some kind has stood here since the 6th century, but the Norman castle was damaged during the 15th century and the central tower is all that remains intact. Much of the structure—the home of the Armstrong family since 1894—was restored during the 18th and 19th centuries. The interior is mostly late Victorian (most impressively, the Great Hall), although a few rooms, such as the small but alarmingly well-stocked armory, have a more authentically medieval feel. The breathtaking view across the North Sea is worth the trip much as anything else; bring a picnic if the weather's good (or order to-go sandwiches at the café). ✉ *Off B1340* ☎ *01668/214515* 🌐 *www.bamburghcastle.com* 🎟 *£10* 🕒 *Mid-Feb.–Oct., daily 10–5; Nov.–mid-Feb., weekends 11–4:30; last admission 1 hr before closing.*

WHERE TO STAY

$$ HOTEL 🏨 **Lord Crewe Hotel.** This cozy, stone-walled inn with oak beams sits in the heart of the village, close to Bamburgh Castle. **Pros:** in the center of the village; good restaurant. **Cons:** pub can get quite crowded. [$] *Rooms from: £115* ✉ *Front St.* ☎ *01668/214243* 🌐 *www.lordcrewe.co.uk* 🛏 *18 rooms* 🍴 *Breakfast.*

WALES

WELCOME TO WALES

TOP REASONS TO GO

★ **Castle country:** Wales doesn't quite have a castle in each town, but there is a greater concentration than almost anywhere else in Europe—more than 600 in all.

★ **The Gower Peninsula:** This stretch of coastland near Swansea includes some of the region's prettiest beaches, as well as spectacular coastal views and medieval ruins.

★ **Snowdonia:** The biggest of the country's three national parks contains its highest mountain, Snowdon, as well as villages that recall the past.

★ **Brecon Beacons:** Moorlands, mountains, and valleys make up this rough and wild stretch of the Welsh midlands, as popular with hikers as it is with those who are just happy to take in the stunning views from the road.

★ **Hay-on-Wye:** This pretty village on the Welsh-English border has become world famous as a book lover's paradise; every street is lined with secondhand bookstores.

1 **South Wales.** Cardiff, the lively young capital city, is here, as are two very different national parks: the green, swooping hills of the Brecon Beacons and, in the far west, the sea cliffs, beaches, and estuaries of the Pembrokeshire Coast. Both are excellent for outdoor activities such as walking and mountain biking. Pembrokeshire has some of the region's best beaches.

2 **Mid-Wales.** The quietest part of Wales is home to scenic countryside, from rolling hills to more rugged mountains. Aberystwyth is a Victorian resort town on the coast, and Hay-on-Wye is a magnet for lovers of antiquarian bookstores.

3 **North Wales.** Wales's most famous castles are in its northern region. The cream of the crop is Caernarfon, a medieval palace dominating the waterfront on the Menai Strait. Conwy (castle and town) is popular, too. Snowdonia's mountains are a major draw, as is the quirky, faux-Italian village of Portmeirion.

GETTING ORIENTED

Wales has three main regions: South, Mid-, and North. South Wales is the most varied and in just a few miles you can travel from Wales's bustling and cosmopolitan capital city, Cardiff, to the most enchanting old villages and historical sights. Mid-Wales is almost entirely rural (its largest town has a population of just 16,000), and it's fringed on its western shores by the arc of Cardigan Bay. Here you'll find mountain lakes, quiet roads, hillside sheep farms, and traditional market towns. North Wales is a mixture of mountains, popular sandy beaches, and coastal hideaways. Although dominated by the rocky Snowdonia National Park, the north has a gentler, greener side along the border with England.

CASTLES IN WALES

You can't go far in Wales without seeing a castle: there are more than 600 of them. From crumbling ruins in fields to vast medieval fortresses with rich and violent histories, these castles rank among the most impressive in the world.

(above) The marquess of Bute transformed Cardiff Castle into a Victorian extravaganza; (right, top) Caerphilly Castle's romantic moat; (right, bottom) Raglan Castle's impressive ruins

The first great wave of castle building arrived in England with the Norman Conquest in 1066. When the descendants of those first Anglo-Norman kings invaded Wales 200 years later, they brought with them their awesome skill and expertise. Through deviousness and brutal force, King Edward I (1239–1307) won control over the Welsh lords in the north and wasted no time in building mighty castles, including Caerphilly and Conwy, to consolidate his power. These became known as his "ring of iron." Wars came and went over the next few centuries, until, rendered obsolete by gunpowder and the changing ways of warfare, castles were destroyed or fell into disrepair. Only in the Victorian age, when castles became hugely fashionable, was there widespread acceptance of how important it was to save these historic structures for the nation.

CASTLE GLOSSARY

Bailey: open grounds within a castle's walls.

Battlements: fortified ledge atop castle walls.

Keep: largest, most heavily defended castle building.

Moat: water-filled ditch around castle.

Motte: steep man-made hill on which a castle was often built.

Portcullis: iron drop-gate over entrance.

12

With such a dizzying array of castles, it can be hard to know where to start. Here are six of the best to help you decide. At the larger sites, buy a guidebook or take an audio or other tour so that you can best appreciate the remains of a distant era.

CAERNARFON CASTLE

Welsh naturalist Thomas Pennant (1726–98) called Caernarfon Castle "that most magnificent badge of our subjection." Built in 1283 on the site of an earlier castle, it's the most significant symbol of Edward I's conquest of Wales. It's also the best preserved of his "ring of iron" and, along with Edward's Beaumaris, Harlech, and Conwy castles in North Wales, is a UNESCO World Heritage Site. *North Wales*

CAERPHILLY CASTLE

Near Cardiff, this is the largest castle in Wales, and the second largest in Britain after Windsor Castle. Caerphilly's defenses included a man-made island and two huge lakes. The castle was ruined by centuries of warfare, although modern renovations have recaptured much of its former glory. Kids love it. *South Wales*

CARDIFF CASTLE

Though the capital's titular castle has medieval sections, most of it is, in fact, a Victorian flight of fancy. Its most famous occupant, the 3rd Marquess of

Bute (1847–1900), was once the richest man in the world, and his love of the exotic led to the bizarre mishmash of styles. *South Wales*

CARREG CENNEN CASTLE

The great views over the countryside are worth the steep hike to this bleak, craggy cliff-top fortress in the Brecon Beacons. This medieval stronghold was partially destroyed during the Wars of the Roses in the 15th century. Some interior rooms, hollowed out from the mountain itself, survive intact. *South Wales*

CONWY CASTLE

Imposing, if partially ruined, Conwy Castle with its eight towers captures like no other the feeling of sheer dominance that Edward I's citadels must have had over the landscape. The approach by foot over the River Conwy, along a 19th-century suspension bridge designed by Thomas Telford, makes for an awesome view. You can walk the ancient walls of Conwy town, which has places to eat and shop. *North Wales*

RAGLAN CASTLE

The boyhood home of Henry VII, the first Tudor king, Raglan is a small but impressive 15th-century castle, surrounded by a steep moat (one of the few in Wales that's still filled with water). Largely a ruin, it's relatively complete from the front, making for some irresistible, fairy-tale photo ops. *South Wales*

Updated by
Jack Jewers

Wales is a land of dramatic national parks, plunging, unspoiled coastlines, and awe-inspiring medieval castles. Its ancient history and deep-rooted Celtic culture makes Wales similar in many ways to its more famous Celtic neighbors, Scotland and Ireland; and yet it doesn't attract the same hordes of visitors, which is another part of the country's appeal.

Vast swaths of Wales were untouched by the industrial boom of the 19th century. Although pockets of the country were given over to industries such as coal mining and manufacturing (both of which have all but disappeared), most of Wales remained unspoiled. Brecon Beacons, Snowdonia, and Pembroke Coast are stunning national parks, and the Gower Peninsula and Cardigan Bay offer beautiful coast. The country is largely rural, and there are more than 10 million sheep—but only 3 million people. It has a Britain-as-it-used-to-be feel that can be hugely appealing.

Now is a great time to visit Wales. The country is reveling in a new political autonomy, just a decade-and-a-half old, that's brought with it a flourish of optimism and self-confidence. Cardiff, the capital, is thriving. Welsh culture has undergone something of a renaissance, and its culinary traditions are being reinvented by an enthusiastic new generation of chefs and artisan foodies. Simply put, Wales loves being Wales, and that enthusiasm is infectious to the visitor. It also means that the tourism industry has grown, including some truly unique places to stay.

Although Wales is a small country—on average, about 60 miles wide and 170 miles north to south—looking at it on a map is deceptive. It can be a difficult place to get around, with a distinctly old-fashioned road network and poor public transportation connections. To see it properly, you really need a car. The good news is that along the way you'll experience some beautiful drives. There are rewards to be found in the gentle folds of its valleys and in the shadows of its mountains.

Were some of the more remote attractions in Wales in, say, the west of Ireland, they'd be world famous and overrun with millions of visitors. Here, if you're lucky, you can almost have them to yourself—for now.

WALES PLANNER

WHEN TO GO

The weather in Wales, as in the rest of Britain, is a lottery. It can be hot in summer or never stop raining. Generally it's cool and wet in spring and autumn, but could also be surprisingly warm and sunny. The only surefire rule is that you should be prepared for the unexpected.

Generally speaking, southwest Wales tends to enjoy a milder climate than elsewhere in Britain, thanks in part to the moderating effects of the Gulf Stream. In contrast, mountainous areas like Snowdonia and the Brecon Beacons can be chilly at any time of the year. Book far ahead for major festivals such as the literary Hay Festival, Brecon Jazz, and the Abergavenny Food Festival.

PLANNING YOUR TIME

First-time visitors often try to cover too much ground in too little time. It's not hard to spend half your time traveling between points that look close on the map, but take the better part of a day to reach. From Cardiff, it's easy to visit the Wye Valley, Brecon Beacons, and the Gower Peninsula. Along the North Wales coast, Llandudno and Lake Vyrnwy make good bases for the Snowdonia National Park.

The location of Wales lends itself to a border-hopping trip—in both directions. Well-known locations like Bath (near South Wales) and Chester (near North Wales) are no more than an hour from the Welsh border, and you can even take a ferry to Ireland if you want to go farther afield.

GETTING HERE AND AROUND

AIR TRAVEL

If you're arriving from the United States, London's Heathrow and Gatwick airports are generally the best options because of their large number of international flights. Heathrow (2 hours) is slightly closer than Gatwick (2½ hours), but both have excellent motorway links with South Wales. For North Wales, the quickest access is via Manchester Airport, with a travel time of less than an hour to the Welsh border.

Cardiff International Airport, 19 miles from downtown Cardiff, is the only airport in Wales with international flights, but these are mostly from Europe and Canada. A bus service runs from the airport to Cardiff's central train and bus stations.

Airports Cardiff International Airport ✉ *A4226, Rhoose* ☎ *01446/711111* ⊕ *www.cwlfly.com.* **Manchester Airport** ✉ *M56, Near Junctions 5 and 6* ☎ *08712/710711* ⊕ *www.manchesterairport.co.uk.*

BUS TRAVEL

Most parts of Wales are accessible by bus, but long-distance bus travel takes a long time. National Express travels to all parts of Wales from London's Victoria Coach Station and also direct from London's

Heathrow and Gatwick airports. The company also has routes into Wales from many major towns and cities in England and Scotland. Average travel times from London are 3½ hours to Cardiff, 4 hours to Swansea, 7 hours to Aberystwyth, and 4½ hours to Llandudno.

Wales's three national parks run summer bus services. In the North, the excellent Snowdon Sherpa runs into and around Snowdonia and links with main rail and bus services. The Pembrokeshire Coastal Bus Service operates in the Pembrokeshire Coast National Park, and the Beacons Bus serves the Brecon Beacons National Park.

Bus Contacts Beacons Bus ☎ *0871/200–2233* ⊕ *www.travelbreconbeacons. info.* **National Express** ☎ *0871/781–8178* ⊕ *www.nationalexpress.com.* **Pembrokeshire Coastal Bus** ☎ *0845/345–7275* ⊕ *www.pembrokeshirecoast. org.uk.* **Snowdon Sherpa** ☎ *01286/870880* ⊕ *www.gwynedd.gov.uk.*

CAR TRAVEL

To explore the Welsh heartland properly, you really need a car. Be prepared to take the scenic route: there are no major highways north of Swansea (which means virtually all of Wales). For the most part it's all back roads, all the way. There are some stunning routes to savor: the A487 runs along or near most of the coastline, while the A44 and A470 both wind through mountain scenery with magnificent views.

FERRY TRAVEL

Two ferry ports that connect Britain with Ireland are in Wales. Regular daily ferries with Stena Line and Irish Ferries sail from Fishguard, in the southwest, and Holyhead, in the northwest. Celtic Link runs some ferries between Rosslare and Cherbourg in France.

Ferry Contacts Celtic Link ⊕ *www.celticlinkferries.com.* **Irish Ferries** ☎ *0818/300–400* ⊕ *www.irishferries.com.* **Stena Line** ☎ *0844/770–7070* ⊕ *www.stenaline.co.uk.*

TRAIN TRAVEL

Travel time on the First Great Western rail service from London's Paddington Station is about two hours to Cardiff and three hours to Swansea. Trains connect London's Euston Station with Mid-Wales and North Wales, often involving changes in cities such as Birmingham. Travel times average between three and five hours. Regional train service covers much of South and North Wales but, frustratingly, there are virtually no direct connections between these regions. For example, to make the 73-mile trip between Cardiff and Aberystwyth you have to make a connection in Shrewsbury, lengthening the trip to 147 miles. North Wales has a cluster of steam railways, but these are tourist attractions rather than a practical way of getting around. The mainline long-distance routes can be very scenic indeed, such as the Cambrian Coast Railway, running between Machynlleth and Pwllheli, and the Heart of Wales line, linking Swansea with London, Bristol, and Manchester.

Train Contacts National Rail Enquiries ☎ *0845/748–4950* ⊕ *www. nationalrail.co.uk.*

DISCOUNTS AND DEALS

For travel within Wales, ask about money-saving unlimited-travel tickets (such as the Freedom of Wales Flexi Pass, the North and Mid-Wales Rover, and the South Wales Flexi Rover), which include the use of bus services. A discount card offering a 20% reduction on each of the steam-driven Great Little Trains of Wales is also available. It costs £10 and is valid for 12 months.

The Cadw/Welsh Historic Monuments Explorer Pass is good for unlimited admission to most of Wales's historic sites. The seven-day pass costs £20 per person, £32 per couple, or £39 per family; the three-day pass costs £13.50, £20.50, and £28.30, respectively. Passes are available at any site covered by the Cadw program. All national museums and galleries in Wales are free.

Discount Information Cadw/Welsh Historic Monuments ✉ *Plas Carew, Unit 5–7 Cefn Coed, Parc Nantgarw, Treforest* ☎ *01443/336000* ⊕ *www.cadw.wales. gov.uk.* **Flexi Pass information** ☎ *0845/606–1660* ⊕ *www.nationalrail.co.uk.* **Great Little Trains of Wales** ⊕ *www.greatlittletrainsofwales.co.uk.* **National Museums and Galleries of Wales** ⊕ *www.museumwales.ac.uk.*

TOURS

In summer there are all-day and half-day tour-bus excursions to most parts of the country. In major resorts and cities, ask for details at a tourist information center or bus station.

The Wales Official Tourist Guide Association (WOTGA) uses only guides recognized by VisitWales and will create tailor-made tours. You can book a driver-guide or someone to accompany you as you drive.

Tour Information Wales Official Tourist Guide Association ☎ *01633/774796* ⊕ *www.walestourguides.com.*

RESTAURANTS

Wales has developed a thriving restaurant scene over the last decade or so, and not just in major towns. Some truly outstanding food can be found in rural pubs and hotel restaurants. More and more restaurants are creating dishes using fresh local ingredients—Welsh lamb, Welsh Black beef, Welsh cheeses, and seafood from the Welsh coast—that show off the best of the region's cuisine.

HOTELS

A 19th-century dictum, "I sleeps where I dines," still holds true in Wales, where good hotels and good restaurants often go together. Castles, country mansions, and even disused railway stations are being transformed into interesting hotels and restaurants. Traditional inns with low, beamed ceilings, wood paneling, and fireplaces are often the most appealing places to stay. The best ones tend to be off the beaten track. Cardiff and Swansea have some large chain hotels, and, for luxury, some excellent spas have cropped up in the countryside. An added bonus is that prices are generally lower than they are for equivalent properties in the Cotswolds, Scotland, or southeast England. *Hotel reviews have been shortened. For full information, visit Fodors.com.*

WHAT IT COSTS IN POUNDS			
$	$$	$$$	$$$$
Restaurants	under £15	£15–£19	£20–£25	over £25
Hotels	under £100	£100–£160	£161–£220	over £220

Restaurant prices are the average cost of a main course at dinner or, if dinner isn't served, at lunch. Hotel prices are the lowest cost of a standard double room in high season, including 20% V.A.T.

VISITOR INFORMATION
Contacts **VisitWales Centre** ☎ *08708/300306* ⊕ *www.visitwales.com.* **Wales in Style** ⊕ *www.walesinstyle.com.*

SOUTH WALES

The most diverse of Wales's three regions, the south covers the area around Cardiff that stretches southwest as far as the rugged coastline of Pembrokeshire. It's the most accessible part of the country, as the roads are relatively good and the rail network is more extensive than it is elsewhere in Wales. Pleasant seaside towns such as Tenby are within a four- to five-hour drive of London; from Cardiff and Swansea you're never more than a half hour away from some gorgeous small villages.

Cardiff has had limited success in reinventing itself as a cultured, modern capital, but Swansea and neighboring Newport have struggled to find their place in this postindustrial region. With a few exceptions, it's better to stick to the countryside in South Wales. The heart-stopping Gower Peninsula stretches along 14 miles of sapphire-blue bays and rough-hewn sea cliffs, and the Brecon Beacons National Park is an area of grassy mountains and craggy limestone gorges.

CARDIFF CAERDYDD

20 miles southwest of the Second Severn Bridge.

With a population of around 330,000, Cardiff is the largest and most important city in Wales. It's also one of the youngest capitals in Europe: although a settlement has existed here since Roman times, Cardiff wasn't declared a city until 1905, and didn't become the capital until 50 years later. This is an energetic, youthful place, keen to show its new-found cosmopolitanism to the world. Cardiff is experiencing something of a cultural renaissance with the opening of the Wales Millennium Centre in Cardiff Bay.

For all its urban optimism, however, Cardiff is still a rather workaday town, with little to detain you for more than a day. See Cardiff Castle and the National Museum, wander Cardiff Bay, and maybe catch a show. Otherwise, it's a convenient base for exploring the nearby countryside.

Castell Coch looks medieval but don't be fooled: it's a delightful Victorian-Gothic fantasy.

GETTING HERE AND AROUND

The capital is a major transportation hub with good connections to other parts of South Wales and with England. Getting to Mid-Wales and North Wales is more difficult, as there's no direct north–south train route (you'll have to connect in Bristol or Shrewsbury) and north–south buses are painfully slow. From London, trains from Paddington to Cardiff Central take about two hours; National Express coaches take about three hours. Cardiff is easily accessible by the M4 motorway. You must pay a £6.20 toll to cross the Severn Bridge between England and Wales (though crossing back is free).

TIMING

If you don't like crowds, avoid Cardiff during international rugby tournaments or other major sporting events.

ESSENTIALS

Visitor and Tour Information Cardiff Bay Visitor Centre ⊠ *Wales Millennium Centre, Bute Pl.* ☎ *029/2087–3573* ⊕ *www.visitcardiff.com.* **Cardiff Tourist Information Centre** ⊠ *The Old Library, The Hayes* ☎ *029/2087–3573* ⊕ *www. visitcardiff.com.*

EXPLORING
TOP ATTRACTIONS

FAMILY

Fodor's Choice

★

Caerphilly Castle. One of the largest and most impressive fortresses in Wales, Caerphilly was remarkable at the time of its construction in the 13th century. Built by an Anglo-Norman lord, the concentric fortification contained powerful inner and outer defenses. It was badly damaged during the English Civil War, although extensive 20th-century renovations have restored much of its former glory. The original Great Hall is still intact, and near the edge of the inner courtyard there's a replica of a trebuchet—a giant catapult used to launch rocks and other projectiles at the enemy. Kids love exploring this castle, which is 7 miles north of Cardiff. ⊠ *Castle St., Caerphilly* ☏ *029/2088–3143* ⊕ *www.cadw.wales. gov.uk* ▣ *£4* ☉ *Mar.–June, Sept., and Oct., daily 9:30–5; July and Aug., daily 9:30–6; Nov.–Feb., Mon.–Sat. 10–4, Sun. 11–4. Last admission 30 mins before closing.*

Cardiff Bay. Perhaps the most potent symbol of Cardiff's 21st-century rebirth, this upscale district is a 10-minute cab ride from Cardiff Central Station. Its museums and other attractions are clustered around the bay itself. The area can seem rather tranquil during the day, but buzzes with activity at night.

Techniquest. A large science-discovery center for children, Techniquest has 160 interactive exhibits, a planetarium, and a science theater. ⊠ *Stuart St., Cardiff Bay* ☏ *029/2047–5475* ⊕ *www.techniquest.org* ▣ *£7; planetarium £1.30* ☉ *Jan.–mid-July and Sept.–Dec., weekends 9:30–4:30; mid-July–Aug., daily 10–5.*

Wales Millennium Centre. Inviting comparisons to Bilbao's Guggenheim, Cardiff's main arts complex (known locally as "The Armadillo" for its coppery, shingled exterior) is an extraordinary building, inside and out. The materials used in the construction are intended to represent "Welshness." (Slate is for the rocky coastline, for example, while wood is for its ancient forests.) The massive words carved into the curving facade read "In These Stones Horizons Sing" in English and Welsh. Inside there's a maritime feel, from the curving wooden stairs to balconies evoking the bow of a ship. A broad range of cultural programs take place on the various stages, from ballet and opera to major touring shows. Guided tours (£5.50) depart about every hour. ⊠ *Bute Pl., Cardiff Bay* ☏ *029/2063–6464* ⊕ *www.wmc.org.uk*

Fodor's Choice   **Cardiff Castle.** A higgledy-piggledy mishmash of styles, from austere Norman keep to over-the-top Victorian mansion, Cardiff Castle is an odd but beguiling place, located right in the middle of the city. Take the tour of the Victorian portion to discover the castle's exuberant side. William Burges (1827–81), an architect obsessed by the Gothic period, transformed the castle into an extravaganza of medieval color for the 3rd Marquess of Bute. The result was the Moorish-style ceiling in the Arab Room, the intricately carved shelves lining the Library, and gold-leaf murals everywhere. Look for the painting of *The Invisible Prince* in the Day Nursery; on first glance it's just a tree, but stare long enough and a man takes shape in the branches. Note the not-so-subtle rejection of Darwin's theory of evolution, represented by monkeys tearing up his book around the library's doorway. The vast grounds, which include beautiful rhododendron gardens and a habitat for owls and falcons, are sometimes the setting for jousting in summer. ⊠ *Castle St.* ☏ *029/2087–8100* ⊕ *www.cardiffcastle.com* ▣ *£11, £14 with guided tour* ☉ *Mar.–Oct., daily 9–6; Nov.–Feb., daily 9–5. Last admission 1 hr before closing.*

Castell Coch. Perched on a hillside is this fairy-tale castle. The turreted Red Castle was built on the site of a medieval stronghold in the 1870s,

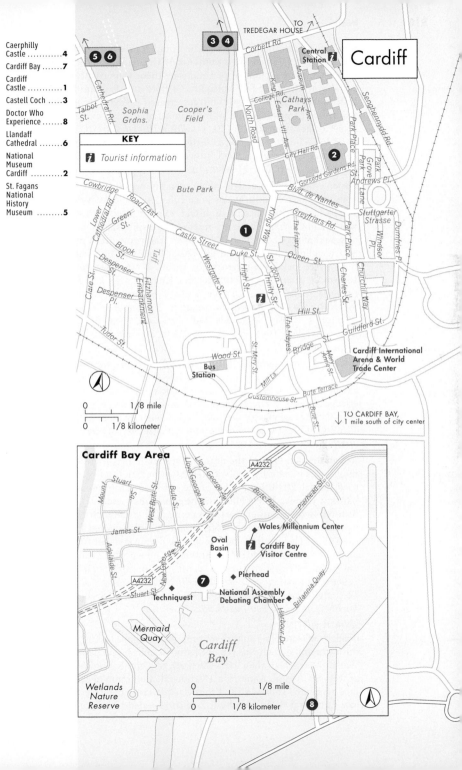

Cardiff

KEY

🛈 *Tourist information*

Cardiff Bay Area

Cardiff Bay

about the time that the "Fairytale King" Ludwig II of Bavaria was creating his castles in the mountains of Germany. This Victorian fantasy wouldn't look out of place among them. The castle was another collaboration of the 3rd Marquess of Bute and William Burges, who transformed Cardiff Castle. Burges created everything, including the whimsical furnishings and murals, in a remarkable exercise in Victorian-Gothic whimsy. ⊠ *A470, 4 miles north of Cardiff, Tongwynlais* ☎ *029/2081–0101* ⊕ *www.cadw.wales.gov.uk* 🖾 *£3.80* ⊘ *Mar.–June, Sept., and Oct., daily 9:30–5; July and Aug., daily 9:30–6; Nov.–Feb., Mon.–Sat. 10–4, Sun. 11–4; last admission 30 mins before closing.*

FAMILY **Doctor Who Experience.** The phenomenally popular BBC TV series— which has been made in Wales since 2005—marked its 50th anniversary in 2013, and this suitably high-tech exhibit celebrates its weird and wonderful charms. There are interactive displays, specially re-created sets, and a huge collection of costumes and props from the show, plus an exceedingly well-stocked gift shop. Fans will be in heaven. Entry is by timed ticket, so try to book ahead. ■**TIP**→ Reserve online and save more than £10 on family tickets. Kids get a pack of *Doctor Who*-related goodies, too. ⊠ *Discovery Quay, Butetown* ☎ *0844/801–2279 box office, 0844/801–3663 information* ⊕ *www.doctorwhoexperience. com* 🖾 *£13* ⊘ *Mar.–mid-July and Sept.–Jan., Wed.–Mon. 10–5; mid-July–Aug., daily 10–5; Feb., Thurs.–Mon. 10–5; last admission 90 mins before closing.*

National Museum Cardiff. At this splendid museum you can learn about the story of Wales through its archaeology, art, and industry. The Evolution of Wales gallery uses inventive robotics and audiovisual effects. There's a fine collection of modern European art, including works by Daumier, Renoir, Van Gogh, and Cézanne. ⊠ *Cathays Park* ☎ *029/2057–3000* ⊕ *www.museumwales.ac.uk* 🖾 *Free* ⊘ *Tues.–Sun. and holidays 10–5.*

Tredegar House. One of the grandest stately homes in Wales, Tredegar House was bought by the National Trust in 2011 and opened its doors to visitors in 2013. Highlights of the self-guided tour include the grand baroque Jacobean New Hall and the enormous Victorian kitchens, both restored to their former glory. Don't miss the lavish Victorian Side Hall, lined with portraits of the Morgan family, which owned Tredegar until the 1950s. The grounds include immaculately laid-out formal gardens and an orangery. Tredegar is just outside Newport, 12 miles northwest of Cardiff. ⊠ *Tredegar House Dr., off A48, Newport* ☎ *01633/815880* ⊕ *www.nationaltrust.co.uk* 🖾 *£6.80* ⊘ *House: Mar.–Oct., weekends 11–5; mid–late Feb., weekends 11–4:30. Gardens: Mar.–Oct., weekends 10:30–5, mid–late Feb., weekends 11–4:30.*

WORTH NOTING

Llandaff Cathedral. In a suburb that retains its village feeling, you can visit this cathedral, which was repaired after serious bomb damage in World War II. The cathedral includes the work of a number of Pre-Raphaelites as well as *Christ in Majesty,* a 15-foot-tall aluminum figure by sculptor Jacob Epstein (1880–1959). From Cardiff, cross the River Taff and follow Cathedral Road for about 2 miles. Guided tours are available by

WALES: COUNTRY WITHIN A COUNTRY

Is Wales a nation, a state, or a country? The answer—confusingly—is yes, kind of, and yes and no. This requires some untangling.

Wales is a country within the United Kingdom, the same as Scotland and England. It has its own language—which you'll see on every signpost, though everybody also speaks English—its own flag, and sends its own teams to international sporting events like soccer's World Cup (but not the Olympics).

Although Wales has the right to pass some of its own laws, it isn't a sovereign nation. It shares the same head of state and has the same central government as England, Scotland, and Northern Ireland. It uses the same currency, and there are no restrictions for travelers who cross the English border.

In medieval times Wales was an independent nation, but lacked a single government or ruler. It was slowly annexed by England in a drawn-out series of wars and skirmishes. Although the Welsh retained a strong sense of their own national identity, by the middle of the 16th century their land was effectively part of England.

This was the case until 1997, when Tony Blair was elected prime minister on a platform that included semiautonomous legislatures for Wales and Scotland. Two years later, the Welsh Assembly passed the first laws made solely by and for Wales in more than 400 years.

You should always refer to Wales as a separate country. Be respectful of the fact that when you cross the border you're entering a place with a rich and proud history of its own.

arrangement. ⊠ *Cathedral Close, Llandaff* ☎ *029/2056–4554* ⊕ *www.llandaffcathedral.org.uk* ⊠ *Free* ☉ *Mon., Fri. and Sat., 9–7; Tues. and Thurs., 7–7; Wed., 7–8; Sun., 7–7:30.*

FAMILY **St. Fagans National History Museum.** On 100 acres of gardens, this excellent open-air museum celebrates the region's architectural history with a collection of farmhouses, cottages, shops, chapels, a school, and a 16th-century manor house. All but two of the structures were brought here from around Wales. Of special note are the ironworkers' cottages; a string of attached structures each reflecting a different era from 1805, 1855, 1925, 1955, and 1985 from the decor to the technology to the gardening methods. Galleries display clothing and other articles from daily life, and special events highlight local customs. ⊠ *Off A4232, St. Fagans* ☎ *029/2057–3500* ⊕ *www.museumwales.ac.uk* ⊠ *Free* ☉ *Daily 10–5.*

WHERE TO EAT

$$ × **Bayside Brasserie.** With its gorgeous view over Cardiff Bay, this unde-
FRENCH niably romantic restaurant is one of the most popular in Cardiff. The classic bistro menu has few surprises, but the kitchen serves up some tasty fare. Fish is a particular specialty—start with an appetizer of mussels, scallops, or smoked salmon before moving on to fillet of sea bass stuffed with citrus fruit, or a simple Welsh sirloin from the grill. The extensive wine list includes organic and fair-trade labels. $ *Average*

main: £16 ✉ *Mermaid Quay, Bute Pl.* ☎ *029/2035–8444* ⊕ *www.baysidebrasserie.com.*

$ ✕ **The Clink.** Well, this is unusual: a trendy new restaurant in which all
BRITISH the food is prepared by prisoners. The idea behind the Clink (British slang for jail) is that those serving time for minor crimes are given the chance to turn their lives around by gaining experience as gourmet chefs. The restaurant (just outside the prison grounds) is a bright, modern space, and the Modern British food is genuinely delicious. You might try shoulder of lamb with lemon, olive, and caper tapenade, or the wild boar and venison ragout with grilled polenta. At the time of writing, the restaurant is open for lunch all week, plus a single dinner sitting on Wednesday. This is likely to change, however. $ *Average main: £10* ✉ *Knox Rd., in front of Cardiff Prison* ☎ *029/2092–3130* ⊕ *www.theclinkcharity.com/cardiff.*

$$ ✕ **The Potted Pig.** Vaulted ceilings and exposed brick walls provide a
BRITISH dramatic backdrop to this restaurant down the block from Cardiff
Fodor'sChoice Castle. Formerly a bank vault, the Potted Pig turns out superb Welsh
★ dishes. Starters like duck hash with fried egg and entrees such as Devonshire brown crab with chips and mayonnaise keep diners satisfied. Popular desserts like the jelly roll can run out by the end of the night. Servers are warm and attentive and knowledgeable about wine. The underground atmosphere and candlelight make this a romantic dinner choice. $ *Average main: £17* ✉ *27, High St.* ☎ *029/2022–4817* ⊕ *www.thepottedpig.com* ☽ *Closed Mon. No dinner Sun.*

$ ✕ **Restaurant Minuet.** A longtime favorite with locals, Restaurant Minuet
PIZZA serves simple, fresh Italian lunches at decidedly ungourmet prices. The simple menu won't win any prizes for originality—a simple *Capricciosa* pizza, perhaps, with pepperoni and artichokes, or pasta with prawns, garlic, and chili—but the cooking is excellent and the atmosphere homey. Kids are well cared for, with junior-size pizzas and calzones, all for around £5. $ *Average main: £7* ✉ *42 Castle Arcade* ☎ *029/203–41794* ⊕ *www.restaurantminuet.co.uk* ⌂ *Reservations not accepted* ☽ *No dinner. Closed Sun.*

$ ✕ **Valentino's.** With its nicely understated rustic decor and friendly Italian
ITALIAN staff, this restaurant drips with authenticity. In addition to pizzas and pastas, there is an ever-changing selection of fresh, locally sourced meat and fish dishes. $ *Average main: £12* ✉ *5 Windsor Pl.* ☎ *029/2022–9697* ⊕ *www.valentinocardiff.co.uk* ☽ *Closed Sun.*

WHERE TO STAY

$ ⊡ **Jolyons Boutique Hotel.** This town house, a hop and a skip from the
B&B/INN Wales Millennium Centre in Cardiff Bay, bucks the trend in a city where big, modern hotels are usually a safer bet than boutique places. **Pros:** loads of character; comfortable bar; good online discounts. **Cons:** 10-minute drive from the city center; no parking. $ *Rooms from: £76* ✉ *Bute Crescent* ☎ *029/2048–8775* ⊕ *www.jolyons.co.uk* ⇱ *6 rooms* ⎹⊙⎸ *Breakfast.*

$ ⊡ **Lincoln House Hotel.** Perhaps the best of the many B&Bs on Cathe-
B&B/INN dral Road—a handsome enclave of Victorian houses—this place close to the city center is a great find. **Pros:** good service; handy location; free parking. **Cons:** attractive road is spoiled by traffic; no restaurant.

12

$ Rooms from: £90 ⊠ 118 Cathedral Rd. ☎ 029/2039–5558 ⊕ www. lincolnhotel.co.uk ↪ 24 rooms ⊙ Breakfast.

$$
HOTEL ⛩ **Park Plaza.** Just off Cardiff's main shopping street, this contemporary hotel is popular with business travelers for its luxurious feel and convenient downtown location. **Pros:** central location; good spa; stainless-steel pool. **Cons:** a bit sterile. $ Rooms from: £110 ⊠ Greyfriars Rd. ☎ 029/2011–1111 ⊕ www.parkplaza.com ↪ 129 rooms ⊙ Breakfast.

$
HOTEL ⛩ **St. David's Hotel and Spa.** Natural light from a glass atrium floods this starkly modern luxury hotel overlooking Cardiff Bay. **Pros:** a bit like staying on a cruise ship; relaxing spa; good deals. **Cons:** out-of-the-way location; service can be patchy; breakfast is pricey. $ Rooms from: £95 ⊠ Havannah St. ☎ 029/2045–4045 ⊕ www.thestdavidshotel.com ↪ 132 rooms ⊙ Multiple meal plans.

NIGHTLIFE AND THE ARTS
NIGHTLIFE
Café Jazz. With live jazz five nights a week, Café Jazz has video monitors in the bar and restaurant so you can enjoy the on-stage action. ⊠ 21 St. Mary St. ☎ 029/2038–7026 ⊕ www.cafejazzcardiff.com.

Clwb Ifor Bach. This hot spot, whose name means "Little Ivor's Club," has three floors of eclectic music, from funk to folk to rock. ⊠ 11 Womanby St. ☎ 029/2023–2199 ⊕ www.clwb.net.

THE ARTS
Motorpoint Arena Cardiff. This huge venue is Cardiff's premier location for big-ticket music acts and other touring shows. ⊠ Mary Ann St. ☎ 029/2022–4488 ⊕ www.livenation.co.uk.

New Theatre. This refurbished Edwardian playhouse presents big names, including the Royal Shakespeare Company, the National Theatre, and the Northern Ballet. ⊠ Park Pl. ☎ 029/2087–8889 ⊕ www. newtheatrecardiff.co.uk.

SHOPPING
Canopied Victorian and Edwardian shopping arcades lined with specialty stores weave in and out of the city's modern shopping complexes.

Cardiff Antiques Centre. In an 1856 arcade, the Cardiff Antiques Centre is a good place to buy vintage jewelry and accessories. ⊠ Royal Arcade ☎ 029/2039–8891 ⊕ www.royalarcadecardiff.com.

Cardiff Market. The traditional Cardiff Market sells tempting fresh foods beneath its Victorian glass canopy. ⊠ St. Mary St. ☎ 029/2087–1214 ⊕ www.cardiff-market.co.uk.

Melin Tregwynt. This elegant shop sells woolen clothing, bags, and cushions woven in an old Pembrokeshire mill. ⊠ 26 Royal Arcade ☎ 029/2022–4997 ⊕ www.melintregwynt.co.uk.

ABERGAVENNY Y FENNI

28 miles north of Cardiff.

The market town of Abergavenny, just outside Brecon Beacons National Park, is a popular base for walkers and hikers. It has a ruined castle and is near the industrial-history sites at Blaenavon.

GETTING HERE AND AROUND

Abergavenny is on the A40 road, about an hour's drive from Cardiff. Direct trains connect with Cardiff about every half hour and take about 40 minutes.

ESSENTIALS

Visitor Information Abergavenny Tourist Information Centre ⊠ *24 Monmouth Rd.* ☎ *01873/853254* ⊕ *www.visitabergavenny.co.uk.*

EXPLORING

TOP ATTRACTIONS

Abergavenny Castle. Built early in the 11th century, this castle witnessed a tragic event on Christmas Day, 1176: the Norman knight William de Braose invited the neighboring Welsh chieftains to a feast, and in a crude attempt to gain control of the area, had them all slaughtered as they sat to dine. The Welsh retaliated and virtually demolished the castle. Most of what now remains dates from the 13th and 14th centuries. The castle's 19th-century hunting lodge houses an excellent museum of regional history. The re-creation of a Victorian Welsh farmhouse kitchen includes old utensils and butter molds. ⊠ *Castle St.* ☎ *01873/854282* ⊕ *www.abergavennymuseum.co.uk* ☒ *Free* ☉ *Mar.–Oct., Mon.–Sat. 11–1 and 2–5, Sun. 2–5; Nov.–Feb., Mon.–Sat. 11–1 and 2–4.*

FAMILY
Fodor'sChoice
★
Big Pit: National Coal Museum. For hundreds of years, South Wales has been famous for its mining industry. Decades of decline—particularly during the 1980s—left only a handful of mines in business. The mines around Blaenavon, a small town 7 miles north of Abergavenny, have been designated a UNESCO World Heritage Site, and this fascinating museum is the centerpiece. Ex-miners lead you 300 feet underground into a coal mine. You spend just under an hour examining the old stables, machine rooms, and exposed coalfaces. Afterward you can look around an exhibition housed in the old Pithead Baths, including an extraordinary section on child labor in British mines. ∎TIP➜ Children under 3½ feet tall are not allowed on the underground portion of the tour. ⊠ *Off A4043, Blaenavon* ☎ *01495/790311* ⊕ *www.museumwales. ac.uk* ☒ *Free* ☉ *Feb.–Dec., daily 9:30–4:30; Jan., weekends 9:30–4:30. Last admission 1 hr before closing.*

Blaenavon Ironworks. A UNESCO World Heritage Site, the 1789 Blaenavon Ironworks traces the entire process of iron production in the late 18th century. Well-preserved blast furnaces, a water-balance lift used to transport materials to higher ground, and a terraced row of workers' cottages show how the business operated. ⊠ *A4043, Blaenavon* ☎ *01495/792615* ⊕ *www.cadw.wales.gov.uk* ☒ *Free* ☉ *Apr.–Oct., daily 10–5; Nov.–Mar., Fri. and Sat. 9–4, Sun. 11–4; last admission 30 mins before closing.*

Fodor'sChoice
★
Raglan Castle. Impressively complete from the front, majestically ruined within, Raglan was built in the 15th century and was the childhood home of Henry Tudor (1457–1509), who seized the throne of England in 1485 and became Henry VII. Raglan's heyday was relatively short-lived. The castle was attacked by Parliamentary forces during the English Civil War, and has lain in ruins ever since. The hexagonal Great Tower survives in reasonably good condition, as do a handful of

South Wales

rooms on the ground floor. ✉ *A40, Raglan* ☎ *01291/690228* ⊕ *www.cadw.wales.gov.uk* 💷 *£4* ⊙ *Mar.–June, Sept., and Oct., daily 9:30–5; July and Aug., daily 9:30–6; Nov.–Feb., Mon–Sat. 10–4, Sun. 11–4; last admission 30 mins before closing.*

OFF THE
BEATEN
PATH

Tintern Abbey. Literally a stone's throw from the English border, Tintern is one of the region's most romantic monastic ruins. Founded in 1131 and dissolved by Henry VIII in 1536, it has inspired its fair share of poets and painters over the years—most famously J.M.W. Turner, who painted the transept covered in moss and ivy, and William Wordsworth, who idolized the setting in his poem "Lines Composed a Few Miles above Tintern Abbey." ■TIP→ Come early or late to avoid the crowds. The abbey, 5 miles north of Chepstow and 19 miles southeast of Abergavenny, is on the banks of the River Wye. ✉ *A466, Tintern* ☎ *01291/689251* ⊕ *www.cadw.wales.gov.uk* 💷 *£3.80* ⊙ *Mar.–Jun., Sept., and Oct., daily 9:30–5; July and Aug., daily 9:30–6; Nov.–Feb., Mon.–Sat. 10–4, Sun. 11–4; last admission 30 mins before closing.*

WORTH NOTING

Tretower Court. A rare surviving example of a fortified medieval manor house, Tretower Court dates mostly from the 15th century. Buildings such as these were huge status symbols in their day, as they combined the security of a castle with the luxury of a manor house. On the grounds are the ruins of an earlier Norman castle. Tretower Court, restored in the 1930s, is outside the idyllic village of Crickhowell, 5 miles northwest of Abergavenny. ⊠ *A479, Crickhowell* ☎ *01874/730279* ⊕ *www.cadw. wales.gov.uk* 🎫 *£4.50* ⊘ *Apr.–Oct., daily 10–5; Nov.–Mar., Fri. and Sat. 10–4, Sun. 11–4.; last admission 30 mins before closing.*

WHERE TO EAT AND STAY

$ ✕ **Clytha Arms.** On the banks of the River Usk between Abergavenny
MODERN BRITISH and Raglan, this restaurant serves imaginative Modern Welsh dishes in a relaxed setting. The menu makes great use of local Welsh ingredients in the cider-roasted ham with parsley sauce and the wild boar and duck cassoulet. There's a cheaper menu at the bar. $ *Average main: £14* ⊠ *Off B4598* ☎ *01873/840206* ⊕ *www.clytha-arms.com* ⊘ *Closed Mon.*

$ 🏨 **Bear Hotel.** In the middle of town, this coaching inn is full of char-
HOTEL acter. **Pros:** friendly bar; good food. **Cons:** some rooms overlook the road; rooms vary in size; can get busy on weekends. $ *Rooms from: £95* ⊠ *High St., Crickhowell* ☎ *01873/810408* ⊕ *www.bearhotel.co.uk* 🛏 *35 rooms* ⏐⊘⏐ *Breakfast.*

$ 🏨 **The Lamb and Flag Inn.** This inn on the outskirts of Abergavenny
HOTEL embodies what the British like to call "cheap and cheerful," meaning good-quality accommodations that cover all the basics. **Pros:** excellent value; good restaurant; free parking. **Cons:** a little way from the town center; few amenities. $ *Rooms from: £60* ⊠ *Brecon Rd.* ☎ *01873/857611* ⊕ *www.lambflag.co.uk* 🛏 *5 rooms* ⏐⊘⏐ *Breakfast.*

$$ 🏨 **Llansantffraed Court Hotel.** Dating from 1400, this grand country
HOTEL house 4 miles southeast of Abergavenny is set on 20 acres of well-
Fodor's Choice tended grounds with lovely views of the Brecon Beacons. **Pros:** excellent
★ food; peaceful setting; great for anglers. **Cons:** tired decor; out-of-the-way location. $ *Rooms from: £115* ⊠ *Old Raglan Rd., Clytha* ☎ *01873/840678* ⊕ *www.llch.co.uk* 🛏 *21 rooms* ⏐⊘⏐ *Breakfast.*

NIGHTLIFE AND THE ARTS

Abergavenny Food Festival. Held over a weekend in September, the Abergavenny Food Festival is a celebration for foodies and a symbol of the growing interest in Welsh cuisine. There are demonstrations, lectures, special events, and, of course, a food market. Be sure to sample the local cheese called Y Fenni, flavored with a piquant combination of mustard seeds and ale. ☎ *01873/851643* ⊕ *www.abergavennyfoodfestival.com.*

BRECON ABERHONDDU

19 miles northwest of Abergavenny, 41 miles north of Cardiff.

The historic market town of Brecon is known for its Georgian buildings, narrow passageways, and pleasant riverside walks. It's also the gateway to Brecon Beacons National Park. The town is particularly appealing on Tuesday and Friday, which are market days. You may want to purchase a hand-carved wooden "love spoon" similar to those on display in the Brecknock Museum.

One of three national parks in Wales, Brecon Beacons offers some panoramic mountain views, whether you're on foot or in a car.

GETTING HERE AND AROUND

Brecon's nearest railway stations are at Merthyr Tydfil and Abergavenny (both about 19 miles away). Beacons Bus service runs to many parts of Brecon Beacons National Park. Brecon is a handsome town to explore on foot—especially the riverside walk along the promenade.

ESSENTIALS

Visitor Information Brecon Beacons Tourism ⊠ *Market Car Park, Church La.* ☎ *01874/622485* ⊕ *www.breconbeaconstourism.co.uk.*

EXPLORING

TOP ATTRACTIONS

Fodor's Choice ★ **Brecon Beacons National Park.** About 5 miles southwest of Brecon you encounter mountains and wild, windswept uplands that are tipped by shafts of golden light when the weather's fine, or fingers of ghostly mist when it's not. This 519-square-mile park is one of Wales's most breathtaking areas, perfect for a hike or scenic drive. Start at the visitor center on Mynydd Illtyd, a grassy stretch of upland west of the A470. It's an excellent source of information about the park, including maps and advice on the best routes (guided or self-guided). There's also an excellent Tea Room where you can fuel up for the journey or reward yourself with an indulgent slice of cake afterwards. If you want to see it all from your car, any road that crosses the Beacons will reward you with beautiful views, but the most spectacular is the high and undulating A4069, between Brynamman and Llangadog in the park's western end. ■TIP→ To explore the moorlands on foot, come prepared. Mist and rain descend quickly, and the summits are exposed to high winds. ⊠ *Off A470, Libanus* ☎ *01874/623366* ⊕ *www.breconbeacons.org* ⌖ *Free,* *parking £1 for 2 hrs, £2.50 all day* ☉ *Visitor Center: Mar.–Jun., Sept. and Oct., daily 9:30–5; July–Aug., daily 9:30–5:30; Nov.–Feb., daily 9:30–4:30.*

Fodor's Choice
★
Carreg Cennen Castle. On the edge of Brecon Beacons National Park, about 30 miles west of Brecon, this decaying cliff-top fortress was built in the 12th century, and remains of earlier defenses have been found dating back to the Iron Age. The castle, though a ruin, has a partially intact barbican (fortified outer section) and some inner chambers hewn dramatically from the bedrock. The climb up is somewhat punishing—you have to trudge up a steep, grassy hill—but the views of the valley, with its patchwork of green fields framed by the peaks of the Black Mountains, are enough to take away whatever breath you have left. ✉ *Off Derwydd Rd., Trapp* ☎ *01443/336000* ⊕ *www.cadw.wales.gov.uk* 🖾 *£4* ☉ *Apr.–Oct., daily 9:30–6:30; Nov.–Mar., daily 9:30–4; last admission 45 mins before closing.*

> ## LOVE SPOONS
>
> The rural Welsh custom of giving the object of your affection a "love spoon" dates from the mid-17th century. Made from wood, the spoons are elaborately hand-carved with tokens of love, including hearts, flowers, doves, intertwined vines, and chain links. These days you can barely turn around in a Welsh souvenir shop without seeing one.

WORTH NOTING

Brecon Cathedral. Modest on the outside but surprisingly cavernous on the inside, this cathedral stands on the hill above the middle of town. Its heritage center does a good job of telling the building's history, and there's also a handy café. Local choirs perform concerts here regularly. ✉ *Cathedral Close* ☎ *01874/623857* ⊕ *www.breconcathedral.org.uk* 🖾 *Free* ☉ *Daily 8–6.*

FAMILY
National Show Caves of Wales. This underground cave system was discovered by two local men in 1912—make that rediscovered, as one of the caves contained 42 human skeletons that had lain undisturbed for up to 7,000 years. The main cave system, Dan Yr Ogof (Welsh for "beneath the cave"), is an impressive natural wonder, particularly the Cathedral Cave with natural stone archways and a dramatic waterfall. The whole thing is pitched at kids, with "dramatic" piped music to "enhance" the atmosphere, and a park featuring life-size models of prehistoric creatures. There's also a petting zoo and playground. The caves are 17 miles southwest of Brecon. ✉ *Off A48 or B4310, Abercrave* ☎ *01639/730284* ⊕ *www.showcaves.co.uk* 🖾 *£14* ☉ *Apr.–early Nov., daily 10–3.*

WHERE TO EAT AND STAY

$$
BRITISH
✕ **Felin Fach Griffin.** Old and new blend perfectly in this modern country-style inn with old wood floors, comfy leather sofas, and stone walls hung with bright prints. The excellent menu makes use of fresh local produce, much of it coming from the Griffin's own organic garden, in dishes such as monkfish with pancetta and parsley butter, or shin of beef with cep risotto, asparagus, and wet garlic. The inn is in Felin Fach, 5 miles northeast of Brecon. 🖸 *Average main: £18* ✉ *A470, Felin Fach* ☎ *01874/620111* ⊕ *www.eatdrinksleep.ltd.uk.*

HIKING AND BIKING IN WALES

Opened to much fanfare in 2012, the Wales Coast Path is an 870-mile walking path that snakes along the entire coastline. Linking existing routes like the Pembrokeshire Coast Path in southeast Wales with new sections, it passes as close to the coastline as possible. Managed by the Welsh government, the route can be pretty wild in places and there isn't always a guardrail, so keep a close eye on small children. Work is currently under way to link it up with other popular routes, which should create an unbroken system of walking trails extending for more than 1,000 miles within a couple of years.

Other long-distance paths include north–south Offa's Dyke Path, based on the border between England and Wales established by King Offa in the 8th century, and the Glyndr Way, a 128-mile-long highland route that traverses Mid-Wales from the border town of Knighton via Machynlleth to Welshpool. Signposted footpaths in Wales's forested areas are short and easy to follow. Dedicated enthusiasts might prefer the wide-open spaces of Brecon Beacons National Park or the mountains of Snowdonia.

Wales's reputation as both an on-road and off-road cycling mecca is well established. There's an amazing choice of scenic routes and terrain from challenging off-road tracks (🌐 *www.mbwales.com* is for the serious cyclist) to long-distance road rides and gentle family trails; VisitWales has information to get you started.

CONTACTS AND RESOURCES

Cycling Wales 🌐 *www.cycling.visitwales.com.*

Offa's Dyke Centre ☎ *01547/528753* 🌐 *www.offasdyke.demon.co.uk.*

Pembrokeshire Coast Path 🌐 *www.nationaltrail.co.uk.*

Ramblers' Association in Wales ☎ *029/2064–4308* 🌐 *www.ramblers.org.uk/wales.*

Wales Coast Path 🌐 *www.walescoastpath.gov.uk.*

$ HOTEL 🏨 **Coach House.** This former coach house in the center of Brecon has been converted into a luxurious place to stay. **Pros:** lovely staff; central location; private parking. **Cons:** on a main road. [$] *Rooms from: £81* ✉ *Orchard St.* ☎ *01874/620043* 🌐 *www.coachhousebrecon.com* 🛏 *7 rooms* 🍴 *Breakfast.*

$ B&B/INN 🏨 **Felin Glais.** In the 17th century Felin Glais was a barn; enlarged but without losing its ancient character, it provides spacious and comfortable accommodations. **Pros:** beautiful building; spacious rooms; good food. **Cons:** dog-friendly environment won't please everyone; no credit cards; 48-hours notice required for dinner. [$] *Rooms from: £85* ✉ *Aberysycir* ☎ *01874/623107* 🌐 *www.felinglais.co.uk* 🛏 *4 rooms* 💳 *No credit cards* 🍴 *Breakfast.*

NIGHTLIFE AND THE ARTS

Brecon Jazz. For a weekend every August, Brecon Jazz, an international music festival, takes over the town. It attracts an increasingly high-profile list of performers and includes a parade through the town on the Sunday morning. ☎ *01874/611622 box office* 🌐 *www.breconjazz.com.*

Theatr Brycheiniog. On the canal, Theatr Brycheiniog is the town's main venue for music, plays, and comedy. It also has a waterfront bistro. ⊠ *Canal Wharf* ☎ *01874/611622* ⊕ *www.brycheiniog.co.uk.*

SPORTS AND THE OUTDOORS

Biped Cycles. The Brecon Beacons contain some of the best cycling routes in Britain. Biped Cycles will rent you the right bike and equipment. ⊠ *10 Ship St.* ☎ *01874/622296* ⊕ *www.bipedcycles.co.uk.*

Crickhowell Adventure Gear. This shop sells outdoor gear and climbing equipment. ⊠ *21 Ship St.* ☎ *01874/611586* ⊕ *www.crickhowell adventure.co.uk.*

MERTHYR MAWR

45 miles south of Brecon, 22 miles west of Cardiff.

As you cross over an ancient stone bridge into Merthyr Mawr, you feel as if you've entered another world. From stone cottages with beehive-shape thatched roofs to the Victorian-era Church of St. Teilo, with the pieces of its long-gone 5th-century predecessor lined up in its churchyard, it's an idyllic place to wander around. The picturesque ruin of Ogmore Castle is just off the B4524, but the most memorable way to reach it is via the walking path that starts in the car park at the very southern tip of the village. The mile-long route goes through a farm and a Shetland pony stables.

GETTING HERE AND AROUND

Merthyr Mawr is signposted from the A48 and B4524, 7 miles southwest of junction 35 on the M4. The nearest train station is in Bridgend. There's no bus service to the village.

EXPLORING

Nash Point. Just a few miles south of Merthyr Mawr is this stunning promontory overlooking the Bristol Channel. Twin lighthouses stand guard against the elements; one is still operational, but the other is open for tours. This is also a popular picnic spot, and a small snack kiosk is open during summer months. Nothing beats this place at sunset, when the evening sky ignites in a riot of color. It's one of the most romantic spots in South Wales. ■ TIP➜ There's no guardrail on the cliff, so keep a close eye on children. ⊠ *Marcross* ☎ *01225/245011* ⊡ *Free; lighthouse £3.50* ⊙ *Mid-Mar.–Oct., weekends 2–5.*

Ogmore Castle. Just south of the village are these atmospheric ruins, nestled by a river that can only be crossed via stepping-stones. A number of legends are associated with the castle, one concerning a ghost that supposedly forces passersby to embrace a large rock known as the "Goblin Stone." When you try to draw back, so the story goes, you find that your hands and feet have become part of the rock. ⊠ *Ogmore Rd.* ⊡ *Free.*

QUICK BITES

The Pelican in Her Piety. Up a small hill next to Ogmore Castle, The Pelican in Her Piety stands like a mirage. This friendly and fabulously named little pub is a welcome spot for a snack or restorative pint after the

long walk from Merthyr Mawr. ✉ *Ogmore Rd.* ☎ *01656/880049* 🌐 *www.pelicanpub.co.uk.*

WHERE TO EAT

$ BRITISH 🍴 **The Plough and Harrow.** A short drive from Nash Point is this friendly local pub, on the edge of the tiny cliff-top village of Monknash. The food is delicious and unfussy, mostly pub classics like steaks and grilled fish. Everything is served in a cozy dining room with a fireplace. There's a small but decent wine list, and an even better selection of real ales. This place is popular locally, so call ahead or be prepared to wait. [$] *Average main: £13* ✉ *Off Hoel Las, Monknash* ☎ *01656/890209* 🌐 *www.ploughandharrow.org.*

SWANSEA ABERTAWE

22 miles northwest of Merthyr Mawr, 40 miles west of Cardiff.

The birthplace of poet Dylan Thomas (1914–53), Swansea adores its native son. It honors him throughout the year, especially at the Dylan Thomas Festival in October and November. But Swansea no longer seems like a place that would inspire poetry. Heavily bombed in World War II, it was clumsily rebuilt. Today it merits a stop primarily for a couple of good museums. But the surrounding countryside tells a different story. The National Botanic Gardens and Neath Abbey make for interesting diversions, and the stunning Gower Peninsula contains some of the region's best beaches.

GETTING HERE AND AROUND

There's a half-hourly rail service from London's Paddington Station. The city has direct National Express bus connections to other parts of Wales, as well as to London and other cities.

ESSENTIALS

Visitor Information Swansea Tourist Information Centre ✉ *Plymouth St.* ☎ *01792/468321* 🌐 *www.visitswanseabay.com.*

EXPLORING

TOP ATTRACTIONS

Dylan Thomas Centre. Situated on the banks of the Tawe close to the Maritime Quarter, the Dylan Thomas Centre serves as the National Literature Centre for Wales. The center houses a permanent Dylan Thomas exhibition, art gallery, restaurant, and café-bookshop, and hosts the annual Dylan Thomas Festival. ■ **TIP→ The poet's fans can buy a booklet that outlines the Dylan Thomas Trail around South Wales. It includes the Boathouse (now a museum), in Laugharne, where the poet lived and wrote the last four years of his life.** ✉ *Somerset Pl.* ☎ *01792/463980* 🌐 *www.dylanthomas.com* 🎫 *Free* 🕒 *Daily 10–4:30.*

FAMILY Fodor's Choice ★ **Gower Peninsula.** This peninsula, which stretches westward from Swansea, was the first part of Britain to be designated an Area of Outstanding Natural Beauty. Its shores are a succession of sheltered sandy bays and awesome headlands. The seaside resort of Mumbles, on the outskirts of Swansea, is the most famous town along the route. It's an elegantly faded place to wander on a sunny afternoon, with an

Stretching west of Swansea, the Gower Peninsula has some stunning beaches, including Rhossili.

amusement pier and seaside promenade. Farther along the peninsula, the secluded Pwlldu Bay can only be reached on foot from nearby villages like Southgate. A few miles westward is the more accessible (and very popular) Three Cliffs Bay, with its sweeping views and wide, sandy beach. At the far western tip of the peninsula, Rhossili has perhaps the best beach of all. Its unusual, snaking causeway—known locally as the Worm's Head—is inaccessible at high tide. ⊕ *www.enjoygower.com.*

Fodor's Choice **National Botanic Garden of Wales.** This 568-acre, 18th-century estate is
★ dotted with lakes, fountains, and a Japanese garden. The centerpiece is the Norman Foster–designed Great Glass House, the largest single-span greenhouse in the world, which blends into the curving landforms of the Tywi Valley. The greenhouse's interior landscape includes a 40-foot-deep ravine and thousands of plants from all over the world. The garden, 20 miles northwest of Swansea, is signposted off the main road between Swansea and Carmarthen. ⊠ *Off A48 or B4310, Llanarthne* ☎ *01558/668–7688* ⊕ *www.gardenofwales.org.uk* ⊠ *£8.50* ☉ *Apr.–Sept., daily 10–6; Oct.–Mar., daily 10–4:30.*

FAMILY **National Waterfront Museum.** Housed in a construction of steel, slate, and glass grafted onto a historic redbrick building, the National Waterfront Museum's galleries have 15 theme areas. State-of-the-art interactive technology and a host of artifacts bring Welsh maritime and industrial history to a 21st-century audience. ⊠ *Oystermouth Rd., Maritime Quarter* ☎ *029/2057–3600* ⊕ *www.museumwales.ac.uk* ⊠ *Free* ☉ *Daily 10–5.*

WORTH NOTING

5 Cwmdonkin Drive. Dylan Thomas was born in this suburban Edwardian house, which remains a place of pilgrimage for the poet's devotees. Tours (which must be booked in advance) are tailored according to how much time you want to spend here; devoted fans can hang around for hours. The house can be rented as self-catering accommodations for around £130 per night or £530 per week. ✉ *5 Cwmdonkin Dr.* ☎ *01792/405331* 🌐 *www.5cwmdonkindrive.com* 🎟 *£5* ⏲ *Call ahead for tours.*

Maritime Quarter. Swansea was extensively bombed during World War II, and its old dockland has reemerged as the splendid Maritime Quarter, a modern marina with attractive housing and shops and a seafront that commands views across the sweep of Swansea Bay.

Neath Abbey. Built in the 12th century, this abbey was, in its day, one of the largest and most important in the British Isles. Though just a shell, the main church gives an impressive sense of scale, with its tall buttresses and soaring, glassless windows. Here and there small sections of the original building have survived unscathed, including an undercroft with a vaulted stone ceiling. Neath Abbey is 9 miles northeast of Swansea. ✉ *Monastery Rd., Neath Abbey* 🌐 *www.cadw.wales.gov.uk* 🎟 *Free* ⏲ *Daily 10–4.*

Richard Burton Trail. Two new walking trails celebrate the early life of the revered Welsh actor, who was born in the village of Pontrhydyfen, 13 miles northeast of Swansea. The tours cover significant places from his childhood, in addition to some beautiful Welsh countryside. Illustrated maps detailing the tours can be downloaded on the Visit Neath Port Talbot website. ✉ *B4286, Pontrhydyfen* 🌐 *www.visitnpt.co.uk.*

Swansea Museum. Founded in 1841, this museum contains a quirky and eclectic collection that includes an Egyptian mummy, local archaeological exhibits, and the intriguing Cabinet of Curiosity, which holds artifacts from Swansea's past. The museum is close to the Maritime Quarter. ✉ *Victoria Rd.* ☎ *01792/653763* 🌐 *www.swanseaheritage.net* 🎟 *Free* ⏲ *Tues.–Sun. 10–5.*

WHERE TO EAT AND STAY

$$ SPANISH 🍴 **La Braseria.** Lively and welcoming, this spot resembles a Spanish *bodega* (wine cellar), with its flamenco music, oak barrels, and whitewashed walls. Among the house specialties are sea bass in rock salt, roast suckling pig, and pheasant (in season, of course). There's a good choice of 140 Spanish and French wines. [$] *Average main: £15* ✉ *28 Wind St.* ☎ *01792/469683* 🌐 *www.labraseria.com* ⏲ *Closed Sun.*

$ ITALIAN 🍴 **Verdi's.** This family-run ice-cream parlor, café, and restaurant sits right on the seafront. Homemade pizza is a specialty, or you could just join the queue for the delicious fresh gelato. Every indoor and outdoor table has panoramic views of Swansea Bay. It's in The Mumbles, a resort town southwest of Swansea. [$] *Average main: £7* ✉ *Off Pier Rd., The Mumbles* ☎ *01792/369135* 🌐 *www.verdis-cafe.co.uk.*

$$$ HOTEL Fodor's Choice ★ 🏨 **Fairyhill.** Luxuriously furnished public rooms, spacious bedrooms, and delicious cooking make this 18th-century country house a restful retreat. **Pros:** peaceful surroundings; good restaurant. **Cons:** you must buy dinner on Friday and Saturday night stays; restaurant always busy.

[$] *Rooms from: £180* ✉ *Off B4295, 11 miles southwest of Swansea, Reynoldston* ☎ *01792/390139* 🌐 *www.fairyhill.net* 🛏 *8 rooms* 🍴 *Some meals.*

$ HOTEL 🏨 **Morgans.** Now a hotel, the Victorian-era Port Authority building in the Maritime Quarter has lost none of its period features: moldings, pillars, stained glass, and wood floors. **Pros:** near the marina; short walk to shops; maritime flair. **Cons:** no room service in Townhouse. [$] *Rooms from: £65* ✉ *Somerset Pl.* ☎ *01792/484848* 🌐 *www.morganshotel.co.uk* 🛏 *41 rooms* 🍴 *No meals.*

TENBY DINBYCH-Y-PYSGOD

53 miles west of Swansea.

Fodor's Choice ★ Pastel-color Georgian houses cluster around a harbor in this seaside town, which became a fashionable resort in the 19th century and is still popular. Two golden sandy beaches stretch below the hotel-lined cliff top. Medieval Tenby's ancient town walls still stand, enclosing narrow streets and passageways full of shops, inns, and places to eat. From the harbor you can take a short boat trip to Caldey Island, with its active Cistercian community.

GETTING HERE AND AROUND

Tenby is on the southwest Wales rail route from London's Paddington Station. You have to change trains at Swansea or Newport. The center of Tenby, a maze of narrow medieval streets, has parking restrictions. In summer, downtown is closed to traffic, so park in one of the lots and take the shuttle buses.

ESSENTIALS

Visitor Information **Tenby Information Centre** ✉ *Unit 2, Upper Park Rd.* ☎ *01834/842402* 🌐 *www.pembrokeshire.gov.uk.*

EXPLORING

Fodor's Choice ★ **Caldey Island.** This beautiful little island off the coast at Tenby has whitewashed stone buildings that lend it a Mediterranean feel. The island is best known for its Cistercian order, whose black-and-white-robed monks make a famous perfume from the local plants. You can visit tiny St. Illtud's Church to see the Caldey Stone, an early Christian artifact from circa AD 600, engraved in Latin and ancient Celtic. St. David's Church, on a hill above the village, is a simple Norman chapel noted for its art deco stained glass. The monastery itself isn't open to the public, but its church has a public viewing gallery if you want to observe a service. Boats to Caldey Island leave from Tenby's harbor every 20 minutes or so between Easter and September. ✉ *Caldey Island* ☎ *01834/844453* 🌐 *www.caldey-island.co.uk* 🎟 *Free, boats £11 round-trip* 🕒 *Boats Easter–Oct., weekdays (also Sat. May–Sept) 10–3. Last return usually 5.*

Pembroke Castle. About 10 miles east of Tenby is this remarkably complete Norman fortress dating from 1190. Its walls remain stout, its gatehouse mighty, and the enormous cylindrical keep proved so impregnable to cannon fire in the civil war that Cromwell's men had to starve out its Royalist defenders. Climb the towers and walk the walls for fine views. A well-stocked gift shop sells faux-medieval knickknacks.

✉ *Westgate Hill, Pembroke* ☎ *01646/681510* 🌐 *www.pembroke-castle.co.uk* 🎫 *£5.50* ⏲ *Apr.–Aug., daily 9:30–6; Sept.–Oct. and Mar., daily 10–5; Nov.–Feb., daily 10–4; last entry 45 mins before closing.*

Pembrokeshire Coast National Park. By far the smallest of the country's three national parks, Pembrokeshire Coast is no less strikingly beautiful than the other two. The park has 13 blue flag beaches and a host of spectacular cliff-top drives and walks, including some of the most popular stretches of the Wales Coast Path. The park has a smattering of historic sites, including the impossibly picturesque St. David's Cathedral, built in a Viking-proof nook by the Irish Sea. The information center in Tenby is a good place to start. ✉ *Tenby National Park Centre, South Parade* ☎ *01834/845040* 🌐 *www.pembrokeshirecoast.org.uk* 🎫 *Free* ⏲ *Apr.–Sept., daily 9:30–5; Oct.–Mar., Mon.–Sat. 10:30–3:30.*

FAMILY **Tenby Museum and Art Gallery.** Close to the castle, this small but informative museum recalls the town's maritime history and its growth as a fashionable resort. Kids will appreciate the section on Tenby's role in the golden age of piracy. Two art galleries feature works by local artists. ✉ *Castle Hill* ☎ *01834/842809* 🌐 *www.tenbymuseum.org.uk* 🎫 *£4* ⏲ *Oct.–Mar., Tues.–Sat. 10–5; Apr.–Sept., daily 10–5; last admission 30 mins before closing.*

FAMILY **Tudor Merchant's House.** This late-15th-century home shows how a prosperous trader would have lived in Tudor times. Kids can try on Tudor-style costumes. ✉ *Quay Hill* ☎ *01834/842279* 🌐 *www.nationaltrust.org.uk* 🎫 *£3.20* ⏲ *Mid-Feb.–Mar., Nov. and Dec. weekends 11–3; Apr.–mid-Jun., Sept. and Oct. Wed.–Mon. 11–5; mid-July–Aug., daily 11–5; last admission 30 mins before closing.*

WHERE TO EAT AND STAY

$$ BRITISH 🍴 **Plantagenet House.** Flickering candles, open fireplaces, exposed stone walls, and top-notch locally sourced food are hallmarks of this popular restaurant and bar. The menu contains a selection of Welsh-reared steaks and other meat dishes, but seafood is the specialty. The romantic setting is as much of a draw as the food. Check out the huge stone "Flemish chimney," a distinctive style popularized by immigrants during the 16th century. [$] *Average main: £18* ✉ *Quay Hill* ☎ *01834/842350* 🌐 *www.plantagenettenby.co.uk* ⏲ *Closed Jan.–mid-Feb.*

$ B&B/INN 🏨 **Ivy Bank Guest House.** This comfortable and immaculate Victorian house sits across from the train station, a five-minute stroll from the sea. **Pros:** cozy and simple; close to beach; seniors discounts. **Cons:** you have to park at the train station; color scheme not for everyone. [$] *Rooms from: £36* ✉ *Harding St.* ☎ *01834/842311* 🌐 *www.ivybanktenby.co.uk* 🛏 *5 rooms* 🍽 *Breakfast.*

$$ HOTEL 🏨 **Penally Abbey.** Built on the site of a 6th-century abbey in 5 acres of lush forest overlooking Camarthen Bay, this dignified 18th-century house is awash with period details. **Pros:** informal luxury; great views; friendly hosts. **Cons:** small pool. [$] *Rooms from: £148* ✉ *Off A4139, 2 miles west of Tenby, Penally* ☎ *01834/843033* 🌐 *www.penally-abbey.com* 🛏 *17 rooms* 🍽 *Breakfast.*

$$ HOTEL 🏨 **St. Brides Spa Hotel.** Between Amroth and Tenby, this luxury hotel is perched on a breathtaking location above Carmarthen Bay; most of

the superbly appointed rooms have stunning sea views. **Pros:** amazing views; wonderful spa; fantastic restaurant. **Cons:** steep walk from the beach; minimum stay on weekends. $ *Rooms from: £150* ✉ *St. Brides Hill, Saundersfoot* ☎ *01834/812304* ⊕ *www.stbridesspahotel. com* ⤳ *35 rooms* ⊚| *Breakfast.*

SPORTS AND THE OUTDOORS

The town's beaches are hugely popular in summertime. North Beach is the busiest, with shops and a little café along the promenade. The adjoining Harbour Beach is prettier and more secluded. Castle Beach is in a little cove where you can walk out to a small island at low tide. Past that is South Beach, which stretches for more than a mile.

ST. DAVID'S TYDDEWI

35 miles northwest of Tenby.

Despite its miniscule size, this community of fewer than 1,800 people isn't a village or a hamlet—it's actually Britain's smallest city. Historically, little St. David's has punched above its weight due to the presence of St. David's Cathedral, the resting place of the patron saint of Wales and once a major destination for pilgrims. These days, visitors with time on their hands might want to consider approaching the city via the Wales Coast Path, around the St. David's headland from St. Justinian to Caerfai Bay. In May and June the town's hedgerows and coastal paths are ablaze with wildflowers. The town's visitor center also has a small collection of art and artifacts drawn from the collection of the National Museum of Wales.

GETTING HERE AND AROUND

St. David's is on the A487. The nearest train station is 14 miles southeast in Haverfordwest. Bus 411 travels from Haverfordwest to St. David's every hour or so.

ESSENTIALS

Visitor Information Oriel y Parc Gallery and Visitor Centre ✉ *1 High St.* ☎ *01437/720392* ⊕ *www.pembrokeshirecoast.org.uk.*

EXPLORING

Fodor's Choice ★ **St. David's Cathedral.** The idyllic valley location of this cathedral helped protect the church from Viking raiders by hiding it from the view of invaders who came by sea. Originally founded by St. David himself in around AD 600, the current building dates from the 12th century, although it has been added to at various times since. You must climb down 39 steps (known locally as the Thirty-Nine Articles) to enter the grounds; then start at the Gatehouse, with its exhibition on the history of the building. In the cathedral itself, the 15th-century choir stalls still have their original floor tiles, while the Holy Trinity Chapel contains an intricate fan-vaulted ceiling and a casket said to contain the patron saint's bones. ■ **TIP→ Don't miss the Treasury and its illuminated gospels, silver chalices, and 700-year-old golden bishop's crosier.** In August, guided tours costing £4 begin Monday at 11:30 and Friday at 2:30, and on other days by arrangement. The cathedral has a good café. ✉ *The Close* ☎ *01437/720202* 🌐 *www.stdavidscathedral.org.uk* 🎫 *Free* 🕒 *Daily 8:40–5.*

Bishop's Palace. At the rear of the grounds of St. David's Cathedral are the ruins of the 13th-century Bishop's Palace, particularly beautiful at dusk. ✉ *The Close* ☎ *01437/720517* 🌐 *www.cadw.wales.gov.uk* 🎫 *£3.50* 🕒 *Mar.–June, Sept., and Oct., daily 9:30–5; July and Aug., daily 9:30– 6; Nov.–Feb., Mon.–Sat. 10–4, Sun. 11–4; last admission 30 mins before closing.*

WHERE TO STAY

$$ HOTEL 🏨 **Warpool Court Hotel.** Overlooking a stunning stretch of coastline, this hotel sits on a bluff above St. Non's Bay. **Pros:** beautiful sea views; peaceful gardens; good food. **Cons:** unattractive entrance; few restaurants nearby. [$] *Rooms from: £140* ✉ *Off Goat St.* ☎ *01437/720300* 🌐 *www.warpoolcourthotel.com* 🛏 *25 rooms* 🍴 *Breakfast.*

MID-WALES

Traditional market towns and country villages, small seaside resorts, quiet roads, and rolling landscapes filled with sheep farms, forests, and lakes make up Mid-Wales, the country's green and rural heart. There are no cities here—the area's largest town is barely more than a big village. Outside of one or two towns, such as Aberystwyth and Llandrindod Wells, accommodations are mainly country inns, small hotels, and rural farmhouses. This area also has some splendid country-house hotels.

There are no motorways through Mid-Wales, and the steam railways that once linked this area with Cardiff are long gone. Getting around requires a bit of advance planning, but it's worth the trouble. The bibliophilic charms of Hay-on-Wye have made the town world-famous, while the countryside around Abertystwyth is peppered with peaceful sandy beaches and dramatic beauty spots.

HAY-ON-WYE Y GELLI GANDRYLL

109 miles northeast of St. David's, 57 miles north of Cardiff, 25 miles north of Abergavenny.

Fodor's Choice ★ With its crumbling old castle and low-slung buildings framed by lolloping green hills, Hay-on-Wye is a beautiful little place. In 1961 Richard Booth established a small secondhand bookshop here. Other booksellers soon got in on the act, and now there are dozens of shops. It's now the largest secondhand bookselling center in the world, and priceless 14th-century manuscripts rub spines with "job lots" selling for a few pounds.

For 10 days every May and June, Hay-on-Wye is taken over by its Literary Festival, a celebration of literature that attracts famous writers from all over the world. (Bill Clinton, himself an attendee, once called it "the Woodstock of the mind.") Plan ahead if you want to attend, as hotels get booked several months in advance.

GETTING HERE AND AROUND

You'll need a car to get to Hay. Use one of the public lots of the outskirts of town and walk—the whole town is accessible on foot. The nearest train stations are Builth Wells in Wales (19 miles) and Hereford in England (22 miles).

ESSENTIALS

Visitor Information **Hay-on-Wye Tourist Information Bureau** ✉ *Oxford Rd.* ☎ *01497/820144* 🌐 *www.hay-on-wye.co.uk/tourism.*

EXPLORING

Hay Castle. On a hilltop are the handsome remains of a 12th-century castle keep, jutting out from behind a 16th-century manor house. ✉ *Castle St.* 🎟 *Free* 🕒 *Late Mar.–Oct., daily 9:30–6; Nov.–late Mar., daily 9:30–5:30.*

QUICK BITES

Shepherd's. The delicious ice cream at Shepherd's is legendary in these parts. Produced at a local farm, its distinct, creamy flavor comes from the fact that it's made from sheep's milk. ✉ ***9 High Town*** ☎ ***01497/821898*** 🌐 ***www.shepherdsicecream.co.uk.***

WHERE TO EAT AND STAY

$$ BRITISH

🍴 **Old Black Lion.** A 17th-century coaching inn close to Hay's center is ideal for a lunch break while you're ransacking the bookshops. The oak-beamed bar serves food, and the breakfasts are especially good. The restaurant's sophisticated cooking has an international flavor and emphasizes local meats and produce. You can even opt for an overnight stay in one of the country-style rooms (from about £90 per night). [$] *Average main: £15* ✉ *Lion St.* ☎ *01497/820841* 🌐 *www.oldblacklion.co.uk.*

$$ HOTEL

🏨 **Llangoed Hall.** This magnificent Jacobean mansion on the banks of the River Wye, about 7 miles west of Hay-on-Wye, has beautiful fabrics and furnishings, open fireplaces, a sweeping carved staircase, and a paneled library dating back to 1632. **Pros:** secluded setting by River Wye; wonderful art collection. **Cons:** often filled with wedding parties; minimum stay sometimes required; no attractions within walking distance. [$] *Rooms from: £160* ✉ *A470, Llyswen* ☎ *01874/754525* 🌐 *www.llangoedhall.co.uk* 🛏 *23 rooms* 🍽 *Breakfast.*

$$ HOTEL

🏨 **The Swan.** Once a coaching inn, this sophisticated lodging on the edge of town retains its sense of history. **Pros:** atmospheric building; friendly staff; good food. **Cons:** wedding parties dominate in summer; beds a bit creaky. [$] *Rooms from: £100* ✉ *Church St.* ☎ *01497/821188* 🌐 *www.swanathay.co.uk* 🛏 *17 rooms* 🍽 *Breakfast.*

SHOPPING

The Thursday Market takes over much of the town center every Thursday morning. Traders sell everything from antiques to home-baked cakes.

Boz Books. The kind of dusty old bookshop you see in movies, Boz Books has an impressive range of 19th-century first editions, including many by Dickens. ✉ *13A Castle St.* ☎ *01497/821277* 🌐 *www.bozbooks.demon.co.uk.*

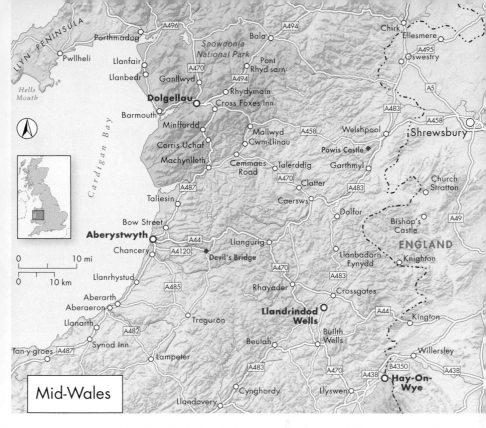

Murder and Mayhem. True to its name, this shop specializes in crime and horror. Head upstairs for a cheaper and more eclectic selection, including old pulp novellas. ✉ *5 Lion St.* ☎ *01497/821613.*

Richard Booth Books. Shopkeeper Richard Booth once tried to declare Hay an independent kindgom—with himself as king. His bookstore has a huge collection from all over the world, piled haphazardly across two labyrinthine floors. ✉ *44 Lion St.* ☎ *01497/820322* ⊕ *www.boothbooks.co.uk.*

Rose's Books. Easy to spot for its fuchsia-pink front, Rose's Books is devoted entirely to children's books, including rare first editions. ✉ *14 Broad St.* ☎ *01497/820013* ⊕ *www.rosesbooks.com.*

LLANDRINDOD WELLS LLANDRINDOD

27 miles north of Hay-on-Wye, 67 miles north of Cardiff.

Also known as Llandod, the old spa town of Llandrindod Wells preserves its Victorian look with turrets, cupolas, loggias, and balustrades everywhere. Cross over to South Crescent, passing the Glen Usk Hotel with its wrought-iron balustrade and the Victorian bandstand in the gardens opposite, and you reach Middleton Street, a Victorian thoroughfare. From there, head to Rock Park and the path that leads to the

Hay-on-Wye's claims to fame are its many secondhand bookstores and the annual Literary Festival.

Pump Room. This historic building is now an alternative health center, but visitors can freely "take the waters."

GETTING HERE AND AROUND
There are about half a dozen trains daily from Cardiff's Craven Arms Station and the journey takes around three hours. Direct trains from Swansea and Shrewsbury also stop here, but they're less frequent.

ESSENTIALS
Visitor Information Llandrindod Wells Tourist information Centre ⊠ *Temple St.* ☎ *01597/822600* ⊕ *www.llandrindod.co.uk.*

EXPLORING

OFF THE BEATEN PATH

Powis Castle. Continuously occupied since the 13th century, Powis Castle rises above the town of Welshpool. One of the most elegant residential castles in Britain, Powis is equally renowned for its magnificent terraced gardens. The interior contains an outstanding art collection, from Greek vases to paintings by Thomas Gainsborough and Joshua Reynolds. The **Clive of India Museum** contains perhaps the most extensive private collection of antique Indian art in Britain. Powis Castle is north of Llandrindod Wells on the A483. ⊠ *A483, Welshpool* ☎ *01938/551944* ⊕ *www.nationaltrust.org.uk* ⊠ *£12; castle only £6; garden only £9* ⊙ *Castle: Mar.–Oct., daily 12:30–5; Nov.–Feb., weekends 12:30–3:30. Museum: Mar.–Oct., daily 12:30–5. Gardens: Mar.–Sept., daily 11–5:30; Oct. daily 11–4:30; Nov. daily 11–3:30.*

Radnorshire Museum. In Memorial Gardens, this museum tells the story of the town's development from prehistory onwards, and includes a small collection of Roman and medieval artifacts. The largest and most interesting section is devoted to the town's Victorian heyday, with some of the "cures" at the spa explained in gruesome detail. ✉ *Temple St.* ☎ *01597/824513* 🎟 *£1* 🕑 *Apr.–Sept., Tues.–Sat. 10–4; Oct.–Mar., Tues.–Fri. 10–4, Sat. 10–1.*

Royal Welsh Show. The town of Llanelwedd, 7 miles south of Llandrindod, comes to life in late July for the Royal Welsh Show. The old-school livestock judging, sheepdog competitions, and craft demonstrations are spiced up with events such as vintage air displays and motorbike stunt shows. ✉ *Llanelwedd* ☎ *01982/553683* 🌐 *www.rwas.co.uk.*

Victorian Festival. The Victorian Festival takes over Llandrindod Wells for a week in late August. Everyone from shopkeepers to hotel clerks dresses up in period costume for events from tea dances to street parades. ☎ *01597/823441* 🌐 *www.victorianfestival.co.uk.*

WHERE TO EAT AND STAY

$ BISTRO 🍴 **Jules.** Cheerful and family-run, this bar and bistro in the middle of town offers a small but well-edited menu of bistro cooking, such as fried tilapia with coconut curry, or slow-baked chicken with chorizo, couscous, and olives. Traditional Sunday roast lunches are delicious and popular. [$] *Average main: £11* ✉ *Temple St.* ☎ *01597/824642* 🌐 *jules-restaurant.blogspot.com.*

$ B&B/INN 🏨 **Brynhir Farm.** A friendly welcome awaits at this cozy farmhouse 2 miles outside Llandrindod. **Pros:** lovely house; peaceful location; charming hosts. **Cons:** lacks modern extras; remote location is not in walking distance to town. [$] *Rooms from: £70* ✉ *Chapel Rd., Howey* ☎ *01597/822425* 🌐 *www.brynhirfarm.co.uk* 🛏 *3 rooms* 🍽 *Breakfast.*

$$ HOTEL 🏨 **Metropole.** This grand-looking hotel from 1896 is surprisingly contemporary on the inside, with modern furnishings that complement the original architectural flourishes. **Pros:** very central; good service; inexpensive spa. **Cons:** lacks character; can be taken over by conferences. [$] *Rooms from: £126* ✉ *Temple St.* ☎ *01597/823700* 🌐 *www.metropole.co.uk* 🛏 *120 rooms* 🍽 *Breakfast.*

ABERYSTWYTH

41 miles northwest of Llandrindod Wells, 118 miles northwest of Cardiff.

A pleasingly eccentric combination of faded Victorian seaside resort and artsy college town, Aberystwyth is the largest community in Mid-Wales, with a population of barely 16,000. When the weather's fine, the beaches along the bay fill up with sunbathers; when it's not, waves crash so ferociously against the sea wall that even the hotels across the street get soaked. To the east of the town are the Cambrian Mountains and the Veil of Rheidol, which can be visited by steam train.

GETTING HERE AND AROUND

All journeys from South Wales are routed through Shrewsbury and take four to five hours. From London, the trip here takes five to six hours. Long-distance buses are infrequent and painfully slow, though the local bus system is good. There are two roads to Aberystwyth, both of them among the most scenic in Wales: the coastal A487 and the mountainous A44.

ESSENTIALS

Visitor Information Aberystwyth Tourist Information Centre ✉ *Lisburn House, Terrace Rd.* ☎ *01970/612125.*

EXPLORING

TOP ATTRACTIONS

FAMILY **Constitution Hill.** At the northern end of the beach promenade, Constitution Hill dominates the skyline. From the top you can see much of the Welsh coastline (and, on *exceptionally* clear days, Ireland). There's a small café at the top and plenty of space for a picnic. If you're feeling hale and hearty, there's a long footpath that zigzags up to the 430-foot summit. From there a 5-mile-long coastal path stretches to the village of Borth, a smaller, sleepier resort north of Aberystwyth where the remains of a 3,000-year-old petrified forest may be seen on the beach at low tide.

Aberystwyth Cliff Railway. The Victorian-era Aberystwyth Cliff Railway deposits you at the top of Constitution Hill. Opened in 1896, it's the longest electric cliff railway in Britain. ✉ *Cliff Terr.* ☎ *01970/617642* ⊕ *www.aberystwythcliffrailway.co.uk* 🎫 *£4 round-trip* ⊙ *Apr.–Oct., daily 10–5; Nov.–Mar. Wed.–Sun. 10–5. Times vary in winter.*

Great Aberystwyth Camera Obscura. A modern version of a Victorian amusement, Great Aberystwyth Camera Obscura is a massive 14-inch lens that gives you a bird's-eye view of Cardigan Bay and 26 Welsh mountain peaks. It's reached via the Aberystwyth Cliff Railway. ✉ *Cliff Terr.* ☎ *01970/617642* 🎫 *Free* ⊙ *Mar.–Oct., daily 10–5.*

National Library of Wales. This massive neoclassical building next to the University of Wales houses notable Welsh and other Celtic literary works among its more than 4.5 million volumes. The cache of public records makes it an invaluable tool if you're tracing your family tree. Also here is the **National Screen and Sound Archive of Wales**, which hosts lunchtime and evening film screenings. ✉ *Off Penglais Rd.* ☎ *01970/632800* ⊕ *www.llgc.org.uk* 🎫 *Free* ⊙ *Weekdays 9:30–6, Sat. 9:30–5.*

FAMILY **Vale of Rheidol Railway.** At Aberystwyth Station you can hop on the steam-powered Vale of Rheidol Railway for an hour-long ride to the **Devil's Bridge** (*Pont y Gwr Drwg*, or, literally, "the Bridge of the Evil One") where the rivers Rheidol and Mynach meet in a series of spectacular falls. Clamped between two rocky cliffs where a torrent of water pours unceasingly, there are actually three bridges, one built on top of the other. The oldest bridge is about 800 years old. ✉ *Park Ave.* ☎ *01970/625819* ⊕ *www.rheidolrailway.co.uk* 🎫 *£16 round-trip* ⊙ *Easter–Oct.; call for schedule.*

WORTH NOTING

Aberystwyth Castle. At the southern end of the bay, a little way down from the pier, are the crumbling remains of this castle. Built in 1277, it was one of the key strongholds captured in the early 15th century by Owain Glyndwr, a Welsh prince who led the country's last serious bid for independence from England. Today it's a romantic, windswept ruin. ✉ *New Promenade* 🖼 *Free.*

Ceredigion Museum. Housed in a flamboyant 1905 Edwardian theater, the Ceredigion Museum has collections related to folk history and the building's own music hall past. Highlights include a reconstructed mud-walled cottage from 1850 and items illustrating the region's seafaring, lead-mining, and farming history. ✉ *Terrace Rd.* ☎ *01970/633088* ⊕ *museum.ceredigion.gov.uk* 🖼 *Free* ⊙ *Apr.–Sept., Mon.–Sat. 10–5; Oct.–Mar., Mon.–Sat. noon–4:30.*

WHERE TO EAT

$ ✕ **Gannets.** A simple but friendly bistro, Gannets specializes in hearty
BRITISH roasts and traditional Welsh-style dishes that use local meat and fish. Organically grown vegetables and a good wine list are further draws for a university crowd. This place is popular with locals, and you're likely to hear Welsh being spoken at the next table. $ *Average main: £11* ✉ *7 St. James's Sq.* ☎ *01970/617164* ⊙ *No lunch. Closed Sun.–Tues.*

$ ✕ **Ultracomida.** This lively, modern Spanish eatery brings a splash of
SPANISH Mediterranean color to the Mid-Wales coastline. The lunch menu is served tapas style: hake with lentils and Serrano ham, squid fried in garlic with salsa verde, or maybe just some fresh hummus and toast. Or you could just put together an upscale picnic hamper from the in-house deli. Light meals are available in the evening. $ *Average main: £5* ✉ *31 Pier St.* ☎ *01970/630686* ⊕ *www.ultracomida.co.uk* ⊙ *No dinner Sun. and Mon.*

WHERE TO STAY

$ 🛏 **Gwesty Cymru.** This seafront Edwardian house has been converted
HOTEL into one of Aberystwyth's more stylish lodgings. **Pros:** contemporary
Fodor'sChoice design; beautiful location. **Cons:** seafront can be noisy at night; lim-
★ ited parking. $ *Rooms from: £87* ✉ *19 Marine Terr.* ☎ *01970/612252* ⊕ *www.gwestycymru.com* ⟿ *8 rooms* ⊙| *Breakfast.*

$$ 🛏 **Harbourmaster Hotel.** A drive south on the coast road from Aberys-
HOTEL twyth brings you to this early-19th-century Georgian-style building, right on the harbor among colorfully painted structures. **Pros:** good food; stunning harbor location; friendly hosts. **Cons:** difficult parking; often booked up; minimum stay on weekends. $ *Rooms from: £110* ✉ *Pen Cei, 15 miles south of Aberystwyth, Aberaeron* ☎ *01545/570755* ⊕ *www.harbour-master.com* ⟿ *13 rooms* ⊙| *Breakfast.*

$$$ 🛏 **Ynyshir Hall.** This luxurious Georgian mansion is *the* place to stay in
HOTEL this part of Wales if money is no object—as the photos of its world-
Fodor'sChoice famous guests on the lobby walls will attest. **Pros:** artsy ambience;
★ unabashed luxury; great food. **Cons:** isolated location; impossible to reach without a car. $ *Rooms from: £205* ✉ *Off A487, southwest of Machynlleth, Eglwysfach* ☎ *01654/781209* ⊕ *www.ynyshir-hall.co.uk* ⟿ *9 rooms* ⊙| *Breakfast.*

NIGHTLIFE AND THE ARTS

Aberystwyth Arts Centre. In addition to a cinema, the Aberystwyth Arts Centre has a theater, gallery, shops, and a good café and bar. The list of movies is varied, including an international horror movie festival every fall. ✉ *Bridge St.* ☎ *01970/623232* ⊕ *www.aberystwythartscentre.co.uk.*

OUTDOORS

Glyndwr's Way. To the east of Aberystwyth, the 128-mile Glyndwr's Way walking route passes through the Cambrian Mountains before turning north through the town of Machynlleth. From there it veers east to climb above the River Dovey, with wonderful views north to Cadair Idris. ⊕ *www.nationaltrail.co.uk/glyndwrsway.*

DOLGELLAU

34 miles northeast of Aberystwyth.

A solidly Welsh town with dark-stone buildings and old coaching inns made of the local gray dolerite and slate, Dolgellau (pronounced dol-*geth*-lee) thrived with the wool trade until the mid-19th century. Prosperity left striking architecture, with buildings of different eras side by side on crooked streets that are a legacy from Norman times.

Dolgellau has long been a popular base for people eager to walk the surrounding countryside, which forms the southern tip of Snowdonia National Park. To the south of Dolgellau rises the menacing bulk of 2,927-foot Cadair Idris. The name means "the Chair of Idris," a reference to a giant from ancient Celtic mythology.

GETTING HERE AND AROUND

Dolgellau's nearest railway station is at the town of Barmouth, about 10 miles away. The town is small and full of interesting nooks and crannies easily explored on foot. To discover the surrounding area you'll need a car.

ESSENTIALS

Visitor Information Dolgellau Tourist Information Centre ⊠ *Ty Meirion, Eldon Sq.* ☎ *01341/422888* ⊕ *www.visitmidwales.co.uk.*

EXPLORING

Quaker Heritage Centre. In the town square, this museum commemorates the area's strong links with the Quaker movement and the Quakers' emigration to the American colonies. ⊠ *Eldon Sq.* ☎ *01341/424680* ▣ *Free* ☉ *Easter–Oct., daily 10–6; Nov.–Easter, Thurs.–Mon. 10–5.*

FAMILY **Ty Siamas.** The National Centre for Welsh Folk Music is in the converted Victorian Market Hall and Assembly Rooms. It has a fascinating interactive folk-music exhibition, performance auditorium, and café and bar. ⊠ *Neuadd Idris, Eldon Sq.* ☎ *01341/421800* ⊕ *www. tysiamas.com* ▣ *Free* ☉ *Easter–Sept., Wed.–Fri. 10–4, Sat. 10–1. Call for off-season hrs.*

NORTH WALES

Wales masses its most dramatic splendor and fierce beauty in the north. Dominating the area is Snowdon, at 3,560 feet the highest peak in England and Wales. The peak gives its name to the 840-square-mile Snowdonia National Park, which extends southward all the way to Machynlleth in Mid-Wales. As in other British national parks, much of the land is privately owned, so inside the park are towns, villages, and farms, in addition to some spectacular mountain scenery.

The mock-Italianate village of Portmeirion is an extraordinary architectural flight of fancy, and the seaside resort of Llandudno is as popular today as it was during its Victorian heyday. And scattered across the countryside are a ring of mighty medieval castles, built by King Edward I (1239–1307) at the end of a bloody war to bring the population under English rule.

Although North Wales is more popular with travelers than Mid-Wales, the road network is even more tortuous. In fact, you haven't really experienced North Wales until you've spent a maddening hour snaking along a narrow mountain road, all the while with your destination in plain view.

LLANGOLLEN

39 miles northeast of Dolgellau, 23 miles southwest of Chester, 60 miles southwest of Manchester.

Llangollen's setting in a deep valley carved by the River Dee gives it a typically Welsh appearance. The bridge over the Dee, a 14th-century stone structure, is named in a traditional Welsh folk song as one of the "Seven Wonders of Wales." In July the very popular International Musical Eisteddfod brings crowds to town.

For a particularly scenic drive in this area, head for the Horseshoe Pass. For other views, follow the marked footpath from the north end of the canal bridge up a steep hill to see Castell Dinas Bran, the ruins of a 13th-century castle built by a native Welsh ruler. The views of the town and the Vale of Llangollen are worth the 45-minute (one-way) walk.

GETTING HERE AND AROUND

You'll need a car to get here, but once you arrive you can take a trip on the Llangollen Railway. Along the Llangollen Canal, longboat tours head both west and east. The town itself is easy to explore on foot.

ESSENTIALS

Visitor Information Llangollen Tourist Information Centre ⊠ *Y Capel, Castle St.* ☎ *01978/860828* ⊕ *www.llangollen.org.uk.*

EXPLORING

Chirk Castle. This impressive medieval fortress has evolved from its 14th-century origins into a grand home complete with an 18th-century servants hall and interiors furnished in 16th- to 19th-century styles. Nevertheless, it still looks satisfyingly medieval from the outside—and also below ground, where you tour the original dungeons. Surrounding the castle are beautiful formal gardens and parkland. Chirk Castle is 5 miles southeast of Llangollen. ⊠ *Off B4500, Chirk* ☎ *01691/777701* ⊕ *www.nationaltrust.org.uk* ☒ *£9.50* ☉ *Castle: Apr.–Sept., daily 10–4; Mar. and Oct., daily 10–4; Nov.–mid-Dec. and Feb., weekends 10–4. Gardens: Apr.–Sept., daily 10–5; Oct.–Mar., daily 10–4.*

FAMILY **Llangollen Railway.** This restored standard-gauge steam line runs for 7 miles along the scenic Dee Valley. The terminus is near the town's bridge. ⊠ *Abbey Rd.* ☎ *01978/860979* ⊕ *www.llangollen-railway.co.uk* ☒ *£12 round-trip* ☉ *Apr.–Oct., daily 10:30–5; Nov.–Mar., some weekends.*

WELSH: A SHORT PRIMER

The native language of Wales, Welsh (or *Cymraeg*, as it's properly called) is spoken fluently by around a quarter of the population. (The vast majority, however, speaks a little.) Not legally recognized in Britain until the 1960s, it was suppressed beginning in the time of Henry VIII and blamed for poor literacy during the reign of Queen Victoria. Today Welsh children under 17 are required to take classes to learn the language.

Welsh may look daunting to pronounce, but it's a phonetic language, so pronunciation is fairly easy once the alphabet is learned. Remember that "dd" is sounded like "th" in *they*, "f" sounds like "v" in *save*, and "ff" is the equivalent of the English "f" in *forest*. The "ll" sound has no English equivalent; the closest match is the "cl" sound in *close*.

Terms that crop up frequently in Welsh are *bach* or *fach* (small; also a common term of endearment similar to *dear*), *craig* or *graig* (rock), *cwm* (valley; pronounced coom), *dyffryn* (valley), *eglwys* (church), *glyn* (glen), *llyn* (lake), *mawr* or *fawr* (great, big), *pentre* (village, homestead), *plas* (hall, mansion), and *pont* or *bont* (bridge).

Plas Newydd. From 1778 to 1828 Plas Newydd (not to be confused with the similarly named Isle of Anglesey estate) was the home of Lady Eleanor Butler and Sarah Ponsonby, the eccentric Ladies of Llangollen, who set up a then-scandalous single-sex household, collected curios and magnificent carvings, and made it into a tourist attraction even during their lifetimes. You can take tea there, as did Wordsworth and the Duke of Wellington, and stroll in the attractively terraced gardens. ⌧ *Hill St.* ☎ *01978/862834* ⊕ *www.denbighshire.gov.uk* ⌧ *£5.50* ☉ *Apr.–Sept., Wed.–Sun., 10:30–5; last admission 45 mins before closing.*

Pontcysyllte. From the Llangollen Canal Wharf you can take a horse-drawn boat or a narrow boat (a slender barge) along the canal to the world's longest and highest navigable cast-iron aqueduct: Pontcysyllte (Welsh for "the bridge that connects"), a UNESCO World Heritage Site. The aqueduct is more than 1,000 feet long. The aqueduct is 3 miles east of Llangollen. ⌧ *Llangollen Canal Wharf, Wharf Hill,* ☎ *01978/860702 Llangollen Wharf* ⊕ *www.horsedrawnboats.co.uk* ⌧ *£12.50.*

Vale of Ceiriog. Near Llangollen is this verdant valley, known locally as "Little Switzerland." The B4500, running between Chirk and the village of Glyn Ceiriog, at the foothills of the Berwyn Mountains, is one of the region's great drives. It's just remote enough that you can often have the road to yourself.

WHERE TO EAT AND STAY

$

BRITISH

✕ **The Corn Mill.** In a converted mill on the River Dee, this pub and restaurant has an old water wheel that turns behind the bar. Dine on the open-air deck or in the cozy dining room, sampling stylishly updated pub fare, from smoked salmon and haddock fish cakes to chicken with grilled truffle polenta. There are light bites, too, and dessert classics such as pecan and toffee cheesecake. Several of the ales are from Welsh microbreweries. Service can be slow when things get busy, but this is a good place to unwind. $ *Average main: £12* ✉ *Dee La.* ☎ *01978/869555* ⊕ *www.cornmill-llangollen.co.uk.*

$ 📷 **Cornerstones Guesthouse.** Made up of three 16th-century cottages with
B&B/INN   views over the River Dee, this little B&B mixes period charm with modern comfort. **Pros:** spacious bedrooms; free passes for town parking lots. **Cons:** directly on the street; two-night minimum stay. $ *Rooms from: £80* ✉ *15 Bridge St.* ☎ *01978/861569* ⊕ *www.cornerstones-guesthouse. co.uk* ⌁ *3 rooms, 2 suites* ⦿ *Breakfast.*

NIGHTLIFE AND THE ARTS
International Musical Eisteddfod. The six-day International Musical Eisteddfod, held in early July, brings together amateur choirs and dancers—more than 12,000 participants in all—from all corners of the globe for a colorful folk festival. The tradition of the *eisteddfod,* held throughout Wales, goes back to the 12th century. Originally gatherings of bards, the *eisteddfodau* of today are more like national festivals. ☎ *01978/862001* ⊕ *www.international-eisteddfod.co.uk.*

EN
ROUTE   **Pistyll Rhaeadr.** The peat-brown water of Pistyll Rhaeadr, the highest waterfall in Wales, thunders down a 290-foot double cascade. When you're driving on the B4500 between Llangollen and Llanwddyn, take the road leading northwest from the town of Llanrhaeadr ym Mochnant, in the peaceful Tanat Valley. It was near here that, in 1588, the Bible was translated into Welsh—one of the key moments that helped to ensure the survival of the language. The waterfall is 4 miles up the road.

LAKE VYRNWY LLYN EFYRNWY

18 miles southwest of Llangollen.

This beautiful lake has a sense of tranquillity that doesn't entirely befit its history. Lake Vyrnwy was created in the 1880s to provide water for the people of Liverpool, 80 miles north. Unfortunately, this meant forcibly evicting the residents of a small town—an act that's still controversial in Wales. Today it's a peaceful spot surrounded by a thriving nature reserve. The closest settlement is tiny Llanwddyn, and a bit farther away is Bala, a pretty town with an almost-as-lovely natural lake of its own.

GETTING HERE AND AROUND
Rural bus service is infrequent, so you need a car to explore the area. The B4393 circles Lake Vyrnwy itself; from here, Bala is a 14-mile drive over hair-raising Bwlch y Groes pass or a circuitous drive along the B4391. Llangollen is 28 miles northeast of Lake Vyrnwy on the B4396.

EXPLORING
FAMILY   **Bala Lake Railway.** The steam-powered train runs along the southern shores of Bala Lake (Llyn Tegid, or "Lake of Beauty"), a large natural reservoir just northeast of Lake Vyrnwy. Bala Lake is also popular for kayaking and other water sports. ✉ *Off B4403, Llanuwchllyn* ☎ *01678/540666* ⊕ *www.bala-lake-railway.co.uk* ⌁ *£9.50 round-trip* ⊙ *Late Apr., weekends; May, late June, and Sept., Sat.–Thurs; early June, July, and Aug., daily; call for departure times.*

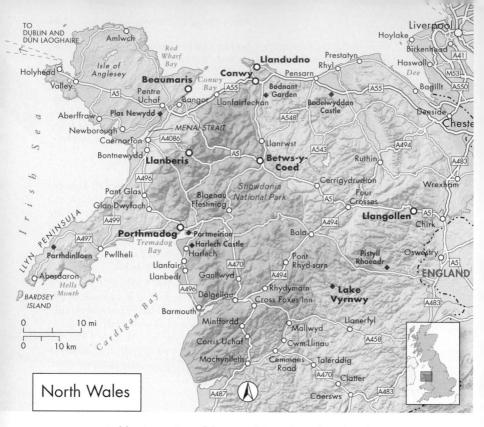

North Wales

Bwlch y Groes. One of the great drives of North Wales, the sweeping, vertiginous panoramas of Bwlch y Groes (Pass of the Cross) form the highest mountain pass accessible by road in the country. From Lake Vyrnwy, drive for a mile on B4393 before heading west on the mountain road.

FAMILY **Lake Vyrnwy Nature Reserve.** Bordered by lush forest and emerald green
Fodor's Choice hills, Lake Vyrnwy is a haven for wildlife. It's rich in rare bird species,
★ from falcons to siskins and curlews. Stretching out along the shores of the lake near the visitor center, the Lake Vyrnwy Sculpture Park is a collection of pieces by the talented local artist Andy Hancock. Arranged along a paved walking trail, many of the wooden sculptures resemble oversize versions of the lake's wildlife, including a 15-foot-long dragonfly. It's an extremely popular cycling route, and there's a bike shop and coffee shop near the visitor center. ⊠ *Off B4393, Llanwddyn* ☎ *01691/870278* ⊕ *www.lake-vyrnwy.com* ☝ *Free* ☉ *Visitor Center: Apr.–Oct., daily 10:30–5:30; Nov.–Mar., weekdays 10:30–4; weekends 10:30–4:30. Park: daily year-round.*

WHERE TO STAY

$$ ☑ **Cyfie Farm.** This ivy-clad 17th-century farmhouse sits in a tranquil
B&B/INN area 5 miles from Lake Vyrnwy. **Pros:** in-room fireplaces; outdoor hot tub; hosts are trained chefs; discounts for longer stays. **Cons:** remote location; need a car to get around. $ *Rooms from: £125* ⊠ *Off B4393,*

Llanfihangel-yng-Ngwynfa ☎ *01691/648451* ⊕ *www.cyfiefarm.co.uk* ⇔ *4 suites* ⁐⃝ *Breakfast.*

$$
B&B/INN ▦ **Lake Vyrnwy Hotel.** Awesome views of mountain-ringed Lake Vyrnwy are just one asset of this country mansion on a 24,000-acre estate. **Pros:** perfect for outdoor pursuits; luxurious spa; excellent package deals. **Cons:** too remote for some; minimum stay on some summer weekends. Ⓢ *Rooms from: £135* ✉ *Off B4393, Llanwddyn* ☎ *01691/870692* ⊕ *www.lakevyrnwy.com* ⇔ *52 rooms* ⁐⃝ *Breakfast.*

12

PORTHMADOG

35 miles southeast of Lake Vyrnwy, 16 miles southeast of Caernarfon.

The little seaside town of Porthmadog, built as a harbor to export slate from nearby Blaenau Ffestiniog, stands at the gateway to the Llŷn Peninsula (pronounced like "lean," with your tongue touching your palate), with its virtually unspoiled coastline and undulating, wildflower-covered hills. It's also near the town of Harlech, which contains one of the great castles of Wales, and the weird and wonderful Portmeirion.

GETTING HERE AND AROUND

The picturesque Cambrian Coast Railway runs from Machynlleth, near Aberystwyth, up the coast to Porthmadog. When you arrive you can take a scenic trip on the town's "little railways." Porthmadog is a stop on the excellent Snowdon Sherpa bus service. The town itself is totally walkable and has good access to coastal trails.

ESSENTIALS

Visitor Information Porthmadog Tourist Information Centre ✉ *High St.* ☎ *01766/512981* ⊕ *www.visitsnowdonia.info.*

EXPLORING

TOP ATTRACTIONS

FAMILY **Ffestiniog Railway.** Founded in the early 19th century to carry slate, the Ffestiniog Railway starts at the quayside and climbs up 700 feet through a wooded vale, past a waterfall, and across the mountains. The northern terminus is in Blaenau Ffestiniog, where you can visit an old slate mine. The Ffestiniog Railway is perhaps the best of several small steam lines in this part of the country. ■**TIP➜** **Porthmadog gets very crowded in summer, and parking is limited, so you might want to make this journey from Blaenau Ffestiniog to Porthmadog instead.** ✉ *Harbour Station, High St.* ☎ *01766/516000* ⊕ *www.festrail.co.uk* 🎫 *£20.20 round-trip* ⏱ *Mid-Mar.–Oct., daily; call for times.*

Harlech Castle. A wealth of legend, poetry, and song is conjured up by the 13th-century Harlech Castle, built by Edward I to help subdue the Welsh. Its mighty ruins, visible for miles, are as dramatic as its history (though you have to imagine the sea, which used to crash against the rocks below but receded in the 19th century). Harlech was occupied by the Welsh Prince Owain Glyndwr from 1404 to 1408 during his revolt against the English. The music of the traditional folk song "Men of Harlech" refers to the heroic defense of this castle in 1468 by Dafydd ap Eynion, who, summoned to surrender, is alleged to have replied: "I held a castle in France until every old woman in Wales heard of

EATING WELL IN WALES

Talented chefs making use of the country's bountiful resources have put Wales firmly on the culinary map. Welsh Black beef and succulent Welsh lamb are world renowned, and the supply of fish and seafood (including mussels and oysters) from coasts and rivers is excellent. Organic products are available to restaurants and the public from specialty companies, farm shops, and farmers' markets.

Ty Nant Welsh spring water graces restaurant tables worldwide, and there are a few small vineyards in the south. There's even a Welsh whisky that's won awards at international tastings.

You can try traditionally named cheeses such as Llanboidy and Caws Cenarth or an extra-mature cheddar called Black Bomber.

Contemporary cuisine is more fashionable, but traditional dishes are worth seeking out. Cawl, for example, is a nourishing broth of lamb and vegetables, and laverbread is a distinctive puréed seaweed that's usually fried with eggs and bacon.

it, and I will hold a castle in Wales until every old woman in France hears of it." On a clear day you can climb the battlements for a spectacular view of the surrounding countryside. The castle dominates the coastal town of Harlech, 12 miles south of Porthmadog. ⊠ *Off B4573, Harlech* ☎ *01443/336000* ⊕ *www.cadw.wales.gov.uk* ⊠ *£4.50* ☉ *Mar.– Jun., daily 9:30–5; July and Aug., daily 9:30–6; Nov.–Feb., Mon.–Sat. 10–4; Sun. 11–4. Last admission 30 mins before closing.*

Fodor's Choice **Portmeirion.** One of the true highlights of North Wales is Portmeirion,
★ a tiny fantasy-Italianate village on a private peninsula surrounded by hills, which is said to be loosely modeled after Portofino. Designed in the 1920s by architect Clough Williams-Ellis (1883–1978), the village has a hotel and restaurant among its multicolored buildings, and gift shops sell a distinctive local pottery. On the edge of town is a peaceful woodland trail punctuated here and there by such flourishes as a red iron bridge and a miniature pagoda. William-Ellis called it his "light-opera approach to architecture," and the result is magical, though distinctly un-Welsh. Portmeirion is about 2 miles east of Porthmadog. ⊠ *Off A487, Portmeirion* ☎ *01766/772311* ⊕ *www.portmeirion-village.com* ⊠ *£10* ☉ *Daily 9:30–7:30.*

Fodor's Choice **Tre'r Ceiri.** Remote, atmospheric, and astoundingly little known, Tre'r
★ Ceiri is one of the most impressive ancient monuments in Wales. Today parts of the 4th-century fort's outer walls are still intact (rising more than 18 feet in places), and within are the ruins of 150 stone huts. They were inhabited by a Celtic tribe known as the Ordovices, and may have survived as a settlement for up to 700 years. From Porthmadog, take the A497 west, then turn left onto the A499 just before Pwllheli. At the village of Llanaelhaearn, turn left onto the B4417. Less than a mile down this road is an unmarked footpath on the right leading straight up a hill to Tre'r Ceiri. ⊠ *B4417, Llanaelhaearn* ⊠ *Free.*

12

WORTH NOTING

FAMILY **Llechwedd Slate Caverns.** At these caverns you can take two trips: a tram ride through floodlighted tunnels where Victorian working conditions have been re-created, and a ride on Britain's deepest underground railway to a mine where you can walk by an eerie underground lake. Either tour gives a good idea of the difficult working conditions the miners endured. Above are a re-created Victorian village and slate-splitting demonstrations. ⚠ Wear sturdy footwear—during busy times you may have to climb 70 steps as part of the tour. ⊠ *Off A470, Blaenau Ffestiniog* ☎ *01766/830306* ⊕ *www.llechwedd-slate-caverns.co.uk* 🚃 *Tram ride or deep mine tour £10.50; both tours £17* ⊙ *Mid-Mar.–Sept., daily 9:30–5:30; Oct.–mid-Mar., daily 10–5; last admission 45 mins before closing.*

Porthdinllaen. On the very tip of a thumb-shape peninsula jutting out into the Irish Sea, this miniscule but gorgeous little harbor community is 20 miles from Porthmadog. There's a wide, sheltered beach where the sand is so fine that it squeaks underfoot, and whitewashed cottages line the curving seafront. Park at the nearby visitor center. ⊠ *Porthdinllaen.*

WHERE TO EAT AND STAY

$$$$ ✗ **Castle Cottage.** Close to Harlech's mighty castle, this friendly "res-
BRITISH taurant with rooms" is a wonderful find. The emphasis is on the exceptional cuisine of chef-proprietor Glyn Roberts, who uses locally sourced ingredients from lobster to lamb to create imaginative, beautifully presented contemporary dishes. There's a fixed-price dinner menu (£39.50). There are three spacious, modern rooms (from £135) in the main house and four more in the annex, a 16th-century coaching inn. Ⓢ *Average main: £39* ⊠ *Near B4573, Harlech* ☎ *01766/780479* ⊕ *www.castlecottageharlech.co.uk* ⊙ *No lunch.*

$ ✗ **Ty Coch Inn.** In a seafront building in picture-postcard Porthdinllaen,
BRITISH this pub has what is undoubtedly one of the best locations in Wales. The lunches are honest and unpretentious: pies, sandwiches, bangers and mash, or perhaps a plate of local mussels in garlic butter. Everything is delicious and reasonably priced. The atmosphere is friendly and slightly bohemian; this is the kind of place where they're pleasantly surprised you've managed to find it. Ⓢ *Average main: £9* ⊠ *Off B4417, Porthdinllaen* ☎ *01758/720498* ⊕ *www.tycoch.co.uk* ⊙ *No dinner.*

$ 🏨 **Hotel Maes-y-Neuadd.** Eight acres of gardens and parkland create a
B&B/INN glorious setting for this luxurious manor house dating from the 14th century. **Pros:** magnificent location above Tremadog Bay; great restaurant. **Cons:** low ceilings in some rooms. Ⓢ *Rooms from: £90* ⊠ *Off B4573, Talsarnau* ☎ *01766/780200* ⊕ *www.neuadd.com* ⤳ *15 rooms* ⍩ *Breakfast.*

$$ 🏨 **Hotel Portmeirion.** One of the most elegant and unusual places to
HOTEL stay in Wales, this waterfront mansion is located at the heart of Portmeirion. **Pros:** unique location; beautiful building; woodland walks. **Cons:** gets crowded with day-trippers; minimum stay on weekends. Ⓢ *Rooms from: £139* ⊠ *A487, Portmeirion* ☎ *01766/770000* ⊕ *www.portmeirion-village.com* ⤳ *42 rooms, 11 suites* ⍩ *Multiple meal plans.*

For a touch of whimsy, visit the mock-Italianate village of Portmeirion, set on the coast.

BETWS-Y-COED

25 miles northeast of Porthmadog, 19 miles south of Llandudno.

The rivers Llugwy and Conwy meet at Betws-y-Coed, a popular village surrounded by woodland with excellent views of Snowdonia. It can be used as a base to explore the national park, although its diminutive size means that it can get overcrowded in summer. The most famous landmark in the village is the ornate iron Waterloo Bridge over the River Conwy, designed in 1815 by Thomas Telford.

GETTING HERE AND AROUND

The town is easy to reach on the Conwy Valley Railway that runs from Llandudno to Blaenau Ffestiniog. Betws-y-Coed is also a hub for the excellent Snowdon Sherpa bus service that covers most of Snowdonia's beauty spots, so it's feasible to explore this part of Wales without a car.

ESSENTIALS

Visitor Information Betws-y-Coed Tourist Information Centre ⊠ *Royal Oak Stables, Station Rd.* ☎ *01690/710426* ⊕ *www.betws-y-coed.co.uk.*

EXPLORING

FAMILY
Fodor's Choice
★

Snowdonia National Park. Stretching from the Welsh midlands almost to its northern coast, Snowdonia National Park covers a vast swath of North Wales. The park consists of 840 square miles of rocky mountains, valleys clothed in oak woods, moorlands, lakes, and rivers, all guaranteeing natural beauty and, to a varying extent, solitude. Its most famous attraction, by far, is the towering peak of Mt. Snowdon. The view from the top is jaw-dropping: to the northwest you can see the

Menai Strait and Anglesey; to the south, Harlech Castle and the Cadair Idris mountain range. To the southwest, on an exceedingly clear day, you can make out the distant peaks of Ireland's Wicklow Mountains. There are six different walking paths to the top, but a far less punishing way is via the Snowdon Mountain Railway, in nearby Llanberis.

Perched at the top of Snowdon is Hafod Eryri, an eco-friendly replacement for the previous visitor center (once described by Prince Charles as "the highest slum in Wales"). The granite-roof building, which blends beautifully into the rocky landscape, has a café and exhibitions about the mountain, its ecology, and its history. If you're planning to make the ascent, the visitor center in Betws-y-Coed is the best place to stop for information. ✉ *Royal Oak Stables, Station Rd.* ☎ *01690/710426* 🌐 *www.eryri-npa.gov.uk/home.*

Swallow Falls. Betws-y-Coed is bordered by Gwydyr Forest, which has several well-marked walking trails. The forest also contains a half dozen or so mines, the last of which was abandoned in the 1940s. On the western approach to the village you'll find Swallow Falls, where the River Llugwy tumbles down through a wooded chasm. **■ TIP→ Be careful on the footpath: there's no guardrail.** ✉ *Off A5.*

WHERE TO EAT AND STAY

$$ BRITISH 🍴 **Ty Gwyn.** This coaching inn, built in 1636, is one of the best places to eat in Snowdonia. The food is traditional Welsh fare, beautifully prepared with local ingredients. Standouts include steak with cream of Stilton cheese and coriander, or lobster with a prawn and crayfish thermidor. Vegetarians are well cared for with such dishes as Thai-style vegetable curry with fresh lime and chili. The inn also has simple, cozy bedrooms starting at £30 per night. [$] *Average main: £16* ✉ *A5* ☎ *01690/710383* 🌐 *www.tygwynhotel.co.uk.*

$ B&B/INN 🏨 **Aberconwy House.** This luxurious Victorian house has panoramic views over Betws-y-Coed. **Pros:** beautiful countryside views; great breakfasts. **Cons:** no bar or evening meal. [$] *Rooms from: £70* ✉ *Lôn Muriau, off A470* ☎ *01690/710202* 🌐 *www.aberconwy-house.co.uk* 🛏 *8 rooms* 🍽 *Breakfast.*

$ B&B/INN Fodor's Choice ★ 🏨 **Pengwern Country House.** Hosts Ian and Gwawr Mowatt are charmingly adept at making their guests feel at home in this former Victorian artists' colony. **Pros:** woodland location; wealth of Victorian details; lovely hosts. **Cons:** close to main road; car is essential. [$] *Rooms from: £72* ✉ *A5, Allt Dinas* ☎ *01690/710480* 🌐 *www.snowdoniaaccommodation.co.uk* 🛏 *3 rooms* 🍽 *Breakfast.*

$$ B&B/INN 🏨 **Tan-y-Foel Country House.** Hidden away on a wooded hillside outside Betws-y-Coed, this quiet, contemporary hideaway has views over the Conwy Valley. **Pros:** striking decor; inventive cuisine. **Cons:** meals must be arranged in advance; too far to walk into town. [$] *Rooms from: £125* ✉ *Off A5, Capel Garmon* ☎ *01690/710507* 🌐 *www.tyfhotel.co.uk* 🛏 *6 rooms* 🍽 *Breakfast.*

The Llanberis Path is one route to the top of Snowdon, the highest peak in Wales, in Snowdonia National Park.

LLANBERIS

17 miles west of Betws-y-Coed.

Like Betws-y-Coed, Llanberis is a focal point for people visiting Snowdonia National Park.

GETTING HERE AND AROUND

Llanberis is accessible by bus. The most convenient service, targeted at visitors, is the Snowdon Sherpa bus route.

ESSENTIALS

Visitor Information Llanberis Tourist Information Centre ⊠ *Electric Mountain, Off A4086* ☎ *01286/870765.*

EXPLORING

Fodor'sChoice **Caernarfon Castle.** The grim, majestic mass of Caernarfon Castle, a
★ UNESCO World Heritage Site, looms over the waters of the River Seiont. Numerous bloody encounters were witnessed by these sullen walls, erected by Edward I in 1283 as a symbol of his determination to subdue the Welsh. The castle's towers, unlike those of Edward I's other castles, are polygonal and patterned with bands of different-color stone. In 1284 the monarch thought of a scheme to steal the Welsh throne. Knowing that the Welsh chieftains would accept no foreign prince, Edward promised to designate a ruler who could speak no word of English. Edward presented his infant son to the assembled chieftains as their prince "who spoke no English, had been born on Welsh soil, and whose first words would be spoken in Welsh." The ruse worked, and on that day was created the first Prince of Wales of English lineage. In the Queen's Tower, a museum charts the history of the local regiment, the

Royal Welsh Fusiliers. The castle is in the town of Caernarfon, 7 miles west of Llanberis. ✉ *Castle Hill, Caernarfon* ☎ *01286/677617* 🌐 *cadw.wales.gov.uk* 🎫 *£5.50* 🕒 *Mar.–June, Sept., and Oct., daily 9:30–5; July and Aug., daily 9:30–6; Nov.–Feb., Mon.–Sat. 10–4, Sun. 11–4; last admission 30 mins before closing.*

National Slate Museum. In Padarn Country Park, this museum in the old Dinorwig Slate Quarry is dedicated to what was once an important industry for the area. The museum has quarry workshops and slate-splitting demonstrations, as well as restored worker housing, all of which convey the development of the industry and the challenges faced by those who worked in it. The narrow-gauge Llanberis Lake Railway departs from here. ✉ *Padarn Country Park, A4086* ☎ *029/2057–3700* 🌐 *www.museumwales.ac.uk* 🎫 *Free* 🕒 *Easter–Oct., daily 10–5; Nov.–Easter, Sun.–Fri. 10–4.*

FAMILY
Fodor's Choice ★

Snowdon Mountain Railway. One of the region's most famous attractions is the rack-and-pinion Snowdon Mountain Railway, with some of its track at a thrillingly steep grade; the train terminates within 70 feet of the 3,560-foot-high summit. Snowdon—*Yr Wyddfa* in Welsh—is the highest peak south of Scotland and lies within the 840-square-mile national park. Weather permitting, trains go all the way to the summit; on a clear day you can see as far as the Wicklow Mountains in Ireland, about 90 miles away. You can take two types of train: a modern diesel-driven version, or the brand-new "heritage" version, complete with restored carriages and working steam engine. ✉ *A4086* ☎ *0844/493–8120* 🌐 *www.snowdonrailway.co.uk* 🎫 *Diesel service: £27 round-trip. Heritage service: £35 round-trip* 🕒 *Mid-Mar.–Oct., daily; call for schedule.*

WHERE TO STAY

$
HOTEL

🏨 **Meifod Country House.** Former home of the high sheriff of Caernarfon, this opulent Victorian house has polished tile floors, wood-burning fireplaces, and bedrooms with features such as Victorian claw-foot baths and chandeliers. **Pros:** authentic atmosphere; good restaurant. **Cons:** often booked with wedding parties; not walking distance to town. [$] *Rooms from: £90* ✉ *Off A487, Bontnewydd* ☎ *01286/673351* 🌐 *www.meifodcountryhouse.com* 🛏 *5 rooms* 🍴 *Breakfast.*

BEAUMARIS BIWMARES AND ANGLESEY YNYS MÔN

14 miles north of Llanberis.

Elegant Beaumaris is on the Isle of Anglesey, the largest island directly off the shore of Wales. It's linked to the mainland by the Britannia road and rail bridge and by Thomas Telford's remarkable chain suspension bridge, built in 1826 over the Menai Strait. Though its name means "beautiful marsh," Beaumaris has become a town of pretty cottages, Georgian houses, and bright shops; it also has Plas Newydd, one of the grandest stately homes in Wales.

Around 70% of Anglesey's 60,000 or so inhabitants speak Welsh, so you'll probably hear it more than English.

GETTING HERE AND AROUND

Anglesey is linked to the mainland by the A55 and A5. The roads on the island are in good condition, and there's a relatively extensive bus network. Ferries and catamarans to Ireland leave from Holyhead, on the island's western side.

EXPLORING

Beaumaris Castle. The town of Beaumaris dates from 1295, when Edward I commenced work on this impressive castle, the last and largest link in an "iron ring" of fortifications around North Wales built to contain the Welsh. Guarding the western approach to the Menai Strait, the unfinished castle (a World Heritage Site) is solid and symmetrical, with concentric lines of fortification, arrow slits, and a moat: a superb example of medieval defensive planning. ✉ *Castle St.* ☎ *01248/810361* 🌐 *www.cadw.wales.gov.uk* 🎟 *£4* 🕐 *Mar.–Jun., Sept. and Oct., daily 9–5; July and Aug., daily 9:30–6; Nov.–Feb., Mon.–Sat. 10–4, Sun. 11–4; last admission 30 mins before closing.*

Fodor's Choice ★ **Bryn Celli Ddu.** Dating from around 3000 BC, this megalithic passage tomb is the most complete site of its kind in Wales. You enter via a narrow opening built into a burial mound. The passage extends for around 25 feet before opening out into a wider burial chamber. The far wall, made of quartz, is illuminated at dawn on the summer solstice. ■ **TIP→ Bring a flashlight, as the tomb has no artificial lighting.** Next to the entrance is a replica of a stone pillar carved with Celtic spirals, found here in 1928. The original is in the National Museum in Cardiff. The site is 7 miles southwest of Beaumaris. ✉ *Off A4080, Llanddaniel Fab* 🎟 *Free* 🕐 *Daily, dawn–dusk.*

Plas Newydd. Some historians consider Plas Newydd to be the finest mansion in Wales. Remodeled in the 18th century by James Wyatt (1747–1813) for the Marquesses of Anglesey (whose descendants still live here), it stands on the Menai Strait about 7 miles southwest of Beaumaris. The interior has some fine 18th-century Gothic Revival decorations. Between 1936 and 1940 the society artist Rex Whistler (1905–44) painted the mural in the dining room. A museum commemorates the Battle of Waterloo, where the first marquess led the cavalry. The woodland walk and rhododendron gardens are worth exploring, and it's sometimes possible to take boat trips on the strait. ✉ *Off A4080, southwest of Britannia Bridge, Llanfairpwll* ☎ *01248/714795* 🌐 *www.nationaltrust.org.uk* 🎟 *House and garden £9; garden only £7* 🕐 *House: mid-Mar.–early Nov., Sat.–Wed. noon–4:30. Garden: mid-Mar.–early Nov., Sat.–Wed. 10–5:30.*

WHERE TO STAY

$ B&B/INN 🏨 **Cleifiog.** This cozy manor house, mostly Georgian in style, is on the banks of the Menai Strait a short stroll from Beaumaris Castle. **Pros:** seafront location; close to town; interesting history. **Cons:** minimum stay on weekends. [$] *Rooms from: £90* ✉ *A454* ☎ *01248/811507* 🌐 *www.cleifiogbandb.co.uk* 🛏 *3 rooms* 🍴 *Breakfast.*

$$ B&B/INN 🏨 **Ye Olde Bull's Head and Townhouse.** These twin hotels, a stone's throw away from each other, could hardly be more different: one is a restored 15th- century coaching inn, the other a contemporary lodging. **Pros:** lovely blend of historic and contemporary; good food. **Cons:** Bull's Head

has low ceilings. $ *Rooms from: £100* ✉ *Castle St.* ☎ *01248/810329* ⊕ *www.bullsheadinn.co.uk* ⟳ *13 rooms* ⟊ *Breakfast.*

SPORTS AND THE OUTDOORS
Anglesey is a great place to get outdoors.

Isle of Anglesey Coastal Path. Extending 125 miles around the island, this path leads past cliffs, sandy coves, and plenty of scenic variety. Pick up information at tourist offices and choose a section; the west coast has the most dramatic scenery. ⊕ *www.angleseycoastalpath.co.uk.*

12

CONWY

23 miles east of Beaumaris, 48 miles northwest of Chester.

The still-authentic medieval town of Conwy grew up around its castle on the west bank of the River Conwy. A ring of ancient but well-preserved walls, built in the 13th century to protect the English merchants who lived here, enclose the Old Town and add to the pervading sense of history. Sections of the walls, with their 21 towers, can still be walked. The impressive views from the top take in the castle and the estuary, with mountains in the distance.

GETTING HERE AND AROUND
The A55 expressway links Conwy into the central U.K. motorway system via the M56. The town is also on the North Wales coast rail route, which ends at Holyhead on Anglesey. The town itself—surrounded by its wonderfully preserved walls—is perfect for pedestrians.

ESSENTIALS
Visitor Information Conwy Town Tourism Association ✉ *Muriau Buildings, Rosehill St.* ☎ *01492/577566* ⊕ *www.visitconwytown.co.uk.*

EXPLORING
Aberconwy House. In what is thought to be the oldest complete medieval house in Wales, Aberconwy House's rooms have been restored to reflect three distinct periods in its history: medieval, Jacobean, and Victorian. It's a diverting and atmsopheric little place, which also holds the distinction of (supposedly) being one of the most haunted buildings in North Wales. ✉ *Castle St.* ☎ *01492/592246* ⊕ *www.nationaltrust. org.uk* ✑ *£3.50* ⊙ *Mid-Mar.–June, Sept., and Oct., Wed.–Mon. 11–5; July and Aug, daily 11–5.*

Bodnant Garden. Undoubtedly one of the best gardens in Wales, Bodnant Garden is something of a pilgrimage spot for horticulturists from around the world. Laid out in 1875, the 87 acres are particularly famed for rhododendrons, camellias, and magnolias. ■TIP➜ **Visit in May to see the laburnum arch that forms a huge tunnel of golden blooms.** The mountains of Snowdonia form a magnificent backdrop to the Italianate terraces, rock and rose gardens, and pinetum. The gardens, which are closed mid-November to late December, are about 5 miles south of Conwy. ✉ *Off A470, Tal-y-Cafn* ☎ *01492/650460* ⊕ *www. nationaltrust.org.uk* ✑ *Mar.–Oct., £8.50; Nov.–Feb., £4.60* ⊙ *Mar.– mid-Oct., daily 10–5; mid-Oct.–mid-Nov. and late Dec.–Feb., daily 11–3; winter times may vary.*

Fodor's Choice ★ **Conwy Castle.** Of all Edward I's Welsh strongholds, it is perhaps Conwy Castle that best preserves a sheer sense of power and dominance. The eight large round towers and tall curtain wall, set on a rocky promontory, provide sweeping views of the area and the town walls. Although the castle is roofless (and floorless in places), the signage does a pretty good job of helping you visualize how rooms such as the Great Hall must once have looked. Conwy Castle can be approached on foot by a dramatic suspension bridge completed in 1828; engineer Thomas Telford designed the bridge with turrets to blend in with the fortress's presence. ✉ *Rose Hill St.* ☎ *01492/592358* 🌐 *www.cadw.wales.gov.uk* 🎟 *£5* 🕒 *Mar.–Jun., Sept. and Oct., daily 9:30–5; July and Aug., daily 9:30–6; Nov.–Feb., Mon.–Sat. 10–4, Sun. 11–4; last admission 30 mins before closing.*

Plas Mawr. Dating from 1576, Plas Mawr is one of the best-preserved Elizabethan town houses in Britain. Richly decorated with ornamental plasterwork, it gives a unique insight into the lives of the Tudor gentry and their servants. ✉ *High St.* ☎ *01492/580167* 🌐 *www.cadw.wales.gov.uk* 🎟 *£5.85* 🕒 *Mar.–Sept., Tues.–Sun. 9–5; Oct., Tues –Sun., 9:30–4; last admission 45 mins before closing.*

Smallest House in Britain. What is said to be Britain's smallest house is furnished in mid-Victorian Welsh style. The house, which is 6 feet wide and 10 feet high, was reputedly last occupied in 1900 by a fisherman who was more than 6 feet tall. ✉ *Lower Gate St.* ☎ *01492/593484* 🎟 *£1* 🕒 *Apr.–Oct., Mon.–Sat. 10–5:30; Sun. 11–4.*

WHERE TO EAT AND STAY

$ MODERN BRITISH 🍴 **The Mulberry.** This family-run restaurant overlooking the boats bobbing in Conwy Marina is popular with families for its jovial, laid-back atmosphere. The menu consists of classic dishes like rack of lamb, burgers, curries, and pizzas. Sunday lunch is served buffet style. [$] *Average main: £11* ✉ *Morfa Dr.* ☎ *01492/583350* 🌐 *www.mulberryconwy.com.*

$$ BRITISH 🍴 **Watson's Bistro.** This popular bistro in central Conwy combines traditional Welsh flavors with accents of the Mediterranean. You may start with *Y fenni* mustard cheese and Parmesan beignets served with chorizo and mozzarella, before moving on to poached prawns in a sparkling wine sauce with lime fritters, or shoulder of lamb with minted garlic and honey. ■ **TIP→ The £10 two-course lunch menu is an exceptional value.** [$] *Average main: £16* ✉ *Chapel St.* ☎ *01492/596326* 🌐 *www.watsonsbistroconwy.co.uk* 🕒 *Closed Mon.*

$$ HOTEL 🏨 **Castle Hotel.** Nestled within Conwy's medieval walls, this former coaching inn has wood beams, stone fireplaces, and plenty of antiques. **Pros:** oozes history; in the heart of Conwy; good food. **Cons:** small rooms; noisy seagulls. [$] *Rooms from: £140* ✉ *High St.* ☎ *01492/582800* 🌐 *www.castlewales.co.uk* 🛏 *28 rooms* 🍽 *Breakfast.*

$$ HOTEL 🏨 **Sychnant Pass House.** On a peaceful wooded hillside 2 miles west of Conwy, this country-house hotel has a laid-back atmosphere. **Pros:** great indoor pool and hot tub; beautiful grounds; unforced hospitality. **Cons:** far outside Conwy. [$] *Rooms from: £135* ✉ *Sychnant Pass Rd.* ☎ *01492/596868* 🌐 *www.sychnant-pass-house.co.uk* 🛏 *12 rooms* 🍽 *Breakfast.*

LLANDUDNO

3 miles north of Conwy, 50 miles northwest of Chester.

This engagingly old-fashioned North Wales seaside resort has a wealth of well-preserved Victorian architecture and an ornate amusement pier with entertainments, shops, and places to eat. Grand-looking small hotels line the wide promenade with a view of the deep-blue waters of the bay. The shopping district beyond retains its original canopied walkways.

12

GETTING HERE AND AROUND

Llandudno is on the North Wales railway line, with fast access from London and other major cities. By road, it's connected to the motorway system via the A55 expressway. The scenic Conwy Valley rail line runs to Blaenau Ffestiniog, and the town is also on the network covered by the Snowdon Sherpa bus service.

ESSENTIALS

Visitor Information Llandudno Tourist Information Centre ✉ *Library Building, Mostyn St.* ☎ *01492/577577* ⊕ *www.visitllandudno.org.uk.*

EXPLORING

EN ROUTE

Bodelwyddan Castle. Between Abergele and St. Asaph, this castle is the Welsh home of London's National Portrait Gallery. Paintings on display include works by John Singer Sargent, Dante Gabriel Rossetti, and Edwin Landseer. The castle grounds contain a fascinating, if somber historical footnote: a network of overgrown World War I trenches, used by the army to train new recruits. Also on the grounds are a maze, an aviary, and pretty woodland walks. The castle is 16 miles east of Llandudno. ✉ *Off A55, Bodelwyddan* ☎ *01745/584060* ⊕ *www. bodelwyddan-castle.co.uk* ☜ *£6.50; park only £4* ☉ *Jan.–late Mar. and Nov.–mid-Dec., weekends 10:30–4; late Mar.–Oct., Wed.–Sun. 10:30–5; last admission 30 mins before closing.*

Great Orme. Named for the Norse word meaning "sea monster," the 679-foot headland called Great Orme towers over Llandudno, affording extraordinary views over the bay.

Grand Orme Aerial Cable Car. This cable car zips you one mile to the top of Grand Orme. At the summit there's an artificial ski slope and a toboggan run, both usable all year. ✉ *Happy Valley Rd.* ☎ *01492/879306* ☜ *£7 round-trip* ☉ *Mid-Mar.–Oct., daily 10–4:30.*

Great Orme Tramway. The most picturesque way to reach the summit of Grande Orme is the Great Orme Tramway. Trips depart about every 20 minutes. The summit is a sylvan spot, with open grassland, fields of wildflowers, and rare butterflies. ✉ *Victoria Station, Church Walks* ☎ *01492/577877* ⊕ *www.greatormetramway.co.uk* ☜ *£6 round-trip* ☉ *Late Mar. and Oct., daily 10–5; Apr.–Sept. daily 10–6.*

FAMILY **Great Orme Mines.** Discovered in 1987, these mines date back 4,000 years to when copper was first mined in the area. You can take a tour and learn about the technology that ancient people used to dig the tunnels. ✉ *Pyllau Rd.* ☎ *01492/870447* ⊕ *www.greatormemines.info* ☜ *£6.75* ☉ *Mid-Mar.–Oct., daily 10–5; last admission 1 hr before closing.*

WHERE TO STAY

$$$
HOTEL
Fodor's Choice
★

⬛ **Bodysgallen Hall.** Tasteful antiques, polished wood, and comfortable chairs by cheery fires distinguish one of Wales's most luxurious country-house hotels. **Pros:** superb spa and pool; rare 17th-century knot garden; elegant dining. **Cons:** too formal for some; hard to get to without a car. $ *Rooms from: £189* ✉ *Off A470* ☎ *01492/584466* ⊕ *www.bodysgallen.com* ➪ *15 rooms, 16 cottage suites* ⍩ *Breakfast.*

$
HOTEL

⬛ **Bryn Derwen Hotel.** This immaculate, impeccably run Victorian hotel is traditional in style, but has a contemporary edge. **Pros:** historic building; gracious touches; close to the beach. **Cons:** no sea views. $ *Rooms from: £84* ✉ *34 Abbey Rd.* ☎ *01492/876804* ⊕ *www.bryn-derwen.co.uk* ➪ *9 rooms* ⍩ *Breakfast.*

$$
HOTEL

⬛ **St. Tudno Hotel.** Perfectly situated on the seafront promenade overlooking the beach and pier, this hotel has been run by the same family for nearly 40 years. **Pros:** ocean views; swimming pool; good food. **Cons:** some rooms are snug; overly fussy decor. $ *Rooms from: £104* ✉ *Promenade* ☎ *01492/874411* ⊕ *www.st-tudno.co.uk* ➪ *18 rooms* ⍩ *Breakfast.*

EDINBURGH

WELCOME TO EDINBURGH

TOP REASONS TO GO

★ **Kaleidoscope of culture:** The city's calendar of cultural festivals, including the famous Edinburgh International Festival, is outstanding.

★ **The Royal Mile:** Along the Royal Mile. Edinburgh Castle and the Palace of Holyroodhouse were the locations for some of the most important struggles between Scotland and England.

★ **Awe-inspiring architecture:** From the Old Town's medieval streets to the neoclassical New Town to modern developments like the Scottish Parliament building, the city's architecture spans the ages.

★ **Food, glorious food:** Edinburgh attracts celebrity chefs serving up dishes from around the world. Perhaps the most exotic, however, is genuine Scottish cuisine, with its classic dishes like Cullen skink and haggis with neeps and tatties.

★ **Handcrafted treasures:** Scotland has a strong tradition of distinctive furniture makers, silversmiths, and artists.

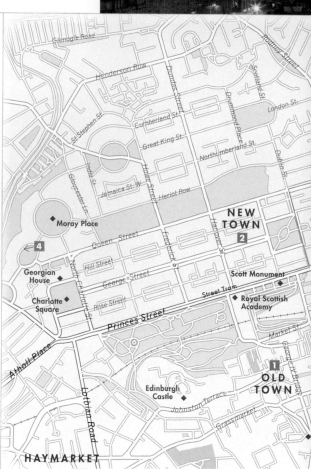

1 Old Town. The focal point of Edinburgh for centuries, the Old Town is a picturesque jumble of medieval tenements. Here are prime attractions such as Edinburgh Castle and the newer symbol of power, the Scottish Parliament. Amid the historic buildings you will find everything from buzzing nightclubs and bars to ghostly alleyways where the spirits of the past often make their presence felt.

2 New Town. Built in the 18th and 19th century, the

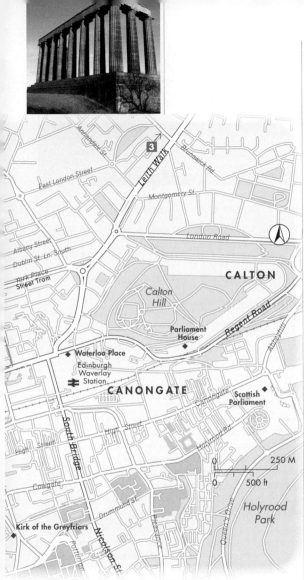

GETTING ORIENTED

13

For all its steep roads and hidden alleyways, Edinburgh is not a difficult place to navigate. Most newcomers gravitate to two areas, the Old Town and the New Town. The former funnels down from the castle on either side of the High Street, better known as the Royal Mile. Princes Street Gardens and Waverly Station separate the oldest part of the city from the stately New Town, known for its neoclassical architecture and verdant gardens. To the north, the city sweeps down to the Firth of Forth. It is here you will find the port of Leith with its trendy pubs and fine restaurants. The southern and western neighborhoods are mainly residential, but are home to such attractions as the Edinburgh Zoo.

neoclassical sweep of the New Town is a masterpiece of city planning. Significant sights include the National Gallery of Scotland and Calton Hill. The city's main shopping thoroughfares, Princes Street and George Street, are also found here.

3 Leith. On the southern shore of the Firth of Forth, Edinburgh's port of Leith is where you'll find the former royal yacht *Britannia*. These days it's also filled with smart bars and restaurants.

4 Side Trips. Historic houses, museums, and attractions in the green countryside of the Lothians, outside Edinburgh, can be reached quickly by bus or car. These day trips are a welcome escape from the festival crush at the height of summer.

Updated by
Nick Bruno
and Mike
Gonzalez

One of the world's stateliest cities and proudest capitals, Edinburgh is built—like Rome—on seven hills, giving the city a striking backdrop for the ancient pageant of history revealed in its architecture. In a skyline of sheer drama, Edinburgh Castle watches over the capital city. Despite its rich past, the city's famous festivals, excellent museums and galleries, as well as the modern Scottish Parliament building, are reminders that Edinburgh has its feet firmly in the 21st century.

Nearly everywhere in Edinburgh (the *burgh* is always pronounced *burra* in Scotland) there are spectacular buildings, whose Doric, Ionic, and Corinthian pillars add touches of neoclassical grandeur to the largely Presbyterian backdrop. Arthur's Seat, a mountain of bright green and yellow furze, rears up behind the spires of the Old Town. Appropriately, these theatrical elements match Edinburgh's character—after all, the city has been a stage that has seen its fair share of romance, violence, tragedy, and triumph.

Modern Edinburgh has become a cultural capital, staging the Edinburgh International Festival and the Fringe Festival in every possible venue each August. The stunning National Museum of Scotland complements the city's wealth of galleries and artsy hangouts. Add Edinburgh's growing reputation for food and nightlife and you have one of the world's most beguiling cities.

Today the city is the second most important financial center in the United Kingdom, and the fifth most important in Europe. In some senses it is showy and materialistic, but Edinburgh still supports learned societies, some of which have roots in the Scottish Enlightenment.

Even as Edinburgh moves through the 21st century, its tall guardian castle remains the focal point of the city and its venerable history. Take time to explore the streets—peopled by the spirits of Mary, Queen of Scots, Sir Walter Scott, and Robert Louis Stevenson—and pay your respects to the world's best-loved terrier, Greyfriars Bobby. In the evenings you can enjoy candlelit restaurants or a folk *ceilidh* (pronounced *kay-lee*, a traditional Scottish dance with music), though you should remember that you haven't earned your porridge until you've climbed Arthur's Seat. Should you wander around a corner, say, on George Street, you might see not an endless cityscape, but blue sea and a patchwork of fields. This is the county of Fife, beyond the inlet of the North Sea called the Firth of Forth—a reminder, like the mountains to the northwest that can be glimpsed from Edinburgh's highest points, that the rest of Scotland lies within easy reach.

13

EDINBURGH PLANNER

WHEN TO GO

Scotland's reliably inclement weather means that you could visit at the height of summer and be forced to wear a scarf. Conversely, conditions can be balmy in early spring and late autumn. You may want to avoid the crowds during July and August, but you'd also miss the famed Edinburgh International Festival and other summer celebrations. May, June, and September are probably the most-hassle-free months in which to visit. Short days and grim conditions make winter less appealing, but Edinburgh's New Year celebrations are justly renowned.

PLANNING YOUR TIME

One of Edinburgh's greatest virtues is its compact size, which means that it is possible to pack a fair bit into even the briefest of visits. The two main areas of interest are the Old Town and the New Town, where you'll find Edinburgh Castle, the Scottish Parliament, Princes Street Gardens, and the National Gallery of Scotland. You can cover all four attractions in one day, but two days is more realistic. You can also choose between the Palace of Holyroodhouse and the important museums of Edinburgh, as well as entertaining sights such as the Real Mary King's Close. Or, explore the Royal Botanic Gardens and Holyrood Park. Head down to leafy, villagelike Stockbridge, then immerse yourself in the greenery along the Water of Leith, visiting the Gallery of Modern Art along the way.

Getting out of town is also an option for stays of more than a few days, depending on your interests: hop on a bus out to Midlothian to see the magnificent Rosslyn Chapel at Roslin (it's of interest to more than *Da Vinci Code* fans). Consider spending another half day traveling out to South Queensferry to admire the Forth rail and road bridges; then visit palatial Hopetoun House, with its wealth of portraits and fine furniture.

GETTING HERE AND AROUND
AIR TRAVEL

Edinburgh Airport, 7 miles west of the city center, offers only a limited number of transatlantic flights. It does, however, have good air connections throughout the United Kingdom as well as with a number of European cities. Flights bound for Edinburgh depart virtually every hour from London's Gatwick and Heathrow airports.

Glasgow Airport, 50 miles west of Edinburgh, serves as the major point of entry into Scotland for transatlantic flights. Prestwick Airport, 30 miles southwest of Glasgow, after some years of eclipse by Glasgow Airport, has grown in importance, not least because of the activities of Ryanair.

Airport Information Edinburgh Airport ✉ *Glasgow Rd., Ingliston* ☎ *0844/481–8989* ⊕ *www.edinburghairport.com.* **Glasgow Airport** ✉ *Caledonia Way, Paisley* ☎ *0844/481–5555* ⊕ *www.glasgowairport.com.* **Prestwick Airport** ✉ *A79, Prestwick* ☎ *0871/223–0700* ⊕ *www.gpia.co.uk.*

TRANSFERS FROM EDINBURGH AIRPORT There are no rail links to the city center, even though the airport sits between two main lines. By bus or car you can usually make it to Edinburgh in a half hour, unless you hit the morning (7:30 to 9) or evening (4 to 6) rush hours. Lothian Buses runs between Edinburgh Airport and the city center every 15 minutes daily from 9 to 5 and roughly every hour during off-peak hours. The trip takes about 40 minutes, or up to an hour during peak traffic times. A single-fare ticket costs £1.50. Lothian Buses runs an Airlink express service to Waverley Station via Haymarket that takes 25 minutes. Buses run every 10 minutes, and single-fare tickets cost £3.50. The new tram service to the airport costs £4.50.

You can arrange for a chauffeur-driven limousine to meet your flight at Edinburgh Airport through Transvercia Chaffeur Drive, Little's Chauffeur Drive, or W L Sleigh Ltd., for about £50.

Taxis are readily available outside the terminal. The trip takes 20 to 30 minutes to the city center, 15 minutes longer during rush hour. The fare is roughly £22. Note that airport taxis picking up fares from the terminal are any color, not the typical black cabs.

Airport Transfer Contacts Little's Chauffeur Drive ✉ *1282 Paisley Rd. W, Paisley* ☎ *0141/883–2111* ⊕ *littles.co.uk.* **Transvercia Chauffeur Drive** ✉ *6/19 Pilrig Heights, Leith* ☎ *0131/555–0459* ⊕ *www.transvercia.co.uk.* **W L Sleigh Ltd.** ✉ *11A W. Craigs Ave., off Turnhouse Rd.* ☎ *0131/339–9607* ⊕ *sleigh.co.uk.*

TRANSFERS FROM GLASGOW AIRPORT Scottish Citylink buses leave Glasgow Airport and travel to Glasgow's Buchanan Street (journey time is 25 minutes), where you can transfer to an Edinburgh bus (leaving every 20 minutes). The trip to Edinburgh takes around two hours and costs £13.20 one-way. ■ **TIP➜ A far more pleasant option is to take a 20-minute cab ride from Glasgow Airport to Glasgow's Queen Street train station (about £20) and then take the train to Waverley Station in Edinburgh.** Trains depart about every 30 minutes; the trip takes 50 minutes and costs £13 to £20. Another, less expensive alternative—best for those with little luggage—is to take the bus from Glasgow Airport to Glasgow's Buchanan bus station, walk five minutes to the Queen Street train station, and catch the train to Edinburgh. Taxis from Glasgow Airport to downtown Edinburgh take about 70 minutes and cost around £100.

Glasgow Transfer Contact Scottish Citylink ☎ *0871/2663333* ⊕ *www.citylink.co.uk.*

BUS TRAVEL

National Express provides bus service to and from London and other major towns and cities. The main terminal, St. Andrew Square bus station, is a short walk north of Waverley Station, immediately east of St. Andrew Square. Long-distance coaches must be booked in advance online, by phone, or at the terminal. Edinburgh is approximately eight hours by bus from London.

Lothian Buses provides much of the service between Edinburgh and the Lothians and conducts day tours around and beyond the city. First runs buses out of Edinburgh into the surrounding area. Megabus offers dirt-cheap fares to selected cities if you book in advance.

Bus Contacts First ☎ *0871/2002233* ⊕ *www.firstgroup.com.* **Lothian Buses** ☎ *0131/555–6363* ⊕ *www.lothianbuses.com.* **Megabus** ☎ *0900/160– 0900* ⊕ *uk.megabus.com.* **National Express** ☎ *08717/818178* ⊕ *www. nationalexpress.co.uk.*

TRAVEL WITHIN EDINBURGH

Lothian Buses is the main operator within Edinburgh. You can buy tickets on the bus. The Day Ticket (£3.50), allowing unlimited one-day travel on the city's buses, can be purchased in advance or from the driver on any Lothian bus (exact fare is required when purchasing on a bus). The Ridacard (for which you'll need a photo) is valid on all buses for seven days (Sunday through Saturday night) and costs £17; the four-week Rider costs £51. ■ **TIP→** Buses are great for cheap daytime travel, but in the evening you'll probably want to take a taxi.

Information Lothian Buses ✉ *Waverley Bridge, Old Town* ☎ *0131/555–6363* ⊕ *www.lothianbuses.com.*

CAR TRAVEL

Driving in Edinburgh has its quirks and pitfalls, but don't be intimidated. Metered parking in the city center is scarce and expensive, and the local traffic wardens are a feisty, alert bunch. Note that illegally parked cars are routinely towed away, and getting your car back will be expensive. After 6 pm the parking situation improves considerably, and you may manage to find a space quite near your hotel, even downtown. If you park on a yellow line or in a resident's parking bay, be prepared to move your car by 8 the following morning, when the rush hour gets under way. Parking lots are clearly signposted; overnight parking is expensive and not always permitted.

TAXI TRAVEL

Taxi stands can be found throughout the downtown area. The following are the most convenient: the west end of Princes Street; South St. David Street and North St. Andrew Street (both just off St. Andrew Square); Princes Mall; Waterloo Place; and Lauriston Place. Alternatively, hail any taxi displaying an illuminated "for hire" sign.

TRAIN TRAVEL

Edinburgh's main train hub, Waverley Station, is downtown, below Waverley Bridge and around the corner from the unmistakable spire of the Scott Monument. Travel time from Edinburgh to London by train is as little as 4½ hours for the fastest service.

PARLIAMENT AND POWER

Three centuries after the Union of Parliaments with England in 1707, Edinburgh is once again the seat of a Scottish parliament. A new parliament building, designed by the late Spanish architect Enric Miralles, stands adjacent to the Palace of Holyroodhouse, at the foot of the Royal Mile.

The first-time visitor to Scotland may be surprised that the country still has a capital city at all, perhaps believing the seat of government was drained of its resources and power after the union with England—but far from it. The Union of Parliaments brought with it a set of political partnerships—such as separate legal, ecclesiastical, and educational systems—that Edinburgh assimilated and integrated with its own surviving institutions.

Scotland now has significantly more control over its own affairs than at any time since 1707, and the 129 Members of the Scottish Parliament (MSPs), of whom 40% are women, have extensive powers in Scotland over education, health, housing, transportation, training, economic development, the environment, and agriculture. Foreign policy, defense, and economic policy remain under the jurisdiction of the U.K. government in London. A September 2014 referendum (results not known at the time of this writing) has allowed voters to decide whether Scotland should remain in the United Kingdom or go it alone as an independent state.

Edinburgh's other main station is Haymarket, about four minutes (by rail) west of Waverley. Most Glasgow and other western and northern services stop here.

Train Contacts National Rail Enquiries ☎ *08457/484950* ⊕ *www.nationalrail. co.uk.* **ScotRail** ☎ *0845/601–5929* ⊕ *www.scotrail.co.uk.*

TRAM TRAVEL
Absent since 1956, trams returned to the streets of Edinburgh in mid-2014. After much delay, disruption, and controversy a 14-km (8.5-mile) stretch of track is completed from Edinburgh Airport in the west to York Place in the east. Useful stops for travelers include Haymarket, Princes Street, and St. Andrew Square (near Waverley Station). Tickets are £1.50 for a single journey and £3.50 for a day ticket, which includes buses as well. The airport service is a little more expensive than the Airlink bus (£4.50 one-way).

Tram Contact Edinburgh Trams ☎ *0800/328–3934* ⊕ *www.edinburghtrams. co.uk.*

TOURS
ORIENTATION TOURS
The best way to get oriented in Edinburgh is to take a bus tour, most of which are operated by Lothian Buses. Its City Sightseeing open-top bus tours include multilingual commentary; its MacTours are conducted in vintage open-top vehicles. All tours take you to the main attractions, including Edinburgh Castle, the Royal Mile, Palace of Holyroodhouse,

and museums and galleries. Buses depart from Waverley Bridge, and are hop-on/hop-off services, with tickets lasting 24 hours. Lothian Buses' 60-minute Majestic Tour operates with a professional guide and takes you from Waverly Bridge to the New Town, past Charlotte Square, the Royal Botanic Garden, and Newhaven Heritage Museum until it reaches the royal yacht *Britannia* moored at Leith. Tickets cost £13 and are available from ticket sellers on Waverley Bridge or on the buses themselves.

If you want to get to know the area around Edinburgh, Rabbie's Trail Burners leads small groups on several different excursions, including a one-day trip to Rosslyn Chapel.

Orientation Tours Contacts Edinburgh Bus Tours ☎ *0131/220–0770* ⊕ *www. edinburghtour.com.* **Rabbie's Trail Burners** ☎ *0131/226–3133* ⊕ *www.rabbies. com.*

PERSONAL GUIDES

Scottish Tourist Guides can supply guides (in 19 languages) who are fully qualified and will meet clients at any point of entry into the United Kingdom or Scotland. They can also tailor tours to your interests.

Personal Guide Contact Scottish Tourist Guides ☎ *01786/451953* ⊕ *www. stga.co.uk.*

WALKING TOURS

Cadies and Witchery Tours, a member of the Scottish Tourist Guides Association, has built a reputation for combining entertainment and historical accuracy in its lively and enthusiastic Ghosts & Gore Tour and Murder & Mystery Tour (£8.50), which take you through the narrow Old Town alleyways and closes. Costumed guides and other theatrical characters show up en route. The Scottish Literary Pub Tour takes you around Edinburgh's Old Town or New Town (£12), with guides invoking Scottish literary characters.

Walking Tour Contacts Cadies and Witchery Tours. ☎ *0131/225–6745* ⊕ *www.witcherytours.com.* **Scottish Literary Pub Tour** ☎ *0800/169–7410* ⊕ *www.edinburghliterarypubtour.co.uk.*

VISITOR INFORMATION

The Edinburgh and Scotland Information Centre, next to Waverley Station (follow the "tic" signs in the station and throughout the city), offers an accommodations-booking service in addition to the more typical services. Complete information is also available at the information desk at the Edinburgh Airport. Information centers also sell the Edinburgh Pass, which offers free admission to more than 30 attractions, rides on Airlink express buses, and lots of discounts. Prices start at £30 for a one-day pass.

Visitor Information Edinburgh and Scotland Information Centre ✉ *3 Princes St., East End* ☎ *0131/473–3868* ⊕ *www.visitscotland.com.*

EXPLORING EDINBURGH

Edinburgh's Old Town, which bears a great measure of symbolic weight as the "heart of Scotland's capital," is a boon for lovers of atmosphere and history. In contrast, if you appreciate the unique architectural heritage of the city's Enlightenment, then the New Town's for you. If you belong to both categories, don't worry—the Old and New towns are only yards apart. Princes Street runs east–west along the north edge of the Princes Street Gardens. Explore the main thoroughfares but don't forget to get lost among the tiny *wynds* and *closes*: old medieval alleys that connect the winding streets.

Like most cities, Edinburgh incorporates small communities within its boundaries, and many of these are as rewarding to explore as Old Town and New Town. Dean Village, for instance, even though it's close to the New Town, has a character all its own. Duddingston, just southeast of Arthur's Seat, has all the feel of a country village. Then there's Corstorphine, to the west of the city center, famous for being the site of Murrayfield, Scotland's international rugby stadium. Edinburgh's port, Leith, sits on the shore of the Firth of Forth, and throbs with smart bars and restaurants.

OLD TOWN

East of Edinburgh Castle, the historic castle esplanade becomes the street known as the Royal Mile, leading from the castle down through Old Town to the Palace of Holyroodhouse. The Mile, as it's called, is actually made up of one thoroughfare that bears, in consecutive sequence, different names—Castlehill, Lawnmarket, Parliament Square, High Street, and Canongate. The streets and passages winding into their tenements, or "lands," and crammed onto the ridge in back of the Mile really *were* Edinburgh until the 18th century saw expansions to the south and north. Everybody lived here, the richer folk on the lower floors of houses, with less well-to-do families on the middle floors—the higher up, the poorer.

Time and progress (of a sort) have swept away some of the narrow closes and tall tenements of the Old Town, but enough survive for you to be able to imagine the original profile of Scotland's capital. There are many guided tours of the area, or you can walk around on your own. The latter is often a better choice in summer when tourists pack the area and large guided groups have trouble making their way through the crowds.

PLANNING YOUR TIME An exploration of the Old Town could be accomplished in a day, but to give the major sights—Edinburgh Castle, the Palace of Holyroodhouse, and the National Museum of Scotland—their due, you should allow more time. ■TIP→ Don't forget that some attractions have special hours during the Edinburgh International Festival. If you want to see something special, check the hours ahead of time.

TOP ATTRACTIONS

FAMILY
Fodor's Choice
★

Edinburgh Castle. The crowning glory of the Scottish capital, Edinburgh Castle is popular not only because it's the symbolic heart of Scotland but also because of the views from its battlements: on a clear day the vistas—stretching to the "kingdom" of Fife—are breathtaking. ■ TIP→ **There's so much to see that you need at least three hours to do the site justice, especially if you're interested in military sites.**

You enter across the **Esplanade,** the huge forecourt built in the 18th century as a parade ground. The area comes alive with color and music each August when it's used for the Military Tattoo, a festival of magnificently outfitted marching bands and regiments. Heading over the drawbridge and through the gatehouse, past the guards, you can find the rough stone walls of the **Half-Moon Battery,** where the one-o'clock gun is fired every day in an impressively anachronistic ceremony; these curving ramparts give Edinburgh Castle its distinctive appearance from miles away. Climb up through a second gateway and you come to the oldest surviving building in the complex, the tiny 11th-century **St. Margaret's Chapel,** named in honor of Saxon queen Margaret (1046–93), who had persuaded her husband, King Malcolm III (circa 1031–93), to move his court from Dunfermline to Edinburgh. Edinburgh's environs—the Lothians—were occupied by Anglian settlers with whom the queen felt more at home, or so the story goes (Dunfermline was surrounded by Celts). The **Crown Room,** a must-see, contains the "Honours of Scotland"—the crown, scepter, and sword that once graced the Scottish monarch. Upon the **Stone of Scone,** also in the Crown Room, Scottish monarchs once sat to be crowned. In the section now called **Queen Mary's Apartments,** Mary, Queen of Scots, gave birth to James VI of Scotland. The **Great Hall** displays arms and armor under an impressive vaulted, beamed ceiling. Scottish Parliament meetings were conducted here until 1840.

Military features of interest include the **Scottish National War Memorial,** the **Scottish United Services Museum,** and the famous 15th-century Belgian-made cannon *Mons Meg.* This enormous piece of artillery has been silent since 1682, when it exploded while firing a salute for the duke of York; it now stands in an ancient hall behind the Half-Moon Battery. Contrary to what you may hear from locals, it's not *Mons Meg* but the battery's gun that goes off with a bang every weekday at 1 pm, frightening visitors and reminding Edinburghers to check their watches. ✉ *Castle Esplanade and Castlehill, Old Town* ☎ *0131/225–9846 Edinburgh Castle, 0131/226–7393 War Memorial* ⊕ *www.edinburghcastle. gov.uk* ☞ *£14* ⊙ *Apr.–Sept., daily 9:30–6; Oct.–Mar., daily 9:30–5; last entry 1 hr before closing.*

High Kirk of St. Giles. Sometimes called St. Giles's Cathedral, this is one of the city's principal churches. But anyone expecting a rival to Paris's Notre Dame or London's Westminster Abbey will be disappointed: St. Giles is more like a large parish church than a great European cathedral. There has been a church here since AD 854, although most of the present structure dates from either 1120 or 1829, when the church was restored.

13

Edinburgh

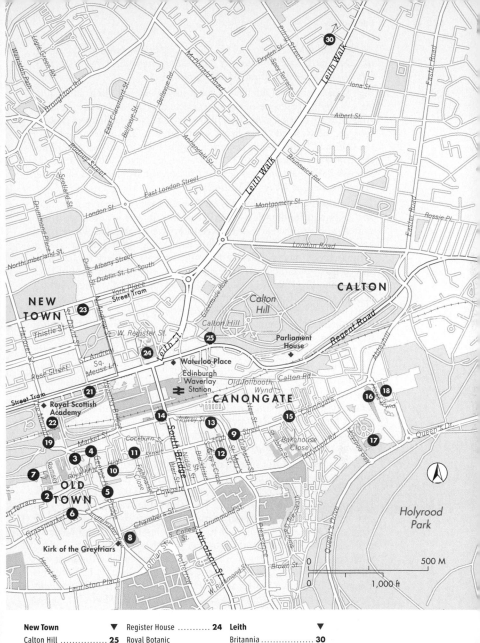

✉ *High St., Old Town* ☎ *0131/225–9442* ⊕ *www.stgilescathedral.org. uk* ✑ *£3 suggested donation* ⊙ *May–Sept., weekdays 9–7, Sat. 9–5, Sun. 1–5; Oct.–Apr., Mon.–Sat. 9–5, Sun. 1–5.*

High Street. Some of Old Town's most impressive buildings and sights are on High Street, one of the five streets making up the Royal Mile. Also here are other, less obvious historic relics. Near Parliament Square, look on the west side for a **heart** set in cobbles. This marks the site of the vanished Tolbooth, the center of city life from the 15th century until the building's demolition in 1817. The ancient civic edifice housed the Scottish Parliament and was used as a prison—it also inspired Sir Walter Scott's novel *The Heart of Midlothian.*

Just outside Parliament House is the **Mercat Cross** (*mercat* means "market"), a great landmark of Old Town life. It was an old mercantile center, where in the early days executions were held, and where royal proclamations were—and are still—read. Most of the present cross is comparatively modern, dating from the time of William Ewart Gladstone (1809–98), the great Victorian prime minister and rival of Benjamin Disraeli (1804–81). Across High Street from the High Kirk of St. Giles stands the **City Chambers,** now the seat of local government. Built by John Fergus, who adapted a design of John Adam in 1753, the chambers were originally known as the Royal Exchange and intended to be where merchants and lawyers could conduct business. Note how the building drops 11 stories to Cockburn Street on its north side.

A *tron* is a weigh beam used in public weigh houses, and the **Tron Kirk** was named after a salt tron that used to stand nearby. The kirk itself was built after 1633, when St. Giles's became an Episcopal cathedral for a brief time. In this church in 1693, a minister offered an often-quoted prayer for the local government: "Lord, hae mercy on a' [all] fools and idiots, and particularly on the Magistrates of Edinburgh." ✉ *Between Lawnmarket and Canongate, Old Town.*

John Knox House. It's not certain that Scotland's severe religious reformer John Knox ever lived here, but there's evidence that he died here in 1572. Mementos of his life are on view inside, and the distinctive dwelling gives you a glimpse of what Old Town life was like in the 16th century. The projecting upper stories were once commonplace along the Royal Mile, darkening and further closing in the already narrow passage. Look for the initials of former owner James Mossman and his wife, carved into the stonework on the marriage lintel. Mossman was goldsmith to Mary, Queen of Scots, and was hanged in 1573 for his allegiance to her. ✉ *45 High St., Old Town* ☎ *0131/556–9579* ⊕ *www. scottishstorytellingcentre.co.uk* ✑ *£5* ⊙ *Sept.–June, Mon.–Sat. 10–6; July and Aug., Mon.–Sat. 10–6, Sun. 10–6; last admission ½ hr before closing.*

FAMILY
Fodor'sChoice
★
National Museum of Scotland. This museum traces the country's fascinating story from the oldest fossils to the most recent popular culture, making it a must-see for first-time visitors to Scotland or anyone interested in history. One of the most famous treasures is the Lewis Chessmen, 11 intricately carved ivory chess pieces found in the 19th century on one of Scotland's Western Isles. An extensive renovation of the basement

THE BUILDING OF EDINBURGH

Towering over the city, Edinburgh Castle was actually built over the plug of an ancient volcano. Many thousands of years ago, an eastward-grinding glacier encountered the tough basalt core of the volcano and swept around it, scouring steep cliffs and leaving a trail of matter. This material formed a ramp gently leading down from the rocky summit. On this *crag* and *tail* would grow the city of Edinburgh and its castle.

CASTLE, WALLED TOWN, AND HOLYROODHOUSE

By the 12th century Edinburgh had become a walled town, still perched on the hill. Its shape was becoming clearer: like a fish with its head at the castle, its backbone running down the ridge, and its ribs leading briefly off on either side. The backbone gradually became the continuous thoroughfare now known as the Royal Mile, and the ribs became the closes (alleyways), some still surviving, that were the scene of many historic incidents.

By the early 15th century Edinburgh had become the undisputed capital of Scotland. The bitter defeat of Scotland at Flodden in 1513, when Scotland aligned itself with France against England, caused a new defensive city wall to be built. Though the castle escaped destruction, the city was burned by the English Earl of Hertford under orders from King Henry VIII (1491–1547) of England. This was during a time known as the "Rough Wooing," when Henry was trying to coerce the Scots into allowing the young Mary, Queen of Scots (1542–87) to marry his son Edward. The plan failed and Mary married Francis, the Dauphin of France.

By 1561, when Mary returned from France already widowed, the guesthouse of the Abbey of Holyrood had grown to become the Palace of Holyroodhouse, replacing Edinburgh Castle as the main royal residence. Mary's legacy to the city included the destruction of most of the earliest buildings of Edinburgh Castle; she was eventually executed by Elizabeth I.

ENLIGHTENMENT AND THE CITY

In the trying decades after the union with England in 1707, many influential Scots, both in Edinburgh and elsewhere, went through an identity crisis. Out of the 18th-century difficulties, however, grew the Scottish Enlightenment, during which educated Scots made great strides in medicine, economics, and science.

Changes came to the cityscape, too. By the mid-18th century it had become the custom for wealthy Scottish landowners to spend the winter in the Old Town of Edinburgh, in town houses huddled between the high Castle Rock and the Royal Palace below. Cross-fertilized in coffeehouses and taverns, intellectual notions flourished among a people determined to remain Scottish despite their parliament's having voted to dissolve itself. One result was a campaign to expand and beautify the city, to give it a look worthy of its future nickname, the Athens of the North. Thus was the New Town of Edinburgh built, with broad streets and gracious buildings creating a harmony that even today's throbbing traffic cannot obscure.

13

has created a dramatic, cryptlike entrance. Visitors now rise to the light-filled, birdcage wonders of the Victorian grand hall and the upper galleries in glass elevators. Highlights include the hanging hippo and sea creatures of the Wildlife Panorama, a life-size skeleton cast of a *Tyrannosaurus rex*, Viking brooches, Pictish stones, Jacobite relics, the Stevenson family's inventions, including lighthouse optics, and Queen Mary's *clarsach* (harp). ✉ *Chambers St., Old Town* ☎ *0300/123–6789* ⊕ *www.nms.ac.uk* ⌐ *Free* ⊙ *Daily 10–5.*

FAMILY **Our Dynamic Earth.** Using state-of-the-art technology, the 11 theme galleries at this interactive science gallery educate and entertain as they explore the wonders of the planet, from polar regions to tropical rain forests. Geological history, from the big bang to the unknown future, is also examined. ✉ *Holyrood Rd., Old Town* ☎ *0131/550–7800* ⊕ *www. dynamicearth.co.uk* ⌐ *£11.50* ⊙ *Apr.–June, Sept., and Oct., daily 10–5:30; July and Aug., daily 10–6; Nov.–Mar., Wed.–Sun. 10–5:30; last admission 90 mins before closing.*

Fodor'sChoice **Palace of Holyroodhouse.** Once the haunt of Mary, Queen of Scots, and
★ the setting for high drama—including at least one notorious murder, several major fires, and centuries of the colorful lifestyles of larger-than-life, power-hungry personalities—this is now Queen Elizabeth's official residence in Scotland. A doughty and impressive palace standing at the foot of the Royal Mile in a hilly public park, it's built around a graceful, lawned central court at the end of Canongate. When the Queen or Royal Family is not in residence you can take a tour. The free audio guide is excellent. Many monarchs have left their mark on its rooms, but it's Mary whose spirit looms largest. For some visitors, the most memorable room here is the little chamber in which Mary's secretary, the ambitious and unpopular David Rizzio, met an unhappy end in 1566 when Mary's second husband, Lord Darnley, burst into the queen's rooms with his henchmen, dragged Rizzio into an antechamber, and stabbed him more than 50 times; a bronze plaque marks the spot. Darnley himself was murdered the next year, which made way for the queen's marriage to her lover, the Earl of Bothwell.

■TIP➔ There's plenty to see here, so make sure you have at least two hours to tour the palace, gardens, and the ruins of the 12th-century abbey. The **King James Tower,** the oldest surviving section, contains the rooms of Mary, Queen of Scots and Lord Darnley. Though much has been altered, there are fine fireplaces, paneling, plasterwork, tapestries, and 18th- and 19th-century furnishings throughout. At the south end of the palace front you can find the **Royal Dining Room,** and along the south side are several drawing rooms used for social and ceremonial occasions.

At the back of the palace is the **King's Bedchamber.** The 150-foot-long **Great Picture Gallery,** on the north side, displays the portraits of 110 Scottish monarchs commissioned by Charles II, who was eager to demonstrate his Scottish ancestry. All the portraits were painted by a Dutch artist, Jacob de Witt, in 1684–5. The **Queen's Gallery,** in a former church and school at the entrance to the palace, holds rotating exhibits from the Royal Collection. There is a separate admission charge.

The Palace of Holyroodhouse, now the Queen's official residence in Scotland, contains the rooms of Mary, Queen of Scots.

Holyroodhouse was originally an Augustinian monastery, founded in 1128. In the 15th and 16th centuries Scottish royalty, preferring the comforts of the abbey to the drafty rooms of Edinburgh Castle, settled there, expanding and altering the buildings until the palace eventually eclipsed the monastery. You can still walk around some ruins though.

After the Union of the Crowns in 1603, when the Scottish royal court packed its bags and decamped for England, the building fell into decline. It was Charles II (1630–85) who rebuilt Holyrood in the architectural style of Louis XIV (1638–1715), and this is the style you see today. Behind the palace lie the open grounds and looming crags of Holyrood Park, the hunting ground of early Scottish kings. From the top of Edinburgh's mini mountain, **Arthur's Seat** (822 feet), views are breathtaking. ⊠ *Abbey Strand, Old Town* ☎ *0131/556–5100* ⊕ *www.royalcollection. org.uk* ⊠ *£11, £15.50 includes the Queen's Gallery* ☉ *Apr.–Oct., daily 9:30–6; Nov.–Mar., daily 9:30–4:30; last admission 1 hr before closing. Closed during royal visits.*

FAMILY
Fodor's Choice
★

Real Mary King's Close. Hidden beneath the City Chambers, this narrow, cobbled *close*, or lane, named after a former landowner, is said to be one of Edinburgh's most haunted sites. The close was sealed off in 1645 to quarantine residents who became sick when the bubonic plague swept through the city, and many victims were herded there to die. After the plague passed, the bodies were removed and buried, and the street was reopened. A few people returned, but they soon reported ghostly goings-on and departed, leaving the close empty for decades. In 1753 city authorities built the Royal Exchange (later the City Chambers) directly over the close, sealing it off and, unwittingly, ensuring it remained intact, except for the buildings' upper stories, which were destroyed. Today you can walk among the remains of the shops and houses. People still report ghostly visions and eerie sounds, such as the crying of a young girl. Over the years visitors have left small offerings for her, such as dolls, pieces of ribbon, or candy. ■TIP➜ **Although kids like the spookiness of this attraction, it's not for the youngest ones. In fact, children under age five are not admitted.** ⊠ *Writers' Court, Old Town* ☎ *0845/070–6244* ⊕ *www.realmarykingsclose.com* ☜ *£12.95* ⊗ *Apr.–Oct., daily 10–9; Nov.–Mar., weekdays 10–5, weekends 10–9.*

Scottish Parliament. Scotland's somewhat controversial Parliament building is dramatically modern, with irregular curves and angles that mirror the twisting shapes of the surrounding landscape. The structure's artistry is most apparent when you step inside, where the gentle slopes, forest's worth of oak, polished concrete and granite, and walls of glass create an understated magnificence. It's worth taking a free tour to see the main hall and debating chamber, a committee room, and other areas. ■TIP➜ **Call well in advance to get a free ticket to view Parliament in action.** Originally conceived by the late Catalan architect Enric Miralles, who often said the building was "growing out of the ground," the design was completed by his widow, Benedetta Tagliabue, in August 2004. ⊠ *Horse Wynd, Old Town* ☎ *0131/348–5200* ⊕ *www.scottish.parliament.uk* ☜ *Free* ⊗ *Mon.–Sat. 10–5:30.*

WORTH NOTING

Canongate Tolbooth. Nearly every city and town in Scotland once had a tolbooth. Originally a customhouse where tolls were gathered, a tolbooth came to mean town hall and later prison because detention cells were in the basement. The building where Canongate's town council once met now has a museum, the **People's Story Museum,** which focuses on the lives of "ordinary" people from the 18th century to today. Exhibits describe how Canongate once bustled with the activities of the tradespeople needed to supply life's essentials in the days before superstores. Special displays include a reconstruction of a cooper's workshop and a 1940s kitchen. ⊠ *163 Canongate, Old Town* ☎ *0131/529–4057* ⊕ *www.edinburghmuseums.org.uk* ☜ *Free* ⊗ *Mon.–Sat. 10–5.*

Fruitmarket Gallery. This contemporary art gallery behind Waverley Station showcases world-renowned artists like Louise Bourgeois and Turner Prize–winning artist Martin Creed. Don't miss Creed's colorful yet subtle marbled transformation of the once-dilapidated Scotsman Steps nearby. ⊠ *45 Market St., Old Town* ☎ *0131/225–2383* ⊕ *www.fruitmarket.co.uk* ☜ *Free* ⊗ *Mon.–Sat. 11–6, Sun. noon–5.*

George IV Bridge. It's not immediately obvious that this is, in fact, a bridge, as buildings are closely packed most of the way along both sides. At the corner of the bridge stands one of the most photographed sculptures in Scotland, *Greyfriars Bobby.* This statue pays tribute to the legendary Skye terrier who kept vigil beside his master John Gray's grave in the Greyfriar's churchyard for 14 years after Gray died in 1858. The 1961 Walt Disney film *Greyfriars Bobby* tells a version of the heartrending tale that some claim to be a shaggy-dog story. ⊠ *Bank St. and Lawnmarket, Old Town.*

Gladstone's Land. This narrow, six-story tenement, next to the Assembly Hall, is a survivor from the 17th century. Typical Scottish architectural features are evident on two floors, including an arcaded ground floor (even in the city center, livestock sometimes inhabited the ground floor). The house has magnificent painted ceilings and is furnished in the style of a 17th-century merchant's home. ⊠ *477B Lawnmarket, Old Town* ☎ *0844/493–120* ⊕ *www.nts.org.uk/property/gladstones-land* ☞ *£6.50* ⊙ *Apr.–Oct., daily 10–5; July and Aug., daily 10–6:30; last admission 30 mins before closing.*

13

Grassmarket. For centuries an agricultural marketplace, Grassmarket now is the site of numerous shops, bars, and restaurants, making it a hive of activity at night. Sections of the Old Town wall can be traced on the north side by a series of steps that ascend from Grassmarket to Johnston Terrace. The best-preserved section of the wall can be found by crossing to the south side and climbing the steps of the lane called the Vennel. Here the 16th-century **Flodden Wall** comes in from the east and turns south at Telfer's Wall, a 17th-century extension.

From the northeast corner of the Grassmarket, **Victoria Street,** a 19th-century addition to the Old Town, leads to the George IV Bridge. Shops here sell antiques and designer clothing. ⊠ *Grassmarket.*

FAMILY **Museum of Childhood.** Even adults tend to enjoy this cheerfully noisy museum—a cacophony of childhood memorabilia, vintage toys, antique dolls, and fairground games such as "Sweeney Todd." There are also a reconstructed schoolroom, street scene, a fancy-dress party, and a nursery. The museum claims to have been the first in the world devoted solely to the history of childhood. It's two blocks past the North Bridge–South Bridge junction on High Street. ⊠ *42 High St., Old Town* ☎ *0131/529–4142* ⊕ *www.edinburghmuseums.org.uk* ☞ *Free* ⊙ *Sept.– July, Mon.–Sat. 10–5, Sun. noon–5.*

National Library of Scotland. Founded in 1689, the library has a superb collection of books and manuscripts on the history and culture of Scotland, and also mounts regular exhibitions. Genealogists investigating family trees come here, and amateur family sleuths will find the staff helpful in their research. ⊠ *George IV Bridge, Old Town* ☎ *0131/623– 3700* ⊕ *www.nls.uk* ☞ *Free* ⊙ *Mon., Tues., Thurs., and Fri. 9:30–8:30, Wed. 10–8:30, Sat. 9:30–1. Exhibitions: weekdays 10–8, Sat. 10–5, Sun. 2–5.*

Scotch Whisky Experience. Transforming malted barley and spring water into one of Scotland's most important exports is the subject of this popular museum. Although the process is not packed with drama, the center manages an imaginative presentation that you take in while riding in low-speed barrel cars. Explore Scotland's diverse whisky regions and the flavors they impart. Sniff the various aromas and decide whether you like fruity, sweet, or smoky, and afterward experts will help you select your perfect dram. Your guide will then allow you access to a vault containing the Diageo Claive Vidiz Scotch Whisky Collection, the world's largest collection of Scotch whiskies. ⊠ *354 Castlehill, Old Town* ☎ *0131/220–0441* ⊕ *www.whisky-heritage.co.uk* ☞ *£12.75* ⊙ *Tours daily 10:20–5.*

Writers' Museum. Down a close off Lawnmarket is the 1662 Lady Stair's House, a fine example of 17th-century urban architecture. Inside, the Writer's Museum evokes Scotland's literary past with such exhibits as the letters, possessions, and original manuscripts of Sir Walter Scott, Robert Louis Stevenson, and Robert Burns. The Stevenson collection is particularly compelling. ⊠ *Lady Stair's Close, Old Town* ☎ *0131/529–4901* ⊕ *www.edinburghmuseums.org.uk* ✉ *Free* ☽ *Sept.–July, Mon.–Sat. 10–5; Aug., Mon.–Sat. 10–5, Sun. noon–5.*

NEW TOWN

It was not until the Scottish Enlightenment, a civilizing time of expansion in the 1700s, that the city fathers decided to break away from the Royal Mile's rocky slope and create a new Edinburgh below the castle. This was to become the New Town, with elegant squares, classical facades, wide streets, and harmonious proportions. Clearly, change had to come. At the dawn of the 18th century Edinburgh's unsanitary conditions—primarily a result of overcrowded living quarters—were becoming notorious. To help remedy this sorry state of affairs, in 1767 the town council held a competition to design a new district for Edinburgh. The winner was an unknown young architect named James Craig (1744–95). His plan called for a grid of three main east–west streets, balanced at either end by two grand squares. These streets survive today: Princes Street is the southernmost, with Queen Street to the north and George Street as the axis, punctuated by St. Andrew and Charlotte squares. A look at the map will reveal a geometric symmetry unusual in Britain. Even the Princes Street Gardens are balanced by the Queen Street Gardens, to the north. Princes Street was conceived as an exclusive residential address, with an open vista facing the castle. It has since been altered by the demands of business and shopping, but the vista remains.

PLANNING
YOUR TIME   If you want to get the most out of the museums of the New Town, take a whole day and allow at least an hour for each one.

TOP ATTRACTIONS

Fodor's Choice
★   **National Gallery of Scotland.** Opened to the public in 1859, the National Gallery presents a wide selection of paintings from the Renaissance to the postimpressionist period within a grand neoclassical building. Most famous are the old-master paintings bequeathed by the Duke of Sutherland, including Titian's *Three Ages of Man.* Many masters are here; works by Velázquez, El Greco, Rembrandt, Goya, Poussin, Turner, Degas, Monet, and Van Gogh, among others, complement a fine collection of Scottish art, including Sir Henry Raeburn's *Reverend Robert Walker Skating on Duddingston Loch* and other works by Ramsay, Raeburn, and Wilkie. The Weston Link connects the National Gallery of Scotland to the Royal Scottish Academy and includes a restaurant, bar, café, shop, and information center. ⊠ *The Mound, New Town* ☎ *0131/624–6336* ⊕ *www.nationalgalleries.org* ✉ *Free* ☽ *Fri.–Wed. 10–5, Thurs. 10–7.*

OFF THE
BEATEN
PATH
FAMILY
Fodor's Choice
★

Royal Botanic Garden Edinburgh. Britain's largest rhododendron and aza-lea gardens are part of this 70-acre garden just north of the city center. An impressive Chinese garden has the largest collection of wild-origin Chinese plants outside China. There's a cafeteria, a visitor center with exhibits exploring biodiversity, and a fabulous gift shop selling plants, books, and gifts. Handsome 18th-century Inverleith House hosts art exhibitions. ■TIP→ Don't miss the soaring palms in the glass-domed Temperate House and the steamy Tropical Palm House. The hilly rock garden and stream are magical on a sunny day. Guided tours are available. Take a taxi to the garden, or ride Bus 27 from Princes Street or Bus 23 from Hanover Street. To make the 20-minute walk from the New Town, take Dundas Street (the continuation of Hanover Street) and turn left at the clock tower onto Inverleith Row. ⊠ *23 Inverleith Row, Inver-leith* ☎ *0131/552–7171* ⊕ *www.rbge.org.uk* ⊠ *Free; greenhouses £4.50* ⊙ *Nov.–Jan., daily 10–4; Feb. and Oct. 10–5; Mar.–Sept., daily 10–6.*

13

Scott Monument. What appears to be a Gothic cathedral spire chopped off and planted in the east end of the Princes Street Gardens is the nation's tribute to Sir Walter—a 200-foot-high monument looming over Princes Street. Built in 1844 in honor of Scotland's most famous author, Sir Walter Scott, the author of *Ivanhoe, Waverley,* and many other novels and poems, it's centered on a marble statue of Scott and his favorite dog, Maida. It's worth taking the time to explore the immediate area, including Princes Street Gardens, one of the prettiest city parks in Brit-ain. In the open-air theater, amid the park's trim flower beds, stately trees, and carefully tended lawns, brass bands occasionally play. Here, too, is the famous **monument to David Livingstone,** whose African meeting with H. M. Stanley is part of Scots-American history. ⊠ *Princes St., New Town* ☎ *0131/529–4068* ⊕ *www.edinburghmuseums.org.uk* ⊠ *£4* ⊙ *Apr.–Sept., Mon.–Sat. 10–7, Sun. 10–6; Oct.–Mar., Mon.–Sat 9–4, Sun. 10–6.*

OFF THE
BEATEN
PATH

Scottish National Gallery of Modern Art. This handsome former school building, close to the New Town, displays paintings and sculptures by Pablo Picasso, Georges Braque, Henri Matisse, and André Derain, among others. The gallery houses an excellent restaurant in the base-ment and lavender-filled garden. Across the street in a former orphanage is the **Gallery of Modern Art Two** (formerly the Dean Gallery), which has Scots-Italian Sir Eduardo Paolozzi's intriguing re-created studio and towering sculpture *Vulcan.* ⊠ *Belford Rd., Dean Village* ☎ *0131/624–6200* ⊕ *www.nationalgalleries.org* ⊠ *Free* ⊙ *Daily 10–5.*

Scottish National Portrait Gallery. A magnificent red-sandstone Gothic building dating from 1889 houses this must-see institution. Conceived as a gift to the people of Scotland, the gallery is organized under five broad themes: Reformation, Enlightenment, Empire, Modernity, and Contemporary. The refurbished complex features a photography gallery, a gallery for contemporary art, and a fancy glass elevator. New spaces hold exhibits on various aspects of Scots history and life, including "The Visual Culture of the Jacobite Cause" and "Playing for Scotland: The Making of Modern Sport," plus excellent temporary exhibitions. ⊠ *1 Queen St., New Town* ☎ *0131/624–6200* ⊕ *www.nationalgalleries.org* ⊠ *Free* ⊙ *Fri.–Wed. 10–5, Thurs. 10–7.*

WORTH NOTING

Calton Hill. Robert Louis Stevenson's favorite view of his beloved city was from the top of this hill. The architectural styles represented by the extraordinary collection of monuments here include mock Gothic—the Old Observatory, for example—and neoclassical. Under the latter category falls the monument by William Playfair (1789–1857) designed to honor his talented uncle, the geologist and mathematician John Playfair (1748–1819), as well as his cruciform **New Observatory.** The piece that commands the most attention, however, is the so-called **National Monument.** Intended to mimic Athens' Parthenon, this monument to the dead of the Napoleonic Wars was started in 1822. But in 1830, only 12 columns later, money ran out, and the facade became a monument to high aspirations and poor fundraising. The tallest monument on Calton Hill is the 100-foot-high **Nelson Monument,** completed in 1815 in honor of Britain's naval hero Horatio Nelson (1758–1805); you can climb its 143 steps for sweeping city views. The **Burns Monument** is the circular Corinthian temple below Regent Road. ⊠ *Bounded by Leith St. to the west and Regent Rd. to the south, New Town* ☎ *0131/556–2716* ⊕ *www.edinburghmuseums.org.uk* ⧈ *Nelson Monument £4* ⊙ *Nelson Monument: Oct.–Mar., Mon.–Sat. 10–3; Apr.–Sept., daily 10–7.*

Charlotte Square. At the west end of George Street is the New Town's centerpiece—an 18th-century square with one of the proudest achievements of Robert Adam, Scotland's noted neoclassical architect. On the north side, Adam designed a palatial facade to unite three separate town houses of such sublime simplicity and perfect proportions that architects come from all over the world to study it. Happily, the Age of Enlightenment grace notes continue within, as the center town house is now occupied by the **Georgian House** museum. ⊠ *West end of George St., New Town.*

OFF THE BEATEN PATH

Edinburgh Zoo. Children love to visit the some 1,000 animals that live in Edinburgh Zoo, especially the two giant pandas—Tian Tian and Yang Gaung—that were flown in from China. Free 20-minute viewing sessions must be booked in advance. The ever-popular Penguin Parade begins at 2:15 (but since penguin participation is totally voluntary, the event is unpredictable). You can even handle some of the animals from April to September. The zoo spreads over an 80-acre site on the slopes of Corstorphine Hill. Take buses 12, 26, or 31. ⊠ *Corstorphine Rd., 3 miles west of city center, Corstorphine* ☎ *0131/334–9171* ⊕ *www.edinburghzoo.org.uk* ⧈ *£16* ⊙ *Apr.–Sept., daily 9–6; Oct. and Mar., daily 9–5; Nov.–Feb., daily 9–4:30.*

The Mound. This rising street originated from the need for a dry-shod crossing of the muddy quagmire left behind when Nor' Loch, the body of water below the castle, was drained (the railway now cuts through this area). Work is said to have been started by a local tailor, George Boyd, who tired of struggling through the mud en route to his Old Town shop. The building of a ramp was under way by 1781, and by the time of its completion, in 1830, "Geordie Boyd's mud brig," as it was first known, had been built up with an estimated 2 million cartloads of earth dug from the foundations of the New Town. ⊠ *From Princes St. to George IV Bridge, New Town.*

In the Old Town, shops and restaurants keep the Grassmarket lively day and night, especially during Edinburgh's August festivals.

Princes Street. The south side of this well-planned street is occupied by the well-kept Princes Street Gardens, which act as a wide green moat to the castle on its rock. The north side is now one long sequence of chain stores with unappealing modern fronts apart from the handsome Victorian facade of Jenners department store. ⊠ *Waterloo Pl. to Lothian Rd., New Town.*

Register House. Scotland's first custom-built archives depository, Register House, designed by the great Robert Adam, was partly funded by the sale of estates forfeited by Jacobite landowners after their last rebellion in Britain (1745–46). Work on the Regency-style building, which marks the end of Princes Street, started in 1774. The statue in front is of the first duke of Wellington (1769–1852). The recently installed **ScotlandsPeople Centre** lets you conduct genealogical research. Free weekday research sessions, from 10 to 2 and 2 and 4, meet growing interest in Scots family history. Access to public records and the library is £15 per day. ⊠ *2 Princes St., New Town* ☏ *0131/314-4300* ⊕ *www. scotlandspeoplehub.gov.uk* ⎙ *Free* ☉ *Weekdays 9–4:30.*

LEITH

Just north of the city is Edinburgh's port, a place brimming with seafaring history and undergoing a slow revival after years of postwar neglect. It may not be as pristine as much of modern-day Edinburgh, but there are plenty of cobbled streets, dockside buildings, and bobbing boats to capture your imagination. Here along the lowest reaches of the Water of Leith (the river that flows through town), you'll find plenty of shops, pubs, and restaurants. Leith's major attraction is the former royal yacht

Ancestor Hunting

Are you a Cameron or a Campbell, Mackenzie or Macdonald? If so, you may be one of the more than 25 million people of Scottish descent around the world. It was the Highland clearances of the 18th and 19th century, in which tenant farmers were driven from their homes and replaced with sheep, that started the mass emigration to North America and Australia. Before or during a trip, you can do a little genealogical research or pursue your family tree more seriously.

VisitScotland (⊕ www.ancestralscotland.com) has information about clans and surnames, books, and family-history societies. At the Register House, the new ScotlandsPeople Centre (⊕ www.scotlandspeople.gov.uk) is the place to dip into the past or conduct in-depth genealogical research.

Willing to pay for help? Companies such as Scottish Ancestral Trail (⊕ www.scottish-ancestral-trail.co.uk) do the research and plan a trip around your family history. Throughout Scotland, you can check bookstores for information and visit clan museums and societies.

Britannia, moored outside the huge Ocean Terminal shopping mall. Reach Leith by walking down Leith Street and Leith Walk, from the east end of Princes Street (20 to 30 minutes), or take Lothian Bus 22 (marked Britannia Ocean Drive, Leith).

EXPLORING

Britannia. Moored on the waterfront at Leith, Edinburgh's port north of the city center, is the former Royal Yacht *Britannia,* launched in Scotland in 1953 and now retired to her home country. The Royal Apartments and the more functional engine room, bridge, galleys, and captain's cabin are all open to view. The land-based visitor center within the huge Ocean Terminal shopping mall has exhibits and photographs about the yacht's history. ⊠ *Ocean Terminal, Leith* ☎ *0131/555–5566* ⊕ *www.royalyachtbritannia.co.uk* ⊠ *£12* ⊙ *Mar.–Oct., daily 9:30–4; Nov.–Feb., daily 10–3:30.*

WHERE TO EAT

Edinburgh's eclectic restaurant scene has attracted a brigade of well-known chefs, including the award-winning trio of Martin Wishart, Tom Kitchin, and Paul Kitching. They and dozens of others have abandoned the tried-and-true recipes for more adventurous cuisine. Of course, you can always find traditional fare, which usually means the Scottish French style that harks back to the historical "Auld Alliance" of the 13th century. The Scots element is the preference for fresh and local foodstuffs; the French supply the sauces. In Edinburgh you can sample anything from Malaysian *rendang* (a thick, coconut-milk stew) to Kurdish kebabs, while the long-established French, Italian,

Chinese, Pakistani, and Indian communities ensure that the majority of the globe's most treasured cuisines are well represented.

PRICES AND HOURS

It's possible to eat well in Edinburgh without spending a fortune. Multicourse prix-fixe options are common, and almost always less expensive than ordering à la carte. Even at restaurants in the highest price category, you can easily spend less than £30 per person. People tend to eat later in Scotland than in England—around 8 pm on average—or rather they finish eating and then drink on in leisurely Scottish fashion.

WHAT IT COSTS IN POUNDS				
	$	$$	$$$	$$$$
Restaurants	under £15	£15–£19	£20–£25	over £25

Prices are the average cost of a main course at dinner or, if dinner is not served, at lunch.

OLD TOWN

Use the coordinate (⊕ B2) at the end of each listing to locate a site on the corresponding map.

The most historic part of the city houses the grander restaurants that many people associate with this city. It is also home to some of Edinburgh's oldest pubs, which serve informal meals.

$$ MODERN BRITISH 🍴 **Angels with Bagpipes.** The name may amuse or bemuse you, but there's no doubt this relaxed spot with windows overlooking the Royal Mile provides good-value, refined dining. Within the 16th-century building the understated decor includes a sculptural centerpiece of an angel with bagpipes copied from a carving in nearby St. Giles Cathedral. Menus are straightforward and not overlong, the service is slick, and the atmosphere is warm. Seafood and game dominate, with dishes such as hake with chorizo and venison with red cabbage. For the best value, opt for the table d'hôte menu, available between noon and 6, with two courses for £13.95 and three for £17.95. [$] *Average main: £18* ✉ *343 High St., Old Town* ☎ *0131/220–1111* 🌐 *www.angelswithbagpipes.co.uk* ⊕ *F4.*

$ MODERN BRITISH 🍴 **David Bann.** In the heart of the Old Town, this ultrahip eatery serving vegetarian and vegan favorites attracts young locals with its light, airy, modern dining room. Drinking water comes with mint and strawberries; the sizable and creative dishes include mushroom risotto and Jerusalem artichoke in puff pastry. The food is so flavorful that carnivores may forget they're eating vegetarian, especially with dishes like mushroom strudel with celeriac sauce. [$] *Average main: £12* ✉ *56–58 St. Mary's St., Old Town* ☎ *0131/556–5888* 🌐 *www.davidbann.com* ⊕ *G5.*

$ BRITISH 🍴 **Doric Tavern.** Edinburgh's original gastro-pub offers a languid bistro environment and serves reliable Scots favorites. The menu has such daily-changing items as honey-baked salmon with oatcakes, and specialties include haggis, neeps and tatties, and grilled steaks. Try the creamy Cullen skink soup for a filling, good-value lunchtime choice. The stripped-wood interiors upstairs have been spruced up. The Doric is handy for rail travelers, as it's near Waverley Station. Sunday lunch includes a traditional roast of Border beef with all the trimmings. [$] *Average main: £13* ⊠ *15/16 Market St., Old Town* ☎ *0131/225–1084* ⊕ *www.the-doric.com* ⚑ *Reservations essential* ✛ *F4.*

$
MIDDLE EASTERN

✕ **Hanam's.** A stone's throw from the castle, this enticing place transports you to the Middle East. Kurdish cuisine may not be as exalted as others in that region, but the *bayengaan surocrau* (marinated eggplant) and the lamb *tashreeb* (a kind of casserole) will convince you that it's among the best. There's also a great range of kebabs and more familiar Lebanese options. The deep-red interiors have a relaxed Middle Eastern vibe. It's possible to smoke a hookah pipe on the heated terrace, and you can bring your own alcohol. [$] *Average main: £12* ⊠ *3 Johnston Terr., Old Town* ☎ *0131/225–1329* ⊕ *www.hanams.com* ✛ *E5.*

$$
MODERN BRITISH

✕ **Michael Neave.** Young chef Michael Neave delivers fine food at reasonable prices in his restaurant just off the Royal Mile. Down an old close is this modern edifice with tranquil terrace. The downstairs dining area lacks much warmth, but the whisky bar upstairs sparkles. Quality Scots produce stars in dishes influenced by Asian and European cuisines: the west coast scallops with celeriac purée, black pudding, and caviar butter makes a wonderful starter. Meaty mains match Aberdeen Angus steaks, Perthshire venison, and roasted duck breast with imaginative sauces and beautifully cooked vegetables. Seafood lovers will enjoy the sea bass with crab and crayfish. Desserts inlcude a delicious pear tarte tatin with whisky marmalade ice cream. ■ TIP→ Two-course express lunches are a bargain at £7.95 [$] *Average main: £15* ⊠ *21 Old Fishmarket Close, Old Town* ☎ *0131/226–4747* ⊕ *www.michaelneave.co.uk* ☉ *Closed Sun. and Mon.* ✛ *F5.*

$
INDIAN

✕ **Mother India Cafe.** Despite its popularity, good Indian food is hard to find in Scotland. Not so at this humble eatery, where the emphasis is on home-style cooking. A good selection of small dishes means you can sample the myriad flavors. The lamb *karahi* (a Pakistani curry made in a woklike pot) is particularly recommended, as are any of the fish dishes. The split-level dining area is smart and contemporary. [$] *Average main: £12* ⊠ *3–5 Infirmary St., Old Town* ☎ *0131/524–9801* ⊕ *www. motherindiaglasgow.co.uk* ✛ *E5.*

$$$
SEAFOOD

✕ **Ondine.** This fabulous seafood restaurant off the Royal Mile is making waves with its expertly prepared dishes from sustainable fishing sources. A wall of windows shines bountiful amounts of sunlight on an attractive monochromatic dining room and an art deco oyster bar. Standout starters include smoked salmon with horseradish cream and squid tempura with a tasty Vietnamese dipping sauce. Other briny delights include the juicy Shetland mussel *marinière*, Isle of Skye lobster thermidor, and wild Cornish sea bass. Traditional puddings include a treacle tart with clotted cream. The wine list is strong on old-world whites. [$] *Average main: £20* ⊠ *2 George IV Bridge, Old Town* ☎ *0131/226 1888* ⊕ *www. ondinerestaurant.co.uk* ⚑ *Reservations essential* ☉ *Closed Sun.* ✛ *E5.*

$
THAI

✕ **Thai Orchid.** A golden Buddha, beautiful flowers, a traditionally dressed staff, and spicy cuisine transport you to Thailand, if only for a few hours. To start, try the *todd mun kao pode* (deep-fried corn cakes with a sweet-and-sour peanut-and-coriander dip). Tasty main

BEST BETS FOR EDINBURGH DINING

Fodor's Choice★

Galvin Brasserie de Luxe, $$, p. 586
Kalpna, $, p. 591
Mark Greenaway, $$$, p. 587
Martin Wishart, $$$$, p. 592
Number One, $$$$, p. 587
Wedgwood, $$, p. 585

By Price

$

Chop Chop, p. 590
David Bann, p. 583
Kalpna, p. 591

$$

Galvin Brasserie De Luxe, p. 586
Michael Neave, p. 584
Wedgwood, p. 585

$$$

Mark Greenaway, p. 587

$$$$

21212, p. 586
Martin Wishart, p. 592
Number One, p. 587

By Cuisine

FRENCH

The Kitchin, $$$$, p. 592
L'escargot Bleu, $$, p. 587
Martin Wishart, $$$$, p. 592

INDIAN

Kalpna, $, p. 591
Mother India Cafe, $, p. 584

SEAFOOD

The King's Wark, $, p. 592
Ondine, $$$, p. 584

VEGETARIAN

David Bann, $, p. 583
Henderson's, $, p. 587

courses include *pla priew wan* (monkfish poached with coconut milk) or *pedt Orchid,* duck stir-fried with mango, chili, garlic, and red peppers. The sticky rice with coconut milk and mango is a dessert not to be missed. The decor is contemporary, with banquette seating and lots of natural wood. [$] *Average main: £12* ✉ *5A Johnston Terr., Old Town* ☎ *0131/225–6633* 🌐 *www.thaiorchid.uk.com* ✣ *E5.*

$$ MODERN BRITISH Fodor's Choice ★

🍴 **Wedgwood.** Rejecting the idea that fine dining should be a stuffy affair, owners Paul Wedgwood and Lisa Channon opened this Royal Mile gem. The dining space is smart but informal, and the professional staff has mastered the tricky task of giving guests space to relax while remaining attentive. But Wedgwood's food is the standout. Flavorful local produce and some unusual foraged fronds enliven the taste buds. Asian, European, and traditional Scottish influences are apparent in dishes such as monkfish tail with shellfish paella and ham, and braised beef and mushroom ballotine. Save space for seasonal sweets like rhubarb-and-blackcurrant fool and sticky toffee pudding. Consider the great two- and three-course lunch deals (£12 and £16). [$] *Average main: £18* ✉ *267 Canongate, Old Town* ☎ *0131/558–8737* 🌐 *www.wedgwoodtherestaurant.co.uk* ✍ *Reservations essential* ✣ *G4.*

$$$$ MODERN BRITISH

🍴 **The Witchery.** The hundreds of "witches" who were executed on Castlehill, just yards from where you'll be seated, are the inspiration for this outstanding and atmospheric restaurant. The cavernous interior, complete with flickering candlelight, is festooned with cabalistic insignia and tarot-card characters. Gilded and painted ceilings reflect the close links between France and Scotland, as does the menu, which includes steak tartare, roasted quail with braised endive, shellfish bisque, and herb-baked scallops. Two-course pre- and posttheater (5:30–6:30 and 10:30–11:30) specials let you sample the exceptional cuisine for just £15.95. [$] *Average main: £27* ✉ *Castlehill, Old Town* ☎ *0131/225–5613* 🌐 *www.thewitchery.com* ✍ *Reservations essential* ✣ *E5.*

NEW TOWN

Use the coordinate (✣ B2) at the end of each listing to locate a site on the corresponding map.

The New Town, with its striking street plan, ambitious architecture, and professional crowd, has restaurants where you can get everything from a quick snack to a more formal dinner.

$$$$ MODERN BRITISH

🍴 **21212.** Paul Kitching is one of Britain's most innovative chefs, and the theatrical dining experience at 21212 delivers surprises galore. In a grand Georgian house, the restaurant is sumptuously appointed. Belle époque decor and quirky cutlery make this a perfect destination for couples, who should ask for a romantic alcove window table. On display behind a large glass screen is a small army of chefs assembling the intricate dishes. On the fixed-price menus you can expect creative takes on old classics, such as deconstructed fish-and-chips and intriguing desserts such as a layered banana trifle with apricot compote. [$] *Average main: £67* ✉ *3 Royal Terr., New Town* ☎ *0131/523–1030* 🌐 *www.21212restaurant.co.uk* ✍ *Reservations essential* ✣ *G3.*

$$$ MODERN BRITISH

🍴 **Forth Floor.** Harvey Nichols has become synonymous with chic shopping, so it stands to reason that the department store's restaurant is no slouch when it comes to style. The decor pulls off the trick of being minimalist without being too severe. Factor in a glorious view over Princes Street Gardens and Edinburgh Castle and it's a winner from the moment you walk in the door. The imaginative menu devised by chef Stuart Muir lives up to the lofty location. Scallops served with spring cabbage and pea mousse and clam-and-cider chowder make for healthy starters, while the roast saddle of Highland venison and North Atlantic halibut with langoustines are memorable mains. ■ **TIP→ Ask for a window or terrace table—weather permitting, of course.** [$] *Average main: £23* ✉ *Harvey Nichols, 30–34 St. Andrew Sq., New Town* ☎ *0131/524–8350* 🌐 *www.harveynichols.com* ✍ *Reservations essential* ⏲ *No dinner Sun. and Mon.* ✣ *E3.*

$$ BRASSERIE FAMILY Fodor's Choice ★

🍴 **Galvin Brasserie de Luxe.** This Parisian-style brasserie combines handsome surroundings with first-class cuisine from London brothers Chris and Jeff Galvin. Dapper waiters glide around the cavernous dining area with a central bar and blue banquette seating. The menu stars such classic French dishes as steak tartare, duck confit, and pork cassoulet alongside Scots staples like Loch Creran oysters, smoked salmon, and haggis. On Sunday, expect hearty, traditional options like slow roast beef brisket with trimmings for £15. Desserts include the melt-in-the-mouth meringue *oeuf a la neige* (eggs in snow). The wine list is extensive, and the staff knowledgable. ■ **TIP→ A decent children's menu makes this a popular spot for families.** [$] *Average main: £18*

✉ *The Caledonian, Princes St., New Town* ☎ *0131/222 8988* ⊕ *www. galvinrestaurants.com* ✛ *C5.*

$ ✕ **Henderson's.** Edinburgh's pioneering canteen-style vegetarian restaurant opened in 1962, long before it was fashionable to serve healthy, meatless creations. The salad bar has more than a dozen different offerings each day, and a massive plateful costs £8. Tasty hot options include Moroccan stew with couscous and moussaka. Live mellow music plays six nights a week, and there's an art gallery as well. Around the corner on Thistle Street is the Bistro, from the same proprietors; it serves snacks, meals, and decadent desserts such as chocolate fondue. ■ TIP➔ Drop by the fabulous deli for picnic supplies, including wonderful organic bread and pastries. $ *Average main: £8* ✉ *94 Hanover St., New Town* ☎ *0131/225–2605* ⊕ *www.hendersonsofedinburgh.co.uk* ☾ *Closed Sun* ✛ *E4.*

VEGETARIAN

$$$ ✕ **Le Café St Honoré.** Chef Neil Forbes's quintessentially Parisian-style café champions sustainable local produce. From the moment you enter the beautifully lighted room you're transported into the decadently stylish belle époque. A concise menu that changes daily leaves more time for chatting. You might start off with a warm salad of scallops, monkfish, chorizo, and pine nuts, followed by Perthshire venison, North Sea hake, or Scotch shepherd's pie. $ *Average main: £20* ✉ *34 N.W. Thistle Street La., New Town* ☎ *0131/226–2211* ⊕ *www.cafesthonore.com* ✛ *D4.*

FRENCH

$$ ✕ **L'escargot Bleu.** Anyone still laboring under the misconception that French cuisine is pretentious should pay a visit to this gem. In one of the city's trendiest quarters, this venture from the former co-owner of Petit Paris would make anyone from France feel at home. The welcome is warm, the stripped wooden floors and period French posters add to a convivial atmosphere that is loud and proud, and the food is as authentic as gendarme whistling "La Marseillaise." Classic dishes like snails in parsley butter and beef bourguignon certainly fly the tricolor. ■ TIP➔ Follow your nose to the French deli in the basement. $ *Average main: £18* ✉ *56A Broughton St., New Town* ☎ *0131/557–1600* ⊕ *www.lescargotbleu.co.uk* ⌕ *Reservations essential* ☾ *Sun.* ✛ *F2.*

FRENCH

$$$ ✕ **Mark Greenaway.** Run by the talented star of the BBC's *Great British Menu*, this restaurant offers wonderful seasonal dishes and indulgent desserts. Greenaway's culinary style is perfectly reflected by the elegant Georgian dining room's fireplace and gleaming brass chandeliers. For an affordable introduction to his cooking, try the market menu (£16.50 and £20 for two or three courses); main dishes might include slow-roast pork or pan-seared cod fillet. Go à la carte for dishes like pan-roasted hake fillet with lobster tortellini. The signature desserts include his famed knot chocolate tart with popping candy. ■ TIP➔ Ask the sommelier for a tour of the wine cellar, in an old bank vault. $ *Average main: £23* ✉ *69 N. Castle St., New Town* ☎ *0131/226–1155* ⊕ *www. markgreenaway.com* ⌕ *Reservations essential* ✛ *D4.*

MODERN BRITISH
Fodor'sChoice
★

$$$$ ✕ **Number One.** Clublike but unstuffy, this basement restaurant with a thoughtful layout perfect for intimate dining serves the best of Scottish seafood and meat within the Edwardian splendor of the Balmoral Hotel. The regular three-course prix-fixe is £68; for special occasions, choose the chef's six-course tasting menu with amuse-bouche delights, gourmet

BRITISH
Fodor'sChoice
★

13

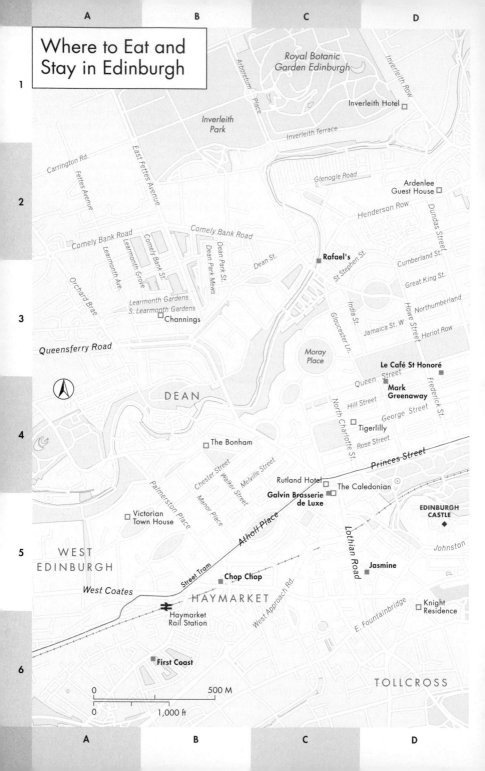

Where to Eat and Stay in Edinburgh

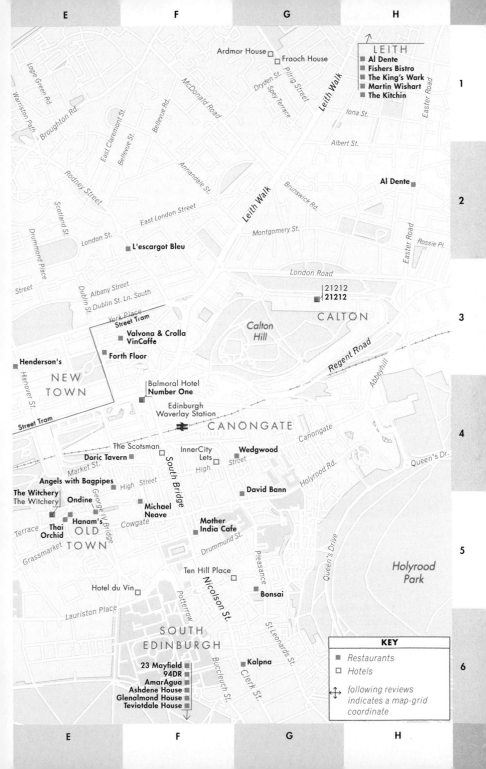

E   **F**   **G**   **H**

Ardmor House

Fraoch House

Dryden St.

Pilrig Street

Spey Terrace

Leith Walk

McDonald Road

LEITH
- Al Dente
- Fishers Bistro
- The King's Wark
- Martin Wishart
- The Kitchin

Easter Road

1

Iona St.

Albert St.

East Claremont St.

Bellevue St.

Bellevue Rd.

Annandale St.

Logie Green Rd.

Warriston Path

Broughton Rd.

Al Dente

Brunswick Rd.

Easter Road

Rossie Pl.

2

Rodney Street

East London Street

Scotland St.

London St.

L'escargot Bleu

Montgomery St.

Drummond Place

Street

Dublin St.

Dublin St. Ln. South

Albany Street

Street Tram

York Place

Leith Walk

London Road

21212
21212

CALTON

Calton Hill

3

Valvona & Crolla
VinCaffe

Forth Floor

Henderson's

Hanover St.

NEW
TOWN

Regent Road

Abbeyhill

Balmoral Hotel
Number One

Edinburgh
Waverley Station

CANONGATE

Canongate

Queen's Dr.

4

The Scotsman

Doric Tavern

Market St.

InnerCity
Lets

High

Street

Wedgwood

Holyrood Rd.

Angels with Bagpipes

High Street

George IV Bridge

South Bridge

David Bann

The Witchery
The Witchery

Ondine

Michael
Neave

Cowgate

Thai
Orchid

Hanam's

OLD
TOWN

Terrace

Mother
India Cafe

Drummond St.

Queen's Drive

Holyrood
Park

5

Grassmarket

Ten Hill Place

Pleasance

Hotel du Vin

Lauriston Place

Potterrow

Nicolson St.

Bonsai

Queen's Drive

St Leonards St.

SOUTH
EDINBURGH

23 Mayfield
94DR
AmarAgua
Ashdene House
Glenalmond House
Teviotdale House

Buccleuch St.

Kalpna

Clerk St.

KEY
- ■ Restaurants
- □ Hotels

↕ following reviews
indicates a map-grid
coordinate

6

E   **F**   **G**   **H**

breads, and exquisite creations highlighting west coast scallops, halibut, monkfish, beef, and lamb for £75. Desserts include a rich, bitter chocolate and orange soufflé and the lighter, candy-store-inspired hibiscus panna cotta. Service is impeccable and friendly. $ *Average main: £68* ⊠ *Balmoral Hotel, Princes St., New Town* ☎ *0131/557–6727* ⊕ *www. restaurantnumberone.com* ⚃ *Reservations essential* ✆ *No lunch* ✣ *F4.*

$$ ✕ **Rafael's.** In a pink-hued basement room replete with eccentric trinkets,
SPANISH the quaint restaurant is clearly not in thrall to prevailing trends, and is all the better for it. Not only does chef/proprietor/all-around-good guy Rafael Torrubia create affordably priced masterpieces with an Iberian twist, he's also likely to deliver dishes such as a sea bass and salmon duo with pesto or a wonderfully authentic tortilla with chorizo to your table himself. Despite his Spanish background, Torrubia's use of ingredients such as curry in his sauces shows that as well as being a man of the people, he is also a man of the world. $ *Average main: £16* ⊠ *2 Deanhaugh St., New Town* ☎ *0131/332–1469* ⊕ *www.rafaels-bistro. wikidot.com* ✆ *Closed Sun. and Mon. No lunch* ✣ *C3.*

$$ ✕ **Valvona & Crolla VinCaffe.** Every Scot with a passion for food knows
ITALIAN Valvona & Crolla, the country's first Italian delicatessen and wine merchant. This eatery of the same name may lack the old-world feel of the original on Elm Row, but the menu created by food writer and cook Mary Contini is as wonderful as you would expect. The fare is relatively simple, but the quality of the ingredients ensures that treats such as the pizza *Capricciosa*, fried calamari, and linguine with crabmeat do nothing to tarnish the brand's reputation. $ *Average main: £15* ⊠ *11 Multrees Walk, New Town* ☎ *0131/557–0088* ⊕ *www.valvonacrolla. co.uk* ✆ *No dinner Sun.* ✣ *F3.*

HAYMARKET

Use the coordinate (✣ B2) at the end of each listing to locate a site on the corresponding map.

This area southwest of the Old Town has many restaurants that tend to be more affordable than those in the center of town.

$ ✕ **Chop Chop.** Authentic Chinese cuisine created by skilled chefs and
CHINESE served in a friendly dining room make this place especially popular. Since arriving in Edinburgh from northern China, Jian Wang has won many awards. Expect flavorful, robust creations like the trademark dumplings with spiced minced meat or vegetables, spicy squid with garlic, and lamb with cumin. The large eatery has splashes of Chinese red and is suitably relaxed. $ *Average main: £11* ⊠ *248 Morrison St., Haymarket* ☎ *0131/221–1155* ⊕ *www.chop-chop.co.uk* ✣ *B5.*

$ ✕ **First Coast.** This laid-back bistro, just a few minutes from Haymarket
BRITISH Station, has won a loyal following. Hardwood floors, stone walls, soft blue hues, and seaside paintings add to the coastal theme. Savory temptations include roasted butternut squash with chestnut-and-apple salad; panfried sea bass with fennel, mustard, and ginger; and Aberdeen Angus sirloin with tomato-and-red-onion salad. The international wine list is as varied as the daily specials. $ *Average main: £13* ⊠ *99–101 Dalry Rd., Haymarket* ☎ *0131/313–4404* ⊕ *www.first-coast.co.uk* ✆ *Closed Sun.* ✣ *A6.*

WEST END

Use the coordinate (⊕ B2) at the end of each listing to locate a site on the corresponding map.

Even after business hours the city's commercial center, west of the Old Town, is the place to find a variety of international restaurants.

$ CHINESE 🍴 **Jasmine.** Seafood matched with just the right spices is the main attraction of this small, friendly Cantonese restaurant. Standout dishes at the long-established place include steamed sea bass with ginger and spring onions, and chicken with peanut sauce. Flickering candles add a relaxing feel to the interior, although the tables are quite closely spaced and the decor is looking a little dated. Prix-fixe lunches, starting at £9.50 for three courses, are a good value. A take-out menu is available. [$] *Average main: £13* ✉ *32 Grindlay St., West End* ☎ *0131/229–5757* 🌐 *www.jasminechinese.co.uk* ⊕ *D5.*

SOUTH SIDE

Use the coordinate (⊕ B2) at the end of each listing to locate a site on the corresponding map.

The presence of university professors and students means eateries that are both affordable and interesting.

$ JAPANESE 🍴 **Bonsai.** The owners of Bonsai regularly visit Tokyo to research the casual dining scene, and their expertise is setting a high standard for Japanese cuisine in Edinburgh. The succulent *gyoza* (steamed dumplings) are pliant and tasty, while the wide variety of noodle and teriyaki dishes and the classy sushi balance sweet and sour deliciously. Try the raw prawns and scallops served with radish noodles and wasabi for refreshing, briny mouthfuls with a kick. The dining area has a bright informality, but the tiny tables may be a tad cramped for some, and the service can be patchy. [$] *Average main: £13* ✉ *46 West Richmond St., South Side* ☎ *0131/668–3847* 🌐 *www.bonsaibarbistro.co.uk* ⊕ *G5.*

$ INDIAN Fodor's Choice ★ 🍴 **Kalpna.** Amid an ordinary row of shops, the facade of this vegetarian Indian restaurant may be unremarkable, but the food is exceptional and a superb value. Try the *dam aloo kashmiri,* a medium-spicy potato dish with a sauce made from honey, pistachios, and almonds. *Bangan mirch masala* has more of a kick, with eggplant and red chili peppers. Thaali, a variety of dishes served in bowls on a tray, is particularly appetizing, and a bargain at £13.95. The interior is enlivened by exotic Indian mosaics. Check out the lunchtime buffet for £8. With lots of meatless options on the menu, veggies and vegans flock here. [$] *Average main: £9* ✉ *2–3 St. Patrick Sq., South Side* ☎ *0131/667–9890* 🌐 *www.kalpnarestaurant.com* ⊗ *Closed Sun. Jan.–Mar.* ⊕ *G6.*

LEITH

Use the coordinate (⊕ B2) at the end of each listing to locate a site on the corresponding map.

Seafood lovers are drawn to the old port of Leith to sample the freshest seafood and to admire the authentic seafaring feel of the docklands.

$ ITALIAN 🍴 **Al Dente.** This friendly neighborhood favorite serves authentic Italian cuisine in homey surroundings. Chef Graziano Spano, from Puglia, is attuned to the freshness and flavors that typify food from the Bel Paese. Fresh pasta and local produce feature prominently. Try the Puglian favorite, pasta *orecchiette* (little-eared pasta), served with lamb ragu, or sample classic dishes from the regions of Sardinia, Liguria, Lazio, Emilia-Romagna, and Tuscany. [$] *Average main: £14* ✉ *139 Easter Rd., Leith* ☎ *0131/652–1932* 🌐 *www.al-dente-restaurant.co.uk* ✍ *Reservations essential* ⏲ *Closed Sun. No lunch Mon.* ✣ *H2.*

$$ SEAFOOD 🍴 **Fishers Bistro.** Locals and visitors flock to this laid-back pub-cum-bistro down on the waterfront, and to its sister restaurant, **Fishers in the City,** at 58 Thistle Street in the New Town. The menu is the same, but Fishers Leith has the better reputation and vibe. Bar meals are served, although for more comfort and elegance sit in the cozy, blue-walled dining room. Seafood is the specialty—the Loch Fyne oysters and queenie scallops from Tarbert are wonderful. Watch for the daily specials: perhaps a seafood or vegetarian soup followed by huge North African prawns. It's wise to reserve ahead. [$] *Average main: £16* ✉ *1 The Shore, Leith* ☎ *0131/554–5666* 🌐 *www.fishersbistros.co.uk* ✣ *H1.*

$ BRITISH 🍴 **The King's Wark.** Along the shoreline at Leith is a gastro-pub with a pleasant atmosphere and quality food that continues to win plaudits. At lunchtime the dark-wood bar does a roaring trade in simple fare such as gourmet burgers and fish cakes, but in the evening the kitchen ups the ante with such dishes as sea trout stuffed with smoked mackerel risotto. Old stone walls attest to the building's 15th-century origins. ■ **TIP→ Book early to sample the legendary breakfast menu.** [$] *Average main: £13* ✉ *36 The Shore, Leith* ☎ *0131/554–9260* 🌐 *www.thekingswark.com* ✣ *H1.*

$$$$ FRENCH 🍴 **The Kitchin.** One of the Edinburgh's most popular eateries, Tom Kitchin's award-winning venture packs in the crowds. It's not difficult to see why. Kitchin, who trained in France, runs a tight ship, and his passion for using seasonal and locally sourced produce to his own creative ends shows no sign of waning. Unfashionable ingredients such as ox tongue, tripe, and pig's head emerge heroic after Kitchin's alchemy, and he works his magic equally dexterously on more familiar elements such as seafood and venison. To sample this verified culinary world affordably, try the three-course lunch for £26.50. [$] *Average main: £35* ✉ *78 Commercial Quay, Leith* ☎ *0131/555–1755* 🌐 *www.thekitchin.com* ✍ *Reservations essential* ⏲ *Closed Sun. and Mon.* ✣ *H1.*

$$$$ FRENCH Fodor's Choice ★ 🍴 **Martin Wishart.** Slightly out of town but worth every penny of the taxi fare, this restaurant's well-known chef woos diners with an impeccable and varied menu of beautifully presented, French-influenced dishes. Shoulder fillet of beef with Devonshire snails, chervil root, and parsley typify the cuisine, which costs £75 for three courses. For the very sweet of tooth there's a dessert tasting menu combing all three daily choices for an extra £7.50. On weekdays the three-course lunch is £28. Reservations are essential on Friday and Saturday night. [$] *Average main: £65* ✉ *54 The Shore, Leith* ☎ *0131/553–3557* 🌐 *www.martin-wishart.co.uk* ⏲ *Closed Sun. and Mon.* ✣ *H1.*

13

WHERE TO STAY

From stylish boutique hotels to homey B&Bs, Edinburgh has a world-class array of accommodations to suit every taste. Its status as one of Britain's most attractive and fascinating cities ensures a steady influx of visitors, but the wealth of overnight options means there's no need to compromise on where you stay. Grand old hotels are rightly renowned for their regal bearing and old-world charm. If your tastes are a little more contemporary, the city's burgeoning contingent of chic design hotels offers an equally alluring alternative. For those on a tighter budget, the town's B&Bs are the most likely choice. If you feel B&Bs can be restrictive, keep in mind that Scots are trusting people—many proprietors provide front-door keys and few impose curfews.

Rooms are harder to find in August and September, when the Edinburgh International Festival and the Fringe Festival take place, so reserve at least three months in advance. Bed-and-breakfast accommodations may be harder to find in December, January, and February, when some proprietors close for a few weeks.

PRICES

Weekend rates in the larger hotels are always much cheaper than midweek rates, so if you want to stay in a plush hotel, come on the weekend. To save money and see how local residents live, stay in a B&B in one of the areas away from the city center, such as Pilrig to the north, Murrayfield to the west, or Sciennes to the south. Public buses can whisk you to the city center in 10 to 15 minutes. *Hotel reviews have been shortened. For more information and additional options, visit Fodors.com.*

	WHAT IT COSTS IN POUNDS			
	$	$$	$$$	$$$$
Hotels	under £100	£100–£160	£161–£220	over £220

Prices are the lowest cost of a standard double room in high season, including 20% V.A.T.

OLD TOWN

Use the coordinate (✣ B2) at the end of each listing to locate a site on the corresponding map.

The narrow *pends* (alleys), cobbled streets, and steep hills of the Old Town remind you that this is a city with many layers of history. Medieval to modern, these hotels all are within a stone's throw of the action.

$$ HOTEL Fodor's Choice ★ 🏨 **Hotel du Vin.** Leave it to one of the U.K.'s most forward-thinking chains to convert a Victorian-era asylum into this understated luxury property that feels steeped in history and lore despite its contemporary decor and trappings, like the hip bar and restaurant. **Pros:** very unique and historical building; trendy design; youthful feel; lively on-site dining and drinking. **Cons:** some rooms are better than others; in a noisy neighborhood. [$] *Rooms from: £160* ✉ *11 Bristo Pl., Old Town*

BEST BETS FOR EDINBURGH LODGING

Fodor's Choice ★

21212, $$$, p. 595
Balmoral Hotel, $$$$, p. 595
The Bonham, $$$, p. 596
Hotel du Vin, $$, p. 593
Rutland Hotel, $$, p. 596
The Scotsman, $$$$, p. 594

By Price

$

Ardenlee Guest House, p. 595
AmarAgua, p. 597

$$

Hotel du Vin, p. 593
Rutland Hotel, p. 596

$$$

21212, p. 595
The Bonham, p. 596

$$$$

Balmoral Hotel, p. 595
The Caledonian, p. 595
The Scotsman, p. 594

By Experience

BEST CONCIERGE

Balmoral Hotel, $$$$, p. 595

BEST HISTORIC HOTELS

Balmoral Hotel, $$$$, p. 595

BEST SPAS

Balmoral Hotel, $$$$, p. 595
The Scotsman, $$$$, p. 594

MOST KID-FRIENDLY

Knight Residence, $$$ p. 594

MOST ROMANTIC

The Witchery, $$$$, p. 594

☎ *0131/247–4900* 🌐 *www.hotelduvin.com* 🛏 *37 rooms, 10 suites* 🍴 *Breakfast* ✥ *F5.*

$$$ RENTAL FAMILY 🏨 **Knight Residence.** About 10 minutes from the Grassmarket, the Knight is made up of 19 different apartments that offer good value and convenient locations. **Pros:** comfortable apartments; secure location; good for families needing space and privacy. **Cons:** lack of staff won't suit everyone; better for stays of two or more nights. [$] *Rooms from: £168* ✉ *12 Lauriston St., Old Town* ☎ *0131/622–8120* 🌐 *www.theknightresidence.co.uk* 🛏 *19 apartments* 🍴 *No meals* ✥ *D5.*

$$$$ HOTEL Fodor's Choice ★ 🏨 **The Scotsman.** A magnificent turn-of-the-20th-century building, with a marble staircase and a fascinating history—it was once the headquarters of the *Scotsman* newspaper—now houses this modern, luxurious hotel. **Pros:** gorgeous surroundings; personalized service. **Cons:** no air-conditioning; spa can be noisy. [$] *Rooms from: £270* ✉ *20 N. Bridge, Old Town* ☎ *0131/556–5565* 🌐 *www.thescotsmanhotel.co.uk* 🛏 *56 rooms, 13 suites* 🍴 *Multiple meal plans* ✥ *F4.*

$$$$ HOTEL 🏨 **The Witchery.** This lavishly theatrical lodging promises a night to remember. **Pros:** the Gothic drama and intriguing antiques; sumptuous dining. **Cons:** can be noisy at night; rooms may feel too cluttered for some. [$] *Rooms from: £325* ✉ *Castlehill, Royal Mile, Old Town* ☎ *0131/225–5613* 🌐 *www.thewitchery.com* 🛏 *9 suites* 🍴 *Breakfast* ✥ *E5.*

NEW TOWN

Use the coordinate (✛ B2) at the end of each listing to locate a site on the corresponding map.

The New Town is filled with gorgeous 18th- and 19th-century architecture but is close to main shopping streets. Also here is Calton Hill, offering some of the best views of the city from its summit.

$$$
HOTEL
Fodor's Choice
★

21212. In this handsome Royal Terrace town house, the spacious rooms are beautifully designed with an eye for detail: an enormous bed sits on a raised platform facing a stylish seating area with a flat-screen TV. **Pros:** stylish decor and service worthy of a special getaway; above a fab restaurant; huge beds. **Cons:** pricey add-ons. $ *Rooms from: £200* ✉ *3 Royal Terr., New Town* ☎ *0131/523 1030* ⊕ *www.21212restaurant. co.uk* ↝ *4 rooms* ⦿| *No meals* ✛ *G3.*

$
B&B/INN

Ardenlee Guest House. An exquisite Victorian-tile floor is one of many original features at this dependable guesthouse tucked away from the hustle and bustle of the city center. **Pros:** family-run establishment; good value, especially for long-term stays. **Cons:** few amenities; uphill walk to the city center. $ *Rooms from: £95* ✉ *9 Eyre Pl., New Town* ☎ *0131/556–2838* ⊕ *www.ardenlee.co.uk* ↝ *9 rooms, 7 with bath* ⦿| *Breakfast* ✛ *D2.*

$$$$
HOTEL
Fodor's Choice
★

Balmoral Hotel. The attention to detail in the elegant rooms—colors were picked to echo the country's heathers and moors—and the sheer élan that has re-created the Edwardian splendor of this grand, former railroad hotel make staying at the Balmoral a special introduction to Edinburgh. **Pros:** big and beautiful building; top-hatted doorman; quality bathroom goodies. **Cons:** small pool; spa books up fast; restaurants can be very busy. $ *Rooms from: £380* ✉ *1 Princes St., New Town* ☎ *0131/556–2414* ⊕ *www.thebalmoralhotel.com* ↝ *168 rooms, 20 suites* ⦿| *Breakfast* ✛ *F4.*

$$$$
HOTEL

The Caledonian, a Waldorf Astoria Hotel. An imposing block of red sandstone beyond the west end of West Princes Street Gardens, "The Caley" has imposing Victorian decor and beautifully restored interiors. **Pros:** service with a smile; good breakfast choice. **Cons:** Internet access is extra; may lack the "wow factor" for some. $ *Rooms from: £240* ✉ *Princes St., New Town* ☎ *0131/222–8888* ⊕ *www.thecaledonian. waldorfastoria.com* ↝ *241 rooms, 20 suites* ⦿| *Breakfast* ✛ *C4.*

$
B&B/INN

Inverleith Hotel. Across from the Royal Botanical Gardens, this renovated Victorian town house has cozy, well-lighted rooms with velour bedspreads, dark-wood furniture, and pale-gold curtains. **Pros:** quiet surroundings; knowledgeable staff. **Cons:** some rooms are small; narrow passageways; uphill walk to the city center. $ *Rooms from: £99* ✉ *5 Inverleith Terr., New Town* ☎ *0131/556–2745* ⊕ *www.inverleithhotel. co.uk* ↝ *12 rooms, 2 apartments* ⦿| *Breakfast* ✛ *D1.*

$$$$
HOTEL

Tigerlilly. On hip George Street, this boutique hotel has everything a girl could imagine—bowls of fresh fruit, designer candles, hair straighteners—for a night away from home. **Pros:** chic yet not intimidating; laid-back but efficient staff. **Cons:** no views; can be noisy and very busy. $ *Rooms from: £294* ✉ *125 George St., New Town* ☎ *0131/225– 5005* ⊕ *www.tigerlilyedinburgh.co.uk* ↝ *33 rooms* ⦿| *Breakfast* ✛ *D4.*

13

HAYMARKET

Use the coordinate (✣ B2) at the end of each listing to locate a site on the corresponding map.

Close to one of the main train stations, Haymarket can make a good base for exploring the city if you're staying in one of the hotels beyond the west end of Princes Street.

$$ B&B/INN **Victorian Town House.** In a leafy crescent, this handsome house once belonged to a cousin of Robert Louis Stevenson, and the celebrated writer would doubtless be happy to lay his head in this good-value B&B. **Pros:** serene surroundings near Water of Leith; gracious staff. **Cons:** no parking nearby; distance from Old Town. [$] *Rooms from: £110* ✉ *14 Eglinton Terr., Haymarket* ☎ *0131/337–7088* 🌐 *www.thevictoriantownhouse.co.uk* 🛏 *3 rooms* 🍴 *Breakfast* ✣ *A5.*

WEST END

Use the coordinate (✣ B2) at the end of each listing to locate a site on the corresponding map.

With easy access to some of the city's trendiest shops and cafés, the West End has lodgings that take advantage of the neighborhood's handsome Georgian-style town houses.

$$$ HOTEL Fodor's Choice ★ **The Bonham.** There's a clubby atmosphere throughout this hotel, which carries on a successful, sophisticated flirtation with modernity. **Pros:** thorough yet unobtrusive service; excellent restaurant. **Cons:** few common areas; can feel like a business hotel. [$] *Rooms from: £165* ✉ *35 Drumsheugh Gardens, West End* ☎ *0131/226–6050* 🌐 *www.thebonham.com* 🛏 *42 rooms, 6 suites* 🍴 *Multiple meal plans* ✣ *B4.*

$$ HOTEL Fodor's Choice ★ **Rutland Hotel.** The building may have once been the residence of Sir Joseph Lister—known as the "father of antiseptic surgery"—but there's nothing clinical about this acclaimed boutique hotel at the west end of Princes Street. **Pros:** friendly staff; not pretentious; great bar and restaurant. **Cons:** decor may be too loud for some. [$] *Rooms from: £150* ✉ *1–3 Rutland St., West End* ☎ *0131/229–3402* 🌐 *www.therutlandhotel.com* 🛏 *12 rooms, 1 apartment* 🍴 *Breakfast* ✣ *C4.*

SOUTH SIDE

Use the coordinate (✣ B2) at the end of each listing to locate a site on the corresponding map.

The B&Bs and restaurants in this residential area offer good value.

$$ B&B/INN **23 Mayfield.** A self-styled "boutique guesthouse," 23 Mayfield is a cut above your average B&B: the Victorian villa features many original elements expertly complemented by dark-wood furniture, lovely artwork, and antiquarian books to create a sumptuous atmosphere. **Pros:** relaxing atmosphere; helpful yet unobtrusive service; gourmet breakfast featuring famed porridge. **Cons:** need to book well in advance. [$] *Rooms from: £150* ✉ *23 Mayfield Gardens, South Side* ☎ *0131/667–5806* 🌐 *www.23mayfield.co.uk* 🛏 *9 rooms* 🍴 *Breakfast* ✣ *F6.*

$$ B&B/INN **94DR.** Like owners Paul Lightfoot and John MacEwan—a self-described "high-octane" couple—94DR reaches for the stars with its stylish decor and contemporary trappings. **Pros:** warm welcome; gay-friendly vibe; smashing breakfast. **Cons:** modern design may not please everyone; a long walk to the city center. [$] *Rooms from: £120* ✉ *94 Dalkeith Rd., South Side* ☎ *0131/662–9265* 🌐 *www.94dr.com* 🛏 *7 rooms* 🍴 *Breakfast* ✥ *F6.*

$ B&B/INN **AmarAgua.** Four-poster beds, a tranquil location, and bountiful breakfasts set this Victorian town house B&B apart. **Pros:** quiet setting; snug rooms; wonderful breakfasts. **Cons:** far from the city center; minimum two-night stay. [$] *Rooms from: £94* ✉ *10 Kilmaurs Terr., Newington* ☎ *0131/667–6775* 🌐 *www.amaragua.co.uk* 🛏 *5 rooms, 4 with bath* 🕓 *Closed Jan.* 🍴 *Breakfast* ✥ *F6.*

$$ B&B/INN **Ashdene House.** On a quiet residential street sits this Edwardian house, one of the city's best-value B&Bs. **Pros:** homemade breads at breakfast; spacious rooms. **Cons:** not within walking distance of the center. [$] *Rooms from: £115* ✉ *23 Fountainhall Rd., The Grange* ☎ *0131/667–6026* 🌐 *www.ashdenehouse.com* 🛏 *5 rooms* 🍴 *Breakfast* ✥ *F6.*

$ B&B/INN **Glenalmond House.** Longtime hoteliers Jimmy and Fiona Mackie are well schooled in delighting guests, which makes elegant Glenalmond House a reliable choice. **Pros:** knowledgeable owners; nice furnishings; superb breakfasts. **Cons:** smallish bathrooms; a bit of a walk to the New Town. [$] *Rooms from: £92* ✉ *25 Mayfield Gardens, South Side* ☎ *0131/668–2392* 🌐 *www.glenalmondhouse.com* 🛏 *9 rooms* 🍴 *Breakfast* ✥ *F6.*

$ B&B/INN **Teviotdale House.** The interior of this 1848 town house—including canopy beds and miles of festive fabrics—makes it a special B&B option. **Pros:** owners take pride in their hospitality; wide range of breakfast items. **Cons:** a long walk from the city center; not all bathrooms have tubs. [$] *Rooms from: £94* ✉ *53 Grange Loan, The Grange* ☎ *0131/667–4376* 🌐 *www.teviotdalehouse.com* 🛏 *7 rooms* 🍴 *Breakfast* ✥ *F6.*

LEITH

Use the coordinate (✥ B2) at the end of each listing to locate a site on the corresponding map.

Staying here means you'll be away from the Old Town and New Town sights, but you can find reasonable prices—and good restaurants.

$$ B&B/INN **Ardmor House.** This excellent guesthouse combines the original features of a Victorian home with stylish contemporary furnishings. **Pros:** warm and friendly owner; decorated with great style; gay-friendly environment. **Cons:** a bit out of the way; double room on the ground floor is tiny. [$] *Rooms from: £140* ✉ *74 Pilrig St., Leith* ☎📠 *0131/554–4944* 🌐 *www.ardmorhouse.com* 🛏 *5 rooms* 🍴 *Breakfast* ✥ *G1.*

$ B&B/INN **Fraoch House.** This popular option manages to combine a homey feel and stylish decor without leaning too far in either direction. **Pros:** a warm welcome; great DVD library; free Wi-Fi. **Cons:** uphill walk to the city center. [$] *Rooms from: £95* ✉ *66 Pilrig St., Leith* ☎ *0131/554–1353* 🌐 *www.fraochhouse.com* 🛏 *9 rooms* 🍴 *Breakfast* ✥ *G1.*

NIGHTLIFE AND THE ARTS

THE ARTS

Those who think Edinburgh's arts scene consists of just the elegiac wail of a bagpipe and the twang of a fiddle or two will be proved wrong by the hundreds of performing-arts options. The jewel in the crown, of course, is the famed Edinburgh International Festival, which now attracts the best in music, dance, theater, painting, and sculpture from all over the globe during three weeks from mid-August to early September. The *Scotsman* and *Herald*, Scotland's leading daily newspapers, carry listings and reviews in their arts pages every day, with special editions during the festival. Tickets are generally sold in advance; in some cases they're also available from certain designated travel agents or at the door, although concerts by national orchestras often sell out long before the day of the performance.

DANCE

Festival Theatre. Scottish Ballet productions and other dance acts appear at the Festival Theatre. ⊠ *13–29 Nicolson St., Old Town* ☎ *0131/529–6000* ⊕ *www.edtheatres.com.*

Royal Lyceum. Visiting contemporary dance companies perform in the Royal Lyceum. ⊠ *Grindlay St., West End* ☎ *0131/248–4848* ⊕ *www.lyceum.org.uk.*

FESTIVALS

Fodor's Choice
★ **Edinburgh Festival Fringe.** While the world's largest fringe festival is going on, most of the city center becomes one huge performance area, with fire eaters, sword swallowers, unicyclists, jugglers, string quartets, jazz groups, stand-up comics, and magicians all thronging into High Street and Princes Street. Every available performance space—church halls, community centers, parks, sports fields, putting greens, and nightclubs—is utilized for every kind of event, with something for all tastes. Many events are free, while others cost £2 to £15. During festival time—roughly the same as the Edinburgh International Festival—it's possible to arrange your own entertainment program from morning to midnight. ⊠ *Edinburgh Festival Fringe Office, 180 High St., Old Town* ☎ *0131/226–0026* ⊕ *www.edfringe.com.*

Fodor's Choice
★ **Edinburgh International Festival.** Running from early August through early September, the flagship arts event of the year attracts international performers to a celebration of music, dance, theater, and art. Programs, tickets, and reservations are available from the Hub, within the impressive Victorian-Gothic Tolbooth Kirk. Tickets for the festival go on sale in April, and many sell out within the month. However, you may still be able to purchase tickets, which range from £4 to £60, during the festival. ⊠ *Edinburgh Festival Centre, Castlehill, Old Town* ☎ *0131/473–2000* ⊕ *www.eif.co.uk.*

Edinburgh Military Tattoo. The Edinburgh Military Tattoo may not be art, but it is certainly Scottish culture. It's sometimes confused with the Edinburgh International Festival, partly because both events take place in August (though the Tattoo starts and finishes a week earlier).

This celebration of martial music features bands, gymnastics, and stunt motorcycle teams on the castle esplanade. Dress warmly for late-evening performances. Even if it rains, the show most definitely goes on. ⊠ *Edinburgh Military Tattoo Office, 32 Market St., Old Town* ☎ *0131/225–1188* ⊕ *www.edintattoo.co.uk.*

Hogmanay. Other places in Scotland have raucous New Year's celebrations, but Edinburgh's multiday Hogmanay is famous throughout Europe and beyond, with something for everyone. Yes, it's still winter and cold, but joining the festivities with up to 80,000 other people can be memorable. ⊠ *Princes St., Old Town* ⊕ *www.edinburghshogmanay. com* ⊠ *£20.*

FILM

Cameo. The Cameo has one large and two small auditoriums, both of which are extremely comfortable, plus a bar with late-night specials. ⊠ *38 Home St., Tollcross* ☎ *0871/902–5723* ⊕ *www.picturehouses. co.uk.*

Fodor's Choice ★ **Filmhouse.** The excellent three-screen Filmhouse is the best venue for modern, foreign-language, offbeat, or simply less commercial films. The café and bar are open late on the weekend. ⊠ *88 Lothian Rd., West End* ☎ *0131/228–2688* ⊕ *www.filmhousecinema.com.*

MUSIC

Playhouse. The Playhouse leans toward popular artists, comedy acts, and musicals. ⊠ *Greenside Pl., East End* ☎ *0131/524–3333* ⊕ *www. edinburghplayhouse.org.uk.*

Queen's Hall. The intimate Queen's Hall hosts small musical recitals. ⊠ *Clerk St., Old Town* ☎ *0131/668–2019* ⊕ *www.thequeenshall.net.*

Usher Hall. Edinburgh's grandest venue, Usher Hall hosts national and international performers and groups, including the Royal Scottish National Orchestra. ⊠ *Lothian Rd., West End* ☎ *0131/228–1155* ⊕ *www.usherhall.co.uk.*

THEATER

MODERN **Traverse Theatre.** With its specially designed space, the Traverse Theatre has developed a solid reputation for new, stimulating Scottish plays and dance performances. ⊠ *10 Cambridge St., West End* ☎ *0131/228–1404* ⊕ *www.traverse.co.uk.*

TRADITIONAL **Royal Lyceum.** The Royal Lyceum presents traditional plays and contemporary works, often transferred from or prior to their London West End showings. ⊠ *Grindlay St., West End* ☎ *0131/248–4848* ⊕ *www. lyceum.org.uk.*

NIGHTLIFE

The nightlife scene in Edinburgh is vibrant—whatever you're looking for, you'll most certainly find it here, and you won't have to go far. Expect old-style pubs as well as cutting-edge bars and clubs. Live music pours out of many watering holes on weekends, particularly folk, blues, and jazz. Well-known artists perform at some of the larger venues.

Edinburgh's 400-odd pubs are a study in themselves. In the eastern and northern districts of the city you can find some grim, inhospitable-looking places that proclaim that drinking is no laughing matter. But throughout Edinburgh many pubs have deliberately traded in their old spit-and-sawdust images for atmospheric revivals of the warm, oak-paneled, leather-chaired howffs of a more leisurely age. Most pubs and bars are open weekdays and Saturday from 11 am to midnight, and from 12:30 to midnight on Sunday.

The List and The Skinny carry the most up-to-date details about cultural events. The List is available at newsstands throughout the city, while The Skinny is free and can be picked up at a number of pubs, clubs, and shops around town. The Herald and Scotsman newspapers are good for reviews and notices of upcoming events throughout Scotland.

OLD TOWN

BARS AND PUBS **Canons' Gait.** The Canons' Gait has a fine selection of local real ales and malts. It stages live jazz and blues performances, as well as edgy comedy shows in the cellar bar. ⊠ 232 Canongate, Old Town ☎ 0131/556–4481.

Whiski. With 300-plus malts, this cheerful place is known for its haggis burger. Foot-stomping fiddle, bluegrass, and country music plays most nights. ⊠ 119 High St., Old Town ☎ 0131/556–3095 ⊕ www.whiskibar.co.uk.

FOLK CLUBS You can usually find folk musicians performing in pubs throughout Edinburgh, although there's been a decline in the live-music scene because of dwindling profits and the predominance of popular theme bars.

Royal Oak. With a piano in the corner, this cozy bar presents live blues and folk music most nights. ⊠ 1 Infirmary St., Old Town ☎ 0131/557–2976 ⊕ www.royal-oak-folk.com.

Whistle Binkies Pub. This friendly basement bar presents rock, blues and folk music every night of the week. ⊠ 4–6 South Bridge, Old Town ☎ 0131/557–5114 ⊕ www.whistlebinkies.com.

NIGHTCLUBS **Bongo Club.** The bohemian Bongo Club stages indie, rockabilly, dub, and techno gigs, as well as various club and comedy nights. ⊠ 66 Cowgate, Old Town ☎ 0131/558–7604 ⊕ www.thebongoclub.co.uk.

Cabaret Voltaire. This vaulted ceilings of this subterranean club reverberates with music most nights. You'll find everything from cheesy raves to cutting-edge indie bands to trendy DJs. ⊠ 36–38 Blair St., Old Town ☎ 0131/247–4704 ⊕ www.thecabaretvoltaire.com.

NEW TOWN

BARS AND PUBS **The Basement.** A longtime favorite with the younger crowd, the Basement is a good stopover before heading out to the clubs. The Hawaiian-shirted bar staff adds to the general amiability. ⊠ 10A–12A Broughton St., New Town ☎ 0131/557–0097.

Bramble. You could easily miss this basement bar on Queen Street—look for a spray-painted sign below a clothing alteration shop. Friendly barmen, superb cocktails, eclectic music (DJs spin most nights), and lots of nooks and crannies in the whitewashed space make for late-night shenanigans that attract a young crowd. ⊠ *16A Queen St., New Town* ☎ *0131/226–6343* ⊕ *www.bramblebar.co.uk.*

Fodor's Choice ★ **Café Royal Circle Bar.** Famed for its atmospheric Victorian interiors— think ornate stucco, etched mirrors, tiled murals, stained glass, and leather booths—the Café Royal Circle Bar draws a cast of Edinburgh characters for its drinks (seven real ales and more than 30 whiskies) and tasty seafood platters. ⊠ *19 W. Regent St., New Town* ☎ *0131/556– 1884* ⊕ *www.caferoyaledinburgh.co.uk.*

Cask and Barrel. A spacious, busy pub, the Cask and Barrel lets you sample hand-pulled ales at the horseshoe-shaped bar ringed by a collection of brewery mirrors. ⊠ *115 Broughton St., New Town* ☎ *0131/556–3132.*

Guildford Arms. This place is worth a visit just for its interior: ornate plasterwork, elaborate cornices, and wood paneling. The bartender serves some excellent draft ales, including Orkney Dark Island. ⊠ *1 W. Register St., east end of Princes St., New Town* ☎ *0131/556–4312.*

FAMILY **Fodor's** Choice ★ **Joseph Pearce's.** One of four Swedish-owned pubs in Edinburgh, Joseph Pearce's has a Continental feel, thanks to the cosmopolitan staff. Scandinavian-themed cocktails are popular, as are meatballs and other Swedish dishes. There's a children's corner with toys to keep the small fry occupied. ⊠ *23 Elm Row, New Town* ☎ *0131/556–4140.*

Milne's Bar. This spot is known as the poets' pub because of its popularity with Edinburgh's literati. Pies and baked potatoes go well with seven real ales and various guest beers (meaning anything besides the house brew). Victorian advertisements and photos of old Edinburgh give the place an old-time feel. ⊠ *35 Hanover St., New Town* ☎ *0131/225–6738.*

Teuchters. With more than 80 whiskies, a cozy fire, and comfy sofas, Teuchters is a fine place to relax with a dram. ⊠ *26 William St., West End* ☎ *0131/226–1036* ⊕ *www.aroomin.co.uk.*

CEILIDHS AND SCOTTISH EVENINGS **Thistle King James Hotel.** For those who feel a trip to Scotland is not complete without hearing the "Braes of Yarrow" or "Auld Robin Gray," several hotels present traditional Scottish-music evenings in the summer season. Head for the Thistle King James Hotel to see *Jamie's Scottish Evening,* an extravaganza of Scottish song, tartan, plaid, and bagpipes that takes place nightly from April to October. The cost is £60, including a four-course dinner. ⊠ *Thistle King James Hotel, 107 Leith St., New Town* ☎ *0131/200–7758* ⊕ *www.thistle.com.*

GAY AND LESBIAN There's a burgeoning gay and lesbian scene in Edinburgh, and the city has many predominantly gay clubs, bars, and cafés. But don't expect the scene to be as open as in London, New York, or even Glasgow. *The List* and *The Skinny* have sections that focus on gay and lesbian venues.

CC Blooms. Modern and colorful, CC Blooms plays a mix of musical styles. Open nightly, it's been a mainstay on the gay scene since the early '90s. ⊠ *23–24 Greenside Pl., New Town* ☎ *0131/556–9331* ⊕ *ccbloomsedinburgh.com.*

GHQ. This stylish gay spot has glam contemporary decor and state-of-the-art sound and lighting. The DJ nights are very popular. ⊠ *4 Picardy Pl., New Town* ☎ *0845/166–6024.*

13

NIGHTCLUBS   **Liquid Room.** Top indie bands and an eclectic mix of club nights (techno, hip-hop, and alternative, to name a few) make the Liquid Room a superb venue. ⊠ *9C Victoria St., New Town* ☎ *0131/225–2564* ⊕ *www. liquidroom.com.*

SOUTH SIDE

BARS AND   **Cloisters.** The Cloisters prides itself on the absence of music, gaming
PUBS   machines, and all other modern pub gimmicks. Instead, it specializes in real ales, malt whiskies, and good food, all at reasonable prices. ⊠ *26 Brougham St., Tollcross* ☎ *0131/221–9997.*

Under the Stairs. As you might guess from the name, Under the Stairs is below street level. This cozy, low-ceilinged place with quirky furniture and art exhibits serves specialty cocktails and decent bar food. ⊠ *3A Merchant St., Old Town* ☎ *0131/466–8550* ⊕ *www.underthestairs.org.*

LEITH

BARS AND   **Bond No 9.** This stylish bar with hidden corners specializes in cool cock-
PUBS   tails and exotic liquors, including absinthe. There's also excellent bistro food. ⊠ *84 Commercial St., Leith* ☎ *0131/555–5578* ⊕ *www.bondno9. co.uk.*

Fodor'sChoice   **The King's Wark.** A 15th-century building houses the popular King's
★   Wark, renowned for its excellent food and good ales. Breakfasts are legendary, and are worth booking in advance. In warm weather you can snag a table on the sidewalk. ⊠ *36 The Shore, Leith* ☎ *0131/554–9260* ⊕ *www.thekingswark.com.*

Malt and Hops. Having opened its doors in 1749, Malt and Hops has a resident ghost. With a fine spot on the waterfront, the place serves microbrewery cask ales. ⊠ *45 The Shore, Leith* ☎ *0131/555–0083* ⊕ *www.barcalisa.com.*

EAST END

COMEDY   **Stand.** Throughout the year you can laugh until your sides split at the
CLUBS   Stand, which hosts both famous names and up-and-coming acts. ⊠ *5 York Pl., East End* ☎ *0131/558–7272* ⊕ *www.thestand.co.uk.*

SHOPPING

Despite its renown as a shopping street, **Princes Street** in the New Town may disappoint some visitors with its dull modern architecture, average chain stores, and fast-food outlets. One block north of Princes Street, **Rose Street** has many smaller specialty shops; part of the street is a pedestrian zone, so it's a pleasant place to browse. The shops on **George Street** in New Town tend to be fairly upscale. London names, such as Laura Ashley and Penhaligons, are prominent, though some of the older independent stores continue to do good business.

The streets crossing George Street—Hanover, Frederick, and Castle— are also worth exploring. **Dundas Street,** the northern extension of Hanover Street, beyond Queen Street Gardens, has several antiques shops. **Thistle Street,** originally George Street's "back lane," or service area, has several boutiques and more antiques shops.

As may be expected, many shops along the **Royal Mile** in Old Town sell what may be politely or euphemistically described as tourist-ware— whiskies, tartans, and tweeds. Careful exploration, however, will reveal some worthwhile establishments. Shops here also cater to highly specialized interests and hobbies. Close to the castle end of the Royal Mile, just off George IV Bridge, is **Victoria Street,** with specialty shops grouped in a small area. Follow the tiny West Bow to **Grassmarket** for more specialty stores.

Stafford and William streets form a small, upscale shopping area in a Georgian setting. Walk to the west end of Princes Street and then along its continuation, Shandwick Place, then turn right onto Stafford Street. William Street crosses Stafford halfway down.

North of Princes Street, on the way to the Royal Botanic Garden Edinburgh, is **Stockbridge,** an oddball shopping area of some charm, particularly on St. Stephen Street. To get here, walk north down Frederick Street and Howe Street, away from Princes Street, then turn left onto North West Circus Place.

13

OLD TOWN

SPECIALTY SHOPS

Fodor's Choice
★

BOOKS,
PAPER, MAPS,
AND GAMES

Analogue Books. This bookshop and gallery has a wonderful and ever-changing selection of stimulating reads—books and magazines covering lots of genres—mostly from small publishers. There are also eye-catching prints to adorn your walls. ⊠ *39 Candlemaker Row, Old Town* ☎ *0131/220–0601* ⊕ *www.analoguebooks.co.uk.*

Main Point Books. This bibliophile's haven is stacked high with obscure first editions and bargain tomes. ⊠ *77 Bread St., Old Town* ☎ *0131/228–4837.*

CLOTHING
BOUTIQUES

Bill Baber. One of the most imaginative of the many Scottish knitwear designers, Bill Baber is a long way from the conservative pastel woolies sold at some of the large mill shops. ⊠ *66 Grassmarket, Old Town* ☎ *0131/225–3249.*

Ragamuffin. Hailing from the Isle of Skye, Ragamuffin sells the funkiest and brightest knits produced in Scotland. ⊠ *278 Canongate, Old Town* ☎ *0131/557–6007.*

JEWELRY

Clarksons. A family firm, Clarksons handcrafts a unique collection of jewelry, including Celtic styles. The pieces here are made with silver, gold, platinum, and precious gems, with a particular emphasis on diamonds. ⊠ *87 W. Bow, Old Town* ☎ *0131/225–8141.*

Fodor's Choice
★

SCOTTISH
SPECIALTIES

Cranachan & Crowdie. On Edinburgh's Royal Mile, this gourmet shop is brimming with the finest Scottish food and drink. There's even a chocolate counter for those with a sweet tooth, as well as shortbread and oatcakes. The staff is happy to put together hampers of food for any occasion—including an impromptu picnic back in your room. ⊠ *263 Canongate, Old Town* ☎ *0131/556–7194* ⊕ *www.cranachan andcrowdie.com.*

Edinburgh Old Town Weaving Company. At the Edinburgh Old Town Weaving Company, you can chat with the cloth and tapestry weavers as they work, then buy the products. The company can also provide information on clan histories and which tartan to wear. ⊠ *555 Castlehill, Old Town* ☎ *0131/226–1555.*

Geoffrey (Tailor) Highland Crafts. This shop can clothe you in full Highland dress, with kilts made in its own workshops. ⊠ *57–59 High St., Old Town* ☎ *0131/557–0256* ⊕ *www.geoffreykilts.co.uk.*

NEW TOWN

ARCADES AND SHOPPING CENTERS
St. James Centre. The St. James Centre has John Lewis, River Island, Thorntons, Wallis, and other chain stores. ⊠ *Leith St., New Town.*

DEPARTMENT STORES
Harvey Nichols. Affectionately known as Harvey Nicks, this high-style British chain has opened a Scots outpost. ⊠ *30–34 St. Andrew Sq., New Town* ☎ *0131/524–8388* ⊕ *www.harveynichols.com.*

Fodor's Choice ★ **Jenners.** Traditional china and glassware are a specialty here, as are Scottish tweeds and tartans. Its famous food hall, run by Valvona & Crolla, stocks Scots staples like shortbread, marmalade, and honey, alongside quality Continental groceries. ⊠ *48 Princes St., New Town* ☎ *0844/800–3725.*

John Lewis. Part of a U.K.–wide chain, John Lewis specializes in furnishings and household goods, but also stocks designer clothes. ⊠ *69 St. James Centre, New Town* ☎ *0131/556–9121* ⊕ *www.johnlewis.com.*

Marks & Spencer. Fairly priced, stylish clothes and accessories are on offer at Marks & Spencer. You can also buy quality food and household goods. ⊠ *54 Princes St., New Town* ☎ *0131/225–2301* ⊕ *www. marksandspencer.com.*

SPECIALTY SHOPS
ANTIQUES **Elaine's Vintage Clothing.** This wee boutique on beguiling St. Stephen Street is crammed full of vintage threads for women and men. The finds span the 20th century, but most are from the '40s to the '70s. The friendly owner shares her knowledge of the many elegant and quirky outfits on her rails. ⊠ *55 St. Stephen, New Town* ☎ *0131/225–5783.*

Fodor's Choice ★ **Unicorn Antiques.** This basement is crammed with fascinating antiques, including artworks, ornaments, and drawerfuls of aged cutlery. ⊠ *65 Dundas St., New Town* ☎ *0131/556–7176.*

JEWELRY **Joseph Bonnar.** Tucked behind George Street, Joseph Bonnar stocks Scotland's largest collection of antique jewelry, including 19th-century agate jewels. ⊠ *72 Thistle St., New Town* ☎ *0131/226–2811* ⊕ *www. josephbonnar.com.*

HOME FURNISHINGS **Hannah Zakari.** Quirky handmade pieces, including embroidered cushions, are a specialty at Hannah Zakari. Also look for unusual jewelry, artwork, and accessories. ⊠ *43 Candlemaker Row, New Town* ☎ *0131/516–3264* ⊕ *www.hannahzakari.co.uk.*

Studio One. This basement shop has a well-established and comprehensive inventory of jewelry, accessories, housewares, and more. ⌧ *10–16 Stafford St., New Town* ☎ *0131/226–5812* ⊕ *www.studio-one.co.uk.*

OUTDOOR SPORTS GEAR **Tiso.** This shop stocks outdoor clothing, boots, and jackets ideal for hiking or camping in the Highlands. There's another branch at 41 Commercial Street. ⌧ *123–125 Rose St., New Town* ☎ *0131/225–9486* ⊕ *www.tiso.com*

WEST END

13

SPECIALTY SHOPS

CLOTHING BOUTIQUES **Concrete Wardrobe.** For an eclectic mix of quirky knitwear and accessories, dive into Concrete Wardrobe. You can also find vintage furnishings. ⌧ *50a Broughton St., West End* ☎ *0131/558–7130* ⊕ *www. concretewardrobe.com.*

Extra Inch. This shop stocks a full selection of clothing in larger sizes. ⌧ *12 William St., West End* ☎ *0131/226–3303* ⊕ *www.extrainch.co.uk.*

Herman Brown's. This secondhand clothing store is where cashmere twinsets and classic luxe labels are sought and found. ⌧ *151 W. Port, West End* ☎ *0131/228–2589* ⊕ *www.hermanbrown.co.uk.*

SOUTH SIDE

SPECIALTY SHOPS

ANTIQUES **Courtyard Antiques.** This lovely shop stocks a mixture of high-quality antiques, toys, and militaria. ⌧ *108A Causewayside, Sciennes* ☎ *0131/662–9008* ⊕ *www.edinburghcourtyardantiques.co.uk.*

LEITH

ARCADES AND SHOPPING CENTERS

Ocean Terminal. The Ocean Terminal houses a large collection of shops, as well as bars and eateries. Here you can also visit the former royal yacht *Britannia.* ⌧ *Ocean Dr., Leith.*

SPECIALTY SHOPS

SCOTTISH SPECIALTIES **Clan Tartan Centre.** For the tartan and clan curious, there's database containing details of all known designs, plus information on clan histories. ⌧ *70–74 Bangor Rd., Leith* ☎ *0131/553–5161.*

SPORTS AND THE OUTDOORS

GOLF

In Scotland, SSS indicates the "standard scratch score," the score a scratch golfer could achieve in ideal conditions.

Braid Hills. Known to locals and many others as Braids (no connection with golfer James Braid), this course is beautifully laid out over a rugged range of small hills in the southern suburbs of Edinburgh. The views to the south and the Pentland Hills and north over the city skyline toward the Firth of Forth are worth a visit in themselves. The city built this course at the turn of the 20th century after urban development forced golfers out of the city center. The 9-hole Princes Course was completed in 2003. Reservations are recommended for weekend play. ⊠ *27 Braids Hill Approach* ☎ *0131/447–6666 for Braids, 0131/666–2210 for Princes* ⊕ *www.edinburghleisuregolf.co.uk* ⊠ *Green fee: Braids weekdays £22, weekends £24.75; Princes weekdays £12.50, weekends £14* ⚑ *Braids: 18 holes, 5865 yds, par 71; Princes: 9 holes* ⊙ *Daily.*

Bruntsfield Links. The British Seniors and several other championship tournaments are held at this Willie Park–designed course, 3 miles west of Edinburgh. The course meanders among 155 acres of mature parkland and has fine views over the Firth of Forth. Bruntsfield takes its name from one of the oldest (1761) golf links in Scotland, in the center of Edinburgh—now just a 9-hole pitch-and-putt course—where the club used to play. A strict dress code applies. ⊠ *32 Barnton Ave., Davidson's Mains* ☎ *0131/336–1479* ⊕ *www.sol.co.uk/b/bruntsfieldlinks* ⊠ *Green fee: weekdays £65; weekends £70* ⚑ *Reservations essential* ⚑ *18 holes, 6446 yds, par 71* ⊙ *Daily.*

Royal Burgess Golfing Society. Dating to 1735, this is one of the world's oldest golf clubs. Its members originally played on Bruntsfield Links; now they and their guests play on elegantly manicured parkland in the city's northwestern suburbs. It's a challenging course with fine greens. ⊠ *181 Whitehouse Rd., Barnton* ☎ *0131/339–2075* ⊕ *www. royalburgess.co.uk* ⊠ *Green fee: weekdays £65; weekends £85* ⚑ *Reservations essential* ⚑ *18 holes, 6511 yds, par 71* ⊙ *Daily.*

RUGBY

Murrayfield Stadium. At Murrayfield Stadium, home of the Scottish Rugby Union, matches are played in early spring and fall. Crowds of good-humored rugby fans from all over the world add greatly to the sense of excitement in the streets of Edinburgh. ⊠ *Roseburn Terr., Murrayfield* ☎ *0131/346–5000* ⊕ *www.scottishrugby.org.*

SOCCER

Like Glasgow, Edinburgh is soccer-mad, and there's an intense rivalry between the city's two professional teams. Remember, the game is called football in Britain.

Heart of Midlothian Football Club. The Heart of Midlothian Football Club, better known as the Hearts, plays in maroon and white and is based at Tynecastle. ⊠ *Tynecastle Stadium, McLeod St.* ☎ *0871/663–1874* ⊕ *www.heartsfc.co.uk.*

Hibernian Club. Known as the Hibs, the green-bedecked Hibernian Club plays its home matches at Easter Road Stadium. ⊠ *Easter Road Stadium, 12 Albion Pl.* ☎ *0131/661–2159* ⊕ *www.hibernianfc.co.uk.*

SIDE TRIPS FROM EDINBURGH

The Lothians is the collective name given to the swath of countryside south of the Firth of Forth and surrounding Edinburgh. Many courtly and aristocratic families lived here, and the region still has the castles and mansions to prove it.

Although the region has always provided rich pickings for historians, it also used to offer even richer pickings for coal miners. Although some black spots still remain, most of the rural countryside is once again a lovely setting for excursions.

13

You can explore a number of historic houses and castles of West Lothian and the Forth Valley, and territory north of the River Forth, in a day or two, or you can just pick one excursion. Stretching east to the sea and south to the Lowlands from Edinburgh, Midlothian is no more than one hour from Edinburgh: Rosslyn Chapel is a highlight.

WEST LOTHIAN AND THE FORTH VALLEY

West Lothian comprises a good bit of Scotland's central belt. The River Forth snakes across a widening floodplain on its descent from the Highlands, and by the time it reaches the western extremities of Edinburgh, it has already passed below the mighty Forth bridges and become a broad estuary. Castles and stately homes sprout thickly on both sides of the Forth.

GETTING HERE AND AROUND

BUS TRAVEL First Bus and Lothian Buses link most of this area, but working out a detailed itinerary by bus isn't always easy.

CAR TRAVEL The Queensferry Road, also known as the A90, is the main thoroughfare running through this region. North of the Forth Bridge, the A985 goes to Culross.

TRAIN TRAVEL Dalmeny and Linlithgow both have rail stations and can be reached from Edinburgh stations.

VISITOR INFORMATION

VisitScotland has an information center about West Lothian in the town of Bo'ness. It's open April to October. Visit West Lothian runs an information center at Burgh Halls in Linlithgow.

ESSENTIALS

Visitor Information VisitScotland ⊠ *Bo'ness Station, Union St., Bo'ness* ☎ *0845/225–5121* ⊕ *www.visitscotland.com/en-us/destinations-maps/ edinburgh-lothians.* **Visit West Lothian** ⊠ *Burgh Halls, The Cross, Linlithgow* ☎ *01506/282720* ⊕ *www.visitwestlothian.co.uk.*

SOUTH QUEENSFERRY
7 miles west of Edinburgh.

This pleasant little waterside community, a former ferry port, is completely dominated by the Forth Bridges, dramatic structures of contrasting architecture that span the Firth of Forth at this historic crossing point. It's near a number of historic and other sights.

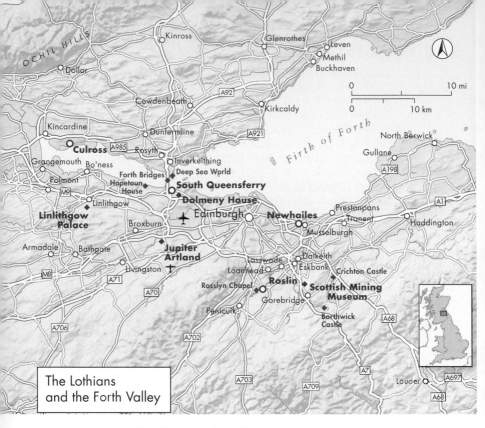

GETTING HERE AND AROUND

The Queensferry Road, also known as the A90, is the main artery north toward the Forth Bridge heading to Hopetoun House.

EXPLORING

Dalmeny House. The first of the stately houses clustered on the western edge of Edinburgh, Dalmeny House is the home of the Earl and Countess of Rosebery. This 1815 Tudor Gothic mansion displays among its sumptuous contents the best of the family's famous collection of 18th-century French furniture. Highlights include the library, the Napoléon Room, the Vincennes and Sevres porcelain collections, and the drawing room, with its tapestries and intricately wrought French furniture. Admission is only by guided tour. ✉ B924 ☎ 0131/331–1888 ⊕ www. dalmeny.co.uk ☑ £8.50 ☉ Tours June–July, Sun.–Wed. 2:15 and 3:30.

FAMILY **Deep Sea World.** The former ferry port in North Queensferry dropped almost into oblivion after the Forth Road Bridge opened, but was dragged abruptly back into the limelight by the hugely popular Deep Sea World. This sophisticated aquarium on the Firth of Forth offers a fascinating view of underwater life. Go down a clear acrylic tunnel for a diver's-eye look at more than 5,000 fish, including 250 sharks (some over 9 feet long); and visit the exhibition hall, which has an Amazon-jungle display and an audiovisual presentation on local marine life. Ichthyophobes will feel more at ease in the adjacent café and gift shop. ✉ *Forthside Terr., North Queensferry* ☎ *01383/411880* ⊕ *www. deepseaworld.com* 💷 *£13* ☉ *Weekdays 10–5, weekends 10–6; last admission 1 hr before closing.*

Forth Rail Bridge. The Forth Rail Bridge was opened in 1890 and at the time hailed as the eighth wonder of the world, at 2,765 yards long; on a hot summer's day it expands by about another yard. Its neighbor is the 1,993-yard-long Forth Road Bridge, in operation since 1964. ✉ *Edinburgh Rd.*

Hopetoun House. The palatial premises of Hopetoun House, probably Scotland's grandest courtly seat and home of the Marquesses of Linlithgow, are considered to be among the Adam family's finest designs. The enormous house was started in 1699 to the original plans of Sir William Bruce (1630–1710), then enlarged between 1721 and 1754 by William Adam (1689–1748) and his sons Robert and John. There's a notable painting collection, and the house has decorative work of the highest order, plus all the trappings to keep you entertained: a nature trail, a restaurant in the former stables, farm shop, and a museum. Much of the wealth that created this sumptuous building came from the family's mining interests in the surrounding regions. ✉ *Off A904, 6 miles west of South Queensferry* ☎ *0131/331-2451* ⊕ *www.hopetoun. co.uk* 💷 *£9.20; grounds only £4.25* ☉ *Apr.–Sept., daily 10:30–5, last admission at 4.*

WHERE TO EAT

$$ × **The Boat House.** Scotland's natural larder is on display at this romantic
MODERN BRITISH restaurant on the banks of the Forth. Seafood is the star of the show, and chef Paul Steward is the man behind the imaginative yet unfussy recipes. Standouts include halibut with an orange, ginger, and peppercorn reduction, panfried Oban scallops, and choice of cuts of steak. If you want a less formal affair, the bistro and cocktail bar next door has a friendly buzz. $ *Average main: £18* ✉ *22 High St.* ☎ *0131/331-5429* ⊕ *www.theboathouse-sq.co.uk.*

JUPITER ARTLAND
10 miles west of Edinburgh.

For anyone drawn to interesting art and beautiful open spaces, a visit to this open-air collection of sculptures by world-renowned artists is a must.

GETTING HERE AND AROUND
To reach Jupiter Artland from Edinburgh, take the A71 toward Kilmarnock. Just after Wilkieston, turn right onto the B7015.

EXPLORING

Fodor'sChoice **Jupiter Artland.** The beautiful grounds of a Jacobean manor house have
★ been transformed by an art-loving couple, Robert and Nicky Wilson, into a sculpture park. With the aid of a map you can explore the magical landscapes and encounter artworks by Andy Goldsworthy, Anya Gallaccio, Jim Lambie, Nathan Coley, Iam Hamilton Finlay, and Anish Kapoor, among many others. A highlight is walking around Charles Jencks's *Cells of Life,* a series of shapely, grass-covered mounds. Run

by First Bus, the 27 and X27 direct buses depart from Regent Road and Dalry Road in Haymarket. ✉ *Bonnington House Steadings, off B7015, Wilkieston, Edinburgh* ☎ *01506/889900* ⊕ *www.jupiterartland.org* ✏ *£8.50* ⊗ *Mid-May–Sept., Thurs.–Sun. 10–5.*

LINLITHGOW PALACE
12 miles west of Edinburgh.

These loch-side ruins retain impressive remnants of what was once the seat of the Stewart kings.

GETTING HERE AND AROUND
From Edinburgh, take the M9 westward to Linlithgow Palace. You can also board a train to Linlithgow Station, a short walk from the palace.

EXPLORING
Linlithgow Palace. On the edge of Linlithgow Loch stands the splendid ruin of Linlithgow Palace, the birthplace of Mary, Queen of Scots in 1542. Burned, perhaps accidentally, by Hanoverian troops during the last Jacobite rebellion in 1746, this impressive shell stands on a site of great antiquity, though it's not certain anything survived an earlier fire in 1424. The palace gatehouse was built in the early 16th century, and the central courtyard's elaborate fountain dates from around 1535. The halls and great rooms are cold, echoing stone husks now in Historic Scotland's care. ✉ *A706, south shore of Linlithgow Loch* ☎ *01506/842896* ⊕ *www.historic-scotland.gov.uk/places* ✏ *£5.50* ⊗ *Apr.–Sept., daily 9:30–5:30; Oct.–Mar., daily 9:30–4:30.*

CULROSS
17 miles northwest of Edinburgh.

The town is a fascinating open-air museum that gives you a feel for life in the 17th and 18th centuries.

GETTING HERE AND AROUND
To get here by car, head north of the Forth Bridge on the A90, then westward on the A985.

EXPLORING
Fodor's Choice ★ **Culross.** With its Mercat Cross, cobbled streets, tolbooth, and narrow wynds (alleys), Culross, on the muddy shores of the Forth, is now a living museum of a 17th-century town and one of the most remarkable little towns in Scotland. It once had a thriving industry and export trade in coal and salt (the coal was used in the salt-panning process). It also had, curiously, a trade monopoly in the manufacture of baking *girdles* (griddles). As local coal became exhausted, the impetus of the industrial revolution passed Culross by, and other parts of the Forth Valley prospered. Culross became a backwater town, and the merchants' houses of the 17th and 18th centuries were never replaced by Victorian developments or modern architecture. In the 1930s the National Trust for Scotland started to buy up the decaying properties. With the help of other agencies, these buildings were brought to life. Today ordinary citizens live in many of the National Trust properties. A few—the Palace, Study, and Town House—are open to the public. ✉ *Off A985, 8 miles south of Dollar* ☎ *0844/493–2189* ⊕ *www.nts.org.uk/visits*

⌨ *£10 ⊙ June–Aug., daily noon–5; Apr., May and Sept., Thurs.–Mon. noon–5; Oct., Fri.–Mon. noon–4; last admission 1 hr before closing.*

MIDLOTHIAN

In spite of the finest stone carving in Scotland at Rosslyn Chapel and miles of rolling countryside, this area immediately south of Edinburgh remained off the beaten path for years. The renewed interest in Rosslyn is changing that, and the fascinating Scottish Mining Museum gives an insight into a harsher aspect of the area's history.

13

GETTING HERE AND AROUND

BUS TRAVEL First buses serve towns and villages throughout Midlothian. For details of all services, inquire at the St. Andrew Square bus station in Edinburgh.

CAR TRAVEL A quick route to Rosslyn Chapel follows the A701, while the A7 heads toward Gorebridge and the Scottish Mining Museum.

TRAIN TRAVEL There is no train service in Midlothian.

ROSLIN

7 miles south of Edinburgh.

Although the town is overshadowed by its chapel, Roslin is a pleasant place to while away some time. There are some nice walks by the North River Esk.

GETTING HERE AND AROUND

By car take the A701 south. Lothian buses also shuttle passengers from Edinburgh.

EXPLORING

Fodor'sChoice **Rosslyn Chapel.** Rosslyn Chapel has always beckoned curious visitors
★ intrigued by the various legends surrounding its magnificent carvings, but today it pulses with tourists as never before. Dan Brown's bestselling novel *The Da Vinci Code* has made visiting this Episcopal chapel (services continue to be held here) an imperative stop for many of its enthusiasts. Whether you're a fan of the book or not—and of the book's theory that the chapel has a secret sign that can lead you to the Holy Grail—this is a site of immense interest. Originally conceived by Sir William Sinclair (circa 1404–80) and dedicated to St. Matthew in 1446, the chapel is outstanding for the quality and variety of the carving inside. Covering almost every square inch of stonework are human figures, animals, and plants. The meaning of these remains subject to many theories; some depict symbols from the medieval order of the Knights Templar and from Freemasonry. The chapel's design called for a cruciform structure, but only the choir and parts of the east transept walls were completed. ⊠ *Chapel Loan* ☎ *0131/440–2159* ⊕ *www. rosslynchapel.com* ⌨ *£9 ⊙ Mon.–Sat. 9:30–5:30, Sun. noon–4:45.*

SCOTTISH MINING MUSEUM •

9 miles southeast of Edinburgh.

The museum provides a sobering look into the lives of coal miners and the conditions they endured down Scotland's mines.

GETTING HERE AND AROUND

To get here by car, head south on the A7 to Newtongrange. You can also take Lothian buses 33 or 29 or First buses 95 or X95.

EXPLORING

Scottish Mining Museum. In the former mining community of Newtongrange, the Scottish Mining Museum provides a good introduction to the history of Scotland's mining industry. With the help of videos you can experience life deep below the ground. There are also interactive displays and "magic helmets" that bring the tour to life and relate the power that the mining company had over the lives of the individual workers here, in Scotland's largest planned mining village. This frighteningly autocratic system survived well into the 1930s—the company owned the houses, shops, and even the pub. The scenery is no more attractive than you would expect, with the green Pentland Hills hovering in the distance. ⊠ *A7* ☎ *0131/663–7519* ⊕ *www.scottishminingmuseum.com* ✉ *£7.50* ☉ *Apr.–Sept., daily 10–5; Oct.–Mar., daily 10–4; last admission 1½ hrs before closing. Guided tours daily at 11:30, 1:30, and 3.*

GLASGOW

WELCOME TO GLASGOW

TOP REASONS TO GO

★ **Design and architecture:** The Victorians left a legacy of striking architecture, and Glasgow's buildings manifest the city's love of grand artistic statements. The Arts and Crafts buildings by Charles Rennie Mackintosh are reason alone to visit.

★ **Art museums:** Some of Britain's best museums and art galleries are in Glasgow, including the Burrell Collection and the Kelvingrove.

★ **Gorgeous parks and gardens:** From Kelvingrove Park to the Botanic Gardens, Glasgow has more parks per square mile than any other city in Europe.

★ **Retail therapy:** The city has become known for cutting-edge design. Look for everything from Scottish specialties to stylish fashions on Ingram and Buchanan streets, or at the elegant Princes Square.

★ **Burns country:** Scotland's national poet lived, wrote, and drank in Ayrshire, a great place to appreciate his work.

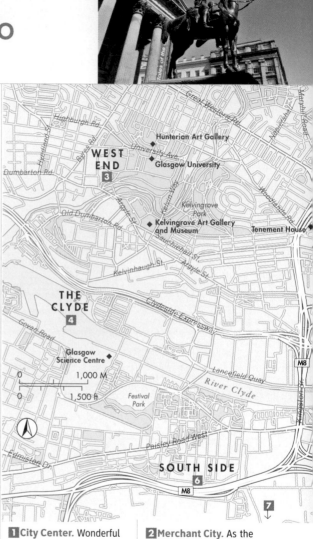

1 City Center. Wonderful Victorian buildings recall the confidence of a burgeoning industrial capital. George Square's City Chambers are worth a visit before you trawl the shops along Buchanan Street, duck into one of the eateries, or explore bars and music venues.

2 Merchant City. As the city expanded along with the growing transatlantic trade, wealthy traders built their palatial houses here. Today the area is busy with restaurants, clubs, and shops.

3 West End. Glasgow University is in this quieter, slightly hillier western part

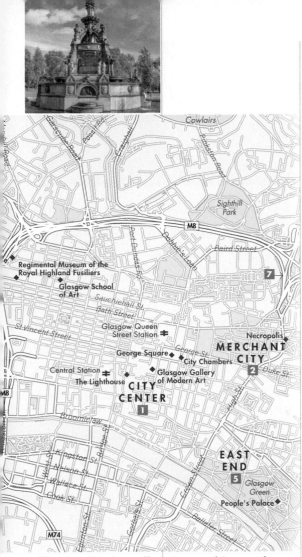

GETTING ORIENTED

Glasgow's layout is hard to read in a single glance. The City Center is roughly defined by the M8 motorway to the north and west, the River Clyde to the south, and High Street to the east. Glaswegians tend to walk a good deal, and the relatively flat and compact City Center, most of which follows a grid pattern, is perfect for pedestrians. The West End has Glasgow University and lovely Kelvingrove Park. The River Clyde, around which Glasgow grew up as a trading city, runs through the center of the city—literally cutting it in two.

14

of the city, which shows off a more bohemian side of Glasgow. Treasures include the Botanic Gardens and the Kelvingrove Art Gallery and Museum.

4 **The Clyde.** Once lined with shipyards, the Clyde has been reborn as a relaxing destination. The Glasgow Science Centre and the Museum of Transport face each other across the water.

5 **East End.** Glasgow Green's wonderful People's Palace draws visitors, and on weekends the nearby Barras market is a reminder of the area's past.

6 **South Side.** Often overlooked, this less visited side of the city has two world-class museums in beautiful Pollok Park: the handsome Burrell Collection and Pollok House, with its art collection.

7 **Side Trips.** An hour or less from Glasgow are some fascinating day trips. Check out Robert Burns sites in Ayr and Alloway, or visit castles, museums, and historic sites.

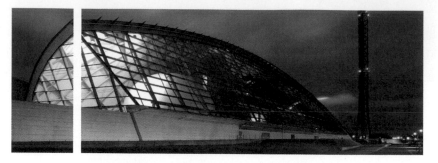

Updated
by Mike
Gonzalez

Trendy stores, a booming cultural life, fascinating architecture, and stylish restaurants reinforce Glasgow's claim to being Scotland's most exciting city. After decades of decline, it has experienced an urban renaissance uniquely its own. The city's grand architecture reflects a prosperous past built on trade and shipbuilding. Today buildings by Charles Rennie Mackintosh hold pride of place along with the Zaha Hadid–designed Riverside Museum.

Glasgow (the "dear green place," as it was known) was founded some 1,500 years ago. Legend has it that the king of Strathclyde, irate about his wife's infidelity, had a ring he had given her thrown into the River Clyde. (Apparently she had passed it on to an admirer.) When the king demanded to know where the ring had gone, the distraught queen asked the advice of her confessor, St. Mungo. He suggested fishing for it—and the first salmon to emerge had the ring in its mouth. The moment is commemorated on the city's coat of arms.

The medieval city expanded when it was given a royal license to trade; the current High Street was the main thoroughfare at the time. The vast profits earned in Glasgow from trading American cotton and tobacco paid for the grand mansions of the Merchant City in the 18th century. In the 19th century the River Clyde became the center of a shipbuilding industry, fed by the city's iron and steel works. The city grew again, but its internal divisions grew at the same time. The West End harbored the elegant homes of the shipyard owners. Down by the river, areas like the infamous Gorbals, with its crowded slums, sheltered the laborers who built the ships.

During the 19th century the population grew from 80,000 to more than a million. The new prosperity gave Glasgow its grand neoclassical buildings, such as those built by Alexander "Greek" Thomson, as well as the adventurous visionary buildings designed by Charles Rennie Mackintosh and others who produced Glasgow's Arts and Crafts movement. The City Chambers, built in 1888, are a proud statement in marble and gold sandstone, a clear symbol of the wealthy and powerful Victorian industrialists' hopes for the future.

The decline of shipbuilding and the closure of the factories led to much speculation as to what direction the city would take. The curious thing is that, at least in part, the past gave the city a new lease on life. It was as if people looked at their city and saw Glasgow's beauty for the first time: its extraordinarily rich architectural heritage, its leafy parks, its artistic heritage, and its complex social history. Today Glasgow is a vibrant cultural center and a commercial hub, as well as a launching pad from which to explore the rest of Scotland. In fact, it takes only 40 minutes to reach Loch Lomond, where the other Scotland begins.

14

GLASGOW PLANNER

WHEN TO GO

The best times to visit Glasgow are spring and summer. Although you may encounter crowds, the weather is more likely to be warm and dry. In summer the days are long and pleasant—that is, if the rain holds off—and festivals and outdoor events are abundant. Fall can be nice, although cold weather begins to set in after mid-September.

PLANNING YOUR TIME

You could quite easily spend five comfortable days here, although in a pinch, two would do and three would be pleasant. On the first day explore the city's medieval heritage, taking in Glasgow Cathedral, the Museum of Religious Life, and Provand's Lordship, as well as the Necropolis with its fascinating crumbling monuments. It is a gentle walk from here to the Merchant City and George Square, around which spread the active and crowded shopping areas. The Mackintosh Trail will take you to the many buildings designed by this outstanding Glasgow designer and architect. Another day could be well spent between the Kelvingrove Art Gallery (you can lunch here and listen to the daily concert on its magnificent organ) and the nearby Hunterian Art Gallery. From here it's only minutes to lively Byres Road and its shops, pubs, and cafés. Another option for art lovers is to go to the South Side and make a beeline for the Burrell Collection and the House for an Art Lover.

If you have a few extra days, head out to Burns country and the extraordinary Burns Birthplace Museum in Ayrshire. It's a scenic 45-minute drive from Glasgow. Most destinations on the Clyde Coast are easily accessible from Glasgow. Direct trains from Central Station take you to a variety of top sights in less than an hour.

GETTING HERE AND AROUND
AIR TRAVEL
Airlines flying from Glasgow Airport to the rest of the United Kingdom and to Europe include Aer Lingus, Air Malta, British Airways, easyJet, Icelandair, and KLM. Several carriers fly from North America, including Air Canada, American Airlines, United, and Icelandair (service via Reykjavík).

Ryanair offers rock-bottom airfares between Prestwick and London's Stansted Airport. Budget-minded easyJet has similar services from Glasgow to London's Stansted and Luton airports. Loganair flies to the islands.

Air Contacts Aer Lingus ☎ *0871/718–2020* ⊕ *www.aerlingus.com.* **Air Canada** ☎ *0871/220–1111* ⊕ *www.aircanada.com.* **Air Malta** ☎ *00356/607–3710* ⊕ *www.airmalta.com.* **American Airlines** ☎ *0844/499–7300* ⊕ *www.americanairlines.co.uk.* **BMI Regional** ☎ *0844/848–4888* ⊕ *www.bmiregional.com.* **British Airways** ☎ *0844/493–0787* ⊕ *www.britishairways.com.* **easyJet** ☎ *0871/244–2366* ⊕ *www.easyjet.com.* **Icelandair** ☎ *0844/811–1190* ⊕ *www.icelandair.com.* **KLM** ☎ *0871/231–0000* ⊕ *www.klm.com.* **Loganair** ☎ *0871/848–7594* ⊕ *www.loganair.co.uk.* **Ryanair** ☎ *0871/246–0000* ⊕ *www.ryanair.com.* **United** ☎ *0845/844–4777* ⊕ *www.united.com.*

AIRPORTS Glasgow Airport is about 7 miles west of downtown on the M8 to Greenock. The airport serves international and domestic flights, and most major European carriers have frequent and convenient connections (some via airports in England) to many cities on the continent. Prestwick Airport sits on the Ayrshire coast about 30 miles southwest of Glasgow. Eclipsed for some years by Glasgow Airport, Prestwick has grown in importance, not least because of lower airfares from Ryanair.

Airport Contacts Glasgow Airport ✉ *Caledonia Way, Paisley* ☎ *0844/481–5555* ⊕ *www.glasgowairport.com.* **Prestwick Airport** ✉ *A79, Prestwick* ☎ *0871/223–0700* ⊕ *www.gpia.co.uk.*

TRANSFERS Although there's a railway station about 2 miles from Glasgow Airport (Paisley Gilmour Street), most people travel downtown by bus or taxi. It takes about 20 minutes, slightly longer at rush hour. Metered taxis are available outside domestic arrivals, and cost around £22.

Express buses run from Glasgow Airport (outside departures lobby) to Central and Queen Street stations and to the Buchanan Street bus station. They depart every 15 minutes throughout the day. The fare is £6.

The drive from Glasgow Airport into the center of the city is normally quite easy, even if you're used to driving on the right. The M8 motorway runs beside the airport (Junction 29) and takes you straight into the Glasgow's downtown core. Thereafter Glasgow's streets follow a grid pattern, at least in the City Center. A map is useful—get one from the car-rental company.

Most companies that provide chauffeur-driven cars and tours will also do limousine airport transfers. A company that is currently a member of the Greater Glasgow and Clyde Valley Tourist Board is Charlton.

An hourly coach service makes trips to Glasgow from Prestwick Airport, but takes much longer than the train. There's a rapid half-hourly train service (hourly on Sunday) direct from the terminal to Glasgow Central. Strathclyde Passenger Transport and ScotRail offer a discount ticket that allows you to travel for half the standard fare; just show a valid airline ticket for a flight to or from Prestwick Airport.

By car, the City Center is reached via the fast M77 in about 40 minutes (longer in rush hour). Metered taxis are available at the airport. The fare to Glasgow is about £40.

Airport Transfer Contacts Charlton ☎ *0870/058–9500* ⊕ *www.charltonlimo. com.* **ScotRail** ☎ *0845/601–5929* ⊕ *www.scotrail.co.uk.*

BUS TRAVEL

The main intercity operators are National Express and Scottish City-link, which serve numerous towns and cities in Scotland, Wales, and England, including London and Edinburgh. Glasgow's bus station is on Buchanan Street, not far from Queen Street Station.

When traveling from the City Center to either the West End or the South Side, it's easy to use the city's integrated network of buses, subways, and trains. Service is reliable and connections are convenient from buses to trains and the subway. Many buses require exact fare, which is usually around £1.75.

14

Traveline Scotland provides information on schedules and fares, as does the Strathclyde Passenger Transport Travel Centre, which has an information center.

Bus Contacts Buchanan Street Bus Station ✉ *Killermont St., City Center* ☎ *0141/333–3708* ⊕ *www.spt.co.uk.* **National Express** ☎ *0871/781–8181* ⊕ *www.nationalexpressgroup.com.* **Scottish Citylink** ☎ *0871/266–3333* ⊕ *www.citylink.co.uk.* **Strathclyde Passenger Transport Travel Centre** ✉ *12 W. George St., City Center* ☎ *0141/332–6811* ⊕ *www.spt.co.uk* ◷ *Mon.– Thurs. 8:30–4:45, Fri. 8:30–4.* **Traveline Scotland** ☎ *0871/200–2233* ⊕ *www. travelinescotland.com.*

CAR TRAVEL

If you're driving to Glasgow from England and the south of Scotland, you'll probably approach the city via the M6, M74, or A74. Downtown is clearly marked from these roads. From Edinburgh, the M8 leads to the center of the city. From the north, the A82 from Fort William and the A82/M80 from Stirling join the M8 downtown.

You don't need a car in Glasgow, and you're probably better off without one. Although most modern hotels have their own lots, parking can be trying. In the City Center meters are expensive, running about £2.40 per hour during the day. In the West End they cost 40 pence per hour, but you often have to feed the meter until 10 pm. Don't even consider parking illegally, as fines are upward of £30. Multistory garages are open 24 hours a day at the following locations: Anderston Centre, George Street, Waterloo Place, Mitchell Street, Cambridge Street, and Concert Square. Rates run between £1 and £2 per hour. More convenient are the park-and-ride operations at some subway stations (Kelvinbridge, Bridge Street, and Shields Road). You'll be downtown in no time.

SUBWAY TRAVEL

Glasgow's small subway system—with 15 stations—is useful for reaching all the City Center and West End attractions. Stations are marked by a prominent letter "S." You can choose between flat fares (£1.40) and a one-day pass (£2.60). Trains run regularly from Monday through Saturday, with more limited Sunday service. The distance between many central stops is no more than a 10-minute walk. More information is available from Strathclyde Passenger Transport Travel Centre.

TAXI TRAVEL

Taxis are a fast and cost-effective way to get around. You'll find metered taxis (usually black and of the London sedan type) at stands all over downtown. Most have radio dispatch. Some have also been adapted to take wheelchairs. You can hail a cab on the street if its "for hire" sign is illuminated. A typical ride from the City Center to the West End or the South Side costs around £6.

Taxi Contact Glasgow Taxis ☎ *0141/429–7070* ⊕ *www.glasgowtaxisltd.co.uk.*

TRAIN TRAVEL

Glasgow has two main rail stations: Central and Queen Street. Central serves trains from London's Euston station (five hours), which come via Crewe and Carlisle in England. East Coast trains run from London's Kings Cross to Glasgow's Queen Street Station. Central also serves other cities in the northwest of England and towns in the southwest of Scotland. Trains run from here to Prestwick Airport.

Queen Street Station has frequent connections to Edinburgh (50 minutes), from where you can head south to Newcastle, York, and King's Cross. Other trains from Queen Street head north to Stirling, Perth, Dundee, Aberdeen, Inverness, Kyle of Lochalsh, Wick, and Thurso, and on the scenic West Highland line to Oban, Fort William, and Mallaig. For details contact National Rail.

A regular bus service links the Queen Street and Central stations (although you can easily walk if you aren't too encumbered). Queen Street is near the Buchanan Street subway station, and Central is close to St. Enoch. Taxis are available at both stations.

The Glasgow area has an extensive network of suburban railway services. Locals still call them the Blue Trains, even though most are now painted maroon and cream. For more information and a free map, contact the Strathclyde Passenger Transport Travel Centre or National.

Train Contacts National Rail ☎ *08457/484950* ⊕ *www.nationalrail.co.uk.*

TOURS

You can sign on for a sightseeing tour to get a different perspective on the city and the surrounding area.

BOAT TOURS

Cruises are available on Loch Lomond and to the islands in the Firth of Clyde; contact the Greater Glasgow and Clyde Valley Tourist Board for details. Contact Waverley Excursions for a ride on the *Waverley* paddle steamer from June through August.

Contacts Waverley Excursions ✉ *36 Lancefield Quay* ☎ *0845/221–8152* ⊕ *www.waverleyexcursions.co.uk.*

BUS TOURS

The popular City Sightseeing bus tours leave daily from the west side of George Square. The Greater Glasgow and Clyde Valley Tourist Board can give information about city tours and about longer tours northward to the Highlands and Islands.

Day trips in minivans (16 people maximum) to the surrounding areas, including Loch Lomond and Oban, are available from Rabbie's Trail Burners.

Contacts City Sightseeing ✉ *153 Queen St.* ☎ *0141/204–0444* ⊕ *www. citysightseeingglasgow.co.uk* 🎫 *£12.* **Rabbie's Trail Burners** ☎ *0845/643–2248* ⊕ *www.rabbies.com.*

PRIVATE GUIDES

Little's Chauffeur Drive arranges personally tailored car-and-driver tours, both locally and throughout Scotland. The Scottish Tourist Guides Association also provides a private-guide service.

Glasgow Taxis offers city tours. If you allow the driver to follow a set route, the cost is £38 for up to five people and lasts around an hour. A two-hour tour costs £59. You can book tours in advance and be picked up and dropped off wherever you like.

Contacts Glasgow Taxis ☎ *0141/429–7070* ⊕ *www.glasgowtaxisltd.co.uk* 🚕 *A city tour costs £38 per taxi (1hr 20mins).* **Little's Chauffeur Drive** ☎ *0141/883–2111* ⊕ *www.littles.co.uk.* **Scottish Tourist Guides Association** ☎ *01786/447784* ⊕ *www.stga.co.uk.*

WALKING TOURS

The Greater Glasgow and Clyde Valley Tourist Board can provide information on special walks on a given day. Glasgow Walking Tours organizes specialized tours of the city's architectural treasures.

Contacts Glasgow Walking Tours ☎ *07751/978935* ⊕ *www.greetin glasgow.com.*

VISITOR INFORMATION

The Greater Glasgow and Clyde Valley Tourist Board provides information about different types of tours and has an accommodations-booking service, a currency-exchange office, and a money-transfer service. Books, maps, and souvenirs are also available. The tourist board has a branch at Glasgow Airport, too.

Contact Greater Glasgow and Clyde Valley Tourist Board ✉ *170 Buchanan St., City Center* ☎ *0845/859–1006* ⊕ *www.visitscotland.com/glasgow* ⊙ *Daily 9–5.*

EXPLORING GLASGOW

As cities go, Glasgow is contained and compact. It's set up on a grid system, so it's easy to navigate and explore, and the best way to tackle it is on foot. In the eastern part of the city, start by exploring Glasgow Cathedral and other highlights of the oldest section of the city, then wander through the rest of the Merchant City. From there you can just continue into the City Center with its designer shops, art galleries, and eateries. From here you can either walk (it takes a good 45 minutes) or take the subway to the West End. There, visit the Botanic Gardens, Glasgow University, and the Kelvingrove Art Gallery and Museum. Then take a taxi to the South Side to experience the Burrell Collection and Pollok House. For Glasgow's East End, walk down High Street

14

from the Cathedral to the Tron Cross; from there you can walk to the Barras and Glasgow Green.

If you break your sightseeing up into neighborhoods, it's completely manageable to explore a variety of places in three days. Glasgow's pubs and clubs serve up entertainment until late in the evening; there's something for everyone.

CITY CENTER

Along the streets of this area are some of the best examples of the architectural confidence and exuberance that so characterized the burgeoning Glasgow of the turn of the 20th century. There are also plenty of shops, trendy eateries, and pubs.

GETTING HERE   Every form of public transportation can bring you here, from bus to train to subway. Head to George Square and walk from there.

TOP ATTRACTIONS

City Chambers. Dominating the east side of George Square, this exuberant expression of Victorian confidence, built by William Young in Italian Renaissance style, was opened by Queen Victoria in 1888. Among the interior's outstanding features are the entrance hall's vaulted ceiling, sustained by granite columns topped with marble, the marble-and-alabaster staircases, and Venetian mosaics. The enormous banqueting hall has murals illustrating Glasgow's history. Free guided tours lasting about an hour depart weekdays at 10:30 and 2:30. ■TIP→ The building is closed to visitors during civic functions. ⊠ 80 George Sq., City Center ☎ 0141/287–4020 ⊕ www.glasgow.gov.uk ☑ Free ⊙ Weekdays 9–5 Ⓜ Buchanan St.

George Square. The focal point of Glasgow is lined with an impressive collection of statues of worthies: Queen Victoria; Scotland's national poet, Robert Burns (1759–96); the inventor and developer of the steam engine, James Watt (1736–1819); Prime Minister William Gladstone (1809–98); and towering above them all, Scotland's great historical novelist, Sir Walter Scott (1771–1832). The column was intended for George III (1738–1820), after whom the square is named, but when he was found to be insane toward the end of his reign, his statue was never erected. ⊠ Between St. Vincent and Argyle Sts., City Center Ⓜ Buchanan St.

Fodor's Choice   **Glasgow School of Art.** This is the most stunning example of the genius
★   of architect Charles Rennie Mackintosh, who was only 28 when he won the commission. He worked on every detail—down to the interior design, furnishings, and lighting—to make this iconic art nouveau building, built between 1897 and 1909, a unified whole. The building still functions as an art school. A major fire in May 2014 damaged the historic building; call or check the website for visiting and tour updates. The School of Art also organizes walking tours of Mackintosh's Glasgow that cost £19.50. ⊠ 11 Dalhousie St., City Center ☎ 0141/353–4526 ⊕ www.gsa.ac.uk/tours ☑ Tours £9.75 ⊙ Building daily 10:30–5. Exhibitions Mon.–Sat. 10:30–4:30, Sat. 10–2. Due to the fire, check ahead for visiting and tour schedule. Ⓜ Cowcaddens.

Glasgow Gallery of Modern Art. One of Glasgow's boldest, most innovative galleries occupies the neoclassical former Royal Exchange building. The modern art, craft, and design collections include works by Scottish conceptual artists such as David Mach, and also paintings and sculptures from around the world, including Papua New Guinea, Ethiopia, and Mexico. Each floor of the gallery reflects one of the elements—air, fire, earth, and water—which creates some unexpected juxtapositions and also allows for various interactive exhibits. In the basement are a café and an extensive library. The exchange building, designed by David Hamilton (1768–1843) and finished in 1829, was a meeting place for merchants and traders; later it became Stirling's Library. ⊠ *Queen St., City Center* ☎ *0141/229–1996* ⊕ *www.glasgowmuseums.com* ✉ *Free* ☉ *Mon.–Wed. 10–5, Thurs. 10–8, Fri.–Sun. 11–5* Ⓜ *Buchanan St.*

The Lighthouse. Charles Rennie Mackintosh designed these former offices of the *Glasgow Herald* newspaper in 1893, with its emblematic Mackintosh Tower. Today it serves as Scotland's **Centre for Architecture, Design and the City,** which celebrates all facets of the architectural field. On the third floor the **Mackintosh Interpretation Centre** is a great starting point for discovering more about this groundbreaking architect's work, illustrated in a glass wall with alcoves containing models of his buildings. From here you can climb the more than 130 steps up the tower and, once you have caught your breath, look out over Glasgow. The fifth-floor Doocot Cafe is a great place to take a break from sightseeing. Building tours cost £5. ⊠ *11 Mitchell La., City Center* ☎ *0141/271–5365* ⊕ *www.thelighthouse.co.uk* ✉ *Free* ☉ *Mon–Sat. 10:30–5* Ⓜ *St. Enoch.*

WORTH NOTING

Tenement House. This ordinary first-floor apartment is anything but ordinary inside: it was occupied from 1937 to 1982 by Agnes Toward (and before that by her mother), who seems never to have thrown anything away. Her legacy is this fascinating time capsule, painstakingly preserved with her everyday furniture and belongings. The red-sandstone building dates from 1892 and can be found in the Garnethill area north of Charing Cross station. A small museum explores the life and times of its careful occupant. ⊠ *145 Buccleuch St., City Center* ☎ *0844/493–2197* ⊕ *www.nts.org.uk* ✉ *£6.50* ☉ *Mar.–Oct., daily 1–5; last admission at 4:30* Ⓜ *Cowcaddens.*

MERCHANT CITY

Near the remnants of medieval Glasgow is the Merchant City, with some of the city's most important Georgian and Victorian buildings, many of them built by prosperous tobacco merchants. Today the area is noted for its trendy eateries and for the designer stores that line Ingram Street and others. Many of Glasgow's young and upwardly mobile make their home here, in converted buildings ranging from warehouses to the old Sheriff's Court. Shopping here is expensive, but the area is worth visiting if you're seeking the youthful Glasgow style. Stick to well-lit, well-traveled areas after sunset.

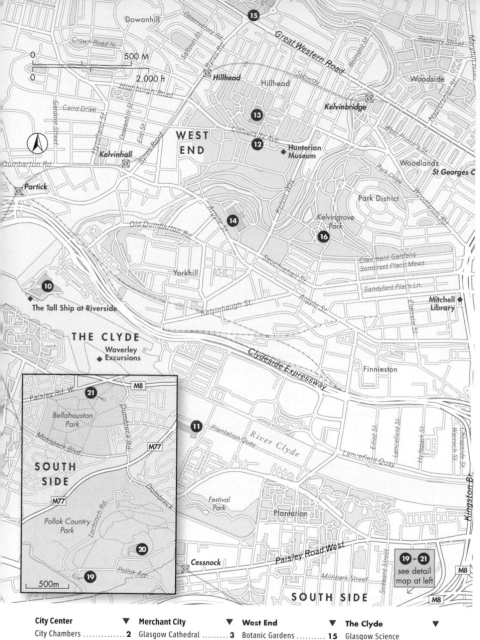

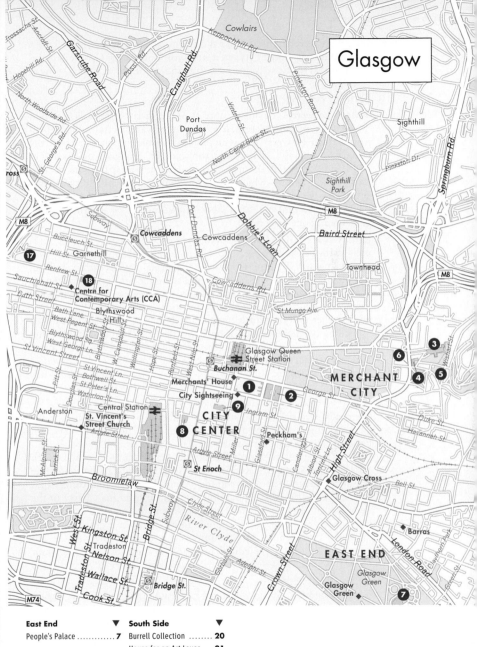

Glasgow

GETTING HERE Buchanan Street is the handiest subway station when you want to explore the Merchant City, as it puts you directly on George Square. You can also easily walk from Central Station or the St. Enoch subway station.

TOP ATTRACTIONS

Fodor's Choice **Glasgow Cathedral.** The most complete of Scotland's cathedrals (it would
★ have been more complete had 19th-century vandals not pulled down its two rugged towers), this is an unusual double church, one above the other, dedicated to Glasgow's patron saint, St. Mungo. Consecrated in 1136 and completed about 300 years later, it was spared the ravages of the Reformation—which destroyed so many of Scotland's medieval churches—mainly because Glasgow's trade guilds defended it. A late-medieval open-timber roof in the nave and lovely 20th-century stained glass are notable features.

In the lower church is the splendid crypt of St. Mungo, who was originally known as St. Kentigern (*kentigern* means "chief word"), but who was nicknamed St. Mungo (meaning "dear one") by his early followers. The site of the tomb has been revered since the 6th century, when St. Mungo founded a church here. Mungo features prominently in local legends; one such legend is about a pet bird that he nursed back to life, and another tells of a bush or tree, the branches of which he used to miraculously relight a fire. The bird, the tree, and the salmon with a ring in its mouth (from another story) are all found on the city's coat of arms, together with a bell that Mungo brought from Rome. ⊠ *Cathedral St., Merchant City* ☎ *0141/552–8198* 🖃 *Free* ☉ *Apr.–Sept., Mon.–Sat. 9:30–5:30, Sun. 1–5; Oct.–Mar., Mon.–Sat. 9:30–4:30, Sun. 1–4:30* Ⓜ *Buchanan St.*

Fodor's Choice **Necropolis.** A burial ground since the beginning of recorded history, the
★ large Necropolis, modeled on the famous Père-Lachaise Cemetery in Paris, contains some extraordinarily elaborate Victorian tombs. A great place to take it all in is from the monument of John Knox (1514–72), the leader of Scotland's Reformation, which stands at the top of the hill at the heart of the Necropolis. Around it are grand tombs that resemble classical palaces, Egyptian tombs, or even the Chapel of the Templars in Jerusalem. The Necropolis was designed as a place for meditation, which is why it is much more than just a graveyard. The main gates are behind the St. Mungo Museum of Religious Art and Life. Call ahead for free guided tours. ⊠ *70 Cathedral Sq., Merchant City* ☎ *0141/287–5064* ⊕ *www.glasgownecropolis.org* 🖃 *Free* ☉ *Daily 7–dusk* Ⓜ *Buchanan St.*

Provand's Lordship. Glasgow's oldest house was built in 1471 by Bishop Andrew Muirhead. Before it was rescued by the Glasgow City Council, this building had been a pub, a sweetshop, and a soft drinks factory. It is now a museum that shows the house as it might have looked when it was occupied by officers of the church. The top floor is a gallery with prints and paintings depicting the characters who might have lived in the surrounding streets. ⊠ *3 Castle St., Merchant City* ☎ *0141/552–8819* ⊕ *www.glasgowmuseums.com* 🖃 *Free* ☉ *Tues.–Thurs. and Sat. 10–5, Fri. and Sun. 11–5* Ⓜ *Buchanan St.*

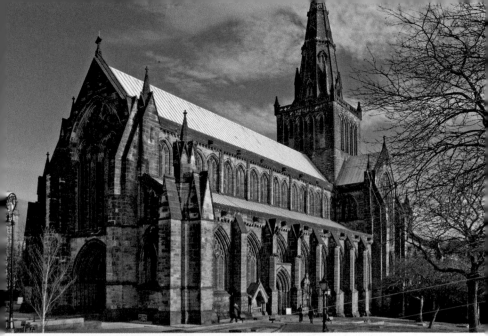

Medieval Glasgow Cathedral has the crypt of St. Mungo and a magnificent open-timber roof in the nave.

WORTH NOTING

St. Mungo Museum of Religious Life and Art. An outstanding collection of artifacts, including Celtic crosses and statuettes of Hindu gods, reflects the many religious groups that have settled throughout the centuries in Glasgow and the west of Scotland. A Zen Garden creates a peaceful setting for rest and contemplation, and elsewhere stained-glass windows include a depiction of St. Mungo himself. Pause to look at the beautiful Chilkat Blanketwofven, made from cedar bark and wool by the Tlingit people of North America. ⊠ *2 Castle St., City Center* ☎ *0141/276–1625* ⊕ *www.glasgowmuseums.com* 🖃 *Free* ☉ *Tues.–Thurs. and Sat. 10–5, Fri. and Sun. 11–5* Ⓜ *Buchanan St.*

WEST END

Glasgow University dominates the West End, creating a vibrant neighborhood. Founded in 1451, the university is the third oldest in Scotland, after St. Andrews and Aberdeen. The industrialists and merchants who built their grand homes on Great Western Road and the adjacent streets endowed museums and art galleries and commissioned artists to decorate and design their homes, as a stroll around the area will quickly reveal. In summer the beautiful Botanical Gardens, with the iconic glasshouse that is the Kibble Palace, become a stage for new and unusual versions of Shakespeare's plays. A good way to save money is to picnic in the park (weather permitting, of course).

GETTING HERE The best way to get to the West End from the City Center is by subway; get off at the Hillhead station. A taxi is another option.

TOP ATTRACTIONS

FAMILY **Botanic Gardens.** When the sun shines, the Botanics (as they're known to locals) quickly fill up with people enjoying the extensive lawns, beautiful flower displays, and herb garden. At the heart of the gardens is the spectacular circular glasshouse, the **Kibble Palace**, a favorite haunt of Glaswegian families. Originally built in 1873, it was the conservatory of a Victorian eccentric named John Kibble. Its domed, interlinked greenhouses contain tree ferns, palm trees, and the Tropicarium, where you can experience the lushness of a rain forest and briefly forget the weather outside. Another greenhouse holds a world-famous collection of orchids. ⊠ *730 Great Western Rd., West End* ☎ *0141/276–1614* ⊕ *www.glasgow.gov.uk* ✉ *Free* ⊙ *Gardens daily 7–dusk; Kibble Palace Mar.–mid-Oct., daily 10–6; mid-Oct.–Feb., daily 10–4:15* Ⓜ *Hillhead.*

MACKINTOSH TRAIL
Mackintosh Trail Ticket. If you're interested in architect Charles Rennie Mackintosh, this is an excellent and economical way of seeing his work. Tickets cost £16 and include admission to all Mackintosh sites across Glasgow, as well as transportation on subways or buses. Tickets can be purchased online or at the individual sites. ☎ *0141/946–6600* ⊕ *www.crmsociety.com.*

Glasgow University. Gorgeous grounds and great views of the city are among the many reasons to visit this university. The Gilbert Scott Building, the university's main edifice, was built more than a century ago and is a lovely example of the Gothic Revival style. **Glasgow University Visitor Centre,** near the main gate on University Avenue, has exhibits on the university, a small coffee bar, and a gift shop; it's the starting point for one-hour guided walking tours of the campus. A self-guided tour starts at the visitor center and takes in the east and west quadrangles, the cloisters, Professor's Square, Pearce Lodge, and the not-to-be-missed University Chapel. ⊠ *University Ave., West End* ☎ *0141/330–5511* ⊕ *www.glasgow.ac.uk* ✉ *Tour £10* ⊙ *Tours on Thurs., Fri., and weekends* Ⓜ *Hillhead.*

Hunterian Art Gallery. Opposite Glasgow University's main gate, this gallery houses William Hunter's (1718–83) collection of paintings. You'll also find prints, drawings, and sculptures by Tintoretto, Rembrandt, and Auguste Rodin, as well as a major collection of paintings by James McNeill Whistler, who had a great affection for the city that bought one of his earliest paintings. Also in the gallery is a replica of **Charles Rennie Mackintosh's town house,** which once stood nearby. The rooms contain Mackintosh's distinctive art nouveau chairs, tables, beds, and cupboards, and the walls are decorated in the equally distinctive style devised by him and his artist wife Margaret. ⊠ *Hillhead St., West End* ☎ *0141/330–5431* ⊕ *www.hunterian.gla.ac.uk* ✉ *Free* ⊙ *Tues.–Sat. 10–5, Sun. 11–4* Ⓜ *Hillhead.*

FAMILY
Fodor's Choice
★
Kelvingrove Art Gallery and Museum. Worthy of its world-class reputation, the Kelvingrove attracts local families as well as international visitors. The stunning red-sandstone edifice is an appropriate home for works by Botticelli, Rembrandt, Monet, and others, and its Glasgow Room houses extraordinary works by local artists. Whether the subject is

The outstanding Kelvingrove Art Gallery and Museum presents engaging displays focusing on Scottish art, design, and culture.

Scottish culture, design, or storytelling, every wall and room begs you to look deeper; labels are thought provoking and sometimes witty. You could spend a weekend here, but in a pinch three hours would do one level justice—there are three. Leave time to visit the gift shop and the attractive basement restaurant. Daily recitals on the massive organ (usually at 1) are well worth the trip. ⊠ *Argyle St., West End* ☎ *0141/276–9599* ⊕ *www.glasgowmuseums.com* ⊠ *Free* ☺ *Mon.–Thurs. and Sat. 10–5, Fri. and Sun. 11–5* Ⓜ *Kelvinhall.*

FAMILY **Kelvingrove Park.** A peaceful retreat, the park was purchased by the city in 1852 and takes its name from the River Kelvin, which flows through it. Among the numerous statues of prominent Glaswegians is one of Lord Kelvin (1824–1907), the Scottish mathematician and physicist who pioneered a great deal of work in electricity. The shady park has a massive fountain commemorating a lord provost of Glasgow from the 1850s, a duck pond, and playground, as well as an excellent eatery. ⊠ *Bounded by Sauchiehall St., Woodlands Rd., and Kelvin Way, West End* Ⓜ *Kelvinhall.*

THE CLYDE

The Clyde River has long been the city's main artery, first as a trading route and later as the place where massive shipyards built everything from warships to ocean liners. The cranes can still be seen today. The Riverside Museum commemorates the great days of shipbuilding, while the Glasgow Science Centre proclaims Glasgow's more modern offerings.

Charles Rennie Mackintosh

Not so long ago, the furniture of innovative Glasgow-born architect Charles Rennie Mackintosh (1868–1928) was broken up for firewood. Today art books are devoted to his distinctive, astonishingly elegant Arts and Crafts– and art nouveau–influenced interiors.

Early influences on his work included the Pre-Raphaelites, James McNeill Whistler (1834–1903), Aubrey Beardsley (1872–98), and Japanese art. But by the 1890s a distinct Glasgow style developed.

The building for the *Glasgow Herald* newspaper, which he designed in 1893, and which is now the Lighthouse Centre for Architecture, Design and the City, was soon followed by other major Glasgow buildings: Queen Margaret's Medical College; the Martyrs Public School; tearooms including the Willow Tearoom (still open); the Hill House, in Helensburgh, now owned by the National Trust for Scotland; and Queen's Cross Church, completed in 1899 and now the headquarters of the Charles Rennie Mackintosh Society. In 1897 Mackintosh began work on a new home for the Glasgow School of Art, recognized as one of his major achievements. A severe fire in 2014 damaged the historic school building; check ahead before you visit.

Mackintosh married Margaret Macdonald in 1900, and in later years her decorative work enhanced the buildings' interiors. Mackintosh died in London in 1928.

After 1904 architectural taste had turned against Mackintosh's style; his work was seen as strange. His reputation revived only in the 1950s with the publication of his monographs, and has continued to grow over time.

HOW TO SEE HIS WORK
Glasgow is the best place in the world to admire Mackintosh's work: in addition to the buildings mentioned above, most of which can be visited, the Hunterian Art Gallery contains magnificent reconstructions of the principal rooms at 78 Southpark Avenue, Mackintosh's Glasgow home. Original drawings, documents, and records, plus the re-creation of a room at 78 Derngate, Northampton are also on display. The Kelvingrove Art Gallery and Museum also has exhibits of his creations in several galleries. A Mackintosh Trail Ticket, purchased online or at various sites, is a good deal if you're visiting multiple sites: see ⊕ *www.crmsociety.com.*

GETTING HERE   From the Partick subway station it's a 10-minute walk to the Riverside Museum. From there it's a short stroll along the river to the Glasgow Science Centre.

TOP ATTRACTIONS

FAMILY   **Glasgow Science Centre.** Families with children love this museum, which has a fun-packed interactive Science Mall, an IMAX theater, and the futuristic Glasgow Tower. In the three-level Science Mall, state-of-the-art displays educate kids and adults about exploration, discovery, and the environment. The ScottishPower Planetarium has a fantastic Zeiss Starmaster projector, which allows you to gaze at the glittering stars. Set aside half a day to see everything. The museum's setting, on the banks of the Clyde, sets it off beautifully. ✉ *50 Pacific Quay, Clyde* ☎ *0141/420–5000* ⊕ *www.glasgowsciencecentre.org* ✆ *£9.95; planetarium £2.50* ⊙ *Apr.–Oct., daily 10–5; Nov.–Mar., Wed.–Sun. 10–5* Ⓜ *Cessnock.*

FAMILY

Fodor's Choice

★

Riverside Museum: Scotland's Museum of Transport and Travel. Designed by Zaha Hadid to celebrate the area's industrial heritage, this huge metal structure with curving walls echoes the covered yards where ships were built on the Clyde. Glasgow's shipbuilding history is remembered with a world-famous collection of ship models. You can wander down Main Street, circa 1930, without leaving the building: the pawnbroker, funeral parlor, and Italian restaurant are all frozen in time. Relax with a coffee in the café, wander out onto the expansive riverside walk, or board the Tall Ship that is moored permanently behind the museum. Bus 100 from George Square brings you here, or you can walk from the Partick subway station in 10 minutes. ✉ *100 Poundhouse Pl., Clyde* ☎ *0141/287–2720* ⊕ *www.glasgowlife.org.uk/museums/riverside* ✆ *Free* ⊙ *Mon.–Thurs. and Sat. 10–5, Fri. and Sun. 11–5* Ⓜ *Partick.*

14

EAST END

Glasgow Green has always been the heart of Glasgow's East End, a formerly down-at-heel neighborhood that has seen many changes over the past several years. One of the top attractions is the People's Palace, which tells the story of daily life in the city. On Sunday head to the nearby Barras market *(see Shopping, below)* to hunt for bargains.

GETTING HERE

To get to the East End, take the subway to the St. Enoch station and walk along Argyle Street to the Tron Cross. From there, London Road takes you to Glasgow Green.

TOP ATTRACTIONS

FAMILY

People's Palace. An impressive Victorian red-sandstone building dating from 1894 houses an intriguing museum dedicated to the city's social history. Included among the exhibits is one devoted to the ordinary folk of Glasgow, called the *People's Story.* Also on display are the writing desk of John McLean (1879–1923), the "Red Clydeside" political activist who came to Lenin's notice, and the famous banana boots worn on stage by Glasgow-born comedian Billy Connolly. On the top floor a sequence of fine murals by Glasgow artist Ken Currie tells the story of Glasgow's working-class citizens. Behind the museum are the restored Winter Gardens and a popular café. To get here from the St. Enoch subway station, walk along Argyle Street past Glasgow Cross. ✉ *Glasgow Green, Monteith Row, East End* ☎ *0141/276–0788* ⊕ *www. glasgowmuseums.com* ✆ *Free* ⊙ *Tues.–Thurs. and Sat. 10–5, Fri. and Sun. 11–5* Ⓜ *St. Enoch.*

SOUTH SIDE

Just southwest of the City Center in the South Side are two of Glasgow's dear green spaces—Bellahouston Park and Pollok Country Park—which have important art collections: Charles Rennie Mackintosh's House for an Art Lover in Bellahouston, and the Burrell Collection and Pollok House in Pollock Country Park.

GETTING HERE   Both parks are off Pollokshaws Road, about 3 miles southwest of downtown. You can take a taxi or car, city bus, or a train from Glasgow Central Station to Pollokshaws West Station or Dumbreck.

TOP ATTRACTIONS

Fodor's Choice   **Burrell Collection.** An elegant, ultramodern building of pink sandstone
★   and stainless steel houses thousands of items of all descriptions, from ancient Egyptian, Greek, and Roman artifacts to Chinese ceramics, bronzes, and jade. You can also find medieval tapestries, stained-glass windows, Rodin sculptures, and exquisite French-impressionist paintings. Eccentric millionaire Sir William Burrell (1861–1958) donated this collection of some 8,000 pieces to the city in 1944. The 1983 building was designed with large glass walls so that the items on display could relate to their surroundings in Pollok Country Park: art and nature, supposedly in perfect harmony. You can get here via Buses 45, 48, and 57 from Union Street, or it's a leisurely 15-minute walk from the Pollokshaws West rail station. ⊠ *2060 Pollokshaws Rd., South Side* ☎ *0141/287–2550* ⊕ *www.glasgowmuseums.com* ⊡ *Free* ⊗ *Mon.– Thurs. and Sat. 10–5, Fri. and Sun. 11–5.*

House for an Art Lover. Within Bellahouston Park is a "new" Mackintosh house, based on a competition entry Charles Rennie Mackintosh submitted to a German magazine in 1901. The house was never built in his lifetime, but took shape between 1989 and 1996. The building houses the Glasgow School of Art's postgraduate study center, and exhibits designs for the various rooms and decorative pieces by Mackintosh and his wife Margaret. The main lounge is spectacular. There's also a café and shop filled with art. Buses 9, 53, and 54 from Union Street will get you here. Call ahead, as opening times can vary. ⊠ *Bellahouston Park, 10 Dumbreck Rd., South Side* ☎ *0141/353–4770* ⊕ *www. houseforanartlover.co.uk* ⊡ *£4.50* ⊗ *Apr.–Sept., Mon.–Wed. 10–4, Thurs.–Sun. 10–1; Oct.–Mar., weekends 10–1* Ⓜ *Ibrox.*

WORTH NOTING

Pollok House. This classic Georgian house, dating from the mid-1700s, sits amid landscaped gardens and avenues of trees that are now part of Pollok Country Park. The Stirling Maxwell Collection includes paintings by Blake and a strong grouping of Spanish works by El Greco, Murillo, and Goya. Lovely examples of 18th- and early-19th-century furniture, silver, glass, and porcelain are also on display. The house has beautiful gardens that overlook the White Cart River. The downstairs servants' quarters house the restaurant's kitchen, still hung with the cooking implements of its times. You can take Buses 45, 47, or 57 to the gate of Pollok County Park. ⊠ *Pollok County Park, 2060 Pollokshaws Rd., South Side* ☎ *0844/616–6410* ⊕ *www.nts.org.uk* ⊡ *Apr.– Oct. £6.50, Nov.–Mar. free* ⊗ *Daily 10–5.*

WHERE TO EAT

In the past few years, restaurants have been popping up all around Glasgow that emphasize the best that Scotland has to offer: grass-fed beef, free-range chicken, wild seafood, venison, duck, and goose—not to mention superb fruits and vegetables. The growing emphasis on organic food is reflected on menus that increasingly provide detailed information about the source of their ingredients.

You can eat your way around the world in Glasgow. Chinese and Indian foods are longtime favorites, and Thai and Japanese restaurants have become popular. Spanish-style tapas are now quite common, and the "small plate" craze has extended to every kind of restaurant. Glasgow has a large Italian community, and its traditional cafés have been joined by a new generation of eateries serving updated versions of the classics. And seafood restaurants have moved well beyond the fish-and-chips wrapped in newspaper that were always a Glasgow staple.

PRICES

Eating in Glasgow can be casual or lavish. For inexpensive dining, consider the benefit of lunch or pretheater set menus. Beer and spirits cost much the same as they would in a bar, but wine is relatively expensive in restaurants. An increasing number of pubs offer food, but their kitchens usually close early. ■ **TIP→ Some restaurants allow you to bring your own bottle of wine, charging just a small corkage fee. It's worth the effort.**

WHAT IT COSTS IN POUNDS

	$	$$	$$$	$$$$
Restaurants	under £15	£15–£19	£20–£25	over £25

Prices are the average cost of a main course at dinner or, if dinner isn't served, at lunch.

CITY CENTER

Use the coordinate (⊕ B2) at the end of each listing to locate a site on the corresponding map.

This area has restaurants catering to the 9-to-5 crowd, meaning there are a lot of fine-dining establishments as well as good restaurants catching people as they leave work, drawing them in with pretheater menus. The choice of eateries is extensive.

$$ SPANISH

🍴 **Arta.** The narrow entrance doesn't prepare you for this huge spacious venue—restaurant, bar, dance club—nor for its extravagant decor. The interior is like an enormous hacienda somewhere in southern Spain, and the menu is made to match. There's an elaborate tapas menu, accentuated by resident musicians and salsa dancing. Paellas (with the usual meat and seafood though there's also a vegetarian version) are substantial and delicious. [$] *Average main: £16* ✉ *13–19 Wallis St., East End* ☎ *0845/166-6018* ⏲ *No lunch. Closed Sun.–Wed.* ⊕ *G5.*

BEST BETS FOR GLASGOW DINING

Fodor's Choice★

Bistro du Vin, $$$, p. 638
The Corinthian Club, $$, p. 634
Crabshakk, $, p. 639
Mother India's Cafe, $ p. 640
Mussel Inn, $, p. 634
Number Sixteen, $$, p. 640
Opium, $$, p. 635
Rogano, $$$, p. 635
The Sisters, $$, p. 640
Stravaigin, $$, p. 640
Ubiquitous Chip, $$$, p. 640

By Price

$

Café Gandolfi, p. 635
Crabshakk, p. 639
Hanoi Bike Shop, p. 639
Kool Ba, p. 638
Mother India's Cafe, p. 640
Mussel Inn, p. 634

$$

City Merchant, p. 638
The Corinthian Club, p. 634
Number Sixteen, p. 640
Opium, p. 635
The Sisters, p. 640
Stravaigin, p. 640

$$$

Bistro du Vin, p. 638
Rogano, p. 635
Two Fat Ladies, p. 635
Ubiquitous Chip, p. 640

By Cuisine

INDIAN

Kool Ba, $, p. 638
Mother India's Cafe, $, p. 640

MODERN BRITISH

Café Gandolfi, $, p. 635
City Merchant, $$, p. 638
Number Sixteen, $$, p. 640
Rogano, $$$ p. 635
Stravaigin, $$, p. 640

SEAFOOD

Crabshakk, $, p. 639
Mussel Inn, $, p. 634
Rogano, $$$, p. 635
Two Fat Ladies, $$$, p. 635

$$
MODERN BRITISH
Fodor's Choice ★

🍴 **The Corinthian Club.** Inside what was once the mansion of tobacco merchant George Buchanan, the Corinthian has an ostentatiously elegant restaurant where you can dine under a 26-foot-high glass dome as classical statues stare in your direction. The menu offers a good selection of seafood and steaks from the standard to the enormous. The gloomy basement, once a criminal court, now houses a beer and champagne bar. Among the other on-site drinking establishments is the Prohibition Bar, which uses teacups rather than glasses. You can also enjoy afternoon tea in an elegant dining room. [$] *Average main: £16* ✉ *191 Ingram St., City Center* ☎ *0141/552–1101* 🌐 *www.thecorinthianclub.co.uk* ✍ *Reservations essential* ✣ *G5.*

$
SEAFOOD
Fodor's Choice ★

🍴 **Mussel Inn.** West coast shellfish farmers own this restaurant and feed their customers incredibly succulent oysters, scallops, and mussels. The pots of mussels, steamed to order and served with any of a number of sauces, are revelatory. The surroundings are simple but stylish, with cool ceramic tiles, wood floors, and plenty of sleek wooden furniture. Another plus is the staff, which is helpful yet unpretentious. The £7.50 lunch menu includes a bowl of mussels and either salad or fries. A pre-theater meal is £10.95 for two courses, £13.95 for three. [$] *Average main: £13* ✉ *157 Hope St., City Center* ☎ *0141/572–1405* 🌐 *www.mussel-inn.com* ⏲ *No lunch Sun.* ✣ *F5.*

$$ ASIAN Fodor's Choice ★ 🍴 **Opium.** This eatery has completely rethought Asian cuisine, taking Chinese, Malaysian, and Thai cooking in new directions. Sauces are fragrant and spicy, but never overpowering. The specialty of the house is dim sum, prepared by a chef who knows his dumplings. The wontons are fresh and crisp, with delicious combinations of crab, shrimp, and chicken peeking through the almost transparent pastry. But leave room for the main dishes, especially the tiger prawns and scallops in a sauce made from dried shrimp and fish. The vegetarian menu is adventurous, too. There are also captivating cocktails. [$] *Average main: £15* ✉ *191 Hope St., City Center* ☎ *0141/332–6668* ⊕ *F4.*

$$$ MODERN BRITISH Fodor's Choice ★ 🍴 **Rogano.** Modeled after the *Queen Mary,* this restaurant's spacious art deco interior—maple paneling, chrome trim, and dramatic ocean murals—is enough to recommend it. Portions are generous in the main dining area, where you'll find impeccably prepared seafood dishes like pan-seared scallops, as well as classics like roast rack of lamb. You can eat very well in the less expensive Cafe Rogano, where the brasserie-style food is more modern and imaginative. The gorgeous bar serves wonderful cocktails along with elegant sandwiches and a lovely fish soup. Few people know that between 3 and 6 you get a free starter or dessert with a main dish. [$] *Average main: £22* ✉ *11 Exchange Pl., City Center* ☎ *0141/248–4055* 🌐 *www.roganoglasgow.com* ✍ *Reservations essential* ⊕ *F5.*

$$$ SEAFOOD 🍴 **Two Fat Ladies.** It might have the same name as the owner's other restaurants at 88 Dumbarton Road and 652 Argyle Street, but this branch of Two Fat Ladies deserves a visit because it has more space, more light, and a better location. The menu is predominantly fish, from the delicate smoked salmon, crab, and asparagus salad to the whole sea bass stuffed with tomatoes, red onions, and thyme to the cod with a chorizo and bean cassoulet. But if fish doesn't rock your boat, then the Angus beef au jus with wild mushrooms and spinach is also delicious. [$] *Average main: £20* ✉ *118A Blythswood St., City Center* ☎ *0141/847–0088* 🌐 *www.twofatladiesrestaurant.com* ⏲ *No lunch Sun.* ⊕ *E4.*

MERCHANT CITY

Use the coordinate (⊕ B2) at the end of each listing to locate a site on the corresponding map.

Despite covering a relatively small area, Merchant City has a wide variety of restaurants. The selection of cafés and restaurants includes many budget-friendly options that cater to the working population.

$ MODERN BRITISH 🍴 **Café Gandolfi.** Occupying what was once the tea market, this trendy café draws the style-conscious crowd. Wooden tables and chairs crafted by Scottish artist Tim Stead are so fluidly shaped it's hard to believe they're inanimate. The café opens early for breakfast, serving croissants, eggs *en cocotte* (casserole-style), and strong espresso. Don't miss the smoked venison or the finnan haddie (smoked haddock). There are daily specials, too, like the John Dory fillets served with clams and garlic butter. The bar on the second floor is more intimate and much less busy—and lets you order from the same menu. [$] *Average main:*

14

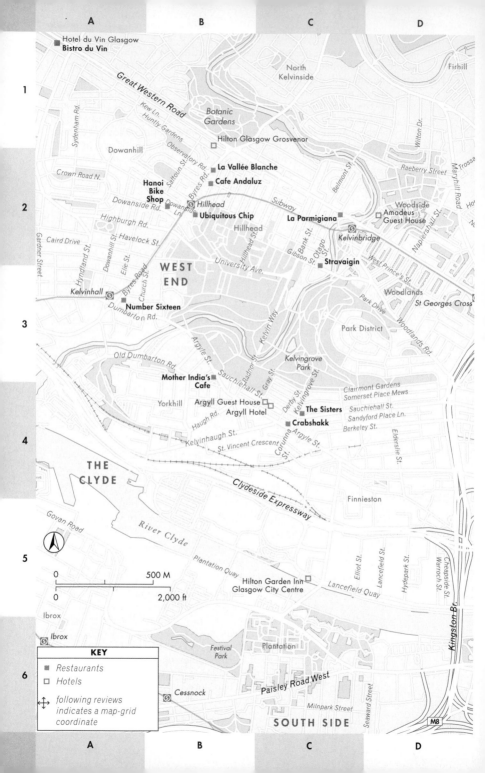

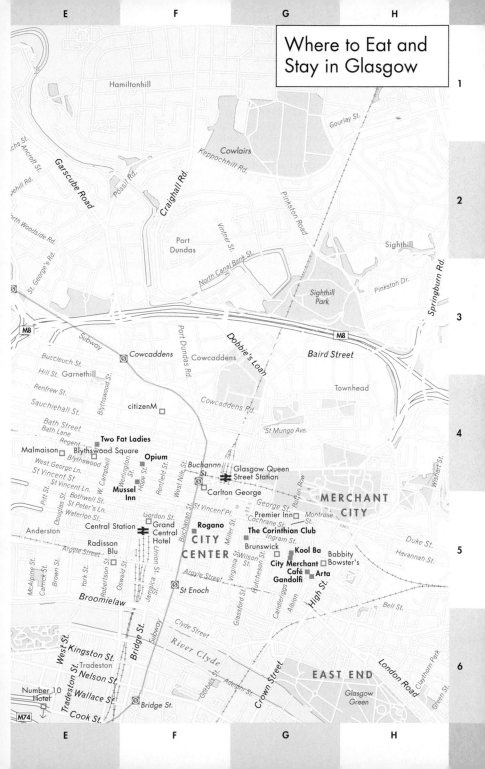

Where to Eat and Stay in Glasgow

£14 ⊠ 64 Albion St., Merchant City ☎ 0141/552–6813 ⊕ www. cafegandolfi.com ✛ G5.

$$
MODERN BRITISH
✕ **City Merchant.** If you have a penchant for fresh and flavorful cuisine, head to this welcoming spot with simple but traditional furnishings, including white tablecloths, dark wood, soft lighting, and tartan carpets. The secret is the kitchen's use of only local ingredients. You can sample the tasty cuts of venison and beef (including a fillet with haggis mousse), but seafood remains the star attraction. The mussels and oysters from Loch Etive are wondrous, as is the sea bass. There's a relatively inexpensive selection of wines and a wonderful cheese board. A two-course lunch special is a bargain at £12.50. $ Average main: £19 ⊠ 97–99 Candleriggs St., Merchant City ☎ 0141/553–1577 ⊕ www.citymerchant.co.uk ☉ No lunch Sun. ✛ G5.

> **TAKE TIME FOR TEA**
>
> In the Victorian tradition, while men went to pubs, Glasgow women's social interaction would take place in the city's many tearooms and cafés. Today everyone goes to the cafés. Glaswegians have succumbed to the worldwide love for Italian-style, espresso-based coffees, but they'll never give up the comfort of a nice cup of tea, so you'll find both at most tearooms, along with scones, Scottish pancakes, other pastries, and light lunch fare like sandwiches and soup.

$
ECLECTIC
✕ **Kool Ba.** This atmospheric haven serves an intriguing mix of Indian and Persian fare. It's all about healthy, flavorful cooking: chicken tikka masala in a yogurt sauce or lamb korma with coconut cream and fruit are good picks. Accompany your meal with bowls of basmati saffron rice and fluffy naan bread. Thick wooden tables, Persian tapestries, and soft candlelight make you feel at home in the small, comfortable dining room. This popular place continues to win award after award; reserve ahead on Friday and Saturday. $ Average main: £14 ⊠ 109–113 Candleriggs, Merchant City ☎ 0141/552–2777 ⊕ www.koolba. com ⚠ Reservations essential ✛ G5.

WEST END

Use the coordinate (✛ B2) at the end of each listing to locate a site on the corresponding map.

Because of Glasgow University, the eateries in this area were once just the domain of students and professors. In recent years, many fine restaurants have opened in this elegant residential area, attracting a wide range of visitors.

$$$
FRENCH
Fodor's Choice
★
✕ **Bistro du Vin.** A kilted doorman and stylish blue-and-green tartan carpets beckon you into the city's most elegant eatery. The service is impeccable from beginning to end, and all the food is locally sourced from a 35-mile radius. It's the perfect place for cold, wet days, as romantic fires flicker in the background, and stained-glass murals twist the natural light into colorful new shades. From the menu of French and Scottish fare, try the venison or the halibut with asparagus and herb gnocchi. The starters are seductive, and the coffee-and-chocolate soufflé with caramel ice cream is a tempting dessert. For serious indulgence,

there's a seven-course taster menu for £69. Ask for a tour of the superb wine cellar. Sunday brunch is popular. $ *Average main: £24* ⊠ *Hotel du Vin, 1 Devonshire Gardens, West End* ☎ *0141/339–2001* ⊕ *www. hotelduvin.com* ⚲ *Reservations essential* ✣ *A1.*

$$
TAPAS

✕ **Cafe Andaluz.** With its Spanish flair, this beautifully designed basement eatery is always busy and lively. The first tapas place to make an impact in Glasgow, it has been followed by others (and has opened a second location of its own in the City Center) but remains the most successful. This is an ideal way to dine with friends: sharing the dishes as they arrive and as you down some good Spanish wine. Booking ahead is strongly advised. $ *Average main: £15* ⊠ *2 Cresswell La., West End* ☎ *0141/339–1111* ⊕ *www.cafeandaluz.com* ⊙ *Mon–Thurs. noon–10, Fri. and Sat. noon–11, Sun. noon–10* Ⓜ *Hillhead* ✣ *B2.*

$
SEAFOOD
Fodor'sChoice
★

✕ **Crabshakk.** This place is anything but a shack. The intimate dining room has heavy wooden tables and chairs and a bar so shiny and inviting that it seems to almost insist you have a drink. The lamps are like half-moons, and the ceiling is elegantly ornate. The food comes from the sea—oysters, lobster, and squid—and you can have your choice served iced, grilled, roasted, or battered. The fish sandwich and crab cakes (no fillers, just the real stuff) are favorites on the lunch menu. In the evening, mussels and scallops draw the eye. Only local and sustainably sourced Scottish seafood is featured. The buzz of conversation and the perfectly modulated music creates the right atmosphere. $ *Average main: £12* ⊠ *1114 Argyle St., West End* ☎ *0141/334–6127* ⊕ *www.crabshakk. com* ⚲ *Reservations essential* ⊙ *Closed Mon.* ✣ *C4.*

$
VIETNAMESE

✕ **Hanoi Bike Shop.** Glasgow's first Vietnamese canteen offers a different style of dining, which is apparent from the moment you walk through the door. There are no starters or mains as such—couples are advised to share three dishes. It could be roast pigeon with bok choy, hot-and-sour fish soup, or rice noodles in a savory broth. The setting is rustic, the tables are low, and the seating, mostly stools, takes a little getting used to, but it's also part of the experience. $ *Average main: £14* ⊠ *8 Ruthven La., West End* ☎ *0141/334–7165* ⊕ *www.thehanoibikeshop. co.uk* ✣ *B2.*

$$
ITALIAN

✕ **La Parmigiana.** The refreshing elegance of the surroundings is mirrored by the consistently exquisite fare at this longtime favorite. The Giovanazzis pride themselves on using the freshest ingredients—this means you may be able to enjoy simply prepared sea bass or veal one day, guinea fowl or scallops the next. Expertise in the kitchen is reflected in the well-balanced wine list and the impeccable attentiveness of the black-jacketed waiters in this small restaurant. $ *Average main: £19* ⊠ *447 Great Western Rd., West End* ☎ *0141/334–0686* ⊕ *www.laparmigiana. co.uk* ⚲ *Reservations essential* ⊙ *Closed Sun.* ✣ *C2.*

$$
FRENCH

✕ **La Vallée Blanche.** Above a record store, this fine-dining restaurant has an alpine atmosphere, with the dark wood eaves that you might find in a chalet. The theme is rustic, and the food is hearty and adventurous: veal osso buco comes with foie gras and a port velouté, while the sea bream is accompanied by razor clams and bok choy. Good lunch and pretheater menus are £12.95 for two courses. $ *Average main: £18*

14

✉ *360 Byres Rd., West End* ☎ *0141/334–3333* 🌐 *www.lavalleeblanche.com* ⏲ *Closed Mon.* ✣ *B2.*

$ INDIAN Fodor's Choice ★ 🍴 **Mother India's Cafe.** Overlooking the Kelvingrove Art Gallery and Museum, this quaint, casual eatery has a spectacular view as well as an impressive menu. It's usually quite crowded, so don't expect much intimacy. The food is served tapas-style in small dishes—the idea is that you get to try lots of different flavors. Chili-flavored king prawns, chicken cooked with lime, and *aloo saag dosa* (potato and spinach stuffed in a rice-and-lentil pancake) are all rich in flavor and presentation. The popular café doesn't accept reservations, so be prepared for a (fast-moving) line. It's worth bringing your own wine; there's a small corkage charge. [$] *Average main: £14* ✉ *1355 Argyle St., West End* ☎ *0141/339–9145* 🌐 *www.motherindiaglasgow.co.uk* ✣ *B3.*

$$ BRITISH Fodor's Choice ★ 🍴 **Number Sixteen.** This tiny, intimate restaurant serves only the freshest ingredients, superbly prepared. Seared mullet is served with risotto, chorizo, broad beans, and artichokes—a typically unpredictable meeting of flavors. The pork belly with black pudding, white-onion marmalade, and spiced applesauce is tantalizing, and desserts are equally seductive. There's room for only 40 diners, and the result is cozy but never cramped. Book ahead, particularly on weekends. [$] *Average main: £17* ✉ *16 Byres Rd., West End* ☎ *0141/339–2544* 🌐 *www.number16.co.uk* ✍ *Reservations essential* ✣ *A3.*

$$ BRITISH Fodor's Choice ★ 🍴 **The Sisters.** Walk up the smooth sandstone steps to this restaurant, which aims to inspire both your palate and your heart. The menu is locally sourced and always changing: a typical dish is chicken with haggis in a whisky-mustard cream. No matter what you choose, it will be served in generous portions. The homegrown Arran gooseberry fool is the ultimate Scottish dessert. Douglas Gray tartan pads the pristine room, and polished floorboards reflect the natural light shining in from the long windows around the unusual oval-shape room. Wild seascape paintings are a nice touch in a space that feels both wide open and contained. [$] *Average main: £19* ✉ *36 Kelvingrove St., West End* ☎ *0141/564–1157* 🌐 *www.thesisters.co.uk* ✣ *C4.*

$$ ECLECTIC Fodor's Choice ★ 🍴 **Stravaigin.** A genuinely cosmopolitan menu that changes regularly, a wine list that is long but economical, and reasonably priced cocktails, all served in a warm and inviting interior buzzing with conversation, explain Stravaigin's popularity. Wooden tables, booths, and assorted chairs in the bar create an informal atmosphere. Stravaigin takes pride in its well-traveled menu, with regular nights featuring less familiar cuisines. Look for fine fish dishes like hake and mussels in a lemongrass broth. There's always a curry plate on the menu, as well as Scottish favorites like haggis and neeps and beer-battered fish-and-chips. If you prefer a quieter atmosphere, the downstairs restaurant serves the same menu. [$] *Average main: £16* ✉ *28 Gibson St., West End* ☎ *0141/334–2665* 🌐 *www.stravaigin.com* ✍ *Reservations essential* ✣ *C2.*

$$$ BRITISH Fodor's Choice ★ 🍴 **Ubiquitous Chip.** Occupying a converted stable behind the Hillhead subway station, this restaurant is an institution among members of Glasgow's media and theater communities, who most days can be found in the busy bar. The more informal upstairs brasserie serves haggis with neeps and tatties (turnips and potatoes) or slow-roasted pork shoulder.

The ground-floor restaurant has a cobbled courtyard with a glass roof. The more expensive menu offers fish and game dishes that vary from week to week. Try the roast saddle of rabbit or the monkfish with pork belly. There's an excellent lunch and pretheater menu for £15.95. [$] *Average main: £24* ✉ *12 Ashton La., West End* ☎ *0141/334–5007* 🌐 *www.ubiquitouschip.co.uk* ✍ *Reservations essential* ✥ *B2.*

WHERE TO STAY

14

Glasgow's City Center never sleeps, so central hotels will be noisier than those in the leafy and genteel West End. Downtown hotels are within walking distance of all the main sights, while West End lodgings are more convenient for museums and art galleries. Over the past few years the hotel scene has become noticeably more stylish with new hotels opening, including Blythswood Square and Grand Central Hotel.

Although big hotels are spread out all around the city, B&Bs are definitely a more popular, personal, and cheaper option. Regardless of the neighborhood, hotels are about the same in price. Some B&Bs as well as the smaller properties may also offer discounts for longer stays. Make your reservations in advance, especially in summer and when there's a big concert, sporting event, or holiday. If you arrive in town without a place to stay, contact the Glasgow Tourist Board.

PRICES AND MONEY-SAVING OPTIONS

It is always worthwhile to inquire about special deals or discounted rates, especially if you book online and in advance. Another money-saving option is to rent an apartment. B&Bs are the best-priced short-term lodging option, and you're sure to get breakfast.

Most smaller hotels and all guesthouses include breakfast in the room rate. Larger hotels usually charge extra for breakfast. Also note that the most expensive hotels often exclude the tax in the initial price quote, but budget places usually include it. *Hotel reviews have been shortened. For full information and additional options, visit Fodors.com.*

WHAT IT COSTS IN POUNDS

	$	$$	$$$	$$$$
Hotels	under £100	£100–£160	£161–£220	over £220

Prices are the lowest cost of a standard double room in high season, including 20% V.A.T.

CITY CENTER

Use the coordinate (✥ B2) at the end of each listing to locate a site on the corresponding map.

Here you'll be close to everything: the main sights, shops, theaters, restaurants, and bars—the pulse of the city. You don't have to worry about transportation in the center of town, but it can get noisy on weekend nights.

BEST BETS FOR GLASGOW LODGING

Fodor's Choice ★

Blythswood Square, $$$
p. 642

citizenM, $ p. 642

Grand Central Hotel,
$$$$, p. 643

Hotel du Vin Glasgow,
$$$, p. 644

Malmaison, $$,
p. 643

By Price

$

Amadeus Guest House,
p. 644

Argyll Hotel, p. 644

Babbity Bowster's,
p. 643

Brunswick, p. 643

citizenM, p. 642

$$

Carlton George, p. 642

Hilton Garden Inn, p. 644

Hilton Glasgow Grosve-
nor, p. 644

Malmaison, p. 643

$$$

Blythswood Square,
p. 642

Hotel du Vin Glasgow,
p. 644

Radisson Blu, p. 643

$$$$

Grand Central Hotel,
p. 643

By Experience

BEST CONCIERGE

Hotel du Vin Glasgow,
$$$, p. 644

Radisson Blu, $$$, p. 643

BEST HISTORIC HOTELS

Blythswood Square, $$$,
p. 642

Hotel du Vin Glasgow,
$$$, p. 644

MOST ROMANTIC

citizenM, $, p. 642

Grand Central Hotel,
$$$$, p. 643

Hotel du Vin Glasgow,
$$$, p. 644

Malmaison, $$, p. 643

$$$
HOTEL
Fodor's Choice
★
Blythswood Square. History and luxury come together at this smart conversion of the former headquarters of the Royal Automobile Club of Scotland, which occupies a classical building on peaceful Blythswood Square. **Pros:** airy and luxurious; glorious bathrooms; lovely common areas that retain the original gold-topped columns. **Cons:** room lighting may be too dim for some; some street noise. $ *Rooms from: £200* ⊠ *11 Blythswood Sq., City Center* ☎ *0141/248–8888* ⊕ *www.blythswoodsquare.com* ↪ *100 rooms, 6 suites* ⦿| *Breakfast* ✛ *E4.*

$$
HOTEL
Carlton George. A narrow revolving doorway, a step back from busy West George Street, creates the illusion of a secret passageway leading into this lavish boutique hotel. **Pros:** near city-center attractions; discounted parking nearby. **Cons:** breakfast is extra during the week. $ *Rooms from: £154* ⊠ *44 W. George St., City Center* ☎ *0141/353–6373* ⊕ *www.carltonhotels.co.uk/george* ↪ *64 rooms* ⦿| *Multiple meal plans* ✛ *F5.*

$
HOTEL
Fodor's Choice
★
citizenM. There's no lobby at the futuristic citizenM—no reception area at all, because you can only book online—but there are chic "living rooms" with ultramodern furnishings where guests congregate. **Pros:** wonderful design; all the creature comforts; central location. **Cons:** not for the claustrophobic. $ *Rooms from: £90* ⊠ *60 Renfrew St., corner of Hope St., City Center* ☎ *01782/488–3490* ⊕ *www.citizenm.com/glasgow* ↪ *198 rooms* ⦿| *Some meals* ✛ *F4.*

$$$$ HOTEL Fodor's Choice ★ 🏨 **Grand Central Hotel.** This hotel certainly deserves its name, as everything about it, from the magnificent marble-floor champagne bar to the ballroom fully restored to its original glory, is grand. **Pros:** a real air of luxury; most rooms are quite spacious; champagne bar is a wonderful place to linger. **Cons:** some noise from street; parking is a couple of blocks away; some rooms are small. [$] *Rooms from: £289* ✉ *99 Gordon St., City Center* ☎ *0141/240–3700* 🌐 *www.principal-hayley.com/grandcentralhotel* 🛏 *230 rooms, 3 suites* 🍴 *Multiple meal plans* ✢ *F5.*

$$ HOTEL Fodor's Choice ★ 🏨 **Malmaison.** Housed in a converted church, this modern boutique hotel prides itself on personal service and outstanding amenities like plasma televisions and high-end stereo systems. **Pros:** stunning lobby; attention to detail; five-minute walk to Sauchiehall Street. **Cons:** bland views; dark hallways; no on-site parking. [$] *Rooms from: £129* ✉ *278 W. George St., City Center* ☎ *0141/572–1000* 🌐 *www.malmaison.com* 🛏 *64 rooms, 8 suites* 🍴 *Breakfast* ✢ *E4.*

14

$$$ HOTEL 🏨 **Radisson Blu.** You can't miss this eye-catching edifice behind Central Station: its glass facade makes the interior, particularly the lounge, seem as though it were part of the street. **Pros:** kilted doorman; impeccable service; free Wi-Fi and other amenities. **Cons:** neighborhood can get noisy; most rooms have poor views; no on-site parking. [$] *Rooms from: £205* ✉ *301 Argyle St., City Center* ☎ *0141/204–3333* 🌐 *www.radissonblu.co.uk/hotel-glasgow* 🛏 *247 rooms, 3 suites* 🍴 *No meals* ✢ *E5.*

MERCHANT CITY

Use the coordinate (✢ B2) at the end of each listing to locate a site on the corresponding map.

The hotels in the Merchant City are best for those who plan to spend most of their time out and about. In general, this busy area is not the place to come if you want peace and quiet.

$ B&B/INN 🏨 **Babbity Bowster's.** Babbity Bowster's is a welcoming pub in an old merchant's house in the heart of the Merchant City. **Pros:** couldn't be more central; good food; great atmosphere. **Cons:** a bit noisy; finding parking can be difficult; no elevator. [$] *Rooms from: £60* ✉ *16–18 Blackfriars St., Merchant City* ☎ *0141/552–5055* 🌐 *www.babbitybowster.com* 🛏 *6 rooms* 🍴 *Breakfast* ✢ *G5.*

$ HOTEL 🏨 **Brunswick.** This modest but comfortable six-story hotel sits at the heart of Glasgow's nightlife. **Pros:** excellent value; lively downstairs café; very central. **Cons:** area can be noisy on weekends; some rooms are very small; rooms at the back have unappealing views over neighboring roofs. [$] *Rooms from: £65* ✉ *106–108 Brunswick St., Merchant City* ☎ *0141/552–0001* 🌐 *www.brunswickhotel.co.uk* 🛏 *18 rooms, 1 suite* 🍴 *Breakfast* ✢ *G5.*

$ HOTEL 🏨 **Premier Inn.** It may be part of a chain, but this hotel's bright rooms and reasonable prices appeal to savvy travelers. **Pros:** great location; bargain rates; modern rooms. **Cons:** some front rooms are noisy; extra charges for parking and Internet access. [$] *Rooms from: £70* ✉ *187 George St., Merchant City* ☎ *0870/238–3320* 🌐 *www.premierinn.com* 🛏 *239 rooms* 🍴 *No meals* ✢ *G5.*

WEST END

Use the coordinate (✥ B2) at the end of each listing to locate a site on the corresponding map.

Many lodgings are on quieter Great Western Road, set apart from busy Byres Road. There are a number of hotels on the other side of Kelvingrove Park in a lively area.

$ B&B/INN **Amadeus Guest House.** This adorable Victorian town house sits on a leafy residential street overlooking the River Kelvin. **Pros:** near West End attractions; two-minute walk from subway; kids under six stay free. **Cons:** some rooms are small; finding parking can be difficult. [$] *Rooms from: £60* ✉ *411 N. Woodside Rd., West End* ☎ *0141/339–8257* 🌐 *www.amadeusguesthouse.co.uk* *9 rooms* 🍴 *Breakfast* ✥ *D2.*

$ B&B/INN **Argyll Guest House.** In this budget-minded annex to the Argyll Hotel, across the road on Sauchiehall Street, the rooms are plainly furnished but scrupulously clean. **Pros:** close to Kelvingrove Park; near public transportation; bargain prices. **Cons:** front rooms noisy on weekends; decor is bland and uninspiring; no elevator. [$] *Rooms from: £60* ✉ *966–970 Sauchiehall St., West End* ☎ *0141/357–5155* 🌐 *www.argyllhotelglasgow.co.uk* *20 rooms* 🍴 *Breakfast* ✥ *C4.*

$ HOTEL **Argyll Hotel.** The tartan in the reception area reflects the clan theme throughout the hotel. **Pros:** centrally located; comfortable rooms; reasonable price. **Cons:** the pub next door can get very noisy; street parking is metered (there is a small hotel car park).[$] *Rooms from: £80* ✉ *973, Sauchiehall St., West End, Glasgow* ☎ *0141/337-3313* 🌐 *www.argyllhotelglasgow.co.uk* *38 rooms* 🍴 *Breakfast* ✥ *C4.*

$$ HOTEL **Hilton Glasgow Grosvenor.** Behind a row of grand terrace houses, this modern hotel overlooks the Botanical Gardens. **Pros:** close to Byres Road; some rooms have good views; tasty eatery. **Cons:** rooms at the back overlook a parking lot; a rather institutional feel. [$] *Rooms from: £109* ✉ *1–9 Grosvenor Terr., West End* ☎ *0141/339–8811* 🌐 *www.hilton.com/glasgowgrosvenor* *96 rooms* 🍴 *Breakfast* ✥ *B2.*

$$$ HOTEL Fodor's Choice ★ **Hotel du Vin Glasgow.** Once the legendary One Devonshire Gardens, frequented by such celebrities as Luciano Pavarotti and Elizabeth Taylor, the Hotel Du Vin Glasgow is still a destination for those in search of luxury. **Pros:** stunning Scottish rooms; doting service; complimentary whisky on arrival. **Cons:** no elevator; on-street parking can be difficult after 6 pm. [$] *Rooms from: £180* ✉ *1 Devonshire Gardens, West End* ☎ *084473/339–2001* 🌐 *www.hotelduvin.com/glasgow* *41 rooms, 8 suites* 🍴 *Breakfast* ✥ *A1.*

THE CLYDE

Use the coordinate (✥ B2) at the end of each listing to locate a site on the corresponding map.

Besides a handful of interesting museums and a cluster of busy bars and restaurants, this up-and-coming area also has a few well-regarded lodgings.

$$ HOTEL **Hilton Garden Inn Glasgow City Centre.** Overlooking the Clyde, this hotel is a short walk along the riverside to Riverside Museum and other

popular destinations. **Pros:** relaxing lounge area; lovely terrace; some great views. **Cons:** isolated from the rest of the city. $ *Rooms from: £119* ✉ *Finnieston Quay, Clyde* ☎ *0141/240–1002* 🌐 *hiltongardeninn3.hilton.com* 🛏 *164 rooms* 🍴 *Breakfast* ✥ *C5.*

SOUTH SIDE

Use the coordinate (✥ B2) at the end of each listing to locate a site on the corresponding map.

This residential area near the center of the city has some lovely parks; there's not much to do at night, though.

$$ HOTEL **Number 10 Hotel.** In one of the grand houses overlooking Queens Park, this elegant hotel's guest rooms are quite large and are decorated in pleasantly muted colors. **Pros:** nice setting; ample parking; pretty garden. **Cons:** can be crowded with wedding parties on weekends. $ *Rooms from: £100* ✉ *10–16 Queens Dr., South Side* ☎ *0141/424–0160* 🌐 *www.10hotel.co.uk* 🛏 *26 rooms* 🍴 *No meals* ✥ *E6.*

14

NIGHTLIFE AND THE ARTS

Glasgow's music scene is vibrant and creative, and many successful pop artists began their careers in its pubs and clubs. Celtic Connections is probably one of the world's most important festivals of its kind, and the city's summer jazz festival has attracted some of the world's finest players.

When it comes to nightlife, the City Center and West End are alive with pubs and clubs offering an eclectic mix of everything from bagpipes to salsa to punk. The biweekly magazine the *List,* available at newsstands and many cafés and arts centers, is an indispensable guide to Glasgow's bars and clubs.

THE ARTS

Because the Royal Scottish Conservatoire is in Glasgow, there is always a pool of impressive young talent that's pressing the city's artistic boundaries in theater, music, and film. The city has a well-deserved reputation for its theater, with everything from cutting-edge plays to over-the-top pantomimes

Scottish Music Centre. Besides having a library, the Scottish Music Centre serves as the main ticket office for all music events at venues like the Royal Concert Hall and for annual events like the Glasgow Jazz Festival. ✉ *Candleriggs, City Center* ☎ *0141/353–8000* 🌐 *www.glasgowconcerthalls.com.*

ARTS CENTERS

Trongate 103. This vibrant contemporary arts center, housed in a converted Edwardian warehouse, is home base for diverse groups producing film, photography, paintings, and prints. It contains the Russian Cultural Centre and the Sharmanka Kinetic Theatre, as well as the Glasgow Print Studio, Street Level Photoworks, and the Transmission

Gallery. Part of the complex, the well-established Street Level Photoworks aims at making photography more accessible. ⊠ *103 Trongate, Merchant City* ☎ *0141/276–8380* ⊕ *www.trongate103.com.*

CONCERTS

Glasgow Royal Concert Hall. The 2,500-seat Glasgow Royal Concert Hall is the venue for a wide range of concerts, from classical to pop. It also hosts the very popular late-night club. ⊠ *2 Sauchiehall St., City Center* ☎ *0141/353–8000* ⊕ *www.glasgowconcerthalls.com.*

The Old Fruitmarket. A wonderful venue for almost every type of music, this was once the city's fruit and vegetable market. The first-floor balcony, with its intricate iron railings, still carries some of the original merchants' names. It's adjacent to City Halls. ⊠ *Candleriggs, Merchant City* ☎ *0141/353–8000* ⊕ *www.glasgowconcerthalls.com.*

SSE Hydro. The newest addition to Glasgow's list of concert venues, the SSE Hydro can accommodate 12,000 people underneath its huge silver dome. ⊠ *SECC Exhibition Way, The Clyde* ☎ *0141/248–3000* ⊕ *www. thehydro.com.*

DANCE AND OPERA

Theatre Royal. Glasgow is home to the Scottish Opera and Scottish Ballet, both of which perform at the Theatre Royal. Visiting dance and theater companies from many countries appear here as well. ⊠ *282 Hope St., City Center* ☎ *0141/332–9000.*

FESTIVALS

Fodor's Choice
★

Celtic Connections. This ever-expanding music festival is held in the second half of January in a number of venues across the city. Musicians from Scotland, Ireland, and other countries celebrate Celtic music, both traditional and contemporary. There are a series of hands-on workshops and a popular late-night club at the Royal Concert Hall. ☎ *0141/353–8000* ⊕ *www.celticconnections.com.*

Glasgay. Held between November and December, Glasgay is the United Kingdom's largest arts festival focusing on LGBT culture. The international lineup is always impressive and draws a huge audience. ☎ *0141/552–7575* ⊕ *www.glasgay.co.uk.*

Glasgow Jazz Festival. In late June and early July, Glasgow hosts jazz musicians from around the world in venues throughout the city, though mainly in the City Center. ⊠ *81 High St., City Center* ☎ *0141/552–3552* ⊕ *www.jazzfest.co.uk.*

FILM

Centre for Contemporary Arts. The center screens classic, independent, and children's films, mounts major art exhibitions and other arts events. It also has a restaurant and an upstairs bar and a very good small bookshop. ⊠ *350 Sauchiehall St., City Center* ☎ *0141/352–4900* ⊕ *www. cca-glasgow.com.*

Glasgow Film Theatre. An independent operation, the three-screen Glasgow Film Theatre hosts the best new releases, documentaries, and classic films. It has several programs for young people and hosts the annual Glasgow Film Festival. ⊠ *12 Rose St., City Center* ☎ *0141/332–6535* ⊕ *www.glasgowfilm.org.*

Grosvenor. This popular, compact cinema has two screens and extremely comfortable leather seats (some of them big enough for two). It's part of a small complex that includes two street-level bars and a spacious upstairs café and bar. ⊠ *Ashton La., West End* ☎ *0845/339–8444* ⊕ *www.grosvenorcafe.co.uk.*

THEATER

Ticketmaster. Tickets for theatrical performances can be purchased at theater box offices or online through Ticketmaster. ⊕ *www.ticketmaster. co.uk.*

Fodor'sChoice
★
Arches. The labyrinth of passageways under Central Station has become the Arches, a flexible space for theater and music. It hosts various festivals through the year, including October's Glasgay celebration of gay arts. There's also a basement café-bar that's open throughout the day and into the evening. ⊠ *253 Argyle St., City Center* ☎ *0141/565–1000* ⊕ *www.thearches.co.uk.*

Fodor'sChoice
★
Citizens' Theatre. Some of the most exciting theatrical performances take place at the internationally renowned Citizens' Theatre, where productions are often of hair-raising originality. Behind the theater's striking contemporary glass facade is a glorious red-and gold Victorian-era auditorium. ⊠ *119 Gorbals St., East End* ☎ *0141/429–0022* ⊕ *www. citz.co.uk.*

Fodor'sChoice
★
Òran Mór. Head to Òran Mór at lunchtime for the hugely successful series called "A Play, Pie and Pint" (and you do get all three). The series, which showcases new writing from Scotland and elsewhere, has included more than 250 works. It sells out quickly, particularly late in the week, so book well in advance. ⊠ *731 Great Western Rd., West End* ☎ *0141/357–6200* ⊕ *www.playpiepint.com.*

FAMILY
Fodor'sChoice
★
Sharmanka Kinetic Theatre. This unique spectacle is the brainchild of Eduard Bersudsky, who came to Glasgow from Russia in 1989 to continue making the mechanical sculptures that are his stock in trade. They are witty and sometimes disturbing, perhaps because they are constructed from scrap materials. They move in a kind of ballet to haunting, specially composed music punctuated by a light show. Kids under 15 get in free when accompanied by an adult. ⊠ *103 Trongate, Merchant City* ☎ *0141/552–7080* ⊕ *www.sharmanka.com* ✉ *£5–£8* ⊗ *Wed. at 3, Thurs. and Fri. at 3 and 7, Sat. at 1 and 3, Sun. at 1, 3, and 7.*

Tron Theatre. Come here for contemporary theater from Scotland and around the world. ⊠ *63 Trongate, Merchant City* ☎ *0141/552–4267* ⊕ *www.tron.co.uk.*

NIGHTLIFE

Glasgow's busy nightlife scene is impressive and varied. Bars and pubs often close at midnight on weekends, but nightclubs often stay open until 3 or 4 am. Traditional *ceilidh* (a mix of country dancing, music, and song; pronounced *kay*-lee) is not as popular with locals as it used to be (except at weddings), but you can still find it at many more tourist-oriented establishments.

Glasgow's pubs were once hangouts for serious drinkers who demanded few comforts. Times have changed, and many gritty establishments have been transformed into trendy cocktail bars or cavernous spaces with video monitors, though a few traditional bars do survive. Bars and pubs vary according to location; many in the City Center cater to business types, although some still draw a more traditional clientele.

> ## WHAT TO ORDER
>
> First-timers to Glasgow should order a pint, meaning a pint of lager. Bottled beers are available, but draft beer is the most popular beverage for men; women tend to drink wine or cocktails (yes, this gender difference is extremely obvious).

As elsewhere in Britain, electronic music—from house to techno to drum and bass—is par for the course in Glasgow's dance clubs. Much of the scene revolves around the City Center, as a late-night walk down Sauchiehall Street on Friday or Saturday will reveal.

CITY CENTER
BARS AND PUBS

Baby Grand. One of Glasgow's best-kept secrets, this intimate piano bar is hidden behind the King's Theatre. It serves good food all day, and it somehow manages to be crowded but never overcrowded, even at the busiest times. The pretheater menu is a good value, and there are tapas available on weekends. ⊠ *3 Elmbank Gardens, City Center* ☎ *0141/248–4942* ⊕ *www.babygrandglasgow.com.*

Black Sparrow. A cool Charles Bukowski theme bar named after the American writer's publishing company, the Black Sparrow serves potent cocktails and sophisticated bar food. There's also a great outdoor beer garden. ⊠ *241 North St., City Center* ☎ *0141/221–5530* ⊕ *www.theblacksparrow.co.uk.*

Fodor's Choice **Sloans.** One of Glasgow's oldest and most beautiful pubs, the wood-pan-
★ eled Sloans is always lively and welcoming and serves traditional pub food like fish-and-chips throughout the day. The upstairs ballroom is a magnificent mirrored affair, and on the floor above that is a dance floor where there's traditional music every Friday night. There's a good selection of beers and spirits, and the outdoor area is always lively when the weather cooperates. ⊠ *108 Argyle St., City Center* ☎ *0141/221–8886* ⊕ *www.sloansglasgow.com.*

CLUBS

Arches. One of the city's largest arts venues, the Arches thumps with house and techno on Friday and Saturday nights. A few times a month, it holds dressed-up gay nights. ⊠ *253 Argyle St., City Center* ☎ *0141/565–1000* ⊕ *www.thearches.co.uk.*

Sub Club. This atmospheric underground venue has staged cutting-edge music events since its jazz club days in the '50s. Legendary favorites like Saturday's SubCulture (house) and Sunday's Optimo (a truly eclectic mix for musical hedonists) pack in friendly and sweaty crowds. ⊠ *22 Jamaica St., City Center* ☎ *0141/248–4600* ⊕ *www.subclub.co.uk.*

MERCHANT CITY

BARS AND PUBS

Babbity Bowster's. A busy, friendly spot, Babbity Bowster's serves real ales and excellent, mainly Scottish food, prepared for more than a decade now by a French chef who adds his own very special touch. There is an outdoor terrace in summer and a fireplace in winter. If you like traditional music, make a point of coming on Saturday and Wednesday afternoon. ✉ *16–18 Blackfriars St., Merchant City* ☎ *0141/552–5055* ⊕ *www.babbitybowster.com.*

Fodor's Choice ★ **Scotia Bar.** The Scotia Bar serves up a taste of an authentic, old-time Glasgow pub, with some traditional folk music occasionally thrown in. ✉ *112 Stockwell St., Merchant City* ☎ *0141/552–8681* ⊕ *www. scotiabar.net.*

CLUBS

Polo Lounge. Oozing with Edwardian style, the Polo Lounge is Glasgow's largest gay club. Upstairs is a bar that resembles an old-fashioned gentlemen's club. On the two dance floors downstairs, the DJs spin something for everyone. ✉ *84 Wilson St., Merchant City* ☎ *0141/553–1221* ⊕ *www.pologlasgow.co.uk.*

WEST END

BARS AND PUBS

78. The 78 has cozy sofas, a real coal fire, and tasty vegan food. There's live music every night, with jazz on Sunday. ✉ *10–14 Kelvinhaugh St., West End* ☎ *0141/576–5018* ⊕ *www.the78cafebar.com.*

Dram. With mismatched furnishings and the odd stag's head on the wall, Dram's four large rooms are decorated in a style that can only be described as "ultra eclectic." There's a wide range of beers, but the place takes special pride in the 75 whiskies. On Thursday and Sunday, musicians gather in an informal jam session. Food is served every night until 9. ✉ *232–246 Woodlands Rd., West End* ☎ *0141/332–1622* ⊕ *www. dramglasgow.co.uk.*

Òran Mór. At the top of Byres Road, Òran Mór is in a massive church that still has its beautiful stained-glass windows. The beer garden fills up quickly in good weather. The place caters to different crowds at different times, and is open until the wee hours. ✉ *731 Great Western Rd., West End* ☎ *0141/357–6200* ⊕ *www.oran-mor.co.uk.*

COMEDY CLUBS

Stand Comedy Club. With live shows every night of the week, the Stand Comedy Club is most popular on Thursday and Friday. Prices vary according to who is appearing, and the doors open at 7:30. ✉ *333 Woodlands Rd., West End* ☎ *0844/335–8879* ⊕ *www.thestand.co.uk.*

SHOPPING

You'll find the mark of the fashion industry on downtown's hottest shopping streets. In Merchant City, Ingram Street is lined on either side by high-fashion and designer outlets like Cruise and Agent Provocateur. Buchanan Street, in the City Center, is home to many chains geared toward younger people, including Diesel, Monsoon, and USC, and malls like the elegant Princes Square and Buchanan Galleries. The adjacent Argyle Street Arcade is filled with jewelry stores. Antiques tend be found on and around West Regent Street in the City Center.

The West End has a number of small shops selling crafts, vintage clothing, and trendier fashions—punctuated by innumerable cafés and restaurants. The university dominates the area around the West End, and many shops cater to students. The easiest way to get here is by taking the subway to Hillhead.

CITY CENTER

ARCADES AND SHOPPING CENTERS

Argyll Arcade. An interesting diversion off Argyle Street is the covered Argyll Arcade, the region's largest collection of jewelers under one roof. The L-shape edifice, built in 1904, houses several locally based jewelers and a few shops specializing in antique jewelry. ⊠ *Buchanan St., City Center* ⊕ *www.argyll-arcade.com.*

Fodor's Choice ★ **Princes Square.** The city's best shopping center is the art nouveau Princes Square, a lovely space filled with high-quality shops and pleasant cafés and restaurants. A stunning glass dome was fitted over the original building, which dates back to 1841. ⊠ *48 Buchanan St., City Center* ☎ *0141/221–0324* ⊕ *www.princessquare.co.uk.*

DEPARTMENT STORES

Fodor's Choice ★ **House of Fraser.** A Glasgow institution, the House of Fraser stocks wares that reflect the city's material aspirations, including European designer clothing. There are also home-produced articles, such as tweeds, tartans, glass, and ceramics. The magnificent interior, set off by the grand staircase rising to various floors and balconies, is itself worth a visit. ⊠ *21–45 Buchanan St., City Center* ☎ *0141/221–3880* ⊕ *www. houseoffraser.co.uk.*

John Lewis. This shop is a favorite for its stylish mix of clothing, household items, electronics, and practically everything else. John Lewis claims to have "never been knowingly undersold" and prides itself on its customer service. It has a very elegant second-floor balcony café. ⊠ *Buchanan Galleries, 220 Buchanan St., City Center* ☎ *0141/353–6677* ⊕ *www.johnlewis.com/glasgow.*

SHOPPING DISTRICTS

Argyle Street. On the often-crowded pedestrian area of Argyle Street you'll find chain stores like Debenham's.

Buchanan Street. The usual suspects are clustered on this pedestrian-only street: Monsoon, Topshop, Burberry, Jaeger, and other chain stores. There are usually plenty of street entertainers to accompany you from shop to shop.

West Regent Street. If you love art or antiques, a walk along West Regent Street is highly recommended. Look for vintage jewelry and other collectibles at Victorian Village.

SPECIALTY SHOPS

ANTIQUES AND FINE ART

Compass Gallery. The gallery is something of an institution, having opened in 1969 to provide space for young and unknown artists. It shares space with Cyril Gerber Fine Arts, which specializes in British paintings from 1880 to the present. ✉ *178 W. Regent St., City Center* ☎ *0141/221–3095* ⊕ *www.compassgallery.co.uk.*

BOOKS, PAPER, AND MUSIC

Art Store. Selling cards, books, and games, the Art Store has a wonderful array of all things connected with art—paper, paints, pens—as well as craft items like beads for stringing. ✉ *94 Queen St., City Center* ☎ *0141/221–1101* ⊕ *www.artstore.co.uk.*

Waterstone's. In an age of online sales, bookstores seem to be becoming scarcer. Waterstone's remains, and it has an excellent selection on its four floors. There's also a good basement café. ✉ *153-57 Sauchiehall St., City Center* ☎ *0141/248–4814* ⊕ *www.waterstones.com.*

CLOTHING

Cruise. Male and female fashionistas shouldn't miss Cruise, which caters to those at the high end of fashion. ✉ *180 Ingram St., City Center* ☎ *0141/572–3200* ⊕ *www.cruisefashion.co.uk.*

SCOTTISH SPECIALTIES

Catherine Shaw. For high-quality gifts in Charles Rennie Mackintosh style, head to Catherine Shaw. ✉ *32 Argyll Arcade, City Center* ☎ *0141/221–9038.*

Hector Russell Kiltmakers. This shop specializes in Highland outfits, wool and cashmere clothing, and women's fashions. ✉ *110 Buchanan St., City Center* ☎ *0141/221–0217* ⊕ *www.hector-russell.com.*

SPORTS GEAR

Tiso Glasgow Outdoor Experience. You'll find good-quality outerwear at Tiso Glasgow Outdoor Experience, handy if you're planning some Highland walks. ✉ *129 Buchanan St., City Center* ☎ *0141/248–4877* ⊕ *www.tiso.com.*

14

MERCHANT CITY

Many of Glasgow's young and upwardly mobile types make their home in Merchant City. Shopping here is expensive, but the area is worth visiting if you're seeking youthful Glasgow styles. You'll find Cruise, Jigsaw, and Agent Provocateur here, among many others.

SPECIALTY SHOPS

ANTIQUES AND FINE ART

Fodor'sChoice **Glasgow Print Studio.** Essentially an artists' cooperative, the Glasgow ★ Print Studio's facilities launched a generation of outstanding painters, printers, and designers. The work of members past and present can be seen (and bought) at the Print Studio Gallery on King Street. ✉ *103 Trongate, Merchant City* ☎ *0141/552–0704* ⊕ *www.gpsart.co.uk* ☻ *Tues.–Sat. 10–5:30.*

WEST END

SPECIALTY SHOPS

BOOKS, PAPER, AND MUSIC

Fopp. This funky shop is an extravaganza of music, books, and DVDs. It's a small space, but the selection is huge. The prices are a lot more reasonable than those at most chain stores. ⊠ *358 Byres Rd., West End* ☎ *0141/222–2128* ⊕ *www.foppreturns.com* ☉ *Mon.–Sun. 9–6.*

CLOTHING

Strawberry Fields. Full of darling designs, Strawberry Fields sells colorful, high-end children's wear. ⊠ *517 Great Western Rd., West End* ☎ *0141/339–1121.*

FOOD

Iain Mellis Cheesemonger. This shop has a superb, seemingly endless selection of fine Scottish cheeses, as well as others from England and across Europe. ⊠ *492 Great Western Rd., West End* ☎ *0141/339–8998* ⊕ *www.mellischeese.net.*

Peckham's Delicatessen. This deli is *the* place for Continental sausages, cheeses, and anything else you'd need for a delicious picnic, including wine and beer. The sandwiches are also outstanding. ⊠ *61–65 Glassford St., West End* ☎ *0141/553–0666* ⊕ *www.peckhams.co.uk.*

EAST END

ARCADES AND SHOPPING CENTERS

Barras. This indoor market, on London Road in the Glasgow Cross neighborhood east of the City Center, prides itself on selling everything "from a needle to an anchor." Stalls hawk antique (and not-so-antique) furniture, bric-a-brac, good and not-so-good jewelry, and textiles—you name it, it's here. ⊠ *Gallowgate, East End.*

SPORTS AND THE OUTDOORS

FOOTBALL

The city has been sports mad, especially for football (soccer), for more than 100 years. The historic rivalry between its two main football clubs, the Rangers and Celtic, is legendary. Partick Thistle, another football team, is a less contentious alternative for football fans. Matches are held usually on Saturday or Sunday in winter. Admission prices start at about £20. Don't go looking for a family-day-out atmosphere; football remains a fiercely contested game attended mainly by males, though the stadiums at Ibrox and Celtic Park are fast becoming family-friendly.

Celtic. This famous football club wears white-and-green stripes and plays in the east at Celtic Park. There are regular stadium tours, which must be booked ahead. The stadium is known locally as Parkhead, which refers to the area where it is located. ⊠ *Celtic Park, 18 Kerrydale St., East End* ☎ *0871/551–4308* ⊕ *www.celticfc.net* ☑ *Tours £8.50* ☉ *Tours daily at 11, noon, 1:45, and 2:30, except game days.*

Partick Thistle. Soccer in Glasgow isn't just blue or green, nor is it dominated by international players and big money. Partick Thistle Football Club, known as the Jags, wears red and yellow, and its home field is Firhill Park. ⊠ *80 Firhill Rd., West End* ☎ *0141/579–1971* ⊕ *www. ptfc.co.uk.*

Rangers. The Rangers wear blue and play at Ibrox, on the south side of the Clyde. Stadium tours on Friday, Saturday, and Sunday cost £8, and booking ahead is essential. ⊠ *Ibrox, 150 Edmiston Dr., South Side* ☎ *0871/702–1972* ⊕ *www.rangers.co.uk* 🖃 *Tours £8.*

SIDE TRIPS: AYRSHIRE

The jigsaw puzzle of firths and straits and interlocking islands that you see as you fly into Glasgow Airport harbors numerous tempting one-day excursion destinations. For many people a highlight of this region is Robert Burns country, a 40-minute drive from Glasgow. The poet was born in Alloway, beside Ayr, and the towns and villages where he lived and loved make for an interesting day out. As time goes by, Burns and his work have increased in stature. When you plunge into Burns country, don't forget that he's held in extreme reverence by Scots of all backgrounds. They may argue about Sir Walter Scott and Bonnie Prince Charlie, but there's no disputing the merits of the author of "Bonnie Doon" and "Auld Lang Syne."

GETTING HERE AND AROUND

From Glasgow you can travel by bus or train to Ayr for the Burns Heritage Trail, and to Troon and Ayr to play golf. Bus companies also operate one-day guided excursions; for details, contact the tourist information center in Glasgow or the Strathclyde Passenger Transport Travel Centre. Traveline Scotland has helpful information.

If you're driving from Glasgow, there are two main routes to Ayr. The quickest is to take the M77 to the A77, which takes you all the way to Ayr. Alloway is well signposted when you get to Ayr. The alternative and much slower route is the coast road; take the M8 to Greenock and continue down the coast on the A78 until you meet the A77 and continue on into Burns Country.

IRVINE

24 miles south of Glasgow.

Beyond Irvine's cobbled streets and grand Victorian buildings, look for a peaceful crescent-shape harbor and fishermen's cottages huddled in solidarity against the Atlantic winds. The Scottish Maritime Museum pays homage to the town's seafaring past. Scotland's national poet, Robert Burns, lived here in 1781.

GETTING HERE AND AROUND

By car, take the M8 from Glasgow, then the A726 and the A736 to Irvine. By rail, it's a 40-minute journey from Glasgow Central Station.

14

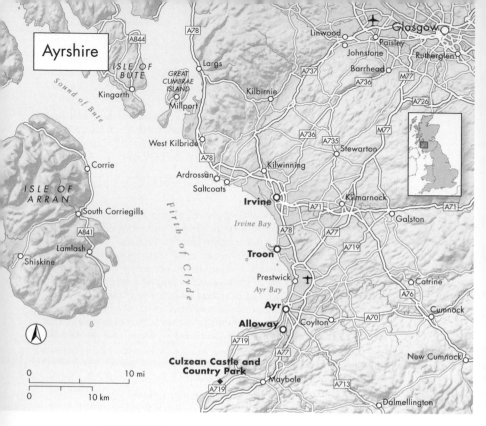

ESSENTIALS

Visitor Information Irvine Tourist Information Centre ☒ *New St.*
☏ *01294/313886.*

EXPLORING

Scottish Maritime Museum. On the waterfront in the coastal town of Irvine,
this museum brings together ships and boats—both models and the real
thing—to tell the tale of Scotland's maritime history, as well as chronicle
the lives of its boatbuilders, its fishermen, its sailors. The atmospheric
Linthouse Engine Building, part of a former shipyard, hosts most of
the displays. The museum also includes a shipyard worker's tenement
home that you can explore. ☒ *6 Gottries Rd.* ☏ *01294/278283* ⊕ *www.
scottishmaritimemuseum.org* ☒ *£7* ☉ *Mar.–Oct., daily 10–5.*

GOLF

Fodor's Choice **Western Gailes Golf Club.** Known as the finest natural links course in
★ Scotland, Western Gailes is entirely nature-made, and the greens are
kept in truly magnificent condition. This is the final qualifying course
when the British Open is held at Royal Troon or Turnberry. Tom
Watson lists the par-5 sixth hole as one of his favorites. ☒ *Gailes Rd.*
☏ *01294/311649* ⊕ *www.westerngailes.com* ☒ *Green fee: Apr.–Sept.,
Mon., Wed., and Fri. £130, Sat. £125, Sun. £130. Mar. and Oct. £85;*

Nov.–Feb. £60 ⛳ *18 holes, 6640 yds, par 71* 🕓 *Mon., Wed., Fri., and weekend afternoons.*

TROON

4 miles south of Irvine, 30 miles south of Glasgow, 6 miles north of Ayr.

The small coastal town of Troon is famous for its outstanding golf course, Royal Troon. You can easily see that golf is popular here and in this area: at times the whole 60-mile-long Ayrshire coast seems one endless course. The town's several miles of sandy beaches provide other diversions. It's easy to get to Troon by train or bus from both Glasgow and Ayr.

14

GETTING HERE AND AROUND

From Glasgow Central Station, board an Ayr-bound train and get off at Troon. By car, take the M77/A77 toward Prestwick Airport and follow the signs to Troon.

WHERE TO EAT

$$ SEAFOOD Fodor's Choice ★ 🍴 **MacCallums Oyster Bar.** Located in Troon Harbor, this outstanding seafood restaurant's menu varies according to the day's catch, but you can usually count on lobster in garlic butter, seared scallops, or grilled langoustines that taste of the sea. The fish pie is justly famous, and excellent light white wines match the freshness of the food. Solid wooden tables and other simple furnishings add a rustic touch to the dining room. For a more modest price, try the adjacent Wee Hurrie, possibly one of the best fish-and-chips shops in Scotland, serving monkfish and oysters with chips as well as the usual fare. Finding McCallums is a bit of an adventure, but it's well worth the trek. [$] *Average main: £17* ✉ *Harbour Rd.* ☎ *01292/319339* 🕓 *Closed Mon. No dinner Sun.*

GOLF

Royal Troon Golf Club. Of the two courses at Royal Troon, it's the Old Course—a traditional links course with superb sea views—that's frequently used for the British Open. Visitor season tee times are limited to certain days from spring through early fall, and change each year according to the tournament program. **■TIP→ Advance payment and a deposit are required, as is a handicap certificate.** ✉ *Craigend Rd.* ☎ *01292/311555* 🌐 *www.royaltroon.com* 🎫 *Green fee: Old Course £180 (includes one round on Portland Course)* ⛳ *Old Course: 18 holes, 6641 yds, SSS 73; Portland Course: 18 holes, 6289 yds, SSS 71* 🕓 *Mid-Apr.–early Sept. and mid-Sept.–mid-Oct., Mon., Tues., and Thurs. for visitors.*

AYR AND ALLOWAY

6 miles south of Troon, 34 miles south of Glasgow.

Robert Burns described Ayr as a town unsurpassed "for honest men and bonny lasses." If he were to visit today, he might also mention the good shopping, from clothing to jewelry. If you're on the Robert Burns trail, head for Alloway, on B7024 in Ayr's southern suburbs. A number of sights here are part of the **Burns National Heritage Park**, including the magnificent Robert Burns Birthplace Museum.

GETTING HERE AND AROUND

From Glasgow you can take the bus or train to Ayr; travel time is about an hour (a bit less by train). Drivers can use the A78 and A77 near the coast; a car would provide more flexibility to see the Burns sites around Alloway.

ESSENTIALS

Visitor Information Ayr Visitor Information Centre ✉ *22 Sandgate* ☎ *01292/288688* ⊕ *www.ayrshire-arran.com.*

EXPLORING

Burns Cottage. In the delightful Burns Heritage Park, this thatched cottage is where Scotland's national poet lived for his first seven years. It has a living room, a kitchen, and a stable, one behind the other. The life and times of Burns, born in 1759, are beautifully and creatively illustrated, particularly in the videos of daily life in the 18th century ✉ *Greenfield Ave., Alloway* ☎ *0844/493–2601* ⊕ *www.burnsmuseum.org.uk* 💰 *£8, includes Burns Monument and Robert Burns Birthplace Museum* ☉ *Apr.–Sept., daily 10–5:30; Oct.–Mar., daily 10–5.*

Fodor's Choice ★ **Robert Burns Birthplace Museum.** Besides being a poet of delicacy and depth, Robert Burns was also a rebel, a thinker, a lover, a good companion, and a man of the countryside. This wonderful museum explains why the Scots so admire this complex "man o' pairts." The imaginative museum presents each of his poems in context, with commentaries sensitively written in a modern version of the Scots language in which he spoke and wrote. Headsets let you hear the poems sung or spoken. The exhibit is vibrant and interactive, with touch screens that allow you to debate his views on politics, love, taxation, revolution, and Scottishness. An elegant café offers a place to pause, while the kids can play in the adjoining garden. ✉ *Murdoch's Lone, Alloway* ☎ *0844/493–2601* ⊕ *www.burnsmuseum.org.uk* 💰 *£8, includes Burns Cottage and Burns Monument* ☉ *Apr.–Sept., daily 10–5:30; Oct.–Mar., daily 10–5.*

WHERE TO EAT

$$
BRITISH
✕ **Brig o' Doon House.** Originally built in 1827, this attractive restaurant often has a piper by the door to greet hungry travelers. The setting is very Scottish, with tartan carpets, dark-wood paneling, and buck heads mounted on the walls. The bar is a shrine to Robert Burns, and the surrounding gardens overlook the Brig o' Doon as well as a small, rushing river. The food keeps to the Scottish theme: try panfried scallops with citrus butter to start, and venison casserole with juniper berries and creamed potatoes or the haggis with neeps and tatties (served with

> ### REMEMBERING MR. BURNS
>
> Born in Ayrshire, Robert Burns (1759–96) is one of Scotland's treasures. The poet and balladeer had a style that was his and his alone. His most famous song, "Auld Lang Syne," is heard everywhere on New Year's Day. Burns's talent, charisma, and good looks made him an icon to both the upper and lower classes (and made him quite popular with the ladies). Today his birthday (January 25) is considered a national holiday; on "Burns Night" young and old alike get together for Burns Suppers and recite his work over neeps, tatties, and drams of the country's finest whisky.

a dram) as a main course. There are several rooms for rent upstairs. [$] *Average main: £16* ✉ *High Maybole Rd., Alloway* ☎ *01292/442466.*

GOLF

Fodor's Choice ★ **Turnberry.** One of the most famous links courses in Scotland, the Ailsa Course is open to the elements, and the 9th hole requires you to hit the ball over the open sea. The British Open was hosted here in 1977, 1986, 1994, and 2009. A second course, the Kintyre, is more compact, with tricky sloped greens. Five of the holes have sea views. ✉ *Turnberry Resort, Maidens Rd., off A719, Turnberry* ☎ *01655/331000* 🌐 *www.turnberryresort.co.uk* 🎟 *Green fee: Ailsa Course: £165 for hotel guests, £199 for nonguests; Kintyre Course: £105 for hotel guests, £135 for nonguests* ⛳ *Ailsa Course 18 holes, 7217 yds, par 70; Kintyre Course 18 holes, 6921 yds, par 72* 🕒 *Daily.*

14

CULZEAN CASTLE AND COUNTRY PARK

12 miles south of Ayr, 50 miles south of Glasgow.

There's plenty to do at this popular spot between visiting the Adam-designed house and touring the extensive grounds.

GETTING HERE AND AROUND

Stagecoach buses run from Ayr to the park entrance; the nearest train station from Glasgow is at Maybole, 4 miles to the east, but there is Stagecoach bus service to the park entrance. Note that the park entrance is a mile from the castle visitor center.

EXPLORING

FAMILY Fodor's Choice ★ **Culzean Castle and Country Park.** The dramatic cliff-top castle of Culzean (pronounced ku-*lain*) is the National Trust for Scotland's most popular property. Robert Adam designed the neoclassical mansion, complete with a walled garden, in 1777. The grounds are enormous, combining parkland, forests, and a beach looking out over the Atlantic Ocean; the lush shrubberies reflect the warm currents that explain the mild climate. In the castle itself you can visit the armory, luxuriously appointed salons and bedchambers, and a nursery with its lovely cradle in a boat. Adams's grand double spiral staircase is the high point of its design. There's a free audio tour, and guided tours are available daily at 11 and 2:30. A short walk through the woods brings you to the visitor center with shops and a restaurant. ✉ *A719, Maybole* ☎ *0844/493–2149* 🌐 *www.culzeanexperience.org* 🎟 *Park £10, park and castle £15* 🕒 *Park: daily 9:30–sunset. Castle: Apr.–Oct., daily 10:30–5; last admission at 4.*

WHERE TO STAY

$$$$ HOTEL 🏨 **Eisenhower Hotel.** It would be hard to imagine a more spectacular location than the upper floors of Culzean Castle, which looks out towards Arran and the Atlantic Ocean. **Pros:** beautiful setting; luxurious lodging; a strong sense of history. **Cons:** a little remote; rather formal; not for minimalists. [$] *Rooms from: £250* ✉ *Culzean Castle, A719, Maybole* ☎ *01655/884455* 🌐 *www.culzeanexperience.org* 🛏 *6 rooms* 🍴 *No meals.*

SIDE TRIPS: THE CLYDE VALLEY

The River Clyde is (or certainly was) famous for its shipbuilding, yet its upper reaches flow through some of Scotland's most fertile farmlands, rich with crops of tomatoes and fruit. It's an interesting area with some museums, most notably at New Lanark, that tell the story of the growth of manufacturing.

GETTING HERE AND AROUND

If you're driving from Glasgow, head south on the M74 and turn on to the A72. This is the main road through the Clyde Valley, ending at Lanark. Train service runs from Glasgow Central Station to Hamilton (near Blantyre) and Lanark; for details, check National Rail.

BLANTYRE

8 miles southeast of Glasgow.

Blantyre, a suburb of Hamilton, is not a pretty town. The explorer David Livingstone was born here and a center devoted to his travels is the main draw.

GETTING HERE AND AROUND

From Glasgow, drive along the M74, then transfer to the A725 at junction 5. The train from Glasgow Central takes just 20 minutes.

EXPLORING

David Livingstone Centre. Set among gardens above the riverbank, the David Livingstone Centre is based partly in the tiny one-room tenement apartment where the explorer-missionary (1813–73) spent his first 23 years. The rest of the museum is devoted to his travels across Africa, depicted in small, framed tableaux that light up as you walk past them. His meeting with Henry Stanley, sent by the *New York Times* to find him and bring him back, is commemorated. On meeting him, Stanley famously said, "Dr Livingstone, I presume." Livingstone refused the invitation and died in Africa. Copies of Livingstone's letters are displayed, and there is plenty of opportunity for youngsters to interact with the exhibits. ✉ *165 Station Rd.* ☎ *0844/493–2207* ⊕ *www.nts. org.uk* ✆ *£6.50* ⊗ *Mar.–Oct., Mon.–Sat. 10–5:30, Sun. 12:30–5:30.*

NATIONAL MUSEUM OF RURAL LIFE

9 miles south of Glasgow.

The effect of farming on the land and on people's lives is the focus of this museum near Glasgow.

EXPLORING

FAMILY   **National Museum of Rural Life.** This lovely museum, a 20-minute drive from Glasgow, is slightly off the beaten track but well worth the trip. Set in a rural area, it explores every aspect of the country's agricultural heritage. In a modern building resembling a huge barn, you learn about how farming transformed the land, experience the life and hardships of those who worked it, and see displays of tools and machines from across the ages. Take a tractor ride to a fully functioning 1950s

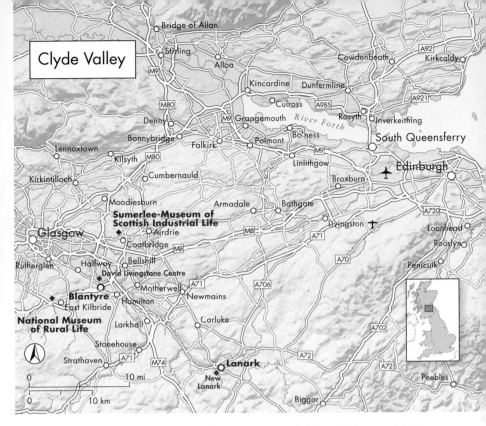

Clyde Valley

farmhouse. There are also some great exhibits geared toward children. ✉ *Philipshill Rd., East Kilbride* ☎ *0300/123–6789* ⊕ *www.nms.ac.uk/ rural* ⛁ *£6.50* ⊙ *Daily 10–5.*

SUMMERLEE–MUSEUM OF SCOTTISH INDUSTRIAL LIFE

10 miles east of Glasgow.

A former ironworks is now a museum with a re-created mine and exhibits that document industrial history and the lives of former workers.

EXPLORING

FAMILY **Summerlee–Museum of Scottish Industrial Life.** On the site of the old Summerlee Ironworks, this vast and exciting museum re-creates a mine and the miners' rows (the cottages where miners and their families lived). An electric tram transports you here from the huge hall where industrial machines vie with exhibits about ordinary life. Later you can stroll along the canal and take the kids to a fine playground. The drive from Glasgow takes less than 15 minutes. ✉ *Heritage Way, Coatbridge* ☎ *01236/638460* ⊕ *www.visitlanarkshire.com/summerlee* ⛁ *Free.*

LANARK

19 miles east of Glasgow.

Set in pleasing, rolling countryside, Lanark is a typical old Scottish town. It's now most often associated with its unique neighbor New Lanark, a model workers' community about a mile to the south.

GETTING HERE AND AROUND

If you're driving, take the M74 to the A72. The train from Glasgow Central Station takes 50 minutes or so.

ESSENTIALS

Visitor Information Lanark Visitor Information Centre ⊠ *Horsemarket, Ladyacre Rd.* ☎ *01555/661661.*

EXPLORING

FAMILY

Fodor's Choice

★

New Lanark. Now a World Heritage Site, New Lanark was home to a social experiment at the beginning of the Industrial Revolution. Robert Owen (1771–1858), together with his father-in-law David Dale (1739–1806), set out to create a model industrial community with well-designed worker homes, a school, and public buildings, as well as cotton mills. Owen went on to establish other communities on similar principles, both in Britain and in the United States. After many changes of fortune, the mills eventually closed. One of the buildings has been converted into a visitor center that tells the story of this brave social experiment. You can also explore Robert Owen's house, the school, and a mill worker's house, and enjoy the Annie McLeod Experience, a fairground ride that takes you through the story of one mill worker's life. Other restored structures hold various shops and eateries; one has a rooftop garden.

The River Clyde powers its way through a beautiful wooded gorge here, and its waters were once harnessed to drive textile-mill machinery. Upstream it flows through some of the finest river scenery anywhere in Lowland Scotland, with woods and spectacular waterfalls. ⊠ *New Lanark Rd., New Lanark* ☎ *01555/661345* ⊕ *www.newlanark.org* ⊠ *£8.50* ⊗ *Oct.–Mar., daily 11–5; Apr.–Sept., daily 10–5.*

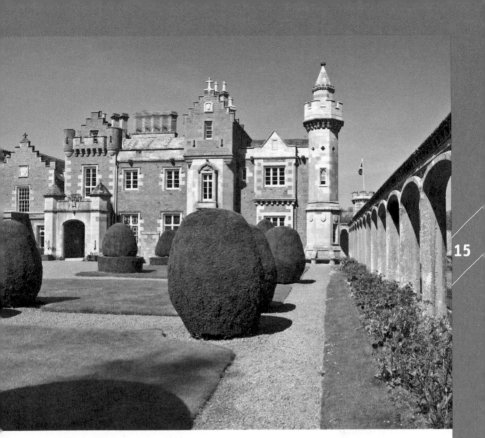

15

THE BORDERS AND
THE SOUTHWEST

WELCOME TO THE BORDERS AND THE SOUTHWEST

TOP REASONS TO GO

★ **Ancient abbeys:** The great abbeys of the Border regions, and the Whithorn Priory and the wonderful Sweetheart Abbey in the southwest, are in ruins, but they retain hints of their former grandeur.

★ **Outdoor activities:** You can walk, bicycle, or even ride horses across Galloway or through the Borders. Abandoned railway tracks make good paths, and there are forests and moorlands.

★ **Stately homes and castles:** The landed aristocracy still lives in these grand mansions, and most of the homes are open to visitors. Try Floors Castle or Traquair House in the east. Threave, Drumlanrig, and Caerlaverock Castle near Dumfries evoke grander times.

★ **Literary Scotland:** Sir Walter Scott's Abbotsford House is unmissable, and poet Robert Burns spent much of his working life in Dumfries.

★ **Shopping:** Mill shops are abundant, and are well worth a visit for their wonderful woolens.

1 The Borders. Borders towns cluster around and between two rivers—the Tweed and its tributary, the Teviot. These are mostly textile towns with plenty of personality, where residents take fierce pride in their local municipalities. The area's top attractions include Jedburgh Abbey, Floors Castle in Kelso, and Abbotsford House just outside Melrose.

2 Dumfries and Galloway. Easygoing and peaceful, towns in this southwestern region are usually very attractive, with wide streets and colorful buildings. The Solway Firth is a vast nature preserve, and the climate of the west sustains the surprising tropical plants at the Logan Botanic Gardens and the gardens at Threave Castle.

15

GETTING ORIENTED

Once a battleground region separating Scotland and England, the Borders area today is a gateway between the two countries. This is a place of upland moors and hills, fertile farmland, and forested river valleys. Yet it also embraces the rugged coastline between Edinburgh and Berwick. It's rustic and peaceful, with century-old textile mills, abbeys, castles, and gardens. The area is a big draw for hikers and walking enthusiasts, too. The Borders region is also steeped in history, with Mary, Queen of Scots a powerful presence despite the relatively short time she spent here.

Updated by Mike Gonzalez

The Borders region, south of Edinburgh, has more stately homes, fortified castles, and medieval abbeys than any other part of Scotland. This is also Sir Walter Scott territory, including his pseudo-baronial home at Abbotsford. The area embraces the whole 90-mile course of one of Scotland's greatest rivers, the Tweed. Passing woodlands luxuriant with game birds, the river flows in rushing torrents through this fertile land. Southwest of the Borders is Dumfries and Galloway, a low-key area with gentle coastal and upland areas.

For centuries the Borders was a battlefield, where English and Scottish troops remained locked in a struggle for its possession. At different times, parts of the region have been in English hands, just as slices of northern England (Berwick-upon-Tweed, for example) have been in Scottish hands. The castles and fortified houses across the Borders are the surviving witnesses to those times. After the Union of 1707, fortified houses gradually gave way to the luxurious country mansions that pepper the area. And in the 19th century the area began to collect grand country houses built by fashionable architects.

All the main routes between London and Edinburgh traverse the Borders, whose hinterland of undulating pastures, woods, and valleys is enclosed within three lonely groups of hills: the Cheviots, the Moorfoots, and the Lammermuirs. Hamlets and prosperous country towns dot the land, giving valley slopes a lived-in look, yet the total population is still sparse. The sheep that are the basis of the region's prosperous textile industry vastly outnumber the human population.

To the west is the region of Dumfries and Galloway, on the shores of the Solway Firth. It might appear to be an extension of the Borders, but the southwest has a history all its own. From these ports ships sailed to the Americas, carrying country dwellers driven from their land to make room for the sheep that still roam the hills across southern Scotland. Inland, the earth rises toward high hills, forest, and bleak but captivating moorland, whereas nearer the coast you can find pretty farmlands, small villages, and unassuming towns. The shoreline is washed by the North Atlantic Drift (Scotland's answer to the Gulf Stream), and first-time visitors are always surprised to see palm trees and exotic plants thriving in gardens and parks along the coast.

At the heart of the region is Dumfries, the "Queen o' the South." Once a major port and commercial center, its glamour is now slightly faded. But the memory of poet Robert Burns, who spent several years living and working here and who is buried in the town, shines as bright as ever.

THE BORDERS AND THE SOUTHWEST PLANNER

WHEN TO GO

Because many lodgings and some sights are privately owned and shut down from early autumn until early April, the area is less suited to off-season touring than some other parts of Scotland. The best time to visit is between Easter and late September. The region also looks magnificent in autumn, especially along the wooded river valleys of the Borders. Late spring is the time to see the rhododendrons in the gardens of Dumfries and Galloway.

PLANNING YOUR TIME

If you're driving north along the A1 toward Edinburgh, take a tour around the prosperous Borders towns. Turn onto the A698 at Berwick-upon-Tweed, which will take you along the Scottish–English border to Kelso, Jedburgh, and Melrose. It's 36 miles from Jedburgh to Peebles, a good place to stay overnight. Another day might begin with a visit to Walter Scott's lovely Abbotsford House, and then some shopping in any of these prosperous towns.

To the west, Dumfries and Galloway beckon. Travel east on the A708 to Moffat and across the A74 toward Dumfries. Two days would give you time to explore Burns sites and more in Dumfries. From Dumfries you can visit Sweetheart Abbey (8 miles away), Caerlaverock Castle (9 miles away), and Threave Gardens (20 miles away). Castle Douglas is a good place to stop for lunch. The A710 and A711 take you along the dramatic coastline of the Solway Firth.

Soon you will be able to travel by train to the Borders from Edinburgh; in 2015, a new rail line from Edinburgh's Waverley Station to Tweedbank, in the heart of the Borders, is set to begin service.

GETTING HERE AND AROUND

AIR TRAVEL

The nearest Scottish airports are at Edinburgh, Glasgow, and Prestwick (outside of Glasgow).

BOAT AND FERRY TRAVEL

P&O European Ferries and Stena Line operate from Larne, in Northern Ireland, to Cairnryan, near Stranraer, several times daily. The crossing takes one hour on the Superstar Express, two hours on other ferries.

Boat and Ferry Contacts P&O European Ferries ☎ *08716/642020* ⊕ *www. poferries.com.* **Stena Line** ☎ *08447/707070* ⊕ *www.stenaline.co.uk.*

BUS TRAVEL

If you're approaching from the south, check with Scottish Citylink, National Express, or First about buses from Edinburgh and Glasgow. In the Borders, Munro's of Jedburgh and Perryman's Buses offer service within the region. Stagecoach Western is the main bus company serving Dumfries and Galloway.

Bus Contacts First ☎ *08708/727271* ⊕ *www.firstgroup.com.* **Munro's of Jedburgh** ☎ *01835/862253* ⊕ *www.munrosofjedburgh.co.uk.* **National Express** ☎ *08717/818178* ⊕ *www.nationalexpress.com.* **Perryman's Buses** ☎ *01289/308719* ⊕ *www.perrymansbuses.co.uk.* **Scottish Citylink** ☎ *0871/266–3333* ⊕ *www.citylink.co.uk.* **Stagecoach Western** ☎ *01387/253496 in Dumfries, 01563/525192 in Kilmarnock, 01776/704484 in Stranraer* ⊕ *www.stagecoachbus.com.*

CAR TRAVEL

Traveling by car is the best way to explore the area. The main route into both the Borders and Galloway from the south is the M6, which becomes the M74 at the border. You can also take the scenic and leisurely A7 northwestward toward Edinburgh, or the A75 and other parallel routes westward into Dumfries, Galloway, and the ferry ports of Stranraer and Cairnryan.

There are several other possible routes: starting from the east, the A1 brings you from the English city of Newcastle to the border in about an hour. The A1 has the added attraction of Berwick-upon-Tweed, on the English side of the border, but traffic on the route is heavy. Moving west, the A697, which leaves the A1 north of Morpeth (in England) and crosses the border at Coldstream, is a leisurely back-road option. The A68 is probably the most scenic route to Scotland: after climbing to Carter Bar, it reveals a view of the Borders hills and windy skies before dropping into the ancient town of Jedburgh.

The best way to explore the region is to get off the main, and often crowded, arterial roads and onto the little back roads. You may occasionally be delayed by a herd of cows on their way to the milking parlor, or a pheasant fluttering across the road, but this is often far more pleasant than, for example, tussling on the A75 with heavy-goods vehicles rushing to make the Irish ferries.

TRAIN TRAVEL

At the time of this writing, a rail link from Edinburgh to Tweedbank was scheduled to start service by summer 2015; check ⊕ *www.bordersrailway.co.uk* for updates. In the southwest, trains headed from London's Euston to Glasgow stop at Carlisle, just south of the border, and some also stop at Lockerbie. Trains between Glasgow and Carlisle stop at Dumfries. From Glasgow there is service on the coastal route to Stranraer.

First Edinburgh has buses linking towns in the region with train service at Carlisle, Edinburgh, and Berwick.

Train Contacts First Edinburgh ☎ *0131/663–9233, 0871/200–2233* ⊕ *www.firstgroup.com.* National Rail ☎ *08457/484950* ⊕ *www.nationalrail.co.uk.* ScotRail ☎ *08457/550033* ⊕ *www.scotrail.co.uk.*

RESTAURANTS

Until recently, most good restaurants in the region were located in hotels, but today things are beginning to change. Good independent eateries are popping up in small (and sometime unlikely) towns and villages, and many of these new establishments specialize in fresh local ingredients. Seasonal menus are now popular in the area.

HOTELS

From top-quality, full-service hotels to quaint 18th-century drovers' inns to cozy bed-and-breakfasts, the Borders has all manner of lodging options. Choices in Dumfries and Galloway may be a little less expensive than in the Borders (with the same full range of services). These days many establishments have a shifting scale and are willing to lower their rates depending on availability. *Hotel reviews have been shortened. For full information, visit Fodors.com.*

WHAT IT COSTS IN POUNDS			
$	**$$**	**$$$**	**$$$$**
Restaurants	under £15	£15–£19	£20–£25	over £25
Hotels	under £100	£100–£160	£161–£220	over £220

Restaurant prices are the average cost of a main course at dinner or, if dinner is not served, at lunch. Hotel prices are the lowest cost of a standard double room in high season, including 20% V.A.T.

VISITOR INFORMATION

Visit Scottish Borders has offices in Jedburgh and Peebles. The Dumfries & Galloway Tourist Board can be found in Dumfries and Stranraer. Seasonal information centers are at Castle Douglas, , Kelso, Kirkcudbright, Langholm, Melrose, and Selkirk.

THE BORDERS

Although the Borders has many attractions, it's most famous for being the home base for Sir Walter Scott (1771–1832), the early-19th-century poet, novelist, and creator of *Ivanhoe*, who single-handedly transformed Scotland's image from that of a land of brutal savages to one of romantic and stirring deeds and magnificent landscapes. The novels of Scott are not read much nowadays—frankly, some of them are difficult to wade through—but the mystique that he created, the aura of historical romance, has outlasted his books. The ruined abbeys, historical houses, and grand vistas of the Borders provide a perfect backdrop.

A visit to at least one of the region's four great ruined abbeys makes the quintessential Borders experience. The monks in these powerful, long-abandoned religious orders were the first to work the fleeces of their sheep flocks, thus laying the groundwork for what is still the area's main manufacturing industry.

15

Borders folks take great pride in the region's fame as Scotland's main woolen-goods manufacturing area. Its main towns—Jedburgh, Selkirk, Peebles, Kelso, and Melrose—retain an air of prosperity and confidence with their solid stone houses and elegant town squares. Although many of the mills have closed in recent years, the pride in local identity is evident in the fiercely contested Melrose Sevens rugby competition in April and the annual Common Ridings—local events commemorating the time when towns needed to patrol their borders—throughout June and July.

JEDBURGH

50 miles south of Edinburgh, 95 miles southeast of Glasgow.

The town of Jedburgh (*burgh* is always pronounced *burra* by Scots) was for centuries the first major Scottish target of invading English armies. In more peaceful times it developed textile mills, most of which have since languished. The large landscaped area around the town's tourist information center was once a mill but now provides an encampment for the armies of modern tourists. The past still clings to this little town, however. The ruined abbey dominates the skyline, a reminder of the formerly strong governing role of the Borders abbeys.

GETTING HERE AND AROUND

The best and easiest way to travel in this region is by car. From Edinburgh you can take the A68 (about 45 minutes) or the A7 (about an hour). From Glasgow take the M8, then the A68 direct to Jedburgh (about two hours).

There are fairly good bus connections from all major Scottish cities to Jedburgh. From Edinburgh, direct routes to Melrose take about two hours. From Glasgow it takes 3½ hours to reach Melrose. From Melrose it's just 20 minutes to Jedburgh.

A new rail link between Edinburgh and Tweedbank, about 15 miles northwest of Jedburgh, is scheduled to be completed in summer 2015.

ESSENTIALS

Visitor Information Jedburgh Visitor Centre ✉ *Abbey Pl.* ☎*01835/863170* ⊕ *www.visitscotland.com/jedburgh.*

EXPLORING

FAMILY   **Harestanes Countryside Visitor Centre.** Housed in a former farmhouse 3 miles north of Jedburgh, this visitor center portrays life in the Scottish Borders through art exhibitions and natural history displays. Crafts such as woodworking and tile making are taught here, and finished projects are often on display. There's a gift shop and tearoom, and outside are meandering paths, quiet roads for bike rides, and the biggest children's play area in the Borders. It is also on one of the best-known walking routes in the Borders, the St. Cuthbert's Path. ✉ *Junction of A68 and B6400, 4 miles north of Jedburgh, Ancrum* ☎*01835/830306* 🖾 *Free* ☉ *Apr.–Oct., daily 10–5.*

Fodor'sChoice   **Jedburgh Abbey.** The most impressive of the Borders abbeys towers above
★   Jedburgh. The abbey was nearly destroyed by the English Earl of Hertford's forces in 1544–45, during the destructive time known as the Rough

Wooing. This was English King Henry VIII's (1491–1547) armed attempt to persuade the Scots that it was a good idea to unite the kingdoms by the marriage of his young son to the infant Mary, Queen of Scots (1542–87); the Scots disagreed and sent Mary to France instead. The story is explained in vivid detail at the visitor center, which also has information about the ruins and an audio tour. Ground patterns and foundations are all that remain of the once-powerful religious complex. ✉ *High St.* ☎ *01835/863925* 🌐 *www.historic-scotland.gov.uk/places* 🎟 *£5.50* 🕓 *Apr.–Sept., daily 9:30–5:30; Oct.–Mar., daily 9:30–4:30.*

THE COMMON RIDINGS

Borders communities have reestablished their identities through the gatherings known as the Common Ridings. Long ago it was essential that each town be able to defend its area, and this need became formalized in mounted gatherings to "ride the marches," or patrol the boundaries. The Common Ridings, which celebrate this history, possess much more authenticity than the concocted Highland Games so often taken to be the essence of Scotland. You can watch the excitement of clattering hooves and banners proudly displayed, but this is essentially a time for native Borderers.

Jedburgh Castle Jail. This was the site of the Howard Reform Prison, established in 1820. It sits behind the front of the castle that previously stood in the same spot. Today you can inspect prison cells, rooms arranged with period furnishings, and costumed figures. Audiovisual displays recount the history of the Royal Burgh of Jedburgh. It's reputedly one of the most haunted buildings in the area. ✉ *Castlegate* ☎ *01835/864750* 🎟 *Free* 🕓 *Mar.–Oct., Mon.–Sat. 10–4:30, Sun. 1–4; last admission ½ hr before closing.*

Mary, Queen of Scots House. This *bastel* (from the French *bastille*) was the fortified town house in which, as the story goes, Mary stayed before embarking on her famous 20-mile ride to Hermitage Castle to visit her wounded lover, the Earl of Bothwell (circa 1535–78). Interesting displays relate the tale and illustrate other episodes in her life. Some of her possessions are on display, as are tapestries and furniture of the period. The ornamental garden surrounding the house has ranks of pear trees leading down to the river. ✉ *Queen St.* ☎ *01835/863331* 🎟 *Free* 🕓 *Mar.–Nov., Mon.–Sat. 10–4:30, Sun. 11–4.*

WHERE TO EAT AND STAY

$$ SPANISH 🍴 **Vino y Tapas.** Mediterranean colors are splashed across the interior of this Spanish-style eatery, where a modern tapas menu was inspired by the years that the Scottish owners spent in Spain. The simple and authentic dishes have an occasional dramatic touch, like the *carne de chocolate* (literally, chocolate meat), a beef stew with a touch of cocoa. Tapas are generous, and cost between £5 and £6. There's a good, if modest, wine list. [$] *Average main: £15* ✉ *23 Castlegate* ☎ *01835/862380* 🌐 *www.theforrestersrestaurantsb.com* 🕓 *No lunch.*

$ B&B/INN FAMILY 🏨 **Hundalee House.** This 18th-century manor house has richly decorated Victorian-style rooms with nice touches like four-poster beds and cozy fireplaces. **Pros:** fantastic views of apple orchards; hearty breakfasts;

good children's facilities. **Cons:** farm aromas; far from shops and restaurants. $ Rooms from: £60 ⊠ Off A68, 1 mile south of Jedburgh ☎ 01835/863011 ⊕ www.accommodation-scotland.org ⇶ 5 rooms ▭ No credit cards ⊘ Closed Christmas, Jan.–Mar. ❑ Breakfast.

$ ▦ **Meadhon House.** On a row of medieval buildings, Meadhon House
B&B/INN   is a charming 17th-century house with a history to match. **Pros:** central; pleasant rooms; welcoming atmosphere. **Cons:** rooms on the small side. $ Rooms from: £65 ⊠ 48 Castlegate ☎ 01835/862504 ⊕ www. meadhon.co.uk ⇶ 5 rooms ❑ Breakfast.

SHOPPING
Jedburgh Woollen Mill. This shop has shelves bursting with sweaters, kilts, tartan knitwear, and scarves. It's a good place to stock up on gifts. ⊠ Bankend North, Edinburgh Rd. ☎ 01835/863585 ⊕ www.ewm. co.uk.

KELSO

12 miles northeast of Jedburgh.

One of the most charming Borders burghs, Kelso is often described as having a continental flavor—some people think its broad, paved square makes it resemble a Belgian market town. The community has some fine examples of Georgian and Victorian Scots town architecture.

GETTING HERE AND AROUND
There are direct bus routes from Jedburgh to Kelso. Edinburgh has direct buses to Jedburgh; buses from Glasgow aren't direct. Your best option is to travel by car. From Jedburgh to Kelso take the A698, which is 12 miles, or about 20 minutes. Alternatively, the A699 is a scenic half-hour drive.

ESSENTIALS
Visitor Information Kelso Tourist Information Centre ⊠ The Square ☎ 01835/863170 ⊕ www.visitscotland.com.

EXPLORING
Fodor's Choice   **Floors Castle.** The palatial Floors Castle, the largest inhabited castle in
★   Scotland, is an architectural extravagance bristling with pepper-mill turrets. Not so much a castle as the ancestral seat of a wealthy and powerful landowning family, the Roxburghes, it stands on the "floors," or flat terrain, on the banks of the River Tweed. The enormous home was built in 1721 by William Adam (1689–1748) and modified by William Playfair (1789–1857), who added the turrets and towers in the 1840s. The interior rooms are crowded with valuable furniture, paintings, porcelain, and a strangely eerie circular room full of stuffed birds. Each room has a knowledgeable guide at the ready. The surrounding 56,000-acre estate is home to more than 40 farms. ⊠ A6089 ☎ 01573/223333 ⊕ www.floorscastle.com ⊠ Grounds £4,50, castle and grounds £8.50 ⊘ May.–Sept., daily 10:30–5; Oct. 10:30-3:30. Last admission ½ hr before closing.

Kelso Abbey. The least intact ruin of the four great abbeys, Kelso Abbey is just a bleak fragment of what was once the largest of the group. It was here in 1460 that the nine-year-old James III was crowned king of

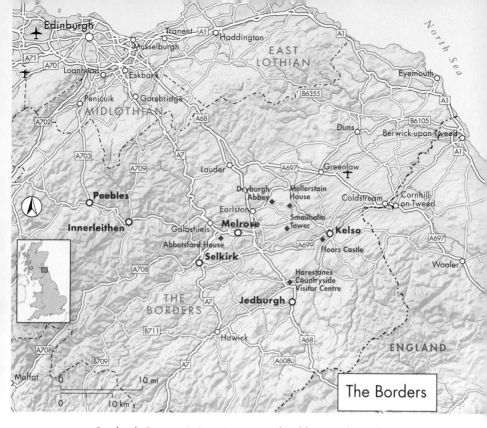

The Borders

Scotland. On a main invasion route, the abbey was burned three times in the 1540s alone, on the last occasion by the English Earl of Hertford's forces in 1545, when the 100 men and 12 monks of the garrison were butchered and the structure all but destroyed. ⊠ *Bridge St.* ☎ *0131/668–8800* ⊕ *www.kelso.bordernet.co.uk* ✉ *Free* ☉ *Apr.–Dec., daily 24 hrs.*

Mellerstain House. One fine example of the Borders area's ornate country homes is Mellerstain House. Begun in the 1720s, it was finished in the 1770s by Robert Adam (1728–92) and is considered one of his finest creations. Sumptuous plasterwork covers almost all interior surfaces, and there are outstanding examples of 18th-century furnishings, porcelain and china, and paintings and embroidery. The beautiful terraced gardens (open an hour before the house itself) are as renowned as the house. ⊠ *Off A6089, 7 miles northwest of Kelso, Gordon* ☎ *01573/410225* ⊕ *www.mellerstain.com* ✉ *Gardens £5, house and gardens £8.50* ☉ *May–Sept., Fri.–Mon. 12:30–5; last admission ½ hr before closing.*

Fodor's Choice
★

Smailholm Tower. The characteristic Borders structure Smailholm Tower stands uncompromisingly on top of a barren, rocky ridge in the hills south of Mellerstain. The 16th-century peel was built solely for defense, and its unadorned stones contrast with the luxury of Mellerstain House. If you let your imagination wander in this windy spot, you can almost

Scotland's largest inhabited castle, topped with 19th-century towers, Floors brims with family treasures.

see the flapping pennants and rising dust of an advancing raiding party and hear the anxious securing of doors and bolts. Sir Walter Scott found this spot inspiring. His grandfather lived nearby, and the young Scott visited the tower often during his childhood. A museum displays costumed figures and tapestries relating to Scott's folk ballads. A free audio tour is available. ⊠ *Off B6404, 4½ miles south of Mellerstain House* ☎ *01573/460365* ⊕ *www.historic-scotland.gov.uk* ☜ *£4.50* ⊙ *Apr.–Sept., daily 9:30–5:30; Oct.–Mar., weekends 9:30–4:30; last admission ½ hr before closing.*

WHERE TO EAT AND STAY

$$
BRITISH
✕ **Cobbles Inn.** A lively bar and restaurant off the town square, Cobbles is much favored by locals. The bar menu is an excellent value, and includes such dishes as breaded pork fillets with perfectly prepared root vegetables in a red wine sauce. The dinner menu features a savory cheesecake starter made with chestnuts and balsamic vinegar, and lamb cutlets with parsnips and artichokes. Vegetarian dishes are also on offer. Desserts are well made and come in generous portions. $ *Average main: £16* ⊠ *7 Bowmont St.* ☎ *01573/223548* ⊕ *www.thecobbleskelso.co.uk.*

$$
HOTEL
Fodor's Choice
★
☷ **Ednam House Hotel.** People return again and again to this large, stately hotel on the banks of the River Tweed, close to Kelso's grand abbey and sprawling market square. **Pros:** great outdoor activities; atmospheric lobby; impressive restaurant. **Cons:** some rooms need a makeover. $ *Rooms from: £159* ⊠ *Bridge St.* ☎ *01573/224168* ⊕ *www.ednamhouse.com* ⬅ *32 rooms* ⊙ *Closed late Dec. to early Jan.* ⦿ *Breakfast.*

SHOPPING

John Moody. This shop sells soft cashmere and lambswool sweaters, along with purses, scarves, and gloves. It's a real treat for knitwear fanatics, or those simply looking for something Scottish to keep them warm. ✉ *38 The Square* ☎ *01573/224400* ⊕ *www.johnmoodyknitwear. co.uk.*

MELROSE

15 miles west of Kelso.

Though it's small, there is nevertheless a bustle about Melrose, the perfect example of a prosperous Scottish market town and one of the loveliest in the Borders. It's set around a square lined with 18th- and 19th-century buildings housing myriad small shops and cafés. Despite its proximity to the much larger Galashiels, which has knitwear factories, Melrose has rejected industrialization. You'll likely hear local residents greet each other by first name in the square.

15

GETTING HERE AND AROUND

Buses do go to Melrose. However, driving is the easiest, fastest, and most efficient way to travel here. From Kelso, head to the A6091 (30 minutes).

ESSENTIALS

Visitor Information Melrose Tourist Information Centre ✉ *Abbey St.* ☎ *01896/822283* ⊕ *www.visitscottishborders.com.*

EXPLORING

Fodor's Choice **Abbotsford House.** In this great house overlooking the Tweed, Sir Walter ★ Scott lived, worked, and received the great and the good in luxurious salons. In 1811 the writer bought a farm on this site named Cartleyhole, which was a euphemism for the real name, Clartyhole (*clarty* is Scots for "muddy" or "dirty"). The name was surely not romantic enough for Scott, who renamed the property after a ford in the nearby Tweed used by the abbot of Melrose. Scott eventually had the house entirely rebuilt in the Scots baronial style. It was, of course, an expensive project, and Scott wrote feverishly to keep his creditors at bay. John Ruskin, the art critic, disapproved, calling it an "incongruous pile," but most contemporary visitors find it fascinating, particularly because of its expansive views and delightful gardens. A free audio tour guides you around the salon, the wonderful circular study, and the library with its 9,000 leather-bound volumes. The newly built visitor center houses displays about Scott's life, a gift shop, and an upstairs restaurant serving lunch. To get here, take the A6091 from Melrose and follow the signs for Abbotsford. ✉ *B6360, Galashiels* ☎ *01896/752043* ⊕ *www. scottsabbotsford.co.uk* 🎫 *House and gardens £8.75; gardens only £3.50* ⊙ *Apr.–Sept., daily 10–5; Oct.–Mar., daily 10–4.*

Dryburgh Abbey. The final resting place of Sir Walter Scott and his wife, and the most peaceful and secluded of the Borders abbeys, the "gentle ruins" of Dryburgh Abbey sit on parkland in a loop of the Tweed. The abbey, founded in 1150, suffered from English raids until, like Melrose, it was abandoned in 1544. The style is transitional, a mingling of rounded Romanesque and pointed early English. The north transept, where the Haig and Scott families lie buried, is lofty and pillared, and once formed part of the abbey church. ⊠ *B6404* ☎ *01835/822381* ⊕ *www.historic-scotland.gov.uk/places* ▧ *£5* ⊘ *Apr.–Sept., daily 9:30– 5:30; Oct.–Mar., daily 9:30–4:30; last entry ½ hr before closing.*

Fodor's Choice
★
Melrose Abbey. Just off Melrose's town square sit the ruins of Melrose Abbey, one of the four Borders abbeys. "If thou would'st view fair Melrose aright, go visit it in the pale moonlight," wrote Scott in *The Lay of the Last Minstrel*, and so many of his fans took the advice literally that a sleepless custodian begged him to rewrite the lines. Today the abbey is still impressive: a red-sandstone shell with slender windows, delicate tracery, and carved capitals, all carefully maintained. Among the carvings high on the roof is one of a bagpipe-playing pig. An audio tour is included in the admission price. The heart of Robert the Bruce is rumored to be buried here. ⊠ *Abbey St.* ☎ *01896/822562* ⊕ *www. historic-scotland.gov.uk* ▧ *£5.50* ⊘ *Apr.–Sept., daily 9:30–5:30; Oct.– Mar., daily 9:30–4:30; last entry ½ hr before closing.*

Priorwood Gardens. The National Trust for Scotland's Priorwood Gardens, next to Melrose Abbey, specializes in flowers for drying. Dried flowers are on sale in the shop. Next to the gardens is an orchard with some old apple varieties. The nearby walled Harmony Garden is also included in the entry price. ⊠ *Abbey St.* ☎ *0844/4932257* ⊕ *www.nts. org.uk* ▧ *£6.50* ⊘ *Mar.–Oct., Mon.–Sat. 10–5, Sun. 1–5; Nov. and Dec., Mon.–Sat. 10–4.*

WHERE TO EAT AND STAY

$$
BRITISH
Fodor's Choice
★
✕**Hoebridge Inn.** Whitewashed walls, oak-beamed ceilings, and an open fire welcome you into this converted 19th-century bobbin mill. The cuisine is a blend of British and Mediterranean styles with occasional Asian influences. Rabbit and guinea fowl also appear regularly on the menu. The inn lies in Gattonside, Melrose's across-the-river neighbor, but a 2-mile drive is required to cross to the other side; you can reach the inn more easily via a footbridge. ⓢ *Average main: £17* ⊠ *B6360, Gattonside* ☎ *01896/823082* ◿ *Reservations essential* ⊘ *Closed Sun. and Mon.*

$$
HOTEL
🛏 **Burts Hotel.** This charming whitewashed building dating from the 18th century sits in the center of Melrose. **Pros:** walking distance to restaurants and pubs; good menu in restaurant. **Cons:** some rooms are tiny; bland room decor. ⓢ *Rooms from: £133* ⊠ *Market Sq.* ☎ *01896/822285* ⊕ *www.burtshotel.co.uk* ◄ *20 rooms* ⊠ *Breakfast.*

$$
HOTEL
🛏 **Dryburgh Abbey Hotel.** Mature woodlands and verdant lawns surround this imposing, 19th-century mansion, which is adjacent to the abbey ruins on a sweeping bend of the River Tweed. **Pros:** beautiful grounds; romantic setting. **Cons:** some rooms need to be freshened up; service can be on the slow side. ⓢ *Rooms from: £140* ⊠ *Off B6404, St. Boswells* ☎ *01835/822261* ⊕ *www.dryburgh.co.uk* ◄ *36 rooms, 2 suites* ⊠ *Breakfast.*

Of the ruined abbeys in the Borders, Melrose is notable for its red-sandstone architecture and carvings.

SHOPPING

Abbey Mill. Take a break from sightseeing at Abbey Mill, where you'll find hand-woven knitwear as well as homemade jams and fudge. There's also a wee tearoom. ⊠ *Annay Rd.* ☏ *01896/822138.*

SELKIRK

9 miles southwest of Melrose.

Selkirk is a hilly outpost with a smattering of antiques shops and an assortment of bakers selling Selkirk bannock (fruited sweet bread) and other cakes. It is the site of one of Scotland's iconic battles, Flodden Field, commemorated here with a statue in the town. Sir Walter Scott was sheriff (judge) of Selkirkshire from 1800 until his death in 1832, and his statue stands in Market Place. The town is also near Bowhill, a stately home.

GETTING HERE AND AROUND

If you're driving, take the A699 south from Melrose. The scenic journey is less than 10 miles and takes around 15 minutes. First Edinburgh Bus offers a regular service between Melrose and Selkirk.

ESSENTIALS

Visitor Information Selkirk Visitor Information Centre ⊠ *Halliwell's House, Market Pl.* ☏ *08706/080404* ⊕ *www.visitscotland.com.*

EXPLORING

Halliwell's House Museum. Tucked off the main square, Halliwell's House Museum was once an ironmonger's shop, which is now re-created downstairs. Upstairs, an exhibit tells the town's story, illustrates the

CLOSE UP

The World of Sir Walter Scott

Sir Walter Scott (1771–1832) was probably Scottish tourism's best propagandist. His long narrative poems—such as "The Lady of the Lake"—and historical novels including *Ivanhoe* and *Rob Roy* created the image of heroic Scotland that so many people have fallen in love with. Scott's Scotland is a place of Highland wildernesses and warring clans, a romantic creation that many visitors hope to rediscover.

Scott was born in College Wynd, Edinburgh. A lawyer by training, he was an assiduous collector of old ballads and tales. "The Lay of the Last Minstrel," a romantic poem published in 1805, brought him fame. In 1811 Scott bought the house that was to become Abbotsford, his Borders mansion near Melrose.

Scott started on his Waverley novels in 1814, and by 1820 he had produced five of them. There followed a further 11 titles, including *Ivanhoe*. He used real-life settings, in particular the Trossachs, northwest of Stirling, for his novels and poetry, ensuring that they would attract visitors for years to come.

SCOTT SIGHTS

Abbotsford, Scott's home near Melrose in the Borders, is well worth a visit. Other houses associated with Scott can be seen in Edinburgh: 25 George Square, which was his father's house, and 39 Castle Street, where he lived from 1801 to 1826. The site of his birthplace, in College Wynd, is marked with a plaque. The most obvious structure associated with Scott in Edinburgh is the Scott Monument on Princes Street, which looks like a Gothic rocket ship with a statue of Scott and his pet dog as passengers.

working lives of its inhabitants, and provides useful background information on the Common Ridings. ✉ *Market Pl.* ☎ *01750/20096* 🌐 *www.scotborders.gov.uk* 🎟 *Free* 🕒 *Apr.–Oct., Mon.–Sat. 10–5, Sun. noon–3.*

Lochcarron of Scotland Cashmere and Wool Centre. Love tartans and tweeds? The Lochcarron of Scotland Cashmere and Wool Centre houses a museum where you can tour a mill and learn about the manufacturing process. The shop also sells Scottish jewelry. ✉ *Waverley Mill, Dinsdale Rd.* ☎ *01750/726000* 🌐 *www.lochcarron.com* 🎟 *Museum free, tour £2.50* 🕒 *Mon.–Sat. 9–5. Guided tours Mon.–Thurs. at 10:30, 11:30, 1:30, and 2:30.*

Waverly Mill. You can take an informative tour of this world-renowned mill and also purchase some of the best woolen goods on offer, from knitwear to tartans and tweeds. The shop also sells Scottish jewelry. ✉ *Dinsdale Rd., Selkirk* ☎ *01750/726100.*

WHERE TO STAY

$$ HOTEL 🏨 **Best Western Philipburn House Hotel.** West of Selkirk, this alpine-style hotel enjoys a lovely setting among the woods and hills. **Pros:** pleasant rural setting; bright rooms; on-site parking. **Cons:** no elevator; restaurant closes rather early. [$] *Rooms from: £135* ✉ *Off A708* ☎ *01750/720747* 🌐 *www.bw-philipburnhousehotel.co.uk* 🛏 *12 rooms, 4 lodges* 🍴 *Breakfast.*

INNERLEITHEN

11 miles northwest of Selkirk.

Innerleithen is one of the larger Borders towns; you'll feel that you've entered a hub of activity when you arrive. It's also dramatically beautiful. Surrounded by hills and glens, the town is where the Tweed and Leithen rivers join, then separate. Historically, Innerleithen dates back to pre-Roman times, and there are artifacts all around for you to see. Once a booming industrialized town of wool mills, today it's a great destination for outdoor activities including hiking, biking, and fly-fishing.

GETTING HERE AND AROUND

To drive to Innerleithen, take the A707/A72 northwest from Selkirk. There are no trains between the two towns.

EXPLORING

FAMILY **Robert Smail's Printing Works.** Try your hand at printing the way it used to be done: painstakingly setting each letter by hand. This print shop, founded more than a century ago to produce materials for nearby factories, boat tickets, theater posters, and the local newspaper, Robert Small's is still a working print shop as well as a museum. Two great waterwheels once powered the presses, and they are still running. The guided tour, which includes making your own bookmark, takes 90 minutes. ⌂ *7–9 High St.* ☎ *01896/830206* ⊕ *www.nts.org.uk/Visits* 🎫 *£6.50* ⊙ *Apr.–Oct., Thurs.–Mon. noon–5, Sun. 1–5; last admission at 4:15.*

Fodor's Choice **Traquair House.** Said to be the oldest continually occupied home in Scot-
★ land, Traquair House has secret stairways and passages, a library with more than 3,000 books, and a bed said to be used by Mary, Queen of Scots in 1566. The 18th-century brew house still makes highly recommended ale. You may even spend the night, if you wish. Outside you'll find a maze and extensive gardens. Traquair Fair in August is a major event in the regional calendar. ⌂ *B709* ☎ *01896/830323* ⊕ *www. traquair.co.uk* 🎫 *Grounds £4, house and grounds £8* ⊙ *Apr.–Sept., daily noon–5; Oct., daily 11–4; Nov., weekends 11–3; last admission ½ hr before closing.*

WHERE TO STAY

$$$ 🏨 **Traquair House.** Staying in one of the guest rooms in the 12th-century
B&B/INN wing of Traquair House is to experience a slice of Scottish history. **Pros:** stunning grounds; spacious rooms; great breakfast. **Cons:** nearly 2 miles to restaurants and shops; rooms fill up quickly in summer. $ *Rooms from: £180* ⌂ *B709* ☎ *01896/830323* ⊕ *www.traquair.co.uk* 🛏 *3 rooms* ⋈ *Breakfast.*

$$ 🏨 **Windlestraw Lodge.** This elegant bed-and-breakfast occupies a
B&B/INN grand country home surrounded by extensive gardens. **Pros:** beautifully designed rooms; excellent dining. **Cons:** a bit expensive for what you get. $ *Rooms from: £160* ⌂ *A72, St. Boswells* ☎ *01896/870636* ⊕ *www.windlestraw.co.uk* 🛏 *5 rooms* ⋈ *Breakfast.*

15

PEEBLES

6 miles west of Innerleithen.

Thanks to its excellent though pricey shopping, Peebles gives the impression of catering primarily to leisured country gentlefolk. Architecturally, the town is nothing out of the ordinary, just a very pleasant burgh. Don't miss the splendid dolphins ornamenting the bridge crossing the River Tweed.

> ### SELKIRK'S PRIDE
>
> The little town of Selkirk claims its Common Riding is the largest mounted gathering anywhere in Europe. More than 400 riders take part in the event. It's also the oldest Borders festival, dating back to the Battle of Flodden in 1513.

GETTING HERE AND AROUND

Because of its size and location, direct buses run from both Edinburgh and Glasgow to Peebles. There are also buses here from Innerleithen, though driving here is more direct. (Take the A72; it's about a 10-minute drive.)

ESSENTIALS

Visitor Information Peebles Visitor Information Centre ⊠ *23 High St.* ☎ *01721/723159* ⊕ *www.scot-borders.co.uk.*

EXPLORING

Neidpath Castle. A 15-minute walk upstream along the banks of the Tweed, Neidpath Castle perches artistically above a bend in the river. It comes into view as you approach through the tall trees. The castle is a medieval structure remodeled in the 17th century, with dungeons hewn from solid rock. You can return on the opposite riverbank after crossing an old, finely skewed railroad viaduct. Call ahead to arranged visits to the interior. ⊠ *Off A72* ☎ *01875/870201* ⊕ *www.neidpathcastle.com* ⊠ *£3* ⊙ *By appointment only.*

WHERE TO EAT AND STAY

$

BRITISH

✕ **Adam Room.** With a minstrels' gallery, crystal chandeliers, and tall windows with views over the Tweed, the dining room at the Tontine Hotel has a grand feel. It's a bit surprising, therefore, that it also serves good home cooking at very reasonable prices. Local produce is used for all the dishes, including the appetizing steak pie and the lamb rump. There is also a good wine list. Bring along the kids, as they have their own menu. $ *Average main: £12* ⊠ *Tontine Hotel, High St.* ☎ *01721/720892* ⊕ *www.tontinehotel.com.*

$$$

HOTEL

ALL-INCLUSIVE

Peebles Hydro. One of the great "hydro hotels" built in the 19th century for those anxious to "take the waters," Peebles Hydro has something for everyone, and in abundance: pony rides, a putting green, and a giant chess game are just a few of the diversions. **Pros:** plenty of activities; good children's programs; delicious breakfast. **Cons:** can feel impersonal; some rooms have bland decor. $ *Rooms from: £198* ⊠ *Innerleithen Rd.* ☎ *01721/720602* ⊕ *www.peebleshotelhydro.com* ⊠ *132 rooms* ⊙ *All-inclusive.*

$$

HOTEL

Tontine Hotel. A small and charming facade hides a spacious hotel that stretches back from Peebles High Street. **Pros:** centrally located; pleasant rooms; welcoming staff. **Cons:** some rooms in the rear are quite small; decor in some areas feels old-fashioned. [$] *Rooms from: £100* ✉ *High St.* ☎ *01721/729732* 🌐 *www.tontinehotel.com* 🛏 *36 rooms* 🍴 *Breakfast.*

SHOPPING

Be prepared for temptations at every turn as you browse the shops on High Street and in the courts and side streets leading off it.

Caledonia. For all things Scottish, look no further than Caledonia, where you'll find everything from kilts to throws, and jams to tablecloths. ✉ *61 High St.* ☎ *01721/722343.*

Head to Toe. This shop stocks natural beauty products, handmade pine furniture, and handsome linens—from patchwork quilts to silk flowers. ✉ *43 High St.* ☎ *01721/722752.*

Keith Walter. Among the many jewelers on High Street is Keith Walter, a master of gold and silver who makes his creations on the premises. He also stocks jewelry made by other local designers. ✉ *28 High St.* ☎ *01721/720650* 🌐 *www.keithwalter28.com.*

15

DUMFRIES AND GALLOWAY

Galloway covers the southwestern portion of Scotland, west of the main town of Dumfries. Here a gentle coastline gives way to farmland and then breezy uplands that gradually merge with coniferous forests. Use caution when negotiating the A75—you're liable to find trucks bearing down on you as these vehicles race for the ferries at Stranraer and Cairnryan. Things are far more relaxed once you leave the main highway; take the coastal A710/A711 instead. Dumfries and Galloway offer some of the most pleasant drives in Scotland—though the occasional herd of cows on the way to be milked is a potential hazard.

DUMFRIES

54 miles south of Peebles, 76 miles southeast of Glasgow, 81 miles southwest of Edinburgh.

The River Nith meanders through Dumfries, and the pedestrian-only town center makes wandering and shopping a pleasure. Author J. M. Barrie (1860–1937) spent his childhood in Dumfries, and the garden of Moat Brae House is said to have inspired his boyish dreams in *Peter Pan.* But the town also has a justified claim to Robert Burns, who lived and worked here for several years. His house and his favorite *howff* (pub), the Globe Inn, are here, too, as is his final resting place in St. Michael's Churchyard.

The Dumfries & Galloway Tourist Board has a lodging service, and also sells golf passes for the region at £60 for three rounds.

GETTING HERE AND AROUND

Public transportation is a good option for reaching Dumfries—there's a good train station here, and most major Scottish cities have regular daily bus routes to the town. If you're driving from Glasgow, take the M74 to the A701. From Edinburgh, take the A701.

ESSENTIALS

Visitor Information Dumfries & Galloway Tourist Board ✉ *64 Whitesands* ☎ *01387/245550* ⊕ *www.visitdumfriesandgalloway.co.uk.*

EXPLORING

TOP ATTRACTIONS

Burns House. Poet Robert Burns lived here, on what was then called Mill Street, for the last three years of his life, when his salary from the customs service allowed him to improve his living standards. Many distinguished writers of the day visited him here, including William Wordsworth. The house contains some of his writings and letters, a few pieces of furniture, and some family memorabilia. ✉ *Burns St.* ☎ *01387/255297* ⊕ *www.dumgal.gov.uk/museums* ▦ *Free* ⊙ *Apr.– Sept., Mon.–Sat. 10–5, Sun. 2–5; Oct.–Mar., Tues.–Sat. 10–1 and 2–5.*

Fodor's Choice ★ **Caerlaverock Castle.** The stunningly beautiful, moated Caerlaverock Castle stands in splendid isolation amid the surrounding wetlands that form the Caerlaverock Nature Reserve. Built in a unique triangular design, this 13th-century fortress has solid-sandstone masonry and an imposing double-tower gatehouse. King Edward I of England (1239– 1307) besieged the castle in 1300, when his forces occupied much of Scotland at the start of the Wars of Independence. A splendid residence was built inside in the 1600s. ✉ *Off B725, 10 miles south of Dumfries* ☎ *01387/770244* ⊕ *www.historic-scotland.gov.uk/places* ▦ *£5.50* ⊙ *Apr.–Sept., daily 9:30–5:30; Oct.–Mar., daily 9:30–4:30.*

Fodor's Choice ★ **Caerlaverock Wildfowl and Wetlands Centre.** You can observe wintering wildfowl, including various species of geese, ducks, swans, and raptors on the wetlands surrounding atmospheric Carlaverock Castle. In summer, ospreys patrol the waters of this wild and beautiful place, the northernmost outpost of the Wildfowl and Wetlands Trust. Free guided walks are available in the afternoons throughout the year. ✉ *Eastpark Farm, off B725, Dumfries* ☎ *01387/770200* ▦ *Free* ⊙ *Daily 24 hrs.*

▌OFF THE BEATEN PATH

Drumlanrig Castle. This spectacular estate is as close as Scotland gets to the treasure houses of England—which is not surprising, since it's owned by the dukes of Buccleuch, one of the wealthiest British peerages. Resplendent with romantic turrets, this pink-sandstone palace was constructed between 1679 and 1691 by the first Duke of Queensbury, who, after nearly bankrupting himself building the place, stayed one night and never returned. The Buccleuchs inherited the palace and soon filled the richly decorated rooms with a valuable collection of paintings by Holbein, Rembrandt, and Murillo. Because of the theft of a Leonardo da Vinci painting in 2003, all visits are conducted by guided tour. There's also a playground, a gift shop, and a tearoom. ✉ *Off A76, 18 miles northwest of Dumfries, Thornhill* ☎ *01848/600283* ⊕ *www. drumlanrig.com* ▦ *Park £6, castle and park £10* ⊙ *Grounds Apr.–Sept., daily 10–5. Castle Mar.–Aug., daily 11–4.*

Robert Burns Centre. Not surprisingly, Dumfries has its own Robert Burns Centre, housed in a sturdy former mill overlooking the river. The center has an audiovisual program and an extensive exhibit on the life of the poet. There's a restaurant upstairs. ✉ *Mill Rd.* ☎ *01387/264808*

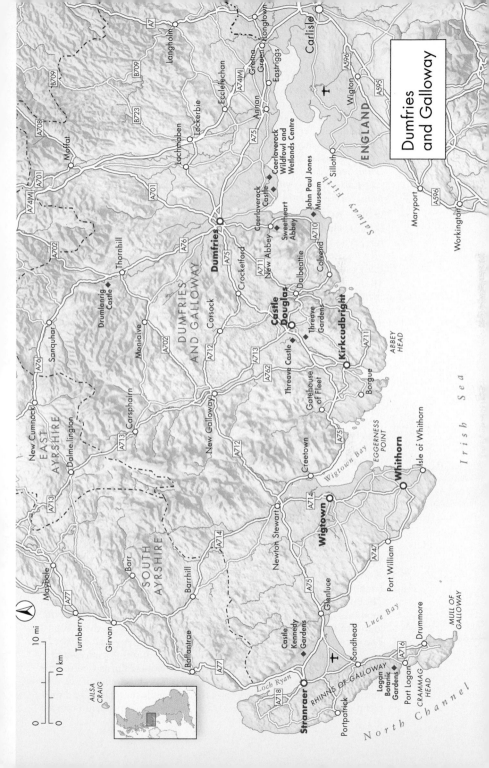

Dumfries and Galloway

🎟 Free ⏲ Apr.–Sept., Mon.–Sat. 10–5, Sun. 2–5; Oct.–Mar., Tues.–Sat. 10–1 and 2–5.

Sweetheart Abbey. At the center of the village of New Abbey is the red-tinted and roofless Sweetheart Abbey. The odd name is a translation of the abbey's previous name, St. Mary of the Dolce Coeur. The abbey was founded in 1273 by the Lady of Galloway, Devorgilla (1210–90), who, it is said, had her late husband's heart placed in a tiny casket that she carried everywhere. After she died, she was laid to rest in Sweetheart Abbey with the casket resting on her breast. *✉ A710, 7 miles south of Dumfries, New Abbey ☎ 01387/253849 🌐 www.historic-scotland.com 🎟 £4.50 ⏲ Apr.–Sept., daily 9:30–5:30; Oct., daily 9:30–4:30; Nov.–Mar., Mon.–Wed. and weekends 9:30–4:30.*

WORTH NOTING

Dumfries Museum and Camera Obscura. A camera obscura is essentially a huge reflecting mirror that projects an extraordinarily clear panoramic view of the surrounding countryside onto an internal wall. The one at the Dumfries Museum is housed in the old Windmill Tower, built in 1836. The museum itself covers the culture and daily life of the people living in the Dumfries and Galloway region from the earliest times. *✉ Rotchell Rd. ☎ 01387/253374 🎟 £2.30 ⏲ Apr.–Sept., Mon.–Sat. 10–5; Oct.–Mar., Tues.–Sat. 10–1 and 2–5.*

Globe Inn. Poet Robert Burns spent quite a lot of time at the Globe Inn, where he frequently fell asleep in the tack room beside the stables. He later graduated to the upstairs bedroom where he slept with his wife, Jean Armour, and scratched some lines of poetry on the window. The room is preserved (or at least partly re-created) and the bar staff will happily show you around if you ask. *✉ 56 High St. ☎ 01387/252335 🌐 www.globeinndumfries.co.uk.*

John Paul Jones Museum. It was in a cottage, in the little community of Kirkbean, now the John Paul Jones Museum, that John Paul (1747–92), the son of an estate gardener, was born. He eventually left Scotland, added "Jones" to his name, and became the founder of the U.S. Navy. The cottage where he was born is furnished as it would have been when he was a boy. Jones returned to raid the coastline of his native country in 1778, an exploit recounted in an adjoining visitor center. *✉ Off A710, 12 miles south of Dumfries, Kirkbean ☎ 01387/880613 🎟 £3.50 ⏲ Apr.–June and Sept., Tues.–Sun. 10–5; July and Aug., daily 10–5.*

WHERE TO EAT AND STAY

$ BRITISH 🍴 **Cavens Arms.** This lively, welcoming, traditional pub has a separate bar and dining area, comfortable seating, and a large selection of beers. The restaurant seems to always be busy, a testimony to the quality of its food (as well as the large portions). As for favorite dishes, grilled pork loin with fruity red cabbage vies with panfried sea bass with couscous. The excellent desserts are made on the premises. *[$] Average main: £11 ✉ 20 Buccleuch St. ☎ 01387/252896 ✍ Reservations not accepted.*

$$ BRITISH 🍴 **Hullabaloo.** Occupying the top floor of the Robert Burns Centre, this restaurant serves a substantial and varied lunch and dinner menu. The lunch menu is imaginative and very tasty, especially the melts. The dinner menu is ambitious and equally varied, ranging from pistachio-crusted

chicken to rack of lamb stuffed with anchovies to grilled sea bass in a ginger and coconut sauce. Try to snag a window table overlooking the River Nith. $ *Average main: £16 ⊠ Robert Burns Centre, Mill Rd.* ☎ *01387/259679 ⊕ www.hullabaloorestaurant.co.uk ⚖ Reservations essential* ⊘ *No dinner Sun. and Mon.*

$$ ⊡ **Aston Hotel.** With the secluded feel of a grand country hotel, the Aston **HOTEL** Hotel is less than 2 miles from the center of Dumfries. **Pros:** beautiful setting; easy access to Dumfries; rooms for people with disabilities. **Cons:** slightly institutional feel. $ *Rooms from: £119 ⊠ Bankend Rd., Crichton* ☎ *01387/272410 ⊕ www.astonhotels.co.uk/dumfries ⌁ 71 rooms* ⦿ *Breakfast.*

THE ARTS

Dumfries & Galloway Arts Festival. This festival, celebrated every year since 1979, is usually held at the end of May at several venues throughout the region. ☎ *01387/260447 ⊕ www.dgartsfestival.org.uk.*

Gracefield Arts Centre. With galleries hosting constantly changing exhibits, Gracefield Arts Centre also has a well-stocked crafts shop. A café serves lunch and snacks. ⊠ *28 Edinburgh Rd.* ☎ *01387/262084* ⊘ *Tues.–Sat. 10–5.*

SHOPPING

Dumfries is the main shopping center for the region, with all the big-name chain stores as well as specialty shops.

Greyfriars Crafts. This shop sells mainly Scottish goods, including glass, ceramics, and jewelry. ⊠ *56 Buccleuch St.* ☎ *01387/264050.*

Fodor'sChoice **Loch Arthur Creamery and Farm Shop.** This lively and active farm in the
★ charmingly named village of Beeswing has organic foods of the highest quality, particularly the award-winning dairy products. If you can't wait to eat your purchases, there's a café. ⊠ *A711, 6 miles from Dumfries, Beeswing* ☎ *01387/760296 ⊕ www.locharthur.org.uk.*

CASTLE DOUGLAS

17 miles southwest of Dumfries, 84 miles south of Glasgow, 90 miles southwest of Edinburgh.

A quaint town that sits beside Carlingwark Loch, Castle Douglas is a popular base for exploring the surrounding countryside. The loch sets off the city perfectly, reflecting its dramatic architecture of sharp spires and soft sandstone arches. Its main thoroughfare, King Street, has unique shops and eateries.

GETTING HERE AND AROUND

There's no train station in Castle Douglas, and buses from Dumfries make several stops along the way. The best way to get to Castle Douglas is by car. From Glasgow, take the A713 (just under two hours). From Edinburgh, take the A70 (2 hours).

ESSENTIALS

Visitor Information Castle Douglas ⊠ *Market Hill* ☎ *01556/502611* ⊕ *www. visitdumfriesandgalloway.co.uk.*

15

EXPLORING

Threave Castle. This castle was an early home of the Black Douglases, who were the earls of Nithsdale and lords of Galloway. Not to be confused with the mansion in Threave Gardens, the castle was dismantled in the religious wars of the mid-17th century, though enough of it remains to have housed prisoners from the Napoleonic Wars of the 19th century. It's a few minutes from Castle Douglas by car and is signposted from the main road. To get here, leave your car in a farmyard and make your way down to the edge of the river. Ring a bell, and, rather romantically, a boatman will come to ferry you across to the great stone tower looming from a marshy island in the river. ✉ *A75, 3 miles west of Castle Douglas* ☎ *07711/223101* 🌐 *www.historic-scotland.gov.uk* 🎫 *£4.50, includes ferry* 🕒 *Apr.–Sept., daily 9:30–4:30.*

Threave Gardens. The National Trust for Scotland cares for the gently sloping parkland around the 1867 mansion built by William Gordon, a Liverpool businessman. The house, fully restored in the 1930s, gives a glimpse into the daily life of a prosperous family in the 19th century. The foliage demands the employment of many gardeners—and it's here that the gardeners train, thus ensuring there's always some fresh development or experimental planting. Entry to the house is by timed guided tour, and it's wise to book ahead. There's an on-site restaurant. ✉ *South of A75, 1 mile west of Castle Douglas* ☎ *0844/493–2245* 🌐 *www.nts.org.uk/Visits* 🎫 *Gardens £7, house and gardens £12* 🕒 *House: Apr.–Oct., Wed.–Fri. and Sun. 11–3:30. Visitor center: Feb., Mar., Nov., and Dec., Fri.–Sun. 10–5; Apr.–Oct., daily 10–5.*

WHERE TO EAT

$ CAFÉ 🍴 **The Café at Designs Gallery.** For a good balance of art and food, look no further. You'll find the freshest ingredients here, from soup to salads, sandwiches to quiches. Everything is made on-site, including the bread, and it's all organic. The soup of the day is always a good choice, as are the seasonal fruit pies. The café is downstairs, beneath the shop and gallery, and is full of light and wooden tables and chairs. You can also choose to sit in the well-kept garden or conservatory when weather permits. [$] *Average main: £7* ✉ *179 King St.* ☎ *01556/504552* 🌐 *www.designsgallery.co.uk* 🕒 *No dinner. Closed Sun.*

SHOPPING

Galloway Gems. This glittery shop sells mineral specimens, polished stone slices, and a range of Celtic- and Nordic-inspired jewelry. ✉ *130–132 King St.* ☎ *01556/503254.*

KIRKCUDBRIGHT

9 miles southwest of Castle Douglas, 89 miles south of Glasgow, 99 miles southwest of Edinburgh.

Kirkcudbright (pronounced kir-*coo*-bray) is an 18th-century town of Georgian and Victorian houses, some of them washed in pastel shades and roofed with the blue slate of the district. In the early 20th century it became a haven for artists, and its L-shaped main street is full of crafts and antiques shops.

GETTING HERE AND AROUND

Driving is your best and only real option. From Castle Douglas, take the A711 (15 minutes). From Glasgow, take the A713 (about two hours). From Edinburgh, take the A701 (about 2½ hours).

ESSENTIALS

Visitor Information Kirkcudbright Tourist Information Centre ✉ *Harbour Sq.* ☎ *01557/330494* 🌐 *www.visitdumfriesandgalloway.co.uk.*

EXPLORING

Broughton House. The 18th-century Broughton House was once the home of the artist E.A. Hornel, one of the "Glasgow Boys" of the late 19th century. Many of his paintings hang in the house, which is furnished in period style and contains an extensive library specializing in local history. There's also a Japanese garden. ✉ *12 High St.* ☎ *0844/493–2246* 🌐 *www.nts.org.uk* 🎟 *£6.50* 🕒 *House and Garden: Apr.–Oct., daily noon–5. Garden: Feb. and Mar., weekdays 11–4.*

Tolbooth Arts Centre. In the 17th-century tolbooth (a combination town hall–courthouse–prison), the Tolbooth Arts Centre tells about the town's most famous artists, including E.A. Hornel, Jessie King, and Charles Oppenheimer. Some of their paintings are on display, as are works by modern artists. ✉ *High St.* ☎ *01557/331556* 🌐 *www.kirkcudbright.co.uk* 🎟 *Free* 🕒 *Oct.–May, Mon.–Sat. 11–4; June–Sept., Mon.–Sat. 11–4, Sun. 2–5.*

15

WHERE TO EAT AND STAY

$$ MODERN BRITISH

🍴 **Artistas.** Paintings of Scotland, starched white tablecloths, and giant windows overlooking the well-kept garden beckon you into this highly praised eatery. Locals love that the food is locally sourced and full of imagination. In season, try the globe artichoke and asparagus salad, then the braised fillet of turbot over saffron-and-shrimp quinoa. The "posh" fish-and-chips is one of the best around. For a less expensive, more casual dining experience try the hotel's bistro, where the à la carte menu is delicious. [$] *Average main: £17* ✉ *Best Western Selkirk Arms, High St.* ☎ *01557/330402* ✍ *Reservations essential.*

$$ HOTEL

🏨 **Best Western Selkirk Arms.** Bursting with charm, this elegant 18th-century hotel has a lot going for it—spacious rooms are individually decorated with cozy beds, contemporary wood furniture, and soft lighting. **Pros:** attentive service; massive breakfast; lively traditional pub. **Cons:** rooms closest to restaurant can be noisy; bar gets crowded during sporting events. [$] *Rooms from: £110* ✉ *High St.* ☎ *01557/330402* 🌐 *www.selkirkarmshotel.co.uk* 🛏 *17 rooms* 🍽 *Breakfast.*

WIGTOWN

19 miles west of Kirkcudbright, 28 miles west of Castle Douglas, 84 miles southwest of Glasgow, 111 miles southwest of Edinburgh.

More than 20 bookshops, mostly antiquarian and secondhand stores, have sprung up on the brightly painted main street of Wigtown, voted Scotland's national book town. The 10-day Wigtown Book Festival is held in late September and early October.

GETTING HERE AND AROUND

There is no train station in Wigtown, and you must make several transfers when traveling by bus to and from Scotland's larger cities. Driving is your best option. From Glasgow, take the A77 (about two hours). From Edinburgh, take the A702 (about three hours).

EXPLORING

Bladnoch Distillery. On the banks of the River Bladnoch, this is Scotland's southernmost malt-whisky producer and one of just six remaining Lowlands distilleries. It has been closed for much of the last 50 years, but was revived by enthusiasts in 2000. It now takes pride in being a small, locally run distillery. Tours are given on the hour between 10 and 4. There's also a visitor center and a gift shop. ⊠ *Bladnoch* ☎ *01988/402605* ⊕ *www.bladnoch.co.uk* 🖾 *£4* ⊙ *July and Aug., weekdays 9–5, Sat. 11–5, Sun. noon–5; Sept.–June, weekdays 9–5.*

Fodor'sChoice ★ **Wigtown Book Festival.** The 10-day Wigtown Book Festival, held in late September and early October, has readings, performances, and other events around town. ☎ *01988/402036* ⊕ *www.wigtown-booktown. co.uk.*

SHOPPING

Bookshop. One of the country's largest secondhand bookstores, the Bookshop offers temptingly full shelves. The narrow entrance, flanked by two tottering towers of books, belies the huge stock within, both upstairs and through to the rear of the shop. ⊠ *17 N. Main St.* ☎ *01988/402499.*

> ### GOLF GETAWAYS
>
> There are more than 30 courses in Dumfries and Galloway and 21 in the Borders. The Freedom of the Fairways Pass (five-day pass, £120; three-day pass, £88) allows play on all 21 Borders courses and is available from the Scottish Borders Tourist Board. The Gateway to Golf Pass (six-round pass, £120; three-round pass, £80) is accepted by all clubs in Dumfries and Galloway.

WHITHORN

11 miles south of Wigtown, 94 miles southwest of Glasgow, 121 miles southwest of Edinburgh.

Known for its Early Christian settlement, Whithorn is full of history. The main street is notably wide, with cute pastel buildings nestled up against each other, their low doorways and small windows creating images of years long past. It's still mainly a farming community, but is fast becoming a popular tourist destination. Several scenes from the original *Wicker Man* were shot in and around the area. During the summer months, it's a popular place for festivals. The Isle of Whithorn, just beyond the town, is not an island at all but a fishing village of great charm.

GETTING HERE AND AROUND

There's no train station in Whithorn, and most of the buses are local (getting to main Scottish cities from Whithorn takes careful planning and several transfers). To drive from Wigtown, take the A746 (about

20 minutes). From Glasgow, take the A77 (about 2½ hours). From Edinburgh, take the A702 (about three hours).

EXPLORING

Whithorn Priory. The road that is now the A746 was a pilgrims' path that led to the royal burgh of Whithorn, where sat Whithorn Priory, one of Scotland's great medieval cathedrals, now an empty shell. It was built in the 12th century and is said to occupy the site of a former stone church, the Candida Casa, built by St. Ninian in the 4th century. As the story goes, the church housed a shrine to Ninian, the earliest of Scotland's saints, and kings and barons sought to visit the shrine at least once in their lives. As you approach the priory, observe the royal arms of pre-1707 Scotland—that is, Scotland before the Union with England—carved and painted above the *pend* (covered walkway). ✉ *Off A746* 🌐 *www.whithornpriorymuseum.gov.uk* 🎫 *£4.50* 🕐 *Apr.–Oct., daily 10:30–5.*

15

WHERE TO EAT

$ BRITISH 🍴 **Steam Packet Inn.** This lovely, old-fashioned inn is always full, mainly because of its hearty, well-cooked food and good beer. Patrons also love the location, on the harbor of this quaint fishing village. You can walk the headland behind the pub to the rocky shore of the Solway Firth. Fish-and-chips and lamb shanks can be followed by some excellent house-made desserts. When weather permits, you can eat at tables in the garden. If you like it so much you want to stay, there are also a couple of rooms. [$] *Average main: £13* ✉ *Harbour Row, Isle of Whithorn* ☎ *01988/500334* 🌐 *www.steampacketinn.co.uk.*

STRANRAER

31 miles northwest of Whithorn, 86 miles southwest of Glasgow, 131 miles southwest of Edinburgh.

Stranraer has a lovely garden and is also the main ferry port to Northern Ireland—if you make a purchase in one of its shops, you may wind up with some euro coins from Ireland in your change.

GETTING HERE AND AROUND

Stranraer has a busy train station that serves all major lines, and the bus connections are good as well (with many links to smaller towns). If you're driving, take the A747 from Whithorn (about 45 minutes). From Glasgow, take the M77/A77 (two hours), and from Edinburgh, take the A77 (three hours).

ESSENTIALS

Visitor Information Stranraer Visitor Information Centre ✉ *28 Harbour St.* ☎ *01776/702595* 🌐 *www.dumfriesandgalloway.co.uk.*

EXPLORING

Fodor's Choice ★ **Castle Kennedy Gardens.** The lovely Castle Kennedy Gardens surround the shell of the original Castle Kennedy, which was burned in 1716. Parks scattered around the property were built by the 2nd Earl of Stair in 1733. The earl was a field marshal and used his soldiers to help with the heavy work of constructing banks, ponds, and other major landscape features. When the rhododendrons are in bloom, the effect is kaleidoscopic. There's also a pleasant tearoom. ⊠ *North of A75, 3 miles east of Stranraer* ☎ *01776/702024* ⊕ *www.castlekennedygardens. co.uk* ▱ *£5* ⊙ *Easter–Oct., daily 10–5.*

Logan Botanic Gardens. The spectacular Logan Botanic Gardens, one of the National Botanic Gardens of Scotland, are a must-see for garden lovers. Displayed here are plants that enjoy the prevailing mild climate, especially tree ferns, cabbage palms, and other Southern Hemisphere exotica. There are free guided walks every second Tuesday of the month at 10:30 am; at other times there is a free audio guide. The gardens are 14 miles south of Stranraer. ⊠ *B7065, Port Logan* ☎ *01776/860231* ▱ *£5.50* ⊙ *Feb., Sun. 10–5; Mar.–Oct., daily 10–5.*

Mull of Galloway. If you wish to visit the southern tip of the Rhinns of Galloway, called the Mull of Galloway, follow the B7065/B7041 until you run out of land. The cliffs and seascapes here are rugged, and there's a lighthouse and a bird reserve.

Southern Upland Way. The village of Portpatrick, 8 miles southwest of Stranraer, is the starting point for Scotland's longest official long-distance footpath, the Southern Upland Way, which runs a switchback course for 212 miles to Cockburnspath, on the east side of the Borders. The path begins on the cliffs just north of the town and follows the coastline for 1½ miles before turning inland. ⊕ *www.southernuplandway. gov.uk/cms/.*

THE CENTRAL HIGHLANDS, FIFE, AND ANGUS

WELCOME TO THE CENTRAL HIGHLANDS, FIFE, AND ANGUS

TOP REASONS TO GO

★ **From Loch Lomond to the sea:** The sparkling waters of Scotland's largest loch reflect its surrounding hills. The Fife and Angus coasts, by contrast, look out on to the North Sea.

★ **Castles:** Among the highlights are Stirling Castle and Scone Palace, near Perth, with its grand aristocratic air.

★ **Great golf:** Golf was born here, near the famous Royal and Ancient at St. Andrews. Small wonder then that the region has such varied and challenging courses.

★ **Great hikes and bike rides:** This varied landscape offers walkers and bikers everything from "Munros" (hills over 3,000 feet) to gentler rambles through the Trossachs. Another popular option is the network of bicycle tracks near Loch Lomond.

★ **East Neuk:** The beautiful fishing villages of the East Neuk, along the Fife coast, are working harbors. Winding cobbled streets and smooth golden beaches add appeal.

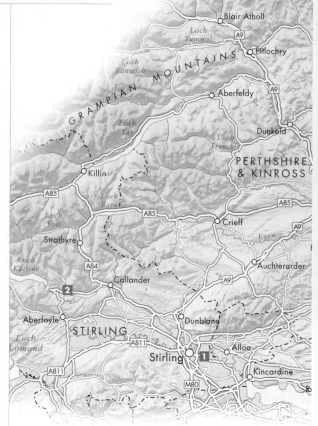

1 Stirling. A city vibrant with history, Stirling has a small Old Town on the hill that can be easily covered on foot. The town is a good center from which to explore central Scotland.

2 The Trossachs and Loch Lomond. Now a National Park, this relatively small area embraces mountain peaks that attract walkers and climbers and the gentler slopes and forests that stretch from Perth westward to Aberfoyle.

3 Perthshire. From the prosperous city of Perth, once the capital of Scotland, the route northward leads across the Highland Boundary and into the changing landscapes beyond Pitlochry to Rannoch Moor.

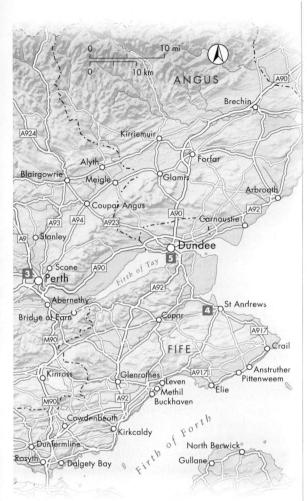

GETTING ORIENTED

The reference points for your trip are Stirling, an ancient historic town with a castle that affords great views of central Scotland; Perth, 36 miles northeast, the gateway to the Highlands; the city of Dundee, on the river Tay; and the historic center and home of golf, St. Andrews, in Fife. North from Stirling, you cross the fertile open plain (the Carse of Stirling) dotted with historic towns. The Trossachs represent the Scotland of the Romantic imagination: lochs and woodland glens, drovers' inns, and grand country houses. The small towns of the region, like Callander, Aberfoyle, and Pitlochry, are bases from which to explore this changing countryside. To the west lies Loch Lomond, whose banks stretch from Glasgow to the hills and glens of the Highlands.

4 St. Andrews and East Neuk. St. Andrews isn't just a playground for golfers. This religious and academic center is steeped in history and prestige, with grand buildings. Beyond St. Andrews, the colorful fishing villages of the East Neuk are a day-tripper's delight.

5 Dundee and Angus. Dundee has a knockout setting beside Britain's mightiest river, historical sights and a vibrant social life. The country roads of the Angus heartlands roll through fields to busy market towns, wee villages, and Glamis Castle.

Updated by
Shona Main
and Mike
Gonzalez

The Central Highlands are home to superb castles, moody mountains, and gorgeous glens, as well as the waters of Loch Lomond. Beyond Scotland's first national park, Loch Lomond and the Trossachs, is the wide plain guarded by Stirling Castle, scene of key moments in Scotland's history. East of the Central Highlands, toward the North Sea, are Fife and Angus, with attractions as varied as golf mecca St. Andrews and scenic fishing villages.

North from Stirling are the hills and valleys of the Trossachs, whose high peaks attract walkers and cyclists. On a good day you can see Edinburgh Castle to the east and the towers of Glasgow's housing projects to the west from there. For many years Stirling was the starting point for visitors setting out to explore these wilder landscapes, with their lochs and hills hung with shaggy birch, oak, and pinewoods.

Perth, overlooking the River Tay, can claim to be the gateway to the Highlands, sitting as it does on the Highland Fault that divides Lowlands from Highlands. Its mansions reflect the prosperous agricultural land surrounding the city. From Perth, the landscape changes on the road to Pitlochry. And farther north, more dramatic landscapes appear in the high, rough country of Rannoch Moor and toward Ben Lawers.

To the east, along the shores of the North Sea, lie Angus and the ancient kingdom of Fife. The East Neuk, or eastern corner, of Scotland has been shaped by the sea and fishing. Charming villages, like Crail, remain working ports, their houses crowded into steep narrow streets (wynds) around the harbor. But for visitors the ancient university town of St. Andrews, with its grand ruined cathedral and castle, evokes Fife's medieval past, though it also remains a mecca for the golf enthusiast.

Across the Tay is the city of Dundee, once a hub for a textile industry based on jute and now seeking a new identity as a city of culture. Beyond the Firth of Tay, the Angus coast marries glens and fishing towns, and on the horizon the outer edges of the Grampian Highlands.

THE CENTRAL HIGHLANDS, FIFE, AND ANGUS PLANNER

WHEN TO GO

The Trossachs and Loch Lomond are in some ways a miniature Scotland, from the tranquil east shore of Loch Lomond to the hills and glens of the Trossachs and the mountains of the Arrochar Alps to the west— and all within a few hours' drive. To the east, the very different, mainly flat kingdom of Fife has always looked toward the sea. It is mainly a place for spring and summer visits, while the west—always crowded in summer—is dramatic and beautiful when the trees are turning red and brown in autumn, and has spectacular evening skies. Scotland in winter has a different kind of beauty, especially for skiers and climbers. ■TIP➔ Carry clothes for wet and dry weather, as the weather can change quickly. Summer evenings attract midges; take some repellent.

PLANNING YOUR TIME

Scotland's beautiful interior is excellent touring country, though the cities of Stirling and Perth are worth your time, too; Stirling in particular is worth a day. Two (slightly rushed) days would be enough to explore the Trossachs loop and to gaze into the waters of Loch Venachar and Loch Achray. The glens, in some places, run parallel to the lochs, including those along Lochs Earn, Tay, and Rannoch, making for satisfying loops and round-trips. Loch Lomond is easily accessible from either Glasgow or Stirling, and is well worth exploring. Don't miss the opportunity to take a boat trip on a loch, especially on Loch Lomond or on Loch Katrine. In Fife, Dundee and St. Andrews reward a day's exploring each, and a day's drive along the A917 (allow for exploring and stops for ice cream and fish) will let you climb the steep narrow streets of East Neuk fishing villages like Crail. The small towns of Angus are a fascinating drive from Dundee; give yourself two or three hours to explore the grand castle of Glamis.

16

GETTING HERE AND AROUND

AIR TRAVEL

Perth and Stirling, and St. Andrews and the East Neuk, can be reached easily from the Edinburgh, Dundee, and Glasgow airports by train, car, or bus. Dundee Airport is off A85, 2 miles west of the city center. Air France operates a popular direct flight from London City Airport. If you are traveling to St. Andrews directly from Edinburgh Airport, the St. Andrews Shuttle offers transfers from £18.

BUS TRAVEL

A good network of buses connects with the central belt via Edinburgh and Glasgow. For more information, contact Scottish Citylink or National Express. Stagecoach connects St. Andrews and Dundee to smaller towns in the area, while Megabus has a regular service to Dundee from Edinburgh and Glasgow.

First, Scottish Citylink, and Stagecoach organize reliable service on routes throughout the Central Highlands, Fife, and Angus. A Day Rover ticket (£8 for Fife only) is a good value. Traveline Scotland is a service that helps you plan all public-transport journeys.

Bus Contacts First ☎ *08708/727271* ⊕ *www.firstgroup.com*. **Megabus** ☎ *0900/160–0900* ⊕ *www.uk.megabus.com*. **National Express** ☎ *08717/818181* ⊕ *www.nationalexpress.com*. **Scottish Citylink** ☎ *0871/2663333* ⊕ *www.citylink.co.uk*. **Stagecoach** ☎ *01292/613502* ⊕ *www. stagecoachbus.com*.**St. Andrews Shuttle** ⊕ *www.standrewsshuttle.com*. **Traveline Scotland** ☎ *08706/200–2233* ⊕ *www.travelinescotland.com*.

CAR TRAVEL

You'll find easy access to the area from the central belt of Scotland via the motorway network. The M80 connects Glasgow to Stirling, and then briefly joins the M9 from Edinburgh, which runs within sight of the walls of Stirling Castle. From there the A9 runs from Stirling to Perth, and onward to Pitlochry; it is a good road but a little too fast for its own good, so take care. The M90 motorway over the Forth Bridge from Edinburgh is the fastest route to Angus and northeast Fife. At the Perth roundabout you can exit to the A90 for the town or continue to Dundee or St. Andrews. Three signed touring routes are useful: the Perthshire Tourist Route, the Deeside Tourist Route, and the Pitlochry Tourist Route, a beautiful and unexpected trip via Loch Tay. Eastern Fife is served by a network of country roads. Local tourist information centers can supply maps of these routes. Once you leave the major motorways, roads become narrower and slower, with many following the contours of the lochs. Be prepared for your journey to take longer than distances might suggest.

TRAIN TRAVEL

The Central Highlands are linked to Edinburgh and Glasgow by rail, with through routes to England (some direct-service routes from London take less than five hours). Several discount ticket options are available, although in some cases on the ScotRail system a discount card must be purchased before your arrival in Britain. Families with children and travelers under 26 or over 60 are eligible for discounts. Contact Trainline, National Rail, or ScotRail for details.

The West Highland Line runs through the western portion of the area. Services also run to Stirling, Perth, and Gleneagles; stops on the Inverness–Perth line include Dunkeld, Pitlochry, and Blair Atholl. In the east, ScotRail stops at Kirkcaldy, Leuchars (for St. Andrews), and Dundee.

Train Contacts National Rail Enquiries ☎ *08457/484950* ⊕ *www.trainline. co.uk*. **ScotRail** ☎ *08457/550033* ⊕ *www.scotrail.co.uk*. **Trainline** ⊕ *www. thetrainline.com*.

RESTAURANTS

Regional country delicacies—loch trout, river salmon, lamb, and venison—appear regularly on even modest menus in restaurants across the region. In all the towns and villages in the area, you will find simple pubs, often crowded and noisy, many of them serving substantial food at lunchtime and in the evening until about 9 (eaten balanced on your knee, perhaps, or at a shared table). It can be difficult to find a place to eat later than that, so plan ahead. With an affluent population and university, St. Andrews supports stylish hotel restaurants and good cafés and bistros. Bar lunches are the rule in large and small hotels throughout the region, and in seaside places the carry-*oot* (to-go) meal of fish-and-chips is an enduring tradition.

HOTELS

There is a wide selection of accommodations throughout the region. They range from bed-and-breakfasts to private houses with a small number of rooms to rural accommodations (often on farms). The grand houses of the past—family homes to the landed aristocracy—have for the most part become country-house hotels. But there are also modern hotels in the area. If you're staying in Fife, the obvious choice for a base is St. Andrews. Dundee and its hinterlands have a number of diverse accommodations, all of which offer good value. *Hotel reviews have been shortened. For full information, visit Fodors.com.*

WHAT IT COSTS IN POUNDS				
	$	$$	$$$	$$$$
Restaurants	under £15	£15–£19	£20–£25	over £25
Hotels	under £100	£100–£160	£161–£220	over £220

Restaurant prices are the average cost of a main course at dinner or, if dinner is not served, at lunch. Hotel prices are the lowest cost of a standard double room in high season, including 20% V.A.T.

16

TOURS

From June to August, Scottish Express, run by Fishers Tours, operates bus tours both within and outside Fife and Angus. Links Golf St. Andrews tailors tours to individual requirements.

Bus Tours Fishers Tours ✉ *16 W. Port, Dundee* ☎ *01382/227290* ⊕ *www.fisherstours.co.uk.*

Golf Tours Links Golf St. Andrews ✉ *7 Pilmour Links, St. Andrews* ☎ *01334/478639* ⊕ *www.linksgolfstandrews.com.*

VISITOR INFORMATION

The tourist offices in Stirling and Perth, Dundee and St. Andrews, are open year-round, as are offices in larger towns; others are seasonal (generally from April to October).

STIRLING

26 miles northeast of Glasgow, 36 miles northwest of Edinburgh.

Stirling is one of Britain's great historic towns. An impressive proportion of the Old Town walls can be seen from Dumbarton Road, a cobbled street leading to Stirling Castle, built on a steep-sided plug of rock. From its esplanade there is a commanding view of the surrounding Carse of Stirling. The guns on the castle battlements are a reminder of the military advantage to be gained from its position.

GETTING HERE AND AROUND

Stirling's central position in the area makes it an ideal point for travel to and from Glasgow and Edinburgh (or north to Perth and the Highlands) by rail, train, or bus. The town itself is compact and easily walkable, though a shuttle bus travels to and from the town center up the steep road to Stirling Castle every 20 minutes. The Back Walk takes the visitor on a circuit around the base of the castle walls—set aside at least 30 minutes for a leisurely walk.

TIMING

The historic part of town is tightly nestled around the castle—everything is within easy walking distance. The National Wallace Monument (2 miles away) is on the outskirts of the town and can be reached by taxi or, for the more energetic, on foot.

ESSENTIALS

Stirling Visitor Information Centre ✉ *Old Town Jail, St. John St.* ☎ *01786/465019.*

EXPLORING

TOP ATTRACTIONS

Fodor'sChoice
★
Bannockburn Heritage Centre. Opening in 2014, this museum uses cutting-edge technology to help you take part in Scotland's greatest battle, where Robert the Bruce defeated King Edward II at Bannockburn in 1314. The beautifully designed Bannockburn Heritage Centre celebrates the cunning of Robert the Bruce, who chose this site because its boggy ground would impede the English horses. The fields that surround the museum were the battlefield, and interactive displays re-create the sights and sounds of that great medieval encounter. ✉ *Glasgow Rd., Bannockburn* ☎ *0844/493–2139* ⊕ *www.nts.org.uk/Visits* 💷 *£20.*

National Wallace Monument. It was near Old Stirling Bridge that William Wallace (circa 1270–1305), with his ragged army of Scots, won a major victory against the English in 1297. This Victorian-era shrine to the Scottish freedom fighter (reborn as "Braveheart" in Mel Gibson's film of the same name) was built between 1856 and 1869. A less flamboyant version of Wallace's life is told in an exhibition and audiovisual presentation in this pencil-thin museum on the Abbey Craig. To reach the monument, follow the Bridge of Allan signs (A9) northward, crossing the River Forth by the New Bridge of 1832, next to the old one. The National Wallace Monument is signposted at the next traffic circle. ✉ *Abbey Craig, Hillfoot Rd.* ☎ *01786/472140* ⊕ *www.nationalwallacemonument.com* 💷 *£8.50* ⊗ *Apr.–June, Sept. and Oct., daily 10–5; July and Aug., daily 10–6; Nov.–Mar., daily 10:30–4.*

Fodor'sChoice
★
Stirling Castle. Its magnificent strategic position on a steep-sided crag made Stirling Castle the grandest prize in the Scots Wars of Independence in the late 13th and early 14th centuries. The Battle of Bannockburn in 1314 was fought within sight of its walls, and the victory by Robert the Bruce won both the castle and freedom from English subjugation for almost four centuries. Take time to visit the **Castle Exhibition** in the Queen Anne Garden beyond the lower gate to get an overview of its long history and evolution as a stronghold and palace.

The daughter of King Robert I (Robert the Bruce), Marjory, married Walter Fitzallan, the high steward of Scotland. Their descendants included the Stewart dynasty of Scottish monarchs (Mary, Queen of

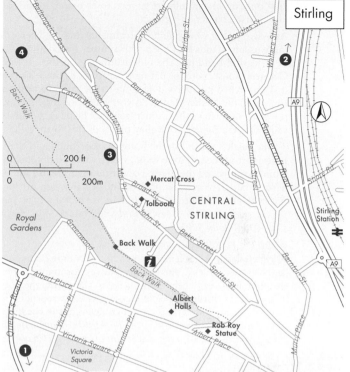

Scots was a Stewart, though she preferred the French spelling, *Stuart*). They made Stirling Castle their court and power base, creating fine Renaissance-style buildings that were never completely obliterated, despite reconstruction for military purposes.

Enter the castle through its outer defenses, which consist of a great curtained wall and batteries from 1708, built to bulwark earlier defenses by the main gatehouse. From this lower square the most conspicuous feature is the **Palace,** built by King James V (1512–42) between 1538 and 1542. The decorative figures festooning the ornate outer walls show the influence of French masons. An orientation center in the basement lets you try out the clothes and musical instruments of the time. Then you are led across a terrace to the **Royal Apartments,** where the furnishings and tapestries of the reign of James V and his French queen, Mary of Guise are re-created. The queen's bedchamber contains copies of the beautiful tapestries in which the hunt for the white unicorn is clearly an allegory for the persecution of Christ. Overlooking the upper courtyard is the **Great Hall,** built by King James IV (1473–1513) in 1503 and now returned to its original splendor. Before the Union of Parliaments in 1707, when the Scottish aristocracy sold out to England, this building had been used as one of the seats of the Scottish Parliament. Here the king once ordered a full-size galleon to be placed in the hall during the fish course of a major banquet.

Among the later works built for regiments stationed here, the **Regimental Museum** stands out; it's a 19th-century baronial revival on the site of an earlier building. The oldest building on the site is the **Mint,** or **Coonzie Hoose,** perhaps dating as far back as the 14th century. Below it is an arched passageway leading to the westernmost section of the ramparts, the **Nether Bailey.** As you walk along the high walls beyond the arch, you'll have the distinct feeling of being in the bow of a warship sailing up the *carselands* (valley plain) of the Forth Valley.

To the castle's south lies the hump of the Touch and the Gargunnock Hills (part of the Campsie Fells), which diverted potential direct routes from Glasgow and the south. For centuries all roads into the Highlands across the narrow waist of Scotland led through Stirling. ✉ *Castlehill* ☎ *01786/450000* 🌐 *www.historic-scotland.gov.uk/places* 🎟 *£14, includes admission to Argyll's Lodging* 🕒 *Apr.–Sept., daily 9:30–5:30; Oct.–Mar., daily 9:30–4:15.*

WORTH NOTING

Argyll's Lodging. A nobleman's town house built in three phases from the 16th century onward, this building served for many years as a military hospital. It has now been refurbished to show how the nobility lived in 17th-century Stirling. Specially commissioned reproduction furniture and fittings are based on the original inventory of the house's contents at that time. ✉ *Castle Wynd* ☎ *01786/450000* 🌐 *www.historic-scotland.gov.uk/places* 🎟 *£14, includes Stirling Castle* 🕒 *Hrs vary.*

WHERE TO EAT

$$ ECLECTIC

🍴 **Hermann's Restaurant.** Run by Austrian Hermann Aschaber and his Glaswegian wife, the restaurant presents the cuisines of both countries. The Black Watch–tartan carpet and alpine murals are as successfully matched as the signature Scottish dishes like *cullen skink* (a fish-and-potato soup) and chicken with Stornaway black pudding and Drambuie cream, and Austrian staples like Wiener schnitzel and cheese spaetzle. [$] *Average main: £19* ✉ *58 Broad St.* ☎ *01786/450632* 🌐 *www.hermanns-restaurant.co.uk.*

$$ ECLECTIC

🍴 **River House.** Behind Stirling Castle, this restaurant sits by its own tranquil little loch and is built in the style of a Scottish *crannog* (ancient loch dwelling). It's relaxed and friendly, with tables on a deck overlooking the water. Local produce dominates the menu, yet the food reflects French and Mediterranean influences. Try the curried Scottish lamb with lime yogurt. You can get here directly from the M9 motorway: follow the Stirling sign at Junction 10. From Aberfoyle it's on A84, or follow B8051 around the castle toward the Castle Business Park. [$] *Average main: £16* ✉ *The Castle Business Park, B8051* ☎ *01786/465577* 🌐 *www.riverhouse-restaurant.co.uk.*

WHERE TO STAY

$ B&B/INN 🏨 **Castlecroft.** Tucked beneath Stirling Castle, this comfortable modern house welcomes you with freshly cut flowers and homemade breakfasts. **Pros:** great location; lovely views; hearty breakfasts. **Cons:** a little hard to find if you are not arriving directly from the motorway. [$] *Rooms from: £70* ✉ *Ballengeich Rd.* ☎ *01786/474933* 🌐 *www.castlecroft-uk.com* 🛏 *5 rooms* 🍴 *Breakfast.*

$$ HOTEL 🏨 **Park Lodge Hotel.** This elegant 18th-century country-house hotel gives you a taste of French-inspired design and cuisine. **Pros:** great views of park; homey feel; recently renovated. **Cons:** too many floral prints. [$] *Rooms from: £108* ✉ *32 Park Terr.* ☎ *01786/474862* 🌐 *www.parklodge.net* 🛏 *9 rooms* 🍴 *Breakfast.*

$ B&B/INN 🏨 **West Plean.** More than 200 years old, this handsome, rambling B&B is part of a working farm. **Pros:** beautiful gardens; plenty of peace and quiet; huge and hearty breakfast. **Cons:** a little off the beaten track; a long walk to Stirling. [$] *Rooms from: £90* ✉ *Denny Rd.* ☎ *01786/812208* 🌐 *www.westpleanhouse.com* 🛏 *4 rooms* ⏲ *Closed Dec.* 🍴 *Breakfast.*

THE ARTS

Tolbooth. Built in 1705, the Tolbooth has been many things: courthouse, jail, and meeting place. At one time the city's money was kept here. It has retained its traditional Scottish steeple and gilded weathercock, and a newer tower lets you survey the surrounding country. Today it serves as an art gallery and a 200-seat theater. The bar is open for performances. ✉ *Broad St.* ☎ *01786/274000* 🌐 *www.stirling.gov.uk/tolbooth.*

SHOPPING

SHOPPING CENTERS

Stirling Arcade. Built in the 19th century, Stirling Arcade has about 20 shops. You'll find everything from toys to fine clothing. ✉ *King St.* ☎ *01786/450719.*

CERAMICS AND GLASSWARE

Barbara Davidson Pottery. South of Stirling, Barbara Davidson Pottery is run by one of the best-known potters in Scotland. Demonstrations can be arranged by appointment. Signs point the way from the A9. ✉ *Muirhall Farm, Muirhall Rd., Larbert* ☎ *01324/554430* 🌐 *www.barbara-davidson.com.*

CLOTHING

House of Henderson. A Highland outfitter, House of Henderson sells tartans, woolens, and accessories, and offers a made-to-measure kilt service. ✉ *6–8 Friars St.* ☎ *01786/473681* 🌐 *www.houseofhenderson.co.uk* ⏲ *Mon.–Sat. 9:30–5:30.*

Mill Trail. East of Stirling is Mill Trail country, along the foot of the Ochil Hills. A leaflet from any local tourist information center will lead you to the delights of a real mill shop and low mill prices—even on cashmere—at Tillicoultry, Alva, and Alloa.

SIDE TRIPS FROM STIRLING

FALKIRK WHEEL
15 miles southeast of Stirling.

FAMILY **Falkirk Wheel.** The only rotating boatlift in the world, the Falkirk Wheel links two major waterways, the Forth and Clyde Canal and the Union Canal, between Edinburgh and Glasgow. This extraordinary engineering achievement lifts and lowers boats using four giant wheels shaped like Celtic axes; it can transport eight or more boats at a time from one canal to the other in about 45 minutes. As the wheel turns, you're transported up or down to the other canal. The Falkirk Wheel replaced 11 locks that were once the only way of moving between the two bodies of water. The site offers children's play areas, as well as canoes and bicycles rentals. From Stirling, take the M9 toward Edinburgh, exit at Junction 8 and follow signs for the Falkirk Wheel. ✉ *Lime Rd., Tamfourhill* ☎ *08700/500208* ⊕ *www.thefalkirkwheel.co.uk* ⊡ *£8.95* ⊗ *Apr.–Oct., daily 10–5:30; Nov.–Mar., Wed.–Sun. 11–4.*

DOUNE CASTLE
9 miles north of Stirling.

Doune Castle. One of the best-preserved medieval castles in Scotland, Doune is grim and high-walled, with a daunting central keep and echoing, drafty stairways up to the curtain-wall walk. The views make the climb well worthwhile. It's also a place of pilgrimage for fans of *Monty Python and Holy Grail*, which was filmed here. There is a good audio guide narrated by Monty Python's Terry Gilliam. ✉ *Castle Rd., Doune* ☎ *01786/841742* ⊕ *www.historic-scotland.gov.uk* ⊡ *£5* ⊗ *Apr.–Sept., daily 9:30–5:30; Oct., daily 9:30–4; Nov.–Mar., Sat.–Wed. 9:30–4.*

THE TROSSACHS AND LOCH LOMOND

Immortalized by Wordsworth and Sir Walter Scott, the Trossachs (the name means "bristly country") contains some of Scotland's loveliest forests, hills, and glens, well justifying the area's designation as a national park. The area has a special charm, combining the wildness of the Highlands with the vegetation of an old Lowland forest. Its open ground is a dense mat of bracken and heather, and its woodland is of silver birch, dwarf oak, and hazel. There are also many small towns, some with castles, to visit along the way. Some towns have their roots in a medieval world; others sprang up and expanded in the wake of the first when the 19th-century tourists came in search of wild country or healing waters. The most colorful season is fall, particularly October, a lovely time when most visitors have departed, and the hares, deer, and game birds have taken over. The best way to explore this area is by car, by bike, or on foot; the latter two depend, of course, on the weather. Keep in mind that roads in this region of the country are narrow and winding.

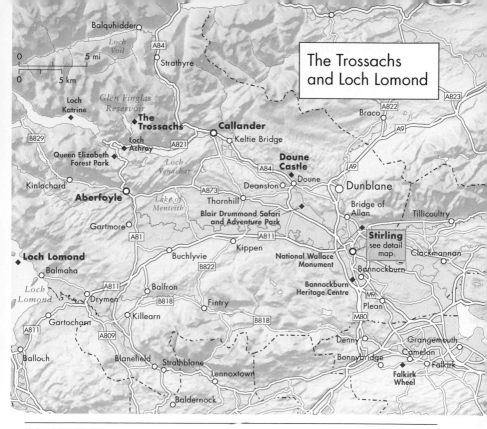

CALLANDER

14 miles northwest of Stirling.

A traditional Highland-edge resort, the little town of Callander bustles throughout the year, even during off-peak times, simply because it's a gateway to Highland scenery and Loch Lomond and the Trossachs National Park. As a result, there's plenty of window-shopping here, plus pub nightlife and a good selection of accommodations.

GETTING HERE AND AROUND

You can access Callander by bus from Stirling, Glasgow, or Edinburgh. If you're traveling by car from Stirling, take the M8 to Dunblane, then the A820 (which becomes the A84) to Callander. If you are coming from Glasgow, take the A81 through Aberfoyle to Callander; an alternative route (longer but more picturesque) is to take the A821 around Loch Venachar, then the A84 east to Callander.

ESSENTIALS

Visitor Information Callander Visitor Information Centre ✉ *Ancaster Sq.* ☎ *01877/330342* ⊕ *www.visitscotland.com.*

EXPLORING

FAMILY **Blair Drummond Safari and Adventure Park.** As unlikely as it might seem in this gentle valley, the Blair Drummond Safari and Adventure Park is the place to see sea lions bobbing their heads above the water or monkeys swinging from the branches. Take a footbridge to Lemur Land or watch hawks and falcons in the "Birds of Prey" exhibit. **■TIP→ Beware the llamas, who are more bad-tempered than they may appear.** The enclosures are spacious, so the place doesn't feel like a zoo. There are rides, slides, and an adventure playground for the kids. ✉ *Blair Drummond, Doune* ☎ *01786/841456* 🌐 *www.blairdrummond.com* 🎟 *£13.50* 🕒 *Mar.–Oct., daily 10–5:30.*

FAMILY **Hamilton Toy Collection.** Here you'll find one of the most extensive toy collections in Britain, with all conceivable types of toys grouped throughout the house, ranging from teddy bears to porcelain dolls, toy soldiers to Matchbox cars. There's a wonderful selection of model railways and an Edwardian nursery complete with dollhouses. The shop is defiantly divided into sections for girls and boys. ✉ *111 Main St.* ☎ *01877/330004* 🎟 *£2* 🕒 *Apr.–Oct., Mon.–Sat. 10–4:30, Sun. noon–4:30.*

WHERE TO EAT AND STAY

$ CAFÉ 🍴 **Pip's Coffee House.** Come to this cheerful little place just off the main street for imaginative soups and salads, as well as exquisite Scottish home baking, including fresh scones. And then, of course, there's great coffee. [$] *Average main: £7* ✉ *21–23 Ancaster Sq.* ☎ *01877/330470* 💳 *No credit cards* 🕒 *No dinner.*

$$$ HOTEL Fodor's Choice ★ 🏨 **Monachyle Mhor.** Twelve miles north of Callander, and set in Balquhidder Glen amid 2,000 acres of forests and moorland, this beautifully converted farmhouse sits in splendid isolation against a backdrop of mountains and views over Lochs Voil and Doine. **Pros:** stunning scenery; delicious food; complimentary salmon and trout fishing. **Cons:** you're isolated; rooms are on the small side. [$] *Rooms from: £195* ✉ *Off A84, Balquhidder* ☎ *01877/384622* 🌐 *www.mhor.net* 🛏 *14 rooms* 🍽 *Breakfast.*

$$ B&B/INN Fodor's Choice ★ 🏨 **Roman Camp.** Within a hundred yards of Callander's main street, pass through an unpretentious arch and you'll find this 17th-century hunting lodge surrounded by ornate gardens. **Pros:** beautiful grounds; luxurious rooms; close to everything in town. **Cons:** restaurant is expensive; no Internet in rooms. [$] *Rooms from: £155* ✉ *Off Main St.* ☎ *01877/330003* 🌐 *www.romancamphotel.co.uk* 🛏 *12 rooms, 3 suites* 🍽 *Breakfast.*

SPORTS AND THE OUTDOORS

BIKING

Wheels. This friendly firm rents bikes of every sort by the hour, the half day, or the day. Most popular are the mountain bikes, which go for £18 per day. The staff will help you find the best mountain-bike routes around the Trossachs. ✉ *Invertrossachs Rd.* ☎ *01877/331100* 🌐 *www.wheelscyclingcentre.com.*

HIKING

Bracklinn Falls. A walk is signposted from the east end of Callander's main street to the Bracklinn Falls, over whose lip Sir Walter Scott once rode a pony to win a bet.

Callander Crags. It's a 1½-mile walk through the woods up to the Callander Crags, with views of the Lowlands as far as the Pentland Hills behind Edinburgh. The walk begins at the west end of Callander's main street.

Pass of Leny. Just north of Callander, the mountains squeeze both the road and rocky river into the narrow Pass of Leny. An abandoned railway—now a pleasant walking or biking path—also goes through the pass, past Ben Ledi and Loch Lubnaig.

> ## GOLF IN THE TROSSACHS
>
> There are many beautiful golf courses within the Loch Lomond area and the Trossachs National Park. The National Park Golf Pass (£50 for three rounds, £80 for five) allows play at Callander, St. Fillans, Aberfoyle, Killin, and Buchanan Castle. The Loch Lomond Pass (£90 for three rounds) covers the Cardos, Helensburgh, and Buchanan Castle courses.

SHOPPING

Trossachs Woollen Mill. The Edinburgh Woollen Mill Group owns this mill shop in Kilmahog. It has a vast selection of woolens on display, including luxurious cashmere and striking tartan throws, and will provide overseas mailing and tax-free shopping. ⊠ *Trossachs Woollen Mill, Main St., Kilmahog* ☎ *01877/330268* ⊕ *www.ewm.co.uk* ⊗ *Mar.–Oct. daily 9–5; Nov. daily 9–4:30; Dec.–Feb. daily 9–4.*

THE TROSSACHS

10 miles west of Callander.

With its harmonious scenery of hill, loch, and wooded slopes, the Trossachs has been a popular touring region since the late 18th century. Early visitors from the central belt came in search of "wild" Scotland. Perhaps because the Trossachs represent the very essence of what the Highlands are supposed to be—birch and pine forests creeping down to loch shores, peaks that rise high enough to be called mountains—the whole of this area, including Loch Lomond, is now protected as a national park.

GETTING HERE AND AROUND

To reach the Trossachs, take the A84 from Callander through the Pass of Leny, then on to Crianlarich on the A85; from here you can take the western shore of Loch Lomond or continue on toward Fort William. Alternately, turn onto the A821 outside Callander and travel past Loch Katrine through the Duke's Pass to Aberfoyle.

EXPLORING

Fodor'sChoice ★ **Ben An.** The parking lot by Loch Achray is the place to begin the ascent of steep, heathery Ben An, which affords some of the best Trossachs views. The climb requires a couple of hours and good lungs. The beginning of the path is near Loch Achray. ⊠ *A821, Aberfoyle.*

16

Loch Achray. Stretching west of the village of Brig o' Turk, on the A821, Loch Achray dutifully fulfills expectations of what a verdant Trossachs loch should be: small, green, reedy meadows backed by dark plantations, rhododendron thickets, and lumpy hills, thickly covered with heather. ⊠ *A821, Brig o' Turk.*

Fodor'sChoice   **Loch Katrine.** This loch was a favorite ★   among Victorian visitors—mysterious and wide and, at times, quite wild. Take a cruise around the loch if time permits, as the shores remain undeveloped and scenic. The steamship *Sir Walter Scott* and the motor launch *Lady of the Lake* sail from here several times a day. You can make the round-trip journey around the loch, or head directly across to Stronlachlachlar and return by bicycle on the loch-side road. Boats depart several times a day between April and October. There are café facilities and cycle-hire shops at the head of the loch. ⊠ *Trossachs Pier, off A821, Aberfoyle* ☎ *01877/376316* ⊕ *www.lochkatrine.com* ⊙ *Apr.–late Oct., daily 9–5.*

> **SCOTLAND BY BIKE**
>
> The region's big attraction for cyclists is the **Lowland/Highland Trail**, which stretches more than 60 miles and passes through Drymen, Aberfoyle, the Trossachs, Callander, and Lochearnhead. This route runs along former railroad-track beds, as well as minor roads, to reach well into the Central Highlands. Another almost completely traffic-free option is the roadway around Loch Katrine. Mountain bikes can tackle many forest roads and trails enjoyed by walkers. Almost every town along the route has cycle-hire shops.

ABERFOYLE

11 miles south of Loch Katrine, in the Trossachs.

This small tourist town has a somewhat faded air, and several of its souvenir shops have closed their doors. But the surrounding hills (some snowcapped) and the green slopes visible from the town are the reason so many visitors pause here before continuing up to Duke's Pass or on to Inversnaid on Loch Lomond. Access to nearby Queen Elizabeth Forest Park is another reason to visit.

GETTING HERE AND AROUND
The main route out of Glasgow, the A81, takes you through Aberfoyle and on to Callander and Stirling. There are regular buses from Stirling and Glasgow to Aberfoyle.

ESSENTIALS
Visitor Information Trossachs Discovery Centre ⊠ *Main St.* ☎ *01877/382352* ⊕ *www.visitscotland.com.*

EXPLORING
Fodor'sChoice   **Inchmahome.** The ruined priory on the tiny island of Inchmahome, on the ★   Lake of Menteith, is a lovely place for a picnic. It was a place of refuge in 1547 for the young Mary, Queen of Scots. Between April and September, a ferry takes passengers to the island, now owned by the National Trust for Scotland. To get here, take the A81 to the B8034. The ferry

jetty is just beyond the Port of Menteith. **TIP→ If the boat is not there when you arrive, turn the board so that the white side faces the island. The boat will come and collect you.** ✉ *Off A81, 4 miles east of Aberfoyle* ☎ *01786/450000* 🎟 *Ferry £5.50* 🕐 *Apr.–Sept., daily 9:30–5:30.*

Queen Elizabeth Forest Park. For exquisite nature, drive north from Aberfoyle on the A821 and turn right at signposts to Queen Elizabeth Forest Park. Along the way you'll be heading toward higher moorland blanketed with conifers. Ben Ledi and Ben Venue can be seen over the spiky green waves of trees as the road snakes around heathery knolls and hummocks. There's another viewing area, and a small parking lot, at the highest point of the road. Soon the road swoops off the Highland edge and leads downhill. At the heart of the Queen Elizabeth Forest Park, the **David Marshall Lodge** leads to four forest walks, a family-friendly bicycle route, and the 7-mile 3 Lochs Forest Drive, open April to October. Or you can sit on the terrace of the Bluebell Cafe and scan the forests and hills of the Trossachs. The visitor center has a wildlife-watch room where you can follow the activities of everything from ospreys to water voles. ✉ *Off A821, 1 mile north of Aberfoyle* ☎ *01877/382383* 🌐 *www.forestry.gov.uk/qefp.*

16

FAMILY **Scottish Wool Centre.** With a vast range of woolen garments and knitwear, the Scottish Wool Centre also has a small café. Three times a day from April to September, it presents an interactive "gathering," when dogs herd sheep and ducks in the large amphitheater, with a little help from the public. Miniature horses watch from a nearby paddock. ✉ *Off Main St.* ☎ *01877/382850* 🎟 *Free* 🕐 *Feb.–Dec., daily 9:30–5:30; Jan., daily 10–4:30.*

WHERE TO STAY

$$ HOTEL Fodor's Choice ★ 🏨 **Lake of Menteith Hotel.** With its muted colors and simple but elegant rooms, this restful hotel emphasizes peace and quiet. **Pros:** elegant, unpretentious bedrooms; beautiful setting. **Cons:** not well signposted; not all rooms have lake views and those that do are more expensive. [$] *Rooms from: £120* ✉ *Off A81* ☎ *01877/385258* 🌐 *www.lake-hotel.com* 🛏 *17 rooms* 🍴 *Breakfast.*

$$ HOTEL 🏨 **Macdonald Forest Hills Hotel.** A traditional Scottish country-house theme pervades this hotel, from the rambling white building itself to the wood-paneled lounges, log fires, and numerous sporting activities. **Pros:** stunning views; log fires; good children's programs. **Cons:** restaurant is pricey and food is average; some of the building looks run-down. [$] *Rooms from: £145* ✉ *B829, Kinlochard* ☎ *08448/799057* 🌐 *www.macdonaldhotels.co.uk/foresthills* 🛏 *56 rooms* 🍴 *Breakfast.*

SPORTS AND THE OUTDOORS

GOLF **Aberfoyle Golf Club.** This hilly course is set against the backdrop of Queen Elizabeth Forest Park. One of the area's many James Braid–designed parkland courses, it dates back to 1890. ✉ *Braeval* ☎ *01877/382493* 🌐 *www.aberfoylegolf.co.uk* 🎟 *Green fee: weekdays £20, weekends £25* ⛳ *18 holes, 5218 yds, par 66.*

LOCH LOMOND

14 miles west of Aberfoyle.

The waters of Scotland's largest loch, which also happens to be one of its most beautiful, create a perfect reflection of the surrounding hills. You can cruise among its small islands by boat or follow the low road along its shores that carries you from Glasgow to the beginning of the Highlands.

GETTING HERE AND AROUND

To reach Loch Lomond's eastern shore from Aberfoyle, take the A81 toward Glasgow, the A811 to Drymen, and then the B837. For its western bank, take the A82 from Glasgow and follow the signs for Crianlarich.

> ### HIKE THE HIGHLAND WAY
>
> **West Highland Way.** The long-distance walkers' route, the West Highland Way, begins in Glasgow, running 96 miles (154 km) from the Lowlands of Central Scotland to the Highlands at Fort William. This is not a difficult walk, but keep Scotland's ever-changing weather in mind. From Milngavie, in Glasgow, the route passes along the banks of Loch Lomond before snaking northward into more demanding hills and finishing at Fort William. ⊕ *www.west-highland-way.co.uk.*

ESSENTIALS

Visitor Information Loch Lomond and the Trossachs National Park Headquarters ✉ *The Old Station, Balloch* ☎ *01389/722600* ⊕ *www.lochlomond-trossachs.org* ⊗ *Weekdays 8:30–5.*

EXPLORING

Fodor's Choice ★ **Loch Lomond.** Known for its "bonnie, bonnie banks," Loch Lomond is Scotland's largest loch in terms of surface area, and its waters reflect the crags that surround it. On the western side of the loch, the A82 follows the shore for 31 miles to Crianlarich, passing picturesque Luss, which has a pier where you can hop aboard boats cruising along the loch, and Tarbert, the starting point for the *Maid of the Loch*. You can drive, cycle, or walk along the 32 miles of Loch Lomond along its western shores, and watch the changing face of the loch as you go, or look up toward the shifting slopes of Ben Lomond.

On the eastern side of the loch, take the A81 to Drymen, and from there the B837 signposted toward Balmaha, where you can hire a boat or take the ferry to the island of Inchcailloch. Once you're there, a short walk takes you to the top of the hill and a spectacular view of the loch. Equally spectacular, but not as wet, is the view from Conic Hill near Balmaha. If you continue along the B837 beyond Rowardennan to where it ends at a car park, you can join the walkers at the beginning of the path up Ben Lomond. Don't underestimate this innocent looking hill; go equipped for sudden changes in the weather.

WHERE TO EAT AND STAY

$ **BRITISH**
Fodor's Choice ★
✕ **Coach House Coffee Shop.** This lively restaurant and café fits perfectly into its surroundings with its cheerful over-the-top Scottishness. Long wooden tables, a large chimney with an open fire in the winter months, and a cabinet full of mouthwatering cakes baked by the owner create the atmosphere. Favorites include rich homemade soups and stokies

(large round rolls filled to overflowing), as well as the ubiquitous haggis, served in king-size quantities. It's worth asking for tea served in ceramic teapots representing everything from dining rooms to telephone boxes (the pots are for sale in the shop). [$] *Average main: £11* ✉ *Church Rd., Luss* ☎ *01436/860341* ⏲ *No dinner.*

$ BRITISH 🍴 **Drovers Inn.** The portions at this noisy, friendly inn are enormous, which is just as well because many customers have returned from a day's walking on the nearby West Highland Way. Scottish staples like sausage and mash, minced beef, and haggis with mash and neeps (turnips) jostle for a place beside occasionally more adventurous dishes. This is a genuine traveler's pub, hearty rather than elegant, with an appropriate range of whiskies. There is traditional music every weekend, and there are 26 rooms for rent. The bear at the door should not put you off (it is stuffed and very old). [$] *Average main: £11* ✉ *A82, north of Ardlui, Inverarnan* ☎ *01301/704234* 🌐 *www.thedroversinn.co.uk.*

$ HOTEL 🏨 **Balloch House.** Cute, cozy, and very Scottish, this small hotel offers tasty breakfasts and hearty pub meals like fish-and-chips and local smoked salmon for reasonable prices. **Pros:** beautiful building; recently refurbished; near shopping. **Cons:** noisy pinball machine next to bar; not all rooms have views. [$] *Rooms from: £84* ✉ *Balloch Rd., Balloch* ☎ *01389/752579* 🌐 *www.innkeeperslodge.com/loch-lomond* 🛏 *12 rooms* 🍽 *Breakfast.*

$$$$ HOTEL 🏨 **Cameron House.** There is little that you cannot do at this luxury resort hotel beside Loch Lomond, including taking to the water in a motorboat or riding a seaplane above the trees. **Pros:** beautiful grounds; away-from-it-all feel; good dining. **Cons:** prices are high; slightly difficult access from A82. [$] *Rooms from: £320* ✉ *Loch Lomond, off A82, Alexandria* ☎ *01389/755565* 🌐 *www.devere.co.uk* 🛏 *96 rooms, 7 suites* 🍽 *Breakfast.*

16

SHOPPING

Loch Lomond Shores. This lakeside shopping complex contains restaurants, pubs, and a visitor center. ✉ *Ben Lomond Way, Balloch* ☎ *01389/751031* 🌐 *www.lochlomondshores.com.*

SPORTS AND THE OUTDOORS

BOATING

FAMILY **Cruise Loch Lomond.** You can take tours year-round with Cruise Loch Lomond. From April to October boats depart from various ports around the loch, including Tarbet, Luss, Balmaha, and Inversnaid. From November to March the boats operate on demand. ✉ *A82, Tarbet* ☎ *01301/702356* 🌐 *www.cruiselochlomond.co.uk* ☞ *£9.50–£12.50.*

Macfarlane and Son. At this longtime favorite, boats with outboard motors rent for £20 per hour or £60 per day. Rowboats rent for £10 per hour or £40 per day. From Balmaha it is a short trip to the lovely island of Incailloch. Macfarlane's also runs a ferry to the island for £5 per person. ✉ *Balmaha Boatyard, B837, Balmaha* ☎ *01360/870214* 🌐 *www.balmahaboatyard.co.uk.*

PERTHSHIRE

Perthshire's castles evoke memories of past conflicts, while its grand houses bear witness to its wealthy landed gentry. In some ways Perthshire is a crossing point between different Scottish landscapes and histories. Its woodlands, rivers, and glens (and agreeable climate and strategic position) drew the Romans and later Celtic missionaries, just as today they draw walkers, cyclists, and water-sports enthusiasts.

PERTH

36 miles northeast of Stirling, 43 miles north of Edinburgh, 52 miles east of Loch Lomond, 61 miles northeast of Glasgow.

For many years Perth was Scotland's capital, and it's central to the nation's history. One king (James I) was killed here, and the Protestant reformer John Knox preached his fiery sermons in the town. Perth's local whisky trade and the productive agriculture that surrounds the town have sustained it through the centuries. The open parkland within the city (the Inches) gives the place a restful air, and shops range from small crafts boutiques to department stores. Impressive Scone Palace is nearby.

GETTING HERE AND AROUND

Perth is served by the main railway line to Inverness, and regular and frequent buses run here from Glasgow, Edinburgh, and Stirling. The central artery, the A9, passes through the city en route to Pitlochry and Inverness, while a network of roads opens the way to the glens and hills around Glen Lyon. The A85 leads to Loch Lomond via Crianlarich.

ESSENTIALS

Visitor Information Perth Visitor Centre ✉ *Lower City Mills, West Mill St.* ☎ *01738/450600* ⊕ *www.visitscotland.co.uk.*

EXPLORING

Perth Art Gallery and Museum. The wide-ranging collection here includes exhibits on natural history, local history, archaeology, and art—including work by the great painter of animals Sir Edwin Landseer and some botanical studies of fungi by Beatrix Potter. ✉ *78 George St.* ☎ *01738/632488* ⊕ *www.pkc.gov.uk/perthmuseum* 🎟 *Free* ☉ *Tues–Sat. 10–5.*

FAMILY
Fodor's Choice
★
Scone Palace. The current residence of the Earl of Mansfield, Scone Palace (pronounced *skoon*) is much more cheerful than the city's other castles. Although it incorporates earlier works, today's palace is mainly 19th century. There's plenty to see if you're interested in the acquisitions of an aristocratic Scottish family: magnificent porcelain, furniture, ivory, clocks, and 16th-century needlework. A coffee shop, restaurant, gift shop, and play area are on-site, and the extensive grounds have a pine plantation. Nearby **Moot Hill** was the ancient coronation place of the Scottish kings. To be crowned, they sat on the Stone of Scone, which was seized in 1296 by Edward I of England, Scotland's greatest enemy, and placed in the coronation chair at Westminster Abbey, in London. The stone was returned to Scotland in November 1996 and is

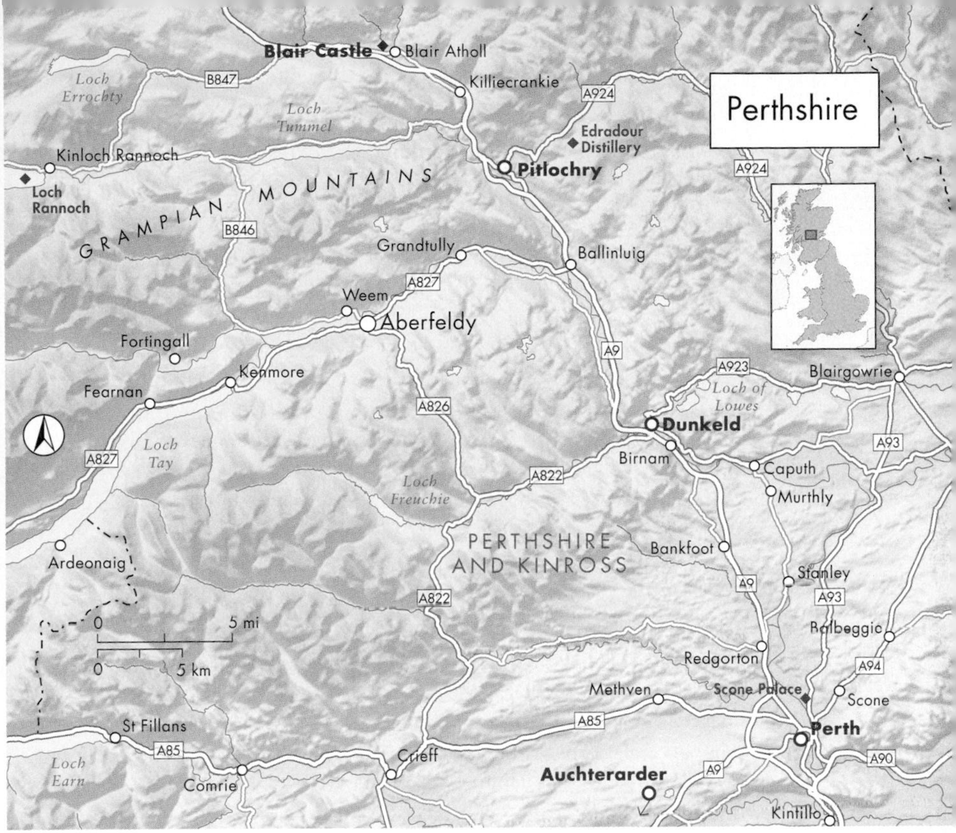

now on view in Edinburgh Castle. ✉ *Braemar Rd., 2 miles from Perth* ☎ *01738/552300* 🌐 *www.scone-palace.co.uk* 🎟 *£9.40* ⏲ *Apr.–Oct., daily 9:30–5:30, last admission at 5; Nov–Mar., Fri. 10–4.*

WHERE TO EAT AND STAY

$$ BRITISH 🍴 **Let's Eat.** The varied clientele reflects the broad appeal of noted chef Willie Deans's imaginative menu. The dinner menu combines some creative starters with earthy dishes with a Scottish flavor (venison with a bitter chocolate and red wine sauce, for example, or Blairgowrie beef fillet). All the ingredients are locally sourced. The restaurant is airy and comfortable, merging warm colors and rich woods. [$] *Average main: £18* ✉ *77–79 Kinnoull St.* ☎ *01738/643377* 🌐 *letseatperth.co.uk* ⏲ *Closed Sun. and Mon.*

$$$$ HOTEL 🏨 **Crieff Hydro.** One of Scotland's great Victorian hydropathy centers, this grand hotel 12 miles west of Perth has been owned and run by the same family for more than 100 years. **Pros:** extensive grounds; variety of activities; particularly good for children. **Cons:** rooms are rather dull; some activities are quite expensive. [$] *Rooms from: £245* ✉ *Off A85Crief* ☎ *01764/655555* 🌐 *www.crieffhydro.com* 🛏 *216 rooms* 🍽 *Multiple meal plans.*

$$ B&B/INN 🏨 **Parklands.** This stylish Georgian town house overlooks lush woodland. **Pros:** lovely rooms; lovely setting; superb restaurants. **Cons:** some rooms have better views than others; restaurants closed on Sunday. $ Rooms from: £129 ⌧ 2 St. Leonard's Bank ☎ 01738/622451 ⊕ www. theparklandshotel.com ⌁ 14 rooms ¦◯¦ Breakfast.

$ 🖫 **Sunbank House Hotel.** This early Victorian gray-stone mansion near
B&B/INN   Perth's Branklyn Gardens overlooks the River Tay and the city of Perth. **Pros:** reasonably priced; friendly staff; delicious local cuisine. **Cons:** some rooms are very small; you can hear traffic from the main road. $ Rooms from: £99 ⌧ 50 Dundee Rd. ☎ 01738/624882 ⊕ www. sunbankhouse.com ⌁ 9 rooms ¦◯¦ Multiple meal plans.

SHOPPING

CERAMICS   Perth is an especially popular hunting ground for china and glass.

Watsons of Perth. This shop has sold exquisite bone china and cut crystal since 1900. The staff can pack your purchase for shipment overseas. ⌧ 163–167 High St. ☎ 01738/639861 ⊕ www.watsonsofperth.co.uk.

CLOTHING   **C & C Proudfoot.** This shop sells a comprehensive selection of sheepskins, leather jackets, rugs, slippers, and handbags. ⌧ 104 South St. ☎ 01738/632483.

JEWELRY AND   **Cairncross of Perth.** The Romans coveted freshwater pearls from the
ANTIQUES   River Tay. If you do, too, then head to Cairncross of Perth, where you can admire a display of some of the more unusual shapes and colors. Some of the delicate settings take their theme from Scottish flowers. ⌧ 18 St. John's St. ☎ 01738/624367 ⊕ www.cairncrossofperth.co.uk ⊙ Weekdays 9:30–5, Sat 9:30–4:30.

Whispers of the Past. The lovely Whispers of the Past has a collection of jewelry, china, and other gift items. ⌧ 15 George St. ☎ 01738/635472.

DUNKELD

14 miles north of Perth.

The ruined cathedral above the town of Dunkeld marks its historic beginnings. The present town grew up around the main square, built by the Atholl family in the wake of the 1689 defeat of the Jacobite army (following its earlier victory in the Battle of Killiecrankie). The National Trust for Scotland has helped to maintain the houses with its Little Houses Project; it has a small exhibition above the Dunkeld and Birnam Tourist Information Centre (ask for the Heritage Trail leaflet). Crafts and interior-design shops dominate Atholl Street, which leads down to the River Tay.

The bridge across the River Tay takes you to Birnam Wood, where Shakespeare's Macbeth met the three witches who issued the prophecy about his death. Witty wooden notices lead you to the right tree, a gnarled hollow oak.

GETTING HERE AND AROUND
Dunkeld is on the A9 between Perth and Pitlochry. The town is also on the main train line to Inverness.

ESSENTIALS

Visitor Information Dunkeld and Birnam Tourist Information Centre ✉ *The Cross* ☎ *01350/727688* ⊕ *www.visitscotland.com* ⊗ *Apr.–June, daily 10–4:30; July and Aug., Mon.–Sat. 9:30–5:30, Sun. 10:30–5; Sept. and Oct., Mon.–Sat. 10–4:30, Sun. 11–4; Nov.–Mar., Fri.–Sun. 11–4.*

EXPLORING

FAMILY **Beatrix Potter Garden.** This garden celebrates the life and work of this much-beloved children's book writer who, for many years, spent her family holidays in the area. An enchanting garden walk allows you to peep into the homes of Peter Rabbit and Mrs. Tiggy-Winkle, her best-known characters. The visitor center has a well-stocked shop, a small café, and an imaginative exhibition on the writer's life and work (£1.50). ✉ *Birnam Arts Centre, Station Rd., Birnam* ☎ *01350/727674* ⊕ *www.birnamarts.com* ⊗ *Museum daily 10–5.*

WHERE TO EAT

$ ✕ **Taybank Hotel.** This spot overlooking the river is a musical meeting
BRITISH place owned by Scottish singer Dougie MacLean. Of course there's live music several nights a week. The walls are lined with instruments, which you're welcome to play. The bar serves good solid Scottish food, including chicken breast cooked with bacon and kale and "stovies," an oven baked dish of meat, onions, and potatoes. $ *Average main: £9* ✉ *Tay Terr.* ☎ *01350/727340* ⊕ *www.taybank.com.*

16

SHOPPING

Dunkeld Antiques. Housed in a former church facing the river, Dunkeld Antiques stocks mainly 18th- and 19th-century items, including books and prints that make great souvenirs. ✉ *Tay Terr.* ☎ *01350/728832* ⊕ *www.dunkeldantiques.co.uk.*

Jeremy Law of Scotland's Highland Horn and Deerskin Centre. Here you can purchase stag antlers and cow horns shaped into walking sticks, cutlery, and tableware. Deerskin shoes and moccasins and a collection of more than 200 different whiskies are also on offer. ✉ *City Hall, Atholl St.* ☎ *0800/146780* ⊕ *www.moccasin.co.uk.*

PITLOCHRY

15 miles north of Dunkeld.

In the late 19th century Pitlochry was an elegant Victorian spa town, famous for its mild microclimate and beautiful setting. Today it is a busy tourist town, with wall-to-wall gift shops, cafés, B&Bs and large hotels, and a huge golf course. The town itself is oddly nondescript, but it's a convenient base from which to explore the surrounding hills and valleys.

GETTING HERE AND AROUND

The main route through central Scotland, the A9, passes through Pitlochry, as does the main railway line from Glasgow/Edinburgh to Inverness. From here the B8019 connects to the B846 west to Rannoch Moor.

ESSENTIALS

Visitor Information **Pitlochry Visitor Information Centre** ✉ *22 Atholl Rd.* ☎ *01796/472215* 🌐 *www.visitscotland.com* 🕒 *Apr.–June, Sept., and Oct., daily 9–5:30; July and Aug., daily 9–6:30; Nov.–Mar., daily 9:30–4:30.*

EXPLORING

Edradour Distillery. If you have a whisky-tasting bent, visit Edradour Distillery, which claims to be the smallest single-malt distillery in Scotland (but then, so do others). There's a fun, informative tour of the distillery where you get to see how the whisky is made; you also get to savor a free dram at the end of the tour. ✉ *A924, 2½ miles east of Pitlochry* ☎ *01796/472095* 🌐 *www.edradour.com* 🎟 *Tours £7.50* 🕒 *May–Oct., Mon.–Sat. 10–5, Sun. noon–5; Nov.–Mar., and Apr., Mon.–Sat. 10–4, Sun. noon–4.*

Loch Rannoch. With its shoreline of birch trees framed by dark pines, Loch Rannoch is the quintessential Highland loch. Fans of Robert Louis Stevenson (1850–94), especially of *Kidnapped* (1886), will not want to miss the last, lonely section of road. Stevenson describes the setting: "The mist rose and died away, and showed us that country lying as waste as the sea, only the moorfowl and the peewees crying upon it, and far over to the east a herd of deer, moving like dots." Loch Rannoch is off B846, 20 miles west of Pitlochry.

WHERE TO STAY

$$$ HOTEL 🏨 **Atholl Palace Hotel.** A grand hotel in the best Victorian style, the Atholl Palace is a 19th-century vision of a medieval castle. **Pros:** lovely grounds; lots for kids to do; high comfort. **Cons:** old-fashioned feel; long anonymous corridors. [$] *Rooms from: £189* ✉ *A924* ☎ *01796/472400* 🌐 *www.athollpalace.com* 🛏 *106 rooms* 🍴 *Breakfast.*

$$$ HOTEL 🏨 **Killiecrankie House Hotel.** This neat oasis is set amid the wooded hills and streams of the Pass of Killiecrankie. **Pros:** lovely location; pleasant rooms. **Cons:** books up fast. [$] *Rooms from: £210* ✉ *B8079, 3 miles north of Pitlochry, Killiecrankie* ☎ *01796/473220* 🌐 *www.killiecrankiehotel.co.uk* 🛏 *10 rooms* 🍴 *Some meals.*

NIGHTLIFE AND THE ARTS

Pitlochry Festival Theatre. This theater presents six plays each season, hosts Sunday concerts, and holds art exhibitions. It also has a café and restaurant overlooking the River Tummel. ✉ *Port Na Craig* ☎ *01796/484626* 🌐 *www.pitlochry.org.uk.*

SPORTS AND THE OUTDOORS

Pitlochry Golf Course. A decent degree of stamina is needed for the first three holes at Pitlochry, where steep climbs are involved. The reward is magnificent Highland scenery. Despite its relatively short length, this beautiful course has more than its fair share of surprises. ✉ *Golf Course Rd.* ☎ *01796/472792* 🌐 *www.pitlochrygolf.co.uk* 🎟 *Green fee: Mar., Apr., Oct., and Nov.: weekdays £32; weekends £40. May–Sept.: weekdays £37; weekends £42* ⛳ *18 holes, 5681 yds, par 69* 🕒 *Daily.*

BLAIR CASTLE

7 miles north of Pitlochry.

GETTING HERE AND AROUND

Popular Blair Castle is just off the A9 Pitlochry-to-Inverness road, beyond the village of Blair Atholl. The village has a railway station that is on the main Inverness line.

EXPLORING

Fodor's Choice ★ **Blair Castle.** Home to successive dukes of Atholl and their families, the Murrays, until the death of the 10th duke, Blair Castle is one of Scotland's most highly rated sights. One of the castle's fascinating details is a preserved piece of floor still bearing marks of the red-hot shot fired through the roof during the 1745 Jacobite rebellion—the last occasion in Scottish history that a castle was besieged. The duke was allowed to keep a private army, the Atholl Highlanders, so the castle exhibits military artifacts as well as a rich collection of furniture, china, and paintings. The Hercules Gardens is a 9-acre Victorian walled garden, and the extensive grounds have woodland and river walks. ✉ *Off B8079, Blair Atholl* ☎ *01796/481207* 🌐 *www.blair-castle.co.uk* 🎫 *Castle and gardens: Apr.–Oct., £9.90, Nov.–Mar., £7.40. Grounds only: Apr.–Oct., £5.45; Nov.–Mar., free* ⏲ *Apr.–Oct., daily 9:30–5:30; Nov.–Mar., weekends 10–4.*

16

AUCHTERARDER

45 miles south of Blair Castle, 13 miles southwest of Perth.

Famous for the Gleneagles Hotel and nearby golf courses, Auchterarder also has a flock of tiny antiques shops to amuse those left behind by Gleneagles' golfers.

GETTING HERE AND AROUND

Gleneagles Station is on the main Inverness line, while the A9 gives direct access to Gleneagles and Auchterarder via the A823.

ESSENTIALS

Visitor Information Auchterarder Visitor Information Centre ✉ *90 High St.* ☎ *01764/663450* 🌐 *www.perthshire-scotland.co.uk.*

WHERE TO STAY

$$$$ HOTEL Fodor's Choice ★ 🏨 **Gleneagles Hotel.** One of Britain's most famous hotels, Gleneagles is the very essence of modern grandeur. **Pros:** luxe rooms; numerous amenities; the three courses are a golfer's paradise. **Cons:** all this comes at a steep price. [$] *Rooms from: £455* ✉ *Off A823* ☎ *01764/662231* 🌐 *www.gleneagles.com* 🛏 *216 rooms, 13 suites* 🍴 *Multiple meal plans.*

GOLF

Fodor's Choice ★ **Gleneagles.** A part of golfing history, this sprawling resort hosted the Ryder Cup in 2014. The 18 holes of the King Course, designed by James Braid in 1919, have quirky names—many golfers have grappled with the tough 17th hole, known as the Warslin' Lea (Wrestling Ground). The beguiling Queen's Course mixes varied terrain, including woods and moors. Jack Nicklaus designed the PGA Centenary Course, which sweeps into the Ochil Hills and has views of the Grampians. The

9-hole Wee Course provides challenges for beginners and pros alike. This is also where you'll find the PGA National Academy, a good place to improve your skills. ⊠ *A823* ☎ *01764/662231* ⊕ *www.gleneagles. com* ✉ *Green fee: Kings, Queens, and PGA Centenary courses: £175; 9-hole PGA course £32* ⚐ *Kings: 18 holes, 6790 yds, par 71. Queens: 18 holes, 5968 yds, par 68. PGA Centenary: 18 holes, 7296 yds, par 72* ⊙ *Daily.*

ST. ANDREWS AND EAST NEUK

St. Andrews is unlike any other Scottish town. It was once Scotland's most powerful ecclesiastical center and now it's well known as the seat of the country's oldest university and the symbolic home of golf. The town has a comfortable, well-groomed air, sitting a bit apart from the rest of Scotland.

Fishing has always been a major industry in the pretty villages of East Neuk, which traded across the North Sea. Today the legacy of Dutch-influenced architecture, such as crowstep gables—the stepped effect on the ends of the roofs—gives these villages a distinctive character.

ST. ANDREWS

47 miles east of Auchterader, 52 miles northeast of Edinburgh, 83 miles northeast of Glasgow.

Fodor's Choice ★ It may have a ruined cathedral and a grand university—the oldest in Scotland—but the modern claim to fame for St. Andrews is mainly its status as the home of golf. Forget that Scottish kings were crowned here, or that John Knox preached here, or that Reformation reformers were burned at the stake here. Thousands flock to St. Andrews to play at the Old Course, home of the Royal & Ancient Club, the hub of world golf. The layout is pure Middle Ages: its three main streets—North, Market, and South—converge on the city's earliest religious site, near the cathedral. Like most of the ancient monuments, the cathedral ruins are impressive in their desolation—but this town is no dusty museum. The streets are busy, the shops are stylish, the gray houses sparkle in the sun, and the scene is particularly brightened during the academic year by bicycling students in scarlet gowns.

GETTING HERE AND AROUND

If you arrive by car, be prepared for an endless drive around the town as you look for a parking space. The parking lots around Rose Park (behind the bus station and a short walk from the town center) are your best bet. If you arrive by local or national bus, the bus station is a five-minute walk from town. The nearest train station, Leuchars, is 10 minutes away by taxi (£15) or bus (£2.70), both of which can be found outside the station.

ESSENTIALS

Visitor Information St. Andrews ⊠ *70 Market St.* ☎ *01334/472021* ⊕ *www. visitfife.com.*

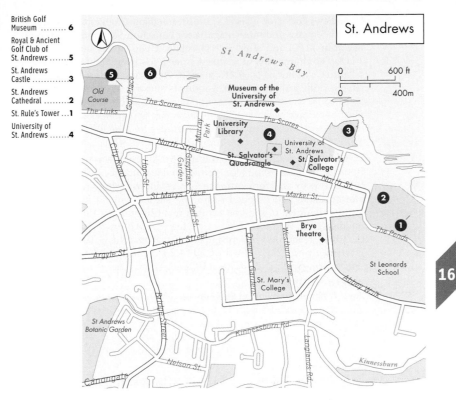

EXPLORING

TOP ATTRACTIONS

British Golf Museum. This museum explores the centuries-old relationship between St. Andrews and golf and displays golf memorabilia from the 18th century to the 21st century. It's just opposite the Royal & Ancient Golf Club. ⊠ *Bruce Embankment* ☎ *01334/460046* ⊕ *www.britishgolfmuseum.co.uk* 🎫 *£6.50* ⏱ *Apr.–Oct., Mon.–Sat. 9:30–5, Sun. 10–5; Nov.–Mar., daily 10–4.*

St. Andrews Castle. On the shore north of the cathedral stands ruined St. Andrews Castle, begun at the end of the 13th century. The remains include a rare example of a cold and gruesome bottle-shape dungeon, in which many prisoners spent their last hours. Even more atmospheric is the castle's mine and countermine. The former was a tunnel dug by besieging forces in the 16th century; the latter, a tunnel dug by castle defenders in order to meet and wage battle belowground. You can stoop and crawl into this narrow passageway—an eerie experience, despite the addition of electric light. The visitor center has a good audiovisual presentation on the castle's history. ⊠ *N. Castle St.* ☎ *01334/477196* ⊕ *www.historic-scotland.gov.uk* 🎫 *£5.50, £7.20 with St. Andrews Cathedral and St. Rule's Tower* ⏱ *Apr.–Sept., daily 9:30–5:30; Oct.–Mar., daily 9:30–4:30.*

St. Andrews Cathedral. This is a ruined, poignant fragment of what was once the largest and most magnificent church in Scotland. Work on it began in 1160, and after several delays it was finally consecrated in 1318. The church was subsequently damaged by fire and repaired, but fell into decay during the Reformation. Only ruined gables, parts of the nave's south wall, and other fragments survive. The on-site museum helps you interpret the remains and gives a sense of what the cathedral must once have been like. ✉ *Off Pends Rd.* ☎ *01334/472563* 🌐 *www.historic-scotland.gov.uk* 🎟 *£4.50, includes St. Rule's Tower* 🕒 *Apr.–Sept., daily 9:30–5:30; Oct.–Mar., daily 9:30–4:30.*

St. Rule's Tower. Local legend has it that St. Andrews was founded by St. Regulus, or Rule, who, acting under divine guidance, carried relics of St. Andrew by sea from Patras in Greece. He was shipwrecked on this Fife headland and founded a church. The holy man's name survives in the cylindrical tower, consecrated in 1126 and the oldest surviving building in St. Andrews. Enjoy dizzying views of town from the top of the tower, reached via steep stairs. ✉ *Off Pends Rd.* ☎ *01334/472563* 🌐 *www.historic-scotland.gov.uk* 🎟 *£4.20, includes St. Andrews Cathedral* 🕒 *Apr.–Sept., daily 9:30–5:30; Oct.–Mar., daily 9:30–4:30.*

WORTH NOTING

Royal & Ancient Golf Club of St. Andrews. The ruling house of golf worldwide is the spiritual home of all who play or follow the game. Founded in 1754, its clubhouse on the dunes—open to members only, who must be male—is a mix of classical, Victorian, and neoclassical styles; it's adjacent to the famous Old Course. ✉ *The Scores* ☎ *01334/460000* 🌐 *www.randa.org.*

University of St. Andrews. Scotland's oldest university is the *alma mater* of John Knox (Protestant reformer), King James II of Scotland, the Duke and Duchess of Cambridge (William and Kate), and Chris Hoy, Scotland's Olympic cyclist. Founded in 1411, the university's buildings pepper the town. For the quintessential University of St. Andrews experience, **St. Salvator's Quadrangle** reveals the magnificence of this historic institution. Looking out onto this impressive college green is the striking St. Salvator's Chapel, founded in 1450. It bears the marks of a turbulent past: the initials PH, carved into the paving stones under the bell tower, are those of Patrick Hamilton, who was burned alive outside the chapel for his Protestant beliefs. ✉ *St Mary's Pl.*

WHERE TO EAT

$ BRASSERIE 🍴 **The Doll's House.** Spilling out onto the pavement, this colorful and lively eatery offers reliably good food at a reasonable price. Using locally sourced meats, the kitchen is especially good at sauces, such as brandy and mixed peppercorn for beef or delicately scented wine and herb for fish. The tables upstairs offer a slightly more relaxed atmosphere. [$] *Average main: £14* ✉ *3 Church St.* ☎ *01334/477422* 🌐 *www.dollshouse-restaurant.co.uk.*

$$$$ SEAFOOD Fodor's Choice ★ 🍴 **The Seafood Restaurant.** This stunning glass-walled building is perched on the banks of the West Sands. Once an open-air theater, the kitchen radiates a confidence and calm that contributes to the easy atmosphere. The food is adventurous without being flashy: start with fat, juicy Shetland mussels, then move on to bream with peas. [$] *Average main: £38*

St. Andrews is famous for golf, but its ruined castle by the sea and other sights are well worth a look.

✉ *Bruce Embankment* ☎ *01334/479475* 🌐 *www.theseafoodrestaurant.com* ✍ *Reservations essential.*

$ MODERN BRITISH 🍴 **West Port Bar & Kitchen.** It's easy to forget that St. Andrews is a university town when the students are on summer break, but this modern bar and eatery remains vibrant and youthful year-round. The reasonably priced menu offers nicely prepared pub grub—everything from gourmet burgers to smoked haddock fish cakes—making this a satisfying stop for lunch or dinner. Upstairs are four bright B&B rooms that go for £95. [$] *Average main: £9* ✉ *170 South St.* ☎ *01334/473186* 🌐 *www.thewestport.co.uk.*

WHERE TO STAY

$ B&B/INN Fodor's Choice ★ 🏨 **Aslar Guest House.** This terraced town house dating from 1865 has large rooms with ornate cornicing and antique reproduction furniture. **Pros:** homey feel; great location; exceptional breakfast. **Cons:** books up quickly. [$] *Rooms from: £96* ✉ *120 North St.* ☎ *01334/473460* 🌐 *www.aslar.com* 🛏 *6 rooms* 🍽 *Breakfast.*

$$$$ HOTEL 🏨 **Fairmont St Andrews.** Two miles from St. Andrews, this modern hotel has spectacular views of the bay and two superb golf courses. **Pros:** spacious feel; excellent spa; golf at your doorstep. **Cons:** the huge atrium feels like a shopping center; paintings made to match the decor. [$] *Rooms from: £260* ✉ *A917, St. Andrews Bay* ☎ *01334/837000* 🌐 *www.fairmont.com/standrews* 🛏 *192 rooms, 17 suites* 🍽 *Breakfast.*

$$$$ HOTEL Fodor's Choice ★ 🏨 **Old Course Hotel.** Regularly hosting international golf stars and jet-setters, the Old Course Hotel recently underwent a renaissance—the guest rooms and public spaces have been reinvigorated, and the service has warmed up. **Pros:** fabulous location and lovely views; unpretentious

service; golfer's heaven. **Cons:** all the golf talk might bore nongolf-ers; spa is on the small side. $ *Rooms from: £350* ⊠ *Old Station Rd.* ☎ *01334/474371* ⊕ *www.oldcoursehotel.co.uk* ⟿ *109 rooms, 35 suites* ⏀ *Breakfast.*

$$$
B&B/INN
Fodor's Choice
★

✆ **The Peat Inn.** With eight bright and contemporary two-room suites, this popular "restaurant with rooms" 10 miles west of St. Andrews is perhaps best known for its outstanding, modern, Scottish-style restaurant. **Pros:** exceptional restaurant; efficient but easygoing staff. **Cons:** booking ahead is essential; you need a car to get here. $ *Rooms from: £195* ⊠ *B941, Cuparat intersection of B940* ☎ *01334/840206* ⊕ *www.thepeatinn.co.uk* ⟿ *8 suites* ⊘ *Closed Sun. and Mon.* ⏀ *Breakfast.*

$$$$
HOTEL

✆ **Rufflets Country House Hotel.** Ten acres of formal and informal gardens surround this creeper-covered country house just outside St. Andrews. **Pros:** attractive gardens; cozy drawing room; great restaurant. **Cons:** too far to walk to St. Andrews; teddy bears in the guest rooms are a bit twee. $ *Rooms from: £245* ⊠ *Strathkinness Low Rd.* ☎ *01334/472594* ⊕ *www.rufflets.co.uk* ⟿ *24 rooms, 4 suites* ⏀ *Breakfast.*

$$
HOTEL

✆ **Scores Hotel.** Overlooking the St. Andrews shoreline, this pair of town houses keeps good company—they sit next to the Royal & Ancient Golf Club of St. Andrews. **Pros:** rooms are from big to vast; the staff is motivated and happy to oblige. **Cons:** reception area is uninspir-ing. $ *Rooms from: £140* ⊠ *76 the Scores* ☎ *01334/472451* ⊕ *www.scoreshotel.co.uk* ⟿ *36 rooms* ⏀ *Breakfast.*

NIGHTLIFE AND THE ARTS

PUBS **Central Bar.** Unlike a lot of local places, the Central Bar hasn't gone down the minimalist-decor-and-cocktails road. You'll find a good range of beers (bottled and on tap) and decent pub food. ⊠ *77 Market St.* ☎ *01334/478296.*

GOLF

What serious golfer doesn't dream of playing at world-famous St. Andrews? Seven St. Andrews courses, all part of the St. Andrews Trust, are open to visitors, and more than 40 other courses in the region offer golf by the round or by the day.

St. Andrews Links Trust. For information about availability—there's usu-ally a waiting list, which varies according to the time of year—contact St. Andrews Links Trust. Green fees range from £75 to £155 for a round on the Old Course and from £8 to £120 for a round on the six other courses. Balgrove and the Strathtyrum Course are beginner-friendly, and the Eden Course is a bit more forgiving than others. The Castle Course (2008) has jaw-dropping views of the coast. ☎ *01334/466666* ⊕ *www.standrews.org.uk.*

SHOPPING

Artery. Artery sells work by local, Scottish, and British artists, includ-ing jewelry, ceramics, paintings, and intriguing handmade clocks. ⊠ *43 South St.* ☎ *01334/478221.*

Mellis. Mellis is a cheese lover's mecca. Look for a soft, crumbly local cheese called Anster. ⊠ *149 South St.* ☎ *01334/471410* ⊕ *www.mellischeese.net.*

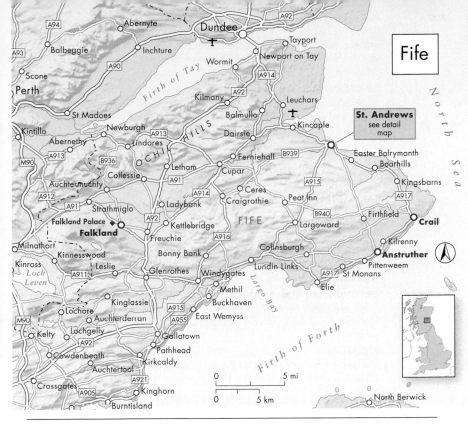

CRAIL

Fodor's Choice

★

10 miles south of St. Andrews.

The oldest and most aristocratic of East Neuk burghs, pretty Crail is where many fish merchants retired and built cottages. The town landmark is a picturesque Dutch-influenced town house, or *tolbooth*, which contains the oldest bell in Fife, cast in Holland in 1520. Crail may now be full of artists, but it remains a working harbor; take time to walk the streets and beaches and to sample fish by the harbor. ■ TIP➔ As you head into East Neuk from this tiny port, look about for market crosses, merchant houses, and little doocots (dovecotes, where pigeons were kept)—typical picturesque touches of this region.

GETTING HERE AND AROUND

Stagecoach bus number 63 operates between Crail and St. Andrews. However, the number 95 is more regular and also takes you to Anstruther and Pittenweem. Crail is about 15 minutes from St. Andrews by car via A917.

EXPLORING

Crail Museum and Heritage Centre. The story of this trading and fishing town can be found in the delightfully crammed Crail Museum and Heritage Centre, entirely run by local volunteers. There is a small tourist information desk within the center. ✉ *62–64 Marketgate* ☎ *01333/450869* 🌐 *www.crailmuseum.org.uk* 🎟 *Free* 🕒 *June–Sept., Mon.–Sat. 11–4, Sun. 1–5.*

WHERE TO STAY

$ B&B/INN 🏨 **Hazelton.** Beautifully polished wood, exquisitely restored period features, and gentle hues put the Hazelton head and shoulders above the typical seaside B&B. **Pros:** handsome building; excellent location; nothing is too much of a problem for the generous-spirited staff. **Cons:** you have to be a meat eater to make the most of the breakfast. [$] *Rooms from: £90* ✉ *29 Marketgate N.* ☎ *01333/450250* 🌐 *www.thehazelton.co.uk* 🛏 *5 rooms* 🕒 *Closed Jan.* 🍴 *Breakfast.*

ANSTRUTHER

4 miles southwest of Crail.

Anstruther, locally called Ainster, has a lovely waterfront with a few shops brightly festooned with children's pails and shovels—a gesture to summer vacationers.

GETTING HERE AND AROUND

Stagecoach bus number 95 operates between St. Andrews, Crail, Pittenweem, and Anstruther. The latter is 5 to 10 minutes from Crail by car via A917.

ESSENTIALS

Visitor Information Anstruther Tourist Information ✉ *Scottish Fisheries Museum, Harbour Head* ☎ *01333/311073* 🌐 *www.visitfife.com.*

EXPLORING

Pittenweem Arts Festival. There is nothing quite like August's Pittenweem Arts Festival. Exhibitions, which involve hundreds of local and international artists, take place in the town's public buildings and in private homes and gardens. It's a week of events, workshops, and live music. The town is 1.5 miles southwest of Anstruther. ☎ *01333/313903* 🌐 *www.pittenweemartsfestival.co.uk.*

Scottish Fisheries Museum. Facing Anstruther Harbor, the Scottish Fisheries Museum is inside a colorful cluster of buildings, the earliest of which dates from the 16th century. The museum illustrates the life of Scottish fisherfolk through documents, artifacts, model ships, paintings, and displays (complete with the reek of tarred rope and net). There are also floating exhibits at the quayside. There's a small desk here with tourism information. ✉ *Harbourhead* ☎ *01333/310628* 🌐 *www.scotfishmuseum.org* 🎟 *£7* 🕒 *Apr.–Sept., Mon.–Sat. 10–5:30, Sun. 11–5; Oct.–Mar., Mon.–Sat. 10–4:30, Sun. noon–4:30; last admission 1 hr before closing.*

NEED A BREAK?

Anstruther Fish Bar and Restaurant. Next door to the Scottish Fisheries Museum, this popular fish-and-chips shop has space to eat, but most people order take-out. Try Pittenweem-landed prawns in batter or the catch of the day, which could be mackerel (line caught by the owners), hake, or local crab. ✉ *42–44 Shore St.* ☎ *01333/310518* 🌐 *www.anstrutherfishbar.co.uk.*

WHERE TO EAT

$$$$ EUROPEAN 🍴 **The Cellar.** Entered through a cobbled courtyard, this unpretentious, old-fashioned restaurant is hugely popular. The low ceiling and exposed beams make for a cozy atmosphere. Specializing in seafood, as well as local beef and lamb, owner and chef Peter Jukes serves three-course meals cooked simply in modern Scottish style. The crayfish bisque served with Gruyère is known all over the region, as is the excellent wine list. [$] *Average main: £40* ✉ *24 E. Green* ☎ *01333/310378* ✍ *Reservations essential* ⏲ *Closed Sun. and Mon. Nov.–Easter.*

> **FIFE COASTAL PATH**
>
> The Fife Coastal Path can be bracing or an amble. The 7-mile stretch between East Wemyss to Lower Largo (four to six hours) is the easiest going, with some of it along the beaches south of Crail. The 8-mile route between Pittenweem to Fifeness (four to six hours) can be rougher in patches, but takes you through Anstruther and Crail. For more information, visit 🌐 *www.fifecoastalpath.co.uk.*

$ BRITISH 🍴 **Ship Inn.** Sports lovers visit Elie, 10 miles west of Anstruther, on Sunday to watch cricket matches played on the beach outside the Ship Inn. The staff fires up a barbecue and cooks simple fare, including burgers and chicken. On the side are salads and lots of chips. The relaxed atmosphere and the beauty of this slow, cerebral game makes for an afternoon you'll never forget, especially if the sun shines. [$] *Average main: £12* ✉ *The Toft, Elie* ☎ *01333/330246* 🌐 *www.ship-elie.com.*

NIGHTLIFE

Dreel Tavern. A 16th-century coaching inn, the Dreel Tavern is famous for its hand-drawn ales. ✉ *16 High St. W* ☎ *01333/310727.*

16

FALKLAND

25 miles west of Anstruther.

Fodor's Choice ★ One of the loveliest communities in Scotland, Falkland is a royal burgh of twisting streets and crooked stone houses.

GETTING HERE AND AROUND

Stagecoach bus number 64A connects Falkland to St. Andrews as well as Cupar and Ladybank (both of which are train stations on the Edinburgh to Dundee line). Falkland is about 15 minutes from Cupar and a half hour from St. Andrews by car via A91 and A912, or A91 to A914 to A912.

EXPLORING

Falkland Palace. A former hunting lodge of the Stewart monarchs, Falkland Palace dominates the town. The castle is one of the country's earliest examples of the French Renaissance style. It was built by French masons in the 1530s for King James V (1512–42), who died here. The palace was a favorite resort of his daughter, Mary, Queen of Scots (1542–87). The beautiful gardens behind Falkland Palace contain a rare survivor: a royal tennis court, built in 1539. It's not at all like its modern counterpart. Look out for the four *lunes* (holes in the wall) and the *ais* (a vertical green board), both of which are featured in the *jeu* *quarré* (square-court) version of the game. ⊠ *Main St.* ☎ *0844/4932186* ⊕ *www.nts.org.uk* ✉ *£12* ⊘ *Mar.–Oct., Mon.–Sat. 10–5, Sun. 1–5.*

DUNDEE AND ANGUS

The small city of Dundee sits near the mouth of the River Tay surrounded by the farms and glens of rural Angus and the coastal grassy banks and golf courses of northeastern Fife. A vibrant, industrious city that's off the main tourist track, Dundee plays a significant role in the biotech and computer-games industries. Dundee has a large student population, a lively arts and nightlife scene, and several historical and nautical sights. In 2014 the city's waterfront transformation began when construction started on the first outpost of London's Victoria and Albert Museum, a repository of decorative arts scheduled to open in 2016. ■TIP→ The main road from Dundee to Aberdeen—the A90— requires special care with its mix of fast cars and unexpectedly slow farm traffic.

DUNDEE

15 miles north of Falkland, 14 miles northwest of St. Andrews, 58 miles north of Edinburgh, 79 miles northeast of Glasgow.

Dundee makes an excellent base for exploring Fife and Angus at any time of year. The West End—especially its main thoroughfare, Perth Road—pulses with life, intimate cafés, and excellent bars. The Dundee Contemporary Arts center has gained the city some attention. D.C. Thomson began publication of his popular comic strips *The Beano* and *The Dandy* here in the 1930s, which explains the statues of some of his best-known characters by the Scottish sculptor Antony Morrow that stand in the City Square.

GETTING HERE AND AROUND

The East Coast train line runs through the city, linking it to Edinburgh (and beyond, to London), Glasgow (and the West Coast of England), and Aberdeen, with trains to all every hour or half hourly at peak times. Cheaper bus service is available to all of these locations, as well as St. Andrews and several other towns in Fife and Angus.

If you're traveling by car, the A92 will take you north from Fife to Abroath and the Angus coast towns. The A90, from Perth, heads north to Aberdeen. Most of the sights in Dundee are clustered together, so you can easily walk around the city. You can also hail one of the many cabs on the easy-to-find taxi ranks for little more than a few pounds.

ESSENTIALS

Visitor Information Angus and Dundee Tourist Board ⊠ *Discovery Point, Riverside Dr.* ☎ *01382/527527* ⊕ *www.angusanddundee.co.uk.*

EXPLORING
TOP ATTRACTIONS

Fodor's Choice ★ **Dundee Botanic Garden.** This renowned botanical garden contains an extensive collection of native and exotic plants outdoors and in tropical and temperate greenhouses. There are some beautiful areas

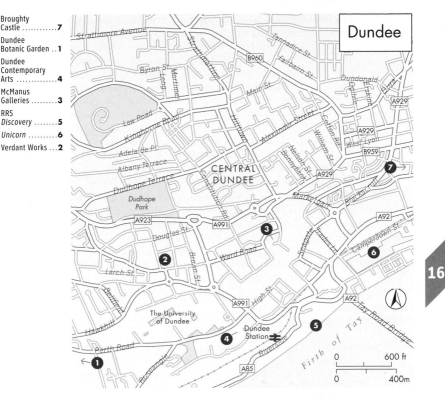

Dundee

16

for picnicking, as well as a visitor center, an art gallery, and a coffee shop. ⊠ *Riverside Dr.* ☎ *01382/381190* ⊕ *www.dundee.ac.uk/botanic* ⊡ *£3.90* ⊙ *Mar.–Oct., daily 10–4:30; Nov.–Feb., daily 10–3:30.*

FAMILY **Dundee Contemporary Arts.** Located between a 17th-century mansion and a cathedral, this strikingly modern building houses one of Britain's most exciting artistic venues. The huge gallery houses up to six shows a year by internationally acclaimed contemporary artists. There are children's workshops and meet-the-artist events throughout the year. Two movie theaters screen mainly independent, revival, and children's films. There's also a craft shop and a buzzing café-bar that's open until midnight. ⊠ *152 Nethergate* ☎ *01382/909900* ⊕ *www.dca.org.uk* ⊡ *Free* ⊙ *Fri.–Wed. 11–8, Thurs. 11–8.*

Fodor'sChoice **McManus Galleries.** Dundee's principal museum and art gallery, housed
★ in a striking Gothic Revival–style building, has an engaging collection of artifacts that document the city's history and the working, social, and cultural lives of Dundonians throughout the 19th and the 20th centuries. Its varied fine art collection includes paintings by Rossetti, Raeburn, and Peploe as well as thought-provoking yet accessible contemporary works and visiting exhibitions, often in conjunction with London's Victoria and Albert Museum. ⊠ *Albert Sq.* ☎ *01382/432350* ⊕ *www.mcmanus.co.uk* ⊡ *Free* ⊙ *Mon.–Sat. 10–5, Sun. 12:30–4:30.*

FAMILY
Fodor's Choice
★

RRS *Discovery*. Dundee's urban-renewal program—the city is determined to celebrate its industrial past—was motivated in part by the arrival of the RRS (Royal Research Ship) *Discovery*, the vessel used by Captain Robert F. Scott (1868–1912) on his polar explorations. The steamer was originally built and launched in Dundee; now it's a permanent resident. At Discovery Point, under the handsome cupola, the story of the ship and its famous expedition unfold; you can even feel the Antarctic chill as if you were there. The ship, berthed outside, is the star: wander the deck, then explore the quarters to see the daily existence endured by the ship's crew and captain. ⊠ *Discovery Quay, Riverside Dr.* ☎ *01382/309060* ⊕ *www.rrsdiscovery.com* ✉ *£8.50, £15 includes Verdant Works.* ☉ *Apr.–Sept., Mon.–Sat. 10–6, Sun. 11–6; Oct.–Mar., Mon.–Sat. 10–5, Sun. 11–5; last admission 1 hr before closing.*

FAMILY

Verdant Works. In a former jute mill, Verdant Works houses a multifaceted exhibit on the story of jute and the town's involvement in the jute trade. Restored machinery, audiovisual displays, and tableaux all bring to life the hard, noisy life of the jute worker. A light and airy café serves lovely cakes. ⊠ *W. Hendersons Wynd* ☎ *01382/309060* ⊕ *www.verdantwork.co.uk* ✉ *£8:50, £15 includes RRS Discovery* ☉ *Apr.–Oct., Mon.–Sat. 10–6, Sun. 11–6; Nov.–Mar., Wed.–Sat. 10:30–4:30, Sun. 11–4:30.*

WORTH NOTING

OFF THE BEATEN PATH

Broughty Castle. Originally built to guard the Tay Estuary, Broughty Castle is now a museum focusing on fishing, ferries, and the history of the area's whaling industry. Four floors of displays include the art collection of Victorian inventor and engineer Sir James Orchar. To the north of the castle lies beautiful Broughty Ferry Beach, which even in midwinter is enjoyed by the locals; there is a regular bus service from Dundee's city center. ⊠ *Castle Approach, 4 miles east of city center, Broughty Ferry* ☎ *01382/436916* ⊕ *www.dundeecity.gov.uk/broughtycastle* ✉ *Free* ☉ *Apr.–Sept., Mon.–Sat. 10–4, Sun. 12:30–4; Oct.–Mar., Tues.–Sat. 10–4, Sun. 12:30–4.*

FAMILY

Unicorn. It's easy to spot this 46-gun wood warship, as it's fronted by a figurehead of a white unicorn. This frigate has the distinction of being the oldest British-built warship afloat, having been launched in 1824 at Chatham, England. You can clamber right down into the hold, or see the models and displays about the Royal Navy's history. In the summer there are often jazz nights onboard. The ship's hours vary in winter, so call ahead. ⊠ *Victoria Dock, east of Tay Rd. bridge* ⊕ *www.frigateunicorn.org* ✉ *£5.25* ☉ *Apr.–Oct., daily 10–5; Nov.–Mar., Wed.–Fri. noon–4, weekends 10–4; last admission 30 mins before closing.*

WHERE TO EAT AND STAY

$$
MODERN BRITISH

✕ **Jute.** Part of Dundee Contemporary Arts, this lively eatery serves breakfast at the bar, cocktails and snacks on the terrace in fine weather, or dinner in the modish dining area with its huge windows that offer views of artists at work in the printmakers studio. There are plenty of handsomely presented dishes, including teriyaki salmon with spring-onion noodles and rhubarb tart tatin. The pretheater meal is a fabulous value: £15.50 for three courses. $ *Average main: £15* ✉ *152 Nethergate* ☎ *01382/909246* 🌐 *www.jutecafebar.co.uk.*

$$$ MODERN BRITISH 🍴 **Playwright.** This stylish restaurant is one of the city's more expensive, but it's worth the price to see the glass floor that looks into the wine cellar. The menu is well put together, offering interesting combinations of seasonal flavors—start with watermelon and fig salad, then move on to a perfectly presented seared salmon with prawn risotto. There's a beautiful bar, too, for pre- or postdinner tippling. The staff is laid-back but totally efficient. $ *Average main: £25* ✉ *11 Tay Sq.* ☎ *01382/223113* 🌐 *www.theplaywright.co.uk* ✍ *Reservations essential* 🕒 *Closed Sun.*

$$ HOTEL 🏨 **Apex City Quay.** Scandinavian-style rooms with easy chairs, plump bedding, and flat-screen TVs with DVD players help you unwind at this contemporary quayside hotel. **Pros:** stylish rooms; excellent brasserie; sleek rooms. **Cons:** outside is popular with seagulls, too; the bar is often mobbed. $ *Rooms from: £150* ✉ *1 W. Victoria Dock Rd.* ☎ *01382/202404* 🌐 *www.apexhotels.com* 🛏 *145 rooms, 8 suites* 🍽 *Breakfast.*

$ HOTEL 🏨 **Shaftsbury Lodge.** Just off the Perth Road, this Victorian-era villa set among well-tended shrubs is a find for those who like smaller, more intimate hotels. **Pros:** first-rate service; pretty rooms; close, but not too close, to the city. **Cons:** some bathrooms are a little dated. $ *Rooms from: £80* ✉ *I Hyndford St.* ☎ *01382/669216* 🌐 *www.shaftesburylodge.co.uk* 🛏 *12 rooms* 🍽 *Breakfast.*

NIGHTLIFE AND THE ARTS

BARS AND PUBS Dundee's pub scene, centered in the West End–Perth Road area, is one of the liveliest in Scotland.

Speedwell Bar. Called Mennie's by locals, the Speedwell Bar is in a mahogany-paneled building brimming with Dundonian characters. It's renowned for its superb cask beers and its whalebonelike Armitage Shanks urinals. ✉ *165–168 Perth Rd.* ☎ *01382/667783* 🌐 *www.speedwell-bar.co.uk.*

THEATER **Dundee Repertory Theatre.** This is home to the award-winning Dundee Rep Ensemble and to Scotland's preeminent contemporary-dance group, Scottish Dance Theatre. Popular with locals, the restaurant and bar welcome late-night comedy shows and jazz bands. ✉ *Tay Sq.* ☎ *01382/223530* 🌐 *www.dundeerep.co.uk.*

SPORTS AND THE OUTDOORS

GOLF East of Perthshire, near the city of Dundee, lies a string of demanding courses along the shores of the North Sea and inland into the foothills of the Grampian Mountains. Golfers who excel in windy conditions particularly enjoy the breezes blowing westward from the sea.

Fodor's Choice ★ **Carnoustie Golf Links.** The venue for the British Open in 1999 and 2007, the coastal links around Carnoustie have challenged golfers since at least 1527. There are three courses, the most famous of which is the breathtaking Championship Course, ranked among the very best in the world. The choice Burnside course is full of historical interest and local color, as well as being tough and interesting. The Buddon course, designed by Peter Allis and Dave Thomas, is recommended for links novices. ✉ *20 Links Parade, Carnoustie* ☎ *01241/802270* 🌐 *www.*

carnoustiegolflinks.co.uk 🎫 *Green fee: Championship £147; Burnside £40; Buddon £30* ✍ *Reservations essential* ⛳ *Championship course: 18 holes, 6941 yds, par 72; Burnside: 18 holes, 6028 yds, par 68; Buddon: 18 holes, 5420 yds, par 66* 🕒 *Daily.*

SHOPPING

HOME FURNISHINGS **Westport Gallery.** This shop stocks contemporary designer housewares, including ceramics and glass, plus highly stylized clothing and jewelry. ✉ *44 West Port* ☎ *01382/221751.*

JEWELRY **Queen's Gallery.** The Queen's Gallery has a compelling selection of jewelry, ceramics, and paintings by Scottish artists. ✉ *160 Nethergate* ☎ *01382/220600.*

THE ANGUS GLENS

20 miles north of Dundee.

The five Angus Glens are often described as being like the spread fingers of a hand reaching up into the countryside of Angus, with their tips touching the edges of the Grampian hills. The town of Kirriemuir is the threshold of Glenisla, Glen Proven, and the dramatic and beautiful Glen Clova. The town of Edzell will be your gateway to Glen Lethnot and Glen Esk. These glens offer all sorts of opportunities for adventurous visitors—rugged hikes or gentle strolls, streams for the fishing enthusiast, and flower and plants to delight the amateur botanist.

Be aware that Thursday is a half day in Angus; many shops and attractions close at lunch.

GETTING HERE AND AROUND

You really need a car to reach the Angus Glens. Travel north from Dundee along the busy A90; for Kirriemuir, turn onto the A926, then onto the A928. Turn right for Kirriemuir or left for Glamis. You can also take the B955 out of Kirriemuir, which loops around at Glen Clova. It's one of the loveliest Scottish roads to drive along, especially when the heather is blooming in late summer. For Edzell, continue up the A90 and then take the B966.

WHERE TO STAY

$ B&B/INN 🏨 **Glen Clova Hotel.** Since the 1850s the hospitality of this hotel has lifted the spirits of many a bone-tired hill walker. **Pros:** stunning location; great base for outdoor pursuits; spacious accommodations. **Cons:** lack of decent public transportation; rooms are booked well in advance. [$] *Rooms from: £90* ✉ *B955, Glen Clova* ☎ *01575/550350* 🌐 *www.clova.com* 🛏 *10 rooms* 🍴 *Breakfast.*

KIRRIEMUIR

18 miles north of Dundee.

Kirriemuir stands at the heart of Angus's red-sandstone countryside and was the birthplace of the writer J.M. Barrie (1860–1937), best known abroad as the author of *Peter Pan* (a statue of whom you can see in the town's square).

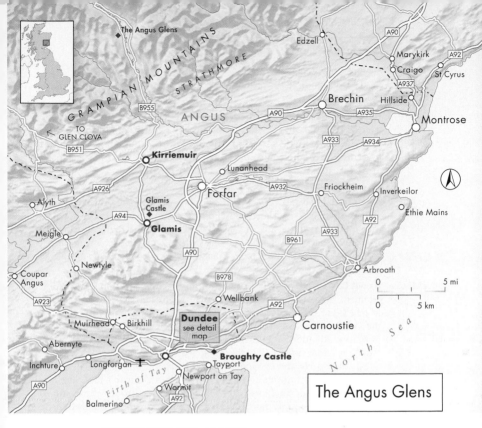

The Angus Glens

GETTING HERE AND AROUND

A number of roads lead to Kirriemuir, but A928 (off A90), which also passes Glamis Castle, is one of the loveliest. Stagecoach Strathtay runs buses to this area; the 20 and 22 from Dundee are the most regular.

EXPLORING

J.M. Barrie's Birthplace. At the J. M. Barrie's Birthplace, the National Trust pays tribute to the man who sought to preserve the magic of childhood more than any other writer of his age. The house's upper floors are furnished as they might have been in Barrie's time, complete with domestic necessities, while downstairs is his study, replete with manuscripts and personal mementos. The outside washhouse is said to have served as Barrie's first theater. ⊠ *9 Brechin Rd.* ☎ *0844/4932142* ⊕ *www.nts.org. uk/visits* ☎ *£6.50, includes Camera Obscura* ☉ *Apr.–June, Sept., and Oct., Sat.–Wed. noon–5; July and Aug., daily 11–5.*

Kirriemuir Gateway to the Glens Museum. As is the style in Angus, the local museum doubles as the visitor center, meaning you can get all the information you need and admire a few stuffed birds and artifacts at the same time. Rock fans will appreciate the exhibit celebrating local lad made good (or rather bad), the late Bon Scott, lead singer of the rock band AC/DC. ⊠ *32 High St.* ☎ *01575/575479* ⊕ *www.angus.gov.uk/ history/museums/kirriemuir* ☎ *Free* ☉ *Tues.–Sat. 10–5.*

GLAMIS

6 miles south of Kirriemuir.

Set in rolling countryside is the little village of Glamis (pronounced *glahms*).

GETTING HERE AND AROUND

The drive to Glamis Castle, along beech- and-yew-lined roads, is as majestic as the castle itself. Take the A90 north from Dundee, then off onto the A928. The village of Glamis can be reached by the Stagecoach Strathtay number 22, but service is rather infrequent.

EXPLORING

Angus Folk Museum. A row of 19th-century cottages with unusual stone-slab roofs makes up the Angus Folk Museum, whose exhibits focus on the tools of domestic and agricultural life in the region during the past 200 years. ⊠ *Off A94* ☎ *0844/4932141* ⊕ *www.nts.org.uk/visits* 🎫*£6.50* ⊘ *Apr.–June and Sept.–Oct., weekends noon–5; July and Aug., daily noon–5.*

Fodor'sChoice
★ **Glamis Castle.** One of Scotland's best-known and most beautiful castles, Glamis Castle connects Britain's royalty through 10 centuries, from Macbeth (Thane of Glamis) to the late Queen Mother and her daughter, the late Princess Margaret, born here in 1930 (the first royal princess born in Scotland in 300 years). The property of the earls of Strathmore and Kinghorne since 1372, the castle was largely reconstructed in the late 17th century; the original keep, which is much older, is still intact. One of the most famous rooms in the castle is Duncan's Hall, the legendary setting for Shakespeare's *Macbeth*. Guided tours allow you to see fine collections of china, tapestries, and furniture. Within the castle is the delightful Castle Kitchen restaurant; the grounds contain a huge gift shop, a shop selling local produce, and a pleasant picnic area. ⊠ *A94, 1 mile north of Glamis* ☎ *01307/840393* ⊕ *www.glamis-castle. co.uk* 🎫*£10.75* ⊘ *Mar.–Oct., daily 10-6.*

ABERDEEN AND
THE NORTHEAST

WELCOME TO ABERDEEN AND THE NORTHEAST

TOP REASONS TO GO

★ **Glorious castles:** With more than 75 castles, some Victorian and others dating back to the 13th century, this area has everything from ruins like Dunnottar to opulent Fyvie Castle.

★ **Fine distilleries:** The valley of the River Spey is famous for its single-malt distilleries. You can choose from bigger operations such as Glenfiddich to the iconic Strathisla, where Chivas Regal is blended.

★ **Seaside cities and towns:** The big-city port of Aberdeen and the colorful smaller fishing towns of Stonehaven and Cullen in the northeast are great places to soak up the seagoing atmosphere.

★ **Great walking:** There are all types of walking, from the bracing inclines of the Grampian Hills to the wooded grounds of Balmoral and Haddo House, to golden sands near towns such as Cullen.

★ **Superb golf:** The northeast has more than 50 golf clubs, some of which have championship courses.

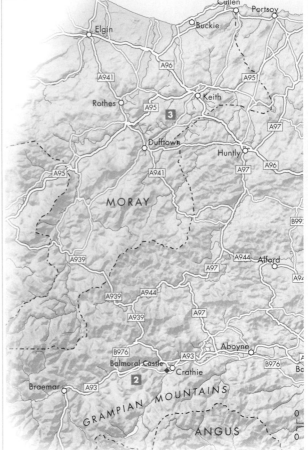

1 Aberdeen. Family connections or Royal Deeside often take travelers to this part of Scotland, but many are surprised by how grand and rich in history Aberdeen is. The august granite-turreted buildings and rose-lined roads make this a surprisingly pleasant city to explore; don't miss Old Aberdeen in particular.

2 Royal Deeside and Castle Country. Prince Albert designed Balmoral Castle for Queen Victoria, and so began the Royal family's love affair with

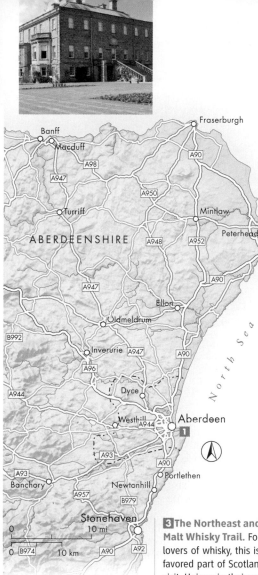

Banff
Macduff
A98
A947
A950
Turriff
ABERDEENSHIRE
A948
A947
Ellon
Oldmeldrum
B992
Inverurie A947
A96
Dyce
A944
Westhill A944
Aberdeen
1
A93
A93
Banchory
A957
Newtonhill
B979
Stonehaven
0   10 mi
0   B974   10 km   A90   A92

Fraserburgh
A90
Mintlaw
Peterhead
A952
A90
A90
A90
Portlethen

North Sea

GETTING ORIENTED

Aberdeen, on the North Sea in the eastern part of the region, is Scotland's third-largest city; many people start a trip here. Once you have spent time in the city, you may be inclined to venture west into rural Deeside, with its royal connections and looming mountain backdrop. To the north of Deeside is Castle Country, with many ancient fortresses. Speyside and its distilleries lie at the western edge of the region, and are equally accessible from Inverness. From Speyside you might travel back east along the pristine coastline at Scotland's northeastern tip.

17

Deeside. However, this area has long been the retreat or the fortress of distinguished families, as the clutter of castles shows. The majesty of the countryside also guarantees a superlative stop for anyone interested in history and romance.

3 The Northeast and the Malt Whisky Trail. For lovers of whisky, this is a favored part of Scotland to visit. Unique in their architecture, their ingredients, and the end product, the distilleries of Speyside are keen to share with you their passion for "the water of life." This region also has rolling hills and, to the north, the beautiful, wild coastline of the North Sea.

Updated by
Shona Main
and Mike
Gonzalez

Here, in this granite shoulder of Grampian, are some of Scotland's most enduring travel icons: Royal Deeside, the countryside that Queen Victoria made her own; the Castle Country route, where fortresses stand hard against the hills; and the Malt Whisky Trail, where peaty streams embrace the country's greatest concentration of distilleries. The region's gateway is the city of Aberdeen, constructed of granite and now aglitter with new wealth and new blood drawn together by North Sea oil.

Because of its isolation, Aberdeen has historically been a fairly autonomous place. Even now it's perceived by many British people as lying almost out of reach in the northeast. In reality, it's a 90-minute flight from London or a little more than two hours by car from Edinburgh. Its magnificent 18th- and early-19th-century city center amply rewards exploration. Yet even if this popular base for travelers vanished from the map, an extensive portion of the northeast would still remain at the top of many travelers' wish lists.

Balmoral, the Scottish baronial–style house built for Queen Victoria as a retreat, is merely the most famous castle in the area, and certainly not the oldest. In some structures, such as Castle Fraser, you can trace the changing styles and tastes of each of their owners over the centuries. Grand mansions such as 18th-century Haddo House, with its symmetrical facade and elegant interior, surrender any defensive role entirely.

A trail leading to a more ephemeral kind of pleasure can be found south of Elgin and Banff, where the glens embrace Scotland's greatest concentration of malt-whisky distilleries. With so many in Morayshire, where the distilling is centered on the valley of the River Spey and its tributaries, there's now a Whisky Trail. Follow it, and visit other distilleries as well, to experience a surprising wealth of flavors.

The northeast's chief topographical attraction lies in the gradual transition from high mountain plateau—by a series of gentle steps through hill, forest, and farmland—to the Moray Firth and North Sea coast, where the word "unadulterated" is redefined. Here you'll find some of the United Kingdom's most perfect wild shorelines, both sandy and sheer cliff, and breezy fishing villages like Cullen on the Banffshire coast and Stonehaven, south of Aberdeen. The Grampian Mountains, to the west, contain some of the highest ground in the nation, in the area of the Cairngorms. In recognition of this area's special nature, Cairngorms National Park was created in 2003.

ABERDEEN AND THE NORTHEAST PLANNER

WHEN TO GO
May and June are probably the loveliest times to visit, but many travelers arrive from late spring to early fall. The National Trust for Scotland tends to close its properties in winter, so many of the northeast's castles are not open for off-season travel, though you can always see them from the outside. The distilleries are open much of the year, but check for the "silent month" when they close down for a holiday. That's often in August, but may vary.

PLANNING YOUR TIME
How you allocate your time may depend on your special interests—castles or whisky, for example. But even if you can manage only a morning or an afternoon in Aberdeen, do not miss a walk around the granite streets of Old Aberdeen, a trip to Aberdeen Art Gallery, as well as a pint in the Prince of Wales pub. A trip southward to the fishing town of Stonehaven and the breathtaking cliff-top fortress of Dunnottar makes a rewarding afternoon. Royal Deeside, with a good sprinkling of castles and grandeur, needs a good two days; even this might be tight for those who want to lap up every moment of majesty at Balmoral, Crathes, Fraser, and Fyvie—the best of the bunch. A visit to malt-whisky country should include tours of Glenfiddich, Glenfarclas, Glenlivet, and Glen Grant distilleries, and although it's not technically a maker of malt whisky, Strathisla. Real enthusiasts should allot two days for the distilleries, and they shouldn't pass up a visit to Speyside Cooperage, one of the few remaining cooperages in Scotland. Cullen and Duff House gallery in Banff, on the coast, can be done in a day before returning to Aberdeen.

GETTING HERE AND AROUND
AIR TRAVEL
Aberdeen is easy to reach from other parts of the United Kingdom as well as Europe. British Airways, bmi, EasyJet, and Flybe are some of the airlines with service to other parts of Britain. Aberdeen Airport—serving both international and domestic flights—is in Dyce, 7 miles west of the city center on the A96 (Inverness). The drive to the center of Aberdeen is easy via the A96 (which can be busy during rush hour).

Airport Contact Aberdeen Airport ✉ *Dyce Dr., Dyce* ☎ *0844/481–6666* ⊕ *www.aberdeenairport.com.*

17

BOAT AND FERRY TRAVEL

Northlink Ferries has service between Aberdeen, Lerwick (Shetland), and Kirkwall (Orkney).

Boat and Ferry Contact Northlink Ferries ✉ *Jamieson's Quay, Aberdeen* ☎ *0845/600–0449* ⊕ *www.northlinkferries.co.uk.*

BUS TRAVEL

Long-distance buses run to Aberdeen from most parts of Scotland, England, and Wales. Contact Megabus, National Express, and Scottish Citylink for bus connections with English and Scottish towns. There's a network of local buses throughout the northeast run by Stagecoach, but they can take a long time and connections are not always well timed.

Bus Contacts Megabus ☎ *0900/160–0900* ⊕ *www.megabus.com.* **National Express** ☎ *08717/818178* ⊕ *www.nationalexpress.com.* **Scottish Citylink** ☎ *0871/266–3333* ⊕ *www.citylink.co.uk.* **Stagecoach** ✉ *Union Square Bus Station, Guild St., Aberdeen* ☎ *01224/591381* ⊕ *www.stagecoachbus.com.*

CAR TRAVEL

A car is the best way to see the northeast. If you are coming from the south, take the A90, continuing on from the M90 (from Edinburgh) or the M9/A9 (from Glasgow), which both stop at Perth. The coastal route, the A92, is a more leisurely alternative, with its interesting resorts and fishing villages. The most scenic route, however, is the A93 from Perth, north to Blairgowrie and into Glen Shee. The A93 then goes over the Cairnwell Pass, the highest main road in the United Kingdom. This route isn't recommended in winter, when snow can make driving difficult.

Around the northeast roads can be busy, with speeding and erratic driving a problem on the main A roads.

TRAIN TRAVEL

You can reach Aberdeen directly from Edinburgh (2½ hours), Inverness (2½ hours), and Glasgow (3 hours). ScotRail timetables have full details. There are also London–Aberdeen routes that go through Edinburgh and the east-coast main line connecting Aberdeen to all corners of the United Kingdom.

Train Contact ScotRail ✉ *Aberdeen Railway Station, Guild St., Aberdeen* ☎ *08457/484950* ⊕ *www.scotrail.co.uk.*

RESTAURANTS

Partly in response to the demands of workers in the oil industry, restaurants have cropped up all over the northeast, and the quality of the food improves yearly. As in the rest of Scotland, this region is rediscovering the quality and versatility of the local produce. Juicy Aberdeen Angus steaks, lean lamb, and humanely reared pork appear on local menus, but despite this being the center of the fishing industry, most seafood available is still of the fish-and-chips variety. Restaurants like the Silver Darling in Aberdeen are spearheading a new interest in fish dishes, though, and old standards like Cullen skink (a creamy smoked-fish soup) are increasingly on menus.

HOTELS

The northeast has some splendid country hotels with log fires and old Victorian furnishings, where you can also be sure of eating well. Many hotels in Aberdeen are in older buildings that have a baronial feel. The trend for serviced apartments has caught on here, with some extremely modish and good-value options for those who want a bit more privacy. This trend is now extending into Deeside, where it's been notoriously difficult to find good accommodations beyond some country-house hotels, even though it's a popular tourist spot. *Hotel reviews have been shortened. For full information, visit Fodors.com.*

WHAT IT COSTS IN POUNDS				
	$	$$	$$$	$$$$
Restaurants	under £15	£15–£19	£20–£25	over £25
Hotels	under £100	£100–£160	£161–£220	over £220

Restaurant prices are the average cost of a main course at dinner or, if dinner is not served, at lunch. Hotel prices are the lowest cost of a standard double room in high season, including 20% V.A.T.

VISITOR INFORMATION

The tourist information center in Aberdeen has a currency exchange, Internet access, and information about all of Scotland's northeast. There are also year-round tourist information offices in Braemar and Elgin. In summer, also look for tourist information centers in Alford, Ballater, Banchory, Braemar, Dufftown, Elgin, and Stonehaven.

Contact Aberdeen Visitor Information Centre ⊠ *23 Union St., Aberdeen* ☎ *01224/288828* ⊕ *www.aberdeen-grampian.com.*

ABERDEEN

As a gateway to Royal Deeside and the Malt Whisky Trail, Aberdeen attracts visitors, though many are eager to get out into the countryside. Today, though, the city's unique history is finally being recognized as more impressive than many Scots had previously realized, and Aberdeen is being rediscovered. Distinctive architecture, some fine museums, universities, and good restaurants, nightlife, and shopping add to the appeal of Scotland's third-largest city (population 217,000). Union Street is the heart of the city, but take time to explore the university and the pretty streets of Old Aberdeen.

In the 18th century local granite quarrying produced a durable silver stone that would be used boldly in the glittering blocks, spires, columns, and parapets of Victorian-era Aberdonian structures. The city remains one of the United Kingdom's most distinctive, although some would say it depends on the weather and the brightness of the day. The mica chips embedded in the rock look like a million mirrors in the sunshine. In rain (and there is a fair amount of driving rain from the North Sea) and heavy clouds, however, their sparkle is snuffed out.

The city lies between the Dee and Don rivers, with a working harbor that has access to the sea; it has been a major fishing port and is the main commercial port in northern Scotland. The North Sea has always been important to Aberdeen. In the 1850s the city was famed for its sleek, fast clippers that sailed to India for cargoes of tea. In the late 1960s the course of Aberdeen's history was unequivocally altered when oil and gas were discovered offshore, sparking rapid growth, prosperity, and further industrialization.

GETTING HERE AND AROUND

AIR TRAVEL   Stagecoach Bluebird Jet Service 727 and First Aberdeen Bus 27 operate between the airport terminal and Union Square in the center of Aberdeen. Buses (£2.70) run frequently at peak times, less often at midday and in the evening; the journey time is approximately 40 minutes. Stagecoach Bluebird Bus 10 stops at Aberdeen Airport, either taking you into the city center or northwest to Elgin.

Dyce is on ScotRail's Inverness–Aberdeen route. The rail station is a short taxi ride from the terminal building. The ride takes 12 minutes, and trains run approximately every two hours.

BUS TRAVEL   First Aberdeen has easy and reliable service within the city of Aberdeen. Timetables are available from the tourist information center in Union Street.

CAR TRAVEL   Aberdeen is a compact city with good signage. Its center is Union Street, the main east–west thoroughfare, which tends to get crowded with traffic. Anderson Drive is an efficient ring road on the city's west side; be extra careful on its many traffic circles. It's best to leave your car in one of the parking garages (arrive early to get a space) and walk around, or use the convenient park-and-ride stop at the Bridge of Don, north of the city. Street maps are available from the tourist information center, newsstands, and booksellers.

TAXI TRAVEL   You can find taxi stands throughout the center of Aberdeen: along Union Street, at the railway station at Guild Street, at Back Wynd, and at Regent Quay. The taxis have meters and might be saloon cars (sedans) or black cabs. They are great ways to travel between neighborhoods.

TRAIN TRAVEL   Aberdeen has good ScotRail service from major cities in Scotland and Britain.

ESSENTIALS

Bus Contacts First Aberdeen ☎ *01224/650000* ⊕ *www.firstaberdeen.co.uk.*

AROUND UNION STREET

Aberdeen centers on Union Street, with its many fine survivors of the Victorian and Edwardian streetscape. Marischal College, dating from the late 16th century, has many grand buildings that are worth exploring.

TIMING

You can explore the center of Aberdeen in half a day, but you'll probably want to devote a full day to poking around its interesting old buildings.

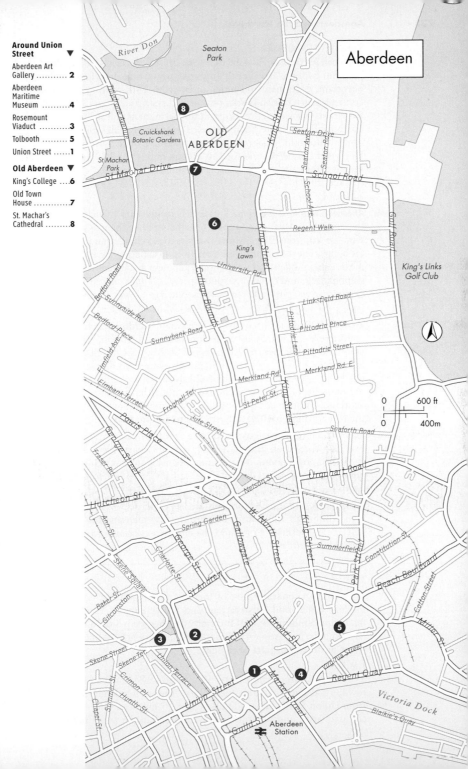

Aberdeen

River Don

Seaton Park

Cruickshank Botanic Gardens

OLD ABERDEEN

St Machar Park

St Machar Drive

Seaton Drive

Seaton Ave

Seaton Dr

School Ave

School Road

Gulf Road

Regent Walk

King's Lawn

University Rd.

King's Links Golf Club

Cattle Burns

Bedford Road

Sunnyside Rd.

Bedford Place

Linksfield Road

Pittodrie Lane

Pittodrie Place

Pittodrie Street

Elmbank Ave.

Elmbank Terrace

Sunnybank Road

Merkland Rd.

Merkland Rd. E.

Froghall Ter.

Hyde Street

St Peter St.

King Street

Seaforth Road

0   600 ft

0   400m

Paris Place

George Street

Fraser Rd.

Nelson St.

Urquhart Road

Hutcheon St.

Ann St.

Spring Garden

Catto Road

Summerfield

Constitution St.

Beach Boulevard

Cotton Street

Charlotte St.

George St.

St Andrew

Baker St.

Skene Square

Gilcomston

King Street

School Hill

Broad St.

Regent Quay

Victoria Dock

Blaikie's Quay

Skene Street

Skene Ter.

Union Terrace

Cannon Pl.

Union Street

Huntly St.

Chapel St.

Guild St.

Virginia Street

Market Street

8

7

6

3 **2**

1 **4**

5

Aberdeen Station

TOP ATTRACTIONS

Aberdeen Art Gallery. Housed in a 19th-century neoclassical building, the museum contains excellent paintings, prints, and drawings, sculpture, porcelain, costumes, and much else—from 18th-century art to major contemporary British works by Lucien Freud and Henry Moore. Scottish artists are well represented in the permanent collection and special exhibits. Local stone has been used in interior walls, pillars, and the central fountain, designed by the acclaimed British sculptor Barbara Hepworth. ■TIP➔ Look for the unique collection of Aberdeen silver on the ground floor. The museum also has a cake-filled café and well-stocked gift shop. ✉ *Schoolhill* ☎ *01224/523700* ⊕ *www.aagm.co.uk* ✎ *Free* ☉ *Tues.–Sat. 10–5, Sun. 2–5.*

FAMILY   **Aberdeen Maritime Museum.** This excellent museum, which incorporates the 1593 Provost Ross's House, tells the story of the city's involvement with the sea, from early inshore fisheries to tea clippers and the North Sea oil boom. The information-rich exhibits, fascinating for kids and adults, include ship models, paintings, and equipment associated with the fishing, shipbuilding, and oil and gas industries. ✉ *Ship Row* ☎ *01224/337700* ⊕ *www.aagm.co.uk* ✎ *Free* ☉ *Tues.–Sat. 10–5, Sun. noon–3.*

WORTH NOTING

Rosemount Viaduct. Three silvery, handsome buildings on this bridge are collectively known by all Aberdonians as Education, Salvation, and Damnation. The **Central Library** and **St. Mark's Church** date from the last decade of the 19th century, and **His Majesty's Theatre** (1904–08) has been restored inside to its full Edwardian splendor. If you're taking photographs, you can choose an angle that includes the statue of Scotland's first freedom fighter, Sir William Wallace (1270–1305), in the foreground pointing majestically to Damnation.

FAMILY   **Tolbooth.** The city was governed from this 17th-century building, which was also the burgh court and jail, for 200 years. Now a museum of crime and punishment, it is as amusing as it is stomach churning—making it a must-see for older kids. ✉ *Castle St.* ☎ *01224/621167* ⊕ *www.aagm.co.uk* ✎ *Free* ☉ *July–Sept., Mon.–Sat. 10–5.*

Union Street. This great thoroughfare is to Aberdeen what Princes Street is to Edinburgh: the central pivot of the city plan and the product of a wave of enthusiasm to rebuild the city in a contemporary style in the early 19th century.

OLD ABERDEEN

Very much a separate area of the city, Old Aberdeen is north of the modern center and clustered around St. Machar's Cathedral and the many fine buildings of the University of Aberdeen. Take a stroll on College Bounds; handsome 18th- and 19th-century houses line this cobbled street in the oldest part of the city.

TIMING

The neighborhood is a 20- to 30-minute walk north of the center of town; it's also easily reachable by First Aberdeen bus numbers 1 and 20 from Union Street. The ride takes 5 to 15 minutes. Old Aberdeen is a compact area, and will take you no more than a few hours to explore.

TOP ATTRACTIONS

Fodor's Choice ★ **King's College.** Founded in 1494, King's College is now part of the University of Aberdeen. Its **chapel,** built around 1500, has an unmistakable flying (or crown) spire. That it has survived at all was because of the zeal of the principal, who defended his church against the destructive fanaticism that swept through Scotland during the Reformation, when the building was less than a century old. Today the renovated chapel plays an important role in university life. **■TIP→ Don't miss the tall oak screen that separates the nave from the choir, the ribbed wooden ceiling, and the stalls, as these constitute the finest medieval wood carvings found anywhere in Scotland.** The **King's College Centre** has more information about the university. ✉ *High St.* ☎ *01224/272660* 🌐 *www.abdn.ac.uk* ⏲ *Weekdays 10–3:30.*

Old Town House. Serving as a gateway to Aberdeen University, this plain but handsome Georgian building is a great place to learn about this ancient seat of learning. The building was the center of all trading activity in the city before it became a grammar school, a Masonic lodge, and then a library. ✉ *High St.* ☎ *01224/273650* 🌐 *www.abdn.ac.uk/oldtownhouse* 🎟 *Free* ⏲ *Mon.–Sat. 9–5.*

St. Machar's Cathedral. It's said that St. Machar was sent by St. Columba to build a church on a grassy platform near the sea, where a river flowed in the shape of a shepherd's crook. This spot fits the bill. Although the cathedral was founded in AD 580, most of the existing building dates from the 15th and 16th centuries. The central tower collapsed in 1688, reducing the building to half its original length. The nave is thought to have been rebuilt in red sandstone in 1370, but the final renovation was completed in granite by the middle of the 15th century. Along with the nave ceiling, the twin octagonal spires were finished in time to take a battering in the Reformation, when the barons of the Mearns stripped the lead off the roof and stole the bells. The cathedral suffered further mistreatment until it was fully restored in the 19th century. ✉ *Chanonry* ☎ *01224/485988* 🌐 *www.stmachar.com* ⏲ *Apr.–Oct., daily 9:30–4:30; Nov.–Mar., daily 10–4.*

17

WHERE TO EAT

$ MODERN BRITISH 🍴 **Café 52.** Right in the historic Grassmarket, this café-restaurant has taken a few years to find its niche but now serves up lovely homemade dishes at pocket-friendly prices. Creamy fish pie filled with juicy chunks of smoked haddock and bramble panna cotta are just a few of the options. No matter what you order, local produce makes it tasty and fresh. The handsome restaurant is in a silvery granite building with exposed-stone walls, huge windows, and shiny black tables. [$] *Average main: £12* ✉ *52 The Green* ☎ *01224/590094* 🌐 *www.cafe52.net* ⏲ *No dinner Sun.*

$$$ SEAFOOD Fodor's Choice ★ 🍴 **Silver Darling.** Huge windows overlook the harbor and beach at this quayside favorite in a former customs house, long one of Aberdeen's most acclaimed restaurants. As the name implies, the French-inspired fare focuses on fish: a silver darling is a herring. Try the langoustine ravioli with hazelnut velouté for a starter, then move on to wild halibut

steamed in seaweed, or sea bass with crushed ginger potatoes. $ *Average main: £25* ✉ *North Pier, Pocra Quay* ☎ *01224/576229* ⊕ *thesilverdarling.co.uk* ⚲ *Reservations essential* ☾ *Closed Sun. No lunch Sat.*

$$ ✗ **Yatai.** It might seem odd ordering Japanese food in Aberdeen, but
JAPANESE   considering the quality and quantity of fresh fish being landed on the
Fodor'sChoice   quayside each day it makes perfect sense. The slick facade and glowing
★   red interior might be a little intimidating at first, but the smiling staff
is approachable, and, for the uninitiated, is happy to help you choose
the right blend of flavors and textures. The place isn't cheap, but as
far as Japanese food is concerned, it's not extortionate either: £12 for
seared beef salad, £15 for six pieces of sushi. Japanese saki and beer
are a treat. $ *Average main: £15* ✉ *53 Langstane Pl.* ☎ *01224/592355*
⊕ *www.yatai.co.uk* ⚲ *Reservations essential* ☾ *Closed Sun. and Mon.*

WHERE TO STAY

$$ ⊞ **Atholl Hotel.** With its many turrets and gables, this granite hotel recalls
HOTEL   a bygone era but has modern amenities. **Pros:** family-run establish-
ment; tasty restaurant; very pleasant staff. **Cons:** some rooms are a
little generic; some bathrooms need updating. $ *Rooms from: £145*
✉ *54 Kings Gate* ☎ *01224/323505* ⊕ *www.atholl-aberdeen.com* ⇆ *34
rooms* ⦿ *Breakfast.*

$$ ⊞ **Bauhaus Hotel.** When the owner got his hands on this 1960s-era
HOTEL   granite office block, he decided to pay homage to Walter Gropius, the
founder of the Bauhaus movement. **Pros:** great design; comfortable
rooms; tasty eatery. **Cons:** beware the furniture's sharp corners; fake
art on the walls—in a city with a great art school. $ *Rooms from:
£130* ✉ *52–60 Langstane Pl.* ☎ *01224/212122* ⊕ *www.thebauhaus.
co.uk* ⇆ *34 rooms, 5 suites* ⦿ *Multiple meal plans.*

$$ ⊞ **The Jays Guest House.** Alice Jennings or her husband George will greet
B&B/INN   you at the front door of this granite house, a homey bed-and-break-
Fodor'sChoice   fast. **Pros:** immaculate rooms; expert advice on city's sites; near shops
★   and restaurants. **Cons:** no public areas; incredibly popular, so book
in advance. $ *Rooms from: £100* ✉ *422 King St.* ☎ *01224/638295*
⊕ *www.jaysguesthouse.co.uk* ⇆ *10 rooms* ⦿ *Breakfast.*

NIGHTLIFE AND THE ARTS

Aberdeen has a fairly lively nightlife scene revolving around pubs and
clubs. Theaters, concert halls, arts centers, and cinemas are also well
represented. The principal newspapers—the *Press and Journal* and the
Evening Express—and *Aberdeen Leopard* magazine can fill you in on
what's going on anywhere in the northeast. Aberdeen's tourist information center has a monthly publication with an events calendar.

THE ARTS
Aberdeen is a rich city, both financially and culturally.

ARTS CENTERS   **Aberdeen Arts Centre.** The Aberdeen Arts Centre hosts plays, musicals,
poetry readings, and exhibitions by local and Scottish artists. ✉ *33 King
St.* ☎ *01224/635208* ⊕ *www.aberdeenartscentre.org.uk.*

Lemon Tree. The Lemon Tree has an innovative and international program of dance, stand-up comedy, and puppet theater, as well as folk, jazz, and rock music. ⊠ *5 W. North St.* ☎ *0845/270–8200* ⊕ *www. boxofficeaberdeen.com.*

CONCERT HALLS **Music Hall.** The Scottish National Orchestra, the Scottish Chamber Orchestra, and other major groups perform at the Music Hall. Events also include folk concerts, crafts fairs, and exhibitions. ⊠ *Union St.* ☎ *01224/632080* ⊕ *www.boxofficeaberdeen.com.*

FILM **The Belmont.** Independent and classic films are screened at the Belmont. ⊠ *49 Belmont St.* ☎ *0871/902–5721* ⊕ *www.picturehouses.co.uk.*

NIGHTLIFE

With a greater club-to-clubber ratio than either Edinburgh or Glasgow, Aberdeen offers plenty of loud music and dancing for a night out. There are also pubs and pool halls for those with two left feet. Pubs close at midnight on weekdays and 1 am on weekends; clubs go until 2 or 3 am.

BARS AND PUBS **Fittie Bar.** Some pubs spend a fortune trying to re-create the warm atmosphere that the Fittie Bar comes by naturally. Located where the harbor stops and the old fishing village of Footdee (Fittie) begins, the pub tells the story of Aberdeen's fishing past, as will any of the salty dogs who drink there. ⊠ *18 Wellington St.* ☎ *01224/582911.*

Fodor's Choice
★ **The Prince of Wales.** Dating from 1850, the Prince of Wales has retained its paneled walls and wooden tables. Still regarded as Aberdeen's most traditional pub, it's hardly regal, but good-quality food and reasonable prices draw the regulars back. ⊠ *7 St. Nicholas La.* ☎ *01224/640597.*

Soul. In a converted church that still has stained-glass windows and ecclesiastical furnishings, Soul is popular with young, upwardly mobile Aberdonians. The eclectic menu includes everything from chicken satay to mussels. ⊠ *333 Union St.* ☎ *01224/211150.*

DANCE CLUBS People tend to dress up a bit to go clubbing, and jeans or sneakers might get you turned away at the door. Clubs are open until 2 am during the week and until 3 am on Friday and Saturday nights.

SPORTS AND THE OUTDOORS

GOLF

Northeast Scotland is known for good golf. Just north of Aberdeen is Donald Trump's controversial International Golf Links, while to the south a new championship course to be designed by Jack Nicklaus will open at Ury Castle (date not set at this writing). Expect to pay £15 to £120 per round at courses in and around Aberdeen. Make reservations at least 24 hours in advance and check that the course you wish to play is open when you want to play it.

Royal Aberdeen Golf Club. This venerable club, founded in 1780, is the archetypal Scottish links course: tumbling over uneven ground, with the frequently added hazard of sea breezes. Prickly gorse is inclined to close in and form an additional hurdle. The two courses are tucked behind the rough, grassy sand dunes, and there are surprisingly few views of the sea. One historical note: in 1783 this club originated the

17

five-minute-search rule for a lost ball. A handicap certificate and letter of introduction are required. ■TIP➔ Visitors are allowed only on
weekdays. ✉ *Links Rd., Bridge of Don* ☎ *01224/702571* ⊕ *www.
royalaberdeengolf.com* ✉ *Green fee: Balgownie £120; Silverburn £60*
⚑ *Reservations essential* ⚑. *Balgownie: 18 holes, 6900 yds, par 71;
Silverburn: 18 holes, 4021 yds, par 64* ◯ *Daily.*

SHOPPING

You can find most of the large national department stores in Union
Square. Bon Accord, St. Nicholas, and Trinity shopping malls are along
Union Street, but Aberdeen has a few good specialty shops as well.

SPECIALTY SHOPS

Aitkins. You can't leave Aberdeen without trying one of its famous *row-
ies* (or *butteries*), the fortifying morning roll. Aitkins Bakery is considered the finest purveyor of this local speciality. ✉ *202 Holburn St.*
☎ *01224/582567.*

Books and Beans. This secondhand bookshop has its own little café.
You're welcome to browse and sip at the same time. ✉ *22 Belmont St.*
☎ *01224/646438* ⊕ *www.booksandbeans.co.uk.*

Candle Close Gallery. This shop has some strange and wonderful mirrors, clocks, ceramics, and jewelry that you're unlikely to see elsewhere.
✉ *123 Gallowgate* ☎ *01224/624940* ⊕ *www.candleclosegallery.co.uk.*

Colin Wood. This shop is the place to go for small antiques, interesting
prints, and regional maps. ✉ *25 Rose St.* ☎ *01224/643019.*

ROYAL DEESIDE AND CASTLE COUNTRY

Deeside, the valley running west from Aberdeen down where the River
Dee flows, earned its "royal" appellation when discovered by Queen
Victoria. To this day, where royalty goes, lesser aristocracy and freshly
minted millionaires follow. You may appreciate this yearning when you
see the piney hills, purple moors, and blue river intermingling. As you
travel deeper into the Grampian Mountains, Royal Deeside's gradual
scenic change adds a growing sense of excitement.

There are castles along the Dee as well as to the north in Castle Country, another region that illustrates the gradual geological change in
the northeast: uplands lapped by a tide of farms. All the Donside and
Deeside castles are picturesquely sited, with most fitted out with tall
slender turrets, winding stairs, and crooked chambers that epitomize
Scottish baronial style. Many were tidied up and "domesticated" during the 19th century. Although best toured by car, much of this area is
accessible either by public transportation or on tours from Aberdeen.

STONEHAVEN

15 miles south of Aberdeen.

This historic town near splendid Dunnottar Castle was once a popular
holiday destination, with people including Robert Burns enjoying walks

A cliff-top setting by the North Sea gives ruined Dunnottar Castle spectacular views.

along the golden sands. The surrounding red-clay fields were made famous by Lewis Grassic Gibbon (real name James Leslie Mitchell), who attended school in the town and who wrote the seminal Scottish trilogy, *A Scots Quair*, about the people, the land, and the impact of World War I. The decline of the fishing industry emptied the harbor, but the town, being so close to Aberdeen, has begun to thrive again. It's now famous for its Hogmanay (New Year) celebrations, where local men swing huge balls of fire on chains before tossing them into the harbor.

GETTING HERE AND AROUND

Stagecoach Bluebird runs a number of buses to Stonehaven from Aberdeen, but numbers 107 and 109 are the fastest (50 minutes). Most trains heading south from Aberdeen stop at Stonehaven; there's at least one per hour making the 15-minute trip. Drivers should take A90 south and turn off at A957.

ESSENTIALS

Visitor Information Stonehaven Visitor Information Centre ✉ *66 Allardyce St., Stonehaven* ☎ *01569/762806* ⊕ *www.aberdeen-grampian.com* ⊙ *Apr.–Oct.*

EXPLORING

Fodor'sChoice ★ **Dunnottar Castle.** It's hard to beat the magnificent cliff-top ruins of Dunnottar Castle, especially with the panoramic views of the North Sea. Building began in the 14th century, when Sir William Keith, Marischal of Scotland (keeper of the king's mares), decided to build a tower house to demonstrate his power. Subsequent generations added to the structure, and important visitors included Mary, Queen of Scots. The castle is most famous for holding out for eight months against Oliver Cromwell's army in 1651 and 1652, and thereby saving the Scottish crown

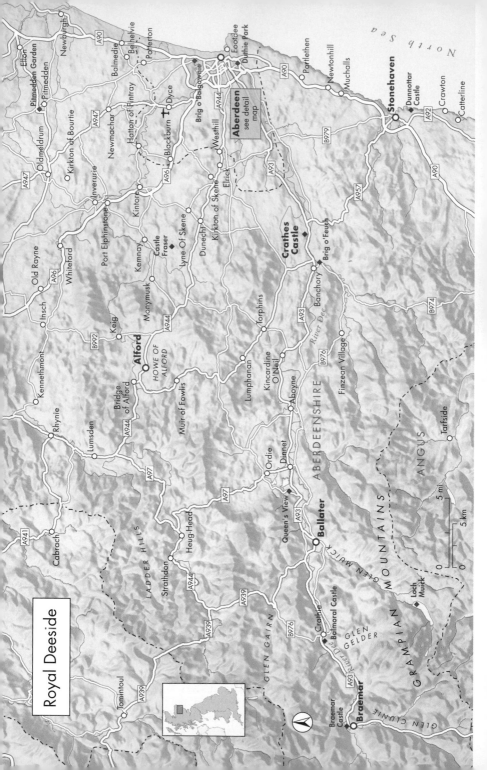

Royal Deeside

jewels, which had been stored here for safekeeping. Reach the castle via the A90; take the Stonehaven turnoff and follow the signs. **■ TIP→ Wear sensible shoes, and allow about two hours.** ✉ *Off A92, Stonehaven* ☎ *01569/762173* 🌐 *www.dunnottarcastle.co.uk* 🎟 *£6* 🕐 *Easter–Sept., daily 9–6; Nov.–Easter, daily 10–sunset.*

WHERE TO EAT AND STAY

$ BRITISH 🍴 **Carron Art Deco Restaurant.** For an outstanding meal of classic Scottish dishes served in the most splendid surroundings, try this longtime favorite. Evoking the style and class of the 1930s, it's a must for both lovers of architecture and food. Look out for the rather risqué figure of a woman etched onto a mirror between two dazzlingly tiled columns. The cuisine is not diminished by the surroundings: try the Aberdeen Angus roast beef with a Drambuie (a honey-flavor whisky liqueur) gravy and the sticky pear and carrot pudding. [$] *Average main: £14* ✉ *Cameron St., Stonehaven* ☎ *01569/760460* 🌐 *www.carron-restaurant.co.uk* 🕐 *Closed Sun.*

$ B&B/INN Fodor'sChoice ★ 🏨 **Bayview B&B.** On the beach and down the lane from the town square, this contemporary bed-and-breakfast couldn't be in a more convenient location—or have better views. **Pros:** spic-and-span rooms; walk to restaurants and shops; eccentric design. **Cons:** standard rooms are smallish; breakfast room is windowless. [$] *Rooms from: £95* ✉ *Beachgate La., Stonehaven* ☎ *07791/224227* 🌐 *www.bayviewbandb.co.uk* 🛏 *3 rooms, 2 suites* 🍽 *Breakfast.*

17

CRATHES CASTLE

15 miles west of Stonehaven, 16 miles west of Aberdeen.

The house and gardens at Crathes Castle are well worth a look. It's 3 miles northeast of Banchory, an immaculate town filled with pinkish granite buildings.

GETTING HERE AND AROUND

A car is by far the best way to get around the area; A93 is one of the main roads connecting the towns.

For those reliant on public transport, Stagecoach buses operate a number of services for towns along or just off A93 (Banchory, Kincardine, Aboyne, Ballater, Balmoral, and Braemar).

ESSENTIALS

Visitor Information Banchory Visitor Information Centre ✉ *Bridge St.* ☎ *01330/822000* 🌐 *www.aberdeen-grampian.com* 🕐 *Apr.–Oct.*

EXPLORING

FAMILY **Crathes Castle.** About 16 miles west of Aberdeen, Crathes Castle was once the home of the Burnett family and is one of the best-preserved castles in Britain. Keepers of the Forest of Drum for generations, the family acquired lands here by marriage and later built a castle, completed in 1596. The National Trust for Scotland cares for the castle, which is furnished with many original pieces and family portraits. Outside are grand gardens with calculated symmetry and clipped yew hedges. Make sure you browse the Horsemill bookshop and sample the tasty baked goods in the tearoom. There's an adventure park for kids,

CLOSE UP

Which Castle Is Right for You?

Because it's nearly impossible to see all the castles in this area, we've noted the prime characteristics of some key places to help you decide which to visit.

■ **Balmoral:** The Queen's home, this is where Queen Victoria and the Royal Family fell in love with Scotland and all things Scottish. Expect baronial largesse and groomed grounds, though you don't see much inside.

■ **Braemar:** Offering memorable insight into the lives of the Scottish landed gentry, this recently restored castle heaves with memorabilia and mementos of the fascinating Farquharsons, who still hold their clan gathering here.

■ **Crathes:** Expect tight quarters, notable family portraits, and a network of walled gardens at this well-preserved seat of the Burnett family. Its adventure park keeps the kids occupied.

■ **Dunnottar:** The dramatic, scene-stealing, cliff-top location of Mel Gibson's *Hamlet* (1991), the ruins of this 14th-century tower house by the sea are unbeatable.

■ **Fraser:** Considered the grandest castle in Aberdeenshire, Castle Fraser has opulent period furnishings and woodland walks that make for a rewarding day.

■ **Fyvie:** This 14th-century castle underwent a luxurious Edwardian makeover. Come here for an awesome art collection, rich interiors, and haunting history.

and the staff organizes activities that are fun and educational. ✉ *Off A93Banchory* ☎ *0844/493–2166* 🌐 *www.nts.org.uk* 🎟 *£12* 🕒 *Apr.–Oct., daily 10–4:45; Nov.–Mar., weekends 10:30–3:45; last admission 45 mins before closing.*

OFF THE BEATEN PATH

Queen's View. To reach one of the most spectacular vistas in northeast Scotland—stretching across the Howe of Cromar to Lochnagar—take the B9094 due north from Aboyne (12 miles west of Banchory), then turn left onto the B9119 for 6 miles.

WHERE TO STAY

$$$ HOTEL

🏨 **Raemoir House Hotel.** Dating from the 16th to 19th centuries, this baronial home 2 miles north of Banchory makes you feel as if you're on the set of a period drama. **Pros:** charming old building; extensive grounds; staff is informal and efficient. **Cons:** pricey rates. [$] *Rooms from: £165* ✉ *Off A980, Raemoir* ☎ *01330/824884* 🌐 *www.raemoir.com* 🛏 *17 rooms, 3 suites* 🍴 *Breakfast.*

BALLATER

20 miles west of Crathes Castle, 43 miles west of Aberdeen.

The handsome holiday resort of Ballater, once noted for the curative properties of its waters, has profited from the proximity of the royals, nearby at Balmoral Castle. You might be amused by the array of "by royal appointment" signs proudly hanging from many of its various shops (even monarchs need bakers and butchers). Take time to stroll around this well-laid-out community. The railway station houses the tourist information center and a display on the glories of the Great North of Scotland branch railway line, closed in the 1960s along with so many others in this country.

The locals have long taken the town's royal connection in stride. To this day, the hundreds who line the road when the queen and her family arrive for services at the family's parish church at Crathie are invariably visitors to Deeside—one of Balmoral's attractions for the monarch has always been the villagers' respect for royal privacy.

GETTING HERE AND AROUND

There's good train service to Aberdeen, but you'll need to catch a bus to get to this and other towns near A93. Stagecoach Bluebird buses numbers 201 and 202 operate hourly to all the main towns, including Ballater. Otherwise, it's an easy car trip.

ESSENTIALS

Visitor Information Ballater Visitor Information Centre ⊠ *Old Royal Station, Station Sq.* ☎ *01339/755306.*

EXPLORING

Balmoral Castle. The enormous parking lot is indicative of the public's appreciation of Balmoral Castle, one of Queen Elizabeth II's favorite family retreats. Only the formal gardens, the ballroom, and the carriage hall are on view, with their exhibitions of royal artifacts, commemorative china, and native wildlife. Thanks to Victoria and Albert, who built the house to Prince Albert's design, stags' heads abound, the bagpipes wailed incessantly, and the garish Stewart tartan was used for everything from carpets to chair covers. A more somber Duff tartan, black and green to blend with the environment, was later adopted.

Queen Elizabeth II follows her predecessors' routine in spending a holiday of about six weeks in Deeside, usually from mid-August to the end of September. During this time Balmoral is closed to visitors, including the grounds. You can take a guided tour in November and December; if the weather is crisp and bright, the estate is at its most dramatic and romantic. You're only allowed a peek inside, but the Royal Cottage is where Queen Victoria spent much of her time. You can see the table where she took breakfast and wrote her correspondence.

Around and about Balmoral, which is 7 miles west of Ballater, are some notable spots—Cairn O'Mount, Cambus O'May, and the Cairngorms from the Linn of Dee—and some of them may be seen on pony-trekking expeditions, which use Balmoral stalking ponies and go around the grounds and estate. Tempted by the setting? Balmoral Castle has five cottages (some very large) for rent by the week at certain times. They are atmospheric but can be basic. ⊠ *A93* ☎ *01339/742534* ⊕ *www. balmoralcastle.com* 🖻 *£10* ⊙ *Apr.–July, daily 10–5; last admission 1 hr before closing. Guided tours on certain dates in Nov. and Dec.*

17

CLOSE UP

Balmoral, Queen Victoria's Retreat

Some credit Sir Walter Scott with having opened up Scotland for tourism through his poems and novels. But it was probably Queen Victoria (1819–1901) who gave Scottish tourism its real momentum when, in 1842, she first came to Scotland and when, in 1847—on orders of a doctor, who thought the relatively dry climate of upper Deeside would suit her—she bought Balmoral. The pretty little castle was knocked down to make room for a much grander house in full-blown Scottish baronial style, designed by her husband, Prince Albert (1819–61), in 1855. It had a veritable rash of tartanitis. Before long the entire Deeside and the region north were dotted with country houses and mock-baronial châteaux.

"It seems like a dream to be here in our dear Highland Home again," Queen Victoria wrote. "Every year my heart becomes more fixed in this dear Paradise." Victoria loved Balmoral more for its setting than its house, so be sure to take in its pleasant gardens. Year by year Victoria and Albert added to the estate, taking over neighboring houses, securing the forest and moorland around it, and developing deer stalking and grouse shooting here.

WHERE TO EAT AND STAY

$$$$ MODERN EUROPEAN 🍴 **Darroch Learg.** On a rise that gives you an unobstructed view of the majestic Grampian Mountains, this restaurant has an old country charm. The food, however, fuses Scottish classics with modern touches: ravioli with smoked haddock, loin of local venison with goat cheese gnocchi, and warm chocolate cake with Deeside cream are a few of the creations. The staff is unpretentious and efficient, all the while keeping a quiet eye on your needs. There are more than 200 wines in the cellar. [$] *Average main: £43* ✉ *Braemar Rd.* ☎ *01339/755443* 🌐 *www.darrochlearg.co.uk.*

$$ B&B/INN 🏨 **Deeside Hotel.** With plenty of period charm, this Victorian-era house offers old-fashioned hospitality and simple, understated comfort. **Pros:** unpretentious feel; good price; forever-cheerful staff. **Cons:** a few bedrooms on the small side; restaurant can get very busy. [$] *Rooms from: £120* ✉ *45 Braemar Rd.* ☎ *01339/755420* 🌐 *www.deesidehotel.co.uk* 🛏 *9 rooms* 🍽 *Breakfast.*

SHOPPING

Countrywear. At either location of Countrywear, men can find everything that's necessary for Highland country living, including fishing tackle, natty tweeds, and that flexible garment popular in Scotland between seasons: the body warmer. ✉ *15 and 35 Bridge St.* ☎ *01339/755453* 🌐 *www.countrywearballater.co.uk.*

McEwan Gallery. A mile west of Ballater, the McEwan Gallery displays fine paintings, watercolors, prints, and books (many with a Scottish or golf theme) in an unusual house built by the Swiss artist Rudolphe Christen in 1902. ✉ *A939* ☎ *01339/755429* 🌐 *www.mcewangallery.com.*

BRAEMAR

17 miles west of Ballater, 60 miles west of Aberdeen, 51 miles north of Perth via A93.

Synonymous with the British monarchy, due to its closeness to Balmoral, this village is popular year-round as a base for walkers and climbers enjoying the Grampian Mountains. There isn't really much else going on in Braemar, although the castle is well worth a couple of hours and the famous Highland Gathering every year is a big draw.

GETTING HERE AND AROUND

The town is on A93; there's bus service here, as to other towns on the road, but the closest train station is Aberdeen.

ESSENTIALS

Visitor Information Braemar Visitor Information Centre ⊠ *The Mews, Mar Rd.* ☎ *01339/741600* ⊕ *www.braemarscotland.co.uk.*

EXPLORING

Braemar Castle. On the northern outskirts of town, Braemar Castle dates from the 17th century, although its defensive walls, in the shape of a pointed star, came later. At Braemar (the *braes,* or slopes, of the district of Mar), the standard, or rebel flag, was first raised at the start of the unsuccessful Jacobite Rebellion of 1715. About 30 years later, during the last Jacobite rebellion, Braemar Castle was strengthened and garrisoned by government troops. From the early 1800s the castle was the clan seat of the Farquharsons, who hold their clan reunion here every summer.

Thanks to the commitment of local volunteers, a remarkable 2008 renovation restored Braemar back to the home it would have been in the early 20th century, complete with all the necessary comforts and family memorabilia. A dozen rooms are on view, including the Laird's dayroom with a plush daybed and the kitchen. ⊠ *Off A93* ☎ *01339/741219* ⊕ *www.braemarcastle.co.uk* ⚑ *£6* ☉ *Apr.–June, Sept., and Oct., weekends 11–4; July and Aug., Wed. 11–4 and weekends 11–4.*

Braemar Highland Gathering. The village of Braemar is associated with the Braemar Highland Gathering, held the first Saturday in September. Although there are many such gatherings celebrated throughout Scotland, this one is distinguished by the presence of the Royal Family. Competitions and events include hammer throwing, caber tossing, and bagpipe playing. If you plan to attend, book your accommodations months in advance. ■ TIP→ Be sure to buy tickets about six months in advance, as they do sell out. ⊠ *Princess Royal and Duke of Fife Memorial Park, Broombank Terr.* ⊕ *www.braemargathering.org.*

Braemar Highland Heritage Centre. You can find out more about local lore at the Braemar Highland Heritage Centre, in a converted stable block in the middle of town. The center tells the history of the village with displays and a film. The tourist office and a gift shop are here, too. ⊠ *The Mews, Mar Rd.* ☎ *01339/741944* ⚑ *Free* ☉ *Jan.–May, Nov., and Dec., Mon.–Sat. 10:30–1:30 and 2–5, Sun. 1–4; June, Sept., and Oct., daily 9–5; July and Aug., daily 9–6.*

17

WHERE TO EAT AND STAY

$$
BRITISH
✕ **Moorfield House.** Although the dining room may be underwhelming and the menu limited, when your plate is set before you, you'll understand why this is considered one of the best eateries in Braemar. The chef—who learned his craft by catering for big groups—offers unpretentious yet superb home-style cooking. Simple main dishes like panfried fish with garden vegetables, followed by a dessert like a seasonal crumble, will satisfy even the most exacting gourmand. ⓢ *Average main: £16 ⊠ Moorfield House Hotel, Chapel Brae* ☎ *013397/41244* ⊕ *www. moorfieldhousehotel.com.*

$
CAFÉ
✕ **Taste.** It's strangely difficult to eat like a queen in Braemar, but this chalet-style café serves her subjects well, with the tastiest, freshest soups and sandwiches (Scottish cheddar and homemade meat loaf are two options). You can order moist cakes and tasty lattes here, too. ⓢ *Average main: £6 ⊠ Auchendryne Sq.* ☎ *01339/741425* ⊕ *www.taste-braemar.co.uk* ⊟ *No credit cards* ⊙ *No dinner. Closed Sun.*

$
B&B/INN
Fodor's Choice
★
⛉ **Ivy Cottage.** A relative newcomer in Braemar, this B&B should up the game of its competitors. **Pros:** relaxing rooms; owners who go out of their way to make you feel at home. **Cons:** next to the church, so expect bells on Sunday morning. ⓢ *Rooms from: £70 ⊠ Cluniebank Rd.* ☎ *01339/741642* ⊕ *www.ivycottagebraemar.co.uk* ⇋ *3 rooms, 2 self-catering flats* ⦿*Multiple meal plans.*

GOLF

Braemar Golf Course. The tricky 18-hole Braemar Golf Course, founded in 1902, is laden with foaming waters. Erratic duffers, take note: the compassionate course managers have installed, near the water, poles with little nets on the end for those occasional shots that may go awry. ⊠ *Cluny Bank Rd.* ☎ *01339/741618* ⊕ *www.braemargolfclub.co.uk* ⛳ *Green fee: £25* ⚐ *18 holes, 4935 yds, SSS 64.*

ALFORD

29 miles east of Braemar, 28 miles west of Aberdeen.

A plain and sturdy settlement in the Howe (Hollow) of Alford, this town gives those who have grown somewhat weary of castle hopping a break: it has a museum instead. Castle Fraser is nearby, though.

GETTING HERE AND AROUND

The town is on A944.

ESSENTIALS

Visitor Information Alford Visitor Information Centre ⊠ *Grampian Transport Museum, Montgarrie Rd.* ☎ *01975/562052* ⊕ *www.aberdeen-grampian.com* ⊙ *Apr.–Sept., daily 10–5, Oct., daily 10–4.*

EXPLORING

Fodor's Choice
★
Castle Fraser. The massive Castle Fraser is the ancestral home of the Frasers and one of the largest of the castles of Mar; it's certainly a contender as one of the grandest castles in the northeast. Although the well-furnished building shows a variety of styles reflecting the taste of its owners from the 15th through the 19th centuries, its design is typical of the cavalcade of castles in the region, and for good reason.

CLOSE UP

Language and the Scots

"Much," said Doctor Johnson, "may be made of a Scotchman if he be caught young." This quote sums up, even today, the attitude of some English people—confident in their English, the language of parliament and much of the media—toward the Scots language. The Scots have long been made to feel uncomfortable about their mother tongue, and until the 1970s (and in some private schools, even today) they were encouraged to mimic the dialect of the Thames Valley ("standard English") in order to "get on" in life.

LOWLAND SCOTS

The Scots language (that is, Lowland Scots, not Gaelic) was a northern form of Middle English and in its day was the language used in the court and in literature. It borrowed from Scandinavian, Dutch, French, and Gaelic. After a series of historical blows—such as the decamping of the Scottish court to England after 1603 and the printing of the King James Bible in English but not in Scots—it declined as a literary or official language. It survives in various forms but is virtually an underground language, spoken among ordinary folk, especially in its heartland, in the northeast.

You may even find yourself exporting a few useful words, such as *dreich* (gloomy), *glaikit* (acting and looking foolish), or *dinna fash* (don't worry), all of which are much more expressive than their English equivalents.

Some Scottish words are used and understood across the entire country (and world), such as *wee* (small), *aye* (yes), *lassie* (girl), and *bonny* (pretty). Regional variations are evident even in the simplest of greetings. When you meet someone in the Borders, *Whit*

fettle? (What state are you in?) or *Hou ye lestin?* (How are you lasting?) may throw you for a loop; elsewhere you could hear *Hoo's yer doos?* (How are your pigeons?). If a group of Scots takes a fancy to you at the pub, you may be asked to *Come intil the body o the kirk,* and if all goes well, your departure may be met with a jovial farewell, *haste ye back* (return soon).

GAELIC

Scottish Gaelic, an entirely different language, is still spoken across the Highlands and Hebrides. There's also a large Gaelic-speaking population in Glasgow as a result of the Celtic diaspora—islanders migrating to Glasgow in search of jobs in the 19th century. Speakers of Gaelic in Scotland were once persecuted, after the failure of the 18th-century Jacobite rebellions. Official persecution has now turned to enthusiastic support, as the Gaelic lobby has won substantial public funds to underwrite television programming, public signage, and language classes for new learners.

One of the joys of Scottish television is watching Gaelic news programs on BBC Alba to see how the ancient language copes with such topics as nuclear energy, the Internet, and the latest band to hit the charts. A number of Gaelic words have been absorbed into English: *banshee* (a wailing female spirit), *galore* (plenty), *slob* (a slovenly person), and *brat* (a spoiled or unruly child).

To experience Gaelic language and culture in all its glory, you can attend the Royal National Mod—a competition-based festival with speeches, drama, and music, all in Gaelic—held in a different location every year.

17

This—along with many others, including Midmar, Craigievar, Crathes, and Glenbuchat—was designed by a family of master masons called Bell. There are plenty of family items, but don't miss the two Turret Rooms—one of which is the trophy room—and Major Smiley's Room. He married into the family but is famous for having been one of the escapees from Colditz (a high-security prisoner of war camp) during World War II. The walled garden includes a 19th-century knot garden, with colorful flower beds, box hedging, gravel paths, and splendid herbaceous borders. Have lunch in the tearoom or the picnic area. ⊠ *Off A944, 8 miles southeast of Alford* ☎ *0844/493–2164* ⊕ *www.nts.org. uk* ⊠ *£10* ⊙ *Apr.–June, Sept., and Oct., Wed.–Sat. noon–5; July and Aug., daily 11–5; last admission 45 mins before closing.*

FAMILY **Grampian Transport Museum.** The entertaining and enthusiastically run Grampian Transport Museum specializes in road-based means of locomotion, backed up by an archives and library. Its collection of buses and trams is second to none, but the Craigievar Express, a steam-driven creation invented by the local postman to deliver mail more efficiently, is the most unusual. There's a small café that offers tea, baked goods, and ice cream. ⊠ *Montgarrie Rd.* ☎ *01975/562292* ⊕ *www.gtm.org.uk* ⊠ *£9.50* ⊙ *Apr.–Sept., daily 10–5; Oct., daily 10–4.*

THE NORTHEAST AND THE MALT WHISKY TRAIL

North of Deeside lies Speyside—the valley, or strath, of the River Spey—famed for its whisky distilleries, some of which it promotes in a signposted trail. Distilling scotch is not an intrinsically spectacular process. It involves pure water, malted barley, and sometimes peat smoke, then a lot of bubbling and fermentation, all of which cause a number of odd smells. The result is a prestigious product with a fascinating range of flavors that you may either enjoy immensely or not at all.

Instead of closely following the Malt Whisky Trail, dip into it and blend visits to distilleries with some other aspects of the county of Moray, particularly its coastline. Whisky notwithstanding, Moray's scenic qualities, low rainfall, and other reassuring weather statistics are worth remembering. You can also sample the northeastern seaboard, including some of the best but least-known coastal scenery in Scotland.

DUFFTOWN

22 miles northwest of Alford, 54 miles west of Aberdeen.

On one of the Spey tributaries, Dufftown was planned in 1817 by the Earl of Fife. Its simple cross layout with a square and a large clock tower (originally from Banff and now the site of the visitor center) is typical of a small Scottish town built in the 19th century. Its simplicity is made all the more stark by the brooding, heather-clad hills that rise around it. Dufftown is convenient to a number of distilleries.

Tours at Glenfiddich Distillery include older buildings and a modern visitor center—plus a wee dram.

GETTING HERE AND AROUND

To get here from Aberdeen, drive west on A96 and A920; then turn west at Huntly. It's not easy or quick, but you can take the train to Elgin or Keith and then the bus to Dufftown.

ESSENTIALS

Visitor Information Dufftown Visitor Information Centre ⊠ *The Square* ☎ *01340/820501* ⊘ *Apr.–Oct.*

EXPLORING

Fodor's Choice
★

Balvenie Distillery. Offering just a handful of tours each week, you'd think that Balvenie Distillery didn't want visitors. Yet as soon as you step into the old manager's office—now gently restored and fitted with knotted-elm furniture—you realize Balvenie just wants to make sure that all visitors get to see, smell, and feel the magic of the making of this malt. Balvenie is unusual because it has its own cooperage with six coopers hard at work turning the barrels. During the three-hour tour you'll see the mashing, fermentation, and distillation process, culminating in a five-malt tasting session. ⊠ *Balvenie St.* ☎ *01340/822062* ⊕ *www.thebalvenie.com* 🎫 *£35* ⊘ *Tours Mon.–Thurs. at 10 and 2, Fri. at 10.*

Glenfiddich Distillery. Many make Glenfiddich Distillery their first stop on the Malt Whisky Trail. The independent company of William Grant and Sons Limited was the first to realize the tourist potential of the distilling process. The company began offering tours around the typical pagoda-roof malting buildings and subsequently built an entertaining visitor center. Besides a free 20-minute tour of the distillery there's a two-hour in-depth Connoisseurs' Tour (£20; reserve ahead in summer) that includes a special nosing and tasting session. Check out the

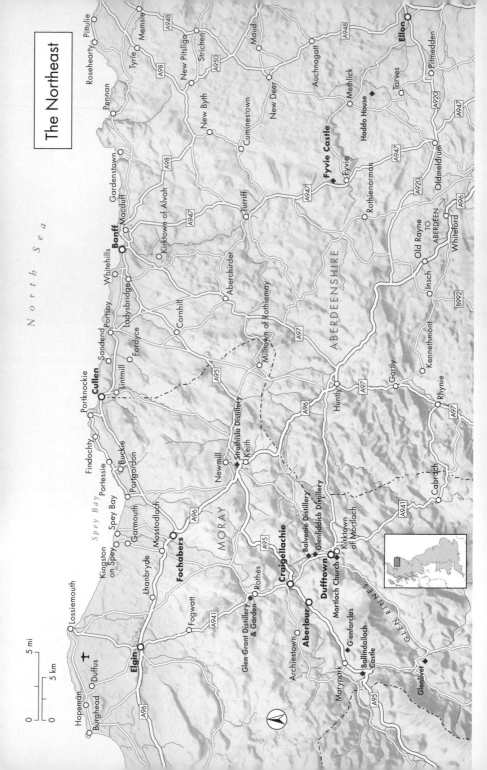

The Northeast

North Sea

Glenfiddich Distillery Art Gallery, showing the work of international artists. ✉ *A941, ½ mile north of Dufftown* ☎ *01340/820373* 🌐 *www.glenfiddich.com* 🎟 *Free* 🕒 *Easter–mid-Oct., daily 9:30–4:30; mid-Oct.–Easter, weekends 9:30–4:30.*

Keith and Dufftown Railway. Leaving from Dufftown twice a day on weekends, this restored locomotive chugs 11 miles around forests, fields, and rivers. It passes Drummuir Castle on its way to Keith, home of the Strathisla Distillery. The Buffer Stop restaurant car at the Dufftown Station serves snacks, scones, and tea. Reservations are a good idea. ✉ *Dufftown Station, Station Rd.* ☎ *01340/821181* 🌐 *www.keith-dufftown-railway.co.uk* 🎟 *£6.50* 🕒 *Easter–Sept., weekends.*

Strathisla Distillery. Whisky lovers should take the B9014 11 miles northeast from Dufftown—or alternatively, ride the Keith Dufftown Railway—to see one of Scotland's most iconic distilleries, the Strathisla Distillery, with its cobblestone courtyard and famous double pagoda roofs. Stretching over the picturesque River Isla, the Strathisla Distillery was built in 1786 and now produces the main component of the Chivas Regal blend. Guided tours take you to the mash house, tun room, and still house—all pretty much the same as they were when production began. The tour ends with a tasting session. ✉ *Seafield Ave., Keith* ☎ *01542/783044* 🌐 *www.chivas.com* 🎟 *£6* 🕒 *Apr.–Oct., Mon.–Sat. 9:30–4, Sun. noon–4.*

WHERE TO EAT AND STAY

$$$ FRENCH Fodor's Choice ★

🍴 **La Faisanderie.** Gourmands from around the region descend on La Faisanderie for a truly French gastronomic experience. A large, distillery-inspired fresco in the plain dining room adds some panache to the tall windows, creaky wood floors, and crisp white tablecloths. The French and English owners use fine cuts of local beef and game and seafood caught on the coast to create classic dishes with not-too-heavy sauces. Worth trying is the lamb with pinhead oatmeal risotto served with a honey and whisky sauce, and the chanson of russet apples with cinnamon ice cream. [$] *Average main: £20* ✉ *2 Balvenie St.* ☎ *01340/821273* 🌐 *www.lafaisanderie.co.uk* 🕒 *Closed Tues. and Wed. in Oct.–Mar.*

$ B&B/INN

🏨 **Castleview.** Next to the babbling Burn of Mackalea, the tranquil Castleview has rooms that are quite small but beautifully dressed and well maintained. **Pros:** colorful garden; fabulous views; bountiful breakfasts. **Cons:** half-hour walk into town; not for anyone with a cat allergy. [$] *Rooms from: £70* ✉ *A920, 2½ miles east of Dufftown, Auchindoun* ☎ *01340/820941* 🌐 *www.castleviewdufftown.com* 🛏 *3 rooms* 🍽 *Breakfast.*

SHOPPING

Collector's Cabin. Two adjoining shops—one with Scottish silver, fossils, and book illustrations, the other with kilts, ceramics, and other curiosities—are filled with conversation starters. This is truly a trove worth delving into. ✉ *22 and 24 Balvenie St.* ☎ *01340/821393.*

17

Whisky, the Water of Life

Conjured from an innocuous mix of malted barley, water, and yeast, malt whisky is for many synonymous with Scotland. Clans produced whisky for hundreds of years before it emerged as Scotland's national drink and major export. Today those centuries of expertise result in a sublimely subtle drink with many different layers of flavor. Each distillery produces a malt with—to the expert—instantly identifiable, predominant notes peculiarly its own.

WHISKY TYPES AND STYLES

There are two types of whisky: malt and grain. Malt whisky, generally acknowledged to have a more sophisticated bouquet and flavor, is made with malted barley—barley that is soaked in water until the grains germinate and then is dried to halt the germination, all of which adds extra flavor and a touch of sweetness to the brew. Grain whisky also contains malted barley, but with the addition of unmalted barley and maize.

Blended whiskies, which make up many of the leading brands, usually balance malt- and grain-whisky distillations; deluxe blends contain a higher percentage of malts. Blends that contain several malt whiskies are called "vatted malts." Whisky connoisseurs often prefer to taste the single malts: the unblended whisky from a single distillery.

In simple terms, malt whiskies may be classified into "eastern" and "western" in style, with the whisky made in the east of Scotland, for example in Speyside, being lighter and sweeter than the products of the western isles, which often have a taste of peat smoke or even iodine.

The production process is, by comparison, relatively straightforward: just malt your barley, mash it, ferment it and distill it, then mature to perfection. To find out the details, join a distillery tour, and be rewarded with a dram. Check out ⊕ *www.scotlandwhisky.com* for more information.

TASTING WHISKY

When tasting whisky, follow these simple steps. First, pour a dram. Turn and tilt the glass to coat the sides. Smell the whisky, "nosing" to inhale the heady aromas. If you want, you can add a little water and turn the glass gently to watch it "marry" with the whisky, nosing as you go. Take a wee sip and swirl it over your tongue and sense what connoisseurs call the "mouthfeel." Swallow and admire the finish. Repeat until convinced it's a good malt!

CRAIGELLACHIE

4 miles northwest of Dufftown via A941.

Renowned as an angling resort, Craigellachie, like so many settlements on the River Spey, is sometimes enveloped in the malty reek of the local industry. Glen Grant is one of the distilleries nearby. The Spey itself is crossed by a handsome suspension bridge, designed by noted engineer Thomas Telford (1757–1834) in 1814 and now bypassed by the modern road.

GETTING HERE AND AROUND

The town is on A491; it's best to drive here, as public transportation is infrequent and complicated.

EXPLORING

Glen Grant Distillery & Garden. James Grant founded a distillery in 1840 when he was only 25, and it was the first in the country to be electrically powered. This place will come as a welcome relief to companions of dedicated Malt Whisky Trail followers, because in addition to the distillery there's a large and beautiful garden. It's planted and tended as Grant envisioned, with orchards and woodland walks, log bridges over waterfalls, a magnificent lily pond, and azaleas and rhododendrons in profusion. Using peculiarly tall stills and special purifiers that follow a design introduced over a century ago, Glen Grant produces a distinctive pale-gold whisky with an almost floral or fruity finish. The tour is excellent value, with perhaps the friendliest guides and certainly the most generous tastings. ⊠ *A941, Rothes* ☎ *01340/832118* ⊕ *www. glengrant.com* ✉ *£3.50* ⊗ *Apr–Oct., daily 9:30–4; Nov.–Mar., Mon.– Sat. 9:30–4, Sun. noon–5.*

Speyside Cooperage and Visitor Centre. A major stop on the Malt Whisky Trail, the huge Speyside Cooperage and Visitor Centre is a must for all whisky fans. Retired coopers will talk you through the making of the casks, a surprisingly physical and dramatic process that uses the same tools and skills employed for hundreds of years. Inside you can watch highly skilled craftspeople make and repair oak barrels used in the local whisky industry. The Acorn to Cask exhibit tells all about the ancient craft of coopering. There's a cottage café with huge cakes and sandwiches for those in need of fortification. ⊠ *Dufftown Rd.* ☎ *01340/871108* ⊕ *www.speysidecooperage.co.uk* ✉ *£3.50* ⊗ *Weekdays 9–4.*

WHERE TO STAY

$$
B&B/INN

☷ **Highlander Inn.** Don't be fooled by the rather alpine exterior: this very Scottish hotel prides itself on its whisky bar and its friendly welcome. **Pros:** simple accommodations; warm atmosphere; great bar. **Cons:** dated decor. Ⓢ *Rooms from: £103* ⊠ *Victoria St.* ☎ *01340/881446* ⊕ *www.whiskyinn.com* ⇥ *5 rooms* ❙❍❙ *Breakfast.*

ABERLOUR

2 miles southwest of Craigellachie.

Aberlour, often listed as Charlestown of Aberlour on maps, is a handsome little burgh, essentially Victorian in style, though actually founded in 1812 by the local landowner. The names of the noted local whisky stills are Cragganmore, Aberlour, and Glenfarclas; Glenlivet and Cardhu are also nearby. Also in Aberlour is Walkers, famous for producing tins of buttery, crumbly shortbread since 1898.

GETTING HERE AND AROUND

Aberlour is on A95; public transportation here is infrequent.

CHOOSING A DISTILLERY TOUR

Like whiskies, distillery tours are not the same, though you'll usually spend about an hour or two at each place. The company's history, size, and commercial savvy create different experiences. You should also investigate any special in-depth tours if you're willing to pay extra.

Balvenie: This distillery's tour is for those who want to understand the details of distilling. No other distillery lets you see and smell the malting floor before watching the coopers turn their barrels.

Glen Grant: The distillery tour is good, but the gardens of Major Grant are sublime. He traveled the world collecting species and created a Victorian garden that has been gloriously restored.

Glenfarclas: This proud family-owned still may not provide the slickness of the Glenfiddich tour, but the quiet passion of the still workers

is more powerful than a dram of the stuff.

Glenfiddich: Owned by the same family since day one, this distillery offers both entry-level and enthusiasts' tours that cover the older buildings and the swankier visitor center.

Glenlivet: It's a beautiful drive to this, the first licensed distillery in the Highlands. You'll learn the fascinating story of Glenlivet's founder, George Smith.

Speyside Cooperage: Although this isn't a distillery, real whisky enthusiasts shouldn't miss a visit to one of the few remaining cooperages in Scotland. See just how much craft goes into making and treating these precious barrels.

Strathisla: Home of Chivas, not a malt but a fine blended whisky, this is perhaps one of the prettiest and most compact distilleries in the northeast.

EXPLORING

Ballindalloch Castle. The family home of the Macpherson-Grants since 1546, Ballindalloch Castle—known as the Pearl of the North—is the quintessential castle you've probably seen in a miniseries made by the BBC. You can wander around the beautifully kept rooms and meticulously tended gardens at your leisure; you may even bump into the lord and lady of the manor, who live here all year. There's also a splendid tea shop offering large slices of cake. Anglers take note: The estate offers a limited number of permits for fishing on the banks of the Spey and the Avon. It's 8 miles southwest of Craigellachie. ⊠ *Off A95* ☏ *01807/500205* ⊕ *www.ballindallochcastle.co.uk* 🎫 *£10* ⊙ *Easter–Sept., Sun.–Fri. 10:30–5:30.*

Glenfarclas. In an age when most small distilleries have been taken over by multinationals, Glenfarclas remains family-owned, passed down from father to son since 1865. That link to the past is most visible among its low buildings, where the retired still sits outside: if you didn't know what it was, you could mistake it for part of a submarine. The tours end with tastings in the superlative Ship Room, the intact lounge of an ocean liner called the *Empress of Australia*. An in-depth Connoisseur's Tour and tasting is available for £25. ⊠ *Off A95, Ballindalloch*

☎ 01807/500345 🌐 www.glenfarclas.co.uk 🎟 £5 ⏲ Oct.–Mar., weekdays 10–4; Apr.–Jun., weekdays 10–5; July–Sept., weekdays 10–5, Sun. 10–4.

Glenlivet. The famous Glenlivet was the first licensed distillery in the Highlands, founded in 1824 by George Smith. Today it produces one of the best-known 12-year-old single malts in the world. The free distillery tour reveals the inside of the huge bonded warehouse where the whisky steeps in oak casks. The tour has two aspects: the Spirit of the Glen examines how unique factors come together to make this nectar, and the Glenlivet Legacy looks at the dream of the distillery's founder. There are two other tours—Spirit of the Malt (£30) and the Legacy Experience (£60)—for those who can't get enough. There's a coffee shop with baked goods and, of course, a whisky shop. Glenlivet is 10 miles southwest of Aberlour via A95 and B9008. *✉ Off B9008, Ballindalloch ☎ 01340/821720 🌐 www.glenlivet.com 🎟 Free ⏲ Apr.–Oct., Mon.–Sat. 9:30–5, Sun. noon–5.*

WHERE TO EAT AND STAY

$ CAFÉ 🍴 **Old Pantry.** This pleasantly rustic corner restaurant and gift shop overlooks Aberlour's tree-shaded central square. The kitchen serves—albeit sometimes slowly—everything from a cup of coffee with a sticky cake at teatime to a three-course spread of soup, roasted meat, and traditional pudding. *[$] Average main: £9 ✉ The Square ☎ 01340/871617 ⏲ No dinner Oct.–May.*

$$ B&B/INN Fodor's Choice ★ 🏨 **Cardhu Country House.** This once-abandoned manse (minister's house) looks as if it has always been loved and lived in: huge bedrooms with wooden floors, antique fireplaces, and large beds dressed in Harris tweed throws are married to contemporary bathrooms. **Pros:** period charm and modern comforts; tasty meals. **Cons:** you need a car to get here. *[$] Rooms from: £120 ✉ Off B9102, Knockando ☎ 01340/810895 🌐 www.cardhucountryhouse.co.uk 🛏 6 rooms 🍽 Breakfast.*

$ B&B/INN 🏨 **Mash Tun.** Curvy yet sturdy, this former station hotel harks back to a time when Aberlour was a busy holiday destination on the Aberdeen–Aviemore train line. **Pros:** superb accommodations; tasty meals; great atmosphere in the restaurant and bar. **Cons:** book well ahead in summer. *[$] Rooms from: £97 ✉ 8 Broomfield Sq. ☎ 01340/881771 🌐 www.mashtun-aberlour.com 🛏 4 rooms, 1 suite 🍽 Breakfast.*

ELGIN

13 miles north of Aberlour, 69 miles northwest of Aberdeen, 41 miles east of Inverness.

As the center of the fertile Laigh (low-lying lands) of Moray, Elgin has been of local importance for centuries. Sheltered by great hills to the south, the city lies between two major rivers, the Spey and the Findhorn. Beginning in the 13th century, Elgin became an important religious center, a cathedral city with a walled town growing up around the cathedral and adjacent to the original settlement.

Elgin prospered, and by the early 18th century it became a mini-Edinburgh of the north and a place where country gentlemen spent their winters. It even echoed Edinburgh in carrying out wide-scale reconstruction in the 18th century. Many fine neoclassical buildings survive today despite much misguided demolition in the late 20th century for better traffic flow. But the central main-street plan and some of the older little streets and *wynds* (alleyways) remain. You can also see Elgin's past in the arcaded shop fronts—some of which date from the late 17th century—on the main shopping street.

GETTING HERE AND AROUND
Elgin is on the A96 road from Aberdeen to Inverness. The A941 runs north from the distillery area to the city. There's a train stop here on the line that links Aberdeen and Inverness: Aberdeen is 90 minutes away.

ESSENTIALS
Visitor Information Elgin Visitor Information Centre ⊠ *Cooper Park* ☎ *01343/562608* ○ *Mon.–Sat. 10–4.*

EXPLORING
Elgin Cathedral. Cooper Park contains a magnificent ruin, the Elgin Cathedral, consecrated in 1224. Its eventful story included devastation by fire: a 1390 act of retaliation by bandit Alexander Stewart (circa 1343–1405), the Wolf of Badenoch. The illegitimate son of King David II (1324–71) had sought revenge for his excommunication by the bishop of Moray. The cathedral was rebuilt but finally fell into disuse after the Reformation in 1560. By 1567 the highest authority in the land, the Regent Earl of Moray, had stripped the lead from the roof to pay for his army. Thus ended the career of the religious seat known as the Lamp of the North. Some traces of the cathedral settlement survive—the gateway Pann's Port and the Bishop's Palace—although they've been drastically altered. ⊠ *Cooper Park* ☎ *01343/547171* ⊕ *www.historic-scotland.gov. uk* ⊠ *£5.50; £7.20 with Spynie Palace* ○ *Apr.–Sept., daily 9:30–5:30; Oct.–Mar., Sat.–Wed. 9:30–4:30; last admission ½ hr before closing.*

GOLF
Moray Golf Club. Discover the relatively mild microclimate of what vacationing Victorians dubbed the Moray Riviera, as Tom Morris did in 1889 when he was inspired by the lay of the natural links. Henry Cotton's New Course (1979) has tighter fairways and smaller greens. ■TIP➔ A handicap certificate is required for the Old Course. ⊠ *Stotfield Rd., Lossiemouth* ☎ *01343/812018* ⊕ *www.moraygolf.co.uk* ⊠ *Green fee: Old Course £70; New Course £30; joint ticket £80* ⚐ *Old Course: 18 holes, 6995 yds, par 71; New Course: 18 holes, 6008 yds, par 69* ○ *Daily.*

SHOPPING
Gordon and MacPhail. An outstanding delicatessen and wine merchant, Gordon and MacPhail also stocks rare malt whiskies. This is a good place to shop for gifts for your foodie friends. ⊠ *58–60 South St.* ☎ *01343/545110* ⊕ *www.gordonandmacphail.com.*

Johnstons of Elgin. This woolen mill has a worldwide reputation for its luxury fabrics, especially cashmere. The large shop stocks not only the firm's own products, but also top-quality Scottish crafts. There's a coffee shop on the premises. Free tours of the mill must be booked in advance. ✉ *Newmill Rd.* ☎ *01343/554094* ⊕ *www.johnstonscashmere.com.*

FOCHABERS

9 miles east of Elgin.

With its hanging baskets of fuchsia in summer and its perfectly mowed village square, Fochabers has a cared-for charm that makes you want to stop here, even just to stretch your legs. Lying just to the south of the River Spey, the former market town was founded in 1776 by the Duke of Gordon. The duke moved the village from its original site because it was too close to Gordon Castle. Famous today for being home to the Baxters brand of soups and jams, Fochabers is near some of the best berry fields: come and pick your own in the summer months.

GETTING HERE AND AROUND

Fochabers is not on the Inverness-to-Aberdeen train line, but there is an hourly bus service (Stagecoach Bluebird number 10) from Fochabers to Elgin. It's near the junction of A98 and A96.

EXPLORING

Fochabers Folk Museum. Once over the Spey Bridge and past the cricket ground (a very unusual sight in Scotland), you can find the symmetrical, 18th-century Fochabers village square lined with antiques dealers. Through one of these shops, Pringle Antiques, you can enter the Fochabers Folk Museum, a converted church with a fine collection of items relating to past life in the village and surrounding area. Exhibits include carts and carriages, farm implements, domestic laborsaving devices, and an exquisite collection of Victorian toys. ✉ *High St.* ☎ *01343/821204* ⊕ *www.fochabers-heritage.org.uk* ▨ *Free* ☉ *Easter–Oct., Tues.–Fri. 11–4, weekends 2–4.*

Gordon Chapel. One of the village's lesser-known treasures is the Gordon Chapel, which has an exceptional set of stained-glass windows by Pre-Raphaelite artist Sir Edward Burne-Jones. ✉ *Castle St., just off The Square.*

SHOPPING

Just Art. If you're interested in works by local artists, head to Just Art, a fine gallery with imaginative, often fun contemporary ceramics and paintings. ✉ *64 High St.* ☎ *01343/820500* ⊕ *www.justart.co.uk.*

The Quaich. At The Quaich you can stock up on cards and small gifts, then sit with a cup of tea and a home-baked snack. ✉ *85 High St.* ☎ *01343/820981.*

Watts Antiques. This shop has small collectables, jewelry, ornaments, and china. ✉ *45 High St.* ☎ *01343/820077* ⊕ *www.wattsantiques.com.*

CULLEN

13 miles east of Fochabers, 3 miles east of Findochty.

Fodor's Choice ★ Look for some wonderfully painted homes at Cullen, in the old fishing town below the railway viaduct. The real attractions of this charming little seaside resort, however, are its white-sand beach (the water is quite cold, though) and the fine view west toward the aptly named Bow-fiddle Rock. In summer Cullen bustles with families carrying buckets and spades. A stroll past the small but once busy harbor reveals fishers' cottages, huddled together with small yards where they dried their nets. Beyond these, the beach curves gently round the bay. Above are the disused Victorian viaduct—formerly the Peterhead train line—and the 18th-century town.

GETTING HERE AND AROUND
Cullen is on A98, on Cullen Bay.

EXPLORING
Seafield Street. The town has a fine *mercat* (market) cross and one main street—Seafield Street—that splits the town. It holds numerous specialty shops—antiques and gift stores, an ironmonger, a baker, a pharmacy, and a locally famous ice-cream shop among them—as well as cafés.

WHERE TO EAT AND STAY
$

SEAFOOD

Fodor's Choice

★

✕ **Rockpool.** A newer addition to the Cullen scene, this modish fish restaurant has remarkably reasonable prices for the quality of the food and size of the servings. Try the rich cullen skink (a creamy smoked haddock soup), a pint glass of fat prawns served with mayo and oat bread, or some freshly fried squid with a limey sauce, all beautifully presented on wooden boards. It's also worth mentioning the lovingly crafted cupcakes and the happy staff that takes great delight in serving you your food. $ *Average main: £8* ⊠ *10 The Square* ☎ *01542/841397* ⊕ *www.rockpool-cullen.co.uk* ✆ *Closed Mon. No dinner.*

$

B&B/INN

Fodor's Choice

★

⊞ **Academy House.** About 10 minutes from the seaside town of Cullen, this luxurious bed-and-breakfast in a handsome Victorian house was once the headmaster's house for the local secondary school. **Pros:** good home cooking; delightful setting. **Cons:** rooms book up fast; there's little to do in Fordyce. $ *Rooms from: £80* ⊠ *School Rd., Fordyce* ☎ *01261/842743* ⊕ *www.fordyceaccommodation.com* ⤴ *2 rooms* ▭ *No credit cards* ⵘ *Breakfast.*

BANFF

10 miles east of Cullen, 36 miles east of Elgin, 47 miles north of Aberdeen.

Midway along the northeast coast, overlooking Moray Firth and the estuary of the River Deveron, Banff is a fishing town of considerable elegance that feels as though it's a million miles from tartan-clad Scotland. Part Georgian, like Edinburgh's New Town, and part 16th-century small burgh, Banff is an exemplary east-coast salty town, with a tiny harbor and fine architecture. It's also within easy reach of plenty of unspoiled coastline—cliff and rock to the east, at Gardenstown (known as Gamrie) and Pennan, or beautiful little sandy beaches westward toward Sandend and Cullen.

GETTING HERE AND AROUND
Banff is on the A98 coastal road and at the end of the tree-lined A947 to Aberdeen. If you are relying on public transportation, Bus 325 from Aberdeen Bus Station takes two hours and gets you into Low Street, just five minutes from Duff House.

ESSENTIALS
Visitor Information Banff Visitor Information Centre ⊠ *Collie Lodge, Low St.* ☎ *01261/812419* ⊙ *Apr.–Sept.*

EXPLORING

Fodor's Choice ★ **Duff House.** The jewel in Banff's crown is the grand mansion of Duff House, a splendid William Adam–designed (1689–1748) Georgian mansion. Used as a swish hotel in the Roaring Twenties before becoming a sanitarium and then a military base, it lay empty and moldering for years before it was restored in 1995 by the National Galleries of Scotland. It exhibits many fine paintings, including works by El Greco, Sir Henry Raeburn, and Thomas Gainsborough. A good tearoom and a gift shop are on the ground floor. ⊠ *Off A98* ☎ *01261/818181* ⊕ *www.duffhouse.org.uk* ⊠ *£7.10* ⊙ *Apr.–Oct., daily 11–5; Nov.– Mar., Thurs.–Sun. 11–4.*

FAMILY **Macduff Marine Aquarium.** Across the river in Banff's twin town, Macduff, on the shore east of the harbor, stands the conical Macduff Marine Aquarium. A 250,000-gallon central tank and many smaller display areas and touch pools show the sea life of the Moray Firth and North Atlantic. The staff is knowledgeable and engaging, especially with children, and there's always some creature to touch in the shallow pool or being fed by divers. ⊠ *11 High Shore* ☎ *01261/833369* ⊕ *www.macduff-aquarium.org.uk* ⊠ *£6.20* ⊙ *Apr.–Oct., weekdays 10–4; weekends 10–5; Nov.–Mar., Sat.–Wed. 11–4.*

FYVIE CASTLE

18 miles south of Banff, 18 miles northwest of Ellon.

This castle mixes ancient construction with Edwardian splendor and includes excellent art. The grounds are also worth exploring.

GETTING HERE AND AROUND
If you're driving from Banff, take the A947 south for 20 minutes or so until you see the turnoff.

EXPLORING
Fyvie Castle. In an area rich with castles, Fyvie Castle stands out as the most complex. Five great towers built by five successive powerful families turned a 13th-century foursquare castle into an opulent Edwardian statement of wealth. Some superb paintings are on view, including 12 works by Sir Henry Raeburn. There are myriad sumptuous interiors— the circular stone staircase is considered one of the best examples in the country—and delightfully laid-out gardens. A former lady of the house, Lillia Drummond, was apparently starved to death by her husband, who entombed her body inside the walls of a secret room. In the 1920s, when the bones were disrupted during renovations, a string of such terrible misfortunes followed that they were quickly returned

17

and the room sealed off. Her name is carved into the windowsill of the Drummond Room. ⊠ *Off A947, Turriff* ☎ *0844/493–2182* ⊕ *www. nts.org.uk* ✉ *£12* ⊙ *Apr.–June and Sept., Sat.–Wed. noon–5; July and Aug., daily 11–5; last admission 45 mins before closing.*

ELLON

12 miles southeast of Fyvie Castle, 32 miles southwest of Banff, 14 miles north of Aberdeen.

Formerly a market center on what was then the lowest bridging point of the River Ythan, Ellon, a suburb of Aberdeen, is a small town at the center of a rural hinterland. It's also well placed for visiting Fyvie Castle and Haddo House.

GETTING HERE AND AROUND
To get to Ellon, take the A947 from Banff or the A90 from Aberdeen; both routes take half an hour.

EXPLORING
Fodor's Choice   **Haddo House.** Built in 1732, this elegant mansion has a light and grace-
★   ful Georgian design, with curving wings on either side of a harmoni-
ous, symmetrical facade. The interior is late-Victorian ornate, filled with magnificent paintings (including works by Pompeo Batoni and Sir Thomas Lawrence) and plenty of objets d'art. Pre-Raphaelite stained-glass windows by Sir Edward Burne-Jones grace the chapel. Outside is a terrace garden with a fountain, and few yards farther is Haddo Country Park, which has walking trails leading to memorials about the Gordon family. Visits are by prebooked tour only. ⊠ *Off B999, 8 miles northwest of Ellon* ☎ *0844/493–2179* ⊕ *www.nts.org.uk* ✉ *£10* ⊙ *Easter–June. and Sept.–Oct., Fri.–Mon., tours at 11:30, 1:30, and 3:30; July and Aug., daily, guided tours at 11:30, 1:30, and 3:30.*

GOLF
Cruden Bay Golf Club. Sheltered behind extensive sand dunes, Cruden Bay offers a typical Scottish golf experience. The narrow channels and deep valleys on the challenging fairways ensure plenty of excitement. Like Gleneagles and Turnberry, this course owes its origins to an association with the grand railway hotels built in the heyday of steam. The hotel may be gone, but the course remains in fine shape. ■**TIP→** Weekend tee times are extremely limited; book months in advance. ⊠ *Aulton Rd., Cruden Bay* ☎ *01779/812285* ⊕ *www.crudenbaygolfclub.co.uk* ✉ *Green fee: Championship £90; St. Olaf weekdays £20, weekends £30* ⚑ *Reservations essential* ⛳ *Championship: 18 holes, 6287 yds, par 70; St. Olaf: 9 holes, 2463 yds, par 32* ⊙ *Daily.*

ARGYLL AND
THE ISLES

WELCOME TO ARGYLL AND THE ISLES

TOP REASONS TO GO

★ **Whisky, whisky, whisky:** The peaty smell of the whiskies of Islay yields to the lighter whiskies of Arran and Oban.

★ **Iona and its abbey:** This was an early center of Scottish Christianity from the 6th century onward and also the burial place of Scottish kings, including Macbeth.

★ **The great outdoors:** Salmon and trout fill the lochs and rivers. If it's golf you prefer, there are two-dozen golf courses, including fine coastal links like Machrihanish. For the cyclist there's every kind of terrain.

★ **Cool castles:** Often dramatically located on cliffs overlooking the sea, the region's castles tell their own stories of occupations, sieges, and conflicts over eight centuries. Vikings, Scots, and the English fought for their possession.

★ **Glorious gardens:** Plants flourish in the mild Gulf Stream. For flowers, trees, birds, and butterflies, visit Crarae Garden, southwest of Inveraray.

1 Argyll. The twin peninsulas of Kintyre are thickly wooded areas broken up by long lochs. From Inverarary at the head of Loch Fyne, you can take in Auchindrain's re-created fishing village on the way to the Arran ferry. Or turn west toward Crinan and the prehistoric sites around Kilmartin, then travel northward toward Loch Awe. A short drive away is Oban, a ferry port.

2 Arran. The island's wilder west coast attracts birdwatchers and naturalists, while the fertile south of the island contains nine lovely golf courses, leisurely walks, and Brodick Castle.

3 Islay and Jura. The smell of peat that hangs in the air on Islay is bottled in its famous whiskies. Aside from distilleries, the island has historical sites, and the whitewashed cottages along its coast line clean and beautiful beaches.

4 Isle of Mull and Iona. The pretty harbor of Tobermory, with its painted houses, is a relaxing base from which to explore the varied and beautiful island of Mull. You can also take the ferry to the meditative island of Iona.

Kilchoan
Salen
Strontian
Onich
Tobermory
Kentallen
Duror
A884
A828
Loch Linnhe
A849
Salen
Lochaline
Achnacroish
Barcaldine
Fishnish
Benderloch
ISLE OF
MULL Craignure
Connel
4
Oban
Taynuilt
1
Kilmore
A85
Firth of Lorn
Knipoch
Balvicar
Ellenabeich
A816
A819
Kilmelford
Arduaine
Inveraray
Ardfern
A83
Ford
Furnace
Kilmartin
Crinan
Minard
A816
Lochgair
JURA Carsaig
Lochgilphead
A886
Ardrishaig
A846
Achahoish
Colintraive
A83
Kames
A886
Feolin Ferry
Tarbert
Tighnabruaich
Craighouse
Portavadie
Loch Fyne
Rothesay
Sound of Jura
Clachan
Cloonaig
Kilchattan Bay
GIGHA
ISLAND
A83
Lochranza
Ardminish
Firth of Clyde
Tayinloan
ARRAN
Glenbarr
Carradale
Brodick
KINTYRE
2
A841
A83
Blackwaterfoot
Kilchenzie
Peninver
Whiting Bay
Machrihanish
Campbeltown
Drumlemble
Southend
SANDA
ISLAND
AILSA CRAIG
ISLAND

GETTING ORIENTED

With long sea lochs carved into its hilly, wooded interior, Argyll is a beguiling interweaving of water and land. The Kintyre Peninsula stretches between the islands of the Firth of Clyde (including Arran) and the islands of the Inner Hebrides. Ferry services allow all kinds of interisland tours. On land, you can take the A85 to Oban (a ferry port) past barren hills and into the forest of Argyll after Loch Lomond (and the A82) ends. The roads grow narrower as they wind around the banks of Loch Awe and Loch Etive. Alternatively, you can turn off the A82 at Arrochar and trace the longer route around Loch Fyne, to Inveraray and down the Argyll peninsula to Campbeltown. Along the way you'll pass Kennacraig, where ferries sail to Islay and Jura.

18

Updated
by Mike
Gonzalez

Argyll's rocky seaboard looks out onto islands that were once part of a single prehistoric landmass. Here narrow, winding roads slow travel but force you to see and admire the lochs, the woods, and the ruins that hint at the region's dramatic past. Highlights include everything from grand houses such as Brodick and Inveraray castles to gardens such as Crarae. This is whisky country, too: the distilleries on Islay should not be missed. Distances are relatively small, as the area is within three hours of Glasgow.

Divided in two by the long peninsula of Kintyre, western Scotland has a complicated, splintered coastline. Looking out onto the islands and the Atlantic Ocean beyond, it is breathtakingly beautiful, though it often catches wet ocean weather. Oak woods and bracken-covered hillsides dot the region, and just about everywhere you'll encounter the bright interplay of sea, loch, and rugged green peninsula.

Ancient castles like Dunstaffnage and the towers on the islands of Loch Awe give testimony to the region's past importance. The stone circles, carved stones, and Bronze and Iron Age burial mounds around Kilmartin and on Islay and Arran are reminders of the prehistoric peoples who left their mark here. The grounds of Inveraray and Brodick Castles, nourished by the temperate west-coast climate, contain great gardens that are the pride of Argyll.

Western Scotland's small islands have jagged cliffs or tongues of rock, long white-sand beaches, fertile pastures where sheep and cattle graze, fortresses, and shared memories of clan wars. Their cliff paths and lochside byways are a paradise for walkers and cyclists, and their whisky the ideal reward after a long day outside. While the islands' western coasts are dramatic, their more sheltered eastern seaboards are the location for the pretty harbor towns like the brightly painted Tobermory on Mull, or Port Ellen, with its neat rows of low whitewashed houses, on Islay.

ARGYLL AND THE ISLES PLANNER

WHEN TO GO

This part of the mainland is close enough to Glasgow to make it accessible year-round. Oban is just over two hours from the city by car (three hours by bus), but getting to the isles via ferries takes longer, and the crossings are less frequent. You can take advantage of quiet roads and plentiful accommodations in early spring and late autumn. The summer months of July and August can get very busy indeed; book accommodations and restaurants in advance during high season, or you might miss out. In winter, short daylight hours and winds can make island stays rather bleak.

This is a coastal region, buffeted by Atlantic winds and rains. Come prepared with adequate clothing for the changing weather, including good walking shoes, waterproof outerwear, and sunscreen.

PLANNING YOUR TIME

You could easily spend a week exploring the islands alone, so consider spending at least a few nights in this region. Argyll and some island excursions make pleasant and easy side trips from Glasgow and Loch Lomond. Driving anywhere here takes a little longer than you'd think, so allow ample travel time. A leisurely day will take you to Inveraray, its castle, and the surrounding gardens (don't miss the folk museum at Auchindrain) before driving on to Kennacraig to take the ferry to Islay and Jura. Two or three days here will give you a sense of the history and varied landscapes of these stunning islands—and time for a distillery or two. If time is a constraint, begin in Oban and sail to Mull, returning the same day or the next to take in the Scottish Sea Life Sanctuary. If you can, drive around the beautiful Loch Awe on your way back to Glasgow.

Plan ahead: ferries fill up in the summer months, and some of the smaller islands are served only once or twice a week. Bear in mind that it is not easy to find places to eat after 9 pm at any time of year—though you can usually find a place that will sell you a whisky.

GETTING HERE AND AROUND

AIR TRAVEL

Flybe operates flights from Glasgow to Campbeltown, Islay, and Mull. Hebridean Air Services flies between the small islands out of Oban.

Air Travel Contacts Flybe ☎ *0871/700–2000* ⊕ *www.flybe.com.* **Hebridean Air Services** ✉ *Lochranza* ☎ *0845/805–7465* ⊕ *www.hebrideanair.co.uk.*

BOAT AND FERRY TRAVEL

Caledonian MacBrayne (CalMac) operates car-ferry services to and from the main islands. It is important to plan ahead when traveling to the islands in order to coordinate the connecting ferries; CalMac can advise you on this. Multiple-island tickets are available and can significantly reduce the cost of island-hopping, and give you a memorable trip.

CalMac ferries run from Oban to Mull and Lismore; from Kennacraig to Islay, Jura, and Gigha; and from Ardrossan to Arran as well as a number of shorter routes. Western Ferries operate between Dunoon, in Argyll, and Gourock, west of Glasgow. The ferry passage between

18

Dunoon and Gourock is one frequented by locals; it saves a lot of time, and you can take your car across as well. Jura Passenger Ferry operates between Tayvallich and Craighouse.

Ferry reservations are needed if you have a car; passengers traveling by foot do not need to make reservations.

Boat and Ferry Travel Contacts Caledonian MacBrayne (*CalMac*). ☎ *0800/066–5000* ⊕ *www.calmac.co.uk.* **Jura Passenger Ferry** ☎ *07768/450000* ⊕ *www.jurapassengerferry.com* ⊠ *£20.* **Western Ferries** ⊠ *Hunter's Quay, Dunoon* ☎ *01369/704452* ⊕ *www.western-ferries.co.uk.*

BUS TRAVEL

You can travel throughout the region by bus, but service here tends to be less frequent than elsewhere in Scotland. Scottish Citylink runs daily service from Glasgow's Buchanan Street Station to the mid-Argyll region and Kintyre; the trip to Oban takes about three hours. Several other companies provide local services within the region.

Bus Contacts Bowman's Tours ☎ *01631/566809* ⊕ *www.bowmanscoaches. co.uk.* **Islay Coaches** ☎ *01496/840273.* **Jura Bus** ☎ *01496/820314.* **Royal Mail** ☎ *08457/740740.* **Scottish Citylink** ☎ *0871/266–3333* ⊕ *www.citylink.co.uk.* **Stagecoach West Scotland** ☎ *01292/613502* ⊕ *www.stagecoachbus.com.* **West Coast Motors** ☎ *01586/552319* ⊕ *www.westcoastmotors.co.uk.*

CAR TRAVEL

Negotiating this area is easy except in July and August, when the roads around Oban may be congested. There are a number of single-lane roads, especially on the east side of the Kintyre Peninsula and on the islands that require special care. Remember that white triangles indicate places where you can pass. You'll probably have to board a ferry at some point during your trip; nearly all ferries take cars as well as pedestrians.

From Glasgow, take the A82 and the A85 to Oban, the main ferry terminal for Mull and the islands (about 2½ hours by car). From the A82, take the A83 at Arrochar; it rounds Loch Fyne to Inveraray. From there you can take the A819 from Inveraray around Loch Awe and rejoin the Glasgow–Oban road. Alternatively, you can stay on the A83 and head down Kintyre to Kennacraig, the ferry terminal for Islay. Farther down the A83 is Tayinloan, the ferry port for Gigha. You can reach Brodick on Arran by ferry from Ardrossan, on the Clyde coast (M8/A78 from Glasgow); in summer you can travel to Lochranza from Claonaig on the Kintyre Peninsula, but there are very few crossings.

TRAIN TRAVEL

Oban and Ardrossan are the main rail stations; it's a three-hour trip from Glasgow to Oban. For information, call ScotRail. All trains connect with ferries.

Train Contact ScotRail ☎ *0845/601–5929* ⊕ *www.scotrail.co.uk.*

RESTAURANTS

Until recently this part of Scotland had few restaurants of distinction. That has changed, and more and more quality restaurants are opening and using excellent local produce—fine fish and shellfish, lamb, and venison, as well as game of many kinds. Most hotels and many guesthouses offer evening meals, though the quality can vary. Bear in mind that most restaurants and pubs stop serving food by 9 pm; lunch usually ends at 2:30.

HOTELS

Accommodations in Argyll and on the isles range from country-house hotels to private homes offering a bed and breakfast. Most small, traditional, provincial hotels in coastal resorts have been updated and modernized, while still retaining personalized service. And though hotels often have a restaurant offering evening meals, the norm is to offer breakfast only. *Hotel reviews have been shortened. For full information, visit Fodors.com.*

WHAT IT COSTS IN POUNDS				
	$	**$$**	**$$$**	**$$$$**
Restaurants	under £15	£15–£19	£20–£25	over £25
Hotels	under £100	£100–£160	£161–£220	over £220

Restaurant prices are the average cost of a main course at dinner or, if dinner is not served, at lunch. Hotel prices are the lowest cost of a standard double room in high season, including 20% V.A.T.

TOURS

BOAT TOURS

Getting out on the water is a wonderful way to see the landscape of the islands and also sea life.

Gordon Grant Tours leads an excursion from Oban to Mull, Iona, and Staffa and leaves Mull on other trips to Treshnish Isles and Staffa. From Taynuilt, near Oban, boat trips are available from Loch Etive Cruises Easter through October. Sea Life Surveys offers four- and six-hour whale-watching and wildlife day trips from Tobermory, on the Isle of Mull. Turas-Mara runs daily excursions in summer from Oban and Mull to Staffa, Iona, and the Treshnish Isles and specializes in wildlife tours.

Boat Tour Contacts Gordon Grant Tours ✉ *Railway Pier, Achavaich, Isle of Iona* ☎ *01681/700338* ⊕ *www.staffatours.com.* **Loch Etive Cruises** ✉ *Kelly's Pier, Etive View, Taynuilt* ☎ *01866/822430.* **Sea Life Surveys** ✉ *A848, Tobermory* ☎ *01688/302916* ⊕ *www.sealifesurveys.com.* **Turus-Mara** ✉ *Penmore Mill, Dervaig* ☎ *01688/400242* ⊕ *www.turusmara.com.*

BUS TOURS

Many of the bus companies in the area also arrange sightseeing tours, so check with them *(see Getting Here and Around, above).* Bowman's Tours runs trips from Oban.

Bus Tour Contact Bowman's Tours ✉ *Queens Park, Oban* ☎ *01631/563221* ⊕ *www.bowmanstours.co.uk.*

VISITOR INFORMATION

The tourist offices in Tarbert and Tobermory (Mull) are open April through October only; other offices are open year-round.

Contact Visit Scottish Heartlands ⊕ *www.visitscottishheartlands.com.*

18

ARGYLL

Topographical grandeur and rocky shores are what make Argyll special. Try to take to the water at least once, even if your time is limited. The sea and the sea lochs have played a vital role in the history of western Scotland since the time of the war galleys of the clans. Oban is the major ferry gateway and transport hub, with a main road leading south into the Kintyre Peninsula.

OBAN

96 miles northwest of Glasgow, 125 miles northwest of Edinburgh, 50 miles south of Fort William, 118 miles southwest of Inverness.

It's almost impossible to avoid Oban when touring the west. Its waterfront has some character, but the town's main role is as a launch point for excursions into Argyll and for ferry trips to the islands. A traditional Scottish resort town, Oban has many music festivals, *ceilidhs* with Highland dancing, as well as all the usual tartan kitsch and late-night revelry in pubs and hotel bars. The Oban Distillery is on Stafford Street in town, offering tours and a shop. Still, there are more exciting destinations just over the horizon, on the islands and south to Kintyre.

GETTING HERE AND AROUND

From Glasgow, the A82 along Loch Lomond meets the A85 at Crianlarich. Turn left and continue to Oban. In summer the center of Oban can become gridlocked with ferry traffic, so leave yourself time for the wait. Alternatively, the A816 from Lochgilphead enters Oban from the less crowded south. Train services run from Glasgow to Oban (ScotRail); bus services from Glasgow to Oban by Scottish Citylink run several times a day.

ESSENTIALS

Visitor Information Oban Tourist Informaton Centre ⊠ *Argyll Sq.*
☏ *08707/200630* ⊕ *www.visitscotland.com.*

EXPLORING

Fodor's Choice **Dunstaffnage Castle.** Standing high atop volcanic rock, Dunstaffnage
★ commands the hills and lochs that surround it. That is why this 13th-century castle was so strategic and fought over between those battling for control of the kingdom of Argyll. From the walk along the walls, you have outstanding views across the **Sound of Mull** and the **Firth of Lorne.** A small well-illustrated guidebook (£2.50) lets you take your own guided tour, but there are storyboards throughout the building that give you a sense of how it was used across the ages. In the woods is the ruined chapel of St. Cuthbert, built by the Macdougall clan at the same time as the castle. ⊠ *Off A85* ☏ *01631/562465* ⊕ *www.historic-scotland.gov.uk/places* 💷 *£4.50* ☉ *Apr.–Sept., daily 9:30–5:30; Oct., daily 9:30–4:30; Nov.–Mar., Mon.–Wed. and weekends 9:30–4:30.*

FAMILY **Scottish Sea Life Sanctuary.** On the shores of Loch Creran, this marine sanctuary is part aquarium where you can get an up-close look at everything from sharks to stingrays, and part animal rescue facility. Adorable otters and seals receive rehabilitation here before being released

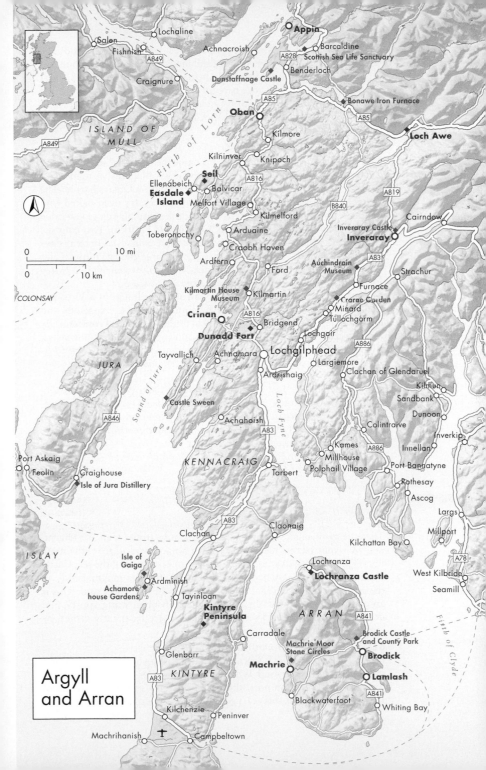

back into the wild. Kids will appreciate the adventure playground. The restaurant serves morning coffee, a full lunch menu, and afternoon tea. To get here, drive north from Oban for 10 miles on the A828; West Coast Motors also provides a regular bus service. ✉ *Barcaldine, off A828, Connel* ☎ *01631/720386* 🌐 *www.sealsanctuary.co.uk* 🎟 *£13.20* 🕒 *Apr.–Oct., daily 10–5; Nov.–Mar, daily 10–4; last admission 1 hr before closing.*

WHERE TO EAT AND STAY

$$ SEAFOOD 🍴 **Ee-usk.** This clean-lined restaurant's name means "fish" in Gaelic, and it has earned quite a reputation for serving excellent dishes made with the freshest fish and shellfish delivered directly from Oban's harbor. The signature creations use appealingly simple sauces; try oven-baked wild halibut with creamed leeks or the full-scale seafood platter. Good-value options include fixed-price menus for lunch (£11.50 for two courses) and dinner (£15.95 or £17.95 for two or three courses). On clear days there are nice views of the islands through the large glass windows. Children under 12 not admitted for dinner. [$] *Average main: £19* ✉ *North Pier* ☎ *01631/565666* 🌐 *www.eeusk.com* 🕒 *Closed Sun.*

$$ B&B/INN 🏨 **Glenburnie House.** At this typical seafront guesthouse in a Victorian house with fine views over Oban Bay, most rooms are spacious and comfortable, if slightly overdecorated in traditional style. **Pros:** centrally located; good sea views. **Cons:** too many flowery fabrics for some tastes; slightly expensive for what you get; no elevator. [$] *Rooms from: £110* ✉ *Esplanade* ☎📠 *01631/562089* 🌐 *www.glenburnie.co.uk* 🛏 *12 rooms* 🕒 *Closed Dec.–Feb.* 🍽 *Breakfast.*

$ B&B/INN 🏨 **Kilchrenan House.** Just a few minutes from the town center, this Victorian-era stone house has been transformed into a lovely bed-and-breakfast. **Pros:** great sea views; tasteful attention to detail. **Cons:** some bedrooms may be too colorfully decorated for some tastes; attic rooms have a slanting roof. [$] *Rooms from: £80* ✉ *Corran Esplanade* ☎📠 *01631/562663* 🌐 *www.kilchrenanhouse.co.uk* 🛏 *10 rooms* 🕒 *Closed Dec. and Jan.* 🍽 *Breakfast.*

APPIN

10 miles north of Oban.

The little peninsula of Appin, a 20-minute drive from Oban, is a charming, well-kept secret. Just 2 miles along a narrow road from the main Fort William route (A828), the bay opens to Lismore and the sea. Castle Stalker, a privately owned castle on the water, sits magnificently in the center of the picture, a symbol of ancient coastal Scotland. This is an excellent, uncrowded base for walking, fishing, water sports, and cycling. The Appin Rocks on the headland are frequently visited by seals.

GETTING HERE AND AROUND

From Oban, follow the A828 around Loch Creran and take the left turn to Port Appin just beyond Tynribbie. Continue for just over 2 miles to the old pier. From the port, the passenger ferry runs to the island of Lismore throughout the year; steamers once plied the waters of Loch

Linnhe, but today the largest boats here are those taking workers to the quarries of Kingairloch.

WHERE TO STAY

$$$$ **Airds Hotel and Restaurant.** The old ferry inn for travelers visiting Lismore now houses this luxurious small hotel; rooms are stylish and restrained, with superb views either toward the sea or the woods behind. **Pros:** fabulous views from the breakfast room; spare boots for the unprepared; beautiful location. **Cons:** an expensive option. *$ Rooms from: £315 ⊠ A828, Port Appin ☎ 01631/730236 ⊕ www. airds-hotel.com ⤳ 9 rooms, 2 suites, 1 cottage ❑ Some meals.*

HOTEL
Fodor's Choice
★

$$ **Pierhouse Hotel.** The round towers of the old pier mark the entrance to this hotel and restaurant, appealingly situated on the water's edge beside the jetty. **Pros:** breathtaking view across the loch; lively, warm atmosphere; good restaurant. **Cons:** rooms are a little small; not all rooms have views of the water; prices rise on weekends. *$ Rooms from: £160 ⊠ Port Appin ☎ 01631/730302 ⊕ www.pierhousehotel. co.uk ⤳ 12 rooms ❑ Breakfast.*

HOTEL

LOCH AWE

18 miles east of Oban.

Measuring more than 25 miles long, Loch Awe is Scotland's longest stretch of freshwater. Its northwest shore is quiet; forest walks crisscross the Inverliever Forest here. At the loch's northern end, tiny islands, many with ruins, pepper the water. One, Inishail, is home to a 13th-century chapel.

GETTING HERE AND AROUND

From Oban the A85 will bring you to the head of Loch Awe and the small town of the same name. Turn onto the B845 at Taynuilt to reach the loch's northern shore, or continue through the forbidding Pass of Brander and turn onto the A819 to get to the southern shore. From here you can continue on to Inveraray, or drive along the loch on the B840.

EXPLORING

Bonawe Iron Furnace. This beautifully reconstructed site shows a different face of this mainly agricultural region. The ironworks were very advanced for their time, and an elaborate exhibit takes you through the different stages of the production process. During the Napoleonic Wars it began making cannonballs, and these provided firepower for Admiral Lord Nelson's ships at the Battle of Trafalgar in 1805. The local graveyard, at Taynuilt, has a monument to Nelson raised by the workers. The majority of the workers were Gaelic-speaking peasants who were responsible for collecting the wood from the surrounding forests to make charcoal. ⊠ *Off B845, Bonawe ☎ 01866/822432 ⊕ www. historic-scotland.gov.uk ⤳ £4.50 ☼ Apr.–Sept., Mon.–Sun. 9:30–5:30.*

Cruachan. This "hollow mountain" is a fascinating engineering achievement, all the more dramatic for being hidden in a landscape that gives no hint of its presence. A bus takes you the 1 km (mile) into Ben Cruachan where you find yourself in a massive man-made cavern containing the vast turbines that supply so much of western Scotland's

18

electricity. Take in the hands-on exhibit at the visitor center. ✉ *A85, Dalmally* ☎ *01866/822618* 🌐 *www.visitcruachan.co.uk* 🎟 *£6.50* 🕒 *Apr.–Oct., 9:30–4:45; Nov.–Mar., 9:30–3:45.*

St. Conan's Kirk. This striking stone-built church on the banks of Loch Awe has a medieval air about it, but in fact it was completed in 1930 by amateur architect Walter Campbell. It was built with the boulders strewn across the area, rather than quarried stone, and it looks rough and almost incomplete. But its interior is impressive. Light filters in through modern stained-glass windows, and wood and stone carvings are scattered throughout, not to mention the effigy of Robert the Bruce lying on a stone catafalque that contains a fragment of bone taken from Bannockburn. It's on the A85, about 18 miles from Oban. ✉ *A85, Lochawe* ☎ *01838/200298* 🌐 *www.stconanskirk.org.uk* 🎟 *Free.*

WHERE TO STAY

$$$ HOTEL Fodor's Choice ★

🏨 **Taychreggan Hotel.** The tranquillity of this lovely country-house hotel echoes the stillness of nearby Loch Awe. **Pros:** lovely setting; high level of comfort; wonderful meals. **Cons:** Wi-Fi only in public rooms; off the beaten track. [$] *Rooms from: £154* ✉ *Off B845, Kilchrenan* ☎ *01866/833211* 🌐 *www.taychregganhotel.co.uk* 🛏 *18 rooms* 🍴 *Breakfast.*

EN ROUTE

The A819 south to Inveraray initially runs alongside Loch Awe, then joins the A83, which carries traffic from Glasgow and Loch Lomond by way of the high **Rest and Be Thankful Pass**. This quasi-alpine pass, set among high green slopes and gray rocks, is one of the most scenic points along the road.

INVERARAY

21 miles south of Loch Awe, 61 miles north of Glasgow, 29 miles west of Loch Lomond.

Fodor's Choice ★

The town is a sparkling fishing village with cute shops, attractions, and the haunted Campbell Castle all within walking distance. There are lovely views of the water and plenty of fishing boats to watch; several worthwhile gardens and museums are nearby, too. On the approaches to Inveraray, note the ornate 18th-century bridgework that carries the road along the loch side. This is your first sign that much of Inveraray was planned by the 3rd Duke of Argyll in the mid-18th century.

GETTING HERE AND AROUND

If you're driving from Oban, take the A85 and the A819 beyond Loch Awe (the village). From Glasgow, take the A82, turn on to the A83 at Arrochar, and make the long drive around Loch Fyne.

ESSENTIALS

Visitor Information Inveraray Tourist Information Centre ✉ *Front St.* ☎ *01499/302063* 🌐 *www.visitscotland.com.*

EXPLORING

Fodor's Choice ★

Auchindrain Museum. Step a few centuries back in time at this open-air museum, a rare surviving example of an 18th-century communal tenancy farm. About 250 years ago, there were several thousand working communities like Auchendrain. It was the last of them, its final tenant leaving in 1963. Today the bracken-thatch and iron-roof buildings, about 20 in all, give you a feel for early farming life in the Highland communities. Several houses are furnished and tell the story of their occupants. A tearoom is open morning to afternoon. ✉ *Off A83, 6 miles south of Inveraray* ☎ *01499/500235* 🌐 *www.auchindrain.org.uk* 🎫 *£6.30* 🕒 *Apr.–Oct., daily 10–5; last admission 4.*

Crarae Garden. Well worth a visit for plant lovers is this 100-acre garden, where magnolias, azaleas, and rhododendrons flourish in the moist, lush environment around Crarae Burn (a burn is a small stream). A rocky gorge and waterfalls add appeal, and the flowers and trees attract several different species of birds and butterflies. The gardens are 10 miles southwest of Inveraray off the A83. ✉ *Off A83* ☎ *0844/493–2210* 🌐 *www.nts.org.uk/Visits* 🎫 *£6.50* 🕒 *Garden daily 9:30–sunset. Visitor center Apr.–Oct., daily 10–5:45; last admission at 5.*

Inveraray Castle. The current seat of the Chief of the Campbell clan is a smart, grayish-green turreted stone house with a self-satisfied air. This 18th century construction, set among extensive and well-tended grounds, contains displays of luxurious furnishings and interesting art, as well as a huge armory. Tours of the castle follow the history of the powerful Campbell family and how it acquired its considerable wealth. There is a tearoom for snacks and light lunches. You can hike around the extensive estate grounds, but wear sturdy footwear. ✉ *Off A83* ☎ *01499/302203* 🌐 *www.inveraray-castle.com* 🎫 *£9* 🕒 *Apr.–Oct., daily 10–5:45, last admission at 5.*

FAMILY **Inveraray Jail.** In this old jail, realistic courtroom scenes, carefully re-created cells, and other paraphernalia give you a glimpse of life behind bars in Victorian times—and today. Actors represent some of the jail's most famous occupants. ✉ *Main St.* ☎ *01499/302381* 🌐 *www.inverarayjail.co.uk* 🎫 *£8.95* 🕒 *Apr.–Oct., daily 9:30–6; Nov.–Mar., daily 10–5; last admission 1 hr before closing.*

18

WHERE TO EAT AND STAY

$$ SEAFOOD 🍴 **Loch Fyne Oyster Bar and Restaurant.** This well-regarded seafood spot sits surrounded by hills at the head of Loch Fyne, 10 miles northeast of Inveraray. Polished wood and maritime artworks help set the mood. The dishes are generally simple and unpretentious—try the fish and shellfish soup, or the roast salmon with asparagus, broad beans, and pea salad. Don't miss the oysters, either in the restaurant or in the adjacent shop. Arrive early, as the place closes at 8, and reserve in advance. [$] *Average main: £17* ✉ *Clachan Farm, A83, Cairndow* ☎ *01499/600482* 🌐 *www.lochfyne.com* ✍ *Reservations essential.*

$ HOTEL Fodor's Choice ★ 🏨 **The George Hotel.** The Clark family has run this 18th-century former coaching inn at the heart of Inveraray for six generations, and that's reflected in the warmth of the welcome you'll receive. **Pros:** excellent restaurant; atmospheric bars; hotel Scottish in every way. **Cons:** too much tartan for some; unattractive reception area; Wi-Fi in public areas only. [$] *Rooms from: £75* ✉ *Main St. E* ☎ *01499/302111* 🌐 *www.thegeorgehotel.co.uk* 🛏 *17 rooms* 🍽 *Breakfast.*

CRINAN

15 miles south of Inverary.

Crinan is synonymous with its canal, the reason for this tiny community's existence and its mainstay. The narrow road beside the Crinan Hotel bustles with yachting types waiting to pass through the locks, bringing a surprisingly cosmopolitan feel to such an out-of-the-way corner of Scotland.

GETTING HERE AND AROUND

To reach Crinan, take the A816 Oban road north from Lochgilphead for about a mile, then turn left on to the B841 at Cairnbaan.

EXPLORING

Crinan Canal. This canal opened in 1801 to let fishing vessels reach Hebridean fishing grounds without making the long haul south around the Kintyre Peninsula. At its western end the canal drops to the sea in a series of locks, the last of which is beside the Crinan Hotel. Today it's popular with pleasure boats traveling to the west coast.

Fodor's Choice ★ **Kilmartin House Museum.** For an exceptional encounter with early Scottish history, start at this museum 8 miles north of Crinan and then explore some of the more than 300 nearby ancient monuments. Exhibits provide information about the stone circles and avenues, burial mounds, and carved stones dating from the Bronze Age and earlier that are scattered nearby. There is also a nice tearoom in the museum. Nearby **Dunadd Fort,** a rocky hump between Crinan and Kilmartin, was once the capital of the early kingdom of Dalriada, founded by the first Scots migrants from Ireland around AD 500. ✉ *A816, Kilmartin* ☎ *01546/510278* 🌐 *www.kilmartin.org* 🎟 *£5* 🕒 *Mar.–Oct., daily 10–5:30; Nov. and Dec., daily 11–4.*

WHERE TO STAY

$$$ HOTEL 🏨 **Crinan Hotel.** One of a group of houses around the last lock of the Crinan Canal, the hotel has a dramatic setting overlooking the Sound of Jura and Craignish Point; it echoes the style of the boats on the canal in its use of wood. **Pros:** elevator to rooms on upper floors; good restaurants. **Cons:** Wi-Fi in public areas only. [$] *Rooms from: £180* ✉ *Off B841* ☎ *01546/830261* 🌐 *www.crinanhotel.com* 🛏 *20 rooms* 🍴 *Breakfast.*

KINTYRE PENINSULA

62 miles south of Crinan (to Campbeltown).

Rivers and streams crisscross this long, narrow strip of green pasturelands and hills.

GETTING HERE AND AROUND

Continue south on the A83 (the road to Campbeltown) to Tarbert. Some 4 miles farther along the A83 is Kennacraig, where you catch the ferry to Islay. Beyond that is the pier at Tayinloan; CalMac ferries run from here to the Isle of Gigha.

Flybe operates flights from Glasgow to Campbeltown.

ESSENTIALS

Air Travel Contact Campbeltown Airport ⊠ *Off A83, Kintyre* ☎ *01586/553797* ⊕ *www.hial.co.uk.*

Visitor Information Campbeltown Information Centre ⊠ *Mackinnon House, The Pier, Campbeltown* ☎ *01586/552056* ⊕ *www.visitscotland.com.* **Tarbert Information Centre** ⊠ *Harbour St., Tarbert* ☎ *01880/820429* ⊕ *www. visitscotland.com.*

EXPLORING

Isle of Gigha. Barely 7 miles long, this sheltered island between Kintyre and Islay has sandy beaches and rich wildlife. Achamore House Gardens is here as well. The island was long favored by British aristocrats as a summer destination. Ferries make the 20-minute trip from Tayinloan on the mainland. ⊠ *Isle of Gigha* ☎ *01583/505392* ⊕ *www.gigha.org.uk.*

GOLF

Machrihanish Golf Club. Many enthusiasts discuss this course in hushed tones—its out-of-the-way location, around the sandy Machrihanish Bay, has made it something of a golfer's Shangri-la. The drive off the first tee is across the beach to reach the green—an intimidating start to a memorable series of holes. ⊠ *Off B843, Machrihanish* ☎ *01586/810277* ⊕ *www.machgolf.com* ▨ *Green fee: £65* ⌕ *Reservations essential* ⚑ *18 holes, 6235 yds, par 70* ☼ *Daily.*

ARRAN

Approaching Arran by sea, you'll first see the forbidding Goatfell (2,868 feet) in the north, then the green fields of the south. It is this contrast and varied geography that has led visitors to describe Arran as "Scotland in Miniature." The island's temperate climate allows tropical plants to grow, and this relative warmth probably attracted the ancient cultures whose stone circles still stand. This weather also explains why it has always been a favorite getaway for Glasgow's residents, who come here to walk, play golf, observe the rich birdlife, and simply enjoy the sea.

GETTING HERE AND AROUND

Caledonian MacBrayne runs regular car and passenger ferries that cross the Firth of Clyde from Ardrossan (near Saltcoats) to Brodick through-out the year (crossing takes just under an hour). There is also a small ferry from Claonaig on the Kintyre Peninsula to Lochranza during the summer months.

Connecting trains run to the ferry at Ardrossan from Glasgow's Queen Street station. Stagecoach runs regular local bus services around the island. Exploring the island by car is easy, as the A841 road circles it.

BRODICK

1 hour by ferry from Ardrossan.

Arran's largest village, Brodick, has a main street that is set back from the promenade and the lovely bay beyond.

GETTING HERE AND AROUND

You can reach Brodick from Ardrossan by ferry. From Brodick the A841 circles the island; head north to reach Lochranza. The String Road crosses the island between Brodick and Machrie.

ESSENTIALS

Visitor Information Brodick Information Centre ✉ *The Pier* ☎ *01770/303774* 🌐 *www.visitscotland.com.*

EXPLORING

Fodor's Choice ★ **Brodick Castle and Country Park.** On the north side of Brodick Bay, this reddish sandstone structure is surrounded by lush woods, gardens, and parks. Several rooms are open to the public between March and October, both in the original 16th-century castle and in the Victorian additions that nicely illustrate the Hamilton family's opulent lifestyle. The 87 stag heads on the stairs are a disturbing reminder of how the aristocracy spent their leisure time. The vast gardens, open all year, are filled with rhododendrons and azaleas. A café serves homemade cakes and coffee for breakfast as well as a light lunch menu. The country park here includes the 2,867-foot **Goatfell,** the highest peak in Arran. The beautiful upland landscape is more challenging than it seems, so go prepared, but the views from the peak make the effort worthwhile. Year-round access is from the country park or from Cladach on the A841. ✉ *Off A841, 1 mile north of Brodick Pier* ☎ *0844/4932152* 🌐 *www.nts.org.uk* 🎟 *Castle and gardens £12* 🕒 *Castle: Apr. and Oct., daily 11–3; May–Sept, daily 11–4. Garden: Apr. and Oct., daily 10–4; May–Sept., daily 10–5.*

Isle of Arran Heritage Museum. The museum documents life on the island from ancient times to the present. Several buildings, including a cottage and *smiddy* (smithy), have period furnishings as well as displays on prehistoric life, farming, fishing, and other aspects of the island's social history. ✉ *Rosaburn, A841* ☎ *01770/302636* 🌐 *www.arranmuseum.co.uk* 🎟 *£3* 🕒 *Apr.–Oct., daily 10:30–4:30.*

WHERE TO EAT

$$ SEAFOOD 🍴 **Creelers.** It would be hard to find fresher seafood than at Creelers. The shellfish served in the restaurant will often have been caught that day by the owners' own boat. The restaurant's name comes from the "creels," or baskets, used to gather shellfish. The restaurant serves a range of delicious smoked fish from its own smokery next door, as well as other fish and meat dishes. Try the Arran scallops with monkfish and pesto, or the cod with Arran mustard. [$] *Average main: £18* ✉ *Home Farm, A841* ☎ *01770/302810* 🌐 *www.creelers.co.uk* ✍ *Reservations essential.*

$ ITALIAN 🍴 **Eilean-Mor Bar Bistro.** Painted a bright shade of red, this unpretentious Italian bar and bistro has a friendly and attentive staff. The substantial pastas, pizzas, and burgers are nicely prepared—even the haggis ravioli in whisky sauce is startlingly tasty. [$] *Average main: £11* ✉ *Shore Rd.* ☎ *01770/302579.*

SHOPPING

Arran's shops are well stocked with locally produced goods. The Home Farm off A841 is a popular shopping area with several shops and a small restaurant.

MACHRIE

10 miles west of Brodick, 11 miles north of Lagg.

The area surrounding Machrie, home to a popular beach, is littered with prehistoric sites: chambered cairns, hut circles, and standing stones dating from the Bronze Age.

GETTING HERE AND AROUND

The quick route to Machrie is via the String Road (B880) from Brodick; turn off onto the Machrie Road 5 miles outside Brodick. A much longer but stunning journey will take you from Brodick, north to Lochranza, around the island to Machrie, and down the island's dramatic west coast, a distance of some 28 miles.

EXPLORING

Machrie Moor Stone Circles. From Machrie, a well-surfaced track takes you to a grassy moor by a ruined farm, where you can see the Machrie Moor Stone Circles: small, rounded granite-boulder circles and much taller, eerie red-sandstone monoliths. Out on the bare moor, the lost and lonely stones are very evocative, well worth a walk to see if you like the feeling of solitude. The stones are about 1 miles outside of Machrie; just follow the "Historic Scotland" sign pointing the way. The ground is boggy, so go prepared. 🌐 *www.stonesofwonder.com.*

SHOPPING

Old Byre Showroom. This shop sells sheepskin goods, hand-knit sweaters, leather goods, and rugs. ✉ *Auchencar Farm, A841, 2 miles north of Machrie, Auchencar* ☎ *01770/840227* 🌐 *www.oldbyre.co.uk.*

18

LOCHRANZA CASTLE

11 miles north of Brodick via A841.

EXPLORING

Lochranza Castle. This picturesque ruined castle is said to have been the landing place of Robert the Bruce when he returned from Rathlin Island in 1307 to start the campaign that won Scotland's independence. The ground-floor rooms and a few upstairs can be visited during the summer months. A sign indicates where you can pick up the key to get in. You'll often see deer grazing nearby or seals swimming in the bay. ✉ *Off A841* ☎ *0131/668–8800* 🌐 *www.historic-scotland.gov.uk* 🎟 *Free* 🕓 *Apr.–Sept., daily 9:30–5:30.*

WHERE TO STAY

$ B&B/INN 🏨 **Apple Lodge.** A charming whitewashed building that once served as a pastor's house, Apple Lodge sits beneath the hills at the edge of Lochranza. **Pros:** lovely setting on the outskirts of Lochranza; charming gardens. **Cons:** dinner not always available; no children under 12; credit cards not accepted. [$] *Rooms from: £78* ✉ *A841* ☎ *01770/830229* 🌐 *www.applelodgearran.co.uk* 🛏 *4 rooms* 💳 *No credit cards* 🕓 *Closed mid-Dec.–mid-Jan.* 🍴 *Breakfast.*

ISLAY AND JURA

Known for its whiskies, Islay (population 3,200) has a character distinct from that of the rest of the islands that make up the Hebrides. In contrast to areas where most residents live on crofts (small plots generally worked by people in their spare time), Islay's western half in particular has large, self-sustaining farms. The southeast, by contrast, is mainly an extension of the island of Jura's inhospitable quartzite hills. Although it's possible to meet an Islay native in a local pub, such an event is less likely on tiny Jura (population 200), given the island's one road, one distillery, one hotel, and six sporting estates.

ISLAY

2½ hours by ferry from Kennacraig to Port Ellen.

Several distilleries produce Islay's famous and characteristically peaty malt whiskies, and most welcome visitors. They charge a fee for tours, which you can usually credit toward any whisky purchases. Islay is also known for its birds, including the rare chough (a crow with red legs and beak) and, in winter, its barnacle geese. Many of the island's wildlife preserves, historical sites, and beautiful beaches are on the western side of the island. It's dangerous to swim at the coastal beaches, but the white-sand beaches around Loch Indaal are safe and clean.

BOWMORE
11 miles north of Port Ellen.

Compact Bowmore is a good base for touring because it's central to Islay's main routes. Sharing a name with the whisky made in the distillery by the shore, Bowmore is a tidy town, its grid pattern having been laid out in 1768 by the local landowner Daniel Campbell of Shawfield. Main Street stretches from the pier head to the commanding parish church, built in 1767 in an unusual circular design—so the devil could not hide in a corner.

GETTING HERE AND AROUND
Flybe flights from Glasgow to Islay take 40 minutes; the airport is 5 miles north of Port Ellen. The trip by CalMac ferry from Kennacraig to Port Ellen takes about 2½ hours; ferries also travel less frequently to Port Askaig. From Port Ellen you'll need to travel 10 miles on the A846 to reach Bowmore; drivers should use caution during the first mile out of Port Ellen, as the road is filled with sharp turns. The rest of the route is straight but bumpy, because the road is laid across peat bog. The ferry to Feolin on Jura departs from Port Askaig; the crossing takes five minutes.

Bus service is available on the island through Islay Coaches and Royal Mail; comprehensive timetables are available from the tourist information center.

ESSENTIALS
Air Travel Contact Glenegedale Airport ⊠ *A846, Glenegadale, Albania* ☎ *01496/302022* ⊕ *www.hial.co.uk.*

Visitor Information **Bowmore Information Centre** ✉ *The Square* ☎ *08707/200617* 🌐 *www.visitscotland.com.*

ISLAY'S WHISKIES

Islay has nine major whisky producers. Which local whisky you prefer depends on how fond you are of the scent of peat, the boggy material used instead of coal, whose smoke tints the island's air. The distilleries on the southeast coast—Laphroaig, Lagavulin, and Ardbeg—have the strongest taste of peat. You can add a little water when you enjoy a dram. The western distilleries—Bowmore, Bunnahabhain, and Bruichladdich—are lighter and more flowery. Each distillery offers basic tours for a few pounds and more expensive specialized tours for connoisseurs.

EXPLORING

Bowmore Distillery. Whisky lovers can tour this 1779 distillery, which has an appealing spot near the water's edge. The more expensive Craftsman's Tour, costing £45 per person, is best for those who fancy themselves experts. Tours must be booked in advance. ✉ *School St.* ☎ *01496/810671* 🌐 *www.bowmore.com* 🎟 *£6 tour* 🕓 *Visitor center: Easter–June, Mon.–Sat. 9–5; July–Sept., Mon.–Sat. 9–5, Sun. noon–4; Oct.–Easter, Mon.–Sat. 9–noon. Tours: Easter–Aug., Mon.–Sat. at 10, 11, 2, and 3; Sept.–Easter, weekdays at 10:30 and 3; Sat. at 10.*

Islay Woollen Mill. In a wooded hollow by the river, this mill has a fascinating array of machinery that proud owners Gordon and Sheila Covell will be happy to show you. A shop sells high-quality products that were woven on the premises. All the tartans and tweeds worn in the film *Braveheart* were woven here. ✉ *A846, 3 miles outside Bridgend* ☎ *01496/810563* 🌐 *www.islaywoollenmill.co.uk* 🎟 *Free* 🕓 *Mon.–Sat. 10–5.*

18

WHERE TO EAT

$$$ SEAFOOD

🍴 **Harbour Inn.** The cheerfully noisy bar of this harborside inn is frequented by off-duty distillery workers who are happy to rub elbows with travelers and exchange island gossip; the superb restaurant has expansive views over the water and serves morning coffee, lunch, and dinner. Menus highlight local lobster, crab, and prawns, as well as island lamb and beef. If you can't bear to leave, the inn's bedrooms are bright and contemporary, with simple wood or velvet-upholstered furniture. [$] *Average main: £22* ✉ *The Square, Bowmore* ☎ *01496/810330* 🌐 *www.harbour-inn.com* 🛏 *7 rooms* 🍽 *Breakfast.*

PORT CHARLOTTE

11 miles west of Bowmore.

A delightful conservation village (meaning an area of architectural or historical interest) at the head of Loch Indaal on Islay, Port Charlotte is home to the Museum of Islay Life, the charming Natural History Trust, and safe, sandy beaches.

GETTING HERE AND AROUND

To reach Port Charlotte from Bowmore, take the A846 via Bridgend and then the A847, Portnahaven Road. Islay Coaches and Royal Mail buses also travel here from Bowmore.

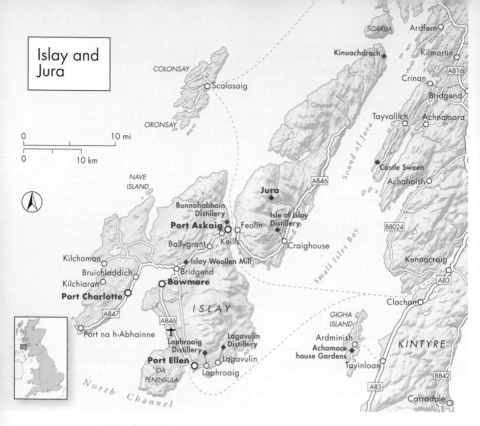

EXPLORING

Museum of Islay Life. A converted church is home to this local museum, a haphazard but authentic collection of local artifacts, photographs, and memorabilia. There is also a local history archive. ⊠ *A847* ☎ *01496/850358* ⊕ *www.islaymuseum.org* ✉ *£3* ⊙ *Apr.–Oct., Mon.–Sat. 10–5.*

Rhinns of Islay. South of Port Charlotte, the A847 continues along the wild landscape of the Rhinns of Islay. The road ends at **Portnahaven** and its twin, **Port Wemyss**, where pretty white cottages built in a crescent around the headland belie the harsh lives of the fisher families who live and work here. Return to Port Charlotte via the bleak, unclassified road that loops north and east, passing by the recumbent stone circle at Coultoon and the ruined chapel at Kilchiaran along the way. The strange whooping sound you may hear as you turn away from Portnahaven comes from Scotland's first wave-powered generator, sucking and blowing as it supplies electricity for both villages. It's well worth the climb down to the shore to see it in action.

WHERE TO STAY

$$$
HOTEL
🏨 **Port Charlotte Hotel.** Once a row of fishermen's cottages and with views over a sandy beach, this whitewashed Victorian hotel has been lovingly restored. **Pros:** beautiful location; lovely restaurant; views over

the water. **Cons:** slightly expensive; rooms are quite small; can be a little noisy from the bar. $ *Rooms from: £190* ⊠ *Main St.* ☎ *01496/850360* ⊕ *www.portcharlottehotel.co.uk* ↬ *10 rooms* ❙⦿❙ *Breakfast.*

PORT ELLEN

11 miles south of Bowmore.

Islay's sturdy community of Port Ellen was founded in the 1820s, and much of its architecture dates from the following decades. It has a harbor (ferries stop here), a few shops, and a handful of inns. The road traveling east from Port Ellen (the A846 to Ardbeg) passes three top distilleries and makes a pleasant afternoon's "whisky walk." All three distilleries offer tours, but you should call ahead for an appointment; there may be no tours on weekends at times.

GETTING HERE AND AROUND

It is likely that Port Ellen will be your port of arrival on Islay. From here you can travel north to Bowmore, along the A846, before turning northwest towards Bridgend and Port Askaig.

EXPLORING

Lagavulin Distillery. The whisky produced here is certainly distinctive—it has the strongest peaty scent (the mark of Islay whisky) of all the island malts. At 10:30 on Tuesday and Thursday are special warehouse tours; call ahead to reserve this and other tours. ⊠ *A846* ☎ *01496/302400* ⊕ *www.malts.com* ⌑ *£6; warehouse tours £15* ☉ *Jan.–Apr., Nov., and Dec., weekdays 9–12:30; May, June, Sept., and Oct., weekdays 9–5, Sat. 9–12:30; July and Aug., weekdays 9–7, Sat. 9–5, Sun. 12:30–4:30.*

Laphroaig Distillery. The whisky produced here is one of the most unusual in the Western Isles, with a tangy, peaty, seaweed-and-iodine flavor. The visitor center is free, and a basic tour costs £5. Call ahead for these and more expensive tour options. The distillery is a little less than a mile from Port Ellen. ⊠ *A846* ☎ *01496/302418* ⊕ *www.laphroaig.com* ⌑ *£5* ☉ *Mar.–Oct., weekdays 9:45–5:30, weekends 10–4; Nov.–Feb., daily 9:45–4:30.*

PORT ASKAIG

11 miles northeast of Bowmore.

Serving as the ferry port for Jura and receiving ferries from Kennacraig, Port Askaig is a mere cluster of cottages. Uphill, just outside the village, a side road travels along the coast, giving impressive views of Jura on the way. There are distilleries near here, too; make appointments for tours.

GETTING HERE AND AROUND

Traveling from Bowmore, you can reach Port Askaig (where the road ends) via A846. The village is also served by local buses.

EXPLORING

Bunnahabhain Distillery. Established in 1881, the Bunnahabhain (pronounced Boon-a-hain) Distillery sits on the shore, with great water views. This is one of the milder single malts on Islay. You can upgrade to a more elaborate tour when you reserve ahead. ⊠ *A846* ☎ *01496/840646* ⊕ *www.bunnahabhain.com* ⌑ *£6* ☉ *Mar.–Oct., weekdays 10–4:30; tours at 10:30, 1:30, and 3:15.*

18

WHERE TO STAY

$$ 🏠 **Kilmeny Country House.** This luxurious bed-and-breakfast is on a
B&B/INN   300-acre farm. **Pros:** elegant and quiet; great breakfast. **Cons:** easy
to miss; up a farm road. $ *Rooms from: £125* ✉ *A846, Ballygrant*
☎ *01496/840668* ⊕ *www.kilmeny.co.uk* ⇢ *4 rooms* ⭐ *Breakfast.*

JURA

5 minutes by ferry from Port Askaig.

The rugged, mountainous landscape of the island of Jura looms immediately east of Port Askaig, across the Sound of Islay. Jura has only one single-track road (the A846), which begins at Feolin, the ferry pier. It climbs across moorland, providing scenic views of the island's most striking feature, the Paps of Jura, three beastlike rounded peaks. The ruined Claig Castle, on an island just offshore, was built by the lords of the Isles to control the Sound.

Jura House lies between Feolin and Craighouse, the island's only village, some 8 miles away (its walled gardens are open to the public for part of the year). Jura's solitude attracted George Orwell to the remote farmhouse at Barnhill, where he completed his famous novel *1984*.

GETTING HERE AND AROUND

The Port Askaig–Feolin car ferry takes five minutes to cross the Sound of Islay. Bus service is also available from Craighouse and Inverlussa.

EXPLORING

Isle of Jura Distillery. The community of Craighouse has the island's only distillery, producing malt whisky since 1810. Phone ahead to reserve your place on a tour. ✉ *A846* ☎ *01496/820385* ⊕ *www.isleofjura.com* 💷 *Free* ⊙ *Apr.–Sept, weekdays10–4, Sat. 10–2; tours weekdays at 11 and 2. Oct.–Mar., weekdays 11–2; tour at 11.*

WHERE TO STAY

$ 🏠 **Jura Hotel.** In spite of its monopoly on Jura, this hotel has a lot going
HOTEL   for it, including great views, a handy location, and pleasant gardens.
Pros: good views across the bay; spacious rooms; next door to distillery.
Cons: room decor is tired, to say the least; you may have to share a
bathroom. $ *Rooms from: £95* ✉ *A846, Craighouse* ☎ *01496/820243*
⊕ *www.jurahotel.co.uk* ⇢ *17 rooms, 11 with bath* ⭐ *Breakfast.*

ISLE OF MULL AND IONA

Though its economy has historically been built on agriculture, fishing, and whisky distilling, today the Isle of Mull relies on tourism dollars—which makes sense, because there are many wonderful things to see here. The landscapes range from the pretty harbor of Tobermory to the dramatic Atlantic beaches on the west. In the south, the long road past the sweeping green slopes of the Ross of Mull leads to Iona, a year-round attraction.

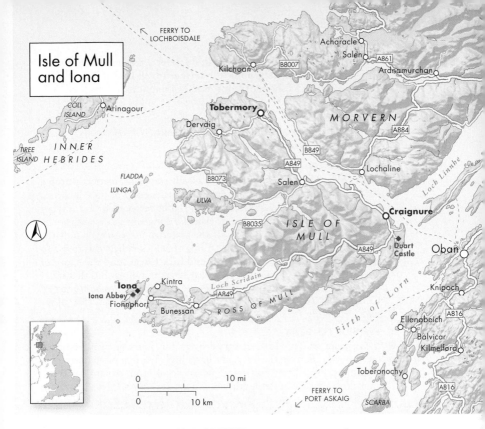

GETTING HERE AND AROUND

Ferries to Mull are run by the ubiquitous Caledonian MacBrayne. Its most frequent car-ferry route to Mull is from Oban to Craignure (45 minutes). Two shorter routes are from Lochaline on the Morvern Peninsula to Fishnish (15 minutes), or Kilchoan (on the Adrnamurchan Peninsula) to Tobermory (15 minutes). These ferries do not accept reservations, and the Lochaline ferry does not run on Sunday. Bowman's Coaches serves the east coast, running between Tobermory and Fionnphort (for the ferry to Iona).

CRAIGNURE

On Mull: 40-minute ferry crossing from Oban, 15-minute ferry crossing to Fishnish (5 miles northwest of Craignure) from Lochaline.

Craignure, little more than a pier and some houses, is close to the well-known Duart Castle. Reservations for the year-round ferries that travel from Oban to Craignure are advisable in summer. The ferry from Lochaline to Fishnish, just northwest of Craignure, does not accept reservations and does not run on Sunday.

GETTING HERE AND AROUND

The arrival point for the 40-minute ferry crossing from Oban, Craignure is the starting point for further travel on Mull northwest toward Salen and Tobermory, or toward Fionnphort and the Iona ferry to the southwest.

ESSENTIALS

Visitor Information **Craignure Information Centre** ✉ *The Pierhead* ☎ *01680/812377* 🌐 *www.visitscotland.com.*

EXPLORING

Duart Castle. The 13th-century Duart Castle stands dramatically atop a cliff overlooking the Sound of Mull. The ancient seat of the Macleans, it was ruined by the Campbells in 1691 but restored by Sir Fitzroy Maclean in 1911. Inside you can visit the dungeons and state rooms, then climb the keep for a view of the waterfront. Nearby stands the **Millennium Wood,** planted with groups of Mull's indigenous trees. To reach Duart by car, take the A849 and turn left around the shore of Duart Bay. From Craignure's ferry port, there is a direct bus that takes you to the castle in about 10 minutes. ✉ *A849, 3 miles southeast of Craignure* ☎ *01680/812309* 🌐 *www.duartcastle.com* 🎟 *£5.75* ⏲ *May–mid-Oct., daily 10:30–5:30.*

WHERE TO STAY

$ B&B/INN 🏨 **Craignure Inn.** This 18th-century drovers' inn, in a whitewashed building a short walk from the ferry pier, has a lively bar that often hosts local musicians. **Pros:** lively bar scene; hearty local food; expansive views. **Cons:** live music can get loud; bar can get very busy. [$] *Rooms from: £82* ✉ *A849, near the ferry pier* ☎ *01680/812305* 🌐 *www.craignure-inn.co.uk* 🛏 *3 rooms* 🍴 *Breakfast.*

TOBERMORY

5 miles northeast of Dervaig, 21 miles north of Craignure.

Fodor's Choice ★ Founded as a fishing station, Tobermory is now a lively tourist center and a base for exploring Mull. The town is famous for its crescent of brightly painted houses around the harbor.

GETTING HERE AND AROUND

The most frequent service to Mull is via the Oban-Craignure ferry. Tobermory is 21 miles from Craignure along the A849/848 (via Salen). Bowman's Coaches runs services between Tobermory and Craignure.

ESSENTIALS

Visitor Information **Mull Information Centre** ✉ *Pierhead, Craignure* ☎ *01680/812377* 🌐 *www.visitscotland.com.*

WHERE TO EAT AND STAY

$$ SEAFOOD Fodor's Choice ★ ✕ **Café Fish.** This restaurant's location has certainly contributed to its success—it's perched on the pier at the end of Tobermory. The owners pride themselves on the freshness of their fish; they have their own boat and bring in their own seafood each day. The fish is served simply, grilled with a slice of lemon, to let the natural flavors speak for themselves. Diver-harvested scallops are served with vermouth and orange

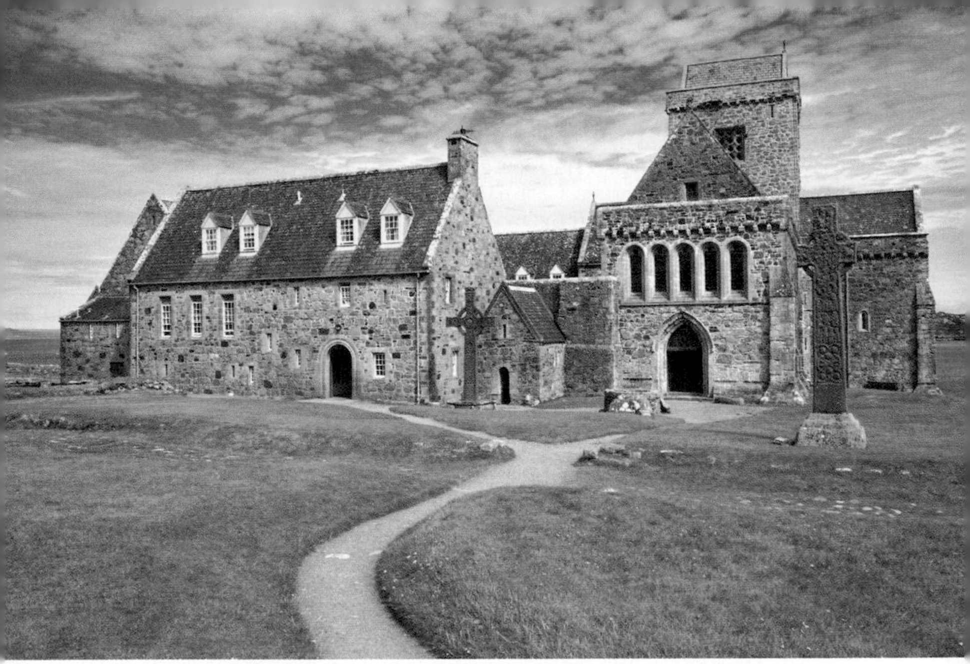

Once a key center of Christianity in Scotland, Iona Abbey still serves an ecumenical religious community.

juice over rice. Other popular dishes include fish stew and the langoustines and squat lobster (not really a lobster—it's related to crab) served with garlic butter and granary bread. [$] *Average main: £17* ✉ *The Pier* ☎ *01688/301253* 🌐 *www.thecafefish.com* ✍ *Reservations essential* 🕓 *Closed Jan.–mid-Mar.*

18

$ HOTEL 🏨 **Tobermory Hotel.** Made up of five former fishermen's cottages, this lodging on Tobermory's waterfront has a warm, intimate feel. **Pros:** adorable cottage setting with fireplace; toys for children. **Cons:** small rooms; small bathrooms. [$] *Rooms from: £98* ✉ *Main St.* ☎ *01688/302091* 🌐 *www.thetobermoryhotel.com* 🛏 *18 rooms* 🕓 *Closed Nov.–Mar.* 🍴 *Breakfast.*

$$ HOTEL 🏨 **Western Isles Hotel.** This grand hotel from the Victorian era looks down on Tobermory from its wonderful location overlooking the Sound of Mull; it suffered a period of neglect, but is now being refurbished and restored to its former elegance. **Pros:** the view is brilliant; spacious public rooms; great food. **Cons:** outmoded plumbing; occasional lack of hot water; still being renovated. [$] *Rooms from: £150* ✉ *Off B882* ☎ *01688/302012* 🌐 *www.westernisleshotel.co.uk* 🛏 *26 rooms* 🍴 *Breakfast.*

THE ARTS

Mull Theatre. The renowned Mull Theatre, founded in 1966, once prided itself on being the smallest theater in the United Kingdom. Today it has grown in size and in stature, and its productions tour not only the islands but the whole of Scotland. It's wise to book ahead. ✉ *Druimfin, Salen Rd.* ☎ *01688/302828* 🌐 *www.mulltheatre.com.*

IONA

5 minutes by ferry from Fionnphort (Mull).

The ruined abbey on Iona gives little hint that this was once one of the most important Christian religious centers in the land. The priceless Book of Kells (now in Dublin) was illustrated here, and it was the monks of Iona who spread Christian ideas across Scotland and the north. The abbey was founded in the year 563 by the fiery and argumentative Columba (circa 521–97) after his expulsion from Ireland. Until the 11th century, many of Scotland's kings and rulers were buried here, their tombstones still visible inside the abbey.

GETTING HERE AND AROUND

Caledonian MacBrayne's ferry from Fionnphort departs at regular intervals throughout the year (£4.50 round-trip). Timetables are available on the Caledonian MacBrayne website. Note that cars are not permitted; there's a parking lot by the ferry at Fionnphort.

EXPLORING

Fodor's Choice ★ **Iona Abbey.** Overseen by St. Columba, who traveled here from Ireland, Iona was the birthplace of Christianity in Scotland in the 6th century. It survived repeated Norse sackings before falling into disuse around the time of the Reformation. Restoration work began at the beginning of the 20th century. Today the restored buildings serve as a spiritual center under the jurisdiction of the Church of Scotland. Guided tours by the Iona Community, an ecumenical religious group, begin every half hour in summer and on demand in winter. ✉ *Isle of Iona* ☎ *01681/700793* 🌐 *www.iona.org.uk* 🎟 *£7.10* ⏲ *Apr.–Sept., daily 9:30–5:30; Oct.–Mar., daily 9:30–4:30.*

WHERE TO STAY

$$ HOTEL 🏨 **St. Columba Hotel.** Rooms in this 1846 manse are very simply decorated, but all those on the front have glorious views across the Sound of Iona to Mull. **Pros:** it's all about what's good for the earth and soul; nice log fires; Wi-Fi throughout the hotel. **Cons:** no TVs; basic decor. [$] *Rooms from: £146* ✉ *Next to cathedral, about ¼ mile from the ferry pier* ☎ *01681/700304* 🌐 *www.stcolumba-hotel.co.uk* 🛏 *27 rooms* ⏲ *Closed Nov.–Mar.* 🍴 *Breakfast.*

THE GREAT GLEN, SKYE, AND THE NORTHERN HIGHLANDS

WELCOME TO THE GREAT GLEN, SKYE, AND THE NORTHERN HIGHLANDS

TOP REASONS TO GO

★ **Castles, fortresses, and battlefields:** History is felt keenly at Cawdor, Dunvegan, and other castles, Augustus and other fortresses, and the battlefields of Glencoe and Culloden Moor.

★ **Isle of Skye:** The landscape of Skye ranges from lush, undulating hills to the deep glens that cut into the saw-toothed peaks of the Cuillin Mountains.

★ **Hill walking and outdoor activities:** The Great Glen is renowned for its hill walking, with routes around Glen Nevis, Glencoe, and on Ben Nevis. The landscapes of Skye and the Northern Highlands are stunning.

★ **Whisky tours:** The two westernmost distilleries on the Malt Whisky Trail are in Forres. Benromach has excellent tours; Dallas Dhu is preserved as a museum.

★ **Single-track roads:** In the Northern Highlands, take a drive on single-track roads, such as Destitution Road north of Gairloch, which lead through primeval terrain.

1 Inverness and Environs. From Inverness, just about anywhere in the Great Glen is a day trip. Spend your days exploring Culloden Moor, Brodie Castle, or Cawdor Castle. There are long, walkable beaches at Nairn and Findhorn.

2 Speyside and the Cairngorms. The long River Spey threads the northern section of Cairngorms National Park, Great Britain's largest national park. Mountains, lochs, and river scenery fills the view here.

North Atlantic Ocean

GETTING ORIENTED

The Great Glen spreads out to the east, south, and west of Inverness. To the east beckons the Morayshire coast and its castles, distilleries, and beaches. Southeast lie Cairngorms National Park and other nature preserves. The A82 heads southwest from Inverness, hugging the west side of Loch Ness to Fort William. Continue west on the Road to the Isles (A830) to reach the Isle of Skye. Or follow the A835 northwest into the Northern Highlands to Ullapool, perhaps detouring south (on the A832) into Gairloch, in the Torridon Hills, before swinging back north past Ullapool on the coastal roads that lead to Lochinver, Scourie, and eventually John o'Groats. The A99 leads south from here back to Inverness.

19

3 Loch Ness, Fort William, and Environs. You may prefer to go in search of the Loch Ness Monster, in which case visit romantic Urquhart Castle. For history, head to Glenfinnan Monument and other spots associated with the Jacobite rebellion.

4 Isle of Skye. The largest and most famous of the Outer Hebrides, also known as the Western Isles, is home to the dramatic jagged peaks of the Cuillin Mountains, the quiet gardens of Sleat, and the peninsulas of Waternish and Trotternish.

5 The Northern Highlands. Northwestern Scotland is known for its dramatic coastline and beautifully desolate interior landscapes.

Updated by
Jack Jewers
and Mike
Gonzalez

The ancient rift valley of the Great Glen formed when two tectonic plates collided, then widened into a glen, or valley, punctuated by a thin line of lochs. The most famous is mysterious Loch Ness. To the north lie the rugged Northern Highlands; to the west, the Isle of Skye. This wild country delights nature lovers, but there are also reminders of often tragic history: Glencoe, where two families warred, and Culloden Moor, where the Jacobite rebellion came to its end.

Fort William and Inverness provide twin starting points from which to explore this expansive and varied region. South from Fort William the A82 runs through Glencoe, between its steep mountains, and toward Argyll. West from Fort William the Road to the Isles (A830) follows the coast, passing Glenfinnan Monument where the Bonnie Prince rallied his troops in 1745 for the short-lived Jacobite rebellion.

North of Fort William on the A82 is Fort Augustus, with the first of the 29 locks of the Caledonian Canal linking Inverness to Fort William and ending near the foot of Ben Nevis (4,406 feet), Great Britain's highest mountain. To the west of Fort Augustus on the A87, across the bridge from Kyle of Lochalsh, lies the Isle of Skye; the brooding Cuillin Mountains on its northern coast suggest its prehistoric past.

North of Fort Augustus and south of Inverness, the 13th-century ruined Urquhart Castle provides a perfect spot from which to view Loch Ness before traveling its length in search of the monster first sighted (or invented?) 70 years ago. From Inverness to the east along the A96, the sandy beaches of Nairn and Findhorn beckon the visitor towards the Malt Whisky Trail that begins at Forres and follows the River Spey. Here too, are the opulent Cawdor and Brodie castles.

The alternative is to follow the coastal routes (the A9 and later A99) of Sutherland and Caithness north from Inverness as they dip and curve around rocks and beaches. It is wise to drive slowly here, in case you catch a glimpse of an eagle or a deer, or simply to appreciate the rugged beauty of these landscapes before they continue to Cape Wrath and John o'Groats and the shores of the northern sea.

THE GREAT GLEN, SKYE, AND THE NORTHERN HIGHLANDS PLANNER

WHEN TO GO

The Great Glen, Skye, and the Northern Highlands are best seen from May through September. Summer days can be glorious, though even at this time of year the weather can be erratic, and you might find yourself confronted by tiny biting insects called midges. (Keep walking to outpace them—they can't move very fast—and bring protection.) The earlier in the spring or later in the autumn you visit, the greater the chances of your encountering the elements in their extreme form, and the fewer attractions and accommodations you will find open. Even tourist-friendly Skye and the islands close down almost completely by October, and the weather in winter can be fierce.

PLANNING YOUR TIME

The single-track roadways, undulating landscapes, and eye-popping views will slow your journey through the Northern Highlands. Leave sufficient time for car travel, and remain aware of timetables if traveling by ferry. The Great Glen is an enormous area best visited in two stages, with Inverness or Fort William as your base; you can access Northern Highland regions from either as well. If you have limited time, head to Skye. It attracts many tourists in summer, but it's easy to access more isolated areas. Sunday is a day of minimal activity throughout this region; restaurants, bars, and shops are closed, as are many sights.

GETTING HERE AND AROUND

AIR TRAVEL

The main airports for this region are Inverness and Wick, both on the mainland. The larger Inverness Airport, with direct links to London, Edinburgh, Glasgow, and Amsterdam, is served by easyJet, Flybe/Loganair, and KLM. Wick John o'Groats Airport is served by Flybe/Loganair. Trains and buses connect Fort William with Glasgow, making Glasgow Airport (see Air Travel in Travel Smart Great Britain) a feasible alternative.

Airport Contact Inverness Airport ✉ Old Military Rd., Dalcross ☎ 01667/464000 ⊕ www.hial.co.uk/inverness-airport.

Wick John o'Groats Airport ✉ Airport Rd., off A99, Caithness ☎ 01955/602215 ⊕ www.hial.co.uk.

BOAT AND FERRY TRAVEL

Ferry services are generally reliable, weather permitting. Caledonian MacBrayne (known locally as CalMac) provides ferry service from the mainland to the islands and has a page on its website of day trips to wildlife areas and historic sites. Ferries to Skye depart from Mallaig. *For information about ferries and discount passes, see Boat Travel in Travel Smart Great Britain.*

19

Boat and Ferry Contact Caledonian MacBrayne ☎ *08000/665000* ⊕ *www. calmac.co.uk.*

BUS TRAVEL

Scottish Citylink and National Express run buses to Inverness and Wick. Discount carrier Megabus (book online to avoid phone charges) has service to Inverness. Stagecoach Highland serves the Great Glen and Fort William. Bus travel to sights within northern Scotland is spotty (or nonexistent), but Traveline Scotland (⊕ *www.travelinescotland. com)* has a journey planner to help you navigate Skye and other areas. There's an app, too.

Bus Contacts Megabus ☎ *0900/160–0900* ⊕ *www.megabus.com.* **Royal Mail Post Buses** ☎ *0845/7740740* ✎ *www.royalmail.com.* **Scottish Citylink** ☎ *0871/266–3333* ⊕ *www.citylink.co.uk.* **Stagecoach Highlands** ☎ *01463/233371* ⊕ *www.stagecoachbus.com.*

CAR TRAVEL

A car is definitely the best way to explore the Great Glen, Skye, and Northern Highlands. You can use the main A82 from Inverness to Fort William, or use the smaller B862/B852 roads to explore the much quieter east side of Loch Ness. In the Great Glen the best sights are often hidden from the main road, a reason to favor peaceful rural byways and to avoid as much as possible the busy A96 and A9, which carry much of the traffic in the area.

The winding single-lane roads in the entire region demand a degree of driving dexterity, however. Local rules require that when two cars meet, whichever driver reaches a passing place first must stop and allow the oncoming car to continue (this sometimes entails backing up). Cars driving uphill have priority, and small cars tend to yield to large commercial vehicles. Never park in passing places, and remember that these sections of the road can also be used to allow traffic behind you to pass.

In sparsely populated areas, distances between gas stations can be considerable, so it is wise to fill your tank when you see a station.

TRAIN TRAVEL

ScotRail has connections from London to Inverness and Fort William (including overnight sleeper service), as well as reliable links from Glasgow and Edinburgh. There's train service between Glasgow (Queen Street) and Inverness, via Aviemore, which provides access to the heart of Speyside.

Although there's no rail connection among towns within the Great Glen, this area has the West Highland Line, which links Fort William to Mallaig. This train, run by ScotRail, remains the most enjoyable way to experience the rugged hills and loch scenery between these two places. From mid-May to mid-October, the Jacobite Steam Train is an exciting option on the same route. Main railway stations in the area include Inverness for the entire region and Kyle of Lochalsh for Skye. There's a direct service from London to Inverness and connecting service from Edinburgh and Glasgow. For information, contact National Rail or ScotRail.

Train Contacts **Jacobite Steam Train** ☎ *0844/850–4685* ⊕ *www. westcoastrailways.co.uk.* **National Rail** ☎ *08457/484950, 4420/7278–5240 from abroad* ⊕ *www.nationalrail.co.uk.* **ScotRail** ☎ *0845/755–0033* ⊕ *www. scotrail.co.uk.*

RESTAURANTS

You can find tasty meals almost everywhere in the area, though in remote areas you might have to drive some distance. Inverness has diverse dining options, and Aviemore and Fort William have cafés and restaurants in all price ranges. Most pubs and country-house inns (a good choice if you're looking for a restaurant) serve reliable, hearty seafood and meat-and-potatoes meals, some quite good. Skye has very good, sometimes expensive, restaurants. Locals eat early, and few restaurants serve dinner after 9 or 9:30.

HOTELS

Inverness has a varied lodging selection conveniently located for day trips, though you might find the nearby countryside more enchanting. The Northern Highlands and Skye have many small inns, along with some larger, upscale properties. It's wise to book well ahead in summer. *Hotel reviews have been shortened. For full information, visit Fodors.com.*

WHAT IT COSTS IN POUNDS			
	$	$$	$$$	$$$$
Restaurants	under £15	£15–£19	£20–£25	over £25
Hotels	under £100	£100–£160	£161–£220	over £220

Restaurant prices are the average cost of a main course at dinner or, if dinner is not served, at lunch. Hotel prices are the lowest cost of a standard double room in high season, including 20% V.A.T.

TOURS

The Highland Countryside Rangers (⊕ *www.outdoorhighlands.co.uk/ your-countryside-rangers)* lead guided walks and conduct wildlife talks and other events in the Great Glen, on Skye, and throughout the Northern Highlands. The rangers' yearly, downloadable booklet lists Top 5 Must Sees for each area covered.

Among the private companies, Inverness Tours runs the occasional boat cruise but is mainly known for tours around the Highlands led by expert guides and heritage enthusiasts. Jim Johnstone, a personal guide, and his drivers are well versed in local history and lore and give excellent tours.

Tour Contacts **Inverness Tours** ☎ *01667/455699* ⊕ *www.invernesstours.com.* **J.A. Johnstone Chauffeur Drive** ☎ *01463/798372* ⊕ *www.jajcd.com.*

VISITOR INFORMATION

Great Glen: Aviemore, Fort William, and Inverness have year-round tourist offices. Seasonal tourist centers include those at Fort Augustus, Kingussie, Mallaig, and Nairn.

Skye: A year-round center operates in Portree, and seasonal ones in Broadford, Uig, and other towns, including Kyle of Lochalsh, the mainland gateway.

Northern Highlands: the centers in Dunvegan, Durness, Portree, and Ullapool are open year-round, though with limited winter hours. Seasonal centers can be found in Gairloch, Helmsdale, John o'Groats, Lairg, Lochinver, and elsewhere.

Information Highlands of Scotland Tourist Board ☎ *08452/255121* ⊕ *www. visithighlands.com.* **Visit Highlands** ⊕ *www.visithighlands.com.*

INVERNESS AND ENVIRONS

A small but appealing city, Inverness makes a useful gateway to the Great Glen. It has good dining and lodging options, though cultural offerings are more or less limited to the Eden Court Theatre and live music at a few good pubs. East of Inverness, Culloden Moor looks desolate on many days, and you can easily imagine the bloody battle here in 1746 that concluded in catastrophic defeat for the Jacobites, ending their quest to restore the Stuart monarchy. You will find echoes of Bonnie Prince Charlie's rebellion throughout the area.

Beyond Culloden the Morayshire coast contains long beaches and some refined castles (Cawdor and Brodie) definitely worth a visit. Continuing east, you might be tempted by Benromach distillery in Forres, a taste of what you can find farther south if you follow the Malt Whisky Trail along the River Spey.

INVERNESS

172 miles north of Glasgow, 105 miles northwest of Aberdeen, 157 miles northwest of Edinburgh.

The city makes a great base for exploring the region, and you can fan out in almost any direction from Inverness for interesting day trips: east to Moray and the distilleries near Forres, southeast to the Cairngorms, and south to Loch Ness. Throughout its history, the town was burned and ravaged by Highland clans competing for dominance, but compared with other towns in these parts it has less to offer visitors interested in Scottish history.

GETTING HERE AND AROUND
You can easily fly into Inverness Airport, as there are daily flights from London, Bristol, Birmingham, and Manchester. ScotRail runs trains here from London, Edinburgh, Glasgow, and other cities. Scottish Citylink has service here, and Megabus serves Inverness from Edinburgh and Glasgow. You can explore much of Inverness on foot. A rental car makes visiting the surrounding areas easier, but bus and boat tours depart from the city center to key Great Glen spots.

ESSENTIALS
Airport Contact Inverness Airport ✉ *Dalcross* ☎ *01667/464000* ⊕ *www.hial. co.uk/inverness-airport.*

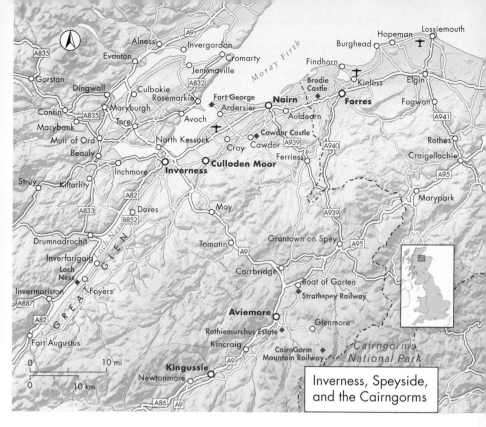

Inverness, Speyside, and the Cairngorms

Boat Contact John o'Groats Ferries ☎ 01955/611353 ⊕ www.jogferry.co.uk/ tours.aspx .

Bus Contact Inverness Coach Station ✉ Margaret St. ☎ 01463/233371.

Visitor Information Inverness ✉ Castle Wynd ☎ 01463/252401 ⊕ www. inverness-scotland.com.

EXPLORING

Fort George. After the fateful battle at Culloden, the nervous government in London ordered the construction of a large fort on a promontory reaching into the Moray Firth. Fort George was started in 1748 and completed two decades later. It's one of the best-preserved 18th-century military fortifications in Europe. Exhibits at the on-site museum chronicle the fort's history. ✉ *Old Military Rd., 14 miles northeast of Inverness*Ardersier ☎ *01667/460232* ⊕ *www.historic-scotland.gov.uk* ☞ *£8.90* ⊙ *Apr.–Sept., daily 9:30–5:30; Oct.–Mar., daily 10–4:30; last admission 45 mins before closing.*

FAMILY **Inverness Museum and Art Gallery.** Lively displays at this small but excellent facility cover archaeology, art, local history, and the natural environment. The Highland Photographic Archive, with many area photographs, is also here. ✉ *Castle Wynd* ☎ *01463/237114* ⊕ *inverness. highland.museum* ☞ *Free* ⊙ *Tues.–Sat. 10–5.*

Phoenix Boat Trips. This company's boat excursions from Inverness harbor into the Moray Firth provide a chance to see dolphins in their breeding areas. When demand is sufficient, trips to Fort George (£25) take place. ✉ *Inverness Marina, Longman Dr.* ☎ *0770/316–8097* 🌐 *www.inverness-dolphin-trips.co.uk* 🎟 *£16* 🕒 *Daily 10:30, noon, 1:30, and 3 in summer, weather permitting.*

FISHING

The Great Glen is laced with rivers and lochs where you can fly-fish for salmon and trout. The fishing seasons are as follows: salmon, from early February through September or early October (depending on the area); brown trout, from March 15 to September 30; sea trout, from May through September or early October; rainbow trout year-round. Sea angling from shore or boat is also possible. Tourist centers can provide information on locations, permits, and fishing rights.

WHERE TO EAT

$$ MODERN BRITISH

🍴 **Cafe 1.** Locals recommend this restaurant before any other, so it's no surprise that a well-dressed and diverse crowd fills the dining room. The decor is refined, with thin-legged metal chairs, lacquered wood-topped tables, and Celtic knot mirrors. The menu includes bistro-style dishes such as sea bass with rosemary and garlic polenta chips, and classic Angus steak with peppercorn sauce. The tiny bar at the front has a great view of the castle. [$] *Average main: £18* ✉ *75 Castle St.* ☎ *01463/226200* 🌐 *www.cafe1.net.*

$ BRITISH

🍴 **Dores Inn.** Off a pretty country road on the eastern shore of Loch Ness, this low-slung, white-stone eatery is the perfect place to stop for lunch or dinner. The menu is a combination of well-prepared old favorites—fish-and-chips, perhaps, or neeps and tatties (turnips and potatoes)—together with steaks, lamb, and seafood. It's busy during the summer and on weekends, so book ahead. [$] *Average main: £12* ✉ *Off B862, Dores* ☎ *01463/751203* 🌐 *www.thedoresinn.co.uk.*

$ ITALIAN

🍴 **Riva.** Facing Inverness Castle, Riva has views over the River Ness from its window seats. The dining room has subtly lighted deep-red walls lined with black-and-white photographs of Italian cityscapes. Tasty Italian dishes include pasta carbonara (with eggs, cream, and pancetta), as well as more unusual concoctions such as tagliatelle with smoked salmon and a tomato cream sauce. A separate pizzeria is upstairs from the main dining room. [$] *Average main: £14* ✉ *4–6 Ness Walk* ☎ *01463/237377* 🌐 *www.rivarestaurant.co.uk* 🕒 *No lunch Sun.*

$$$ BRASSERIE

🍴 **Rocpool Restaurant.** Highly recommended by locals, the Rocpool has a frequently changing menu of modern bistro classics, with a few modern twists. Main dishes could include sea bream fillet with a roasted pepper salad, or lamb cutlets with polenta cakes. The early evening menu is an excellent value. [$] *Average main: £20* ✉ *1 Ness Walk* ☎ *01463/717274* 🌐 *www.rocpoolrestaurant.com* 🕒 *Closed Sun.*

WHERE TO STAY

There are many places to stay in Inverness, but if your goal is to explore the countryside, a hotel outside the center might be a better choice.

$$$ HOTEL **Bunchrew House Hotel.** This 17th-century baronial mansion, its turrets reflected in a glassy lake, looks like something from a Scottish fairytale. **Pros:** beautiful setting; atmospheric building; good restaurant. **Cons:** some rooms could use refurbishment. [$] *Rooms from: £165* ✉ *Of A862, about 3 miles west of Inverness* ☎ *01463/234917* 🌐 *www.bunchrew-inverness.co.uk* 🛏 *16 rooms* 🍴 *Breakfast.*

$ B&B/INN **Moyness House.** Scottish author Neil M. Gunn (1891–1973), known for Highlands-based short stories and novels, among them *Morning Tide and Butcher's Broom,* once lived in this Victorian villa. **Pros:** relaxing interiors; lovely garden; great location near the river. **Cons:** public rooms a bit fussy for some; books up quickly. [$] *Rooms from: £80* ✉ *6 Bruce Gardens* ☎ *01463/233836* 🌐 *www.moyness.co.uk* 🛏 *6 rooms* 🍴 *Breakfast.*

$ B&B/INN **Pottery House.** This well-run modern lodging, about 8 miles south of Inverness, provides lovely extras like having jugs of ice water and fresh milk for tea or coffee in the refrigerator. **Pros:** great location; spacious rooms; delicious breakfasts. **Cons:** some decor could use updating; no public rooms. [$] *Rooms from: £88* ✉ *Off B862, Dores* ☎ *01463/751267* 🌐 *www.potteryhouse.co.uk* 🛏 *3 rooms* 🍴 *Breakfast.*

$ B&B/INN **Strathness House.** A guesthouse on the banks of the River Ness, the Strathness is a quick walk from the Eden Court Theatre and other city center attractions. **Pros:** overlooks the river; close to the city center; free Wi-Fi. **Cons:** parking can be difficult. [$] *Rooms from: £80* ✉ *4 Adross Terr.* ☎ *01463/232765* 🌐 *www.strathnesshouse.com* 🛏 *12 rooms* 🍴 *Breakfast.*

$$ B&B/INN **Trafford Bank.** This delightful little B&B that's a 15-minute walk from downtown Inverness makes a fine base. **Pros:** welcoming atmosphere; stylish rooms; relaxing vibe. **Cons:** rooms on the small side. [$] *Rooms from: £110* ✉ *96 Fairfield Rd.* ☎ *01463/241414* 🌐 *www.traffordbankguesthouse.co.uk* 🛏 *5 rooms* 🍴 *Breakfast.*

19

NIGHTLIFE AND THE ARTS

BARS AND PUBS **Blackfriars Pub.** The Blackfriars prides itself on its cask-conditioned ales. You can enjoy one to the accompaniment of live entertainment including jazz nights and *ceilidhs* (a traditional mix of country dancing, music, and song). ✉ *93–95 Academy St.* ☎ *01463/233881* 🌐 *www.blackfriarshighlandpub.co.uk.*

Hootenany. An odd combination of Scottish pub, concert hall, and Thai restaurant, this excellent pub has a warm atmosphere and serves food locals recommend highly. ✉ *67 Church St.* ☎ *01463/233651* 🌐 *www.hootanannyinverness.co.uk.*

ARTS CENTER **Eden Court Theatre.** The varied program at this popular local venue includes films, music, comedy, ballet, and even pantomime. Check out the art gallery and the bright café, and take a walk around the magnificent, Victorian-era Bishop's Palace, part of the complex. ✉ *Bishops Rd.* ☎ *01463/234234* 🌐 *www.eden-court.co.uk.*

SPORTS AND THE OUTDOORS

Fodor's Choice ★ **Castle Stuart Golf Links.** Opened in 2009, this course overlooking the Moray Firth is already considered one of Scotland's finest, hosting the Scottish Open in 2011. Expect undulating fairways and extensive bunkers that test your mettle. The 210-yard 17th hole provides perilous—and windy, cliff-top play. The art deco–inspired clubhouse provides stunning water views. ⊠ *B9039* ☎ *01463/796111* ⊕ *www.castlestuartgolf. com* ⊠ *£175 May–Oct., £130 Apr. and Nov.* ⚑ *18 holes, 6553 yards, par 72* ☉ *Apr.–Nov., daily.*

Torvean Golf Course. This municipal course has one of the longest par-5 holes (565 yards) in northern Scotland. The many water hazards include the Caledonian Canal. ⊠ *Glenurquhart Rd.* ☎ *01463/225651* ⊕ *www. torveangolfclub.co.uk* ⊠ *Green fee: £30 weekdays, £37 weekends* ⚑ *18 holes, 5784 yards, par 68.*

SHOPPING

Although Inverness has the usual indoor shopping malls and department stores, the most interesting goods are in the specialty outlets in and around town.

BOOKSTORES **Leakey's Secondhand Bookshop.** When you get tired of leafing through the 100,000 or so titles sold inside the former Gaelic Church (1793), climb to the mezzanine café and study the cavernous interior. Antique prints and maps are housed on the balcony. ⊠ *Greyfriars Hall, Church St.* ☎ *01463/239947* ☉ *Closed Sun.*

CLOTHING **Duncan Chisholm and Sons.** Highland dress and tartans are the specialty here; made-to-measure services are available. ⊠ *47–51 Castle St.* ☎ *01463/234599* ⊕ *www.kilts.co.uk.*

GALLERIES **Castle Gallery.** This excellent gallery sells contemporary paintings, sculpture, prints, and crafts. Exhibitions often feature the works of up-and-coming artists. ⊠ *43 Castle St.* ☎ *01463/729512* ⊕ *www.castlegallery. co.uk.*

SHOPPING **Victorian Market.** Don't miss this colorful market, built in 1870. The CENTER atmospheric indoor space houses more than 40 privately owned specialty shops. ⊠ *Academy St.* ☎ *01463/724273.*

CULLODEN MOOR

8 miles east of Inverness.

Culloden Moor was the scene of the last battle fought on British soil and to this day its name is enough to invoke raw and tragic feelings in Scotland. Austere and windswept, it's also a place of outstanding natural beauty.

GETTING HERE AND AROUND

Driving along the B9006 from Inverness is the easiest way to Culloden Moor, and there's a large car park to handle many visitors. Local buses also run from Inverness to the battlefield.

EXPLORING

Fodor's Choice **Culloden Moor.** Here, on a cold April day in 1746, the outgunned Jacobite forces of Bonnie Prince Charlie were destroyed by George II's army. The victorious commander, the Duke of Cumberland (George II's son), earned the name of "Butcher" for the bloody reprisals carried out by his men on Highland families, Jacobite or not. In the battle itself, the duke's army—greatly outnumbering the Jacobites—killed up to 2,000

Bonnie Prince Charlie

His life became the stuff of legends. Charles Edward Stuart—better known as Bonnie Prince Charlie, or the Young Pretender—was born in Rome in 1720. The grandson of ousted King James II of England, Scotland, and Ireland (King James VII of Scotland) and son of James Stuart, the Old Pretender, he was the focus of Jacobite hopes to reclaim the throne of Scotland. Charles was charming and attractive, and he enjoyed more than the occasional drink.

In 1745 Charles led a Scottish uprising to restore his father to the throne. He sailed to the Outer Hebrides with only a few men but with promised support from France. When that support failed to arrive, he sought help from the Jacobite supporters, many from the Highland clans, who were faithful to his family. With 6,000 men behind him, Charles won victories at

Prestonpans and Falkirk, but the tide turned when he lied to his men about additional Jacobite troops waiting south of the border. When these fictitious troops did not materialize, his army retreated to Culloden where, on April 16, 1746, they were massacred.

Charles escaped to the Isle of Benbecula where he met and is rumored to have fallen in love with Flora MacDonald. After he had hidden there for a week, Flora dressed him as her maid and brought him to sympathizers on the Isle of Skye, who helped him escape to France.

Scotland endured harsh reprisals from the government after the rebellion. Charles spent the rest of his life in drunken exile. In 1772 he married Princess Louise of Stolberg-Gedern, only to separate from her eight years later. He died a broken man in Rome in 1788.

soldiers. (The victors lost just 50). The National Trust for Scotland has reproduced a slightly eerie version of the battlefield as it looked in 1746 that you can explore with a guided audio tour. Exhibits at the innovative visitor center re-create the Gaelic dialect, song, and music of the time and simulate the sights and sounds of the battle. There's also a good on-site café. ⊠ *B9006, Culloden* ☎ *0844/4932159* ⊕ *www.nts.org.uk/ Culloden* ⤳*£10* ☉ *Apr., May, Sept., and Oct., daily 9–5:30; June–Aug., daily 9–6; Nov.–late Dec., Feb., and Mar. daily 10–4.*

19

NAIRN

12 miles east of Culloden Moor, 17 miles east of Inverness, 92 miles west of Aberdeen.

This once-prosperous fishing village has something of a split personality. King James VI (1566–1625) once boasted of a town so large the residents at either end spoke different languages. This was a reference to Nairn, whose fisherfolk lived by the sea and spoke Lowland Scots, whereas its uptown farmers and crofters spoke Gaelic. Nearby is Nairn Castle, loaded with history. East of Nairn pier is a long beach, great for a stroll.

GETTING HERE AND AROUND

A car gives you the most flexibility, but Nairn is close to Inverness (via B9006/B9091) and regular local buses serve the town.

EXPLORING

FAMILY Fodor's Choice ★ **Cawdor Castle.** Shakespeare's Macbeth was the Thane of Cawdor (a local officer of the crown), but the sense of history that exists within the turreted walls of Cawdor Castle is certainly more than fictional. Cawdor is a lived-in castle, not an abandoned, decaying structure. The earliest part is the 14th-century central tower; the rooms contain family portraits, tapestries, fine furniture, and paraphernalia reflecting 600 years of history. Outside the walls are sheltered gardens and woodland walks. Children will have a ball exploring the lush and mysterious Big Wood, with its wildflowers and varied wildlife. There are lots of creepy stories and fantastic tales amid the dank dungeons and drawbridges. If you like it here, the estate has cottages to rent. ✉ *B9090, 5 miles southwest of Nairn, Cawdor* ☎ *01667/404401* 🌐 *www.cawdorcastle.com* 🎫 *Castle £10; grounds only £5.50* 🕒 *May–early Oct. daily 10–5:30.*

WHERE TO STAY

$$$$ B&B/INN Fodor's Choice ★ 🏨 **Boath House.** Built in the 1820s, this stunning Regency manor house is surrounded by 20 acres of lovingly nurtured gardens. **Pros:** excellent dining; well-kept grounds; relaxed atmosphere. **Cons:** some airplane noise can puncture the silence. [$] *Rooms from: £230* ✉ *A96, Auldearn* ☎ *01667/454896* 🌐 *www.boath-house.com* 🛏 *8 rooms* 🍴 *Multiple meal plans.*

GOLF

Nairn Golf Club. Well regarded in golfing circles, the Nairn Golf Club dates from 1887 and is the regular home of Scotland's Northern Open. Huge greens, aggressive gorse, a beach hazard for five of the holes, a steady prevailing wind, and distracting views across the Moray Firth make play on the Championship Course unforgettable. The adjoining 9-hole Cameron course is ideal for a warm-up or a fun round for the family. ✉ *Seabank Rd.* ☎ *01667/453208* 🌐 *www.nairngolfclub.co.uk* 🎫 *Green fee: Championship £95; Cameron £15* ✍ *Reservations essential* 🏌 *Championship: 18 holes, 6774 yards, par 72; Cameron: 9 holes, 1634 yards, par 29* 🕒 *Daily.*

SHOPPING

Auldearn Antiques. It's easy to spend an hour wandering around an old church filled with furniture, fireplaces, architectural antiques, and linens. The converted farmsteads have tempting antique (or just old) chinaware and textiles. ✉ *Dalmore Manse, Lethen Rd., 3 miles east of Nairn, Auldearn* ☎ *01667/453087* 🌐 *www.auldearnantiques.co.uk.*

Brodie Countryfare. Visit Brodie only if you're feeling flush: you may covet the unusual knitwear, quality designer clothing and shoes, gifts, and toys, but they are *not* cheap. The excellent restaurant, on the other hand, is quite inexpensive. ✉ *On A96, 6 miles east of Nairn, Brodie* ☎ *01309/641555* 🌐 *www.brodiecountryfare.com.*

FORRES

10 miles east of Nairn.

The burgh of Forres is everything a Scottish medieval town should be, with a handsome tolbooth (the former courthouse and prison) and impressive gardens as its centerpieces. It's remarkable how well the old buildings have adapted to their modern retail uses. With two distilleries—one still operating, the other preserved as a museum—Forres is a key point on the Malt Whisky Trail. Brodie Castle is also nearby. Just 6 miles north you'll find Findhorn Ecovillage and a sandy beach that stretches along the edge of the semi-enclosed Findhorn Bay, which is excellent bird-watching territory.

GETTING HERE AND AROUND

Forres is easy to reach by car from Inverness on the A96. Daily ScotRail trains run here from Inverness and Aberdeen.

EXPLORING

Benromach Distillery. Moray's smallest facility was founded in 1898. Now owned by whisky specialist Gordon and MacPhail, it stocks many malts. An informative hourly tour ends with a tutored nosing and tasting. ⊠ *Invererne Rd.* ☎ *01309/675968* ⊕ *www.benromach.com* ⌑ *£5* ⊗ *May and Sept., Mon.–Sat. 9:30–5; June–Aug., Mon.–Sat. 9:30–5, Sun. noon–4; Oct.–Dec. and Feb.–Apr., weekdays 10–4; last tour 1 hr before closing.*

Brodie Castle. This medieval castle was rebuilt and extended in the 17th and 19th centuries. Fine examples of late-17th-century plasterwork are preserved in the Dining Room and Blue Sitting Room; an impressive library and a superb collection of pictures extend into the 20th century. The castle is about 24 miles east of Inverness, making it a good day trip. ⊠ *Off A96, 2 miles west of Forres, Brodie* ☎ *0844/493–2156* ⊕ *www.nts.org.uk* ⌑ *Castle £10, grounds free* ⊗ *Grounds: daily 10:30–sunset. Castle: late Mar., Apr., Sept., and Oct., daily 10:30–4:30; May and June, Sun.–Thurs. 10:30–4:30; July and Aug., daily 10:30–5. Last tour 1 hr before closing.*

19

Dallas Dhu Historic Distillery. The final port of call on the Malt Whisky Trail, this was the last distillery built in the 19th century. These days distillery structure houses a small museum that tells the story of Scotland's national drink. ⊠ *Mannachie Rd.* ☎ *01309/676548* ⊕ *www.dallasdhu.com* ⌑ *£6* ⊗ *Apr.–Sept., daily 9:30–5:30; Oct., daily 9:30–4:30; Nov.–Mar., Sat.–Wed. 9:30–4:30.*

Findhorn Ecovillage. This education center is dedicated to developing "new ways of living infused with spiritual values." Drawing power from wind turbines, locals farm and garden to sustain themselves. A tour affords a thought-provoking glimpse into the lives of the ultra-independent villagers. See homes made out of whisky barrels, and the Universal Hall, filled with beautiful engraved glass. The Phoenix Shop sells organic foods and handmade crafts, and the Blue Angel Café serves organic and vegetarian fare. ⊠ *The Park, off B9011, 6 miles north of Forres, Findhorn* ☎ *01309/690311* ⊕ *www.findhorn.org* ⌑ *Free; tours £5* ⊗ *Visitor center: May–Sept., weekdays 10–5, weekends 1–4;*

Oct.–Apr., weekdays 10–5. Tours: Apr., Oct., and Nov., Mon., Wed., and Fri. at 2; May–Sept., Fri.–Mon. and Wed. at 2.

SPEYSIDE AND THE CAIRNGORMS

The Spey is a long river, running from Fort Augustus to the Moray Firth, and its fast-moving waters make for excellent fishing. They also give Speyside malt whiskies a softer flavor than those made with peaty island water. The area's native and planted pine forests draw many birds each spring and summer, among them capercaillies and ospreys.

Defining the eastern edge of the Great Glen, Cairngorms National Park provides sporty types with all the adventure they could ask for, including walking, kayaking, rock climbing, and even skiing, if the winter is cold enough. The park has everything but the sea: craggy mountains, calm lochs, and swift rivers. This area can become very cold above 3,000 feet, and weather conditions can change rapidly, even in midsummer.

AVIEMORE

57 miles southwest of Forres, 30 miles south of Inverness.

At the foot of the Cairngorms, Aviemore has all the brashness of a year-round holiday resort. In summer it's filled with walkers, cyclists, and rock-climbers, and in winter with skiers. It's a convenient place for stocking up on supplies, though the smaller villages nearby provide quieter places to stay.

GETTING HERE AND AROUND

From Inverness take the A9 to Aviemore; from Forres head west on A96 and then south on A9.

Trains and buses serve Aviemore from Inverness, Glasgow, and Edinburgh.

ESSENTIALS

Visitor Information Aviemore Visitor Information Centre ⊠ *7 Grampian Rd.* ☎ *01479/810930* ⊕ *www.visitcairngorms.com.*

EXPLORING

Fodor'sChoice **CairnGorm Mountain Railway.** A funicular to the top of Cairn Gorm, the
★ mountain that gives the region its name, the railway affords sweeping views across the Cairngorms and the broad valley of the Spey. At the peak are a visitor center and restaurant. The round-trip journey takes about half an hour. Reservations are recommended. ⊠ *B970* ☎ *01479/861261* ⊕ *www.cairngormmountain.co.uk* ⊠ *£10.30* ⊙ *Daily 10:20–4.*

Fodor'sChoice **Cairngorms National Park.** A rugged wilderness of mountains, moorlands,
★ glens, and lochs, the sprawling national park, established in 2003, encompasses small towns as well as countryside. Past Loch Morlich, at the high parking lot on the exposed shoulders of the Cairngorm Mountains, lie dozens of hiking and cycling trails. A good place to start exploring is the main visitor center in Aviemore, whose staff

CLOSE UP

Cairngorms National Park

At the heart of Britain's largest national park (nearly 1,750 square miles of countryside) is a wild arctic landscape that sits on a granite plateau. Five of Scotland's nine 4,000-feet-high mountains are in this range, and there are 13 more over 3,000 feet. These rounded mountains, including Cairn Gorm (meaning "blue hill" in Gaelic) and Ben Macdui, the second highest in Britain at 4,295 feet, were formed at the end of the last ice age. The Larig Ghru Pass, a stunning U-shape glen, was carved by the retreating glacier.

The park is a haven for rare wildlife: a full 25% of Britain's endangered species reside here, including flora such as the least willow and alpine blue-sow thistle, and birds such as the ptarmigan, Scottish crossbill, and dotterel. Lower down the slopes what was once woodland is now open country where you might glimpse golden eagles or red deer. The remaining fragments of the ancient Caledonian forest are home to pine martens, red squirrels, and capercaillie (a large grouse), and in the rivers Spey, Don, and Dee live salmon, otters, and freshwater pearl mussels.

Fierce conditions on the Cairngorms plateau have claimed many lives. If you hike here, prepare well and inform someone of your planned route and estimated return time.

members dispense maps, trail advice, and information about guided walks and other activities. Additional Cairngorms visitor centers are in Glenmore, Newtonmore, and other towns. Because much of the park's best scenery—including ancient pine forests and open moorland— is off-road, a good way to cover ground here is on horseback. Guides at **Rothiemurchus Estate** conduct pony treks and hacks for riders of all levels of ability. ⚠ Weather conditions in the park change abruptly, so be sure to bring cold-weather gear, particularly if you plan on hiking long-distance. ✉ *Visitor Information Centre, Grampian Rd.* ☎ *0845/225–5121* ⊕ *www.cairngorms.co.uk* ⊗ *Mon.–Sat. 9–5, Sun. 10–4.*

19

FAMILY **Cairngorm Reindeer Centre.** On the high slopes of the Cairngorms you may see the reindeer herd that was introduced in the 1950s. The reindeer are docile creatures that seem to enjoy human company. Ranger-led visits to the herd are offered at least once a day from February to December, weather permitting. Bring waterproof gear, as conditions can be wet and muddy. ✉ *Glenmore Forest Park, B970, 6 miles east of Aviemore* ☎ *01479/861228* ⊕ *www.cairngormreindeer.co.uk* ☎ *£12* ⊗ *Visitor center: Feb.–Dec., daily 10–5. Visits to herd: Feb.–Apr. and Sept.–Dec. at 11; May and June at 11 and 2:30; July and Aug. 11, 2:30 and 3:30.*

FAMILY **Strathspey Steam Railway.** The oily scent of smoke and steam hangs faintly in the air near the authentically preserved train station in Boat of Garten, 6 miles northeast of Aviemore. Travel in old-fashioned style and enjoy superb views of the high and often white domes of the Cairngorm Mountains. Breakfasts, lunches, and special dinners are served on board from March to mid-September. ✉ *Boat of Garten Station,*

Spey Ave., Boat of Garten ☎ *01479/810725* ⊕ *www.strathspeyrailway. co.uk* ✉ *£13.*

WHERE TO EAT AND STAY

$ ✕ **Mountain Café.** On the main street in Aviemore, the café is a useful
CAFÉ   pit stop for a hearty lunch or afternoon snack—sandwiches, burgers, salads, and the like. The all-day breakfasts are famed locally. Leave room for the cakes, which are made on the premises. There are great views of the Cairngorm Mountains from the dining room. Service can be slow, so you may have to wait for a table. $ *Average main: £9* ⊠ *111 Grampian Rd.* ☎ *01479/812473* ⊕ *www.mountaincafe-aviemore.co.uk* ⊘ *No dinner.*

$$ ✕ **Old Bridge Inn.** Across a pedestrian bridge from Aviemore Station,
MODERN BRITISH   this old-style bar and conservatory restaurant serves what many locals deem Aviemore's best pub food. The simple fare includes favorites such as Shetland halibut and Speyside beef, and the roasted potatoes are a good side for any main dish. The bar serves many local brews, and often hosts live music. Roaring fires are very welcome in a place where nights can be cool at anytime of year. $ *Average main: £17* ⊠ *Dalfaber Rd.* ☎ *01479/811137* ⊕ *www.oldbridgeinn.co.uk* ⚠ *Reservations essential.*

$$ ☖ **Mountview Hotel.** An old hunting lodge perched in the hills of
HOTEL   Nethybridge, this hotel has great views out over the valley. **Pros:** stunning setting; pretty views; good restaurant. **Cons:** some rooms have separate bathrooms. $ *Rooms from: £120* ⊠ *B970, Nethy-bridge* ☎ *01479/821515* ⊕ *www.mountviewhotel.co.uk* ⤴ *12 rooms* ⦿ *Breakfast.*

SPORTS AND THE OUTDOORS

Fodor'sChoice   **Boat of Garten Golf Club.** This is one of Scotland's greatest "undiscovered"
★   courses, and each of its 18 holes has a strong Highland feel. Some cut through birch wood and heathery rough, and most have long views to the Cairngorms. An unusual feature is the preserved steam railway that runs alongside part of the course. The course, which dates to the late 19th century, was redesigned and extended by James Braid in 1932. ⊠ *Nethybridge Rd., Boat of Garten* ☎ *01479/831282* ⊕ *www.boatgolf. com* ✉ *£41–£46* ⚠ *Reservations essential* ⚑ *18 holes, 5876 yards, par 70* ⊘ *Daily.*

G2 Outdoor. The adventures you can arrange through G2 include white-water rafting, gorge walking, and rock climbing. The company offers a family float trip on the River Spey in summer, and in winter runs ski courses. ⊠ *Dalfaber Industrial Estate, off Dalfaber Dr.* ☎ *01479/811008* ⊕ *www.g2outdoor.co.uk.*

Glenmore Lodge. Inside Cairngorms National Park, this is a good center for courses on rock and ice climbing, hiking, kayaking, ski touring, mountain biking, and other sports. The superb facilities include an indoor climbing wall. ⊠ *Signposted on B970, about 5 miles west of Glenmore* ☎ *01479/861256* ⊕ *www.glenmorelodge.org.uk.*

KINGUSSIE

13 miles southwest of Aviemore.

Kingussie is a pretty town east of the Monadhliadh Mountains. With great distant views of the Cairngorms, it's a good fit for those who would prefer to avoid the bustle of Aviemore.

GETTING HERE AND AROUND

From Aviemore, Kingussie is easy to reach by car via the A9 and the A86.

EXPLORING

FAMILY **Highland Folk Museum.** At the museum you can explore reconstructed Highland buildings, including a Victorian-era schoolhouse, and watch tailors, clockmakers, and joiners demonstrating their trades. Walking paths (or old-fashioned buses) take you to an 18th-century township that includes a feal house, made of turf, and a weaver's house. Throughout the museum are hands-on exhibits, among them a working quern stone for grinding grain, that make this a great outing for kids. Newtonmore is 5 miles west of Kingussie. ⊠ *Kingussie Rd., Newtonmore* ☎ *01540/673551* ⊕ *www. highlandfolk.com* ⊠ *Free* ⊙ *Late Mar.–Aug., daily 10:30–5:30; Sept. and Oct., daily 11–4:30.*

> ### BIKING THE GLEN
>
> A dedicated bicycle path runs from Glasgow to Inverness, passing through Fort William and Kingussie. Additionally, a good network of back roads snakes around Inverness and toward Nairn. The B862/B852, which runs by the southeastern side of Loch Ness, has little traffic and is a good bet for cyclists. Stay off the A9, though—it's busy with vehicular traffic on both sides of Aviemore.

WHERE TO EAT AND STAY

$$$$ ✕ **The Cross at Kingussie.** This former tweed mill, with a narrow river
BRITISH running alongside its stone walls, is set in 4 acres of woodlands. The
Fodor's Choice intimate dining room, whose stone walls have been painted a creamy
★ white, is warmed by a crackling fireplace. The fixed-price menus are smart and bold, with dishes such as local lamb with truffle gnocchi, or halibut with samphire and shrimp butter. Each dish reveals an intimate knowledge of textures and flavors. You can also spend the night; rooms start at £100. $ *Average main: £60* ⊠ *Tweed Mill Brae, Ardbroilach Rd.* ☎ *01540/661166* ⊕ *www.thecross.co.uk* ⊙ *Closed Jan. No dinner Sun. and Mon.*

$ ✕ **The Potting Shed.** Seasonal fruits and smooth cream top many of the
CAFÉ delectable desserts at this Kingussie cake shop. Taught by his Norwe-
FAMILY gian mother, John Borrowman makes sponges that are rich and light
Fodor's Choice and contain no butter or fat (although you can't say the same thing
★ about the rich cream they're topped with). The shop also offers gluten-free options that use almonds in place of flour. $ *Average main: £5* ⊠ *Main St.* ☎ *01540/651287* ⊕ *www.inshriachnursery.co.uk* ⊙ *Closed Tues. and Wed.*

$ ⬚ **Coig Na Shee.** This century-old Highland lodge has a warm and cozy
B&B/INN atmosphere. **Pros:** excellent rooms; quiet location; great walks from house. **Cons:** a bit out of the way. $ *Rooms from: £70* ⊠ *Laggan Rd., Newtonmore* ☎ *01540/670109* ⊕ *www.coignashee.co.uk* ⬚ *5 rooms* ⊙ *Breakfast.*

19

LOCH NESS, FORT WILLIAM, AND ENVIRONS

Loch Ness draws attention for its famous monster, but it also has its own dramatic beauty. Heading south from Inverness, you can travel along the loch's quiet east side or the more touristy west side. A pleasant morning can be spent at Urquhart Castle, in the tiny town of Drumnadrochit, or a bit farther south in the pretty town of Fort Augustus, where the Caledonian Canal meets Loch Ness. As you travel south and west, the landscape opens up and the Nevis Range comes into view.

A more leisurely alternative to the fast-moving traffic on the busy A82 from Inverness to Fort William is to take the B862 south from Inverness and follow the eastern bank of Loch Ness. Take the opportunity to view the waterfalls at Foyers and the peaceful, reedy Loch Tarff. Descend through forests and moorland until the road runs around the southern tip of Loch Ness.

From Fort William you can visit the dark, cloud-laden mountains of Glencoe and the desolate stretch of moors and lochans at Rannoch Moor. Travelers drive through this region to experience the landscape, which changes at nearly every turn. It's a brooding, haunting area that's worth a visit in any season.

The Road to the Isles, less romantically known as the A830, leads from Fort William to the coastal towns of Arisaig, Morar, and Mallaig, with ferry access to Skye as well as some smaller isles.

DRUMNADROCHIT

58 miles northwest of Kingussie, 14 miles south of Inverness.

A tourist hub at the curve of the road, Drumnadrochit attracts hordes of monster hunters. There aren't many good restaurants, but there are decent enough hotels.

GETTING HERE AND AROUND

It's easy to get here from Fort Augustus or Inverness via the A82, either by car or by local bus.

EXPLORING

Loch Ness. The A82 provides many views of this formidable and famous lake, whose waters, at maximum more than 800 feet deep, are reputedly home to the Loch Ness Monster. Don't let the tales of the monster distract you from enjoying the scenery. The English lexicographer Dr. Samuel Johnson (1709–84) and his guide and biographer, James Boswell (1740–95), passed the loch on their way to the Hebrides in 1783, and commented on the poverty of the population and their squalid living conditions. Starting in the 1720s, the English General George Wade oversaw the construction of military roads along the eastern shore. None of these visitors mentioned a monster.

FAMILY **Loch Ness Centre & Exhibition.** The center documents the fuzzy photographs, unexplained sonar readings, and sincere testimony of eyewitnesses regarding the Loch Ness Monster. It has been said that the warm local climate produces mirages on the water, but you'll have to make up your own mind. Whether the *bestia aquatilis* lurks in the depths

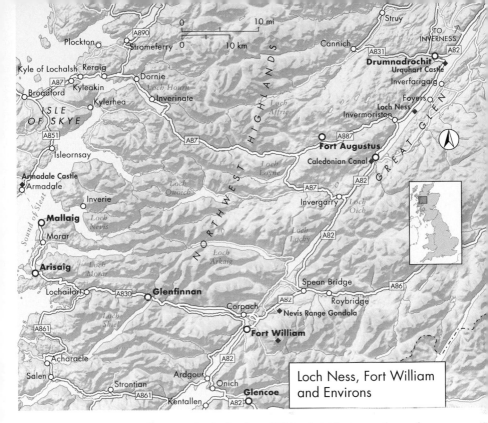

Loch Ness, Fort William
and Environs

is more than ever in doubt since 1994, when the man who took one
of the most convincing photos of Nessie confessed on his deathbed
that it was a fake. From late spring to early fall you can take a cruise
of the loch. ⊠ *On A82* ☎ *01456/450573* ⊕ *www.lochness.com* 📧 *£7*
☉ *Easter–June, daily 10–4:15; July and Aug., daily 9:30–6:45; Sept.
and Oct., daily 9:30–5:45; Nov.–Easter, daily 10–4:15; last admission
45 mins before closing.*

Urquhart Castle. About 2 miles southeast of Drumnadrochit, this castle
is a favorite Loch Ness Monster–watching spot. This romantically bro-
ken-down 13th-century fortress stands on a promontory overlooking
the loch, a strategic position in the Great Glen line of communication
that made it the focus of assault and occupation over the years. The
castle was destroyed before the end of the 17th century to prevent
its use by the Jacobites. Exhibits at the visitor center provide an idea
of what life was like here in medieval times. ⊠ *A82* ☎ *01456/450551*
⊕ *www.historic-scotland.gov.uk/places* 📧 *£8* ☉ *Apr.–Sept., daily 9:30–
6; Oct., daily 9:30–5; Nov.–Mar., daily 9:30–4:30; last admission 45
mins before closing.*

WHERE TO STAY

$$$ 🖼 **Loch Ness Lodge.** Run by siblings Scott and Iona Sutherland, the lodge
B&B/INN is opulent, classy, and welcoming. **Pros:** excellent staff; superb views;
Fodor'sChoice nice touches in rooms. **Cons:** near a busy road; no restaurant. $ *Rooms*
★ *from: £210* ✉ *A82, Brachla* ☎ *01456/459469* ⊕ *www.loch-ness-lodge.*
com ⇄ *7 rooms* 🍽 *Some meals.*

FORT AUGUSTUS

19 miles south of Drumnadrochit, 33 miles south of Inverness.

The best place to see the locks of the Caledonian Canal is at Fort
Augustus, at the southern tip of Loch Ness. The small town is a great
place to begin walking and cycling excursions, or to sit by the canal
watching the locks fill and empty as boats sail between Loch Ness and
Loch Laggan. The Jacobite clans captured Fort Augustus during the
1745 rebellion. The fort was later rebuilt as a Benedictine abbey, but
the monks no longer live here.

GETTING HERE AND AROUND

Fort Augustus is an easy drive from Inverness or Drumnadrochit on the
A82. Buses run frequently here.

EXPLORING

Caledonian Canal. The link between the lochs of the Great Glen—Loch
Lochy, Loch Oich, and Loch Ness—originated at the time of the Napo-
leonic Wars with France, when Great Britain needed a faster way to
move naval vessels from one side of Scotland to the other. The canal,
which took 19 years to complete, has 29 locks and 42 gates. Thomas
Telford (1757–1834), the great Scottish engineer, ingeniously took
advantage of the Great Glen's three lochs. With their length a combined
45 miles, only 22 miles of canal had to be constructed to complete the
waterway from coast to coast. Stunning vistas open up along the canal:
mountains, lochs, and glens, and to the south, the profile of Ben Nevis.
✉ *Ardchattan House, Canalside* ⊕ *www.scottishcanals.co.uk* ☉ *Visitor
center: Apr.–Oct., 10–1:30 and 2–5:30.*

WHERE TO STAY

$$ 🖼 **Glengarry Castle Hotel.** Tucked away in Invergarry, this rambling baro-
HOTEL nial mansion is just south of Loch Ness and within easy reach of the
Fodor'sChoice Great Glen's most popular sights. **Pros:** atmospheric building and gar-
★ dens; good-value takeout lunches; family rooms available. **Cons:** no
elevator. $ *Rooms from: £124* ✉ *On A82, Invergarry* ☎ *01809/501254*
⊕ *www.glengarry.net* ⇄ *26 rooms* ☉ *Closed mid-Nov.–mid-Mar.*
🍽 *Breakfast.*

FORT WILLIAM

*31 miles southwest of Fort Augustus, 69 miles southwest of Inverness,
108 miles northwest of Glasgow, 135 miles northwest of Edinburgh.*

Fort William is the southern gateway to the Great Glen and the far west.
It's not Scotland's most charming or authentic town, but it's got several
good hotels and makes a convenient base for exploring the surrounding

countryside. As its name suggests, Fort William originated as a military outpost, first established by Oliver Cromwell's General Monk in 1655 and refortified by George I (1660–1727) in 1715 to combat an uprising by the turbulent Jacobites.

GETTING HERE AND AROUND

From Inverness and Fort Augustus to the north and Glasgow to the south, the A82 takes you the entire way. From Edinburgh, take the M9 to the A84. This empties into the A85, which connects to the A82. Roads around Fort William are well maintained, but mostly one lane in each direction. They can be busy in summer.

A Scottish Citylink bus connects Glasgow and Fort William. ScotRail has trains from London, as well as connections from Glasgow and Edinburgh. It also operates a train service three times a day between Fort William and Mallaig.

ESSENTIALS

Visitor Information Fort William Tourist Information Centre ✉ *15 High St.* ☎ *01397/701801* ⊕ *www.visitscotland.com.*

EXPLORING

Ben Nevis. The tallest mountain in the British Isles, 4,406-foot Ben Nevis looms over Fort William, less than 4 miles from Loch Linnhe. A trek to its summit is a rewarding experience, but you should be fit and well prepared: bring food and water, a map and a compass, a first-aid kit, a whistle, a hat, gloves, a mobile phone with tracker, and warm clothing (yes, even in summer). It's wise to seek weather and other advice at the local tourist office before you begin.

Fodor'sChoice ★ **Jacobite Steam Train.** The most relaxing way to take in the landscape of birch- and bracken-covered wild slopes is by rail, and the best ride is on the steam train's famously scenic 84-mile round-trip between Fort William and Mallaig. You'll see mountains, lochs, beaches, and islands along the way. ✉ *Station Square* ☎ *0844/850–4685* ⊕ *www. westcoastrailways.co.uk* 🎫 *£33* ⊙ *Mid-May–June and late Sept.–late Oct., weekdays; July and Aug., daily.*

Nevis Range Gondola. An enjoyable way to ascend a mountain—in this case Aonach Mor, part of the Nevis range—is by gondola. The cable cars here rise nearly 610 meters (2,000 feet) to the summit. The journey takes about 15 minutes, and needless to say the views of the Great Glen are incredible—but definitely not for those without a head for heights. ✉ *Off A82, 3 miles north of A830, Fort William* ☎ *01397/705825* ⊕ *www.nevisrange.co.uk* 🎫 *£11.50* ⊙ *Apr.–June and Sept., daily 10–5; July–Aug., daily 9:30–6; Oct.–mid-Nov. and Jan.–Mar., weekdays 9–5. Hours may change according to daylight and weather conditions.* ⊙ *Closed mid-Nov.–Dec.*

WHERE TO EAT AND STAY

$$ SEAFOOD ✕ **Crannog Seafood Restaurant.** Loch Linnhe fishing boats deliver their catch straight to the kitchen of this seafood restaurant perched on the town pier. The menu changes daily, but you could find salmon with fennel and orange salad, or hake with a peppercorn crust served with samphire. From the window seats you can watch the sun setting on the

19

far side of the loch. Reservations are recommended. The restaurant also runs daily, 90-minute cruises (£12.50) of Loch Linnhe during summer. $ *Average main: £18* ☒ *The Pier* ☎ *01397/705589* ⊕ *www.crannog.net.*

$$
B&B/INN

☷ **Crolinnhe.** An elegant Victorian house with colorful gardens, this exceptionally comfortable B&B overlooks Loch Linnhe, yet is only a 10-minute walk from town. **Pros:** stunning loch views; great breakfasts; comfortable rooms. **Cons:** final payment only by cash or check. $ *Rooms from: £130* ☒ *Grange Rd.* ☎ *01397/702709* ⊕ *www.crolinnhe.co.uk* ➥ *3 rooms* ▭ *No credit cards* ☉ *Closed Nov.–Easter* ❍ *Breakfast.*

$$
B&B/INN
Fodor'sChoice
★

☷ **The Grange.** This meticulously renovated Victorian villa stands in pretty gardens a 10-minute walk from downtown. **Pros:** lots of little extras; great attention to detail; elegant lounge with plenty of books. **Cons:** no restaurant; not suitable for families with younger children. $ *Rooms from: £126* ☒ *Grange Rd.* ☎ *01397/705516* ⊕ *www.thegrange-scotland.co.uk* ➥ *3 rooms* ☉ *Closed Oct.–Mar.* ❍ *Breakfast.*

SPORTS AND THE OUTDOORS

This area—especially around Glen Nevis, Glencoe, and Ben Nevis—is popular with hikers; however, routes are not well marked, so contact the Fort William tourist information center before you go. The center will provide you with expert advice based on your interests, level of fitness, and hiking experience.

Glen Nevis. For a walk in Glen Nevis, drive north from Fort William on the A82 toward Fort Augustus. On the outskirts of town, just before the bridge over the River Nevis, turn right up the road signposted Glen Nevis. About 8 miles farther along is a parking lot where a footpath leads to waterfalls and a steel-cable bridge (1 mile), and then to Steall, a ruined croft beside a boulder-strewn stream. It's a good picnic place. You can continue up the glen for some distance without danger of becoming lost, so long as you stay on the path and keep the river to your right. Watch your step going through the tree-lined gorge. Reverse course to return to your car.

SHOPPING

Most shops here are along High Street, which in summer attracts crowds intent on stocking up for excursions to the west.

Ellis Brigham Mountain Sports. This shop can help you get kitted out for your outdoor adventures. ☒ *St. Marys Hall, Belford Rd.* ☎ *01397/706220* ⊕ *www.ellis-brigham.com.*

Nevisport. This shop has been selling outdoor supplies, maps, and travel books for more than 40 years. ☒ *High St.* ☎ *01397/704921* ⊕ *www.nevisport.com.*

GLENCOE

16 miles south of Fort William, 92 miles north of Glasgow, 44 miles northwest of Edinburgh.

Fodor'sChoice
★

Glencoe is both a small town and a region of awesome beauty, with high peaks and secluded glens. The area, where wild, craggy buttresses loom darkly over the road, has a special place in the folk memory of Scotland. The glen was the site of an infamous massacre in 1692, still remembered in the Highlands for the treachery with which soldiers of the Campbell clan, acting as a government militia, treated their hosts, the MacDonalds. According to Highland code, in his own home a clansman should give shelter even to his sworn enemy. In the face of bitter weather, the Campbells were accepted as guests by the MacDonalds. Apparently acting on orders from the British crown, the Campbells turned on their hosts and murdered them.

GETTING HERE AND AROUND

Glencoe is easily accessed by car via the A82. ScotRail trains and regional buses arrive from most of Scotland's major cities.

EXPLORING

FAMILY **Glencoe Visitor Centre.** Exhibits here describe the MacDonald massacre, and there are excellent interactive displays about the area's history and wilderness. Staff members provide advice about walking and other activities, and there's a café. ✉ *Off A82, 1 mile east of Glencoe Village* ☎ *0844/493–2222* 🌐 *www.glencoe-nts.org.uk* 🎟 *Exhibition £6.50* 🕒 *Late Mar.–Oct., daily 9:30–5:30; Nov.–late Mar., Thurs.–Sun. 10–4.*

WHERE TO STAY

$$$$ B&B/INN 🏨 **Glencoe House.** Peaceful surroundings, incredible views, and the friendliest of welcomes await you at this former Victorian hunting lodge. **Pros:** beautiful landscape; superb restoration; lovely hosts. **Cons:** no proper restaurant; pricey given the lack of facilities. [$] *Rooms from: £240* ✉ *Glencoe Lochan* ☎ *01855/811179* 🌐 *www.glencoe-house.com* 🛏 *7 rooms* 🍴 *No meals.*

GLENFINNAN

30 miles northwest of Glencoe, 10 miles west of Fort William, 26 miles southeast of Mallaig.

Perhaps the most visitor-oriented stop on the route between Fort William and Mallaig, Glenfinnan has much to offer if you're interested in Scottish, especially Jacobite, history.

GETTING HERE AND AROUND

If you're driving from Fort William, travel via the A830. For great views, take a ride in the Jacobite Steam Train, which you can catch in Fort William.

EXPLORING

Glenfinnan Monument. It was at Glenfinnan that the rash adventurer Bonnie Prince Charlie gathered his meager forces for the final Jacobite Rebellion of 1745–46. This commemorative tower, built in 1815, overlooks Loch Shiel; the figure at the top, however, is a Highlander and not the ill-fated prince. Exhibits at the visitor center convey the romantic and ultimately tragic story of the Jacobites' attempts to return a Stuart monarch and the Roman Catholic religion to a country that had become staunchly Protestant. You have to pay a small access fee when the center is open, but in truth it's just as picturesque when seen from the car park. ■ **TIP→ The view down Loch Shiel from the Glenfinnan Monument is one of the most photographed in Scotland.** ✉ *A830* ☎ *0844/493–2221* 🌐 *www.nts.org.uk* 🎟 *£3.50* 🕒 *Late Mar.–Oct., daily 10–5.*

The scenic Jacobite Steam Train between Fort William and Mallaig provides a ride over the 21 arches of the Glenfinnan Viaduct.

Glenfinnan Viaduct. The 1,248-foot-long Glenfinnan Viaduct was a genuine wonder when it was built in 1897, and remains so today. The railway's contractor, Robert MacAlpine—known among locals as "Concrete Bob"—pioneered the use of concrete for bridges when his company built the Mallaig extension, which opened in 1901. In more recent times the viaduct became famous for its appearance in the Harry Potter films. The viaduct can be seen on foot; about half a mile east of the railway station in Glenfinnan, on the A830 road, is a small parking lot. Take the footpath from here; you'll reach the viaduct in about ½ mile. ✉ *A380.*

WHERE TO STAY

$$ HOTEL 🏨 **Glenfinnan House.** This handsome hotel on the shores of Loch Shiel was built in the 18th century as the home of Alexander MacDonald VII of Glenaladale, who was wounded fighting for Bonnie Prince Charlie; it was transformed into an even grander mansion in the 19th century. **Pros:** fabulous setting; atmospheric dining experience. **Cons:** not all guest rooms have private bathrooms. [$] *Rooms from: £140* ✉ *A830* ☎ *01397/722235* 🌐 *www.glenfinnanhouse.com* 🛏 *14 rooms* 🕓 *Closed mid-Nov.–mid-Mar.* 🍴 *Breakfast.*

EN ROUTE

As you get closer to **Arisaig** along A830, you'll be able to spot Eigg, a low island marked by the dramatic black peak of An Sgurr. Beyond Eigg is the larger Rum, with its range of hills and the Norse-named, cloud-capped Rum Coullin looming over the island. The breathtaking seaward views should continue to distract you from the road beside Loch nan Uamh (from Gaelic, meaning "cave," and pronounced *oo*-am). This loch is associated with Prince Charles Edward Stuart's nine-month stay on the mainland, during which he gathered a small army, marched as far south as Derby in England, alarmed the king, retreated to unavoidable defeat at Culloden in the spring, and then spent a few months as a fugitive in the Highlands. A cairn by the shore marks the spot where the prince was rescued by a French ship; he never returned to Scotland.

ARISAIG

15 miles west of Glenfinnan.

Considering its small size, Arisaig, gateway to the **Small Isles,** offers a surprising choice of high-quality options for dining and lodging. To the north of Arisaig the road cuts across a headland to reach a stretch of coastline where silver sands glitter with the mica in the local rock when the sun is shining.

From Arisaig try to visit a couple of the Small Isles: **Rum, Eigg, Muck,** and **Canna,** each tiny and with few or no inhabitants. Rum serves as a wildlife reserve, while Eigg has the world's first solely wind-, wave-, and solar-powered electricity grid.

GETTING HERE AND AROUND

From Glenfinnan, you reach Arisaig on the A830, the only road leading west. The Fort William–Mallaig train also stops here.

EXPLORING

Arisaig Marine. Along with whale-, seal-, and bird-watching excursions, Arisaig Marine runs a boat service from the harbor at Arisaig to the islands from May to September. You can also charter a fast motor yacht. ✉ *Arisaig Harbour* ☎ *01687/450224* 🌐 *www.arisaig.co.uk* 🎟 *£18.*

WHERE TO EAT AND STAY

$$$ FRENCH — 🍴 **Old Library.** On the waterfront, this 1722 barn has been converted into a fine, reasonably priced restaurant. Local fish and other fare is prepared French-bistro style and served in the whitewashed, airy dining room. Six cozy rooms with contemporary furnishings are available starting at around £50. [$] *Average main: £22* ✉ *A30* ☎ *01687/450651.*

$$ HOTEL — Fodor's Choice ★ — 🏨 **Arisaig House.** An open-arms welcome and amazing views of the Isle of Skye await you at this wonderful mansion. **Pros:** amazing views; gracious hosts; outstanding food. **Cons:** a bit isolated. [$] *Rooms from: £145* ✉ *Beasdale* ☎ *01687/450730* 🌐 *www.arisaighouse.co.uk* 🛏 *4 rooms, 6 suites* 🍽 *Multiple meal plans.*

MALLAIG

8 miles north of Arisaig, 44 miles northwest of Fort William.

After the approach along the coast, the workaday fishing port of Mallaig itself is slightly anticlimactic. It has a few shops, and there's some bustle by the quayside when fishing boats unload or the ferry departs for the Isle of Skye, the largest island of the Inner Hebrides.

Mallaig is also the starting point for day cruises up the Sound of Sleat, which separates Skye from the mainland. The sound offers views into the rugged Knoydart region and its long, fjordlike sea lochs: Lochs Nevis and Hourn. The area to the immediate north and west beyond

Loch Nevis, one of the most remote in Scotland, is often referred to as the Rough Bounds of Knoydart.

GETTING HERE AND AROUND

The Fort William–Mallaig train is by far the best way to travel to Mallaig, because you can relax and enjoy the incredible views. By car take the A830.

EXPLORING

Caledonian MacBrayne. CalMac runs scheduled service and cruises from Mallaig to Skye. The ferries depart from several different points along the coast; the port at Mallaig also has a booking office. ⊠ *Mallaig Harbour* ☎ *0800/066–5000* ⊕ *www.calmac.co.uk.*

MV Western Isles Cruises. This company runs year-round Loch Nevis and other cruises. ⊠ *Mallaig Harbour* ☎ *01687/462233* ⊕ *www.westernislescruises.co.uk.*

ISLE OF SKYE

Fodor's Choice
★

Skye is full of romance and myth, lush gardens, and steep, magnetic mountains (a compass is useless in the Cuillin range). It ranks near the top of most visitors' must-see lists: the romance of Bonnie Prince Charlie and the wild beauty of the Cuillin Mountains contribute to its popularity. Skye remains dramatic and mysterious, an island of magical mists and sunsets that linger brilliantly until late at night. Much photographed are the old crofts, one or two of which are still inhabited. It also has some impressive accommodations and restaurants.

To reach Skye, you can cross over the bridge spanning the narrow channel of Kyleakin, between Kyle of Lochalsh and Kyleakin; in summer you can take the more romantic trip via boats between Mallaig and Armadale, or the little old ferry between Glenelg and Kylerea. You can easily see the island's sights in two or three days, but a bit longer would allow time for some hiking or kayaking.

Orientation is easy: in the north, follow the roads that loop around the peninsulas of Waternish and Trotternish; in the south, take the road running the length of the Sleat Peninsula. There are some stretches of single-lane road, but with attention and care none pose a problem.

KYLE OF LOCHALSH

28 miles (ferry crossing) north of Mallaig, 55 miles west of Inverness.

This little town is the mainland gateway to Skye. The bridge linking Kyle to Skye opened in 1995, transforming not only travel to Skye but also the very seascape itself. The most noticeable attraction, though (in fact, almost a cliché), is not in Kyle at all, but 8 miles farther east at Dornie—Eilean Donan Castle.

GETTING HERE AND AROUND

From the north, you reach Kyle of Lochalsh via the A890 or A896; from the south, take the A87. From Mallaig, take the Armadale ferry to Skye and follow the A851 to the A87.

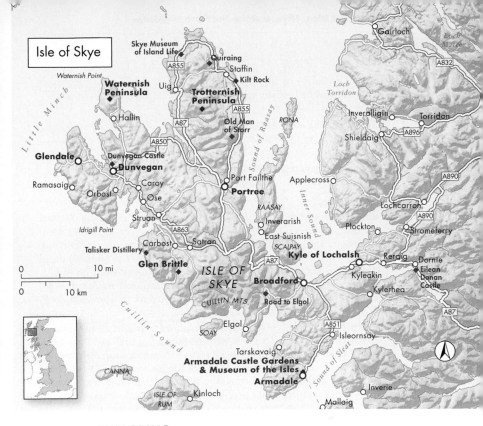

Isle of Skye

Waternish Point, Little Minch, Waternish Peninsula, Hallin, Uig, Skye Museum of Island Life, Quiraing, Staffin, Kilt Rock, Trotternish Peninsula, A855, A855, A87, Old Man of Storr, RONA, Sound of Raasay, Gairloch, Loch Maree, A832, Loch Torridon, Inveralligin, Torridon, A896, Shieldaig, Glendale, A850, Dunvegan Castle, Dunvegan, Ramasaig, Orbost, Caroy, Ose, Struan, A87, Port Failthe, Portree, RAASAY, Applecross, Inner Sound, Lochcarron, A890, A890, Stromeferry, Plockton, Idrigill Point, A863, Satran, Carbost, Inverarish, East Suisnish, SCALPAY, Kyle of Lochalsh, Reraig, Dornie, Eilean Donan Castle, Talisker Distillery, Glen Brittle, ISLE OF SKYE, A87, Broadford, Kyleakin, Kylerhea, A87, CUILLIN MTS., Road to Elgol, Cuillin Sound, Elgol, SOAY, A851, Isleornsay, Tarskavaig, Armadale Castle Gardens & Museum of the Isles, Armadale, Inverie, CANNA, ISLE OF RUM, Kinloch, Sound of Sleat, Mallaig

0 10 mi
0 10 km

EXPLORING

Eilean Donan Castle. Guarding the confluence of lochs Long, Alsh, and Duich stands the most picturesque of all Scottish castles, Eilean Donan, perched on an islet connected to the mainland by a stone-arched bridge. Dating from the 14th century, this romantic icon has all the massive stone walls, timber ceilings, and winding stairs that you could ask for. Empty and neglected for years after being bombarded by frigates of the Royal Navy during an abortive Spanish-Jacobite landing in 1719, it was almost entirely rebuilt in the early 20th century. The kitchen re-creates the busy scene before a grand banquet, and the upper floors show how the castle was transformed into a grand house. ⊠ *A87, 8 miles east of Kyle of Lochalsh, Dornie* 📠 *01599/555202* ⊕ *www. eileandonancastle.com* 🎫 *£6.50* ☉ *Feb.–May and Oct.–Dec., daily 10–6; June and Sept., daily 9:30–6; July and Aug., daily 9–6.*

WHERE TO STAY

$$
B&B/INN **Glenelg Inn.** Looking out over the Sound of Sleat, the Glenelg Inn's pleasant, contemporary rooms are furnished in wood and cane and are bright and clean. **Pros:** lively atmosphere; nice views; pleasant rooms. **Cons:** only some rooms have sea views; out-of-the-way location. $ *Rooms from: £120* ⊠ *Kirkton* 📞 *01599/522273* ⊕ *www.glenelg-inn. com* 🛏 *7 rooms* ⎟◎⎟ *Breakfast.*

BROADFORD

8 miles west of Kyle of Lochalsh via Skye Bridge.

One of the larger of Skye's settlements, Broadford lies along the shore of Broadford Bay, which has on occasion welcomed whales to its sheltered waters.

GETTING HERE AND AROUND

Broadford is on the main road crossing the Isle of Skye, the A87.

ESSENTIALS

Visitor Information Broadford Tourist Information Centre ✉ *Off A87* ☎ *08452/255121* 🌐 *www.visithighlands.com.*

EXPLORING

FAMILY Fodor's Choice ★ **Misty Isle Boat Trips.** For fantastic views of the Cuillin Mountains and the Inner Hebrides, take one of these boat trips. The expansive scenery around Loch Coruisk is some of the most spectacular in Scotland. Round-trip journeys depart from the town of Elgol, and booking ahead is essential. Prices vary, but a cruise to a seal colony costs around £15. Private charters are available. ✉ *Elgol jetty, Sealladh na Mara, Elgol* ☎ *01471/866288* 🌐 *www.mistyisleboattrips.co.uk* 🕒 *Mon.–Sat. at 9, 11, 2:15, and 5:15.*

OFF THE BEATEN PATH **Road to Elgol.** The B8083 leads from Broadford to one of the finest views in Scotland. This road passes through **Strath Suardal** and little **Loch Cill Chriosd** (Kilchrist) by a ruined church. You can appreciate breathtaking views of the mountain called **Bla Bheinn** as the A881 continues to Elgol, a gathering of crofts along this road that descends to a pier. Admire the heart-stopping profile of the Cuillin peaks from the shore, or, at a point about halfway down the hill, you can find the path that goes toward them across the rough grasslands.

Bella Jane. Take a boat trip on the *Bella Jane* toward Loch Coruisk, where you'll be able to see seals. The three-hour round-trip excursions, available April to October (and sometimes beyond), cost £24 per person. ✉ *Elgol jetty, B8083, Elgol* ☎ *01471/866244* 🌐 *www.bellajane.co.uk*

WHERE TO STAY

$$ HOTEL 🏨 **Broadford Hotel.** Though few of the rooms look directly out to sea, this comfortable hotel's dining room does have fine views of Broadford Bay. **Pros:** good base for touring the island; near the village; free Wi-Fi throughout. **Cons:** no elevator; rather dark public areas. [$] *Rooms from: £149* ✉ *Torrin Rd.* ☎ *01471/822204* 🌐 *www.broadfordhotel.co.uk* 🛏 *11 rooms* 🍴 *Breakfast.*

ARMADALE

17 miles south of Broadford, 43 miles south of Portree, 5 miles (ferry crossing) west of Mallaig.

Rolling moorlands, scattered with rivers and lochans, give way to enchanting hidden coves and scattered waterside communities here in the southernmost part of Skye.

GETTING HERE AND AROUND

The Mallaig-Armadale ferry arrives here. There's a short (and beautiful) road to the southwest, while the main road heads east following the stunning coast.

EXPLORING

Clan Donald Skye. Walk the lush, extensive gardens at Armadale Castle Gardens and the Museum of the Isles and you take in magnificent view across the Sound of Sleat to Knoydart and the Mallaig Peninsula. The museum tells the story of the Macdonalds and their proud title—the Lords of the Isles—with the help of an excellent audiovisual presentation. In the 15th century the clan was powerful enough to threaten the authority of the Stewart monarchs of Scotland. There's a gift shop, restaurant, library, and center for genealogy research. Also on the grounds are high-quality accommodations in seven cottages with kitchen facilities. Access is from Armadale Pier, where signs indicate the different forest walks that are available. ✉ *Off A851, ½ mile north of Armadale Pier* ☎ *01471/844305* 🌐 *www.clandonald.com* 🎟 *Gardens free, museum £7.50* ⏲ *Gardens: daily dawn–dusk. Museum: Apr.–Oct., daily 9:30–5:30; last entry 30 mins before closing.*

WHERE TO STAY

$$$ HOTEL 🏨 **Hotel Eilean Iarmain.** Built on a small peninsula with a quiet lighthouse, this hotel has an unforgettable location. **Pros:** wonderful waterfront location; plenty of sporting activities, superb wine list. **Cons:** some unattractive renovations. [$] *Rooms from: £170* ✉ *Off A851* ☎ *01471/833332* 🌐 *www.eileaniarmain.co.uk* 🛏 *12 rooms, 4 suites* 🍴 *Breakfast.*

$$$$ HOTEL 🏨 **Kinloch Lodge.** Overlooking the tidal Loch na Dal, this historic lodge has buildings that date from the 17th century. **Pros:** historic property; interior full of character; great afternoon tea. **Cons:** rooms and dining are pricey. [$] *Rooms from: £320* ✉ *Off A851, Sleat* ☎ *01471/833333* 🌐 *www.kinloch-lodge.co.uk* 🛏 *15 rooms* 🍴 *Some meals.*

SHOPPING

Fodor's Choice ★ **Ragamuffin.** A friendly place, this well-stocked shop specializes in designer knitwear. In winter the staff might make you a cup of coffee while you browse, then mail your purchases back home for you. ✉ *Armadale Pier, off A851* ☎ *01471/844217* 🌐 *www.ragamuffinloves.blogspot.co.uk.*

PORTREE

43 miles north of Armadale.

Portree, the population center of the island, is a pleasant place clustered around a small and sheltered bay. Although not overburdened by historical features, it's a good touring base with a number of great shops and an excellent bakery.

GETTING HERE AND AROUND

The biggest town on Skye, Portree is well served by local buses and by a well-maintained road, the A87.

ESSENTIALS

Visitor Information **Portree Information Centre** ✉ *Bayfield House, Bayfield Rd.* ☎ *01478/614906* 🌐 *www.visithighlands.com.*

WHERE TO EAT

$$ MODERN BRITISH 🍴 **Bistro at Bosville.** This pleasant eatery overlooks Portree Harbour and its colorful row of waterfront houses. It can get busy, so you may have to wait a while in the bar next door. The kitchen serves basic dishes, well prepared and presented, with imaginative touches; try the sole on green lentils with chorizo, or the mackerel on a Niçoise salad. The portions are generous, though the wine is a little overpriced. The staff are cheerful and welcoming. [$] *Average main: £15* ✉ *9–11 Bosville Terr.* 🌐 *www.bosvillehotel.co.uk.*

$ BRITISH 🍴 **Café Arriba.** Up a steep flight of stairs, the laid-back café has window seats with great views over Portree Harbour. Using only local produce (whatever is "fresh, local, and available"), this is a good option for no-frills eating. Good choices include scallops, creamy summer risotto, and, on the lighter side, salad with freshly baked bread. [$] *Average main: £10* ✉ *Quay Brae, Quay St.* ☎ *01478/611830* 🕐 *No dinner.*

WHERE TO STAY

$$$ HOTEL 🏨 **Cuillin Hills Hotel.** This Victorian-era hunting lodge looks down on Portree and the brightly painted houses around the harbor. **Pros:** Portree is a short stroll away; good breakfast menu; attentive service. **Cons:** rooms at back overpriced; restaurant can get very busy; no elevator. [$] *Rooms from: £200* ✉ *Off A855* ☎ *01478/612003* 🌐 *www.cuillinhills-hotel-skye.co.uk* 🛏 *29 rooms* 🍽 *Breakfast.*

$$ B&B/INN Fodor's Choice ★ 🏨 **The Spoons.** After years of running a luxury estate for others, Marie and Ian Lewis put their considerable talents to work at the Spoons. **Pros:** top-notch breakfasts; perfect base for exploring; bucolic setting. **Cons:** books up quickly. [$] *Rooms from: £140* ✉ *75 Aird Bernisdale* ☎ *01470/532217* 🌐 *www.thespoonsonskye.com* 🛏 *3 rooms* 🍽 *Breakfast.*

$ B&B/INN 🏨 **Viewmount Guest House.** This pink house stands out on the main road near the southern entrance of Portree. **Pros:** cheerful owners; unpretentious but comfortable rooms; ample parking. **Cons:** Close to the main road; not good if you're not fond of animals. [$] *Rooms from: £76* ✉ *Viewfield Rd.* ☎ *01478/612570* 🌐 *www.viewmount-skye.co.uk* 🛏 *5 rooms* 🍽 *Breakfast.*

SHOPPING

Isle of Skye Soap Company. This shop stocks soaps, essential oils, and other nice-smelling gifts. ✉ *Somerled Sq.* ☎ *01478/611350* 🌐 *www.skye-soap.co.uk.*

TROTTERNISH PENINSULA

16 miles north of Portree.

As A855, the main road, goes north from Portree, cliffs rise to the left. They're actually the edge of an ancient lava flow, set back from the road and running for miles. Fossilized dinosaur bones have been uncovered

Clans and Tartans

The origins of the clans are diverse; some had Norman roots, some Norse—the product of Viking raids on Scotland. Others are traceable to the monastic system, while yet others may have descended from Pictish tribes. But by the 13th century the clan system was at the heart of Gaelic tribal culture. By the 15th century the clan chiefs of the Scottish Highlands were a threat even to the authority of the Stewart monarchs.

The word *clann* means "family" or "children" in Gaelic, and it was the custom for clan chiefs to board out their sons among nearby families, a practice that helped to bond the clan unit and create strong allegiances.

THE CLAN SYSTEM

The clan chiefs' need for strong men-at-arms, fast-running messengers, and bards for entertainment, and the preservation of clan genealogy, was the probable origin of the Highland Games, still celebrated in many Highland communities each year, and which are an otherwise rather inexplicable mix of sports, music, and dance.

Gradually, by the 18th century increasing knowledge of Lowland agricultural improvements, and better roads into the Highlands that improved communication of ideas and "southern" ways, began to weaken the clan system. The Battle of Culloden marked its death throes, as the victorious English armies banned the kilt and the pipes and claimed the land of the rebellious clan chiefs. And when the new landowners introduced the hardy Cheviot breed of sheep and changed farming activity, the Highlands were transformed forever and the Highlanders, and especially the islanders, began the long journey to emigration in the 1750s.

TARTAN REVIVAL

Tartan's own origins as a part of the clan system are disputed; the Gaelic word for striped cloth is *breacan*—piebald or spotted—so even the word itself is not Highland. However, when cloth was locally spun, woven, and dyed using plant derivatives, each neighborhood would have different dyestuffs. In this way, particular combinations of colors and favorite patterns of the local weavers could become associated with a particular area and therefore clan. Between 1746 and 1782 the wearing of tartan was generally prohibited. By the time the ban was lifted, many recipes for dyes and weaving patterns had been forgotten.

It took the influence of Sir Walter Scott, with his romantic (and fashionable) view of Highland history, to create the "modern myth" of clans and tartan. Sir Walter engineered George IV's visit to Scotland in 1822, which turned into a tartan extravaganza. The idea of one tartan or group of tartans "belonging" to one particular clan was created at this time—literally created, with new patterns and colorways dreamed up and "assigned" to particular clans. Queen Victoria and Prince Albert reinforced the tartan culture later in the century and with it the revival of the Highland Games.

Tartan Centre. You may be able to find a clan connection with expertise such as that available at the Clan Tartan Centre. ✉ *70–74 Bangor Rd., Leith, Edinburgh* ☎ *0131/5535161* ⊕ *www.ewm.co.uk.*

19

The Old Man of Storr, a volcanic pinnacle, is part of the dramatic scenery on Skye's Trotternish Peninsula.

at the base of these cliffs. Don't forget to look up: you might spot a sea eagle, identifiable by the flash of its white tail.

GETTING HERE AND AROUND

From Portree, take the twisting, undulating A855 as it follows the coast.

EXPLORING

Kilt Rock. From Portree, the A855 travels past neat white croft houses and forestry plantings to Kilt Rock, which got its odd name because the sheer rock is ridged like a pleated kilt. Everyone on the tour circuit stops here to peep over the edge at the viewing platform.

Old Man of Storr. Along the dramatic road around the Trotternish Peninsula, a gate beside a car park marks the beginning of the climb to the Old Man of Storr. Give yourself at least three hours to explore this 2,000-foot-high volcanic pinnacle with spectacular views from the top. The weather here changes very quickly, so be prepared.

Quiraing. A geological formation of rocky crags and stacks, the spectacular Quiraing dominates the horizon about 5 miles beyond Kilt Rock. For a closer view of this area's strange pinnacles, make a left onto a small road at Brogaig by Staffin Bay. There's a parking lot near the point where this road breaches the ever-present cliff line. The road is very narrow and rough, so drive cautiously. The rambler's trail is on uneven, stony ground, and it's a steep scramble up to the rock formations. In ages past, stolen cattle were hidden deep within the Quiraing's rocky jaws.

Skye Museum of Island Life. Not far from the tip of the Trotternish Peninsula, the Skye Museum of Island Life brings the old crofting ways vividly to life. Included in the displays and exhibits are documents and photographs, reconstructed interiors, and implements. Flora Macdonald, who assisted Bonnie Prince Charlie, is buried nearby. ✉ *Off A855, Kilmuir* ☎ *01470/552206* 🌐 *www.skyemuseum.co.uk* 🎟 *£2.50* 🕐 *Easter–Oct., Mon.–Sat. 9–5.*

Staffin Museum. Built on the foundations of an 1840s schoolhouse, this single-room museum is a labor of love of builder Dugald Ross, who first saw the fossilized dinosaur prints as a boy and as an adult saved them from rough seas. You'll also find objects saved from shipwrecks, agricultural implements, and some old photographs. ✉ *6 Ellishadder, Staffin* ☎ *01470/562321* 🌐 *www.borve.net/staffin-museum.co.uk* 🎟 *£2* 🕐 *Apr.–Sept., Mon.–Sat. 9–5.*

WHERE TO EAT AND STAY

$$$ BRITISH 🍴 **The Glenview.** On the Trotternish Peninsula between Portree and Staffin, a renovated croft building houses this gem of a "restaurant with rooms." With wood floors and cheerfully painted walls, the simple, chic decor allows the older building's charms to flourish. The well-considered menu (£29 for two courses, £35 for three) includes offerings like Skye shellfish broth and poached Uist salmon. If you like the place so much you want to stay, rooms are available from £110. [$] *Average main: £20* ✉ *A855, Culnacnoc* ☎ *01470/562248* 🌐 *www.glenviewskye.co.uk* ✍ *Reservations essential* 🕐 *No lunch. Closed Sun. and Mon.*

$$$$ HOTEL Fodor's Choice ★ 🏨 **Flodigarry Country House Hotel.** With spectacular coastal views, Flodigarry retains the feel of a grand country house, with antique furnishings and beautifully finished wood throughout. **Pros:** spectacular views; a good base for walking. **Cons:** the road down is steep; expensive rates; no room TVs. [$] *Rooms from: £250* ✉ *A855, Staffin* ☎ *01470/552203* 🌐 *www.flodigarry.co.uk* 🛏 *15 rooms* 🍽 *Breakfast.*

WATERNISH PENINSULA

19

20 miles northwest of Portree.

The northwestern corner of Skye has scattered crofting communities, magnificent coastal views, and a few good restaurants worth the trip in themselves. In the Hallin area look westward for an islet-scattered sea loch with small cliffs rising from the water—looking like miniature models of full-size islands.

GETTING HERE AND AROUND

From Portree, follow the A850 to the Waternish Peninsula.

WHERE TO EAT AND STAY

$$$$ SEAFOOD 🍴 **Loch Bay Seafood Restaurant.** The island's top chefs unwind at this black-and-white waterfront restaurant on their nights off, so you know the food must be good. The seafood is freshly caught and simply prepared, the goal being to enhance the natural flavors of the ingredients rather than overwhelm the senses with extraneous sauces. The many fish dishes include halibut, sea bass, and Western Ross salmon. At dinner you must order two courses. [$] *Average main: £26* ✉ *Off B886, near fishing jetty, Stein* ☎ *01470/592235* 🌐 *www.lochbay-seafood-restaurant.co.uk* ✍ *Reservations essential* 🕐 *Closed Sun. and Mon. No lunch Tues. and Fri.*

$$ B&B/INN **Greshornish House.** Set above a sea loch, this pretty white house stands among mature trees and beside a nurtured, but not tame, walled garden filled with raspberries and gooseberries. **Pros:** ideal setting; pretty gardens; great walks at the doorstep. **Cons:** reserved welcome may not suit everyone. [$] *Rooms from: £150* ✉ *Off A850, Greshornish* ☎ *01470/582266* 🌐 *www.greshornishhouse.com* *8 rooms* 🍴 *Some meals.*

DUNVEGAN

7 miles south of the Waternish Peninsula.

Dunvegan Castle is the big star here, but for some nature you can take a Dunvegan Sea Cruises boat trip from the castle to the nearby seal colony.

GETTING HERE AND AROUND

EXPLORING

Fodor's Choice ★ **Dunvegan Castle.** In a commanding position above a sea loch, Dunvegan Castle has been the seat of the chiefs of Clan MacLeod for more than 700 years. Though the structure has been greatly changed over the centuries, a gloomy ambience prevails, and there's plenty of family history on display, notably the Fairy Flag—a silk banner, thought to be originally from Rhodes or Syria and believed to have magically saved the clan from danger. Guides take you through several rooms, and an interesting collection of photos hangs in the lower corridors. Make time to visit the gardens, with their water garden and falls, fern house, a walled garden, and viewing points. There's a café beside the car park. ✉ *Junction of A850 and A863, Dunvegan* ☎ *01470/521206* 🌐 *www.dunvegancastle.com* 🎫 *Garden £7.50, castle and garden £9.50* ⏲ *Late Mar.–mid-Oct., daily 10–5:30, last entry 30 mins before closing.*

WHERE TO EAT

$$$$ MODERN BRITISH Fodor's Choice ★ ✕ **Three Chimneys.** On Loch Dunvegan, this old building with thick stone walls holds a restaurant that has become a top destination for serious foodies. The kitchen serves consistently daring, well-crafted food, and the chef's belief in Scottish ingredients is clear in what is on offer: Glendale salad leaves, panfried Mallaig skate, and Esk salmon. Dinner is a three- or seven-course fixed-price extravaganza; lunch is shorter but has an equally tempting menu. If you love the food so much you want to stay here, there are six comfortable rooms at the nearby House Over-By. [$] *Average main: £60* ✉ *B884, Colbost* ☎ *01470/511258* 🌐 *www.threechimneys.co.uk* ✍ *Reservations essential* ⏲ *No lunch Sun.*

GLEN BRITTLE AND THE CUILLIN MOUNTAINS

24 miles southeast of Dunvegan.

Fodor's Choice ★ The gentle slopes of the valley called Glen Brittle are a gateway to the dramatic peaks and ridges of the Cuillin Mountains. The lower slopes are fine for walkers and weekend climbers, but the higher ridges are strictly for the serious mountaineer.

GETTING HERE AND AROUND
Glen Brittle extends off the A863/B8009 on the west side of the island.

EXPLORING

Glen Brittle. You can safely enjoy spectacular mountain scenery in Glen Brittle, with some fine views of the Cuillin Mountains (which are not for the casual walker, as there are many steep and dangerous cliff faces). The drive from Carbost along a single-track road is one of the most dramatic in Scotland and draws outdoorsy types from throughout the world. At the southern end of the glen is a murky-color beach, a campground, and the chance for a gentle stroll amid the foothills. ⊠ *Off A863 and B8009.*

Talisker Distillery. The only distillery on the Isle of Skye, Talisker produces a sweet, light single malt that has the typical peaty aroma of island whiskies, but is a bit less intense. Robert Louis Stevenson called Talisker "the king of drinks." Classic tours take about 45 minutes, while two-hour tasting tours are usually available Monday, Wednesday, and Friday. ■TIP➔ **Book ahead, as the tours are very popular.** ⊠ *B8009, Carbost* ☎ *01478/614308* ⊕ *www.discovering-distilleries.com/talisker* ⊠ *£7* ⊙ *Apr., May, and Oct., Mon.–Sat. 9:30–5; June and Sept., Mon.–Sat., 9:30–5, Sun. 11–5; July and Aug., weekdays 9:30–5:30, Sat. 9:30–5, Sun. 11–5; Nov.–Mar., daily 10–4:30.*

THE NORTHERN HIGHLANDS

Wester Ross and Sutherland, the northernmost part of Scotland, have some of the most distinctive mountain profiles and coastal stretches in all of Scotland. Starting at Gairloch and moving north, then east, and finally south, you can experience the wild inland interior, the mountains, and the coast, before ending just north of Inverness. The rim roads around the wilds of Durness overlook rocky shores, and the long beaches are as dramatic as the awe-inspiring and desolate cross-country routes like Destitution Road in Wester Ross.

19

GAIRLOCH

103 miles northeast of Glen Brittle, 70 miles west of Inverness.

Aside from its restaurants and lodgings, peaceful Gairloch has one further advantage: lying just a short way from the mountains of the interior, this small oasis often escapes the rain clouds that can cling to the high summits. You can enjoy a round of golf here and perhaps stay dry, even when the nearby Torridon Hills are deluged.

GETTING HERE AND AROUND
From Inverness head west on the A9 to A835 to A832. North of Glen Brittle in Carbost, head east on B8009 to A863 to A87; then go north at A890 and west at A832.

EXPLORING

Fodor'sChoice **Destitution Road.** The road between Gairloch and the Corrieshalloch ★ Gorge initially heads north and passes coastal scenery with views of Gruinard Bay and its white beaches, then woodlands around Dundonnell and Loch Broom. Soon the route traverses wild country: the toothed ramparts of the mountain known as An Teallach (pronounced tyel-lack) are visible on the horizon. The moorland route you travel is known chillingly as Destitution Road. At Corrieshalloch the road, A832, joins the A835 for Inverness.

Fodor's Choice ★ **Inverewe Gardens.** A highlight of the area, Inverewe Gardens has lush plantings tucked away behind a dense barrier of trees and shrubs, all courtesy of the warm North Atlantic Drift, which takes the edge off winter frosts. Inverewe is sometimes described as subtropical, but do not expect coconuts and palm trees here. Instead, look for rarities such as the blue Himalayan poppy. ✉ *A832, 6 miles northeast of Gairloch, Poolewe* ☎ *01445/781200* 🌐 *www.nts.org.uk* 🎟 *£10* 🕘 *Easter–Oct., daily 9:30–9; Nov.–Mar., daily 9:30–5.*

Fodor's Choice ★ **Loch Maree.** Southeast of Gairloch stretches scenic Loch Maree. Its harmonious environs, with tall Scots pines and the mountain Slioch looming as a backdrop, witnessed the destruction of much of the tree cover in the 18th century. Iron ore was shipped in and smelted using local oak to feed the furnaces. Oak now grows here only on the northern limits of the range. Scottish Natural Heritage has an information center and nature trails by the loch and in the Beinn Eighe Nature Reserve. Red-deer sightings are virtually guaranteed; locals say the best place to spot another local denizen, the endangered pine marten (a member of the weasel family), is around the trash containers in the parking turnoffs.

WHERE TO STAY

$$ HOTEL 🏨 **Dundonnell Hotel.** This family-run hotel, set on the roadside by Little Loch Broom, has a solid reputation for hospitality. **Pros:** fabulous scenery; outdoor activities; good dining options. **Cons:** bland exterior; so-so decor. [$] *Rooms from: £120* ✉ *A832, 30 miles northeast of Gairloch, Dundonnell* ☎ *01854/633204* 🌐 *www.dundonnellhotel.com* 🛏 *28 rooms* 🍴 *Breakfast.*

ULLAPOOL

55 miles north of Gairloch, 57 miles west of Inverness.

Ullapool is an ideal base for hiking throughout Sutherland and taking wildlife and nature cruises, especially to the Summer Isles. The town, by the shores of salty Loch Broom, was founded in 1788 as a fishing station to exploit the local herring stocks. Some fishing vessels remain, and yachts and foreign ships visit as well. When their crews fill the pubs and local ferries arrive and depart, Ullapool has a lively, cosmopolitan feel.

GETTING HERE AND AROUND

From Gairloch take the A832 to the A835. The A835 will deliver you here from Inverness.

ESSENTIALS

Visitor Information Ullapool Visitor Centre ✉ *7 and 8 W. Argyle St.* ☎ *01854/612486* 🌐 *www.visitscotland.com* 🕘 *Apr.–Oct., Mon.–Sat. 10–5.*

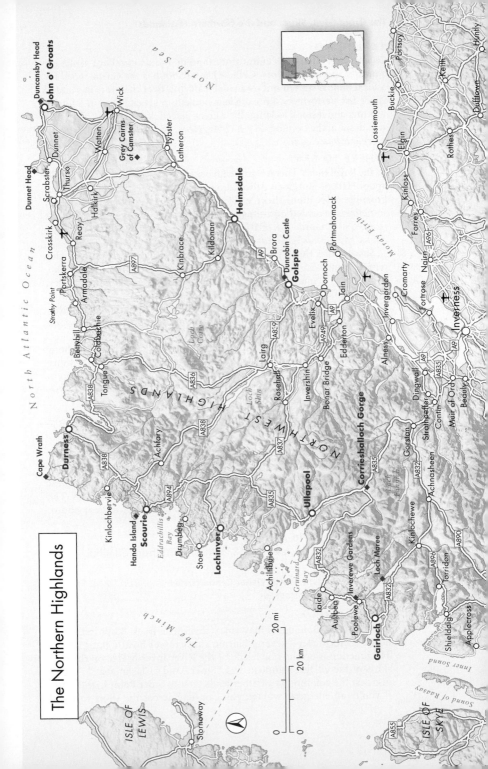

EXPLORING

Ceilidh Place. Ullapool's cultural focal point and an excellent venue for concerts and other events, Ceilidh Place (*ceilidh* is the Gaelic word for a local dance) started out as a small café and over the years has added space for performers, an excellent bookshop specializing in Scottish writing, and a small lodging. It's a great place for afternoon coffee or a wee dram in the evening. ✉ *14 W. Argyle St.* ☎ *01854/612103* 🌐 *www.theceilidhplace.com.*

WHERE TO STAY

$ HOTEL — 🏨 **The Royal Hotel.** This longtime favorite has beautiful views over Ullapool Harbor and Loch Broom, so be sure to request a balcony room. **Pros:** great location; short walk to Ullapool; good breakfasts. **Cons:** sometimes crowded and noisy; rear rooms have no views. [$] *Rooms from: £99* ✉ *Garve Rd.* ☎ *01854/612181* 🌐 *www.royalhotel-ullapool.com* 🛏 *55 rooms* 🍴 *Breakfast.*

$$ HOTEL Fodor's Choice ★ — 🏨 **Summer Isles Hotel.** Halfway along a road that ends at the sea, this remote gem, a 25-mile drive from Ullapool in the town of Achiltibuie, is built into a small hill and contemplates the mystical Summer Isles. **Pros:** Highlands chic; stunning views; peaceful location; good food. **Cons:** not much to do nearby. [$] *Rooms from: £155* ✉ *Achiltibuie Rd., Achiltibuie* ☎ *01854/622282* 🌐 *www.summerisleshotel.com* 🛏 *6 rooms* ⏲ *Closed Nov–Mar.* 🍴 *Breakfast.*

$$ B&B/INN — 🏨 **Tanglewood House.** On a headland overlooking Loch Broom, this hotel a mile from Ullapool feels much more remote. **Pros:** comfortable rooms; 4 acres of gardens. **Cons:** a steep drive down to the house. [$] *Rooms from: £104* ✉ *Off A835* ☎ *01854/612059* 🌐 *www.tanglewoodhouse.co.uk* 🛏 *3 rooms* 🍴 *Breakfast.*

LOCHINVER

38 miles north of Ullapool.

A splendid base for exploring Sutherland, Lochinver is a quiet shoreside community of whitewashed cottages, with a harbor used by the west coast fishing fleet, and a couple of good dining and lodging options. The mountain Suilven rises abruptly behind the town. For a great photo, take **Baddidarroch Road,** a cul-de-sac.

GETTING HERE AND AROUND

To get to Lochinver, take the A835/A837 north from Ullapool.

ESSENTIALS

Visitor Information **Assynt Visitor Centre** ✉ *Main St.* ☎ *01571/844654* 🌐 *www.discoverassynt.com.*

EXPLORING

Drumbeg Loop. Bold souls may enjoy this single-track B869 loop road north of Lochinver—several hairpin turns reveal breathtaking views. The junction is on the north side of the River Inver bridge on the outskirts of the village, signposted as "Stoer" and "Clashnessie." A road just past the community of Stoer leads west to **Stoer Point Lighthouse.** If you're an energetic walker, you can hike across the short turf and heather along the cliff top for fine views west over toward Skye. There's also a red-sandstone sea stack: the **Old Man of Stoer.**

WHERE TO EAT AND STAY

$ BRITISH 🍴 **Lochinver Mission.** An abandoned fishermen's mission—a place where fishermen stayed while in port—houses this cafeteria-style restaurant that dishes out top-notch fare. Hot breakfasts are served, and for lunch and dinner come expertly prepared langoustines and other local seafood, as well as soups and burgers. The restaurant can get crowded on weekends. The building also contains the local archives, a marine center, and three basic guest rooms. [$] *Average main: £9* ✉ *Culag Park* ☎ *01571/844324* 🌐 *www.lochinvermission.org.uk.*

$ B&B/INN 🏨 **Tigh Na Sith.** This B&B above the bay earns rave reviews for its owners' warm welcome; they'll pack lunches for your day excursions and provide binoculars so you can fully enjoy the views down to the loch and over the hills. **Pros:** great hosts; fantastic views. **Cons:** room at back doesn't have a view; shared dining table for breakfast may not suit everyone. [$] *Rooms from: £79* ✉ *A837* ☎ *01571/844352* 🌐 *www.tighnasith.com* 🛏 *3 rooms* 🍽 *Breakfast.*

SHOPPING

Achins Book & Craft Shop. On the Lochinver-Achiltibuie road, this shop carries Scottish fiction and books on natural history, hill walking, and trout fishing. It also sells craft items—knitwear, tweeds, and pottery—along with works by local artists and recordings of traditional music. The shop and pleasant café are open daily from 10 to 5 (except on Sunday from October to March). ✉ *Off B869, Inverkirkaig* ☎ *01571/844262* 🌐 *www.scotbooks.freeuk.com.*

SCOURIE

19

44 miles north of Lochinver, 66 miles north of Ullapool.

Bay-side Scourie is a small settlement catering to visitors—fisherfolk especially—with a range of accommodations. The town is a good base for a trip to the bird sanctuary on Handa Island.

GETTING HERE AND AROUND

From Lochinver, take the A837, which becomes the A894 as you turn north.

EXPLORING

Fodor's Choice ★ **Handa Island.** Just off the coast of Scourie is Handa Island, a huge bird sanctuary that shelters guillemots, razorbills, great skuas, kittiwakes, and even the odd puffin. At nesting time more than 200,000 birds gather on spectacular cliffs. The best view is from the towering sandstone vantage point of Stack an Seabhaig (Hawk's Stack). A remarkable reserve administered by the Scottish Wildlife Trust, Handa is open only in spring and summer. It can be reached by a small open boat from Tarbet; contact the tourist information center in Lochinver or Durness for details. ■ **TIP→ Sturdy boots, a waterproof jacket, and a degree of fitness are needed to walk the path around the island.**

WHERE TO STAY

$$ B&B/INN 🏨 **Eddrachilles Hotel.** The hotel's views—toward the tiny islands of Badcall Bay—are among the best of any lodging in Scotland. **Pros:** attractive garden; stunning shoreline nearby; close to bird sanctuary. **Cons:** restaurant's quality can vary; service sometimes disappoints. [$] *Rooms from: £110* ✉ *Off A894* ☎ *01971/502080* 🌐 *www.eddrachilles.com* 🛏 *11 rooms* 🕒 *Closed early Oct.–late Mar.* 🍴 *Breakfast.*

$$ HOTEL 🏨 **Kylesku Hotel.** This charming hotel looks out over Loch Glendhu and toward Eas Coul Aulin, Scotland's highest waterfall. **Pros:** stunning views; great staff; delicious food. **Cons:** some old-building quirks; two attic rooms are small, but cheaper. [$] *Rooms from: £115* ✉ *Off A894, Kylesku* ☎ *01971/502231* 🛏 *8 rooms* 🍴 *Breakfast.*

DURNESS

27 miles north of Scourie.

The sudden patches of green surrounding the village of Durness, on the north coast, are caused by the richer limestone outcrops among the acid moorlands. Here you'll find the country's highest cliff, Clo Mor.

GETTING HERE AND AROUND

Past Scourie, the A894 becomes the A838 as you head north. The road to Durness is often a single lane in each direction.

ESSENTIALS

Visitor Information Durness Information Centre ✉ *Sangomore* ☎ *01971/511368* 🌐 *www.durness.org.*

EXPLORING

Cape Wrath. If you've made it this far north, you'll probably want to go all the way to Cape Wrath, a rugged headland at Scotland's northwestern tip. The white-sand beaches, impressive dunes covered in marram grass, and crashing seas of nearby Balnakeil Bay make the cape an exhilarating place to visit. As this land is owned by the Ministry of Defence, you can't drive your own vehicle. From May through September a small boat ferries people here from Keoldale, 2 miles outside Durness; once you're across the sea inlet called the Kyle of Durness, a minibus will then take you to the lighthouse. Call ahead or check departure times on the board at the jetty. ☎ *01971/511284* 🌐 *www.capewrath.org.uk.*

WHERE TO STAY

$$ HOTEL 🏨 **Tongue Hotel.** With open fireplaces in its public areas and hunting lodge–style rooms, the Tongue makes a great base for exploring the northernmost coast of the Scottish mainland. **Pros:** welcoming atmosphere; stunning views; relaxing public rooms. **Cons:** you'll need a car to make the most of this area. [$] *Rooms from: £110* ✉ *On A838, near Lairg, Tongue* ☎ *01847/611206* 🌐 *www.tonguehotel.co.uk* 🛏 *19 rooms* 🍴 *Breakfast.*

SHOPPING

Balnakeil Craft Village. Artisans sell pottery, weavings, paintings, and other works from their studios, housed inside former military buildings. Cocoa Mountain, which serves up world-class truffles and rich hot chocolate, is a treat for those with a sweet tooth. ⊠ *Balnakeil* ☎*01971/511777* ⊙ *Village Apr.–Oct., most shops daily 10–5, later in summer.*

JOHN O'GROATS

130 miles northeast of Ullapool, 119 miles northwest of Inverness.

The windswept outpost of John o'Groats is usually credited as the northernmost community on the Scottish mainland, though this is not strictly accurate, as an exploration of the roads between Dunnet Head and the town will confirm. From the harbor you can take a boat to see the dolphins and seals that live beneath the coastal cliffs. Or you can seek out Duncansby Head, where you can watch the puffins and guillemots. This is nature, wild and untouched. The little town has charms of its own, including a crafts center with high-quality shops.

GETTING HERE AND AROUND

Traveling east from Durness, take the A838 and then the coast-hugging A836. From Inverness follow A9 and A99 north.

EXPLORING

Duncansby Head. Head to Duncansby Head for spectacular views of cliffs and sea stacks by the lighthouse—and puffins, too. It's on the coastal road east of town.

Dunnet Head. Many people make the trip to the northernmost point of mainland Britain, where the Dunnet Head Lighthouse, built in 1831, still stands. As a bonus, there are fine views over the sea to Orkney. ⊠ *Off B855.*

John o'Groats Ferries. Sailing from John o'Groats Harbor, this company conducts 90-minute cruises past spectacular cliff scenery and bird life into the Pentland Firth, to Duncansby Stacks, and to the island of Stroma. Trips cost £17 and take place daily at 2:30 between June and August. Between May and September the company runs day trips to Orkney for £47. ⊠ *County Rd.* ☎*01955/611353* ⊕ *www.jogferry. co.uk.*

THE ARTS

Lyth Arts Centre. A Victorian-era school building houses this cultural hub inland between John o'Groats and Wick. From April to November, professional music and theater companies fill the schedule. There are also exhibitions of contemporary fine art. ⊠ *Off A9, Lyth* ☎*01955/641434* ⊕ *www.lytharts.org.uk.*

EN
ROUTE

Grey Cairns of Camster. The extraordinary Grey Cairns of Camster, two Neolithic chambered cairns dating from 4000 BC to 3000 BC, are among the best preserved in Britain. **Camster Round Cairn** is 20 yards in diameter and 13 yards high, and **Camster Long Cairn** reaches nearly 77 yards in length. Some 19-century excavations revealed skeletons, pottery, and flint tools in the round cairn's internal chamber. You can crawl into the chambers in both cairns, which are 27 miles south of John o'Groats. ⊠ *Off A9* ☎*01667/460232* ⊕ *www.historic-scotland. gov.uk* ⊠ *Free* ⊙ *Open all yr.*

19

HELMSDALE

50 miles south of John o'Groats.

Helmsdale is a fascinating fishing village with a checkered past. It was a busy Viking settlement and then the scene of an aristocratic poisoning plot before it was transformed into a 19th-century village to house some of the people removed from their land to make way for sheep. These "clearances," perpetrated by the Duke of Sutherland, were among the area's most inhumane.

GETTING HERE AND AROUND

Helmsdale is one of the only towns on this part of the coast that has daily train service from Inverness. But a car will allow you to see more in the surrounding area. Get here via the coastal A9 or the inland A897.

EXPLORING

FAMILY **Timespan Heritage Centre.** This thought-provoking mix of displays, artifacts, and audiovisual materials portrays the history of the area from the Stone Age to the 1869 gold rush in the Strath of Kildonan. The garden contains a geology exhibit, and you can tour the Kildonan gold rush site. The complex also includes a café and an art gallery. ⊠ *Dunrobin St.* ☎ *01431/821327* ⊕ *www.timespan.org.uk* 🎫 *£4* ☉ *Mar–Oct., Mon.–Sat. 10–5, Sun. noon–5; Nov.–Feb., Sat. 11–4, Tues. 2–4; last admission 1 hr before closing.*

GOLSPIE

18 miles south of Helmsdale.

The little coastal town of Golspie is worth a stop if you're heading for Dunrobin Castle. There are several places to stop for a bite and some shops to poke around in.

GETTING HERE AND AROUND

Golspie can be reached by train from Inverness; in summer the train also stops at Dunrobin Castle. Drivers should use the A9.

EXPLORING

Dunrobin Castle. The Scottish home of the dukes of Sutherland is flamboyant Dunrobin Castle, an ancient seat developed by the first duke into a 19th-century white-turreted behemoth. As well as lavish interiors, there are Versailles-inspired gardens. Trains so fascinated the duke that he built his own railroad in the park and staffed it with his servants. ⊠ *Off A9* ☎ *01408/633177* ⊕ *www.dunrobincastle.co.uk* 🎫 *£10* ☉ *Apr., May, Sept., and early Oct., Mon.–Sat. 10:30–4:30, Sun. noon–4:30; June–Aug., daily 10–5.*

TRAVEL SMART
GREAT BRITAIN

GETTING HERE AND AROUND

■ AIR TRAVEL

Flying time to London and Glasgow is about 6½ hours from New York, 7½ hours from Chicago, 9½ hours from Dallas, 10 hours from Los Angeles, and 21½ hours from Sydney. Direct flights into Edinburgh or Manchester take a half hour or so longer. Not all airlines offer direct flights to Scotland; many go via London. For those flights, allow an extra four to five hours of travel (two to three for the layover in London plus an additional hour or two for the flight itself).

When flying from Britain, plan to arrive at the airport 90 minutes in advance for flights to Europe, 2 hours for the United States. Security at British airports is always fairly intense. Most people can expect to be patted down after they pass through metal detectors. Travelers are randomly searched again at the gate before transatlantic flights.

Airline Security Issues Transportation Security Administration ☎ 866/289–9673 in U.S. ⊕ www.tsa.gov.

AIRPORTS

England: Most international flights to London arrive at either Heathrow Airport (LHR), 15 miles west of London, or at Gatwick Airport (LGW), 27 miles south of the capital. Most flights from the United States go to Heathrow. Gatwick is London's second gateway, serving many U.S. destinations. Heathrow and Gatwick are enormous. Both have bars and pubs and dining options, and both are near hotels that run airport shuttles or buses, some of them free. Manchester (MAN), in northwestern England, handles some flights from the United States, as does Birmingham (BHX).

Smaller Stansted (STN), 40 miles northeast of London, handles mainly European and domestic traffic. London City Airport (LCY), a small airport inside the city near Canary Wharf, has twice-daily

business-class flights to New York on British Airways, as well as flights to European destinations. Luton Airport (LLA), 32 miles north of the city and the hub for low-cost easyJet, serves British and European destinations. These smaller airports have fewer amenities than at Heathrow and Gatwick.

Airport Information: England Birmingham Airport ☎ 0871/222–0072 ⊕ www.birminghamairport.co.uk. **Gatwick Airport** ☎ 0844/892–0322 ⊕ www.gatwickairport.com. **Heathrow Airport** ☎ 0844/335–1801 ⊕ www.heathrowairport.com. **London City Airport** ☎ 0207/646–0088 ⊕ www.londoncityairport.com. **Luton Airport** ☎ 01582/405100 ⊕ www.london-luton.co.uk. **Manchester Airport** ☎ 0871/271–0711 ⊕ www.manchesterairport.co.uk. **Stansted Airport** ☎ 0844/355–1803 ⊕ www.stanstedairport.com.

Scotland: The major international gateways to Scotland are Glasgow Airport (GLA), about 7 miles outside Glasgow, and Edinburgh Airport (EDI), 7 miles from the city. Both offer connections for dozens of European cities and regular flights to London's Gatwick (LGW) and Heathrow (LHR) airports, as well as Luton and Stansted. Aberdeen Airport (ABZ) has direct flights to most major European cities. Prestwick (PIK) has direct flights to most major British and European cities at discounted rates. Inverness (INV) offers direct flights in and around the United Kingdom.

All Scottish airports offer typical modern amenities: restaurants, cafés, pubs, shops, pharmacies, bookshops, and newsstands; some even have spas and hair salons. There are plenty of hotels near all airports, and all airports have Internet access.

Airport Information: Scotland Aberdeen Airport ☎ 0844/481–6666 ⊕ www.aberdeenairport.com. **Edinburgh Airport** ☎ 0844/444–8833 ⊕ www.edinburghairport.

com. **Glasgow Airport** ☎ *0844/481-5555*
⊕ *www.glasgowairport.com.* **Glasgow
Prestwick Airport** ☎ *0871/223-0700*
⊕ *www.glasgowprestwick.com.* **Inverness
Airport** ☎ *01667/464000* ⊕ *www.hial.co.uk/
inverness-airport.*

GROUND TRANSPORTATION—LONDON

London has excellent bus and train connections between its airports and downtown. Train service can be the fastest, but the downside is that you must get yourself and your luggage to the terminal, often via a series of escalators and connecting trams. Airport buses (generally run by National Express) may be located nearer to the terminals and drop you closer to central hotels, but they're subject to London traffic, which can be a problem at rush hour. Taxis can be more convenient than buses, but prices can go through the roof.

The Transport for London website has helpful information, as does Airport Travel Line. The official sites for Gatwick, Heathrow, and Stansted are useful resources for transportation options.

FROM HEATHROW TO CENTRAL LONDON		
Travel Mode	Time	Cost
Taxi	40–80 minutes	£50–£80
Heathrow Express Train	15 minutes	£20 one-way
Underground	50 minutes	£5.70 one-way
National Express Bus	45–80 minutes	£6 one-way

Heathrow by Bus: National Express buses take around 90 minutes (longer at peak time) to reach the city center (Victoria Coach Station) and cost £6 to £8.50 one-way and £13.20 round-trip. Buses leave every 30 to 75 minutes from 4:20 am to 10 pm. The National Express Hotel Hoppa service runs from all terminals to around 20 hotels near the airport (£4). Alternatively, nearly every hotel in London is served by the Hotel By Bus service. Fares to Central London begin at

£22.50. SkyShuttle also offers a minibus service between Heathrow and any London hotel. The N9 night bus runs every 20 minutes from 11:45 pm to 5 am to Kensington, Trafalgar Square, and Aldwych; it takes about 75 minutes and costs £2.20.

Heathrow by Train: The cheap, direct route into London is via the Piccadilly line of the Underground (London's extensive subway system, or "Tube"). Trains normally run every three to seven minutes from all terminals from around 5 am until just before midnight. The 50-minute trip into central London costs £5 and connects with other central Tube lines. The Heathrow Express train is comfortable and very convenient, if costly, speeding into London's Paddington Station in 15 minutes. Standard one-way tickets cost £20, or £28 for first class. Book online for the lowest fares. If you arrive without tickets you should purchase them at a kiosk before you board, as they're more expensive on the train. There's daily service from a little after 5 am until a quarter to midnight, with departures every 15 minutes. A less expensive option is the Heathrow Connect train, which stops at local stations between the airport and Paddington. Daily service is every half hour from 5:23 am (6:07 am on Sunday) to 12:01 am. The journey takes about 30 minutes and costs £9.50 one-way.

Gatwick by Bus: Hourly bus service runs from Gatwick's north and south terminals to Victoria Coach Station with stops at Hooley, Coulsdon, Mitcham, Streatham, Stockwell, and Pimlico. The journey takes two hours and costs between £6.50 and £8 one-way. Make sure you get on a direct bus not requiring a change; otherwise the journey could take much longer. The easyBus service runs a service to Earls Court in west London from as little as £2; the later the ticket is booked online, the higher the price (up to £10 on board).

Gatwick by Train: The fast, nonstop Gatwick Express leaves for Victoria Station every 15 minutes from 4:35 am to 1:35 am. The 30-minute trip costs £19.90

one-way. Tickets cost more on board than when booked in advance. The First Capital Connect rail company's nonexpress services are cheaper. Trains runs regularly throughout the day until midnight to St. Pancras International, London Bridge, and Blackfriars stations; daytime departures are every 10 to 25 minutes (hourly between 1:30 am and 5 am), and the journey takes 30 to 45 minutes. Tickets cost from £10 one-way to St. Pancras. You can also reach Gatwick by First Capital Connect coming from Brighton in the opposite direction. First Capital Connect service is on commuter trains, and during rush hour trains can be crowded, with little room for baggage and seats at a premium.

Stansted by Bus: Hourly service on National Express Airport bus A6 (24 hours a day) to Victoria Coach Station costs from £10 one-way, and takes about an hour and a half. Stops include Golders Green, Finchley Road, St. John's Wood, Baker Street, Marble Arch, and Hyde Park Corner. The easyBus service to Victoria via Baker Street costs from £2. The Terravision bus goes to Liverpool Street station and costs £8. Travel is extended to Victoria Coach Station between 8 pm and 6 am, and the fare is £9. Travel time is 60 minutes.

Stansted by Train: The Stansted Express to Liverpool Street Station (with a stop at Tottenham Hale) runs every 15 minutes from 5:30 am to 12:30 am daily (until 1:30 am Friday and Saturday). The 45-minute trip costs £23.40 each way if booked online. Tickets cost more on board.

Luton by Bus and Train: A free airport shuttle runs from Luton Airport to the nearby Luton Airport Parkway Station, where you can take a train or bus into London. From there, the First Capital Connect train service runs to St. Pancras, Farringdon, Blackfriars, and London Bridge. The journey takes about 40 minutes. Trains leave every 10 minutes or so from 5 am until midnight, hourly at other times. One-way tickets begin at £13.50.

The Terravision Shuttle bus runs from Luton to Victoria Coach Station, with departures every 20 to 30 minutes during peak hours. The journey takes around an hour, with fares from £10 each way. The Green Line 757 bus service from Luton to Victoria Station runs every 15 to 30 minutes between 7 am and midnight, takes 60 to 90 minutes, and costs from £10, while an easyBus shuttle has tickets starting from £2. National Express runs coaches from Victoria Coach Station to Luton for £15.

Heathrow, Gatwick, Stansted, and Luton by Taxi: This is an expensive and time-consuming option. If your destination is within the city's congestion zone, £10 will be added to the bill during charging hours. If you get stuck in traffic, a taxi from the rank (stand) will be even more expensive; a cab booked ahead is a set price. A taxi trip from Heathrow to Victoria, for example, can take more than an hour and cost more than £58. Private hire cars may be the same price or even less—at this writing, the fee to Victoria Station is about £50 from Heathrow and £100 from Gatwick and Stansted, not including the congestion charge. Another option, if you have friends in the London area, is to have them book a reputable minicab firm to pick you up. The cost of a minicab from Heathrow to central London is approximately £47. Your hotel may also be able to recommend a car service.

TRANSFERS BETWEEN LONDON AIRPORTS

Allow two or three hours for transferring between airports.

National Express Bus: The National Express Airport bus is the most direct option between Gatwick and Heathrow. Buses depart from Gatwick every 5 to 35 minutes between 5:35 am and 1:35 am (then once an hour until 5:35 am) and from Heathrow every 5 to 35 minutes from 2:35 am to 12:35 am. The trip takes from 45 to 95 minutes, and the fare is £27.50 each way. Book tickets in advance. National Express buses between Stansted and Gatwick depart every 30 to 75 minutes and take between 3 and 4½ hours. The one-way fare is from £18 to £31.50. Some airlines may offer shuttle services as well—check with your airline before your journey.

Public Transportation: The cheapest option—but most complicated—is public transportation: from Gatwick to Stansted, for instance, catch the Gatwick Express train from Gatwick to Victoria Station, take the Tube to Liverpool Street Station, then hop on the train to Stansted. Alternatively, take the Thameslink train to Farringdon and transfer to the Tube bound for Liverpool Street. From Heathrow to Gatwick, take the Tube to King's Cross/St. Pancras, then take the Thameslink train to Gatwick, or else transfer from the Piccadilly Line to the District/Circle Line at Hammersmith, head to Victoria Station, and take the Gatwick Express.

Later this decade when the Crossrail train system is completed, transfers between airports using public transportation will become much easier.

Contacts Crossrail ☎ *0345/602-3813* ⊕ *www.crossrail.co.uk.* **easyBus** ⊕ *www. easybus.co.uk.* **First Capital Connect** ☎ *0845/748-4950* ⊕ *www.firstcapitalconnect. co.uk.* **Gatwick Express** ☎ *0845/850-1530* ⊕ *www.gatwickexpress.com.* **Green Line** ☎ *0844/800-4411* ⊕ *www.greenline.co.uk.* **Heathrow Connect** ☎ *0845/678-6975* ⊕ *www.heathrowconnect.com.* **Heathrow Express** ☎ *0845/600-1515* ⊕ *www. heathrowexpress.com.* **Hotel By Bus** ☎ *0845/850-1900* ⊕ *www.hotelbybus. com.* **National Express** ☎ *0871/781-8178* ⊕ *www.nationalexpress.com.* **SkyShuttle** ☎ *0845/481-0960* ⊕ *www.skyshuttle. co.uk.* **Stansted Express** ☎ *0845/600-7245* ⊕ *www.stanstedexpress.com.* **Terravision** ☎ *01279/662-931* ⊕ *www.terravision. eu/london.html.* **Transport for London** ☎ *0843/222-1234* ⊕ *www.tfl.gov.uk.* **Traveline** ☎ *0871/200-2233* ⊕ *www.traveline.info.*

GROUND TRANSPORTATION—SCOTLAND

Taxi: The best way to get to and from the airports based on speed and convenience is by taxi. Stands are just outside the airports' front doors and are well marked with clear signs. Most taxis have a set price when going to and from the airport to the city center, but the driver will turn on the meter at your request to confirm the flat-rate price. Luggage is included in the taxi fare; you should not be charged extra for it.

Public Transportation: If you're traveling alone, a more economical transfer option is public transportation. Buses travel between city centers and Glasgow, Edinburgh, Aberdeen, and Inverness airports. Trains go direct to Prestwick Airport from Glasgow's Central Station every half hour. All are fast, inexpensive, and reliable. *For more information and specific contacts, refer to the planning sections at the beginning of chapters.*

TRANSFERS BETWEEN SCOTTISH AIRPORTS

Public Transportation: You must take a combination of bus and train to transfer between the major Scottish airports, but it's easily done. From Edinburgh Airport, for instance, you can take a bus to the city center (£3.50) and then a train from Waverley station to Glasgow's Queen Street station(£12.50) and then a bus to Glasgow Airport (£4.50) from the bus terminal just a few minutes walk from Queen Street. This journey generally takes less than two hours.

Taxi or Car: Taxis are fast but costly. A taxi ride from Edinburgh Airport to Glasgow Airport runs about £85, not bad if you are traveling with a few people, whereas renting a car might be a better choice for trips between Edinburgh and Aberdeen Airport. Otherwise, take a bus to the city center and then take a train. *For specific information, see the planning section at the start of appropriate chapters.*

FLIGHTS

The least expensive airfares to Great Britain are often priced for round-trip travel and must usually be purchased in advance. Airlines generally allow you to change your return date for a fee; most low-fare tickets, however, are nonrefundable.

British Airways offers mostly nonstop flights from 28 U.S. cities to Heathrow, along with flights to Manchester and Birmingham and a vast program of discount airfare–hotel packages. Britain-based Virgin Atlantic is a strong competitor in terms of packages. London is a very popular destination, so many U.S. carriers have flights and packages, too.

If you intend to fly to Scotland from London, take advantage of fare wars on internal routes—notably among London's airports and between Glasgow and Edinburgh. Among the cheapest fares are those from easyJet, which offers bargain fares from London Luton/Gatwick/Stansted (all with good rail links from central London) to Glasgow, Edinburgh, Aberdeen, and Inverness. Larger British Airways now offers competitive fares on some flights, especially those booked well in advance. For trips within Great Britain of less than 200 miles, though, trains are often quicker because rail stations are more centrally located (book online and in advance to save money).

Airport tax is included in the price of your ticket. Generally the tax for economy tickets within the United Kingdom from European Union countries is £13. For all other flights it runs from £67 to £69. For first- and club-class flights from the United Kingdom and European Union the tax is £26; for all other destinations it costs between £134 and £188.

Air Passes: Oneworld's Visit Europe Pass offers packages, based on mileage, that allow travel throughout Europe on airlines that include British Airways (which has an extensive network of European flights). You must purchase this pass online before you leave home through Oneworld (⊕ *www.oneworld.com*). In Britain the best place to search for consolidator tickets, or so-called bucket-shop tickets, is through Cheap Flights (⊕ *www. cheapflights.com*), a website that pools all flights available and then directs you to a phone number or site to purchase tickets.

Major Airline Contacts American Airlines ☎ *800/433–7300, 0844/499–7300 in U.K.* ⊕ *www.aa.com.* **British Airways** ☎ *800/247–9297, 0844/493–0787 in U.K.* ⊕ *www.britishairways.com.* **Delta Airlines** ☎ *800/241–4141 international reservations, 0871/221–1222 in U.K.* ⊕ *www.delta.com.* **KLM** ☎ *866/434–0320 in U.S., 0 871/231–0000 in U.K.* ⊕ *www.klm.com.* **United Airlines** ☎ *800/864–8331 in U.S., 0845/607–6760 in U.K.* ⊕ *www.united.com.* **US Airways** ☎ *800/428–4322 for U.S. and Canada reservations, 0845/600–3300 in U.K.* ⊕ *www. usairways.com.* **Virgin Atlantic** ☎ *800/862–8621, 0800/874–7747 in U.K.* ⊕ *www.virginatlantic.com.*

Within England and to Europe easyJet ☎ *0871/244–2377* ⊕ *www.easyjet. com.* **Ryanair** ☎ *0871/246–0000* ⊕ *www.ryanair.com.*

▌ BOAT TRAVEL

Ferries and other boats travel regular routes to France, Spain, Ireland, and Scandinavia. P&O runs ferries to Belgium, Spain, Ireland, and the Netherlands. DFDS Seaways serves France and the Netherlands, and Stena Line serves Ireland, Northern Ireland, and the Netherlands. Prices vary; booking early ensures cheaper fares, but also ask about special deals. Seaview is a comprehensive online ferry- and cruise-booking portal for Britain and continental Europe. Ferry Cheap is a discount website.

WITHIN SCOTLAND

Because Scotland has so many islands, plus the river Clyde, ferry services—some passengers-only, others also for cars—are of paramount importance. Though not required, making a reservation is a good idea. The main ferry operator is Caledonian MacBrayne— CalMac for short. Services extend from the Firth of Clyde in the south to northwestern Scotland and all the Hebrides. CalMac sells an 8-day or 15-day Island Rover runabout ticket, which is ideal for touring holidays in the islands, as well as an island-hopping plan called Island Hopscotch. Fares can range from £4 to £5 for a short trip to almost £50 for a longer trip with several legs. Western Ferries and Northlink also operate ferries (they can be busy in summer) to destinations of interest to tourists. Traveler's checks (in pounds), cash, and major credit cards are accepted for payment.

European Ferry Information DFDS Seaways ☎ *0871/574-7235* ⊕ *www.dfdsseaways. co.uk.* **Ferry Cheap** ☎ *01304/501100* ⊕ *www. ferrycheap.com.* **P&O** ☎ *0871/664-2121* ⊕ *www.poferries.com.* **Seaview** ☎ *01442/843-050* ⊕ *www.seaview.co.uk.* **Stena Line** ☎ *0137/040-100* ⊕ *www.stenaline.co.uk.*

Scottish Ferry Operators Caledonian MacBrayne ☎ *0800/066-5000* ⊕ *www. calmac.co.uk.* **Northlink Ferries** ☎ *0845/600-0449* ⊕ *www.northlinkferries.co.uk.* **Western Ferries** ☎ *01369/704452* ⊕ *www.western-ferries.co.uk.*

TRANSATLANTIC AND OTHER CRUISES

Most cruise ships leave from southern England—particularly Southampton and Portsmouth. Some ships leave from Liverpool and Dover as well, or from Harwich, near Cambridge.

Cruise Lines Cunard Line ☎ *800/728-6273 in U.S., 0843/374-0033 in U.K* ⊕ *www.cunard. co.uk.* **Holland America Line** ☎ *0843/374-2300* ⊕ *www.hollandamerica.com.* **Norwegian Cruise Line** ☎ *0845/201-8900 in U.K, 866/234-7350 in U.S.* ⊕ *www.ncl.co.uk.* **Princess Cruises** ☎ *800/774-6237 in U.S., 0843/374-4444 in U.K.* ⊕ *www.princess.com.* **Royal Caribbean International** ☎ *866/562-7625 in U.S., 0844/493-4005 in U.K.* ⊕ *www. royalcaribbean.com.*

▌BUS TRAVEL

Throughout Great Britain: Long-distance buses usually provide the cheapest way to travel between England and Scotland; fares can run as little as a third of the rail fares for comparable trips. Nevertheless, the trip is not always as comfortable as by train (no dining cart, smaller bathrooms, less spacious seats), and travel takes longer. The trip between Glasgow and London by nonstop bus takes nearly 9 hours, as opposed to about 5½ hours by train.

National Express is the major coach operator; Victoria Coach Station, near central London's Victoria Station, is its regional hub, and there are offices in the Heathrow and Gatwick airport coach stations. On its Gold Service routes to Scotland, Megabus, a budget option for long-distance travel, has seats that convert into bunk beds. Greyhound operates long-distance bus service to five destinations in Wales.

Private companies offer local service on double-decker buses in cities and regions. Check with the local bus station or tourist information center for routes and schedules. Most companies offer daylong or weeklong unlimited-travel tickets and in popular tourist areas operate special scenic tours in summer. The top deck of a double-decker bus is a great perch from which to view the countryside.

Within Scotland: Scotland's bus (short-haul) and coach (long-distance) network is extensive. Bus service is comprehensive within cities, less so in country districts. Express service links main cities and towns, connecting, for example, Glasgow and Edinburgh to Inverness, Aberdeen, Perth, Skye, Ayr, Dumfries, and Carlisle; or Inverness with Aberdeen, Wick, Thurso, and Fort William. Express service is very fast, and fares are reasonable. Scottish Citylink, National Express, and Megabus are among the main operators; there are about 20 in all.

DISCOUNTS AND DEALS

Book online to receive the lowest fares on National Express, and check the Offers section of its website for CoachCard and other discounts. Young Persons Coach-Cards, for instance, provide discounts of up to a third for students age 16 to 26 and Senior CoachCards do the same for passengers 60 or older. The cards, valid for a year, cost £10. Family CoachCard and Brit Xplorer discounts are also available. Midweek fares for all travelers are generally less expensive than those on weekends and holidays. Megabus (order tickets online) offers competitive discounts on its fares between major cities.

Scottish Citylink's Explorer Passes provide discounts for travel on three out of five days, five out of 10 days, or eight out of 16 days. Available through Citylink offices, they cost £41, £62, and £93 respectively. The line's Apex (advance purchase) tickets are good for savings of up to 20%.

FARES AND SCHEDULES

You can find schedules online, pick them up from tourist information offices, or get them by phone from the bus companies. Contact Traveline Scotland for information about all Scottish public transportation and timetables.

PAYING

Tickets for National Express can be bought from the Victoria, Heathrow, or Gatwick coach stations, by phone, online, or from most British travel agencies. Tickets for Megabus must be purchased online or by phone (avoid calling, as there's a surcharge). Most companies accept credit cards for advance purchases, but onboard transactions usually require cash. For town, suburban, or short-distance journeys in Scotland, you can buy your ticket on the bus, from a pay box, or from the driver. Exact change is required.

RESERVATIONS

Book in advance, as buses on busy routes fill up quickly. With most bus companies (National Express, Megabus, Green Line), advance payment means you receive an email receipt and your name is placed on a list given to the bus driver. Scottish Citylink has several delivery methods, including by email (you're required to print the ticket) and text.

Bus Contacts Green Line ☎ *0844/800–4411* ⊕ *www.greenline.co.uk.* **Greyhound** ☎ *0900/096–0000* ⊕ *www.greyhounduk.com.* **Megabus** ☎ *0900/160–0900* ⊕ *uk.megabus. com.* **National Express** ☎ *0871/781–8178* ⊕ *www.nationalexpress.com.* **Scottish Citylink** ☎ *0871/266–3333* ⊕ *www.citylink.co.uk.* **Traveline** ☎ *0871/200–2233* ⊕ *traveline.info.* **Victoria Coach Station** ✉ *164 Buckingham Palace Rd., London* ☎ *0207/027–2520* ⊕ *www.tfl.gov.uk.*

▌ CAR TRAVEL

Driving in Britain can be a challenge, especially if you aren't used to driving on the left side of often disconcertingly narrow roads. Many rental cars have standard transmissions, and the gears are shifted with the left hand, not the right. If you are driving for the first time this way, take the time to acclimate yourself to the difference before entering heavy traffic.

There's no reason to rent a car for a stay in London. The city and its suburbs are well served by public transportation, and traffic is desperately congested. Here and in other major cities, it's best to rely on public transportation.

Outside the cities, a car can be handy. Many sights aren't easily reached without one—castles, for example, are rarely connected to any public transportation system. Small villages might have only one or two buses a day pass through them. If you're comfortable on the road, the experience of driving between the tall hedgerows or on country roads is a truly English experience.

Throughout Great Britain your own driver's license is acceptable. Nevertheless, you may choose to get an International Driving Permit (IDP), which can be used only in conjunction with a valid driver's license. Check the Automobile

Association of America website for more info as well as for IDPs ($15) themselves. These permits are universally recognized, and having one may save you a problem with the local authorities.

GASOLINE

Gasoline is called petrol in Britain and is sold by the liter. The price you see posted at a petrol station is the price of a liter, and there are about 4 liters in a U.S. gallon. Petrol is expensive; it was around £1.35 per liter, or $2.10 per liter, at the time of this writing. Supermarket pumps just outside city centers frequently offer the best prices. Premium and superpremium—aka unleaded and super unleaded respectively—are the two main varieties; most cars run on premium. Diesel is widely available; be sure not to use it by mistake. Along busy motorways, most large service stations are open 24 hours a day, 7 days a week. In rural areas, hours can vary. Most service stations accept major credit cards, and most are self-service.

PARKING

Parking regulations are strictly enforced, and fines are high. In the cities you often must pay for on-street parking by purchasing a sticker from a parking machine—these machines are clearly marked with a large "P"—and displaying the sticker on your car. Exact change is usually required. In London's City of Westminster (⊕ *www.westminster.gov.uk/parking*) and some other boroughs, parking machines have been replaced by a pay-by-phone plan, enabling you to pay by cell phone if you've preregistered. There's even an app to help drivers find parking. In town centers your best bet is to park in a public lot marked with a square blue sign with a white "P" in the center. Visit the website of ParkMark (⊕ *www.parkmark.co.uk*) to find lots in England, Scotland, and Wales that have taken measures to create a safe parking environment.

If you park on the street, follow these basic rules: Do not park within 15 yards of an intersection. Never park in bus lanes or on double yellow lines, and do not park on single yellow lines when parking meters are in effect. On busy roads with red lines painted on the street or on the zigzag lines near traffic lights, you cannot park or even stop to let a passenger out of the car.

RENTALS

Rental rates are generally reasonable, and insurance costs are lower than in the United States. If you want a car only for country trips, consider renting outside London. Rates are cheaper, and you'll avoid having to navigate London's notoriously complex road system. Standard rates begin at around £25 a day and £130 a week for a midsize car, usually with manual transmission. When booking, be aware that vehicle and other fees and V.A.T. add substantially to the base rental price. As in the United States, prices rise in summer and during holidays. Car seats for children cost from £10 to £30, and GPS usually costs about £14.

Major car-rental agencies are much the same in Britain as in the United States: Alamo, Avis, Budget, Enterprise, Hertz, and National all have offices in Britain. Europcar (⊕ *www.europcar.com*) is another large company. Companies frequently restrict rentals to people over age 23 and under age 75. If you are over 70, some companies require you to have your own insurance. If you are under 25, a surcharge of £16 per day will apply.

Major Agencies Avis ☎ *0844/581–0147* ⊕ *www.avis.co.uk*. **Budget** ☎ *0844/581–2231* ⊕ *www.budget.co.uk*. **Hertz** ☎ *0843/309–3099* ⊕ *www.hertz.co.uk*. **National Car Rental** ☎ *0871/384–1140* ⊕ *www.nationalcar.co.uk*.

Manchester and Scotland Arnold Clark ☎ *0141/237–4374* ⊕ *www.arnoldclarkrental.com*.

Wholesalers Auto Europe ☎ *0800/358–1229* ⊕ *www.auto-europe.co.uk*. **Europe by Car** ☎ *0141/531–5220 in Glasgow* ⊕ *www.ebctravel.com*. **Eurovacations** ☎ *877/471–3876 in U.S.* ⊕ *www.eurovacations.com*. **Kemwel** ☎ *877/820–0668 in U.S.* ⊕ *www.kemwel.com*.

ROAD CONDITIONS

A good network of superhighways, known as motorways, and divided highways, known as dual carriageways, extends throughout Britain. Motorways (with the prefix "M"), shown in blue on most maps, are mainly two or three lanes in each direction. Other major roads (with the prefix "A") are shown on maps in green and red. Sections of fast dual carriageways (with black-edged, thick outlines on maps) have both traffic lights and traffic circles. Turn-offs are often marked by highway numbers, rather than place names. An exit is called a junction in Britain.

Lesser roads, for the most part old coach and turnpike roads, might make your trip twice as long but reveal twice as much of the countryside. Minor roads are drawn in yellow or white on maps, the former prefixed by "B," the latter unlettered and unnumbered. On single-track (one-lane) roads, there's no room for two vehicles to pass, and you must use a passing place if you meet an oncoming car or tractor, or if a car behind wishes to overtake you. Never hold up traffic on single-track roads.

ROADSIDE EMERGENCIES

On major highways emergency roadside telephone booths are positioned at regular intervals. Contact your car-rental company or call the police. You can also call the Automobile Association (AA) toll-free. You can join and receive assistance from the AA or the RAC on the spot, but the charge is higher than a simple membership fee. If you're a member of the American Automobile Association, check before you travel; reciprocal agreements may provide you free roadside aid.

Emergency Services Ambulance, fire, police ☎ *999 emergency, 101 police non-emergency.* **Automobile Association** ☎ *0800/887–766 emergency service, 0800/085–2721 general calls* ⊕ *www.theaa. com.* **RAC** ☎ *0333/200–0999 emergency service, 0844/891–3111 general inquiries* ⊕ *www.rac.co.uk.*

RULES OF THE ROAD

The most noticeable difference for most visitors is that when in Britain, you drive on the left and steer the car on the right. Speed limits are complicated, and there are speed cameras everywhere. The speed limit (shown on circular red signs) is generally 20 or 30 mph in towns and cities, 40 to 60 mph on two-lane highways, and 70 mph on motorways. At traffic circles (called roundabouts), you turn clockwise. As cars enter the circle, drivers must yield to those already in the circle. If you're taking an exit all the way around the circle, signal right as you enter, stay to the center, and then signal and move left just before your own exit.

Driving while using a cell phone is illegal, and the use of seat belts is mandatory, as is the use of appropriate child seats up to the age of 12 (the exceptions are taxis and emergency situations). Service stations and newsstands sell copies of the Highway Code (£2.50), which lists driving rules and has pictures of signs. It's also available online at ⊕ *www.direct.gov.uk.*

Pedestrians have the right-of-way on "zebra" crossings (black-and-white-stripe crosswalks between two orange-flashing globe lights). At other crossings, pedestrians must yield to traffic, but they do have the right-of-way over traffic turning left.

Drunk-driving laws are strictly enforced. The legal limit is 80 milligrams of alcohol per 100 milliliters of blood, which means two units of alcohol—two glasses of wine, one pint of beer, or four shots of whisky—but amounts vary, depending on your weight or what you've eaten that day. If you drink, take a taxi.

▌ TRAIN TRAVEL

Operated by several different private companies, the train system in Britain is extensive and useful, though less than perfect. Some regional trains are old, and virtually all lines suffer from occasional delays, schedule changes, and periodic repair work that runs over schedule. All major cities and many small towns are served by trains, and despite the difficulties, rail travel is the most pleasant way to cover long distances.

On long-distance runs some rail lines have buffet cars; on others you can purchase snacks from a mobile snack cart. Most train companies have "quiet cars" where mobile-phone use is forbidden.

CLASSES

Most rail lines have first-class and second-class cars. In virtually all cases, second class is perfectly comfortable. First class is quieter and less crowded, has better furnishings, and marginally larger seats. It usually costs from two to three times the price of second class, but not always, so it's worth comparing prices. Most train operators offer a Weekend First ticket. Available on weekends and holidays, these tickets allow you to upgrade for as little as £5.

FARES AND SCHEDULES

National Rail Enquiries is a helpful, comprehensive, and free service that covers all of the country's rail lines. National Rail will help you choose the best train, and then connect you with the right ticket office. You can also book tickets online. A similar service is offered by the Trainline, which provides online train information and ticket booking for all rail services. The Man in Seat 61, a website, has information and advice about train–ferry connections, along with booking facilities.

It is advisable to book online, and as far in advance as you can for long-distance travel; you will save a considerable amount if you do, perhaps up to 50%. Ticket prices are higher during rush hour.

■ TIP➔ Ask the local tourist board about hotel and local transportation packages that include tickets to major events.

Information National Rail Enquiries
☎ *0845/748–4950, 020/7278–5240 outside U.K.* ⊕ *www.nationalrail.co.uk.* **The Man in Seat 61** ⊕ *www.seat61.com.* **Trainline** ☎ *0871/244–1545* ⊕ *www.thetrainline.com.*

PASSES

National Rail Enquiries has information about rail passes such as Rovers, which save you money on individual trips; these are well worth a look. If you plan to travel a lot by train, consider purchasing a BritRail Pass, which allows unlimited travel over the entire British rail network and can save you money. If you don't plan to cover many miles, you may come out ahead by buying individual tickets. Buy your BritRail Pass before you leave home—it's not sold in Britain. The pass is available from most U.S. travel agents or from ACP Rail International, Flight Centre, or VisitBritain. BritRail passes come in two basic varieties: the Consecutive Pass and the FlexiPass. You can get a Consecutive Pass good for 3, 4, 8, 15, 22, or 31 consecutive days starting at $215 standard and $319 first-class for 3 days. The FlexiPass for 3, 4, 8, or 15 days of travel in two months costs $269 standard and $395 first class for 3 days. BritRail's Scottish Freedom Pass allows transportation on all Caledonian MacBrayne and Strathclyde ferries in addition to major bus lines and the Glasgow underground. You can travel any 4 days in an 8-day period for $239 or any 8 days in a 15-day period for $319.

A rail pass does not guarantee you a seat on a particular train. Book seats even if using a rail pass, especially in summer on popular routes. Note that Eurail Passes aren't honored in Britain.

Discount Passes ACP Rail International ☎ *866/938–7245 in U.S., 0207/953–4062 in U.K.* ⊕ *www.acprail.com.* **BritRail** ☎ *866/938–7245 in U.S.* ⊕ *www.britrail.com.* **Flight Centre** ☎ *0870/499–0040 in U.K., 866/938–7245 in U.S.* ⊕ *www.flightcentre.com.* **VisitBritain** ☎ *877/992–4732 in U.S.* ⊕ *www. visitbritainshop.com.*

PAYING

Cash and credit cards are accepted by all train ticket offices; credit cards are accepted over the phone and online.

RESERVATIONS

Ticket reservations are recommended—even ones made just 24 hours ahead can provide a substantial discount. Look into cheap day returns if you plan to travel a round-trip in one day.

CHANNEL TUNNEL

The Eurostar through the Channel Tunnel is a fast way to cross the English Channel. Travel time is 2¼ hours from London's St. Pancras Station to Paris's Gare du Nord. Trains also travel to Lyon (5½ hours) and Aix-en-Provence (6¼ hours) on Saturday in May and June, and to Avignon (6 hours), on Saturday from July to September. Early risers can easily take a day trip to Paris if time is short. If purchased in advance, round-trip tickets to Paris start at £98.

Channel Tunnel Car Transport Eurotunnel
☎ 0844/335–3535 ⊕ www.eurotunnel.com.
French Motorail/Rail Europe ☎ 0844/848–4064 ⊕ www.raileurope.co.uk.

Channel Tunnel Passenger Service
Eurostar ☎ 0843/218–6186 ⊕ www.eurostar.com. **Rail Europe** ☎ 800/622–8600 in U.S., 0844/848–4064 in U.K. ⊕ www.raileurope.com.

FROM ENGLAND TO SCOTLAND

There are two main rail routes to Scotland from the south of England. The first, the west-coast main line, runs from London Euston to Glasgow Central; it takes under 5 hours to make the 400-mile trip. Useful for daytime travel to the Scottish Highlands is the direct train to Stirling and Aviemore, terminating at Inverness. For a restful route to the Scottish Highlands, take the overnight sleeper service, with soundproof sleeping carriages. It runs from London Euston, departing in late evening, to Perth, Stirling, Aviemore, and Inverness.

The east-coast main line from London King's Cross to Edinburgh provides the quickest trip to the Scottish capital. Between 8 am and 6 pm there are 16 trains to Edinburgh, three of them through to Aberdeen. Limited-stop expresses like the Flying Scotsman make the 393-mile London-to-Edinburgh journey in about four hours. Connecting services to most parts of Scotland—particularly the Western Highlands—are often better from Edinburgh than from Glasgow.

Trains from elsewhere in England are good: regular service connects Birmingham, Manchester, Liverpool, and Bristol with Glasgow and Edinburgh. From Harwich (the port of call for ships from Holland, Germany, and Denmark), you can travel to Glasgow via Manchester. But it's faster to change at Peterborough for the east-coast main line to Edinburgh.

SCENIC ROUTES

Although many routes in Scotland run through extremely attractive countryside, several stand out: from Glasgow to Oban via Loch Lomond; to Fort William and Mallaig via Rannoch (ferry connection to Skye); from Edinburgh to Inverness via the Forth Bridge and Perth; from Inverness to Kyle of Lochalsh and to Wick; and from Inverness to Aberdeen.

A private train, the Royal Scotsman, does all-inclusive scenic tours, partly under steam power, with banquets en route. This is a luxury experience: some evenings require formal wear. You can choose itineraries from two nights (£2,350 per person) to seven nights (£6,990).

Train Tours The Royal Scotsman
☎ 0845/217–0799 in the U.K., 800/524–2420 in the U.S. ⊕ www.royalscotsman.com.

ESSENTIALS

■ ACCOMMODATIONS

Hotels, bed-and-breakfasts, rural inns, or luxurious country houses—there's a style and price to suit most travelers. Wherever you stay, make reservations well in advance.

Our local writers vet every hotel to recommend the best overnights in each price category, from budget to expensive. Unless otherwise specified, you can expect private bath, phone, and TV in your room. *Hotel reviews have been shortened. For full information, visit Fodors.com.*

Lodgings are indicated in the text by ⊡. Throughout Britain, lodging prices often include breakfast of some kind, but this is generally not the case in London.

CATEGORY	LONDON	ELSEWHERE
$	under £100	under £100
$$	£100–£200	£100–£160
$$$	£201–£300	£161–£220
$$$$	over £300	over £220

Prices are the lowest cost of a standard double room in high season, including 20% V.A.T.

APARTMENT AND HOUSE RENTALS

Rental houses and flats (apartments) are becoming more popular lodging choices for travelers visiting Britain, particularly for those staying in one place for more than a few days. Some places may rent only by the week. Prices can be cheaper than a hotel (though perhaps not less than a bed-and-breakfast), and the space and comfort are much better than what you'd find in a typical hotel. Such rentals also provide more privacy than a hotel or B&B. Because they're often in isolated locations, however, a car is vital.

Living Architecture offers stays in one-of-a-kind architect-designed country houses. Lists of rental properties are available free of charge from VisitBritain *(see Visitor Information, below)*. You may find discounts of up to 50% on rentals during the off-season (from October through March).

BED-AND-BREAKFASTS

A British tradition, B&Bs are the backbone of budget travel. Typical prices outside London range from £40 to £100 a night. B&Bs vary in style and grace, but these days most have private bathrooms. More upscale B&Bs, along the line of their American counterparts, can be found throughout Britain. The line between B&Bs and guesthouses is growing increasingly blurred, but the latter are often larger.

Some Tourist Information Centres in cities and towns can help you find and book a B&B (there may be a small charge for this service), even on the day you arrive. Many private services also deal with B&Bs.

Reservation Services Bed & Breakfast.com ☎ *512/322-2710* ⊕ *www. bedandbreakfast.com.* **The Bed and Breakfast Club** ☎ *01243/370692* ⊕ *www. thebedandbreakfastclub.co.uk.* **Wolsey Lodges** ☎ *01473/822058* ⊕ *www.wolseylodges.com.*

COTTAGES

Renting a cottage in the country is a good option for longer stays if you prefer to have one base. Several online resources can help you locate one.

Contacts Classic Cottages ☎ *01326/555555* ⊕ *www.classic.co.uk.* **National Trust** ☎ *0844/800-2070* ⊕ *www. nationaltrustcottages.co.uk.* **Rural Retreats** ☎ *01386/701177* ⊕ *www.ruralretreats.co.uk.* **VisitBritain** ☎ *0207/578-1000* ⊕ *www. visitbritain.com.*

FARMHOUSES

A popular option for families with children is a farmhouse holiday, combining the freedom of B&B accommodations with the hospitality of British family life.

Consider this option only if you are touring by car, though, because farmhouses may be in remote locations. Prices are generally reasonable.

Contacts Farm & Cottage Holidays UK
☎ 01237/459–888 ⊕ www.holidaycottages.
co.uk. **Farm Stay UK** ☎ 024/7669–6909
⊕ www.farmstayuk.co.uk. **Scottish Farmhouse Holidays** ☎ 01334/476370 ⊕ www.
scottishfarmhouseholidays.com.

HISTORIC BUILDINGS

Several organizations, such as the Landmark Trust, National Trust, National Trust for Scotland, English Heritage, and Vivat Trust, have specially adapted historic buildings to rent. Many of these have kitchens. For some homes a minimum stay of two or more days (or a week or more) is required.

Contacts Celtic Castles ☎ 01422/323200
⊕ www.celticcastles.com. **English Heritage**
☎ 0870/333–1181 ⊕ www.english-heritage.
org.uk. **Landmark Trust** ☎ 01628/825925
⊕ www.landmarktrust.org.uk. **National Trust** ☎ 0844/800–2070 ⊕ www.
nationaltrustcottages.co.uk. **National Trust for Scotland** ☎ 0131/458–0303, 866/211–7573 in U.S. ⊕ www.nts.org.uk.**Portmeirion Cottages** ☎ 01766/770000 ⊕ www.
portmeirion-village.com. **Rural Retreats**
☎ 01386/701177 ⊕ www.ruralretreats.co.uk.
Stately Holiday Cottages ☎ 01638/674756
⊕ www.statelyholidaycottages.co.uk.
Unique Home Stays ☎ 01637/881183
⊕ ww.uniquehomestays.com. **Vivat Trust**
☎ 0845/090–0194 ⊕ www.vivat-trust.org.

HOME EXCHANGES

With a direct home exchange you stay in someone else's home while they stay in yours. Some outfits handle vacation homes, so you're staying in someone's vacant weekend place. Home Exchange.com offers a one-year membership for $101; HomeLink International costs $119 for an annual online membership, which includes a directory listing; and Intervac U.S. offers international membership for $100.

Exchange Clubs Home Exchange.com
☎ 800/877–8723 ⊕ www.homeexchange.com.
HomeLink International ☎ 800/638–3841
⊕ www.homelink.org. **Intervac.** ☎ 800/756–4663 ⊕ www.intervac-homeexchange.com.

HOTELS

Your stay in Britain can take place in everything from a room in budget chain hotel to one in a luxurious retreat in a converted country house. In many towns and cities you'll find old inns that are former coaching inns; these served travelers as they journeyed around the country in horse-drawn carriages and stagecoaches.

Most hotels have rooms with "ensuite" bathrooms—as private bathrooms are called—although bathrooms in older hotels may have only washbasins; in this case, showers and toilets are usually down the hall. Especially in London, rooms and bathrooms may be smaller than those you find in the United States.

Besides familiar international chains, Britain has some local chains that are worth a look; they provide rooms from the less expensive (Travelodge and Premier Inn are the most widespread; Jurys Inns offer good value in city centers) to the trendy (ABode, Apex, Hotel du Vin, Malmaison).

Local Chains ABode ⊕ www.abodehotels.
co.uk. **Apex Hotels** ⊕ www.apexhotels.co.uk.
Hotel du Vin ☎ 0871/943–0345 ⊕ www.
hotelduvin.com. **Jurys Inn** ☎ 0870/410–0800 ⊕ www.jurysinn.com. **Malmaison**
☎ 0871/943–0350 ⊕ www.malmaison.com.
Premier Inn ☎ 0871/527–9222 ⊕ www.
premierinn.com. **Travelodge** ☎ 0800/835–2424 in U.K., 800/525–4055 in U.S. ⊕ www.
travelodge.com.

HOTEL GRADING SYSTEM

Hotels, guesthouses, inns, and B&Bs in the United Kingdom are all graded from one to five stars by the tourism board, VisitBritain. Basically, the more stars a property has, the more amenities it has, and the higher the standard of the facilities. The most luxurious hotels will have five stars; a simple, clean, acceptable hostelry will have one star.

Online Booking Resources

Contacts		
The Apartment Service	0208/944–1444	www.apartmentservice.com
At Home Abroad	212/421–9165	www.athomeabroadinc.com
English Country Cottages	0845/268–0785	www.english-country-cottages.co.uk
In the English Manner	01559/371600 or 800/422–0799	www.english-manner.com
Interhome	800/882–6864	www.interhome.us
Living Architecture	07734/323464	www.living-architecture.co.uk
National Trust	0844/800–2070	www.nationaltrustcottages.co.uk
Suzanne B. Cohen & Associates	207/622–0743	www.villaeurope.com
Vacation Rentals By Owner	877/228–3145	www.vrbo.com
Villanet	877/250–4366 or 206/417–3444	www.rentavilla.com
Villas International	415/499–9490 or 800/221–2260	www.villasintl.com

DISCOUNTS AND DEALS

Hotel rates in major cities tend to be cheapest on weekends, whereas rural hotels are cheapest on weeknights. The lowest occupancy is between November and April, so hotels lower their prices substantially during these months. It is always worthwhile to ask if there are discounts available, or to seek them out online.

Lastminute.com offers deals on hotel rooms all over Great Britain. VisitLondon.com, London's official website, has some good deals.

Local Resources Lastminute.com ☎ 0800/083–4000 ⊕ www.lastminute.com.

▌ COMMUNICATIONS

INTERNET

Wi-Fi is increasingly available in hotels, and broadband coverage is widespread in cities. Many London Underground stations now have Wi-Fi (for a fee). All hotels and many B&Bs have facilities for computer users, such as dedicated computer rooms and wired or wireless connections for Internet access. Most cafés offer free Wi-Fi access. Cybercafes lists more than 4,000 Internet cafés worldwide.

Contacts Cybercafes ⊕ www.cybercafes.com. **Wi-Fi Freespot** ⊕ www.wififreespot.com.

PHONES

All calls (including local calls) made within Great Britain are charged according to the time of day. The standard landline rate applies weekdays 7 am to 7 pm; a cheaper rate is in effect weekdays 7 pm to 7 am and all day on weekends, when it's even cheaper.

A word of warning: 0870 numbers are *not* toll-free numbers in Britain; in fact, numbers beginning with this or the 0871, 0844, or 0845 prefixes cost extra to call. The amount varies and is usually relatively small—except for numbers with the premium-rate 090 prefix, which cost £1 per minute when dialed from within the country—but can be excessive when dialed from outside Britain.

LOCAL DOS AND TABOOS

CUSTOMS OF THE COUNTRY

In general, British and American rules of etiquette are much the same. Differences are subtle. British people find Americans' bluntness somewhat startling from time to time, but are charmed by their friendliness.

Many British people still tend to take politeness extremely seriously, but younger people and urbanites have a more casual approach. Self-deprecating humor, however, always goes down well. The famous British reserve is still in place, but on social occasions it's best to observe what the others do, and go with the flow. If you're visiting a family home, a gift of flowers is welcome, as is a bottle of wine.

DOING BUSINESS

Punctuality is of prime importance; if you anticipate a late arrival, call ahead. For business dinners, if you proffered the invitation, it's usually assumed that you'll pick up the tab. If you're the visitor, however, it's good form for the host to pay the bill. Alternatively, play it safe and offer to split the check.

GREETINGS

Older British people will shake hands on greeting old friends or acquaintances; female friends may greet each other with a kiss on the cheek. In Britain, you can never say "please," "thank you," or "sorry" too often; to thank your host, a phone call or thank-you card does nicely. Email and other electronic messages are fine for younger hosts.

OUT ON THE TOWN

Etiquette in restaurants is much the same as in any major U.S. city. In restaurants you hail a waiter by saying, "Excuse me . . ." as one passes by, or by politely signaling with subtle hand signals (but no snapping fingers). It's common to have drinks before dinner, and wine with dinner. Friends and co-workers frequently gather in pubs, but you don't have to drink alcohol—some people in the pub drink juice or sodas. Nonetheless, drunkenness can be common in major cities after 10 pm.

"Smart casual" is fine for the theater, and those going to nightclubs will dress just the same here as they would in New York or Chicago—the flashier the better. Pubs are very casual places, however.

Smoking is forbidden in all public places, including bars and restaurants.

SIGHTSEEING

As in the United States, in public places it's considered polite to give up your seat to an elderly person, to a pregnant woman, or to a parent struggling with children and bags. Jaywalking isn't illegal in Britain and everybody does it. But since driving is on the left here, the traffic flow may be confusing; use caution.

British people used to take waiting in line (called queuing) incredibly seriously, but, especially in London bus queues, line discipline is breaking down. Nevertheless, many still highly value patience, and will turn on "queue jumpers" who try to cut in line.

The single thing you can do that will most mark you as a tourist—and an impolite one—is fail to observe the written and spoken rule that, on virtually all escalators but especially those in Tube stations, you stand on the right side of the escalator and leave room for people to walk past you on the left.

CALLING BRITAIN

The country code for Great Britain is 44. When dialing a British number from abroad, drop the initial 0 from before the local area code. For example, let's say you're calling Buckingham Palace—0207/7930–4832—from the United States. First, dial 011 (the international access code), then 44 (Great Britain's country code), then 207 (London's center-city code—without its initial 0), then the remainder of the number.

CALLING WITHIN BRITAIN

For all calls within Britain, dial the area code (which usually begins with 01, except in London), followed by the telephone number.

There are two types of pay phones: those that make calls to landlines or mobiles and those that also let you send texts or email. Most coin-operated phones take 10p, 20p, 50p, and £1 coins. SIM cards for your own cell phone and inexpensive pay-as-you-go cell phones are widely available from mobile network retailers such as 3, O2, T-Mobile, Vodaphone, and Virgin, as well as the Carphone Warehouse chain.

For pay and other phones, if you hear a repeated single tone after dialing, the line is busy; a continuous tone means the number didn't work.

To call the operator, dial 100; directory inquiries (information), 118–500; international directory inquiries, 118–505. For genuine emergencies, dial 999. For nonurgent police matters, dial 101.

CALLING OUTSIDE BRITAIN

For direct overseas dialing from Britain, dial 00, then the country code, area code, and number. For the international operator, credit card, or collect calls, dial 155; for international directory assistance, dial 118505. The country code for the United States is 1.

Access Codes AT&T Direct ☎ *0800/890–0011.* **MCI WorldPhone** ☎ *0800/279–5088.* **Sprint International Access** ☎ *817/698–4199.*

CALLING CARDS

Public card phones operate with special cards you can buy from post offices, some newsstands, or on the Internet. Ideal for longer calls, the cards are composed of units of 10p, and come in values of £3, £5, £10, and more. To use a card phone, lift the receiver, insert your card, and dial the number. An indicator panel shows the number of units used. At the end of your call, the card will be returned. Where credit cards are taken, slide the card in as indicated.

MOBILE PHONES

Any cell phone can be used in Europe if it's tri-band, quad-band, or GSM. Ask your home cell-phone company if your phone fits in this category and make sure it's activated for international calling before leaving your home country. Roaming fees can be steep, however: $1 a minute is considered reasonable. And overseas you normally pay the toll charges for incoming calls. It's almost always cheaper to send a text message than to make a call, since text messages have a low set fee (often less than 25¢).

If you just want to make local calls, consider buying a new SIM card (your provider may have to unlock your phone for you) and a prepaid local service plan. You'll then have a local number and can make local calls at local rates. You can also rent a cell phone from most major car-rental agencies. Some upscale hotels now provide loaner cell phones to their guests. Beware, however, of the per-minute rates charged. Alternatively, you may want to buy a basic pay-as-you-go phone for around £15.

Contacts Carphone Warehouse
☎ *0870/087–0870* ⊕ *www.carphonewarehouse.com.* **Cellular Abroad**
☎ *800/287–5072* ⊕ *www.cellularabroad.com.*
Mobal ☎ *888/888–9162* ⊕ *www.mobal.com.*

▌ CUSTOMS AND DUTIES

You're always allowed to bring goods of a certain value back home without having to pay any duty or import tax. But there's a limit on the amount of tobacco and liquor you can bring back duty-free, and some countries have separate limits for perfumes; for exact figures, check with your customs department. The values of so-called duty-free goods are included in these amounts. When you shop abroad, save all your receipts, as customs inspectors may ask to see them as well as the items you purchased. If the total value of your goods is more than the duty-free limit, you'll have to pay a tax (most often a flat percentage) on the value of everything beyond that limit.

Fresh meats, plants and vegetables, controlled drugs, and firearms (including replicas) and ammunition may not be brought into Great Britain, nor can dairy products from non-EU countries. Pets from the United States with the proper documentation may be brought into the country without quarantine under the U.K. Pet Travel Scheme (PETS). The process takes about four months to complete and involves detailed steps.

Information in Great Britain Department for Environment, Food and Rural Affairs
☎ *08459/335577* ⊕ *www.defra.gov.uk.* **HM Revenue and Customs** ☎ *0845/010 9000* ⊕ *www.hmrc.gov.uk.* **Pet Travel Scheme** ☎ *0845/933–5577 in U.K., 207/238–6951 in U.S.* ⊕ *www.gov.uk.*

U.S. Information U.S. Customs and Border Protection ☎ *877/228–5511 in U.S.* ⊕ *www.cbp.gov.*

▌ EATING OUT

The stereotypical notion of British meals as parades of roast beef, overcooked vegetables, and stodgy puddings has largely been replaced—particularly in London, Glasgow, other major cities, and some country hot spots—with an evolving picture of the country as foodie territory. From trendy gastro-pubs to interesting ethnic-fusion restaurants to see-and-be-seen dining shrines, British food is becoming known for having an international approach.

In general, restaurant prices are high. If you're watching your budget, seek out pubs and ethnic restaurants.

CATEGORY	LONDON	ELSEWHERE
$	under £16	under £15
$$	£16–£23	£15–£19
$$$	£24–£32	£20–£25
$$$$	over £32	over £25

Prices are the average cost of a main course at dinner or, if dinner isn't served, at lunch.

DISCOUNTS AND DEALS

Eating out in Britain's big cities in particular can be expensive, but you can do it cheaply. Try local cafés, where heaping plates of comfort food (bacon sandwiches and stuffed baked potatoes, for example) are served. Britain has plenty of the big names in fast food, as well as smaller places selling sandwiches, fish-and-chips, burgers, falafels, kebabs, and the like. Marks & Spencer, Sainsbury's, Morrison's, Tesco, and Waitrose are chain supermarkets with outlets throughout the country. They're good choices for groceries, premade sandwiches, and picnic fixings.

MEALS AND MEALTIMES

Cafés serving the traditional English breakfast (called a fry-up) of eggs, bacon, sausage, beans, mushrooms, half a grilled tomato, toast, and strong tea are often the cheapest places for breakfast. The Scottish variation goes like this: bacon and eggs served with sausage, fried mushrooms, and tomatoes, and usually fried bread or potato scones. For lighter morning fare (or real brewed coffee), try the Continental-style sandwich bars and coffee shops—the Pret-a-Manger chain being one of the largest—offering croissants and other pastries.

At lunch you can grab a sandwich between sights, pop into the local pub, or sit down in a restaurant. Dinner, too, has no set rules, but a three-course meal is standard in most midrange or high-end restaurants. Pre- or post-theater menus, offering two or three courses for a set price, are usually a good value.

Most traditional pubs don't have any waiters, and you're expected to order beverages or meals at the bar. Many pubs in cities don't serve food after 3 pm, so they're usually a better lunch option than dinner. In rural areas it's not uncommon for pubs to stop serving dinner at 9 pm.

Breakfast is generally served between 7:30 and 9, lunch between noon and 2:30, dinner or supper between 7:30 and 9:30, sometimes earlier, seldom later except in large cities. These days late-afternoon high tea is rarely a proper meal anymore, and tearooms are often open all day in touristy areas (they're not found at all in nontouristy places). So you can have a cup and pastry or sandwich whenever you feel you need it. Sunday roasts at pubs last from 11 am or noon to 3 pm.

Smoking is banned in pubs, clubs, and restaurants throughout Britain.

PAYING

Credit cards are widely accepted in restaurants and pubs, though some require a minimum charge of around £10. Be sure that you don't double-pay a service charge. Many restaurants exclude service charges from the printed menu (which the law obliges them to display outside), and then add 10% to 15% to the check. Others will stamp "Service not included" along the bottom of the bill, in which case you should add 10% to 15%. Cash is always appreciated, as it's more likely to go to the specific waiter.

PUBS

A common misconception among visitors to Britain is that pubs are simply bars. Pubs are, generally speaking, where people go to meet their friends and catch up on one another's lives. In small towns pubs act almost as town halls. Traditionally pub hours are from 11 am to 11 pm, with last orders called about 20 minutes before closing time, but pubs can choose to stay open until midnight or 1 am, or later.

Some pubs are child-friendly, but others have restricted hours for children. If a pub serves food, it will generally allow children in during the day with adults. Some pubs are stricter than others, though, and won't admit anyone younger than 18. If in doubt, ask the bartender.

RESERVATIONS AND DRESS

It's a good idea to make a reservation if you can. We mention them specifically only when they're essential or not accepted. For popular restaurants, book as far ahead as you can (often 30 days), and reconfirm as soon as you arrive. Large parties should always call ahead to check the reservations policy. We mention dress only when men are required to wear a jacket or a jacket and tie.

You can make reservations online through Square Meal and Toptable.

Contacts **Square Meal** ☎ *0207/582–0222* ⊕ *www.squaremeal.co.uk.* **Toptable** ☎ *0207/299–2949* ⊕ *www.toptable.co.uk.*

WINES, BEER, AND SPIRITS

Although hundreds of varieties of beer are brewed around the country, the traditional brew is known as "bitter" in England and Wales, and "heavy" in Scotland, and isn't carbonated; it's usually served at room temperature. Fizzy American-style beer is called lager. There are also plenty of other potations: stouts like Guinness and Murphy's are thick, pitch-black brews; ciders, made from apples, are alcoholic in Britain (Bulmer's and Strongbow are the big names, but look out for local microbrews); shandies are a low-alcohol mix of lager and lemon soda. Real ales, which have a natural second fermentation in the cask, have a shorter shelf life (so many are brewed locally) but special flavor; these are worth seeking out. You can order Scotland's most famous beverage—whisky (most definitely spelled without an *e*)—at any local pub. All pubs serve single-malt and blended whiskies. Generally the selection and quality of cocktails is higher in a wine bar or café than in a pub. The legal drinking age is 18.

ECOTOURISM

Ecotourism is an emerging trend in Great Britain. The Shetland Environmental Agency Ltd. runs the Green Tourism Business Scheme, a program that evaluates lodgings in England, Scotland, and Wales and gives them gold, silver, or bronze ratings. You can find a list of green hotels, B&Bs, and apartments on the GTBS website.

Contacts **Green Tourism Business Scheme** ☎ *01738/632162* ⊕ *www.green-business.co.uk.*

ELECTRICITY

The electrical current in Great Britain is 220–240 volts, 50 cycles alternating current (AC); wall outlets take three-pin plugs, and shaver sockets take two round, oversize prongs. British bathrooms aren't permitted to have 220–240 volt outlets in them. Consider making a small investment in a universal adapter, which has several types of plugs in one lightweight, compact unit. Most laptops and mobile phone chargers are dual voltage (i.e., they operate equally well on 110 and 220 volts) and require only an adapter. The same is true of newer small appliances such as hair dryers. Always check labels and manufacturer instructions. Don't use 110-volt outlets marked "For shavers only" for high-wattage appliances such as hair dryers.

Contacts **Walkabout Travel Gear** ☎ *800/852–7085* ⊕ *www.walkabouttravelgear.com.*

EMERGENCIES

If you need to report an emergency, dial 999 for police, fire, or ambulance. Be prepared to give the telephone number you're calling from. The number for nonurgent police calls, such as reporting a stolen car, is 101. You can get 24-hour medical treatment at British hospitals. Prescriptions are valid only if made out by doctors registered in the United Kingdom. Treatment from the National Health Service is free to British citizens; as a foreigner, you will be billed after the fact for your care. Check with your health-insurance company to make sure you're covered. Some British hospitals now require a credit card or other payment before they'll offer treatment.

U.S. Embassies American Consulate General ✉ *3 Regent Terr., Calton, Edinburgh* ☎ *0131/556–8315* ⊕ *edinburgh.usconsulate. gov.* **American Embassy** ✉ *24 Grosvenor Sq., London* ☎ *0207/499–9000* ⊕ *london. usembassy.gov.* **U.S. Passport Unit** ✉ *55/56 Upper Brook St., London* ☎ *0207/499–9000.*

▌ HEALTH

SPECIFIC ISSUES IN GREAT BRITAIN

If you take prescription drugs, keep a supply in your carry-on luggage and make a list of all your prescriptions to keep on file at home while you're abroad. You won't be able to renew a U.S. prescription at a pharmacy in Britain. Prescriptions are accepted only if issued by a U.K.-registered physician. If traveling in the Scottish Highlands and islands in summer, when insects called midges are out biting, pack some repellent—and antihistamine cream to reduce swelling if you do get bitten. Check with ⊕ *www.midgeforecast.co.uk* for updates on these pests.

OVER-THE-COUNTER REMEDIES

Over-the-counter medications in Britain are similar to those in the United States, with a few differences. Headache medicine is usually filed under "painkillers." You can buy generic ibuprofen or a popular European brand of ibuprofen, Nurofen. Tylenol isn't sold, but its main ingredient, acetaminophen, is found in brands such as Panadol. Clarityn (spelled here with a y) is the main anti-allergy option; instead of Nyquil cold medicine, there's Sudafed or Lemsip. The most popular cough medicine is Benylin.

Drugstores are generally called pharmacies, but sometimes referred to as chemists' shops. The country's biggest drugstore chain, Boots, has outlets everywhere, except for the smallest towns. If you're in a rural area, look for shops marked with a sign of a green cross.

If you can't find what you want, ask at the counter; many over-the-counter medicines are kept behind the register.

MEDICAL INSURANCE AND ASSISTANCE

Consider buying trip insurance with medical-only coverage. Neither Medicare nor some private insurers cover medical expenses anywhere outside the United States. Medical-only policies typically reimburse you for medical care (excluding that related to preexisting conditions) and hospitalization abroad, and provide for evacuation. You still have to pay the bills and await reimbursement from the insurer, though.

Another option is to sign up with a medical-evacuation assistance company. A membership in one of these companies gets you doctor referrals, emergency evacuation or repatriation, 24-hour hotlines for medical consultation, and other assistance. International SOS Assistance Emergency and AirMed International provide evacuation services and medical referrals. MedjetAssist offers medical evacuation.

Medical Assistance Companies AirMed International ⊕ *www.airmed.com.* **International SOS** ⊕ *www.internationalsos. com.* **MedjetAssist** ⊕ *www.medjetassist.com.*

Medical-Only Insurers International Medical Group ☎ *800/628–4664* ⊕ *www.imglobal.com.* **Wallach & Company** ☎ *800/237–6615, 540/687–3166* ⊕ *www.wallach.com.*

SHOTS AND MEDICATIONS

No special shots are required or suggested for Great Britain.

Health Warnings National Centers for Disease Control & Prevention (*CDC*). ☎ *800/232–4636 travelers' health line* ⊕ *wwwnc.cdc.gov/travel.* **World Health Organization** (*WHO*). ⊕ *www.who.int.*

▌ HOURS OF OPERATION

Most banks are open on weekdays at least from 9:30 until 3:30; some open at 9 and close as late as 5. Some have Thursday evening hours, and a few are open on Saturday morning. The larger banks are increasingly open on Saturday. Normal office hours for most businesses are weekdays from 9 to 5.

The major national museums and galleries are open daily from 9 to 6, including lunchtime, but have shorter hours on Sunday. Regional museums are usually closed on Monday and have shorter hours in winter. In London many museums are open late one evening a week.

Independently owned pharmacies are generally open on weekdays and Saturday between 9:30 and 5:30, although in larger cities some stay open until 10 pm; local newspapers list which pharmacies are open late.

Usual retail business hours are weekdays and Saturday from 9 to 5:30 or 10 to 6:30, and Sunday from noon to 4. Shops in small villages shops may close at 1 pm once a week, often on Wednesday or Thursday. They may also close for lunch and not open on Sunday at all. In large cities—especially London—department stores stay open late (usually until 7:30 or 8) one night a week, usually Thursday. On national holidays most stores are closed, and over the Christmas holidays most restaurants are closed as well.

Service stations are at regular intervals on motorways and are usually open 24 hours a day, though stations elsewhere are open 7 am to 9 pm; in rural areas many close at 6 pm and on Sunday.

HOLIDAYS

Holidays are January 1, New Year's Day; Good Friday and Easter Monday; May Day (first Monday in May); spring and summer bank holidays (last Monday in May and August respectively); December 25, Christmas Day; and December 26, Boxing Day (day after Christmas). If these holidays fall on a weekend, the holiday is observed on the following Monday. During the Christmas holidays many restaurants, as well as museums and other attractions, may close for at least a week—call to verify hours. Book hotels for Christmas travel well in advance.

▮ MAIL

Stamps can be bought from post offices (the usual opening hours are weekdays from 9 to 5:30, Saturday from 9 to noon), from stamp machines outside post offices, and from newsagents. Some post offices are located within supermarkets or general stores. Specialized shipping shops like Mail Boxes Etc. also sell stamps. Mailboxes, known as post or letter boxes, are painted bright red. Allow seven days for a letter to reach the United States and about 10 days to two weeks to reach Australia or New Zealand. The useful Royal Mail website has information on everything from buying stamps to finding a post office.

Airmail letters up to 10 grams (0.35 ounce) to North America cost 88p. Letters within Britain weighing up to 100 grams (3.5 ounces) are 60p for first class, 50p for second class. Rates for envelopes larger than 353 mm (13.9 inches) long, 250 mm (9.84 inches) wide, and 25 mm (1 inch) deep are higher.

Contact Royal Mail ☎ *0845/577–4040* ⊕ *www.royalmail.com.*

SHIPPING PACKAGES

Most department stores and retail outlets can ship your goods home. You should check your insurance for coverage of possible damage. Private delivery companies such as Federal Express and DHL provide two-day delivery service to the United States, but you'll pay a considerable amount for the privilege.

Express Services DHL ☎ *0800/316–0498* ⊕ *www.dhl.co.uk.* **Federal Express** ☎ *0845/607–0809* ⊕ *www.fedex.com.* **Mail Boxes Etc.** ☎ *0800/623123* ⊕ *www.mbe. co.uk.* **Parcelforce** ☎ *0844/800–4466* ⊕ *www. parcelforce.com.* **UPS** ☎ *0845/787–7877* ⊕ *www.ups.com.*

▮ MONEY

Prices in Britain can seem high because of the exchange rate. London remains one of the most expensive cities in the world. But travelers can get breaks: staying in bed-and-breakfasts or renting a city apartment brings down lodging costs, and national museums are free. *The chart below gives some ideas of the prices you can expect to pay for day-to-day life.*

ITEM	AVERAGE COST
Cup of Coffee	£2–£3
Glass of Wine	£3.50 in a pub or wine bar, £5.50 or more in a restaurant
Glass of Beer	£3 or more
Sandwich	£3.50
One-Mile Taxi Ride in London	£5.50–£8.60
Museum Admission	National museums free; others £5–£10

Prices throughout this guide are given for adults. Substantially reduced fees—generally referred to as "concessions" throughout Great Britain—are almost always available for children, students, and senior citizens.

■TIP→ Banks have limited amounts of foreign currencies on hand, and it may take as long as a week to order. If you're planning to exchange funds before leaving home, don't wait until the last minute.

ATMS AND BANKS

Make sure before leaving home that your credit and debit cards have been programmed for ATM use abroad—ATMs in Great Britain accept PINs of four or fewer digits only. If you know your PIN as a word, learn the numerical equivalent. Most keypads show numbers only, not letters. Most ATMs are on both the Cirrus and Plus networks. ATMs are available at most main-street banks, large supermarkets such as Sainsbury's and Tesco, some Tube stops in London, and many rail stations. Major banks include Barclays, HSBC, and NatWest, and Bank of Scotland, Royal Bank of Scotland, and Clydesdale in Scotland.

Your own bank will probably charge a fee for using ATMs abroad (unless you use your bank's British partner); the foreign bank you use may also charge a fee. Nevertheless, you'll usually get a better rate of exchange at an ATM than you will at a currency-exchange office or even when changing money in a bank. And extracting funds as you need them is a safer option than carrying around a large amount of cash.

CREDIT CARDS

The Discover card isn't accepted throughout Britain. Other major credit cards, except Diners Club and American Express, are accepted virtually everywhere in Britain; however, you're expected to know and use your pin number for all transactions—even for credit cards, so it's a good idea to do some quick memorization for whichever card you intend to use.

Most European credit cards store information in microchips, rather than magnetic strips. Although some banks in the United States, such as Chase and Wells Fargo, are starting to adopt this system, you may find some places in Britain that can't process your credit card. It's a good idea to carry enough cash to cover small purchases.

Inform your credit-card company before you travel, especially if you're going abroad and don't travel internationally very often. Otherwise, the credit-card company might put a hold on your card owing to unusual activity. Record all your credit-card numbers in a safe place. Both MasterCard and Visa have general numbers you can call (collect if you're abroad) if your card is lost, but you're better off calling the number of your issuing bank, since MasterCard and Visa usually just transfer you to your bank; your bank's number is usually printed on your card.

If you plan to use your credit card for cash advances, you'll need to apply for a PIN at least two weeks before your trip. Although it's usually cheaper (and safer) to use a credit card abroad for large purchases (so you can cancel payments or be reimbursed if there's a problem), some credit-card companies *and* the banks that issue them add substantial percentages to all foreign transactions, whether they're in a foreign currency or not. Check on these fees before traveling.

Reporting Lost Cards American Express
☎ 336/393–1111 collect from abroad
⊕ www.americanexpress.com. **Diners Club**
☎ 514/881–3735 collect from abroad ⊕ www.
dinersclubus.com. **MasterCard** ☎ 636/722–
7111 collect from abroad ⊕ www.mastercard.
com. **Visa** ☎ 800/847–2911 collect from
abroad ⊕ usa.visa.com.

CURRENCY AND EXCHANGE

The unit of currency in Great Britain is
the pound sterling (£), divided into 100
pence (p). Bills (called notes) are issued in
the values of £50, £20, £10, and £5. Coins
are £2, £1, 50p, 20p, 10p, 5p, 2p, and
1p. Scottish coins are the same as English
ones, but have a thistle on them. Scottish
notes have the same face values as English
notes, and English notes are interchange-
able with them in Scotland.

At the time of this writing, the exchange
rate was about U.S. $1.70 to £1.

British post offices exchange currency
with no fee, and at decent rates.

■TIP➔ Even if a currency-exchange
booth has a sign promising no commission, rest assured that there's some kind
of huge, hidden fee. As for rates, you're
almost always better off getting foreign
currency at an ATM or exchanging money
at a bank.

Currency Conversion
Google ⊕ www.google.com. **Oanda.com**
⊕ www.oanda.com. **XE.com** ⊕ www.xe.com.

∎ PACKING

Great Britain can be cool, damp, and over-
cast, even in summer. You'll want a heavy
coat for winter and a lightweight coat or
warm jacket for summer. There's no time
of year when a raincoat or umbrella won't
come in handy. For the cities, pack as you
would for an American city: coats and ties
for expensive restaurants and nightspots,
casual clothes elsewhere. It can be a good
idea to take a washcloth. Pack insect
repellent if you plan to hike.

∎ PASSPORTS

U.S. citizens need only a valid passport
to enter Great Britain for stays of up to
six months. Travelers should be prepared
to show sufficient funds to support and
accommodate themselves while in Britain
(credit cards will usually suffice for this)
and to show a return or onward ticket.
If you're within six months of your passport's expiration date, renew it before
you leave—nearly expired passports
aren't strictly banned, but they make
immigration officials anxious, and may
cause you problems. Health certificates
aren't required.

If only one parent is traveling with a child
under 17 and his or her last name differs from the child's, then he or she will
need a signed and notarized letter from
the parent with the same last name as the
child authorizing permission to travel.
Airlines, ferries, and trains have different
policies for children traveling alone, so if
your child must travel alone, make sure to
check with the carrier prior to purchasing
your child's ticket.

**U.S. Passport Information U.S. Department
of State** ☎ 877/487–2778 ⊕ www.travel.state.
gov/passport.

∎ RESTROOMS

Public restrooms are sparse in Britain,
although most big cities maintain public
facilities that are clean and modern. Train
stations and department stores have public restrooms that occasionally charge a
small fee, usually 30p. Most pubs, restaurants, and even fast-food chains reserve
their bathrooms for customers. Hotels
and museums are usually a good place to
find clean, free facilities. On the road, gas-
station facilities are usually clean and free.

The Bathroom Diaries rates toilets and
has an iTunes find-a-loo app called
Toiletocity.

Find a Loo The Bathroom Diaries
⊕ www.thebathroomdiaries.com.

▌ SAFETY

Great Britain has a low incidence of violent crime. But petty crime, mostly in urban areas, is on the rise, and tourists can be the targets. Use common sense: when in a city center, if you're paying at a shop or a restaurant, never put your wallet down or let your bag out of your hand. When sitting on a chair in a public place, keep your purse on your lap or between your feet. Don't wear expensive jewelry or watches, and don't flash fancy smart phones outside Tube stations, where there have been some thefts. Store your passport in the hotel safe, and keep a copy with you. Don't leave anything in your car.

Although scams do occur in Britain, they aren't pervasive. If you're getting money out of an ATM, beware of someone bumping into you to distract you. You may want to use ATMs inside banks rather than those outside them. In London scams are most common at ATMs on Oxford Street and around Piccadilly Circus. Watch out for pickpockets, particularly in London. They often work in pairs, one distracting you in some way.

Always take a licensed black taxi or call a car service (sometimes called minicabs) recommended by your hotel. Avoid drivers who approach you on the street, as in most cases they'll overcharge you. Always buy theater tickets from a reputable dealer. If you're driving in from a British port, beware of thieves posing as customs officials who try to "confiscate illegal goods."

While traveling, don't leave any bags unattended, as they may be viewed as a security risk and destroyed by the authorities. If you see an unattended bag on the train, bus, or Tube, find a worker and report it. Never hesitate to get off a Tube, train, or bus if you feel unsafe.

■TIP➔ Distribute your cash, credit cards, IDs, and other valuables between a deep front pocket, an inside jacket or vest pocket, and a hidden money pouch. Don't reach for the money pouch once you're in public.

General Information and Warnings **Transportation Security Administration** (*TSA*). ☏ *866/289–9673* ⊕ *www.tsa.gov*. **U.K. Foreign & Commonwealth Office** ☏ *0207/008–1500* ⊕ *www.gov.uk/foreign-travel-advice*. **U.S. Department of State** ⊕ *www.travel.state.gov*.

▌ SIGHTSEEING PASSES

DISCOUNT PASSES

If you plan to visit castles, gardens, and historic houses during your stay in Britain, look into discount passes or memberships that offer significant savings. Just be sure to match what the pass or membership offers against your itinerary to see if it's worthwhile.

The British monarchy has an official website with information about visiting royal homes and more. English Heritage, the Historic Houses Association, the National Trust (and its U.S. affiliate, the Royal Oak Foundation), and VisitBritain all offer discount passes for structures throughout England.

If you're heading to Scotland, look into the Scottish Explorer Ticket, available from any staffed Historic Scotland (HS) property and from many tourist information centers. Another worthwhile pass, called Discover Scotland, allows access to all National Trust for Scotland properties. It's available to overseas visitors only and can be purchased online and by phone, or at properties and some of the main tourist information centers.

For information about sightseeing passes in Wales, see the Wales Planner in Chapter 12.

Contacts British Monarchy ☏ *0207/930–4832* ⊕ *www.royal.gov.uk*.

Information English Heritage ☏ *0870/333–1181* ⊕ *www.english-heritage.org.uk*. **Historic Houses Association** ☏ *0207/259–5688* ⊕ *www.hha.org.uk*. **Historic Scotland** ☏ *0131/668–8831* ⊕ *www.historic-scotland.gov.uk/explorer*. **London Pass** ☏ *0870/242–9988* in U.K., *01664/485020* from U.S. ⊕ *www.londonpass.com*. **National Trust**

☎ 0844/800–1895 ⊕ www.nationaltrust.org.
uk. **National Trust for Scotland** ☎ 0131/458–
0303 ⊕ www.nts.org.uk.**Royal Oak Foundation** ☎ 212/480–2889, 800/913–6565 ⊕ www.
royal-oak.org.

▌ SPORTS AND THE OUTDOORS

VisitBritain and local Tourist Information
Centres can recommend places to enjoy
your favorite sport.

BIKING

The national body promoting cycle touring is the Cyclists' Touring Club (£39 a
year). Members get free advice and route
information and a magazine. Transport
for London publishes maps of recommended routes across the capital and British Cycling has online route maps. The
CTC organizes cycling vacations.

Contacts British Cycling ☎ 0161/274–2000
⊕ www.britishcycling.org.uk. **Cyclists' Touring
Club** ☎ 0844/736–8450 ⊕ www.ctc.org.uk.

BOATING

Boating—whether on bucolic rivers or
industrial canals—can be a leisurely way
to explore the British landscape. For boat-
rental operators along Britain's several
hundred miles of historic canals and waterways, contact the Association of Pleasure
Craft Operators or Waterway Holidays.
The Canal and River Trust has maps and
other information. Waterway Holidays
arranges boat accommodations from traditional narrow boats to wide-beam canal
boats, motorboats, and sailboats.

**Contacts Association of Pleasure Craft
Operators** ☎ 01784/223603 ⊕ www.apco.org.
uk. **Canal and River Trust** ☎ 0303/040–4040
⊕ www.canalrivertrust.org.uk. **Waterways
Holidays** ☎ 0845/127–1020 in U.K. ⊕ www.
waterwaysholidays.com.

GOLF

Invented in Scotland, golf is a beloved
pastime all over Britain. The website
English Golf Courses has general information about courses, fees, and locations.

The Golf in Scotland section on VisitScot-
land.com website provides comprehensive information. You can gain access to
famous private and public courses on
package tours arranged by companies
such as Golf International and Owenoak
International Golf Travel. *For information about golf tours in Scotland, see
Tours in this chapter.*

Contacts English Golf Courses
☎ 0141/353–2222 ⊕ www.englishgolf-courses.
co.uk. **Golf International** ☎ 212/986–9176,
800/833–1389 ⊕ www.golfinternational.
com. **Owenoak International Golf Travel**
☎ 203/854–9000, 800/426–4498 ⊕ www.
owenoak.com.

WALKING AND HIKING

Walking and hiking—from a slow ramble
to a challenging mountainside climb—are
enormously popular in Britain. National
Trails is a great online resource, as is The
Ramblers, which maintains a list of B&Bs
close to long-distance footpaths. The Ordnance Survey (⊕ *www.ordnancesurvey.
co.uk*) produces the very fine Explorer
Maps for walkers.

Contacts National Trails
⊕ www.nationaltrail.co.uk. **The Ramblers**
☎ 0207/339–8500 ⊕ www.ramblers.org.uk.

▌ TAXES

Air Passenger Duty (APD) is a tax included
in the price of your ticket. The U.K.'s APD
fees, currently the highest in the world, are
divided into four bands, based on cabin
class and distance traveled, that range from
£13 per person in economy for 2,000 miles
flown to £376 first and business class for
more than 6,000 miles.

The British sales tax (Value Added Tax, or
V.A.T.) is 20%. The tax is usually included
in quoted prices in shops, hotels, and restaurants. The most common exception
is at high-end hotels, where prices often
exclude V.A.T. Outside of hotels and
rental-car agencies, which have specific
additional taxes, there is no other sales
tax in Britain.

Refunds apply for V.A.T. only on goods being taken out of Britain. Many large stores provide a V.A.T.–refund service, but only if you request it. You must ask the store to complete Form V.A.T. 407, to be given to customs at departure along with a V.A.T. Tax Free Shopping scheme invoice. Fill in the form at the shop, have the salesperson sign it, have it stamped by customs when you leave the country, then mail the stamped form to the shop or to a commercial refund company. Alternatively, you may be able to take the form to an airport refund-service counter after you're through passport control for an on-the-spot refund. There is an extra fee for this service, and lines tend to be long.

Global Blue is a Europe-wide service with 270,000 affiliated stores. It has refund counters in the U.K. at Heathrow and Gatwick, as well as on Oxford Street and in the Westfield Shopping Centre. There's also one in Edinburgh. Global Blue's refund form, called a Tax Free Check, is the most common across the European continent. The service issues refunds in the form of cash, check, or credit-card adjustment. The latter is useful for small purchases, as the cost of cashing a foreign-currency check may exceed the amount of the refund.

V.A.T. Refunds Global Blue ☎ *866/706–6069* ⊕ *www.globalblue.com.* **HM Revenue and Customs** ☎ *0845/010–9000* ⊕ *www.hmrc.gov. uk/customs.*

∎ TIME

Britain sets its clocks by Greenwich Mean Time, five hours ahead of the U.S. East Coast. British summer time (GMT plus one hour) generally coincides with American daylight saving time adjustments.

Time Zones Timeanddate.com ⊕ *www.timeanddate.com.*

∎ TIPPING

Tipping is done in Britain just as in the United States, but at a lower level, generally 12.5% to 15%. Tipping more can look like you're showing off. Don't tip bar staff in pubs—although you can always offer to buy them a drink. There's no need to tip at clubs (it's acceptable at posher establishments, though) unless you're being served at your table. Rounding up to the nearest pound or 50p is appreciated.

TIPPING GUIDELINES FOR BRITAIN	
Bartender	£1–£2 per round of drinks, depending on the number of drinks, except in pubs, where tipping isn't the custom
Bellhop	£1 per bag, depending on the level of the hotel
Hotel Concierge	£5 or more, if he or she performs a service for you
Hotel Doorman	£1 if he helps you get a cab
Hotel Maid/ Housekeeping	£1 or £2 per day
Hotel Room-Service Waiter	Same as a waiter, unless a service charge has been added to the bill
Porter at Airport or Train Station	£1 per bag
Skycap at Airport	£1 per bag checked
Taxi Driver	10p per pound of the fare, then round up to nearest pound
Tour Guide	Tipping optional: £1 or £2 is generous
Waiter	12.5%–15%, with 15% being the norm at high-end London restaurants; nothing additional if a service charge is added to the bill, unless you want to reward particularly good service. Tips in cash preferred
Other	Restroom attendants in more expensive restaurants expect some small change or £1. Tip coat-check personnel £1 unless there's a fee, then nothing. Hairdressers and barbers get 10%–15%

▌ TOURS

Visiting London on a fully escorted tour is unnecessary because of its extensive public transport and wide network of taxicabs. Many tour companies offer day tours to the main sights, and getting around is fairly easy.

If you're traveling beyond London, packaged tours can be very useful, particularly if you don't want to rent a car. Because many sights are off the beaten track and not accessible by public transportation—particularly castles, great houses, and small villages—tour groups make the country accessible to all. There are a few downsides to escorted tours: rooms in castles and medieval houses tend to be small and can feel overrun when tour groups roll in. And as on a cruise, your traveling companions are inescapable.

Dozens of companies offer fully guided tours in Britain. Most of these are full packages including lodging, food, and transportation costs in one flat fee. Do a bit of research before booking. You'll want to know about the hotels you'll be staying in, how big your group is likely to be, how your days will be structured, and who the other people are likely to be.

Among the most reliable tour companies, two U.S.–based companies—Trafalgar Tours and Globus & Cosmos Tours—specialize in moderately priced trips that feature plenty of sights. Tauck is another well-established company. At the high end of the price scale is Abercrombie & Kent, known for luxurious tours that include everything from castle hotels to journeys on vintage railways.

Contacts Abercrombie & Kent ☎ 800/554–7016 ⊕ www.abercrombiekent.com. **Globus & Cosmos Tours** ☎ 877/245–6287 in U.S. ⊕ www.globusandcosmos.com. **Tauck** ☎ 0800/931-834 in U.K., 203/899-6500 in U.S. ⊕ www.tauck.co.uk. **Trafalgar Tours** ☎ 0800/533–5616 ⊕ www.trafalgar.com/uk.

SPECIAL-INTEREST TOURS

CULINARY

Britain's foodie culture is increasingly rich and thriving. Gourmet on Tour, a U.S.–based tour company, offers vacations that focus on cooking, eating, and fine wine.

Contact Gourmet on Tour ☎ 646/461–6088 in U.S., 0207/558–8796 in U.K. ⊕ www. gourmetontour.com.

GARDENS

Britain is a land of garden lovers, and its gardens are varied and impressive. The British companies Adderley and Flora conduct tours, as do the U.S.-based Coopersmiths and Lynott Tours. Tools on the website of the National Gardens Scheme and Gardenvisit.com can help you decide which gardens in England, Scotland, and Wales to tour; the website Scottish Gardens (⊕ *www.scottishgardens.org*) focuses solely on Scotland.

Contacts Adderley Travel Ltd. ☎ 01953/606706 ⊕ www.adderleytravel. com. **Coopersmiths** ☎ 415/669–1914 in U.S. ⊕ www.coopersmiths.com. **Flora Garden Tours** ☎ 01366/328946 ⊕ www.flora-garden-tours.co.uk. **Lynott Tours** ☎ 800/221–2474 ⊕ www.lynotttours.com.**National Gardens Scheme** ☎ 01483/211535 ⊕ www.ngs.org.uk.

GOLF TOURS

Scotland has fabulous golf courses; a tour can help enthusiasts make the most of their time. Golf Scotland, Scotland for Golf, and Thistle Golf arrange golfing packages and full vacations. VisitScotland has information about discount passes and other deals.

Contacts Golf Scotland ☎ 866/875–4653 ⊕ www.golfscotland.com. **Scotland for Golf** ☎ 01334/460762 ⊕ www.scotlandforgolf. co.uk. **Thistle Golf** ☎ 0141/942-4043 ⊕ www. thistlegolf.co.uk. **VisitScotland** ✉ Proces Mall, 3 Princes St., Edinburgh ☎ 0845/473–3868 ⊕ www.visitscotland.com.

HISTORY

Britain is rich in history and culture, to the point where it's developed what's known as the "heritage industry." Celtic Dream Tours, which specializes in Celtic-inspired excursions, as well as golf and whisky tours. Classic England specializes in private tours to castles, cathedrals, and areas of historic interest. Classic Scotland offers tours of castles and gardens as well as a literary tour that takes in the homes of Robert Louis Stevenson, Robert Burns, Walter Scott, and J.M. Barrie. Inscape offers tours of four days or less, oriented toward fine art and architecture led by knowledgeable academics.

Contacts Celtic Dream Tours ☎ *813/317–6039* ⊕ *www.celticdreamtours.com.* **Classic England** ☎ *01277/841651 in U.K., 866/464–7389 in U.S.* ⊕ *www.classic-england.com.* **Classic Scotland** ☎ *01866/464–7389* ⊕ *www.classic-scotland.com.* **Inscape Fine Art Study Tours** ☎ *0208/566-7539* ⊕ *inscapestudytours.wordpress.com.*

WALKING AND HIKING

Many visitors prefer to amble through their vacations. You can arrange walking tours through Adventure Sports Holidays (which also books surfing, kayaking, and paragliding trips), Adventureline, and the U.S.-based Country Walkers and England Lakeland Ramblers. For specialized tours, such as walks through Brontë Country, look into The Wayfarers.

Contacts Adventureline ☎ *01209/820847* ⊕ *www.adventureline.co.uk.* **Adventure Sports Holidays** ☎ *01273/358092* ⊕ *www.adventuresportsholidays.com.* **Country Walkers** ☎ *800/464–9255 in U.S.* ⊕ *www.cwadventures.com.* **English Lakeland Ramblers** ☎ *800/724–8802 in U.S.* ⊕ *www.ramblers.com.* **The Wayfarers** ☎ *01242/620871* ⊕ *www.thewayfarers.com.*

FODORS.COM CONNECTION

Before your trip, be sure to check out what other travelers are saying in the forums on ⊕ *www.fodors.com.*

▌ VISITOR INFORMATION

ONLINE TRAVEL TOOLS

GENERAL INFORMATION

VisitBritain, the country's official tourism website and a good first stop for British-bound U.S. travelers, provides practical information. You can find money-saving deals on the site. VisitEngland (⊕ *www.visitengland.com*), Visit Wales (⊕ *www.visitwales.com*), and VisitScotland (⊕ *www.visitscotland.com*) are also useful resources. *For information about discounts, see Sightseeing Passes in this chapter.*

In the U.S.
VisitBritain ⊕ *www.visitbritain.com.*

MUSEUMS AND THE ARTS

The well organized Culture 24 website has up-to-date information about publicly funded museums, art galleries, and historic sights.

Contact Culture 24 ☎ *01273/623266* ⊕ *www.culture24.org.uk.*

INDEX

PHOTO CREDITS